Dictionary of British Literary Characters:
20th-Century Novels

Dictionary of British Literary Characters:
20th-Century Novels

Edited by
John R. Greenfield

Associate Editors
John Rogers
Arlyn Bruccoli

A Bruccoli Clark Layman Book

☑ Facts On File®

AN INFOBASE HOLDINGS COMPANY

Dictionary of British Literary Characters: 20th-Century Novels

Facts On File, Inc.
460 Park Avenue South
New York, NY 10016

Library of Congress Cataloging-in-Publication Data

Dictionary of British literary characters : 20th-century novels /
   edited by John R. Greenfield ; associate editors, John Rogers, Arlyn
Bruccoli.
     p. cm.
   "A Bruccoli Clark Layman book."
   Includes index.
   ISBN 0-8160-2180-5 (alk. paper). — ISBN 0-8160-2178-3 (set : alk.
paper) : $115.00
   1. English fiction—20th century—Dictionaries. 2. Characters and
characteristics in literature—Dictionaries. I. Greenfield, John
R. II. Rogers, John.   III. Bruccoli, Arlyn.
PR888.C47D53 1994   94-26620
823'.910927'03—dc20

Manufactured by the Maple-Vail Book Manufacturing Group
Printed in the United States of America

VP PKG 10 9 8 7 6 5 4 3 2 1

This book is printed on acid-free paper.

To my teachers, students, and colleagues

Preface

The Dictionary of British Literary Characters: The Novel is a two-volume compendium representing over a thousand novels and more than twenty thousand characters. As the most comprehensive reference on characters in the English novel, these volumes may have implications for the current controversy over what constitutes the canon of the English novel. The editors' approach concerning the selection of novels has been as democratic and as inclusive as space permits. In addition to comprehensive coverage of established British novelists, the editors have sought to include a representative sampling of novels by lesser-known authors. In general, three broad criteria were followed in selecting the novels included herein: (1) has the novelist or the novel become established so as to have achieved a degree of permanence? (2) has the novelist or the novel received scholarly or critical attention? (3) has the novel achieved a degree of popularity in its own time or in later times? A novel or novelist that meets two or in some cases only one of these general criteria may qualify for inclusion.

Volume two posed special problems and considerations because some of the novels are too recent to have achieved a degree of permanence. We tried to err on the side of inclusion, but there are so many writers in the contemporary period that we could not possibly include them all. With a few exceptions, volume two does not attempt to include novels published after 1980. In addition, there are many genre writers, such as mystery, thriller, and humor writers, who, if we gave them the thoroughness of coverage that we did traditional novelists, would add enough to make yet a third volume. Accordingly, we have sought to include only those genre writers whose novels merit consideration either as "literature" or as cultural phenomena. (John le Carré and P. D. James are examples of the former; Agatha Christie and P. G. Wodehouse — from whose scores of novels a handful were selected as representative — are examples of the latter).

In order of chronology, volume one begins with *The Pilgrim's Progress* and includes a strong representation of eighteenth-century and nineteenth-century novels, 486 novels in all and more than eleven thousand characters. Volume two continues with novelists who published the bulk of their work after 1900 and includes some novels published in the contemporary period. In all, volume two includes 686 novels and nearly ten thousand characters. Although there is some inevitable overlapping of different novels written by the same author and published in the nineteenth and twentieth centuries, the two volumes are divided so that all the novels written by a particular novelist are included in the same volume. To take two examples, both George Moore and H. G. Wells published in both the nineteenth and twentieth centuries, but Moore's novels are included in volume one while Wells's are in volume two, the consensus being that Moore is considered to be a Victorian novelist while Wells is usually identified with the twentieth century.

Generally speaking, an effort has been made to include all major characters and all other characters who contribute to the plot or themes of the novel in any significant way. Characters who appear in more than one novel are listed in the *Dictionary* only once with their roles for all the novels in which they appear described in that single entry. Each character is listed alphabetically by surname (when the surname is available). Characters with only first names or with no names are listed alphabetically by first names or, in cases of those with no name, by some identifying designation, as for example, Prisoner No. 402 in Arthur Koestler's *Darkness at Noon.*

In addition to providing the author and title within each character entry, volume two provides two indices for reference. The alphabetical index of all included novels (from both volumes) supplies alternative titles under which the novels were published, as well as the titles of original British publication, the latter being almost invariably the ones used throughout the text. The alphabetical index of authors is the more comprehensive. It includes birth and death dates, and each author's name is followed by an alphabetical list of his or her included titles with dates of first publication, initials identifying the contributors who wrote the entries, and under each title an alphabetical listing of characters. This index makes it possible for the *Dictionary* user to study in any desired order all the included characters from a particular novel. It also assists the reader who remembers from a novel the first but not the surname of a character, or who is puzzled by apparent inconsistencies of alphabetical ordering. (In ordering, the *de* or *von* prefix is disregarded in alphabetizing if the character is, respectively, French or German; Mitzi von Kessen in Richard Hughes's *The Fox in the Attic,* for example, can be found in the K section. If the character is English or American, the connotation "of " has been lost, and the *de* or *von* has become part of the name; Adelaide de Crecy in Iris Murdoch's *Bruno's Dream* is in the D section.)

Those consulting the *Dictionary* may find useful information about characters' occupations, family relations, relations with other characters, class, and gender roles as well as the characters' contributions to the novels' plots and themes. In addition to providing students and others with factual information about the characters, the *Dictionary* may provide scholars and critics with data for various historical, sociological, or thematic studies of the English novel.

A project of this magnitude could never have been accomplished without the help and cooperation of many people. I would especially like to thank John Rogers, Associate Editor of volume two, for his help in getting this project started in the summer of 1989, and of course for all the work he has done on the project. David Brailow, who is the Associate Editor of volume one, also helped in securing contributors for volume two. The *Dictionary* could never have been completed without the participation of the many contributors, some few of whom are friends or acquaintances of mine and most of whom I have never met. These contributors deserve and have my gratitude for their promptness in meeting deadlines, for their conscientiousness in compiling their character entries, for their willingness to make revisions, and most of all, for their cooperation and patience over the long duration of this project. I would also like to thank Danyelle Warden for her valuable editorial assistance performed under the auspices of the McKendree College internship program. Four secretaries at McKendree College, Naomia Severs, Linda Gordon, Ella Doty, and Nancy Ferguson, deserve thanks for the help they gave me in handling the correspondence associated with this project. Finally, as the dedication suggests, I would like to thank all my best students, teachers, and colleagues for helping to keep me continually and vitally interested in the English novel.

—John R. Greenfield

A

Michael Aaronson Barbara Vaughan's Jewish cousin in Muriel Spark's *The Mandlebaum Gate.*

AbathVasidol MetyVasidol's daughter, who has an affair with RobaydayAnganol and later falsely testifies against him in Brian W. Aldiss's *Helliconia Summer.*

The Abbess Mother Superior at Imber Abbey and spiritual adviser to Michael Meade in Iris Murdoch's *The Bell.*

Richard Abbot Down-to-earth romantic friend of Jane Weatherby; he takes up with Liz Jennings when Jane dismisses him for John Pomfret in Henry Green's *Nothing.*

Abbott Midshipman who fails at his duties during an attack on a fort in C. S. Forester's *Lieutenant Hornblower.*

Caroline Abbott Conventional, agreeable, romantic young woman, who chaperones Lilia Herriton to Italy, where she too falls in love with Gino Carella in E. M. Forster's *Where Angels Fear to Tread.*

General Abdul Turkish ambassador in Tunis and friend of Aunt Augusta Bertram; he helps her with shady investment deals in Graham Greene's *Travels with My Aunt.*

Abdulla Arab trader to whom Willems betrays the navigation of the River Pantai in Joseph Conrad's *An Outcast of the Islands.*

Abdullam An Arab merchant in Luxor who sells Jane Mallory the head that looks like Jimmy Assad in John Fowles's *Daniel Martin.*

Mr. Abel (Abel Guevez de Argensola) Venezuelan adventurer in W. H. Hudson's *Green Mansions.*

Rowland, Lord Aberavon Deceased shipping magnate and art patron and the maternal grandfather of both Barbara Goring and Eleanor Walpole-Wilson in Anthony Powell's *A Buyer's Market.* Paintings from his collection — by Isbister, Deacon, and others — unvalued and dispersed at the time of his death, are sought by collectors in *Hearing Secret Harmonies.*

Mrs. Aberdeen Rickie Elliott's servant at Cambridge in E. M. Forster's *The Longest Journey.*

Abou Tired "aged negro with haunted sin-sick eyes" who helps deliver bouquets for Bachir from the Duchess of Varna's flower shop in Ronald Firbank's *The Flower Beneath the Foot.*

Captain Abraham Captain of the *Patricia,* sent to tow the crippled *Archimedes* to safety after the hurricane; he resolves an impasse over authority with Captain Edwardes by kneeling to make his assurances in Richard Hughes's *In Hazard.*

Mrs. Abramowitz An effusive button-shop proprietor in Joe's neighborhood with a knack for cheek-pinching unparalleled in Wolf Mankowitz's *A Kid for Two Farthings.*

David Abravanel Egyptian Jewish lawyer to Mrs. Khoury and father of Leah Strauss; he advises Mrs. Khoury to put her possessions in his name to avoid their confiscation by the Egyptian government; he dies in his sleep in P. H. Newby's *Something to Answer For.*

Paul Abreskov Young, elegant Russian turned Bolshevik; he is determined to capture Princess Sakskia and her jewels and take her back to Russia; he drowns in a storm in John Buchan's *Huntingtower.*

AbstrogAthenat JanolAngand's personal priest who advocates the union with Oldorando in Brian W. Aldiss's *Helliconia Summer.*

Achon Emperor Seth's uncle who, although the legitimate heir to the throne, has been kept prisoner for many years in a remote monastery; when he is released by the combined military forces of General Connolly and the Earl of Ngumo and is crowned Emperor, the strain becomes so great that he collapses and dies in Evelyn Waugh's *Black Mischief.*

Mrs. Cecil Ackroyd Roger Ackroyd's widowed sister-in-law; she and her daughter, Flora, live in financial dependence upon him at Fernly Park in Agatha Christie's *The Murder of Roger Ackroyd.*

Flora Ackroyd Niece of Roger Ackroyd, whose will leaves her £20,000 in Agatha Christie's *The Murder of Roger Ackroyd.*

Roger Ackroyd Successful manufacturer turned country squire; he is murdered in his study at Fernly Park in Agatha Christie's *The Murder of Roger Ackroyd.*

Acky Mercenary unfrocked clergyman and owner of a "short-time" house who finds consolation for his betrayals through his grotesque wife's genuine affection for him in Graham Greene's *A Gun for Sale.*

Ada Servant girl; having grown up in Hilda Lessways

Clayhanger's service, she criticizes her demanding mistress and leaves with no notice, confirming Edwin Clayhanger's judgment of Hilda as an incompetent household manager in Arnold Bennett's *These Twain*.

Ada   Manager of the seedy Golden Peach Club, where Arthur Blearney gives Charles Lumley a job as a bouncer when he is down on his luck in John Wain's *Hurry On Down*.

Aunt Ada   Arthur Seaton's aunt, who tells him what to tell a woman to do to have a miscarriage in Alan Sillitoe's *Saturday Night and Sunday Morning*.

Queen of Adalantaland   A ruler who lives no better than her subjects; she tells Ambien II all that she knows of her people's history and their many laws — most of which were given them by the Canopians in Doris Lessing's *The Sirian Experiments*.

Father Adam   Constant companion of Dean Jocelin, who refers to him as "Father Anonymous" in William Golding's *The Spire*.

Miss Adam   The young lecturer in history at the women's college that Dolores Hutton attends in Ivy Compton-Burnett's *Dolores*.

Sir Adam   A rich Jew whom Lucy, Sebastian's mother, considers marrying in Vita Sackville-West's *The Edwardians*.

Adams   Coroner's Clerk who investigates the death of Percy Higgins in David Lodge's *Ginger, You're Barmy*.

Dr. Adams   Country physician who drives the child Lucy Cane to take Hazel back from Nuthanger Farm to the Down in Richard Adams's *Watership Down*.

Geoffrey Adams   Cousin of Elizabeth Trelone; he is an East End preacher who befriends Sirius, broadens his experience with human nature, and allows him to sing in his church; Adams is later killed in the World War II bombing of London in Olaf Stapledon's *Sirius: A Fantasy of Love and Discord*.

George Adams   Handiman afflicted by advancing age and senility in Henry Green's *Concluding*.

Robin Adams   Fiancé of Angela Crevy; he is jealous of and disgusted by Angela's wealthy new friends in Henry Green's *Party Going*.

Ken Adamson   Attractive, well-mannered patient in Clive Ward who is popular with other patients and the nursing staff; in the hospital because of a car accident, he is concerned about his souring marriage to Maevis

and his dubious involvement in the traffic accident that resulted in the death of a motorcyclist in John Berger's *The Foot of Clive*.

Maevis (Maeve) Adamson   Beautiful model and wife of Ken Adamson; pampered, indolent, and self-centered, she visits Ken only once in the hospital in John Berger's *The Foot of Clive*.

(Sparks) Adcock   The radio operator who signs on with Captain Bennett to go on an unknown mission for good pay and is the only person who survives the experience; he is narrator of Alan Sillitoe's *The Lost Flying Boat*.

Charles Addinsell   Arthur Middleton's oldest friend; he becomes successively involved with Arthur's wife Diana, Arthur's younger love interest Annabel Paynton, and Annabel's close friend Clair Belaine in Henry Green's *Doting*.

Adela   The nurse for Sefton and Clemence Shelley; she is kind, trustworthy, and attached to the children in Ivy Compton-Burnett's *Two Worlds and Their Ways*.

Adela   Josephine Napier's maid in Ivy Compton-Burnett's *More Women Than Men*.

Adela   Emma Greatheart's maid who says that she never lays a finger on anything dead in Ivy Compton-Burnett's *Mother and Son*.

Aderyn the Bird Queen   Llewellyn's apparent mother, a Welsh women famous for her trained bird act in a traveling circus; she is uneducated but shrewd and ambitious in Anthony Burgess's *MF*.

Max Adey   Fabulously wealthy young man, who plans and pays for the fog-delayed holiday of his friends; he is torn between loving Julia Wray and Amabel in Henry Green's *Party Going*.

Adlan   Supernormal being, an Egyptian who lives nearly four hundred years and, thirty-five years after his death, makes telepathic contact with John Wainwright, influencing the establishment of John's colony in Olaf Stapledon's *Odd John: A Story Between Jest and Earnest*.

Joe Adler   An American looking for a good time and finding it with Laurie Gaynor in Jean Rhys's *Voyage in the Dark*.

Adolph   Servant who accompanies Swithin Forsyte on a drive with Irene Forsyte to the site of Soames Forsyte's country house in John Galsworthy's *The Man of Property*.

Monsieur Adolphe Perfectly attired, rosy-cheeked, cosmopolitan Reception-Manager in Arnold Bennett's *Imperial Palace*

Andy Adorno Weekend guest of Celia and Quentin Villiers and boyfriend of Diane Parry; he is rowdy, aggressive, and obsessed with his macho image; a number of perverse and violent acts, culminating in murder, are committed during a decadent weekend in the country, and Andy turns out to be the perpetrator in Martin Amis's *Dead Babies*.

Adrian Man involved in a brief relationship with Kate Fletcher Armstrong in Margaret Drabble's *The Middle Ground*.

Adrian Friend of Imogene King in Isabel Colegate's *Orlando at the Brazen Threshold*. Adrian becomes Imogene's lover in *Agatha*.

Irene Aldwinkle Lilian Aldwinkle's frank but naïve niece, to whom Lord Hovenden proposes in Aldous Huxley's *Those Barren Leaves*.

Colonel Adye Port Burdock Chief of Police and friend of Dr. Kemp; he is shot by Griffin while trying to prevent Griffin's murder of Kemp in H. G. Wells's *The Invisible Man: A Grotesque Romance*.

A. E. See George Russell.

A Few Fleas Son of Roman Diosdado and barman at the Farolito in Malcolm Lowry's *Under the Volcano*.

Jackie Afflick Good-humoredly vulgar owner of a coach-tour business in Agatha Christie's *Sleeping Murder*.

Colonel the Right Honourable Sir Rupert Afflock, M.P., J.P., F.R.S. Eminently versatile Secretary of War; he is humiliated by Lord Raingo and schemes to bring about Raingo's defensive speech in the House of Lords which seriously taxes Raingo's heart in Arnold Bennett's *Lord Raingo*.

Africana The somewhat physically disadvantaged kid goat passed off as a wish-granting, magical unicorn; it becomes the source of fantasy-play and the imaginary panacea to more mature, adult wants and aspirations in young Joe's world in Wolf Mankowitz's *A Kid for Two Farthings*.

Sergeant Julian Agate Flagrantly homosexual soldier in Sergeant Richard Ennis's unit; he becomes Ennis's friend and roommate but not lover; upbeat and irresponsible, Agate flaunts his homosexuality in Anthony Burgess's *A Vision of Battlements*.

Agnes The Heriots' under-housemaid who fell because of the broken back steps in Ivy Compton-Burnett's *The Last and the First*.

Agnew Mortuary superintendent who helps Morgan perform the autopsy on the body of Lady Ashbrook in C. P. Snow's *A Coat of Varnish*.

Agrippinilla Claudius's niece and mother of Nero; after marrying Claudius, she rules Rome in his stead, finally poisoning him to make way for Nero's accession in Robert Graves's *Claudius, the God and His Wife Messalina*.

The Agronomist Friend of the Colonel; given custody of the Cartographer ostensibly because of his horticultural skills, he sets him free to spare the Colonel the difficulty of a trial at which the Cartographer was to be the principal witness in Nigel Dennis's *A House in Order*.

Ahmed A Turkish man working at the hotel in Istanbul where the Global Foods conference is going on; assigned to assist Kate Brown, he innately understands her role as "nanny" and its similarity to his own role in Doris Lessing's *The Summer Before the Dark*.

Godfrey Ailwyn Priest who notifies Lewis and Margaret (Hollis) Eliot that Maurice Hollis plans to marry in C. P. Snow's *Last Things*.

Ainger The sometimes facetious butler to the Middletons; he gossips and eavesdrops on the family in Ivy Compton-Burnett's *The Mighty and Their Fall*.

Alfred Ainger The butler to the Clare family; he identifies with Cassius Clare, the master, and advises the family not to call for a doctor when Cassius seems to be making a second pseudo-suicide attempt in Ivy Compton-Burnett's *The Present and the Past*.

Air Vice Marshall Structured, determined, controlling speaker; glimpses of humanity show through his intimidating exterior in Rex Warner's *The Aerodrome: A Love Story*.

Alice Aisgill Handsome, passionate, affectionate, empty woman, whose husband no longer loves her but will not divorce her; she is lonely until she meets Joe Lampton; their breakup results in her suicidal death by auto "accident" in John Braine's *Room at the Top*. She is the subject of talk in *Life at the Top*.

George Aisgill Controlling, conservative, sarcastic woolman; he does not like his wife Alice's friends and does not love her in John Braine's *Room at the Top*. He is an upstanding and strange man in the community in *Life at the Top*.

Aïssa Malay mistress of Peter Willems; she murders him out of jealousy over his wife in Joseph Conrad's *An Outcast of the Islands*.

Mr. Aitken Scots landing agent for a mining firm in Africa; he helps subdue the native uprising and finds the diamond pipe in John Buchan's *Prester John*.

Ajali Store clerk in Sergeant Gollup's General Store who likes and at the same time despises Johnson; he is a witness against Johnson in the murder of Gollup in Joyce Cary's *Mister Johnson*.

Adeline Aked Small, dark-haired, grey-eyed orphan; her solitary youth and her inheritance from an uncle give her an independence of mind which surprises Richard Larch when he fails her test of love in Arnold Bennett's *A Man From the North*.

Richard Aked Elderly, thin, intense former solicitor's clerk and uncle of Adeline Aked; his erratic enthusiasms fire Richard Larch's literary ambitions until Larch recognizes that neither the old man nor he will ever achieve significant authorship in Arnold Bennett's *A Man From the North*.

Professor Alabaster Art critic who plans to write a biography of Gulley Jimson in Joyce Cary's *The Horse's Mouth*.

Alamanack Jack Former wealthy textile designer who chooses to become a street philosopher and is befriended by Michael Cullen in Alan Sillitoe's *A Start in Life*.

Catharine Alan Elderly spinster who travels to Italy with her sister, Teresa, in E. M. Forster's *A Room with a View*.

Teresa Alan Elderly spinster who travels to Italy with her sister, Catharine, in E. M. Forster's *A Room with a View*.

Alastair ("Long Al") Charlie's alcoholic, chauvinistic lover, who physically and mentally abuses her and is mysteriously summoned back to England by an Israeli device so that Gadi Becker can entice Charlie away from her theatrical family in John le Carré's *The Little Drummer Girl*.

Frank Alban Jacqueline Armine's brother; he leaves his slum parish in Birkpool for a pulpit guaranteed to make him an "important figure in the Church" in John Buchan's *A Prince of the Captivity*.

Captain Alberic The estranged husband, a reported "wrong 'un", of Eustace Cherrington's old friend, Nancy Steptoe, from whom she is separated when Eustace meets her again in Venice in L. P. Hartley's *Eustace and Hilda*.

Albert One of the circle of Hunt's people whom Kate Fletcher (Armstrong) found interesting when she was aged sixteen; he is "lank, silent, vain" in Margaret Drabble's *The Middle Ground*.

Mr. d'Alcacer Embassy official who loved a young woman who died; he accompanies Mr. and Mrs. Travers on the *Hermit* to Batavia and secretly admires Edith Travers in Joseph Conrad's *The Rescue: A Romance of the Shallows*.

François Alcasan French radiologist, executed for poisoning his wife; his head is recused by the N.I.C.E. (National Institute for Coordinated Experiments) and becomes the medium of communication between the Macrobes and the inner circle of the N.I.C.E. in C. S. Lewis's *That Hideous Strength*.

Aldom The manservant of the Shelleys; he mimics family visitors for the children's amusement; he is the unacknowledged natural son of Sir Roderick Shelley in Ivy Compton-Burnett's *Two Worlds and Their Ways*.

Mrs. Aldom The mother of the Shelleys' manservant by Sir Roderick Shelley; she is now willing to sell back the Shelleys' farm in order to be able to move to town in Ivy Compton-Burnett's *Two Worlds and Their Ways*.

Lillian Aldwinkle Aging, self-styled patron of the arts and hostess in her Italian villa to a myriad of guests; after rescuing the poet Francis Chelifer from a water accident, she makes preposterous advances to him which he skillfully avoids in Aldous Huxley's *Those Barren Leaves*.

Alehaw Yuli's father, who teaches Yuli to hunt and is killed by the phagors in Brian W. Aldiss's *Helliconia Spring*.

Alex Working-class graduate of a Corrective School; ignorant and violent, yet surprisingly intelligent and sensitive to serious music, he is the leader of a gang of young delinquents specializing in crimes of violence; he speaks a futuristic, degraded English intermixed with slang and vulgarized foreign words; extremely anti-social, he is temporarily reformed by a psychological treatment while in prison in Anthony Burgess's *A Clockwork Orange*.

Alex A friend of Rosamund Stacey; he writes copy

for an advertising agency in Margaret Drabble's *The Millstone*.

Alex Alexander   One of the wealthy socialites trapped in a fog-bound London railway station; his rudeness and lack of tact frequently annoy Angela Crevy and his other friends in Henry Green's *Party Going*.

F. Alexander   Upper-class author of the fictional book *A Clockwork Orange* and a slightly demented intellectual fanatically opposed to the current government; he and his wife have been the victims of robbery and rape at the hands of a gang of delinquests, and he rightly suspects Alex of having been the gang's leader in Anthony Burgess's *A Clockwork Orange*.

Mr. Lord Alexander   Singer and songwriter from Trinidad; he successfully performs on the radio and in cabarets in Colin MacInnes's *City of Spades*.

Alexandra   The daughter of Beatrice and Hallam and the niece of Rosamund Stacey in Margaret Drabble's *The Millstone*.

Sister Alexandra   Charismatic candidate in the election for Abbess who represents the old order even as she uses electronic devices to track her competitors in Muriel Spark's *The Abbess of Crewe*.

Dr. Paul Alexis   Official of the German Ministry of Interior and an Israeli sympathizer; he investigates the bombing at Bad Godesberg and is surprised when Marty Kurtz magically unravels the atrocity in John le Carré's *The Little Drummer Girl*.

Jeremy Alford   Rose Vassiliou's solicitor, who acts promptly to prevent the carrying out of Christopher Vassiliou's threat to take his children out of the country in Margaret Drabble's *The Needle's Eye*.

Alfred   Old professional waiter at Rules restaurant; he knew Sarah Miles and Maurice Bendrix from the days when their affair was active and they met at Rules in Graham Greene's *The End of the Affair*.

Alfred   A power-hungry fanatic; he is a leader of the rebellion whose jealousy leads to doubts about his goals in Rex Warner's *The Wild Goose Chase: An Allegory*.

Ali   House steward and manservant of Henry Scobie for fifteen years and brother of Vande; he serves Scobie well but provides Vande and thus Wilson with information about Scobie's affairs; he is murdered after Scobie informs Yusef of this in Graham Greene's *The Heart of the Matter*.

Mahmoud Ali   Pleader for Dr. Aziz's case at the trial in E. M. Forster's *A Passage to India*.

Alibai   An Indian graduate student in Adam Appleby's department; he is trying to decide on a thesis topic in David Lodge's *The British Museum Is Falling Down*.

Alice   A servant at Manderly in Daphne Du Maurier's *Rebecca*.

Alice   The Lovats' upper-housemaid, not as likeable as Tabitha; she is censorious about Sir Ransome Chace's having an illegitimate daughter in Ivy Compton-Burnett's *Darkness and Day*.

Alice   Dalby's secretary; her knowledge of espionage and W.O.O.C.(P.) documents and procedures helps the narrator piece together Dalby's duplicity in Len Deighton's *The Ipcress File*.

Alice   A widowed cousin of the Lovatt family; she acts as the children's short-term nanny in Doris Lessing's *The Fifth Child*.

Alice   Caroline Knowell's African nurse in Doris Lessing's *A Proper Marriage*.

Alice   The daughter of Lady O.; she is considered an acceptable marriage partner for Sebastian, master of Chevron, in Vita Sackville-West's *The Edwardians*.

Sophy Alingsby   A tall, weird, intense, colorful, well-connected friend of Lucia Lucas in E. F. Benson's *Lucia in London*.

Mr. Alington   Sophisticated, well-to-do wool merchant of Bruddersford, Yorkshire, who introduces Gregory Dawson to art, music, and literature in J. B. Priestley's *Bright Day*.

Mrs. Alington   Sophisticated, well-to-do wife of Mr. Alington; she and her husband introduce Gregory Dawson to art, music, and literature in J. B. Priestley's *Bright Day*.

Bridget Alington   A daughter of Mr. and Mrs. Alington in J. B. Priestley's *Bright Day*.

David Alington   The precocious son of Mr. and Mrs. Alington in J. B. Priestley's *Bright Day*.

Eva Alington   A daughter of Mr. and Mrs. Alington; she is revealed to have been pushed to death by her sister Joan in J. B. Priestley's *Bright Day*.

Joan Alington   The Alington daughter responsible

for the death of her sister Eva in J. B. Priestley's *Bright Day.*

Oliver Alington   Mr. and Mrs. Alington's son who dies in World War I in J. B. Priestley's *Bright Day.*

Lady Alison   Dean Jocelin's "courtesan" aunt, who has sacrificed herself sexually to obtain royal favors so that her nephew can achieve his goal of building a spire on Salisbury cathedral in William Golding's *The Spire.*

Al-Ith   The Queen of Zone Three who is told by the Providers that she must marry the savage King of Zone Four, whom she learns to love and respect, and with whom she has several children in Doris Lessing's *The Marriages Between Zones Three, Four, and Five.*

Aliu   Brave, stout brother of Bamu; he bargains with Johnson for his sister's hand in marriage, brings her back home after Johnson loses his government job, and turns Johnson over to the police for the murder of Gollup in Joyce Cary's *Mister Johnson.*

Miss Allan   Contented elderly teacher engaged in writing a short *Primer of English Literature* while on vacation at the Santa Marina Hotel; she offers Rachel Vinrace books, ginger, and conversation to no avail in Virginia Woolf's *The Voyage Out.*

Henry Allègre   Millionaire art connoisseur who establishes Doña Rita de Lastaola in Paris society, then dies, willing her his fortune in Joseph Conrad's *The Arrow of Gold: A Story Between Two Notes.*

Sir Percy Alleline (codename "Tinker")   Scottish-born, Cambridge-educated career spy and Operational Director who takes over as chief after Control's resignation in John le Carré's *Tinker, Tailor, Soldier, Spy.*

Allen   Lonely barrister who shares Lewis Elliot's room in Herbert Getliffe's chambers in C. P. Snow's *Time of Hope.*

Vera Allen   Secretary to Lewis Eliot; she asks Eliot to testify on behalf of the father of her lover, Norman Lacey, in C. P. Snow's *Homecomings.*

Major Allerton   A guest at Styles; attractive to women, he is detested by Arthur Hastings in Agatha Christie's *Curtain: Hercule Poirot's Last Case.*

Mr. Allington   Maurice Allington's common-sensical father; he sees that Joyce is unhappy in her marriage to Maurice and suspects that Maurice is interested in Diana Maybury; he dies of a cerebral hemorrhage after seeing an apparition in Kingsley Amis's *The Green Man.*

Amy Allington   The lonely, depressed, and withdrawn thirteen-year-old daughter of Maurice Allington by his first marriage; after her father saves her from the green man, a creature sent by Dr. Underhill to kill her, she wants to participate in life again in Kingsley Amis's *The Green Man.*

Joyce Allington   Maurice Allington's second wife, who feels that he has used and neglected her; after Allington arranges an orgy with her, Diana Maybury, and himself as participants, Joyce divorces him and leaves with Diana in Kingsley Amis's *The Green Man.*

Lucy Allington   Maurice Allington's daughter-in-law; she is practical and unemotional but believes that people can see ghosts in Kingsley Amis's *The Green Man.*

Margaret Allington   Maurice Allington's first wife and Amy Allington's mother; she was hit and killed by a car while crossing a street several months after a man with whom she was having an affair refused to leave his wife for her; Maurice's guilt over her death helps him to identify with Dr. Underhill, who killed his wife in Kingsley Amis's *The Green Man.*

Margaret Allington (Mrs. William Grey)   Lower-class, middle-aged married woman; blunt, maternal, practical, sympathetic, sallow-faced and poorly clothed, she is remembered by amnesiac Chris Baldry as beautiful and twenty-one; she reluctantly forces Chris to lose false happiness by recalling him to the reality of his son's death and to his marriage to a demanding and materialistic woman in Rebecca West's *The Return of the Soldier.*

Maurice Allington   The middle-aged proprietor of the Green Man inn and a manipulative, selfish adulterer who drinks excessively; he has difficulty relating to his wife and daughter and is afraid of death; after his encounters with God and the ghost of Thomas Underhill, he learns to be more sensitive to his daughter and accepts death in Kingsley Amis's *The Green Man.*

Nick Allington   Maurice Allington's son and an assistant lecturer in French literature at a university; he advises his wife, Lucy, to stop encouraging his father's interest in ghosts in Kingsley Amis's *The Green Man.*

Sigismund Allins   Confidential secretary of Thomas Carlyle Craw; he is a rogue and a gambler who boasts of his power with the Craw Press while doublecrossing the Evallonian Monarchists in John Buchan's *Castle Gay.*

Colonel Allison   The squeamish Chief Constable of Southbourne, where the murder takes place; he is nauseated by Jacko Jaques's betrayal of his friend Hugo Chesterton in Nicholas Blake's *A Tangled Web*.

Captain Allistoun   Captain of the *Narcissus* who survives a great storm off the Cape of Good Hope and confronts the rebellion of his crew in Joseph Conrad's *The Nigger of the "Narcissus"*.

Charlie Allnutt   A cockney mechanic in German-occupied Central Africa during World War I; he accompanies Rose Sayer on a boat down the Ulanga River on a doomed mission to torpedo a German ship in C. S. Forester's *The African Queen*.

Cassie Allsop   Visitor who jolts Alvina Houghton into realizing that she herself seems destined to be an old maid in D. H. Lawrence's *The Lost Girl*.

Mrs. Almayer   Malayan woman who betrays her husband, Kaspar Almayer, by arranging for their daughter Nina's marriage to a local rajah and deserts her husband in Joseph Conrad's *Almayer's Folly: A Story of an Eastern River*.

Kaspar Almayer   Dutch trader who marries Lingard's adopted Malay daughter for her dowry and dreams of finding a gold mine, but loses his daughter to Dain Maroola and ends his days in a half-finished mansion smoking opium in Joseph Conrad's *Almayer's Folly: A Story of an Eastern River*. He enters into an unsuccessful partnership with Peter Willems, who betrays the navigation of the River Pantai to the Arab trader Abdulla in *An Outcast of the Islands*.

Nina Almayer   Beautiful Eurasian daughter of Kaspar Almayer; she rejects the prejudiced society and education of white Europeans, marrying a Malayan rajah, Dain Maroola, and abandoning her father in Joseph Conrad's *Almayer's Folly: A Story of an Eastern River*.

Jackie Almond   John Connell's school friend who meets Sarah Bennett at a party and gallantly drives her home; he provides a potential but never an actual romantic affair for Sarah in Margaret Drabble's *A Summer Bird-Cage*.

Alsi   An eleven-year-old girl who shows extraordinary courage and willingness to survive the Ice; she assists the older representatives in trying to save the people and in assessing the progress of the glaciers in Doris Lessing's *The Making of the Representative for Planet 8*.

Herbert Alton   Famous caricaturist whose drawings of Philip and Lucia Lucas are exhibited at the Rutland Gallery in E. F. Benson's *Lucia in London*.

Don Julian (El Supremo) Maria de Jesus de Alvarada y Moctezuma   Tyrannical, crazed leader of Spanish rebel forces with whom Hornblower is to create an alliance and whom he later faces as an enemy in C. S. Forester's *The Happy Return*.

Amabel   The young, dramatically beautiful French girl Miriam Henderson meets at the women's club she has joined, who shows a decided (even slightly alarming) interest in a relationship with Miriam in Dorothy Richardson's *Dawn's Left Hand*. She moves into Mrs. Bailey's house and becomes the center of Miriam's emotional life, with the result that Miriam begins to feel the need to escape from intense involvements in *Clear Horizon*. Her marriage to Michael Shatov takes place in *Dimple Hill*, and Miriam sees that it is not altogether successful in *March Moonlight*.

Amabel   Incredibly rich and beautiful London socialite; she loves Max Adey and, though not asked, joins his fog-delayed holiday party in Henry Green's *Party Going*.

Claude Amaril   A womanizing doctor in Alexandria; he falls helplessly in love with a woman at a masquerade; unmasked, she proves to have lost her nose to disease; he determines to use his surgical skill to construct a nose for her and to make her his wife in Lawrence Durrell's *Mountolive*. The operation and marriage are successful; he also constructs a serviceable mechanical hand for Clea Montis in *Clea*.

Semira Amaril   Wife of the doctor Claude Amaril, whose wedding present to her is a rebuilt nose in Lawrence Durrell's *Mountolive*. She becomes a trained doll surgeon in *Clea*.

Amarylis   Art student with whom Stuart Armstrong had an affair that led to his divorce from Kate Fletcher Armstrong in Margaret Drabble's *The Middle Ground*.

Stephen Ambedkar   Rector of St. Luke's in Ranpur who also serves once a month as chaplain of St. John's Church in Pankot, where Frank Bhoolabhoy and Susy Williams are members; Ambedkar is on the verge of being replaced by Father Sebastian in Paul Scott's *Staying On*.

Hermes Ambelas   The donkey driver who works for Maurice Conchis at Bourani in John Fowles's *The Magus*.

Mary Amberley   Promiscuous mother of Helen Ledwidge and first lover of Anthony Beavis; her life is a chronicle of increasing decadence in Aldous Huxley's *Eyeless in Gaza*.

Gertrude Amberly Mark's puritanical wife with intellectual pretensions; Hugo Chesterton points a gun at her when she refuses to apologize for calling his lover a "moronic shop girl" in Nicholas Blake's *A Tangled Web*.

Mark Amberly The estranged brother of Hugo Chesterton; an extension lecturer at London University and a chaser of lost causes, he wishes to reform his brother in Nicholas Blake's *A Tangled Web*.

Cornelia, Lady Ambermere Arrogant, patronizing, aristocratic widow; she expects everyone to be silent when she speaks in E. F. Benson's *"Queen Lucia"*. Only Lucia Lucas dares to assume the task of rejecting her gift to the Riseholme Museum of the stuffed body of her dead lapdog in *Lucia in London*.

Richard (Dicky) Ambermere Aristocrat and friend of Sebastian in Vita Sackville-West's *The Edwardians*.

Ambien I Ambien II's mate who was on the committee to decide what work the Sirians should be doing on Rohanda (Shikasta); he goes on a spy tour across Rohanda, looking for any information that he can find about Canopian progress on the planet in Doris Lessing's *The Sirian Experiments*.

Ambien II One of the five rulers of the Sirian Empire; before becoming a great expert on Canopian wisdom, she must first learn from the Canopian agent Klorathy to understand that Canopus is not only a planet with high intentions and morals, but one which the Sirians should trust and follow in Doris Lessing's *The Sirian Experiments*.

Ambrose The Lovats' sententious butler with a gray face and jutting bones; he tries to be the authority to and moral arbiter of the Lovats' servants in Ivy Compton-Burnett's *Darkness and Day*.

Ambrose Alienated, expatriate, homosexual Englishman who builds a house on a Greek island and tries to establish a homosexual enclave in Christopher Isherwood's *Down There on a Visit*.

Ambrose Petty officer aboard the *Renown* in C. S. Forester's *Lieutenant Hornblower*.

Detective-Sergeant Ambrose Impassive police investigator who arrests Cliff Sanders for trying to exploit his sister Julia Delmore's absence by claiming to be a go-between in a kidnapping plot; he is a character in the story novelist Giles Hermitage writes in John Wain's *The Pardoner's Tale*.

Helen Ambrose Rachel Vinrace's aunt, surrogate mother, dream lover/confidante/friend, and guide; Helen, the "angel of the house", orchestrates the Villa Santa Gervasio and Rachel's world in Santa Marina; vacillating between roles as omniscient, omnipotent visionary deity and human with limited insight evidenced by her rejection of ideal or religion, Helen is the creator of one path to vision for Rachel with enough foresight to foretell her tragic end in Virginia Woolf's *The Voyage Out*.

Ridley Ambrose Rachel Vinrace's scholarly, self-absorbed uncle, with whom she lives in South America; translating Pindar's odes in his private room/world, Ridley represents single-minded, obsessive devotion to thought and to cold fact in contrast to the imaginative vision embodied by his wife, Helen, in Virginia Woolf's *The Voyage Out*.

Amelie Half-caste servant of Antoinette Cosway after Antoinette's marriage to Mr. Rochester; she brings Daniel Cosway's letters to Rochester and sleeps with Rochester in Jean Rhys's *Wide Sargasso Sea*.

Mrs. Amerson Mother of Jerrard Amerson; she lives with her son and his family in Frank Swinnerton's *The Happy Family*.

Alice Rodwell Amerson Demanding and unsympathetic wife of Jerrard Amerson and mother of five children; she is condemned by her mother-in-law for killing Jerrard by turning him into a machine to satisfy her demands at the end of Frank Swinnerton's *The Happy Family*.

Edward (Teddy) Amerson Youngest son of Jerrard and Alice Amerson; he divides his time between his work as an invoice clerk at Tremlett & Grove's, a publishing firm, and his amateur theatricals in Frank Swinnerton's *The Happy Family*.

Grace Amerson Eldest daughter of Jerrard and Alice Amerson; Grace has made a respectable match with Edwin Gower, son of a prosperous local builder, at the opening of Frank Swinnerton's *The Happy Family*.

Jerrard Amerson Self-educated and self-reliant manager at the printing firm Dickertons, who began as a messenger boy; his marriage to his cousin Alice, after its first bloom, is joyless; he has thrown himself into his work and dies prematurely in Frank Swinnerton's *The Happy Family*.

Mabel Amerson Middle daughter of Jerrard and Alice Amerson; she becomes sexually involved with Bert Moggerson, her fiancé, alienating her family in Frank Swinnerton's *The Happy Family*.

Mary Amerson   Youngest of the Amerson children; she gets the brunt of the family criticism; she becomes engaged to Septimus Bright to escape her family, but later chooses Roger Dennett, whom she really loves, in Frank Swinnerton's *The Happy Family*.

Tom Amerson   Eldest of the Amerson children; like his father, he works at Dickertons printing firm; he becomes head of the household after his father's death in Frank Swinnerton's *The Happy Family*.

Father Amerton   Hypocritical, prurient-minded clergyman who denounces the Utopians as promiscuous sinners and becomes a vocal supporter of Rupert Catskill's plan to conquer them in H. G. Wells's *Men Like Gods*.

Lieutenant Amin   Seemingly mild and controlled police officer who is well liked by Jack Townrow even though he arrests Townrow on charges of espionage and murder; he jumps from a train window and is killed by a British soldier in P. H. Newby's *Something to Answer For*.

Martin Amis   A struggling author and screenwriter in Martin Amis's *Money*.

Ammatter   German scholar who arranges for Roy Calvert's lecture in Berlin in C. P. Snow's *The Light and the Dark*.

Andrew Amos   Loyal Scots patriot and pillar of an intelligence service in World War I; he is Richard Hannay's intelligence contact in Glasgow and the Scottish Highlands in John Buchan's *Mr. Standfast*. He is one of Adam Melfort's instructors and a "watch-dog" in his intelligence training as an undercover agent in World War I in *A Prince of the Captivity*.

Amy   Sarah and William's youngest child, a Down's Syndrome victim, who is loved and cared for by the entire family in Doris Lessing's *The Fifth Child*.

Ana   The church-going secretary of Dr. Eduardo Plarr in Graham Greene's *The Honorary Consul*.

Bettie Mae Anapoupolis   Friend of Elsinore briefly encountered by Eva Trout in a midwestern American city; her father, who is also present, knows of Willy Trout by reputation; he also delivers a prophetic tirade against the questionable practice of adoption rings on the eve of Eva's adoption of Jeremy in Elizabeth Bowen's *Eva Trout, or Changing Scenes*.

Anatole   Tom and Dahlia Travers's French cook, for whose art Bertie Wooster is readily corrupted in P. G.

Wodehouse's *The Code of the Woosters* and in *Aunts Aren't Gentlemen*. He appears in four other novels.

Colonel Anderson   Pessimistic Chief Constable in Agatha Christie's *The A.B.C. Murders*.

Mr. Anderson   A silent, morose hypochondriac, who is a past government official in Doris Lessing's *Martha Quest*.

Mrs. Anderson   Donovan Anderson's mother, who knew Martha Quest's mother; she is patronized by Donovan in Doris Lessing's *Martha Quest*.

Crispin (Smog) Anderson   Son of Bridgitte Appledore's former husband; he attaches himself to Bridgitte and Michael Cullen in Alan Sillitoe's *A Start in Life*.

Donovan Anderson   A young man from a wealthy family who becomes Martha Quest's first serious romantic interest in Doris Lessing's *Martha Quest*. He also appears in *A Proper Marriage*.

Dr. Gilbert Anderson   Specialist in shell-shock who recognizes that Chris Baldry's unconscious refuses to admit the truth of the last fifteen years; his cure forces Chris into a life of suffering in Rebecca West's *The Return of the Soldier*.

Hubert Anderson   Acquaintance of the Westons; he marries Cicely Carmichael in Isabel Colegate's *Statues in a Garden*.

Nick (Nicky) Anderson   Francis Coldridge's school friend who, after being brutally beaten by police at a demonstration, becomes politically active before his entire family is killed in Doris Lessing's *The Four-Gated City*.

Palmer Anderson   An American psychoanalyst of independent means; he is Honor Klein's half brother and lover, the lover of his patient Antonia Lynch-Gibbon, and the protector of Georgie Hands, with whom he leaves for America at the end of Iris Murdoch's *A Severed Head*.

Steve Anderson   An American film star who tries to seduce Jenny McNeil and figures in her fictional account of her experiences in Hollywood in John Fowles's *Daniel Martin*.

Andrea   A Polish production secretary with whom Daniel Martin has a two-year affair; she commits suicide several years later in John Fowles's *Daniel Martin*.

Andrea Servant in Count Caloveglia's household in Norman Douglas's *South Wind.*

Andrei Andreiech Narrator of the novel; once Nina Bursanov's fiancé, he has enlisted in the Navy and is a friend and frequent guest of the Bursanov family in William Gerhardie's *Futility: A Novel on Russian Themes.*

Countess Helena (Elena) Andrenyi Beautiful, exotic passenger on the Calais Coach; she is proved to be the daughter of Caroline Martha Hubbard and the aunt of Daisy Armstrong in Agatha Christie's *Murder on the Orient Express.*

Count Rudolph Andrenyi Hungarian husband of Helena in Agatha Christie's *Murder on the Orient Express.*

Lieutenant Andrews Young officer who is attacked by one of his own men after brutally interrogating three black political suspects caught in a military police operation in an African colony experiencing Mau Mau-like activities; he sustains a fractured skull, from which injury he dies in Roy Fuller's *The Father's Comedy.*

Francis Andrews Smuggler on the run from his gang after he has informed on them, having been continually ridiculed for his lack of daring, especially as compared to his father, now deceased; he falls in love with Elizabeth and testifies against the smugglers, but later saves the smugglers' leader, Carlyon, by falsely confessing to the murder of Elizabeth in Graham Greene's *The Man Within.*

Hamish Andrews Cambridge student and old boy-friend of Rosamund Stacey; he once attempted to check into a hotel with Rosamund in Margaret Drabble's *The Millstone.*

Milly Andriadis An often-married society hostess with a cockney accent; said to have been a king's mistress, she is briefly Charles Stringham's in Anthony Powell's *A Buyer's Market.* She is thought to be having an affair with the German Trotskyist Guggenbühl in *The Acceptance World.* Her goings on are discussed in *Casanova's Chinese Restaurant,* in *The Kindly Ones,* in *The Valley of Bones,* and in *The Military Philosophers.* Her death is mentioned in *Hearing Secret Harmonies.*

Angel Chief of a British broadcasting group that comes to interview Gilbert Pinfold at his home; he is later identified by Pinfold as the leader of the hallucinatory voices in Evelyn Waugh's *The Ordeal of Gilbert Pinfold.*

Angela A blonde, beautiful, virtuous Catholic; she marries Dennis after a long engagement and has sev-

eral children, one of whom has Down's Syndrome and another of whom is killed by a van; she first breaks with and then forgives Dennis after he has an affair in David Lodge's *How Far Can You Go?.*

Angela A relative of the Lovatts who is married and has three children in Doris Lessing's *The Fifth Child.*

Angelina Flirtatious fifteen-year-old beauty who serves as the Duchess's handmaiden in Norman Douglas's *South Wind.*

Anna Servant in the Hanover school run by Fraulein Pfaff; she is dismissed under a cloud and in a violent scene in Dorothy Richardson's *Pointed Roofs.*

Anna Niece of the Butcher (Giorgio) and lover of and co-terrorist with Robert Leaver in Muriel Spark's *Territorial Rights.*

Lady Crystabel Annable An earl's niece once sexually infatuated with the curate Frank Annable; her humiliating indifference after three years of marriage has driven him to flight in D. H. Lawrence's *The White Peacock.*

Frank Annable An educated ex-parson, now a gamekeeper; he is an embittered misogynist hated by the countryfolk; his "death by misadventure" may be an act of revenge in D. H. Lawrence's *The White Peacock.*

Poll Annable Frank Annable's second wife and widow, a slatternly but devoted countrywoman and mother of several small children in D. H. Lawrence's *The White Peacock.*

Sam Annable One of the many young children of the gamekeeper's union to an uneducated countrywoman; after his discovery of his father's body he becomes recklessly delinquent until befriended by Emily Saxton in D. H. Lawrence's *The White Peacock.*

Anne The more frankly sexual and less talented of the two girls who live with Henry Breasley, who has nicknamed her "the Freak" in John Fowles's *The Ebony Tower.*

Anne Marie Young peasant-girl friend of Orlando King while he lives with Professor King on the remote French island in Isabel Colegate's *Orlando King.*

Annie Daughter/serving girl in the Collopy household who may be leading a double life in Flann O'Brien's *The Hard Life.*

Aunt Annie Ferdinand Clegg's aunt, whose stifling moral attitudes have helped to mold him into the repressed deviant he has become in John Fowles's *The Collector*.

Count Ann-Jules   Dark-featured young courtier of Pisuerga and brother of Blanche de Lambese; Olga Blumenghast pines in vain for him in Ronald Firbank's *The Flower Beneath the Foot*.

Leonard Anquetil   A traveler and explorer invited into the Chevron circle; he becomes the confidant of both Viola and Sebastian, encouraging both to break free of the demands of Chevron and live a wider life; he becomes engaged to Viola in Vita Sackville-West's *The Edwardians*. He and his wife, Viola, visit Miles Vane-Merrick in Kent in *Family History*.

Lesley Anquetil   Daughter of Viola and Leonard Anquetil; she comes with her family to visit Miles Vane-Merrick in Kent; calm and self-contained at eighteen, she is a detached critic of society; Miles is attracted to her and confides in her after the end of his affair with Evelyn Jarrold in Vita Sackville-West's *Family History*.

Paul Anquetil   Son of Viola and Leonard Anquetil; Paul, who is Dan Jarrold's age, comes with his parents to visit Miles Vane-Merrick in Kent in Vita Sackville-West's *Family History*.

Viola Anquetil   See Viola.

Maud Ansell   Stewart Ansell's kind, helpful sister in E. M. Forster's *The Longest Journey*.

Stella Ansell   A balding Lesbian painter who mistakes Daniel Boleyn for a model and forces him to strip and pose; she is a typical illustration of Pierpoint's "Apes of God" theory in Wyndham Lewis's *The Apes of God*.

Stewart Ansell   Rickie Elliott's scholarly Cambridge friend in E. M. Forster's *The Longest Journey*.

Father Anselm   The sacristan of Salisbury Cathedral and an old friend of Dean Jocelin, although their "rope of friendship has grown thin" in William Golding's *The Spire*.

Ansit   Wife of Bardia, Captain of the Royal Guard in the land of Glome; she confronts Orual after Bardia's death and castigates Orual for her possessiveness of Bardia; her criticism contributes to Orual's self-knowledge in C. S. Lewis's *Till We Have Faces*.

Wilfred Anstey   Mystically inclined, charismatic, but ultimately shallow warden of Toynton Grange, a private nursing home; he believes himself to have been miraculously cured of multiple sclerosis at Lourdes,

although in fact he was misdiagnosed in P. D. James's *The Black Tower*.

Anthony   Adela Quested's rude servant, who tries to blackmail her in E. M. Forster's *A Passage to India*.

Father Anthony   Priest who takes a disliking to Tarry Flynn and urges him to confession, where he recommends that Tarry stop reading Shaw in Patrick Kavanagh's *Tarry Flynn*.

Mrs. Anthony   A Bestwood neighbor of the Morels; she makes money by seaming stockings; after William Morel tears her son Alfy's collar, she complains, triggering a domestic quarrel between Mr. and Mrs. Morel in D. H. Lawrence's *Sons and Lovers*.

Mrs. Anthony   Cook and housekeeper for Godfrey and Charmian Colston in Muriel Spark's *Memento Mori*.

Alfred (Alfy) Anthony   A Bestwood child who steals a "cobbler" from young William Morel; his mother complains to the Morels that William has retaliated by tearing her son's collar in D. H. Lawrence's *Sons and Lovers*.

Campbell Anthony   Young poet in whom Annabel Paynton is mildly interested; he is editing a volume of love poetry entitled "Doting" in Henry Green's *Doting*.

Flora de Barral Anthony   Daughter of the banker de Barral; rescued from suicidal despondency, she marries Captain Roderick Anthony, whom her father attempts unsuccessfully to poison, but loses him in a storm in Joseph Conrad's *Chance: A Tale in Two Parts*.

Roderick Anthony   Ship's captain who rescues Flora de Barral from suicide, marries her, and escapes poisoning by her jealous father, but dies in a shipwreck in Joseph Conrad's *Chance: A Tale in Two Parts*.

Mr. Antoine   A fair-haired dancing partner, colleague to the late Paul Alexis Goldschmidt; he consoles Flora Weldon with courtship in Dorothy L. Sayers's *Have His Carcase*.

Antoinette   A shallow art student, who introduces Miranda Grey to George Paston and sleeps with Paston in John Fowles's *The Collector*.

Antonia   Irishwoman long in love with her cousin Guy; she inherited not only his estate, Montefort, when he died in France but also responsibility for his fiancée in Elizabeth Bowen's *A World of Love*.

Antonio   A perverted philosophical historian; he

tries to create his own culture with cruelty and hypocrisy in Rex Warner's *The Wild Goose Chase: An Allegory.*

Mrs. Antrobus Hard-of-hearing mother of Goosie and Piggy Antrobus; she wields an ear trumpet in E. F. Benson's *"Queen Lucia"* and in *Lucia in London.* She is called Mrs. Arbuthnot in *Mapp and Lucia.* Mrs. Antrobus has taken up sign language in *Trouble for Lucia.*

Goosie Antrobus Energetic unmarried daughter of Mrs. Antrobus; she and her sister, Piggy, gambol on the town green in the hope of attracting Colonel Boucher in E. F. Benson's *"Queen Lucia".* She also appears in *Lucia in London,* in *Mapp and Lucia,* and in *Trouble for Lucia.*

Piggy Antrobus Mrs. Antrobus's unmarried daughter who once pursued Georgie Pillson; she and her sister, Goosie, attempt to attract Colonel Boucher in E. F. Benson's *"Queen Lucia".* She also appears in *Lucia in London,* in *Mapp and Lucia,* and in *Trouble for Lucia.*

David ("Red Davie") Antropus Militant pacifist, nihilist, and Clydeside Member of Parliament; he identifies Anton Mastrovin for John Galt, "Jaikie", in John Buchan's *Castle Gay.*

Anya An Austrian girl training in the hotel business and acting as nurse to Kate Brown at the London hotel where Kate stays after leaving Spain in Doris Lessing's *The Summer Before the Dark.*

Ao Ling Rebellious young Chinese who, having found meaning in Communism and having served in the Red Army, has shipped aboard the *Archimedes* with forged identification to evade capture by the authorities; so informed, Captain Edwardes has him arrested during the hurricane to help quell a mutiny imagined by Mr. Soutar in Richard Hughes's *In Hazard.*

Mrs. Ape A hypocritical American evangelist whose principal interest is financial gain in Evelyn Waugh's *Vile Bodies.*

Adam Appleby A Catholic graduate student in English married to Barbara Appleby; he is having trouble completing his dissertation at the British Museum and lives in fear that his wife is pregnant for the fourth time, since the Safe Method has failed them so far; he resists the temptation of Virginia Rottingdean, causes a fire scare at the British Museum, and is offered a job by Bernie Schnitz in David Lodge's *The British Museum Is Falling Down.*

Barbara Appleby The Catholic wife of graduate student Adam Appleby and a mother of three; she fears that the Safe Method has failed them again and that she may be pregnant a fourth time; she goes in search of Adam at the British Museum when she hears it is on fire in David Lodge's *The British Museum Is Falling Down.*

Clare Appleby The precocious and talkative three-year-old daughter of Adam and Barbara Appleby in David Lodge's *The British Museum Is Falling Down.*

Bridgitte Appledore Dutch au pair girl who becomes Michael Cullen's lover and eventually his wife in Alan Sillitoe's *A Start in Life.*

Applethwaite Sculptress from whose studio Jeremy Trout is taken by Iseult Arble in a kidnapping scare in Elizabeth Bowen's *Eva Trout, or Changing Scenes.*

Mrs. Appleton Percy's inflexible, straight-laced mother, who accuses the schoolmaster Anthony Neale of putting ideas into her boy's head; she finally complains to the headmaster about him in C. Day Lewis's *Starting Point.*

Percy Appleton An aggressive and well-read Communist student who succeeds, with his brother Ted, in persuading his schoolmaster Anthony Neale to join the Party in C. Day Lewis's *Starting Point.*

Ted Appleton Percy's brother and fellow Communist in C. Day Lewis's *Starting Point.*

Appleyard Gunner on the flying boat who is shot as the plane ascends with the gold by another treasure hunter on the search for Nazi gold in Alan Sillitoe's *The Lost Flying Boat.*

Aqil One of three soldiers who accompany Robert Winter into the desert in P. H. Newby's *A Journey to the Interior.*

Aquino Member of Leon Rivas's guerrilla band who has lost two fingers in a Paraguayan prison; he is almost tricked into letting Charley Fortnum escape in Graham Greene's *The Honorary Consul.*

Koré ("Corrie") Arabin A "modern" girl; she confides to Sir Edward Leithen her fear of what she must endure as heiress to the Greek island of Plakos with its corrupt House; she and Vernon Milburne survive a test which saves both their lives and makes them aware of their mutual love in John Buchan's *The Dancing Floor.*

Arachnoids A crab-like alien species, most adept at engineering and other activities that involve practical intelligence, who eventually form a telepathic union with the Ichthyoids to create a symbiotic species in Olaf Stapledon's *Star Maker*.

Aragorn (Strider)   Young, brave friend of Gandalf who befriends Frodo Baggins and joins the fellowship of the rings; he leads the group after Gandalf is killed in the mines of Moria in J. R. R. Tolkien's *The Fellowship of the Ring*. He helps defeat Sauron's armies and claims his rightful title of King Elessar and marries Lady Arwen in *The Return of the King*.

Second-Lieutenant Aranjuez   Son of a Protestant minister; he serves in Major Christopher Tietjens's battalion; his eye is shot out as Tietjens carries him to safety through enemy bullets in Ford Madox Ford's *A Man Could Stand Up* —.

Peregrine Arbelow   An alcoholic Irish actor, now playing fat TV villains; he has long concealed his jealous hatred of Charles Arrowby, who broke up his first marriage in Iris Murdoch's *The Sea, the Sea*.

Eric Arble   Unsuccessful fruit farmer turned garage foreman; he is the husband of Iseult in Elizabeth Bowen's *Eva Trout, or Changing Scenes*.

Iseult (Smith) Arble   Former teacher at Lumleigh, a school for girls, whose special interest in Eva Trout continues after Lumleigh; following the death of Eva's father, she is asked by Eva's guardian, Constantine Ormeau, to take Eva into her house as a paying guest in Elizabeth Bowen's *Eva Trout, or Changing Scenes*.

Colonel Arbuthnot   The only pipe smoker on the Calais Coach; he was the devoted friend of Daisy Armstrong's father in Agatha Christie's *Murder on the Orient Express*.

Alexander ("Sandy") Arbuthnot (Lord Clanroyden) Effervescent Scot, bold man of genius and action and of chameleonic disguises; recruited by Richard Hannay for an assignment in the Foreign Office, he travels disguised as the leader of the Companions of the Rosy Hours and at Erzerum as the prophet "Greenmantle" leads the Cossack attack which defeats the evil German war machine in John Buchan's *Greenmantle*. Suspicious of the popular Dominick Medina, he investigates Medina's evil past; hearing Medina's plan to conquer the heart of society by controlling human souls, he thwarts Medina and returns the hostages to their families in *The Three Hostages*. As "El Obro Gris" he guides John S. Blenkiron and Blenkiron's niece, Barbara Dasent, in a revolt against the wicked conspirators and then leads the rebel army into Olifa City; he returns to his estates in Scotland with Barbara Dasent as his affianced bride in *The Courts of the Morning*. As husband and father, he assumes with Hannay the protec-

tion of Valdemar Haraldsen, and, in disguise as Martel the Belgian arranges for the children, Anna Haraldsen and Peter John Hannay, to escape from the trawler on which they have been held as hostages in *The Island of Sheep*. In a last appearance "Sandy" bids farewell to the terminally ill Sir Edward Leithen, who leaves London for New York and a final adventure in *Sick Heart River*.

Freddy Arbuthnot   Lord Peter Wimsey's fellow clubman; he is a suitor of Rachel Levy in Dorothy L. Sayers's *Whose Body?*. He is one of the Duke of Denver's houseguests when the Duke is arrested for Denis Cathcart's murder in *Clouds of Witness*. He attends Harriet Vane's first trial with Lord Peter Wimsey in *Strong Poison*.

Karen Arbuthnot   Gracie Tisbourne's friend, who angles for both Richard Pargeter and Sebastian Odmore and marries the latter in Iris Murdoch's *An Accidental Man*.

Archie   Unemotional sailor on the *Narcissus* in Joseph Conrad's *The Nigger of the "Narcissus"*.

Captain Jim Arcoll   Intelligence officer who traces John Laputa from the Limpopo to a meeting of the Royal Geographical Society in London and back to the kraal; he helps to defeat Laputa in John Buchan's *Prester John*. As a police officer in Rhodesia he sends Peter Pienaar, the scout, to warn Richard Hannay of a suspicious group of men converging on Haraldsen's gold claim in *The Island of Sheep*.

Arden   Utopian scientist who dies in the experiment which transports several Earthlings to the perfect world of Utopia in H. G. Wells's *Men Like Gods*.

Deborah Arden   Daughter of John and Patty Arden, with whom she shares a strong love of nature; hysterical after rejection by her husband, Stephen Southernwood, and his desertion of her, she burns down their home in the shadow of an ominous rock formation called Devil's Chair and almost dies wandering in a snow storm in Mary Webb's *The Golden Arrow*.

Joe Arden   Son of John and Patty Arden and brother of Deborah Arden (Southernwood); he disastrously marries the deceptive and selfish Lily Huntbatch in Mary Webb's *The Golden Arrow*.

John Arden   Shepherd and common countryman; he is husband of Patty Arden and father of Deborah Arden (Southernwood) and Joe Arden; he shares mystic beliefs with Deborah, whom he saves from death in a snow storm and later unites with her husband, Stephen Southernwood, and their baby in Mary Webb's *The Golden Arrow*.

Patty Arden A midwife; she is wife of John Arden and mother of Joe and Deborah Arden in Mary Webb's *The Golden Arrow*.

Bijou, Countess of Ardglass A fashionable, beautiful, promiscuous divorcée, who is the daughter of theatrical parents in Anthony Powell's *A Buyer's Market*. Her affair with Bob Duport is discussed in *The Acceptance World*. Her war work and her death are mentioned in *The Soldier's Art*.

James Argyle One of Aaron Sisson's friends in Florence, Italy; James, Angus Guest, and Francis Dekker are examples of jaded cosmopolitan travellers in D. H. Lawrence's *Aaron's Rod*.

Mavis Argyll The unmarried elder sister of Dorina Gibson Grey; after Dorina's death she becomes the dutiful caretaker of Austin Gibson Grey, sacrificing her romance with Matthew Gibson Grey in Iris Murdoch's *An Accidental Man*.

Aristides Shrewd organizer of the successful effort to smuggle arms to the Greek Cypriot rebels; because he thought Jack Townrow was a British spy he twice threatened him with death in P. H. Newby's *Something to Answer For*.

Angela d'Arivée Friend of Ethan and Jacqueline Llewelyn; she recommends that they consider settling on Gabriola Island In Malcolm Lowry's *October Ferry to Gabriola*.

Arlette Mute orphan of the French revolution who serves the sans-culotte farmer Scevola Bron until Peyrol helps her regain her speech; she marries Lieutenant Eugene Réal in Joseph Conrad's *The Rover*.

Arlova Nicolas Rubashov's private secretary and former mistress; she is called under suspicion of oppositional conspiracy, falsely confesses, and is sacrificed by Rubashov to save his own position in Arthur Koestler's *Darkness at Noon*.

Armatage Gunner on the flying boat; he deserts the treasure hunt because he is sure that they will all be killed and is killed by explosives thrown by another group of treasure hunters in Alan Sillitoe's *The Lost Flying Boat*.

Armgardson The piccolo and bass-flute player in the orchestra expropriated in wartime by the enemy; he plans to escape in Alan Sillitoe's *The General*.

Superintendant Armstrong A huge, direct, abrupt police official, who has formidable intelligence in his small eyes; he is an unscrupulous if clumsy tactician in Nicholas Blake's *A Question of Proof*.

Alex Armstrong Stuart Armstrong's elder brother, who helped Kate Fletcher Armstrong launch her career in journalism in Margaret Drabble's *The Middle Ground*.

Daisy Armstrong Kidnapped child whose death resulted in a string of tragedies, motivating the action in Agatha Christie's *Murder on the Orient Express*.

David Armstrong A young British army officer garrisoned in Ireland during the Anglo-Irish War (1919–21); he falls in love with Ascendancy-class Livvy Thompson in Elizabeth Bowen's *The Last September*.

Dr. Edward Armstrong Eminent physician whose inebriation once caused the death of a patient; he is drowned in Agatha Christie's *And Then There Were None*.

Jackie Armstrong Young girlfriend of Alec Gooch; because of her love for Alec she sees with new eyes that the world is a dangerous place; she later marries Alec and has a child in John Berger's *Corker's Freedom*.

Kate Armstrong Young housemaid whose loneliness and jealousy of her friend Edith's romance drive her into the arms of the uncouth Paddy O'Conor in Henry Green's *Loving*.

Kate Fletcher Armstrong Ex-wife of Stuart Armstrong, mother of their three children, journalist, and feminist; at age forty she is suffering through a midlife crisis, examining her experiences with men, with herself and others; she sees herself as a "marginal person" in Margaret Drabble's *The Middle Ground*.

Luisa Armstrong Wife to Michael Armstrong and mother of their five children; she is a Portuguese Jew; she appears in minor artistic works of the 1930s and 1940s in Margaret Drabble's *The Middle Ground*.

Mark Armstrong The eighteen-year-old eldest child of Kate (Fletcher) and Stuart Armstrong in Margaret Drabble's *The Middle Ground*.

Michael Armstrong Husband to Luisa Armstrong and father of their five children; he is half Scottish, half Irish and is an unemployed journalist who had worked as a theatre and art reviewer for a left-wing daily that went out of business in Margaret Drabble's *The Middle Ground*.

Paul Armstrong One of the sons of Luisa and Michael Armstrong; he is a writer of a political gossip column for a weekly in Margaret Drabble's *The Middle Ground*.

Reuben Armstrong Youngest of three children of Kate (Fletcher) and Stuart Armstrong; his parents are divorced and he lives with his mother in Margaret Drabble's *The Middle Ground*.

Ruth Armstrong Second of the three children of Kate (Fletcher) and Stuart Armstrong; her parents are divorced and she lives with her mother in Margaret Drabble's *The Middle Ground*.

Stella Armstrong Confidante of Tom Thirkill; she is his chief political adviser in C. P. Snow's *A Coat of Varnish*.

Stuart Armstrong Ex-husband to Kate Fletcher Armstrong and father of their three children; he is an unsuccessful painter; he was irresponsible with money and unfaithful to his wife, who found him unsatisfactory sexually in Margaret Drabble's *The Middle Ground*.

Father Arnall Teacher at the Clongowes School in whose class Father Dolan pandies Stephen Dedalus; he delivers the hellfire sermon to the school retreat in James Joyce's *A Portrait of the Artist as a Young Man*.

[Child] Arnauti Young daughter of the first marriage of Justine (Hosnani); she vanished and is the constant object of Justine's searching; she appears, a dying child prostitute, but is not identified in Lawrence Durrell's *Justine*. Financial support of the search is offered as an inducement in Justine's marriage to Nessim Hosnani in *Balthazar*. Justine reveals to Darley her long-past discovery of the dying child; Balthazar has assisted in her denial of the discovery in *Clea*.

Jacob Arnauti First husband of Justine Hosnani; he has written a novel called *Moeurs* that is a Freudian study of her character in Lawrence Durrell's *Justine*. He is mentioned in *Balthazar*, in *Mountolive*, and in *Clea*.

Ida Arnold Ample, friendly, determined, life-loving, free and easy, inexorable, early-middle-aged woman; nicknamed "Lily" by the pub's regulars because of her singing, she is loyal and has a strong sense of right and wrong; befriended by Charles Hale as a protective measure against Pinkie Brown's gang, she feels a duty to find out what happened to him; intending to "see justice done", she performs an opposite function and is ultimately responsible for Rose Wilson's marriage to Pinkie, for tracking down Hale's killers, and for Pinkie's exposure and death in Graham Greene's *Brighton Rock*.

John Arnold A philanderer who inherited from his father the company that owns Captain William Russell's ship; he plans to seduce Sylvia Russell during a sea voyage; she misjudges him as superior to her husband and is later unnerved that she so narrowly escaped his advances; he continues to send her birthday gifts each year and offers her stock in his shipping business, which she declines in Storm Jameson's *Farewell, Night; Welcome, Day*.

Philip Arnold Sammy Mountjoy's unscrupulous rival, as child and man, in William Golding's *Free Fall*.

Abel Arrowby Adam's brother, who became a barrister and married an American heiress; James Arrowby is his son in Iris Murdoch's *The Sea, the Sea*.

Adam Arrowby Charles's now-deceased unambitious, unadventuresome, affectionate father; Charles reflects on his father with respect and affection and still suppresses his resentment of the advantages enjoyed by his richer cousin, James Arrowby, in Iris Murdoch's *The Sea, the Sea*.

Charles Arrowby A retired actor, director, and playwright, who meets again with unfortunate consequences the girl he loved as a youth; he is narrator of Iris Murdoch's *The Sea, the Sea*.

Estelle Arrowby James's American mother, now deceased; Charles Arrowby's mother concealed her resentment of Estelle's wealth behind a façade of quiet contempt in Iris Murdoch's *The Sea, the Sea*.

James Arrowby Charles Arrowby's first cousin and only living kinsman, whose relationship with Charles has always been characterized by tension; a bachelor, a career army officer, and of late a Buddhist, he visits Charles and happens upon an unfolding tragedy; he rescues Charles from drowning in Iris Murdoch's *The Sea, the Sea*.

Marian Arrowby Charles's puritanical, loving mother, who died before her son achieved professional success in Iris Murdoch's *The Sea, the Sea*.

Arsene Watt's predecessor as Mr. Knott's servant in Samuel Beckett's *Watt*.

Melissa Artemis An inept dancer and beautiful prostitute; mistress of the dying furrier Cohen, she falls gratefully and slavishly in love with Darley; neglected by him during his affair with Justine Hosnani, she seduces Justine's husband, Nessim, and gives birth to Nessim's daughter before dying of tuberculosis in Lawrence Durrell's *Justine*. Her affair with Cohen resulted in her knowledge of the gunrunning conspiracy, of which she informs Pursewarden in *Mountolive*. She is mentioned in *Balthazar* and in *Clea*.

Almidano Artifoni   Italian music teacher who befriends Stephen Dedalus in James Joyce's *Ulysses*.

Sheila ("Sheikie" Beaker) Artworth   One of three women in their sixties who at the age of eleven were "best friends" at a school in Kent; now the attractive wife of a successful local businessman and stepmother to his two children, Sheila dreads that gossip will result from the cryptic ads Diana Delacroix has placed to call them all together in Elizabeth Bowen's *The Little Girls*.

Arvanitaki   Foreman of the Rasuka oil well; Ford heavily relies on him in P. H. Newby's *A Journey to the Interior*.

Lady Arwen   Beautiful young daughter of Elrond and Lady Galadriel; she marries King Elessar (Aragorn) in J. R. R. Tolkien's *The Return of the King*.

Asano   Graham's Japanese valet and guide, who betrays him to the revolutionary leader Ostrog in H. G. Wells's *When the Sleeper Wakes: A Story of the Years to Come*.

Alice Ascher   The first murder victim, a tobacconist in Andover, in Agatha Christie's *The A.B.C. Murders*.

Franz Ascher   Drunkard, abusive husband of Alice in Agatha Christie's *The A.B.C. Murders*.

Captain Asfur   Police captain who wrongly arrests Edgar Perry for starting a student demonstration in P. H. Newby's *The Picnic at Sakkara*.

Janice Ash   One of the "old guard" at the day-care center where Evelyn Morton Stennett volunteers some of her time in Margaret Drabble's *The Middle Ground*.

Walter Ash   Clara Maugham's marginally satisfactory secondary-school boyfriend; she breaks with him before starting her university career in Margaret Drabble's *Jerusalem the Golden*.

Madge, Lady Ashbrook   Old lady in her eighties who disapproves of Lancelot Loseby's relationship with Susan Thirkill; she is murdered, apparently for money, in C. P. Snow's *A Coat of Varnish*.

Mrs. Ashburnham   Edward's mother, who arranges his marriage to Leonora, daughter of her Irish-Catholic friend Mrs. Powys in Ford Madox Ford's *The Good Soldier: A Tale of Passion*.

Captain Edward Ashburnham   An English officer and a gentleman; a brave and decorated soldier, the Protestant Ashburnham is married by parental arrangement to a Catholic wife; his predilection for passionate love affairs leads to his mental and emotional bankruptcy and finally to his suicide in Ford Madox Ford's *The Good Soldier: A Tale of Passion*.

Leonora Ashburnham   The beautiful, gracious, Irish-Catholic wife of Edward Ashburnham; she manages his estates and his love affairs in the vain hope that he will return to her in recognition and gratitude; she tortures him and destroys his pride, driving him to suicide in Ford Madox Ford's *The Good Soldier: A Tale of Passion*.

Beatrice Ashby   Simon Ashby's unmarried aunt, a professional horse breeder and trainer, who runs the Ashby household with affection and competence in Josephine Tey's *Brat Farrar*.

Charles Ashby   Younger brother of Beatrice Ashby's father; he inherits the estate after Simon Ashby's death in Josephine Tey's *Brat Farrar*.

Derek Ashby   A forty-five-year-old architect; he divorces his wife, Evelyn, to marry Maureen Kirby, with whom his relations progressed from employer to lover in Margaret Drabble's *The Ice Age*.

Eleanor Ashby   Simon Ashby's sister, who realizes as she falls in love with Brat Farrar that he cannot be her brother in Josephine Tey's *Brat Farrar*.

Evelyn Ashby   Wife to Derek Ashby, who divorces her to marry Maureen Kirby; following the divorce she leads an eccentric, solitary existence, refusing to see her children in Margaret Drabble's *The Ice Age*.

Jane Ashby   Ten-year-old sister of Simon and Eleanor Ashby; she is the tomboy of a pair of twins in Josephine Tey's *Brat Farrar*.

Patrick Ashby   The elder Ashby brother, long believed to have committed suicide by drowning in Josephine Tey's *Brat Farrar*.

Ruth Ashby   Jane's dainty, ladylike twin sister in Josephine Tey's *Brat Farrar*.

Simon Ashby   The charming, vicious younger twin brother and heir of Patrick Ashby; he alone knows that the unexpectedly returned Patrick must be an imposter in Josephine Tey's *Brat Farrar*.

William Ashe (Bill; covername: Murphy)   Effeminate GDR intelligence mercenary who makes first contact with Alec Leamas for Abteilung in John le Carré's *The Spy Who Came In from the Cold*.

William Ashenden Critical, realistic, cultured novelist and narrator of the story; William meets Edward Driffeld when he is a boy, but as William matures his ties to Driffeld are insignificant compared to his knowledge of Rose Driffeld in W. Somerset Maugham's *Cakes and Ale: Or the Skeleton in the Cupboard*. As a British agent he enjoys the excitement and mystery of his travels yet wishes he could see the result of his work; he relates to people well, using measured amounts of sincerity and falsehood; he sees people as puzzles and tries to decode them in *Ashenden: or The British Agent*.

Hamilton Ashinow Johnny Fortune's good-natured childhood classmate, who came from Lagos to London as a stowaway; he is a hustler and drug addict; he dies of a drug overdose in Colin MacInnes's *City of Spades*.

Dr. Ashley-Densley An elegantly handsome physician called in to treat a group of nurses; one of them, Eleanor Dear, thereafter assumes him to be on call at demand; he sees through her desperate maneuverings but looks after her anyway in Dorothy Richardson's *The Tunnel*. He becomes Miriam Henderson's friend and potential suitor in *The Trap*. He reports Eleanor Dear's death to Miriam in *Dawn's Left Hand*. Miriam refuses his proposal of marriage in *Clear Horizon*.

Ashok An eight-year-old Indian boy who is befriended by Barbara Batchelor, the retired missionary teacher, in Paul Scott's *The Towers of Silence*.

Sir Harold Ashton Determined teetotaller, chartered accountant, and vice-chairman of the Saddleford Building Society in Northern England in Roy Fuller's *Image of a Society*.

Archpriest-Militant Devit Asperamanka Leader of the Church of the Formidable Peace and commander of the Sibornalese forces; he eventually becomes the Supreme Oligarch in Brian W. Aldiss's *Helliconia Winter*.

Connie Aspinall "Dreary" spinster relation of Edith Liversidge; she plays the harp and pines away in a small village for the scenes of her former glory when she was companion to a lady in Belgrave Square in Barbara Pym's *Some Tame Gazelle*.

Jimmy Assad An Egyptian in the film business who hosts Daniel Martin and Jane Mallory in Cairo and arranges their trip to Palmyra in John Fowles's *Daniel Martin*.

Assistant Commissioner Opportunistic police official who oversees the bungling of Chief Inspector Heat in Joseph Conrad's *The Secret Agent: A Simple Tale*.

Assistant Commissioner Police official in his fifties, lately returned from long service in the East; though he sees his job as stopping when the "right man" is caught, he is asked to find out the possible reaction to the execution of Jim Drover and is followed by Conrad Drover, who tries to shoot him, in Graham Greene's *It's a Battlefield*.

Laurence Astill Scientist who serves on the advisory committee for nuclear weapons and is included among those investigated for security reasons in C. P. Snow's *Corridors of Power*.

Ben Ata The King of Zone Four who is told by the Providers that he must marry Al-Ith; though he does so unwillingly, he learns to love her; later he must leave her behind and marry the savage Queen of Zone Five in Doris Lessing's *The Marriages Between Zones Three, Four, and Five*.

Sally Athelney Healthy, well-made, practical, and sensible young girl who waits patiently for the maturing Philip Carey to realize her worth in W. Somerset Maugham's *Of Human Bondage*.

Thorpe Athelney The highly intelligent, well-educated father of nine who toils in a mundane, badly paid job, befriends Philip Carey, and demonstrates what a loving family can be in W. Somerset Maugham's *Of Human Bondage*.

Mrs. Atherton Julia Martin's landlady in Jean Rhys's *After Leaving Mr. Mackenzie*.

Athy Stephen Dedalus's companion in the school infirmary in James Joyce's *A Portrait of the Artist as a Young Man*.

Harry Atkins Sally Atkins's simple and pleasure-loving husband, who drinks too often and beats her in W. Somerset Maugham's *Liza of Lambeth*.

Mollie Atkins A married woman who runs a money-losing shop and has had affairs with numerous men, including Roger Micheldene; after he admits to her that he loves Helene Bang, Mollie gives him the key to her New York apartment, where he finds Helene with Irving Macher in Kingsley Amis's *One Fat Englishman*.

Sally Atkins Liza Kemp's simple, good-hearted friend, who marries Harry Atkins in W. Somerset Maugham's *Liza of Lambeth*.

Strode Atkins A New York literary agent and horrible Anglophile, who accompanies Roger Micheldene back to England; he illegally obtained Swinburne's notebooks, which Micheldene steals after finding them in Atkins's New York apartment in Kingsley Amis's *One Fat Englishman*.

Atkinson Manservant of Colonel Boucher; his engagement to Jane Weston's maid, Elizabeth Luton, poses servant problems that require as solution the marriage of their employers in E. F. Benson's *"Queen Lucia"*.

Bill Atkinson Insurance salesman, ex-Army major, and Jim Dixon's dependable friend, who resides in the rooming house where Jim lives; he pretends to faint in order to draw attention away from Jim when Jim has difficulties presenting his "Merrie England" speech in Kingsley Amis's *Lucky Jim*.

Aubrey Ernest Freeman's solicitor; he negotiates with Charles Smithson following the jilting of Ernestina Freeman in John Fowles's *The French Lieutenant's Woman*.

Clare Keith Aubrey A former well-established concert pianist who met her husband, Piers Aubrey, in Ceylon; thin and nervous and desolate and betrayed in her marriage, she insists on the extraordinary and wonderful possibilities of life to her children, Cordelia, Rose, Mary, and Richard Quin Aubrey; Cordelia's lack of musicianship disappoints her in Rebecca West's *The Fountain Overflows*.

Cordelia Aubrey The eldest Aubrey child, who resembles her father in appearance and in lack of musical talent; to the chagrin of her mother and of her more gifted sisters, her eccentric teacher, Miss Beevor, insists that she has great talent and must continue to practice her violin in Rebecca West's *The Fountain Overflows*.

Mary Aubrey Second child in the Aubrey family; she is a pianist in Rebecca West's *The Fountain Overflows*.

Piers Aubrey Father of the four Aubrey children and husband of Clare; a gambler and an attractive and lovable but irresponsible parent, he joins the family in a house on the edge of London about 1900 after they have lived in South Africa and in Edinburgh; he frequently changes jobs because he annoys people, and he gambles in stocks; he sells his wife's furniture in her absence to meet his debts, and he leaves the family and does not communicate for months at a time in Rebecca West's *The Fountain Overflows*.

Richard Quin Aubrey Youngest and only male Aubrey child, adored by the other members of the family; he is destined to die young in World War I in Rebecca West's *The Fountain Overflows*.

Rose Aubrey Third child of the Aubrey family; she is ten when her father leaves the family; a pianist, she is the child closest to the mother in understanding; she envies and dislikes Cordelia for her closeness to their father and her inability to achieve musical success; Rose is narrator of Rebecca West's *The Fountain Overflows*.

Rose Auburn Beautiful, virginal, hard, materialistic "harlot"; she went from one rich lover to the next in W. Somerset Maugham's *Ashenden: or The British Agent*.

Audrey University of London student of history who becomes Arthur Miles's lover for several years; she marries Charles Sheriff and welcomes Miles's offers to help advance Sheriff's scientific career in C. P. Snow's *The Search*.

Mallam Audu Road treasurer in Fada who is arrested, without understanding why, for misappropriating funds; he is later rehired by Officer Rudbeck to complete the road in Joyce Cary's *Mister Johnson*.

Augray A sorn, one of the native species of Malacandra (Mars), who meets Ransom on his journey to meet Oyarsa of Malacandra; Augray carries Ransom to Oyarsa's habitation in C. S. Lewis's *Out of the Silent Planet*.

St. Augustine Saint conjured up by De Selby; he voices various complaints and opinions in a Dublin accent in Flann O'Brien's *The Dalkey Archive*.

Augustus Caesar First emperor of Rome; he rules according to the will of his wife, Livia, who eventually poisons him in Robert Graves's *I, Claudius*.

Aulus Military commander sent by Claudius to conquer Britain; following the Roman victory, he nobly offers his friendship to the vanquished Caractacas in Robert Graves's *Claudius, the God and His Wife Messalina*.

Auntie A senile retired theatrical-lodging-house keeper; her boasts of her Czarist-regime past and of her jewels are laughed at by her friend-caretaker-tenant Will Boase, but they unexpectedly enrich him in Iris Murdoch's *Bruno's Dream*.

Marcus Aurelius Well-known critic, who thinks Janos Lavin's work is worthy but boring in John Berger's *A Painter of Our Time*.

Concetta Auronzo   Widowed mother of Don Carlo and Domenico Campanati; she is an American transplanted to Europe; intelligent and well-read, she involves herself deeply in the effort to save the Jews from extermination in Nazi Germany in the 1930's in Anthony Burgess's *Earthly Powers*.

Austin   Professor of physics who directs Arthur Miles's research at King's College, University of London; he chairs the committee which establishes the National Institute for Biophysical Research in C. P. Snow's *The Search*.

Mrs. Austin   Wife of Professor Austin; she is hostess for dinner parties attended by Arthur Miles in C. P. Snow's *The Search*.

Antonia Avellanos   Costaguanan patriot who falls in love with Martin Decoud but loses him in Joseph Conrad's *Nostromo: A Tale of the Seaboard*.

Don José Avellanos   Costaguanan patriot and father of Antonia in Joseph Conrad's *Nostromo: A Tale of the Seaboard*.

Miss Avery   Mysterious old charwoman at the farms attached to Howards End in E. M. Forster's *Howards End*.

John Somerton Avery   Youthful, unassertive aide to Director Leclerc; he befriends Fred Leiser but ignominiously sacrifices him to Operation Mayfly in John le Carré's *The Looking-Glass War*.

Sarah Avery   John Avery's lonely, anxious wife; her bitterness drives her husband further into Leclerc's Neverneverland of outdated espionage threats in John le Carré's *The Looking-Glass War*.

Awad   Lawyer hired to take care of Abravanel's and Mrs. Khoury's estates after Abravanel's death in P. H. Newby's *Something to Answer For*.

Axel Axel (covernames: "Poppy," "Greensleeves", Herr König)   Magnus Pym's Czechoslovakian controller and beloved second father-figure; he introduces Magnus to culture, literature, and philosophy; he offers Magnus sanctuary when British Intelligence unearths him, but, even with Mary Pym's help, he is unable to prevent Magnus's suicide in John le Carré's *A Perfect Spy*.

Alan Axwick   Dull and witless Member of Parliament for whom Owen Tuby and Cosmo Sultana form a more exciting image in J. B. Priestley's *The Image Men*.

Laintal Ay   Yuli's great-great-great grandson, who is destined to become king of Oldorando and lead the country into a new era in Brian W. Aldiss's *Helliconia Spring*.

Ayesha   Pakistani woman with a Danish husband; she works for International Family Planning; she is present at an Evelyn (Morton) and Ted Stennett gathering in Margaret Drabble's *The Middle Ground*.

Joe Ayida   An art historian and sculptor who is Minister of Culture of Adra; Frances Wingate's long-time professional friend, he is her host at the conference from which she is summoned home following the discovery of Constance Ollerenshaw's death in Margaret Drabble's *The Realms of Gold*.

Mr. Aymer (alias Mr. Vallance)   An evil accomplice of Squire Cranmer in John Buchan's *The Free Fishers*.

Major William ("Willie") Ayscue   Self-doubting chaplain, who is generally ineffective when called upon in professional capacities and more interested in pursuing interests in music in Kingsley Amis's *The Anti-Death League*.

Aziz   Mabel Layton's Indian servant who has been with the family for many years; when Mabel dies at Rose Cottage, he returns to his home village in the mountains in Paul Scott's *The Towers of Silence*.

Dr. Aziz   Muslim Indian doctor who is optimistically friendly to the sympathetic English: Henry Fielding, Mrs. Moore, and Adela Quested; Adela's accusation against him of attempted rape in the Marabar Caves he perceives as insulting and maliciously false; he is acquitted when Adela withdraws her accusation at his trial, but he has become hostile to the British in E. M. Forster's *A Passage to India*.

Abdul Aziz   Instigator of the Fouad University student uprising against the British in P. H. Newby's *The Picnic at Sakkara*.

B

B An artist who is a friend of DeSilva in Doris Lessing's *The Golden Notebook*.

Mr. B. GESS (Global-Equip Security Services) agent consulted by Anthea Leaver in Muriel Spark's *Territorial Rights*.

Babalatchi Aid to Lakamba, Rajah of Sambir; he helps Kaspar Almayer's daughter elope in Joseph Conrad's *Almayer's Folly: A Story of an Eastern River*. He thwarts Peter Willems and Almayer in *An Outcast of the Islands*.

Mrs. Babbacombe Evie's mother and the town of Stilbourne's "only Roman Catholic"; she does not know her place in the social structure of the town and is ridiculed by its inhabitants in William Golding's *The Pyramid*.

Sergeant Babbacombe Town crier and brutal father of Evie Babbacombe; he has an incestuous relationship with his daughter in William Golding's *The Pyramid*.

Evie Babbacombe The sexual "local phenomenon" of Stilbourne; she makes her body accessible to Oliver as well as to others in William Golding's *The Pyramid*.

Dr. Arthur Amos Cuncliffe Babcock Protective English physician to the royal court of Pisuerga and lover of royal governess Aggie Montgomery in Ronald Firbank's *The Flower Beneath the Foot*.

Anne Baberton Resident of the May of Teck Club and owner of a coveted Schiaparelli taffeta evening dress in Muriel Spark's *The Girls of Slender Means*.

Nan Babington A suburban middle-class friend of the Henderson girls in Dorothy Richardson's *Backwater*. She makes a brief reappearance in *Clear Horizon*.

Tommy Babington Nan's brother, also a friend of the Henderson girls, in Dorothy Richardson's *Backwater*.

Bachir Cheerful, hardworking young Tunisian manager of the Duchess of Varna's exotic but discreet flower shop "Haboubet of Egypt" in Ronald Firbank's *The Flower Beneath the Foot*.

Felix Bacon A man who lives with Jonathan Swift, dances with him, and sits on his knee; he becomes a drawing master at Josephine Napier's school and marries Helen Keats after his father, Sir Robert, dies in Ivy Compton-Burnett's *More Women Than Men*.

Francis Bacon A very intelligent eleven-year-old pupil at Lucius Cassidy's school in Ivy Compton-Burnett's *Two Worlds and Their Ways*.

Sir Robert Bacon Felix's father, who disapproves of his way of life; when he is dying, he makes Felix promise to marry and continue the family and protect the estate in Ivy Compton-Burnett's *More Women Than Men*.

Father Michael Baddeley Chaplain at Toynton Grange, a private home for the disabled; he writes to Adam Dalgliesh, whom he knew as a child, requesting a visit, but is murdered before Dalgliesh can arrive in P. D. James's *The Black Tower*.

Captain Baddlestone Rude merchant captain of the "Princess"; he is good in battle alongside Hornblower but shows contempt for the navy in C. S. Forester's *Hornblower And the Crisis: An Unfinished Novel*.

Badger Kindly and wise creature, experienced in the ways of both the Wild Wood and the Wide World; with the help of Water Rat and Mole he decides to take the irresponsible Toad in hand and make him learn the error of his ways in Kenneth Grahame's *The Wind in the Willows*.

Miss Badsen A thin, dark lady, who teaches music and French at Mr. Herrick's school; she is a feminist in Ivy Compton-Burnett's *Pastors and Masters*.

Arnold Baffin A successful and prolific novelist, who is the father of Julian Baffin; his wife, Rachel Baffin, murders him out of sexual jealousy in Iris Murdoch's *The Black Prince*.

Julian Baffin Arnold and Rachel Baffin's student daughter, with whom the fifty-eight-year-old Bradley Pearson falls joyously and disastrously in love in Iris Murdoch's *The Black Prince*.

Rachel Baffin Wife of Arnold and mother of Julian; her unimportance to both her husband and to Bradley Pearson so enrages her that she kills the former with a poker and frames the latter for the murder in Iris Murdoch's *The Black Prince*.

Bilbo Baggins Formerly comfort-loving, unambitious hobbit who travels with Gandalf to rescue the Mountain and its treasure from the dragon and finds the One Ring in J. R. R. Tolkien's *The Hobbit; or There and Back Again*. He leaves his home and the ring to his nephew Frodo Baggins in *The Fellowship of the Ring*. He and Frodo depart over the Sea for eternity in *The Return of the King*.

Frodo Baggins   Young, brave hobbit who accepts the responsibility for the One Ring from his uncle Bilbo Baggins in J. R. R. Tolkien's *The Fellowship of the Ring*. He manages to take the ring to the Mountain of Doom; paralyzed by the spider Shelob, he is left for dead by his companion Sam Gamgee in *The Two Towers*. Reunited with Sam, he destroys Sauron's power in *The Return of the King*.

Mr. Bagshaw   An English gentleman who reveals to John Dowell that Florence Dowell had an affair before their marriage; his arrival in Bad Nauheim precipitates Florence's suicide in Ford Madox Ford's *The Good Soldier: A Tale of Passion*.

Lindsay ("Books-Do-Furnish-a-Room") Bagshaw Seedy left-wing journalist given to drink and rows; his nickname derives from an apocryphal statement attributed to him at University; he is a founder of the progressive weekly *Fission* in Anthony Powell's *Books Do Furnish a Room*. He is a television personality with a house and a large family in *Temporary Kings*.

Florence (Florrie) Bagster   Young servant of Carolyn Lessways; she joins Hilda Lessways in George Cannon's Brighton boarding house, where her physical charms soon make her the mistress of the newly widowed boarder Mr. Boutwood in Arnold Bennett's *Hilda Lessways*.

Freddie Bagster   Young man with a crush on Helen Rolt in Graham Greene's *The Heart of the Matter*.

Sir Ahmed Ali Gaffus Kasim Bahadur   The Nawab of Mirat, a Muslim Prince, in Paul Scott's *The Jewel in the Crown*. He graciously offers a guest house on his estate to Susan Layton and her family so that she may be married to Edward Bingham in Mirat in *The Day of the Scorpion*. His presence continues to be felt in *The Towers of Silence* and in *A Division of the Spoils*.

Mrs. Bailey   Miriam Henderson's widowed landlady on the edge of London's Bloomsbury in Dorothy Richardson's *The Tunnel*. She has decided to take boarders rather than merely lodgers but allows Miriam to stay on as lodger, with the option of paying for a meal when she wishes in *Interim*. She astonishes Miriam by agreeing to marry a young man half her age in *Deadlock*.

Polly Bailey   Sissie Bailey's sister in Dorothy Richardson's *Interim*.

Sissie Bailey   One of two young daughters on whose behalf Mrs. Bailey has decided to convert 7 Tansley Street to a boarding-house, in the hope of providing social opportunities for them in Dorothy Richardson's *Interim*. Sissie grows "from an elderly schoolgirl into a young housekeeper" and disapproves of Amabel's flirtatious behavior in *Clear Horizon*.

Nanette de Bailly   Dark, high-colored Frenchwoman, of good family, from Provence; her engagement to Colonel Stanley Levin is announced in Ford Madox Ford's *No More Parades*.

Vesta Bainbridge   Glamorous, opportunistic features editor of a women's magazine who attempts to reform F. X. Enderby as well as capitalize on his literary reputation in Anthony Burgess's *Inside Mr. Enderby* and in *Enderby Outside*.

Miss Baines   Timberwork secretary who is somewhat incompetent in Isabel Colegate's *Orlando King*.

Constance Baines   Placid, custom-bound oldest daughter of John Baines; she spends her life maintaining her parents' standards in her marriage to their clerk Cyril Povey, in her parenthood of Samuel Povey, and in her attitude toward her wayward sister, Sophia, in Arnold Bennett's *The Old Wives Tale*.

Hattie Baines   Anthony Keating's first girlfriend, whom he sees years later at the Mike Morgan comedy performance in Margaret Drabble's *The Ice Age*.

John Baines   Long-paralyzed and bed-ridden proprietor of Bursley's best dry-goods store; his death by his daughter Sophia's negligence precipitates her renunciation of a teaching career and her repentant clerking in the store where she meets the traveling salesman Gerald Scales, with whom she disastrously elopes to Paris in Arnold Bennett's *The Old Wives Tale*.

Mrs. John Baines   Widow of John Baines and confident mother of Constance and Sophia; she finds she cannot control the circumstances of her maturing daughters' lives and withdraws in defeat to live with her widowed sister in her birthplace, Axe, in Arnold Bennett's *The Old Wives Tale*.

Sophia Baines   Beautiful, intelligent, impetuous younger daughter of John Baines; by deceiving her family and negligently causing her father's death, she is precipitated into an elopement and psychically wounding experiences in Paris with her insensitive husband, Gerald Scales, and she is abandoned there; she ruthlessly sets up the Bursley standards she had run from and lives a repressed life in the Paris commune until age and strain force her return to her birthplace, where she struggles with her sister's customs and dies of the shock sustained by having to view her late husband's body in Arnold Bennett's *The Old Wives Tale*.

Rosemary Bains   An elderly ex-school mistress who is deeply inspired by one of Charles Watkins's lectures; she very much wants to meet him in Doris Lessing's *Briefing for a Descent into Hell*.

Corporal Baker   The cruel, spiteful N.C.O. at the Basic Training camp; he is hostile to Jonathan Browne; he is assaulted by Mike Brady for having hounded Percy Higgins to his death; he is demoted in David Lodge's *Ginger, You're Barmy*.

Dr. Baker   Physician whom Rebecca de Winter visited the day of her death, according to her journal; his surprising evidence concludes the investigation into Rebecca's death in Daphne duMaurier's *Rebecca*.

Mr. Baker   Beleaguered first mate of the *Narcissus* in Joseph Conrad's *The Nigger of the "Narcissus"*.

Hermione Baker   Slightly less sinister of the two evil principals of the state educational institution for women in Henry Green's *Concluding*.

Tracy Baker   Ex-pupil of Romley Fourways', the school Kate Fletcher (Armstrong) attended; years later she is seen in Majorca in Margaret Drabble's *The Middle Ground*.

Earl of Balcairn   A young aristocrat whose financial difficulties force him to become a newspaper gossip writer; he eventually commits suicide when he is ostracized by the high-society set in Evelyn Waugh's *Vile Bodies*.

Guiseppe (Pepino) Baldino   Italian patient in Clive Ward who loses his right hand after a fiery bus crash; unable to speak or understand English, he frantically tries to find out if his pregnant wife in Italy has borne him a son in John Berger's *The Foot of Clive*.

Christopher (Chris) Baldry   Thirty-six-year-old amnesiac soldier and successful businessman; he returns from service in World War I to his fine country estate and his wife, Kitty, and cousin, Jenny, who pride themselves on having provided him with a "gracious life"; he recalls only the sweetheart of his youth, Margaret Allington, daughter of an innkeeper, and he blocks out fifteen years of memory in Rebecca West's *The Return of the Soldier*.

Kitty Baldry   Wife of amnesiac Chris Baldry; she is a rich, materialistic woman who thinks Chris should remember her because he gave her the beautiful neck-laces she fingers as she welcomes him home; she expresses anger at his refusal to recall their marriage and at his pursuit of a dowdy, uneducated, and unattractive woman, Margaret Allington, whom he met at an inn fifteen years earlier in Rebecca West's *The Return of the Soldier*.

Mr. Baldwin   The mysterious British financier who travels to Ishmaelia and helps defeat the Russian coup d'état in Evelyn Waugh's *Scoop*.

Leonard Bale   Chief Inspector who is the senior policeman working with Frank Briers investigating the murder of Lady Ashbrook; he travels to New York for evidence in C. P. Snow's *A Coat of Varnish*.

Denise (Scooter) Ball   Schoolmate of Kate Fletcher (Armstrong); she worked hard to become a nurse; she becomes Terry Ball's wife; her story is used by Kate in the television film Kate is making in Margaret Drabble's *The Middle Ground*.

Terry Ball   Electrical engineer, married to Denise (Scooter); their story is used by Kate Fletcher Armstrong in the television film she is making in Margaret Drabble's *The Middle Ground*.

Rozina (Rozzie) Balmforth   Strong-willed, independent, life-long friend of Sara Monday; she advises Sara on how to handle Gulley Jimson's advances in Joyce Cary's *Herself Surprised* and in *The Horse's Mouth*.

Joseph Balterghen   Small, moustached, Armenian-born, conscienceless man; chairman of Pan-Eruasian Petroleum and a shareholder in Cator and Bliss munitions firm, he employs Stefan Saridza to steal the B2 plans in Eric Ambler's *Uncommon Danger*.

S. Balthazar   A homosexual physician and a leading student of the Cabala; he is a friend of L. G. Darley, of Justine Hosnani, and of Clea Montis in Lawrence Durrell's *Justine*. He expands upon Darley's version of Justine's private life in *Balthazar*. He helplessly attends the dying Narouz Hosnani in *Mountolive*. He recovers from a passion for a Greek actor in *Clea*.

Bamboo   Cheerful young fisherman in the village of Mediaville and lover of Miami Mouth; he is eaten by a shark after Miami moves away to the city in Ronald Firbank's *Sorrow in Sunlight*.

Bamu   Beautiful daughter of Brimah; she becomes Johnson's wife, serves him faithfully but will not adopt his civilized nature, and later leaves him after he loses his job in Joyce Cary's *Mister Johnson*.

Acheson Bandicott   American millionaire and amateur archaeologist, who discovers the Viking burial barrow and treasure of "Harold Blacktooth"; he behaves in a sportsmanlike manner when "John Macnab" succeeds in killing a salmon in Strathlarrig waters in John Buchan's *John Macnab*.

Junius Theodore Bandicott   Son of a wealthy American who has rented Strathlarrig, a great house and estate bordering the property of Sir Archibald Roylance; he meets and falls in love with Agatha Raden, elder daughter of Colonel Alastair Raden and Janet's sister, in John Buchan's *John Macnab*.

Dai Bando   A disreputable former prizefighter who teaches Huw Morgan to box, attacks Mr. Jonas when he beats Huw, and, despite his blindness, helps Huw to search the mine for his father's body in Richard Llewellyn's *How Green Was My Valley*.

Bane   Chair of Absurdist Drama in Adam Appleby's department; he has been promoted over the head of Briggs, Adam's supervisor, in David Lodge's *The British Museum Is Falling Down*.

Jill Banford   A moralistic, selfishly dependent, tiny woman, who lives with her Lesbian lover Nellie March on an unproductive Berkshire farm during World War I; she is deliberately killed by a tree felled by Henry Grenfel in D. H. Lawrence's *The Fox*.

Arthur Bang   The seven-year-old son of Helene and Ernst Bang; his presence makes it difficult for Roger Micheldene to get together with Helene; Micheldene mistakenly blames him for taking his lecture notes, and after Arthur beats Micheldene at Scrabble, Micheldene reveals his childishness by breaking one of Arthur's toys in Kingsley Amis's *One Fat Englishman*.

Dr. Ernst Bang   A Danish philologist who comes to an American college for one year as a Visiting Fellow from the University of Copenhagen; he knows and accepts the fact that his wife, Helene, has meaningless affairs and plans to move with her to Chicago, where he has been offered a job in the linguistics department in Kingsley Amis's *One Fat Englishman*.

Helene Bang   Danish wife of Ernst Bang; she renews her affair with Roger Micheldene while he is in Pennsylvania and then has an affair with Irving Macher during the weekend she promised to spend with Micheldene; she realizes that Micheldene is hostile and loves her but does not like her in Kingsley Amis's *One Fat Englishman*.

William Bankes   Long-time bachelor friend of the Ramsays; he walks with Lily Briscoe, and Mrs. Ramsay

tries to match them romantically in Virginia Woolf's *To the Lighthouse*.

Major Banks   Douglas Knowell's superior who confirms that Douglas can no longer serve in active duty because of his ill health in Doris Lessing's *A Proper Marriage*.

Sir Gerald Banks   Intelligent, wealthy aristocrat with impeccable taste and a fabulous art collection who offends Janos Lavin with his cold, "dead" art collection; he later buys one of Lavin's paintings in John Berger's *A Painter of Our Time*.

Joey Banks   An enervated society woman, who is described by Miriam Henderson as "an Oriental princess" in Dorothy Richardson's *Honeycomb*.

Bannister   Thomas Carlyle Craw's butler and a born organizer who loves mystery and secrecy in John Buchan's *Castle Gay*.

Auriol Bannister   Bookstore proprietor and employer of Agatha (King) Field in Isabel Colegate's *Agatha*.

Dolly Bantry   Jane Marple's closest friend in St. Mary Mead; she appears in Agatha Christie's *Sleeping Murder* and in two other novels.

Count Banubula   A decrepit nobleman; he is in the employ of Countess Hippolyta, sporadically cataloguing her library in Lawrence Durrell's *Tunc*.

Baptiste   Male servant in Rochester's island home who serves Antoinette Cosway rum which contributes to her ultimate decline into madness in Jean Rhys's *Wide Sargasso Sea*.

Senor Barasi   Unctuous, wealthy Gibraltar businessman who marries Richard Ennis's mistress, Conception Gomez, while still remaining on friendly terms with Ennis himself in Anthony Burgess's *A Vision of Battlements*.

Barbara   Orlando King's secretary; Judith (Gardner) King finds out about Barbara's affair with him in Isabel Colegate's *Orlando King*.

Barbara (the witch)   A depressingly wholesome and efficient secretary who is one of Billy Fisher's three fiancées in Keith Waterhouse's *Billy Liar*.

Mrs. Barbazon   Stella Mathews's mother who interferes in her daughter's life after the baby is born in Doris Lessing's *A Proper Marriage*.

Mr. Barbecue-Smith   Pretentious writer of popular philosophy; briefly joining the houseparty at Crome estate, he attempts to offer his hackneyed advice on writing to Denis Stone in Aldous Huxley's *Crome Yellow.*

Frederick ("Freddy") Barbon   Thomas Carlyle Craw's confidential secretary in John Buchan's *Castle Gay.*

Nosy Barbon   Aspiring young artist who worships Gulley Jimson and later helps Gulley paint the Creation in Joyce Cary's *The Horse's Mouth.*

Elizabeth Barclay   The long-suffering wife of Wilfred Barclay; she sees him clearly for what he is in William Golding's *The Paper Men.*

Emily Barclay   The daughter of Elizabeth and Wilfred Barclay; she has little more than contempt for her father, who sees himself as the protagonist of his own religious tragedy but whom she sees as an egocentric monster in William Golding's *The Paper Men.*

Wilfred Townsend Barclay   The dipsomaniac novelist and narrator; he believes he is a penitent undergoing a religious crisis but is simply a sadistic prig experiencing a kind of literary delirium tremens in William Golding's *The Paper Men.*

Bard   Grim but wise man of Lake-town Esgaroth who kills Smaug the dragon after he is chased out by Bilbo Baggins and his companions in J. R. R. Tolkien's *The Hobbit; or There and Back Again.*

Bardia   Captain of the Royal Guard in the land of Glome; he teaches Orual swordsmanship and becomes a trusted counsellor after her ascension to the throne; he is the object of Orual's possessiveness which is revealed to her after his death in C. S. Lewis's *Till We Have Faces.*

Dr. Margaret Baring   Warden of Shrewsbury College, Oxford University; she wants to expose the anonymous mischief maker without embarrassing the college in Dorothy L. Sayers's *Gaudy Night.*

Barker   Former chauffeur to Lilian Portway and Canon Portway; he blackmailed the Canon with knowledge of Gilbert Stokesay's practical joke in the Melpham discovery; he dies after years as a mute in the care of his daughter, Alice Cressett, in Angus Wilson's *Anglo-Saxon Attitudes.*

Israel Barker   Walter Morel's "fellow-butty" in the mines in D. H. Lawrence's *Sons and Lovers.*

James Barker   Government official who becomes

Lord High Provost of South Kensington and spokesman for the other borough leaders; their desire to build a road through Notting Hill leads to war with the borough of Notting Hill in G. K. Chesterton's *The Napoleon of Notting Hill.*

Jean Barker   A Communist Party member, married to a minor party official and considered a "clown" by other party members because she never thinks before speaking in Doris Lessing's *The Golden Notebook.*

Bessie Barleymoon   English captain's widow with means and resident of Pisuerga who, in the opinion of her friend Mrs. Bedley, doesn't get enough respect for her noble background in Ronald Firbank's *The Flower Beneath the Foot.*

Anthea Barlow   An emissary from the pastorate whose repeated efforts to see the new rector, Carel Fisher, are blocked by Pattie O'Driscoll; recognized by Marcus Fisher, she is revealed to have been the girl with whom he, Carel, and their late brother Julian were simultaneously in love in Iris Murdoch's *The Time of the Angels.*

Dennis Barlow   A young, cynical English author who comes to Hollywood to write films; lack of success forces him to take a job at a pet cemetery; he courts Aimée Thanatogenos, but after her death he returns to England with money obtained from Mr. Joyboy for secretly cremating Aimée at the pet cemetery in Evelyn Waugh's *The Loved One.*

Eli Barlow   Elderly director of the Saddleford Building Society who finds it convenient to turn off his hearing device in Roy Fuller's *Image of a Society.*

Barman   Brighton bartender who supplies information to Ida Arnold about Kite, Colleoni, and Pinkie Brown in Graham Greene's *Brighton Rock.*

Eustace Barnack   Epicurean patron of the arts whose scandalous enjoyment of life's many pleasures is an embarrassment to his relations; himself childless, he dotes on his nephew Sebastian Barnack, on whom he showers expensive gifts; after his sudden death he hovers in the after-life bemused by his random memories and observations of the living in Aldous Huxley's *Time Must Have a Stop.*

John Barnack   Sebastian's often-absent father, an upper-class Socialist whose politics cause Sebastian many unnecessary embarrassments in Aldous Huxley's *Time Must Have a Stop.*

Sebastian Barnack   Sensitive and socially insecure youth who writes clever verse chiefly for the amusement of his Uncle Eustace Barnack; his immaturity leads him into various intrigues at his uncle's Florentine home and though aided in his difficulties after Eustace's death by Bruno Rontini, he fails to develop a sense of equanimity until after many years of unhappiness in Aldous Huxley's *Time Must Have a Stop.*

Jessie ("Granny") Barnacle   Noisy, cantankerous resident patient of the old women's hospital ward; when the transfer of the bullying nurse, Sister Burstead, removes the stimulation of her hatred, she dies in Muriel Spark's *Memento Mori.*

Elizabeth (Betty) Barnard   Young woman murdered on a beach at Bexhill-on-Sea in Agatha Christie's *The A.B.C. Murders.*

Harold Barnard   Constance Ollerenshaw's solicitor, an agreeable, sensible, happily married man whom Frances Wingate admires and likes in Margaret Drabble's *The Realms of Gold.*

Henry D. Barnard   See Chalmers Bryant.

Megan Barnard   Betty's intelligent, observant sister; she joins forces with Hercule Poirot to find her sister's killer in Agatha Christie's *The A.B.C. Murders.*

Ralph Barnby   Third-generation painter of talent; he is Edgar Deacon's tenant in Anthony Powell's *A Buyer's Market.* He is a well-known womanizer, involved amicably with Lady Anne Stepney, among others, in *The Acceptance World.* He is discussed in *Casanova's Chinese Restaurant,* in *The Kindly Ones,* and in *The Valley of Bones.* His murals for the Donners-Brebner building are destroyed by a bomb, and he is killed when his plane is shot down in *The Soldier's Art.*

Barnes   A soldier who thinks "The Lady of the Lake" is "good po'try", and tells Mike Brady and Jonathan Browne the story of his brother-in-law, the Jehovah's Witness, in David Lodge's *Ginger, You're Barmy.*

Lieutenant Barney Barnes   Black CIA agent who warns the narrator about bureaucratic traps being set for him; he is murdered for his loyalty in Len Deighton's *The Ipcress File.*

Cissie Barnes   General Curzon's abandoned but not forgotten old flame in C. S. Forester's *The General.*

June Barnes   Schoolmate of Kate Fletcher (Armstrong); upon leaving school, she took a lackluster position in an estate office in Margaret Drabble's *The Middle Ground.*

Sergeant Ruby Barnes   A sailing master on Earth who pilots the raft with which the explorers get to the Raman island and with which they rescue Lieutenant Pak in Arthur C. Clarke's *Rendezvous with Rama.*

Barney   A dwarf member of Nick Ollanton's magic act who grows more and more irresponsible; enticed and then insulted by Nonie Colmar, he strangles her but escapes the clutches of the law through an elaborate scheme devised by Nick, who has his own sense of justice in J. B. Priestley's *Lost Empires.*

William Barnstaple   Disillusioned Victorian socialist and journalist who crosses into another dimension, the perfect world of Utopia, where he resists attempts by other Earthlings to overthrow the Utopian system; in Utopia he learns that humanity's only hope of developing an equally mature society is through the persistence of ethical men like himself in H. G. Wells's *Men Like Gods.*

Robbie Barraclough   Academic sociologist in his late twenties; he is a resident in the West Oxfordshire village where Emma Howick has come to stay in Barbara Pym's *A Few Green Leaves.*

Tamsin Barraclough   Academic sociologist wife of Robbie; she is a resident in the West Oxfordshire village where Emma Howick has come to stay in Barbara Pym's *A Few Green Leaves.*

Lord Barralonga   Gnomish land baron whose automotive rampage across Utopia confounds its peaceful inhabitants and who supports Rupert Catskill's plan to overthrow Utopian rule in H. G. Wells's *Men Like Gods.*

Joseph Bannatyne Barralty   "Half-adventurer, half squire" but "ugly as sin"; he proposes to Lancelot Troth the enterprise to seek revenge on Valdemar Haraldsen in John Buchan's *The Island of Sheep.*

Barras   Belgian soldier and friend of Pierre Lavendie; he is a painter driven near to madness by his experiences on the battlefield in World War I in John Galsworthy's *Saint's Progress.*

Charlie Barrett   Singer for whom Bertram Verren provides piano accompaniment on a twenty-week provincial tour in Frank Swinnerton's *The Young Idea: A Comedy of Environment.*

Daisy Barrett   Tim Reede's lover, a fiercely honest, vituperative, harmless painter who no longer paints; after Tim returns to Gertrude Openshaw, she leaves for California in Iris Murdoch's *Nuns and Soldiers.*

Mabel Barrett   Wife of the singer Charlie Barrett; she has an affair with Bertram Verren, her husband's piano accompanist, in Frank Swinnerton's *The Young Idea: A Comedy of Environment.*

Barrios   Brave Costaguanan general in Joseph Conrad's *Nostromo: A Tale of the Seaboard.*

Mr. Barrow   Discretionary associate of Mr. Marsden; he is good at deception and convinces Hornblower to spy in C. S. Forester's *Hornblower And the Crisis: An Unfinished Novel.*

Dr. Barry   The Hall family's well-meaning neighbor, whose attempts to play the role of father and advisor to Maurice Hall are unsuccessful in E. M. Forster's *Maurice.*

Major Barry   Tiresome storyteller with an abnormal interest in gossip in Agatha Christie's *Evil Under the Sun.*

Clyde Barstow   British consul at Wallacia who represents Jane Murray at her trial; she is convicted, and he is assassinated later in Margaret Drabble's *The Ice Age.*

Bart   Ellie O'Grady's fiancé in Mary Lavin's *Mary O'Grady.*

Hussell Barter   Rector of Worsted Skeynes who opposes Gregory Vigil's efforts to secure a divorce for Helen Bellew in John Galsworthy's *The Country House.*

Rose Barter   Wife of the Rector Hussell Barter; she delivers her eleventh child in John Galsworthy's *The Country House.*

Tom Barter   An employee of Philip Crow and, later, of Johnny Geard; his profligacy produces twins and then marriage to their mother, Tossie Stickles; his homosexual love for John Crow culminates in his death, defending John, at the hands of Finn Toller in John Cowper Powys's *A Glastonbury Romance.*

Mr. Bartholomew   Ninety-year-old, eccentric, well-traveled gentleman with excellent manners; living on a Caribbean island, he gives parties in the kitchen and on the beach for all visitors and residents in Rosamond Lehmann's *A Sea-Grape Tree.*

Bartle   The seventeen-year-old irrepressible "boy" servant of the Lovats; he eavesdrops on the servants to discover the latest gossip in Ivy Compton-Burnett's *Darkness and Day.*

Bartlett   The Westons' butler in Isabel Colegate's *Statues in a Garden.*

Charlotte Bartlett   Lucy Honeychurch's well-meaning but troublesome cousin and chaperone on a trip to Italy; she tries to keep Lucy and George Emerson apart, only to turn around and unite them in E. M. Forster's *A Room with a View.*

Evie Bartlett   Mousey wife of the vicar in E. F. Benson's *Miss Mapp,* in *Mapp and Lucia,* in *The Worshipful Lucia,* and in *Trouble for Lucia.*

Hector Bartlett   Hanger-on of the novelist Emma Loy, member of a radionics-blackmail group, and "pisseur de copie" according to Nancy Hawkins in Muriel Spark's *A Far Cry from Kensington.*

Kenneth (Padre) Bartlett   Card-playing vicar of Tilling; though he comes from Birmingham, he speaks in a distinctive combination of Elizabethan English and Scottish dialect in E. F. Benson's *Miss Mapp,* in *Mapp and Lucia,* in *The Worshipful Lucia,* and in *Trouble for Lucia.*

Paul A. Bartlett   Large, self-confident scientist of about forty who is appointed leader of the group of scientists who will populate a new colony in space; his brittle inflexibility leads to an intense conflict with his group in Anthony Burgess's *The End of the World News.*

Miss Barton   A Fellow at Shrewsbury College, Oxford; her book attacking the subjugation of women is burnt in Dorothy L. Sayers's *Gaudy Night.*

Ivy Barton   Twenty-year-old country girl who was a model for Bianca Dallison; she copies old Mr. Stone's book manuscript and unsuccessfully tries to persuade Hilary Dallison to take her with him when he leaves in John Galsworthy's *Fraternity.*

Basil   A fictional character in the writing of the Unnamable; he is later called Mahood in Samuel Beckett's *The Unnamable.*

Mrs. Basil   The wife of an officer in Burma; her prolonged affair with Edward Ashburnham leads to her husband's blackmailing Edward for years in Ford Madox Ford's *The Good Soldier: A Tale of Passion.*

Wilfred Bason   Fussy, spinsterish, gossipy housekeeper and gourmet cook for the celibate priests in the St. Luke's clergy house in Barbara Pym's *A Glass of Blessings.* His menus are still remembered and discussed in *A Few Green Leaves.*

Bassett   A worker on the country estate of Chevron in Vita Sackville-West's *The Edwardians.*

Madeline Bassett   Golden-haired, baby-talking girl who perceives Bertie Wooster as an acceptable fall-back suitor in P. G. Wodehouse's *The Code of the Woosters* and in four other novels.

Sir Watkyn Bassett   Madeline's father, who competes with Tom Travers for possession of a silver cow-creamer and for the services of the French cook Anatole in P. G. Wodehouse's *The Code of the Woosters*. He appears in two other novels.

Myra Bassingfield   Frank Dawley's girlfriend and mother of his infant son, Mark; she left her husband to live with Frank in Algeria until Frank left on an idealistic gun-running mission for the Algerian guerillas in Alan Sillitoe's *The Death of William Posters*. She returns to England and becomes involved with the family of Frank's best friend, Albert Handley; when their house burns down she invites them to live with her on the large estate left to her when her husband died in *A Tree on Fire*.

Jacky Bast   Leonard's uncultured wife; brought with Leonard to a Wilcox family event by the restitution-seeking Helen Schlegel, Jacky recognizes Henry Wilcox as her old lover; Helen's sympathetic but extreme response brings more disaster upon the Basts in E. M. Forster's *Howards End*.

Leonard Bast   Poor clerk whose aspirations for culture lead to his involvement with the Schlegel sisters and consequently, through a series of misunderstandings and mishaps, to his economic ruin and death; he is the father of Helen Schlegel's baby and is killed by Charles Wilcox in E. M. Forster's *Howards End*.

Bastaki   Son of a Rumanian industrialist; a corrupt businessman, he is Stefan Saridza's contact man in Prague in Eric Ambler's *Uncommon Danger*.

Mrs. Bas-Thornton   A well-read, well-intending woman incapable of understanding her children or of being an object of interest to them in Richard Hughes's *A High Wind in Jamaica*.

Edward Bas-Thornton   Younger brother of Emily Bas-Thornton; he enjoys being aboard the pirate ship in Richard Hughes's *A High Wind in Jamaica*.

Emily Bas-Thornton   Ten-year-old girl who, en route with her siblings to the safety of England after a hurricane in Jamaica, is accidentally captured by pirates; in mistaken fear she kills another captive, a Dutch captain who wants her to help him escape; though her hysterical testimony condemns the pirate captain, Jonsen, to hang, she retains the savage innocence of childhood throughout her adventures in Richard Hughes's *A High Wind in Jamaica*.

Frederick Bas-Thornton   Emily's father, who understands his daughter enough to be afraid of her in Richard Hughes's *A High Wind in Jamaica*.

John Bas-Thornton   The eldest of the Bas-Thornton children; he is killed in an accidental fall, and his name is never again mentioned by his siblings in Richard Hughes's *A High Wind in Jamaica*.

Laura Bas-Thornton   Three-year-old youngest of the Bas-Thornton children; she, Edward, and Rachel are the "Liddlies", for whom John and Emily are expected to be responsible in Richard Hughes's *A High Wind in Jamaica*.

Rachel Bas-Thornton   Younger sister of John and Emily Bas-Thornton in Richard Hughes's *A High Wind in Jamaica*.

Mrs. Batch   Boarding-house landlady who likes to mother her Oxford-undergraduate tenants, especially the Duke of Dorset, in Max Beerbohm's *Zuleika Dobson; or An Oxford Love Story*.

Clarence Batch   Katie's young brother, who returns home to describe the drowning of the Duke of Dorset and the other undergraduates in Max Beerbohm's *Zuleika Dobson; or An Oxford Love Story*.

Katie Batch   The landlady's daughter whose silent love for the Duke of Dorset is rewarded by his giving her, just before his suicide, the earrings Zuleika Dobson gave him in Max Beerbohm's *Zuleika Dobson; or An Oxford Love Story*.

Barbara Batchelor   Retired missionary teacher and companion to Mabel Layton at Rose Cottage; her presence in Rose Cottage is a continuing irritation to Mabel's daughter-in-law, Mildred Layton, who would like to live there herself; within days of Mabel's death, Barbara is forced to find other accommodations in Paul Scott's *The Towers of Silence*. After having been injured in a fall from a small cart, she ends up in hospital unable, or unwilling, to communicate with anyone but Sarah Layton in *A Division of the Spoils*.

Latimer Bateman   Peter's son, constantly humiliated by his father and by Sophia Stace's wounding comments; he obtains a partnership-apprenticeship with the "little house agent" in Ivy Compton-Burnett's *Brothers and Sisters*.

Matilda (Tilly) Bateman   Peter's daughter, who adores her Stace cousins but agrees to marry the "little house agent" so that she and Latimer Bateman can have a future in Ivy Compton-Burnett's *Brothers and Sisters*.

Peter Bateman   A cousin of the Staces; a neighborhood doctor with no tact or discretion, he spreads the news of Christian and Sophia Stace's incest in Ivy Compton-Burnett's *Brothers and Sisters.*

Bates   Miranda Hume's maid who tells Miss Burke of the vacant housekeeper position in the neighborhood in Ivy Compton-Burnett's *Mother and Son.*

Bates   Colonel Calloway's man who is shot by Harry Lime, whom he is tracking in the sewer beneath Vienna in Graham Greene's *The Third Man and the Fallen Idol.*

Miss Bates   Teacher who suggested a job possibility to Kate Fletcher (Armstrong) when she was age sixteen in Margaret Drabble's *The Middle Ground.*

Amy Bates   Young maid who grows old in service to the Baines family; she becomes unprecedentedly critical of old Constance and Sophia and loses her place in Arnold Bennett's *The Old Wives Tale.*

Eliza Bates   A sociable elderly woman in Maudie Fowler's neighborhood; her social rank is better than Maudie's in Doris Lessing's *The Diaries of Jane Somers.*

Ildiko Bates   An Oxford friend of Sarah Bennett; he joins David Vesey and Simon Rathbone in throwing a party, at which Sarah meets Jackie Almond in Margaret Drabble's *A Summer Bird-Cage.*

Joe Bates   Coal workers' union leader in Benditch; D. cannot persuade him to refuse to work for enemy agent L.'s contract in Graham Greene's *The Confidential Agent.*

Louis Bates   An unsophisticated, unconventional, maladroit, self-important student with a possible poetic gift; he falls in love with Emma Fielding, attempts suicide, and ends up in a mental hospital in Malcolm Bradbury's *Eating People Is Wrong.*

Prudence Bates   Twenty-nine-year-old London spinster, who shares her romantic woes and triumphs with Jane Cleveland, her friend and former English tutor at Oxford; she is Arthur Grampian's research assistant and hopelessly devoted lover in Barbara Pym's *Jane and Prudence.* Her "love affairs" are mentioned again in *A Glass of Blessings.*

Theodora Bates   Friend of Orlando King in Italy; she lives near Orlando's villa and takes Agatha King under her protection in Isabel Colegate's *Orlando at the Brazen Threshold.*

Bathkaarnet-she   A half-human Madi who is Sayren Stund's wife and queen of Oldorando in Brian W. Aldiss's *Helliconia Summer.*

Albert Batt   Elevator operator at the residence of Marguerite Vandemeyer; he becomes Tuppence and Tommy Beresford's office boy in Agatha Christie's *The Secret Adversary.* He becomes their butler, appearing in the remaining three Beresford novels, ending with *Postern of Fate.*

Elsie Batt   Mrs. Craddock's chambermaid; she supplies information about Mrs. Craddock's association with Dr. Roberts in Agatha Christie's *Cards on the Table.*

Mrs. Battacharya   Indian woman who invites Mrs. Moore and Adela Quested to her home in E. M. Forster's *A Passage to India.*

Battle   Hyperactive, tap-dancing black man, an ex-sailor committed to a psychiatric hospital after knocking out his second engineer's tooth; he threatens others with "treatment 63" in Malcolm Lowry's *Lunar Caustic.*

Superintendent Battle   Careful, relentless Scotland Yard man, who works with Hercule Poirot and Ariadne Oliver to solve the murder of Mr. Shaitana in Agatha Christie's *Cards on the Table.* He appears in four other novels.

Batty   Colin Saville's childhood friend, who does not escape the poverty of the coalmine family in David Storey's *Saville.*

Father Baudouin   Jesuit confessor and ally of Sister Alexandra in Muriel Spark's *The Abbess of Crewe.*

Mr. Bauersch   Well-dressed book buyer from New York; he deplores Henry Earlforward's refusal to provide even the minimum services for customers, but acknowledges he will continue to seek rarities in the shop in Arnold Bennett's *Riceyman Steps.*

Dr. Bauerstein   A German spy disguised as a convalescent; he is an expert on poisons in Agatha Christie's *The Mysterious Affair at Styles: A Detective Story.*

Mr. Baxter   English pharmaceutical salesman, former air-raid warden, and passenger on the *Medea*; he dies of a heart attack in Graham Greene's *The Comedians.*

Rupert Baxter   Lord Emsworth's suspicious secretary, whose investigations are interpreted as evidence of derangement in P. G. Wodehouse's *Something New.* His dismissal is mourned by Lady Constance Keeble; she hires him to steal and destroy the manuscript of

Galahad Threepwood's almost-completed memoirs in *Fish Preferred*. He appears in three other novels.

Ludwig Bayer Communist Party leader who tells William Bradshaw of Arthur Norris's intrigues and is later assassinated in Christopher Isherwood's *Mr. Norris Changes Trains*.

Mr. Bayliss Penniless, skeleton-like, tubercular young man with costly tastes, the protégé of Mrs. Satterthwaite in Ford Madox Ford's *Some Do Not. . . .*

Louisa Baynes Philip Bosinney's aunt, who cannot tell June Forsyte about Bosinney's relationship with Irene Forsyte in John Galsworthy's *The Man of Property*.

Bazhakuloff (Messiah) Russian ex-monk who moves to Nepenthe; his disciples record his words in the *Golden Book* in Norman Douglas's *South Wind*.

Sebastian Beach Blandings Castle butler, whose appearance bodes imminent apoplexy but who is merely a hypochondriac in P. G. Wodehouse's *Something New*. Endebted to Ronnie Fish for profitable horse-racing tips, he assists Ronnie in kidnapping Lord Emsworth's prize sow, the Empress of Blandings, in *Fish Preferred*. He appears in nine other novels.

Beale Cabinet minister who wishes to find out what the popular reaction will be to Jim Drover's execution in Graham Greene's *It's a Battlefield*.

Mary Beamish "Excellent" woman, devoted to church and social work, who becomes landlady to Father Ransome and considers a vocation in a religious community, once freed from caring for her elderly mother in Barbara Pym's *A Glass of Blessings*.

Tommy Beamish A born comic who is at the top of the bill on the variety circuit; he cannot fully control his sadistic streak and a touch of madness in J. B. Priestley's *Lost Empires*.

Old Bean Solicitor who locates Art Kipps through a newspaper announcement and who handles his inheritance and finances in H. G. Wells's *Kipps: The Story of a Simple Soul*.

"Granny" Bean Resident patient so old as to seem androgynous; her hundredth birthday is celebrated in the old women's hospital ward in Muriel Spark's *Memento Mori*.

Ceridwen Beard Welsh sister of Leonora Beard and sister-in-law of Ronald Beard; she nurses and comforts Beard after the death of his wife in Anthony Burgess's *Beard's Roman Women*.

Leonora Beard Alcoholic, tart-tongued wife of Ronald Beard; she dies of cirrhosis of the liver but remains very much alive in his memory, even to making phantom phone calls to him in Rome in Anthony Burgess's *Beard's Roman Women*.

Ronald Beard Fiftyish film-script writer and heavy drinker; he is a Briton living in Rome more or less permanently; he deludes himself only about important matters, including his love for Paola Belli in Anthony Burgess's *Beard's Roman Women*.

Maudie Beardon A tall, thin, twenty-eight-year-old fellow chorus girl with yellow hair and white skin; she is Anna Morgan's early roommate in Jean Rhys's *Voyage in the Dark*.

Cyril ("Sybil", "Pat") Beardsall Lettie Beardsall's self-effacing bachelor brother; his slow-maturing avowed love is for Emily Saxton, but his most deeply felt affection is for Emily's brother George; he is narrator of D. H. Lawrence's *The White Peacock*.

Frank Beardsall Unkempt, dying father of Lettie and Cyril; he does not identify himself to them when he encounters them after an eighteen-years absence in D. H. Lawrence's *The White Peacock*.

Lettice Beardsall Mother of Lettie and Cyril; her husband left her eighteen years earlier; finding him dead, she regrets that she kept his children from him for so many years in D. H. Lawrence's *The White Peacock*.

Lettie Beardsall Romantic, selfish, charming girl; after considerable vacillation, she marries the more eligible but the less physically compelling of two devoted suitors; the happiness of her successful marriage comes from maternity in D. H. Lawrence's *The White Peacock*.

Beatrice Cynthia, Lady Weston's personal maid, who carries the news of Cynthia's affair with Philip Weston to Sir Aylmer Weston after she is rejected by Ralph Moberly in Isabel Colegate's *Statues in a Garden*.

Beatrice (Trissie) Reuben Egerton's fiancée; the daughter of a clergyman, she is pursued sexually by Hereward Egerton, Reuben's father, in Ivy Compton-Burnett's *A God and His Gifts*.

Beatrice Rosamund Stacey's sister, an Oxford graduate; a pacifist, she is a housewife living with her atomic-scientist husband and her three children in the Midlands in Margaret Drabble's *The Millstone*.

Mrs. Beauchamp Landlady who watches visitors to Lewis Eliot's rooms where he lives alone after his wife's suicide and who gossips with him about them in C. P. Snow's *Homecomings*.

Henri de Beaujolais   Patient, concerned, observant military man and storyteller; he belongs to the Spahis XIXth (African) Army Corps; he uses his reasoning to solve a mystery he narrates to his friend George Lawrence while traveling; he is an inspiration to the Geste brothers in Percival Christopher Wren's *Beau Geste*.

Beauty   Girlfriend of Trevor Lomas in Muriel Spark's *The Ballad of Peckham Rye*.

Mrs. Beaver   John Beaver's unprincipled mother; she is the proprietor of a London interior-decorating business whose sole interest is making money in Evelyn Waugh's *A Handful of Dust*.

John Beaver   Brenda Last's parasitic lover, who deserts her when she is no longer able to finance their affair in Evelyn Waugh's *A Handful of Dust*.

Anthony Beavis   Directionless intellectual who attempts to sort out his spiritual growth in a series of fragmented diary entries, at the center of which are his relationships with Helen Ledwidge, his longtime lover, and with Dr. Miller, an ardent pacifist from whom he discovers something about human decency in Aldous Huxley's *Eyeless in Gaza*.

Gadi Becker ("the Steppenwolf", Jose; covernames: Peter Richthoven, Joseph)   Disillusioned Israeli military hero and skeptical Mossad (Israeli intelligence) operative, who is manipulated by Marty Kurtz into seducing Charlie; he scripts her infiltration into Khalil's inner circle, murders Khalil in her bed, and, after finally rejecting Kurtz's moral uncertainty, returns to Charlie to try to repair their shattered psyches in John le Carré's *The Little Drummer Girl*.

Ralph Becker   Wealthy banker acquaintance of Theodora Bates in Isabel Colegate's *Orlando at the Brazen Threshold*.

Dr. Beckerman   Senior teacher at Petersons School who falls into an insane fit at seeing Bryan Morley's statue of a nude Fay Corrigan exhibited at the school in David Storey's *A Prodigal Child*.

Beautiful Joe Beckett   A cynical, manipulative young thug loved by Cato Forbes; when Joe, who has kidnapped both Cato and his sister, Colette Forbes, in an extortion scheme, is attempting to rape Colette, Cato kills him in Iris Murdoch's *Henry and Cato*.

Mrs. Beddoes   Tom Mallow's wealthy aunt from Belgravia who expresses the family's concern about Tom's living with Catherine Oliphant and gives a coming-out party for her daughter attended by Mark Penfold in Barbara Pym's *Less Than Angels*.

Belinda Bede   The elder of two middle-aged spinsters whose lives center on church activities in a small village; she is harmlessly devoted to the local vicar, with whom she fell in love at Oxford while studying seventeenth-century poetry in Barbara Pym's *Some Tame Gazelle*.

Harriet Bede   Plump spinster sister of Belinda; she plays the piano, flirts with young curates, and has an affinity for colorful clothes in Barbara Pym's *Some Tame Gazelle*.

Bedford   A bankrupt businessman and fledgling playwright who assists Cavor in developing Cavorite and in building the space ship with which they explore the moon; when they become separated there, he is forced to return to Earth alone, where he settles in Italy to write his account of their adventures in H. G. Wells's *The First Men in the Moon*.

Mrs. Bedley   Venerable "Mother of the English Colony" of Kairoulla, the capital of Pisuerga, who operates a combined circulating library and tea-room, provides information to tourists, and resents her lack of social status relative to the Court society of Pisuerga in Ronald Firbank's *The Flower Beneath the Foot*.

Arthur Beebe   Understanding rector of Summer Street who observes and sympathizes with Lucy Honeychurch's dilemma in E. M. Forster's *A Room with a View*.

Lady Beeder   Sir William's wife, an aspiring artist in Joyce Cary's *The Horse's Mouth*.

Sir William Beeder   Wealthy art collector and a benefactor of Gulley Jimson; he wishes to obtain one of Gulley's nudes; Gulley ransacks his apartment while staying there and then sells him a reproduction of one of his nudes in Joyce Cary's *The Horse's Mouth*.

Max Beerbohm   A writer who was once seated next to Zuleika Dobson at a dinner; the literary flavor of her speech was picked up from his example in Max Beerbohm's *Zuleika Dobson; or An Oxford Love Story*.

Alfred Beesley   A member of the university English Department and a resident in the rooming house where Jim Dixon lives; he gives Jim notes on "The Age of Chaucer" to use in Jim's "Merrie England" lecture in Kingsley Amis's *Lucky Jim*.

Mrs. Beetle   The first normal, civil person that Flora

Poste meets at Cold Comfort Farm; she is in contrast with the Starkadder family in Stella Gibbons's *Cold Comfort Farm.*

Agony Beetle   Meriam's normal, civil father in Stella Gibbons's *Cold Comfort Farm.*

Meriam Beetle   Simple, rural hired girl who gives birth once a year as the natural result of springtime passions; she is finally captured by Urk Starkadder as an earthy alternative to the ethereal Elfine Starkadder in Stella Gibbons's *Cold Comfort Farm.*

Miss Beevor   Violin teacher who becomes obsessed with the conviction that the untalented Cordelia Aubrey will become a great musician; she wears huge feathered hats, and she becomes roguish and plump, supposedly because she gains nourishment from her hopes for Cordelia in Rebecca West's *The Fountain Overflows.*

Beguildy   A wizard and an aggressive atheist; Jancis Beguildy's father, he destroys the property of the Sarn family in vengeance against Gideon Sarn's sleeping with Jancis prior to marriage in Mary Webb's *Precious Bane.*

Jancis Beguildy   Daughter of the village wizard, Beguildy; she is beautiful and greatly loved by the Sarn family and by her own; after Beguildy burns Gideon Sarn's crops and Gideon refuses to support her and their baby, Jancis drowns herself and the infant in Mary Webb's *Precious Bane.*

"Missus" Beguildy   Wife of the wizard, Beguildy, and mother of Jancis Beguildy; in her husband's absence she permits Jancis and Gideon Sarn's unlawful wedding night with tragic consequences in Mary Webb's *Precious Bane.*

Michel Behgin   Overweight, intelligent, middle-aged, masterful French agent; a member of the Secret Generale attached to the French Department of Naval Intelligence, he blackmails Josef Vadassy into discovering the identity of the spy who took the photographs, acts as his control, and ultimately corners the real spy and is responsible for his death in Eric Ambler's *Epitaph for a Spy.*

Clair Belaine   Annabel Paynton's close friend and confidante, who becomes involved with Charles Addinsell, in whom Annabel is also interested, in Henry Green's *Doting.*

Belarab   Ousted successor to the rule of Wajo; he leads the settlement of "vanquished fanatics, fugitives, and outcasts" living on the Shore of Refuge in Joseph Conrad's *The Rescue: A Romance of the Shallows.*

Hugo Belfounder   An entrepreneur businessman and patron of the performing arts who befriends Jake Donaghue at a common-cold research establishment and inspires *The Silencer,* Jake's philosophical treatise in dialogue; Hugo's disappointing romantic involvement with the sisters Anna and Sadie Quentin ends in his giving up his theatrical pursuits to become a watchmaker in Iris Murdoch's *Under the Net.*

Sir Henry Belfrage   The British ambassador to Argentina; he would like to be rid of Charley Fortnum, the Honorary Consul, but he offers some help to Dr. Eduardo Plarr when Charley is kidnapped in Graham Greene's *The Honorary Consul.*

Clara (Claribel) Bell   Anna Donne's older cousin, who has been part of the family since Anna's mother died in Ivy Compton-Burnett's *Elders and Betters.*

Edwin Bell   Former headmaster of a foundling boys' school in Greenfield; he is one of the three men who provide commentary on the events in William Golding's *Darkness Visible.*

Mrs. Bellairs   A member of the spy ring "The Free Mothers"; fronting as a fortune teller and medium, she passes along information through specific clients in Graham Greene's *The Ministry of Fear.*

Camilla Bellamy   Divorced wife of Edward Bellamy; she is a femme fatale who pursues Sir Godfrey Haslem when his wife dies, but she becomes engaged to the richer lawyer Dominic Spong in Ivy Compton-Burnett's *Men and Wives.*

Edward Bellamy   The rector of the Haslams' parish; he is a nervous, self-dramatizing man, who divorces Camilla, proposes to Griselda Haslam and, after the Haslam family scandals, proposes to Kate Dabis in Ivy Compton-Burnett's *Men and Wives.*

Tessa Bellamy   Ailing upper-class Englishwoman who, accompanied by her young cousin, Sydney Warren, is wintering at a resort in northern Italy favored by the British in Elizabeth Bowen's *The Hotel.*

Mr. Bellby   Junior barrister who works with Dreamer, Q.C., on Winifred Dartie's divorce case in John Galsworthy's *In Chancery.*

Helen Bellew   Wife of Captain Bellew; she is separated from her husband and is sued for divorce with George Pendyce as co-respondent; she ceases to care for George and leaves him in John Galsworthy's *The Country House.*

Captain Jaspar Bellew Landowner and neighbor of the Pendyces; he sues his wife for divorce, naming George Pendyce as co-respondent, and drops his suit after appeal from Margery Pendyce in John Galsworthy's *The Country House.*

Paola Lucrezia Belli A beautiful, thirtyish, Italian still photographer; separated from her Jamaican husband, she meets Ronald Beard at a Hollywood party and becomes his lover in Anthony Burgess's *Beard's Roman Women.*

Arturo Bellinetti Effusive office assistant to Sidney Arthur Ferning, later to Nick Marlow; an agent of OVRA (Italian secret police), he spies on Marlow and is responsible for the assault on him in Eric Ambler's *Cause for Alarm.*

Oscar Belling Julian Baffin's art-student boyfriend; Julian destroys his letters but eventually marries him in Iris Murdoch's *The Black Prince.*

Christopher Bellman A scholar and antiquarian; the widowed father of Frances, he is in love with Millie Kinnard, whom he assists financially and to whom he becomes briefly engaged; though apolitical, he is killed by a sniper in the 1916 Easter Rising in Iris Murdoch's *The Red and the Green.*

Frances Bellman An Anglo-Irish girl, Christopher Bellman's daughter; though everyone expects her to marry Andrew Chase-White, when his proposal comes she turns it down, being in love with her first cousin Pat Dumay in Iris Murdoch's *The Red and the Green.*

Dr. Bellows Director of the Entrenationo Language Centre in London, where D. meets his contact in Graham Greene's *The Confidential Agent.*

Charles Belrose Hearty wholesaler of cheeses; he discovers the body of the miser Henry Earlforward by his open safe on the evening of his wife's death in hospital, and he discovers Earlforward's servant Elsie Sprickett hiding her beloved Joe upstairs in Arnold Bennett's *Riceyman Steps.*

Mrs. Charles Belrose Large, jolly, compassionate wife of a cheesemaker; she willingly calls the hospital for news of Violet Earlforward for the servant Elsie Sprickett and is informed of Violet's death from undernourishment in Arnold Bennett's *Riceyman Steps.*

Harry, Lord Belses Eldest son of Lord Snowdoun, Minister of Scotland; he is made prisoner by Squire Cranmer, escapes, is injured, and finds succor in the home of the minister Mr. Blackstocks; he joins the Free Fishers and Wyse in saving the lives of the Prime Minister and Gabriel Cranmer, whom he loves and who, one day, will love him and marry him in John Buchan's *The Free Fishers.*

Mrs. Beltane Blue-haired, smug suburban widow who fancies her grey poodle more than her grown children; she lives next door to Dulcie Mainwaring in Barbara Pym's *No Fond Return of Love.*

Paul Beltane Shy young owner of a florist's shop who lives next door to Dulcie Mainwaring and becomes romantically interested in her niece Laurel in Barbara Pym's *No Fond Return of Love.*

Ben Phoebe's husband, who is the caretaker of Daniel Martin's country house, Thorncombe, in John Fowles's *Daniel Martin.*

Ben A refugee who has been rescued by Jahor from a whirlpool; afterwards he is unable to emerge from his state of shock in Doris Lessing's *Re: Colonised Planet 5, Shikasta.*

Ben Mentally handicapped man who lives near the cottage to which Rebecca de Winter used to bring her lovers in Daphne Du Maurier's *Rebecca.*

Albert Benbow A vulgar opportunist who marries Clara Clayhanger; he juggles false camaraderie and reluctant deference to her brother, Edwin, in Arnold Bennett's *Clayhanger.* His treatment of his children, his attempts to be noticed socially, and his financial incompetence cause Edwin to despise him in *These Twain.*

Bert Benbow Cowed eldest son of Albert Benbow in Arnold Bennett's *These Twain.*

Lord Benditch Rose Cullen's father, an English coal magnate whom D. attempts to persuade into providing coal for his government in Graham Greene's *The Confidential Agent.*

Maurice Bendrix Middle-aged, jealous, cynical, self-absorbed, materialistic, intellectual, sexually proficient bachelor and professional writer; a former lover of Sarah Miles, he attempts to resurrect the affair after a two-year hiatus and after engaging a detective to follow Sarah; he asks the dead Sarah to help him avoid starting an affair with Sylvia Black; after the funeral, he moves in with Henry Miles and gradually begins to take care of him just as Sarah did as a means of expiation of guilt in Graham Greene's *The End of the Affair.*

Alice Benedict Kitty Weston's companion/governess, who falls in love with Edmund Weston and is disliked by Cynthia, Lady Weston; Alice is the third-person narrator of Isabel Colegate's *Statues in a Garden*.

Dr. Benevento Dr. Eduardo Plarr's only medical colleague in the northern Argentine city; he regularly "inspects" the girls at Senora Sanchez's brothel in Graham Greene's *The Honorary Consul*.

Flora Beniform Howard Kirk's current lover; she makes a habit of going to bed with men who have troubled marriages in Malcolm Bradbury's *The History Man*.

Gabriel Benito Ishmaelian governmental official engaged in an unsuccessful coup to overthrow the ruling Jackson family and set up a Soviet state in Evelyn Waugh's *Scoop*.

Benjamin Well educated, formal Post Office clerk in Fada and friend of Johnson; although he tries to bring excitement to his life by stealing stamp monies, he rebukes Johnson for stealing from Gollup in Joyce Cary's *Mister Johnson*.

Mrs. Benjamin Maid at Wood Hill from Mount Sorrel in Isabel Colegate's *Agatha*.

Benjie School caretaker who informs the headmaster about the sexual acts committed by Miss Manning and Mr. Carew on school property in William Golding's *Free Fall*.

Lady Eva Bennerley Sir Clifford Chatterley's imperious, elderly aunt; she is one of the Wragby Hall "mental-lifers" who condemn the "life of the body" and the "love-business" in D. H. Lawrence's *Lady Chatterley's Lover*.

Miss Bennet The head nurse to the Clare children; she is kind and interested in others in Ivy Compton-Burnett's *The Present and the Past*.

Bennett Communist Party leader who thinks Conder is following him, while Conder thinks the same of him in Graham Greene's *It's a Battlefield*.

Bennett Ship's boy who recovers from an attack of terror to become wholly possessed by his task of pouring out oil to quiet the waves engulfing the *Archimedes* during the hurricane in Richard Hughes's *In Hazard*.

Captain Bennett Captain of the flying boat who plans to retrieve a hoard of gold left hidden by Nazis at the end of World War II; he goes crazy when the money is found and shoots one of his crew as they load

the gold; he is killed when the plane crashes in Alan Sillitoe's *The Lost Flying Boat*.

Mr. Bennett Father of Sarah and of Louise Halifax in Margaret Drabble's *A Summer Bird-Cage*.

Mrs. Bennett Mother of Sarah and of Louise Halifax in Margaret Drabble's *A Summer Bird-Cage*.

Mrs. Bennett Rose Cullen's childhood nurse; she refuses to help D. when he seeks her out in Benditch in Graham Greene's *The Confidential Agent*.

"Benny" Bennett Aging servant whose deranged religiosity is supposed harmless; she kills Freddy Hamilton's mother in Muriel Spark's *The Mandlebaum Gate*.

Elizabeth Bennett A married woman who is separated from her husband; she has an affair with Colin Saville in David Storey's *Saville*.

Sarah (Sal) Bennett Intellectual and pretty sister of the bride Louise Bennett Halifax; she is at loose ends after graduating from Oxford and waiting for her fiancé to return from America; she finally acquires a sense of self separate from the personality and powers of her sister in Margaret Drabble's *A Summer Bird-Cage*.

Mr. Bensington Timid, nervous scientist, who is both hailed and reviled as the inventor of herakleophorbia, the growth-inducing compound commonly called Boomfood; he first enjoys and then endures his notoriety, and he retires to a Tunbridge Wells sanitorium after a mob attempts to assassinate him in H. G. Wells's *The Food of the Gods, and How It Came to Earth*.

Ted Benskin Barrister who leads in the defense of Cora Ross in C. P. Snow's *The Sleep of Reason*.

Mrs. Benson Disagreeable employer of Anne Meredith; she dies after consuming hat paint instead of Syrup of Figs in Agatha Christie's *Cards on the Table*.

Bill Bent Husband of Karen Michaelis's Aunt Violet in Elizabeth Bowen's *The House in Paris*.

Violet Bent Cork relative with whom Karen Michaelis takes refuge while she tries to sort out her ambivalent feelings about her engagement to Ray Forrestier; Violet's serious illness and pending surgery increase Karen's feeling that before she marries she must know more about life in Elizabeth Bowen's *The House in Paris*.

Mr. Justice Bentham Judge who decides the case

brought by Soames Forsyte against Philip Bosinney in John Galsworthy's *The Man of Property.*

Lord William Bentinck   British Minister in Palmero in C. S. Forester's *Hornblower and the Atropos.*

Delia Bentley   The thirty-year-old daughter of Henry; she is kind to her younger stepbrothers in Ivy Compton-Burnett's *Pastors and Masters.*

Henry Bentley   The father of two boys at Mr. Herrick's school; he berates and badgers his sons and daughter Delia in Ivy Compton-Burnett's *Pastors and Masters.*

Jasper Bentwich   Rather cynical esthete who spends time at Lady Nelly Staveley's Venetian palazzo; he befriends Eustace Cherrington and provides commentary on the characters in L. P. Hartley's *Eustace and Hilda.*

Wilfred Bentworth   Old Squire who accepts the chairmanship of Michael Mont's committee for slum clearance in John Galsworthy's *Swan Song.* He is chairman of Hilary Cherrell's slum-conversion committee in *Maid in Waiting.*

Tegwen Benyon   Oldest of seven children of impoverished parents; she encourages Huw Morgan to witness the birth of her mother's child in Richard Llewellyn's *How Green Was My Valley.*

Bere   An old farmer who is a distant relative of the Forsyte family in John Galsworthy's *Swan Song.*

Beregond   Human friend whom Pippin Took rescues in J. R. Tolkien's *The Two Towers.*

Prudence Cowley (Tuppence) Beresford   Spirited, ingenious young wife and partner in adventure of Tommy Beresford in Agatha Christie's *The Secret Adversary.* The mysteries continue and the family increases and ages through two other novels before the last, *Postern of Fate.*

Thomas (Tommy) Beresford   Red-haired, unimaginative, twice-wounded lieutenant; jobless after World War I, he becomes involved in preventing a plot to take over Britain in Agatha Christie's *The Secret Adversary.* He and his wife, Tuppence, establish the International Detective Agency and continue to solve crime in two other novels before they appear, retired and in their seventies, in *Postern of Fate.*

Alf Bergan   Assistant to the Dublin sub-sheriff's office; he is among the patriotic drinkers in Barney Kiernan's Pub in James Joyce's *Ulysses.*

Astrid Berger (covernames: Helga, Edda, Maria Brinkhausen)   German national and a calculating Palestinian mercenary; she sadistically threatens Charlie should she fail the Palestinian cause, and she suspects Charlie as a double agent in John le Carré's *The Little Drummer Girl.*

Anna Bergfeld   Austrian living in Michael Mont's parliamentary district; after her husband kills himself she becomes cook for Nora Curfew in John Galsworthy's *The Silver Spoon.*

Fritz Bergfeld   German actor who is married to Anna; he is given work on a poultry farm by Michael Mont; he hangs himself in John Galsworthy's *The Silver Spoon.*

Clara Bergmann   South German pupil in the Hanover school in Dorothy Richardson's *Pointed Roofs.*

Emma Bergmann   Younger sister of Clara and, at fourteen, the youngest pupil in the Hanover school; her piano-playing exemplifies German freedom of emotional expression as contrasted with English restraint in Dorothy Richardson's *Pointed Roofs.*

Mrs. Bergstein   A convert to Judaism from Unitarianism whom Miriam Henderson visits at the urging of Michael Shatov in Dorothy Richardson's *Deadlock.*

Berkeley-Tyne   Obnoxious editor of an art monthly; on the pretense of interviewing Janos Lavin at his exhibition, he delivers his own opinions on the modern artist, infuriating Lavin, who brushes him off in John Berger's *A Painter of Our Time.*

Maurice Berkley   The middle-aged, married, bitter manager of the Palladium cinema and former owner of the theater when it was a vaudeville house; he has an affair with the young usher Doreen Higgins, who becomes pregnant by him in David Lodge's *The Picturegoers.*

Commendatore Bernab   The Italian Ordnance Office's go-between for payment and for the Spartacus machinery information exchange between General Vagas and Nicholas Marlow in Eric Ambler's *Cause for Alarm.*

Jacques Bernadet   Stephan Zelli's former jailmate who, after Stephan's release from jail, is Stephan's "benefactor"; Marya Zelli immediately dislikes him in Jean Rhys's *Postures.*

Bernard   Phrasemaker and novelist, who as a child unable to distinguish between the knob of the dresser ("a loop of light") and the horizon, awakens to sensation with Nanny's sponge and fears to lose his self; he attempts to hang on with his beautiful, wise, witty words and to tell the "true" story of his friends' lives; after experiencing a dreaded loss of self during a solar eclipse, he regains his identity and is able at last to write the perfect novel, no longer merely collecting phrases in Virginia Woolf's *The Waves*.

Bernard   A young monk who helps Miles to accept his homosexuality in David Lodge's *How Far Can You Go?*.

Mr. Bernay   Pawnbroker who sells Conrad Drover the rusty gun with blank cartridges with which Conrad tries to kill the Assistant Commissioner in Graham Greene's *It's a Battlefield*.

Sir Paul Berowne   Government minister and baronet; he is murdered in an old church in P. D. James's *A Taste for Death*.

Porfirio Ilyitch Berr (Poor Berr)   Blind servant in the household of the exiled Count Nikolai Diakanov in Paris; Gorin (Monsieur Komensky) almost convinces Vassili Iulievitch Chubinov that Berr is guilty of spying on his master in Rebecca West's *The Birds Fall Down*.

Berry   A crewman aboard the *Renown* in C. S. Forester's *Lieutenant Hornblower*.

Berry   A timid maker of inconsequential remarks during conversations among the Wragby Hall intellectuals who surround Sir Clifford Chatterley in D. H. Lawrence's *Lady Chatterley's Lover*.

Bert   A lazy, completely amoral member of the IRA, highly attracted to terrorist activities as well as to women; Alice Mellings dislikes him in Doris Lessing's *The Good Terrorist*.

Bert   Working-class neighbor and father of five who helps Dan Graveson try to start a small grassroots peace movement in Alan Burns's *Buster*.

Bertha   Wife of "Fido" in Olaf Stapledon's *Odd John: A Story Between Jest and Earnest*.

Edward Berthelin   Idealistic French patriot who believes that after World War II is over a Christian society will be established; he remains in the army for ten years after the war because he thinks the army represents a positive and strong "gathering of men"; he later becomes the manager of Cousin Honoré's ironworks in Storm Jameson's *Cousin Honoré*.

Robert Berthelin   Strongly pro-English son of Edward Berthelin; he lost his mother when he was two years old; now 17, he loves Fanny Siguenau and enlists in the French army in Storm Jameson's *Cousin Honoré*.

Mrs. Bertram   Widowed, refined, money-borrowing mother of Sarah Miles; after Sarah's cremation, she confesses to Maurice Bendrix that she had Sarah baptized (secretly) a Roman Catholic, thereby reinforcing the significance of Sarah's desire to convert in Graham Greene's *The End of the Affair*.

Uncle Bertram   Dulcie Mainwaring's ostentatiously High-Church relation who contemplates entering a monastery in Barbara Pym's *No Fond Return of Love*.

Augusta Bertram   Henry Pulling's supposed aunt, who although in her late seventies continues to live as she always has, traveling from country to country and taking new lovers as she goes; upon the death of Henry's stepmother she takes Henry traveling with her and regales him with many stories about her past lovers and about his family; she winds up settling in Paraguay happily reunited with one of her lovers, Mr. Visconti, and is joined by Henry, who discovers that Aunt Augusta is actually his mother in Graham Greene's *Travels with My Aunt*.

Besi Besamitikahl   Eedam Mun Odin's mistress, who has an affair with Harbin Fashnalgid and eventually dies of the Fat Death in Brian W. Aldiss's *Helliconia Winter*.

Bess   Beautiful, gregarious lover, who makes herself ill over the past in Rex Warner's *The Aerodrome: A Love Story*.

Bessie   Employee at the women's lodging where the nurses live in Margaret Drabble's *The Millstone*.

Dr. Best   Insane psychiatrist in his forties with shining blue eyes and black-edged teeth; he typically diagnoses his patients as having problems with same-sex-sexual-attraction repression; suspected of being a spy, he comes to believe he is a member of the Anti-Death League in Kingsley Amis's *The Anti-Death League*.

Mr. Best   Librarian from the Irish National Library who criticizes Stephen Dedalus's interpretation of Shakespeare in James Joyce's *Ulysses*.

Ann Best   Attractive woman serving in the Wrens whom Alan Percival meets during a radio and radar training course and later marries in Roy Fuller's *The Perfect Fool*.

Margot Beste-Chetwynde   A wealthy socialite who controls a white-slavery ring; deciding to marry to boost her sagging social reputation, she becomes engaged to Paul Pennyfeather and sends her innocent fiancé on a risky mission connected with her business; after Paul's arrest she uses her influence with Humphrey Maltravers, her new husband and head of the prison system, to have Paul freed by faking his death in Evelyn Waugh's *Decline and Fall.*

Peter Beste-Chetwynde Margot's son, who is Paul Pennyfeather's student at Llanabba School; Peter takes a strong liking to Paul and is pleased that Paul may become his stepfather; he is an Oxford student drinking heavily at the end of Evelyn Waugh's *Decline and Fall.*

Gordon Bestwick Cambridge student from a poor background who is a friend of Charles Eliot; he is implicated in the national-security incident in C. P. Snow's *Last Things.*

Bethia The middle-aged maid of the Edgeworths; she declines the family invitation to go to church in Ivy Compton-Burnett's *A House and Its Head.*

Betty Nurse who cared for Gyp Winton (Fiersen) from infancy and then cared for Little Gyp (Fiersen) in John Galsworthy's *Beyond.*

Betty Haggard, vulgar girl who supports herself and her lover Edwin Froulish and pays for the apartment they share with Charles Lumley by prostituting herself to hypocritical Robert Tharkles in John Wain's *Hurry On Down.*

Aunt Betty Aunt of Sarah Bennett and Louise Bennett Halifax and mother of Cousin Michael and Cousin Daphne in Margaret Drabble's *A Summer Bird-Cage.*

Thomas Bevill Tory government minister who chairs committees in charge of atomic-energy research, loses his appointment during the war, and returns to government after the war to continue atomic-energy development; he offers to appoint Martin Eliot as head of research in C. P. Snow's *The New Men.* He becomes Lord Grampound before his death in *Corridors of Power.*

O. Killa Beynon A candidate for the same job that John Lewis wants; he is older than Lewis and has written pamphlets on Welsh antiquities in Kingsley Amis's *That Uncertain Feeling.*

Frank Bhoolabhoy Husband of the owner of Smith's hotel in Pankot; though he is hotel manager, Frank is kept in the dark about most of the hotel's business; he reluctantly composes the letter instructing Colonel

and Mrs. Smalley to vacate the Lodge, also owned by Lila Bhoolabhoy; Frank is a devoted member of St. John's Church, where he is an assistant warden, in Paul Scott's *Staying On.*

Lila Bhoolabhoy Wife of Frank Bhoolabhoy and owner of Smith's Hotel in Pankot; Lila dreams of great financial schemes to transform Smith's into a center of commerce; since part of her current scheme is to tear down The Lodge, where "Tusker" and Lucy Smalley have lived for many years, she makes her husband Frank write the eviction letter which precipitates "Tusker's" death in Paul Scott's *Staying On.*

Bhryeer A phagor who steers the sledge while Uuundaamp drives the dogs; it is he who throws Harbin Fashnalgid from the sledge in Brian W. Aldiss's *Helliconia Winter.*

Count Ricardo Bianco Gentle, sad bachelor, hopelessly devoted to the middle-aged Harriet Bede in Barbara Pym's *Some Tame Gazelle.*

Margo Bickerton The wild, indiscreet, outgoing, once-married aunt of Rita; she does as she pleases; she blames Nellie and Jack for ruining her chances for happiness; though she is fond of Rita, she wants a man and seizes upon Ira when the occasion arises in Beryl Bainbridge's *The Dressmaker.*

Anthony (Tony) Bicket Young worker who is sacked for stealing copies of Wilfred Desert's book to sell; he plans to emigrate to Australia in John Galsworthy's *The White Monkey.* He writes to Michael Mont to complain about Australia in *The Silver Spoon.*

Victorine (Vic) Collins Bicket Wife of Tony; she models nude to earn money for passage to Australia in John Galsworthy's *The White Monkey.*

Mrs. Bidlake Aloof and vague mother of Walter Bidlake and Elinor Quarles and the third wife of John Bidlake, by whom she was abandoned early in their marriage; content with his long absence, she accepts him back for his final illness in Aldous Huxley's *Point Counter Point.*

John Bidlake Robust artist of great renown and father of Walter Bidlake and Elinor Quarles; a life-long philanderer, he returns to his third wife when he learns of his fatal illness, selfishly demanding the attention of the entire household in Aldous Huxley's *Point Counter Point.*

Walter Bidlake Ineffectual literary critic and son of John Bidlake; bored with his mistress Marjorie Carling, he is briefly the object of Lucy Tantamount's amorous interest; he is devastated when she moves on to new amusements in Aldous Huxley's *Point Counter Point.*

Bidwell   Servant who is shared by Lewis Eliot and Roy Calvert in their Cambridge rooms; he is made to answer for his thefts by Calvert in C. P. Snow's *The Light and the Dark.*

Mr. Big   Smuggler who considers himself the "first of the great Negro criminals"; he is James Bond's adversary in Ian Fleming's *Live and Let Die.*

Sir Impey Biggs   Council for the Duke of Denver in his trial for murder in Dorothy L. Sayers's *Clouds of Witness.* He defends Harriet Vane in *Strong Poison.*

Miriam Biggs   The kitchenmaid for the Lambs who is at the bottom of the house's pecking order; she grew up in an orphanage; she offers to teach Miss Buchanan to read in Ivy Compton-Burnett's *Manservant and Maidservant.*

Mr. Bigwell   A master at Lucius Cassidy's school who did not attend Oxford or Cambridge; he teaches the boys Latin and Greek in Ivy Compton-Burnett's *Two Worlds and Their Ways.*

Bigwig (Thlayli)   A junior member of the Sandleford Owsla (rabbit-warren militia) who joins Hazel's pioneers; he plays a critical role in the infiltration of the Efrafa Warren and in the subsequent defense of the new warren from General Woundwort in Richard Adams's *Watership Down.*

Bill   Mean, jealous husband of Winnie; he gets his buddies to help him beat up Arthur Seaton several times for having an affair with his wife in Alan Sillitoe's *Saturday Night and Sunday Morning.*

Bill   A former enlisted man and friend of Gerry; he participates in the kidnaping and firebombing masterminded by Sophy Stanhope in William Golding's *Darkness Visible.*

Bill   Palace of Pleasure shooting-booth attendant; he unwittingly provides an alibi for Pinkie Brown in Graham Greene's *Brighton Rock.*

Bill   "Enlightenment leader" and yin-yang adherent who pursues Lise in Muriel Spark's *The Driver's Seat.*

Bill   The inebriated boyfriend of a young pregnant woman; they are discovered squatting in Anthony Keating's uninhabited London home by Keating; Bill is arrested and the woman dies later in Margaret Drabble's *The Ice Age.*

Bill   An aggressive, cruel, confident farmer in Rex Warner's *The Wild Goose Chase: An Allegory.*

Aunt Bill   A malicious, resentful woman who lived on National Assistance until her death; she took in her orphaned niece and nephew, Crystal and Hilary Burde, but soon sent the troublesome Hilary to an orphanage in Iris Murdoch's *A Word Child.*

Bill (Comrade Bill)   A young, cynical, and wary man in charge of culture in the British Communist Party; he interviews Anna Wulf and admits her into the Party in Doris Lessing's *The Golden Notebook.*

(Commanding Officer, Colonel) Bill   Efficient, careful, gruff friend of McKechnie; overstrained, he becomes drunk and is locked up by Christopher Tietjens, to whom he later confides that he has a fatal cancer in Ford Madox Ford's *A Man Could Stand Up —.*

Old Bill   One of the Gorbals Die-Hards; he guides Dickson McCunn to Sakskia, the Russian princess, in John Buchan's *Huntingtower.*

Isobel Billows   Rich widow and doting paramour of Martin Bowles in Muriel Spark's *The Bachelors.*

Billson   Misanthropic, hysterical parlormaid of the Jenkins family who is mentally unhinged by unrequited passion for Creech, the cook, in Anthony Powell's *The Kindly Ones.*

Billy   Judy's blind, older husband; a member of Pinkie Brown's mob, he owns a boarding house where Pinkie, Spicer, Dallow, and other mob members live in Graham Greene's *Brighton Rock.*

Billyboy   Fat, brutal thug a few years older than Alex; a rival gang leader, he becomes a police officer in order to enable him to even the score with Alex for past humiliations in Anthony Burgess's *A Clockwork Orange.*

Bilson   Maid for Soames and Irene Forsyte; she quietly understands their tensions in John Galsworthy's *The Man of Property.*

Bim   A Russian clown; paired with Bom he comments critically on English Society in the Epilogue to Richard Aldington's *The Colonel's Daughter.*

Harold Binde   Chancellor of Euphoric State University; he tries to handle student protest in David Lodge's *Changing Places: A Tale of Two Campuses.*

Captain Edward (Teddie) Arthur David Bingham
Young British officer of the Muzzafirabad Guides Reg-

iment stationed in Pankot; he marries Susan Layton at the Nawab's palace in Mirat and returns to duty after only a three-day honeymoon; Captain Bingham is killed shortly afterward while trying to locate and restore to duty an Indian soldier of his regiment who has gone over to the INA (the "Indian National Army", a collection of renegade soldiers who allied themselves with the Japanese) in Paul Scott's *The Day of the Scorpion*.

Edward Biranne   Henrietta's twin brother; the children are fond of watching flying saucers in Iris Murdoch's *The Nice and the Good*.

Henrietta Biranne   The nine-year-old daughter of Richard and Paula; she is Edward's twin sister in Iris Murdoch's *The Nice and the Good*.

Paula Biranne   A divorced schoolteacher who is at last reconciled with her errant husband, Richard, in Iris Murdoch's *The Nice and the Good*.

Richard Biranne   Civil servant and colleague of Octavian Gray; before his divorce from Paula he was an unfaithful and violently jealous husband; he and Paula are ultimately reconciled, to the satisfaction of their twins in Iris Murdoch's *The Nice and the Good*.

Janet Ollerenshaw Bird   A young mother who derives little satisfaction from the intelligence and clarity of her perceptions, being ridiculed by a sarcastic husband and suppressed by the conditions of her marriage; her chief solace comes from an emotional readiness for catastrophe until the arrival of her distant cousin, Frances Wingate, brings some diversion in Margaret Drabble's *The Realms of Gold*.

Luke (Preacher) Bird   Temperance reformer and dejected pursuer of Jenny Bunce; he believes that only beasts possess souls worthy of divine recitation; he seeks out the wine merchant Weston to fill his well with wine in order to get the approval of Thomas Bunce in T. F. Powys's *Mr. Weston's Good Wine*.

Mark Bird   Janet's mean-spirited, sarcastic, bullying husband in Margaret Drabble's *The Realms of Gold*.

Rupert Birkin   A school inspector who looks for and finds "star-equilibrium" (togetherness without merging) in his relationship with Ursula Brangwen, but is frustrated in his quest for "Bluterbrüderschaft" (sworn blood-brotherhood) with Gerald Crich; he is given to apocalyptic condemnations of the modern world in D. H. Lawrence's *Women in Love*.

Jacob (Ikey Mo) Birnbaum   Short, fair, stout, and very wealthy admirer of Albert Sanger; Birnbaum loves Sanger's daughter Antonia and after suffering some rejection at her hands eventually marries her in Margaret Kennedy's *The Constant Nymph*.

Sebastian Birt   Young economics tutor having an affair with the mentally disturbed Elizabeth Rock in Henry Green's *Concluding*.

Norman Birtley   Lillian Matfield's suitor in J. B. Priestley's *Angel Pavement*.

Bishop   Titular head of the Order which serves the leproserie in Graham Greene's *A Burnt-Out Case*.

Bishop of El Toboso   Father Quixote's regional bishop; he is the immediate superior to the humble parish priest; when the letter arrives from the Vatican promoting Father Quixote to monsignor, the Bishop informs Father Quixote in a rather uncomplimentary letter, suggesting that his rank is now too great for such a small parish; when word of Father Quixote's escapades reaches El Toboso, the Bishop arranges to have Father Quixote kidnapped and returned to El Toboso; Father Quixote, however, escapes and continues his journey in Graham Greene's *Monsignor Quixote*.

Bishop of Motopo   Cleric sent from Rome on special assignment to Spain; when his car apparently breaks down near El Toboso, he is aided by Father Quixote and invited to lunch; after lunch, Father Quixote "fixes" the car by adding a little petrol to the tank and sends the Bishop on his way; the Bishop is so impressed with Father Quixote that he recommends his promotion to monsignor in Graham Greene's *Monsignor Quixote*.

Bishop of Norchester   Oliver Green's superior; he is a shy man who discourages easy intimacy but has time for everyone and is universally confident and clear visioned in C. Day Lewis's *Child of Misfortune*.

Bismark   Winifred Crich's pet rabbit in D. H. Lawrence's *Women in Love*.

Alexandra (Biscuit) Bisset   The beautiful half-Pakistani servant of Lady Kitty Jopling; she has invented an exotic Indian identity but is in fact a cockney; she carries messages to Hilary Burde from Kitty and attracts his playful amorous attentions; she marries Christopher Cather, who is promoting her career as a model at the end of Iris Murdoch's *A Word Child*.

Rudi Bittesch   Collector of authors' handwritten letters and one of Jane Wright's part-time employers in the period following Germany's surrender in 1945 in Muriel Spark's *The Girls of Slender Means*.

Bitzenko   Former Russian landowner who acts as Otto Kreisler's second in a duel with Louis Soltyk; he insists on the dignity of the duel and flees the country after Soltyk's accidental shooting in Wyndham Lewis's *Tarr.*

Black   Seaman who gets drunk during the advance to Scotchman's Bay in C. S. Forester's *Lieutenant Hornblower.*

Colin Black   Margorie Pratt's suitor, later husband, a civil servant who makes Anton Hesse quite jealous in Doris Lessing's *A Ripple from the Storm.*

Sylvia Black   Young, intelligent aspiring writer and girlfriend of Peter Waterbury; she accompanies Maurice Bendrix to Sarah Miles's cremation and is ready to be seduced by him, but the attempt is aborted when Sarah's mother speaks to Bendrix at Sarah's cremation in Graham Greene's *The End of the Affair.*

Blackavar   Efrafan rabbit mutilated by Council Police for attempting to emigrate; rescued by Bigwig, he becomes a valued member of the band, proving his worth in the defense of the new warren in Richard Adams's *Watership Down.*

Blackberry   Clever rabbit in Hazel's band of pioneers; he is responsible for devising and implementing important stratagems, including the use of boats in Richard Adams's *Watership Down.*

Paul Blackenhurst   English, upper-middle-class pilot (later killed) in Doris Lessing's *The Golden Notebook.*

Rosie Blackledge   Repressed and misunderstood wife of the successful Stuart Blackledge; she has an affair with the aspiring writer and company lawyer Philip Witt in Roy Fuller's *Image of a Society.*

Stuart Blackledge   Mortgage manager of the Saddleford Building Society; a flashy, ambitious man who is considered the executive most likely to succeed the General Manager, he is later detected in what proves to have been a somewhat shady property deal in Roy Fuller's *Image of a Society.*

Mrs. Blacklow   Superficially unimpressive employee; with her husband a prisoner of war, she becomes pregnant by another soldier and impresses Lord Raingo with her attitude toward her situation and condition so that he provides funds for her care in Arnold Bennett's *Lord Raingo.*

Black Rabbit of Inlé   Mythological rabbit responsible for death and disease; El-ahrairah turns to him in desperation in Richard Adams's *Watership Down.*

Blacksmith   Trainer of George Pendyce's horse Ambler in John Galsworthy's *The Country House.*

Melaine Blackwell   A widowed Irish-American painter who befriends and attempts to seduce Dan Boleyn in Wyndham Lewis's *The Apes of God.*

Carrie Blackwood   The religiously doctrinaire, argumentative wife of Herbert; she is competitive with her sister, Sophia Hutton, in Ivy Compton-Burnett's *Dolores.*

Elsa Blackwood   The elder daughter of Herbert and Carrie; more independent and worldly than her sister, she secretly marries Bertram Hutton and waits while he is educated at Oxford in Ivy Compton-Burnett's *Dolores.*

Herbert Blackwood   A hospitable man, the Wesleyan minister, who is an evangelist for temperance; he invites the Huttons to dinner parties in Ivy Compton-Burnett's *Dolores.*

Herbert Blackwood (the younger)   The quiet-mannered son of Herbert and Carrie; he marries Evelyn Hutton in Ivy Compton-Burnett's *Dolores.*

Lettice Blackwood   The younger daughter of Herbert and Carrie; she gives her parents no trouble and is converted at a young age to Wesleyanism in Ivy Compton-Burnett's *Dolores.*

Harold Blade   Artist who paints portraits of Anne Forsyte, Jon Forsyte, and Fleur Mont in John Galsworthy's *Swan Song.*

Captain Robert Blaikie   Old friend of Richard Hannay in Rhodesia; he is in a shell-shock hospital at Isham, where Hannay visits him and first sees Mary Lamington in John Buchan's *Mr. Standfast.*

Maggie Blain   Overtalkative cook at the state educational institution for women in Henry Green's *Concluding.*

Bartholomew Scott Blair (Barley; covername: Mr. Brown)   Individualistic but feckless London publisher and gifted amateur jazz musician; he becomes a reluctant spy, betraying his country for his love, Katya Orlova, when he gives Soviet K.G.B. agents the questions about Soviet military readiness that British Intelligence wants Russian dissident "Goethe" (Yakov Savelyev) to answer in John le Carré's *The Russia House.*

Harriet Blair   An aging actress and the neglectful mother of Theodore Follett; she is an artificial, self-absorbed partygoer and giver; she needs the love and peace which she unexpectedly finds with her son's friend Henry Voyce; in a moment of derangement during an untoward and violent confrontation, Theodore kills her and himself in C. Day Lewis's *Starting Point*.

Robert Blair   Solicitor employed in the defense of Marion Sharpe and her mother; his investigative efforts, deductive powers, and belief in his clients triumph over his inexperience with criminal cases in Josephine Tey's *The Franchise Affair*.

Miss Blake   The third governess of Muriel Ponsonby; she quits her post after Dr. Chaucer proposes to her in Ivy Compton-Burnett's *Daughters and Sons*.

Meredith Blake   Sensitive herbalist, apparently in love with Caroline Crale but actually in love with Elsa Greer; he is suspected of the poisoning of Amyas Crale in Agatha Christie's *Five Little Pigs*.

Philip Blake   Meredith Blake's brother and Amyas Crale's best friend; he was in love with Caroline Crale, although seeming to hate her in Agatha Christie's *Five Little Pigs*.

Laura Blakely   Actress who is falsely characterized in a story made up by Tim and told to Anthony Keating; the story proves to Keating that his suspicions about Tim's credibility are true in Margaret Drabble's *The Ice Age*.

Mrs. Blakeston   Large, strong, blowsy, wronged wife of Jim; she physically fights the pregnant Liza Kemp for her husband in W. Somerset Maugham's *Liza of Lambeth*.

Jim Blakeston   The big, strong married man with whom Liza Kemp enjoys the passionate love she denies Tom; however, the lovers can control neither their physical passion nor events in their lives in W. Somerset Maugham's *Liza of Lambeth*.

Blakey   School boarder at Seaforth House whose parents live in Jamaica in Roy Fuller's *The Ruined Boys*.

Mr. Blamington   A Frobisher dinner-party guest; eighteen years earlier, when he proposed marriage to the Provincial Lady, he was called Bill Ransom in E. M. Delafield's *The Provincial Lady Goes Further*.

Mrs. Blamington   The Provincial Lady's old flame's wife, whose look — lovely hair, Paris frock — the Provincial Lady "does not like at all" in E. M. Delafield's *The Provincial Lady Goes Further*.

Mrs. Blanch   Woman detective assigned by Claude

Polteed to spy on Irene Forsyte for Soames Forsyte in John Galsworthy's *In Chancery*.

Emmy Blanchard   Elder sister of Jenny; she has spent the last ten years taking care of the household and caring for her ailing father; she feels she has lost her youth and her chance for romance, but she finds happiness with Alf Rylett, who originally courted her sister in Frank Swinnerton's *Nocturne*.

Jenny Blanchard   A millinery-shop worker who dreams of romance; at nearly twenty-six, she has begun to feel that life is passing her by until she meets Keith Reddington, captain of a small private yacht, whose rebellious and romantic temperament matches her own in Frank Swinnerton's *Nocturne*.

Pa Blanchard   A semi-invalid who, though he depends on his daughters Emmy and Jenny for his care, is financially stable, having provided for income in addition to his retirement through membership in various beneficent societies in Frank Swinnerton's *Nocturne*.

Mr. Blanchard-White   Uni-European zealot who forces Emile Englander to use the zoo as a source for animal torture and human contests after the victory of the Uni-Europeans in Angus Wilson's *The Old Men at the Zoo*.

Blanche   Common-law wife of Albert Shore; he nurses her with great care through a terminal illness in Roy Fuller's *My Child, My Sister*.

Anthony Blanche   A brilliantly cultured aesthete who is, for a time, a student at Oxford with Charles Ryder and Sebastian Flyte; he leaves Oxford to carry on a homosexual relationship in Munich and later gives a clever and dismissive analysis of Charles Ryder's recent series of paintings in Evelyn Waugh's *Brideshead Revisited*.

Daisy Bland   An extremely naïve and beautiful nineteen-year-old from the Cotswold hills working in a London millinery shop when she meets Hugo Chesterton, a suave criminal, and is soon pregnant with his child; passive and not particularly bright, this "child of nature" is treated as a white goddess among savages in her lover's underworld; she is tricked into giving evidence against him in Nicholas Blake's *A Tangled Web*.

Roy Bland (codename "Soldier")   Working-class Oxford don, ex-Marxist dialectical materialist, and British Intelligence officer who is Bill Haydon's second in command of the London Station; he creates and runs European espionage networks Aggravate, Contemplate, and Plato in John le Carré's *Tinker, Tailor, Soldier, Spy.* He appears in *The Honourable Schoolboy.*

Julie Blane An actress in Tommy Beamish's act who lives with him in a loveless relationship; she seeks solace from the much younger Dick Herncastle, but is thrown out by Beamish, who discovers them together; she continues her second-rate career in South Africa in J. B. Priestley's *Lost Empires.*

Gilbert Blaskin Novelist who befriends Michael Cullen and is discovered to be his father in Alan Sillitoe's *A Start in Life.*

Sister Blatt Deaconess resident of the Malorys' parish and an "excellent" woman acquaintance of Mildred Lathbury in Barbara Pym's *Excellent Women.* She makes a brief appearance in *A Glass of Blessings.*

Horace Blatt Intrusive, irritating vacationer; his snapshot-taking is annoying but helpful to Hercule Poirot in Agatha Christie's *Evil Under the Sun.*

Arthur Blearney Amicable and well-travelled entertainment promoter who introduces Charles Lumley to Bernard and Veronica Roderick and later gives Charles a job as a bouncer in an all-night club in John Wain's *Hurry On Down.*

Bledyard A landscape painter and art master at St. Bride's School and the voice of William Mor's moral conscience in Iris Murdoch's *The Sandcastle.*

Mr. Bleedham A deaf director for the New Collier Company who participates in the General Meeting in John Galsworthy's *The Man of Property.*

Blenkinsop Chauffeur to the Pattersons in Frank Swinnerton's *Some Achieve Greatness.*

Mrs. Blenkinsop A possessive woman who bitterly opposes the marriage of her daughter in E. M. Delafield's *The Diary of a Provincial Lady.* A year later she proudly displays her daughter's baby and insists that the grandchild is an exact replica of her picture of herself as an infant in *The Provincial Lady Goes Further.*

Barbara Blenkinsop Daughter of Old Mrs. Blenkinsop; she repeatedly breaks her engagement to Crosbie Carruthers to placate her dominating mother; she marries just before he leaves for India in E. M. Delafield's *The Diary of a Provincial Lady.*

Heather Blenkinsop Bossy fifty-nine-year-old librarian; she has always taken her holidays with and planned to retire with her old school friend Daphne Dagnall in Barbara Pym's *A Few Green Leaves.*

Cousin Maud Blenkinsop Elderly spinster who comes to the village to be companion of Old Mrs. Blenkinsop; both are cheered as she recklessly drives her tiny Austin about the village in E. M. Delafield's *The Provincial Lady Goes Further.*

John Scantlebury Blenkiron Wealthy American engineer industrialist with a duodenal complaint and the habit of playing Patience in times of stress; gifted with the cool nerve of the ideal counterespionage agent, he moves across enemy lines to solve the cryptic puzzle and defeat the German war machine in John Buchan's *Greenmantle.* He works with Richard Hannay and Mary Lamington under the direction of Sir Walter Bullivant of the Foreign Service in destroying the secret organization of a dangerous German agent in *Mr. Standfast.* Officially dead, but in disguise as "Senor Rosas", he uncovers a new threat against civilization brought by Mr. Castor in Olifa in South America and ends Castor's dictatorship in *The Courts of the Morning.* He urges Sir Edward Leithen to search for the missing Francis Galliard, without knowing that Leithen is terminally ill in *Sick Heart River.*

Ian Bletchley Lifelong friend of Colin Saville; he gets an education and manages to escape the almost inevitable poverty of a coalmine family in David Storey's *Saville.*

Blethyn Husband of Ceridwen Morgan in Richard Llewellyn's *How Green Was My Valley.*

Calvin Blick A blackmailer and an evil manipulator, disliked and feared by others in Iris Murdoch's *The Flight from the Enchanter.*

Danny Blick Boyfriend to Kate Fletcher (Armstrong) during her sexual-awakening year of sixteen; he is a naïve, small-time con man; Kate includes him on her list of possible "marginal people" in Margaret Drabble's *The Middle Ground.*

Ernst Stavro Blofeld Powerful, two-hundred-eighty-pound leader of the international terrorist organization SPECTRE; he steals two atomic bombs in an extortion plot against England and the United States in Ian Fleming's *Thunderball.* Thwarted, he devises a biological-warfare scheme against England from his Alpine fortress in *On her Majesty's Secret Service.* He has become "Dr. Shatterhand", the owner of a Japanese island property stocked with poisonous tropical plants; James Bond succeeds in his mission to kill him in *You Only Live Twice.*

Ellen Bloom   Deceased mother of Leopold Bloom; she is remembered by her son in James Joyce's *Ulysses*.

Leopold Bloom   Apparently insignificant middle-aged Jewish advertising man whose wanderings in Dublin on June 16th, 1904, parallel the homecoming of Homer's Odyseus; he suffers the prejudice of Dublin's Roman Catholic citizens, avoids confronting the infidelity of his wife, Molly, with whom he has not had sex for ten years, and rescues Stephen Dedalus from British soldiers in the brothel district in James Joyce's *Ulysses*.

Marion (Molly) Bloom   Leopold Bloom's voluptuous wife, who has an affair with Blazes Boylan; her stream-of-consciousness monologue, recalling all the men she has ever loved, is the final episode in James Joyce's *Ulysses*.

Milly Bloom   Leopold Bloom's adolescent daughter working in a Mullingar photo shop whose letter home appears in James Joyce's *Ulysses*.

Rudy Bloom   Son whose death in infancy initiated Leopold and Molly Bloom's decade of celibacy in James Joyce's *Ulysses*.

Blore   District Officer in Fada who is ready to press charges against Johnson for stealing government funds; he is released before a trial begins and is replaced by Rudbeck in Joyce Cary's *Mister Johnson*.

Blore   Butler for Sir Lawrence Mont and Aunt Emily Mont; he helps Dinny Cherrell find a pawnbroker in John Galsworthy's *Maid In Waiting*.

William Henry Blore   Retired police detective whose perjured testimony resulted in the prison death of an innocent man in Agatha Christie's *And Then There Were None*.

Colonel Blount   Nina's eccentric father, who supports a movie being filmed on his estate; he purchases the film when it cannot find a commercial outlet and shows it for his own pleasure in Evelyn Waugh's *Vile Bodies*.

Nina Blount   Fiancée of Adam Fenwick-Symes; she eventually marries Eddy Littlejohn; while her husband is away in the army, she renews her relationship with Adam in Evelyn Waugh's *Vile Bodies*.

Bluebell   Rabbit jokester and storyteller who escapes with Captain Holly from the doomed Sandleford Warren and joins Hazel's new colony in Richard Adams's *Watership Down*.

Minna Blum   One of the well-to-do German pupils in the Hanover school; her conventional future life as middle-class wife and mother is pictured by young Miriam Henderson with a mixture of envy and pity in Dorothy Richardson's *Pointed Roofs*.

Olga Blumenghast   Young lady of the court of Pisuerga and friend of Laura de Nazianzi; her "exotic, sexless" nature attracts the amorous interest of the Countess Violet of Tolga, despite Olga's love for the aloof Count Ann-Jules in Ronald Firbank's *The Flower Beneath the Foot*.

Blundell   Joseph Balterghen's innocuous second secretary; he provides insight into Balterghen's character in Eric Ambler's *Uncommon Danger*.

Superintendent Blundell   Official in charge of the investigation into the death of an unknown man; he welcomes Lord Peter Wimsey's assistance in Dorothy L. Sayers's *The Nine Tailors: Changes Rung on an Old Theme in Two Short Touches and Two Full Peals*.

Major Hector Blunt   Taciturn big-game hunter visiting at Fernly Park; he becomes engaged to Flora Ackroyd in Agatha Christie's *The Murder of Roger Ackroyd*.

Captain J. K. Blunt   Affected American supporter of the Spanish royalists who deceitfully wounds Monsieur George in a duel fought over Doña Rita de Lastaola in Joseph Conrad's *The Arrow of Gold: A Story Between Two Notes*.

Mr. Bly   Man who tried to do something to Kate Fletcher (Armstrong) that was embarrassing for her when she was eleven years old in Margaret Drabble's *The Middle Ground*.

Pevensey Blythe   Editor of *The Outpost* who persuades Michael Mont to accept Foggartism in John Galsworthy's *The Silver Spoon*. He is distressed when Michael turns his attention to slum clearance in *Swan Song*. He writes the preface for Hubert Cherrell's diary in *Maid In Waiting*.

Karl Marx Bo   Law student from Sierra Leone in Colin MacInnes's *City of Spades*.

Mr. Board   Rich, drunken bachelor mayor of Maidenbridge who is loved by Nancy Gipps in T. F. Powys's *Mr. Weston's Good Wine*.

Nigel Boase   Bruno Greensleave's mystical nurse-companion; he is Will Boase's twin and Adelaide de Crecy's cousin in Iris Murdoch's *Bruno's Dream*.

Wilfred (Will) Boase A professional actor long enamored of his cousin, Adelaide de Crecy; his duel with Danby Odel results in his marriage to Adelaide; his marriage and career prove unexpectedly successful in Iris Murdoch's *Bruno's Dream*.

Bob Milly's husband, who informs May Quest that her daughter, Martha, is employed in England by a communist writer in Doris Lessing's *The Four-Gated City*.

Bob An old friend of Emma Evans; he helped Emma when she first started modeling and has recently offered her a job on a television news program in Margaret Drabble's *The Garrick Year*.

Bob A frightened, silly musician; George thinks of Bob as a friend but realizes Bob is afraid of being alone in Rex Warner's *The Wild Goose Chase: An Allegory*.

Little Bob Jen's two-year-old brother in Isabel Colegate's *Orlando King*.

Comrade-Editor Bobbe (satirical portrait of D. H. Lawrence) Vain, class-conscious Socialist political writer whom George Winterbourne meets at a London literary evening in Richard Aldington's *Death of a Hero*.

Bobby German bartender and boarder at Fraulein Schroeder's in Christopher Isherwood's *Goodbye to Berlin*.

Doris, Lady Bocastle Wife of Lord Bocastle; she makes Lewis Eliot her confidant in C. P. Snow's *The Light and the Dark*.

Hugh, Lord Bocastle Brother of Lady Muriel Royce; he is crushed by the death of his only child in World War II in C. P. Snow's *The Light and the Dark*.

Henry Boddick Ex-serviceman, out of work, who accepts Michael Mont's offer to start a poultry farm in John Galsworthy's *The Silver Spoon*.

Father Bode Nondescript, good, selfless assistant priest to the parish of St. Luke's, who makes a contrast with the well-heeled connoisseur vicar, Father Thames, in Barbara Pym's *A Glass of Blessings*. His scheduled succession to the retiring Father Thames is mentioned in Edwin Braithwaite's reminiscences about the parish in *Quartet in Autumn*.

Mr. Bode Almeric's father, who has money through his wife's inheritance in Ivy Compton-Burnett's *A House and Its Head*.

Mrs. Bode Almeric's mother; she is embarrassed when he and Alison Edgeworth run away together in Ivy Compton-Burnett's *A House and Its Head*.

Almeric Bode A young man in love with Alison Edgeworth; he runs away with her when Grant Edgeworth is discovered to be the father of her son, Richard, in Ivy Compton-Burnett's *A House and Its Head*.

Dulcia Bode Almeric's sister, a friend of Nance and Sibyl Edgeworth; she is outspoken but warm and cheerful in Ivy Compton-Burnett's *A House and Its Head*.

Else Bode David Parker's housekeeper, who loves Gordon Paget; she leaves the nursery for a while after Meg Eliot arrives to convalesce from her nervous breakdown in Angus Wilson's *The Middle Age of Mrs. Eliot*.

Benjamin ("Fish Benjie") Bogle Scots ragamuffin, an impudent urchin who becomes the resourceful ally and co-conspirator in "John Macnab's" plot to poach the two stags and salmon in John Buchan's *John Macnab*.

Michael (Prisoner No. 38) Bogrov Former sailor on the Battleship Potemkin and Nicolas Rubashov's broken-spirited friend; he is imprisoned, viciously tortured, and executed as a political extremist for opposing No. 1's naval construction plans in Arthur Koestler's *Darkness at Noon*.

Mr. Bojanus Cockney tailor of socialist sympathies who helps the younger Theodore Gumbril perfect his pneumatic pants in Aldous Huxley's *Antic Hay*.

Enid Bolam Abrasive administrative head of Steen Psychiatric Clinic; she is murdered in P. D. James's *A Mind to Murder*.

Marion Bolam Self-effacing cousin of Enid Bolam in P. D. James's *A Mind to Murder*.

Boland Bully from the Belvedere School who interrogates Stephen Dedalus in James Joyce's *A Portrait of the Artist as a Young Man*.

Miss Boland Middle-aged acedemic who becomes involved romantically with F. X. Enderby; she is shy but friendly and masks her self doubts with a confident manner in Anthony Burgess's *Enderby Outside*.

Mr. Boldero Diminutive financier and partner of the younger Theodore Gumbril in the marketing of his pneumatic pants in Aldous Huxley's *Antic Hay*.

Francesco Boldini Tricky, dishonest, experienced

Legionnaire; he is a source of information for the Geste brothers; he plots to steal the jewel Michael Geste supposedly took; he is a spy for Color Sergeant Lejaune in Percival Christopher Wren's *Beau Geste*.

Terence Boles   Mark Coldridge's publisher in Doris Lessing's *The Four-Gated City*.

Daniel Boleyn   A nineteen-year-old homosexual Irish naïf, who has written "one most lovely poem"; under Horace Zagreus's tutelage, he undergoes a course of instruction in the ways of apery; his innocence and naïveté highlight the hypocracies and pretensions of bohemian society in Wyndham Lewis's *The Apes of God*.

Lazarus Bolowski   London music publisher who prints but does not distribute Hugh Firmin's songs in Malcolm Lowry's *Under the Volcano*.

Gwen Bolsover   Real-estate secretary who unwittingly helps Michael Cullen in a shady real-estate deal while becoming his lover in Alan Sillitoe's *A Start in Life*.

Bolt   Master's mate of the English sloop *Amelia* captured by Peyrol while spying for the English in Joseph Conrad's *The Rover*.

Bolt   Chauffeur at Rudge Hall, the estate for which Lester Carmody is trustee in P. G. Wodehouse's *Money for Nothing*.

Myra Bolt   University student who is defended by Lewis Eliot when she is threatened with expulsion for sexual misconduct in C. P. Snow's *The Sleep of Reason*.

The Bolter   Youngest sister of Sadie Radlett and Emily Warbeck and mother of Fanny Logan; married at least three times and the veteran of many love affairs, she has been almost entirely absent from Fanny's life until she returns to England from Europe at the outbreak of World War II in Nancy Mitford's *The Pursuit of Love*.

Bolton   Third lieutenant of the *Indefatigable* in C. S. Forester's *Mr. Midshipman Hornblower*. He has been promoted and is captain of the *Caligula*, though he lacks the manners and elegance that are usually requisite for his station in life in *Ship of the Line*.

Mrs. Bolton   Plain and dowdy wife of Captain Bolton; her appearance somewhat comforts Maria Hornblower in C. S. Forester's *Ship of the Line*.

Ivy Bolton   A gossipy Tevershall parish nurse, who comes to Wragby Hall to care for the crippled Sir Clif-

ford Chatterley; still loving her husband, who died in a mine accident, she inspires Lady Chatterley with her remarks on the lasting value of "touch" between lovers; she enters into "an intimacy of perversity" with Chatterley, who gives over full control to her as a "Magna Mater" figure at the end of D. H. Lawrence's *Lady Chatterley's Lover*.

Jackie Bolton   Founder of the first "true" Communist Party in Martha Quest's town; he scoffs at people like Boris Kruger for organizing ineffective groups like Sympathizers for Russia in Doris Lessing's *A Proper Marriage* and in *A Ripple from the Storm*.

Boltwood   A Church Bishop who is the father of Tess; he is pleased by her announcement of marriage with Stephen Freer in C. P. Snow's *The Malcontents*.

Tess Boltwood   University student who is a member of a Marxist group planning political action; she believes the death of Bernard Kelshall was martyrdom and accepts Stephen Freer's proposal of marriage in C. P. Snow's *The Malcontents*.

Bom   A Russian clown; paired with Bim he comments critically on English society in the Epilogue to Richard Aldington's *The Colonel's Daughter*.

Bom   Tormentor created by and identified with the "I"; his arrival is awaited in the third section of Samuel Beckett's *How It Is*.

Mr. Boms   A clergyman and an obsequious shareholder, who attends the General Meeting of the New Collier Company in John Galsworthy's *The Man of Property*.

Richard (Nick) Bonamy   Jacob Flanders's counterpart, who is attracted to the same women; he is sullen, opportunistic, and meaty where Jacob is bright, beautiful, idealistic, and diaphanous; Jacob writes the saga of his life in letters to Nick in Virginia Woolf's *Jacob's Room*.

Napoleon Bonaparte ("Boney")   French emperor and enemy with whose forces the English navy engages battle in C. S. Forester's *Hornblower and the Hotspur*.

James Bond (Code 007)   British Secret Service agent whose 00 code designation gives him a license to kill; he duels LeChiffre at baccarat in Ian Fleming's *Casino Royale*. He pursues Mr. Big, a USSR agent who is running a gold-smuggling scheme in *Live and Let Die*. He foils Hugo Drax's plot to destroy London in *Moonraker*. He uses the name Francs during his investigation of "The Spangled Mob" in *Diamonds Are Forever*. He is the intended victim of an assassination that he foils, but he is perhaps fatally wounded by a poison-tipped blade in Rosa Klebb's shoe in *From Russia, With Love*. Recovering, he acts as a freelance agent in his investigation into mysterious deaths on Crab Key in *Dr. No*. He blocks a plot to rob Fort Knox in *Goldfinger*. He thwarts Ernst Stavro Blofeld's atomic-bomb extortion plot in *Thunderball*. He is seen through the eyes of Vivienne Michel, whom he rescues from professional arsonists in *The Spy Who Loved Me*. He poses as Sir Hilary Bray to infiltrate Blofeld's Alpine fortress; his marriage to Tracy di Vicenzo ends with her murder by Blofeld in *On Her Majesty's Secret Service*. He takes the identity Taro Todoroki on his Japanese mission; he kills Blofeld but loses his memory in *You Only Live Twice*.

May Bond   Aspiring actress, Oxford student, and part-time lover of the younger Tom Nimmo; she plans to open a burlesque acting company with Tom, but their plans go awry in Joyce Cary's *Prisoner of Grace*.

Father Bondorlonganon   A priest of Wutra, the god worshipped in Oldorando; he conducts the funeral for Laintal Ay's grandfather in Brian W. Aldiss's *Helliconia Spring*.

Mr. Bondy   London pawnbroker who lends money to Dinny Cherrell on Jean Tasburgh Cherrell's pendant in John Galsworthy's *Maid In Waiting*.

Mrs. Bone   Eccentric, energetic, elderly widow whose near-madness takes the form of obsessions about dangerous birds and proselytizing Jesuits; she is the agnostic mother of the devout Everard Bone in Barbara Pym's *Excellent Women*. She is briefly mentioned in *Less Than Angels*.

Everard Bone   Handsome, clever, churchgoing anthropologist with an eccentric mother; he tries to use Mildred Lathbury to extricate him from a nebulous relationship with his married colleague Helena Napier, and then seems to be interested in Mildred herself in Barbara Pym's *Excellent Women*. His further career is mentioned in *Less Than Angels*.

Alfy Bongo   Young homosexual who was raised by Mr. Obo-King; he performs sexual favors in Colin MacInnes's *City of Spades*.

Dr. Gerard Bonnard   French child-care expert; because of his handicap, Jeremy Trout is placed in Dr. Bonnard's care in Elizabeth Bowen's *Eva Trout, or Changing Scenes*.

Mrs. Gerard Bonnard   Dr. Bonnard's wife, who assists with Jeremy Trout's education in Elizabeth Bowen's *Eva Trout, or Changing Scenes*.

Mrs. Booch   Pensioned servant who visits Bladesover; her stereotypical remarks make her disgusting to young George Ponderevo in H. G. Wells's *Tono-Bungay*.

Mr. Booker   A director for the New Collier Company who participates in the General Meeting in John Galsworthy's *The Man of Property*.

Lord Boom   Edward Ponderevo's nemesis; he uses his newspaper to spread rumors concerning Edward in H. G. Wells's *Tono-Bungay*.

Charles Boon   An eccentric, self-confident English graduate student from Rummidge; now at Euphoric State University, he hosts a wildly popular radio talk show in Plotinus; he moves in with Melanie Byrd, Morris Zapp's daughter, and during his on-air interview with Philip Swallow, Hilary Swallow calls and discusses the Swallows' sex life in David Lodge's *Changing Places: A Tale of Two Campuses*.

Danny Boon   Comedian to whom Billy Fisher has sent material and for whom he hopes to work in London in Keith Waterhouse's *Billy Liar*.

Pete Boone   Idealistic young assistant to the cynical scientist Dr. Obispo; in love with the beautiful Virginia Maunciple and unable to reconcile his idealistic view of the world with its sordid reality, he contemplates suicide but is murdered by a jealous Jo Stoyte in Aldous Huxley's *After Many a Summer*.

Mr. Boot   Proprietor of an old, charming sweets factory which is forced out of business by modern property developers in Margaret Drabble's *The Ice Age*.

John Courteney Boot   Popular author who desires to be a war correspondent in Ishmaelia; by mistake another writer with the same last name is chosen; later John becomes a correspondent in Antarctica in Evelyn Waugh's *Scoop*.

Theodore Boot   William Boot's elderly uncle, who takes William's place at the banquet honoring William's journalistic achievement in Evelyn Waugh's *Scoop*.

William Boot   A timid nature writer who, because of mistaken identity, is sent to Ishmaelia to cover the war for a London newspaper; he discovers a Russian plot, reports the scoop, and returns to acclaim in England; he resumes his old position as a rural commentator in Evelyn Waugh's *Scoop*.

Booth   Bulky bosun aboard the *Renown* in C. S. Forester's *Lieutenant Hornblower*.

Mr. Boothby   Owner of a successful hotel in Mashopi; his distrust of Anna Wulf's group of socialist friends is due to their subtle criticisms of him as a colonist in Doris Lessing's *The Golden Notebook*.

Mrs. Boothby   A plain woman who is pleasant and polite but unable to understand why Paul Blackenhurst and Jimmy tease her, or to realize that their maliciousness towards her is due to her treatment of the Africans in Doris Lessing's *The Golden Notebook*.

June Boothby   Mr. and Mrs. Boothby's adolescent daughter, who is sexually aware of the men around her; she eventually meets and marries a man in Mashopi in Doris Lessing's *The Golden Notebook*.

Lieutenant Booth-Henderson   The pudgy, pimply, stupid, nervous, pompous officer in charge of intake at Catterick; he interviews Jonathan Browne as a potential officer candidate during Basic Training in David Lodge's *Ginger, You're Barmy*.

Major Boothroyd   Head of the weapons branch of the British Secret Service; he advises James Bond to change guns in Ian Fleming's *Dr. No*.

Gran Boothroyd   The aged grandmother of Billy Fisher; her death leads to a partial and temporary easing of family problems in Keith Waterhouse's *Billy Liar*.

Akbil Borak   A friendly, conscientious professor of English at the University of Ankara; he and his wife Oya Borak are Philip Swallow's hosts at Ankara in David Lodge's *Small World*.

Oya Borak   Turkish wife of Akbil Borak in David Lodge's *Small World*.

Boris   Moscow Centre agent; investigating him, Ricki Tarr becomes the lover of his common-law wife, Irina, and is told of the existence of a double agent high in British Intelligence in John le Carré's *Tinker, Tailor, Soldier, Spy*.

Boris   Maurice Castle's humane communist controller and confessor, who helps arrange Maurice's defection in Graham Greene's *The Human Factor*.

Boris   The editor of *Lilith* during the 50s; he is supposed to represent "the new wave", but he actually turns out to be highly inefficient in Doris Lessing's *The Diaries of Jane Somers*.

Boromir   Ambitious member of the fellowship whose mission is to destroy the One Ring and its evil power; Boromir desires the power of the ring and attempts to take the ring from Frodo Baggins; he repents of his actions but is killed in a battle with Orcs in J. R. R. Tolkien's *The Fellowship of the Ring*.

borracho ("drunkard")   Unnamed man who beats a blind woman and her dead dog in Malcolm Lowry's *Dark as the Grave Wherein My Friend Is Laid*.

Lieutenant Borthwick   Young officer in General Curzon's regiment; his knowledge of modern weaponry is in contrast to the general's deliberate ignorance of it in C. S. Forester's *The General*.

Clive Bosanquet   Barrister who leads the prosecution in the trial of Cora Ross and Kitty Pateman in C. P. Snow's *The Sleep of Reason*. Now a judge, he decides in favor of Jenny Rastall's challenge to her father's will in 1970; his decision is overturned on appeal in 1972 in *In Their Wisdom*.

Dr. Bose   Ambassador from Mars to the United Planets and chairman of the Rama committee; he approves the expedition in Arthur C. Clarke's *Rendezvous with Rama*.

Joe Bosenby   Agent for many variety artists, including Nick Ollanton, in J. B. Priestley's *Lost Empires*.

Philip (The Buccaneer) Bosinney   Architect engaged to June Forsyte but in love with Irene Forsyte; he loses a lawsuit to Soames Forsyte over the country house he builds; he dies when he is run over by a London omnibus in John Galsworthy's *The Man of Property*.

Herr Bossenberger   Music master in the Hanover school in Dorothy Richardson's *Pointed Roofs*.

Miss Bostock   Alan Percival's teacher at school in Garside in Roy Fuller's *The Perfect Fool*.

Joe Boswell   A darkly handsome Gypsy; he is the social outcast who causes "something [to take] fire" in the breast of Yvette Saywell; he rescues her from raging flood waters and spends the night with her, but his caravan departs at the end in D. H. Lawrence's *The Virgin and the Gipsy*.

Alfie Bottesford   Foundry office clerk and childhood friend of Michael Cullen; Michael seduces his girlfriend in Alan Sillitoe's *A Start in Life*.

Mrs. Bindon Botting   Garrulous Folkestone society matron who hosts the crucial Anagram Tea at which Art Kipps discovers his childhood sweetheart Anne Pornick working as her maid in H. G. Wells's *Kipps: The Story of a Simple Soul*.

Monsieur Bouc   Hercule Poirot's long-time professional friend; he hires Poirot to investigate the murder of Samuel Edward Ratchett in Agatha Christie's *Murder on the Orient Express*.

Colonel Jacob Boucher   An elderly bachelor whose friendship with the widow Jane Weston is of years' standing; the engagement of their servants prompts their own in E. F. Benson's *"Queen Lucia"*. He is her husband in *Lucia in London* and in *Mapp and Lucia*.

Yves Boularis   Versatile, strong, middle-aged Tunisian bodyguard and electronics and demolition expert; Paul Firman's right-hand man and instrumental in saving Paul Firman, he is murdered by Mathew Williamson Tuakana's men in Eric Ambler's *Send No More Roses*.

Ursala Bourne (Mrs. Ralph Paton)   Secret wife of Roger Ackroyd's estranged stepson; employed as parlormaid at Fernly Park, she is fired on the day of Ackroyd's death in Agatha Christie's *The Murder of Roger Ackroyd*.

Mr. Boutwood   Newly widowed boarder; his taking as mistress the flirtatious servant Florrie Bagster disgusts Hilda Lessways as they all try to survive in George Cannon's Brighton boarding house in Arnold Bennett's *Hilda Lessways*.

Miles Bovey   One of the men whom Charles Watkins remembers as having been aboard his ship (in his alternate reality); he was the only person who Charles felt understood him in Doris Lessing's *Briefing for a Descent into Hell*.

Antoine Bowdoin   A musician Miriam Henderson meets through Bernard Mendizabal, one of Mrs. Bailey's boarders; he invites her to hear him play on his own piano in a setting that strikes her as really "bohemian" in Dorothy Richardson's *Interim*.

Dr. Bowen   Physician who oversees the care of Helen Chichester-Redfern during her physical decline and who Giles Hermitage resentfully suspects is engaged sexually with Dinah Redfern at the same time he is himself in John Wain's *The Pardoner's Tale*.

Mrs. Bower   The Morels' neighbor who comes to assist during Gertrude Morel's labor and childbirth and seems antagonistic toward Walter Morel on that occasion in D. H. Lawrence's *Sons and Lovers*.

Humphrey Capstone Bowers   The big-game-hunting pukka chap whom Elizabeth Barclay takes on, briefly, as either lover or husband in William Golding's *The Paper Men*.

Bowles   Master who gives classes in navigation to the mates and to the midshipmen aboard the *Justinian* in C. S. Forester's *Mr. Midshipman Hornblower*.

Magnus Bowles   Blaise Gavender's patient, a painter whose neurotic compulsion prevents his leaving home in the daytime; he is in fact the invention of Monty Small, created as a believable alibi for Blaise's evening absences; he is so real to Harriet Gavender that Monty makes him a suicide to forestall her attempts to consult him in Iris Murdoch's *The Sacred and Profane Love Machine*.

Martin Bowles   Bachelor barrister who lives with his mother and exploits his professional and personal relationship with Isobel Billows in Muriel Spark's *The Bachelors*.

Sally Bowles   Naïve, promiscuous expatriate English cabaret singer, who takes Christopher Isherwood under her wing in Christopher Isherwood's *Goodbye to Berlin*.

George Bowling   A fat, unhappy insurance man, who decides to go back to his old home town and reclaim his youth and memories, telling his wife he is on business; finding that his old love has grown old and fat and his little town has become industrialized and polluted, he decides that his regular life and marriage are really what he wants in George Orwell's *Coming Up for Air*.

Hilda Bowling   The wife of George Bowling; she recognizes when he is trying to get away with something but loves him in spite of her anger in George Orwell's *Coming Up for Air*.

David Bowman   Astronaut and captain of the space ship *Discovery*; he is the only crew member to escape HAL's murder attempt; he destroys HAL's intellectual capacity, goes through the star gate, and becomes the star child in Arthur C. Clarke's *2001: A Space Odyssey*.

Bowshot   Randall Peronett's head gardener in Iris Murdoch's *An Unofficial Rose*.

Nancy Bowshot   The Peronetts' head gardener's wife; yearning for Randall Peronett, she is Ann Peronett's constant companion and silent enemy in Iris Murdoch's *An Unofficial Rose*.

Lady Boxe   Rich woman who flaunts her knowledge of drama, art, and literature; she arrives at parties with an entourage of fashionable friends and waves white-gloved hands as she drops her jeweled bag, lace parasol, and embroidered handkerchief in E. M. Delafield's *The Diary of a Provincial Lady*.

Boxer (satiric representation of the proletariat) A large cart horse; the hardest and most loyal worker in the cooperative of animals, he dies in the midst of his work in George Orwell's *Animal Farm*.

Mrs. Boxer A charwoman employed by Kitty Friedman, who worries that she will not be paid while Mrs. Friedman is in hospital in Margaret Drabble's *The Ice Age*.

boy Unnamed youth on the same bus as Ethan and Jacqueline Llewelyn; he has an uncertain command of Latin but firm opinions of Calgary girls and of Americans; he calls Ethan "Old Somebody" in Malcolm Lowry's *October Ferry to Gabriola*.

Humphrey Boyce Sixtyish widower owner of an antiques shop near Sloan Square who is initiating his nephew into the business; he takes a decided interest in Leonora Eyre in Barbara Pym's *The Sweet Dove Died*.

James Boyce Twenty-four-year-old recent university graduate; the orphan nephew of Humphrey, he works in his uncle's antiques shop while deciding on his sexual preference; he becomes romantically entangled with two women and one man in Barbara Pym's *The Sweet Dove Died*.

Rupert Boyce An extremely wealthy collector of books on the occult in which the Overlords are interested; he holds a séance in which Jean Morrel's psychic powers are revealed in Arthur C. Clarke's *Childhood's End*.

Kenneth Sefton (Kenny) Boyd Aristocratic ne'er-do-well who, as a student, is viciously betrayed by Magnus Pym; as a dissolute adult, he is one of the few who understand and forgive Magnus's duplicity in John le Carré's *A Perfect Spy*.

Philip Boyes A novelist whose love affair with Harriet Vane lasted two years and ended when he proved the insincerity of his principles by wanting her to marry him; Harriet narrowly escapes being convicted of his death by arsenic poisoning in Dorothy L. Sayers's *Strong Poison*.

Hugh (Blazes) Boylan Advertising agent and Casanova who has an affair with Molly Bloom in James Joyce's *Ulysses*.

Captain Boyle "New on the job" police captain who investigates Robert Halliday's bomb-threat report and reception in Eric Ambler's *The Care of Time*.

Janice Brabner Volunteer social worker who comes to check on Marcia Ivory in the aftermath of her operation, ineffectually suggesting a number of activities and improvements for Marcia's life in *Quartet in Autumn*.

Bracegirdle Horatio Hornblower's shipmate aboard the *Indefatigable* in C. S. Forester's *Mr. Midshipman Hornblower*. He has become Admiral Lord St. Vincent's flag lieutenant; he sympathizes with Hornblower but refuses entry to retrieve his watch in C. S. Forester's *Hornblower and the Atropos*.

Mary Bracegirdle Sexually frustrated but naïve guest at the Crome estate; she offers herself to Ivor Lombard but is disappointed by his aloof indifference in Aldous Huxley's *Crome Yellow*.

Olga Bracely Good-natured, popular, refreshingly unconventional, sophisticated woman and an acclaimed and gifted opera star; she settles in Riseholme, makes an immediate conquest of Georgie Pillson, and inadvertently unseats Lucia Lucas as the cultural leader of Riseholme; she is the wife of George Shuttleworth in E. F. Benson's *"Queen Lucia"*. She is Lucia's neighbor and cheerfully allows herself to be used in Lucia's social campaign in *Lucia in London*. She introduces the Duchess of Sheffield to Georgie and Lucia in *Trouble for Lucia*.

Samuel P. Braceweight Wealthy chocolate tycoon who befriends Charles Lumley in the hospital and hires Charles briefly as a chauffeur in John Wain's *Hurry On Down*.

Walter Braceweight Spoiled, mature-looking adolescent hot-rod enthusiast whom George Hutchins unsuccessfully attempts to tutor and whom Charles Lumley shields from Mr. Braceweight's wrath by taking the blame for an auto accident and forfeiting his chauffeur job in John Wain's *Hurry On Down*.

Bracey Captain Jenkins's smartly turned-out, melancholic soldier-servant, who loves the emotionally unstable maid Billson; he is killed in 1914 in Anthony Powell's *The Kindly Ones*.

Gerald Bracher Sensitive boy attending Seaforth House, a second-rate English public school on the brink of financial collapse; consigned to the school after the break up of his parents' marriage, Bracher changes gradually from conformist to rebel in Roy Fuller's *The Ruined Boys*.

Len Bracton Stage comedian for whom Owen Tuby and Cosmo Sultana form a marketable image in J. B. Priestley's *The Image Men*.

Mr. Braddock Barrister who defends the smugglers and makes a mockery of Francis Andrews and his crucial testimony during cross-examination in Graham Greene's *The Man Within.*

Hazel Bradfield Rawley Bradfield's beautiful wife and Leo Harting's mistress; she gives Harting the key to an unused basement office of the Bonn Embassy where Harting stores pilfered documents confirming Karfeld's guilt in John le Carré's *A Small Town in Germany.*

Rawley Bradfield Condescending, dishonest Head of Chancery at the Bonn Embassy; he hides information about Klaus Karfeld's concentration camp experiments on humans from British diplomatic politicians to demean Leo Harting, repress his subordinates, divert and officially terminate Alan Turner's investigation, and compromise democratic principles to current political expediencies in John le Carré's *A Small Town in Germany.*

Isabel Bradley The radiantly healthy young girl who is engaged to marry Larry Darrell; being completely unable to understand Larry's changed thinking after his experiences in World War I, she marries the mundane Gray Maturin although she covertly hankers after Larry; Isabel can love only selfishly, never realizing that Larry will always be out of her reach in W. Somerset Maugham's *The Razor's Edge.*

Louisa Bradley Isabel's pleasant, practical mother, who is perfectly content with her middle-class values that approve of the Gray Maturins of this era but would never comprehend the philosophy of a Larry Darrell in W. Somerset Maugham's *The Razor Edge.*

Laura Bradshaw Gregory Dawson's friend from youth who liberates him to live in the present when she tells him that Joan Alington had been responsible for Eva Alington's death in J. B. Priestley's *Bright Day.*

William Bradshaw Young, gullible English writer who travels to Germany to tutor English and narrates the story of how he became embroiled in Arthur Norris's schemes; he demonstrates how the desire for experience may blind one to reality in Christopher Isherwood's *Mr. Norris Changes Trains.*

Sir William Bradshaw Dr. Holmes's mentor and superior; he is a didactic, sanctimonious medical doctor; his tardy appearance at Clarissa Dalloway's party forges another superficial link between the Dostoevskian doubles, Septimus Smith and Mrs. Dalloway; to her

dismay, Bradshaw describes Septimus's gory impalement in Virginia Woolf's *Mrs. Dalloway.*

Mr. Brady Drunken, abusive father of Caithleen Brady; through his reckless behavior, he loses his wife, his farm, and his daughter's affections in Edna O'Brien's *The Country Girls.*

Mrs. Brady Mother of Caithleen Brady; she tragically drowns on her way to her father's house while trying to escape her abusive, drunken husband in Edna O'Brien's *The Country Girls.*

Caithleen (Cait) Brady Clever and intelligent daughter of Mr. Brady; after her mother's tragic death, she goes to a convent on scholarship; she is later expelled, along with Bridget Brennan, for misconduct, and eventually she follows Bridget to Dublin, where she works as a shop assistant and pursues her affair with the married Mr. Gentleman in Edna O'Brien's *The Country Girls.*

Mike Brady The rebellious, fiercely principled Irish Catholic friend of Jonathan Browne, who shares his hatred of National Service; Brady befriends Percy Higgins and avenges his death by assaulting Corporal Baker; later he joins the Irish Republican Army and is arrested in a raid on Jonathan's camp; he dates Pauline Vickers and introduces her to Jonathan, who later marries her in David Lodge's *Ginger, You're Barmy.*

Molly Brady Young, fleshy, sensual farm girl; she plays flirtatious games with Tarry Flynn and catches his interest, but he later refuses to associate with her in Patrick Kavanagh's *Tarry Flynn.*

"Brahms Four" See Dr. Walter von Munte.

Maurice Braithewaite A star player on the Rugby League team who plays with Arthur Machin, becomes his friend, gets married, and tries to get Arthur to go into business with him in David Storey's *This Sporting Life.*

Mr. Braithwaite The cashier at the colliery who pays out miners' wages when Paul Morel goes to collect his father's pay in D. H. Lawrence's *Sons and Lovers.*

Edwin Braithwaite Sixtyish widower clerk who lives alone in a semi-detached house but vacations with his daughter and her family; his life revolves around his church, where he is Master of Ceremonies, and vague speculation about his co-workers in Barbara Pym's *Quartet in Autumn.*

Bran See Sirius.

The Brand (Individual Four)   A female, once kept in a concentration camp, with whom Individual Five has sexual relations in Doris Lessing's *Re: Colonised Planet 5, Shikasta.*

Bertha Brand   Brittle, sharp-faced elderly spinster who after working all her life solicits a job at Corker's employment agency in order to stay out of a home for the elderly; desperate to continue working and briefly hopeful that Corker will hire her as his housekeeper, she ends up in an "Old People's Home" in John Berger's *Corker's Freedom.*

Gala Brand   An undercover policewoman who helps James Bond avert the destruction of London; she is engaged to be married and has no sexual interest in Bond in Ian Fleming's *Moonraker.*

Augustus (Gussie) Brandon   Arrogant, competitive, aggressive nephew of Sir Hector Brandon; he is too much like his brutal uncle; Michael Geste dislikes but tolerates Augustus in Percival Christopher Wren's *Beau Geste.*

Sir Hector Brandon   A brutal, cruel husband to Patricia; he is hated for squandering money while his estate collapses in Percival Christopher Wren's *Beau Geste.*

Patricia, Lady Brandon   The refined, abused wife of Sir Hector; she cares for her nieces and nephews, including the Geste brothers; she tries to handle the finances of Brandon Abbas; she is the beloved friend of George Lawrence; she is the owner of the sapphire called the "Blue Water" in Percival Christopher Wren's *Beau Geste.*

Thomas Brandwhite   Wealthy financier who gossips about Captain and Mrs. Bellew in John Galsworthy's *The Country House.*

Meriadoc (Merry) Brandybuck   Young, unadventurous hobbit who is a member of the fellowship who travel with Frodo Baggins to destroy the One Ring in J. R. R. Tolkien's *The Fellowship of the Ring.* He fights with Theoden, King of the Mark, and kills Ringwraith in battle in *The Two Towers.* He is reunited with the fellowship to join the rebellion against the invading men in *The Return of the King.*

Mr. Justice Brane   Judge in the libel case brought by Marjorie Ferrar against Fleur Mont in John Galsworthy's *The Silver Spoon.*

Anna Brangwen   Daughter of Lydia Brangwen's first marriage; Anna marries her stepfather's nephew, Will Brangwen; her sensuality is in conflict with his spirituality in D. H. Lawrence's *The Rainbow.*

Gudrun Brangwen   Ursula Brangwen's little sister; she is closest to Ursula in D. H. Lawrence's *The Rainbow.* She emerges, now grown up, as a nihilistic artist and becomes Gerald Crich's demonic and destructive lover and later Loerke's lover in *Women in Love.*

Lydia (Lynsky) Brangwen   An exotic widowed Polish immigrant in England who marries Tom Brangwen, alleviating his sexual repression in D. H. Lawrence's *The Rainbow.*

Tom Brangwen (the elder)   A farmer troubled by conflicts of sensuality and religious fervor; his marriage to Lydia is both liberating and tormented; in old age he drowns in a flood in D. H. Lawrence's *The Rainbow.*

Tom Brangwen (the younger)   Son of Lydia and the elder Tom Brangwen; a colliery manager and Ursula Brangwen's uncle, he marries Winifred Inger in D. H. Lawrence's *The Rainbow.*

Ursula Brangwen   A daughter of Will and Anna; she becomes a teacher who urgently strives for independence and meaning in her life; she has a Lesbian affair with another teacher, Winifred Inger; she has an intense love affair with Anton Skrebensky in D. H. Lawrence's *The Rainbow.* She provides a realistic balance to her lover Rupert Birkin in *Women in Love.*

Will Brangwen   A carpenter and wood-carver with artistic yearnings for the spirituality in church architecture; he becomes submissive and resigned in the warfare engendered by his and his wife Anna's passions in D. H. Lawrence's *The Rainbow.*

Archpriest BranzaBaginut   The Borlienese priest who interrogates Billy Xiao Pin in Brian W. Aldiss's *Helliconia Summer.*

Bratch   The Planet 6 Representative of Health who must decide how the miraculous blue flowering summer plant can be divided among the millions of hungry people and animals in Doris Lessing's *The Making of the Representative for Planet 8.*

Mr. Braun   Multilingual brooding captain's clerk and translator to Hornblower; he steals guns from Hornblower and tries to commit an assassination at the Imperial Palace of Peterhof in C. S. Forester's *Commodore Hornblower.*

Henry Breasley   An English painter now in old age, living in the French countryside with two young girls as companions; he rejects abstract art as a retreat from human reality; he alternately berates and befriends David Williams in John Fowles's *The Ebony Tower*.

Madame Breda   Sinister colleague of Dominick Medina and Dr. Newhover; she purports to be a Swedish masseuse to whom Richard Hannay is sent by Dr. Newhover for "treatment", to determine and increase Hannay's sensitivity to Medina's hypnotic powers in John Buchan's *The Three Hostages*.

Andersen ("Andy") Marathon Bredahl   Chinless ship's cook aboard the *Oedipus Tyrannus* who becomes Dana Hilliot's chief tormenter but eventually accepts him in Malcolm Lowry's *Ultramarine*.

Denis Breen   Dublin eccentric obsessed with discovering the sender of an anonymous, cryptic postcard in James Joyce's *Ulysses*.

Josie Powell Breen   Wife of crazy Denis; she was formerly attracted to Leopold Bloom in James Joyce's *Ulysses*.

Brenda   Well-brought-up, quiet, shy, directionless woman; denominated a "born victim" by Freda, she feels inadequate in coping with the role reversal forced on her by the discovery of Freda's murdered corpse in Beryl Bainbridge's *The Bottle Factory Outing*.

Brenda   Winnie's sister, who is married to Arthur Seaton's friend Jack; she becomes pregnant by Arthur and aborts in Alan Sillitoe's *Saturday Night and Sunday Morning*.

Brenda   Operator of a nursery group that includes Jane Gray's son, Laurie; Jane is critical of Brenda's methods; the women are afraid of each other in Margaret Drabble's *The Waterfall*.

Mr. Brennan   Hard-working veterinary surgeon and father of Bridget Brennan; he watches over Caithleen Brady after her mother's death and tries to protect her from her abusive father in Edna O'Brien's *The Country Girls*.

Bridget (Baba) Brennan   Beautiful, coy, and malicious daughter of Mr. Brennan; she gets herself and Caithleen Brady expelled from the convent so that they can lead wild, free lives in Dublin in Edna O'Brien's *The Country Girls*.

Martha Brennan   Beautiful mother of Bridget Brennan; she desires drink and admiration in life; she is a good friend to Caithleen Brady, especially after Cait's mother dies in Edna O'Brien's *The Country Girls*.

Emily Brent   Self-righteous Puritan who was accused of causing the death of an unfortunate servant girl; Miss Brent is the fatal victim of an apparent bee sting in Agatha Christie's *And Then There Were None*.

Jimmy Brent   Peter Templer's fat, high-voiced City friend, who is immediately disliked by Nicholas Jenkins in Anthony Powell's *A Question of Upbringing*. Jenkins is dismayed to learn that Jean (Templer) Duport ended her affair with him to pursue one with Brent in *The Kindly Ones*. Brent tells Jenkins about his affair with Jean in *The Valley of Bones*.

Sophy Brent   A beautiful and talkative young actress, who has recently finished drama school and is part of the ensemble gathered at Hereford; she has an affair with David Evans in Margaret Drabble's *The Garrick Year*.

Jean Pierre Breteuil   A French novelist who, to the surprise of his English translator Jake Donaghue, wins the Prix Goncourt; *The Wooden Nightingale*, Jake's translation of an earlier novel, is appropriated by Sammy Starfield in Iris Murdoch's *Under the Net*.

Ivan Ivanovitch Bretlev   Moscow Centre agent who probably recruited Nelson Ko for Karla in John le Carré's *The Honourable Schoolboy*.

Dr. Brett   Harriet Lovatt's extremely conventional doctor, who will not admit that something is indeed "wrong" with her fifth child, Ben Lovatt, in Doris Lessing's *The Fifth Child*.

Colonel Humphrey Brett   Husband of Mary Brett and father of Lise Brett; the reckless, talkative commandant of a Prisoner of War camp in Northern Scotland, he is disturbed by trials and executions and suffers guilt for the deaths of six German prisoners killed in an attempted escape and also for the anticipated execution of Emil Gerlach in Storm Jameson's *The Black Laurel*.

Lise Brett   Twelve-year-old neglected child, who cries all night for her mother and is comforted by her eighteen-year-old neighbor, Arnold Coster, in Storm Jameson's *Before the Crossing*. An eighteen-year-old girl in 1945, she lives at a Scottish military installation with her father, Colonel Humphrey Brett, and in London and Berlin with her mother, Mary Brett, and falls in love with Arnold in Storm Jameson's *The Black Laurel*.

Mary Brett   Unfaithful wife of Colonel Brett and neglectful mother of Lise Brett in 1939; she is an actress and musician who arranges concerts for charities, dines with Julian Swan, and frequently has her picture in the London *Tatler* in Storm Jameson's *Before the*

Crossing. She has been the mistress of Lieutenant Edward West for four years when she discovers he is attempting to seduce her eighteen-year-old daughter, Lise, in Storm Jameson's *The Black Laurel.*

Bretton　Political agent for Miles Vane-Merrick in Kent; the son of the local blacksmith, he is described by Miles as "a raging communist" in Vita Sackville-West's *Family History.*

Brewer　Elderly, overweight man; a lower-middle-class pony player, he is behind in "subscription" payments on horse-racing bets to Pinkie Brown's mob; he is roughed up by Pinkie in Graham Greene's *Brighton Rock.*

Emily Brewster　Gruff and hearty spinster; she and Patrick Redfern are the apparent discoverers of Arlena Marshall's body in Agatha Christie's *Evil Under the Sun.*

Alphonse Briac　Pupil of Chopin who is a monk at Shangri-la and teaches Hugh "Glory" Conway an unknown song by Chopin in James Hilton's *Lost Horizon.*

Brian　The group leader of the rebellious teenagers by whom Kate wants to be accepted in Doris Lessing's *The Diaries of Jane Somers.*

Brian　Foul-smelling, marginally human boy whose whole experience is limited to the goings-on in a slaughterhouse; he resists Norah's well-meant but fleeting attempts to improve him in Richard Hughes's *The Wooden Shepherdess.*

Brian　Car salesman with a wealthy family in Isabel Colegate's *Orlando at the Brazen Threshold.*

Lord Brideshead (Bridey)　Lord and Lady Marchmain's oldest son; strait-laced and humorless, he is a strict Roman Catholic who eventually marries a middle-aged widow and enlists in the British army in World War II in Evelyn Waugh's *Brideshead Revisited.*

Arthur Bridge　Works Manager at the Dupret Foundry; his approach to the workers makes him very unpopular with them and with Richard Dupret in Henry Green's *Living.*

Katherine (Kathie) Bridges　"New Woman of the nineties" with radical political views and leanings toward Bernard Shaw and William Morris; she meets Mr. Chips on a rock-climbing expedition at Great Gable; the older Mr. Chips and the beautiful young woman fall in love, marry, and take up residence at Brookfield, where she is well liked by students and staff and has a rejuvenating, tempering effect on Mr. Chips's

character; she and her newly born child die on April 1 in James Hilton's *Good-bye, Mr. Chips.*

Ronald Bridges　Roman Catholic epileptic assistant curator of a handwriting museum whose expertise leads to the downfall of Patrick Seton in Muriel Spark's *The Bachelors.*

Bridget　The loyal, loving fiancée of Len; she has to walk home alone after the movies and is attacked by Harry but escapes him; she marries Len in David Lodge's *The Picturegoers.*

Bridgett　An overworked social worker for the elderly in Doris Lessing's *The Diaries of Jane Somers.*

Bridgett　A schoolgirl from a broken family who takes refuge on her holidays with Harriet and David Lovatt's family until Ben Lovatt is born in Doris Lessing's *The Fifth Child.*

Father Austin Brierly　The Catholic curate of Our Lady and St. Jude's, where the student group attends morning mass; he marries Angela and Dennis, is transferred several times because of his changing attitudes towards doctrine, studies first Biblical scholarship and then psychology, and ends up leaving the priesthood and pairing up with Lynn, Dennis's secretary, in David Lodge's *How Far Can You Go?.*

Betty Briers　Wife of Frank; she is slowly dying of a debilitating disease in C. P. Snow's *A Coat of Varnish.*

Frank Briers　Detective Chief Superintendent who believes that Ralph Perryman is the murderer of Lady Ashbrook but cannot prove it; he asks Humphrey Leigh to work for him in anti-terrorism in C. P. Snow's *A Coat of Varnish.*

H. W. Brigginshaw　Colleague of Cornelius Cardew; he amuses Cardew's wife while Cardew is away in Isabel Colegate's *The Shooting Party.*

Briggs　Adam Appleby's thesis supervisor at the university; he has been working on the same book for twenty years; he halfheartedly tries to help Adam obtain a position in the department in David Lodge's *The British Museum Is Falling Down.*

Jack Briggs　A previous journalist on the *Times* who became involved in leftist politics, found a low-paying job working for a left newspaper, and was forced to resign because of rumors that he was communist, in Doris Lessing's *The Golden Notebook.*

John Briggs　Nicholas Urfe's successor at the Lord Byron School on Phraxos in John Fowles's *The Magus.*

Professor Brigham   English department head at Brockshire University in J. B. Priestley's *The Image Men.*

Agatha Bright   Stepmother of Viola and Septimus; a young and attractive widow, Agatha becomes involved with and ultimately engaged to Robson Joyce, a sales representative for Tremlett & Grove's, the publishing firm where her stepson Septimus works, in Frank Swinnerton's *The Happy Family.*

Septimus Bright   Junior clerk at the publishing house Tremlett & Grove's; engaged to Mary Amerson, he becomes jealous of her attentions to Roger Dennett and conspires to get Dennett dismissed from the publishing firm; the failure of his plan results in his own dismissal in Frank Swinnerton's *The Happy Family.*

Viola Bright   Sister of Septimus Bright; she strives to attract Roger Dennett but loses him to Mary Amerson in Frank Swinnerton's *The Happy Family.*

A. M. Brightman   Retired major who initially tries to help James Latter so that he will file suit against Chester Nimmo; the plan fails, and Jim later realizes that Brightman is out only for personal gain during the General Strike in Joyce Cary's *Not Honour More.*

Brigitta   Impudent seven-year-old bastard daughter of the whiskey priest; growing up in poverty and violence, she is worldly and mature beyond her years and, to her father's grief, is lost utterly in Graham Greene's *The Power and the Glory.*

Brigstock   Member of Benditch's coal board, which votes for L. rather than for D. in Graham Greene's *The Confidential Agent.*

Brimah   Bamu's father; a shrewd bargainer, he continually raises the price Johnson must pay to marry his daughter in Joyce Cary's *Mister Johnson.*

Alisa Brimley   Adrian Fielding's wartime secretary and George Smiley's Intelligence colleague; she edits and writes as Barbara Fellowship the *Christian Voice* before enlisting Smiley's aid to help Stella Rode in John le Carré's *A Murder of Quality.* She operates a safehouse for Smiley in *Tinker, Tailor, Soldier, Spy.*

Roberta Brinklow   Missionary of the Eastern mission who is aboard the highjacked plane and taken to the Tibetan monastery, Shangri-La, with Hugh "Glory" Conway, Henry D. Barnard, and Captain Charles Mallison in James Hilton's *Lost Horizon.*

Brinsley   The narrator's friend and fellow student, who is a voice of common sense in Flann O'Brien's *At Swim-Two-Birds.*

Harriet Westwater Brisbane-Brown   Alison Westwater's clannish and devoted aunt; she falls in love with Thomas Carlyle Craw, the newspaper magnate, in John Buchan's *Castle Gay.* She has married Craw in the beginning of *The House of the Four Winds.*

Colonel Jimmy Briscoe   Dahlia Travers's friend and host, through whom Bertie Wooster rents a seaside cottage; owner of a racing stable, he is Mr. Cook's chief rival in P. G. Wodehouse's *Aunts Aren't Gentlemen.*

Lily Briscoe   A self-described "peevish, ill-tempered dried-up old maid", who represents the questing artist; she brings her androgynous vision as a means to redemptive reunion between conflicting forces; she finally completes her long-unfinished painting, in which Mrs. Ramsay is a "wedge of darkness" in Virginia Woolf's *To the Lighthouse.*

Britannicus   Claudius's son, whose proud refusal to flee incognito to Britain, as Claudius suggests, costs him his life in Robert Graves's *Claudius, the God and His Wife Messalina.*

Edith Britling   Scientific wife of Mr. Britling; she offsets her husband's Hellenistic qualities, yet cannot relate to him on an emotionally intimate level in H. G. Wells's *Mr. Britling Sees It Through.*

Hugh Britling   Bumbling but distinguished philosopher and writer, who questions the Hellenistic attitudes of England in the face of German threat; he views his home, Dower House, as a pampered microcosm of England; he attempts to justify and later condemns the war through his writing; he discovers God and a mutuality with Germany through his son's death in H. G. Wells's *Mr. Britling Sees It Through.*

Hugh Britling (the younger)   Oldest Britling son by a previous marriage; his plans to study science at Oxford are interrupted by World War I; he lies about his age and joins the war at seventeen; his letters home inspire pride and anxiety before he is killed in the trenches in H. G. Wells's *Mr. Britling Sees It Through.*

Sunny Jim Britling   One of two minor Britling sons; he reads American comics and, like his brother, lives the war through toy soldiers in H. G. Wells's *Mr. Britling Sees It Through.*

Jules Briton   Friend of Conder and lover of Kay Rimmer; he thinks anxiously about trying to help Jim Drover, receives a small inheritance from his father, and decides to propose to Kay, taking her for a country outing in Graham Greene's *It's a Battlefield.*

Adele, Lady Brixton   American cousin of Agnes

Sandeman; she becomes the first of many "Luciaphiles", a group of London elite who are captivated by Lucia Lucas's social maneuvers in E. F. Benson's *Lucia in London*. She purchases Lucia's house in Riseholme in *Mapp and Lucia*.

Colonel Broadbury Gentleman who meets Richard Hannay in the Highlands of Scotland where Hannay is again on the run; after checking Hannay's credentials, he takes Hannay home for a civilized twenty-four hours in the company of Broadbury's son, Ted, maimed in the war, in John Buchan's *Mr. Standfast*.

Mr. Brock Effete weekend guest of Margy Stuart; he thinks Georgie Smithers a "fantastic frump" in Richard Aldington's *The Colonel's Daughter*.

Mrs. Brockie Widow who runs an inn whose name attracts Dickson McCunn on the first stage of his journey in John Buchan's *Huntingtower*.

Brod (covernames: Ivlov, Lapin) Moscow Centre operative; during an adulterous affair with Moscow Centre agent Irina, he revealed to her the existence of Karla's double agent Gerald; he is executed with Irina for his betrayal in John le Carré's *Tinker, Tailor, Soldier, Spy*.

Colonel Brodeshaw A wealthy Tory Member of Parliament who appears sympathetic to Anton Hesse's desire to become a citizen in Doris Lessing's *A Proper Marriage* and in *Landlocked*.

Bennett Brodie Medical student and fiancé of Sarah Henderson in Dorothy Richardson's *Backwater*. He marries Sarah and provides a home for his bankrupt father-in-law in *Honeycomb*.

Ian Brodie Officious and censorious doctor, brother-in-law of January Marlowe, and sometime double for Robinson in Muriel Spark's *Robinson*.

Jean Brodie Charismatic, unorthodox teacher at the Marcia Blaine School in Edinburgh; she manipulates the girls who form "the Brodie set" to fulfill her political and sexual fantasies until one of her girls is moved to betray her in Muriel Spark's *The Prime of Miss Jean Brodie*.

Marian Brodie Miriam Henderson's young niece in Dorothy Richardson's *March Moonlight*.

Valentine Brodie Professor of literature in twenty-first-century North America and a writer of science fiction; he is the philandering, shallow, and self-absorbed but charming husband of Vanessa Frame Brodie in Anthony Burgess's *The End of the World News*.

Vanessa Frame Brodie Brilliant, beautiful, unemotional scientist, daughter of Hubert Frame; she is one of the top theoretical physicists of her time; she remains inexplicably in love with Valentine Brodie even after divorcing him in Anthony Burgess's *The End of the World News*.

William Brodie Miriam Henderson's nephew, Marian Brodie's brother, in Dorothy Richardson's *March Moonlight*.

Brodribb Middle-aged secretary of the dock workers' union who encourages Chester Nimmo to start a farm laborers' union in Joyce Cary's *Except the Lord*.

Dr. Brodsky A social scientist and the developer of a method of criminal reform using behavioral conditioning; superficially friendly and possibly well-meaning, he is also coldly scientific and is able to deal ruthlessly with Alex to prove his theory in Anthony Burgess's *A Clockwork Orange*.

Michael Brodzinski Polish scientist who serves on the advisory committee for nuclear weapons; he opposes Roger Quaife's policy on disarmament and impugns the loyalty of scientists and civil servants in C. P. Snow's *Corridors of Power*.

Brome Crazed woman who is after Chester Nimmo for supposedly causing her son's death by not exempting him from war service; after numerous incidents she is committed to an asylum in Joyce Cary's *Not Honour More*.

Bromley Surviving member of the crew of the jolly boat in C. S. Forester's *Mr. Midshipman Hornblower*.

Scevola Bron Bloodthirsty sans-culotte farmer who forces Arlette to participate in the Terror and is killed with Peyrol carrying the false papers to the British blockaders in Joseph Conrad's *The Rover*.

Dmitri Bronowsky A white-Russian emigre who serves as secretary to the Nawab of Mirat, Sir Ahmed Bahadur, a local prince; Bronowsky's network of informants and his participation or connection with events make him an informed commentator in Paul Scott's *The Jewel in the Crown*, in *The Day of the Scorpion*, in *The Towers of Silence*, and in *A Division of the Spoils*.

Lev Davidovich Bronstein (Leon Trotsky) Russian-Jewish politician, one of the intellectual leaders of the Bolshevik wing of the Russian Communist party in the early twentieth century; he seems uncharacteristically frivolous in Anthony Burgess's *The End of the World News*.

Lisa Brooke Seventy-three-year-old woman of

wealth, viciousness, and legendary promiscuity; after her death, her estate prompts discord and discovery among her aged relatives, housekeeper, and old lovers in Muriel Spark's *Memento Mori.*

Florence Broom   One of a pair of sisters who are day-pupils at Wordsworth House, the school in north London where Miriam Henderson teaches in Dorothy Richardson's *Backwater.* They make friendly overtures to Miriam and continue to invite her to their comfortable home for restorative weekends in *Interim* and in *The Trap.* Miriam goes to the Broom sisters from her Swiss holiday before returning to her job in the dental surgery in *Dawn's Left Hand.* Miriam travels on holiday with them to Sussex in *Dimple Hill.*

Grace Broom   Florence Broom's sister in Dorothy Richardson's *Backwater,* in *Interim,* in *The Trap,* in *Dawn's Left Hand,* and in *Dimple Hill.*

Jack Brotherhood (covername: Marlow)   Senior British Intelligence officer; he recruits young Magnus Pym, grooms him for high honors in the "Firm", and becomes one of the two father figures Magnus betrays in John le Carré's *A Perfect Spy.*

Mr. Brough   Barrister who represents Sir Gerald Corven in his divorce suit in John Galsworthy's *Over the River.*

Paul Louis ("Johnnie Vulkan", "King", "Mr. Angle") Broum   Prague-born, half-Jewish agricultural biologist who served as a wartime interpreter for Britain; believed killed at Treblinka, he escaped by impersonating the concentration-camp guard John August Vulkan; as Vulkan he works as Dawlish's Berlin contact and occasional operative; he tries unsuccessfully to collect £250,000 of the Broum family securities by obtaining his true identification from British intelligence and an endorsed claim from the Israeli government; he accidentally dies in a fight with the narrator in Len Deighton's *Funeral in Berlin.*

Brown   Narrator, owner of the Trianon, a hotel above Port-au-Prince, and a lapsed Catholic who distrusts everyone and is committed to no one and nothing; he is the lover of Martha Pineda, an ambassador's wife; he befriends Major Jones and helps him to join Haitian rebels; he becomes an undertaker in Santo Domingo in Graham Greene's *The Comedians.*

Brown   Burly, vulgar, lower-class coxswain, who eventually shows his more reserved, compassionate side in his service to Horatio Hornblower and William Bush in C. S. Forester's *The Happy Return,* in *Ship of the Line,* and in *Flying Colours.* He is the intelligent, resourceful, masterful coxswain and companion who anticipates and fulfills Hornblower's needs in *Commodore Hornblower* and in *Lord Hornblower.*

Brown   One of three English road laborers mistaken by John Lavender for German prisoners of war in John Galsworthy's *The Burning Spear: Being the Experiences of Mr. John Lavender in Time of War.*

Gentleman Brown   Rapacious pirate who raids Patusan and, while fleeing, murders Dain Waris in retribution for Jim's resistance in Joseph Conrad's *Lord Jim.*

Mr. Brown   Master criminal and propagandist for peace during World War I in Agatha Christie's *The Secret Adversary.*

Abe Brown   Rich, self-driven businessman, who loves his daughter, Susan; he makes family and business decisions with brutal force in John Braine's *Room at the Top.* He rules his employees according to his ideas and disregards other opinions in *Life at the Top.*

Arthur Brown   Fellow of the Cambridge college; a Junior Tutor, he helps organize support for the election of Roy Calvert to his college; he informs Lewis Eliot that Calvert is killed in C. P. Snow's *The Light and the Dark.* He helps Chrystal woo an endowment from Sir Horace Timberlake, refuses to stand as a compromise candidate for new Master, and supports Paul Jago to the very end in *The Masters.* He casts the deciding vote for reinstatment of Howard's fellowship in *The Affair.* He delivers the eulogy for Sir Francis Getliffe in *Last Things.*

Eileen Brown   The twenty-two-year-old only daughter of Kate and Michael Brown; she accompanies her father to Boston for the summer and is attempting to decide if she will want her mother's life style for herself, or if she will become radically different in Doris Lessing's *The Summer Before the Dark.*

James Brown   British prime minister who is forced to resign as a consequence of his daughter's giving a party at No. 10 Downing Street in Evelyn Waugh's *Vile Bodies.*

James Brown   The second son of Michael and Kate Brown; he will begin at the university after a summer spent on an archaeological "dig" in the Sudan with his friends in Doris Lessing's *The Summer Before the Dark.*

Kate Ferreira Brown A middle-aged, married woman — the nurturer to her four children, her husband, and her coworkers — who is alone for the first time since she can remember when her husband and children go their separate ways one summer; she begins a deep examination into her past life and her present self in Doris Lessing's *The Summer Before the Dark*.

Kate Brown's Grandfather A kindly, tyrannical man from Lourenço Marques with whom Kate Brown spent a year while a teenager learning Portuguese; he expected her to grow up and become only a wife and mother in Doris Lessing's *The Summer Before the Dark*.

Laurence Brown Frail, hypersensitive tutor of Josephine and Eustace Leonides; he and Brenda Leonides are arrested for the murder of her husband in Agatha Christie's *Crooked House*.

Margaret Brown Overcritical, socially busy wife of Abe and mother of Susan in John Braine's *Room at the Top* and in *Life at the Top*.

Michael Brown Kate Brown's wealthy husband, a neurologist, who has comfortable but increasingly uninvolved relationships with his wife and children; he has had numerous affairs and has grown apart from his wife in Doris Lessing's *The Summer Before the Dark*.

Pinkie Brown (The Boy) Seventeen-year-old, cold, frigid, amoral, calculating bookmakers' extortion-mob leader and killer of Charles Hale; haunted by his lower-class background and Roman Catholic upbringing, he seduces and marries Rose Wilson to keep her from identifying Spicer as posing as Charles Hale in Snow's restaurant; after Rose refuses to kill herself and the police come, he douses himself with vitriol and drowns himself in order to avoid police capture in Graham Greene's *Brighton Rock*.

Puggy Brown Hypocritical, adulterous Benjamite preacher who marries Lucy Wilcher in Joyce Cary's *To Be a Pilgrim*.

Robert Brown Tom Wilcher's nephew; he is a scientific farmer who wants to assume control of Tolbrook Manor; he marries Ann Wilcher but has an affair with Molly Panton in Joyce Cary's *Herself Surprised* and in *To Be a Pilgrim*.

Stephen Brown The oldest son of Kate and Michael Brown; he is in his last year at the university in Doris Lessing's *The Summer Before the Dark*.

Sue Brown A diminutive, adorable chorus girl of resourcefulness and spirit; she is in love with Ronnie Fish in P. G. Wodehouse's *Fish Preferred*. She appears in two other novels.

Susan Brown Young, immature, beautiful, rich girl; although Joe Lampton does not love her, he woos her successfully to win her from her childhood sweetheart, Jack Wales, in John Braine's *Room at the Top*. She proves to be smarter and more passionate than her husband knew in *Life at the Top*.

Ted Brown Working-class Englishman who had won scholarships to Oxford, and who was the only genuine socialist of Anna Wulf's group of friends in Mashopi in Doris Lessing's *The Golden Notebook*.

Tim Brown The nineteen-year-old problem son of Kate and Michael Brown; he causes an emotional crisis in the family by shouting that his mother was suffocating him in Doris Lessing's *The Summer Before the Dark*.

Tommy Brown A young, highly sensitive and sincere member of the Communist Party whom the rest of the members, especially Andrew McGrew, watch out for and protect in Doris Lessing's *A Ripple from the Storm*.

William Brown A young Englishman stationed in Martha Quest's town who leads her to want to become a communist, and who has an extended affair with her in Doris Lessing's *A Proper Marriage* and in *A Ripple from the Storm*.

Yvette Brown (the Comtesse de Lascot-Villiers) The narrator's mother, who left him at a Jesuit school in Monaco; a colorful figure who may have fought in the French resistance, she acquires the Trianon, a Haitian hotel, and leaves it to Brown in Graham Greene's *The Comedians*.

Jonathan Browne The conforming, pragmatic, agnostic narrator; he clings to Mike Brady during the Basic Training portion of his National Service stint out of need for intelligent companionship and moral support; he tries to neither help nor hurt Mike, but feels in the end that he has betrayed him; he marries Mike's former girlfriend, Pauline Vickers, in David Lodge's *Ginger, You're Barmy*.

Leonard Browne Talis Browne's irascible ailing father, who lives with him; Tallis is unable to tell the old man that he is fatally ill in Iris Murdoch's *A Fairly Honourable Defeat*.

Morgan Browne Hilda Foster's younger sister, a linguistics professor; she is the discarded lover of Julius King, whose child she aborted on finding herself pregnant; estranged from her husband, Tallis Browne, she is the supposed lover of Rupert Foster in an elaborate punitive practical joke engineered by Julius in Iris Murdoch's *A Fairly Honourable Defeat*.

Sam Browne   A stereotypic Public School Englishman without intelligence or character; he is Isabel Winterbourne's "sheik" in Richard Aldington's *Death of a Hero*.

Tallis Browne   An adult-education lecturer, who is a morally upright person; he is Julius King's inadequate adversary in Iris Murdoch's *A Fairly Honourable Defeat*.

Yvonne (Velvet) Browning   The pretty accomplice of her beloved houseburglar-boyfriend, Wolf; she goes to Corker's employment agency posing as a jobseeker to case the place; she deceives Corker but winds up in jail unjustly accused of hitting Irene Corker over the head in John Berger's *Corker's Freedom*.

Charles Brownleigh   The rational, no-nonsense attorney for the prosecution in Hugo Chesterton's trial; he is susceptible to Daisy Bland's charm in Nicholas Blake's *A Tangled Web*.

Mr. Brownlie   A banker, the nephew of Lord Port Scatho; he harbors a gloomy passion for Sylvia Tietjens; convinced that she will marry him if she can be got to divorce her husband, he juggles accounts at the bank so that Christopher Tietjens overdraws in Ford Madox Ford's *Some Do Not. . . .*

Mr. Brownlow   Housemaster at Westminster who encourages the theatrical abilities of young Piers Mosson in Angus Wilson's *Setting the World on Fire*.

Pamela Brune   Goddaughter of Sir Edward Leithen; affirming her love and courage, both by precept and example, she overcomes a dangerous illness and is rewarded by joyful union with Charles Ottery in John Buchan's *The Gap in the Curtain*.

Toto de Brunel   A homosexual socialite given to inappropriate word substitutions when speaking English; he wears Justine Hosnani's identifiable ring — at her request — at a masked ball and is murdered in error by Narouz Hosnani in Lawrence Durrell's *Balthazar*.

Irene Brunskill   Woman whose marriage to Martin Eliot is discouraged by Lewis Eliot; she flirts with other men after her marriage, has a son named for Lewis, and breaks with her lover Edgar Hankins to settle into her marriage in C. P. Snow's *The New Men*. She encourages Martin in his advocacy of Donald Howard's reinstatement in *The Affair*. She worries about the financial future of her son, Pat Eliot, in *The Sleep of Reason*.

Alice Brury   Young, spirited hotel housekeeper; having quit her post because of a contretemps with a thieving guest, she begs to be reinstated but is placed in another hotel in Arnold Bennett's *Imperial Palace*.

Brute-men   An alien species whose worship of irrationalism, instinct, and ruthlessness travesties fascism in Olaf Stapledon's *Star Maker*.

Millicent, Lady Bruton   A duchess and a powerful meddler, with whom Richard Dalloway frequently has intimate lunches; Clarissa Dalloway is jealous of her on the day of her party in Virginia Woolf's *Mrs. Dalloway*.

Major Eric E. J. Brutt   Retired British army officer of modest means and no property who lives in inexpensive residential hotels; to Anna Quayne's discomfort, he emerges from her indiscreet past; in his blustering avuncular manner, he becomes an understanding and trusted friend to Portia Quayne in Elizabeth Bowen's *The Death of the Heart*.

Loil Bry   Laintal Ay's grandmother, a sorceress in Brian W. Aldiss's *Helliconia Spring*.

Mr. Bryanston   Rose Vassiliou's abject, irritating, hard father; a self-made man of great wealth, he speaks primarily to impress or be approved of in Margaret Drabble's *The Needle's Eye*.

Inspector Bryant   Scotland Yard officer who uncovers a plot by terrorists using Ralph Tucker's play production as a front and makes arrests during its presentation at Tothill House in Angus Wilson's *Setting the World on Fire*.

Chalmers Bryant   American banker who is traveling under the alias Henry D. Barnard because of business crimes amounting to millions of dollars; he is abducted on a highjacked plane and taken to the Tibetan monastery, Shangri-La, along with Hugh "Glory" Conway, Roberta Brinklow, and Captain Charles Mallinson in James Hilton's *Lost Horizon*.

Elsie Bryant   Mrs. Wilbraham's maid, who was under suspicion when her employer's necklace was stolen some fifteen years earlier in Dorothy L. Sayers's *The Nine Tailors: Changes Rung on an Old Theme in Two Short Touches and Two Full Peals*.

Thomas Bryant   An English R.A.F. pilot stationed in Martha Quest's town; she takes a strong romantic interest in him in Doris Lessing's *A Proper Marriage*.

Miss Buchanan   A woman with a dry sense of humor; she keeps a general shop and conceals the fact that she cannot read in Ivy Compton-Burnett's *Manservant and Maidservant*.

Father Bede Buchanan The college chaplain who officiates at the Paschal Festival which occurs at the end of David Lodge's *How Far Can You Go?*.

Mr. Buck Draper who becomes Lord High Provost of North Kensington; he is killed by Adam Wayne during the last battle in G. K. Chesterton's *The Napoleon of Notting Hill*.

Buckland First lieutenant of the *Renown*; he is a capable seaman, who assumes command and is taken captive during the Spanish prisoners' revolt; he is angered by Hornblower's promotion in C. S. Forester's *Lieutenant Hornblower*.

Ned Buckton A former geography teacher turned warden of the local youth hostel; he is the husband of Sally Buckton and the father of their two children; he meets Anthony Keating at Mrs. Bunney's pub, and they become friends in Margaret Drabble's *The Ice Age*.

Sally Buckton Wife of Ned Buckton and mother of their two children in Margaret Drabble's *The Ice Age*.

Gervaise Bucktrout Estate agent who sells Lady Slane the house in Hampstead and becomes her true companion in Vita Sackville-West's *All Passion Spent*.

Lady Frederica Budd Lord Warminster's eldest daughter, a distinguished-looking, self-controlled, highly respectable widow in Anthony Powell's *The Acceptance World* and in *Casanova's Chinese Restaurant*. Her sister Isobel (Tolland) Jenkins stays with Frederica during the war when she is pregnant in *The Kindly Ones*. Frederica becomes Dicky Umfraville's fifth wife in *The Valley of Bones*. The marriage endures through *Hearing Secret Harmonies*.

Buddy Smart, sly good friend to the Geste brothers; inseparable from his friend Hank, he is an American soldier in the French Foreign Legion in Percival Christopher Wren's *Beau Geste*.

Duke of Bude Father-in-law to General Curzon; his amiable, gentle nature is in contrast to his wife's in C. S. Forester's *The General*.

Duchess of Bude Domineering mother of Lady Emily Winter-Willoughby; she is an intrusive mother-in-law to General Curzon in C. S. Forester's *The General*.

Mrs. Budgen Lame caretaker for the house where Ivy Barton, Joshua Creed, and the Hugheses live in John Galsworthy's *Fraternity*.

Martin Budgen Son of Mrs. Budgen; he makes cynical observations on the visits of the upper crust in John Galsworthy's *Fraternity*.

Sir Henry Budstock Lord Raingo's predecessor as Minister of Records; he recognizes the status of a "mushroom" Ministry in Arnold Bennett's *Lord Raingo*.

Buffles (The Stink Merchant) Pale, lean, and medically unfit science master at Brookfield in James Hilton's *Good-bye, Mr. Chips*.

Mr. Buggins Friend of Art Kipps from the Folkestone Drapery Bazaar who warns Kipps against answering Old Bean's inheritance announcement but whom Kipps later sets up in business as a gentlemen's clothier in H. G. Wells's *Kipps: The Story of a Simple Soul*.

Bulic Gullible, conceited clerk in the Yugoslav Submarine Defence Department; befriended by Wladyslaw Grodek and Dimitrios Makropoulos, who later force him to steal secret information, he is roughed up by Dimitrios and when Grodek informs on him is sent to prison for life in Eric Ambler's *The Mask of Dimitrios*.

Madame Bulic Amiable, pretty, stupid wife of Bulic; her gambling losses as manipulated by Wladyslaw Grodek serve as the means for Bulic's downfall in Eric Ambler's *The Mask of Dimitrios*.

Bull KolobEktofer's aide; he advises against attacking the Draits in Brian W. Aldiss's *Helliconia Summer*.

Bull Tattooed gunner on the flying boat who gets lost in a fog on the first night of the treasure hunt, falls off a cliff, and is decapitated in Alan Sillitoe's *The Lost Flying Boat*.

Dr. Bull Saturday of the General Council of the Anarchists of Europe who is entrusted with the plans to assassinate the Czar and the King of France; he reveals himself to Gabriel Syme and Professor de Worms as a Scotland Yard Detective and travels with them to France to prevent the assassination; he joins with the other Council members in the pursuit of Sunday in G. K. Chesterton's *The Man Who Was Thursday: A Nightmare*.

Mrs. Bull Fat gossip who tells everyone about Arthur Seaton's various affairs and then is shot in the buttocks with an air rifle by Arthur in Alan Sillitoe's *Saturday Night and Sunday Morning*.

Buller Maurice Castle's trusting dog that Castle kills before he defects so his wife Sarah and adopted son Sam can live with his prejudiced mother in Graham Greene's *The Human Factor.*

Bullfry Barrister who represents Marjorie Ferrar in her libel suit against Fleur Mont in John Galsworthy's *The Silver Spoon.*

Bullivant Butler to the Lambs; he has witty talks with Mortimer Lamb but speaks sententiously to the other servants in Ivy Compton-Burnett's *Manservant and Maidservant.*

Sir Walter Bullivant (Lord Artinswell) Permanent Secretary at the Foreign Office who aids Richard Hannay in subverting the villainous plot of enemy agents to steal British naval plans in John Buchan's *The Thirty-Nine Steps.* He recruits Hannay as an intelligence officer to prevent the forming of a jehad in the Near East in *Greenmantle.* He seeks Hannay's undercover abilities to locate and destroy an enemy spy network headed by Moxton Ivery (Graf von Schwabing) in World War I in *Mr. Standfast.* He appeals to Hannay to solve the mysterious disappearance of the three kidnap victims in *The Three Hostages.*

Bulteel Elderly government Resident who helps Rudbeck complete his road by secretly diverting funds from other treasury accounts in Joyce Cary's *Mister Johnson.*

Ethel Bumfrett Devoted assistant to Mary Taylor, matron of a teaching hospital in P. D. James's *Shroud for a Nightingale.*

Richard (Dickie) Bumpus A little, dark man who had meant romance for William Masson in youth; he pretends that a book he wrote years ago is a second, new creation in Ivy Compton-Burnett's *Pastors and Masters.*

Bessy Bunce Thomas Bunce's wife, who pickles onions and supplies the Angel Inn with a grandfather clock in T. F. Powys's *Mr. Weston's Good Wine.*

Jenny Bunce Thomas Bunce's playful daughter, who admires Tamar Grobe, narrowly averts being raped by the Mumby brothers, and marries Luke Bird in T. F. Powys's *Mr. Weston's Good Wine.*

Thomas (Landlord) Bunce Proprietor of the Angel Inn who believes God is to be blamed for everything and sets out to prove God is to blame for the ruin of Folly Down's maidens in T. F. Powys's *Mr. Weston's Good Wine.*

Teddy Bunder Flashy, gangling automobile-export delivery driver who recruits co-worker Charles Lumley for a subsidiary drug-smuggling operation and who shoves Charles from a moving, stolen car while fleeing the police in John Wain's *Hurry On Down.*

Jenny Bunn Slender twenty-year-old beauty with long black hair and darkish coloring who is a grade-school teacher; she falls in love with rake Patrick Standish and after prolonged resistance loses her prized virginity to him on his terms in Kingsley Amis's *Take a Girl Like You.*

Mrs. Bunney Proprietress of a pub Anthony Keating finds a pleasant escape from various pressures at his home, High Rook House, in Margaret Drabble's *The Ice Age.*

Bunny Indo-Chinese hairdresser and associate of William Holmes in Isabel Colegate's *Orlando at the Brazen Threshold.*

Irma Bunt A "toad-like", brutal woman, who is Ernst Stavro Blofeld's secretary and mistress in Ian Fleming's *On Her Majesty's Secret Service.* She has become "Mrs. Shatterhand" in *You Only Live Twice.*

Mervyn Bunter Lord Peter Wimsey's imperturbable, resourceful manservant, whose photography hobby, observation, and adaptability are useful to Lord Peter in Dorothy L. Sayers's *Whose Body?*, in *Clouds of Witness,* in *Unnatural Death,* in *The Unpleasantness at the Bellona Club,* in *Strong Poison,* in *Have His Carcase,* and in *The Nine Tailors: Changes Rung on an Old Theme in two Short Touches and Two Full Peals.*

Mr. Bunting Iping vicar whom Griffin burgles to get needed rent money and whose clothes he later steals in H. G. Wells's *The Invisible Man: A Grotesque Romance.*

Dorothea Bunyan Muriel Ponsonby's first governess; she leaves insulted by Sabine Ponsonby; she is the niece of the Reverend Dr. Chaucer in Ivy Compton-Burnett's *Daughters and Sons.*

Agatha Burbridge Lady Clementina Burbridge's daughter and Margaret Roehampton's cousin in Vita Sackville-West's *The Edwardians.*

Lady Clementina Burbridge Sister to George, Earl of Roehampton; she upholds the traditional values and standards of aristocratic Edwardian society in Vita Sackville-West's *The Edwardians.*

Agatha Burch Housekeeper at the Tennant estate who is disturbed and offended when Charley Raunce becomes head butler in Henry Green's *Loving.*

Caroline Burckheim   Second wife of Honoré Burckheim; considered completely unmanageable by her husband, she struggles to be accepted as a French woman rather than as the daughter of an American senator; the jealous Anne-Marie Eschelmer and later Honoré himself taunt her for her inability to conceive children; she finally returns to America, disillusioned by her husband's intrigues but loyal to France in Storm Jameson's *Cousin Honoré*.

Genevieve Burckheim   Lighthearted first wife of Honoré Burckheim, whom she married at age nineteen and who remembers her as very young when he is over eighty; he also remembers her as a woman who constantly contradicted herself and was the only love of his life in Storm Jameson's *Cousin Honoré*.

Honoré Burckheim   Lusty, cunning, greedy, elderly egoist; he is the independent and self-centered owner of an ancient vineyard in an Alsatian valley and of an ironworks; husband of first Genevieve and then Caroline, he is also the father of an illegitimate daughter, Anne-Marie Eschelmer; he is fiercely anti-German just before the fall of France in World War II; he loves France but is an unheroic and often heartless figure, who is betrayed by relatives who see the financial success of the ironworks as dependent upon covert cooperation with German industrialists in Storm Jameson's *Cousin Honoré*.

Crystal Burde   Hilary Burde's beloved unmarried sister, a dressmaker; she cherishes a selfless, hopeless passion for Gunnar Jopling in Iris Murdoch's *A Word Child*.

Hilary Burde   An orphanage-reared illegitimate child who became a brilliant linguist but is now working as a civil-service clerk in Whitehall; he becomes involved in an emotional triangle that repeats the tragedy that destroyed his career as an Oxford don years before; he is narrator of Iris Murdoch's *A Word Child*.

Burge   Arrogant college acquaintance and physician-in-training whom Charles Lumley encounters at a hospital staff party, where Charles attacks Burge's snobbery head-on in John Wain's *Hurry On Down*.

Mr. Burgess   The undermaster who teaches the older boys in Mr. Herrick's school; he is retained for his image as a man with a degree in Ivy Compton-Burnett's *Pastors and Masters*.

Ted Burgess   Handsome, vital tenant farmer identified with Aquarius who has a clandestine love affair with Marian Maudsley, the wealthy daughter of the resident family at Brandham Hall; he kills himself following discovery of their union in L. P. Hartley's *The Go-Between*.

Sir Thomas Burgh   An aristocratic college friend of Charles Smithson; he accompanies him on a night of debauchery in John Fowles's *The French Lieutenant's Woman*.

Colonel Burgoyne   Chief Constable of the village in Kent where the actress Christine Clay was murdered in Josephine Tey's *A Shilling for Candles*.

Erica Burgoyne   Daughter of Colonel Burgoyne; she befriends Robin Tisdall and clears him as a suspect by recovering an important piece of evidence in Josephine Tey's *A Shilling for Candles*.

Miss Burke   A woman not hired as a companion by Miranda Hume but hired as a housekeeper by Emma Greatheart; Rosebery Hume proposes to her in Ivy Compton-Burnett's *Mother and Son*.

Frederick Burke   David Lovatt's stepfather, an academic who lives in a large, shabby house in Oxford with David's mother in Doris Lessing's *The Fifth Child*.

Molly Burke   David Lovatt's mother, who can never forgive Harriet Lovatt for going to take Ben Lovatt out of the institution where she and her husband had put him in Doris Lessing's *The Fifth Child*.

O'Madden Burke   Newspaperman in James Joyce's *Ulysses*.

Tim Burke   Irishman, goldsmith, and close friend of the Mor family in Iris Murdoch's *The Sandcastle*.

Clare ("Mumbo") Burkin-Jones   One of three women in their sixties who at the age of eleven were "best friends" at a school in Kent; now divorced, childless, and the successful owner of a chain of gift shops, she assumes a half-cynical, half-amused pose toward Diana Delacroix's cryptic ads designed to call them all together in Elizabeth Bowen's *The Little Girls*.

Denis Burlap   Pompous editor of a small literary magazine; his pious devotion to Christian charity is overshadowed by his indifference to his employee Walter Bidlake's financial problems and his calculated seduction of the vulnerable Beatrice Gilray in Aldous Huxley's *Point Counter Point*.

Cecil Burleigh   Conservative politician and supposedly eminent philosopher who first explains human society to the Utopians and who later succumbs to Rupert Catskill's plan to overthrow Utopian rule in H. G. Wells's *Men Like Gods.*

Thomas Burns Dublin shopkeeper who gives Caithleen her job as a shop assistant in Edna O'Brien's *The Country Girls.*

Reggie Burnside Rich young snob engaged in atomic research at Cambridge; he is first Fanny Welford's lover and then Elizabeth Paston's in Richard Aldington's *Death of a Hero.*

Burra Little, demonstrative girl at the north London school, whose affection Miriam Henderson tries to keep within bounds in Dorothy Richardson's *Backwater.*

Harry G. Burrard A variety artist whose day has passed; billed as an "Eccentric Comedian", he sings idiotic songs made up in white face with a red nose and topped with a ginger wig in an embarrassingly bad act; a victim of paranoia, he commits suicide in J. B. Priestley's *Lost Empires.*

Alice Burrell A friend of Martha Quest and Stella Mathews; she works as Dr. Stern's nurse in Doris Lessing's *A Proper Marriage.*

Willie Burrell Alice's husband, a friend of Martha Quest's husband, Douglas Knowell, in Doris Lessing's *A Proper Marriage.*

Magda Nikolaevna Bursanov Nikolai Bursanov's wife; she is the gentle-natured mother of Sonia, Nina, and Vera Bursanov and the lover of, successively, Eisenstein and Cecedek in William Gerhardie's *Futility: A Novel on Russian Themes.*

Nikolai Vasilievich Bursanov Father to Sonia, Nina, and Vera Bursanov; he is married to Magda Bursanov but lives with his long-time mistress Fanny Ivanovna and wishes to marry his new mistress, Zina; he is handsome and somewhat honorable, yet weak and sloppy; he is not rich but owns gold mines in Siberia and another home and is the source of income for his extended family in William Gerhardie's *Futility: A Novel on Russian Themes.*

Nina Bursanov Second eldest of the three Bursanov sisters; she is irresistibly attractive and charming, yet cold, sarcastic, and often childish; she was once the fiancée of Andrei Andreiech in William Gerhardie's *Futility: A Novel on Russian Themes.*

Sonia Bursanov Eldest of the three Bursanov sisters and wife of Baron Wunderhausen; she is very attractive

and well-mannered, yet unmotivated to do anything significant with her life in William Gerhardie's *Futility: A Novel on Russian Themes.*

Vera Bursanov Youngest of the three Bursanov sisters; very attractive like her sisters, she is in other ways quite different from them; she is thought to be the natural daughter of Eisenstein, and she is apparently hated by her sisters and putative father, Nikolai Bursanov, in William Gerhardie's *Futility: A Novel on Russian Themes.*

Sister Burstead ("Sister Bastard") Wrathful, hostile, middle-aged nurse in the old women's hospital ward; her fear of her own approaching old age has made her malicious in Muriel Spark's *Memento Mori.*

Tom Burt Thieving Maidenbridge child who tries to steal from Mr. Weston's Ford and discovers a lion in T. F. Powys's *Mr. Weston's Good Wine.*

Alexander Burtenshaw Rosamund's father, a man who followed no calling in Ivy Compton-Burnett's *A House and Its Head.*

Rosamund Burtenshaw A woman retired from missionary work, active in Oscar Jekyll's church; she is closest to her cousin Beatrice Fellowes in Ivy Compton-Burnett's *A House and Its Head.*

Jack Burton Salesman for a firm selling chair covers; he is an enthusiastic theater goer and culture seeker who falls hopelessly in love with Alan Percival in Roy Fuller's *The Perfect Fool.*

Ted Burton A member of the Henderson girls' social circle who is understood to be "sweet" on Miriam Henderson in Dorothy Richardson's *Backwater.*

Caroline Bury Wealthy, generous old friend of both Philip Surrogate and the Assistant Commissioner; Surrogate persuades her to ask the Assistant Commissioner to help obtain a reprieve for Jim Drover in Graham Greene's *It's a Battlefield.*

John Thomas Buryan A farmer in Cornwall; Richard Lovat Somers helps him harvest corn and do other tasks in D. H. Lawrence's *Kangaroo.*

Bob Busby English lecturer at the University of Rummidge in David Lodge's *Changing Places: A Tale of Two Campuses.* He organizes the University Teachers of English conference at the University of Rummidge and agonizes over arrangements and entertainment in *Small World.*

Bush One of the Homo sapiens tribe given metaphoric names based on botanical resemblances by Lok and Fa as they observe their opponents from up in a tree in William Golding's *The Inheritors*.

William Bush An innately cautious lieutenant aboard the *Renown*; he is injured during a prisoner break in C. S. Forester's *Lieutenant Hornblower*. He is Horatio Hornblower's battle-ready lieutenant in *Hornblower and the Hotspur*. His capability as a seaman and his loyalty continue to be of service to his country and to Captain Hornblower in *The Happy Return* and in *Ship of the Line*. He has lost a foot during battle before they return home in *Flying Colours*. He is an aggressive, out-for-bloodshed captain under Hornblower's command in *Commodore Hornblower*, in *Lord Hornblower*, and in *Hornblower And the Crisis: An Unfinished Novel*.

Bushman Self-proclaimed son of an African chief; he illegally sells government-issued goods on the streets of London in Colin MacInnes's *City of Spades*.

Mrs. Buss The senior secretary for the Robinson, Cohen legal firm; she is completely devoted to mothering Jasper Cohen in Doris Lessing's *Martha Quest*, in *A Proper Marriage* and in *A Ripple from the Storm*. After his departure she transfers her devotion to Mr. Robinson until she and her husband leave the city in *Landlocked*.

Senor Bustamente Manager of the cinema in Malcolm Lowry's *Under the Volcano*.

Guy Butcher A businessman who is sympathetic to Frederick Tarr, listens to his sermon on English humor and its effect on reality, and advises him against marrying Bertha Lunken in Wyndham Lewis's *Tarr*.

Sir Ryland Butcher Senior Council for the defense of Giles Colmore in Roy Fuller's *The Father's Comedy*.

Samuel (Long Sam) Butcher Head night porter of giant size; he appreciates Evelyn Orcham's notice in Arnold Bennett's *Imperial Palace*.

Miss Butler The lecturer in classics with a sense of humor who teaches Dolores Hutton; she is later replaced by Dolores at the women's college in Ivy Compton-Burnett's *Dolores*.

Mrs. Butler Elizabeth's cleaning woman, whose testimony at the trial of the smugglers reveals to them Elizabeth's role in sheltering Francis Andrews in Graham Greene's *The Man Within*.

Admiral Butt Officer who accompanies Andrei Andreiech during the revolution; he is a man of sweeping movements and a war-winning air of confidence in William Gerhardie's *Futility: A Novel on Russian Themes*.

Mr. Buttall Barrister who prosecutes the case against Hubert Cherrell for extradition to Bolivia in John Galsworthy's *Maid In Waiting*.

John Butte A British Communist Party member with whom Anna Wulf has an antagonistic, if not dubious, friendship, in Doris Lessing's *The Golden Notebook*.

Butterfield Insurance corporation clerk who, fired by Robert Elderson, is employed by Michael Mont as a bookseller in John Galsworthy's *The White Monkey*. He helps Soames Forsyte in the libel case against Fleur Forsyte Mont in *The Silver Spoon*. Soames plans for Butterfield to replace old Gradman in *Swan Song*.

Buttermere Sir Godfrey Haslam's butler, who always overhears the family secrets in Ivy Compton-Burnett's *Men and Wives*.

Button Lucy's hairdresser at the country estate of Chevron in Vita Sackville-West's *The Edwardians*.

Harold Butts The Coldridges' gardener who, like his wife, Mary, helps out the family when they need to escape London for the countryside in Doris Lessing's *The Four-Gated City*.

Mary Butts Mark Coldridge's former nanny, who is often called to take care of his children when he is under stress in Doris Lessing's *The Four-Gated City*.

Mr. Buxton First mate of the hurricane-tossed ship *Archimedes*; the experience makes him understand, after twenty-five years of seagoing, that his virtue as a man and his profession are inextricable in Richard Hughes's *In Hazard*.

Marvell Buzhardt A "small owlish American, postgraduate in psychology, anthropology, and environment at Columbia University, underground journalist, film-maker, and cultural entrepreneur", who is the guest of Quentin Villiers and the dispenser of exotic drug combinations in Martin Amis's *Dead Babies*.

Bvalltu One of the Other Men; he is a philosopher who allows his mind and body to serve as a host to the disembodied narrator in Olaf Stapledon's *Star Maker*.

Stephanie ("Stiffy") Byng Madeline Bassett's forthright cousin, whose engagement to "Stinker" Pinker is opposed by Sir Watkyn Bassett in P. G. Wodehouse's *The Code of the Woosters*. She is referred to as Mrs.

Pinker in *Aunts Aren't Gentlemen*. She appears in *Stiff Upper Lip, Jeeves*.

Jessica Byrd   John Ducane's lover, who proves to be the only possible girl for Willy Kost in Iris Murdoch's *The Nice and the Good*.

Melanie Byrd   Morris Zapp's free-spirited daughter from a former marriage; she lives on the ground floor of the house in which Philip Swallow lives in Plotinus, and Philip sleeps with her once; thereafter, she moves in with Charles Boon in David Lodge's *Changing Places: A Tale of Two Campuses*.

Byring   Young, handsome, well-bred diplomat for the British government; Byring could have been ambassador if he had not fallen in love with Rose Auburn in W. Somerset Maugham's *Ashenden: or The British Agent*.

Michael Byrne   Dublin patron of the arts who invites students and budding artists to his home in Flann O'Brien's *At Swim-Two-Birds*.

C

Emma C. Object of Stephen Dedalus's unrequited love; she is admired on the tram at Harold's Cross by Stephen, who ultimately sees her as representing the conformity that he must reject in James Joyce's *A Portrait of the Artist as a Young Man*.

Count Cabinet "Fallen" minister of the Pisuergan Court who lives in exile with his servant Peter Passer on the secluded island of St. Helena; he is visited by the pious Countess Yvorra with religious tracts during his stay at the nearby Summer-Palace in Ronald Firbank's *The Flower Beneath the Foot*.

Mr. Caddles Albert Edward's bumpkin father, the perennial butt of Lady Wondershot's snobbish contempt; she considers him the archetypal selfish, indolent serf in H. G. Wells's *The Food of the Gods, and How It Came to Earth*.

Albert Edward Caddles Boomfood baby from the village of Cheasing Eyebright who lives in ignorance of the other Giants, grows dissatisfied with his serfdom, and travels to London; there he becomes the first giant to be killed by the fearful Little People in H. G. Wells's *The Food of the Gods, and How It Came to Earth*.

Cadman Lucia Lucas's chauffeur, who marries Georgie Pillson's housemaid, Foljambe, in E. F. Benson's *Mapp and Lucia*. He appears in *The Worshipful Lucia*.

Mr. Cadman Minor partner and manager of the publishing house Tremlett & Grove's; though he has no literary training, Cadman knows what sells books and is a good judge of character in Frank Swinnerton's *The Happy Family*.

Cissy Caffrey Companion of Gerty MacDowell observed by Leopold Bloom on the beach in James Joyce's *Ulysses*.

Mr. Cage Intelligent, humorous teacher and friend; he is Ann Veronica Stanley's lover, and he makes a life for Ann and himself in H. G. Wells's *Ann Veronica: A Modern Love Story*.

Percy Cahill Dolly Wilcox's uncle, who marries Evie Wilcox in E. M. Forster's *Howards End*.

Colonel Jean-Baptiste Caillard Proud, cruel aide-de-camp to Napoleon who is ordered to escort Horatio Hornblower, William Bush, and Brown to Paris; they escape, leaving him bound and gagged in C. S. Forester's *Flying Colours*.

Ephraim Caird ("Chasehope") Influential elder of the Kirk in the parish of Woodilee, but also the high priest of the coven in depraved Satanic revels in the Black Wood in John Buchan's *Witch Wood*.

Cairn American writer of short stories; he is an ugly drinking companion to Marya Zelli and an honest appraiser of the Heidlers in Jean Rhys's *Postures*.

Mr. Calamy Rich, handsome amorist, who is a houseguest at Lillian Aldwinkle's Italian villa; after a passionate affair with Mary Thriplow, he retires to a cottage in the mountains to contemplate life in Aldous Huxley's *Those Barren Leaves*.

Calary Aoz Roon's human slave, who is made a ceremonial sacrifice in Brian W. Aldiss's *Helliconia Spring*.

Caldecott Previous captain of the *Atropos* who stripped the captain's quarters bare in C. S. Forester's *Hornblower and the Atropos*.

Calder A mining leader who wants very much to overthrow the tyrannous Volyen Empire but is extremely distrustful of Klorathy's advice; he does heed his suggestion to grow a food source that ultimately gives the planet the power to overthrow both Volyen and Sirius in Doris Lessing's *Documents Relating to the Sentimental Agents in the Volyen Empire*.

Jessica Calderone Terence's mother, who loves him best; she is a deeply meditative, ethical woman, who kills herself when her niece Anna Donne tells her that she is blighting her family's life in Ivy Compton-Burnett's *Elders and Betters*.

Julius Calderone Thomas and Jessica's eleven-year-old son, who is closest to his sister Dora; he gives his father conventional answers when Thomas wants conventional children in Ivy Compton-Burnett's *Elders and Betters*.

Terence Calderone The elder son of Jessica and Thomas; he tutors his cousin Reuben Donne and proposes to his cousin Anna Donne; he is not willing to make his own living in Ivy Compton-Burnett's *Elders and Betters*.

Theodora (Dora) Calderone Thomas and Jessica's ten-year-old daughter who, with her brother Julius, has her own religion, praying to the Great God Chung in Ivy Compton-Burnett's *Elders and Betters*.

Thomas Calderone A journalist and critic, married

to Jessica; after Jessica's death he proposes to Florence Lacey, but he loves his daughter Tullia best in Ivy Compton-Burnett's *Elders and Betters*.

Tullia Calderone   The elder daughter of Jessica and Thomas; she is closest to her father and jealous of his proposed marriage to Florence Lacey in Ivy Compton-Burnett's *Elders and Betters*.

Dora Caldicote   School friend of Mildred Lathbury, with whom she has shared a flat; now a resident schoolteacher, she visits to comment on Mildred's life in Barbara Pym's *Excellent Women*.

William Caldicote   Fussy, epicene civil servant, brother to Dora; his purported passion for Mildred Lathbury has become almost a joke in Barbara Pym's *Excellent Women*. He makes an appearance in *Jane and Prudence*.

Caldwell   Midshipman aboard the *Goliath* in C. S. Forester's *Mr. Midshipman Hornblower*.

Sally Cale   Aging homosexual Hong Kong antiques dealer who introduces Lizzie Worthington to Drake Ko in John le Carré's *The Honourable Schoolboy*.

Calendar   Captain of the fleet who puts on military airs despite his lower-class origin in C. S. Forester's *Flying Colours*.

Caligula   Grandnephew and successor of Tiberius, whose murder he oversees; he eventually goes mad and is assassinated by conspirators in Robert Graves's *I, Claudius*.

Chief Constable Calkin   Detective-Sergeant Mather's weak, place-hunting, bullying superior in Graham Greene's *A Gun for Sale*.

Agatha Calkin   A sixty-year-old widow, who tries to be a mother to Gregory Haslam; she takes over Harriet Haslam's place in the charity sewing circle in Ivy Compton-Burnett's *Men and Wives*.

Christine Callaghan   An intelligent, sensitive woman who leaves Bertrand Welch and becomes romantically involved with Jim Dixon in Kingsley Amis's *Lucky Jim*.

Jack Callcott   A former soldier and now a workman; he tries to lure Richard Lovat Somers into the secret, fascistic "Diggers Clubs" that plan a revolution and a seizing of power in Australia; Callcott shows his pathological mentality when he kills three Socialists during a political rally in D. H. Lawrence's *Kangaroo*.

Victoria Callcott   The bright, attractive wife of Jack Callcott; she seems willing to become Richard Lovat Somers's lover, but Somers typically holds back and does not commit himself in D. H. Lawrence's *Kangaroo*.

Major Callendar   British officer stationed in Chandrapore, India, in E. M. Forster's *A Passage to India*.

Miss Callendar   A recently hired faculty member of the English Department at Howard Kirk's university; she finds herself added to the list of his sexual conquests in Malcolm Bradbury's *The History Man*.

Mark Callendar   Troubled son of Ronald Callendar; he takes a job as a gardener and is murdered in P. D. James's *An Unsuitable Job for a Woman*.

Ronald Callendar   Prominent, cold-hearted scientist; he hires Cordelia Gray to investigate the death of his son, Mark, in P. D. James's *An Unsuitable Job for a Woman*.

Max Callis   Seedy middle-aged Bohemian who is found shot with Harry Sinton's revolver in Roy Fuller's *Fantasy and Fugue*.

Call-me-Cobber   Vain television personality constantly looking for new faces for his television show, *Junction!*; he films the racial riots in Napoli in Colin MacInnes's *Absolute Beginners*.

Calloway   Manservant to Sir Ronald, minister at the British legation in Stockholm; Minty tries to get information on Krogh from him in Graham Greene's *England Made Me*.

Colonel Calloway   British officer, formerly of Scotland Yard, who for a time erroneously believes Harry Lime to be dead; in charge of the investigation into Lime's racketeering, he is the wary narrator of Graham Greene's *The Third Man and the Fallen Idol*.

Count Caloveglia   Polite but poor Italian who forges the *Locri Faun* sculpture to provide a dowry for his daughter in Norman Douglas's *South Wind*.

Calpurnia   A benevolent Roman widow who becomes a close friend of Helena in Evelyn Waugh's *Helena*.

Calvert   Newspaper owner who is the father of Roy; he drops his financial support of Jack Cotery to learn printing when he learns that Roy has a romantic attachment to Jack in C. P. Snow's *Strangers and Brothers*.

Miss Calvert   Jake Richardson's student whom he holds in contempt for her lack of intellectual ability and interest in seeking knowledge in Kingsley Amis's *Jake's Thing*.

Herbert Calvert   Commission agent; his pressure for rent on Ruth Earp involves Denry Machin in saving her from the runaway pantechnicon (furniture van) in which she tries to slip out of town at night in Arnold Bennett's *The Card: A Story of Adventure in the Five Towns*.

Lieutenant Joe Calvert   Pilot of the *Endeavor* and member of the Rama expeditionary group; he first discovers the nature of Rama's propulsion system in Arthur C. Clarke's *Rendezvous with Rama*.

Muriel Calvert   Daughter of Roy and Rosalind (Wykes) Calvert; she is pregnant and engaged to marry Pat Eliot in C. P. Snow's *The Sleep of Reason*. She divorces him after the birth of their daughter; she lives with Charles Eliot as his mistress in *Last Things*. She is a spectator of the court challenge by Jenny Rastall of her father's will and is a guest at Jenny's wedding in *In Their Wisdom*.

Olive Calvert   Roy's cousin, who breaks her relationship with Arthur Morcom, is seduced by Jack Cotery, and is one of the three tried and acquitted for fraud in C. P. Snow's *Strangers and Brothers*. Divorced from Jack Cotery, she is remarried; she hates Lewis Eliot for his political past in *The Sleep of Reason*.

Roy Calvert   Son of a newspaper owner; his romantic attachment to Jack Cotery causes the elder Calvert to drop his financial support for Jack's schooling in C. P. Snow's *Strangers and Brothers*. A scholar learned in ancient Asian languages, he is elected to a fellowship in a Cambridge college, suffers from mania and depression, and demonstrates some enthusiasm for the Nazis in Germany; he marries Rosalind Wykes in order to have a child and dies during a bombing mission during World War II in *The Light and the Dark*. He is active in support of Paul Jago for election as new college Master in *The Masters*.

Robert Calwell   Author and homosexual neighbor of Daniel House; he fought in the Spanish civil war and, with a number of others, is a guest at House's island retreat soon after the arrival there of James Ross in Roy Fuller's *The Carnal Island*.

Camel   A sardonic perpetual graduate student in English, who has been working on his doctoral thesis at the British Museum for years; he amuses Adam Appleby with a game called "When We are in Power," and is the intended recipient of a job in the English department mistakenly offered to Adam in David Lodge's *The British Museum Is Falling Down*.

Cameron   Principal of the school where George Passant teaches nights; he presides at the board meeting at which Calvert drops his subsidy for Jack Cotery; he dismisses Passant from the faculty during the trial in C. P. Snow's *Strangers and Brothers*.

Alec Cameron   Letty Green's brother, down from Oxford; he is a veteran who needs violence, a militant of the Society of Ancient Britain who believes the only way to waken democrats is to kill them in C. Day Lewis's *Child of Misfortune*.

Mrs. Camish   Simon's intelligent, grindingly self-driven mother; the wife of an invalid, she became a radio-script writer to enable her son to escape the poverty of his background in Margaret Drabble's *The Needle's Eye*.

Julie Camish   Simon's socialite wife, whose unhappiness finds expression in scathing criticism of her husband; she improves in cheerfulness and goodwill after she and Rose Vassiliou become friends in Margaret Drabble's *The Needle's Eye*.

Simon Camish   A constrained, self-effacing, embittered barrister; he feels dead inside until he meets Rose Vassiliou; her plight and character rouse his respectful, unconsummated love in Margaret Drabble's *The Needle's Eye*.

Domenico Campanati   Self-indulgent younger brother of Don Carlo Campanati, brother-in-law of Kenneth Toomey, and husband of Hortense Toomey Campanati; he is a successful composer of Hollywood film scores, as well as a successful womanizer in Anthony Burgess's *Earthly Powers*.

Don Carlo Campanati (Pope Gregory XVII)   Aggressive, worldly Catholic priest with a large appetite for food and drink; he befriends Kenneth Toomey when both are in their thirties; Don Carlo ascends to the top of the Church hierarchy by shrewd and subtle machinations and a stroke of luck in Anthony Burgess's *Earthly Powers*.

Hortense Toomey Campanati   Beautiful, willful younger sister of Kenneth Toomey and later wife of Domenico Campanati; she bears twins adulterously; after her divorce from Domenico, she forms a long-standing Lesbian alliance in Anthony Burgess's *Earthly Powers*.

Campbell   An awe-struck crofter who discovers Pincher Martin's body on the Hebrides beach in William Golding's *Pincher Martin*.

Mr. Camperdine   The young squire who Beguildy

hopes will fall in love with his daughter, Jancis, in Mary Webb's *Precious Bane*.

Dorabella Camperdine Young woman of propertied family who is insolently attracted to the handsome Gideon Sarn; his dreams of vengeance fuel his lust for wealth in Mary Webb's *Precious Bane*.

Campion Efrafan rabbit, captain of Woundwort's Owsla (rabbit-warren militia) who succeeds Woundwort as Chief Rabbit of Efrafa in Richard Adams's *Watership Down*.

General Edward, Lord Campion A white-haired, red-cheeked, lame friend of Christopher Tietjens and an admirer of Christopher's wife, Sylvia, in Ford Madox Ford's *Some Do Not.* . . . He believes Sylvia's slander about Christopher until his interrogation of Christopher in *No More Parades*. He distinguishes himself during World War I, and lives at Groby with Sylvia after the war in *A Man Could Stand Up —* and in *The Last Post*.

Lucy Cane Child who rescues Hazel from the cat during his last expedition to Nuthanger farm; driven in Dr. Adams's car, she brings Hazel back to the down in Richard Adams's *Watership Down*.

Peggy Canford Older and less attractive of two concert-party girls performing in Blackpool; intelligent but cynical, she has a brief relationship with the younger Dick Herncastle in J. B. Priestley's *Lost Empires*.

Jimmy Cannibal Former champion boxer who is beaten by Billy Whispers and knifed by Ronson Lighter because they suspect he is a police informant in Colin MacInnes's *City of Spades*.

Cannibal King The alcoholic drifter whose seedy and enigmatic presence inspires Joe to include his adversarial persona in the fantasy game "Africa" in Wolf Mankowitz's *A Kid for Two Farthings*.

George Cannon Thirty-six-year-old hopeful hotel entrepreneur; he loves Hilda Lessways and draws her into his Bursley newspaper project, which fails, then into his Brighton boarding-house venture, and then into a marriage, the bigamous nature of which a servant reveals to her in Arnold Bennett's *Hilda Lessways*. He is an innocent prisoner for theft in Dartmoor; he is discovered there by Hilda and Edwin Clayhanger, and Edwin helps him to a new life in America in *These Twain*.

George Edwin Cannon Illegitimate young son of Hilda Lessways; he charms Edwin Clayhanger before Edwin becomes his stepfather in Arnold Bennett's *Clayhanger*. He adores his stepfather and hopes to become the architect Edwin always wanted to be in *These Twain*.

Hughie Cantrip Manipulative young artist who plans to marry Lady Franklin without giving up his mistress, Constance Copthorne, until his plan is foiled through an anonymous note sent to Lady Franklin by her car-hire driver, Steven Leadbitter; during a chauffeured drive after this note has been received, Leadbitter crashes his for-hire car, killing both himself and Hughie with Constance alone surviving in L. P. Hartley's *The Hireling*.

Johnny Capetenakis An aging Greek who owns a restaurant where Martha Quest and her colleagues often eat and discuss politics in Doris Lessing's *Landlocked*.

Paul Capodistria ("Da Capo") A rich lecher whose rape of Justine Hosnani when she was a girl has resulted in her troubled promiscuity; his apparently accidental death during a shooting party frees her to leave husband and lover in Lawrence Durrell's *Justine*. Evidence that his death was faked is supplied in *Balthazar*. He is proved to be a co-conspirator with Justine and Nessim Hosnani in gunrunning in *Mountolive*. He writes to Balthazar from his hideout in *Clea*.

Cappone Tall, graceful, melancholic manager of the hotel restaurant; he delights in creating unique menus for wealthy patrons and brings an orchid to Gracie Savotte when she first dines in the restaurant in Arnold Bennett's *Imperial Palace*.

Captain/Priest Middle-aged, non-English-speaking priest appointed by the Order to supervise the ship's crew, cargo, and infrequent passengers to and from the leproserie in Graham Greene's *A Burnt-Out Case*.

Cara Lord Marchmain's likeable middle-aged mistress in Evelyn Waugh's *Brideshead Revisited*.

Bardol CaraBansity A dealer in bodies and anatomical specimens; he gives JandolAngand the alien watch and becomes for a short time the king's chancellor in Brian W. Aldiss's *Helliconia Summer*.

Caractacas Noble British king defeated by Claudius's invading army; he is allowed to live freely in Rome as the city's guest in Robert Graves's *Claudius, the God and His Wife Messalina*.

Caradoc A famous architect who designs projects for the Firm; he gives a mighty, drunken lecture on proportion in front of the Parthenon, and escapes to the Cook Islands but is recaptured by the Firm in Lawrence Durrell's *Tunc*.

Lady Barbara (Babs) Carádoc Daughter of Lord and Lady Valleys; she is torn between her love for Charles Courtier and her love for Lord Harbinger; when Courtier leaves England, she marries Harbinger in John Galsworthy's *The Patrician*.

Hubert (Bertie) Carádoc Younger son of the Earl of Valleys; he follows adventure around the world in John Galsworthy's *The Patrician*.

Carberry Insensitive master aboard the *Renown*; he is wounded in C. S. Forester's *Lieutenant Hornblower*.

Mr. Cardan Elderly guest and one-time lover of Lillian Aldwinkle; a social parasite, he proposes marriage to the dull-witted Grace Elver, but her death thwarts his designs in Aldous Huxley's *Those Barren Leaves*.

Jimmy Carde The intelligent, supercilious St. Bride's classmate and closest friend of Donald Mor; when the two boys attempt a forbidden climb of the school tower, Carde is seriously injured in a fall in Iris Murdoch's *The Sandcastle*.

Ada Cardew Cornelius Cardew's wife, who divorces him in Isabel Colegate's *The Shooting Party*.

Cornelius Cardew Radical activist attempting to win Sir Randolph Nettleby's support in his goals of obtaining animals' rights and "free landowning" in Isabel Colegate's *The Shooting Party*.

Mabel Cardew Mrs. Crankshaw's niece, to whom Eustace Cherrington is introduced at the wedding of his sister Barbara to Jimmy Crankshaw; Eustace finds her too inclined to wince and wiggle during their exchange of "almost passionate civilities" in L. P. Hartley's *The Sixth Heaven*.

Imogen Dartie Cardigan Daughter of Montague and Winifred Dartie; she comes out into society in John Galsworthy's *In Chancery*. Fleur Forsyte visits Imogen before meeting her father at the gallery in *To Let*. Imogen goes to the race track to watch Val Dartie's horse in *Swan Song*.

Jack Cardigan Husband of Imogen Dartie; he is devoted to health and physical fitness in John Galsworthy's *To Let*. He introduces Soames Forsyte to golf in *The Silver Spoon*. He tries to interest Soames in betting on horses in *Swan Song*.

Gino Carella Impulsive, good-looking, sexually compelling, jovial young Italian of no background or education; he marries the visiting English widow Lilia Herriton in E. M. Forster's *Where Angels Fear to Tread*.

Mr. Carew Latin teacher and rugby coach who, although married, becomes the lover of Miss Manning in William Golding's *Free Fall*.

Mr. Carey Head of the English and Drama department at a new school at Camden; he is husband to Fiona Macfarlane Carey, long-time teacher at the school that had been attended by Kate Fletcher (Armstrong) in Margaret Drabble's *The Middle Ground*.

Fiona Macfarlane Carey Former teacher of Kate Fletcher Armstrong; years afterward Kate interviews her in Margaret Drabble's *The Middle Ground*.

Louisa Carey Philip Carey's shy, gentle aunt, who is the only person who genuinely loves the lonely boy during his isolated childhood in W. Somerset Maugham's *Of Human Bondage*.

Philip Carey An intelligent, shy boy who is dreadfully sensitive about his club foot; he seeks self-knowledge and worldly experience by attempting to study art in Paris; realizing his own mediocrity, he turns to medicine in London, simultaneously becoming disastrously involved with the deceitful Mildred Rogers; finally, after dire poverty, he finds a gentle peace with Sally Athelney in W. Somerset Maugham's *Of Human Bondage*.

William Carey A weakly hypocritical and mediocre clergyman; convention expects him to bring up his dead sister-in-law's child, Philip Carey, to whom he is neither kind nor cruel but indifferent in W. Somerset Maugham's *Of Human Bondage*.

Cargill A novice who assists in ship operation; later, promoted to officer of the watch, he proves his worth to his commander as he navigates the ship in rough weather in C. S. Forester's *Hornblower and the Hotspur*.

Basil Carlin A married tenant in Milly Sanders's house in Muriel Spark's *A Far Cry from Kensington*.

Eva Carlin Basil's wife; they are childless and secretive tenants in Milly Sanders's house in Muriel Spark's *A Far Cry from Kensington*.

Jemmy Carlin Unsuccessful farmer whose land is supposedly purchased by Mrs. Flynn; he later tells Tarry Flynn that his good fields were not part of the sale, and as a result the Flynns lose money and prestige in Patrick Kavanagh's *Tarry Flynn*.

Tom Carlin Unsuccessful farmer who loses his land, which turns out to be very poor land, to Mrs. Flynn in Patrick Kavanagh's *Tarry Flynn*.

Marjorie Carling   Clinging mistress of Walter Bidlake, by whom she is impregnanted after abandoning her husband; insecure in her relationship, she eventually finds some solace in acquaintance with Rachel Quarles in Aldous Huxley's *Point Count Point*.

Carlo   Left-wing terrorist kidnapper of Morris Zapp; he negotiates with Desiree Zapp for Morris's release in David Lodge's *Small World*.

Carlo   Garage owner and pursuer of Lise in Muriel Spark's *The Driver's Seat*.

Carlyon   Intelligent, charismatic successor to Francis Andrews's father as leader of a smuggling gang; he is protective and compassionate towards Andrews until Andrews informs on and testifies against the gang, whereupon Carlyon seeks revenge against him; he attempts to save Elizabeth from other members of the gang and is himself saved from arrest by Andrews in Graham Greene's *The Man Within*.

Augustus Carmichael   A poet guest stoned on opium and liquor at the Ramsays' summer house in the Hebrides; eventually, during World War I and after Mrs. Ramsay's death, he publishes an acclaimed volume of poetry, much to Mr. Ramsay's chagrin in Virginia Woolf's *To the Lighthouse*.

Cicely Carmichael   Friend of the Westons and of Ida; she hopes to attract Edmund Weston in Isabel Colegate's *Statues in a Garden*.

Captain Lawrence Carmine   Authority on Indian and oriental studies and frequentor of Dower House; he is emotionally scarred by the war in H. G. Wells's *Mr. Britling Sees It Through*.

George Carmody   A student who stands up to Howard Kirk and is forced out of the university by Howard in Malcolm Bradbury's *The History Man*.

Hugo Carmody   Nephew of Lester Carmody, upon whose parsimonious trusteeship he depends; he wants to invest in a nightclub with Ronnie Fish in P. G. Wodehouse's *Money for Nothing*. He is Lord Emsworth's secretary and is in love with Millicent Threepwood in *Fish Preferred*. He appears in *Heavy Weather*.

Lester Carmody   Uncle of both John Carroll and Hugo Carmody; he is the parsimonious trustee of Hugo's estate; he hopes to raise money from inalienable family heirlooms by arranging their theft in conspiracy with "Soapy" Molloy in P. G. Wodehouse's *Money for Nothing*.

Manuel Carmona   Romantic, mystical, vain, self-reli-ant spy, who fascinates Ashenden with his brutal and exotic stories; Ashenden does not trust Carmona but respects his survival instincts in W. Somerset Maugham's *Ashenden: or The British Agent*.

Earl of Carnaby   Wealthy, elderly aristocrat who is Beatrice Normandy's rich lover, much to George Ponderevo's disgust in H. G. Wells's *Tono-Bungay*.

Carol   Student roommate of Melanie Byrd in David Lodge's *Changing Places: A Tale of Two Campuses*.

Carol   Rational secretary for Leclerc's incompetent Department; though ignored by her condescending employers, she accurately diagnoses Leclerc's intelligence operations as chauvinistic fantasies in John le Carré's *The Looking-Glass War*.

Caroline   A plump young student with whom Robin Meadowes is having an affair in David Lodge's *How Far Can You Go?*.

Caroline   Alice Mellings's close friend who later comes to despise the rest of the house members when she is told about their plans to leave a time bomb in a car parked near a busy pavement in Doris Lessing's *The Good Terrorist*.

Caroline   Friend of Agatha King and Imogene King; she is a model who has an affair with Orlando King in Isabel Colegate's *Orlando at the Brazen Threshold*.

Carolo   Violinist and former child prodigy once married to Matilda Wilson; he boards with the Maclinticks and runs away with Audrey Maclintick in Anthony Powell's *Casanova's Chinese Restaurant*. Long parted from Audrey, he appears as a white-haired stand-in violinist at a party in *Temporary Kings*.

Mrs. Carpenter   Secretary to Dr. Bellows at the Entrenationo Language Centre in Graham Greene's *The Confidential Agent*.

Edmund Carpenter   A playwright and friend of Wyndham Farrar in Margaret Drabble's *The Garrick Year*.

Jack Carpenter   Detective-constable who annoys Billy Fisher and ends up in bed with Helen Lightfoot in Keith Waterhouse's *Billy Liar on the Moon*.

Private Carr   Pugnacious cockney soldier who strikes Stephen Dedalus in the brothel district in James Joyce's *Ulysses*.

Dr. Edward Carr   Physician whose reiterated puzzlement over Agatha Dawson's premature death costs him the loss of his practice; his story initiates Lord Peter Wimsey's investigation, which motivates two additional murders and several attempted murders in Dorothy L. Sayers's *Unnatural Death*.

Brent Carradine   Young American scholar who helps Detective Inspector Alan Grant, bedridden with a broken leg, resurrect the reputation of King Richard III by doing the research to prove that Henry Tudor (later King Henry VII) had more to gain by the death of the two Princes in the Tower than did Richard in Josephine Tey's *The Daughter of Time*.

Dona Carlota Carrasco   Don Ramon's Catholic first wife, who dies of fever and shock in D. H. Lawrence's *The Plumed Serpent (Quetzalcoatl)*.

Don Ramon Carrasco   The leader of a religious and political revolution in Mexico resurrecting the old Aztec gods; he assumes the persona of Quetzalcoatl (the "plumed serpent") in D. H. Lawrence's *The Plumed Serpent (Quetzalcoatl)*.

Senor Carreras   Former member of Mr. Castor's Bodyguard in Olifa, now in league with the evil Jacques D'Ingraville and the plot against Valdemar Haraldsen in John Buchan's *The Island of Sheep*.

Henry Carrington, M.A.   The new Vicar of Cleeve, a widower with a private income; he disappoints as a possible husband for Georgie Smithers in Richard Aldington's *The Colonel's Daughter*.

Lukey Carrington   London science teacher and algae specialist who barely survives an attack by giant water-beetle larvae in H. G. Wells's *The Food of the Gods, and How It Came to Earth*.

Rico Carrington   A sophisticated but effeminate would-be artist, the husband of Rachel Witt; he is injured by the great stallion St. Mawr in D. H. Lawrence's *St. Mawr*.

Sir William Boyd Carrington   Recent possessor of a large inherited estate; Hercule Poirot finds him a stupid bore in Agatha Christie's *Curtain: Hercule Poirot's Last Case*.

Iulo Carrino   Fiercely loyal young Gentleman in the Apostolic Chamber whose desire to kill the blackmailers Hadrian VII quells in Frederick William Rolfe's *Hadrian the Seventh*.

John Carroll   Cousin of Hugo Carmody and nephew of Lester Carmody, whose estrangement from his old friend Colonel Wyvern complicates John's romantic attachment to Patricia Wyvern; John wins Patricia by

proving himself intrepid and resourceful when necessary in P. G. Wodehouse's *Money for Nothing*.

Crosbie Carruthers   Impatient fiancé of Barbara Blenkinsop; he spends much of his time reading *The Times of India*; he finally asserts himself, proposing at the zoo, and Barbara chooses to follow him rather than her mother in the struggle for power that has supplied village gossip for months in E. M. Delafield's *The Diary of a Provincial Lady*.

Mr. Carshot   Fat, nagging window dresser who supervises Art Kipps at the Folkestone Drapery Bazaar in H. G. Wells's *Kipps: The Story of a Simple Soul*.

Carslake   The young inexperienced purser of the *Atropos* who finally proves himself capable of his duties in C. S. Forester's *Hornblower and the Atropos*.

Carson   Sympathetic Communist agent who helps Sarah Castle escape South Africa and whose death, allegedly from pneumonia, in a British-South African prison provokes Maurice Castle into betraying Operation Uncle Remus and himself in Graham Greene's *The Human Factor*.

Carson   Crewman aboard the *Indefatigable* and the *Marie Galante* in C. S. Forester's *Mr. Midshipman Hornblower*.

Widow Carson   Martha Quest's landlady, who is petrified of the Africans' breaking into her house and stealing from her in Doris Lessing's *A Ripple from the Storm*.

Alice (Ally) Cartaret   Youngest sister who, pregnant, marries a local farmer, James Greatorex; her confrontation with her sister Mary and her father results in her father's severe stroke and Mary's refusal to associate with her in May Sinclair's *The Three Sisters*.

Gwendolen (Gwenda) Cartaret   Middle sister, who leaves Garth in the hope that her lover, Steven Rowcliffe, will marry her younger sister Alice and thereby cure Alice's hysteria; her sacrifice backfires and she remains unmarried and the caretaker of her father in May Sinclair's *The Three Sisters*.

James Cartaret   Twice-widowed vicar of Garth, abandoned by his third wife; the tyrannical father of Mary, Gwendolen, and Alice, he mellows when a stroke destroys his memory in May Sinclair's *The Three Sisters*.

Mary Cartaret   Eldest sister, who manipulates Steven Rowcliffe into marriage although he loves her sister Gwendolen; she secures her marriage by becoming the perfect Victorian wife and mother in May Sinclair's *The Three Sisters.*

Robina Cartaret James Cartaret's third wife, who leaves him; she later uses her influence to obtain a position for Gwendolen Cartaret when she leaves Garth in May Sinclair's *The Three Sisters.*

Carter Colonel Calloway's young assistant who first suggests that Harry Lime's body be exhumed in Graham Greene's *The Third Man and the Fallen Idol.*

Carter Second officer of the *Hermit,* the stranded schooner that interferes with Lingard's plans to reestablish native succession in Wajo; he attempts to remain dutiful to Mr. and Mrs. Travers but proves to have greater allegiance to Lingard in Joseph Conrad's *The Rescue: A Romance of the Shallows.*

A. Carter Chief of British Intelligence; he commissions Tommy and Tuppence Beresford to find Jane Finn in Agatha Christie's *The Secret Adversary.* Tommy discovers that he is Lord Easterfield in *N or M?.*

Martha Carter Wife of Simon; a wealthy half American, she takes their children to California to be safe during the war; she tries to leave Simon when she learns how the zoo animals are tortured under the administration of Emile Englander in Angus Wilson's *The Old Men at the Zoo.*

Rain Carter A young painter, commissioned to paint Demoyte's portrait, who falls in love with William Mor but refuses to break up his marriage and run away with him, so saving the quality of her art in Iris Murdoch's *The Sandcastle.*

Simon Carter Secretary of the zoological gardens; a young administrator, he helps implement the plan of the removal of animals to the Welsh reserve, takes practical charge of the London zoo during the war, is imprisoned by the conquering Uni-Europeans, and survives to compete for the directorship of the zoo after the fall of the conquerors in Angus Wilson's *The Old Men at the Zoo.*

William Carter Communist agent posing as a slick British representative of Nucleaners Ltd.; he gives James Wormold poisoned whiskey at a vacuum-cleaner convention in Graham Greene's *Our Man in Havana.*

cartero Unnamed postman with a goatee beard who delivers to Geoffrey Firmin a postcard that Yvonne Firmin had mailed to him nearly a year earlier in Malcolm Lowry's *Under the Volcano.*

The Cartographer A cowardly war-time mapmaker

left behind when his colleagues were captured by the enemy; he takes shelter for several months in a greenhouse where he tends to the plants obsessively; he becomes embroiled in the petty rivalries of his enemies and, becoming an embarrassment to them, is eventually reunited with his countrymen, who regard him as a hero in Nigel Dennis's *A House in Order.*

Emily Cartright A child most likely severely neglected as a baby; she is left to go through puberty while living with the narrator in Doris Lessing's *Memoirs of a Survivor.*

Cartwright An artist who explains, at the dinner table, the mystery of the ancient god Pan in D. H. Lawrence's *St. Mawr.*

Joanna Cartwright Freddy Hamilton's friend and frequent hostess in Jordan in Muriel Spark's *The Mandlebaum Gate.*

Matt Cartwright Joanna's husband and Freddy Hamilton's frequent host in Jordan in Muriel Spark's *The Mandlebaum Gate.*

Casabianca Competent, likable, ingenious holiday tutor who accompanies the Provincial Lady's family on a Brittany tour in E. M. Delafield's *The Provincial Lady Goes Further.*

Tiffany Case James Bond's neurotic American ally and eventual lover in Ian Fleming's *Diamonds Are Forever.* She lives with Bond in his London flat but leaves to marry an American serviceman in *From Russia, With Love.*

Catherine Casement Thirty-two-year-old beauty with fair skin, hazel eyes, and dark blond hair who falls in love with Captain James Churchill; she recovers from a cancer operation; she is divorced from her first husband and separated from her second and is a patient of Dr. Best in Kingsley Amis's *The Anti-Death League.*

Dolly Casement Lesbian guest at Margy Stuart's weekend party who embarrasses Georgie Smithers by her attentions in Richard Aldington's *The Colonel's Daughter.*

Jem Casey Poet of the Pick and Bard of Booterstown who writes "A Pint of Plain is Your Only Man" and "The Gift of God is a Working Man" in Flann O'Brien's *At Swim-Two-Birds.*

John Casey An old Fenian who bitterly argues politics with Stephen Dedalus's Aunt Dante Riordan in James Joyce's *A Portrait of the Artist as a Young Man.*

Violet Casey   A shrinking, melancholy, penitential Irish Catholic, prone to nervous breakdowns; she is seduced by her college tutor, Robin Meadowes, and marries him; she is continually troubled by religious doubt and marital difficulties; she becomes first a Jehovah's Witness and then a Sufist in David Lodge's *How Far Can You Go?*.

Dr. Cashmore   Overworked physician; his initial mistake in identifying the master as the valet allows the famous artist Priam Farll to pose as Henry Leek after Leek's death in Arnold Bennett's *Buried Alive: A Tale of These Days*.

Caspar   Bastard mulatto child of Sophia Willoughby's uncle; he is sent to England to become Sophia's ward, follows Sophia to Paris where he becomes a member of the Gardes Mobiles, and is slain by Sophia after he bayonets Minna Lemuel in Sylvia Townsend Warner's *Summer Will Show*.

Miss Cass   Evelyn Orcham's trusted, authoritative, efficient, well-dressed personal secretary; she believes that men lack a sense of actuality; she is considered sufficiently eminent to be invited to the celebratory dinner of the male officials who created the merger of eight luxury hotels in Arnold Bennett's *Imperial Palace*.

Dr. Cassell   The physician of the village, who preaches on religious subjects in the building in the field; he regales people with anecdotes he has read in Ivy Compton-Burnett's *Dolores*.

Mrs. Cassell   The slender, comely, affectionate wife of Dr. Cassell; she knows little about housekeeping in Ivy Compton-Burnett's *Dolores*.

Margarita Cassell   A beautiful, well-dressed performer at the poetry reading that introduces Clara Maugham to Clelia Denham in Margaret Drabble's *Jerusalem the Golden*.

Aldo Cassidy   Successful and overgenerous pram manufacturer and emotionally repressed, naïve lover; he seeks love and escape from his safe, middle-class world through a doubtful affair with a charismatic, failed novelist, Shamus, and Shamus's abused, sexually provocative wife, Helen, but destroys all his loving relationships through inertia and betrayal in John le Carré's *The Naive and Sentimental Lover*.

Eusebius Cassidy   Sentimental poet, farmer, and horse-breeder; Tarry Flynn's best friend, he loves to spread gossip no matter who gets into trouble, including Tarry, in Patrick Kavanagh's *Tarry Flynn*.

Hugo Cassidy   Aldo Cassidy's seven-year-old son; he manipulates his father as obviously and successfully as does the grandfather for whom he is named in John le Carré's *The Naive and Sentimental Lover*.

Hugo ("Old Hugo") Cassidy   Aldo Cassidy's manipulative father; he lives off his son's largesse while draining away Aldo's emotional reserves in John le Carré's *The Naive and Sentimental Lover*.

Juliet Cassidy   A sister of Lesbia Firebrace and of the late Mary Shelley; she is married to Lucius Cassidy; she kindly conceals Maria Shelley's theft of an earring belonging to her father, Oliver Firebrace, and replaces it in Ivy Compton-Burnett's *Two Worlds and Their Ways*.

Lucius Cassidy   Juliet's husband, who runs a school for boys; he reproves Oliver Shelley and Oliver Spode for their conspicuous friendship in Ivy Compton-Burnett's *Two Worlds and Their Ways*.

Mark Cassidy   Aldo Cassidy's eleven-year-old son; he is isolated at Sherborne School because he never receives his father's secret confessional letters in John le Carré's *The Naive and Sentimental Lover*.

Sandra Cassidy   Aldo Cassidy's uncommunicative wife; she refuses to comfort Aldo but overlooks his affairs with Shamus and Helen and accepts him back after his psychic breakdown for the sake of her children in John le Carré's *The Naive and Sentimental Lover*.

Jacqueline Castagnet   French prostitute who is one-hundred-sixty-five years old but appears under thirty; she is a supernormal being discovered telepathically by John Wainwright in Olaf Stapledon's *Odd John: A Story Between Jest and Earnest*.

Lady Casterley   Elderly mother of Lady Valleys; she prevents her grandson, Lord Miltoun, from ruining his political future by persuading Audrey Noel to leave England in John Galsworthy's *The Patrician*.

Mrs. Castle   Maurice Castle's prejudiced mother; she chides Maurice for forgetting his deceased wife and belittles his African family but takes them into her home after Maurice defects in Graham Greene's *The Human Factor*.

Maurice Castle   Emotionally drained espionage analyst; he betrays South Africa maneuvers, particularly the genocidal Operation Uncle Remus, to Soviet Intelligence as emotional repayment for a communist agent's help freeing his African wife from her government's apartheid oppression; he defects without being able to protect her or her young son in Graham Greene's *The Human Factor*.

Sam Castle   Sarah Castle's seven-year-old son, whose love for Arthur Davis and naïve questions torture his adoptive father, Maurice Castle, in Graham Greene's *The Human Factor*.

Sarah MaNkosi Castle   Former M.I.6 agent and Maurice Castle's African wife who, while pregnant, escapes South Africa, marries Maurice despite his family's ostracism, and is trapped without support in Britain after Maurice defects in Graham Greene's *The Human Factor*.

Mr. Castlemaine   Irving Macher's college friend who informs Roger Micheldene that Macher is in New York City, leading Micheldene to find Macher with Helene Bang in Kingsley Amis's *One Fat Englishman*.

Senor Castor   Olifa's dictatorial Gubernado and president of the Gran Seco; when forced by Lord Clanroyden to command the rebel troops, he is captured by a new dream and discovers a more wholesome allegiance to Olifa before he sacrifices his life to save the life of Lady Roylance (Janet Raden) in John Buchan's *The Courts of the Morning*.

Dr. Catafago   Pompous doctor who examines Jack Townrow when he becomes delirious in P. H. Newby's *Something to Answer For*.

Catchpole   Former boyfriend of Margaret Peel; he reveals to Jim Dixon that Margaret is a liar and a manipulator in Kingsley Amis's *Lucky Jim*.

John Caterham   Conservative politician who sees the dangers of Boomfood; his failure to block its development or to effect its containment is due largely to the meddling Dr. Winkles in H. G. Wells's *The Food of the Gods, and How It Came to Earth*.

Denis Cathcart   Fiancé of Lady Mary Wimsey; he is found dead of a gunshot wound in the garden of the Duke of Denver's country place in Dorothy L. Sayers's *Clouds of Witness*.

Lydia Cathcart   Disapproving aunt of Denis Cathcart in Dorothy L. Sayers's *Clouds of Witness*.

Christopher Cather   A handsome bisexual young man whose defunct rock group boasted one hit; he rents a room in Hilary Burde's apartment; after affairs with both Clifford Larr and Laura Impiatt he marries Biscuit Bisset in Iris Murdoch's *A Word Child*.

Catherine   Aunt of Arlette in Joseph Conrad's *The Rover*.

Catherine   Jane Gray's younger sister, who is believed

by Jane to be their parents' favorite in Margaret Drabble's *The Waterfall*.

Mère Catherine   Madam of a Haitian brothel where Brown encounters Captain Concasseur and Major Jones in Graham Greene's *The Comedians*.

Cathy   Book-keeper at Ullswater Press and friend of Nancy Hawkins in Muriel Spark's *A Far Cry from Kensington*.

Miss Caton   Colorless, middle-aged assistant in Humphrey Boyce's antiques shop in Barbara Pym's *The Sweet Dove Died*.

Dr. L. S. Caton   Editor of a scholarly journal; he accepts Jim Dixon's article for publication, becomes evasive when Jim asks when it will be published, and publishes it as his own in Kingsley Amis's *Lucky Jim*.

Cator   Head clerk at the Rasuka oil well; he is a tense man with a prejudice against the Rasuka natives; he is stabbed by Hebechi Effendi but survives in P. H. Newby's *A Journey to the Interior*.

Mrs. Cator   Excitable wife of Cator in P. H. Newby's *A Journey to the Interior*.

Rupert Catskill   Britain's Secretary of State for War who plots to overthrow Utopia, arguing that its inhabitants are a decadent race who should be dominated by the more vital Earthlings in H. G. Wells's *Men Like Gods*.

Catterick   Snobbish gentleman of the Royal Court in C. S. Forester's *Hornblower and the Atropos*.

Mrs. Catterick   The unwilling jailer of Thomas Carlyle Craw; she agrees to provide room and board for Dougal Crombie and John Galt, "Jaikie", in John Buchan's *Castle Gay*.

Miss Cattermole   A Shrewsbury College undergraduate who is resentfully dissatisfied with her academic program and social life in Dorothy L. Sayers's *Gaudy Night*.

Duchess Cavalojos (Her Gaudiness)   Gossipy "Mistress of the Robes" for Queen Lois of Pisuerga and aunt of Laura de Nazianzi, whose court debut she helps to make in Ronald Firbank's *The Flower Beneath the Foot*.

Montagu (Monty) Cave   Conservative Member of Parliament who serves in a ministry with Roger Quaife; he is a competitor with Quaife for high office; his wife leaves him in C. P. Snow's *Corridors of Power*.

Cavendish Proud first lieutenant of the *Pluto* in C. S. Forester's *Ship of the Line.*

John Cavendish Childhood friend whom the convalescing Captain Arthur Hastings visits; he is accused of poisoning his stepmother, Emily Inglethorp, in Agatha Christie's *The Mysterious Affair at Styles: A Detective Story.*

Lawrence Cavendish John's younger brother, an unsuccessful publisher of poetry in Agatha Christie's *The Mysterious Affair at Styles: A Detective Story.*

Mary Cavendish John's wife, who is admired by Dr. Bauerstein and Captain Hastings in Agatha Christie's *The Mysterious Affair at Styles: A Detective Story.*

Anne Cavidge Gertrude Openshaw's old friend, who has for fifteen years been a nun in a closed convent; she leaves the order just before Guy Openshaw's death; she falls unrequitedly in love with "Count" Szczepanski; she leaves for Chicago when it is clear that his dogged devotion to Gertrude will endure despite Gertrude's happy marriage to Tim Reede in Iris Murdoch's *Nuns and Soldiers.*

Cavor Brilliant, eccentric scientist who develops the gravity-repelling alloy Cavorite, with which he builds a spherical spaceship and journeys to the Moon; there he becomes the permanent prisoner of the native Selenites, whose hierarchical, ant-like culture he at first admires, and to whom he appears the ambassador of a savage, dangerous race in H. G. Wells's *The First Men in the Moon.*

Mrs. Caypor Cold, quiet, loyal German wife of Grantley; she sees World War I Germany as the greatest nation in the world; she has a scholarly background, but she discusses only her German speech lesson with Ashenden; her passion is her husband in W. Somerset Maugham's *Ashenden: or The British Agent.*

Grantley Caypor Energetic, vibrant, cheerful, devoted Englishman who is a British and a German spy; Caypor loves his wife more than anything else and works side by side with her; his good-natured side competes with his cold-heartedness in W. Somerset Maugham's *Ashenden: or The British Agent.*

Cecedek Magda Bursavov's latest lover, an Austrian; he is an extraordinarily wealthy man until the Bolshevik Revolution in William Gerhardie's *Futility: A Novel on Russian Themes.*

Peter Cecil An Englishman who shows up at Alice Mellings's door wanting information about Andrew Connors, and to whom, in her hurry, Alice gives in-

criminating evidence in Doris Lessing's *The Good Terrorist.*

Cedar Utopian scientist who houses the infectious Earthlings at Quarantine (Coronation) Crag and is wounded in their attempt to take him hostage in H. G. Wells's *Men Like Gods.*

Ceria Brilliant manager of the grill-room; he is counted among Evelyn Orcham's finest employees; his wistful, appealing smile involves Violet Powler in her second romantic difficulty in Arnold Bennett's *Imperial Palace.*

Juan Cerillo Zapotecan Indian in the employ of the Banco Ejidal who taught Hugh Firmin how to whinney like a horse; he is a symbol of generosity and self-sacrifice in Malcolm Lowry's *Under the Volcano.* He is associated with Juan Fernando Martinez in *Dark as the Grave Wherein My Friend Is Laid.*

Cervantes Cockfighter, friend of Geoffrey Firmin, and bartender from whom Geoffrey orders mescal at the Salon Ofelia in Malcolm Lowry's *Under the Volcano.*

Ann Chace Sir Ransome's middle daughter, shorter and fairer than Emma; she tries to be friendly to Mildred Hallam in Ivy Compton-Burnett's *Darkness and Day.*

Emma Chace Sir Ransome's eldest daughter, who did not want her father to adopt Brigit Hallam (later Brigit Lovat) when Brigit was young; she is never proposed to in Ivy Compton-Burnett's *Darkness and Day.*

Sir Ransome Chace A man eighty years old, chivalrous and affectionate to his daughters Emma and Ann; Brigit Lovat is his secret daughter in Ivy Compton-Burnett's *Darkness and Day.*

Chadd Lieutenant aboard the *Indefatigable* and commander of the first gig in the *Indefatigable*'s surprise attack of the *Papillin* in C. S. Forester's *Mr. Midshipman Hornblower.*

Bernard William Chadwick China buyer for a wholesale firm; his evidence at the Sharpe women's trial contradicts their accuser, Betty Kane, in Josephine Tey's *The Franchise Affair.*

Jocelyn Chadwick English land-agent who watches over Major Jack Thompson's estate; he is ruthless and unkind to the tenant farmers and eventually meets his death at their hands in Liam O'Flaherty's *Famine.*

Mary Francis Chadwick Bernard's wife; her evidence supports his, explains Betty Kane's injuries, and exonerates the Sharpe women at their trial in Josephine Tey's *The Franchise Affair.*

Mrs. Chalfont   Giles Peters's old, elegant ex-mother-in-law; she attends the Mike Morgan comedy performance with Giles and Anthony Keating in Margaret Drabble's *The Ice Age.*

Chalk   Lieutenant of the *Goliath* in charge of impressing men into the navy in C. S. Forester's *Mr. Midshipman Hornblower.*

Alice Challice   Endearing, practical Putney widow; seeking a new husband by advertising, she contacts Henry Leek; she accepts the great artist Priam Farll as Leek, and she insouciantly copes with the series of comical crises the double identity of her new husband brings in Arnold Bennett's *Buried Alive: A Tale of These Days.*

Claude Challoner   The youngest son of Simon and Fanny (Graham); he is a charming little boy who wants to marry his sister Emma in Ivy Compton-Burnett's *A Heritage and Its History.*

Sir Edwin Challoner   Baronet who evicts his nephew, Simon Challoner, from his house when he discovers that Simon has impregnated Rhoda Graham; married to Rhoda, Sir Edwin rears her son, the younger Hamish, as his own in Ivy Compton-Burnett's *A Heritage and Its History.*

Emma Challoner   The younger daughter of Simon and Fanny (Graham); she copies the actions of her brother Claude; she is forgotten by her parents after Sir Edwin's funeral in Ivy Compton-Burnett's *A Heritage and Its History.*

Graham Challoner   A son of Simon and Fanny (Graham); intelligent and ironic, he is kept under constraint by Simon, who begrudges him his financial support in Ivy Compton-Burnett's *A Heritage and its History.*

Hamish Challoner   Brother to Sir Edwin, who is always the center of Hamish's life; Hamish dies in his sixties in Ivy Compton-Burnett's *A Heritage and Its History.*

Hamish Challoner (the younger)   Sir Edwin's legal son; when his wife, Marcia, wants to leave the house, Hamish gives up his inheritance to Simon Challoner, his natural father, in Ivy Compton-Burnett's *A Heritage and Its History.*

Julia Challoner   Hamish's wife, who feels that she gave him up to his elder brother, Sir Edwin; she is

shocked that Simon is the father of the younger Hamish in Ivy Compton-Burnett's *A Heritage and Its History.*

Marcia Challoner   The wife of the younger Hamish; she is charmed by Simon Challoner to influence Hamish to relinquish his claim to the family estate in Ivy Compton-Burnett's *A Heritage and Its History.*

Naomi Challoner   Elder daughter of Simon and Fanny (Graham); she falls in love with and wants to marry her supposed cousin, the younger Hamish Challoner; their mothers are sisters, but his father is not her father's uncle, as publicly believed, but her own father in Ivy Compton-Burnett's *A Heritage and Its History.*

Ralph Challoner   A son of Simon and Fanny (Graham); he is always threatened by his disappointed father with the workhouse as his future in Ivy Compton-Burnett's *A Heritage and Its History.*

Simon Challoner   Hamish's son, reared in expectation of inheriting his uncle's title and estate; he is supplanted by his own natural son, the younger Hamish, when Sir Edwin, married to the mother, Rhoda Graham, assumes paternity; Simon feels his life is ruined and brings up his legitimate children in harsh preparation for penury in Ivy Compton-Burnett's *A Heritage and Its History.*

Walter Challoner   Younger brother of Simon; he does not earn a degree at Oxford and remains in the family home as a dependent in Ivy Compton-Burnett's *A Heritage and Its History.*

Steve Champion   Stylish, flamboyant British agent perceived as an anachronism by his superiors; he is suspected of planning to supply the Arabs with massively destructive weapons in Len Deighton's *Yesterday's Spy.*

Edward, Lord Champneis   Famous explorer and writer who is Christine Clay's husband; he smuggles a well-known Eastern European radical into England under circumstances which suggest opportunity and alibi for the murder of his wife in Josephine Tey's *A Shilling for Candles.*

Miss Chancellor   The mistress who teaches history at Lesbia Firebrace's school; she accompanies the four girls to visit Clemence Shelley at her home in Ivy Compton-Burnett's *Two Worlds and Their Ways.*

Chang   Polite citizen of Shangri-La whose monkhood is pending; he is a diligent and compassionate host to his unwilling guests at the Tibetan monastery in James Hilton's *Lost Horizon.*

Young Chankery   Barrister who represents Philip Bosinney in court in John Galsworthy's *The Man of Property*.

Judy Channing   Mistress of the special school that Molly Murray attends; Channing writes to Molly's mother, Alison Murray, of Molly's unusual, hard-to-control behavior in Margaret Drabble's *The Ice Age*.

Mr. Chaplin   Teacher and house master at Seaforth House school in Roy Fuller's *The Ruined Boys*.

Chapman   A landing-party member who suffers a sprained ankle in C. S. Forester's *Lieutenant Hornblower*.

Mr. Chapman   Fiery and independent Labour Member of Parliament; he rescues Edward Leithin from two murderous plots of the "Power-House" until he himself is hospitalized after being run down by a car in John Buchan's *The Power-House*.

Richard Chapman   Fifteen-year-old boy sentenced to hang on charges of murder and attempted rape; Ethan Llewelyn imagines himself unsuccessfully defending the boy against the charges in Malcolm Lowry's *October Ferry to Gabriola*.

Simone Chardin   Jacques Bernadet's sluttish paramour, who ends up with Stephan Zelli after he deserts Marya Zelli in Jean Rhys's *Postures*.

M. de Charette   Wealthy officer who is attempting to raise armies to turn back rebels in C. S. Forester's *Mr. Midshipman Hornblower*.

Major Charge   Henry Pulling's politically conservative and gruff next-door neighbor, who occasionally watches Pulling's dahlias when he is away in Graham Greene's *Travels with my Aunt*.

Chargut   One of the supernormals of John Wainwright's Pacific island colony; he sacrifices himself to prevent dissolution of the colony in Olaf Stapledon's *Odd John: A Story Between Jest and Earnest*.

Chairman of the Bench   Official who convicts the errant Toad of stealing a motor car, of furious driving, and of the more serious offence of cheeking the police in Kenneth Grahame's *The Wind in the Willows*.

Uncle Charles   Stephen Dedalus's granduncle who smokes in the outhouse and exercises in the park with him in James Joyce's *A Portrait of the Artist as a Young Man*.

Alfred Charlesworth   A colliery manager in Best-wood; he hears Walter Morel mimicking his "squeaky voice" in a pub and then retaliates by assigning Morel unprofitable mine "stalls" to work in D. H. Lawrence's *Sons and Lovers*.

Charley   Inexperienced sailor on the *Narcissus* in Joseph Conrad's *The Nigger of the "Narcissus"*.

Charlie   Reactivated reluctant American World War II spy; he returns to service impersonating a burned-out field agent to investigate his close wartime friend Steve Champion's suspicious liaisons with Egypt but ends up killing his one-time comrade in Len Deighton's *Yesterday's Spy*.

Charlie   A fellow voyager who, in Charles Watkins's hallucination, was snatched up by the Crystal Disc in Doris Lessing's *Briefing for a Descent into Hell*.

Charlie   Inebriated boatman-postilion whose concussion forces Hornblower to assist the crew of the canal boat in C. S. Forester's *Hornblower and the Atropos*.

Charlie   Hard-drinking member of the Alpha and Omega Club in Norman Douglas's *South Wind*.

Charlie   The new, lazy, good-natured editor of *Lilith* whom many of the magazine's employees feel to be a disappointment; he later marries Jane Somers's co-worker Phyllis in Doris Lessing's *The Diaries of Jane Somers*.

Charlie (Charmian, "Charlie the Red"; covernames: Comrade Leila, Fräulein Palme, Imogen Boastrup, Joan, Margaret)   Chameleon-like red-haired British actress, naïve political radical, and Palestinian sympathizer manipulated by the Israelis into espionage; at Marty Kurtz's orders, she infiltrates a Palestinian training camp and, by a supreme performance in the "theatre of the real", sets up the Israeli assassination of Palestinian bomb-maker Khalil and her own psychic death in John le Carré's *The Little Drummer Girl*.

Felix Charlock   An inventor and the central consciousness of the narrative; after an affair with Iolanthe Samiou he marries Benedicta Merlin; he strives to resist the machinations of the Firm in Lawrence Durrell's *Tunc*. He ultimately becomes the Firm's puppet, even after rising to its directorship in *Nunquam*.

Mark Charlock   Young son of Benedicta Merlin and Felix Charlock; he is killed accidentally by a shotgun booby trap Felix plants within the Abel computer in Lawrence Durrell's *Tunc*.

Charlotte   An American nun who runs an institute

for retarded adults in southern California; she takes Ruth (Sister Mary Joseph) to a meeting of charismatic Catholics in David Lodge's *How Far Can You Go?*.

Charlotte (Charley)   George and Jim's friend who allows George to express his grief in Christopher Isherwood's *A Single Man*.

Charrington   An old man who runs an antiques store in the prole section of Oceania when he is in disguise and is actually part of the Thought Police; he sets up the environment where Smith and Julia get caught in George Orwell's *Nineteen Eighty-Four*.

Princess Betsy Charskaya   A penniless Russian princess, incomparably plain but chic; she must attach herself to others to subsist; she receives favors from Mr. Rivers for bringing wealthy women such as Martha Denman to his dress shop in Vita Sackville-West's *Family History*.

Anna Charteris   A nineteen-year-old daughter of a schoolmaster; she communes with her only friend, a tree, until Steve Hallem appears; though attracted to Steve's rebelliousness, she fears the consummation of love; she marries Steve in spite of her father's opposition in C. Day Lewis's *The Friendly Tree*.

Edward Charteris   Anna's gracelessly and rigidly moral father, a schoolmaster, who claims to be a "bit of a socialist himself"; believing that he has devoted his life to Anna and worrying that she will leave him, he plans strategies against her marrying in C. Day Lewis's *The Friendly Tree*.

Robin Charvill   Oxford undergraduate and rugby star; he joins Dougal Crombie and John Galt, "Jaikie", in saving Prince John of Evallonia from the Republican conspirators determined to keep him off the throne in John Buchan's *Castle Gay*.

Warrender Chase   Central and title character in Fleur Talbot's novel in Muriel Spark's *Loitering with Intent*.

Andrew Chase-White   A young, virginal, and decent British cavalry officer stationed in Ireland in 1916; stunned after his proposal of marriage is rejected by Frances Bellman, he becomes briefly involved with his sexually magnetic aunt, Millie Kinnard; the inglorious part he plays in the Easter Rising is redeemed by his hero's death later at Passchendaele in Iris Murdoch's *The Red and the Green*.

Hilda Chase-White   Andrew's widowed Anglo-Irish mother, pleased with her recent purchase of a picturesque house in Ireland; oblivious to the political and familial chaos around her, she is euphoric on the eve of the Easter Rising in Iris Murdoch's *The Red and the Green*.

Mrs. Chattaway   The mistress for English literature in Josephine Napier's school; she is a widow whose chatter is not discreet in Ivy Compton-Burnett's *More Women Than Men*.

Mr. Chatteris   Successor to Mr. Ralston at Brookfield; diabetic and visually impaired, he is unfit for military duty when the war breaks out; the shortage of masters at the school forces him to call back Mr. Chips from retirement; Chatteris dies shortly thereafter, and Mr. Chips serves as Acting Head until the end of the war in James Hilton's *Good-bye, Mr. Chips*.

Lili, Lady Chatterjee   Widow of the late Sir Nello Chatterjee; she is part of that small segment of educated and often Anglicized Indians who form the civil-servant and professional class throughout the Raj; an old friend of Lady Manners, Lady Chatterjee becomes a surrogate "auntie" to Daphne Manners, welcoming her to her home and looking after her interests in Paul Scott's *The Jewel in the Crown*. Lady Chatterjee comments on events, especially in *The Day of the Scorpion*. She appears in *The Towers of Silence* and in *A Division of the Spoils*.

Sir Clifford Chatterley   Constance's husband, who is paralyzed and rendered impotent during World War I; he returns home to run his prosperous Midlands mines and to host gatherings of "highly mental" friends at Wragby Hall in D. H. Lawrence's *Lady Chatterley's Lover*.

Constance (Connie), Lady Chatterley   The daughter of artists and intellectuals whose husband returns from World War I paralyzed and impotent; her sufferings induced by his "life of the mind" are not sufficiently alleviated by a brief sexual affair with a young writer; an affair with the estate's gamekeeper, Mellors, brings her into vital life and closer contact with nature; pregnant by Mellors, she abandons Clifford and plans a life with the gamekeeper at the end of D. H. Lawrence's *Lady Chatterley's Lover*.

Sir Geoffrey Chatterley   A baronet and a wealthy mine owner; he is Clifford's father in D. H. Lawrence's *Lady Chatterley's Lover*.

Dr. Herbert Chaucer   The maternal uncle of Dorothea Bunyan; a clergyman, he proposes to two governesses (Edith Hallam and Miss Blake) and finally successfully to Henrietta Ponsonby in Ivy Compton-Burnett's *Daughters and Sons*.

Chauffeur L.'s unnamed employee, who beats D. at the behest of Captain Currie in Graham Greene's *The Confidential Agent.*

Chayne Private detective who spies on Clare Corven and her activities with Tony Croom to supply evidence for Gerald Corven's divorce proceedings in John Galsworthy's *Over the River.*

Mr. Cheeseman A money-tight bookseller; he starts a two-penny library of cheap paperback books and hires Gordon Comstock after he gets arrested in George Orwell's *Keep the Aspidistra Flying.*

Maria Cheeseman Retired actress and singer whose biography Dougal Douglas is supposed to be writing in Muriel Spark's *The Ballad of Peckham Rye.*

Francis Chelifer Romantic but aloof poet who after being rescued from near drowning by Lillian Aldwinkle holds off her pointed advances; the story of his life is recorded in a series of tedious fragments which he writes before escaping to London to work as editor for the *Rabbit Fancier's Gazette* in Aldous Huxley's *Those Barren Leaves.*

Countess of Chell (Interfering Iris) Pretty, young, philanthropic wife; of poor parentage but successfully groomed for a rich marriage, she involves herself in the social progress of the Five Towns; she appreciates the amusing exploits of Denry Machin to the extent of dancing with him at her annual ball, which starts Denry on his career as a "card" in Arnold Bennett's *The Card: A Story of Adventure in the Five Towns.*

Adrian Cherrell Fiftyish museum curator who is in love with Diana Ferse; he finds Ronald Ferse's body in John Galsworthy's *Maid In Waiting.* He is critical of Wilfred Desert's conversion to Islam in *Flowering Wilderness.* He writes his wife a description of Dinny Cherrell's wedding in *Over the River.*

Lady Alison (Charwell) Cherrell Wife of Michael Mont's young uncle Lionel; she helps Fleur Forsyte Mont with social arrangements in John Galsworthy's *The White Monkey.* She helps Fleur communicate with the Bolivian ambassador on behalf of Dinny and Hubert Cherrell in *Maid In Waiting.*

General Sir Conway Cherrell The sixty-year-old eldest brother of his family, who worries over the fate of his son, Hubert, in John Galsworthy's *Maid In Waiting.* Sixty-two in 1930, he is grieved by Dinny Cherrell's engagement to a man branded as a coward in *Flowering Wilderness.* He stands by his daughter Clare (Corven) during her divorce in John Galsworthy's *Over the River.*

Cuthbert (Cuffs) Cherrell Canon, aged eighty-two, whose death occasions the gathering of his nieces and nephews in John Galsworthy's *Maid In Waiting.*

Elizabeth Frensham, Lady Cherrell Wife of General Sir Conway Cherrell in John Galsworthy's *Maid In Waiting.* She hears her daughter Dinny's problems of love without help for her in John Galsworthy's *Flowering Wilderness.* She offers kindly advice to her daughters Clare (Corven) and Dinny in *Over the River.*

Elizabeth (Dinny) Cherrell Twenty-four-year-old daughter of General Sir Conway and Elizabeth Cherrell; she uses her brother Hubert's diary to prevent his extradition and gives evidence to protect her Uncle Adrian at the coronor's inquest in John Galsworthy's *Maid In Waiting.* She plans to marry Wilfred Desert in 1930, surrenders to him when he decides to leave England again, and returns to her parents in sorrow in John Galsworthy's *Flowering Wilderness.* She helps her sister Clare during the divorce from Sir Gerald Corven; she learns that her dream of Wilfred Desert's death is true, and in 1932 she marries Eustace Dornford, the new Member of Parliament from Oxfordshire, in *Over the River.*

Hilary (Charwell) Cherrell Vicar who persuades his nephew Michael Mont to take up the cause of slum clearance in John Galsworthy's *Swan Song.* He performs the marriage ceremony for his nephew Hubert Cherrell and Jean Tasburgh, and he helps his brother Adrian search for Ronald Ferse in *Maid In Waiting.* He sticks by his niece, Dinny Cherrell, when she decides to marry Wilfred Desert in *Flowering Wilderness.*

Hubert Cherrell Son of General Conway Cherrell; he is a British Army Officer and is liable to extradition to Bolivia for the murder of a half-caste Bolivian Indian in John Galsworthy's *Maid In Waiting.* He attends a family conference on his sister Dinny's problems with Wilfred Desert before taking a foreign post in John Galsworthy's *Flowering Wilderness.*

Jean Tasburgh Cherrell Daughter of the rector near Sir Lawrence Mont's estate; at twenty-one she marries Hubert Cherrell; she plans for him to escape extradition in John Galsworthy's *Maid In Waiting.* She fails to make Wilfred Desert surrender his affections for Dinny Cherrell in *Flowering Wilderness.*

Lionel (Charwell) Cherrell Michael Mont's uncle in John Galsworthy's *The White Monkey.* As a new judge he avoids involvement in Hubert Cherrell's legal problems in *Maid In Waiting.* He joins in family conference about Dinny Cherrell and Wilfred Desert in *Flowering Wilderness.*

May (Charwell) Cherrell Wife of Hilary; she supports her husband's slum-clearance project in John Galsworthy's *Swan Song*. She helps her niece Dinny Cherrell keep in touch with Hilary during the trials of Hubert Cherrell in *Maid In Waiting*. She criticizes Wilfred Desert's conversion in *Flowering Wilderness*.

Alfred Cherrington Widower and rather weak father of Eustace, Hilda, and Barbara; his wife died in childbirth with the latter child in L. P. Hartley's *The Shrimp and the Anemone*.

Barbara Cherrington Youngest sibling in L. P. Hartley's *The Shrimp and the Anemone*. She is the nubile younger sister of Eustance and Hilda when she marries Jimmy Crankshaw in *The Sixth Heaven*. As Barbara Crankshaw, she gives birth to her first child, a boy named after her brother Eustace, as an act of renewal in *Eustace and Hilda*.

Eustace Cherrington A neurotic, sister-dominated boy who becomes the recipient of an old woman's financial largesse in L. P. Hartley's *The Shrimp and the Anemone*. He is an Oxford undergraduate who has refined his earlier capacity to render himself agreeable but possesses an interior life rich in romantic fantasy in *The Sixth Heaven*. As a sensitive young man in Venice, he writes a novella which is accepted for publication; he plunges into the Adriatic sea as a ritual baptism, aids in the recovery of his sister Hilda, and undergoes transfiguration and death in *Eustace and Hilda*.

Hilda Cherrington Eustace's older sister, who is largely responsible for creating his senses of reality and morality in L. P. Hartley's *The Shrimp and the Anemone*. She administers Highcross Hill for Crippled Children with money from Eustace's inheritance and becomes romantically involved with Dick Staveley in *The Sixth Heaven*. Notwithstanding her own rejection of Dick Staveley, she is shocked by the announcement of his engagement and suffers psychosomatic paralysis, only to recover as a result of a shock imposed by Eustace to benefit her; she resumes care of him in *Eustace and Hilda*.

Aunt Sarah Cherrington Strict, puritanical mother-substitute, who presides over the household at Anchorstone and warns the family about presuming beyond one's social and economic class in L. P. Hartley's *The Shrimp and the Anemone*. Resuming her care over her nieces and nephew, she calls Eustace back to England from Venice at the behest of Hilda in *Eustace and Hilda*.

Cherry Brian's girlfriend in Isabel Colegate's *Orlando at the Brazen Threshold*.

Mr. Cherry-Marvel Garrulous English socialite in Paris from whom the writer-narrator learns that his friend Iris Storm is ill and under the obstetric care of Conrad Masters in Michael Arlen's *The Green Hat*.

Hattie Chessman Old friend of Swithin Forsyte in John Galsworthy's *The Man of Property*.

Hugo Chesterton (born Chester Hugo Amberly) A quick-witted, self-assured young man of the public-school type, but a violent-tempered natural anarchist incapable of responding to social values; a manic-depressive thief, he falls totally in love with Daisy Bland's innocence; he is sentenced to die for killing a police inspector in Nicholas Blake's *A Tangled Web*.

Chestnut-head Red-haired Homo sapiens man, metaphorically designated by Lok and Fa; he is the father of Tanakil in William Golding's *The Inheritors*.

Alyn Chetwynd Favorite teacher of Sophia Baines; she encourages Sophia to follow her desire to be a teacher in defiance of her parents' wish in Arnold Bennett's *The Old Wives Tale*.

Mrs. Chetwynd-Smythe An intemperate woman of means who waddles in a big house; Daisy Bland is delivering her hat when she encounters Hugo Chesterton in Nicholas Blake's *A Tangled Web*.

Madame Chevez Rich, overbearing Turkish woman; she introduces Charles Latimer to Colonel Zia Haki at a party at her villa in Eric Ambler's *The Mask of Dimitrios*.

Romola Cheyne A clever woman who maintains a difficult social position as mistress to the King; Sebastian recognizes her great soul despite her materialism and hardness in Vita Sackville-West's *The Edwardians*.

Dinah (Diana) Redfern (Chichester-Redfern) Strong and sensual but ruthlessly independent and controlling professional guitarist, who shares her passions for music, sex, and superficial religious ritual with novelist Giles Hermitage while she lives with and cares for her dying mother in John Wain's *The Pardoner's Tale*.

Helen Chichester-Redfern Terminally ill matron and avid reader of the novels of Giles Hermitage; she asks him to come visit her at her home to help her "make sense of" them and ultimately to indict, in his fiction, her own abandonment years ago by her husband in John Wain's *The Pardoner's Tale*.

Richard Chichester-Redfern Scientist husband who leaves his homemaker-wife Helen and unborn daughter Diana for a more fulfilling relationship with a younger woman colleague; Helen struggles to come to terms with the desertion years later on her deathbed in John Wain's *The Pardoner's Tale*.

Chico   Highly touted, brainy W.O.O.C.(P). agent; he bungles every assignment and has to be rescued by agents working with the narrator in Len Deighton's *The Ipcress File*.

Chief (codename: C)   Bureaucratic-minded head of the Secret Service; he recalls James Wormold to England and rewards his incompetence with a promotion, an O.B.E. (Officer of the Order of the British Empire), and a substantial raise in Graham Greene's *Our Man in Havana*.

Chief of Rostrums   Along with the Chief of Gardens (Fructuoso Sanabria) and the Chief of the Municipality (Zuzugoitea), one of the three fascist militiamen who persecute Geoffrey Firmin at the Farolito; it is he who actually shoots Geoffrey in Malcolm Lowry's *Under the Volcano*.

Simone Chihani   Young, striking, intense Algerian (Berber) woman; a trained terrorist, undercover agent, and security officer for Karlis Zander, she is also his daughter; she protects Robert Halliday and is instrumental in the success of the Ruler-NATO negotiations in Eric Ambler's *The Care of Time*.

Humphrey Chilcox   Political opponent who loses Parliamentary election to Lord Miltoun in John Galsworthy's *The Patrician*.

Joanna Childe   A rector's daughter, elocution teacher, and resident of the May of Teck Club; virginal and ritualistic, she is deficient in the self-centered, life-affirming drives that variously characterize her fellow residents; she dies in the fire after an unrecovered German bomb belatedly explodes in Muriel Spark's *The Girls of Slender Means*.

Harold Chilleywater   First attache to the English Embassy in Pisuerga whose successful diplomatic career becomes less certain when his wife begins publishing "lurid stories of low life" under her maiden name in Ronald Firbank's *The Flower Beneath the Foot*.

Victoria Gellybone Frinton Chilleywater   Aristocratic, Kentish-born wife of an English Embassy official in Pisuerga and a vain, popular romantic novelist in Ronald Firbank's *The Flower Beneath the Foot*.

Teresa Chilton   A woman who rejects Ninian Middleton, rejects Hugo Middleton, and finally accepts Ninian as a husband, saying that she has little feeling for

her life in Ivy Compton-Burnett's *The Mighty and Their Fall*.

Bet (Mad Bet) Chinnock   A madwoman whose unrequited passion for John Crow motivates her conspiracy with Finn Toller to murder him; she kills Toller after his murder attempt goes awry, and her plot is never discovered in John Cowper Powys's *A Glastonbury Romance*.

Mr. Chipping (Mr. Chips)   Classics teacher at Brookfield School who devotes a lifetime to teaching generations of British boys; he witnesses the upheavals in the world and the changes in masters and headmasters through his decades at Brookfield, yet strives for balance between the old world and the new, the young and the old, and earns the love and respect of all with his wisdom and keen sense of humor in James Hilton's *Good-bye, Mr. Chips*.

Mrs. Chirk   A muddleheaded patient taken by Beaufort Mallet from Dr. Towzer's waiting room; "Captain Mallet" recasts her as his own overzealous maid, who also responds to the name of "Mrs. Finch" in Nigel Dennis's *Cards of Identity*.

Monsieur Chiroc   Sensitive, courteous newsman and adventurer; he befriends Sophia Baines after her husband abandons her, falls in love with her, and, after her refusal of him, purposely goes on a dangerous mission from which he never returns in Arnold Bennett's *The Old Wives Tale*.

Chitterlow   Aggressive, overwhelming playwright who befriends Art Kipps and recognizes him as the missing heir in Old Bean's inheritance announcement, and whose play *Pestered Butterfly* is a great success, making Kipps, one of its investors, independently wealthy in H. G. Wells's *Kipps: The Story of a Simple Soul*.

Chlestakon   The covernamed K.G.B. agent who enlists Giles Trent as a minor K.G.B. mole to cover for the real mole, Fiona Samson, in Len Deighton's *Berlin Game*.

Chloe   Barmaid at Pandaemonium Club in Hampstead in Muriel Spark's *The Bachelors*.

Sir Trevor Choape   The London doctor favored by the Duchess of Bude; he assumes Lady Emily (Winter-Willoughby) Curzon's obstetrical care in C. S. Forester's *The General*.

Lionel Cholmley   A young boarder in Mrs. Bailey's house who in the past would have attracted Miriam Henderson, especially with his ambition "to disseminate poetry," but whom she resists taking up in Dorothy Richardson's *Clear Horizon*.

Chopper Member of the regular fire brigade; he is assigned to Richard Roe's auxiliary fire service unit in Henry Green's *Caught*.

Christabel Schoolgirl who finds the young Alfred Polly's impassioned attempts to woo her merely a source of entertainment for herself and her friends; her rejection drives him to marry Miriam Larkins (Polly) in H. G. Wells's *The History of Mr. Polly*.

Annabel Christopher The "English Lady-Tiger" of Italian B Films who breaks free of her public image after the suicide of her husband and his carefully crafted attempt to blacken her with responsibility for his death in Muriel Spark's *The Public Image*.

Carl Christopher Infant son of Annabel and Frederick Christopher; his existence gives purpose to his mother's life after his father's suicide in Muriel Spark's *The Public Image*.

Frederick Christopher Failed actor and screenwriter who tries to destroy his wife through a plot to blame her for his suicide in Muriel Spark's *The Public Image*.

Christou Storyteller, liar, and good-natured owner of the Cyprus Bar; he was a friend and partner of Elie Khoury in arms-smuggling to Cypriot rebels, as well as an acquaintance of Townrow; supposedly he tried to kill Townrow in P. H. Newby's *Something To Answer For*.

Mrs. Christy Camilla Bellamy's mother, who has wars of words with Edward Bellamy; she does much of the charity sewing work in Ivy Compton-Burnett's *Men and Wives*.

Charles P. Chrystal Dean of the Cambridge college who successfully courts Sir Horace Timberlake for a handsome endowment to the college; he joins Arthur Brown to lead in organizing support for Paul Jago as new Master but defects at the last moment to support Crawford instead in C. P. Snow's *The Masters*.

Vassili Iulievitch Chubinov Colorless-appearing anarchist descended from monarchs; he is the son of old friends of Nikolai Diakanov, whose heart attack he causes by reporting that Nikolai was betrayed by his secretary, the double agent Monsieur Kamensky, in Rebecca West's *The Birds Fall Down*.

Chubsalid Priest-Supreme of the Church of the Formidable Peace; he insists the Church must be superior to the State and is executed by the Supreme Oligarch in Brian W. Aldiss's *Helliconia Winter*.

Charles Churchill Plump schoolmaster and father of Florence Churchill; he combines a "gross person" with a "fine delicacy of wits"; he astutely recognizes the error Florence has made in marrying Lewis Dodd in Margaret Kennedy's *The Constant Nymph*.

Evelyn Churchill Albert Sanger's talented, intelligent, beautiful British second wife, who bears him four children; Evelyn loves Sanger "to distraction" but dies early from a heart condition in Margaret Kennedy's *The Constant Nymph*.

Florence Churchill Beautiful, good-humored, intelligent cousin to Albert Sanger's children; she falls in love with Lewis Dodd and determines to marry him; achieving her goal, she is devastated when she discovers the love between Lewis and her cousin Teresa Sanger; losing her good humor, she verbally torments Teresa; when Teresa and Lewis run off together, she sets out to find them, determined not to lose Lewis, in Margaret Kennedy's *The Constant Nymph*.

Captain James Churchill Twenty-four-year-old romantic who falls in love with Catherine Casement; he is easily affected by the pitfalls of the human condition, especially death, in Kingsley Amis's *The Anti-Death League*.

Robert Churchill Evelyn Churchill's unprepossessing, reserved brother, who is the principal at a university in the British midlands; he accompanies his niece Florence Churchill to the Austrian Tyrol to visit the Sanger household and disapproves of most of the people there in Margaret Kennedy's *The Constant Nymph*.

Ghht-Mlark Chzarn Phagor major of the Borlien guard; she reports secretly to the phagor leader in hiding and sets fire to the Borlien palace in Brian W. Aldiss's *Helliconia Summer*.

Ciccio A dark, passionate Italian, who comes to Woodhouse as a member of the Natcha-Kee-Tawara Troupe; he has mesmeric power upon Alvina Houghton, who goes with him to his remote mountain village in southern Italy in D. H. Lawrence's *The Lost Girl*.

Cicely Wife of Otto and sister of Mrs. Pullbody's sister's husband; she attends Otto during John Lavender's visit to the dentist's office in John Galsworthy's *The Burning Spear: Being the Experiences of Mr. John Lavender in Time of War*.

Cifuentes An engineer nearly killed by enemy agents stalking James Wormold because Wormold has taken his identity for an imaginary agent (code identification: 59200/5/2) who allegedly details the mysterious constructions in the Oriente mountains in Graham Greene's *Our Man in Havana*. See also James Wormold.

Cindy An artist's model who is Philip Weston's customary sexual refuge in Isabel Colegate's *Statues in a Garden*.

Lady Circumference Querulous, aggressive noblewoman whose son Lord Tangent dies from an accidental gunshot wound he suffered while attending Llanabba School in Evelyn Waugh's *Decline and Fall*.

The Citizen Bigoted leader of the patriotic drinkers in Barney Kiernan's Pub; he throws a biscuit tin at Leopold Bloom in James Joyce's *Ulysses*.

Cla-cla Runi's mother; she is killed in W. H. Hudson's *Green Mansions*.

Dr. Claggart Sympathetic but pessimistic staff psychiatrist who is forced to discharge Bill Plantagenet from City Hospital without having helped him in Malcolm Lowry's *Lunar Caustic*.

Claire Young, attractive surgeon, who is affianced to Nicholas Marlow; her opened letters to him while he is in Italy serve to confuse the enemy in Eric Ambler's *Cause for Alarm*.

Major Herbert Clandon-Hartley Retired, broke British military officer; he avoids his wife's relatives, who are partly responsible for his financial difficulties; he is wrongly suspected by Vadassy of being a spy in Eric Ambler's *Epitaph for a Spy*.

Maria Clandon-Hartley Dry, austere, Italian-born wife of Major Herbert Clandon-Hartley; having married against her father's wishes, she and her husband have traveled to France in Eric Ambler's *Epitaph for a Spy*.

Lady Clanroyden See Barbara Dasent.

Lord Clanroyden See Alexander ("Sandy") Arbuthnot.

Clara Prostitute who befriended Else Crole and appears in the hotel after her death in Graham Greene's *The Confidential Agent*.

Aunt Clara Thomas Phillips's aunt, a wealthy old woman, who takes care of him financially, sends him to good boarding schools while he is young, lets him visit occasionally when he becomes a sailor, and leaves him all her belongings when she dies in Alan Sillitoe's *Her Victory*.

Clare Agatha (King) Field's old schoolmate in Isabel Colegate's *Agatha*.

Clare A black dancing teacher and gigolo whose life is composed of women and drink; he is a confidant of Herbert Gregory and a denizen of the Regina Hotel in Lawrence Durrell's *The Black Book*.

Mother Clare A member of the Anglican Benedictine convent; she appears surprisingly to assist Dora Greenfield in rescuing Catherine Fawley from drowning in Iris Murdoch's *The Bell*.

Mr. Clare Cassius's father, who says he loved Cassius best in Ivy Compton-Burnett's *The Present and the Past*.

Cassius Clare A self-dramatizing father of five; he is married first to Catherine and then to Flavia; he pretends suicide and then suffers a heart attack that resembles his previous drugged state in Ivy Compton-Burnett's *The Present and the Past*.

Catherine Clare Elton Scrope's sister and Cassius's divorced wife; she returns to get to know her sons, Fabian and Guy, and takes them away with her when Cassius dies in Ivy Compton-Burnett's *The Present and the Past*.

Edward, Lord Clare Tory member of the House of Lords who shows Jenny Rastall about the House, abuses his privilege to claim travel expenses on behalf of charity, and is removed from his board position by Reginald Swaffield in C. P. Snow's *In Their Wisdom*.

Fabian Clare Cassius's eldest son, whose mother, Catherine, left when he was four years old; he is an angry boy in Ivy Compton-Burnett's *The Present and the Past*.

Flavia Clare The present wife of Cassius and the stepmother of Fabian and Guy and the mother of Henry, Megan and Tobias; she treats the children equally, and her friendship with her predecessor, Catherine Clare, makes Cassius jealous in Ivy Compton-Burnett's *The Present and the Past*.

Guy Clare Fabian's full brother, who cannot bear to be parted from him but who loves Flavia Clare as the only mother he has known in Ivy Compton-Burnett's *The Present and the Past*.

Henry Clare Closest child to Megan in age; he is a son who does not glorify his father even after Cassius's death in Ivy Compton-Burnett's *The Present and the Past*.

Megan Clare Cassius's seven-year-old daughter; she

is thoughtful like Fabian and insightful in Ivy Compton-Burnett's *The Present and the Past.*

Tobias (Toby) Clare   A three-year-old boy who pretends to be a minister at the mole's funeral; he is said to have the sense of humor of a savage in Ivy Compton-Burnett's *The Present and the Past.*

Clarence (the ghost)   Sombre, thin man; he is one of Ida Arnold's lovers in Graham Greene's *Brighton Rock.*

Clarice   Woman with whom Steven Leadbitter, the hireling, lived for three years and from whom he disengages himself before beginning to chauffeur Lady Franklin and embarking on the tales of family life which entrap him in L. P. Hartley's *The Hireling.*

Clarice   Helpful and unintimidating young maid who is assigned to Mrs. de Winter in Dapne Du Maurier's *Rebecca.*

G. S. Clark   Modern Languages scholar and Cambridge college fellow; a fierce conservative and anticommunist, he gives hostile testimony against Donald Howard in C. P. Snow's *The Affair.* The new Master of the Cambridge college, he pesters Charles Eliot with talk about college matters at the party given by Charles's parents in *The Sleep of Reason.* He wants to deliver the eulogy for Sir Francis Getliffe but yields the honor to Arthur Brown in *Last Things.*

Major Jimmy Clark   A British officer who pays attention to Sarah Layton while she is visiting her uncle and aunt, Arthur and Fenny Grace, in Calcutta; Sarah becomes pregnant from their single sexual encounter in Paul Scott's *The Towers of Silence.*

Nobby Clark   Impudent and charming Cockney private who teams up with Roger Henderson when they are stranded in France in W. Somerset Maugham's *The Hour Before the Dawn.*

Sir Carmichael Clarke   The third murder victim in Agatha Christie's *The A.B.C. Murders.*

Charlotte, Lady Clarke   Wife of Sir Carmichael; she hires Hercule Poirot to investigate her husband's death in Agatha Christie's *The A.B.C. Murders.*

Franklin Clarke   Sir Carmichael's brother and prospective heir in Agatha Christie's *The A.B.C. Murders.*

St. John Clarke   Immensely popular novelist of waning prestige who employs Mark Members as secretary in Anthony Powell's *A Buyer's Market.* He fires Members, replacing him with Quiggin, who converts him to Marxism, and later with Guggenbühl, who converts

him to Trotskyism, in *The Acceptance World.* He is abandoned by Guggenbühl in *At Lady Molly's.* He backslides politically; at his death he leaves his money to Lord Erridge in *Casanova's Chinese Restaurant.* His books have resisted revival, but he is the subject of a TV documentary in *Hearing Secret Harmonies.*

Archie Clark-Matthew   Boisterous nephew of Lady Spencer; well groomed and superior-acting, he gets somewhat drunk and makes crude remarks at the ball in Rosamond Lehmann's *Invitation to the Waltz.*

Colonel Juan Claros   Lean and considerate yet stubborn and proud leader of the Cape Creux forces who are to aid in the attack on Rosas Bay in C. S. Forester's *Ship of the Line.*

Claudius   Lame, stuttering historian and stepgrandson of Augustus; he is virtually ignored by all until he is chosen to succeed Caligula as emperor in Robert Graves's *I, Claudius.* He is a trepid Roman emperor who intends, following initial reforms, to restore the Republic but is prevented by successive crises from doing so; he eventually surrenders power to his wife and niece, Agrippinilla, dies at her hands, and is subsequently deified in *Claudius, the God and His Wife Messalina.*

Janet Claverhouse   Sigismund's aged mother, who is devoted to him and his writing in Ivy Compton-Burnett's *Dolores.*

Sigismund Claverhouse   A dramatist of genius who lectures at the women's college that Dolores Hutton attends; he is the love of Dolores's life whom she gives up for her friend Perdita Kingsford and for the sake of Dolores's father in Ivy Compton-Burnett's *Dolores.*

Clay   First lieutenant aboard the *Justinian* in C. S. Forester's *Mr. Midshipman Hornblower.*

Father Clay   Lonely, homesick Catholic priest in Bamba with whom Henry Scobie stays during his investigation of Dicky Pemberton's suicide in Graham Greene's *The Heart of the Matter.*

Christine (Gotobed) Clay   Film actress found murdered at a seashore retreat in Josephine Tey's *A Shilling for Candles.*

Lady Claybody   A romantic with social ambitions; she enjoys Haripol for its ancient traditions but also exhibits warmth and the ability to laugh at herself during the recovery of her dog, Wee Roguie, in John Buchan's *John Macnab.*

Charles Johnson Claybody   Son of Lord Claybody;

his capture of Lord Lamancha reveals the scheme and elicits a laugh and admiration for Lamancha's success in John Buchan's *John Macnab.*

Johnson, Lord Claybody   Wealthy, shrewd Scot, owner of Haripol; he exhibits humor and generosity at the unmasking of "John Macnab" in John Buchan's *John Macnab.*

Clara Clayhanger   Pert, vivacious, youngest sister of Edwin Clayhanger; she declines into the fecund, assenting wife of Albert Benbow in Arnold Bennett's *Clayhanger.* A loyal wife, she becomes a prying, embittered sister; her youthful potential has been erased in her submissive wifehood in *These Twain.*

Darius Clayhanger   A successful Bursley printer but an inarticulate, dictatorial father, haunted by his childhood trauma of being driven into the workhouse; his hidden love for and incomprehension of his son, Edwin, and his lingering death form the context of Edwin's conflicts and development in Arnold Bennett's *Clayhanger.*

Edwin (Teddy) Clayhanger   Intelligent, introspective, compassionate, diffident son; his daily conflicts with his tyrannical father, Darius, and his awkwardness with his sisters, aunt, and neighbors provoke his ingenuous astonishment at human behaviour and his constant efforts to adjust his perspective during his coming of age and first love in Arnold Bennett's *Clayhanger.* He attracts Hilda Lessways by his spontaneously stated insights and makes her realize her true love after the disaster of her bigamous marriage to George Cannon in *Hilda Lessways.* His capacity to view daily life with wonder allows him to adjust and to weather the frictions within his marriage and with his relatives in *These Twain.*

Maggie Clayhanger   Older, placid sister of Edwin Clayhanger; she spends her early years as housekeeper for her widowed father and, following his death, keeps house for her brother, Edwin, until his marriage in Arnold Bennett's *Clayhanger.* Maggie's long years of quiet servitude to her relatives are sporadically interrupted with flashes of independent thinking which finally win her brother's respect in *These Twain.*

Imogen Grantley Claymore   The well-placed, vain, and musically unaccomplished young woman whom Oliver unsuccessfully pursues in William Golding's *The Pyramid.*

Norman Claymore   The socially pretentious and arrogant owner of Stilbourne's newspaper; he gets one of the leads opposite his wife in the town opera in William Golding's *The Pyramid.*

Vera Claythorne   Governess who once deliberately allowed a child to drown; she hangs herself in Agatha Christie's *And Then There Were None.*

Miss Clayton   Headmistress of the school Agatha King attends; she writes progress reports to Agatha's father, Orlando King, in Isabel Colegate's *Orlando at the Brazen Threshold.*

Gabriel Clayton   A dipsomaniac sculptor friend of Wilfred Barclay and Johnny St. John John in William Golding's *The Paper Men.*

Arthur Clegg   Property owner whose house is the object of a disputed real-estate transaction, through which Michael Cullen obtains funds to go to London in Alan Sillitoe's *A Start in Life.*

Ferdinand Clegg   A young working-class man who wins a fortune in a football pool, kidnaps Miranda Grey, and holds her prisoner in a cottage basement; his narration reveals the narrowness and deadness of his inner life, epitomized by his butterfly collection and his pathetic attempts to make Miranda fall in love with him in John Fowles's *The Collector.*

Harry Clegg   Barbara Vaughan's lover, an archaeologist working at the Dead Sea excavation sites; his hoped-for marriage to the Roman Catholic Barbara awaits the annulment of his previous marriage to his long-divorced wife in Muriel Spark's *The Mandlebaum Gate.*

Humphrey Clegg   Forty-five-year-old divorced civil servant with the British Foreign and Commonwealth Office; he invites Anthony Keating to go to Wallacia to escort Jane Murray home and also to take and receive some secret papers in Margaret Drabble's *The Ice Age.*

Sylvia Clegg   Ex-wife of Humphrey Clegg, whom she divorced after discovering he was a solitary transvestite in Margaret Drabble's *The Ice Age.*

Dennis Clement   Sixteen-year-old would-be detective and nephew of Leonard Clement in Agatha Christie's *The Murder at the Vicarage.*

Griselda Clement   Leonard Clement's pretty, much younger wife in Agatha Christie's *The Murder at the Vicarage.* She becomes Miss Jane Marple's great friend and appears in two subsequent mysteries.

Leonard (Len) Clement   Vicar and neighbor of Miss Jane Marple; he is bemused by the antics of his much younger wife, Griselda, in Agatha Christie's *The Murder at the Vicarage.* He appears in *The Body in the Library.*

Cleveland   Crewman of the *Justinian* who acts as Simpson's second in C. S. Forester's *Mr. Midshipman Hornblower*.

Flora Cleveland   Competent only child of her absentminded clergyman father and domestically disorganized mother; she toys with romantic possibilities in the village before she goes up to Oxford in Barbara Pym's *Jane and Prudence*.

Jane Cleveland   Forty-one-year-old intellectual eccentric, wife of a country clergyman she met at Oxford; she is a disorganized housewife and mother of a grown daughter; she occupies herself with trying to arrange the life of her protégée Prudence Bates in Barbara Pym's *Jane and Prudence*.

Nicholas Cleveland   Handsome, bespectacled, vague, middle-aged newcomer clergyman to a village parish; he is bemused by parish disputes and by his wife's unpredictable tangents of thought in Barbara Pym's *Jane and Prudence*.

Sir Henry (nickname "D-G") Clevemore   Director-General of British Secret Intelligence who approves Dr. von Munte's defection in Len Deighton's *Berlin Game*. He assists in the search for a mole and Bret Rensselaer's downfall in *London Match*.

Tony Clevering-Haight   Anglican priest who is a friend of Constantine Ormeau in Elizabeth Bowen's *Eva Trout, or Changing Scenes*.

Hasper Clews   Tall, taciturn, hypochondriacal Chancellor of the Exchequor and member of the War Cabinet; he has risen to his post from being the son of a nonconformist professor of theology in a minor college in Arnold Bennett's *Lord Raingo*.

Miss Cliff   The grey-haired lecturer in English literature at the women's college that Dolores Hutton attends in Ivy Compton-Burnett's *Dolores*.

Clifford   One of the circle of Hunt's people whom Kate Fletcher (Armstrong) found interesting when she was sixteen; he is "butch, thick, hairy, squat", and "travels in Oriental fabrics" in Margaret Drabble's *The Middle Ground*.

Martha Clifford   Woman who writes a suggestive letter in response to a classified advertisement placed by Leopold Bloom; he decides not to respond in James Joyce's *Ulysses*.

Lord Clifton   Elderly major-domo to Lady Casterley; he takes great interest in the future of Lord Miltoun in John Galsworthy's *The Patrician*.

Alexandra Climpson   A good-humored, observant middle-aged woman, who works as Lord Peter Wimsey's "inquiry agent" in Dorothy L. Sayers's *Unnatural Death*. She is Katharine Climpson when, as a juror in Harriet Vane's first murder trial, she holds out for a verdict of not guilty in *Strong Poison*.

Clint   Attorney of James Latter; he advises Jim not to go public in a suit against Chester Nimmo because of the damage it may do to Jim's own name in Joyce Cary's *Not Honour More*.

Clive   American millionaire who befriends Sally Bowles and Christopher Isherwood and offers to fly them off to "nowhere" in Christopher Isherwood's *Goodbye to Berlin*.

Clive   Surgeon who is very cautious in assessing Captain Sawyer's sanity in C. S. Forester's *Lieutenant Hornblower*.

Clive   Young, sharp-suited British espiocrat; he cynically questions Niki Landau and Barley Blair, surreptitiously degrades his American counterparts, and helps run the Russia House's compromising Operation Bluebird in John le Carré's *The Russia House*.

Clive   An inside member of the British Communist Party and an acquaintance of Anna Wulf; he is a communist pamphleteer and journalist in Doris Lessing's *The Golden Notebook*.

Maurice Clive   Handsome ex-fiancé of Dulcie Mainwaring in Barbara Pym's *No Fond Return of Love*.

Mary Clothier   The widowed mother of Pierce Clothier; she falls in love with Willy Kost but eventually is happily married to John Ducane in Iris Murdoch's *The Nice and the Good*.

Pierce Clothier   A teenaged schoolboy who has a summer-vacation love affair with Barbara Gray in Iris Murdoch's *The Nice and the Good*.

Clough   A crewman aboard the *Indefatigable* in C. S. Forester's *Mr. Midshipman Hornblower*.

Clout   Gunner's mate aboard the *Atropos* in C. S. Forester's *Hornblower and the Atropos*.

Clover   Hutch doe rabbit liberated by Hazel's pioneers; she is the first to bear a litter in the new warren in Richard Adams's *Watership Down*.

Esther Clovis   Fiercely loyal resident organizing force and research associate of the Learned Society for anthropologists in Barbara Pym's *Excellent Women*. She performs the same functions for the new Research Centre in *Less Than Angels*. Her memorial service occurs in *A Few Green Leaves*.

Arthur Clun   Professor of history who opposes the appointment of Gerald Middleton to the editorship of a new journal; he admires John Middleton's social-welfare activities; he finally supports Gerald after disclosure of the Melpham fraud in Angus Wilson's *Anglo-Saxon Attitudes*.

Major Clutterbuck   Head of a family of eight; his repudiation of the Alpine hotel at which Denry Machin was honeymooning provokes Denry to attempt to draw customers to his hotel from the hotel of their choice in Arnold Bennett's *The Card: A Story of Adventure in the Five Towns*.

Clutton   The sardonic, talented artist who studies at Amitrano's Studio in Paris with Philip Carey in W. Somerset Maugham's *Of Human Bondage*.

Clynes   A crewman of the *Indefatigable* in C. S. Forester's *Mr. Midshipman Hornblower*.

Andrew Clyth   Powerful Prime Minister; he is influenced by his adored mother to appoint his old Eccles schoolmate Sam Raingo to be Minister of Records and impresses Sam with his comradely demeanor but unique genius for chicanery in Arnold Bennett's *Lord Raingo*.

Bill Coade   Resettlement officer when Timberwork shuts down in Isabel Colegate's *Orlando King*.

Father Cobble   Uncomprehending priest with whom Mick Shaughnessy discusses the De Selby problem in Flann O'Brien's *The Dalkey Archive*.

Eric Cobbley   Struggling artist who is the object of June Forsyte's attempts to help bring him before the public in John Galsworthy's *In Chancery*.

Kitty Cobham   An actress who assumes the identity of the recently dead Duchess of Wharfedale in order to help smuggle orders entrusted to Horatio Hornblower before his capture in C. S. Forester's *Mr. Midshipman Hornblower*.

Ben Cobling   Clara Whittaker's old groom, who supplies information about Whittaker/Dawson family affairs in Dorothy L. Sayers's *Unnatural Death*.

Mr. Coburn   Protestant minister; even though falsely accused of proselytism, he charitably helps the poor Catholic farmers during the blight in Liam O'Flaherty's *Famine*.

Lord Cochrane   Englishman ruined by court martial after years of service; Hornblower continually imagines himself victim of the same fate in C. S. Forester's *Ship of the Line*.

Mrs. Cocker   The housekeeper who discovers Helen Halliday's skeleton and recovers from a dose of poisoned brandy in Agatha Christie's *Sleeping Murder*.

Annette Cockeyne   A spoilt young girl at finishing school who attempts suicide when disappointed in love but takes the wrong tablets and survives in Iris Murdoch's *The Flight from the Enchanter*.

Mrs. Codlyne   The stout widow of a chemist; the increase in taxes on her rented cottages angers her against Mr. Duncalf, her collector, so that Duncalf tells her to place her cottages in other hands; she does so after Duncalf fires Denry Machin, who offers to be her rent collector in Arnold Bennett's *The Card: A Story of Adventure in the Five Towns*.

Father Coffey   Taciturn priest at Paddy Dignam's funeral in James Joyce's *Ulysses*.

Cogshill   The new captain of the *Renown*, formerly of the *Buckler*; he sits as a member of the court of inquiry regarding the *Renown*'s voyage in C. S. Forester's *Lieutenant Hornblower*.

Cohen   An elderly furrier who kept the prostitute Melissa Artemis; he dies painfully from uraemia in Lawrence Durrell's *Justine*. Nessim Hosnani's co-conspirator in procuring arms for Palestinian Jews, he has indiscretely confided in Melissa in *Mountolive*.

Dr. Cohen   A medical man discussed by the nurses at St. Andrews, where Rosamund Stacey goes to have her baby in Margaret Drabble's *The Millstone*.

Mr. Cohen   An orthodox Jewish storekeeper in the station neighboring the Quests' farm, with whose boys Martha Quest develops a friendship in Doris Lessing's *Martha Quest*.

Mrs. Cohen   An orthodox, rather sad Jewish woman, wife of the storekeeper; she is friendly to Martha Quest and worries incessantly about her two sons in Doris Lessing's *Martha Quest*.

Bella (Bello) Cohen   Mistress of a brothel who, in the hallucination of the "Circe" episode, transforms Leopold Bloom into a prostitute; she also calls the police on Stephen Dedalus in James Joyce's *Ulysses*.

Jasmine Cohen   Solly and Joss's cousin and Martha Quest's close friend in Doris Lessing's *Martha Quest*.

She works with Martha in the Communist Party in *A Proper Marriage*, in *A Ripple from the Storm*, and in *Landlocked*. She is tried for treason in *The Four-Gated City*.

Jasper Cohen A senior partner in the town law firm who offers Martha Quest a secretarial job, thus giving her the chance to leave behind her parents' farm in Doris Lessing's *Martha Quest*. He later leaves to help run an army in North Africa in *A Ripple from the Storm*.

Joss Cohen A Jewish intellectual friend of Martha Quest; he experiments with socialism and other political philosophies in Doris Lessing's *Martha Quest*, in *A Proper Marriage*, in *A Ripple from the Storm*, and in *Landlocked*. His expulsion from North Africa by the Colonialist government has brought him to London, England, in *The Four-Gated City*.

Max Cohen Jasper Cohen's brother, also a lawyer, whom Martha Quest dislikes because of his disagreeable and overformal nature in Doris Lessing's *Martha Quest*.

Solly Cohen A rebellious Jewish intellectual who leaves his home to study at the university in Cape Town in Doris Lessing's *Martha Quest*. He returns to the city of his province and attempts to bring reforms for the Africans in Doris Lessing's *A Proper Marriage*, in *A Ripple from the Storm*, and in *Landlocked*.

Miss Cohenson A musical-comedy actress; her fabrication of a connection with the famous painter Priam Farll for her reporter friend Charlie Docksay is overheard by Farll, whose reported death is making headlines in Arnold Bennett's *Buried Alive: A Tale of These Days*.

Coker Homely barmaid to whom Gulley Jimson owes money; she tries to get Gulley's paintings from Sara Monday and Mr. Hickson, but her plan fails; having become pregnant, she loses her job and is forced to live with her mother in Gulley's old apartment in Joyce Cary's *The Horse's Mouth*.

Amanda Coldridge Jill's daughter and Francis Coldridge's stepdaughter, to whom Francis leaves his memoirs of life as it was before the Catastrophe in Doris Lessing's *The Four-Gated City*.

Arthur Coldridge Phoebe Coldridge's ex-husband, who is a member of the Labour left Party and a Member of Parliament; Phoebe maintains a good relationship with him in Doris Lessing's *The Four-Gated City*.

Colin Coldridge Mark Coldridge's brother, who is a physicist working at Cambridge on a bomb during the Cold War; accused of spying for the Soviet Union, he decides to flee his country for the Soviet Union in Doris Lessing's *The Four-Gated City*.

Elizabeth Coldridge Daughter of Mark Coldridge's deceased brother; she visits him because she knows it will create havoc among her stepfamily — all of whom see Mark as a traitor; she later becomes involved with Graham Patten and leaves with him in Doris Lessing's *The Four-Gated City*.

Francis Coldridge Mark Coldridge's son, who suffers from a traumatic relationship with his mentally ill mother; he eventually marries Phoebe Coldridge's daughter, Jill, before establishing a farm commune in Doris Lessing's *The Four-Gated City*.

Galina Coldridge Colin Coldridge's Russian wife, whom he marries after fleeing England in Doris Lessing's *The Four-Gated City*.

Gwen Coldridge Phoebe Coldridge's daughter, who rebels against her mother by joining political activities completely at odds with hers; she later moves to the farm commune in Wiltshire in Doris Lessing's *The Four-Gated City*.

Jill Coldridge Phoebe Coldridge's daughter, who rebels against her mother by joining political activities completely at odds with hers; she later marries Francis Coldridge, moving with him to the farm commune in Wiltshire, and ultimately getting a divorce in Doris Lessing's *The Four-Gated City*.

Lynda Coldridge Mark Coldridge's mentally ill wife (later ex-wife), who very slowly gains her independence from the hospital and drugs; she is able to predict the imminent disaster that will eventually strike Great Britain in Doris Lessing's *The Four-Gated City*. Her therapist instructs her to write down her thoughts and to assist other mental patients in *Re: Colonised Planet 5, Shikasta*.

Mark Coldridge A writer for whom Martha Quest works as a secretary and confidante; through Martha's visions, he is able to develop characters and plots for his novels; ultimately he initiates a plan for a rescue mission and rescue points to save people from the destructive environment they have created in Doris Lessing's *The Four-Gated City*.

Paul Coldridge Sally and Colin's son, who suffers miserably because of his mother's suicide and his father's fleeing; he later becomes rich and helps fund Mark Coldridge's rescue enterprise in Doris Lessing's *The Four-Gated City*.

Phoebe Coldridge Martha Quest's connection in

London; she offers Martha a job working for her ex-brother-in-law, Mark Coldridge, as a secretary; she is herself highly devoted to the Labour party, in which she eventually holds a minor office in Doris Lessing's *The Four-Gated City.*

Sally (Sarah Koenig) Coldridge   Colin's wife, a Jewish refugee from Germany, who commits suicide after her husband flees England for the Soviet Union in Doris Lessing's *The Four-Gated City.*

Giles Coldstream   A rich, anxious, and decidedly alcoholic innocuous weekend guest of Celia and Quentin Villiers; he is obsessed with losing his teeth; he wants most to do nothing, but he can be aroused to cautious movement by the promise of gin in Martin Amis's *Dead Babies.*

Brian Cole   Son of Alderman Cole; he is a fat boy at Seaforth House who out of fear of injury hides equipment to prevent a school boxing tournament which would have pitted him against talented boxers in his weight class in Roy Fuller's *The Ruined Boys.*

Elizabeth (Litchfield) Cole   Deeply troubled woman whose sister killed their tyrannical father in Agatha Christie's *Curtain: Hercule Poirot's Last Case.*

Harry Cole   Blue-collar worker in Clive Ward for ulcer surgery who is bitter towards the bosses of the world; he stays busy helping patients, seeks to keep peace when Ken Adamson and Dai Evans fight, and looks forward to returning home to his wife and son in John Berger's *The Foot of Clive.*

Kate Cole   Wife of Stanley Cole and aunt of General Curzon, for whom she is a source of embarrassment in C. S. Forester's *The General.*

Nat King Cole   Hamilton Ashinow's landlord; he joins Hamilton and his friends in drinking and smoking marijuana in Colin MacInnes's *City of Spades.*

Peter Cole   Young son of Harry Cole; he "lacks confidence" and "has too much imagination" in John Berger's *The Foot of Clive.*

Phyl Cole   Small, dark, energetic wife of Harry Cole; a schoolteacher, she is lovingly called a "great agitator" by her husband in John Berger's *The Foot of Clive.*

Corporal Richard Cole   General Curzon's cousin, son of Stanley and Kate Cole; he is killed in military action after Curzon ignores Kate's written plea for her son's withdrawal and civilian reestablishment in C. S. Forester's *The General.*

Stanley Cole   A Radical, who is father of Corporal Richard Cole and husband to Kate; he stands in political opposition to the Victorian conservatism of his celebrated nephew, General Curzon, in C. S. Forester's *The General.*

Coleman   Exploitative cynic and prophet of despair; stabbed by one mistress, he immediately goes to work on and seduces Rosie Shearwater in Aldous Huxley's *Antic Hay.*

Coleman   Surgeon's mate who assists in the repair of Captain Sawyer after his tumble in C. S. Forester's *Lieutenant Hornblower.*

Miss Coleman ("Collie")   One of three aging spinsters who live in the May of Teck Club in Muriel Spark's *The Girls of Slender Means.*

Walter ("Bill") Coleman   Master of Ceremonies at St. Luke's Church, who jealously protects his position and his tailor-made cassock in Barbara Pym's *A Glass of Blessings.*

Arthur Coles   Friend and research partner of Colin Pasmore; he tries to help Colin and his wife, Kay, while they are estranged in David Storey's *Pasmore.*

Irene Coles   Boyish and unconventional artist; Elizabeth Mapp dreads her powers of mimicry in E. F. Benson's *Miss Mapp.* She is one of Lucia Lucas's allies in *Mapp and Lucia* and in *The Worshipful Lucia.* Her satire of Botticelli's Venus in Victorian attire caricatures Elizabeth Mapp and is named "Picture of the Year" at the Royal Academy in *Trouble for Lucia.*

Captain Kevin Coley   Adjutant and frequently the official representative of the prestigious Pankot Rifles in Paul Scott's *The Day of the Scorpion.* He inevitably spends much time with Mildred Layton, wife of the regiment's commander, who is a prisoner of war in Germany, and is revealed to be Mildred's lover in *The Towers of Silence.*

Father Colgate   A Catholic priest and optimist who says Roger Micheldene's soul is at variance with God; Micheldene, under the influence of alcohol, goes to Colgate's residence and immerses the priest's head in a fishtank in Kingsley Amis's *One Fat Englishman.*

Colin   Young, homosexual server in a Kensington snack bar; he is the object of the hopeless devotion of Leonora Eyre's friend and contemporary Meg in Barbara Pym's *The Sweet Dove Died.*

Dr. Colin   Hard-working, dedicated, early-middle-aged physician employed by the Order in charge of the leper colony; a professed atheist motivated by anger and a strong sense of duty, he finds his salvation in helping others; through his example and uncritical acceptance he helps Querry cure himself of spiritual aridity in Graham Greene's *A Burnt-Out Case.*

Ann Colindale   Gracie Tisbourne's friend, who succeeds in marrying Richard Pargeter in Iris Murdoch's *An Accidental Man.*

Tom Collander   Very successful architect in prison for corruption, keeping almost entirely to himself until Len Wincobank speaks to him; he then proceeds to share with Wincobank ideas which Wincobank finds maddening in Margaret Drabble's *The Ice Age.*

Mr. Colleoni   Wealthy, powerful, elegant-appearing Jewish leader of a rival extortion mob; he engineers a takeover of Pinkie Brown's (formerly Kite's) mob after Kite's death in Graham Greene's *Brighton Rock.*

Colley   Red-haired student at Brookfield who has the distinction of being the first boy Mr. Chips punished; he eventually becomes an alderman of the City of London and a baronet whose son and grandson attend Brookfield in James Hilton's *Good-bye, Mr. Chips.*

Colley (the younger)   Grandson of the first boy Mr. Chips punished at Brookfield and son of another Brookfield boy; he is the butt of Mr. Chips's joke about the stupidity of the Colleys in James Hilton's *Good-bye, Mr. Chips.*

Lord Cuthbert Collingwood   Vice Admiral of the Mediterranean; he was promoted after battle victories as Captain of the *Trafalgar* in C. S. Forester's *Hornblower and the Atropos.*

Reginald Collingwood   Cabinet minister who is an ally of Roger Quaife in C. P. Snow's *Corridors of Power.*

Alfred Collins   Alcoholic who stopped drinking for a period but who lost all remission, according to the prison officer Jim in Margaret Drabble's *The Ice Age.*

Josh Collins   Sardonic computer expert at Darlington University who introduces Robin Dempsey to Eliza, the psychiatric program, in David Lodge's *Small World.*

Sam (covername: Mellon) Collins   Bill Haydon's recruit who becomes Operational Director for British Intelligence; he is dismissed when Operation Testify goes sour in John le Carré's *Tinker, Tailor, Soldier, Spy.* Reinstated by George Smiley for Operation Dolphin, he forces Lizzie Worthington to betray her lover Drake

Ko in *The Honourable Schoolboy.* He conspires with Saul Enderby for Smiley's dismissal in *Smiley's People.*

Mr. Colliphant   Dark-haired, dark-faced, heavy-set master of the Works Department; he fails to deal appropriately with the crises created by a visiting Rajah's demand for a special bed in Arnold Bennett's *Imperial Palace.*

Mr. Collopy   A campaigner for public lavatories for women; while in Rome to seek the Pope's assistance for his project, he crashes through a floor because of his enormous weight in Flann O'Brien's *The Hard Life.*

Nonie Colmar   A sexual tease who is part of a company of foreign acrobats; she is murdered by Barney, a dwarf, after she insults his manhood in J. B. Priestley's *Lost Empires.*

Dorothy Colmore   Wife of Harold Colmore in Roy Fuller's *The Father's Comedy.*

Giles Colmore   Harold Colmore's son; he is completing his compulsory military service in an African colony when he is arrested for striking an officer who he thinks has brutally interrogated some political prisoners; the charge of assault turns to one of murder on the death of the officer in Roy Fuller's *The Father's Comedy.*

Harold Colmore   A chartered accountant who has risen from humble social origins to become the complacent assistant secretary of a major London industrial company; poised to replace the company's secretary in a post which will ultimately give him a knighthood, he leaves England for an African colony to help organize the legal defense of his son, Giles, who is charged with assault; he is also involved in a relationship with Giles's young woman friend in Roy Fuller's *The Father's Comedy.*

The Colonel   Ranking enemy officer who holds the Cartographer captive in a greenhouse to spite the prison-camp Commandant; he becomes the subject of an inquiry at which the Cartographer is the principal witness in Nigel Dennis's *A House in Order.*

Mrs. Colston   Widowed mother of Leo Colston; she discourages him from departing Brandham Hall when his own instincts suggest disaster if he remains as go-between in L. P. Hartley's *The Go-Between.*

Eric Colston   Middle-aged failure, who preys on his aged relatives for money in Muriel Spark's *Memento Mori.*

Godfrey Colston   Retired businessman, husband of

Charmian Piper; his sexual voyeurism makes him suseptible to Mabel Pettigrew's control, and his long-past indiscretions make him her blackmail victim; his selfishness makes him obtuse to death's call in Muriel Spark's *Memento Mori*.

Leo Colston   Impressionable narrator who at age thirteen visits his classmate's rented estate in Norfolk during Summer 1900 and finds himself messenger and inadvertent panderer for a love relationship; fifty years later he returns to the scene of early trauma to deliver a final message between survivors and a new generation in L. P. Hartley's *The Go-Between*.

Dame Lettie Colston   Sister of Godfrey Colston and friendless social reformer; her selfishness, isolation, and fear cause her to misinterpret death's telephone warning and lead to her violent death in Muriel Spark's *Memento Mori*.

Ronald Colt   Director of the British Institute in Zagazig; he invites Edgar Perry to Zagazig to give a lecture in P. H. Newby's *The Picnic at Sakkara*.

Geoffrey Coltham   Critic whose review publicizes Wilfred Desert's religious conversion as an act of cowardice in John Galsworthy's *Flowering Wilderness*.

Commandant of German Prisoner-of-war Camp   An unnamed German officer who disagrees with the sadistic Dr. Halde; he says that the psychologist "does not know about peoples" in William Golding's *Free Fall*.

Composite beings   Beings on various planets where the "individual" is a flock of birds or a swarm of insects in Olaf Stapledon's *Star Maker*.

Father Compton   Graceless, overworked Roman Catholic priest to whom Sarah Miles goes for counseling and announces her intention to convert to Roman Catholicism; while having dinner with Henry Miles and Maurice Bendrix, he reveals his understanding that Maurice's feelings about Sarah are reflected in his anger in Graham Greene's *The End of the Affair*.

Private Compton   Cockney soldier and companion of Private Carr; he strikes Stephen Dedalus in the brothel district in James Joyce's *Ulysses*.

Gordon Comstock   A middle-class working man who tries to resist the lure of an easy, unthinking life by writing poetry and working at a bookstore instead of at a "good job"; he spends the money he receives for the sale of a poem to an American magazine on a convivial binge that ends in his being arrested and fired; after he gets Rosemary pregnant, he finally marries her and takes the good job and all that comes with it in George Orwell's *Keep the Aspidistra Flying*.

Julia Comstock   Gordon Comstock's unmarried sister; though she works seventeen hours a day to make her bills, she lends Comstock money when he is low in George Orwell's *Keep the Aspidistra Flying*.

Captain Concasseur   Officer in the Tontons Macoutes, the Haitian secret police; he briefly befriends Major Jones, discovers Jones is trying to trick him, and pursues Jones and Brown; he is killed by Henri Philipot in Graham Greene's *The Comedians*.

Concepta   Housekeeper who serves Geoffrey Firmin both his drinks and his "strychnine" (cure for alcoholism) in Malcolm Lowry's *Under the Volcano*.

Maurice Conchis   The wealthy Greek owner of Bourani, a villa on the island of Phraxos; he lures Nicholas Urfe into his elaborate "god-game", in which he exposes Urfe to a variety of carefully staged experiences using actors and people from Urfe's life in order to teach him his philosophy of life; he half-fabricates long stories about his own past, including one about the Nazi occupation of Phraxos in John Fowles's *The Magus*.

Conder   Short, balding newspaperman, who tells elaborate lies about his life; Milly Drover attempts to persuade him to publish a story about Rose Coney's signing of the petition to save Jim Drover from execution in Graham Greene's *It's a Battlefield*.

Arnold Condorex (Lord Mondh)   Ambitious and hypocritical politician, who achieves some economic and social power and gains a title; he spars ably with Harriet Hume in an unstable relationship over several years; he sometimes tells her that he thinks of marrying Ginevra, a richer woman from a powerful family; both conceited and insecure, he is interested in politics because he enjoys "the struggle for eminence"; he believes Harriet Hume cannot understand him because he is a man and "a man must rise" in Rebecca West's *Harriet Hume, A London Fantasy*.

Rose Coney   Wife of the constable killed by Jim Drover; Milly Drover persuades her to sign the petition for the reprieve of Drover in Graham Greene's *It's a Battlefield*.

Katherine Coniffe   Elegant wife of Theodore Coniffe and mother of fifteen-year-old Theresa and thirteen-year-old Sara; at age thirty-eight she discovers to her dismay that she is once again pregnant; she dies delivering a third daughter, Lily, in Mary Lavin's *The House in Clewe Street*.

Lily Coniffe Youngest of the three daughters of prosperous Theodore Coniffe; her brief marriage to Cornelius Galloway at the age of seventeen is a source of great bitterness to Theresa, her thirty-two-year-old elder sister, in May Lavin's *The House in Clewe Street*.

Sara Coniffe Second daughter of Theodore Coniffe; the gentle and warm but unassertive aunt of Gabriel Galloway, she timidly tries to shield her orphaned nephew from the harsh Puritanism of her elder sister, Theresa, in Mary Lavin's *The House in Clewe Street*.

Theodore Coniffe Prosperous and conservative widower; he is the owner of properties in Castlerampart, many of them on fashionable Clewe Street; he is the father of Theresa, Sara, and Lily and the grandfather of Gabriel Galloway in Mary Lavin's *The House in Clewe Street*.

Theresa Coniffe Eldest and most assertive of the three daughters of Theodore Coniffe; having regarded Cornelius Galloway as her suitor, she was embittered by his marriage to her sister Lily; she is Gabriel Galloway's rigid, Puritanical, class-conscious aunt in Mary Lavin's *The House in Clewe Street*.

John, Lord Coningsby Polly Hampton's rich and handsome "official young man" during her debutante season; that she has no interest in encouraging him outrages her mother, Lady Montdore, in Nancy Mitford's *Love in a Cold Climate*.

Father John Conmee Jesuit rector of Clongowes School who offers to prevent Father Dolan from pandying Stephen Dedalus in James Joyce's *A Portrait of the Artist as a Young Man*. His perambulations transect the nineteen narratives of "The Wandering Rocks" episode in *Ulysses*.

George Kingham Connell Youngish, ambitious social scientist and criminologist; he is the witness chosen by Frits Krom to substantiate his evidence against Paul Firman in Eric Ambler's *Send No More Roses*.

John Connell Lover of Louise Bennett Halifax and a friend of Louise's husband, Stephen Halifax; because he is an actor, Louise doubts his sincerity, although her sister, Sarah Bennett, suspects he truly loves Louise in Margaret Drabble's *A Summer Bird-Cage*.

Maggie Connemara Kind-hearted Dublin prostitute who befriends Gypo Nolan in Liam O'Flaherty's *The Informer*.

Charlie Conner Hired hand on George Whitney's place; a slave to superstition and an ardent "home-ruler", he helps Arthur Green locate Uncle George, missing in Ireland, in C. Day Lewis's *Child of Misfortune*.

Matt Conner Childhood playmate of Arthur Green; he is now an I.R.A. militant, who leads Arthur into the camp where Uncle George Whitney is captive in C. Day Lewis's *Child of Misfortune*.

Connie Editorial colleague of Nancy Hawkins at Mackintosh & Tooley in Muriel Spark's *A Far Cry from Kensington*.

Connie A red-haired machinist at Jordan's surgical appliances factory in Nottingham in D. H. Lawrence's *Sons and Lovers*.

General Connolly Capable head of Emperor Seth's army who defeats a rebellion against the Azanian government; he and Basil Seal later disagree, however, and Connolly and the Earl of Ngumo join and succeed in overthrowing Seth's government in Evelyn Waugh's *Black Mischief*.

Doris Connolly The leering teenaged eldest of a trio collectively known as "the Connollies"; presumed war evacuees of unknown origin, they wreak havoc wherever they are sent; Basil Seal billets them on various rural families and accepts payment from the families to place them elsewhere in Evelyn Waugh's *Put Out More Flags*.

Marlene Connolly Doris's sister, the drooling youngest of "the Connollies" in Evelyn Waugh's *Put Out More Flags*.

Micky Connolly The lowering brother of Doris and Marlene in Evelyn Waugh's *Put Out More Flags*.

Andrew Connors A man involved with the IRA who poses as an American and whom Alice Mellings suspects of being a Russian; he inadvertently makes Alice and her comrades conspicuous to the authorities in Doris Lessing's *The Good Terrorist*.

Wilfred Connybeare Wealthy brewer and cousin to Nina Woodville; he helps Chester Nimmo make a lot of money in stocks, and his advice helps Chester avoid an insider-information scandal in the Contract Case in Joyce Cary's *Prisoner of Grace*.

Cathleen Conran Wife of Jack and mother of Rose; she is a fussy, querulous woman in C. Day Lewis's *Child of Misfortune*.

Jack Conran Irish uncle visited by Arthur and Oliver Green in C. Day Lewis's *Child of Misfortune*.

Rose Conran Cathleen's provocative and deceitful ten-year old daughter, who cries to her mother in order to escape the consequences of her behavior in C. Day Lewis's *Child of Misfortune.*

Conroy Man involved in a brief relationship with Kate Fletcher Armstrong in Margaret Drabble's *The Middle Ground.*

Bill Conroy Husband of Stella Conroy; he works at the Polytechnic in Margaret Drabble's *A Summer Bird-Cage.*

Stella Conroy Cambridge graduate and wife of Bill Conroy; she spends her day in a domestic chaos of crying babies, spilt food, and a cluttered terrace house; she complains that she has no one intelligent to talk to in Margaret Drabble's *A Summer Bird-Cage.*

Conscientious Objector Young Christian Socialist who is recently out of prison; he is defended by John Lavender from attacks by four commercial travellers in John Galsworthy's *The Burning Spear: Being the Experiences of Mr. John Lavender in Time of War.*

Father Consett Perpetually laughing, untidy, dark-haired, clear-sighted Irish priest, who is Mrs. Satterthwaite's friend; he is hanged by British military authorities in Ulster in Ford Madox Ford's *Some Do Not. . . .* The Roman Catholic Sylvia Tietjens sees him as a saint and martyr who directs her life in *No More Parades* and in *The Last Post.*

Donald Consett Kay's sociologist husband, who cannot find an academic appointment; he gives lectures to the workers in Robin Middleton's plant and is fired when he discloses a family confidence during one of his lectures in Angus Wilson's *Anglo-Saxon Attitudes.*

Kay Consett Daughter of Gerald and Ingeborg Middleton; her hand was burned in a fire from an accident caused by her mother when she was a child; she hates her father for reminding her of it in Angus Wilson's *Anglo-Saxon Attitudes.*

Captain Constable Yvonne Firmin's late father in Malcolm Lowry's *Under the Volcano.*

Constance A primitive woman inhabiting the forest where Charles Watkins finds himself after his shipwreck; she is perhaps a hallucinatory version of his former mistress, Constance Maine, in Doris Lessing's *Briefing for a Descent into Hell.*

Cousin Constance Clare Aubrey's cousin, Jock's wife, and Rosamund's mother; she nurtures her unusual child and is patient about Jock's failures and mean spiritedness in Rebecca West's *The Fountain Overflows.*

Constantine Brilliant young physicist who meets Arthur Miles at Cambridge; he is elected to the Royal Society at very young age; he tries to get Miles the directorship of the National Institute in C. P. Snow's *The Search.*

Constantine Son of Helena and Constantius Chlorus; he rises in military and political influence until he becomes the ruler of the Roman Empire in Evelyn Waugh's *Helena.*

Dr. Constantine Physician who examines Samuel Edward Ratchett's body in Agatha Christie's *Murder on the Orient Express.*

Maria Constantinescu Geoffrey's friend who disrupts life at Ambrose's in Christopher Isherwood's *Down There on a Visit.*

Constantius Chlorus Constantine's father, who is an ambitious Roman military officer; he marries Helena and achieves constant governmental promotions; he ultimately divorces Helena in order to become a Caesar under the Emperor Diocletian; he serves as governor of Dalmatia and eventually is put in charge of Gaul in Evelyn Waugh's *Helena.*

Control Otherwise unnamed head of British Intelligence London Station; he and George Smiley instigate a complex double-doublecross to protect Hans-Dieter Mundt in John le Carré's *The Spy Who Came In from the Cold.* On the trail of a double agent within his inner circle, he is lured into launching an espionage operation that is in fact a set-up; utterly discredited, he dies not long after losing his position in *Tinker, Tailor, Soldier, Spy.*

Conway A fierce and dissipated-looking Australian from Oxford; possessing a strong, unsatisfied sense of community, he is a leader desiring to capture the will of the group, any group, although he is himself without basic belief in C. Day Lewis's *Starting Point.*

Hugh ("Glory") Conway Member of H.M. Consul who is abducted with Miss Roberta Brinklow, Henry D. Barnard, and Captain Charles Mallison when their pilot, Fenner, is mysteriously replaced by Talu, a Tibetan, and flown to Shangri-la, a monastery in Tibet whose monks are hundreds of years old in James Hilton's *Lost Horizon.*

General Aylmer Conyers A capable soldier and family friend of Nicholas Jenkins's grandparents; an amateur psychologist, he comments on Widmerpool's broken engagement to his sister-in-law, Mildred Haycock, in Anthony Powell's *At Lady Molly's*. After his wife's death Conyers marries Geraldine Weedon in *The Kindly Ones*. His marriage is successful in *The Valley of Bones*. He dies in *The Military Philosophers*.

Bertha Conyers   General Conyers's wife, who is twenty years younger than he and twenty years older than her sister, Mildred Haycock, in Anthony Powell's *At Lady Molly's*. She dies in *The Kindly Ones*.

Cook   A short, thin woman, employed by the Donnes; she finds the stairs steep and the house eerie in Ivy Compton-Burnett's *Elders and Betters*.

Cook   The Provincial Lady's servant, who takes revenge against an underequipped kitchen and larder with culinary accidents in E. M. Delafield's *The Diary of a Provincial Lady*.

Mr. Cook   Vanessa's father; his trusteeship of Orlo Porter's inheritance gives teeth to his opposition to Vanessa and Orlo's engagement; he owns the racehorse Potato Chip in P. G. Wodehouse's *Aunts Aren't Gentlemen*.

Vanessa Cook   A beautiful art student and an old flame of Bertie Wooster; the radical politics she shares with her fiancé, Orlo Porter, arouse her father's opposition to the engagement in P. G. Wodehouse's *Aunts Aren't Gentlemen*.

Gilbert Cooke   Bureaucrat in government civil service who works under the direction of Lewis Eliot; his gossip about the suicide of Sheila (Knight) Eliot causes Eliot to have him transferred in C. P. Snow's *Homecomings*.

Elsie Cookson   A previously beautiful and now fat and ugly woman; she was George Bowling's lover when he was young in Lower Binfield; she does not recognize him when he sees her on his outing in George Orwell's *Coming Up for Air*.

Mr. Cool   Black teenager living in Napoli; he is attacked by racists and defended by his half brother, Wilf, in Colin MacInnes's *Absolute Beginners*.

Colonel Cooler   Corrupt American officer and Harry Lime's friend who is present at Lime's supposed demise in Graham Greene's *The Third Man and the Fallen Idol*.

Benjamin ("Kangaroo") Cooley   A Jewish lawyer and former army officer; he is the charismatic, powerful leader of the Australian paramilitary "Diggers" group; he preaches the "love-ideal" of "mateship" as a new social principle that will save Australia, but he is shot during a political rally and dies at the end of D. H. Lawrence's *Kangaroo*.

Charlie Cooper   The main translator coordinator for Global Foods, who not only introduces Kate Brown to her job, but also fulfills the role as nanny to the many delegates, in the same way that Kate does for her family in Doris Lessing's *The Summer Before the Dark*.

Effingham (Effie) Cooper   Former student of Max Lejour, to whom he makes an annual visit; he has developed a romantic fixation on Hannah Crean-Smith; he conspires unsuccessfully with Marion Taylor to rescue Hannah from Gaze Castle in Iris Murdoch's *The Unicorn*.

Marlene Cooper   Rich widow and patron of "The Wider Infinity", a setting for séances in Muriel Spark's *The Bachelors*.

Chester Coote   Pallid, class-conscious friend of Helen Walshingham; he becomes Art Kipps's mentor, advising him how to live like a gentleman but ultimately spurning him when Kipps breaks off with Helen in H. G. Wells's *Kipps: The Story of a Simple Soul*.

Cope   A crewman aboard the *Renown* in C. S. Forester's *Lieutenant Hornblower*.

George Coppard   A Nottingham engineer; he is Gertrude Morel's high-minded, stern father in D. H. Lawrence's *Sons and Lovers*.

Lord Copper   English newspaper magnate who sends William Boot as a war correspondent to Ishmaelia; he is confused by Theodore Boot's later substitution at the banquet honoring Boot's journalistic achievement in Evelyn Waugh's *Scoop*.

Stephen Copperwheat   British government official who notifies Bernard Sands of the government's subsidy for Vardon Hall in Angus Wilson's *Hemlock and After*.

Constance Copthorne   Mistress of Hughie Cantrip; following the crash that killed Hughie and Steven Leadbitter, she delivers the latter's truncated final message to Lady Franklin that he loved her in L. P. Hartley's *The Hireling*.

Aunt Cora   Ex-slaveowner who cares for Antoinette Cosway after her brother Pierre's death until Antoinette goes to the Mt. Calvary Convent; she leaves for England for her health and returns for the same reason; she tries to tell Antoinette not to marry Mr. Rochester in Jean Rhys's *Wide Sargasso Sea*.

Mrs. Coral   Diana Delacroix's helpful neighbor in Elizabeth Bowen's *The Little Girls*.

Mr. Corbett   Engineer who came to the mines of the Gran Seco from Rhodesia; he is now in charge of the coast garrison held by the rebels in John Buchan's *The Courts of the Morning*.

Mr. Corcoran   Headmaster of Rawcliff School where Colin Saville gets a teaching job; Corcoran extinguishes the small spark of enthusiasm with which Colin is pursuing his vocation and fires him in David Storey's *Saville*.

Ludovic (Ludo) Corcos   The son of a wealthy Jewish financier; his friend Augustine Penry-Herbert travels with him in Morocco and in Germany in Richard Hughes's *The Wooden Shepherdess*.

Peter Cordwainer   College friend of Ethan Llewelyn, who believes he should have prevented Peter's suicide two decades ago; Ethan thinks of Peter each time he sees a billboard advertisement for Mother Gettle's Kettle Simmered Soups, made by the Cordwainer family, in Malcolm Lowry's *October Ferry to Gabriola*.

Mrs. Cork (Nanny)   Silvia Fox Tebrick's old nurse, who discovers her mistress as a fox dressed in her jacket lying in a chair in the Tebricks' bedroom; she recognizes her instantly but hurries away and leaves the house for a cottage near Tangley because she hears Richard Tebrick shooting the family dogs to protect his wife's safety in their home; she later returns to the house to care for the couple and tries to be a civilizing influence on Silvia Fox Tebrick in David Garnett's *Lady Into Fox*.

Polly Cork   Mrs. Cork's granddaughter, who lives at Cork's cottage in Tangley with her father, Simon, Mrs. Cork's son; she befriends Silvia Fox Tebrick when Richard Tebrick decides to relocate to the secluded cottage as a means of protecting his wife's secret in David Garnett's *Lady Into Fox*.

Simon Cork   Son of Mrs. Cork and father of Polly; the Cork cottage becomes a place of refuge for the Tebricks in David Garnett's *Lady Into Fox*.

Irene Corker   Spiteful invalid sister of William Corker, with whom she has lived for twelve years; she "talks like a wife but isn't"; bitterly resentful of her brother's leaving her, she leaves all of her money and property at her death to the Radley Rheumatism Clinic in John Berger's *Corker's Freedom*.

William Tracey Corker   Nondescript, gullible, sixty-three-year-old bachelor, who owns and manages an employment agency in Clapham, England; giving slide shows and lectures of his travels in his spare time, he lives with and is henpecked by an invalid sister for twelve intolerable years until one day, determined to be happy, he declares his freedom from her and leaves her in John Berger's *Corker's Freedom*.

Phil Corkery   Quiet, spare man; an occasional lover of Ida Arnold, he assists her in her quest to find Charles Hale's killers by acting as confidant and by accompanying her to the police station in Graham Greene's *Brighton Rock*.

Cornblow   Young, amiable interior decorator who believes the work he performs has a "civilizing or priestly function"; he is rejected by Sergeant Jebb because his superior taste makes Jebb recognize that all he himself wants in life is an attic or hotel with no possessions but his books in Storm Jameson's *There Will Be a Short Interval*.

Cecily Corner   Sister-in-law of Mr. Britling's secretary; she reads extensively, is interested in utopias, and longs for a formal education; she is suspicious of marriage and is pursued by the American Mr. Dierck in H. G. Wells's *Mr. Britling Sees It Through*.

Adam Cornford   Psychiatrist who gives expert testimony for the defense in the trial of Cora Ross and Kitty Pateman in C. P. Snow's *The Sleep of Reason*.

Denise Cornwall-Cope   New wife of Mr. Daintry in Isabel Colegate's *Agatha*.

Isabel Cornwallis   Director of a traveling ballet company; she practices voodoo and kills chickens when her performances are not sold out; she is strict with her dancers in Colin MacInnes's *City of Spades*.

William Cornwallis   Admiral of the English naval fleet; he commands Hornblower, offering advice, gratitude, and praise; he finally helps Hornblower get promoted to Captain in C. S. Forester's *Hornblower and the Hotspur*.

Felix Corrie, Q.C.   Wealthy and sophisticated barrister and owner of the country house Newlands; Miriam Henderson's employer, he comes to represent for her narrow and limited masculine logic in Dorothy Richardson's *Honeycomb*.

Julia Corrie   Indulgent mother and bored woman of leisure, whose life-style both attracts and repels Miriam Henderson; she follows the sensational trial of Oscar Wilde with rapt and shocked attention in Dorothy Richardson's *Honeycomb*.

Sybil Corrie   The twelve-year-old privileged daughter of Felix Corrie in Dorothy Richardson's *Honeycomb*.

Miss Corrigan   Red-haired principal of the secretarial school Meg Eliot attends; she helps Meg succeed in her study to find a position in Angus Wilson's *The Middle Age of Mrs. Eliot*.

Mrs. Corrigan   A resident on the street purchased by Hilary Charwell for his clearance project in John Galsworthy's *Swan Song*.

Fay Corrigan   Very wealthy aunt of Margaret Spencer; she takes Bryan Morley into the Corrigan household in order to send him to Petersons School; her relationship with Bryan becomes questionable as he matures, being more that of lover to lover than guardian to child in David Storey's *A Prodigal Child*.

Harold Corrigan   A wealthy furniture retailer and husband to Fay Corrigan; he finances Bryan Morley's education at Petersons School in David Storey's *A Prodigal Child*.

Signor Cortese   The acclaimed Italian composer of the opera *Lucretia*; his presence at Olga Bracely's dinner party exposes Lucia Lucas's ignorance of Italian in E. F. Benson's *"Queen Lucia"*. He appears in *Lucia in London* and in *Trouble for Lucia*.

Dorothea Cortese   English wife of composer Signor Cortese in E. F. Benson's *Trouble for Lucia*.

Cardinal Cortleigh   Elderly prelate who, in reparation for pains suffered at the Church's hands, offers George Arthur Rose Holy Orders in Frederick William Rolfe's *Hadrian the Seventh*.

Clare Cherrell, Lady Corven   Twenty-year-old daughter of General Sir Conway and Elizabeth Frensham Cherrell; she discusses the background of the Tasburghs with Dinny Cherrell in John Galsworthy's *Maid In Waiting*. She marries Sir Gerald (Jerry) Corven, seventeen years older than she, in *Flowering Wilderness*. In 1931, at twenty-four, she flees her sadistic husband in Ceylon, meets Tony Croom returning to England, and is divorced with Croom as co-respondent in *Over the River*.

Sir Gerald (Jerry) Corven   Government official in British Colonial service; at forty he marries Clare Cherrell before taking a post in Ceylon in John Galsworthy's *Flowering Wilderness*. He treats his wife sadistically in Ceylon and divorces her in *Over the River*.

Cosmic Spirit   A composite mind, made up of the minds of innumerable beings from throughout the cosmos, which makes contact with its own past (the nebulae) and develops a vision of its creator, the Star Maker, in Olaf Stapledon's *Star Maker*.

Cossar   Ferociously determined and single-minded civil engineer and friend of Bensington and Redwood; along with Redwood, Cossar acts as mentor and mediator for the Giants, encouraging their creativity and independence, and, ultimately, their rebellion in H. G. Wells's *The Food of the Gods, and How It Came to Earth*.

Cossar's Sons   Three unnamed Giants who become frustrated with the Little People's laws, limits, and fearful narrow-mindedness; Cossar's sons lead the other Giants in rebellion and conquest, refusing to compromise their belief that they are following natural law in claiming the earth for their own in H. G. Wells's *The Food of the Gods, and How It Came to Earth*.

Mr. Cost   An agent for the spy ring "The Free Mothers"; with Willi Hilfe, he schemes to frame Arthur Rowe for the apparent muder of Cost at a seance, sending Rowe into hiding; Cost first appears as Travers, a businessman to whom Rowe delivers a suitcase supposedly filled with books but actually containing a bomb which seriously injures Rowe; he later appears as Ford, a tailor's assistant; he commits suicide in Graham Greene's *The Ministry of Fear*.

Dr. Costam   Young, satiric hotel medical man; his treatments of various women's illnesses and emergencies are based upon his belief that the women must be deceived for their own good in Arnold Bennett's *Imperial Palace*.

Arnold Coster   Eighteen-year-old son of Frances and Stephen Coster in 1939; he admires David Renn, comforts a neglected child, Lise Brett, and very briefly loves Georgina Swan in London in Storm Jameson's *Before the Crossing*. In 1945 he is a twenty-four-year-old discharged Airforce Flight-Lieutenant, the private pilot of William Gary, a close companion of Edward West, and the hesitant but successful lover of Lise Brett in Storm Jameson's *The Black Laurel*.

Frances Coster   Dominating wife of Stephen Coster; she seeks to direct and even to smother their son, Arnold, with her anxious solicitude and desire for his safety; against her husband's wishes, she approaches his financial sponsors, Evelyn Lamb and Sir Thomas and Lady Harben, and arranges for Arnold to avoid military service, but he secretly enlists in the air force in Storm Jameson's *Before the Crossing*.

Stephen Coster   Editor of a conservative paper, *The Order*; he is the husband of Frances Coster in an incompatible marriage and the father of Arnold Coster;

he seeks financial support from Evelyn Lamb and Nancy, Lady Harben in Storm Jameson's *Before the Crossing.*

Johnny Costuopolis   The Greek head waiter at the sports club where all of the young people gather nightly for dinner and dancing in Doris Lessing's *Martha Quest.*

Mrs. Cosway (Mrs. Mason)   Antoinette's unloving, irrational, and helpless mother; a beautiful West Indian Creole, she is the widowed second wife of an impoverished landowner; she marries the wealthy Mr. Mason but becomes slowly, irrevocably insane and dies when Antoinette is sixteen years old in Jean Rhys's *Wide Sargasso Sea.* See Antoinetta Mason in *Dictionary of British Literary Characters 18th- and 19th-Century Novels.*

Antoinette Cosway   Beautiful West Indian Creole of English descent with long, sad, dark, alien eyes, a pleading expression, and a family history of madness; she marries Mr. Rochester, who renames her Bertha; increasingly unhappy and irrational, she is incarcerated in the attic of her husband's English house in Jean Rhys's *Wide Sargasso Sea.* See Bertha Antoinetta Mason Rochester in *Dictionary of British Literary Characters 18th- and 19th-Century Novels.*

Daniel Cosway (Boyd)   Antoinette Cosway's kinsman, who writes letters to Mr. Rochester telling him of Antoinette's true background and inherited tendency toward madness in Jean Rhys's *Wide Sargasso Sea.*

Pierre Cosway   Antoinette's younger broher, who "staggered when he walked and couldn't speak distinctly"; he dies as result of fire at Coulibri, their estate, in Jean Rhys's *Wide Sargasso Sea.*

Jack Cotery   Schoolchum of Lewis Eliot; he urges Eliot not to be hurt by Mr. Peck's insults and warns Eliot in 1925 to stay away from Sheila Knight; he is implicated in the lawsuit for fraud against George Passant in C. P. Snow's *Time of Hope.* He is a businessman and entrepreneur who drops out of the technical school when he loses his subsidy from Calvert to learn printing; he goes into business with financial help from George Passant and seduces Olive Calvert away from Arthur Morcom; he is tried and acquitted of fraud in *Strangers and Brothers.* He is divorced from his second wife; he is religious and tries to convert Eliot in *The Sleep of Reason.*

Cothope   Engineer who assists George Ponderevo in his aeronautical work in H. G. Wells's *Tono-Bungay.*

Councillor Cotterill   Portly, apparently affluent builder; his patronizing responses annoy Denry Machin, and his bankruptcy precipitates Denry's proposal to his daughter, Nellie, in Arnold Bennett's *The Card: A Story of Adventure in the Five Towns.*

Nellie Cotterill   Councillor Cotterill's shy daughter and Ruth Earp's friend; Nellie admires Denry Machin but thinks he will marry Ruth Earp until the day of Nellie's departure as bankrupt for America, when Denry sweeps her off the boat and into an unconventional marriage with him in Arnold Bennett's *The Card: A Story of Adventure in the Five Towns.*

Mr. Cotton   Associate of Mr. Daintry in Isabel Colegate's *Orlando at the Brazen Threshold.*

Miss Counihan   Woman who loves Murphy — as long as he is off seeking his fortune in London — in Samuel Beckett's *Murphy.*

Julius Court   Young, rich, hedonistic owner of a cottage on the grounds of Toynton Grange in P. D. James's *The Black Tower.*

Hubert Courtenay   An elderly, dignified gentlemanly performer; once a Shakespearean actor, he is now a supporting member of Tommy Beamish's act in J. B. Priestley's *Lost Empires.*

Prudence Courteney   Frivolous daughter of the British ambassador to Azania; one of her love affairs is with Basil Seal; later a plane in which she is riding crashes in the jungle, and she is captured and eaten by cannibals and — inadvertently — by Basil in Evelyn Waugh's *Black Mischief.*

Samson Courteney   The imperturbable British minister to Azania who seems to regard his job as a perpetual vacation in Evelyn Waugh's *Black Mischief.*

Charles Courtier   Forty-year-old radical author of books against war; a longtime friend of Audrey Noel, he courts Lady Barbara Carádoc though discouraged by her family; he gives her up to Lord Harbinger when he goes off to Persia in John Galsworthy's *The Patrician.*

Emile Cousin   Sedate, reserved, cigar-smoking hotel manager upon whom Evelyn Orcham relies in Arnold Bennett's *Imperial Palace.*

Dr. Coutras   The French physician who diagnoses Charles Strickland's leprosy and narrates both Strickland's death and the fate of Ata and their young son in W. Somerset Maugham's *The Moon and Sixpence.*

Merle Coverdale   Head of the typing pool at Meadows, Meade & Grindley; her affair with the married Vincent Druce ends with her murder in Muriel Spark's *The Ballad of Peckham Rye.*

Florence ("Florrie") Covert (Mrs. "Jos" Utlaw)   Utlaw's fiancée, daughter of a country clergyman, deeply in love and ambitious for both Utlaw and herself in John Buchan's *A Prince of the Captivity.*

Mr. Justice Covill   Judge who hears the suit of divorce brought by Sir Gerald Corven against his wife, Clare, in John Galsworthy's *Over the River.*

Linda Cowlard   "A vast dazzling blonde" and the resident lover of Albert Sanger; Linda is "splendidly stupid" and indolent, but her great beauty attracts Kiril Trigorin when he comes to visit Sanger, and she has an affair with him in Margaret Kennedy's *The Constant Nymph.*

Sergeant-Major Cowley   Army professional with a walrus moustache and scarlet cheeks who serves under Captain Christopher Tietjens on the Western Front; he watches over his men and over Tietjens with motherly tenderness in Ford Madox Ford's *No More Parades.*

Father Bob Cowley   Debt-ridden priest who owes money to Reuben J. Dodd and accompanies Simon Dedalus in James Joyce's *Ulysses.*

Cecil Cowley   Man who seeks to be with "the right people" in London, Paris, and New York; he is fat, flaccid, coquettish, has a "big snout", and is described as a "cultural insect" with merely superficial interest in the arts; he takes Mary Brett as mistress after she rejects Edward West in Storm Jameson's *The Black Laurel.*

Cowslip   Rabbit who guides conduct in the Warren of the Snares in Richard Adams's *Watership Down.*

Mrs. Coyte   Wealthy landowner who gives the elder Tom Nimmo a job as foreman on her farm in Joyce Cary's *Except the Lord.*

Fred Coyte   Underachieving son of the wealthy landowner Mrs. Coyte; he becomes engaged to Georgina Nimmo but is later rejected and dies a poor man in Joyce Cary's *Except the Lord.*

Norma Cozens   The lecturing and intrusive but essentially good-natured wife of an Oxford colleague of Alfred Wincham; she constantly drops in on the recently married Fanny (Logan) Wincham in Nancy Mitford's *Love in a Cold Climate.*

Crab   Young man with dyed red hair; a former member of Pinkie Brown's mob, he joins Colleoni's mob;

he serves to point out the instability of Pinkie's position as new leader of Kite's mob and thus to further frighten Spicer in Graham Greene's *Brighton Rock.*

Alf Crabb   Scotland Yard inspector who investigates the death of Nonie Colmar; he is finally no match for the shrewder Nick Ollanton, who enables Barney to escape in J. B. Priestley's *Lost Empires.*

Crabbe   The recently deceased old don; he was a friend of Nicholas Herrick, William Masson, and Richard Bumpus in Ivy Compton-Burnett's *Pastors and Masters.*

Lieutenant Crabbe   Aggressive, patriotic fellow army officer who leads a group to dunk Dan Graveson's head in grease for his Marxist discourses in the mess hall in Alan Burns's *Buster.*

Cissie Crabbe   The Provincial Lady's old friend, whose postcards with pictures of exotically distant landmarks have Norwich postmarks in E. M. Delafield's *The Diary of a Provincial Lady.* She also appears in *The Provincial Lady Goes Further.*

Mickey Crabbe   Politically and sexually impotent Bonn Embassy official; he relates Leo Harting's bar fight in Cologne to Alan Turner in John le Carré's *A Small Town in Germany.*

Crabbin   Confused British Council representative who, believing Rollo Martins, whose pseudonym is Buck Dexter, to be the novelist Benjamin Dexter, a stylist in the Henry James tradition, arranges a lecture for the hack writer of westerns in Graham Greene's *The Third Man and the Fallen Idol.*

Arthur Crabtree   Billy Fisher's fellow worker and friend; he is finally put off by Billy's constant lying in Keith Waterhouse's *Billy Liar.*

Mr. Crackamup   News editor for a journal; he is assigned the task of running John Lavender's article on a plan to starve German prisoners in John Galsworthy's *The Burning Spear: Being the Experiences of Mr. John Lavender in Time of War.*

Craddock   Driver for Eustace Cherrington; his mentioning to the youngster that "we shall be losing you before long", on the assumption, unspoken to the boy, that he will be going to boarding school following receipt of his legacy, inspires the boy to think he is facing imminent death in L. P. Hartley's *The Shrimp and the Anemone.*

Mrs. Craddock   Philandering wife of Charles Craddock; she dies in Egypt of an infection in Agatha Christie's *Cards on the Table.*

Alan Craddock　　Eric's older brother, who is a rising Inspector of Education; he tries to dissuade Eric from his life of homosexuality in Angus Wilson's *Hemlock and After.*

Father Brendan Craddock　　Cato Forbes's friend, whose wise advice Cato is too infatuated to take in Iris Murdoch's *Henry and Cato.*

Celia (Mimi) Craddock　　Eric's American mother, who loses her battle to keep Eric with her in Angus Wilson's *Hemlock and After.*

Charles Craddock　　Suspicious husband who dies of anthrax while intending to present a complaint against Dr. Roberts in Agatha Christie's *Cards on the Table.*

Edward Joseph Craddock　　An Oxford University rowing-man whose last will and testament leaves everything to Zuleika Dobson in Max Beerbohm's *Zuleika Dobson; or An Oxford Love Story.*

Eric Craddock　　Twenty-eight-year-old lover of Bernard Sands; he works in a London bookstore and is thought to be a poet; he finally succeeds in breaking from the influence of his mother in Angus Wilson's *Hemlock and After.*

Jack Craddock　　Fifty-nine-year-old, short, stout, shrewd meat buyer for the hotel; he marvels at Evelyn Orcham's knowledge of foods yet lack of pretense, but he is shocked at Orcham's taking Gracie Savotte to the Smithfield market in Arnold Bennett's *Imperial Palace.*

Howard Craggs　　A left-wing publisher; he employs Gypsy Jones, whose duties presumably include sleeping with him in Anthony Powell's *A Buyer's Market.* His publishing career progresses, and he is knighted in *The Military Philosophers.* He becomes J. G. Quiggin's partner; he marries Gypsy and tolerates her infidelity in *Books Do Furnish a Room.* He dies in *Temporary Kings.*

Phil Craigan　　Best moulder in the Dupret foundry; he shares his house with and controls the lives of Joe and Lily Gates until his forced retirement saps his strength and his dominance in Henry Green's *Living.*

Constant Craige　　Factory owner in debt to Sir Horace Stimms; he houses his underpaid workers in two "infamous" blocks of cottages in Richard Aldington's *The Colonel's Daughter.*

Craik (Belfast)　　Sailor on the *Narcissus* in Joseph Conrad's *The Nigger of the "Narcissus".*

Miss Crail　　Supervisory librarian at the Bayswater Library for Psychic Research whose verbal abuse of Alec Leamas helps Liz Gold fall in love with him in John le Carré's *The Spy Who Came In from the Cold.*

Amyas Crale　　Licentious painter, whose wife was convicted of his murder; their daughter, Carla Lemarchant, asks Hercule Poirot to investigate the sixteen-year-old case in Agatha Christie's *Five Little Pigs.*

Caroline Crale　　Wife of Amyas Crale, of whose poisoning she was accused and convicted in Agatha Christie's *Five Little Pigs.*

Olive Cramier　　Four-years-married wife of Robert Cramier; at age twenty-six she begins an affair with Mark Lennon at Monte Carlo and dies of drowning when she and Mark are attacked in a boat while she is leaving her husband in John Galsworthy's *The Dark Flower.*

Robert Cramier　　Forty-two-year-old Member of Parliament who pursues his wife, Olive, when she flees with Mark Lennon and causes her to drown when he attacks them in a boat in John Galsworthy's *The Dark Flower.*

Crane　　Henry Wilcox's chauffeur in E. M. Forster's *Howards End.*

Clarissa Crane　　A popular novelist who is a neighbor of Dollie Stokesay; she is researching medieval history for a new novel but changes her subject after disclosures of truth about the Melpham artifacts in Angus Wilson's *Anglo-Saxon Attitudes.*

Edwina Crane　　Superintendent of the Protestant mission schools in the Mayapore District; she and Mr. D. R. Chaudhuri, an Indian teacher from Dibrapur, are attacked by a mob of locals, and Chaudhuri is killed; though Edwina is not severely injured, she never recovers emotionally from the incident and eventually commits suicide in Paul Scott's *The Jewel in the Crown.*

Evelyn Crane　　Richard's vivacious, irresponsible, irrevocably attached sister; desirous of their "bolshi" friend, Steve Hallem, she intends her brother for an innocent local, Anna Charteris, who is herself taken with Steve; Evelyn manages an affair with Steve in C. Day Lewis's *The Friendly Tree.*

Richard Crane　　Well-born, cynical writer of detective fiction; he is inordinately attached to his sister, Evelyn, with whom he lives in an "agreeable ambiance of privilege"; he is somewhat in love with Anna Charteris in C. Day Lewis's *The Friendly Tree*.

Mrs. Crankshaw Mother of Barbara Cherrington's husband, Jimmy; she tries a bit of futile match-making for Eustace Cherrington at the wedding of her son in L. P. Hartley's *The Sixth Heaven*.

Jimmy Crankshaw Man who marries Barbara Cherrington; he is "a representative of the Better Sort rather than the Finer Grain", but Eustace Cherrington warms to his friendliness and directness in L. P. Hartley's *The Sixth Heaven*. He and Barbara have a young son whom they name Eustace in *Eustace and Hilda*.

Cranly Stephen Dedalus's university friend who circulates a petition for universal peace in James Joyce's *A Portrait of the Artist as a Young Man*.

Faith Cranmer Hope Cranmer's stepdaughter, who opposes fox hunting and other cruelty to animals in Ivy Compton-Burnett's *Parents and Children*.

Gabriel Cornelia Lucy Perceval Cranmer Mistress of Overy Hall and wife of Squire Justin Cranmer of Hungrygrain; she has been the victim of Cranmer's fiendish plot to use her as a decoy in his nightmarish schemes to destroy England and to assassinate her cousin, Spencer Perceval, the Prime Minister; after the death of Cranmer she is restored to health and to hope in a happy future with Lord Belses in John Buchan's *The Free Fishers*.

Hope Cranmer Ridley Cranmer's stepmother and a neighbor of Eleanor Sullivan; there is something second-rate about her in Ivy Compton-Burnett's *Parents and Children*.

Justin Cranmer Squire of Hungrygrain, a justice of the peace, and deputy-lieutenant for the county of Northumberland; his attempt to kill Anthony Lammas and to assassinate Spencer Perceval, the Prime Minister, fails when Sir Turnour Wyse shoots Cranmer in John Buchan's *The Free Fishers*.

Paul Cranmer Ridley's and Faith's quiet father, who is often in the background in Ivy Compton-Burnett's *Parents and Children*.

Ridley Cranmer A lawyer who conceals knowledge of Fulbert Sullivan's return in order to try to marry Eleanor Sullivan in Ivy Compton-Burnett's *Parents and Children*.

Nobby Cranton London jewel thief, a conspirator in the theft of Mrs. Wilbraham's necklace; the body un-

earthed in the Fenchurch St. Paul churchyard is thought to be his in Dorothy L. Sayers's *The Nine Tailors: Changes Rung on an Old Theme in Two Short Touches and Two Full Peals*.

Crashaw One of two cronies on the staff of Lord Raingo's Ministry of Records; Raingo hopes to see them to ease his awkward entry for the first time to the St. James's Club frequented by government members in Arnold Bennett's *Lord Raingo*.

Nurse Craven Opportunistic manhunter who knows that her patient, Barbara Franklin, is not in bad health in Agatha Christie's *Curtain: Hercule Poirot's Last Case*.

Stella Craven Villem Craven's wife, who wants her husband to become thoroughly British and therefore forbids George Smiley any contact, forcing Smiley to interrogate Villem secretly in John le Carré's *Smiley's People*.

Villem (William) Craven Estonian exile and occasional courier for General Vladimir and his freedom movement who risks his British passport and residency to carry Otto Leipzig's clues to Karla's secret to General Vladimir in John le Carré's *Smiley's People*.

Bill Craw Legendary Australian journalist and British Intelligence agent who feeds information on Jerry Westerby's activities to George Smiley and who visibly represents Smiley's disillusion at his betrayal and Westerby's and Luke's death in John le Carré's *The Honourable Schoolboy*.

Thomas Carlyle Craw Scots newspaper magnate who leases Castle Gay; sought by Evallonian conspirators who seek to use Craw and his influence to insure British support, he moves under John Galt's tutelage on their walking tour from childish sulkiness and despair to become a "new man", as he recognizes the inadequacy of his former values in John Buchan's *Castle Gay*.

Myles Crawford Editor of the *Weekly Freeman and National Press* who refuses to give a commission to Leopold Bloom in James Joyce's *Ulysses*.

Redvers T. A. Crawford Scientist and fellow of the Cambridge college who has a strong reputation for the quality of his research in physiology; he is elected as Master in a close vote over Paul Jago in C. P. Snow's *The Masters*. He is nearing the end of his mastership and conducts the deliberations of the Court of Seniors into the affair of Donald Howard's fellowship; he finally votes for restoration of the fellowship in *The Affair*.

David Crawfurd Young, courageous Scots boy-hero; he joins in the effort to combat John Laputa's evil enterprise; later he uses the treasure of Prester John to create a college for black Africans in John Buchan's *Prester John*.

Frank Crawley Maxim de Winter's agent and loyal friend, who also befriends the second Mrs. de Winter in Daphne Du Maurier's *Rebecca*.

Cray The landing-party member who is in charge of swabbing the cannons for precaution against hot shot in C. S. Forester's *Lieutenant Hornblower*.

Hannah Crean-Smith An heiress who made an unhappy marriage to her bisexual, abusive cousin; guilt and religion have made her an accomplice in her imprisonment at Gaze Castle since, seven years ago, she almost killed her husband during a row over her affair with Pip Lejour; believing her husband about to return, she shoots her keeper, Gerald Scottow, and commits suicide in Iris Murdoch's *The Unicorn*.

Peter Crean-Smith Hannah's abusive absent husband, who keeps her imprisoned in their isolated house under the watchful eyes of servants, especially his homosexual lover Gerald Scottow; returning after a seven years' absence, he is deliberately killed in a car crash by Denis Nolan in Iris Murdoch's *The Unicorn*.

Albert Creech The Jenkins family's weary, egotistical, self-taught cook, who is loved by Billson, the emotionally unstable maid; he marries another and leaves the Jenkinses, eventually managing the Bellevue Hotel in Anthony Powell's *The Kindly Ones*. His death is mentioned in *The Military Philosophers*.

Joshua (Westminster) Creed Aged newspaper vender, once a butler, who gives evidence to police after Hughes stabs his wife in John Galsworthy's *Fraternity*.

Warren Creevey Man of misdirected genius and brilliant intellect whose powers are devoted to goals of self-glorification and who is changed by the self-sacrifice of Adam Melfort in John Buchan's *A Prince of the Captivity*.

Mrs. Creevy A disagreeable, selfish old woman who runs the Ringwood House Academy for Girls where Dorothy Hare teaches and who forces Dorothy to stay hungry most of the time and will not let her teach the students anything but basic math and penmanship because that is what parents want to see from their daughters in George Orwell's *A Clergyman's Daughter*.

Creighton Officer on the *Narcissus* wounded during a storm in Joseph Conrad's *The Nigger of the "Narcissus"*.

Crenshaw A shrewd, alcoholic poet; Philip Carey, studying art in Paris, becomes fascinated with Crenshaw, realizing that mediocrity ends in cynical disillusionment in W. Somerset Maugham's *Of Human Bondage*.

Alice Cressett Daughter of Barker and bullying wife of Harold Cressett; she cares for her crippled father in his last years; she helps her father blackmail Canon Portway over the Melpham affair and is convicted of killing her husband in Angus Wilson's *Anglo-Saxon Attitudes*.

Harold Cressett Husband of Alice; he is a victim of British bureaucracy and is made a public cause by John Middleton; he is murdered by his wife in Angus Wilson's *Anglo-Saxon Attitudes*.

Colonel Cresswell Brother of Adele, Lady Brixton; when Adele purchases Lucia Lucas's Riseholme property, he conveniently makes an offer for Georgie Pillson's in E. F. Benson's *Mapp and Lucia*.

Cretha Si's wife and the mother of Orfik and Iyfilka in Brian W. Aldiss's *Helliconia Spring*.

Angela Crevy Young woman who joins an older, more advanced social set; she has a dominating power over her jealous and love-sick fiancé Robin Adams, in Henry Green's *Party Going*.

Arthur Crewe Stepfather of Dixie Morse in Muriel Spark's *The Ballad of Peckham Rye*.

Leslie Crewe Half brother of Dixie Morse and member of Trevor Lomas's loutish gang in Muriel Spark's *The Ballad of Peckham Rye*.

Mavis Crewe First G.I. bride from Peckham and mother of Leslie Crewe and Dixie Morse in Muriel Spark's *The Ballad of Peckham Rye*.

Yod Crewsy Celebrated, loutish pop musician who plagiarizes F. X. Enderby's poetry with the connivance of Vesta Bainbridge in Anthony Burgess's *Inside Mr. Enderby* and in *Enderby Outside*.

Christiana Crich The eccentric, resentful wife of colliery owner Thomas Crich in D. H. Lawrence's *Women in Love*.

Diana Crich Gerald Crich's young sister who drowns in the lake at Shortlands during the water party in D. H. Lawrence's *Women in Love*.

Gerald Crich   Thomas Crich's son and Gudrun Brangwen's lover; he becomes a wealthy and modern industrialist who is driven by an inner emptiness and his destructive relationship with Gudrun to commit suicide; he dies by freezing in the snow in D. H. Lawrence's *Women in Love.*

Laura Crich   Thomas Crich's daughter who is the bride in the wedding scene that opens D. H. Lawrence's *Women in Love.*

Thomas Crich   The paternalistic old colliery owner in D. H. Lawrence's *Women in Love.*

Winifred Crich   Gerald Crich's precocious youngest sister, who has artistic talent in D. H. Lawrence's *Women in Love.*

Crichton   Aide to the British ambassador to Argentina who relieves Charley Fortnum of his position as Honorary Consul in the final pages of Graham Greene's *The Honorary Consul.*

Cricklade   One of a group of Brookfield boys patrolling the railway lines who asks Mr. Chips what he should do should he meet any strikers in James Hilton's *Good-bye, Mr. Chips.*

Crikey   One of a gang of boys in Benditch who blow up an explosives shed with D.'s gun, thus helping D. win a small victory in Graham Greene's *The Confidential Agent.*

Thomas Crimplesham   A solicitor who answers Lord Peter Wimsey's advertisement offering the return of the eyeglasses found on the body in Alfred Thipp's bathtub in Dorothy L. Sayers's *Whose Body?.*

Mr. Critchlow   Harsh realist and Methuselah of St. Luke's Square; his wry criticisms chart the years; he, late in life, marries the desiccated Miss Insull, clerk of Baines's store, in Arnold Bennett's *The Old Wives Tale.*

Mr. Crofts   Solicitor for the defense who thinks his client, Harriet Vane, is guilty in Dorothy L. Sayers's *Strong Poison.*

Dr. Acton Croke   Eminent London medical specialist who diagnoses the unusual weariness of Sir Edward Leithen and Mr. Palliser-Yeates as boredom with life in John Buchan's *John Macnab.* He tells Leithen that he has less than a year to live in John Buchan's *Sick Heart River.*

Else Crole   Fourteen-year-old girl, a servant at D.'s London hotel; she devotedly helps D. until she is mur-

dered by the manageress and K. in Graham Greene's *The Confidential Agent.*

Dougal Crombie   Chieftain and canny leader of the Gorbals Die-Hards; he aids Dickson McCunn in rescuing Sakskia, the Russian princess, and preserving her jewels in John Buchan's *Huntingtower.* He again joins forces with McCunn, his benefactor, and Jaikie (John Galt), another former Die-hard, in teaching self-control and objectivity to his boss, Thomas Carlyle Craw, and the quarreling Evallonian political factions in *Castle Gay.* In the confidence of Craw and gradually taking over the position of general manager of the Craw Press, he realizes that a Royalist rebellion would be upset by the new third party, Juventus, and seeks Dickson McCunn's advice and aid again in *The House of the Four Winds.*

George Crome   Captain of the frigate *Syrtis* who allows Hornblower and the Spaniards to return to Ferrol in accordance with the rules of law in C. S. Forester's *Mr. Midshipman Hornblower.*

Jack Crompton   English consulting engineer who tries to help organize the work-relief effort in Crom during the blight in Liam O'Flaherty's *Famine.*

James Bernard (Tony) Croom   Unemployed young man who meets Clare Corven on a ship from Ceylon; he finds employment caring for Jack Muskham's horses; he becomes co-respondent in Clare's divorce from Sir Gerald Corven in John Galsworthy's *Over the River.*

Cropper   A boarder at Seaforth House school who is in charge of the library in Roy Fuller's *The Ruined Boys.*

Evelyn Gotobed Cropper   Bertha Gotobed's sister and former fellow housemaid in Agatha Dawson's service; she married and emigrated but returns to England for Bertha's funeral in Dorothy L. Sayers's *Unnatural Death.*

Crosby   Servant and housekeeper to the original Pargiter family; Crosby assists Eleanor in her duties as "angel of the house" in Virginia Woolf's *The Years.*

Crosby   Head servant at Anchorstone Hall during the Staveleys' houseparty in L. P. Hartley's *The Sixth Heaven.*

Abel Cross   Guard on the Rover Mail; Sir Turnour Wyse appropriates his coach for the last desperate run to Fenny Horton and the defeat of Squire Cranmer's plan in John Buchan's *The Free Fishers.*

Sir Henry Cross   A supposedly intimidating figure

who proves scarcely a threat to General Curzon or anyone else in C. S. Forester's *The General.*

Mr. Crossby High-spirited journalist and long-distance runner; seeking a story about the archaeological discovery of the Viking barrow of "Harold Blacktooth", he agrees to act as a decoy for Sir Edward Leithen in his attempt to kill a salmon in the waters at Strathlarrig in John Buchan's *John Macnab.*

Superintendent Crosse Policeman who takes the Assistant Commissioner along to make the arrest of a murderer in Graham Greene's *It's a Battlefield.*

Canon Crow John Crow's grandfather, whose death at ninety has brought John back to Glastonbury in John Cowper Powys's *A Glastonbury Romance.*

John Crow A cynical adventurer who returns upon his grandfather's death to Glastonbury after fifteen years in France; he re-encounters and marries his cousin Mary, inveigles a position as Johnny Geard's secretary, and, disdainful of Glastonbury, leaves with Mary for Norfolk in John Cowper Powys's *A Glastonbury Romance.*

Mary Crow A cousin of John Crow employed as the companion of the spinster Euphemia Drew; she and John become lovers, marry, and, contemptuous of Glastonbury's overawing spiritual character, leave for Norfolk in John Cowper Powys's *A Glastonbury Romance.*

Philip Crow John Crow's third cousin, an ambitious Glastonbury industrialist who battles Johnny Geard's efforts to revive the town's religious past and the communists' attempts to collectivize its business and industry; he fails on both counts and goes bankrupt, vowing to "begin again" in John Cowper Powys's *A Glastonbury Romance.*

Lady Crowan A guest at Manderly who asks Maxim de Winter about continuing the tradition of the Manderly costume ball; Maxim's decision to have the ball is the occasion for a public humiliation of his second wife, engineered by Mrs. Danvers in Daphne Du Maurier's *Rebecca.*

Anne Crowder Detective-Sergeant Mather's romantically misled fiancée and James Raven's "moll"; after being terrorized by Raven, she joins him in his search for Davis but betrays him to Mather and his death in Graham Greene's *A Gun for Sale.*

Mrs. Crowe Young woman who travels to interview with the Committee for Aid to the Elderly; she sullenly agrees to accept her aged mother into her home in Angus Wilson's *The Middle Age of Mrs. Eliot.*

Mrs. Crowe Obsessive widow whose desire to be near Hadrian VII impells her to join Jerry Sant's blackmailing scheme in Frederick William Rolfe's *Hadrian the Seventh.*

Old Crowe Old man who lives in the same boarding house as Ida Arnold and partners her as they consult the Ouija Board in Graham Greene's *Brighton Rock.*

Letty Crowe Spinster in her mid-sixties; she is a clerk in an undefined office who lives alone in a bed-sitting room, her retirement plans overthrown by her friend's impending marriage, until her landlady sells the building to an African evangelical pastor in Barbara Pym's *Quartet in Autumn.*

Emily Crowne William's "elusively radiant" twin, who possesses a "divine purity of outline"; the daughter of Norman Crowne, she inherits his dreaminess and childlike attitude but unlike her father and brother consciously defies her fate and marries Philip Luttrell, conceives a child, and becomes blissfully happy in Margaret Kennedy's *Red Sky at Morning.*

Lenina Crowne Attractive genetic worker who after disaffection with Bernard Marx develops an emotional interest in the uncivilized John Savage; conditioned to express affection sexually, she is rebuffed by the naïve youth and eventually brutally murdered by him in Aldous Huxley's *Brave New World.*

Norman Crowne Handsome, well-born, rich, unstable poet who marries and produces two beautiful children, William and Emily; possessing a "dazzling if fitful genius", he lives in a world of fantasy and is eventually implicated in the death of one of his friends; found innocent, he flees England and dies abroad in Margaret Kennedy's *Red Sky at Morning.*

William Crowne Handsome, "elusively radiant" twin of Emily Crowne and son of Norman Crowne; like his father, William has poetical genius and is brilliant and unbalanced; he makes an unfortunate marriage to Tilli Van Tuyl and, like his father, is implicated in the death of a man, his cousin Trevor Frobisher, in Margaret Kennedy's *Red Sky at Morning.*

Irene Crowther One of Evelyn Morton Stennett's "clients"; on one visit to Irene's, Evelyn is injured during a domestic quarrel between Irene and Joseph Leroy in Margaret Drabble's *The Middle Ground.*

Cruddock Sir Edward Leithen's manservant in John Buchan's *Sick Heart River.*

Crum   A twenty-year-old spendthrift chum of Val Dartie; he is out with Val on an evening when Montague Dartie embarrasses his son in John Galsworthy's *In Chancery.*

John Crump   Secretary of the Imperial Palace Hotel Company; his nervousness at the annual meeting makes him read the notice of meeting in a loud, defiant voice in Arnold Bennett's *Imperial Palace.*

Lottie Crump   Eccentric owner of a London hotel where many of the aristocrats gather in Evelyn Waugh's *Vile Bodies.*

Richard (Dicky) Cruyer   German Stations Controller and Bernard Samson's boss, who sends Bernard to Berlin for "Brahms Four" in Len Deighton's *Berlin Game.* He conspires for Bret Rensselaer's position in *Mexico Set* and in *London Match.*

Crystal   Utopian teenager who befriends the isolated William Barnstaple; Crystal's intelligence makes Barnstaple realize how inferior he is to the Utopians in H. G. Wells's *Men Like Gods.*

Cubitt   Slow, large, redheaded man; a member of Pinkie Brown's extortion mob, he witnesses Charles Hale's killing, deserts Pinkie, and tries unsuccessfully to join Colleoni's mob in Graham Greene's *Brighton Rock.*

Alastair Cuff   Director of a family publishing house where George Garner works in Roy Fuller's *The Second Curtain.*

Nigel Cuff   Published critic and cynical friend of Trevor Frobisher; invited by Trevor to join his communal "settlement," Nigel goes with his girlfriend Sally Green to live at the settlement in Margaret Kennedy's *Red Sky at Morning.*

Alice Cullen   Working-class mother of Michael Cullen, whose birth resulted from her liaison with a serviceman during World War II in Alan Sillitoe's *A Start in Life.*

Michael Cullen   Illegitimate youth who seeks love and fortune through illegal real estate deals and smuggling; he is narrator of Alan Sillitoe's *A Start in Life.*

Rose Cullen   Embittered, reckless daughter of Lord Benditch; though at first distrustful of D., she finds new purpose for her life by helping him, falling in love with him, and finally leaving England with him in Graham Greene's *The Confidential Agent.*

Tad Cullen   American pilot and friend of Bill

Kendrick; he identifies the dead man on the train as Kendrick in Josephine Tey's *The Singing Sands.*

Richard Cumberland   Asinine young man who wishes to attend society parties to which he is not invited; Max Adey finally invites him to join his holiday party to occupy Amabel, so that Max will be free to romance Julia Wray in Henry Green's *Party Going.*

Harry Cummings   "Shy youth" who helps his friend Bachir fill orders at the Countess of Varna's flower shop and who complains to an American companion that his position as "Salad-Dresser to the King" affords him no opportunities to rise socially in Ronald Firbank's *The Flower Beneath the Foot*

Ellie Cunningham   Wife of Harold; she has wisdom and insight and believes in miracles; enamoured of Johnny, she feels shy around him in Rosamond Lehmann's *A Sea-Grape Tree.*

Captain Harold Cunningham   Grumpy and unresponsive but curious-minded husband of Ellie; he watches the beach area through binoculars or sits on the veranda keeping a look-out in Rosamond Lehmann's *A Sea-Grape Tree.*

Martin Cunningham   Sympathetic, failing barrister who seeks assistance for Paddy Dignam's widow with Leopold Bloom in James Joyce's *Ulysses.*

Curate   Deranged clergyman whose reckless behavior while hiding from the Martians drives the anonymous narrator, his unwilling companion, to kill him in H. G. Wells's *The War of the Worlds.*

Ernest Curco   A Las Vegas cab driver whom James Bond employs in Ian Fleming's *Diamonds Are Forever.*

Bertie Curfew   Young man who directs Marjorie Ferrar in a Restoration play; she had a liaison with him in Paris in John Galsworthy's *The Silver Spoon.*

Nora Curfew   Sister of Bertie; she wins the admiration of Michael Mont for her social service in John Galsworthy's *The Silver Spoon.* She helps Fleur Mont run the railway canteen during the General Strike in *Swan Song.*

William Curlew   Richard Pulling's partner, who wanted to get rid of his "perfect" wife; with the help of Pulling, Curlew writes a letter to his wife claiming to be unfaithful, but to his distress she forgives him and he is forced to remain with her in Graham Greene's *Travels with My Aunt.*

Dr. Curnow   Disliked but trusted general practitioner; finding no physical reason for Jake Richardson's declining sex drive, he recommends psychological treatment in Kingsley Amis's *Jake's Thing*.

Mr. Curpet A small, round-faced man with a neatly trimmed beard; the senior partner in a law firm, he recognizes Richard Larch's dependability and talent for bookkeeping; he surprises Richard with a promotion enabling him to consider marriage in Arnold Bennett's *A Man From the North*.

Curran Past lover of Aunt Augusta Bertram; after working in a circus he established a church for dogs and was often in trouble with the law in Graham Greene's *Travels with My Aunt*.

Mark Curran Rich art collector, American expatriate, and former lover of Robert Leaver, whose blackmail scheme he foils in Muriel Spark's *Territorial Rights*.

Captain Currie Bigoted restaurant manager whom D. encounters at crucial moments; alternately hostile and friendly, he ultimately tries to turn D. over to the police in Graham Greene's *The Confidential Agent*.

Vera Curry Old woman who is a neighbor of Bernard Sands; she is convicted of blackmail, procuring, and other crimes, largely because of Sands's initiative in Angus Wilson's *Hemlock and After*.

Mrs. Curtis Stubborn landlady to Edgar and Mary Perry; she has owned a beauty parlor in Cairo for twenty years yet is prejudiced against the natives and refuses to learn Arabic in P. H. Newby's *The Picnic at Sakkara*.

Charles Curtis Father of Kate and Olivia in Rosamond Lehmann's *Invitation to the Waltz* and in *The Weather in the Streets*.

Mrs. Charles Curtis Mother of Kate and Olivia; she expects conventional actions of her daughters in Rosamond Lehmann's *Invitation to the Waltz*. Her superficial, domestic perspective makes it impossible for her to understand Olivia's independent nature in *The Weather in the Streets*.

John Curtis Richard Curtis's son who has Down's Syndrome in Doris Lessing's *The Diaries of Jane Somers*.

Kate Curtis Independent, sensible older daughter of Mr. and Mrs. Charles Curtis; she plans to go to Paris to further her education in Rosamond Lehmann's *Invitation to the Waltz*. She is a capable, experienced wife with four children in *The Weather in the Streets*.

Kathleen Curtis Richard Curtis's daughter, a student at the University of London, whose time is spent "secretly" trailing Jane Somers and Richard on their dates in Doris Lessing's *The Diaries of Jane Somers*.

Mathew Curtis Richard Curtis's bright and ambitious son, who looks like his father; he admits to Jane Somers that he is in love with her in Doris Lessing's *The Diaries of Jane Somers*.

Olivia Curtis Naïve, sheltered, seventeen-year-old daughter of Mr. and Mrs. Charles Curtis; she is curious about others and feels that she has had an introduction to life after a party where she meets different characters in Rosamond Lehmann's *Invitation to the Waltz*. At twenty-six she is estranged from her husband, lives an impoverished existence with a cousin, and has an eight-month love affair with Rollo Spencer in *The Weather in the Streets*.

Richard Curtis A middle-aged doctor whom Jane Somers meets at a railroad station, and with whom she falls in love; he must eventually move to Canada for his wife's career in Doris Lessing's *The Diaries of Jane Somers*.

Sylvia Curtis Richard Curtis's hard-working, brilliant wife, a surgeon, who has always allotted only a certain amount of time to her husband in Doris Lessing's *The Diaries of Jane Somers*.

Curtiss Hercule Poirot's manservant in the necessary absence of George in Agatha Christie's *Curtain: Hercule Poirot's Last Case*.

Lieutenant-General Sir Herbert ("Bertie") Curzon Central figure whose ascent from an acclaimed commander of the 22nd Lancers in the Boer War to his final post as a general in charge of 100,000 soldiers in World War I is counterpointed by his increasing blindness to a drastically changing world, particularly with regard to wartime tactics and practices; the social status solidified by his marriage to Lady Emily Winter-Willoughby, daughter of the Duke and Duchess of Bude, is accompanied by internal punishments; Curzon grows to understand the anachronism he and his peers have become only in his final symbolic, and somewhat pathetic, attempt to resuscitate the past in C. S. Forester's *The General*.

Cuss Iping doctor who witnesses Griffin's open invisibility while soliciting his charity at the Coach and Horses, and whose trousers are later stolen by Griffin in H. G. Wells's *The Invisible Man: A Grotesque Romance*.

Alexander Bonaparte Cust Frustrated possessor of a grandiose name; his travels connect with the murder scenes to a degree beyond coincidence in Agatha Christie's *The A.B.C. Murders*.

Alex Custer   British Council Cultural Affairs officer in Turkey; he takes Philip Swallow to a party in Ankara, where Philip re-discovers Joy Simpson in David Lodge's *Small World*.

Primrose Cutbush   Third-year anthropology student who competes for the Foresight Fellowship in Barbara Pym's *Less Than Angels*.

Cutler   Gunner aboard the *Indefatigable* in C. S. Forester's *Mr. Midshipman Hornblower*.

Fiona Cutts   Daughter of Susan Tolland Cutts; a difficult girl, she has run away from various schools before she becomes a disciple of Scorpio Murtlock and a member of his cult; she marries Russell Gwinnett in Anthony Powell's *Hearing Secret Harmonies*.

Roddy Cutts   Smiling, assiduously polite Tory Member of Parliament who becomes engaged to Lady Susan Tolland in Anthony Powell's *At Lady Molly's*. They are married in *Casanova's Chinese Restaurant* and in *The Kindly Ones*. He has a wartime romance with a cypher decoder and wants a divorce in *The Military Philosophers*. Chastened, he submits to his wife's domination in *Books Do Furnish a Room*. He talks about his daughter, Fiona, in *Hearing Secret Harmonies*.

Cynthia   Fickle secretary in Section 6A, Overseas Intelligence, and the unresponsive object of Arthur Davis's infatuation in Graham Greene's *The Human Factor*.

Cynthia   Tall, busty Swedish girl at the convent who befriends Caithleen Brady and teaches her many things about the real world in Edna O'Brien's *The Country Girls*.

Hugo Cypress   Young aristocratic friend and protégé of Guy de Travest; he attends a tension-filled swimming party at Guy's house the night before Iris Storm's death in Michael Arlen's *The Green Hat*.

Shirley Cypress   Well-bred but spirited aristocrat who feels jealous of Iris Storm for saving her girlhood friend Venice Pollen from drowning during their swimming party in Michael Arlen's *The Green Hat*.

Cyril   Cancer-stricken, scripture-quoting elderly patient in Clive Ward who is wracked with guilt because of the memory of his rape of his now-deceased wife; he hopes that his daughter, Dorothy, can still be "saved" and prays for "judgement" in John Berger's *The Foot of Clive*.

Dr. Richard Czinner (covername: Richard John)   Doomed political leader and weary refugee; he is captured and condemned by Subotican military authorities while attempting a return to Belgrade to lead a futile uprising and, after breaking away, is shot by the militia and dies in Coral Musker's arms in Graham Greene's *Stamboul Train*.

D

D. Former scholar of medieval French literature; he is a dogged but disillusioned confidential agent of an unnamed country torn by a civil war in which his wife was killed; sent to buy coal in England, suspicious of everyone, he is thwarted by his enemies, though he wins the love of Rose Cullen in Graham Greene's *The Confidential Agent.*

Duchess of D. An arbiter of social practices for the aristocratic class of Edwardian society; she exercises power to admit or exclude persons from intimate social gatherings on the basis of birth, dignity (virtue), and reserve in Vita Sackville-West's *The Edwardians.*

Dabeeb Jarnti's wife, who becomes Al-Ith's closest friend and confidante in Doris Lessing's *The Marriages Between Zones Three, Four, and Five.*

Geraldine Dabis The hearty sister of Agatha Calkin; she will always be a spinster in Ivy Compton-Burnett's *Men and Wives.*

Kate Dabis Geraldine Dabis's half sister, who accepts Edward Bellamy's proposal after his divorce from Camilla; she is an alert woman with a pleasant face in Ivy Compton-Burnett's *Men and Wives.*

Viola Dace Thirtyish spinster, disappointed in her love for Aylwin Forbes; she works as a researcher and maker of book indices and comes to share Dulcie Mainwaring's suburban house and her voyeuristic interest in people's lives in Barbara Pym's *No Fond Return of Love.*

Reggie Dacker Dandified fellow-director usually referred to as the alter ego of managing-Director Evelyn Orcham; both are involved in an elaborate fighting campaign for the reform of the liquor licensing laws of the country in Arnold Bennett's *Imperial Palace.*

Dad The narrator's father; a mild, middle-aged man, he is estranged from his wife; he spends his time in the attic of his wife's boarding house writing the history of his neighborhood, Pimlico; he dies of an unnamed illness and leaves his life savings and unfinished manuscript to his son in Colin MacInnes's *Absolute Beginners.*

Daphne Dagnall Fifty-five-year-old eager spinster housekeeper to her brother in the village rectory; she cherishes vaguely discontented dreams of retirement in a Greek villa, but she must settle eventually for sharing a dog and a house near Birmingham with her bossy old school friend Heather Blenkinsop in Barbara Pym's *A Few Green Leaves.*

Tom Dagnall Middle-aged widower rector of a West Oxfordshire village church, who lives with his sister whom he takes for granted until she departs; he is an amateur student of local history who hopes to enlist Emma Howick in some of his researches — and who may be interested in Emma herself — in Barbara Pym's *A Few Green Leaves.*

Sir Jehoshophat Dain Aged philanthropist and snob; he is ignored by the Countess of Chell at the opening ceremonies for the Policeman's Institute, while Denry Machin gains her attention and all the limelight in Arnold Bennett's *The Card: A Story of Adventure in the Five Towns.*

Colonel Daintry Psychologically insecure head of British Intelligence security; he argues ineffectually against Dr. Percival's circumstantial evidence condemning Arthur Davis and verifies Maurice Castle as a double agent, but fails to prevent Castle's defection in Graham Greene's *The Human Factor.*

Mr. Daintry Serena Daintry's father; a successful and wealthy businessman, he buys Timberwork and gives Paul Gardner a job in Isabel Colegate's *Orlando at the Brazen Threshold.*

Elizabeth Daintry Colonel Daintry's estranged daughter; during her wedding Daintry and Maurice Castle learn of Arthur Davis's death in Graham Greene's *The Human Factor.*

Serena Daintry Daughter of Paul Gardner's wealthy employer; she marries Paul in Isabel Colegate's *Orlando at the Brazen Threshold.* She is divorced from him in *Agatha.*

Daisy Mark Linkwater's former mistress, to whom he reverts when he becomes tired of Emmeline Summers in Elizabeth Bowen's *To the North.*

Daisy A young married woman with whom Peter Walsh has had a sordid affair in Virginia Woolf's *Mrs. Dalloway.*

Thorin Dakenshield Old, important elf leader whose ancestors were killed, their castle and treasures taken by a dragon; he journeys with Bilbo Baggins and Gandalf to the Mountain to recapture his inheritance and kill the dragon; he is successful in his quest but dies in a battle with the Orcs in J. R. R. Tolkien's *The Hobbit; or There and Back Again.*

Reginald ("Reggie") Daker An admiring suitor of

Pamela Brune and member of the Whitsuntide house party at Flambard; participating in Professor Moe's experiment to gain a brief glimpse of his future, he is saved from an intolerable alliance in John Buchan's *The Gap in the Curtain*.

Brigadier Dalby   Elegant public-school-educated head of W.O.O.C.(P.), a provisional subdivision of M.I.6; a Communist double agent, he is Jay's espionage tool and is exposed by the narrator in Len Deighton's *The Ipcress File*.

Jim Dale   Worker in the Dupret foundry; he lives in Phil Craigan's house and hopes to marry Lily Gates, but when she elopes with Bert Jones, Dale changes his job and his lodgings in Henry Green's *Living*.

Adam Dalgliesh (also Dalgleish)   Introspective, intellectual detective and poet who lost his wife and son in childbirth and who has a variety of unsatisfactory romantic attachments; as Adam Dalgleish he is a Detective Chief Inspector and Metropolitan CID veteran who investigates the murder of a servant and is attracted to Deborah Riscoe in P. D. James's *Cover Her Face*. Adam Dalgliesh thereafter, he finds his courtship of Deborah interrupted while he investigates the murder of the administrative head of a psychiatric clinic in *A Mind to Murder*. His matrimonial plans are ended by Deborah's departure to America after he has solved the murders of two nursing students in *Shroud for a Nightingale*. His investigative methods, inculcated by the late Bernie Pryde, influence Cordelia Gray's solution of the murder of a scientist's son in *An Unsuitable Job For a Woman*. He has become a CID Commander and is a recognized poet during his investigation of the death of a chaplain whom he knew as a child in *The Black Tower*. He investigates the murder of a laboratory pathologist in *Death of an Expert Witness*. He vouches for Cordelia Gray when she is viewed by the police as a suspect in *The Skull Beneath the Skin*. He is assisted by Inspector Kate Miskin in solving the murder of a cabinet minister in *A Taste for Death*. He investigates the murder of an ambitious scientist in *Devices and Desires*.

Bianca Dallison   Artist and estranged wife of Hilary; she paints a portrait of the country girl Ivy Barton and laughs at her when Ivy insists on going with Hilary in John Galsworthy's *Fraternity*.

Cecilia (Cis) Dallison   Wife of Stephen; she spends her time shopping and worrying over her daughter and sister in John Galsworthy's *Fraternity*.

Hilary Dallison   Author and man of letters, brother of Stephen; estranged from his wife, Bianca, he sepa-

rates from her; he rejects the appeals of Ivy Barton to take her with him in John Galsworthy's *Fraternity*.

Stephen (Stevie) Dallison   Attorney brother of Hilary; he attempts to dissuade Hilary from becoming involved with Ivy Barton in John Galsworthy's *Fraternity*.

Thyme Dallison   Seventeen-year-old daughter of Cecilia and Stephen; she fails to help Martin Stone in social rescue projects in John Galsworthy's *Fraternity*.

Dallow   Ugly, coarse, cautious, insensitive man who is a member of Pinkie Brown's mob; trusted by Pinkie, he exercises a calming influence on him; apparently not afraid of capture, he always has his eye on the main chance in Graham Greene's *Brighton Rock*.

Clarissa Dalloway   Young woman who meets Rachel Vinrace aboard the *Euphrosyne* crossing the Atlantic; she serves as a bridge between Rachel and her husband, Richard Dalloway, in Virginia Woolf's *The Voyage Out*. She is the heroine and interval narrator, a middle-aged but still beautiful London matron and the apparent prototype of a society hostess but also the Dostoevskian double of Septimus Smith, whose suicide, although they never meet, reflects the emptiness and paradoxical fullness of her life choices; unlike Septimus, Clarissa survives, is even at home in the world of flux because she can adapt to motion and change; she breaks through to a reality larger than herself in which the moment is enough in *Mrs. Dalloway*.

Elizabeth Dalloway   Clarissa's similarly beautiful seventeen-year-old daughter, presently enamored of her teacher Miss Kilman; engaged in rebellion and identity crises, she is closer to her father than to her mother in Virginia Woolf's *Mrs. Dalloway*.

Richard Dalloway   Masculine, "factual" Member of Parliament, who assaults Rachel Vinrace with kisses and sexual energy on her father's ship; his meticulous appearance represents to Rachel his solidity and favored connections with the objective world; Rachel turns to him for a version of truth only to find physical harassment in Virginia Woolf's *The Voyage Out*. As Clarissa's husband, he is content with lunch at Lady Bruton's and with his wife's party that the Prime Minister attends; in spite of passionately choosing him over his ardent rival Peter Walsh as a young woman, Clarissa now feels she has failed him "through some contraction of this cold spirit" in *Mrs. Dalloway*.

Dorothy (Sister Doll) Dalraye   A Red Cross nurse who wants to train Martha Quest and other young women in care for the wounded in Doris Lessing's *A Proper Marriage*.

Lady Dalrymple   Red-faced, fussy woman who invites Hornblower to dinner in C. S. Forester's *Mr. Midshipman Hornblower*.

Father Daly   Well educated priest who is well liked by his congregation; he preaches sternly on matters of morality and sex but is himself in financial trouble in Patrick Kavanagh's *Tarry Flynn*.

Mr. Dalziel   A tall, thin man who teaches Scripture, history, and English at Lucius Cassidy's school in Ivy Compton-Burnett's *Two Worlds and Their Ways*.

Daman   Malay who arrives at the Shore of Refuge and backs Tengga, not Belarab in Joseph Conrad's *The Rescue: A Romance of the Shallows*.

Achille Dambreuse   One of Aunt Augusta Bertram's many lovers; married with four children, he kept Augusta as his mistress for six months in a Parisian hotel until he was discovered to be keeping another mistress at the same time at the same hotel in Graham Greene's *Travels with My Aunt*.

Fred Danby   Illegitimate cousin of Antonia; by arrangement with her, he has married Lilia and now lives at Montefort with Antonia and with Lilia and their daughter, Jane, in Elizabeth Bowen's *A World of Love*.

Jane Danby   Daughter of Lilia; she reads Guy's letters and becomes infatuated with his memory in Elizabeth Bowen's *A World of Love*.

Lilia Danby   Englishwoman who had been engaged to Guy when he was killed in France; she lives as the dependent of Guy's cousin and heir, Antonia, in Elizabeth Bowen's *A World of Love*.

Philip Norman Danby   Publisher who fires Tony Bicket for stealing books in John Galsworthy's *The White Monkey*.

Mrs. Dancey   Wife of Alaric and mother of Catrina, Henry, Andrew, and Louise; she is always ready to provide a warm welcome for Eva Trout in Elizabeth Bowen's *Eva Trout, or Changing Scenes*.

Alaric Dancey   Vicar of the church near Larkins, the home of the Arbles, in Elizabeth Bowen's *Eva Trout, or Changing Scenes*.

Andrew Dancey   Younger brother of Henry Dancey in Elizabeth Bowen's *Eva Trout, or Changing Scenes*.

Catrina Dancey   Eldest of the children of Alaric Dancey, the vicar near Larkins; she is thirteen when Eva Trout meets her in Elizabeth Bowen's *Eva Trout, or Changing Scenes*.

Henry Dancey   Second oldest of the Dancey children of the vicarage near Larkins; he is twelve when Eva Trout meets him; despite the twelve-year difference in their ages, he becomes Eva's trusted friend and is about to marry her when she is killed in a shocking accident in Elizabeth Bowen's *Eva Trout, or Changing Scenes*.

Louise Dancey   Youngest of the Dancey children of the vicarage near Larkins in Elizabeth Bowen's *Eva Trout, or Changing Scenes*.

Dandelion   Storytelling rabbit whose recounting of the tales of El-ahrairah is critical to morale and suggests stratagems to Hazel's band of pioneers in Richard Adams's *Watership Down*.

Daniel   Miriam's husband; his mother-in-law, Kitty Friedman, thinks him an overcritical father to Jonothan in Margaret Drabble's *The Ice Age*.

Daniel   Writer and friend of Sigbjorn Wilderness in Malcolm Lowry's *Dark as the Grave Wherein My Friend Is Laid*.

Inspector Daniel   Local Dorsetshire policeman who investigates the deaths of Victor Holroyd and Maggie Hewson in P. D. James's *The Black Tower*.

Mr. Daniel   A Brazilian who is part of the Global Foods delegation meeting in Istanbul in Doris Lessing's *The Summer Before the Dark*.

Mr. Daniel   A partner in the legal firm where Martha Quest works; he is also a Member of Parliament in Doris Lessing's *Martha Quest*.

Daniele   A gondolier, "unprostituted" and loyal to the woman he loves; Connie Chatterley and her sister, Hilda Reid, encounter him in Venice in D. H. Lawrence's *Lady Chatterley's Lover*.

Danvers   Master's mate aboard the *Justinian* who acts as Hornblower's second in his duel with Simpson in C. S. Forester's *Mr. Midshipman Hornblower*.

Mrs. Danvers   Family servant who accompanied the newly married Rebecca de Winter to Manderly, where after Rebecca's death she remains as housekeeper; fanatically loyal to Rebecca, she expresses her contempt for the new Mrs. de Winter by intimidating her with accounts of Rebecca's perfection and by manipulating her into humiliating situations in Daphne Du Maurier's *Rebecca*.

Daphne A precocious child whom Miriam Henderson meets on her two-week holiday in the Bernese Alps in Dorothy Richardson's *Oberland*.

Cousin Daphne A schoolteacher and the cousin of Sarah Bennett and Louise Bennett Halifax and the sister of Cousin Michael; she seems destined for spinsterhood, and the course of her life terrifies Sarah and Louise in Margaret Drabble's *A Summer Bird-Cage*.

Darby Vesey's chief in the town-hall education office, where Lewis Eliot works in 1921-22 in C. P. Snow's *Time of Hope*.

Joyce Darby University student who is one of four defended by Lewis Eliot when they are threatened with expulsion for sexual misconduct in C. P. Snow's *The Sleep of Reason*.

Felix D'Arcy Snobbish, unmarried senior yet temporary tutor at Carne School who knows of Stella Rode's extortion and the identity of her murderer in John le Carré's *A Murder of Quality*.

Amber Darke Oldest daughter of Solomon and Rachel Darke; with a grey face and mouse-colored hair, she is a love mystic, whose insights derive from nature and are expressed in nurturing protection of others and in a spirit of laughter; she supports her brother Jasper in his quest for greater psychic understanding and his rejection of Christian theology in Mary Webb's *The House in Dormer Forest*.

Jasper Darke Theology student, dismissed from university for his rejection of Christianity; he achieves mental and emotional transformation through symbolic drowning in an "opaque and fathomless pool" within himself and suffers an emotional isolation from his family and sweetheart, Catherine Velindre, when he returns to Dormer Old House in Dormer Forest in Mary Webb's *The House in Dormer Forest*.

Peter Darke Twenty-year-old brother of Jasper, Ruby, and Amber Darke; he denounces Jasper's loss of religious faith; he appears nervous and always ready to spring but uncertain upon whom he will pounce; he has inherited the farm ahead of the elder son, Jasper; he is almost forced by Enoch Gale to marry Marigold Gosling after he kisses her in Mary Webb's *The House in Dormer Forest*.

Rachel Darke Solomon's unloving wife, who married in order to escape her family; she is so bored by childbirth that she refuses to help her husband select names for their children; she harshly dominates the family in Mary Webb's *The House in Dormer Forest*.

Ruby Darke The tall, plump, and pretty eighteen-year-old younger daughter of Solomon and Rachel Darke; her resentment of her brother Jasper's decision to give up theological studies parallels that of other family members; at her mother's insistence, she marries the Reverend Ernest Swyndal in Mary Webb's *The House in Dormer Forest*.

Solomon Darke Sixty-year-old husband of Rachel Darke; he is the father of Peter, Ruby, Jasper, and Amber Darke in Mary Webb's *The House in Dormer Forest*.

L. G. Darley A writer enmeshed in, and baffled by, the many intrigues of Alexandria; he has affairs with Justine Hosnani and with Melissa Artemis; after Melissa's death he retires to a Greek island with her infant daughter to compile the narrative of his Alexandrian adventures in Lawrence Durrell's *Justine*. Balthazar visits him, bringing corrections and emendations that extend the narrative in *Balthazar*. He is proved to be altogether mistaken and unimportant — taken up by Justine merely in an attempt to discover Melissa's awareness of the gunrunning conspiracy — in *Mountolive*. He returns to Alexandria where he has a love affair with Clea Montis and is again narrator in *Clea*.

Mr. Darlington Secretary for the Committee for Aid to the Elderly who disappoints Meg Eliot when he displays no sense of humor after her widowhood in Angus Wilson's *The Middle Age of Mrs. Eliot*.

Rosamund Darnley A fashionable dressmaker; she is Kenneth Marshall's lifelong devoted friend in Agatha Christie's *Evil Under the Sun*.

Larry Darrell Enigmatic, graceful man with a true sweetness of soul who struggles to find spiritual truth and peace; the quest loses him his fiancée, Isabel Bradley, but finds him Sophie Macdonald; however, he is destined to remain alone in his search in W. Somerset Maugham's *The Razor's Edge*.

Miss Darrington (The Pussum) Julius Halliday's mistress and a member of the London Bohemian set; she also sleeps with Gerald Crich in D. H. Lawrence's *Women in Love*.

Holly Forsyte Dartie Daughter of Young Jolyon and the foreign governess in John Galsworthy's *The Man of Property*. She goes to South Africa with her half sister, June, to be near Val Dartie and her brother, Jolly; she marries Val in 1900 after the death of Jolly in *In Chancery*. She entertains her younger half brother, Jon, and Fleur Forsyte as houseguests in *To Let*. She meets Michael Mont at Winifred Dartie's and tells him the story of Fleur's love for Jon in *The White Monkey*. She entertains Jon and her sister-in-law, Anne Wilmot Forsyte, while they search for a farm to buy in *Swan Song*.

Montague (Monty) Moses Dartie Gambler son-in-law of James Forsyte and husband of Winifred; he drunkenly flirts with Irene Forsyte in John Galsworthy's *The Man of Property*. He gives his wife's pearls to a dancer with whom he flees to Buenos Aires, and he returns to beg Winifred to take him back in *In Chancery*. He dies from a fall in Paris in 1914 in *To Let*.

Publius Valerius (Val) Dartie Seven-year-old son of Montague and Winifred in John Galsworthy's *The Man of Property*. At age nineteen he joins the army for service in the Boer War on a dare from Jolly Forsyte, is wounded, and marries Holly Forsyte (Dartie) in 1900 in *In Chancery*. He does some farming in South Africa and returns to England to train race horses in *To Let*. He objects to Soames Forsyte about the race horses left him by George Forsyte in *The White Monkey*. He gives Soames information about Lord Charles Ferrar in *The Silver Spoon*. He refuses to prosecute Aubrey Stainford after being robbed by him in *Swan Song*.

Winifred (Freddie) Dartie Soames Forsyte's sister, wife of Montague Dartie; she invites Irene Forsyte and Philip Bosinney on a dinner outing in John Galsworthy's *The Man of Property*. She is deserted by her husband and turns to Soames for legal help in divorce; she takes her husband back in *In Chancery*. A sixty-two-year-old widow in 1920, she gives a wedding reception for Fleur Forsyte and Michael Mont in *To Let*. She sells her insurance corporation stock upon Soames's advice in *The White Monkey*. She helps calm Soames during the crisis of the libel suit in *The Silver Spoon*. She is distressed by the theft by Aubrey Stainford of a snuff-box given her by her father in *Swan Song*.

Darvlish the Skull The Driat leader who attacks Borlien and defeats JandolAngand's forces at the battle of the Cosgatt in Brian W. Aldiss's *Helliconia Summer*.

Mr. Das Indian magistrate who presides over the court and controls the English at Dr. Aziz's trial in E. M. Forster's *A Passage to India*.

Barbara Dasent Lovely young American niece of John S. Blenkiron; she courageously assists in the revolt against Senor Castor's enemy forces; she falls in love with "Sandy" (Lord Clanroyden) and agrees to marry him in John Buchan's *The Courts of the Morning*. As Lady Clanroyden, she is hostess at Laverlaw, the Clanroydens' ancestral property, where the Richard Hannays and their guests Valdemar and Anna

Haraldsen move for sanctuary and greater protection in *The Island of Sheep*.

Mary Datchet Katherine Hilbery's friend who runs a London women's suffrage office; she has her work and her principles in the factual world; she is in love with Ralph Denham but gives him up to Katherine, whom he truly loves, because she believes that "whatever happens, I mean to have no pretences in my life" in Virginia Woolf's *Night and Day*.

Dathka A silent and rebellious metal worker who becomes a hunter and Laintal Ay's best friend in Brian W. Aldiss's *Helliconia Spring*.

The Daughter of Man A beautiful multi-racial woman who emerges from the sea during a summit conference on a Pacific island and becomes the mistress of the President of the World State in Olaf Stapledon's *Last and First Men: A Story of the Near and Far Future*.

Mary Daunt Young woman who works with Martin Stone; she shows Thyme Dallison how to study the sanitation needs of the poor in John Galsworthy's *Fraternity*.

Janey Davenant Lady Sylvia Davenant's willful child, who holds the younger Polly Wadamy in contempt in Richard Hughes's *The Fox in the Attic*. An emotionally unstable eighteen-year-old, she follows Polly's lead, especially in developing a crush on Adolf Hitler in *The Wooden Shepherdess*.

Lady Sylvia Davenant London neighbor of Gilbert and Mary Wadamy in Richard Hughes's *The Fox in the Attic*.

Captain Dermot Davenport Lover of Violet Tennant in Henry Green's *Loving*.

David A psychiatrist and husband of Evelyn (Morton) Stennett's sister Isobel (Morton) in Margaret Drabble's *The Middle Ground*.

David Selfish, cultured, philosophical scholar; he travels to the city quickly, thinking it Paradise, while forgetting all else in Rex Warner's *The Wild Goose Chase: An Allegory*.

Lucia ("Loo") Davidge Vacationer in Sweden who meets and falls in love with Anthony Fallant; feeling that his job with Erik Krogh is not respectable, she finally persuades him to give it up and meet her in England, though he is murdered before he can do so in Graham Greene's *England Made Me*.

Davidson   Generous captain of a coastal steamer who regularly visits Axel Heyst at Samburan but is unable to prevent the gamblers, Jones and Ricardo, from murdering Lena in Joseph Conrad's *Victory: An Island Tale.*

Captain Davidson   The royal Navy officer whose duty it is to collect the bodies of drowned sailors; he takes charge of Pincher Martin's body in William Golding's *Pincher Martin.*

Austin Davidson   Art critic who is the father of Margaret Hollis; he interrogates Lewis Eliot about the prosecution of Eric Sawbridge for espionage and offers assistance for Margaret's divorce in C. P. Snow's *Homecomings.* He asks Lewis and Margaret (Hollis) Eliot to help him commit suicide and continues to live when they refuse in *The Sleep of Reason.* He fails to commit suicide and then dies in 1966 of natural causes in *Last Things.*

Helen Davidson   Older sister of Margaret Hollis; married but childless, she opposes Margaret's divorce in C. P. Snow's *Homecomings.*

Professor Olaf Davidson   Chairman of the Space Advisory Council who sees Rama as unimportant in Arthur C. Clarke's *Rendezvous with Rama.*

Mr. Davies   A bus conductor and Edna Davies's husband; he rescues John Lewis when a man is chasing Lewis after he has disguised himself as a woman in order to sneak out of Elizabeth Gruffydd-Williams's house in Kingsley Amis's *That Uncertain Feeling.*

Edna Davies   John Lewis's meddlesome, annoying downstairs neighbor; she lives with her husband and grown son, Ken Davies, in Kingsley Amis's *That Uncertain Feeling.*

Ken Davies   Edna Davies's grown son, who spends his time drinking and frequenting dance halls, where he helps John Lewis when Lewis gets into a fight with some men over Elizabeth Gruffydd-Williams; Lewis later helps Ken home after finding him drunk, beaten, and lying in the street in Kingsley Amis's *That Uncertain Feeling.*

Davin   Nationalist university-student friend of Stephen Dedalus in James Joyce's *Ulysses.*

Davis (covername: Cholmondeley)   Sir Marcus's fat, scheming business associate; he hires James Raven to assassinate the Minister for War in Middle Europe and then lays a trap with stolen bank notes for Raven's capture in Graham Greene's *A Gun for Sale.*

Captain Davis   Drunken, intolerant officer of the *Ipe-cacuanha* who maroons Edward Prendick on Moreau's island and dies at sea himself in H. G. Wells's *The Island of Doctor Moreau.*

Arthur Davis   Maurice Castle's open-hearted, somewhat eccentric assistant; he is wrongly suspected as a double agent and murdered by British Intelligence's Dr. Percival in Graham Greene's *The Human Factor.*

Lavender Davis   A boring and detested acquaintance of Linda Radlett in her girlhood; she is among the English activists who assist the Spanish in the Perpignan refugee camps; the discovery of Christopher Talbot's affair with her partly motivates Linda's departure in Nancy Mitford's *The Pursuit of Love.*

Spunk Davis   "B" actor recruited for John Self's movie in Martin Amis's *Money.*

Alice Dawes   Diabetic coffee-bar waitress whose pregnancy inspires her lover, Patrick Seton, to plan her murder in Muriel Spark's *The Bachelors.*

Baxter Dawes   A sullen, defiant man who is Clara Dawes's estranged husband; he and Paul Morel engage in a bloody fight, and later Paul feels a bond with the other man, eventually helps Dawes find a new job, and helps engineer Clara's return to her husband in D. H. Lawrence's *Sons and Lovers.*

Clara Dawes   A striking blonde woman and a clever advocate of Women's Rights; estranged from her bullying husband, Baxter, she helps Paul Morel achieve his "baptism of fire in passion"; then, "morally frightened" and seeking to do "penance", she returns to her husband in D. H. Lawrence's *Sons and Lovers.*

Gerald Dawes   The fiancé of Agnes Pembroke (later Elliott); he is killed playing football in E. M. Forster's *The Longest Journey.*

Frank Dawley   Young workingman who left his wife, Nancy, and two children to run away with Myra Bassingfield to Algeria; he goes on a gun-running mission to the Algerian guerilla forces against French occupation troups and stays to fight with them in Alan Sillitoe's *The Death of William Posters.* He is found in a hospital cave by John Handley, his friend's brother, and brought back to England, where he is reunited with Myra, their son Mark, and Albert Handley and his family in *A Tree on Fire.*

Nancy Dawley   The wife of Frank Dawley and mother of his two children; he deserts them in Alan Sillitoe's *The Death of William Posters.* They are brought to live on Myra Bassingfield's estate in *A Tree on Fire.*

Dawlish   Eccentric but politically astute chief of W.O.O.C.(P.) who counters Colonel Stok's moves in Len Deighton's *Funeral in Berlin*. He sets up General Midwinter in *The Billion-Dollar Brain*. He guides the narrator with information about Steve Champion's Middle East connections in *Yesterday's Spy*. He explains the true scope of the mission to the narrator in *Spy Story*.

Miss Dawlish ("Bounce")   A spinster of passion and wisdom, as well as Oliver's music teacher and guide in William Golding's *The Pyramid*.

Mr. Dawlish   The father of "Bounce" Dawlish, whom he represses; the town's "failed artist," he has turned himself into "the portrait of a romantic musician" in William Golding's *The Pyramid*.

Agatha Dawson   A wealthy spinster who, though terminally ill, superstitiously refuses to make a will; she expects her great niece, Mary Whittaker, who lives with and cares for her, to inherit in Dorothy L. Sayers's *Unnatural Death*.

Gregory Dawson   Successful, middle-aged film writer who thinks back on his youth in a genteel hotel on the Cornish coast, wondering what has brought him to his present state of disenchantment with his work and his life in J. B. Priestley's *Bright Day*.

Hallelujah Dawson   A mulatto West Indian distant relation of Agatha Dawson and Mary Whittaker in Dorothy L. Sayers's *Unnatural Death*.

Louisa Dawson   Elegant young-woman passenger of the steamship to which the pirates transfer the Bas-Thornton and Fernandez children; Emily Bas-Thornton's romantic crush on her is ended by her invitation to Emily to call her "Lulu" in Richard Hughes's *A High Wind in Jamaica*.

Dawson-Hill   Barrister who serves to represent the case against Donald Howard before the Court of Seniors in C. P. Snow's *The Affair*.

Arthur Dayson   Devious reporter and sub-editor of George Cannon's still-born paper; Hilda Lessways works for him in her first employment as a secretary competent in shorthand in Arnold Bennett's *Hilda Lessways*.

Edgar Bosworth Deacon   A painter once acquainted with Nicholas Jenkins's parents; his canvases — large and classical in theme — evoke past associations for Jenkins in Anthony Powell's *A Buyer's Market*. His oddly borderline criminal activities connected with the sale of illegal erotica are examined in *The Acceptance World*

and in *Casanova's Chinese Restaurant*. His artistic reputation undergoes a rehabilitation in *Hearing Secret Harmonies*.

Jeff Deacon   Sir Charles Thorpe's butler at the time of the theft of a necklace some fifteen years earlier; convicted of complicity in the crime, he later escaped from prison and was identified as an accident victim in Dorothy L. Sayers's *The Nine Tailors: Changes Rung on an Old Theme in Two Short Touches and Two Full Peals*.

Deakin   The Challoner butler, who has an especial regard for Julia Challoner, but who talks familiarly with her son Simon in Ivy Compton-Burnett's *A Heritage and Its History*.

Susie Dean   Soubrette of genuine talent destined for success in London's West End in J. B. Priestley's *The Good Companions*.

The Dean of Studies   English Jesuit and University College professor who discusses Aquinas with Stephen Dedalus in James Joyce's *A Portrait of the Artist as a Young Man*.

Eleanor Dear   An unscrupulous but attractive nurse, suffering from tuberculosis and refusing to admit it, who deftly manipulates everyone (including Miriam Henderson) in Dorothy Richardson's *The Tunnel*. She stays briefly in Mrs. Bailey's house and embarrasses Miriam by trying to extort money from some of the boarders in *Interim*. Enterprising to the end, she succeeds in getting married and actually bears two children in *Revolving Lights*. Miriam learns of her death in *Dawn's Left Hand*.

Garrett Deasy   Prejudiced Protestant headmaster of Dalkey School who pays Stephen Dedalus, gives Stephen a letter on hoof-and-mouth disease, and expounds his theological theory of history in James Joyce's *Ulysses*.

"Deathwish" the Hun   South African photographer who lets Jerry Westerby hide in his lodgings while he is on a photo assignment in Cambodia in John le Carré's *The Honourable Schoolboy*.

Mary Hermione Debanham   Apparently emotionless passenger on the Calais Coach; she is proved to be the former governess of the present Countess Helena Andrenyi in Agatha Christie's *Murder on the Orient Express*.

Charles Debates   Unprepossessing youth, Alan Percival's cousin, who sits out the war as a solicitor with a munitions company and becomes a Labour Member of Parliament, rising to Parliamentary Secretary in the Attlee government in Roy Fuller's *The Perfect Fool.*

Lottie Debates Alan Percival's widowed aunt; she is the mother of Charlie Debates in Roy Fuller's *The Perfect Fool.*

de Barral Banker who builds a large fortune but then becomes bankrupt and imprisoned; feeling betrayed by his daughter Flora's marriage to Roderick Anthony, he attempts to poison Anthony, only to be discovered and to drink his own poison in Joseph Conrad's *Chance: A Tale in Two Parts.*

Mrs. de Barral Wife of the banker de Barral in Joseph Conrad's *Chance: A Tale in Two Parts.*

Lucie Declaux A sophisticated Frenchwoman whom Miriam Henderson meets at a lecture in Dorothy Richardson's *Deadlock.*

Martin Decoud French intellectual who becomes engaged to Antonia Avellanos but commits suicide when trapped, alone in a boat, while helping Nostromo (Gian' Battista) to keep the silver from the Monterists in Joseph Conrad's *Nostromo: A Tale of the Seaboard.*

Adelaide de Crecy Danby Odell's maidservant and lover, over whom Danby fights a duel with Will Boase; she marries Will, eventually becoming Lady Boase, in Iris Murdoch's *Bruno's Dream.*

Dilly Dedalus Stephen Dedalus's impoverished sister, who goes book shopping with him in James Joyce's *Ulysses.*

Mary Dedalus Mother of Stephen Dedalus in James Joyce's *A Portrait of the Artist as a Young Man.* She haunts him for not having prayed at her deathbed in *Ulysses.*

Maurice Dedalus Stephen Dedalus's brother in James Joyce's *A Portrait of the Artist as a Young Man.*

Simon Dedalus Stephen Dedalus's gregarious, once-respectable, bankrupt father, who wants his son to become a gentleman and tours Cork with him in James Joyce's *A Portrait of the Artist as a Young Man.* He is a sort of false father figure, crossing paths with Leopold Bloom in *Ulysses.*

Stephen Dedalus Aspiring Irish artist; he is tyrannized by classmates and teachers at two Jesuit schools and is embarrassed by his father Simon's bankruptcy; he develops an adolescent infatuation for Emma C.; he visits a prostitute and suffers overwhelming remorse; he rejects the call to become a Catholic priest

or an Irish patriot; he determines "to forge in the smithy of my soul the uncreated conscience of my race" in James Joyce's *A Portrait of the Artist as a Young Man.* He is an intellectually tormented schoolteacher who, while dissipating himself with a group of medical students, encounters Leopold Bloom; Bloom rescues him from a fight and takes him home in *Ulysses.*

Mr. Dedekind Member of the governing Republican Party in league with Count Mastrovin; he interrogates John Galt, "Jaikie", in Castle Gay and continues to question and to bully Jaikie in John Buchan's *The House of the Four Winds.*

Private Deering Personal servant to Captain P. B. Leonard; he is described as "untidy and casual and sometimes faintly impertinent"; he is a spy working for the Chinese who is eventually apprehended in Kingsley Amis's *The Anti-Death League.*

Edith de Haviland Sister-in-law of Aristide Leonides; hostility to him has made her the more determined in the supervision of his children and grandchildren after her sister's death in Agatha Christie's *Crooked House.*

Deirdre Student roommate of Melanie Byrd in David Lodge's *Changing Places: A Tale of Two Campuses.*

Francis Dekker One of Aaron Sisson's friends in Florence, Italy; Francis, James Argyle, and Angus Guest are examples of jaded cosmopolitan travellers in D. H. Lawrence's *Aaron's Rod.*

Mat Dekker Clergyman father of Sam Dekker in John Cowper Powys's *A Glastonbury Romance.*

Sam Dekker Son of the clergyman Mat Dekker; his religious struggle prompts him to renounce the married Nell Zoyland, who has borne him a child, and to become an ascetic; his faith is transformed by his vision of the Grail in John Cowper Powys's *A Glastonbury Romance.*

Diana (Dinah, "Dicey" Pigott) Delacroix One of three women in their sixties who at the age of eleven were "best friends" at a school in Kent; there she had persuaded the others to create a fictionalized time capsule; although now a widow with two grown sons and five grandchildren, she is still fascinated with digging up and burying things in Elizabeth Bowen's *The Little Girls.*

Emma Delacroix A granddaughter of Diana in Elizabeth Bowen's *The Little Girls.*

Pamela Delacroix   A granddaughter of Diana in Elizabeth Bowen's *The Little Girls*.

Roland Delacroix   One of Diana's two sons in Elizabeth Bowen's *The Little Girls*.

William Delacroix   One of Diana's two sons in Elizabeth Bowen's *The Little Girls*.

Father Egbart Delaney   Unfrocked priest and member of the Autobiographical Association in Muriel Spark's *Loitering with Intent*.

Gibson Delavacquerie   Poet and critic who works in public relations for Donners-Brebner; he and Nicholas Jenkins award a literary prize to Gwinnett's book on Trapnel; he marries the actress Polly Duport in Anthony Powell's *Hearing Secret Harmonies*.

Juan del Fuego   President of Nicaragua who inspires Auberon Quin in his role as King of England in G. K. Chesterton's *The Napoleon of Notting Hill.*

Delia   Friend of Molly the fat girl in Graham Greene's *Brighton Rock*.

Peter de Lisle   Homosexual Assistant in the General Department and, later, member of the British Diplomatic Chancery in Bonn; he allegedly allows Leclerc to initiate Operation Mayfly in John le Carré's *The Looking-Glass War*. He unsuccessfully attempts to betray his Embassy superior, Rawley Bradfield, and subvert Alan Turner's investigation in *A Small Town in Germany*.

Major Dell   World War II operative; he now manages the Alias Club, a drinking home for other leftover, disillusioned agents like Wilf Taylor and Bruce Woolford in John le Carré's *The Looking-Glass War*.

Julia Delmore   Beautiful actress and estranged wife of actor Jake Driver, whose infidelity and insensitivity trigger her flight to Wales, where she encounters and accepts the help of the sympathetic and lonely Gus Howkins; she is a character in the story novelist Giles Hermitage writes in John Wain's *The Pardoner's Tale*.

Hannah DeLoch   A young, robust Lesbian who joins the editorial staff of *Lilith*; she persuades Jane Somers to allow Kate to move into her commune in Doris Lessing's *The Diaries of Jane Somers*.

Tommy Deloraine   One of Edward Leithen's eminent London friends; he sets off to Russia to find and, ultimately, to save Charles Pitt-Heron after his mysterious disappearance in John Buchan's *The Power-House*.

Juanita del Pablo   A querulous film starlet who treacherously backbites Sir Francis Hinsley when he has been insturmental in establishing and developing her career in Evelyn Waugh's *The Loved One*.

P. R. Deltoid   Alex's Post-Corrective Advisor, a kind of probation officer for juvenile delinquents; he seems genuinely interested in Alex's welfare, but he has become cynical and pessimistic in Anthony Burgess's *A Clockwork Orange*.

Marchesa Del Torre   A spoiled and jaded aristocrat; an unfaithful wife, she sleeps with Aaron Sisson in D. H. Lawrence's *Aaron's Rod*.

Marchese Del Torre   A rich aristocratic Italian in Florence; Aaron Sisson sleeps with his wife, the Marchesa, in D. H. Lawrence's *Aaron's Rod*.

Meli Demetriades   Nicholas Urfe's colleague in English at the Lord Byron School on Phraxos in John Fowles's *The Magus*.

Lazari Demitraki   "Blonde boy with skin of amber" who dawdles as he helps his friend Bachir fill orders in the Countess of Varna's flower shop in Ronald Firbank's *The Flower Beneath the Foot*.

Edgar Demornay   A famous scholar recently returned from America to be Master of an Oxford college; his romantic attachments to women have all been unconsummated; his love for his late long-time friend Sophie Small is complicated by his infatuation with her husband, Monty Small, in Iris Murdoch's *The Sacred and Profane Love Machine*.

Demoyte   The former headmaster of St. Bride's School and a close friend and patron of William Mor; Rain Carter is commissioned to paint his portrait in Iris Murdoch's *The Sandcastle*.

Janet Dempsey   Wife of Robin Dempsey in David Lodge's *Changing Places: A Tale of Two Campuses*. She is divorced from Dempsey but is reunited with him in *Small World*.

Robin Dempsey   Linguistics specialist at the University of Rummidge; he unsuccessfully competes with Philip Swallow for a senior lectureship in David Lodge's *Changing Places: A Tale of Two Campuses*. He is divorced and at the University of Darlington; he pursues Angelica Pabst at the Rummidge conference, becomes obsessed with a psychiatric computer program that increases his jealous rage and despair, and reunites with his wife, Janet Dempsey, in *Small World*.

Dresyl Den   The father of Nahkri and Klils; he and

Little Yuli conquer Embruddock in Brian W. Aldiss's *Helliconia Spring*.

Sar Gotth Den Iyfilka's husband and the father of Dresyl Den in Brian W. Aldiss's *Helliconia Spring*.

Mr. Denby Styles Court accountant, who provides Alfred Inglethorp with an alibi in Agatha Christie's *The Mysterious Affair at Styles: A Detective Story*.

Mr. Denge Partner in the real-estate office of Denge & Donewell through whom Eva Trout purchases her first home, Cathay, on the north foreland of the English Channel in Elizabeth Bowen's *Eva Trout, or Changing Scenes*.

Sergeant Denham Investigator notified by Charlie Slatter that Mary Turner has been murdered; he must depend on Slatter for information and details concerning the events of the slaying in Doris Lessing's *The Grass Is Singing*.

Amelia Denham The only member of the Denham family who eschews family contact; Clelia's eldest sister, she married and "went mad" in Margaret Drabble's *Jerusalem the Golden*.

Annunciata (Nancy) Denham Clelia's youngest sibling; she is so like Clelia that Clara Maugham resents the "dilution" in Margaret Drabble's *Jerusalem the Golden*.

Candida Gray Denham A handsome, successful novelist and mother of five grown children; she is the center of a lively, mutually nourishing, almost exhaustingly embracing family that is extended to include, as well as her daughter Clelia's friend Clara Maugham, Clelia's married lover Martin, complete with infant son, in Margaret Drabble's *Jerusalem the Golden*.

Clelia Denham A creative, charming young painter who lives at home and works in the art gallery of her married lover, Martin; the liveliness and shared intimacy of her large family are a revelation to her friend Clara Maugham in Margaret Drabble's *Jerusalem the Golden*. Her brother Gabriel says he has always been in love with her in *The Middle Ground*.

Danny Denham Youngest son of Gabriel Denham; he is a friend to Reuben Armstrong in Margaret Drabble's *The Middle Ground*.

Gabriel Denham Clelia's pleasant and witty brother, who works in television; his remarkable good looks and sex appeal are irresistible to Clara Maugham; faithful heretofore to his unremittingly unhappy wife, Phillippa, he ventures upon a love affair with Clara in Margaret Drabble's *Jerusalem the Golden*. He is Phillippa's ex-husband and Jessica's husband; Kate Fletcher Armstrong's longtime friend, he has hired Kate to make a film he is producing; he says he has always been in love with his sister Clelia in *The Middle Ground*.

Jessica Denham Second wife of Gabriel Denham; she accuses him of having an affair with Kate Fletcher Armstrong in Margaret Drabble's *The Middle Ground*.

Magnus (Marcus) Denham Clelia's eldest brother, a political economist; he confides to Clara Maugham, whom he has accidentally encountered with his brother, Gabriel, in Paris, that he was once in love with Phillippa Denham; he insists that Clara kiss him in Margaret Drabble's *Jerusalem the Golden*. He is called Marcus in *The Middle Ground*.

Phillippa Denham Gabriel's passive, exhausted wife, who embraces suffering as an indiscriminate response to every frustration and irritation; philosophically as well as constitutionally unhappy, she is indifferent to her husband and children and brightens up only at social gatherings in Margaret Drabble's *Jerusalem the Golden*. She is Gabriel's ex-wife and Danny's mother in *The Middle Ground*.

Ralph Denham Katherine Hilbery's true love, who approaches fact through vision and with whom she can unite both, as he can with her; their relationship hinges upon Katharine's ability to reconcile her love of clean abstractions with the visionary side and upon Ralph's recognizing the reality underlying his dreams; Katherine supplies objectivity, and he provides imagination; he is also loved and altruistically renounced by Mary Datchet, who sees him as "a young Greek horseman who reins his horse back so sharply" in Virginia Woolf's *Night and Day*.

Sebastian Denham An admired fiftyish poet featured at a reading attended by Clara Maugham; he is Candida's husband and the father of Clelia and her siblings in Margaret Drabble's *Jerusalem the Golden*.

Denis A four-year-old boy who started murdering people at the age of three in Doris Lessing's *Memoirs of a Survivor*.

Denise Mother to Johnnie, a nursery-group playmate of Laurie Gray; Jane Gray's attempt at becoming friends with Denise is an early, tentative step in her breaking free of her nearly complete fear of social contact in Margaret Drabble's *The Waterfall*.

Martha Denman A rich, unpleasant widow whom Evelyn Jarrold sees in the exclusive London dress shop of Rivers and Roberts; squat as a toad, she is a vulgar woman whose excessive personal vanity is flattered by Julia Levison in Vita Sackville-West's *Family History*.

Charles Dennett Father of Roger and Edith Dennett; although he is partially paralyzed, he manages to earn an adequate livelihood for his family as an independent journalist and literary critic in Frank Swinnerton's *The Happy Family*.

Edith Dennett Teenaged sister of Roger Dennett; like her mother, she has a tender heart for any troubled person; when Jerrard Amerson dies, Edith and her mother nurse Mary Amerson back to health in Frank Swinnerton's *The Happy Family*.

L. Dennett Mother of Roger and Edith Dennett and wife of Charles; though less well educated than her husband, she too sprang from the class of small tradespeople; even though they are self-reliant and independent thinkers, both are sensitive to those in need; she welcomes Mary Amerson into her home in Frank Swinnerton's *The Happy Family*.

Roger Dennett Confidential clerk to the manager of Tremlett & Grove's, general publishers; formerly a school friend and now a senior colleague of Teddy Amerson, Dennett gradually becomes the object of Mary Amerson's love; he acts as a protector for both Mary and her sister Mabel in Frank Swinnerton's *The Happy Family*.

Dennis The stocky, successful husband of Angela; after their long engagement, including his two years in National Service, he becomes an executive in an electronics firm; he is devastated by the birth of one child with Down's Syndrome and the death of another in an accident, and he has an affair with his secretary, Lynn, but is reconciled with Angela in David Lodge's *How Far Can You Go?*.

Dennis ("Epaulets") Uncooperative doorman in Jake Driver's apartment building who briefly thwarts Gus Howkins's attempts to see Driver concerning his estranged wife, the mysterious Julia Delmore; he is a character in the story Giles Hermitage writes within John Wain's *The Pardoner's Tale*.

Arthur Denniston Sociologist and Fellow of Northumberland College, University of Edgestow; he is husband of Camilla and undergraduate friend of Mark Studdock, with whom he later competes for a fellowship at Bracton College; he is the member of the St. Anne's community who, along with Cecil Dimble and Jane Studdock, searches for Merlin's tomb in C. S. Lewis's *That Hideous Strength*.

Camilla Denniston Wife of Arthur Denniston and the member of the St. Anne's community who attempts to persuade Jane Studdock to join the community in C. S. Lewis's *That Hideous Strength*.

Gerald, Duke of Denver Lord Peter Wimsey's elder brother; arrested for the murder of Denis Cathcart, he refuses to supply an alibi in Dorothy L. Sayers's *Clouds of Witness*. He is shocked by his brother's and sister's matrimonial plans in *Strong Poison*.

Helen, Duchess of Denver The duke's conventional, uninteresting wife in Dorothy L. Sayers's *Clouds of Witness*. She appears in *Strong Poison*.

Lucy, Dowager Duchess of Denver Lord Peter Wimsey's mother, who summons Lord Peter to investigate the unknown corpse discovered in the bathtub of church architect Alfred Thipps in Dorothy L. Sayers's *Whose Body?*. She attends Harriet Vane's first trial and takes a liking to her in *Strong Poison*.

Deo Gratias Mutilated native; a cured leprosy victim, he is a helper of Dr. Colin and later servant to Querry; a burnt-out case himself, he is Querry's loyal ally, especially after Querry sits with him during his night of fear in Graham Greene's *A Burnt-Out Case*.

Horatio Benedict (Harry) dePalfrey British Intelligence's portentously lamenting legal counsel and disillusioned lover; in his recounting of the Russia House's Operation Bluebird, he admits papering over this intricate but ineptly managed operation and offers some insight into Barley Blair's treason in John le Carré's *The Russia House*.

Sir Montague Depleach Barrister who unsuccessfully defended Caroline Crale for the murder of her husband; he argued for suicide although, as he tells Hercule Poirot, he believed his client guilty in Agatha Christie's *Five Little Pigs*.

Robert de Quincey Director of the Garden Gallery and writer on aesthetics who examines Janos Lavin's work and rejects it because of its "desperate optimism" in John Berger's *A Painter of Our Time*.

Nancy Derek Englishwoman who opportunely helps Adela Quested escape the Marabar Caves; she has an affair with Mr. McBryde in E. M. Forster's *A Passage to India*.

Derik A derelict fifteen-year-old to whom eleven-year-old Ben Lovatt attaches himself after John leaves in Doris Lessing's *The Fifth Child*.

Grace Derlanger The middle-aged American wife of

Joe Derlanger; she is the hostess of a party Roger Micheldene attends, and although she does not understand her husband's bad temper, she accepts it in Kingsley Amis's *One Fat Englishman*.

Joe Derlanger   An American who invites Roger Micheldene to his parties; he has a bad temper, often becoming angry at such inanimate objects as his car and destroying them in Kingsley Amis's *One Fat Englishman*.

Mrs. Dermody   Receptionist for the spy ring "The Free Mothers" in Graham Greene's *The Ministry of Fear*.

Lord Derrydown   Chancellor of the Duchy of Lancaster for whom Arnold Condorex serves as secretary; he is the father of "young Ladyday" and is the target of Condorex's aim to topple the elder politicians in Rebecca West's *Harriet Hume, A London Fantasy*.

Mrs. Dersingham (Pongo)   Howard Dersingham's wife in J. B. Priestley's *Angel Pavement*.

Howard Dersingham   Snobbish head of Twigg and Dersingham, dealers in veneers and inlays used in the manufacture of furniture; he is out of touch with the market in a time of general economic depression in J. B. Priestley's *Angel Pavement*.

Walter Derwent   American who gives Sir Edward Leithen the clue he needs to search for Francis Galliard in Northern Canada in John Buchan's *Sick Heart River*.

Peter de Salis   An aspiring young poet who takes Clara Maugham to the poetry reading at which she meets Clelia Denham in Margaret Drabble's *Jerusalem the Golden*.

Lily DeSeitas (alias Julie Holmes)   The twin sister of Rose DeSeitas; she pretends to fall in love with Nicholas Urfe during Maurice Conchis's "god-game" on Phraxos; Urfe falls in love with her and tries to find her after the game is over, but finds only her mother, also named Lily, in John Fowles's *The Magus*.

Lily Montgomery DeSeitas (alias Constance Holmes) Mother of Lily and Rose; she assists Maurice Conchis in his elaborate schemes; Conchis also appropriates her maiden name for his invented boyhood love and fiancée in John Fowles's *The Magus*.

Rose DeSeitas (alias June Holmes)   The twin sister of Lily DeSeitas, with whom Nicholas Urfe falls in love on Phraxos; the elder Lily DeSeitas's daughter, she is an actress employed by Maurice Conchis in John Fowles's *The Magus*.

De Selby   Mad scientist and inventor of the dread DMP in Flann O'Brien's *The Dalkey Archive*. His theories of space, time, matter, and motion are footnoted in *The Third Policeman*.

Wilfred Desert   Successful poet, wounded in World War I, who is published by Michael Mont's firm; he is attracted to Fleur Forsyte and leaves England for Arabia in John Galsworthy's *The White Monkey*. He causes Fleur to feel Michael is ignoring her in *The Silver Spoon*. He returns to London in 1930, plans to marry Dinny Cherrell, is ostracized as a coward, brawls with Jack Muskham, and leaves England and Dinny for Siam in despair in *Flowering Wilderness*. His death by drowing near Bangkok is reported in *Over the River*.

Nick de Silsky   Bill Haydon's protégé and secret courier; he is forced out by George Smiley in John le Carré's *Tinker, Tailor, Soldier, Spy* and in *The Honourable Schoolboy*. He is re-employed by Toby Esterhase to help kidnap and blackmail Anton Grigoriev in *Smiley's People*.

DeSilva   Originally a friend of Molly Jacobs from Ceylon; he abandons his wife and two children; he sleeps once with Anna Wulf and attempts to control her, but Anna firmly rejects him in Doris Lessing's *The Golden Notebook*.

Desmond   Carpenter at Wood Hill, the estate of Conrad, Lord Field in Isabel Colegate's *Orlando King*.

Desmond   Oxford scientist who meets Arthur Miles in Munich; he is the swing vote on the committee to establish the new National Institute, and he turns against Miles after the notoriety of the incorrect research report in C. P. Snow's *The Search*.

Esther De Solla   Painter and ascetic who introduces Marya Zelli to the Heidlers and is uneasy about Marya's living with the Heidlers in Jean Rhys's *Postures*.

Major John Despard   A suspect of the murder of Mr. Shaitana in Agatha Christie's *Cards on the Table*. He has been promoted to Colonel and is called Hugh in *The Pale Horse*.

Rhoda Dawes Despard   Anne Meredith's former roommate and Major John Despard's wife; she becomes Ariadne Oliver's friend in Agatha Christie's *Cards on the Table*. She also appears in *The Pale Horse*.

Albert T. Despard-Smith   Mathematician, clergyman, and Cambridge fellow, who opposes Roy Calvert's election; he delivers the eulogy at Calvert's memorial service in C. P. Snow's *The Light and the Dark*. He nurses an old grievance that he was not elected

Master years ago and supports election of Redvers Crawford as new Master so that Paul Jago will know the same grievance in C. P. Snow's *The Masters*.

Teresa Desterro   A South American who is a physical-education-college graduating senior; her critical assessment of her fellow students alerts Lucy Pym to discord in the school in Josephine Tey's *Miss Pym Disposes*.

Detective-Sergeant   Hard-nosed man who promotes Edward Justice to plain-clothes policeman but then suspends him when he refuses to testify against Frankie Love in Colin MacInnes's *Mr. Love and Justice*.

Evelyn de Tracy   The transvestite professional director hired by the Stilbourne Operatic Society; he tries drunkenly to share some of his perceptions about the town and its inhabitants with Oliver in William Golding's *The Pyramid*.

Guy de Travest   Soldier, family man, and self-possessed guardian of aristocratic values; he is the proper but concerned standard-bearer of discretion and conduct among his social circle in Michael Arlen's *The Green Hat*.

Captain Deverax   Thin, monocle-wearing snob; Denry Machin tricks him into total discomfiture and departure from the Alpine village where Denry is honeymooning in Arnold Bennett's *The Card: A Story of Adventure in the Five Towns*.

De Vere   The Quantocks' parlormaid in E. F. Benson's *"Queen Lucia"* and in *Lucia in London*.

Miss Devi   Beautiful, inscrutable Asiatic Indian secretary to Mr. Theodorescu; she seduces Denis Hillier for her employer, and during their liaison, she drugs him in Anthony Burgess's *Tremor of Intent*.

Miss de Vine   The new Research Fellow at Shrewsbury College, Oxford; a hard-minded, distinguished scholar, she was formerly administrator of a provincial college in Dorothy L. Sayers's *Gaudy Night*.

Dick Devine, Lord Feverstone   Elwin Ransom's former classmate, who is a mysterious financier and a Member of Parliament; he and Edward Weston kidnap Elwin Ransom and take him to Malacandra (Mars); Ransom escapes from Weston and Devine, and in their search for Ransom, they are captured by inhabitants of Malacandra and delivered to Oyarsa of Malacandra; he and Weston are expelled from Malacandra and return to Earth in C. S. Lewis's *Out of the Silent Planet*. As a Fellow of Bracton College, Lord Feverstone is involved in promoting the evil programs of the N.I.C.E. (National Institute for Coordinated Experiments); he

introduces Mark Studdock to the leaders of the N.I.C.E.; he is killed in the destruction of the city of Edgestow in *That Hideous Strength*.

John Devine   Unruly British youth who, brought to the Vatican to build his character, serves as Hadrian VII's Gentleman in Waiting with extreme loyalty in Frederick William Rolfe's *Hadrian the Seventh*.

Tom Devitt   Physician who courts Sheila Knight; he accompanies Sheila when she uses him to embarrass Lewis Eliot at the Edens'; he gives a medical exam to Eliot in C. P. Snow's *Time of Hope*.

Zoë Devlin   Dorothy Mellings's long-time friend, who eventually parts with Dorothy because of their increasingly different political and philosophical outlooks in Doris Lessing's *The Good Terrorist*.

Paul de Vries   Wealthy American idealist whose blind devotion to Veronica Thwale, whom he eventually marries, prevents him from seeing her many deceptions in Aldous Huxley's *Time Must Have a Stop*.

Mrs. de Winter   The young, timid, naïve paid companion of Mrs. Van Hopper; Maxim de Winter meets her in Monte Carlo, marries her, and brings her back to his English estate, Manderly; her jealousy of her predecessor, Rebecca de Winter, is fostered by the housekeeper, Mrs. Danvers, but she grows in strength and resolution; so self-effacing that she never reveals her name, she is the first-person narrator of Daphne Du Maurier's *Rebecca*.

Maxim de Winter   Aristocratic owner of the estate Manderly; he marries — presumably out of pity, as well as loneliness following his beloved first wife's death — a timid, browbeaten young woman, with whom he returns home; he is aloofly unsympathetic to his wife's awkward attempts to fill her predecessor's place; gradually a different picture of his first marriage emerges in Daphne Du Maurier's *Rebecca*.

Rebecca de Winter   Stunningly beautiful and poised late wife of Maxim, who is generally believed to be unmanned by grief at her accidental drowning; a legendary model of perfection as wife and hostess, she is the object of her successor's unhappy jealousy until a different picture of her and of her marriage emerges in Daphne Du Maurier's *Rebecca*.

Violet de Winter (The Countess)   Friend of Mark Curran, agent of GESS (Global-Equip Security Services), and because of wartime treachery in Venice, victim of Robert Leaver's blackmail attempt in Muriel Spark's *Territorial Rights*.

Clive de Wit   A man with an African contact who wants to start a study group with some of Martha Quest's acquaintances; however, he distrusts both Martha and Mrs. Van der Bylt in Doris Lessing's *Landlocked*.

Count Nikolai Nikolaievitch Diakanov   Laura Rowan's grandfather; formerly Russian Minister of Justice, he is now in exile in Paris; after a heart attack he gives a long speech preceding his death in Rebecca West's *The Birds Fall Down*.

Countess Sofia Andreievna Diakanova   Dying wife of Nikolai Diakanov in Rebecca West's *The Birds Fall Down*.

Diana   A talented art-school dropout, who is nicknamed "the Mouse" by Henry Breasley, with whom she lives; she befriends and nearly makes love to David Williams in John Fowles's *The Ebony Tower*.

Diana   Nick's wife and Simon Camish's frequent hostess; she is an old acquaintance of Rose Vassiliou in Margaret Drabble's *The Needle's Eye*.

Diana   Imogene King's roommate in Isabel Colegate's *Agatha*.

Diana   One of Orlando King's secretary/lovers; she is hated by Judith (Gardner) King in Isabel Colegate's *Orlando King*.

Diawl Du ("black devil")   A large and aggressive dog that bullies Sirius and then is nearly killed by him in Olaf Stapledon's *Sirius: A Fantasy of Love and Discord*.

Jeremy Dibden   Augustine Penry-Herbert's Oxford friend who argues that all revolutionary movements are flights from freedom in Richard Hughes's *The Fox in the Attic*. A German-speaking journalist sent to report on Germany in 1938, he is surprised at the ease with which he learns of her rearmament in *The Wooden Shepherdess*.

Joan Dibden   Pretty young aunt of Jeremy Dibden; she falls in love with Augustine Penry-Herbert but tires of his fear of commitment and marries Anthony Fairfax in Richard Hughes's *The Wooden Shepherdess*.

Dick   A writer and friend of Rosamund Stacey in Margaret Drabble's *The Millstone*.

Dick   An Inside member of the British Communist Party and a socialist-realist novelist who does a lot of traveling and has recently returned from Russia in Doris Lessing's *The Golden Notebook*.

Mr. Dickingham   Scrubby little solicitor with a rasping voice; he tries to influence the shareholders' vote in the annual meeting of the Imperial Palace Hotel Company in Arnold Bennett's *Imperial Palace*.

Miss Dickinson   Insinuating head assistant at Baines's drapery shop in Bursley; her gossip embarasses Anna Tellwright in Arnold Bennett's *Anna of the Five Towns*.

Diego   Paraguayan guerrilla, a member of the group that kidnaps Charley Fortnum; he dies trying to escape the police in Graham Greene's *The Honorary Consul*.

Senor Diego   A Galician wine merchant visited by Father Quixote and Enrique Zancas on their way to the Trappist Monastery at Osera; they pause there to buy wine before continuing their journey in Graham Greene's *Monsignor Quixote*.

Mr. Dierck   Salaried secretary of an American society of thought; on his first visit to Europe he researches his ancestry, falls in love with Cecily Corner, criticizes the falseness of English society, and is injured in a car crash; embarrassed by his uninvolvement in the war, he joins the Canadian army in H. G. Wells's *Mr. Britling Sees It Through*.

Hippolyte Dieudonne   Haitian drummer with the Isabel Cornwallis Ballet Company; he practices voodoo in Colin MacInnes's *City of Spades*.

Alastair Digby-Vane-Trumpington   One of the wealthy Oxford fraternity brothers whose drunken antics are responsible for Paul Pennyfeather's expulsion from college; later he and Paul become friendly; he becomes Margot Beste-Chetwynde's lover after she marries Maltravers in Evelyn Waugh's *Decline and Fall*.

Patrick Dignam   Acquaintance of Leopold Bloom, who attends his funeral in James Joyce's *Ulysses*.

Patrick Aloysius Dignam   Son of Patrick Dignam, whose funeral Leopold Bloom attends in James Joyce's *Ulysses*.

Sir George Dillingham   Wealthy and distinguished poet and uncle of Alexis Golightly; when he finds Alexis with Rose Vibert at his villa at Pau, he is at first quite angry, but later, charmed by Mademoiselle Vibert, he leaves the villa reconciled with his nephew; Rose and Sir George become lovers and eventually marry; their daughter, Jenny, is born several years later; the three Dillinghams live at a vineyard near Chinon, although Rose returns to the theater and openly takes a lover, Vincent; Sir George's fatal heart attack occurs fourteen years after Jenny's birth in David Garnett's *Aspects of Love*.

Jeanne (Jenny) Dillingham Daughter of Sir George and Rose Dillingham; somewhat precocious, Jenny at fourteen becomes infatuated and believes herself in love with her cousin Alexis Golightly, more than twenty years her senior; his protective feelings toward her overshadow any romantic attraction that might develop in David Garnett's *Aspects of Love*.

Rose Vibert Dillingham Beautiful and free-spirited French actress who first becomes the lover of the very young and inexperienced Alexander Golightly; later she marries his uncle, Sir George Dillingham, a wealthy widower and poet; after the birth of their daughter, Jenny, Rose and George become reconciled with Alexis, who is visiting them on the night, fourteen years later, of Sir George's fatal heart attack in David Garnett's *Aspects of Love*.

Mr. Dillon Real-estate agent and a director of the Saddleford Building Society in Roy Fuller's *Image of a Society*.

Bernard Dillon An Oxford neighbor of Daniel Martin; he becomes a critic and television personality; he is known to Dan as "Barney"; he becomes the lover of Dan's daughter, Caroline, in John Fowles's *Daniel Martin*.

Dim A descriptively named, large, stupid, and particularly vicious young delinquent and member of Alex's gang; he has a correspondingly large capacity for resentment, which leads him to avenge himself on Alex for the latter's condescending treatment of him in Anthony Burgess's *A Clockwork Orange*.

Cecil Dimble Fellow of Northumberland College, University of Edgestow, tutor to Jane Studdock, and a member of the St. Anne's community; his knowledge of medieval England helps the community search for and communicate with Merlin in C. S. Lewis's *That Hideous Strength*.

Margaret (Mother) Dimble Wife of Cecil Dimble, friend of Jane Studdock, and a member of the St. Anne's community; she encourages Jane to visit St. Anne's and to speak to Grace Ironwood about Jane's troubling dreams in C. S. Lewis's *That Hideous Strength*.

Ramon Diosdado (the Elephant) Father of A Few Fleas; he is owner of the Farolito, the bar where Geoffrey Firmin dies in Malcolm Lowry's *Under the Volcano*.

The Director Belvedere School official who encour-

ages Stephen Dedalus to prepare for the priesthood in James Joyce's *Ulysses*.

"Doc" ("the Mad Jesuit") di Salis Grumbling and grubby former priest, Oriental scholar, fieldman, and recruiter who heads the China surveillance operation for British Intelligence; with Connie Sachs, he educates George Smiley on Nelson Ko's and Drake Ko's motivations in John le Carré's *The Honourable Schoolboy*.

The Discoverer A Chinese physicist who invents, uses, and destroys a superweapon before committing suicide and much later is misconceived as the prophet of the pseudo-scientific religious cult of Gordelpus in Olaf Stapledon's *Last and First Men: A Story of the Near and Far Future*.

Distinguished Professor Competent female Chairman of a debate that forms the entertainment provided at a party given by *Time and Tide,* a publication for which the Provincial Lady also writes; her demeanor makes her contempt for the Provincial Lady's literary efforts clear in E. M. Delafield's *The Provincial Lady Goes Further*.

Lord Dittisham Poet-dramatist who has spent large sums staging his own works; he is the third husband of Elsa Greer in Agatha Christie's *Five Little Pigs*.

The Divine Boy (or, the Boy Who Refused to Grow Up) A religious prophet of the Patagonian civilization who teaches that life must be recognized as a game in Olaf Stapledon's *Last and First Men: A Story of the Near and Far Future*.

John Divney Partner in crime and murderer of the narrator, whose ghostly reappearance after many years causes Divney's own death in Flann O'Brien's *The Third Policeman*.

Lily Divver Max Divver's wife; weary of his neglect, she requests a divorce; she is later unaffected by news of his death in Nigel Dennis's *Boys and Girls Come Out to Play*.

Max Divver The liberal editor of *Forward* magazine whom Mrs. Morgan sends to Poland as a journalist and as her son's guardian; he becomes the lackey of and is later murdered by the tyrannical Larry Streeter in Nigel Dennis's *Boys and Girls Come Out to Play*.

Sandra Dix A beautiful student who seduces and blackmails Philip Swallow and Rodney Wainwright in order to pass her exams in David Lodge's *Small World*.

Jim Dixon A junior lecturer in medieval history at a provincial university; of lower-middle-class origin, he despises insincerity and snobbishness in academia and dislikes his job; he unintentionally imitates Professor Welch during his "Merrie England" lecture, loses his job, and moves toward self-realization in Kingsley Amis's *Lucky Jim.*

Gareth Dobell   Wife of Colonel Felix Dobell, member of the Guardians of Ethics in the United States, and an unexpected visitor to the May of Teck Club in Muriel Spark's *The Girls of Slender Means.*

Colonel G. Felix Dobell   Head of a branch of American Intelligence and the married lover of Selina Redwood in Muriel Spark's *The Girls of Slender Means.*

Jack Dobie   A Socialist Member of Parliament who is later appointed member of a committee on the condition of urban Africans; he wants to have an affair with Martha Quest in Doris Lessing's *A Ripple from the Storm* and in *Landlocked.*

Diana Dobson   Handicapped woman from a poor background; she marries Maurice Hollis and has a baby in C. P. Snow's *Last Things.*

Zuleika Dobson   A "not strictly beautiful" but thoroughly adorable orphan who supports herself by ineptly performing conjuring tricks and is the "toast of two hemispheres"; in honor of her charms the entire undergraduate population of Oxford University commit suicide; she abandons her impulsively remorseful decision to take the veil and orders a special train to Cambridge at the end of Max Beerbohm's *Zuleika Dobson; or An Oxford Love Story.*

Charlie Docksey   A struggling reporter of the *Daily Record*; while he interviews an actress who is his friend, she greets a society priest of her acquaintance who then discusses with them the appropriateness of burying Priam Farll in Westminster Abbey as Farll, sitting nearby, overhears in Arnold Bennett's *Buried Alive: A Tale of These Days.*

Colonel Colin Dodd   Dinner guest at Daniel House's island home; he has written a book about the Sherpas and shows some knowledge of Sanskrit in Roy Fuller's *The Carnal Island.*

Lewis Dodd   Lean, pale, plain-faced, and rude Englishman who nevertheless is irresistible to women; Dodd is a gifted composer and disciple of Albert Sanger; he loves Sanger's daughter Teresa but marries Florence Churchill instead; he finally leaves Florence to run away with Teresa, only to lose her to death in Margaret Kennedy's *The Constant Nymph.*

Millicent Dodd   Lewis Dodd's toothy, pop-eyed sister, who possesses a "tongue like a horse radish" and spreads gossip generously as she climbs in society in Margaret Kennedy's *The Constant Nymph.*

Reuben J. Dodd   Jewish solicitor, agent for the Patriotic Insurance Co., and moneylender, who is the object of anti-Semitic remarks in James Joyce's *Ulysses.*

Mr. Dodge   Chief Superintendent of the fire service in Henry Green's *Caught.*

William Dodge   Self-described clerk carted to Pointz Hall by Mrs. Manresa on the day of the village pageant; Mrs. Manresa describes William as an artist in Virginia Woolf's *Between The Acts.*

Mr. Dodson   Innkeeper in Dalquharter village who refuses to give Dickson McCunn and John Heritage a room; he is captured by the Gorbals Die-Hards and locked in the boiler room at Huntingtower in John Buchan's *Huntingtower.*

Revission Doe   Publisher who contracts for Fleur Talbot's *Warrender Chase* and then refuses to publish it because of Sir Quentin Oliver's blackmail threat in Muriel Spark's *Loitering with Intent.*

Doeg   Planet 8's main representative, who records the story of the planet's sudden shift on its axis, which causes the coming of the Ice (-Age) — an event which destroys people, both physically and emotionally — in Doris Lessing's *The Making of the Representative for Planet 8.*

Miss Doggett   Dogmatic spinster who tyrannizes the parish society, especially her companion Jessie Morrow, in Barbara Pym's *Jane and Prudence.*

Harry Dogson   Persistent tabloid reporter and college acquaintance of Charles Lumley; he discovers the export-delivery drug-smuggling ring in which Charles is involved and, as a result, is beaten up or killed by Teddy Bunder and his cohorts in John Wain's *Hurry On Down.*

Johnnie Doig   The policeman who comes with Dickson McCunn to Castle Gay just in time to overhear Thomas Carlyle Craw and others threatened by Evallonian political intriguers in John Buchan's *Castle Gay.*

Father Dolan   Prefect at the Clongowes School who pandies Stephen Dedalus after unjustly accusing him of breaking his glasses in James Joyce's *Ulysses.*

George Dolgelly   Farmer in Wales with whom the narrator and Emily Cartright can take refuge if they are forced to move; the narrator creates pastoral fantasies about the Dolgellys to help her in crisis situations in Doris Lessing's *Memoirs of a Survivor*.

Mary Dolgelly   Wife of George in Doris Lessing's *Memoirs of a Survivor*.

Dr. Dolling   Exiled Frenchman who is one leader of the Proudham Society; his revolutionary rhetoric has a great influence on the young Chester Nimmo in Joyce Cary's *Except the Lord*.

Dolly   An aging former chorus girl who cleans the Palladium cinema and talks to Gertrude Halibut in David Lodge's *The Picturegoers*.

Luke Dolour   Thickly built, silent fellow with an eye to the bed and the board in Stella Gibbons's *Cold Comfort Farm*.

Mark Dolour   Silent fellow with a penchant for chicken feathers in Stella Gibbons's *Cold Comfort Farm*.

Miss Dolton   The nursery governess to the Challoners; she is loved best by Claude and Emma; her pupils grow beyond her in Ivy Compton-Burnett's *A Heritage and Its History*.

Dominguez   Thomas Fowler's Asiatic informant and newspaper stringer; he sends Fowler to Mr. Heng, a leader in the Vietnamese underground, to discover the nature of Alden Pyle's covert connection to General Thé in Graham Greene's *The Quiet American*.

Raul Dominguez (code identification: 59200/5/4)   See James Wormold.

Dominic   Audacious Corsican who assists Monsieur George in gunrunning in Joseph Conrad's *The Arrow of Gold: A Story Between Two Notes*.

Don   A young English R.A.F. pilot who marries Maisie Gale but is killed in Doris Lessing's *A Proper Marriage*.

James (Jake) Donaghue   A writer who makes a living from translations and other literary odd jobs; his commercially and critically unsuccessful philosophical treatise *The Silencer* owes much to his friend Hugo Belfounder; he is in love with Anna Quentin and is loved by her sister, Sadie; the fruitless result of his energetic efforts at benign extortion convinces him to get a job and to settle himself seriously to his own writing; he is narrator of Iris Murdoch's *Under the Net*.

Donkin   Troublesome cockney sailor who befriends the dying black sailor James Wait and challenges Cap-

tain Allistoun, who recognizes that Wait is dying in Joseph Conrad's *The Nigger of the "Narcissus"*.

Anna Donne   A thirty-year-old woman, bossy and rude; she destroys her Aunt Sukey Donne's real will so that she will inherit, and drives her Aunt Jessica Calderone to suicide in Ivy Compton-Burnett's *Elders and Betters*.

Benjamin Donne   A widower for twelve years; lately retired from a government office, he wishes now to spend time with his sisters in Ivy Compton-Burnett's *Elders and Betters*.

Bernard Donne   The eldest, somewhat stout son of Benjamin Donne; he proposes to his cousin Tullia Calderone in Ivy Compton-Burnett's *Elders and Betters*.

Edgar Donne   The latest curate over whom Harriet Bede has mildly made a fool of herself in Barbara Pym's *Some Tame Gazelle*.

Esmond Donne   The child least liked by his father, Benjamin Donne; he is a young man who makes cynical comments but understands his sister Anna better than the rest of the family do in Ivy Compton-Burnett's *Elders and Betters*.

Reuben Donne   Anna's youngest brother, who is lame from an accident; he is tutored by his cousin Terence Calderone in Ivy Compton-Burnett's *Elders and Betters*.

Susan (Aunt Sukey) Donne   Jessica Calderone's sister; a querulous, self-absorbed invalid, she dies after becoming friendly with her niece Anna Donne in Ivy Compton-Burnett's *Elders and Betters*.

Sir Magnus Donners   Magnate of the City and employer of Bill Truscott and Charles Stringham in Anthony Powell's *A Question of Upbringing*. His business and social prominence and his undisclosed sexual proclivities make him a subject of speculation; he is accompanied by Baby Wentworth in *A Buyer's Market*. He takes up with Matilda Wilson in *The Acceptance World*. After her marriage to Hugh Morland, Donners lends the couple a cottage; he goes about with Lady Anne (Stepney) Umfraville in *The Kindly Ones*. He marries the divorced Matilda in *The Soldier's Art*. His political fortunes change with the times in *The Valley of Bones* and in *The Military Philosophers*. His sexual tastes and voyeurism are analyzed after his death in *Books Do Furnish a Room*. The Magnus Donners Prize is established by his widow fifteen years after his death in *Hearing Secret Harmonies*.

Mr. Donnington   Inn landlord and churchwarden;

he pulls the number six bell, "Dimity", in Dorothy L. Sayers's *The Nine Tailors: Changes Rung on an Old Theme in Two Short Touches and Two Full Peals.*

Aunt Ada Doom   The powerful old matriarch who spends all her time in her room brooding but nevertheless rules the Starkadder family with an iron hand until Flora Poste suggests that a much more pleasant life can be had by a handsome old lady of good fortune and firm will in Stella Gibbons's *Cold Comfort Farm.*

Mrs. Doone   Mother of Sylvia (Lennon) and sister of Gordy Heatherly; in poor health, she travels for therapy with Sylvia as her companion in John Galsworthy's *The Dark Flower.*

Doramin   Malay chief whose son, Dain Waris, is murdered by the rapacious Gentleman Brown; he shoots Lord Jim in retribution in Joseph Conrad's *Lord Jim.*

Doris   Senior waitress at Snow's, the restaurant at which Rose Wilson is employed, in Graham Greene's *Brighton Rock.*

Doris   George's dying friend who some years earlier had seduced Jim in Christopher Isherwood's *A Single Man.*

Ann Dorland   Ward and distant relative of Lady Dormer; she refuses to cooperate with Lord Peter Wimsey when he makes inquiries in Dorothy L. Sayers's *The Unpleasantness at the Bellona Club.*

Margaret Dorman   Neville Stafford's friend, who dates Colin Saville and discusses marriage with him but leaves him for Neville in David Storey's *Saville.*

Felicity, Lady Dormer   Wealthy long-estranged but lately reconciled sister of General Fentiman; their deaths occur on the same morning in Dorothy L. Sayers's *The Unpleasantness at the Bellona Club.*

Eustace Dornford   A nearly middle-aged barrister, a veteran of World War I, and a newly elected Member of Parliament; he marries Dinny Cherrell in John Galsworthy's *Over the River.*

Dorothy   Harriet Lovatt's mother, who believes that her daughter's repeated pregnancies indicate utter irresponsibility; she manages to stay and help Harriet raise her first four children, ultimately leaving her to fend for herself after Ben Lovatt's birth in Doris Lessing's *The Fifth Child.*

Dorothy   Upper-middle-class Englishwoman who travels to Germany to explore Communism and brings her boyfriend, Waldemar, into Britain in Christopher Isherwood's *Down There on a Visit.*

Dorothy   Cyril's red-haired daughter, who conscientiously albeit perfunctorily visits her father in the hospital and who is, according to her father, shameless and fleshy like her mother in John Berger's *The Foot of Clive.*

Miss Dorrington   The ungainly lecturer in German with eruptive skin; she exhibits moral attractiveness at the women's college that Dolores Hutton attends in Ivy Compton-Burnett's *Dolores.*

Tam Dorrit   Member of the secret society the Free Fishers of Forth and loyal ally of Anthony Lammas's applications to join the society in John Buchan's *The Free Fishers.*

John Tanville-Tankerton, Duke of Dorset   Zuleika Dobson's romantic suitor; though he has become disaffected, resolving to spurn her and not to die for love, honor and reputation require that he carry out his pledge of suicide, which the other Oxford undergraduates have pledged to emulate in Max Beerbohm's *Zuleika Dobson; or An Oxford Love Story.*

Dorsey   Elderly, intelligent, reserved clerk; he is an expert with captured dispatches in C. S. Forester's *Hornblower And the Crisis: An Unfinished Novel.*

Countess Dorsoduro   Friend of Lady Nelly Staveley in Venice; she playfully teases Eustace Cherrington during his stay as he embarks on becoming a writer in L. P. Hartley's *Eustace and Hilda.*

Duncan Dott   Lawyer and town-clerk of the burgh of Waucht; he becomes an important ally in the group devoted to saving Lord Belses and bringing Squire Cranmer to justice in John Buchan's *The Free Fishers.*

Dottie   Censorious Catholic and wife of Leslie (lover of Fleur Talbot); she steals her friend Fleur's manuscript in Muriel Spark's *Loitering with Intent.*

Gertrude Doubleday   The mother of Gideon and Magdelen; she receives letters at Miss Buchanan's shop and notices the knife that George, the Lambs' footman, carries in Ivy Compton-Burnett's *Manservant and Maidservant.*

Gideon Doubleday   The tutor for all the Lamb children except Avery; he lives unmarried with his mother and sister in Ivy Compton-Burnett's *Manservant and Maidservant.*

Magdelen Doubleday   Gideon's sister; she finds a letter from Charlotte Lamb to Mortimer Lamb and reveals their planned escape together to Horace Lamb in Ivy Compton-Burnett's *Manservant and Maidservant.*

Lydia Douce Bronze-haired, siren-like barmaid whom Leopold Bloom encounters at the Ormond Hotel in James Joyce's *Ulysses.*

Harvey (Boy) Dougdale Husband of Polly Hampton's aunt, Patricia Dougdale, and lover of Polly's mother, Lady Montdore; known as the Lecherous Lecturer, he is a general Casanova with a penchant for very young girls; his hobbies include needlework and the history of the nobility; he becomes Polly's husband and enters into a homosexual liaison with Cedric Hampton at the end of Nancy Mitford's *Love in a Cold Climate.*

Lady Patricia Dougdale Lord Montdore's sister and Boy Dougdale's sickly wife; she is a beautiful, quiet woman ashamed of her unfaithful husband and relieved when his philandering seems limited to her sister-in-law, Lady Montdore; her death paves the way for his marriage to her niece, Polly Hampton, in Nancy Mitford's *Love in a Cold Climate.*

Beth Doughty Efficient spinster in her mid-forties; she is an administrator of an old-people's home near Letty Crowe's friend Marjorie's country cottage, and rival for Marjorie's fiancé, David Lydell, in Barbara Pym's *Quartet in Autumn.*

Vicar Douglas The rather confused and ineffectual young cleric who performs funeral rites for Elizabeth Barclay in William Golding's *The Paper Men.*

Dougal Douglas (Douglas Dougal) Mysterious (possibly satanic) interloper in the world of Peckham Rye; his persuasive, experimentally manipulative personality is given scope by his employment as Arts man at Meadows, Meade & Grindley — bringing "vision" to industry — and causes class unrest, disrupted relationships, and a brutal murder in Muriel Spark's *The Ballad of Peckham Rye.*

Molly Douglas Commonplace and dowdy-looking wife of the blind Timmy Douglas; she is indifferent to Olivia Curtis in Rosamond Lehmann's *Invitation to the Waltz.*

Monica Douglas The member of "the Brodie set" who is "famous for mathematics" in Muriel Spark's *The Prime of Miss Jean Brodie.*

Timmy Douglas Pale, worn-looking young man, blinded in the war, who dances with Olivia Curtis; in

general he resignedly sits while his wife enjoys the dance in Rosamond Lehmann's *Invitation to the Waltz.*

Dennis Dover ("father") Chairman of the Board of Directors and largest shareholder; he is over seventy, of huge frame, with damaged vocal chords; he implicitly trusts the judgment of his protégé Evelyn Orcham and casts his vote for the merger of his prized hotel with seven other luxury hotels in Arnold Bennett's *Imperial Palace.*

Johnnie Dow Journeying packman who brings news of the other farm towns and Kirk Aller to Woodilee village in John Buchan's *Witch Wood.*

Dowager Duchess Sebastian's grandmother; she believes firmly in the old creed that the people who lead the aristocracy deserve their privileges in Vita Sackville-West's *The Edwardians.*

Florence Hurlbird Dowell Beautiful, upper-class New England wife of John Dowell; her "heart condition" is unmasked as a fraud used to cover her affair with Edward Ashburnham; she commits suicide when an earlier infidelity is uncovered in Ford Madox Ford's *The Good Soldier: A Tale of Passion.*

John Dowell An intelligent, upper-class, well-educated, extremely wealthy American Quaker; he attends his "ailing" wife, Florence, in spas and resorts for ten years; after her suicide, he discovers her prolonged infidelity with his best friend; henceforth he sees the beauty and harmony of upper-class life as deceptions in Ford Madox Ford's *The Good Soldier: A Tale of Passion.*

Sir Lionel Dowling Aristocrat who tries to seduce Sonia Sands at the opening of Vardon Hall in Angus Wilson's *Hemlock and After.*

Roger Emmanuel Downes Moviegoer sitting next to the murdered George Earlsfield; because of the broken alphabetical sequence, Colonel Anderson believes that Downes was the intended victim in Agatha Christie's *The A.B.C. Murders.*

Inspector Doyle Irish local police chief investigating the death of Edwin Lorrimer; he is assisted by Adam Dalgliesh in P. D. James's *Death of an Expert Witness.*

Julia Doyle A young, energetic, worshipful Irish girl, who joins Miriam Henderson as a teacher in the north London school and tries to relieve Miriam's burden with the youngest girls in Dorothy Richardson's *Backwater.*

Ruby Doyle Alexandra McCaffrey's almost life-long

servant, who acted as nurse to George, Brian, and Tom; her increased assertiveness is seen by Alexandra as a symbol of societal breakdown in sense and order in Iris Murdoch's *The Philosopher's Pupil*.

Marc-Ange Draco   Head of the French crime syndicate Union Corse; he becomes James Bond's ally against Ernst Stavro Blofeld, initially because he thinks Bond is the right man for his daughter, Tracy di Vicenzo, in Ian Fleming's *On Her Majesty's Secret Service*.

Princess Natalia Dragomiroff   Fascinatingly ugly, bejewelled passenger on the Calais Coach; she is proved to have been the godmother of Daisy Armstrong's mother in Agatha Christie's *Murder on the Orient Express*.

Drake   The married lover of Sylvia Satterthwaite; her suspicion that she is pregnant is the motive for her marriage to Christopher Tietjens in Ford Madox Ford's *Some Do Not. . . .* Drake takes revenge after Sylvia's marriage by inserting slanderous material into Christopher Tietjens's military file in *A Man Could Stand Up —*.

Elfreda Drake   Widow of an American millionaire attracted to Cosmo Sultana; wishing to put her dead husband's money into sociological studies, she gives Sultana and Owen Tuby sufficient funds to start the Institute of Social Imagistics in J. B. Priestley's *The Image Men*.

Drakefield   One of two cronies on the staff of Lord Raingo's Ministry of Records; Raingo hopes to see them to ease his awkward entry for the first time to the St. James's Club frequented by government members in Arnold Bennett's *Lord Raingo*.

Dravog   The brutal lieutenant of guards who oversees Yuli's work with prisoners in Pannoval in Brian W. Aldiss's *Helliconia Spring*.

Cyril Drawbell   Superintendent of British atomic energy research who is replaced by Walter Luke after World War II; he is disappointed in his hope for knighthood in C. P. Snow's *The New Men*.

Sir Hugo Drax   Supposed English national hero, who awakens M's suspicion because he cheats at cards; backed by the USSR, he has almost ready a weapon to destroy London as a means of avenging Germany; he is foiled by James Bond in Ian Fleming's *Moonraker*.

Dreamer, Q.C.   Senior barrister who takes on Winifred Dartie's divorce case in John Galsworthy's *In Chancery*.

James Dreme   A teen movie-idol whose death is constantly mourned by Hilda Syms in David Lodge's *The Picturegoers*.

Drew   Reporter who helps James Latter escape after he tries to kill Chester Nimmo; later Drew records Jim's story about why he killed his wife, but the newspaper rewrites it and distorts the truth in Joyce Cary's *Not Honour More*.

Lady Drew   The lady of Bladesover estate; she represents the persistence of the Victorian class structure in H. G. Wells's *Tono-Bungay*.

Mr. Drewitt   Middle-aged, tough, shady lawyer paid by Pinkie Brown and other mob members for legal advice; he witnesses Pinkie's and Rose Wilson's wedding; he is arrested as he tries to leave Brighton and tells the police about Pinkie's murder of Charles Hale and Spicer in Graham Greene's *Brighton Rock*.

Amy Driffeld   Determined, forceful, organized hostess and Edward's second wife; she was his nurse when Rose left him; she molded Edward during his later years into a genteel and cultured gentleman in W. Somerset Maugham's *Cakes and Ale: Or the Skeleton in the Cupboard*.

Edward Driffeld (fictionalized portrait of Thomas Hardy)   Irresponsible, sociable, unique, contradictive writer; hailed as a gentleman in his later life, Edward was considered lower class in his hometown when he was young; disliking social convention, Edward did what he liked until his late life, when the world recognized him as a great novelist, with help from his second wife, Amy, in W. Somerset Maugham's *Cakes and Ale: Or the Skeleton in the Cupboard*.

Rose (Gann) Driffeld   Simple, attractive, ambitious, gregarious first wife to Edward; her plain looks are made beautiful by her mischievous personality; Rosie wants to rise above her lower-class status, even though she has sexual relationships with most of her husband's friends in W. Somerset Maugham's *Cakes and Ale: Or the Skeleton in the Cupboard*.

Osyth Drine   Resident of the last cottage in Flittering; near Moze Hall, it is the last outpost against the North Sea and German raiders in Arnold Bennett's *Lord Raingo*.

Mary Driscoll   Leopold Bloom's former maid, whom he allegedly tried to seduce in James Joyce's *Ulysses*.

Fabian Driver   Dark, handsome, self-satisfied, formerly philandering widower resident of the Clevelands' parish who takes up with Prudence Bates in Barbara Pym's *Jane and Prudence*. His obituary appears in *A Few Green Leaves*.

Jake Driver (Delmore) Successful television actor whose insensitivity and infidelity drive away his wife, Julia Delmore, and whom Gus Howkins seeks out in London to discover the cause of Julia's distress; he is a character in the story novelist Giles Hermitage writes in John Wain's *The Pardoner's Tale*.

Johnny Dromore Oxford roommate of Mark Lennon; he is a horseman and a gambler; he introduces his seventeen-year-old daughter, Nell, to Mark in 1906 in John Galsworthy's *The Dark Flower*.

Nell Dromore Johnny's illegitimate daughter, whose mother died in childbirth; at seventeen she meets the forty-six-year-old Mark Lennon and wants him to leave his wife for her; she is courted by her father's cousin, Oliver Dromore, in John Galsworthy's *The Dark Flower*.

Oliver Dromore Twenty-four-year-old cousin of Johnny Dromore; he courts Johnny's daughter, Nell, and wants to marry her in John Galsworthy's *The Dark Flower*.

Amberly Drove Self-important journalist for a London daily; he writes a racist article about unrestricted immigration and the blacks of London in Colin MacInnes's *Absolute Beginners*.

Conrad Drover Brother of Jim Drover; in love with Jim's wife, Milly Drover, he is frustrated by love and resentment for his brother and deep feelings of inadequacy, despite his responsible job; he sleeps with Milly, buys a gun, and is fatally injured trying to shoot the Assistant Commissioner in Graham Greene's *It's a Battlefield*.

Jim Drover Communist bus driver condemned to death for the killing of a policeman who he thought was going to strike his wife, Milly Drover; efforts to gain his reprieve are successful in Graham Greene's *It's a Battlefield*.

Milly Drover Desperate, intelligent wife of Jim Drover; she gets Rose Coney to sign the petition to save Jim, and she sleeps with Conrad Drover, her brother-in-law, in Graham Greene's *It's a Battlefield*.

Druce Police officer who assists Henry Scobie in his investigations in Graham Greene's *The Heart of the Matter*.

Vincent Druce Manager of Meadows, Meade & Grindley and a married man with a well-established

extra-marital affair; his muddled ambition to link Art and Industry leads him to hire Dougal Douglas, whose personality so acts on him that he murders his mistress, Merle Coverdale, in Muriel Spark's *The Ballad of Peckham Rye*.

Barnabas Drumm Hilda Chase-White's brother, a Roman Catholic convert and an ardent though constitutionally ineffectual Irish patriot; his infatuation for Millie Kinnard resulted in his failing to become a priest and has persisted through his unconsummated marriage to Kathleen in Iris Murdoch's *The Red and the Green*.

Kathleen Kinnard Dumay Drumm Sister of Christopher Bellman's late wife and of Millie Kinnard's late husband; herself the widow of Millie's brother, she is the conventional, pious, morally sturdy, unglamorous mother of Pat and Cathal Dumay; her marriage to Hilda Chase-White's brother, Barnabus Drumm, is unconsummated in Iris Murdoch's *The Red and the Green*.

Edward Dryden The rector of the parish, who conducts funerals for Christian and Sophia Stace; he proposes to Dinah Stace but withdraws his offer when the Stace scandal breaks in Ivy Compton-Burnett's *Brothers and Sisters*.

Judith Dryden The younger Andrew Stace's tall, pale, reputedly intellectual fiancée; the engagement ends when the news of his parents' incest is revealed in Ivy Compton-Burnett's *Brothers and Sisters*.

Miss Dubber Shrewish, tyrannical, but unsuspecting landlady; her Devon boarding house serves as Magnus Pym's "safehouse" until he commits suicide in John le Carré's *A Perfect Spy*.

Christophine (Josephine) Dubois Servant and cook to the Cosways; blue-black with thin face and straight features, she has a quiet voice and laugh; she wears her head scarf Martinique style and practices obeah (a type of voodoo) in Jean Rhys's *Wide Sargasso Sea*.

John Ducane Octavian Gray's colleague, who makes an unorthodox but highly competent investigation into an office suicide; he is entangled with both Jessica Byrd and Kate Gray and is pursued by Judy McGrath; he falls in love with Mary Clothier, whose son, Pierce, he saves from drowning in Iris Murdoch's *The Nice and the Good*.

Elspeth Ducayne Miriam Henderson's niece, the small child of Gerald and Harriett (Henderson); they have suffered financial reverses and are running a seaside boarding house in Dorothy Richardson's *Deadlock*.

Gerald Ducayne Well-to-do, appealing, empathic young fiancé of Harriett Henderson in Dorothy Richardson's *Backwater*. He marries Harriett in *Honeycomb*. He has suffered financial reverses in *Deadlock*.

Duchateau French doctor who is convinced that Jack Townrow is a British spy in P. H. Newby's *Something to Answer For*.

Mr. Duchemin A wealthy clergyman, who is prone to fits of violent madness; he attacks his wife, Edith Ethel Duchemin, and is subsequently incarcerated in an insane asylum, where he dies in Ford Madox Ford's *Some Do Not. . . .*

Edith Ethel Duchemin Blue-eyed, black-haired, gracious and cultured woman, who has been "bought", educated, and married by Mr. Duchemin; she marries Vincent Macmaster immediately following Duchemin's death in an insane asylum; her obligations to Christopher Tietjens and to Valentine Wannop make her the enemy of both in Ford Madox Ford's *Some Do Not. . . .* She intrudes into Valentine's employment at school with telephone slander in *A Man Could Stand Up —*. Her mischief continues in *The Last Post*.

Colonel Victor Duck Older aristocratic cad with whom Iris Storm reluctantly appears in Michael Arlen's *The Green Hat*.

Marie Duclos Young and abused French mistress of Captain Tim Hunt; her poverty and dogged loyalty to Hunt, whom she knows to be a murderer, arouse great pity in David Renn and cause him to search across Europe for several years to find and help her; when he locates her at a Prague convent, she refuses to allow him to rescue her by marrying her, but urges him to adopt her son and take him to safety; she plans to accompany an American official and his wife to Wisconsin to find freedom and work in Storm Jameson's *The Black Laurel*.

Robert Duclos White-bearded, mentally unstable, middle-aged French clerk; an inveterate liar, he pretends to be a wealthy businessman during his annual sojourns at the Reserve Hotel, and Joseph Vadassy incorrectly thinks him to be the spy in Eric Ambler's *Epitaph for a Spy*.

Aline Ducorroy French Protestant pupil-teacher in the Hanover school; prim and priggish, she leaves before the end of the term under somewhat mysterious and charged circumstances in Dorothy Richardson's *Pointed Roofs*.

Charles Ducorroy A French Catholic seminarian

whom the Roscorlas take in and with whom Miriam Henderson becomes involved when Rachel Mary Roscorla invites her back to the Sussex farm in Dorothy Richardson's *March Moonlight*.

Monsieur Ducos French captain severely wounded in the battle for the *Amelia Jane* in C. S. Forester's *Hornblower and the Atropos*.

Duddingstone Chandler who gives Hornblower credit, taking his sword as collateral in C. S. Forester's *Ship of the Line*. After Hornblower's return he absolves him from his debt in *Flying Colours*.

William Humble, Earl of Dudley Lord Lieutenant of Ireland whose progress forms one axis of "The Wandering Rocks" episode in James Joyce's *Ulysses*.

John Duerinckx-Williams Nick Allington's former supervisor at Cambridge; he persuades the librarian to show Maurice Allington the journal belonging to Dr. Thomas Underhill in Kingsley Amis's *The Green Man*.

Duff Gun-crew member in C. S. Forester's *Lieutenant Hornblower*.

Mrs. Duff The housekeeper for the Heriots; she is talkative and not as servile as Eliza Heriot would like her to be in Ivy Compton-Burnett's *The Last and the First*.

Dr. Anthony Dufferin A physician who gives Lady Harriet Haslam a suicide pill that is really harmless; he becomes engaged to Camilla Bellamy and later to Griselda Haslam in Ivy Compton-Burnett's *Men and Wives*.

Dug An Australian workman who appears briefly at the opening of D. H. Lawrence's *Kangaroo*.

Mrs. Duke Proprietor of Beacon House who acts as judge in the trial of Innocent Smith in G. K. Chesterton's *Manalive*.

Kenny Duke Bouncer at the strip club who causes Mr. Moggerhanger to fire his chauffeur, Michael Cullen, in Alan Sillitoe's *A Start in Life*.

Tommy Dukes A Brigadier-General in the British army who leads conversations of the Wragby Hall "mental-lifers" and espouses (but does not act upon) the philosophy of "phallic consciousness" in D. H. Lawrence's *Lady Chatterley's Lover*.

Baronne Clotilde du Loiret Member of the Autobiographical Association in Muriel Spark's *Loitering with Intent*.

Cathal Dumay The fourteen-year-old hotheaded brother of Pat, who so loves Cathal that he considers killing him to keep him safe from the planned uprising; with Millie Kinnard's help, Pat leaves Cathal gagged and handcuffed to Andrew Chase-White until the fighting has begun; Cathal becomes an IRA member and is killed in 1921 in Iris Murdoch's *The Red and the Green.*

Pat Dumay An ardent young Irish nationalist who is a romantic focus for his aunt Millie Kinnard and his cousin Frances Bellman but holds women in contempt; his allegiance makes him an enemy of his cousin Andrew Chase-White, whom he neutralizes at the start of the 1916 Easter Rising in which he himself is killed in Iris Murdoch's *The Red and the Green.*

Dumb Man The dumb and faithful mason-artist who produces a sculpted likeness of Dean Jocelin, saves him from falling to his death, and works doggedly to bring their construction project to a conclusion in William Golding's *The Spire.*

Dumetrius Owner of a London gallery where Aubrey Greene's painting "Afternoon of a Dryad" is shown in John Galsworthy's *The White Monkey.*

Mr. Duncalf Town clerk of Bursley; he organizes the invitation list for the Countess of Chell's ball in his office where Denry Machin, working as shorthand clerk, manages to include on the list his own name and those he wishes to favor in Arnold Bennett's *The Card: A Story of Adventure in the Five Towns.*

Dunkel Manager of a traveling circus in which Llewellyn and Aderyn the Bird Queen work; he is motivated almost purely by avarice in Anthony Burgess's *MF.*

Alfred Dunsop Only son of a wealthy cotton man; he is infatuated with the music-hall artist Lilly Farris in J. B. Priestley's *Lost Empires.*

Dunstan Homely middle-aged man who is Henry Miles's superior; he is subject of a nascent but never-realized post-Bendrix affair with Sarah Miles in Graham Greene's *The End of the Affair.*

Colonel Duperrier Athletic and energetic British former army officer who prefers the company of young female guests to that of his dull and complaining wife in Elizabeth Bowen's *The Hotel.*

Mrs. Duperrier Wife of Colonel Duperrier; she is a member of the gossip, needlework, and card-game circles of upper-class Englishwomen in Elizabeth Bowen's *The Hotel.*

Father Duplessis Priest with medical training who has served in the war with Sir Edward Leithen and whom Leithen meets on his way north at Fort Bannerman; he welcomes Leithen when he returns and gives the account of Leithen's last months in his journal in John Buchan's *Sick Heart River.*

Mr. Dupont A guest at the hotel where Adolf Hitler is briefly employed; he pays Adolf to run mysterious errands, involving him unwittingly in embarrasing petty thievery in Beryl Bainbridge's *Young Adolf.*

Clement Dupont Haitian undertaker; he and his twin brother, Hercule, try to bury Dr. Philipot but are stopped by the Tontons Macoutes in Graham Greene's *The Comedians.*

Emile Dupont French companion of Lord Barralonga; he supports Rupert Catskill's plan to overthrow Utopian rule but insists that French interests be considered in the resulting empire in H. G. Wells's *Men Like Gods.*

Hercule Dupont Haitian undertaker and twin brother of Clement in Graham Greene's *The Comedians.*

Polly Duport Daughter of Jean (Templer) and Bob Duport in Anthony Powell's *The Military Philosophers.* She is a successful, dedicated actress; she has an affair with Louis Glober in *Temporary Kings.* Her affair with Delavacquerie is complicated by his involvement with Fiona Cutts, but Polly's marriage to Delavacquerie is imminent in *Hearing Secret Harmonies.*

Robert (Bob) Duport Acquaintance whom Nicholas Jenkins immediately dislikes in Anthony Powell's *A Question of Upbringing.* His marriage to Jean Templer, characterized by infidelities, separations, and ultimately divorce, and his business dealings are detailed in *The Acceptance World,* in *At Lady Molly's,* and in *The Kindly Ones.* He is recalled with admiration by Jimmy Brent in *The Valley of Bones.* He appears in *The Military Philosophers* and is discussed in *Books Do Furnish a Room* and in *Temporary Kings.* A wheelchair-bound invalid, he is disliked less than heretofore by Jenkins in *Hearing Secret Harmonies.*

Marie du Preez A woman who partakes in the socialist movement of Zambesia and is an acquaintance of Martha Quest in Doris Lessing's *A Proper Marriage* and in *A Ripple from the Storm.*

Piet du Preez A prominent official in the white trade union movement and an outspoken socialist in Doris Lessing's *A Ripple from the Storm.*

Jack Dupret   Strong-willed owner of the Dupret foundry; his death enables his son, Richard, to assume control of the business in Henry Green's *Living*.

Richard Dupret   Son of Jack Dupret; after his father's death and a failed attempt at romance with Hannah Glossop, he assumes control of and tries to modernize the Dupret foundry and its workers in Henry Green's *Living*.

Sylvia Dupret   Wife of Jack and mother of Richard Dupret in Henry Green's *Living*.

Captain Duquesne   Owner of the house on Gabriola island that Ethan and Jacqueline Llewelyn consider buying in Malcolm Lowry's *October Ferry to Gabriola*.

Duras (His Britannic Majesty Consul)   A mountainous, clay-colored Mussulman attended by a Negro slave who leads his donkey; he dies of the "black plague" in front of the landing party at Oman in C. S. Forester's *Mr. Midshipman Hornblower*.

Anne Woods Durham   Clive Durham's kind, energetic wife, who tries to befriend Maurice Hall in E. M. Forster's *Maurice*.

Clive Durham   Sincere, sentimental Cambridge scholar, who has a platonic, intimate relationship with Maurice Hall in E. M. Forster's *Maurice*.

Clara Durrant   Timothy Durrant's sister, who has an affair with Jacob Flanders when he comes to visit their summer home in Cornwall in Virginia Woolf's *Jacob's Room*.

Timothy Durrant   College chum of Jacob Flanders at Cambridge; their sailing trip to the Durrants' summer home in Cornwall leads to Jacob's affair with Timothy's sister, Clara, in Virginia Woolf's *Jacob's Room*.

Dutton   Lanky first lieutenant of the flagship; he is rumored to be replacing Cogshill as the new Commander of the *Buckler* in C. S. Forester's *Lieutenant Hornblower*.

Pierre Duval   Chief of the United Nations Science Bureau; he builds a device to discover the Overlords' nature in Arthur C. Clarke's *Childhood's End*.

Dulcie Duveen   Young woman who marries Arthur Hastings in Agatha Christie's *The Murder on the Links*.

Councillor Duxbury   The elderly senior partner in the undertaking firm where Billy Fisher works; he is given to reminiscing about the good old days in Keith Waterhouse's *Billy Liar*.

Dy   Richard Roe's sister-in-law; she takes care of Christopher Roe during the blitz and fails to understand the significance of Richard's fire-fighting experience in Henry Green's *Caught*.

Mrs. Dyer   Grim, censorious, gossiping charwoman at the rectory in Barbara Pym's *A Few Green Leaves*.

Dying Indian   Unnamed victim of robbery by the pelado; his dying word, "Companero", becomes Geoffrey Firmin's dying word in Malcolm Lowry's *Under the Volcano*.

Tam Dyke   A boyhood friend of David Crawfurd's; he serves on the ship which Crawfurd takes to Africa in John Buchan's *Prester John*.

E

Eaden   A businessman friend of Harry Vereker; the child Daphne attaches herself to him exclusively and passionately in Dorothy Richardson's *Oberland*.

Cuthbert Eager   Zealous English clergyman and member of a religious colony who spreads the rumor that Mr. Emerson murdered his wife in E. M. Forster's *A Room with a View*.

Mrs. Eames   Neighbor of Phil Craigan; she expends all her thought and energy on her son and her soon-to-be-born daughter in Henry Green's *Living*.

Ernest Eames   Reclusive bibliographer whose love for Latin inspires him to devote his life to annotating Perrelli's *Antiquities* in Norman Douglas's *South Wind*.

Fred Eames   Neighbor of Phil Craigan in Henry Green's *Living*.

Augustus Earlforward   Stiff, surprised inheritor of his brother Henry's estate; he learns of his good fortune on furlough from a Carribean mission and reservedly permits Elsie Sprickett's ailing fiancé, Joe, to remain in the Earlforward home until after the funeral in Arnold Bennett's *Riceyman Steps*.

Henry Earlforward   Middle-aged miser of a quiet, refined, prosperous appearance with rich, red lips and near-sighted brown eyes; he is the proprietor of a second-hand bookstore inherited from his uncle; his passion for thrift slowly freezes and starves to death him and his new wife, Violet, without destroying their mutual affection in Arnold Bennett's *Riceyman Steps*.

Violet Arb Earlforward   Petite, vivacious, fortyish, lonely, nervous widow; she becomes passionately bound to her new husband, Henry Earlforward; she is overwhelmed by his obsession for thrift; she succumbs to his frugality, having failed to rally from an operation because of undernourishment in Arnold Bennett's *Riceyman Steps*.

Louis Earlham   Husband of Rachel Earlham; he is a friend of David Renn and Mary Hervey Russell in London, 1918, and struggles in poverty to publish a socialist weekly, which advocates assistance for Germany's recovery rather than punishment; he plans to runs as Labour candidate in North London in Storm Jameson's *Company Parade*. In 1939 he is a wealthy and high-ranking member of the Labour Party; he curries favor with elegant and rich Nancy, Lady Harben and powerful Sir Thomas Harben; he loses his commitment to equality, sends his children to exclusive boarding schools, and is no longer respected by David Renn in *Before the Crossing*.

Rachel Earlham   Half-Jewish wife of Louis Earlham; she helps her husband publish a radical socialist newspaper; a friend of David Renn and Mary Hervey Russell in London, 1918, she opposes their newspaper's emphasis on commercial advertising rather than social reform in Storm Jameson's *Company Parade*. In 1939 Rachel remains loyal to Louis but has adjusted only tenuously to the status-conscious life of British Labour Party members in *Before the Crossing*.

George Earlsfield   The fourth murder victim, stabbed in a movie theater in Agatha Christie's *The A.B.C. Murders*.

Sergeant Earnshaw   A soldier on Jonathan Browne's last guard duty in National Service in David Lodge's *Ginger, You're Barmy*.

Ruth Earp (Mrs. Capron-Smith)   Flirtatious, extravagant dancing mistress; she is chronically short of funds; she entices Denry Machin into an early engagement, but eventually her spendthrift ways provoke him to break the engagement in Arnold Bennett's *The Card: A Story of Adventure in the Five Towns*.

Humphrey Chimpden (HCE) Earwicker   Stuttering Dublin pub owner who arrives from overseas, commits some unidentified crime in Phoenix Park, and appears under many names as the patriarch in the archetypal family romance of James Joyce's *Finnegans Wake*.

Primrose East   Former model, a protégé of Owen Tuby; she has an interest in sociology and a fixation on Cosmo Sultana in J. B. Priestley's *The Image Men*.

Mrs. Eastcourt   Spiteful gossip whose victims include all the residents of Cleeve but especially Georgie Smithers in Richard Aldington's *The Colonel's Daughter*.

Martin Eastcourt   Fifty-year-old son still under the domination of his mother, the town busybody, in Richard Aldington's *The Colonel's Daughter*.

Lord Eastlake   Governor-designate of Bombay who, in reward for their efforts in protecting the East India Company's ship, offers a generous reward to the crew of the *Sutherland* in C. S. Forester's *Ship of the Line*.

Major Eastwood   A powerful sportsman who was formerly in the British military; his unconventional union with Mrs. Fawcett inspires Yvette Saywell in D. H. Lawrence's *The Virgin and the Gipsy*.

Christina Eastwood   Philip Witt's girlfriend, supposed euphemistically by his mother to be his fiancée in Roy Fuller's *Image of a Society*.

Easy Walker   An expatriate Briton in Morroco who lives opportunistically and amorally by performing various, mostly illegal services; he accepts F. X. Enderby's British passport in exchange for transportation in Anthony Burgess's *Enderby Outside*.

Jim Eaves   Anthony Keating's assistant in removing a tree from a future garden site at his residence in Margaret Drabble's *The Ice Age*.

Vanessa Eaves   Third-year anthropology student who competes for the Foresight Fellowship in Barbara Pym's *Less Than Angels*.

Mrs. Ebag (alias Mrs. de Rassiter)   Drunken woman; she tries to claim cloakroom furs as hers; she is stopped by Alice Brury, housekeeper, who is chastised for insubordination to a guest and feels she must leave her position in Arnold Bennett's *Imperial Palace*.

Max Ebhart   French-English Jew engaged to marry Naomi Fisher until he has an affair with Naomi's friend Karen Michaelis, quarrels with Mrs. Fisher, and commits suicide; his son, Leopold, is born to Karen after his death in Elizabeth Bowen's *The House in Paris*.

Mr. Eborebelosa   A student from West Africa who carries an ancestor's skull around with him; he proposes marriage to Emma Fielding in Malcolm Bradbury's *Eating People Is Wrong*.

Captain Ebron   A military leader who interrogates Yuli in Pannoval in Brian W. Aldiss's *Helliconia Spring*.

Eccles   Grey-haired, blue-eyed first lieutenant aboard the *Indefatigable* in C. S. Forester's *Mr. Midshipman Hornblower*.

Francis Eccles   Bachelor, dilettante, and amateur critic in Muriel Spark's *The Bachelors*.

Sol Eckland   Senior agent for Drug Enforcement Administration in Southeast Asia who brusquely argues with George Smiley for U.S. priority in interrogating Drake Ko in John le Carré's *The Honourable Schoolboy*.

Ed   Heavily built facilitator of encounter-group workshops attended by Jake Richardson and his wife, Brenda; he is not respected by Jake for his seeming lack of empathy in Kingsley Amis's *Jake's Thing*.

Eddie   Conceited and callow twenty-three-year-old would-be writer, who trades on his Oxford connec-

tions, flatters himself that he has charmed Anna Quayne, and plays with Portia Quayne's affections in Elizabeth Bowen's *The Death of the Heart*.

Mabel Eddison   Ex-pupil of Romley Fourways', the school Kate Fletcher (Armstrong) attended; she works in a drug store in Margaret Drabble's *The Middle Ground*.

Aubrey Eden   Solicitor who is the nephew of Harry Eden; he is bored by Lewis Eliot's enquiries into the case against Cora Ross in C. P. Snow's *The Sleep of Reason*.

Harry Eden   A solicitor who is partner with Howard Martineau; George Passant's employer, he introduces Lewis Eliot to Herbert Getliffe in C. P. Snow's *Time of Hope*. He accepts a gift of the firm from Martineau; disliking Passant, he refuses to offer him a share of the firm; he employs Getliffe to lead in the defense of the accused at the trial for fraud in *Strangers and Brothers*.

Mable Edge   Co-principal of the state educational institute for women who devotes her considerable energies to strictly enforcing state rules and trying to force Mr. Rock from his cottage in Henry Green's *Concluding*.

Sir James Peel Edgerton   Celebrated barrister and criminologist in Agatha Christie's *The Secret Adversary*.

Alison Edgeworth   The second wife of Duncan Edgeworth; she has a son, Richard, by her husband's nephew, Grant Edgeworth, and later a legitimate daughter by her second husband, Almeric Bode, in Ivy Compton-Burnett's *A House and Its Head*.

Duncan Edgeworth   An autocratic father, impatient with his wife Ellen's illness; he later marries Alison and then Cassie Jekyll and has a son by each woman in Ivy Compton-Burnett's *A House and Its Head*.

Ellen Edgeworth   Duncan's first wife, who was always kept short of money by him; she is the mother of Nance and Sibyl in Ivy Compton-Burnett's *A House and Its Head*.

Grant Edgeworth   The son of Duncan Edgeworth's deceased brother; Grant fathers Richard Edgeworth on Alison, Duncan's wife; he marries Sibyl Edgeworth and remains with her when she inherits money from her aunt in Ivy Compton-Burnett's *A House and Its Head*.

Aunt Maria Edgeworth   A relative who extends hospitality to Duncan Edgeworth after his wife Ellen's death; she leaves her money to Sibyl Edgeworth in Ivy Compton-Burnett's *A House and Its Head*.

Nance Edgeworth　　The elder daughter of Duncan and Ellen; sensible and intelligent, she eventually marries the clergyman Oscar Jekyll and gets a home of her own in Ivy Compton-Burnett's *A House and Its Head*.

Richard Edgeworth　　The supposed son of Duncan and Alison Edgeworth; he has a lock of white hair like his natural father, Grant Edgeworth, in Ivy Compton-Burnett's *A House and Its Head*.

Sibyl Edgeworth　　The younger daughter of Duncan and Ellen; devoid of a normal moral sense, she pays a nurse to kill Richard Edgeworth, her father's young presumed son by Alison, his second wife; Sibyl is married to Richard's actual father, Grant Edgeworth, in Ivy Compton-Burnett's *A House and Its Head*.

William Edgeworth　　Son and heir of Duncan Edgeworth by his third wife, Cassandra (Jekyll), in Ivy Compton-Burnett's *A House and Its Head*.

Edith　　Young housemaid who elopes to England with the butler Charley Raunce in Henry Green's *Loving*.

Edith　　Unkempt young housemaid; she is kindly treated by Lord Raingo and develops into an efficient servant who adores him in Arnold Bennett's *Lord Raingo*.

Edmundo　　A hairy Argentinian butcher who guards Adam Appleby while he is reading the Merrymarsh manuscript in David Lodge's *The British Museum Is Falling Down*.

Earl of Edrington　　Heavily built major in command of a wing of the 43rd Foot; his youthfulness indicates that his rank was purchased, although he proves an excellent soldier in C. S. Forester's *Mr. Midshipman Hornblower*.

Edward the Ted (Ed)　　Childhood friend of the narrator; a former member of the Teddy gang and involved in rioting against blacks as a member of Flikker's gang, he attacks the narrator in Colin MacInnes's *Absolute Beginners*.

Captain Edwardes　　Captain of the *Archimedes*; his latent greatness as a seaman is revealed during the hurricane in Richard Hughes's *In Hazard*.

Chief Constable Edwards　　Head of police; he unsympathetically puts down protests by the poor and hungry in Liam O'Flaherty's *Famine*.

Eurydice Edwards　　Vain, affected companion of Madame Ruiz in Ronald Firbank's *Sorrow in Sunlight*.

Julie Eeles　　Aspiring actress and Edward Wilcher's mistress; she is rejected by Edward and becomes Tom Wilcher's mistress until he ends the affair to marry Sara Monday in Joyce Cary's *Herself Surprised* and in *The Horse's Mouth*.

Effendi　　Levantine Greek youth with a "cigarette smouldering at his ear" who sluggishly helps his friend Bachir fill orders at the Countess of Varna's flower shop in Ronald Firbank's *The Flower Beneath the Foot*.

Hebechi Effendi　　Native of Rasuka and an accountant for the oil well who is accused of stealing money from the company; he stabs Cator, believing he is the true robber, and is sentenced to death by the Sultan; he escapes prison and flees into the desert in P. H. Newby's *A Journey to the Interior*.

Effie　　Christopher Tietjens's sister, married to a Yorkshire vicar and mother of several children; she has custody of Tommie Tietjens in Ford Madox Ford's *Some Do Not. . . .*

Henry Egerton　　The adopted son of Hereward and Ada (Merton) Egerton, and the natural child of Hetty Egerton by Hereward; he wants to marry dear little Maud, his half sister, in Ivy Compton-Burnett's *A God and His Gifts*.

Hereward Egerton　　A writer of popular novels, who seduces his wife's sister and his son's fiancée; he is moving in on a second son's fiancée; he fosters his feelings and yields to them in Ivy Compton-Burnett's *A God and His Gifts*.

Hetty Egerton　　An orphan with family money who decides to marry Merton Egerton; she is the mother of Henry Egerton by Hereward, Merton's father in Ivy Compton-Burnett's *A God and His Gifts*.

Joanna, Lady Egerton　　The affectionate wife of her distant cousin, Sir Michael; she respects her husband in Ivy Compton-Burnett's *A God and His Gifts*.

Maud Egerton　　The daughter of Hetty and Merton Egerton; she is not made much of by the grandparents, Hereward and Ada Egerton, in Ivy Compton-Burnett's *A God and His Gifts*.

Merton Egerton　　The middle son of Hereward and Ada (Merton); unlike his father, he writes for the select few; his fiancée, Hetty (Egerton), is impregnated by his father in Ivy Compton-Burnett's *A God and His Gifts*.

Sir Michael Egerton   Hereward's father, who is in debt before the income from Hereward's books; he wishes that his son had kept the human laws in Ivy Compton-Burnett's *A God and His Gifts*.

Reuben Egerton   The youngest son of Hereward and Ada (Merton); he becomes a schoolmaster who, wanting to marry Beatrice, warns his father off in Ivy Compton-Burnett's *A God and His Gifts*.

Salomon Egerton   The eldest son of Hereward and Ada (Merton); a steady, intelligent boy, he falls in love with his cousin, Viola, not knowing that she is also his half sister in Ivy Compton-Burnett's *A God and His Gifts*.

Zillah Egerton   Hereward's sister, who is closer to him than his wife; she says that Hereward is a rule unto himself in Ivy Compton-Burnett's *A God and His Gifts*.

Houston Eggar   Government official in the Foreign Office who writes to warn Lord Bocastle about Roy Calvert's close ties to Nazis; he arranges for Lewis Eliot to accompany Calvert to meet a German spy in Switzerland in C. P. Snow's *The Light and the Dark*.

John Eglinton   Colleague of A. E.; he debates interpretations of Shakespeare with Stephen Dedalus in the Irish National Library in James Joyce's *Ulysses*.

Mr. Ehrlich   The "Portuguese Jew" discovered to be a German professor of Celtic languages; operating as one of Moxon Ivery's agents, he follows Richard Hannay on the train from Scotland back to London and is killed at the Pink Chalet by John S. Blenkiron in John Buchan's *Mr. Standfast*.

Margaret Eichmann (covername: Gerda Eich)   Librarian and Leo Harting's former mistress; she allows Harting access to the library for his assassination attempt on Karfeld but, when caught and tortured, reveals Harting's whereabouts and is murdered by his political enemies in John le Carré's *A Small Town in Germany*.

Eileen   Young, pretty nurse in Clive Ward who serves breakfast and is teased by Dai Evans in John Berger's *The Foot of Clive*.

Hilda von Einem   Mysterious but fascinating "evil she-devil", who seeks to insure a German victory in World War I by persuading the prophet "Greenmantle" to launch a jehad; obsessively drawn to "Sandy" Arbuthnot, in disguise as "Greenmantle", she offers him her love, is rejected by him, and, leaping on the parapet and down the hillside, is killed by a Russian shell in John Buchan's *Greenmantle*.

Baron von Eisenbeiss   High Chamberlain who introduces Hornblower to the Prince of Seitz-Bunau; as surgeon aboard the *Atropos,* he is angered that he is not treated with the respect due his social status; he wounds McCullum in a duel and is forced to treat him; his success demonstrates his skill in C. S. Forester's *Hornblower and the Atropos*.

Eisenstein   Magda Bursanov's lover before she meets Cecedek; he is a Jewish dentist and conjurer, and he could possibly be Vera Bursanov's biological father in William Gerhardie's *Futility: A Novel on Russian Themes*.

El-ahrairah (Prince with a Thousand Enemies)   Mythological hero of rabbit folklore; a consummate trickster, he takes risks on behalf of his followers and ultimately loses his ears and tail in a match with the Black Rabbit of Inlé to save his besieged warren; Frith gives him new ears and a tail, and henceforth El-ahrairah passes back and forth at will between the natural and supernatural worlds in Richard Adams's *Watership Down*.

Elaine   Tom Mallow's faithful, neglected, wealthy former girlfriend, who remains at home, breeding dogs, doing church and volunteer work, and attending the Women's Institute near Tom's family's Shropshire estate in Barbara Pym's *Less Than Angels*.

Elaine   One of the nurses at St. Andrews, where Rosamund Stacey goes to have her baby in Margaret Drabble's *The Millstone*.

Robert Elderson   Manager of P.P.R.S. insurance corporation, who is discovered by Soames Forsyte to have wrongfully managed the firm; he flees the country in John Galsworthy's *The White Monkey*.

Eldon   Deceased butler succeeded by Charley Raunce, who assumes his mannerisms and petty embezzlements in Henry Green's *Loving*.

Eleanor   Ken Adamson's former girlfriend, who made "a fool of him" once in John Berger's *The Foot of Clive*.

Abishai (the shop) Elias   Vindictive shop owner and religious fundamentalist who seeks Mr. Gryffydd's removal; caught stealing Gwilym Morgan's turkeys, he attempts to avenge himself on the Morgans by pressing a suit for assault against Huw Morgan in Richard Llewellyn's *How Green Was My Valley*.

Bertie Eliot   Father of Lewis; he is not yet forty in 1914; he goes bankrupt and moves in with Aunt Milly after Lena Eliot dies in C. P. Snow's *Time of Hope*. He is unwillingly retired as choir secretary and dies shortly afterward in *The Sleep of Reason.*

Bill Eliot   Meg's fifty-five-year-old husband, who is a successful barrister; he is killed while saving the life of a Badai political official in the airport at Srem Panh in Angus Wilson's *The Middle Age of Mrs. Eliot.*

Charles Eliot   Son of Lewis Eliot and Margaret (Hollis) Eliot; he recovers from meningitis in C. P. Snow's *Homecomings.* He visits his grandfather Eliot for only the second time, and is growing detached from his father in *The Sleep of Reason.* He is involved in a national security incident when he breaks into a college office to take a document dealing with biological warfare; he lives with Muriel Calvert for a while, and chooses to make his career as a foreign correspondent in the Middle East in *Last Things.*

Julia Eliot   A reticent painter who observes the tragedy of Jacob Flanders in Virginia Woolf's *Jacob's Room.*

Lena Eliot   Lewis's mother, who urges him to distinguish himself in life; she dies in C. P. Snow's *Time of Hope.*

Lewis Eliot   Youth who works as a clerk and attends night classes in law taught by George Passant; he prepares for the bar in 1924 and is accepted into the chambers of Herbert Getliffe; a long-time obsessive love for Sheila Knight results in their mutually miserable marriage, but he decides against a separation in 1933; he is a junior barrister in the trial of George Passant in C. P. Snow's *Time of Hope.* He defends George Passant's moral character and suggests that Passant jump bond rather than stand trial for fraud in *Strangers and Brothers.* He refuses Ann Simon's invitation to join the Communist Party, leaves Getliffe's chambers to take a position at Cambridge, and enquires of Getliffe and Ronald Porson on behalf of the March family concerning unethical financial investments in *The Conscience of the Rich.* He is active in support of Roy Calvert's election to his college at Cambridge and unknowingly gives Calvert the idea for ending his life by volunteering for bombing missions in World War II in *The Light and the Dark.* He supports Paul Jago for election as new college Master in *The Masters.* He is a temporary civil servant connected with atomic-energy research during World War II; he disapproves of Martin Eliot's marriage to Irene Brunskill; he discourages Martin from publishing a protest against use of the atomic bomb and disapproves Martin's role in the confession of Eric Sawbridge in *The New Men.* He suffers from guilt after his wife's suicide, decides he wishes to write books, and marries Margaret Davidson in 1947 after her divorce from Geoffrey Hollis; he secures the appointment of

George Passant to work for him in the civil service for three years in *Homecomings.* He argues the case for Donald Howard before the Court of Seniors in *The Affair.* He works for Roger Quaife with the advisory committee on nuclear weapons and is subjected to a security interrogation; he plans to resign from government service after the forced resignation of Quaife in *Corridors of Power.* He defends university students threatened with expulsion for sexual misconduct, has surgery for a detached retina, and attends the trial of Cora Ross and Kitty Pateman out of respect for George Passant in *The Sleep of Reason.* He suffers cardiac arrest while undergoing more eye surgery, declines a ministerial appointment with the government, and helps his son, Charles, through a security investigation in *Last Things.*

Lewis Gregory (Pat) Eliot   Son of Martin and Irene (Brunskill) Eliot; he pursues several women, drops his relationship with Vicky Shaw, and is engaged to marry Muriel Calvert after she is pregnant in C. P. Snow's *The Sleep of Reason.* A painter, he is divorced from Muriel after the birth of their daughter, and then finally marries Vicky Shaw in *Last Things.*

Martin Eliot   Younger brother of Lewis; born after Bertie Eliot's bankruptcy, he is unwanted by his mother in C. P. Snow's *Time of Hope.* A physicist, he works at the atomic-energy research facility with Walter Luke, helps persuade Eric Sawbridge to confess he spied for communists, and declines an offer by the government to head the agency for atomic-energy research; he marries Irene Brunskill in *The New Men.* He leads the college supporters of Donald Howard in his appeal for reconsideration of his fellowship in *The Affair.* He is Senior Tutor at a Cambridge college; he confides his worries about his son Pat to Lewis; he is relieved when Pat becomes engaged to Muriel Calvert in *The Sleep of Reason.* He sends warning to Lewis about the national security investigation of Charles Eliot in *Last Things.*

Meg Eliot   Middle-aged woman whose husband is murdered; she has to learn to adjust to reduced income and becomes a secretary; she lives with one friend after another and cannot settle into her brother's lifestyle; she continues without end to leave one secretarial position for another in Angus Wilson's *The Middle Age of Mrs. Eliot.*

Nina Eliot   Daughter of Martin and Irene (Brunskill) Eliot; she loves Guy Grenfell; she carries the message to her uncle, Lewis Eliot, about the security investigation in C. P. Snow's *Last Things.*

Elise   Faithful servant who stays with Koré Arabin and with Mitri brings Vernon Milburne to her mistress in hopes he can save her from the islanders' pagan rituals and death in John Buchan's *The Dancing Floor*.

Elizabeth   Woman who shelters Francis Andrews following the arrest of the smuggling gang at Shoreham; she encourages Andrews to testify against the smugglers and through her love for him encourages him to make a new start in his life, but she commits suicide after brutal treatment by a vengeful smuggler in Graham Greene's *The Man Within*.

Archduchess Elizabeth   Aged aunt to King William of Pisuerga; up until her sudden death she keeps busy swimming and designing aesthetically attractive public toilets in Ronald Firbank's *The Flower Beneath the Foot*.

El Khalil   Charismatic, self-righteous Palestinian terrorist and elusive intelligence agent; he welcomes Charlie as an effective comrade-in-arms and sexual diversion, but he is betrayed by her and murdered in her bed by Gadi Becker in John le Carré's *The Little Drummer Girl*.

Ella   The main character in Anna Wulf's manuscript, *The Shadow of the Third*; she is a single woman working for a woman's magazine, who very much mirrors Anna in her love affairs and in her personal and physical make-up in Doris Lessing's *The Golden Notebook*.

Ellen   A Member of the British Communist Party; she persuades Molly Jacobs to join, simply by accusing her of being an "agent" because of her indecisiveness about signing up in Doris Lessing's *The Golden Notebook*.

Ellen   Kitchenmaid at Charleswood, the Westons' country estate; she is in love with and marries Ralph Moberly in Isabel Colegate's *Statues in a Garden*.

Mr. Ellen   Vicar of Dansby Church and Oliver Green's superior; he is a man of almost boisterous vigor who thrives on Christianity and influences Oliver in C. Day Lewis's *Child of Misfortune*.

Judy Ellerker   Downstairs neighbor of Thomas Phillips and Pam Hargreaves; she becomes lover to each of them and becomes close friends with them as a couple in Alan Sillitoe's *Her Victory*.

Captain Elliot   Captain of the *Pluto*; he is somewhat in awe of Hornblower's voyage on the *Lydia* in C. S. Forester's *Ship of the Line*.

Hughling Elliot   Garrulous, vacationing Englishman at the Santa Marina Hotel in Virginia Woolf's *The Voyage Out*.

Mrs. Hughling Elliot   Silly social butterfly on holiday with her husband at the Santa Marina Hotel in Virginia Woolf's *The Voyage Out*.

Agnes Pembroke Elliott   Rickie Elliott's overbearing wife, who schemes to obtain the Elliott family fortune in E. M. Forster's *The Longest Journey*.

Frederick (Rickie) Elliott   Lame young schoolmaster, who longs to be a writer but lets his wife and brother-in-law run his life; he is Stephen Wonham's half brother in E. M. Forster's *The Longest Journey*.

Miss Ellis   One of the nurses at St. Andrews, where Rosamund Stacey goes to have her baby in Margaret Drabble's *The Millstone*.

Nancy Ellis   Teen-aged member of a variety act with her sister and brother-in-law; she progresses from music halls to pantomimes to musical comedy and eventually marries Dick Herncastle, who has always loved her despite their many misunderstandings stemming from his involvements with other women in J. B. Priestley's *Lost Empires*.

P. W. Ellis   A bigoted cockney who is spiteful and abusive and determined that no natives ever be admitted to the European Club in George Orwell's *Burmese Days*.

Sylvia Ellis   Twenty-two-year-old secretary for solicitors who represent local Conservative politicians; she is in love with Mark Robinson, warns the group it has been spied on, and confides to Stephen Freer that the spy was Bernard Kelshall in C. P. Snow's *The Malcontents*.

Fanny Elmer   Jacob Flanders's London girlfriend in whom he "left his seed somewhere"; Jacob's child lives inside her while the father dies in Virginia Woolf's *Jacob's Room*.

Eloise   An au pair girl who stayed for a time with Anthony and Babs Keating in Margaret Drabble's *The Ice Age*.

Miss Elphinstone   Spunky upper-class young woman who flees to France with her mother and the anonymous narrator's unnamed brother in H. G. Wells's *The War of the Worlds*.

Elrond   Wise, kind halfelven who befriends Bilbo Baggins and Gandalf on their quest to oust the dragon from the Mountain in J. R. R. Tolkien's *The Hobbit; or There and Back Again*. He helps and advises Frodo Baggins and provides him shelter and supplies in *The*

Fellowship of the Ring, in *The Two Towers,* and in *The Return of the King.*

Princess Elsie   The young princess of England and niece of the archduchess Elizabeth of Pisuerga; she is an avid huntress; she courts and wins the favor of Prince Yousef and is ceremoniously married in his homeland with the blessings of both their royal families, much to the despair of jilted Laura de Nazianzi in Ronald Firbank's *The Flower Beneath the Foot.*

Elsinore   Eva Trout's sickly and suicidal roommate at The Castle, a school briefly funded by Eva's father; on the day before her adoption of Jeremy, Eva accidentally meets Elsinore again in a city in the American midwest in Elizabeth Bowen's *Eva Trout, or Changing Scenes.*

Jeremy Elton   A TV producer who marries Polly Elton; he tries to engage in wife-swapping with Michael and Miriam and has an affair with Gertrude, the au pair; Polly divorces him in David Lodge's *How Far Can You Go?.*

Polly Elton   A sexy and dark lapsed Catholic who experiments with sex early; she marries Jeremy Elton, writes an advice column, has several children, and finally divorces Jeremy and joins the women's movement in David Lodge's *How Far Can You Go?.*

Ruth Elton   Wealthy socialite who marries Arthur Miles after his appointment as assistant director of the new National Institute; she supports him in his decision to turn from science to writing in C. P. Snow's *The Search.*

Grace Elver   Moronic heiress who is pursued by the scheming Mr. Cardan; she dies after her betrothal from eating tainted fish in Aldous Huxley's *Those Barren Leaves.*

Elvira   Karl Riemeck's mistress; she encourages her lover to defect to West Berlin and, although he is assassinated, follows him; she is later murdered on Hans-Dieter Mundt's orders in John le Carré's *The Spy Who Came In from the Cold.*

Elvira   Venetian maid who tries to make Eustace Cherrington comfortable at the palazzo of Lady Nelly Staveley in L. P. Hartley's *Eustace and Hilda.*

Elyle   A beautiful, wealthy woman living in Koshi who is highly intrigued by Ambien II's beauty; she is Adalantaland's fallen daughter in Doris Lessing's *The Sirian Experiments.*

Elys   The woman who, although responsible for

teaching Ben Ata many ways of increasing sexual pleasure, is unable to teach him the necessary components of tenderness and passion in Doris Lessing's *The Marriages Between Zones Three, Four, and Five.*

Mr. Emerson   George Emerson's father, a kind, outspoken old man who helps Lucy Honeychurch decide to marry George in E. M. Forster's *A Room with a View.*

George Emerson   Unconventional young man who falls in love with Lucy Honeychurch in Italy; aroused and insulted by his impulsive kiss, Lucy accepts another proposal, but recognizes in time the real suitability of George in E. M. Forster's *A Room with a View.*

George Emerson   Aline Peters's ardent suitor, a young man second in command of the Hong Kong police force but on vacation at home in England in P. G. Wodehouse's *Something New.*

Emilio   Man briefly involved with Kate Fletcher Armstrong in Margaret Drabble's *The Middle Ground.*

"Emily"   The unnamed narrator's hallucinatory projection of her former self in an alternate reality; the narrator is a middle-aged woman who takes in a young girl, Emily Cartright, and attempts to pursue a normal life in her city flat following a catastrophic war in Doris Lessing's *Memoirs of a Survivor.*

Emily   Red-haired young woman of the village of Great Mop with whom Lolly Willowes enjoys dancing at the witches' sabbath in Sylvia Townsend Warner's *Lolly Willowes: or, the Loving Huntsman.*

Emily   Sensitive young woman traumatized by her husband, from whom she is separated; sexually naïve, she offers the younger Theodore Gumbril a sense of hope — dashed when he is delayed in a crucial meeting because of his attentions to Myra Viveash in Aldous Huxley's *Antic Hay.*

Emir   Tribal leader who uses his ministers, especially the Wazari, to spy and scheme for him against the government in Joyce Cary's *Mister Johnson.*

Em'ler   Slow-witted girl who helps Brenda with her "miscarriage recipe" in Alan Sillitoe's *Saturday Night and Sunday Morning.*

Emma   A plain girl who works as a machinist at Jordan's factory in D. H. Lawrence's *Sons and Lovers.*

Miss Emmett   Devoted elderly governess and companion of Kitty Faber; she impulsively murders Llewellyn to defend Kitty from attempted rape and then forgets about it in Anthony Burgess's *MF.*

Emmie Unmarried maid in Clara Hamp's house whose newly discovered pregnancy causes the dying Auntie Hamp's last display of strict Chapel morality in ordering her immediately out of the house, although she has nowhere to go until Maggie and Edwin Clayhanger treat her compassionately in Arnold Bennett's *These Twain*.

Empress of Blandings Lord Emsworth's prize sow and raison d'être in P. G. Wodehouse's *Fish Preferred* and in eight other novels.

Mr. Empson-Courtney Relative of Alvina Smithers; he and his wife own a seashore cottage where Georgie Smithers visits to recover from her desertion by Mr. Purfleet in Richard Aldington's *The Colonel's Daughter*.

Mrs. Empson-Courtney Wife of Mr. Empson-Courtney in Richard Aldington's *The Colonel's Daughter*.

Clarence Threepwood, Lord Emsworth A mild, harmless earl whose absence of mind creates difficulties in P. G. Wodehouse's *Something New*. His constant wish is for uninterrupted serenity for his contemplation of the Empress of Blandings, his prize sow, in *Fish Preferred*. He appears in eight other novels.

Captain Dykes Enderby Master of the local hunt; he is a "vulgar pinheaded bore", who nevertheless provides distraction for Evelyn Crane in C. Day Lewis's *The Friendly Tree*.

F. X. Enderby Eccentric, dyspeptic, middle-aged British poet, who has pleasant manners but grossly unclean personal habits; having impulsively spurned a publisher's award, he becomes the object of various reformation attempts in Anthony Burgess's *Inside Mr. Enderby*. He triumphs over the behaviorists by regaining his lyric gifts but must confront his mediocrity in *Enderby Outside*. Temporarily a professor of literature at an American university out of financial need, he achieves a modest fame which attracts additional deranged attentions in *The Clockwork Testament; Or Enderby's End*.

Sir Saul Enderby Foreign Office expert on Southeast Asian affairs whose undercover deal with the American C.I.A. robs the British Intelligence of its prize catch (Sino-Soviet double agent Nelson Ko), forces Smiley's retirement after Operation Dolphin, and insures his own ascension as the new head of London Station in John le Carré's *The Honourable Schoolboy*. He appears in *Smiley's People*.

Mrs. Enders The woman whose family rents Kate Brown's house while the Brown family all go their separate ways for the summer in Doris Lessing's *The Summer Before the Dark*.

Mr. Endicott Retired barber to the elite; Lord Peter Wimsey traces the provenance of the murder weapon through him in Dorothy L. Sayers's *Have His Carcase*.

Mrs. Endicott Owner of a rooming house in Exeter where Sarah Woodruff and Charles Smithson make love in John Fowles's *The French Lieutenant's Woman*.

Mr. Endon A "schizophrenic of the most amiable variety", the opponent in a non-game of chess in which the object is not to lose a piece or attack in Samuel Beckett's *Murphy*.

Dr. Emile Englander Curator of reptiles at the zoological gardens who is suspected by British police to be a spy for the Uni-Europeans; he builds a reptile house in the Western Islands off Scotland to save his serpents during the war; he becomes zoo director after a victory by the Uni-Europeans and is imprisoned for his complicity in zoo-games after the final defeat of the Uni-Europeans in Angus Wilson's *The Old Men at the Zoo*.

Sophie Englander Wife of Emile; she was helped by Simon Carter when she was jailed before the war in Angus Wilson's *The Old Men at the Zoo*.

Arnold Englehart A member of the Lycurgan [Fabian] Society in Dorothy Richardson's *Dawn's Left Hand*.

Englishman Unnamed benefactor who finds Geoffrey Firmin passed out in the street and gives him a drink of Irish whiskey in Malcolm Lowry's *Under the Volcano*.

Enid A Prince of Wales barmaid, for whom Maureen Kirby's mother sometimes substitutes in Margaret Drabble's *The Ice Age*.

Laurel Ennis Shallow, middle-class wife of Richard; she urges him to try for promotion to officer in order to satisfy her longing for social status in Anthony Burgess's *A Vision of Battlements*.

Sergeant Richard Ennis Liberal, intellectual musician inducted into the British Army in World War II; he haphazardly conducts vocational classes for enlisted men in Gibraltar; out of place and thoroughly muddled, he meets confusion and disaster in all his endeavors, including his affair with Conception Gomez in Anthony Burgess's *A Vision of Battlements*.

Geoffrey Enright Young secretary and catamite of

Kenneth Toomey in the latter's old age; frequently drunk, he is an insolent but amusing companion and a lazy, slovenly secretary in Anthony Burgess's *Earthly Powers*.

Dr. Kenneth Enticott   The psychiatrist who treats Beatrice Ifor; he confesses to Sammy Mountjoy that he would like to marry his wife, Taffy Mountjoy, in William Golding's *Free Fall*.

Mr. Entwhistle   Defrocked clergyman whose drunkenness and irresponsibility have led to his losing his position and create severe problems for his daughter, Joan, in Henry Green's *Blindness*.

Joan Entwhistle   Resentful daughter of a defrocked clergyman; she has a relatively short but deep romantic friendship with John Haye in Henry Green's *Blindness*.

Norman Entwhistle   Brother-in-law of Charles Highway; Norman is a middle-class manager of mediocre intellect, pedestrian views, and disgusting personal habits; it is through Norman that Charles gets at least one view of what an adult male thinks about sex and women in Martin Amis's *The Rachel Papers*.

Lady Sophia Entwistle   Priam Farll's former fiancée, from whose control he has bolted in terror; she is subpoenaed back to London to give evidence in a trial to determine the identity of Priam Farll after his supposed death and burial in Westminster Abbey in Arnold Bennett's *Buried Alive: A Tale of These Days*.

Mendel Ephraim   Non-aligned Israeli who lives in the harmony of a youth-culture underclass with his Palestinian contemporaries, especially Abdul Ramdez, in Muriel Spark's *The Mandlebaum Gate*.

Saul Ephraim   Older brother of Mendel and stern, conservative guide of Barbara Vaughan during her stay in Israel in Muriel Spark's *The Mandlebaum Gate*.

Dolly Ercott   Wife of the Colonel; she chaperones Olive Cramier at Monte Carlo and does not discourage Mark Lennon's attentions in John Galsworthy's *The Dark Flower*.

Colonel John Ercott   Olive Cramier's uncle, a retired soldier, who chaperones her at Monte Carlo; he does not like her husband in John Galsworthy's *The Dark Flower*.

Myra Erdleigh   A large, conspicuous middle-aged widow who is Uncle Giles Jenkins's alarming only woman friend; she tells Nick Jenkins's fortune with the Tarot cards; she has acquired control of Jimmy Strip-

ling; Uncle Giles denies all knowledge of her in Anthony Powell's *The Acceptance World*. She associates with Dr. Trelawney for undiscovered nefarious reasons; she visits Uncle Giles's deathbed and inherits all his money in *The Kindly Ones*. She burns incense and makes dark predictions in *The Military Philosophers*. She reappears with Stripling in *Temporary Kings*. Her spiritual "presence" in supernatural cults of the 1960s somewhat validates her claim that death is insignificant in *Hearing Secret Harmonies*.

Eric   Half of "Sam 'n Eric", a pair of twins always mentioned in tandem; they typify people of good will who behave as decently as possible but eventually capitulate to evil in William Golding's *Lord of the Flies*.

Erikson   Late writer who influenced Sigbjorn Wilderness in Malcolm Lowry's *Dark as the Grave Wherein My Friend Is Laid*.

Ermino   One of the two gondoliers attached to the household of Lady Nelly Staveley in Venice who pilot her and her guests around the city in L. P. Hartley's *Eustace and Hilda*.

Erno   Architect friend of Janos Lavin and Laszlo; he worked with them for the socialist cause in Hungary, dying before Laszlo was executed in John Berger's *A Painter of Our Time*.

Dr. Laura Ernst   Chief surgeon on the *Endeavor*; she is the first to examine a Raman robot in Arthur C. Clarke's *Rendezvous with Rama*.

Alfred, Lord Erridge   Eldest of the ten children of Lord Warminster; he is a misfit at debutante dances in Anthony Powell's *A Buyer's Market*. He inherits the Warminster title in *The Acceptance World*. He is a "red" nobleman of slightly comic proportions who derives pleasure from living simply and professing leftist views; he heavily subsidizes Quiggin's publications before Mona Templer ditches Quiggin to accompany him to China in *At Lady Molly's*. He is abandoned by Mona, goes to Spain, and becomes St. John Clarke's heir in *Casanova's Chinese Restaurant*. In failing health, he is invigorated by his opposition to the military requisition of his estate during World War II in *The Kindly Ones*. His death and funeral occur in *Books Do Furnish a Room*.

Errol   David Mountolive's Head of Chancery in Alexandria in Lawrence Durrell's *Mountolive*.

Angela Errol   Wife of the Head of Chancery in Alexandria; her presenting David Mountolive with a dachshund is a formal recognition of his loneliness in Lawrence Durrell's *Mountolive*.

Major Richard Erskine   Married man in love with Helen Halliday in Agatha Christie's *Sleeping Murder.*

Theodore Ertzberger   Powerful financier; he tells the sympathetic Sir Edward Leithen of Koré Arabin's tragic life in John Buchan's *The Dancing Floor.*

Minna Erve   One of the delegates to the conferences of the planets that are to decide on the fate of Planet Earth in Doris Lessing's *Briefing for a Descent into Hell.*

Anne-Marie Eschelmer   Fifty-year-old illegitimate daughter of Honoré Burckheim; she dotes on her son, Henry; she hates her dead German husband, who abused her and Henry; she is jealous of Honoré's wife, Caroline, and insults her as a childless woman; she pressures Honoré to acknowledge Henry as his grandson; she seems finally to have helped her son escape to Germany after he has killed Ernest Siguenau for referring to him as a German agent in Storm Jameson's *Cousin Honoré.*

Henry Eschelmer   Anne-Marie Eschelmer's son; because of Anne-Marie's illegitimacy, Honoré Burckheim refuses to help him or recognize him as a grandson and despises him because he is born of a German father; Henry works as a clerk in a "dubious" financial house in Metz; he hates his dead German father for his great cruelty to him as a child; he covets the favor of Honoré; his trust is misused by unscrupulous employees of the ironworks; he is paranoid and emotionally unstable and finally commits a double murder in Storm Jameson's *Cousin Honoré.*

Gustavo Escobar   Husband of Margarita Escobar in Graham Greene's *The Honorary Consul.*

Margarita Escobar   One of the rich patients with whom Dr. Eduardo Plarr has had an affair in Graham Greene's *The Honorary Consul.*

Insil Esikananzi   Luterin Shokerandit's betrothed, who eventually marries Asperamanka; she befriends Torress Lahl while Luterin is in prison in Brian W. Aldiss's *Helliconia Winter.*

Umat Esikananzi   Insil's brother and Luterin Shokerandit's best friend in Brian W. Aldiss's *Helliconia Winter.*

Frank Esmay   Rosie O'Grady's husband; the marriage is threatened by eight years of childlessness, but Rosie at last conceives in Mary Lavin's *Mary O'Grady.*

Dr. Esmond   Rosamund Stacey's attending physician at St. Andrews in Margaret Drabble's *The Millstone.*

Alam Esomber   The personal envoy of C'Sarr Kilander IX; he brings the divorce papers to MyrdemInggala and later tries to rape her in Brian W. Aldiss's *Helliconia Summer.*

Essie   The Cartaret family's young servant; she is impregnated by James Greatorex in May Sinclair's *The Three Sisters.*

Toby Esterhaze (codename "Poorman"; covernames: Anselm, Mr. Benati, Hector, Jacobi, Kurt Siebel) Hungarian surveillance operative, head "lamplighter", and Roy Bland's second at the British Intelligence London Station; he is suspected in Operation Witchcraft but clears himself and stays with the Circus in John le Carré's *Tinker, Tailor, Soldier, Spy.* He assists George Smiley's Operation Dolphin by taping Connie Sachs and Doc di Salis's interrogation of Mr. Hibbert in *The Honourable Schoolboy.* Dismissed when the "lamplighters" are disbanded, he becomes an art dealer but emerges from retirement to orchestrate Anton Grigoriev's abduction in *Smiley's People.*

Esther   A fifteen-year-old pupil at Lesbia Firebrace's school who complains of the school food; she is a friend of Clemence Shelley in Ivy Compton-Burnett's *Two Worlds and Their Ways.*

Harold Etches   Bachelor son of a wealthy Hanbridge manufacturer and one of the founders of the Sports Club; he suggests that Denry Machin stand for election to the club in Arnold Bennett's *The Card: A Story of Adventure in the Five Towns.*

Ethel   The tall, dark housemaid of the Donne family; she knows much of what goes on in the family in Ivy Compton-Burnett's *Elders and Betters.*

Eufemia   Co-proprietor of the Villa Sofia and of the half of Victor Pancev's body buried in her part of the garden in Muriel Spark's *Territorial Rights.*

Cousin Eugenia   Sakskia's aged companion; she and Sakskia are sheltered by "Aunt Phemie" Morran in Dalquharter after they are rescued from their imprisonment in Huntingtower House by the resourceful Gorbals Die-Hards in John Buchan's *Huntingtower.*

Kimon Euras   The judge before whom Jandol-Anganol is tried for Simdol Tal's death in Brian W. Aldiss's *Helliconia Summer.*

Europa   A beautiful and wealthy young woman whom John Wainwright courts, only to flee just before having sexual intercourse in Olaf Stapledon's *Odd John: A Story Between Jest and Earnest.*

Evan The dead friend with whom the mad, suicidal Septimus Smith communes in Virginia Woolf's *Mrs. Dalloway*.

Christian Evandale Bradley Pearson's detested ex-wife, now the widow of a wealthy American; she is Francis Marloe's sister and becomes Arnold Baffin's lover in Iris Murdoch's *The Black Prince*.

Secretary Evanporil The Shokerandit family's employee; he oversees the workings of the estate in Brian W. Aldiss's *Helliconia Winter*.

Lieutenant Evans Officer of the Pioneer Battalion for whom George Winterbourne serves as Platoon Runner; although ignorant, inhibited, class-conscious, and complacent, he is honest, kindly, and conscientious and recommends George for officer's training in Richard Aldington's *Death of a Hero*.

Bill Evans A former lover of Elizabeth Gruffydd-Williams; he is still devoted to Elizabeth, who mistreats and exploits him; she makes him babysit for the Lewises so that she can have John Lewis at her party in Kingsley Amis's *That Uncertain Feeling*.

David Evans The Welsh husband of Emma Evans; a television actor, he drags his wife and children out to Hereford so that he can perform with a repertory company; he has a brief affair with Sophy Brent in Margaret Drabble's *The Garrick Year*.

David (Dai) Evans Opportunistic, elderly, ugly patient in Clive Ward because of a growth under his armpit; vulgar and crafty, he fights with Ken Adamson and irritates the other patients, but he is also pitied by them and even admired by Robin Garton in John Berger's *The Foot of Clive*.

Emma Lawrence Evans Wife of David Evans and mother of Flora and Joseph; she resists leaving London for the summer and losing a possible job on a television news program; she does leave, remaining a housewife, but has a mild affair with Wyndham Farrar while in Hereford in Margaret Drabble's *The Garrick Year*.

Flora Evans Young daughter of Emma and David Evans; she courts death by drowning but survives in Margaret Drabble's *The Garrick Year*.

Joseph Evans The infant son of Emma and David Evans in Margaret Drabble's *The Garrick Year*.

Marged Evans Daughter of a long-time friend of Gwilym Morgan; she is engaged to Owen Morgan, who breaks the engagement; she marries the younger Gwilym Morgan, goes mad, and commits suicide in Richard Llewellyn's *How Green Was My Valley*.

Michael Evans A schoolmaster lacking personal initiative; something of a "bolshie" and fatalist, he is a friend of the private eye Nigel Strangeways; his affair with the headmaster's wife makes him a strong suspect of murder in Nicholas Blake's *A Question of Proof*.

Owen Evans A sadistic, guilt-ridden Welsh antiquary; possessed of the cruel urge to witness the murder of his friend John Crow, he glimpses instead Tom Barter's corpse; his sadism is relieved, but he is left a broken, doddering, prematurely white-haired man in John Cowper Powys's *A Glastonbury Romance*.

Yestin Evans The loutish son of a mine owner; he makes an unhappy marriage with Angharad Morgan in Richard Llewellyn's *How Green Was My Valley*.

Evart The orchestra conductor who is apathetic concerning war and is caught by the enemy in the midst of one with his entire orchestra; he is forced to play concerts and is finally killed by the prison firing squad in Alan Sillitoe's *The General*.

Eve The new servant at the Wimpole Street surgery, who came at the time of the unexpected death of Miriam Henderson's sister Eve in Dorothy Richardson's *The Trap*.

Everard The butler for the Mowbray family; he serves them disinterestedly in Ivy Compton-Burnett's *A Father and His Fate*.

Giles Everard ("Revvy Evvy") Demoyte's successor as headmaster at St. Bride's; a clergyman, he values moral character over academic brilliance and is held in contempt by Demoyte and by William Mor in Iris Murdoch's *The Sandcastle*.

Jamesie Evercreech Violet's much younger brother; he acts as chauffeur at Gaze Castle and assists Violet and Gerald Scottow in keeping Hannah Crean-Smith a prisoner; he is Gerald's lover in Iris Murdoch's *The Unicorn*.

Violet Evercreech A family connection of Hannah Crean-Smith; she acts as housekeeper at Gaze Castle and keeps an eye on Hannah in Iris Murdoch's *The Unicorn*.

Christian ("Kirsty") Everdale Much-sought young heiress of Balbarnit whose guardian, Lord Mannour, seeks to wed her to Lord Belses; attracted to Sir Turnour Wyse, she realizes her true love is "Jock" Kinloch in John Buchan's *The Free Fishers*.

Mrs. Everett   Well-intentioned landlady of Gerald Lamont and Albert Sorrell; she helps Sorrell escape to Scotland in Josephine Tey's *The Man in the Queue*.

Evie   A little girl from Rotten Row, remembered mainly for her youthful ability to urinate higher up a toilet wall than any of her male friends in William Golding's *Free Fall*.

Evie   One of the daughters of Kitty Friedman in Margaret Drabble's *The Ice Age*.

Auntie Evie   Maureen Kirby's aunt who works hard and is highly respected in the slum neighborhood that she will eventually be forced to leave by modern property developers in Margaret Drabble's *The Ice Age*.

Robert Ewan   The town physician's son who succeeds in winning Imogen Grantley away from Oliver in William Golding's *The Pyramid*.

Bob Ewart   George Ponderevo's closest friend in early adulthood; he is a socialist who questions the status quo in H. G. Wells's *Tono-Bungay*.

Ex-Deb-of-Last-Year   Call-me-Cobber's lover; she is a fashion model and a subject of the narrator's photography in Colin MacInnes's *Absolute Beginners*.

Exell   Partner with Howard Martineau in an advertising agency; he testifies for the prosecution in the trial of George Passant, Jack Cotery, and Olive Calvert in C. P. Snow's *Strangers and Brothers*.

Mr. Exshaw   Short, spectacled, self-important manager of the Audit Department; he is surprised that Evelyn Orcham brings the housekeeper Violet Powler to visit his office on her first working day and informs her that her eighth floor has more breakages than the restaurant in Arnold Bennett's *Imperial Palace*.

Michael Eyam   Anthony Keating's assistant in removing a tree from a future garden site at Keating's residence in Margaret Drabble's *The Ice Age*.

Leonora Eyre   Elegant, fiftyish, self-satisfied, moneyed spinster who lives alone in her London maisonette and cherishes romantic dreams about the much younger James Boyce while accepting the devotion of his uncle Humphrey in Barbara Pym's *The Sweet Dove Died*.

F

F An American friend of Nelson and Anna Wulf's lover for a brief time; he is boring, calculating, and married in Doris Lessing's *The Golden Notebook.*

Fa The wifely companion of Lok and perhaps the most intelligent and perceptive member of the Neanderthal tribe that is vanquished by their Homo sapiens opponents in William Golding's *The Inheritors.*

Mrs. Faber A hoarder of provisions who warns the Britlings of an impending famine in H. G. Wells's *Mr. Britling Sees It Through.*

Catherine (Kitty) Faber Homely, dull, and normal sister of Miles Faber; she understands little and is interested in little but food; functionally orphaned since early childhood, she has no family but Miss Emmet in Anthony Burgess's *MF.*

Miles Faber Intellectual, aggressive, unconventional son of a wealthy businessman; in order to pursue a scholarly interest in an obscure poet and painter, Sib Legru, he travels to the remote Caribbean island where lives a sister whom he has never seen in Anthony Burgess's *MF.*

Dr. Fagan Owner of Llanabba School who eventually sells the property and buys a private sanatorium where he helps arrange Paul Pennyfeather's fake death in Evelyn Waugh's *Decline and Fall.*

Father Kurt Fahrt A Jesuit who argues theology and church history with Mr. Collopy and accompanies him to Rome in Flann O'Brien's *The Hard Life.*

Anthony Eustace Failing Rickie Elliott's uncle, who is the author of a book of essays in E. M. Forster's *The Longest Journey.*

Emily Failing Rickie Elliott's lame, eccentric aunt, the owner of Cadover farms; she tells Rickie about his illegitimate half brother, Stephen Wonham, in E. M. Forster's *The Longest Journey.*

Faint British soldier who mistakes Jack Townrow for a man named Captain Ferris; he is shot and killed in P. H. Newby's *Something to Answer For.*

Sir Charles Fairbanks Secretary of a major industrial company; his ill health and imminent resignation provide the prospect of promotion and an eventual knighthood for Harold Colmore in Roy Fuller's *The Father's Comedy.*

Mrs. Fairclough Old woman passenger on the plane to Srem Panh who offers religious messages to Bill and Meg Eliot in Angus Wilson's *The Middle Age of Mrs. Eliot.*

Anthony Culpepper Fairfax Conventionally racist South Carolinian with whom Augustine Penry-Herbert becomes friends in Canada, each supposing the other's opinions to be a form of jocularity; he returns to England with Augustine and eventually marries Joan Dibden; he wishes there were such a leader as Adolf Hitler in America in Richard Hughes's *The Wooden Shepherdess.*

Professor Gervase Fairfax Anthropologist in Barbara Pym's *Less Than Angels.*

Charles Fairford Flora Poste's cousin and future husband, who promises to rescue her from the wilds of her relatives' Sussex farmhouse if the going gets too rough in Stella Gibbons's *Cold Comfort Farm.*

Mrs. Fairley Mrs. Poulteney's housekeeper; her reports result in Sarah Woodruff's being fired in John Fowles's *The French Lieutenant's Woman.*

Felicity Fairmead The Provincial Lady's occasional guest, whose charms are the subject of Robert's rare — and irritating — praise in E. M. Delafield's *The Diary of a Provincial Lady.* She reappears in *The Provincial Lady Goes Further.*

Jane Falcon Wife of Sir Robert; she quarrels with Martha Carter after the war begins and gives Martha a place to live when Martha leaves Simon in Angus Wilson's *The Old Men at the Zoo.*

Sir Robert Falcon Curator of mammals at the zoological gardens who helped Simon Carter get his position; he tries to seduce Martha Carter in California; he is planning a grand show of the zoo as its director when bombs hit London; he loses his mind during the war in Angus Wilson's *The Old Men at the Zoo.*

Adam Falconet Multi-millionaire American adventurer; nursed back to physical and mental health by Adam Melfort, he insists on providing unlimited financial backing for Adam's quest for a world leader in John Buchan's *A Prince of the Captivity.*

Josephine Fallon Beautiful nursing student murdered in P. D. James's *Shroud for a Nightingale.*

Fallowfield A National Service draftee from public school who goes on to obtain a commission but shows signs of regret to Jonathan Browne in David Lodge's *Ginger, You're Barmy.*

Mr. Falx Socialist labor leader of generous sentiments; as a companion of Lord Hovenden to Rome, he becomes a guest at Lillian Aldwinkle's Italian houseparty in Aldous Huxley's *Those Barren Leaves.*

Fane Scientist from Manchester who argues against locating the new National Institute in London in C. P. Snow's *The Search.*

Justice Fane Judge who presides at the trial of Cora Ross and Kitty Pateman in C. P. Snow's *The Sleep of Reason.*

Eleanor Fane Widowed mother of Walter, who lives with her in Agatha Christie's *Sleeping Murder.*

Kitty Fane Frivolous, silly wife of Dr. Walter Fane; she falls into futile love with an attractive philanderer but, when forced to accompany her husband to Mei-tan-fu, the scene of a cholera epidemic, begins to discover that she has confused love with passion in W. Somerset Maugham's *The Painted Veil.*

Milo Fane Monty Small's immensely popular fictional detective, a man of ruthless courage, contempt for stupidity, and invariable success; he has cut Monty off from the world of literature in Iris Murdoch's *The Sacred and Profane Love Machine.*

Walter Fane Repressed man, unhappy since his proposal to Helen Spenlove Kennedy (later Halliday) was refused years ago; he lives under the dominion of his mother in Agatha Christie's *Sleeping Murder.*

Dr. Walter Fane The deeply emotional yet repressed bacteriologist who, on discovering that his beloved wife, Kitty, is having an affair, insists upon her accompanying him to Mei-tan-fu, an area of China infested by cholera, in W. Somerset Maugham's *The Painted Veil.*

William Fane The paying guest of Jonathan Swift; he is a local lawyer who unwittingly tells Gabriel Swift that Maria Rosetti is his mother in Ivy Compton-Burnett's *More Women Than Men.*

Sir Timothy Fanfield Retired cavalryman who serves on Michael Mont's committee for slum conversion in John Galsworthy's *Swan Song.*

Fanny An unattractive "hunchback woman"; she is one of the "work-girls" at Jordan's factory in D. H. Lawrence's *Sons and Lovers.*

Miss Fanshawe The nurse for Rose and Viola Lovat; she lets the girls be unconventional and even naughty in Ivy Compton-Burnett's *Darkness and Day.*

Fard Fantil An ironworker from Oldorando who helps make weapons for JandolAngand in Brian W. Aldiss's *Helliconia Summer.*

Amelia, Contessa di Faraglione The monocle-wearing, uninhibited, vivacious wife of an Italian count; her visit to her brother, Algernon Wyse, seems long overdue to the inhabitants of Tilling in E. F. Benson's *Miss Mapp.* She disappoints Elizabeth Mapp's hope that she will expose Lucia Lucas's ignorance of Italian in *Mapp and Lucia.* She appears in *The Worshipful Lucia.*

Sunderland (Sunny) Farebrother Young business associate of Peter Templer's father in Anthony Powell's *A Question of Upbringing.* During World War II he feuds with Widmerpool, his counterpart in another battalion, in *The Kindly Ones,* in *The Valley of Bones,* and in *The Soldier's Art.* His rise and downfall as an undercover officer, his ongoing reciprocated hatred of Widmerpool, and his engagement to General Conyers's widow, the former Geraldine Weedon, occur in *The Military Philosophers.* He gloats over Widmerpool's fall in *Temporary Kings.*

Duncan Farll Lawyer and opportunistic nephew of the artist Priam Farll; taking Farll to be Farll's valet Leek, he unwittingly, in his testimony against his uncle, reveals that two particular moles can identify him in Arnold Bennett's *Buried Alive: A Tale of These Days.*

Priam Farll Pathologically shy, solitary, forty-year-old artist; his work is internationally known while the man is unknown; he seizes the death of his valet, Henry Leek, as an opportunity for anonymity; when posing as Leek, he discovers the practical Putney widow Alice Challice, who becomes his comfortable wife and helps him cope with the court case and notoriety subsequent to the discovery through his new paintings that he is alive and his valet is buried in Westminster Abbey in Arnold Bennett's *Buried Alive: A Tale of These Days.*

Roland Farmer Neighbor of Sir Randolph Nettleby; he often flushes game for Sir Randolph's shooting parties in Isabel Colegate's *The Shooting Party.*

Tommy Farmer Son of Roland Farmer, a neighbor of Sir Randolph Nettleby; he sometimes flushes game for Mr. Glass during Sir Randolph's shooting parties in Isabel Colegate's *The Shooting Party.*

Mr. Farne Barrister assisting Sir Henry Merriman in the prosecution of the smugglers in Graham Greene's *The Man Within.*

Eileen Farnsfield Rich widow who takes in young

Peter Granby because he helped her mother once; she uses Peter as helper, handyman, and lover until he becomes a bore in Alan Sillitoe's *Out of the Whirlpool*.

Charles Farquar   Incompetent sportsman, who is invited to Sir Randolph Nettleby's shooting party to occupy Aline, Lady Hartlip while her husband is participating in the shoot in Isabel Colegate's *The Shooting Party*.

Lois Farquar   Unsophisticated, restless, thoughtful, and observant niece of Sir Richard and Lady Naylor, with whom she has lived since the death of her mother, Sir Richard's sister; in contrast to other members of her Ascendancy-class family, she half enjoys, half fears the liberating changes imposed by the Anglo-Irish War (1919–21) on Irish Big House society, including those that nearly result in her engagement to Gerald Lesworth in Elizabeth Bowen's *The Last September*.

Anthony Farrant   Morally and occupationally adrift twin brother of Kate Farrant; hired by Erik Krogh as a bodyguard, he becomes uneasy about Krogh's business activities, finally agreeing to provide newspaper reporter Minty with paid information; he is persuaded by Lucia Davidge to leave Krogh and join her in England, but he is murdered before he can do so in Graham Greene's *England Made Me*.

Kate Farrant   Stylish, ambitious twin sister of Anthony Farrant and secretary and mistress of Erik Krogh; she manages Krogh's social and business life and acts as his confidante; she tries to persuade Anthony to settle in Sweden and work permanently for Krogh, but when Anthony dies, she leaves Krogh in Graham Greene's *England Made Me*.

Brat Farrar   An orphan whose uncanny resemblance to Simon Ashby results in his cooperation in a scheme to pass himself off as Simon's twin brother, Patrick; Brat must expose his own crime of fraud in exposing Simon's crime of murder in Josephine Tey's *Brat Farrar*.

Marjorie Farrar   Deceased aunt of Wyndham Farrar; she owned the now-closed and for-sale Binneford House, which Emma Evans and Wyndham Farrar visit on their first outing together in Margaret Drabble's *The Garrick Year*.

Percy Edward Farrar   Father of Wyndham Farrar in Margaret Drabble's *The Garrick Year*.

Wyndham (born Grantham) Farrar   Stage, film, and television director of some distinction; he has assembled a group of actors to open the Garrick Theatre in Hereford; while there he patiently courts and finally seduces Emma Evans in Margaret Drabble's *The Garrick Year*.

Miss Farrell   Headmistress of a local school in Anchorstone who helps Eustace Cherrington entertain the numerous Crankshavians at the wedding of Jimmy Crankshaw and Barbara Cherrington in L. P. Hartley's *The Sixth Heaven*.

Cashel Boyle O'Connor Fitzmaurice Tisdall Farrell   Dublin eccentric who wanders the streets in James Joyce's *Ulysses*.

Fiona Farrell   Michael's fifty-year-old single colleague, who takes an indulgent attitude toward student sex in David Lodge's *How Far Can You Go?*.

Nicholas Farringdon   Anarchist/poet, author of *The Sabbath Notebooks*; his experience with the women of the May of Teck Club (especially Jane Wright, Joanna Childe, and Selina Redwood) after Germany's surrender in World War II leads to his conversion to Catholicism which, in turn, leads to religious work and martyrdom in Haiti years later in Muriel Spark's *The Girls of Slender Means*.

Lilly Farris   Top-of-the-bill singer of sentimental ballads, who lures Dick Herncastle into a sordid situation involving a drunken young girl, Phyllis Robinson, in J. B. Priestley's *Lost Empires*.

Mary Farrow   Ernestina Freeman's maid who marries Sam Farrow and discovers the whereabouts of Sarah Woodruff in John Fowles's *The French Lieutenant's Woman*.

Sam Farrow   Charles Smithson's valet, who tries to prevent Charles from breaking off his engagement; he marries Ernestina Freeman's maid Mary Farrow and opens a shop in London in John Fowles's *The French Lieutenant's Woman*.

Captain Harbin Fashnalgid   Leader of the force charged with ambushing and killing Asperamanka; he deserts and with Luterin Shokerandit, Torress Lahl, and Besi Besamitikahl escapes to Chalce; eventually he is murdered in Brian W. Aldiss's *Helliconia Winter*.

Fatmeh   Khalil's and Salim's sister, whose sensitivity and radiant strength enrich the Palestinian cause with humanity; she accepts and loves Charlie but is assassinated by the Israeli operatives controlling Charlie in John le Carré's *The Little Drummer Girl*.

Fatty   Cook's mate aboard the *Atropos* in C. S. Forester's *Hornblower and the Atropos*.

Mrs. Faulkner   The dressmaker for Josephine Napier in Ivy Compton-Burnett's *More Women Than Men*.

Fausta   The scheming, treacherous second wife of the Emperor Constantine; because of her various machinations, she is eventually killed by order of her husband in Evelyn Waugh's *Helena*.

Jack Favell   Drunkard cousin and long-time lover of Rebecca de Winter; when her body is discovered he challenges the new finding of suicide and accuses Maxim de Winter of murder in Daphne Du Maurier's *Rebecca*.

Mrs. Fawcett   A thirty-six-year-old Jewess, who has left her two children and her wealthy engineer husband to live with a penniless younger man named Eastwood; their daring lovers' union fascinates Yvette Saywell in D. H. Lawrence's *The Virgin and the Gipsy*.

Catherine Fawley   Nick Fawley's sister, a postulant nun; an incipient schizophrenic, she tries to drown herself when the concealment of her passion for the homosexual Michael Meade can no longer be sustained in Iris Murdoch's *The Bell*.

Nick Fawley   Catherine Fawley's brother, a drunkard and the former lover of Michael Meade, whose career he destroyed; he commits suicide in Iris Murdoch's *The Bell*.

Fawn   Sado-Masochistic assassin for British Intelligence; he guards Ricki Tarr in John le Carré's *Tinker, Tailor, Soldier, Spy*. He kills Jerry Westerby in *The Honourable Schoolboy*.

Faye   Roberta's childish lover, who is careless in her words and actions; she is killed in the car that she herself helped to fill with explosives in Doris Lessing's *The Good Terrorist*.

Mr. Fearenside   Iping deliveryman who believes that Griffin's bandages hide piebald skin, and whose dog attacks Griffin outside the Coach and Horses, tearing his trousers and partially revealing his invisibility in H. G. Wells's *The Invisible Man: A Grotesque Romance*.

Felena   Prudence Sarn's chief rival for the love of Kester Woodseaves; she has green eyes, a sweet smile, "lips red and pleasant but not kind", and a voice "pretty and slippery, like a grass snake"; gossips contend she sleeps with the tavern keeper, dances naked on the heath, brings food delicacies to Kester, and sings wild songs at night beneath his window in Mary Webb's *Precious Bane*.

Felicity   A savage who indulges in a ritual of eating raw meat; she is perhaps a hallucinatory version of Charles Watkins's wife, Felicity Watkins, in Doris Lessing's *Briefing for a Descent into Hell*.

Felicity   The woman with whom Joyce's husband, Jack, has an affair because he feels cheated in his marriage by his wife's career in Doris Lessing's *The Diaries of Jane Somers*.

Felicity   Philip's old lover, a social worker, on whom Alice Mellings often depends for transportation in Doris Lessing's *The Good Terrorist*.

Sister Felicity   Rebel nun who wants to establish a love abbey and who opposes Sister Alexandra in Muriel Spark's *The Abbess of Crewe*.

Felix   Butler to the Count de Gracay and the Vicomtesse de Gracay in C. S. Forester's *Flying Colours*.

Sir Thomas Fell   Anxious, duty-bound, conscientious captain in C. S. Forester's *Hornblower in the West Indies*.

Fellowes   Initially snobbish but later much humbled sanitary inspector in an African port in Graham Greene's *The Heart of the Matter*.

Beatrice Fellowes   Alexander Burtenshaw's niece; she is an evangelist who is self-conscious about her religious duty to inspire others in Ivy Compton-Burnett's *A House and Its Head*.

May Fellowes   Aunt of Claire Hignam; when a dead pigeon falls at her feet in a London railway station, she washes it and wraps it in a brown paper parcel and then becomes seriously ill, acts which disturb the frivolous young people planning to go on holiday in Henry Green's *Party Going*.

Captain Charles Fellows   Vague, falsely boisterous English banana grower who lives in Mexico with his sickly wife and shrewd young daughter; he discovers the whiskey priest hiding in his shed one night after his daughter shelters the priest in Graham Greene's *The Power and the Glory*.

Coral Fellows   Shrewd, old-before-her-time, thirteen-year-old daughter of Captain and Mrs. Fellows; she takes care of her parents, makes decisions for them and for their banana plantation, and at one point shelters the whiskey priest; she dies at the hands of an American criminal in Graham Greene's *The Power and the Glory*.

Trixy Fellows   Sickly, fearful wife of Captain Fellows; she languishes on their banana plantation in Mexico, hating Mexico and fearing death so much that she retreats from life in Graham Greene's *The Power and the Glory*.

Mrs. Felstead   The prim and proper companion of Princess Popescu; she reports the murder of Police Inspector Herbert Stone in Nicholas Blake's *A Tangled Web*.

Nether Fenman   Hypocritical elder of the Kirk in Woodilee village, member of the vocen, and antagonist to David Sempill, the minister, in John Buchan's *Witch Wood*.

Elsa Freimann Fennan   Samuel Fennan's crippled Jewish wife and a dispirited, apolitical espionage agent for the GDR Intelligence Service, the Abteilung; she steals British and American secrets from her husband for her controller, Dieter Frey, only to be murdered by Frey in John le Carré's *Call for the Dead*.

Samuel Arthur Fennan   Expatriated German Jew, cosmopolitan intellectual, and Foreign Office official; he is murdered by Hans-Dieter Mundt when he discovers that his wife, Elsa Fennan, is stealing Western intelligence secrets for her Communist controller Dieter Frey in John le Carré's *Call for the Dead*.

Fenner   Pilot who was overtaken when Talu highjacked his plane in James Hilton's *Lost Horizon*.

General Fentiman   The ninetyish grandfather of George and Robert; questions of inheritance are raised by the timing of his death in Dorothy L. Sayers's *The Unpleasantness at the Bellona Club*.

Captain George Fentiman   A neurasthenic, unemployed veteran of World War I; he is at the Bellona Club when his apparently sleeping grandfather is discovered to be dead in Dorothy L. Sayers's *The Unpleasantness at the Bellona Club*.

Major Robert Fentiman   George's brother; his grandfather's outliving his great aunt affects his inheritance considerably in Dorothy L. Sayers's *The Unpleasantness at the Bellona Club*.

Sheila Fentiman   George's wife; they live on her income as a tea-shop cashier in Dorothy L. Sayers's *The Unpleasantness at the Bellona Club*.

Boy Fenwick   Successful and dashing young aristocrat of the "Careless-Days-Before-the-War" who commits suicide on the night of his wedding to Iris March, triggering her brother Gerald's ten-year, ultimately fatal plunge into anger and depression in Michael Arlen's *The Green Hat*.

Elizabeth Fenwick   Younger, American wife of Miles Fenwick, whom she accompanies as dinner guest at Compton in John Fowles's *Daniel Martin*.

Michael Fenwick   One of the actors gathered at Hereford; he makes romantic overtures to the young actor Julian in Margaret Drabble's *The Garrick Year*.

Miles Fenwick   Conservative Member of Parliament who comes to dinner at Compton while Daniel Martin is visiting; he engages in a pessimistic discussion of the decline of England in John Fowles's *Daniel Martin*.

Adam Fenwick-Symes   Aspiring author who becomes a gossip columnist; he carries on an affair with Nina Blount and eventually enlists in military service for a new world war occurring in Evelyn Waugh's *Vile Bodies*.

Olga Feodorova   A young Russian woman, enamoured of H. G. Wells's novella *The Sea Lady* and its "better dreams"; she communes also with the Russian anarchists Kropotkin and Stepniak; she shocks Miriam Henderson by committing suicide in Paris in Dorothy Richardson's *March Moonlight*.

Faralin Ferd   A hunter who supports Nahkri and Klils in Brian W. Aldiss's *Helliconia Spring*.

Buddy Ferguson   Swaggering young leader of a street gang; after razing the dwelling of a socially and intellectually superior medical student, he is accosted by James Raven and forced at gun point to strip so that Raven may have a disguise to reach Midland Steel and kill his betrayers in Graham Greene's *A Gun for Sale*.

Detective Inspector Fergusson   Officer in charge of the Patrick Seton case in Muriel Spark's *The Bachelors*.

Mr. Fernandez   Dignified black undertaker from Santo Domingo, a passenger on the *Medea*, who becomes partner of Brown at the end of Graham Greene's *The Comedians*.

Harry Fernandez   Youngest of the Fernandez children; he shares Edward Bas-Thornton's enthusiasm for playing pirate while the children are aboard the pirate ship in Richard Hughes's *A High Wind in Jamaica*.

Jimmie Fernandez   The elder of Margaret's brothers; he remains in Jamaica when she and Harry and the Bas-Thornton children begin their sea voyage in Richard Hughes's *A High Wind in Jamaica*.

Margaret Fernandez   Thirteen-year-old weak-willed Creole child who is sexually used by the pirates and so becomes an object of contempt to both the pirates and the other children; the fact of her abuse is evident to the adults after the children's rescue and arrival in London, but she is unable to answer questions in Richard Hughes's *A High Wind in Jamaica*.

Sidney Arthur Ferning   Deceased former manager of the Spartacus Milan office; the supplier of details about Italian-purchased Spartacus shell-production machinery to what he thinks is the Yugoslav government via General Vagas, he is killed by OVRA agents in Eric Ambler's *Cause for Alarm*.

Charles Ferns   One of the solicitors in Hanbridge; he enjoys surprising the community by hiring a sensual French governess in Arnold Bennett's *The Card: A Story of Adventure in the Five Towns*.

Bobbie Ferrar   Nephew of the Marquess of Shropshire and an official in the British Foreign Office; he helps prevent Hubert Cherrell's extradition in John Galsworthy's *Maid In Waiting*.

Lord Charles Ferrar   Son of the Marquess of Shropshire, from whom he is estranged; he asks Soames Forsyte for an apology to his daughter, Marjorie Ferrar, in John Galsworthy's *The Silver Spoon*.

Marjorie Ferrar   Granddaughter of the Marquess of Shropshire; she rejects the marriage proposal of Francis Wilmot; she refuses to marry her fiancé, Sir Alexander MacGowan, after she loses her libel suit against Fleur Forsyte Mont in John Galsworthy's *The Silver Spoon*.

Mrs. Ashley Ferrars   A widow unofficially betrothed to Roger Ackroyd; she dies of a self-administered overdose of veronal in Agatha Christie's *The Murder of Roger Ackroyd*.

Mrs. Ferreira   Kate Brown's beloved mother; she died in Kate's adolescence in Doris Lessing's *The Summer Before the Dark*.

Mr. Ferrugia   An Italian who is part of the Global Foods delegation meeting in Istanbul in Doris Lessing's *The Summer Before the Dark*.

Diana Montjoy Ferse   Second cousin of Sir Lawrence Mont; she is nearly forty, and her husband, Ronald, has been in a mental home in John Galsworthy's *Maid In Waiting*.

Captain Ronald Ferse   A veteran of World War I who leaves the mental home where he has been treated and commits suicide in John Galsworthy's *Maid In Waiting*.

Festibariyatid   A warrior-priest who founds New Ash-kitosh and the Church of Formidable Peace in Brian W. Aldiss's *Helliconia Spring*.

Beadie Fetherwell   One of the older girls in the north London school in Dorothy Richardson's *Backwater*.

Lord Fetting   Member of Benditch's coal board who sleeps through the meeting with D. and votes against him in Graham Greene's *The Confidential Agent*.

Maurice Ffolliot   A quiet and correct but mentally failing clergyman; he lives with Patricia, Lady Brandon, and is her trusted friend at Brandon Abbas in Percival Christopher Wren's *Beau Geste*.

"Fido"   Journalist given his nickname by John Wainwright; he tries, not altogether successfully, to see John's point of view as he narrates Olaf Stapledon's *Odd John: A Story Between Jest and Earnest*.

Mrs. Fiedke   Travelling and shopping companion of Lise and aunt of Lise's murderer in Muriel Spark's *The Driver's Seat*.

Jens Fiedler   Ideologically loyal Jewish head of Abteilung's Counter Intelligence and deputy head of Security; he suspects Hans-Dieter Mundt is Control's agent but is outmaneuvered by Control's Operation Rolling Stone to protect Mundt and is assassinated by the GDR as a traitor in John le Carré's *The Spy Who Came In from the Cold*.

Alexandria, Lady Field   Wife of Conrad, Lord Field; she dies in childbirth in Isabel Colegate's *Orlando King*.

Conrad, Lord Field   Judith Gardner's brother, who owns Timberwork and lives at Mount Sorrel; he is an active politician and supporter of Orlando King, first as a businessman, and then as a Member of Parliament; Conrad comes to see Orlando in the hospital after his near-fatal accident in Isabel Colegate's *Orlando King*. He is Orlando King's enduring friend, companion, and advisor in *Orlando at the Brazen Threshold*. Conrad outlives his wife Alexandria, Orlando, and his faithful dog Jess; he sees his son, Henry, turn political rebel and wishes to die in *Agatha*.

George Field   Agatha (King) and Henry Field's son in Isabel Colegate's *Agatha*.

Henry Field   Son of Conrad, Lord Field in Isabel Colegate's *Orlando King* and in *Orlando at the Brazen Threshold*. He is Agatha King's husband, who keeps a mistress and becomes a political rebel in *Agatha*.

John Field   An early suitor to Gertrude (Morel); she cherishes his memory and keeps his Bible as a remembrance of what her life might have been in D. H. Lawrence's *Sons and Lovers*.

Lucy Field   Agatha (King) and Henry Field's daughter in Isabel Colegate's *Agatha*.

Adrian Fielding   Oxford don and espionage agent; with Jebedee and Steed-Aspry he recruits George Smiley for British Intelligence in John le Carré's *Call for the Dead*. He is the brother of Terence R. Fielding in *A Murder of Quality*.

Alan Fielding   Dark, handsome painter who attracts Isabelle Terry because he is quiet, kind, and peaceful; she sees in Alan a tempting contrast to her husband, Marc Sallafranque, and briefly intends to leave Marc for Alan in Rebecca West's *The Thinking Reed*.

Emma Fielding   A graduate student who attracts the devoted attentions of Mr. Eborebelosa and Louis Bates; she has an affair with Professor Treece in Malcolm Bradbury's *Eating People Is Wrong*.

Henry Fielding   Open-minded English headmaster of the college in Chandrapore, who is responsive to and understanding of the Indians; though he has steadfastly believed in Aziz's innocence, his protective support of Adela Quested after the trial almost destroys his friendship with Aziz; he marries Stella Moore in E. M. Forster's *A Passage to India*.

Terence R. Fielding   Adrian Fielding's younger, less talented brother and Senior Headmaster yet temporary teacher at Carne School in John le Carré's *A Murder of Quality*.

Ghita (Gyp) Winton Fiersen   Natural daughter of Major Winton; she marries Fiersen when she is twenty-three, has a child by him, leaves him in disgust when he abuses the child, lives unmarried with Bryan Summerhay, and returns to live with her father after Bryan's death in John Galsworthy's *Beyond*.

Gustav Fiersen   Swedish violinist who marries Gyp Winton; he seduces Daphne Wing (Daisy Wagge), drives his wife away in disgust with his drunkenness, indebtedness, and brutality, and refuses to give her a divorce when she tells him she loves Bryan Summerhay in John Galsworthy's *Beyond*.

Little Gyp Fiersen   Baby daughter of Gyp and Gustav Fiersen; she is four years old when Gyp begins living with Bryan Summerhay in John Galsworthy's *Beyond*.

Filby   Particularly unbelieving member of the Time Traveller's skeptical but fascinated audience in H. G. Wells's *The Time Machine: An Invention*.

Prince Filiberto   "Seraphic" child of Victor Emanuel III; he reveals to Hadrian VII what it means to love others in Frederick William Rolfe's *Hadrian the Seventh*.

Professor Filostrato   Physiologist at the N.I.C.E. (National Institute for Coordinated Experiments) who devises the physical apparatus which, he believes, keeps Alcasan's head alive; when a new head is needed to replace Alcasan's, Wither and an accomplice behead Filostrato in C. S. Lewis's *That Hideous Strength*.

Old Filson   Head keeper of birds at the zoological gardens whose son is killed by a giraffe; he asks Simon Carter not to continue investigating the death in Angus Wilson's *The Old Men at the Zoo*.

Finbarr   Younger brother of Manus; he narrates events he does not quite understand in Flann O'Brien's *The Hard Life*.

Finch   Poor, frail simpleton in Hornblower's division who believes he sees God in the mizzen top as well as the devil in the cable tier during dogwatch in C. S. Forester's *Mr. Midshipman Hornblower*.

Humphrey (Humpo) Finch   Mildred's homosexual husband; their marriage is an amicable conspiracy; he lusts for Penn Graham in Iris Murdoch's *An Unofficial Rose*.

Matthew Finch   London correspondent for the *Irish Echo* and suitor of Alice Dawes in Muriel Spark's *The Bachelors*.

Mildred Finch   Humphrey Finch's wife and Felix Meecham's elder half sister; in love with Hugh Peronett, she persuades him to accompany her and Felix to India at the end of Iris Murdoch's *An Unofficial Rose*.

Bill Finchley   Mary Finchley's husband, who divorces her after finding her sexually unfaithful; he returns to her after a year because he could never find a woman whom he liked better than Mary in Doris Lessing's *The Summer Before the Dark*.

Mary Finchley   Kate Brown's radical next-door neighbor, who leads a sexually free and uninhibited existence, and from whom Kate eventually learns much about herself in Doris Lessing's *The Summer Before the Dark*.

Vera Findlater   Mary Whittaker's devoted and dominated young lover; she is found murdered in Dorothy L. Sayers's *Unnatural Death*.

Sir Eric Findlay   Baronet with a nursery fixation; he is a member of the Autobiographical Association in Muriel Spark's *Loitering with Intent.*

Augustus (Gussie) Fink-Nottle   A small, fish-faced, somewhat reclusive newt-keeper; Bertie Wooster, assisted by Jeeves, goes to great lengths to encourage Gussie's engagement to Madeline Bassett because of Madeline's willingness to accept himself as an alternative in P. G. Wodehouse's *The Code of the Woosters.* He appears in three other novels.

Jane Finn (Annette, Janet Vandemeyer)   Young American beauty and *Lusitania* survivor; Tuppence Beresford assumes her identity in searching for a secret document in Agatha Christie's *The Secret Adversary.*

Major Lysander Finn   Nicholas Jenkins's superior officer during World War II; an impressive officer, he is a short, bald man with a grotesque nose in Anthony Powell's *The Soldier's Art* and in *The Military Philosophers.*

Joe Finnegan   Peasant-farmer who gets into a fight with Tarry Flynn over a land-border dispute; he turns many of the townspeople against Tarry because of the fight in Patrick Kavanagh's *Tarry Flynn.*

Larry Finnegan   Peasant-farmer who is a famous footballer and a drunken brawler; he sets out to get even with Tarry Flynn for beating up his brother, Joe Finnegan, in Patrick Kavanagh's *Tarry Flynn.*

Tim Finnegan   Irish hod carrier who gets drunk and falls off a ladder but revives at his own wake; he becomes the archetypal hero whose life, fall, and wake initiate James Joyce's *Finnegans Wake.*

Martin Finnucane   Leader of the one-legged men who tries to come to the narrator's aid in hell in Flann O'Brien's *The Third Policeman.*

Lesbia Firebrace   A daughter of Oliver Firebrace and a sister-in-law of Sir Roderick Shelley; she runs a girls' school to which Clemence Shelley is sent in Ivy Compton-Burnett's *Two Worlds and Their Ways.*

Oliver Firebrace   The late Mary Shelley's father, who lives with Sir Roderick Shelley and his second wife, Maria; he is the secret father of Oliver Spode in Ivy Compton-Burnett's *Two Worlds and Their Ways.*

Paul Firman (aliases: Reinhart Oberholzer, Perrivale Smythson)   Early-middle-aged, intelligent, devious, suave master of crime in the field of international law — the "Able Criminal"; confronted by the team of criminologists and threatened with exposure, he cleverly talks his way free and escapes both from them and

from the assassination attempts of his associate, Mathew Williamson Tuakana, in Eric Ambler's *Send No More Roses.*

Geoffrey Firmin (the Consul)   Ex-British consul to Quauhnahuac and a dabbler in cabbalistic lore; he is a paranoid and self-destructive alcoholic who turns his back on salvation (his ex-wife Yvonne) and indirectly causes both their deaths in Malcolm Lowry's *Under the Volcano.*

Hugh Firmin   Geoffrey Firmin's younger half-brother; a one-time song writer who went to sea to gain experience, he is now a journalist who sympathizes with the Spanish Republican cause but does little to help it in Malcolm Lowry's *Under the Volcano.*

Yvonne Constable Firmin   Former Hollywood starlet and estranged wife of the Consul, Geoffrey Firmin; she returns to him on the Day of the Dead 1938, hoping for a reconciliation, in Malcolm Lowry's *Under the Volcano.*

First Secretary   Embassy official who attempts to persuade Rose Cullen and Forbes that D. is not genuine in Graham Greene's *The Confidential Agent.*

Arthur Fisch   Hilary Burde's colleague who is at the bottom of the office hierarchy; he is Crystal Burde's honest, unmalicious, timid, and eventually successful suitor in Iris Murdoch's *A Word Child.*

Bella Fischer   Henry Marshalson's good friend and professional colleague in America; his affair with her did not threaten her marriage or Henry's friendship with her husband in Iris Murdoch's *Henry and Cato.*

Russell Fischer   Bella's husband, also a close friend and professional colleague of Henry Marshalson in America in Iris Murdoch's *Henry and Cato.*

Lady Julia Fish   A sister of Lord Emsworth and the widowed mother of Ronnie Fish in P. G. Wodehouse's *Fish Preferred* and in *Heavy Weather.*

Ronald Overbury (Ronnie) Fish   Small, solemn friend of Hugo Carmody, who becomes his partner in the nightclub The Hot Spot in P. G. Wodehouse's *Money for Nothing.* The nightclub having failed, Ronnie wants his uncle and trustee, Lord Emsworth, to facilitate his marriage to Sue Brown in *Fish Preferred.* He appears in *Heavy Weather.*

Alderman Fishblick (Fishface)   Burmanley estate agent and important member of the City Council; a teetotaller and non-smoker who is dead set against theaters and music halls, he is the victim of an elaborate practical joke perpetrated by the variety artists in J. B. Priestley's *Lost Empires*.

Mrs. Fisher   Superficially kind but deeply domineering, manipulative, and vengeful mother of Naomi; she owns the house in Paris in which: Karen Michaelis and Max Ebhart first meet, Max later commits suicide, Leopold's history is known, and Ray Forrestier keeps Karen's rendezvous with Leopold in Elizabeth Bowen's *The House in Paris*.

Mrs. Fisher   Sylvia Hervey Russell's neighbor and midwife at Rope Terrace; she attempts to persuade Sylvia to love her children rather than to "shape" them with verbal and physical cruelty; she cares for Jacob Russell so many months that he identifies her as his mother and runs from Sylvia; she refuses to assist Sylvia at the birth of the third child, Carlin, many years after the births of Mary Hervey and Jacob in Storm Jameson's *Farewell, Night; Welcome, Day*.

Mrs. Fisher   The staid, unimaginative mother of Billy Fisher; she unsuccessfully tries to understand her son in Keith Waterhouse's *Billy Liar*. She avoids delicate topics like love and sex but eventually confronts Billy about his marital problems in *Billy Liar on the Moon*.

Carel Fisher   The atheistic, adulterous, and incestuous clergyman who commits suicide at the end of Iris Murdoch's *The Time of the Angels*.

Clara Fisher   Carel's long-dead wife, Muriel's mother, in Iris Murdoch's *The Time of the Angels*.

Elizabeth Fisher   An invalid girl who is seduced by her supposed uncle and guardian, actually her father, Carel Fisher, in Iris Murdoch's *The Time of the Angels*.

Geoffrey Fisher   The auto-mechanic father of Billy Fisher; he has no patience with his son's imaginative vagaries in Keith Waterhouse's *Billy Liar*.

Jeanette Fisher   Tolerant, unappreciated wife of Billy Fisher; she thinks mostly about moving to a bungalow in Mayfield and discontinuing her birth control pills in Keith Waterhouse's *Billy Liar on the Moon*.

Julian Fisher   The supposed father of Elizabeth and the brother of Carel and Marcus; when he ran off with the object of all three brothers' infatuation, Carel took revenge by seducing his wife, Sheila; learning of her pregnancy, Julian killed himself in Iris Murdoch's *The Time of the Angels*.

Marcus Fisher   Carel's youngest brother, on leave as headmaster of an independent school to write a philosophical treatise; he shares legal guardianship of Eliz-

abeth Fisher with Carel Fisher, but is frustrated in his efforts to see either in Iris Murdoch's *The Time of the Angels*.

Muriel Fisher   Elizabeth Fisher's supposed cousin, actually her half sister, who allows their father to die after he takes an overdose of sleeping tablets; her reward and punishment is the exclusive care of Elizabeth after his death in Iris Murdoch's *The Time of the Angels*.

Naomi Fisher   Friend of Karen Michaelis; she remains unmarried and continues to live with her mother in their house in Paris following the suicide of her fiancé, Max Ebhart, in Elizabeth Bowen's *The House in Paris*.

Sheila Fisher   Julian's long-dead wife, Elizabeth's mother, in Iris Murdoch's *The Time of the Angels*.

William (Bill, Billy, Arsehole) Fisher   A young man whose vivid imagination, which he uses to escape the drab routine of his life in Northern England, leads him into a web of deceit and pretense from which he tries to escape in Keith Waterhouse's *Billy Liar*. His dissatisfaction with his marriage and with his job at the Shepford District Council and his vivid imagination and dishonesty, especially about his rendezvous with Helen Lightfoot, lead him into difficult situations which finally cause him to begin to mature in *Billy Liar on the Moon*.

Fitch   Tall, thin, pessimistic Works Manager of the Spartacus Machine Tool Company; he instructs Nicholas Marlow in the intricacies and the protocol of the Milan operation in Eric Ambler's *Cause for Alarm*.

Ben Fitch   Mary Hartley Fitch's husband, a peculiarly tough former soldier known by reputation to James Arrowby; his marriage has been characterized by jealousy and isolation from society in Iris Murdoch's *The Sea, the Sea*.

Lavinia Fitch   Prolific and successful, if not distinguished, author, who invites photographer Leslie Searle to her country estate; local police fear foul play after his disappearance in Josephine Tey's *To Love and Be Wise*.

Mary Hartley Fitch   The object of Charles Arrowby's first and persistent — albeit unconsummated — love; meeting her by accident after many years, he resumes his ardent pursuit; though her marriage is bitter and rarely happy, she emigrates with her husband to Australia to escape Charles's romantic harassment in Iris Murdoch's *The Sea, the Sea*.

Titus Fitch   The estranged, almost grown-up

adopted son of Ben and Hartley Fitch; Ben has always mistakenly suspected that Titus is Charles Arrowby's natural son; Titus visits Charles to determine the truth of the allegation and during his stay is accidentally drowned in Iris Murdoch's *The Sea, the Sea*.

Lord Fittleworth   A South Country Squire whose land adjoins Christopher and Mark Tietjens's cottage; Sylvia Tietjens attempts unsuccessfully to have the earl remove the two brothers from the area by maligning them with slanderous statements in Ford Madox Ford's *The Last Post*.

FitzGeorge   An eccentric millionaire/miser art collector; he harbors a secret infatuation for Lady Slane; dying alone, he leaves his art collection to Lady Slane in Vita Sackville-West's *All Passion Spent*.

Lord Dennis Fitz-Harold   Lady Casterley's seventy-six-year-old brother, who enjoys fishing; he tells Lord Miltoun that he should give up Audrey Noel and remain in Parliament in John Galsworthy's *The Patrician*.

"Skin-the-goat" Fitzharris   A former Fenian terrorist who runs the cabman's shelter in James Joyce's *Ulysses*.

Fiver (Hrairoo)   Rabbit prophet and brother of Hazel; Fiver's visions provide warning, guidance, and contact with the supernatural in Richard Adams's *Watership Down*.

Gavin Fivey (alias Ewan)   John Ducane's personable and thoroughly dishonest manservant; he elopes to Australia with Judy McGrath and some of Ducane's property in Iris Murdoch's *The Nice and the Good*.

Evelyn, Lord Flambard   Comfortable English landowner and generous host of the Whitsuntide house party at Flambard in John Buchan's *The Gap in the Curtain*.

Sally, Lady Flambard   Elegant hostess of Flambard who arranges the Whitsuntide house party at which Professor Moe's psychic experiment exacts a tragic cost in John Buchan's *The Gap in the Curtain*. She is a brilliant London hostess and a bit of a lion-hunter, whose guests include Adam Melfort in *A Prince of the Captivity*.

George Flamson   Detective Inspector who assists Frank Briers in investigating the murder of Lady Ashbrook and discovers an early lead in the case in C. P. Snow's *A Coat of Varnish*.

Betty Flanders   Jacob's mother, who grieves as Jacob grows away from her through college, lovers, travel, and finally death in Virginia Woolf's *Jacob's Room*.

Jacob Flanders   The experimental anti-hero whose tremendous potential as leader makes his senseless death in Greece more tragic in Virginia Woolf's *Jacob's Room*.

Flannagan   The scatter-brained, kind-hearted American who whimsically studies at Amitrano's Studio in Paris with Philip Carey in W. Somerset Maugham's *Of Human Bondage*.

Father Finbar Flannegan   The highly conservative Irish curate of Adam Appleby's parish; he hitches a ride on Adam's scooter and lectures him on birth control in a surgical-goods store in David Lodge's *The British Museum Is Falling Down*.

Sergeant-Major Egbert Flannery   Trim, powerful calesthenics director at Healthward Ho; he is finally at cross purposes with his employer, Alexander Twist, in P. G. Wodehouse's *Money for Nothing*.

Joyce Fleetwood   A noisy, self-opinioned young Conservative Member of Parliament; Polly Hampton's contempt for him infuriates her mother, Lady Montdore, in Nancy Mitford's *Love in a Cold Climate*.

Dr. Fleischer   American specialist who diagnoses Ronald Bridges as an epileptic in Muriel Spark's *The Bachelors*.

Fleming   Student at Clongowes pandied by Father Dolan for failing to decline an irregular Latin noun in James Joyce's *A Portrait of the Artist as a Young Man*.

Bob (Uncle Bob) Fletcher   Brother and fellow sanitation worker of Walter Fletcher; Bob is a happy man who is full of fascinating stories in Margaret Drabble's *The Middle Ground*.

Florrie Fletcher   Wife of Walter Fletcher and mother of their two children, Kate Fletcher Armstrong and Peter Fletcher; she is extremely overweight and agoraphobic in Margaret Drabble's *The Middle Ground*.

Francis Fletcher   Peter's conventional nephew, also a clergyman in Ivy Compton-Burnett's *Pastors and Masters*.

June Fletcher   Wife of Peter Fletcher in Margaret Drabble's *The Middle Ground*.

Lydia (Aunt Lyddie) Fletcher   Peter's sixty-year-old sister; she is a charitable lady with an income of her own in Ivy Compton-Burnett's *Pastors and Masters*.

Peter Fletcher   Son of Florrie and Walter Fletcher, brother of Kate Fletcher Armstrong, and husband of

June Fletcher; his sister believes he sends her anonymous hate mail; he was known as "Stinky Fletcher" as a schoolboy in Margaret Drabble's *The Middle Ground*.

Peter Fletcher   Richard Bumpus's friend and cousin; he is a frail, elderly clergyman about to retire; he is also a kind man who was cheated out of his inheritance in Ivy Compton-Burnett's *Pastors and Masters*.

Theresa Fletcher   Peter's wife, an old woman with fierce eyes; Emily Herrick's friend, she is good and trustworthy in Ivy Compton-Burnett's *Pastors and Masters*.

Walter Fletcher   Husband of Florrie Fletcher and father of their children, Kate Fletcher Armstrong and Peter Fletcher; small and thin, he is a man of many dimensions, a working-class intellectual who is passionate about his work in sewage in Margaret Drabble's *The Middle Ground*.

Flight Lieutenant   Cold, vindictive, strange man who performs as instructed but starts to follow instinct after the villagers' influence in Rex Warner's *The Aerodrome: A Love Story*.

Flikker   Seventeen-year-old brutal delinquent, who has supposedly organized four hundred other teenagers to riot against blacks in Napoli in Colin MacInnes's *Absolute Beginners*.

Sir Henry Flinch-Epworth   Ernest Itterby's opponent for political office for whom Owen Tuby and Cosmo Sultana form an acceptable image in J. B. Priestley's *The Image Men*.

Major Benjamin Flint   Elizabeth Mapp's boastful and often intoxicated neighbor and the object of her matrimonial aspirations; the death of his neighbor and golfing companion Captain Puffin facilitates Miss Mapp's campaign in E. F. Benson's *Miss Mapp*. He becomes engaged to her to atone for his unseemly precipitation as her heir after her presumed drowning in *Mapp and Lucia*. As her husband he assists her in her schemes against Lucia Lucas in *The Worshipful Lucia* and in *Trouble for Lucia*.

Captain Cosmo Flitton   Unscrupulous, heavy-drinking, gambling, one-armed husband of Flavia Stringham in Anthony Powell's *A Question of Upbringing*. His divorce is mentioned in *Casanova's Chinese Restaurant*. His being the father of Pamela Flitton is disputed in *The Valley of Bones*. His affair with Baby Wentworth and his marriage to an American are mentioned in *The Military Philosophers*.

Pamela Flitton   The beautiful daughter of Flavia

(Stringham) Flitton and — probably — of Cosmo Flitton; her cosmic rage against life is manifested in destructive, omnivorous sexual promiscuity; she marries Widmerpool in Anthony Powell's *The Military Philosophers*. She leaves him for the impoverished writer Francis X. Trapnel, whose masterpiece novel she destroys, but returns to Widmerpool in *Books Do Furnish a Room*. Her sexual exploits increase in ferocity and eccentricity until her suicide in *Temporary Kings*. Her childhood passion for her uncle, Charles Stringham, is recalled by her mother in *Hearing Secret Harmonies*.

FloerCrow   A friend of ScufBar; he helps the major domo to transport a body to CaraBansity for sale in Brian W. Aldiss's *Helliconia Summer*.

Stanley Flood   Fun-loving, vulgar, ungentlemanly businessman, who hires Maureen Kirby as his secretary and loses her services to Len Wincobank; Flood later is charged with bribery in Margaret Drabble's *The Ice Age*.

Miss Flora   Sensible governess who tries to protect Mary Hansyke as a child and adolescent from the selfishness and irresponsibility of her parents and uncle in Storm Jameson's *The Lovely Ship*.

Florence   The quiet, passive sister of the squire; she becomes aggressive, outspoken, and fierce, completely changing after the squire's death in Rex Warner's *The Aerodrome: A Love Story*.

Florinda   A lover of Jacob Flanders; she is a flower seller in a London shop in Virginia Woolf's *Jacob's Room*.

John Flory   A thirty-five-year-old, naturally silent and shy timber merchant with a discolored birthmark on his left cheek from the eye to the corner of his mouth; he fits into the Burmese culture better than his European Club mates; he falls in love with a young English visitor, who rejects him in disgust upon discovering that he has had a Burmese lover; he shoots himself rather than live without her in George Orwell's *Burmese Days*.

Freda Flower   Widow who charges Patrick Seton with personal and professional fraud in Muriel Spark's *The Bachelors*.

Andrew Floyd   Minister and mentor to Jacob Flanders; he repeatedly misses the opportunity to prevent Jacob's death with proper speech, warnings, or education in Virginia Woolf's *Jacob's Room*.

Dr. Heywood Floyd   The astronomer and science consultant who is called to investigate the artifact discovered on the Moon in Arthur C. Clarke's *2001: A Space Odyssey*.

Mr. Flushing   English merchant and importer-exporter; a guest at the Santa Marina Hotel, he arranges the practical details of the river expedition his wife Alice has planned; his speech is as eloquent as his wife's conversation is brusque in Virginia Woolf's *The Voyage Out*.

Alice Flushing   Vacationing English matron at the Santa Marina Hotel who exuberantly plans the fatal climactic jungle river expedition, enticing Rachel Vinrace with native treasures and enthusiasm in Virginia Woolf's *The Voyage Out*.

Mrs. Flynn   Mother of Tarry Flynn; she steadfastly clings to her land and tries to increase her family's position in town, loses money on a bad land sale, and then loses her son, Tarry, when he decides to leave town in Patrick Kavanagh's *Tarry Flynn*.

Aggie Flynn   Daughter of Mrs. Flynn; after a pilgrimage to Lough Derg she decides to open an eating house in town to attract potential suitors in Patrick Kavanagh's *Tarry Flynn*.

Bridie Flynn   Wild-tempered youngest daughter of Mrs. Flynn; after a pilgrimage to Lough Derg she decides to leave the farm and open an eating house in town to attract suitors in Patrick Kavanagh's *Tarry Flynn*.

Charlie Flynn   Engineer for the Rasuka oil well; he is in love with Nellie Leader and jealous of Robert Winter because she loves him instead in P. H. Newby's *A Journey to the Interior*.

Mary Flynn   Unattractive oldest daughter of Mrs. Flynn; she rejects a marriage proposal from Petey Meegan in Patrick Kavanagh's *Tarry Flynn*.

Nosey Flynn   One of the patriotic drinkers in Barney Kiernan's Pub in James Joyce's *Ulysses*.

Tarry Flynn   Peasant-farmer, poet, dreamer and individualist; he hopes to find love and happiness on the family farm, but, unable to attain that happiness, he decides to put on his good suit and leave town with his uncle, Petey, in Patrick Kavanagh's *Tarry Flynn*.

Cordelia Flyte   Youngest of Lord and Lady Marchmain's children; she does humanitarian work in Spain during the Civil War, returning to England to care for her dying father; she volunteers for service with the woman's auxiliary of the British army in World War II in Evelyn Waugh's *Brideshead Revisited*.

Julia Flyte   Oldest daughter of Lord and Lady Marchmain; although raised in a Roman Catholic household, she ignores her mother's wishes and marries the divorced Protestant Rex Mottram in a civil ceremony; when the marriage proves a sham, she and Charles Ryder have a long love affair; her father's deathbed return to Catholicism persuades her that her religion is too important to be given up for marriage to the divorced Charles in Evelyn Waugh's *Brideshead Revisited*.

Sebastian Flyte   The Oxford-undergraduate younger son of Lord and Lady Marchmain; his hedonistic and alcoholic bent is in conflict with the behavior required of him by his mother and his Catholicism; he later rebels completely, leaving Oxford to live in northern Africa as the companion of a young German; eventually he is cared for by monks in an African monastery in Evelyn Waugh's *Brideshead Revisited*.

Quentin Fogg, KC   Persistent, successful prosecutor of the murder accusation against Caroline Crale in Agatha Christie's *Five Little Pigs*.

Sir James Foggart   Author of the social and political scheme called "Foggartism" in John Galsworthy's *The Silver Spoon*.

Monsieur Foinet   The irascible art teacher in Paris who cautions Philip Carey that it is better to try one's hand at something else than to discover one's mediocrity too late in W. Somerset Maugham's *Of Human Bondage*.

Foljambe   Georgie Pillson's pretty, intrepid, and indispensable parlormaid in E. F. Benson's *"Queen Lucia"*. She appears in *Lucia in London*. Her engagement to Lucia Lucas's chauffeur, Cadman, complicates Georgie's life in *Mapp and Lucia*. She appears in *The Worshipful Lucia* and in *Trouble for Lucia*.

Mr. Foljambe   Curator from the Victoria and Albert Museum who comes to FitzGeorge's flat to assess the miser's art collection in Vita Sackville-West's *All Passion Spent*.

Mrs. Foljambres   The snobbish and dependably unchanging proprietor of Dunes Hotel where the Green family vacationed; she impresses Arthur and Oliver Green with her stories of "decal days" in C. Day Lewis's *Child of Misfortune*.

Fredigonde, Lady Follett   An ancient "ex-gossip-columnist-belle" who, after killing her husband, succeeds in winning a proposal of marriage from Horace Zagreus before expiring in his arms in Wyndham Lewis's *The Apes of God*.

Sir James Follett Patriarch of the Follett family; he dies in a fit of rage over his wife's insults in Wyndham Lewis's *The Apes of God.*

Theodore (Theo) Follett One of the four Oxford chums; he is Harriet Blair's arrogant, insecure son, a novelist with an aura of inviolability; having grown up in his mother's shade, he assumes a disdain for life's battles; he is monstrously jealous of his mother, killing her and himself in C. Day Lewis's *Starting Point.*

Mr. Folliot Eightyish, mildly catty writer of books of reminiscences of acquaintances of the past fifty years; he first tells Sir Edward Leithen of the sordid Arabin family history in John Buchan's *The Dancing Floor.* He questions Leithen about Sir Robert Goodeve and gossips about the Goodeve family history and character in *The Gap in the Curtain.*

Mrs. Richard Folliott Sister of Ursala Bourne; she disapproves of Ursala's employment and clandestine marriage in Agatha Christie's *The Murder of Roger Ackroyd.*

Dr. Z. Fonanta A physician and the undisclosed grandfather of Miles Faber; he engages in illegal import and export on a remote Caribbean island; he is the unacknowledged author of the poems of Sib Legru in Anthony Burgess's *MF.*

Mr. Fontinay Well-favored, grey-haired second-in-command of the grill-room; Violet Powler maneuvers him to help her have Ceria, manager of the grill-room, reinstated in his post after his illegal two-day absence because of her refusal of marriage to him in Arnold Bennett's *Imperial Palace.*

Nurse Forbes Nurse Philliter's successor in Agatha Dawson's service in Dorothy L. Sayers's *Unnatural Death.*

Forbes Jewish coal magnate in love with Rose Cullen, who calls him "Furt", since his real name is Furtstein; he votes against D. but later helps him and Rose to escape from England in Graham Greene's *The Confidential Agent.*

Aylwin Forbes Featured speaker at a convention where Dulcie Mainwaring and Viola Dace meet; he is a scholar of "neo-metaphysical" seventeenth-century poets and a book-review editor, whose romantic imagination is not matched by his marriage in Barbara Pym's *No Fond Return of Love.*

Cato Forbes Henry Marshalson's boyhood friend, a Roman Catholic priest profoundly disturbed by his sexual infatuation with Joe Beckett; he kills Joe to pro-

tect his sister, Colette Forbes, from rape in Iris Murdoch's *Henry and Cato.*

Colette Forbes Cato Forbes's sister, who has loved Henry Marshalson from childhood; after surviving a kidnapping, a knife slashing, and an attempted rape by Joe Beckett, she becomes Henry's wife in Iris Murdoch's *Henry and Cato.*

Duncan Forbes A modernistic painter whom Connie Chatterley encounters in Venice; later she and her lover, Mellors, visit his London studio in D. H. Lawrence's *Lady Chatterley's Lover.*

Horatia Forbes West-Country hotel proprietor and mother of Neville and Aylwin Forbes; her eccentric, lower-middle-class ways tend to tarnish the brothers' glamorous image in Barbara Pym's *No Fond Return of Love.*

John Forbes The widowed father of Cato and Colette; he is disappointed in his children in Iris Murdoch's *Henry and Cato.*

Marjorie Forbes Unimaginative, conventional wife who deserts Aylwin Forbes at the beginning of Barbara Pym's *No Fond Return of Love.*

Neville Forbes Celibate Anglo-Catholic clergyman; he has his share of problems with women in Barbara Pym's *No Fond Return of Love.*

Ford Manager of the oil well in Rasuka; an uncertain and hesitant man who bends under his wife's direction, he builds a useless machine in his basement and then destroys it when Robert Winter decides to travel into the desert in P. H. Newby's *A Journey to the Interior.*

Ford Captain of the *Nightingale* who foolishly forces immediate battle with the Turkish vessel *Castilla* in C. S. Forester's *Hornblower and the Atropos.*

Arthur Ford Mean-spirited Bayswater grocer who keeps Liz Gold from entering Alec Leamas's apartment until she pays Leamas's bills; he is later beaten by Leamas to convince Abteilung agents of Leamas's corruptibility in John le Carré's *The Spy Who Came In from the Cold.*

Josephine Ford A wealthy and bored *nouveau riche* who seduces Aaron Sisson; Aaron is not deeply affected by her in D. H. Lawrence's *Aaron's Rod.*

Tom Ford Timberwork general manager, who left before Orlando King's arrival; Orlando assumes Tom's position as general manger in Isabel Colegate's *Orlando King.*

Captain Will Ford　Ship captain who has transported munitions from London to Germany in nine trips with Captain Tim Hunt in Storm Jameson's *Before the Crossing*.

Mrs. Will Ford　Owner of the London wharf where Henry Smith was murdered in 1938; she discloses vital information to David Renn in his investigation of Smith's murder in Storm Jameson's *Before the Crossing*.

Yvonne Ford　Cold-hearted wife of Ford, whom she treats like a child; she is bored with life in Rasuka and entertains herself by flirting with her other men in P. H. Newby's *A Journey to the Interior*.

James Fordyce　Minister of the neighboring parish of Cauldshaw; he is an ailing saint who befriends David Sempill and defends him when he is censured by the Presbytery in John Buchan's *Witch Wood*.

Minnie Foresight　Wealthy, unimaginative widow who is cajoled by Professor Mainwaring into endowing a new anthropology Research Centre and several fellowships in Barbara Pym's *Less Than Angels*.

Dr. Forester　An agent for the spy ring "The Free Mothers"; he first appears at a seance, then as Arthur Rowe's psychologist at the asylum, where he becomes nervous as Rowe begins to recover his memory; he is killed by his assistant, Johns, in Graham Greene's *The Ministry of Fear*.

Mr. Forester　The secretary for the communist Zambesia society in Doris Lessing's *Martha Quest*, in *A Proper Marriage*, and in *A Ripple from the Storm*.

Claudine Forks　Office worker and girlfriend of Alfie Bottesford and Michael Cullen; her pregnancy precipitates Michael's flight to London in Alan Sillitoe's *A Start in Life*.

Elsie Forrest　Coffee-bar waitress and friend of Alice Dawes; her theft of letters threatens the fraud trial of Patrick Seton in Muriel Spark's *The Bachelors*.

Lance Forrester　Wealthy member of a Marxist student group who uses drugs; he is among the first suspected of planting drugs in Bernard Kelshall's drink; he is prosecuted for possession and selling drugs after Bernard's death in C. P. Snow's *The Malcontents*.

Ray Forrestier　Fiancé and later husband of Karen Michaelis; he keeps Karen's appointment with Leopold in Paris and there decides to take the nine-year-old boy back to their childless English home in Elizabeth Bowen's *The House in Paris*.

Bettina Forster　Robert Forster's pretty daughter, who likely will become Anton Hesse's wealthy, neurotic mistress in Doris Lessing's *Landlocked*.

Robert Forster　An older, wealthy man who treats Athen Gouliamis as if he were his own son, seeing his communism and poverty-stricken background as traits that go hand in hand in Doris Lessing's *Landlocked*.

Aunt Ann Forsyte　Eldest of the Forsytes, a maiden lady who lives with her brother Timothy and dies at eighty-seven in 1886 in John Galsworthy's *The Man of Property*.

Anne Wilmot Forsyte　Jon Forsyte's wife, a young American from South Carolina, who forgives her husband's affair with Fleur Forsyte Mont in 1926 and announces her pregnancy in John Galsworthy's *Swan Song*.

Annette Lamotte Forsyte　A French girl who marries Soames Forsyte in 1899 though she is twenty-five years younger than he; she cannot bear any more children after she delivers their daughter, Fleur, in John Galsworthy's *In Chancery*. She is carrying on a flirtation with Prosper Profond in *To Let*. She disagrees with Soames over policies on France and Germany after World War I in *The White Monkey*. She advises Soames to press the libel suit against Marjorie Ferrar in *The Silver Spoon*. She contemplates living with her mother in Paris after the death of Soames in *Swan Song*.

Cicely Forsyte　Daughter of James; she makes her social debut at her Uncle Roger Forsyte's dance party in John Galsworthy's *The Man of Property*.

Emily Forsyte　Wife of James; she spends much time in bed with a bad toe in John Galsworthy's *The Man of Property*. She tries to protect James from bad news in John Galsworthy's *In Chancery*.

Euphemia Forsyte　Nicholas's daughter who reports she has seen June Forsyte and Philip Bosinney alone at the theatre in John Galsworthy's *The Man of Property*. She shocks her family when she defends Susan Hayman's cremation as her right over her own body in *In Chancery*.

Fleur Forsyte　See Fleur Forsyte Mont.

Frances (Francie) Forsyte　Roger's daughter who writes music and song lyrics without much art in John Galsworthy's *The Man of Property*.

George Forsyte　Son of Roger; he hates his cousin Soames Forsyte; he hears Philip Bosinney muttering about Soames's rape of Irene Forsyte in John

Galsworthy's *The Man of Property*. He is enriched by the death of his father in 1899; he calls Young Jolyon Forsyte "Three Decker" after the birth of Jolyon's son by Irene in *In Chancery*. He tells Prosper Profond the truth about the relationship of Soames and Irene in *To Let*. He instructs Soames to change his will, leaving a large amount to an unnamed woman; he dies in 1922 in *The White Monkey*.

Hester Forsyte Maiden, middle sister of Ann Forsyte and Juley Forsyte; she lives with them and their brother Timothy Forsyte in John Galsworthy's *The Man of Property*.

Irene Heron Forsyte Wife of Soames; she regrets her marriage and loves her husband's architect Philip Bosinney; she leaves her husband after he rapes her in John Galsworthy's *The Man of Property*. She is divorced with Young Jolyon Forsyte as correspondent; she marries Young Jolyon and bears him a son in *In Chancery*. She tries to conceal her past from her son, Jon; she collects her husband's paintings after his death in 1920 for a show in June Forsyte's gallery before she departs to join her son in Canada in *To Let*. She stays in Paris while her son returns to England with his wife in *Swan Song*.

James Forsyte Seventy-five-year-old twin brother of Swithin and father of Soames and Winifred (Dartie); he has been fifty-four years a solicitor; he is insulted by Philip Bosinney at Soames's country house; he helps to identify the corpse of Bosinney in John Galsworthy's *The Man of Property*. He worries over news of the Boer War in 1899 and dies at ninety on the very day Soames's child is born in 1901 in *In Chancery*.

Jolyon (Old Jolyon) Forsyte The eldest Forsyte brother, who, after being estranged from his son, Young Jolyon, for fourteen years, seeks him out for a reunion on impulse; he tries to buy Soames Forsyte's new country house, Robin Hill, in order to triumph over his brother James's family in John Galsworthy's *The Man of Property*.

Jolyon (Young Jolyon, Jo) Forsyte Old Jolyon's son, a forty-year-old amateur painter; he deserts his wife and daughter, June, for a foreign governess, but he and his father are reconciled in John Galsworthy's *The Man of Property*. A widower in 1894, he inherits Robin Hill; having allowed himself to be named as a correspondent in Soames Forsyte's divorce suit against Irene, he marries Irene after the divorce in *In Chancery*. The father of Jon, he is in uncertain health at age seventy-two in 1920; he writes a letter explaining why Jon should not marry Fleur Forsyte and dies before he knows Jon's decision in *To Let*.

Young Mrs. Jolyon Forsyte A foreign governess who has belatedly become the second wife of Young Jolyon Forsyte in John Galsworthy's *The Man of Property*.

Jolyon (Jolly) "Forsyte" Eight-year-old bastard son of Young Jolyon and the foreign governess in John Galsworthy's *The Man of Property*. He dares Val Dartie to join the army with him for the Boer War, goes to South Africa, and dies of illness there at age twenty in 1900 in *In Chancery*.

Jolyon (Jon) Forsyte Young Jolyon and Irene's son, who is born in 1902 in John Galsworthy's *In Chancery*. He rejects marriage with Fleur Forsyte in 1920 and emigrates to Canada to farm in *To Let*. He returns to England in 1926 and is seduced into a sexual liaison by Fleur; he swears never to see Fleur again when he learns his wife Anne is pregnant in *Swan Song*.

June Forsyte Daughter of Young Jolyon Forsyte and granddaughter and heiress of Old Jolyon; she is eighteen when she is engaged to Philip Bosinney; she accuses Irene Forsyte of ruining her life and Bosinney's as well in John Galsworthy's *The Man of Property*. She devotes herself to helping unknown artists and learns nursing to help in the Boer War in *In Chancery*. She owns the picture gallery visited by Soames Forsyte in 1920; she takes her ailing father under her care in *To Let*. She tells Michael Mont she has seen Fleur Forsyte Mont enter the building where Wilfred Desert lives in *The White Monkey*. She arranges the painting sessions which bring Jon and Fleur together briefly again in *Swan Song*.

Nicholas (Nick) Forsyte Seventy-year-old brother of Old Jolyon in John Galsworthy's *The Man of Property*.

Mrs. Nicholas Forsyte Effete wife of Nick in John Galsworthy's *The Man of Property*.

Very Young Nicholas Forsyte Solicitor grandson of Nicholas; he serves as a trustee for Soames Forsyte's will in John Galsworthy's *The White Monkey*. He represents Fleur Mont in her defense against Marjorie Ferrar's libel suit in John Galsworthy's *The Silver Spoon*.

Rachel Forsyte Daughter of James; she goes with her father and Winifred Dartie to see Old Jolyon Forsyte with his son and grandchildren at the zoo in John Galsworthy's *The Man of Property*.

Roger Forsyte One of Old Jolyon's five brothers; he is father of George and Francie Forsyte; he gives the dancing party where June Forsyte is humiliated by Philip Bosinney and Irene Forsyte in John Galsworthy's *The Man of Property*. When he dies in

1899, only Nick from among his brothers and sisters attends the funeral in *In Chancery*.

Very Young Roger Forsyte Roger's grandson, who is wounded in World War I in John Galsworthy's *The White Monkey*. He is a solicitor for Clare Corven in divorce proceedings brought against her by Sir Gerald in *Over the River*.

Soames Forsyte James's wealthy son, a thirty-one-year-old solicitor, who considers his wife Irene his property; Soames hires Philip Bosinney to build a country house and sues him when he exceeds the budget; after Soames discovers Irene loves Bosinney he rapes his wife in John Galsworthy's *The Man of Property*. He names his nephew Young Jolyon Forsyte as correspondent and divorces Irene; he marries Annette Lamotte (Forsyte) and is disappointed when a daughter instead of a son is born on the day his father dies in *In Chancery*. In 1920 he visits Irene on behalf of his daughter, Fleur; he feels helpless when Fleur marries Michael Mont in *To Let*. He gives the painting of "The White Monkey" to Fleur, investigates an insurance corporation matter, and rejoices at the birth of his grandson, Christopher Mont, in *The White Monkey*. He organizes a defense against the libel suit brought by Marjorie Ferrar in 1924 in *The Silver Spoon*. He deals with Aubrey Stainford's thefts and helps Michael's slum clearance committee with legal matters; he visits the site of his family's origins and dies at age seventy-one in 1926, after being struck by a painting while rescuing Fleur from a fire in *Swan Song*.

(Superior Dosset) Forsyte Stonemason from Dorsetshire who moves to London at the beginning of the nineteenth century; his sons are Old Jolyon, James, Swithin, Nick, Roger, and Timothy; his daughters are Ann, Hester, Juley (Small), and Susan (Haymon) in John Galsworthy's *The Man of Property*.

Swithin Forsyte Bachelor twin brother of James; he takes Irene Forsyte to visit Philip Bosinney; he dies in November 1891 in John Galsworthy's *The Man of Property*.

Timothy Forsyte Youngest of six brothers; a retired publisher, he lives with his sisters Ann, Hester, and the widowed Juley (Small) in John Galsworthy's *The Man of Property*. He shows his map of battle pins during the Boer War in *In Chancery*. He dies in his hundredth year in 1920 in *To Let*.

Rodney Forsyth Unimaginative, agnostic civil servant, who lives with his wife, Wilmet, and his mother, Sybil, in a pleasant, fashionable house in Barbara Pym's *A Glass of Blessings*.

Sybil Forsyth Sixty-nine-year-old widowed volunteer social worker and amateur archaeologist; she is a strong, independent figure who nonetheless shares her house with her son and daughter-in-law, Rodney and Wilmet, and persuades the latter to attend Piers Longridge's Portuguese language classes in Barbara Pym's *A Glass of Blessings*.

Wilmet Forsyth Vaguely unhappily married, elegant, attractive, and relatively rich woman in her mid-thirties who seeks contentment through involvement in her church, but seems more likely to find it in one of two extra-marital romantic possibilities in Barbara Pym's *A Glass of Blessings*. She makes a brief appearance in *No Fond Return of Love*.

Mr. Forsythe Lyme Regis vicar who recommends Sarah Woodruff to Mrs. Poulteney in John Fowles's *The French Lieutenant's Woman*.

Jimmy Fort Wounded veteran of World War I; the lover of Leila Lynch, he marries Noel Pierson in John Galsworthy's *Saint's Progress*.

Fortescue Young man who blunders into the apartment where D. is hiding, tells the police, and later fails to identify D. in Graham Greene's *The Confidential Agent*.

Mr. Fortescue A quick-speaking and witty frequent guest at tea at the Hilberys' house in Virginia Woolf's *Night and Day*.

Mr. Fortescue A clergyman and Master Osbert Nettleby's schoolmaster in Isabel Colegate's *The Shooting Party*.

Charley Fortnum The British Honorary Consul in a small Argentinian city who runs a maté plantation and has fallen in love with and married a very young Argentinian prostitute, Clara (Fortnum); mistaken for the American ambassador, he is kidnapped by a Paraguayan guerrilla band in Graham Greene's *The Honorary Consul*.

Clara Fortnum Very young Argentinian peasant who became a prostitute at Senora Sanchez's brothel and married Charley Fortnum, the Honorary Consul; she has an extended affair with and falls in love with Dr. Eduardo Plarr and is pregnant with his baby in Graham Greene's *The Honorary Consul*.

Mrs. Fortune Devoted mother to Johnny Fortune in Colin MacInnes's *City of Spades*.

Christmas Fortune Johnny Fortune's older brother in Colin MacInnes's *City of Spades*.

David MacDonald Fortune   Johnny Fortune's father; he lived in London as a young man and had an illegitimate son, Arthur Macpherson; he sends money to Mrs. Macpherson at Johnny's urging; he now lives in Nigeria with his family, operating an export and import business in Colin MacInnes's *City of Spades*.

John (Johnny) MacDonald Fortune   Young Nigerian who comes to London with optimism and confidence to study meteorology; he loses his money to gambling and quits his studies; he is framed as a pimp by Detective-Inspector Purity but is not convicted; he has a son with Muriel Macpherson and abandons both of them; he returns to Nigeria as a deck hand, transformed into a cynic by his experiences in Colin MacInnes's *City of Spades*.

Peach Fortune   Sensible, loving sister of Johnny Fortune; she comes to London to train as a nurse; she asks Montgomery Pew to convince Muriel Macpherson to allow William Macpherson Fortune to be raised in Nigeria in Colin MacInnes's *City of Spades*.

William Macpherson Fortune   Illegitimate child of Johnny Fortune and Muriel Macpherson; Johnny does not succeed in taking William back to Africa with him in Colin MacInnes's *City of Spades*.

John, Lord Fort William   A stodgy, unglamorous thirty-nine-year-old bachelor; Louisa Radlett's fear of her father largely motivates her acceptance of his proposal, but the marriage is fruitful and enduring in Nancy Mitford's *The Pursuit of Love*.

Fosca   Pombal's beloved, the pregnant wife of a British soldier; she remains sexually faithful to her husband until he is reported a prisoner of war; her moral dilemma is resolved when she gets in the way of gunfire during a harbor incident in Lawrence Durrell's *Clea*.

Antonio Foscarelli   Voluble, swarthy berth-sharer with Edward Masterman; he is proved to have been the Armstrong family chauffeur in Agatha Christie's *Murder on the Orient Express*.

Sir James Foskisson   Barrister who is a leader in representing Fleur Mont's defense against Marjorie Ferrar's libel suit in John Galsworthy's *The Silver Spoon*.

Foster   One of the captains who examine Hornblower for a lieutenant's commission; he is nicknamed "Dreadnought" because of his ship's name as well as his attitude in C. S. Forester's *Mr. Midshipman Hornblower*.

Hilda Foster   Rupert Foster's wife and Morgan Browne's elder sister; she and they are victims of Julius King's elaborate deceptions; after Rupert's death she goes to live with Morgan in America in Iris Murdoch's *A Fairly Honourable Defeat*.

Ian Foster   Huge, red-faced, witty, and happily married husband of Jane in W. Somerset Maugham's *The Hour Before the Dawn*.

Jane Foster   General Henderson's only daughter and the one member of the Henderson family to dislike the German spy, Dora Friedberg; Jane's grotesque appearance and humour mask an astute and shrewd mind in W. Somerset Maugham's *The Hour Before the Dawn*.

Peter Foster   The disaffected Cambridge-dropout son of Hilda and Rupert; convinced of his father's infidelity with his mother's sister, he angrily destroys the manuscript of his father's almost completed philosophical book in Iris Murdoch's *A Fairly Honourable Defeat*.

Rupert Foster   A civil servant and a self-satisfied amateur philosopher; to demolish his pretensions to goodness Julius King mounts a cunning hoax involving Morgan Browne, but things go badly wrong and Rupert drowns in his own swimming pool in Iris Murdoch's *A Fairly Honourable Defeat*.

Simon Foster   Rupert Foster's homosexual younger brother, a museum employee; he is Axel Nilsson's lover; Julius King almost divides them with planted clues falsely indicating a romance between Simon and himself in Iris Murdoch's *A Fairly Honourable Defeat*.

Agnes Foster-Jones   A suffragette on the run from the police whom Nick Ollanton helps get away after she speaks at a public meeting in Leeds; she is responsible for Dick Herncastle's awareness of and sympathy for the feminist movement in J. B. Priestley's *Lost Empires*.

Sergeant-Major Fotherby   Badmore's strict, supercilious Sergeant-Major, who helps the adjutant, Captain Gresley, arrange a false raid on Jonathan Browne's last-night guard duty in David Lodge's *Ginger, You're Barmy*.

Miss Fothergill   An infirm, wealthy spinster, whom the impressionable nine-year old Eustace Cherrington befriends at his older sister's insistence, despite the old woman's terrifying appearance; she bequeaths him at her death a legacy of £18,000 in L. P. Hartley's *The Shrimp and the Anemone*.

Sergeant Fottrell   Simpleminded policeman who

proposes the "mollycule" theory of interchange of atoms between people and bicycles in Flann O'Brien's *The Dalkey Archive*.

Aimee Foucoult Fat, aging Parisian prostitute; she takes into her apartment the prostrate Sophia Baines following her husband's abandonment of her; then, with the help of another prostitute, over months she nurses Sophia back to health; she is saved from the bailiff by Sophia's buying her possessions; thus begins Sophia's lfe as a boarding mistress in Paris in Arnold Bennett's *The Old Wives Tale*.

Colonel E. St G. Foulkes Authority on Central Asian history who provides strong recommendation for Roy Calvert's scholarship in C. P. Snow's *The Light and the Dark*.

Four Old Men Archetypal authority figures who appear under many names in James Joyce's *Finnegans Wake*.

Bob Fowler Anna Wulf's acquaintance, a communist, in Doris Lessing's *The Golden Notebook*.

Helen Fowler Thomas Fowler's long-suffering wife, who endures her husband's infidelities but refuses to divorce him because of her religious beliefs and their debts in Graham Greene's *The Quiet American*.

Johnnie Fowler Maudie Fowler's only son in Doris Lessing's *The Diaries of Jane Somers*.

Laurie Fowler Maudie Fowler's husband, whom she adores and loves; he sometimes physically abuses her and ultimately leaves her in Doris Lessing's *The Diaries of Jane Somers*.

Leslie Fowler Woman kept by James Horgan; she is taken out dancing by Philip Weston in Isabel Colegate's *Statues in a Garden*.

Lucile Fowler Leslie Fowler's seven-year-old daughter in Isabel Colegate's *Statues in a Garden*.

Maryrose Fowler A member of the Mashopi Communist group who formerly had an incestuous affair with her brother; she is wiser and more experienced in human relationships than Anna Wulf, the only other female member of the organization in Doris Lessing's *The Golden Notebook*.

Maudie Fowler Jane Sommers's ninety-year-old friend, living in abject poverty but tremendously proud, who has an amazing history and a clear head in Doris Lessing's *The Diaries of Jane Somers*.

Norman Fowler An art dealer who is going through a breakdown and a nasty divorce when he meets Kay Pasmore and becomes her lover in David Storey's *Pasmore*.

Thomas Fowler Disillusioned, uncommitted middle-aged British journalist skilled at obscuring family and professional commitments; he betrays Alden Pyle to Mr. Heng and the Vietnamese underground because Pyle has provided General Thé with plastic explosives and bewitched Fowler's mistress Phuong in Graham Greene's *The Quiet American*.

The Fox Greek slave purchased by Trom, King of Glome, to educate his daughters; he educates Orual in Greek thought and is a trusted counsellor after her ascension to the throne in C. S. Lewis's *Till We Have Faces*.

Canon Fox Silvia Fox Tebrick's uncle, who calls on Richard Tebrick at Tangley to inquire about Silvia and leaves convinced of Tebrick's madness and his unfitness for service with the Bible Society in David Garnett's *Lady Into Fox*.

Mr. Fox The seemingly ill-organized but competent vicar who cheerfully satisfies the contradictory burial requirements specified in Constance Ollerenshaw's will in Margaret Drabble's *The Realms of Gold*.

Policeman Fox Third policeman encountered by the narrator in hell; Fox allows him to "escape" back to earth, where he scares his murderer, John Divney, to death in Flann O'Brien's *The Third Policeman*.

Digby Fox Anthropology student in his third year who shares lodgings in Camden Town with Mark Penfold, thinks vaguely of asking out Dierdre Swan, and competes for a Foresight Fellowship in Barbara Pym's *Less Than Angels*. His professional and domestic future are mentioned in *No Fond Return of Love*. He delivers an address in *A Few Green Leaves*.

Katie Fox Slatternly drug addict living in the Dublin slums; she is a friend of Gypo Nolan, but, crazed by drugs and jealousy, she reveals his whereabouts to the revolutionary organization in Liam O'Flaherty's *The Informer*.

Mischa Fox The wealthy and powerful manipulator of others; he is in love with Rosa Keepe in Iris Murdoch's *The Flight from the Enchanter*.

Pauline Fox One of the young women residents of the May of Teck Club; her elaborately staged, publicly unhappy, altogether imaginary dates with the actor

Jack Buchanan are evidence of her acute mental imbalance in Muriel Spark's *The Girls of Slender Means*.

Roderick Fox   Poetaster, "literary politican", and go-between who offers George Garner the editorship of a new literary magazine that is covertly financed by a sinister company in Roy Fuller's *The Second Curtain*.

Miss Foxe   Aged tenant whom Leonora Eyre ruthlessly evicts from the flat above hers so that James Boyce can be moved in under Leonora's watchful eye in Barbara Pym's *The Sweet Dove Died*.

Amy Foxe   Fast-spending double heiress, formerly the widowed Lady Warrington; she is divorced from her second husband, Charles Stringham's father, and is a careless mother in Anthony Powell's *A Question of Upbringing*. Her money-fueled dominance of her third husband, Buster Foxe, continues in *A Buyer's Market*, in *The Acceptance World*, and in *At Lady Molly's*. She falls for a cockney dancer in *Casanova's Chinese Restaurant* and divorces Buster in *The Valley of Bones*. Her money troubles and death are recounted in *The Soldier's Art*.

Brian Foxe   Shy and guilt-ridden youth; the victim of his repressive upbringing, he is so mortified by his friend Antony Beavis's seduction of his fiancée that he kills himself in Aldous Huxley's *Eyeless in Gaza*.

Buster Foxe   Unlikable, vaguely sinister stepfather of Charles Stringham in Anthony Powell's *A Question of Upbringing*. His animosity toward his stepson and Geraldine Weedon's for him are detailed in *At Lady Molly's* and in *Casanova's Chinese Restaurant*. Dicky Umfraville's long hatred of him is recounted in *The Valley of Bones*. He has died in *Temporary Kings*.

Leo Foxe-Donnel   Rebel, born Leo O'Donnell, whose socially confused upbringing has made him antagonistic to British rule; his name being changed after his father's death so that he can be reared by his well-to-do, Protestant aunts, he inherits their estate, Foxehall, but becomes a heavy-drinking and promiscuous rebel; imprisoned for participating in a Fenian rebellion, he continues his subversive activities after his release and eventually joins in the 1916 Easter uprising in Sean O'Faolain's *A Nest of Simple Folk*.

Elizabeth Fox-Milnes   Daughter of Lord Hillmorton; she wants to marry Julian Underwood; she asks her father for a gift of money before his death and is disappointed by Julian and by her father in C. P. Snow's *In Their Wisdom*.

Ferdy Foxwell   Wealthy, highly educated, obese double agent whose humanity derives from his connection to traditional values; he dies by falling from a departing Russian helicopter in Len Deighton's *Spy Story*.

Foxy   Hazel Woodus's pet fox and totem or external soul; Hazel dies in a vain attempt to save Foxy from the squire's hounds in Mary Webb's *Gone to Earth*.

Hubert Frame   Father of Vanessa Frame Brodie; he is the leading physicist of his time; although dying of cancer, he manages to continue his work stoically in Anthony Burgess's *The End of the World News*.

Francesca   Luigi Leopardi's press secretary who creates the public images of the Christophers in Muriel Spark's *The Public Image*.

Don Francesco   Fat, extroverted priest who lends his assistance to the Duchess in Norman Douglas's *South Wind*.

Francine   A young black West Indian cook with a pretty face whom Anna Morgan and her father liked and Hester Morgan didn't face; she explained menstruation to Anna in Jean Rhys's *Voyage in the Dark*.

Francis   Fiancé of Sarah Bennett; he is away in America at Harvard in Margaret Drabble's *A Summer Bird-Cage*.

Dr. Frangcon   Elderly ship's doctor aboard the *Archimedes*; he brings to sea with him his collection of antique musical instruments in Richard Hughes's *In Hazard*.

Frank   A flirtatious man discussed by the nurses at St. Andrews, where Rosamund Stacey goes to have her baby in Margaret Drabble's *The Millstone*.

Serge Frankel   A philosophical Communist stamp dealer; he spied with and against Steve Champion and Charlie during World War II in Len Deighton's *Yesterday's Spy*.

Franklin   Seaman who dies aboard the *Indefatigable* in C. S. Forester's *Mr. Midshipman Hornblower*.

Barbara Franklin   Dr. John Franklin's wife, who feigns ill health and is not so stupid as she appears; she dies from poisoned coffee in Agatha Christie's *Curtain: Hercule Poirot's Last Case*.

Don Franklin   A hypochondriac who is one of the actors performing in Hereford in Margaret Drabble's *The Garrick Year*.

Ernestine, Lady Franklin   Young, aristocratic widow who suffered a breakdown because she was not with her husband at the time of his death; she is restored to life and emotional commitment as a result of identification with a fictional family that her for-hire car driver, Leadbitter, evokes for her in L. P. Hartley's *The Hireling.*

Dr. John Franklin Brilliant medical researcher who argues that most of the world's people are expendable in Agatha Christie's *Curtain: Hercule Poirot's Last Case.*

Arthur Frankly Devout young owner of Frankley's hardware store; he hires and then fires Matty Septimus in William Golding's *Darkness Visible.*

Sir William Franks The aristocratic owner of an estate in Florence, Italy, who argues with Aaron Sisson about money and responsibility in D. H. Lawrence's *Aaron's Rod.*

Donald Fraser Betty Barnard's jealous fiancé in Agatha Christie's *The A.B.C. Murders.*

Ann Frazier Charley Summers's garrulous and inquisitive landlady; she is a former friend of Nancy Whitmore's mother in Henry Green's *Back.*

Mrs. Frean Mother of Harriet Frean; she practices the ideal of self-sacrifice so totally that she chooses to die of cancer rather than spend £100 for an operation in May Sinclair's *Life and Death of Harriet Frean.*

Harriet (Hatty) Frean Repressed Victorian woman who devotes her whole life to the ideal of always behaving properly; to be true to this ideal she refuses marriage to the man she loves and only under the influence of anesthesia does she admit the void her life has been in May Sinclair's *Life and Death of Harriet Frean.*

Hilton Frean Harriet Frean's father, a speculator and sometime writer who submerges Harriet so completely in his own personality that even after his death she introduces herself as Hilton Frean's daughter in May Sinclair's *Life and Death of Harriet Frean.*

Freda Brenda's dramatic, outgoing, pompous, critical, and overbearing roommate; she dreams of a tasteful, elegant life with the romantic, noble Vittorio as her dream lover; the seduction of Vittorio is her goal in organizing the outing, but the event turns nasty, especially for Freda in Beryl Bainbridge's *The Bottle Factory Outing.*

Freddie Jane Somers's husband who dies of cancer, and about whom Jane constantly dreams when she is dating Richard Curtis in Doris Lessing's *The Diaries of Jane Somers.*

Mr. Fredrick (satiric representation of the German government) The farmer of Pinchfield farm; instead of helping the people try to restore Manor Farm to Mr. Jones, he went into trade agreements with the pigs who had control of Manor Farm in George Orwell's *Animal Farm.*

Captain Freeman Stocky, respectful, talented gypsy, who works well with Hornblower; he shows respect without groveling, captains well, and is a good singer in C. S. Forester's *Commodore Hornblower* and in *Lord Hornblower.*

Ernest Freeman Ernestina Freeman's father, an industrialist who wants his prospective son-in-law, Charles Smithson, to work for him; he forces Charles to make a public apology when Charles jilts Ernestina in John Fowles's *The French Lieutenant's Woman.*

Ernestina Freeman The pretty, intelligent daughter of an industrialist; she is engaged to Charles Smithson, who breaks off their engagement after his love affair with Sarah Woodruff in John Fowles's *The French Lieutenant's Woman.*

Sarah Freeman Young woman who is part of the sinister network created by George Perrott in Roy Fuller's *The Second Curtain.*

Stephen Freer University student who is a member of a Marxist group that plans to embarrass a powerful public person; he is a witness to the death of Bernard Kelshall, discovers that Bernard was a spy in their group, offers to testify on behalf of Neil St. John at Neil's trial for possession of drugs, and asks Tess Boltwood to marry him in C. P. Snow's *The Malcontents.*

Thomas Freer Solicitor who is the father of Stephen; he advises his son to consult legal advice during an investigation by authorities into Stephen's political activities in C. P. Snow's *The Malcontents.*

Colin Freestone A teacher whose wife is in an institution for a mental weakness; he becomes involved with a wealthy family and their unusual lifestyle, exchanging beds and insults; he ends by leaving all of it to become a street cleaner in David Storey's *A Temporary Life.*

Yvonne Freestone The institutionalized, mentally ill wife of Colin Freestone in David Storey's *A Temporary Life.*

Sir Julian Freke The surgeon and neurologist who is director of St. Luke's Hospital, the institution that adjoins Alfred Thipp's apartment building; years ago he was the rejected suitor of Christine Ford (Lady Levy) in Dorothy L. Sayers's *Whose Body?*.

Lady Frensham   Arrogant political-discussion antagonist of Mr. Britling; she warns of British civil war in H. G. Wells's *Mr. Britling Sees It Through*.

Hookham Frere   Talkative, cynical political writer, once ambassador to Spain, who escorts Hornblower to London to meet His Royal Highness in C. S. Forester's *Flying Colours*.

Sigmund Freud   Renowned Viennese neurologist, founder of modern psychiatry; he is forced to leave Vienna to avoid persecution as a Jew; a wryly humorous man, he retains his air of calm even in the face of forced emigration and a cancer of the jaw in Anthony Burgess's *The End of the World News*.

Dieter Frey   Handsome, Byronic Jewish-German student recruited for British Intelligence despite his rebellious nature and anti-Nazi views; he joins the GDR Intelligence Service, Abteilung, and, with fellow spy Hans-Dieter Mundt, persuades Elsa Fennan to steal Western secrets; he is ignominiously killed by his former tutor and friend George Smiley in John le Carré's *Call for the Dead*.

Dora Friedberg   The pretty, young German spy who befriends the Henderson family and marries idealistic Jim Henderson to continue her underhand work; she wreaks tragic havoc within the Henderson family before she is murdered by her husband in W. Somerset Maugham's *The Hour Before the Dawn*.

Kitty Friedman   Innocent, optimistic, fifty-eight-year-old friend of Alison Murray and Anthony Keating; her husband died in the bomb explosion that caused her to lose a foot in Margaret Drabble's *The Ice Age*.

Max Friedman   A businessman killed in a bomb explosion that occurred at a restaurant at which he was celebrating his Ruby wedding anniversary with his wife, Kitty Friedman; he was a friend to Anthony Keating in Margaret Drabble's *The Ice Age*.

Miss Frierne   Landlady of Dougal Douglas and Humphrey Place in Muriel Spark's *The Ballad of Peckham Rye*.

Frith   Sun, sun-god, and creator in Richard Adams's *Watership Down*.

Frith   A servant at Manderly in Daphne Du Maurier's *Rebecca*.

Johnny Frizel   Game warden who takes Sir Edward

Leithen to Francis Galliard's homeplace in Clairefontaine and sets out with Leithen to track Lew Frizel and Galliard in John Buchan's *Sick Heart River*.

Lew Frizel   Half-breed Scots trapper and hunter who reads *The Pilgrim's Progress* but is a bit mad; after Sir Edward Leithen finds him and restores his sanity, Frizel nurses Leithen in the valley of the Sick Heart and begs Leithen to return to Europe with him and Francis Galliard in John Buchan's *Sick Heart River*.

Captain Frobisher   Officer in General Curzon's regiment; his humanitarian conscience contrasts with Curzon's Johnny Bull morality in C. S. Forester's *The General*.

Lady Frobisher   Neighbor whose duty it is to open the village fête in E. M. Delafield's *The Diary of a Provincial Lady*. She entertains the Provincial Lady in *The Provincial Lady Goes Further*.

Young Frobisher   Lady Frobisher's Oxford-student son, who lectures the Provincial Lady about the fiscal crisis in E. M. Delafield's *The Provincial Lady Goes Further*.

Catherine Frobisher   Plain, clumsy, idealistic, and romantic widow of Charles Frobisher and mother of Charlotte and Trevor; she helps raise her sister's children, William and Emily Crowne, keeps the memory of her husband alive, irritates her children with her intolerance for modern ways, and deals with her loved ones "with irritable, affectionate inclemency" in Margaret Kennedy's *Red Sky at Morning*.

Charles Frobisher   Deceased husband of Catherine Frobisher; he presided over the 1800s as a good but not great poet and critic, "second rate luminary", and "denominator of late Victorianism"; his wife keeps his memory alive and publishes his biography in Margaret Kennedy's *Red Sky at Morning*.

Charlotte Frobisher   Large, ugly, intelligent daughter of Catherine Frobisher; she wants to make a living by writing; she joins her brother Trevor's communal settlement and tries to write in Margaret Kennedy's *Red Sky at Morning*.

Irma Frobisher   Skeptical wife of blocked novelist Ronald Frobisher in David Lodge's *Small World*.

Ronald Frobisher   A glum British novelist of the Angry Young Men generation who now writes only TV scripts; he meets Persse McGarrigle at a prize ceremony and causes an uproar, and he has an affair with Desiree Zapp at a conference in David Lodge's *Small World*.

Trevor Frobisher Clever, handsome, whiny son of Catherine Frobisher; after serving in World War I, he returns to England and spends his time in London trying to avoid work; he meets Tilli Van Tuyl and is attracted to her but leaves London to form a communal settlement at his Uncle Bobbie Trevor's home; there he dallies with Tilli, taunts his cousin William Crowne, and is killed by him in Margaret Kennedy's *Red Sky at Morning*.

Bernard Froelich An American professor, expert at academic in-fighting, who gets James Walker invited to Benedict Arnold University and who becomes Chair of the English Department in Malcolm Bradbury's *Stepping Westward*.

Miss Frost The white-haired, moralistic governness who exercises a "beautiful, unbearable tyranny" over Alvina Houghton in D. H. Lawrence's *The Lost Girl*.

Mrs. Frost The cook for the Clare family; she is discontented and disputes Ainger's estimation of his importance to the family in Ivy Compton-Burnett's *The Present and the Past*.

Augustus Frost Member of the inner circle at the N.I.C.E. (National Institute for Coordinated Experiments); he is under the control of the Macrobes and starts the fire that destroys N.I.C.E. headquarters and himself in C. S. Lewis's *That Hideous Strength*.

J. Frost Ardent gambler, womanizer, and Deputy Chief Trustee of the Hong Kong South Asian and China Bank; he is blackmailed by Jerry Westerby into revealing Drake Ko's assets and is tortured and murdered by Ko for this betrayal in John le Carré's *The Honourable Schoolboy*.

Uncle Frostia Zina's uncle; he is a middle-aged and very well-respected, though unpublished, writer of history and philosophy; he is clever but untidy and undermotivated in William Gerhardie's *Futility: A Novel on Russian Themes*.

Edwin Froulish Impoverished, eccentric writer and college friend of Charles Lumley with whom Charles shares a ramshackle loft apartment while working as a window-washer; he later introduces Charles to comedy writing in John Wain's *Hurry On Down*.

Terence Frush Executive joke-writer for radio programs who gives Charles Lumley the kind of fulfilling and rewarding job he has long sought: generating joke material in an atmosphere of controlled hysteria alongside Edwin Froulish and five other eccentrics at the conclusion of John Wain's *Hurry On Down*.

Mr. Fry A friendly civilian who shares an office with Jonathan Browne at Badmore in David Lodge's *Ginger, You're Barmy*.

Mr. Fullove An apparently frail, elderly gentleman, actually an agent for "The Free Mothers"; he gives Arthur Rowe a suitcase containing a bomb, telling him it is filled with books to be delivered to "Mr. Travers", actually Mr. Cost, in Graham Greene's *The Ministry of Fear*.

James Furness Keen amateur golfer and a director of the Saddleford Building Society in Roy Fuller's *Image of a Society*.

John Furriskey One of the three Dublin characters held in captivity by the fictional novelist Dermot Trellis in Flann O'Brien's *At Swim-Two-Birds*.

Mr. Fyne Friend of Flora de Barral (Anthony) in Joseph Conrad's *Chance: A Tale in Two Parts*.

Mrs. Fyne Feminist friend of Flora de Barral; she introduces Flora to her brother Captain Roderick Anthony but tries to prevent Anthony's marriage to Flora in Joseph Conrad's *Chance: A Tale in Two Parts*.

G

Gaber Messenger who visits the agent, Jaques Moran, in the second section of Samuel Beckett's *Molloy*.

Gabriel Troubled, hyperactive son of the Israeli Labour Attaché; killed by a Palestinian bomb, he is ironically elevated as both Christian and Jewish martyr by the German press in John le Carré's *The Little Drummer Girl*.

Gadsby ("Gaddie") A schoolmaster and a local bore; once a handsome success in a small, mentally confined circle, he is now a burnt-out inebriate; he is not averse to bragging of former times in Nicholas Blake's *A Question of Proof*.

Bill Gagg Hard-driving employee of a group of property-investment companies who tries to use Alan Percival's cousin in the Ministry to advance his business plans and who runs off with Percival's wife, Ann (Best), in Roy Fuller's *The Perfect Fool*.

Sarah Gaily The ailing half sister of George Cannon, an old friend of Carolyn Lessways, and Hilda Lessways's dancing teacher; her illness draws Carolyn Lessways to Brighton in Arnold Bennett's *Hilda Lessways*.

Mr. Gaitskill Aristide Leonides's cautious, conscientious solicitor in Agatha Christie's *Crooked House*.

Lady Galadriel Beautiful elf who is the wearer of one of the elfen rings and is able to see visions; she shows Frodo Baggins Mount Doom and Sauron's eye, searching for Frodo in her mirrored water in J. R. R. Tolkien's *The Fellowship of the Ring*.

Mrs. Galbraith Mother of Eric Galbraith; she becomes fatally ill shortly after their move next door to the Verrens in Frank Swinnerton's *The Young Idea: A Comedy of Environment*.

Eric Galbraith Progressive, independent young man who takes the flat next door to the Verrens for himself and his mother; he falls in love with Hilda Verren and protects her from Percy Temperton's importunities in Frank Swinnerton's *The Young Idea: A Comedy of Environment*.

Enoch Gale Gardener and handyman for the Darke family and the secret lover of Marigold Gosling; he is an earth mystic who supports Jasper Darke's decision to give up Christian theology for non-Christian mysticism; believing that earth mystics grasp a wilder intuition, he finds strength in soil and gardening; he prophesies the destruction of the Darke family house and the oppressive history and laws that it symbolizes in Mary Webb's *The House in Dormer Forest*.

Maisie Gale Martha Quest's close friend in Doris Lessing's *Martha Quest* and in *A Proper Marriage*. She is involved with the other young communists in the community, especially after Andrew McGrew marries her in order to give her child a father in *A Ripple from the Storm* and in *Landlocked*.

Rita Gale Maisie Gale and Binkie Maynard's child, who grows up in Zambesia in Doris Lessing's *Landlocked*. She ultimately comes to London and stays with Martha Quest and Mark Coldridge, falls in love with Mark, lives with him, and bears him children in *The Four-Gated City*.

Alice Gall Wild, sarcastic, likable friend to the Saxton and Beardsall young people; she moves away and marries beneath her class in D. H. Lawrence's *The White Peacock*.

Dan Gallagher Vicious, nihilistic leader of the Irish revolutionary organization that hunts and kills Gypo Nolan in Liam O'Flaherty's *The Informer*.

Galleon The Egerton family butler, a confidant of Sir Michael Edgerton; he wants the forms of aristocracy preserved in Ivy Compton-Burnett's *A God and His Gifts*.

Felicity Galliard Sister of Lady Clanroyden and niece of John S. Blenkiron; she seeks Sir Edward Leithen's aid in finding her husband, Francis Galliard, who has mysteriously disappeared in John Buchan's *Sick Heart River*.

Francis Galliard French-Canadian of genius; working with Sir Edward Leithen to save the Hare Indians, he conquers the North, saves his sanity and his soul, and returns to his life and his wife, Felicity, in John Buchan's *Sick Heart River*.

Cornelius Galloway Handsome and shrewd solicitor, new to Castlerampart; at the age of forty-four he perceives that any one of the Coniffe sisters would make a good match; he is simultaneously identified as an ideal son-in-law by Theodore Coniffe, but within months of his marriage to Lily he is killed in a fall from a horse in Mary Lavin's *The House in Clewe Street*.

Gabriel Galloway Son of Lily (Coniffe) and Cornelius Galloway; he is orphaned by their deaths and thereafter is left to the care of his two aunts: the domineering, embittered Theresa Coniffe and the gentler, passive Sara Coniffe; as a young man he rebels against Theresa and runs off to Dublin with the intention of marrying Onny Soraghan, the Coniffes' saucy, attractive servant girl, in Mary Lavin's *The House in Clewe Street*.

Mr. Galopalus Secondhand dealer and "fence" who cheats "She" when he buys the purse stolen from an elderly woman in Storm Jameson's *A Day Off*.

Mrs. Galopalus Wife of a cheating secondhand dealer and mother of one child; she cares for her small son and earns money by baking bread and providing both lodging and breakfast for her tenants in Storm Jameson's *A Day Off*.

Pussy Galore A Lesbian gang leader who falls in love with James Bond in Ian Fleming's *Goldfinger*.

John ("Wee Jaikie", "Jaikie") Galt Smallest member of the Gorbals Die-Hards; he assists Dickson McCunn in rescuing Sakskia, the Russian princess, in John Buchan's *Huntingtower*. Now a Cambridge undergraduate and rugby star, he meets and falls in love with Alison Westwater and aids his benefactor, McCunn, in settling the tangled political affairs of Evallonia in *Castle Gay*. Having concluded his university career, he joins McCunn and Alison Westwater in Europe in their efforts to restore Prince John to the throne of Evallonia in *The House of the Four Winds*.

Doctor Galvan Local physician who treats Father Quixote when he is kidnapped and returned to El Toboso by the Bishop in Graham Greene's *Monsignor Quixote*.

Janet ("Kelly") Gambeson Attractive twenty-year-old characterized as a hopeless neurotic who tries to seduce Jake Richardson; she later attempts suicide; she is a patient of psychotherapists who are treating Jake in Kingsley Amis's *Jake's Thing*.

Admiral Lord Gambiar Commander of the channel fleet whose failures are being whitewashed so that he can finish out his term in C. S. Forester's *Flying Colours*.

Mrs. Gamble Sharp-tongued, elderly mother-in-law of Eustace Barnack; her only emotional attachment is to her pet terrier in Aldous Huxley's *Time Must Have a Stop*.

Samwise Gamgee Uncomplicated, loyal hobbit servant to Frodo Baggins in J. R. R. Tolkien's *The Fellowship of the Ring*. He travels with Frodo into Mordor and carries the ring when he believes that Frodo is dead in *The Two Towers*. He rescues Frodo from the Orcs

and leads him to the edge of the Crack of Doom, allowing the ring to be destroyed in *The Return of the King*.

Gandalf Powerful, wise wizard who leads Bilbo Baggins to rescue the Mountain in J. R. R. Tolkien's *The Hobbit; or There and Back Again*. He discovers the power of the ring and guides Frodo Baggins in its destruction in *The Fellowship of the Ring*, in *The Two Towers*, and in *The Return of the King*.

Shri Ganesha The benign, holy man whose teachings include the idea that wisdom is the means to freedom; at his Ashrama Larry Darrell experiences a strange mystical illumination that gives him a profound sense of inner peace in W. Somerset Maugham's *The Razor's Edge*.

Carrie Gardener America tourist who chatters tirelessly in Agatha Christie's *Evil Under the Sun*.

Odell Gardener American tourist frequently roused by his wife, Carrie, to express agreement with her statements and opinions in Agatha Christie's *Evil Under the Sun*.

Major Gardeterark Leader of the Oligarchy's guard in Sibornal and military governor of Koriantura; he orders Eedap Mun Odin not to send ships to foreign ports in an attempt to stem the plague of the Fat Death in Brian W. Aldiss's *Helliconia Winter*.

Eunice Gardiner The member of "the Brodie set" who is "famous for her spritely gymnastics" in Muriel Spark's *The Prime of Miss Jean Brodie*.

Lieutenant Gardner Molly Bloom's girlhood lover who was killed in the Boer War in James Joyce's *Ulysses*.

Jane Gardner A former schoolteacher married to Stephen Gardner in Isabel Colegate's *Orlando at the Brazen Threshold*. She appears in *Agatha*.

Judith Gardner Leonard Gardner's wife, a socialite who enjoys spending money and being successful; she marries Orlando King after Leonard's death; when the truth of Orlando's birth is disclosed, she has a mental breakdown and attempts suicide; Judith is left in an institution for her own safety in Isabel Colegate's *Orlando King*. Judith dies in *Orlando at the Brazen Threshold*.

Leonard Gardner Unsuspecting father of the illegitimate Orlando King (Pauline never having told him she was pregnant); he finds young Orlando a job with his pet project, Timberwork; Leonard blames Orlando for his loss of position and employment and accuses Orlando of stealing the affections of his wife,

Judith; Leonard's unintentional death results from his driving maniacally after his argument with Orlando in Isabel Colegate's *Orlando King*.

Paul Gardner   Leonard and Judith Gardner's oldest son, who causes problems at school and is not able to express himself with his stepfather, Orlando King, in Isabel Colegate's *Orlando King*. He marries Serena Daintry in *Orlando at the Brazen Threshold*. Serena divorces him, and Paul turns traitor to England, selling secrets to the Russians, before he is taken to prison in *Agatha*.

Stephen Gardner   Leonard and Judith Gardner's reasonable and malleable youngest son in Isabel Colegate's *Orlando King*. He marries a school-teacher, Jane, in *Orlando at the Brazen Threshold*. He appears in *Agatha*.

Rupert Gardnor   British consular official in Israel who spies for Egypt in Muriel Spark's *The Mandlebaum Gate*.

Ruth Gardnor   Wife of a British consular official, with whom she spies for Egypt, in Muriel Spark's *The Mandlebaum Gate*.

Leila Garland   Hardboiled former girlfriend of the late Paul Alexis Goldschmidt; she provides Lord Peter Wimsey with crucial information in Dorothy L. Sayers's *Have His Carcase*.

Dr. Mike Garland   Lover of Father Socket and fake clairvoyant; he aids Freda Flower against Patrick Seton in Muriel Spark's *The Bachelors*.

George Garner   Reclusive, middle-aged novelist; he investigates the mysterious disappearance of a boyhood friend and, in the process, uncovers two murders made to look like accidents; he realizes that he has been bribed by the offer of editorship of a new magazine and is ruthlessly beaten by a sinister assailant in Roy Fuller's *The Second Curtain*.

Eben Garnock   The "Chief Fisher" in the secret society of the Free Fishers; he has been sent to the fishing village of Yondermouth by the British Government to watch and report on any secret service activity on the part of French sympathizers in Scotland in John Buchan's *The Free Fishers*.

Mr. Garroby-Ashton   Riseholme's Member of Parliament in E. F. Benson's *Lucia in London*.

Millicent Garroby-Ashton   Wife of Riseholme's Member of Parliament in E. F. Benson's *Lucia in London*.

Elizabeth (Liz) Garrowby   Secretary to Lavinia Fitch and fiancée of Walter Whitmore; she and Leslie Searle are attracted to each other in Josephine Tey's *To Love and Be Wise*.

Emma Garrowby   Stepmother of Liz Garrowby and sister of Lavinia Fitch; her fear of Leslie Searle as a threat to Liz's engagement to Walter Whitmore makes her the initial suspect in the disappearance of Searle in Josephine Tey's *To Love and Be Wise*.

Garry   Delusional boy whom Bill Plantagenet associates with Rimbaud; he is committed to a psychiatric hospital after cutting a little girl's throat with a broken bottle in Malcolm Lowry's *Lunar Caustic*.

General Lord Garsington   Breezy and gallant retired general; he seconds the motion which begins the attack on Lord Raingo's Ministry in the House of Lords in Arnold Bennett's *Lord Raingo*.

Mrs. Garstin   Hard, parsimonious, stupid, and status-seeking wife of Bernard Garstin; she is pleased to marry her twenty-five-year-old daughter Kitty off to Walter Fane in W. Somerset Maugham's *The Painted Veil*.

Bernard Garstin   The gentle father of Kitty Fane and Doris Garstin; his only role is to provide money for his self-centered family while denying his own needs, yet he cares enough for human nature to establish a relationship with the much-changed Kitty at the end of W. Somerset Maugham's *The Painted Veil*.

Doris Garstin   Kitty Fane's younger, less attractive sister, who nevertheless manages to find a husband in her first season, thus providing the impetus for Kitty's acceptance of the strange Walter Fane in W. Somerset Maugham's *The Painted Veil*.

Mark Henry Garton   Uncle of Mary Garton Hansyke; he becomes her guardian when she is eight and employs her as interne in his shipyard but refuses to take the ambitious girl into the firm; his antifeminism is thus responsible for her return to her father, who arranges marriage between the fifteen-year-old and the elderly, sick, and wealthy Archibald Roxby, father of her first child, Richard, in Storm Jameson's *The Lovely Ship*.

Robin Garton   Teenaged patient in Clive Ward for a knee injury after a hurdling accident; attached to his mother and inexperienced, he listens and observes the patients in Clive, treats them kindly, and feels that he has learned from them; he is the son of a twice-divorced woman who "would rather have died than failed him" in John Berger's *The Foot of Clive*.

Mr. Garvace   The stout, choleric partner and director of the Port Burdock Drapery Bazaar; he derides Alfred Polly's friend Parsons's window-decorating attempts and then fires him after the enraged Parsons attacks him in H. G. Wells's *The History of Mr. Polly*.

Archie Garvell   Beatrice Normandy's half brother, who fights with George Ponderevo in H. G. Wells's *Tono-Bungay*.

William Gary   Relative of Georgina Swan, who begs him to use his power to protect her husband, Julian Swan, a suspect in the murder of Henry Smith, in Storm Jameson's *Before the Crossing*. He is a Scotsman educated at Bonn and Oxford; he augments inheritance from family coal and land holdings with his own shrewd interest in investment, shipping, and steel, and with his collaboration with the elderly and powerful head of several companies and munitions suppliers, Sir Thomas Harben; Gary has a big, athletic build, fences daily with his manservant, and has a manner associated with charm, humor, simplicity, energy, and power; in furthering his and Sir Thomas Harben's strategic schemes for European reconstruction, Gary is an enemy of David Renn, and he finally disillusions his loyal pilot, Arnold Coster, by failing to intervene in an execution as he promised he would in *The Black Laurel*.

Toby Gashe   An adolescent who loses his innocence at Imber Court and conspires with Dora Greenfield to raise the ancient bell from the lake in Iris Murdoch's *The Bell*.

Jocelyn Gaster   Lindsay Rimmer's successor as Emma Sands's secretary-companion; her hiring is Emma's final revenge on Hugh Peronett in Iris Murdoch's *An Unofficial Rose*.

Mrs. Gates   The Thorpe housekeeper in Dorothy L. Sayers's *The Nine Tailors: Changes Rung on an Old Theme in Two Short Touches and Two Full Peals*.

Fiona Gates   A feckless eighteen-year-old runaway who became the second wife of Alan McCaffrey; she died when her son, Tom, was three in Iris Murdoch's *The Philosopher's Pupil*.

Joe Gates   Father of Lily Gates; he lives and works with Phil Craigan until both men are forced into retirement in Henry Green's *Living*.

Lily Gates   Daughter of Joe Gates; she lives with her father in Phil Craigan's house; she plans to go to Canada with Bert Jones, but when he deserts her in Liverpool she is happy to return home in Henry Green's *Living*.

Herr Gaudian   Brilliant German patriot and railway engineer; he is kind to Richard Hannay when he is bullied by the evil Colonel von Stumm in John Buchan's *Greenmantle*. He reappears in Merdal, Norway, where Hannay is tracking Lord Mercot, one of the captive hostages, and helps Hannay rescue Mercot in *The Three Hostages*.

Miss Gaunt   A teacher at the Marcia Blaine School and an enemy of Jean Brodie in Muriel Spark's *The Prime of Miss Jean Brodie*.

John Gaunt   Gossipy Bonn Embassy Chancery Guard; he allows Alan Turner access to Leo Harting's possessions but protects Harting's reputation with determined friendship during Turner's interrogation in John le Carré's *A Small Town in Germany*.

Silas Gaunt   Fiona Samson's uncle, a retired British Intelligence officer; he is "Brahms Four's" contact in Len Deighton's *Berlin Game*. He is Bernard Samson's consultant in *Mexico Set* and in *London Match*.

Blaise Gavender   A psychotherapist whose apparently serene marriage to Harriet Gavender exists simultaneously with his decade-long affair with Emily McHugh; aggrieved that Harriet will not continue her role once she understands it, he comes to seek her and is almost killed by her dogs; after her death he marries Emily in Iris Murdoch's *The Sacred and Profane Love Machine*.

David Gavender   Blaise and Harriet's son, whose fastidious nature is in conflict with his adolescent fixation on sex; the revelation of his father's adultery and the subsequent death of his mother are incomprehensible to him in Iris Murdoch's *The Sacred and Profane Love Machine*.

Harriet Gavender   Blaise Gavender's wife, who is devoted to him, to their teenaged son, and to her seven dogs; understanding at last the nature of her marriage, she leaves with the neglected, retarded eight-year-old son of her husband and his mistress; she dies in a terrorist outrage at Hanover airport, Germany, in Iris Murdoch's *The Sacred and Profane Love Machine*.

Aubrey Gaveston   The youngest son of Blanche and Edgar; he studies with a tutor and tries to mask his sensitivity in Ivy Compton-Burnett's *A Family and a Fortune*.

Blanche Gaveston   The long-suffering mother of the family, who gets a high fever and dies suddenly in Ivy Compton-Burnett's *A Family and a Fortune*.

Clement Gaveston   The middle son of Blanche and

Edgar; he plans to be a scholar and don, but he becomes a miser with a mass of gold coins in Ivy Compton-Burnett's *A Family and a Fortune.*

Dudley Gaveston   A kindly and ironic man who shares his fortune with his brother Edgar's family; he loses Maria Sloane to Edgar; he rescues Miss Griffin from cold and despair, and he almost dies alone in Ivy Compton-Burnett's *A Family and a Fortune.*

Edgar Gaveston   The squire of the neighborhood; although he is closer to his brother, Dudley, than to his wife, in his widowhood he marries Dudley's betrothed, Maria Sloane, in Ivy Compton-Burnett's *A Family and a Fortune.*

Justine Gaveston   Opiniated only daughter of Blanche; she assumes that her family will share her Uncle Dudley Gaveston's fortune equally in Ivy Compton-Burnett's *A Family and a Fortune.*

Mark Gaveston   Blanche's and Edgar's eldest son; he helps Edgar in managing the estate and teases his brother Aubrey less than his brother Clement does in Ivy Compton-Burnett's *A Family and a Fortune.*

Misha ("Gavron the Rook") Gavron   Marty Kurtz's Israeli chief, who admires the British Intelligence officers for their understanding of violence, but who fails to curb Kurtz's plans in John le Carré's *The Little Drummer Girl.*

Maurice Gay   Senior fellow of the Cambridge college; an internationally famous authority on Icelandic saga literature, he presides at formal meetings of the college; he changes his vote from Redvers Crawford to Paul Jago in the election for new Master in C. P. Snow's *The Masters.* He threatens legal action against the College and is placated when he is appointed Moderator to the Court of Seniors for its last consideration of Donald Howard's fellowship in *The Affair.*

Laurie Gaynor   A chorus-girl friend of Anna Morgan; she arranges Anna's abortion; she introduces Anna to Carol Redman and arranges for recuperation and medical help for Anna in Jean Rhys's *Voyage in the Dark.*

Johnny ("Bloody Johnny") Geard   A former nonconformist preacher and the late Canon Crow's companion and major beneficiary; he rises to mayor and strives to make Glastonbury the religious epicenter of the Western World by establishing a religious shrine and a "Midsummer Religious Festival"; he drowns himself in a flood in John Cowper Powys's *A Glastonbury Romance.*

Miss Geary   School vice-principal who supports the position of George Passant during the board meeting; she invests money in one of Passant's financial schemes in C. P. Snow's *Strangers and Brothers.*

Denis Geary   Headmaster who serves on the university court hearing charges for dismissal of four students for sexual misconduct; he provides hospitality for Lewis Eliot during the trial of Cora Ross and Kitty Pateman in C. P. Snow's *The Sleep of Reason.*

Don Alejando Gedd   British Vice-Consul of Olifa; he becomes a crusader in the revolution to free Olifa from Senor Castor's dictatorship in John Buchan's *The Courts of the Morning.*

Father Thomas Geelan   Old curate of Crom whose outspoken political views and revolutionary rhetoric keep him from rising to power within the Catholic Church in Liam O'Flaherty's *Famine.*

Gelert   A superior sheepdog created by Thomas Trelone and living with the Trelone family in Olaf Stapledon's *Sirius: A Fantasy of Love and Discord.*

Father Gellibrand   High Anglican celibate vicar of Edwin Braithwaite's church near Clapham Common in Barbara Pym's *Quartet in Autumn* and in *A Few Green Leaves.*

Christabel Gellibrand   The upper-class wife of the senior physician; she is a formidable social force, who functions almost as a lady of the manor in the village and church community in Barbara Pym's *A Few Green Leaves.*

Dr. Luke Gellibrand   Senior physician in the small village practice in Barbara Pym's *Quartet in Autumn.* He is Father Gellibrand's elder brother in *A Few Green Leaves.*

Dave Gellman   A Jewish friend of Jake Donaghue and a philosophy teacher; he is an occasional benefactor and a voice of reasonableness to Jake in Iris Murdoch's *Under the Net.*

Father Egidio Gemini   Roman Catholic missionary and linguistic expert who seeks funding for further research in Africa in Barbara Pym's *Less Than Angels.*

The General   The superior officer in a Gorshek camp who takes command of a captured orchestra during war; he disobeys orders to kill the musicians immediately, instead asking them to play for him and his other officers in Alan Sillitoe's *The General.*

Genoux   Lady Slane's personal maid and her only

female intimate; she is a French peasant sent to England at age sixteen to take service with Lady Slane at her marriage in Vita Sackville-West's *All Passion Spent*.

J. W. Gentleman Wealthy older solicitor who becomes Caithleen Brady's first love; he tries to continue his affair with Cait, but after they are found out by her father he calls off the relationship in Edna O'Brien's *The Country Girls*.

Moscow Gentry American ballet dancer with the Isabel Cornwallis Ballet Company; he temporarily lives with Montgomery Pew in Colin MacInnes's *City of Spades*.

Geoff One of Jen's brothers in Isabel Colegate's *Orlando King*.

Geoffrey Marian Taylor's unloving lover; she takes the job at Gaze Castle to escape their unprofitable relationship; their correspondence becomes the whole of her contact with the outside world in Iris Murdoch's *The Unicorn*.

Geoffrey An Alpine Frenchman in the Natcha-Kee-Tawara Troupe of itinerant theatrical performers who work at Houghton's theater in D. H. Lawrence's *The Lost Girl*.

Geoffrey Worker at Timberwork who quarrels with another worker, Tom; Orlando King is able to help the two workers reach a compromise in Isabel Colegate's *Orlando King*.

Geoffrey Heterosexual Englishman visiting Ambrose in Christopher Isherwood's *Down There on a Visit*.

George A "Proletarian writer" from the 1930s, an inside member of the British Communist Party, and an acquaintance of Anna Wulf in Doris Lessing's *The Golden Notebook*.

George Once the captain on Charles Watkins's voyage; he is captured by the Crystal Disc while Watkins is left behind in Doris Lessing's *Briefing for a Descent into Hell*.

George Logical, thoughtful hero; he is a normal man whose good qualities endear him to many people in Rex Warner's *The Wild Goose Chase: An Allegory*.

George Young bank clerk, one of the trio in the holiday boating experience in Jerome K. Jerome's *Three Men in a Boat (To Say Nothing of the Dog)*.

George Married workman who visits "She" or sends her money weekly for five years and whose impending abandonment of her underlies her meditations throughout her day's journey around London; his callous letter of rejection forces her to face her need to depend only on herself and a few other hardworking women in Storm Jameson's *A Day Off*.

George Middle-aged, grieving expatriate English professor whose lover, Jim, has recently died; he is again attempting to find meaning in life in Christopher Isherwood's *A Single Man*.

George The manager of the theatrical company that Pincher Martin works with in William Golding's *Pincher Martin*.

George An older academic who makes a pass at Tessa O'Brien during her summer course in David Lodge's *How Far Can You Go?*.

George Footman for the Lambs; an ungainly youth born in the workhouse, he steals food and removes the warning sign from the unsafe bridge so that Horace Lamb will be killed in Ivy Compton-Burnett's *Manservant and Maidservant*.

George Hercule Poirot's valet, whose knowledge of the British aristocracy is often useful to Poirot; he is critical of his successor, Curtiss, in Agatha Christie's *Curtain: Hercule Poirot's Last Case*. He appears in twelve earlier novels.

Black George Greek seaman left to guard Vernon Milburne's yacht; he tells Sir Edward Leithen that Vernon Milburne is on the island in John Buchan's *The Dancing Floor*.

Monsieur George Dashing gunrunner for the Spanish royalists who falls in love with Doña Rita de Lastaola; deceitfully wounded in a duel by J. K. Blunt, he is nursed by Rita but loses her in Joseph Conrad's *The Arrow of Gold: A Story Between Two Notes*.

His Royal Highness [George III] King of England who knights Captain Horatio Hornblower and appoints him as a colonel in the marines; the honors, which elevate Hornblower in society, make him a political hero to maintain the popularity of the war in C. S. Forester's *Flying Colours*. See King [George III] in *Dictionary of British Literary Characters 18th- and 19th-Century Novels*.

Georgiana (Georgie) Jane Somers's highly disapproving sister; she has several children, none of whom is disciplined in Doris Lessing's *The Diaries of Jane Somers*.

Georgie   Brother of Percy and foreman of the gasworks in E. F. Benson's *The Worshipful Lucia.*

Georgiou   Tavernkeeper on Phraxos who tells Nicholas Urfe about Maurice Conchis's role during the Nazi occupation in John Fowles's *The Magus.*

Gerald   Ann Walton's intelligent, overbearing fiancé and lover; his leaving for a job in America makes Ann lonely and vulnerable, although he sends her letters and money; Ann's eventual baby has Gerald's brown eyes, not William McClusky's blue eyes in Beryl Bainbridge's *Sweet William.*

Gerald   The twenty-two-year-old man with whom thirteen-year-old Emily Cartright falls in love; he has several other mistresses as well and attempts to take under his wing young children who are without homes in Doris Lessing's *Memoirs of a Survivor.*

Gerard   Second lieutenant who is a capable seaman but has a thirst for violence in C. S. Forester's *The Happy Return* and in *Ship of the Line.* Always a good caretaker of Hornblower, he is his inquisitive, considerate, sharp flag lieutenant in C. S. Forester's *Hornblower in the West Indies.*

Lieutenant Emil Gerlach   Brother of Lucius Gerlach and father of Rudolph Gerlach; he has planned never to return to Germany because he might have to condemn his brother; Emil is sentenced to die for executing two German men who alerted British guards to the prison-escape plans of six other Germans in Storm Jameson's *The Black Laurel.*

Lucius Gerlach   Poet and religious man; he is a German who supports peace, forgiveness, and moderation following World War II and is murdered by his bitter and politically radical nephew who has suffered an amputation in the war in Storm Jameson's *The Black Laurel.*

Rudolph (Rudi) Gerlach   Son of Lieutenant Emil Gerlach and nephew of Lucius Gerlach; he has lost a hand in the German infantry in World War II, and his bitterness about the German defeat draws him to the angry preaching of Dr. Gustav Leist rather than to the political supporters of his uncle, the poet Lucius Gerlach, who looks toward peace in Storm Jameson's *The Black Laurel.*

Germanicus   Brother of Claudius and father of Caligula; a brilliant military leader, he is murdered by a political rival under Tiberius's auspices in Robert Graves's *I, Claudius.*

Gerry   A young ex-army officer who turns petty crim-

inal and becomes the lover and accomplice of Sophy Stanhope in William Golding's *Darkness Visible.*

Lieutenant Gerson   Discreet ex-lawyer and Education Corps officer who presents himself to Dan Graveson as a Communist Party member and recruits Dan to paint subversive graffiti, ruining Dan's army career in Alan Burns's *Buster.*

Arnold Gerson   Accounts manager of the Saddleford Building Society; a chartered accountant, financially conservative, industrious, scrupulous, and dull, he is regarded contemptuously by Stuart Blackledge as a rival, but he ultimately becomes general manager of the company in Roy Fuller's *Image of a Society.*

Gertrude   The Ponsonbys' maid whose name is imposed on her by the family in Ivy Compton-Burnett's *Daughters and Sons.*

Gertrude   A Swedish au pair for Jeremy and Polly Elton; she has an affair with Jeremy in David Lodge's *How Far Can You Go?.*

Sister Gertrude   Travelling missionary-philosopher who advises Sister Alexandra in Muriel Spark's *The Abbess of Crewe.*

Digby Geste   Funny, brave, witty twin brother to Michael; he loves his family enough to leave it; he becomes a bugler with the French Foreign Legion in Percival Christopher Wren's *Beau Geste.*

John Geste   Reliable, smart, loving narrator; a member of the French Foreign Legion in Africa, he loves Isobel Rivers but loves his brothers Michael and Digby more; his friends Hank and Buddy keep him alive; he makes it home to solve the family's jewel mystery in Pervical Christopher Wren's *Beau Geste.*

Michael (Beau) Geste   Lady Patricia Brandon's nephew; he is a sly, charming, generous, brave, tragic hero and an idol to his brothers; a man who lives for romance and adventure, he joins the French Foreign Legion because of a jewel mystery and confuses his family, especially his brother John, in Percival Christopher Wren's *Beau Geste.*

Francis Getliffe   Herbert's brother, who is a scientist at Cambridge University; he marries Katherine March even though he is gentile and she Jewish; he tries to persuade Charles March to intervene with Ann Simon to protect Herbert Getliffe's reputation during the financial scandals reported by a Communist newspaper in C. P. Snow's *The Conscience of the Rich.* He first opposes and then supports Roy Calvert's election to a college fellowship; he works on radars at the start of

World War II and loses influence when he opposes emphasis on bombing missions to fight the war in *The Light and the Dark*. He supports Redvers Crawford for election as new college Master and unsuccessfully attempts to persuade Lewis Eliot to join his side in *The Masters*. He opposes the decision to offer Martin Eliot the job of directing atomic-energy research in *The New Men*. He gives the crucial evidence in favor of Donald Howard and damages his own candidacy for new Master by raising the question of Nightingale's veracity in *The Affair*. The leading scientist on Roger Quaife's advisory committee for nuclear weapons, he is subjected to a security check; he worries about his daughter Penelope in *Corridors of Power*. Chancellor of the university where Leonard March teaches, he disagrees with Lewis Eliot on Arnold Shaw's continuing as vice-chancellor in *The Sleep of Reason*. He turns down a ministerial appointment with the goverment and dies of lung cancer in 1968 in *Last Things*.

Herbert Getliffe   A successful, somewhat greedy barrister, who accepts Lewis Eliot into his chambers after Eliot wins a studentship prize but does little to advance Eliot's career; he takes silk; he leads Eliot in the trial of George Passant, Jack Cotery, and Olive Calvert for fraud in C. P. Snow's *Time of Hope*. He delivers a persuasive closing argument which, while it condemns the life-style of Passant as self-deceptive, wins the case for his clients in *Strangers and Brothers*. He passes on privileged information in 1929 to allow his family to make money from government contracts; he convinces Eliot in 1935 that he had nothing to do with the financial embarrassments to Sir Philip March and other government officials in *The Conscience of the Rich*. He recommends a divorce attorney to Eliot and is disappointed that he will not become a judge in *Homecomings*.

Leonard Getliffe   Physicist who is the son of Francis and Katherine (March); he loves Vicky Shaw, and he leads the movement to press Arnold Shaw into retirement in C. P. Snow's *The Sleep of Reason*.

Penelope Getliffe   Nineteen-year-old daughter of Francis and Katherine (March); she encourages the attentions of Arthur Plimpton but marries someone else while touring America in C. P. Snow's *Corridors of Power*.

Giacinto   Venetian servant who attends Eustace Cherrington during his residence at the palazzo of Lady Nelly Staveley in L. P. Hartley's *Eustace and Hilda*.

Gibbon   Gardener at Charleswood, the Westons' country estate, in Isabel Colegate's *Statues in a Garden*.

Miss Gibbon   The governess of the almost-grown Mowbray daughters; she brings Ellen Mowbray money

and clothes and reveals Ellen's survival to the family in Ivy Compton-Burnett's *A Father and His Fate*.

Gibbs   One of Cavor's laborers who let the laboratory furnaces die, thereby accidentally producing Cavorite amidst a devastating wind-storm in H. G. Wells's *The First Men in the Moon*.

Hugh Gibbs   Husband of Milly Pargiter; an old Oxford friend of her brother Edward, he is more interested in horses and other women than in Milly in Virginia Woolf's *The Years*.

Austin Gibson Grey   Dorina Gibson Grey's husband and Matthew Gibson Grey's younger brother, recently made redundant; an unashamedly self-centered person, he is the "accidental man" who unleashes catastrophe around him in Iris Murdoch's *An Accidental Man*.

Betty Gibson Grey   Austin's first wife, whose drowning was accidental; Austin's jealous hatred of his brother, Matthew, is in part the result of his misguided conviction that she and Matthew were having an affair and that her death was a suicide in Iris Murdoch's *An Accidental Man*.

Dorina Gibson Grey   Austin Gibson Grey's second wife, who is accidentally electrocuted in the bath in Iris Murdoch's *An Accidental Man*.

Garth Gibson Grey   Austin Gibson Grey's son by his first wife; a student of philosophy who is Ludwig Leferrier's friend, he returns home from America with a novel in manuscript that is lost on the journey; he is uneasily attracted to his stepmother, but he recovers from her death to marry Ludwig's former fiancée, Gracie Tisbourne; his manuscript is found and published to critical applause in Iris Murdoch's *An Accidental Man*.

Matthew Gibson Grey   Austin Gibson Grey's elder brother, a retired diplomat; he is an egoist of charm who is attractive and attracted to women and men; he takes Ludwig Leferrier under his wing at the end of Iris Murdoch's *An Accidental Man*.

Giddy   Housekeeper of the apartment occupied by the mentally unbalanced Harry Sinton in Roy Fuller's *Fantasy and Fugue*.

Ekki Giesbrecht   German communist and briefly the lover of Helen Ledwidge; betrayed by political comrades, he is murdered by the fascists in Aldous Huxley's *Eyeless in Gaza*.

Elizabeth Giffard   A friend of Josephine Napier's youth; she thinks that Josephine stole Simon Napier from her; later she is Josephine's housekeeper and Gabriel Swift's mother-in-law in Ivy Compton-Burnett's *More Women Than Men*.

Ruth Giffard   Elizabeth's daughter, who teaches briefly at Josephine Napier's school; she marries Gabriel Swift; her death is hastened by the jealous Josephine in Ivy Compton-Burnett's *More Women Than Men*.

Bert Gifford   Disparager of Maureen Kirby; his nose was broken in retaliation by Len Wincobank in Margaret Drabble's *The Ice Age*.

Lady Bernice Gilbert ("Bucks")   Member of the Autobiographical Association whose suicide confirms Fleur Talbot's suspicions of Sir Quentin Oliver's evil manipulations in Muriel Spark's *Loitering with Intent*.

Lord Gilbey   Minister who is forced to resign after a serious illness and who attacks the defense policy of his successor, Roger Quaife, in C. P. Snow's *Corridors of Power*.

Dr. Gilly   A woman medical specialist in London who is the only doctor to admit that Ben Lovatt is a throwback to a more primitive age in Doris Lessing's *The Fifth Child*.

Beatrice Gilray   Repressed patron of Denis Burlap, by whom she is eventually seduced in Aldous Huxley's *Point Counter Point*.

Gimli   Young, adventurous dwarf who is a member of the fellowship who travel with Frodo Baggins to destroy the One Ring and its terrible power in J. R. R. Tolkien's *The Fellowship of the Ring*, in *The Two Towers*, and in *The Return of the King*.

Lady Ginevra   Foolish rich woman; she is dull and "limp as anchovies in a bottle"; Arnold Condorex considers marrying her to raise his status in politics in Rebecca West's *Harriet Hume, A London Fantasy*.

Giorgio (The Butcher)   Venetian businessman who uses his knowledge of wartime crimes to lure Robert Leaver into a blackmailing plot in Muriel Spark's *Territorial Rights*.

Giovanni   A sensual gondolier whom Connie Chatterley meets in Venice; a cadger and a prostitute, he offers himself to Connie and her sister, but they reject him in D. H. Lawrence's *Lady Chatterley's Lover*.

Nancy Gipps   Young Maidenbridge teacher at Miss Willcox's School; she wants to marry Mr. Board and share his wealth with the less fortunate; she is the first person to acknowledge Mr. Weston in T. F. Powys's *Mr. Weston's Good Wine*.

Julie Girtin   Woman who did a television program on blacks and Asians; Kate Fletcher Armstrong thinks her a "rat bag" in Margaret Drabble's *The Middle Ground*.

Gisele   Anthony and Jane Mallory's French maid in John Fowles's *Daniel Martin*.

Giuseppe   Italian peasant, husband of Nella; he is a servant of Orlando King in Isabel Colegate's *Orlando at the Brazen Threshold*.

Marion Gladwell   Elementary-school teacher who loves Lewis Eliot and remains his confidante after he confesses his love for Sheila Knight; she marries happily and is pregnant in C. P. Snow's *Time of Hope*.

Gladys   Strange younger sister of Charles Lumley's sweetheart Rosa; she fixedly stares at Charles during his visit with Rosa's family in John Wain's *Hurry On Down*.

Glass   Gamekeeper for Conrad, Lord Field and friend of Conrad and Orlando King in Isabel Colegate's *Orlando King*. He is remembered fondly in *Orlando at the Brazen Threshold*. He has died in *Agatha*.

Mr. Glass   Game-master and highly respected servant of Sir Randolph Nettleby; he suspects Tom Harker of poaching but is forced to ask him to work as a game-beater in spite of his misgivings; Mr. Glass does not want his son, Dan, to leave for college, although Sir Randolph has offered to pay the tuition for him in Isabel Colegate's *The Shooting Party*.

Dan Glass   Mr. Glass's intelligent son, who wants to be a scientist; Sir Randolph Nettleby pays his way to college at the end of Isabel Colegate's *The Shooting Party*.

Mrs. Glaze   Cook and cleaner at the vicarage who keeps Jane and Nicholas Cleveland's household supplied with gossip in Barbara Pym's *Jane and Prudence*.

Miss Gleason   Officious airline stewardess on the flight from Los Angeles to Mexico in Malcolm Lowry's *Dark as the Grave Wherein My Friend Is Laid*.

Meldy Glebe   Hollywood starlet infatuated with Owen Tuby; Tuby and Cosmo Sultana form a more commercially viable image for her in J. B. Priestley's *The Image Men*.

Barney Gleeson   Weaver and father who becomes

outraged at the abuse his daughter, Ellie, suffers at the hands of Jocelyn Chadwick; he goes crazy seeking revenge and is finally arrested and sentenced to penal servitude in Liam O'Flaherty's *Famine*.

Ellen Gleeson Beautiful wife of Barney Gleeson; after her husband's transportation, she goes to live, until her death, with her daughter Mary Kilmartin in Liam O'Flaherty's *Famine*.

Ellie Gleeson Daughter of Barney Gleeson; her beauty and sensuality drive Jocelyn Chadwick crazy; her alleged sins with Mr. Chadwick force her to leave the valley in Liam O'Flaherty's *Famine*.

Patrick Gleeson Son of Barney Gleeson; he dies avenging his sister's shame when he kills Jocelyn Chadwick in Liam O'Flaherty's *Famine*.

Comrade Gletkin Ivanov's ruthless prison colleague, who interrogates Nicolas Rubashov; he uses Kieffer's false testimony against him and forces him to confess to a trumped-up charge against the party and its leader, No. 1 [One], in Arthur Koestler's *Darkness at Noon*.

Joseph Glikman Maria Ostrakova's Jewish dissident lover, who encourages Ostrakova to desert her husband and himself and their illegitimate daughter, Alexandra, for freedom in the West in John le Carré's *Smiley's People*.

Louis Glober American film maker, tycoon, and sportsman; he is briefly interested in Pamela Flitton and in Polly Duport; an advocate for the fast life, he is killed in a car crash in Anthony Powell's *Temporary Kings*.

Gloria Married secretary of Felix Skinner; she makes love to him in the basement, where he finds copies of Philip Swallow's book on Hazlitt in David Lodge's *Small World*.

Queen Glory English Queen Mother of Princess Elsie; she visits Pisuerga for her daughter's wedding to Prince Yousef in Ronald Firbank's *The Flower Beneath the Foot*.

Hannah Glossop Supercilious young woman; she is loved by Richard Dupret but spurns him for the uninterested Tom Tyler in Henry Green's *Living*.

Glover The pleasant, sensible fellow passenger who is assigned the cabin next to Gilbert Pinfold's in Evelyn Waugh's *The Ordeal of Gilbert Pinfold*.

Glubose Tempter assigned to the mother of Wormwood's subject; Screwtape encourages Worm-

wood to conspire with Glubose in tempting both their subjects in C. S. Lewis's *The Screwtape Letters*.

Rose Glyn The Sharpe women's former servant; fired for stealing, she gives false evidence supporting their accuser in Josephine Tey's *The Franchise Affair*.

Randall Glynde Cousin of Alison Westwater; his timely arrival results in the defeat of Count Mastrovin and the success of the Monarchists' plot in John Buchan's *The House of the Four Winds*.

Dr. Gobany Physician who attends John Lavender; he pronounces him sane in John Galsworthy's *The Burning Spear: Being the Experiences of Mr. John Lavender in Time of War*.

Dr. Gobian The psychiatrist whom Alison Murray tries to persuade to see her daughter in prison in Margaret Drabble's *The Ice Age*.

God A young, well-dressed man who visits and drinks with Maurice Allington and explains that he (God) has no foreknowledge and that humans have free will; he confides that there is an afterlife and prophesies that Allington will learn to appreciate death in Kingsley Amis's *The Green Man*.

Professor Godbole Imperturbably serene Brahman Minister of Education at the college in Chandrapore, India; his delay at his prayers causes Fielding's dangerous absence from the excursion to the Marabar Caves in E. M. Forster's *A Passage to India*.

Godfrey Old Jamaican servant to Mrs. Cosway; he discovers her poisoned horse in Jean Rhys's *Wide Sargasso Sea*.

Master Godfrey Lady Alison's corresponding secretary in William Golding's *The Spire*.

Jack Godfrey Ringer of the oldest of the Fenchurch St. Paul bells, "Batty Thomas," cast in 1338, in Dorothy L. Sayers's *The Nine Tailors: Changes Rung on an Old Theme in Two Short Touches and Two Full Peals*.

Lady Godmanchester Lord Godmanchester's much younger wife; she is defensive about her artistic taste and insults Madge Leacock in Wales in Angus Wilson's *The Old Men at the Zoo*.

Lord Godmanchester British government minister and president of the zoological society; he uses the London zoo in his political efforts to prevent war, urges Simon Carter to remain as secretary after failure of the experiment in Wales, and dies just before war breaks out in Angus Wilson's *The Old Men at the Zoo*.

Carlos Leonardo Luis Manuel de Godoy y Boegas
First Minister of his Most Catholic Majesty, Prince of Peace; he is the Spanish leader who grants Horatio Hornblower his freedom in C. S. Forester's *Mr. Midshipman Hornblower.*

Jack Godstow   Richard Hannay's gamekeeper; he shares with Peter John Hannay the protection of Valdemar Haraldsen in John Buchan's *The Island of Sheep.*

Angela Godwin   Peregrine Arbelow's second-marriage stepdaughter; she repeatedly writes to Charles Arrowby offering to have a child with him in Iris Murdoch's *The Sea, the Sea.*

Gogol   Tuesday of the General Council of the Anarchists of Europe who is denounced by Sunday as a spy and leaves the Council; he rejoins Council members in the pursuit of Sunday in G. K. Chesterton's *The Man Who Was Thursday: A Nightmare.*

Elizabeth (Liz) Gold   Naïve Jewish Communist Party worker and librarian at the Bayswater Library for Psychic Research; she falls in love with Alec Leamas, is drawn into Control's scheme to protect Hans-Dieter Mundt, and is murdered while escaping with Leamas over the Berlin Wall, causing her lover to reject all ideology, embrace love, and die with her in John le Carré's *The Spy Who Came In from the Cold.*

Rockie Goldenberg   Filmmaker who offers David Evans a part in a sea movie to be filmed in the East Indies in Margaret Drabble's *The Garrick Year.*

Auric Goldfinger   The short, large-headed, sun-seeking richest man in England; he likes to make love once a month to a gold-painted woman; he cheats at cards and golf and plans to rob Fort Knox in Ian Fleming's *Goldfinger.*

Mrs. Goldman   Playwright Sam Goldman's tiny mother, who claims she has never understood or liked any of her son's plays in Margaret Drabble's *The Middle Ground.*

Sam Goldman   South African playwright who is very successful in Margaret Drabble's *The Middle Ground.*

Gertrude Goldring   Australian pupil in the Hanover school who is a gruff, loud-voiced, knowing, outspoken girl in Dorothy Richardson's *Pointed Roofs.*

Paul Alexis Goldschmidt   A young, bearded professional dancing partner of Russian parentage; his murdered body is discovered by Harriet Vane on a solitary sea-side hike in Dorothy L. Sayers's *Have His Carcase.*

Bridget Goldsmith   Sister to Jane Gray's mother and mother to Lucy (Otford); she maintains a close relationship with Jane; her return to England from America at the end of World War II began the intimacy of Jane and Lucy in Margaret Drabble's *The Waterfall.*

Carol Goldsmith   An honest, pragmatic woman who has an affair with Bertrand Welch; she advises Jim Dixon that it is his moral duty to get Christine Callaghan away from Bertrand in Kingsley Amis's *Lucky Jim.*

Cecil Goldsmith   Jim Dixon's colleague at the university; his wife, Carol, has an affair with Bertrand Welch in Kingsley Amis's *Lucky Jim.*

Alexander (Alexis) Golightly   A romantic and wayward youth who falls in love with the French actress Rose Vibert and has an affair with her until she takes up with his uncle, George Dillingham; his now frustrated passion culminates in his accidentally shooting and wounding Rose after she has become Sir George's wife; only after the birth of his cousin, Jenny, does Alexis again become a welcome guest at the home of Sir George and Rose Dillingham; after his uncle's death, Alexis begins a romance with Giulietta (the Marchesa Trampani), his uncle's long-time friend in David Garnett's *Aspects of Love.*

Gollum   Horrible, slimy water creature who used to be rather like a hobbit and was known as Smeagol until he found his "precious", the One Ring, and its power made him evil; Bilbo Baggins finds him in the lowest tunnels of the Orcs mountain and gets possession of the ring in J. R. R. Tolkien's *The Hobbit; or There and Back Again.* He follows Frodo Baggins on his journey and attempts to regain the ring; he is tamed by Frodo and leads Frodo and Sam Gamgee into Mordor; there he reverts to evil and betrays them in *The Two Towers.* On the edge of the Crack of Doom, he bites off Frodo's finger but falls into the crack, holding the finger and destroying Sauron in *The Return of the King.*

Gollup   Retired sergeant and owner of the Fada General Store; a jealous, abusive man who beats his lover and his employees, he is killed by Johnson in Joyce Cary's *Mister Johnson.*

James Golspie   Entrepreneur and adventurer who provides Twigg and Dersingham with a mysterious supply of cheap Baltic veneers and brings the firm to bankruptcy in J. B. Priestley's *Angel Pavement.*

Lena Golspie   James Golspie's young and flirtatious daughter in J. B. Priestley's *Angel Pavement.*

R. Gombauld   Indifferent and temperamental

painter commissioned to paint Anne Wimbush; repulsing Mary Bracegirdle's romantic interest, he pursues Anne, who rejects his advances in Aldous Huxley's *Crome Yellow*.

Conception Gomez Widowed native of Gibraltar; she is the adoring mistress of Richard Ennis, a married soldier, until she despairs of having any sort of a future with him in Anthony Burgess's *A Vision of Battlements*.

Goneril A harsh, vicious woman whose hallucinatory voice causes Gilbert Pinfold much distress in Evelyn Waugh's *The Ordeal of Gilbert Pinfold*.

Dr. Gonzi Eccentric professor of philosophy on an island in the Caribbean; he attempts without apparent motive to kill Miles Faber in Anthony Burgess's *MF*.

Alec Gooch Junior and only clerk in Corker's employment agency who, in love with his girlfriend Jackie and disappointed with his employer's behavior, leaves his position at the agency for another job; he later marries Jackie and has a child in John Berger's *Corker's Freedom*.

Sim Goodchild Owner of a bookstore in the small town of Greenfield; he is one of three elderly men who provide commentary on the events; he eventually becomes a follower of Matty Septimus in William Golding's *Darkness Visible*.

Sir Robert Goodeve A member of the Whitsuntide house party at Flambard, where he participates in Professor Moe's experiment in foreseeing a moment of future time in which Goodeve reads in an obituary details of his death; his subsequent death results from heart failure induced by fear in John Buchan's *The Gap in the Curtain*.

The Good Fairy The Pooka's card-playing travelling companion as they await the birth of Orlick Trellis in Flann O'Brien's *At Swim-Two-Birds*.

Fielding Goodney Urbane, handsome, and rich American financier who gets others to back John Self's movie; he is also both the tall, red-headed "woman" who follows John and "Frank", the voice that torments him on the phone; despite his appearance as John's friend, Goodney in reality is trying to sabotage John's success, and he comes to a violent end when John finds out in Martin Amis's *Money*.

Mary Goodnight Loelia Ponsonby's successor as James Bond's secretary in Ian Fleming's *On Her Majesty's Secret Service* and in *You Only Live Twice*.

Bootham Goold Chester Nimmo's private secretary

who is described by many as Chester's evil genius; he marries Sally Nimmo, and they help run Chester's political and private affairs in Joyce Cary's *Prisoner of Grace* and in *Not Honour More*.

Daisy Goold Free-spirited wife of Ted Goold; she becomes Nina (Woodville) Nimmo's close friend and initially provides her with an escape from political worries in Joyce Cary's *Prisoner of Grace*.

Ted Goold Wealthy grocery-store owner who, initially being Chester Nimmo's good friend, helps him rise to political power in Joyce Cary's *Prisoner of Grace*. He hires but sexually abuses Georgina Nimmo; he ends up in jail for his offenses; he is identified as "Mr. G" in *Except the Lord*.

Bella Gootblatt The jovial wife of Sy Gootblatt; she hosts what Philip Swallow describes as a drunken and disorderly party in David Lodge's *Changing Places: A Tale of Two Campuses*.

Sy Gootblatt A Hooker specialist at Euphoric State University and husband of Bella Gootblatt; he accompanies Philip Swallow during the faculty vigil in David Lodge's *Changing Places: A Tale of Two Campuses*. He has left for Penn State and has switched to literary theory; he has a fling with Fulvia Morgana at a conference in *Small World*.

Gordelpus The god of a pseudo-scientific religious cult that worships energy in Olaf Stapledon's *Last and First Men: A Story of the Near and Far Future*.

Eustace Gordon Idle brother of Rosemary Mosson; he sponges off his sister and her family, embarrasses his nephews with his graceless manners, and plans to leave England for Portugal to escape terrorist bombings in Angus Wilson's *Setting the World on Fire*.

Gordon-Nasmyth The explorer who tells the Ponderevos of the "heaps of quap" (heavy metals) on Mordet Island in H. G. Wells's *Tono-Bungay*

Ben Gore Public-school friend and later correspondent of John Haye in Henry Green's *Blindness*.

Julius Gore-Urquhart A rich patron of the arts and Christine Callaghan's uncle; valuing Jim Dixon's honesty, he hires Jim as his secretary and "boredom sensor" who will prevent boring people from making appointments with him in Kingsley Amis's *Lucky Jim*.

Barbara Goring Pretty, lively granddaughter of Lord Aberavon and cousin of Eleanor Walpole-Wilson; both Nicholas Jenkins and Kenneth Widmerpool are in love with her; Jenkins's eyes are opened at a dance when she dumps a sugar basin on Widmerpool's head; she becomes engaged to Johnny Pardoe in Anthony Powell's *A Buyer's Market*. Her assault on Widmerpool is remembered at intervals therafter; the behavior of the Quiggin twins recalls it in *Hearing Secret Harmonies*.

Hermann Göring   Aviator hero to the youth of Germany and an early supporter of Hitler in Richard Hughes's *The Fox in the Attic*. Regarded with suspicion after his escape to Austria, he works his way back into Hitler's power circle and consolidates his position by helping to engineer the blood purge against Ernst Röhm and others in *The Wooden Shepherdess*.

Lance-Corporal Gorman   NCO who works in Jonathan Browne's office at Catterick during the courtmartial of Mike Brady in David Lodge's *Ginger, You're Barmy*.

Miss Gorres   Antiques dealer who had been in a concentration camp; she suggests a sexual arrangement to Meg Eliot after her widowhood in Angus Wilson's *The Middle Age of Mrs. Eliot*.

Ambrose Gorringe   Eccentric owner of an island castle; he hosts a production of *The Duchess of Malfi* in P. D. James's *The Skull Beneath the Skin*.

Jimmy Gorton   Occasional agent whose misinformed intelligence report to Leclerc initiates Operation Mayfly in John le Carré's *The Looking-Glass War*.

Gosheron   The craftsman who repairs Lady Slane's Hampstead house, wins the approval of Genoux, Lady Slane's maid, and becomes Lady Slane's friend in Vita Sackville-West's *All Passion Spent*.

Giles Gosling   A young architect who wants to marry Colette Forbes in Iris Murdoch's *Henry and Cato*.

Marigold Gosling   Pretty daughter of a serving woman in the home of the Darke family in Mary Webb's *The House in Dormer Forest*.

Frederick (Fred) Gosport   Middle-aged pederast who introduces Ellen Henshaw into prostitution when she is thirteen years old in Anthony Burgess's *The Pianoplayers*.

Bertha Gotobed   A conscientious young housemaid who worked for Agatha Dawson; she later moves with her sister to London; she is found mysteriously dead in Dorothy L. Sayers's *Unnatural Death*.

Harry Gotobed   The sexton, a Fenchurch St. Paul bellringer in Dorothy L. Sayers's *The Nine Tailors:*

Changes Rung on an Old Theme in Two Short Touches and Two Full Peals.

Herbert Gotobed   Christine Clay's unsavory, sneaky older brother; his share of Clay's will is a "shilling for candles" in Josephine Tey's *A Shilling for Candles*.

Leonard Gough   Stone-deaf elderly painter; he teaches at the art school where Janos Lavin teaches and admires Lavin's work in John Berger's *A Painter of Our Time*.

Matthew Gough   Psychiatrist who gives evidence for the prosecution in the trial of Cora Ross and Kitty Pateman in C. P. Snow's *The Sleep of Reason*.

Charles Gould   English owner of the San Tomé mines; he is fixated on the virtue of capitalism, and his wealth underlies the prosperity of the newly founded Occidental Republic in Joseph Conrad's *Nostromo: A Tale of the Seaboard*.

Collie Gould   Member of Trevor Lomas's gang in Muriel Spark's *The Ballad of Peckham Rye*.

Emily Gould   Wife of the mine owner Charles Gould in Joseph Conrad's *Nostromo: A Tale of the Seaboard*.

Jeremiah Gould   Victim of Bess Wrigley's charms; he was blackmailed for a job for Bert Wrigley and a cottage for the Wrigley family in Richard Aldington's *The Colonel's Daughter*.

Moses Gould   Boarder at Beacon House who assists in the prosecution of Innocent Smith at his trial in G. K. Chesterton's *Manalive*.

Athen Gouliamis   A Greek communist guerrilla fighter who is training to be a pilot and who becomes an integral part of Martha Quest's communist group, eventually becoming a close friend of Maisie (Gale) McGrew in Doris Lessing's *A Ripple from the Storm* and in *Landlocked*.

Edwin Gower   Fiancé of Grace Amerson and son of a prosperous family in Frank Swinnerton's *The Happy Family*.

Nat Goya   Biologist assigned to the scientific center whose members will be sent into space to propagate a new colony of humans; he rebels to avoid separation from his pregnant wife in Anthony Burgess's *The End of the World News*.

George Goyles   Socialist agitator with whom Lady Mary Wimsey is in love, even after she becomes engaged to Denis Cathcart in Dorothy L. Sayers's *Clouds of Witness.*

Cyrus P. Goytz   An embalmer at the Toybrook Industrial Complex; he works on the project to fashion an android of Iolanthe Samiou in Lawrence Durrell's *Nunquam.*

Lucien Antoine de Ladon, Count de Gracay   Lonely French nobleman who offers to shelter Horatio Hornblower, William Bush, and Brown for the winter; his reputation protects them from the military in *Flying Colours.* He is Hornblower's quick-witted, compassionate friend and savior; he and Hornblower share an almost familial love in *Lord Hornblower.*

Marie, Vicomtesse de Gracay   Count de Gracay's daughter-in-law, who provides comfort to Horatio Hornblower, William Bush, and Brown and falls passionately in love with Hornblower in C. S. Forester's *Flying Colours.* She is Hornblower's beautiful, unselfish lover; she leads a rebellion through her native French countryside in *Lord Hornblower.*

Auntie Grace   Elderly relative visited in the hospital by Anthony Keating as a boy; until he was thirty-eight he doubted that such visits brought much pleasure to the elderly ill in Margaret Drabble's *The Ice Age.*

Major Arthur Grace   Susan and Sarah Layton's uncle, stationed in Calcutta; he runs a course to recruit promising young officers for civilian duty in the Indian service, one of whom seduces and impregnates Sarah, in Paul Scott's *The Towers of Silence.* Arthur Grace also appears in *The Day of the Scorpion* and in *A Division of the Spoils.*

Fenny Grace   Sister of Mildred Layton and aunt of Sarah and Susan Layton in Paul Scott's *The Day of the Scorpion.* When Sarah becomes pregnant by one of her uncle's officers, Aunt Fenny arranges for an abortion in *The Towers of Silence.* Fenny Grace also appears in *A Division of the Spoils.*

Poppy Grace   Small-time showgirl with whom Keith Rickman has a liberating fling; she represents the sensual side of Rickman's life that he must learn to control in May Sinclair's *The Divine Fire.*

Gracie   A young prostitute who is kept by Herbert Gregory and finally marries him; she flirts with several of the residents of the Regina Hotel before finally dying of tuberculosis in Lawrence Durrell's *The Black Book.*

Gradman   Law clerk for Soames Forsyte; in the firm for fifty years, he helps advise Soames on revisions to

his will for his daughter, Fleur, in John Galsworthy's *To Let.* He is witness to the evidence given by Butterfield in *The White Monkey.* He rushes to the dying Soames in *Swan Song.*

Graham (the Sleeper, the Master)   Young Victorian man who awakens after two centuries in a catatonic state to find himself ruler of much of the world, thanks to the shrewd business manipulations of his estate executors (later called the Council); he dies in an aerial battle against rebel forces who oppose his democratic aspirations in H. G. Wells's *When the Sleeper Wakes: A Story of the Years to Come.*

Alexander Graham   A small, dark, sensual Australian physician who courts — but ultimately is rejected by — Alvina Houghton in D. H. Lawrence's *The Lost Girl.*

Fanny Graham   The orphan sister who was brought up by Rhoda Graham; she marries Simon Challoner, not knowing that he has impregnated Rhoda in Ivy Compton-Burnett's *A Heritage and Its History.*

Herbert (Billy) Graham   "King of the local poachers"; he is hired to steal the cat to which the racehorse Potato Chip has become attached in P. G. Wodehouse's *Aunts Aren't Gentlemen.*

Penn Graham   Hugh Peronett's fifteen-year-old visiting Australian grandson; one of a large, close family, he is repelled by the alienation in the household of his English relations; he falls unrequitedly in love with his cousin Miranda Peronett in Iris Murdoch's *An Unofficial Rose.*

Rhoda Graham   Sir Edwin Challoner's friend, who marries the much older man and preserves the illusion that the younger Hamish is his son, although Sir Edwin's nephew Simon Challoner is the actual father in Ivy Compton-Burnett's *A Heritage and Its History.*

Miss Grainger   Nanny/governess who is replaced by Alice Benedict in Isabel Colegate's *Statues in a Garden.*

Lise Grainger   Deep-voiced, yellow-haired married lover of Bobbie Trevor; she is also secretly loved by Philip Luttrell, the rector where she lives; when her husband dies, she marries Bobbie in Margaret Kennedy's *Red Sky at Morning.*

Arthur Grampian   Married middle-aged author, father of two, and economist, who employs two copy editors and two research assistants, including Prudence Bates, who loves him hopelessly in Barbara Pym's *Jane and Prudence.*

Peter Granby   A young man whose coming to the aid

of an old woman who fell has bizarre consequences; he is taken in, fed, employed, and made love to by her daughter, Eileen Farnsfield; dumped by Eileen, he shoots at her lover with an antique gun and is blinded when it explodes in his face in Alan Sillitoe's *Out of the Whirlpool.*

The Grand Lunar Giant-brained Selenite who rules the moon and to whom Cavor unwittingly portrays the human race as violent and uncivilized and, therefore, as an enemy in H. G. Wells's *The First Men in the Moon.*

Grandmother Maxim de Winter's nearly blind grandmother; when Beatrice Lacy brings Mrs. de Winter to meet her, she repeatedly asks for the dead Rebecca, adding to Mrs. de Winter's insecurities in Daphne Du Maurier's *Rebecca.*

Grandmother Peter Granby's grandmother, with whom he lived until he became Eileen Farnsfield's lover in Alan Sillitoe's *Out of the Whirlpool.*

Mr. Granger Neighbor of Judith (Gardner) King and her family while they vacation in the country; the Grangers have a wireless radio which all the neighbors come to listen to in Isabel Colegate's *Orlando King.*

Mrs. Granger Mr. Granger's wife in Isabel Colegate's *Orlando King.*

Alan Grant Genteel Detective-Inspector of Scotland Yard; his deductive genius combines skepticism and intuition to lead him to the correct solution in spite of overwhelming evidence to the contrary; he investigates the murder of Albert Sorrell, whose body is wedged in a theater-entrance line in Josephine Tey's *The Man in the Queue.* He uncovers evidence solving the murder of actress Christine Clay in *A Shilling for Candles.* He represents the police but is not the primary investigator in *The Franchise Affair.* The complex nature of the apparent victim Leslie Searle is the focus of his attention in *To Love and Be Wise.* Immobilized in a hospital bed, he becomes absorbed in historical research that convinces him of the innocence of King Richard III in *The Daughter of Time.* En route to Scotland for sick leave, he finds a body on the train and subsequently identifies the victim, Bill Kenrick, and his murderer in *The Singing Sands.*

Amy Grant Mother of Charley Summers's dead love, Rose Phillips, in Henry Green's *Back.*

Gerald Grant Father both of Charley Summers's dead love, Rose Phillips, and of Rose's half sister and Charley's new love, Nancy Whitmore, in Henry Green's *Back.*

Red Grant Half-English, half-German psychotic assassin hired by the USSR espionage agency SMERSH to kill James Bond; using the name Captain Nash, he repeatedly addresses Bond as "old man"; Bond unmasks and kills him in Ian Fleming's *From Russia, With Love.*

Charlotte Grantham A matriarch living on a country estate who rules London society with the power and severity of a deposed but tenacious dowager; she disapproves of the rise of persons from the less desirable classes into aristocratic circles in Vita Sackville-West's *The Edwardians.*

Lavinia Grantham Attractive, middle-aged officer in the Wren detachment in Gibraltar with an interest in poetry; she seems interested in the educated Sgt. Richard Ennis, but firmly rejects his efforts to seduce her in Anthony Burgess's *A Vision of Battlements.*

Jock Grant-Menzies Well-to-do aristocrat who is a close friend of Tony and Brenda Last; when his affair with Mrs. Rattery terminates and Tony is declared legally dead, he marries Brenda in Evelyn Waugh's *A Handful of Dust.*

Graphos A Greek politician and ertswhile lover of Countess Hippolyta; he labors unsuccessfully to prevent the Firm from buying the Parthenon in Lawrence Durrell's *Tunc.*

Hannah Graves A teacher of English very interested in theater, especially backstage, who worked at Freddie Wentworth's school; she befriends another teacher, the boring and shy Carroll Pierce, and then falls in love with an aging actor in Penelope Fitzgerald's *At Freddie's.*

Josiah Graves Churchwarden and manager of the local bank in Blackstable in W. Somerset Maugham's *Of Human Bondage.*

Bryan Graveson Daniel Graveson's once-spirited older brother who volunteers for World War II army service, afterwards contracts a lingering illness, and dies while Dan is spending his own military leave in Wales in Alan Burns's *Buster.*

Daniel Graveson Spoiled and irresponsible young college graduate and army officer who, through insubordination and apathy, loses his job and social standing and finally becomes a burden on his family in Alan Burns's *Buster.*

Reginald Graves-Upton A gentle, elderly bachelor friend of the Pinfolds; he puts great faith in the "Box", a therapeutic device that allegedly tunes into the Life

Waves of a patient in Evelyn Waugh's *The Ordeal of Gilbert Pinfold.*

Allegra Gray   Elegant, somewhat manipulative widow who rents the top floor of the Malorys' vicarage and becomes engaged to Julian Malory, to the confusion of the community of churchwomen in Barbara Pym's *Excellent Women.*

Barbara Gray   The teenaged daughter of Octavian and Kate Gray; on vacation from her Swiss finishing school, she loses her virginity to Pierce Clothier in Iris Murdoch's *The Nice and the Good.*

Bianca Gray   Infant daughter to Jane and Malcolm Gray; the event of her birth brings together her mother and James Otford, resulting in an intense affair that dramatically alters her mother's life; Bianca's parents are separated when she is born, and her father does not try to visit his family until she is over six months of age in Margaret Drabble's *The Waterfall.*

Cordelia Gray   Young, stubborn, highly intelligent detective who takes over the Pryde Detective Agency after Bernie Pryde commits suicide; she is both attracted to and repelled by Adam Dalgliesh, Bernie's former chief, in P. D. James's *An Unsuitable Job for a Woman* and in *The Skull Beneath the Skin.*

Jane Gray   A young wife estranged from her husband at the time of the birth of her second child, Bianca; the event of the child's birth leads to her falling in love with James Otford, her cousin Lucy's husband; their affair has a dramatic impact upon her life, helping lead her out of a paralyzing depression; complex and romantic, she is a published poet in Margaret Drabble's *The Waterfall.*

Jennie Gray   The member of "the Brodie set" who is "famous for her prettiness"; she is Sandy Stranger's childhood friend in Muriel Spark's *The Prime of Miss Jean Brodie.*

Kate Gray   Octavian's wife, who presides over their country house; she is for a time infatuated with John Ducane in Iris Murdoch's *The Nice and the Good.*

Laurie Gray   Young son to Jane and Malcolm Gray; he enjoys the sports-car world introduced to him by his mother's lover, James Otford, in Margaret Drabble's *The Waterfall.*

Malcolm Gray   Jane's estranged husband, a successful thirty-one-year-old guitarist and singer; he continues to provide financial support to Jane and their children, Laurie and Bianca, while he lives with another woman; when he tries to reconcile with his wife, she rebuffs him, being deeply involved with another man in Margaret Drabble's *The Waterfall.*

Mary Gray   Wife of Innocent Smith; Innocent Smith's proposal to her in the presence of the people at Beacon House, who are unaware that they are already married, leads to a charge of bigamy at Smith's trial; she reveals herself as Mrs. Smith in G. K. Chesterton's *Manalive.*

Octavian Gray   A senior civil servant and patriarchal figure in Iris Murdoch's *The Nice and the Good.*

Theodore Gray   Octavian's brother; he has returned to England following a scandal in India, where he had taken vows in a Buddhist monastery, in Iris Murdoch's *The Nice and the Good.*

Verena Gray   The scheming orphan ward of Eliza Mowbray; she becomes engaged to Malcolm Mowbray and then to his uncle Miles Mowbray; the young woman, pregnant by Miles, marries Malcolm when Aunt Ellen returns in Ivy Compton-Burnett's *A Father and His Fate.*

Grayson   Normally good student of Mr. Chips who gets his instructor's notice by his carelessness in translation and preoccupation in class; the boy's father had sailed on the *Titanic,* and no one knows his fate in James Hilton's *Good-bye, Mr. Chips.*

Alma Grayson   Actress who provides Rupert Matthews with his first successful acting opportunity in Angus Wilson's *No Laughing Matter.*

Emma Greatheart   An independent woman who has lived with Hester Wolsey for many years; she accepts and then rejects Julius Hume's proposal in Ivy Compton-Burnett's *Mother and Son.*

Eric Greatorex   A famous pianist who is a guest at the houseparty given by Adele, Lady Brixton; he is "the only person who can play Stravinski"; Lucia Lucas intrepidly surmounts the folly of having played Stravinski for him in E. F. Benson's *Lucia in London.*

James (Jim) Greatorex   Yeoman farmer who seduces and finally marries Alice Cartaret, curing her hysteria and his drinking, and creating a successful marriage that survives gossip and ostracism in May Sinclair's *The Three Sisters.*

Doreen Greatton   Young woman Arthur Seaton meets, courts and finally marries in Alan Sillitoe's *Saturday Night and Sunday Morning.*

Dr. Greaving   Unbalanced female reader of Enderby's poetry who poses as a professor of literature to gain entry to his apartment, intending to shoot him in Anthony Burgess's *The Clockwork Testament; Or Enderby's End*.

Mr. Green A lower-middle-class young man on holiday in Brighton; he pairs off with Eve Henderson in Dorothy Richardson's *Backwater*.

Mrs. Green A nosy, compassionate widow who is Adam and Barbara Appleby's landlady in David Lodge's *The British Museum Is Falling Down*.

Arthur Green A temperamental artist who experiences the execution of his uncle, George Whitney, by the I.R.A. and gives up painting for political cartooning; a dreamer like his father, he distorts events; he has an affair with Letty Cameron (Green), who finds his brother Oliver more suitable; he seeks reality in a "maze of mirrors" and becomes committed and dies as result of illness incurred during a peace march in C. Day Lewis's *Child of Misfortune*.

Dan Green Second-rate poet and father of Arthur and Oliver; now deceased, he was a romantic Irishman with a magnificent view of his family's past; he was a popular personality with a stymied career in C. Day Lewis's *Child of Misfortune*.

Dorothea Green Widowed mother of Oliver and Arthur; her emptiness is filled with social causes such as woman's suffrage; she resents her late husband Dan's ineffective life, sympathizes with Oliver's conservative bent, and is uneasy over Arthur's display of his father's traits in C. Day Lewis's *Child of Misfortune*.

Letty Cameron Green The sister of Alec Cameron; she is a self-possessed believer in success and cash and a calculating, raw-boned beauty; she has an affair with Arthur Green but marries Oliver Green in C. Day Lewis's *Child of Misfortune*.

Oliver Green A rational, disciplined vicar with a propensity for external action despite internal misgivings; he sympathizes with his brother Arthur's self-searching; he lives with a farm family whose outrageous sixteen-year-old daughter tempts him; Arthur's death results in Oliver's abandoning his high position and separating from his wife, Letty, in C. Day Lewis's *Child of Misfortune*.

Sally Green Timid, weaselish girl, who loves Nigel Cuff and accompanies him to the communal settlement established by Trevor Frobisher; embittered by the shabby way she is treated, she spreads gossip and makes trouble for William Crowne in Margaret Kennedy's *Red Sky at Morning*.

Saul Green Anna Wulf's most important lover, an expatriate from America; he is a writer who is physically unhealthy in his fear and wariness, but he is the final inspiration and impetus for Anna to compose the "Golden Notebook" and her ultimate novel in Doris Lessing's *The Golden Notebook*.

Sue Greene Helene Bang's friend and neighbor who offers to help Ernst Bang with household chores after he breaks his foot and Helene leaves him for a weekend with Irving Macher in Kingsley Amis's *One Fat Englishman*.

Woodford Green Narrator and friend of Tertius Wyland and Rutherford; he reads Rutherford's account of Hugh Conway's adventure in James Hilton's *Lost Horizon*.

Greena A small girl of Zone Three who shows a great propensity for the art of management in Doris Lessing's *The Marriages Between Zones Three, Four, and Five*.

Aubrey Greene Painter who paints the nude picture of Victorine Bicket in John Galsworthy's *The White Monkey*.

Nicholas Greene A poet who propounds upon life and literature to the heartbroken male Orlando as he pines for the cruel Sasha; excessively grateful, Orlando pensions Greene generously; the poet reciprocates several centuries later when Orlando is a woman and Greene has become a prominent literary critic by offering to have her poem "The Oak Tree" published in Virginia Woolf's *Orlando: A Biography*.

Dora Greenfield An easygoing, generously forgiving young woman of common sense and instinctive goodness; she vacillates but decides to divorce her jealous, contemptuous husband, Paul Greenfield, at the end of Iris Murdoch's *The Bell*.

Paul Greenfield An art historian married to Dora Greenfield, whom he bullies; during their stay at Imber Court he does research on fourteenth-century manuscripts in Iris Murdoch's *The Bell*.

Green Lady (Tinidril) First woman on the new-created world of Perelandra (Venus); she is subjected to continual temptation by Edward Weston, the embodiment of evil; after Elwin Ransom kills Weston, she becomes Queen of Perelandra and is named Tinidril in C. S. Lewis's *Perelandra*.

Greenlake Utopian scientist who dies in the experiment which transports several Earthlings to the perfect world of Utopia in H. G. Wells's *Men Like Gods*.

Miss Greenlow   The middle-aged teacher of mathematics at the women's college that Dolores Hutton attends in Ivy Compton-Burnett's *Dolores*.

The Green Man   A creature that simultaneously resembles a man and a tree; sent by Dr. Underhill to kill Amy Allington, he is stopped and destroyed by Maurice Allington in Kingsley Amis's *The Green Man*.

Greenmantle   Eastern holy man used by Hilda von Einem to rally Turkish support for the Germans against the Allied forces; he dies of cancer at the crucial time he must prepare to lead his forces into battle and is replaced by "Sandy" Arbuthnot in John Buchan's *Greenmantle*.

Dr. Tom Greenslade   Oxfordshire friend of the Richard Hannays; his association of the verse, Hannay's only clue in locating the hostages, with Dominick Medina leads Hannay to the solution of the mystery in John Buchan's *The Three Hostages*.

Bruno Greensleave   A bedridden retired printing-works proprietor and an expert on spiders; his death occurs at the end of Iris Murdoch's *Bruno's Dream*.

Diana Greensleave   Wife of Miles Greensleave; she is attracted to Danby Odell and is profoundly disconcerted to learn that both he and Miles are in love with her sister, Lisa Watkins; she becomes absorbed in her attentive care of the dying Bruno Greensleave in Iris Murdoch's *Bruno's Dream*.

Janie Greensleave   Bruno's long-dead wife, who never forgave him for having a mistress, although her discovery of the affair ended it, in Iris Murdoch's *Bruno's Dream*.

Miles Greensleave   A civil servant of failed literary ambitions; the son of Bruno Greensleave, he is the husband of Diana Greensleave; he falls in love with Lisa Watkins, whose rejection of his advances restores his literary potency in Iris Murdoch's *Bruno's Dream*.

Parvati Greensleave   The young Indian, long dead in an airplane crash, whose marriage to Miles estranged her from her Brahman parents and him from his father; he still grieves for her in Iris Murdoch's *Bruno's Dream*.

Evelyn ("Eve") Greenstreet   Attractive, sexually well-travelled secretary at Oxford University with whom Jake Richardson had a brief affair years before she is seduced at the time of the events occurring in Kingsley Amis's *Jake's Thing*.

Greenwood   Corporal of the marines who reports the events leading up to Captain Sawyer's fall in C. S. Forester's *Lieutenant Hornblower*.

Elsa Greer (Lady Dittisham)   Thrice-married beauty; she is one of many former lovers of Amyas Crale, who is poisoned as he is completing her portrait in Agatha Christie's *Five Little Pigs*.

Abel Greeson   American known as a saboteur, now in Glasgow in league with Moxon Ivery; he is shadowed by Richard Hannay, who saves him when he is attacked after a rally and when they are both in the West Highlands on the Tobermory in John Buchan's *Mr. Standfast*.

George Greggson   Television engineer and husband of Jean Morrel; he is the father of the first children in humanity's next evolutionary step in Arthur C. Clarke's *Childhood's End*.

Jeffrey Greggson   The son of Jean Morrel and George Greggson; he is the first male child in humanity's next evolutionary stage in Arthur C. Clarke's *Childhood's End*.

Jennifer Anne Greggson   The daughter of Jean Morrel and George Greggson; she is the first female child in humanity's next evolutionary stage in Arthur C. Clarke's *Childhood's End*.

Alexander Gregorievitch (aliases: Monsieur Kamensky, Gorin, Kaspar)   Double agent devoted to dehumanized espionage; engineer and bridge builder, he is secretary to Nikolai Diakanov, whom he has admired but betrays; he also casts suspicion on blind Berr; he wants to be a bridge between history and the future but dies disillusioned in Rebecca West's *The Birds Fall Down*.

Senora Gregorio   An elderly widow, owner of The Terminal Cantina El Bosque, who treats Geoffrey Firmin sympathetically in Malcolm Lowry's *Under the Volcano*.

Dr. Gregory   The private physician of Evelyn Jarrold; he misdiagnoses her final illness as bronchitis rather than pneumonia in Vita Sackville-West's *Family History*.

Dr. Gregory   Master of St. Joseph's College, Oxford, where Eustace Cherrington is enrolled; in an interview with Hilda Cherrington which she reports to members of her family, he proposes asking Eustace to give up the monetary portion of his scholarship to a more needy student and explains that Eustace may not be developing exactly as the college might wish, choosing usually to be more agreeable than profound, in L. P. Hartley's *The Sixth Heaven*.

Grace Gregory   Former matron of Ambrose College; she follows her ex-lover Arnold Leaver, headmaster of Ambrose, to Venice and spies on his new affair for his wife in Muriel Spark's *Territorial Rights*.

Herbert ("Death") Gregory   Aimless wanderer about the dives of London; his diary chronicles the doings of the motley crew of lodgers in the Regina Hotel; he marries the short-lived prostitute Gracie before settling ultimately into squalor with his favorite barmaid Kate in Lawrence Durrell's *The Black Book*.

Lucian Gregory   Poet and anarchist who aspires to become the new Thursday on the General Council of the Anarchists of Europe, but is defeated in the election by Gabriel Syme in G. K. Chesterton's *The Man Who Was Thursday: A Nightmare*.

Gregory Gregson   British drinking chum of Ronald Beard from the Middle East whom Beard encounters in Rome; Gregson is fun-loving, uninhibited, and irresponsible in Anthony Burgess's *Beard's Roman Women*.

Henry Grenfel   A young soldier who disrupts the Lesbian relationship of the inhabitants at Bailey Farm; he yearns to possess the farm and Nellie March and kills her lover Jill Banford to achieve his goals in D. H. Lawrence's *The Fox*.

Guy Grenfell   Student at Cambridge who loves Nina Eliot; he serves as the scapegoat for the group involved in the national-security incident in C. P. Snow's *Last Things*.

Captain Gresley   A flamboyant adjutant who arranges a false raid on Badmore during Jonathan Browne's last guard duty in National Service, but is then embarrassed by a real raid by the Irish Republican Army in David Lodge's *Ginger, You're Barmy*.

Gretta   Sister of Wanda Podolak; she collects her sister's things after Wanda's drowning in Muriel Spark's *A Far Cry from Kensington*.

Bob Greville   A middle-aged bachelor friend of Gerald Ducayne in Dorothy Richardson's *Backwater*. He later corresponds with Miriam Henderson and takes her to tea and then to his London flat, where he makes unwelcome advances in *Honeycomb*.

Miss Grey   The headmistress of Brinsley Street School, where Ursula Brangwen teaches in D. H. Lawrence's *The Rainbow*.

Greeta Grey   Beautiful but empty-headed blonde companion of Lord Barralonga; she refuses to accept that they cannot return to Earth in H. G. Wells's *Men Like Gods*.

Miranda Grey   A young art student kidnapped by Ferdinand Clegg and held prisoner in the basement of his country cottage; her diary describes her complex relationship with George Paston, an older painter, and her attempts to teach humanity to Clegg as Paston has taught her; she dies in captivity in John Fowles's *The Collector*.

Thora Grey   Sir Carmichael Clarke's beautiful secretary; his widow dismisses her after he is murdered in Agatha Christie's *The A.B.C. Murders*.

Lord Grice   The Volyen Governor of Volyenadna who is ultimately kidnapped by the planet Motz and then released because they become bored with him; his court case against Volyen is never really resolved in Doris Lessing's *Documents Relating to the Sentimental Agents in the Volyen Empire*.

Compson Grice   Publisher who makes money from Wilfred Desert's notoriety in John Galsworthy's *Flowering Wilderness*.

Neville Grierson   Film star who has joined the ensemble performing in Hereford in Margaret Drabble's *The Garrick Year*.

Major Grieve   Edward Charteris's neighbor, who is disturbed that miners are all "bolshies" who stab the country in the back in C. Day Lewis's *The Friendly Tree*.

Edward Griffen   Short-tempered game master and Michael Evans's best friend among the faculty; he teaches history with flagrant inaccuracy and gross caricaturization in Nicholas Blake's *A Question of Proof*.

Griffin   Captain under Lord Edrington's command in C. S. Forester's *Mr. Midshipman Hornblower*.

Griffin (the Stranger, the Invisible Man)   Lanky albino student and scientist, whose amorality leads him to rob his father to fund his research on invisibility; having become permanently invisible, he menaces the villages of Iping and Port Burdock, ultimately dying at the hands of a mob after declaring a reign of terror and attempting to assassinate the local doctor, his old schoolmate Kemp, in H. G. Wells's *The Invisible Man: A Grotesque Romance*.

Miss Griffin   The kind and patient companion to Matilda Seaton; she faithfully nurses both Blanche and Dudley Gaveston in their life-threatening illnesses in Ivy Compton-Burnett's *A Family and a Fortune*.

Mary Griffith Pathetic land-girl in Mr. Pugh's employ who fixes on Sirius as a lover and charges him with assault when he ignores her in Olaf Stapledon's *Sirius: A Fantasy of Love and Discord*.

Mrs. Griffiths Julia Martin and Nora Griffiths's mother; paralyzed, nearly comatose, and dying, she is still beautiful in the bed in Nora's flat; her death parallels Julia's living death in Jean Rhys's *After Leaving Mr. Mackenzie*.

Uncle Griffiths Julia Martin's father's brother, who is short, broad, white-haired, blue-eyed, solid, and powerful; he rejects abruptly Julia's request for money in Jean Rhys's *After Leaving Mr. Mackenzie*.

Harry Griffiths The kind-hearted but frivolous medical student who cares for Philip Carey when he has influenza but then has no qualms about stealing the besotted Philip's beloved Mildred Rogers in W. Somerset Maugham's *Of Human Bondage*.

Nora Griffiths Julia Martin's good, conformist sister, who stayed at home to care for their mother; she is a tall, dark, strong, straightbacked, scrupulously clean girl with no money in Jean Rhys's *After Leaving Mr. Mackenzie*.

Anton Grigoriev ("Tricky Tony"; covername: Dr. Adolf Glaser) Womanizing Soviet Commercial Counsellor in Berne and Karla's operationally naïve courier who manages the bank account Karla uses to funnel Moscow Centre funds to the Berne clinic treating his daughter, Tatiana; Grigoriev reports weekly to Karla on Tatiana's condition and is easily blackmailed by George Smiley into confirming Karla's secret and revealing Tatiana's whereabouts in John le Carré's *Smiley's People*.

Madame Grigorovitch An exiled Ukrainian and a sympathetic neighbor of Ethan and Jacqueline Llewelyn in Malcolm Lowry's *October Ferry to Gabriola*.

Monsieur Grigorovitch Neighbor of Ethan and Jacqueline Llewelyn; his setter gives birth to a blue dog in one of many events suggesting the influence of a poltergeist in Malcolm Lowry's *October Ferry to Gabriola*.

Mrs. Grimble Harsh employer from whom Jancis Beguildy, her wedding postponed by Gideon Sarn's avarice, runs away in Mary Webb's *Precious Bane*.

Waldo Grimbley Egotistical professor and head of the English Department at Fouad University; he lives the life of a Moslem although truly an Englishman; he is upset by Perry's attempts to improve student housing in P. H. Newby's *The Picnic at Sakkara*.

Grimes An alcoholic, homosexual teacher who is employed at Llanabba School; he marries Dr. Fagan's daughter in a fraudulent ceremony, takes a position working for Margot Beste-Chetwynde's prostitution ring, and is arrested; he attempts to escape from a prison surrounded by a swamp, and his ultimate fate is uncertain in Evelyn Waugh's *Decline and Fall*.

Grimes Hornblower's first personal assistant/servant; he shows Hornblower two rotten eggs to prove his trustworthiness; during an act of cowardice, he refuses to join Hornblower on a French on-board siege mission; he hangs himself to escape further humiliation and punishment in C. S. Forester's *Hornblower and the Hotspur*.

Grimethorpe A hostile, suspicious countryman in Dorothy L. Sayers's *Clouds of Witness*.

Mrs. Grimethorpe The beautiful wife of a brutal, abusive, jealous husband; her life would be endangered if she provided an alibi for the Duke of Denver in Dorothy L. Sayers's *Clouds of Witness*.

Amy Grimstone The fourteen-year-old granddaughter of Jocasta; she has a vein of independent thought and a school and a home personality in Ivy Compton-Burnett's *The Last and the First*.

Erica Grimstone The comely sister of Osbert and Amy in Ivy Compton-Burnett's *The Last and the First*.

Hamilton Grimstone The fifty-year-old son of Jocasta and uncle of Osbert, Amy, and Erica; he unsuccessfully proposes to Hermia Heriot but leaves her his money anyway in Ivy Compton-Burnett's *The Last and the First*.

Jocasta Grimstone The mother of Hamilton and grandmother of Osbert and Amy Grimstone; she is a woman who demands quiet when she becomes fatigued in Ivy Compton-Burnett's *The Last and the First*.

Osbert Grimstone A young man articled to a firm of lawyers nearby; he proposes marriage to Hermia Heriot and is accepted by her in Ivy Compton-Burnett's *The Last and the First*.

Grindlay Leader of a political revolt; five years later Arnold Condorex has not yet decided whether it was good or bad in Rebecca West's *Harriet Hume, A London Fantasy*.

Molly Grinham One of Paul Coldridge's girlfriends; he hopes to turn her into a singer, but she leaves him for another man in Doris Lessing's *the Four-Gated City*.

Griskin Ballerina whom David Mountolive, during a posting to the Soviet Union, impregnates and nearly marries; his love evaporates as her vulgarity is exposed by his improved Russian in Lawrence Durrell's *Mountolive*. She and her child are mentioned in a paragraph appended to *Clea*.

Alice Grobe Deceased wanton wife of Nicholas Grobe; she was crushed by a train rescuing her daughter in T. F. Powys's *Mr. Weston's Good Wine*.

Nicholas Grobe Nihilist pastor of Folly Down rectory who dismisses the existence of God following his wife's death; his relationship with God is restored with Mr. Weston's good wine and he joins his wife in T. F. Powys's *Mr. Weston's Good Wine*.

Tamar Grobe Nicholas Grobe's free-spirited, beautiful daughter, who waits for an angel to marry her and whose final ecstacy of fulfillment kills her in T. F. Powys's *Mr. Weston's Good Wine*.

Wladyslaw Grodek Tall, vigorous Polish retired professional master spy; he employed Dimitrios Makropoulos in 1926 to entrap Bulic into stealing secret information; double-crossed by Dimitrios, Grodek tells Charles Latimer of the affair in Eric Ambler's *The Mask of Dimitrios*.

Ernst Groener Hardworking German in London, who sends money to the wife he abandoned in Germany, and who seduces "She" and treats her as a slave as they work in his café for four years in London before British wartime hostility to Germans embitters him and he leaves, hatefully denouncing the loyal woman in Storm Jameson's *A Day Off*.

Grogan A suspicious I.R.A. man who guides Arthur Green to the camp where Uncle George Whitney is held in C. Day Lewis's *Child of Misfortune*.

Dr. Michael Grogan Physician and Darwinist in Lyme Regis who befriends Charles Smithson and warns him against Sarah Woodruff; he helps Charles aid Sarah but condemns his behavior to Ernestina Freeman in John Fowles's *The French Lieutenant's Woman*.

Calvin Gropius A personally humorless and grim but successful televangelist in Anthony Burgess's *The End of the World News*.

Trudy Gross Jewish refugee working against fascists in England; she jolts Arthur Green's indifference and causes his commitment; Arthur thinks her a rarity among people — truly sane, responsive and responsible; she commits suicide in C. Day Lewis's *Child of Misfortune*.

Sir Denbigh Grote Retired diplomat, friend of Miss Prideaux in Barbara Pym's *A Glass of Blessings*.

Theodore Grote, Bishop of Mbawawa Old acquaintance of Archdeacon Hoccleve and the Bede sisters; he is a sixtyish, self-satisfied bachelor who comes to regale the village with his exploits in the mission field in Barbara Pym's *Some Tame Gazelle*.

Groundsel One of five Efrafan buck rabbits who surrender to Fiver after the dog's attack; he afterwards joins Hazel's warren in Richard Adams's *Watership Down*.

Lord Grove Former Lancashire Trades Union figure; he has worked his way up from warehouse clerk to chairman of a major industrial company in Roy Fuller's *The Father's Comedy*.

Mr. Grove A suffering friend of Gerald Ducayne; he wants to enter a monastery but is being forced by his family to study law instead in Dorothy Richardson's *Honeycomb*. He pays a surprising and disconcerting call on Miriam Henderson in the dental surgery where she works in *The Tunnel*.

Grovesnor Lucia Lucas's parlormaid in E. F. Benson's *"Queen Lucia"*, in *Lucia in London*, in *Mapp and Lucia*, in *The Worshipful Lucia*, and in *Trouble for Lucia*.

Gruber German-Jewish optician and owner of a photographic store where Dr. Plarr buys a present for Clara Fortnum in Graham Greene's *The Honorary Consul*.

Elizabeth Gruffydd-Williams The attractive, calculating, upper-class wife of the Chairman of the Libraries Committee; she tempts John Lewis to have an affair with her, indicating that she will influence her husband to advance Lewis's career in Kingsley Amis's *That Uncertain Feeling*.

Vernon Gruffydd-Williams Chairman of the Libraries Committee and a wealthy businessman who is Elizabeth Gruffydd-Williams's husband; he fixes the job appointment for John Lewis only because he wants to spite Rowlands, who dislikes Lewis in Kingsley Amis's *That Uncertain Feeling*.

Grotrian Grundtvig Celebrated Danish concert pianist with a leonine head; he is a close friend of Lady Nelly Staveley who with his family visits her during Eustace Cherrington's sojourn at her palazzo in L. P. Hartley's *Eustace and Hilda*.

Minerva Grundtvig Pale, nervous, retiring wife of Count Grundtvig, the pianist, and mother of Trudi; she is described as having "piano legs" in L. P. Hartley's *Eustace and Hilda*.

Trudi Grundtvig Eighteen-year-old daughter of Grotrian and Minerva Grundtvig who outswims Eustace Cherrington on the Lido and is supposed to know "everyone and everything and had it all pat" in L. P. Hartley's *Eustace and Hilda*.

Flavia Grundy Elderly spinster churchworker and onetime author, intimidated by the benevolence of Miss Lee, who has taken her in, in Barbara Pym's *A Few Green Leaves*.

Joseph Grünlich (covername: Anton) Cynical, sordid criminal; escaping after robbing and murdering an assistant station-manager, he is detained by military authorities with Richard Czinner and Coral Musker, breaks away to Carleton Myatt's car, and escapes, costing Czinner his life and Musker her future in Graham Greene's *Stamboul Train*.

Mr. Grunter Aging Folly Down rectory clerk who relishes his notoriety as the ruiner of Folly Down's maidens; he recognizes Mr. Weston and exhumes Ada Kiddle's body to retrieve his boot in T. F. Powys's *Mr. Weston's Good Wine*.

Mr. Gryffydd Saintly chapel minister whose love for Angharad Morgan is doomed; he is hated by Abishai Elias in Richard Llewellyn's *How Green Was My Valley*.

Guerini The Italian businessman on holiday whom Miriam Henderson initially mistakes for a Russian and to whom she tries to give instruction in socialistic thought in Dorothy Richardson's *Oberland*.

Angus Guest One of Aaron Sisson's friends in Florence, Italy; Angus, James Argyle, and Francis Dekker are examples of jaded cosmopolitan travellers in D. H. Lawrence's *Aaron's Rod*.

Werner Guggenbühl Dark, irritable, good-looking German Trotskyist who converts his presumed lover Milly Andriadis and later St. John Clarke to Trotskyism in Anthony Powell's *The Acceptance World*. He changes his name to Vernon Gainsborough; his anti-Trotskyism book is published by Quiggin & Craggs in *Books Do Furnish a Room*.

Peter Guillam (covernames: Andrew Forbes-Lisle, Gordon, Lampton, Lofthouse, Will) Wartime espio-

nage agent, covert operations' assassin, British diplomat in France, and George Smiley's chivalric confidant; he captures Samuel Fennan's murderer, Hans-Dieter Mundt, in John le Carré's *Call for the Dead*. He turns Mundt into a British double agent for Control's operation against the GDR Intelligence Service Abteilung in *The Spy Who Came In from the Cold*. He assists Smiley in his investigations of the double agent in *Tinker, Tailor, Soldier, Spy*. He helps Smiley with Operation Dolphin in *The Honourable Schoolboy*. He aids Smiley's inquiry into General Vladimir's murder, assists with Karla's defection, and conceals Marie Ostrakova from Karla's Moscow Center assassins in *Smiley's People*.

Gullie Aide to Sir Ronald at the British legation in Stockholm in Graham Greene's *England Made Me*.

Theodore Gumbril (the elder) Kindly but slightly eccentric father of the younger Theodore Gumbril; an architect, he selflessly sells his prized model of an idealized London to pay the gambling debts of the son of his friend Mr. Porteous in Aldous Huxley's *Antic Hay*.

Theodore Gumbril (the younger) Young dissatisfied prep-school teacher who abruptly quits his job with the idea of perfecting pneumatic pants as a commercial venture; he quickly moves into the empty life of post-World War I London society, self styling himself as the "Complete Man"; a series of meaningless affairs leaves him despondent, unable to consumate a promising relationship with Emily in Aldous Huxley's *Antic Hay*.

Mrs. Gunn Martha Quest's landlady, who at first attempts to follow Mrs. Quest's directives on looking after Martha in Doris Lessing's *Martha Quest*.

Mr. Gunner A sensitive young violinist, who comes to live in Mrs. Bailey's house and gradually attaches himself to her in Dorothy Richardson's *Interim*. He persuades her to marry him in *Deadlock*.

Gunning Bailiff and gardener for Mark and Christopher Tietjens in their South Country cottage in Ford Madox Ford's *The Last Post*.

Mr. Gunning-Forbes Stodgy older member of the Stotwell Literary Society and senior English master at the local grammar school, who heckles the comically avant-garde work in progress Edwin Froulish has been invited to read at the Society's meeting in John Wain's *Hurry On Down*.

Guru A supposed Brahman yoga expert introduced by Daisy Quantock and imperiously taken over by Lucia Lucas; in danger of exposure as a former curry cook at an Indian restaurant, he decamps with treasures from the Quantock, Lucas, and Pillson residences; the victims save face by not disclosing their losses in E. F. Benson's *"Queen Lucia"*.

Gustav   Weak, sly, prolific British agent; flaws in Gustav's comprehensive reports directed Ashenden to rectify the situation in W. Somerset Maugham's *Ashenden: or The British Agent*.

Guy   Irishman from Montefort, a small Irish country estate, who joined the British army and was killed in France; he remains vividly present in the memories of those who survived him and in the letters he wrote to them before he died in Elizabeth Bowen's *A World of Love*.

Lorne Guyland   An aging actor with an ego problem who is recruited for John Self's movie in Martin Amis's *Money*.

Dr. Guzman   Doctor who represents salvation but whom Geoffrey Firmin is unable to reach in Malcolm Lowry's *Under the Volcano*.

Gwendolen   Probably Clemence Shelley's best friend at school; she is told she is not clever in Ivy Compton-Burnett's *Two Worlds and Their Ways*.

Gwilym   Welsh miner's frail, intelligent son whose career as a minister is cut short by the war and by consumption; he is in a sanatorium at the time of his daughter Rachel's death; dying at home, he delightedly imparts his lifetime's learning to his infant son in Richard Hughes's *The Fox in the Attic*.

Russell Gwinnett   An American academic researching biographical information on Francis X. Trapnel; he resists Pamela Flitton's advances, but she dies of a drug overdose in his bed in Anthony Powell's *Temporary Kings*. His biography of Trapnel wins the Donners prize, and he marries Fiona Cutts in *Hearing Secret Harmonies*.

H

Henry H— Fellow exhibitor at Janos Lavin's exhibition who is considered one of England's leading abstract painters and believes that "Art is essentially Play" in John Berger's *A Painter of Our Time*.

Max Habolt (covername: Rudi Hartmann) Czechoslovakian-born British Intelligence agent who serves as Jim Prideaux's contact during Operation Testify in John le Carré's *Tinker, Tailor, Soldier, Spy*.

Bertha Hackbutt Sacrificing, honest wife of Mandy Hackbutt; they and their seven children join Trevor Frobisher's communal settlement in Margaret Kennedy's *Red Sky at Morning*.

Mandy Hackbutt Unsuccessful playwright who with his wife and seven children is invited to join Trevor Frobisher's communal settlement in Margaret Kennedy's *Red Sky at Morning*.

Hackett Mick Shaughnessy's friend and sidekick, and possibly the seducer of Mick's girlfriend in Flann O'Brien's *The Dalkey Archive*.

Hadrian VII See George Arthur Rose.

Walter Haigh Clerk and chairman of the Saddleford Building Society's Christian Union in Roy Fuller's *Image of a Society*.

Haines Patronizing, Oxford-educated English anthropologist who shares the tower with Stephen Dedalus and Buck Mulligan in James Joyce's *Ulysses*.

Miss Haines The fashionable teacher of French at the secondary school Clara Maugham attends; she and the science teacher Mrs. Hill become professional rivals for the talented Clara in Margaret Drabble's *Jerusalem the Golden*.

Rupert Haines Married gentleman farmer with whom Isa Oliver fancies herself in love because she imagines in him the poetic fulfillment she has yet to achieve; he once "handed her a cup and a racquet — that was all. But in his ravaged face she always felt mystery; and in his silence, passion" in Virginia Woolf's *Between The Acts*.

Colonel Zia Haki Tall, slim Turkish head of the secret police; a mystery lover and an aspiring detective-fiction writer, he summarizes the contents of Dimitrios Makropoulos's dossier for Charles Latimer and shows him the body of the man (Manus Visser) believed to be Dimitrios, thereby stimulating Latimer's search for more information in Eric Ambler's *The Mask of Dimitrios*.

Dean Abbas el-Hakim Dean of the Faculty of Arts at Fouad University; he is the first to realize that Muawiya Khaslat tried to murder Edgar Perry in P. H. Newby's *The Picnic at Sakkara*.

HAL 9000 The Heuristically programmed ALgorithmic computer which controls the space ship *Discovery* and which decides that nothing must interfere with the mission, including the survival of the crew; it becomes paranoid and murders most of the crew in Arthur C. Clarke's *2001: A Space Odyssey*.

Adrian Haldane (covername: Captain Hawkins) Snobbish, sarcastic Registry official for Leclerc's Department; as director of Special Section during Operation Mayfly, he refuses to curb Leclerc's fantasies and indifferently sacrifices Fred Leiser in John le Carré's *The Looking-Glass War*.

Dr. Halde The master of torture and brain-washing who tries to break Sammy Mountjoy at a German prisoner-of-war camp in William Golding's *Free Fall*.

Mrs. Haldin Mother of Victor and Nathalie Haldin in Joseph Conrad's *Under Western Eyes*.

Nathalie Haldin Sister of Victor Haldin; she befriends Razumov but discovers he was responsible for her brother's execution in Joseph Conrad's *Under Western Eyes*.

Victor Haldin Acquaintance of Razumov; he assassinates Mr. de P——, a hated goverment minister, and is turned in by Razumov and executed in Joseph Conrad's *Under Western Eyes*.

Charles Hale Frightened early-middle-aged man; an employee of *The Daily Messenger* hired to pose as fictitious Kolley Kibber in the *Messenger's* ongoing promo contest, he is in debt to Pinkie Brown's mob, befriends Ida Arnold, and is killed by Pinkie and his cohorts for failing to "pay up" in Graham Greene's *Brighton Rock*.

Hales Young oarsman subject to noisy fits, one of which occurs during a surprise attack; Hornblower silences him by knocking him unconscious; he is left adrift in the jolly boat in C. S. Forester's *Mr. Midshipman Hornblower*.

Half-caste Whining, toothless beggar who follows the whiskey priest and pesters him until finally turning the priest in for a reward in Graham Greene's *The Power and the Glory*.

Ambrose Halford   Chartered surveyor and chairman of the Saddleford Building Society in Roy Fuller's *Image of a Society*.

Gertrude Halibut   An aging former chorus girl who cleans the Palladium cinema and gossips about her family with Dolly in David Lodge's *The Picturegoers*.

Mrs. Halifax   Family friend of Louise Scobie; she accompanies her to South Africa in Graham Greene's *The Heart of the Matter*.

Louise (Lulu) Bennett Halifax   Strikingly attractive elder sister of Sarah Bennett; she has recently married Stephen Halifax for his money and the security she believes he can provide, although she continues her affair with actor John Connell; she has long acted superior to and disdainful of Sarah in Margaret Drabble's *A Summer Bird-Cage*.

Stephen Halifax   Louise's husband, who writes arid novels of social satire that he attempts to turn into screenplays; he associates mostly with wealthy intellectuals and potential backers of his screenplays; he feigns relationship to the ancient Halifax family, although he is really the son of a successful tobacco businessman; Wilfred Smee suggests that he is mad in Margaret Drabble's *A Summer Bird-Cage*.

Mr. Hall   Slow-witted landlord of Iping's Coach and Horses; his unfocused suspicions of Griffin are prompted by Teddy Henfrey in H. G. Wells's *The Invisible Man: A Grotesque Romance*.

Mrs. Hall   Maurice Hall's overbearing mother, who smothers her son with her blind love in E. M. Forster's *Maurice*.

Mrs. Hall   The Coach and Horses' suspicious landlady, whose interrogation of Griffin forces him to reveal his invisibility and to flee Iping in H. G. Wells's *The Invisible Man: A Grotesque Romance*.

Fred Hall   Suspicious, jealous personal friend of Erik Krogh and rival of Laurin; he monitors Krogh's security investments and keeps watch over Anthony and Kate Farrant; he is responsible for the murder of Anthony Farrant in Graham Greene's *England Made Me*.

Lily Hall   Dick Povey's fiancée; she is condescendingly kind to his old aunts Constance Baines Povey and Sophia Baines Scales in Arnold Bennett's *The Old Wives Tale*.

Maurice Hall   Educated, handsome young man of the suburban class; he comes to terms with his own homosexuality in E. M. Forster's *Maurice*.

Percy Hall   Clerk in Herbert Getliffe's chambers; he is persuaded by Lewis Eliot to send him more briefs in C. P. Snow's *Time of Hope*.

Hallam   The husband of Rosamund Stacey's sister, Beatrice; he is a scientist working at an atomic-research center in the Midlands in Margaret Drabble's *The Millstone*.

Edith Hallam   The second governess of Muriel Ponsonby; she allies herself with the older children and marries John Ponsonby in Ivy Compton-Burnett's *Daughters and Sons*.

Mildred Hallam   The housekeeper for Sir Ransome Chace and for a short time the governess for Rose and Viola Lovat; she is the secret daughter of Edmund Lovat in Ivy Compton-Burnett's *Darkness and Day*.

Robin James Hallam   A homosexual British Civil Service worker who aids Vulkan (Paul Louis Broum) for money and who burns to death in an unsuccessful attempt to kill the narrator in order to obtain authorization to Broum's family fortune in Len Deighton's *Funeral in Berlin*.

Marta Hallard   Well-known actress for whom Detective-Inspector Alan Grant once recovered some valuable pearls, creating a friendship useful to Grant in Josephine Tey's *The Man in the Queue*. She takes over the murdered Christine Clay's starring role in *A Shilling for Candles*. Her friendship with Grant is deepened in *To Love and Be Wise*. She helps him by finding a researcher in *The Daughter of Time*. The friendship continues in *The Singing Sands*.

Stephen Hallem   Richard Crane's old friend from Oxford, a "bolshie" whose grandfather was a miner; he replaces the friendly tree in Anna Charteris's affection; he sees the new society in terms of love and family, but he is jobless and without prospects; eventually he finds employment at an institute and marries Anna, who is hospitalized by an automobile accident; he abandons his affair with Evelyn Crane because his home is with Anna in C. Day Lewis's *The Friendly Tree*.

Mr. Halliday   Respectable Soho bookshop proprietor; he couriers Maurice Castle's purloined intelligence to his Soviet superiors and warns Castle to flee England in Graham Greene's *The Human Factor*.

Mr. Halliday   A reputed billionaire, who foots the bill for Rick Tucker in his biographical pursuit of Wilfred Barclay in William Golding's *The Paper Men*.

Helen Spenlove Kennedy Halliday   Gwenda Reed's stepmother; her disappearance years earlier resulted in her husband's suicide; she becomes a disturbing presence to Gwenda in Agatha Christie's *Sleeping Murder*.

Julius Halliday The leader of a sophisticated but jaded set of London Bohemians who eventually turn against Rupert Birkin in D. H. Lawrence's *Women in Love*.

Major Kelvin Halliday Helen's husband; after her disappearance he believes he murdered her and eventually kills himself in an insane asylum in Agatha Christie's *Sleeping Murder*.

Robert Halliday Ethical, short-tempered, early-middle-aged American journalist, ghostwriter, and one-time CIA agent; ostensibly commissioned to collaborate with Karlis Zander on a spurious Russian memoir, he is instead blackmailed by Zander into providing a fake television interview of a powerful but mentally unstable Middle East potentate (The Ruler) as cover for NATO-Ruler Persian Gulf base negotiations in Eric Ambler's *The Care of Time*.

Thomas Halliday The general man for the Clare family, not thought to be fitted for personal attendance on them in Ivy Compton-Burnett's *The Present and the Past*.

Edward Hallorsen American professor of archaeology who plans to help Hubert Cherrell escape extradition, proposes marriage to Dinny Cherrell, and is refused by her in John Galsworthy's *Maid In Waiting*.

Michael Hallowes Mystic and former teacher of Jasper Darke, whom he saves from drowning after Jasper attempts suicide (or is pushed by Catherine Velindre) in Mary Webb's *The House in Dormer Forest*.

Diana Halvorsen The four-year-old daughter of Ralph Halvorsen; she reveals to Dr. Floyd what the first-generation of space-born human children will be like in Arthur C. Clarke's *2001: A Space Odyssey*.

Ralph Halvorsen Administrator of the Moon's Southern Province; he is responsible for the news blackout and rumors of an epidemic that keep knowledge of the discovery of the artifact from the public in Arthur C. Clarke's *2001: A Space Odyssey*.

Sandra (Patterson) Hamburg A willful and somewhat spoiled young woman of twenty-five, educated at private school and Cambridge; she is the daughter of Sir Roderick and Lady Patterson; her marriage to Trevor Hamburg, on the verge of breakup, is saved when Florence Marvell convinces Trevor to discontinue the divorce proceedings and patch things up with Sandra in Frank Swinnerton's *Some Achieve Greatness*.

Trevor Hamburg Son of a wealthy tradesman who has married outside his class; his difficulties with his wife, Sandra, stem primarily from the tensions created by their different backgrounds; as proud and obstinate as his wife, Trevor can find no way to withdraw his suit for divorce without losing face until Florence Marvell reveals to him what a fool he's being; he and Sandra overcome their differences in Frank Swinnerton's *Some Achieve Greatness*.

Hamid Darley's one-eyed servant in Lawrence Durrell's *Justine*, in *Balthazar*, and in *Clea*.

Hamilton Tea planter in an African colony; he offers advice on how to treat the "natives" in Roy Fuller's *The Father's Comedy*.

Mrs. Hamilton Freddy Hamilton's mother in England; she requires Freddy's constant epistolary adjudication of her grievances against her old servant, and is finally murdered by her in Muriel Spark's *The Mandlebaum Gate*.

Sergeant Hamilton The many-toothed instructor of RAC clerks who gets Jonathan Browne his posting at Badmore in David Lodge's *Ginger, You're Barmy*.

Freddy Hamilton Middle-aged, unmarried British consular official whose adventures with Barbara Vaughan in Israel and Jordan convert him, at least temporarily, from observer and chronicler into a man of action in Muriel Spark's *The Mandlebaum Gate*.

George ("Geordie", "Red Geordie", and "Senor Jorge") Hamilton Member of the Royal Scots Fusiliers who attacks Richard Hannay, disguised as Cornelius Brend at an anti-war rally; shocked to learn he has attacked a commanding officer, he becomes Hannay's batman; he reports the death on the battlefield of Moxon Ivery in John Buchan's *Mr. Standfast*. As "Senor Jorge" in Olifa City, he is recognized by Sir Archibald Roylance and joins in the kidnapping of Mr. Castor, Olifa's sinister dictator, and the rescuing of Janet (Raden), Lady Roylance in *The Courts of the Morning*. Established at Laverlaw, Lord Clanroyden's Scottish estate, as a man of all trades and abilities, he accompanies Clanroyden, Hannay, and others to the Island of Sheep to fight the enemies of Valdemar Haraldsen in John Buchan's *The Island of Sheep*.

Hamit Syrian shopkeeper in Port-au-Prince from whom Brown and Martha Pineda briefly rented a room for their trysts; he is murdered by the Tontons Macoutes in Graham Greene's *The Comedians*.

Professor Hammersten Elderly Swedish language teacher who persuades Erik Krogh to finance a production of his translation of Shakespeare's *Pericles* in Graham Greene's *England Made Me*.

Hammond The middle-aged manservant of the Grimstones; he spreads family gossip in Ivy Compton-Burnett's *The Last and the First*.

Sister Hammond Rosamund Stacey's midwife at St. Andrews in Margaret Drabble's *The Millstone*.

Arnold B. Hammond A writer who thrives among the Wragby Hall "mental-lifers" and, like them, derides the "body" in D. H. Lawrence's *Lady Chatterley's Lover*.

Black Charlie Hammond Captain of the *Calypso* who examines Hornblower for promotion to lieutenant in C. S. Forester's *Mr. Midshipman Hornblower*.

Joyce Emily Hammond A newcomer to the Marcia Blaine School; she goes to her death in Spain after fascist indoctrination by Jean Brodie in Muriel Spark's *The Prime of Miss Jean Brodie*.

Valerie Hammond Arthur Machin's landlady; she refuses to be in love with him and finally forces him to leave, causing Arthur to be distraught and lonely until she dies in the hospital in David Storey's *This Sporting Life*.

Clara Hamps (Auntie Hamps) Splendidly dressed, insinuating widowed sister-in-law of Darius Clayhanger; her treatment of the Clayhanger children is viewed as hypocritical by Edwin Clayhanger who, nevertheless, reluctantly admires her family loyalty in Arnold Bennett's *Clayhanger*. A shrewd and economical strict Wesleyan, Auntie Hamps at her death makes Edwin realize that her nephews and nieces were her passion in *These Twain*.

Cedric Hampton The homosexual heir to the Montdore title and fortune; he meets Lord and Lady Montdore and replaces their daughter, Polly Hampton, in their hearts and their wills; his astonishing eye for beauty in art wins Lord Montdore, and his manipulation of feminine interests wins Lady Montdore; he enters into a well-engineered liaison with Boy Dougdale at the end of Nancy Mitford's *Love in a Cold Climate*.

Leopoldina (Polly) Hampton The beautiful, socially impeccable, and kind but emotionally empty daughter of Lord and Lady Montdore; her mother's overbearing behavior alienates her; she is probably pregnant when she becomes the wife of her uncle by marriage, Boy Dougdale; she marries for love, but when her child is born she is indifferent to its death and has come to detest her husband; she has taken a lover at the end of Nancy Mitford's *Love in a Cold Climate*.

Michael ("the dwarf") Hanbury-Steadly-Heamoor Homosexual head of Asian Press Service who employs Luke in John le Carré's *The Honourable Schoolboy*.

George Hanby Treasurer of the Bayswater South Branch Communist Party; he courts Liz Gold but epitomizes everything pompous and lecherous that she abhors in John le Carré's *The Spy Who Came In from the Cold*.

Mr. Hancock The most professional and skilled of the three dentists in the Wimpole Street surgery in London where Miriam Henderson works in Dorothy Richardson's *The Tunnel* and in *Interim*. Miriam continues to have an uncertain, problem-filled relationship with him in *Revolving Lights*.

Len Hancock Talented friend of Janos Lavin; he greatly admires Lavin's work; a butcher by day, he paints for "pure pleasure" and is technically quite proficient in John Berger's *A Painter of Our Time*.

Vee Hancock Len Hancock's gorgeous wife, who objects to her husband's using models to paint nudes; she later poses nude for her husband in John Berger's *A Painter of Our Time*.

Harriet Hancox The unfaithful wife of Linton Hancox in Margaret Drabble's *The Ice Age*.

Linton Hancox Anthony Keating's friend, an academic traditionalist in conflict with the declining standards in university education and scholarship; he is having an affair in retaliation against his wife's infidelity; he is depressed and considers suicide in Margaret Drabble's *The Ice Age*.

Miss Handforth Mr. Demoyte's observant and vigilant housekeeper in Iris Murdoch's *The Sandcastle*.

Albert Handley Recently successful painter who befriends Frank Dawley in Alan Sillitoe's *The Death of William Posters*. He befriends Frank's girlfriend, Myra Bassingfield, and child, Mark; he moves his family into Myra's large country home when his home burns down in *A Tree on Fire*.

Enid Handley Wife of Albert Handley and mother of six children in Alan Sillitoe's *The Death of William Posters* and in *A Tree on Fire*.

John Handley Albert Handley's brother, whose experiences in a Japanese prison camp have kept him isolated in his radio-equipment-filled room in Alan Sillitoe's *The Death of William Posters*. He decides to go to Algeria to find Frank Dawley; he finds Frank and sends him home but kills himself in *A Tree on Fire*.

Mandy Handley   Albert Handley's daughter, who was once Frank Dawley's lover in Alan Sillitoe's *The Death of William Posters*. She marries Ralph in *A Tree on Fire*.

Georgie Hands   Honor Klein's former pupil, who is a lecturer at the London School of Economics and the lover of first Martin Lynch-Gibbon and then Alexander Lynch-Gibbon; her attempted suicide when abandoned by one lover after the other gathers a sexually interconnected group around her hospital bed in Iris Murdoch's *A Severed Head*.

Dr. Ernst (Putzi) Hanfstaengl   Propertied, Harvard-educated friend and early supporter of Adolf Hitler; his patronage provides Hitler access to influential circles in Richard Hughes's *The Fox in the Attic*. He has become too unimportant to be a target worth pursuing when he fortuitously evades Hitler's blood purge in 1934 in *The Wooden Shepherdess*.

Hank   A large, thick American soldier; though he is a tough man, he needs his friends, including Buddy his caretaker, to survive in Percival Christopher Wren's *Beau Geste*.

Hankey   Ship's surgeon on the *Lydia* until his death mid-journey in C. S. Forester's *The Happy Return*.

Edgar Hankins   Literary critic and journalist who is a lover of Irene (Brunskill) Eliot in C. P. Snow's *The New Men*. He covers the trial of Cora Ross and Kitty Pateman for a Sunday newspaper in *The Sleep of Reason*.

Bill Hannacott   A young farming boy; he courts Nancy Reed, who jilts him for Daniel Martin in John Fowles's *Daniel Martin*.

Beatrice (Bee) Hannafey   Unhappily married Protestant wife of St. John Hogan-Hannafey; she carries on an affair with Frankie Hannafey in Sean O'Faolain's *Come Back to Erin*.

Frankie Hannafey   IRA rebel long active in the revolutionary cause; he becomes disillusioned and ultimately takes a safe job with the government as a cow inspector in Sean O'Faolain's *Come Back to Erin*.

Leonard Hannafey   Conscientious but very strict Roman Catholic priest, who emigrates to New York City and is assigned to a parish there in Sean O'Faolain's *Come Back to Erin*.

Michael Hannafey   Bookish, lonely postal worker in Cork, Ireland; unmarried, he is the main support of the family members remaining at home in Sean O'Faolain's *Come Back to Erin*.

Great Aunt Hannah   Deceased forebear of Sir Randolph Nettleby; she painted melancholy oils that Sir Randolph greatly esteems in Isabel Colegate's *The Shooting Party*.

Peter John Hannay   The adored baby son of Mary (Lamington) and Richard Hannay in John Buchan's *The Three Hostages*. As a boy in his teens, he joins his father and Lord Clanroyden in an adventure of "soul-making" during which Peter John applies his extensive knowledge of birds to enable Anna Haraldsen and him to outwit their pursuers in *The Island of Sheep*.

Richard Hannay   Man of action and gentleman amateur sleuth who has had a distinguished career in the British Army and War Office in World War I; having made a fortune in Rhodesia, he returns to London and finds himself drawn into international intrigue by a love of adventure and a strong sense of duty; pursued by the police, the military, and the enemy across upland Scotland, he must solve in twenty-one days a plot to steal British naval plans in John Buchan's *The Thirty-Nine Steps*. He moves across Europe to Asia Minor to thwart Germany's plan to use the prophet "Greenmantle" to unite the Turks for a joint attack against the Allied forces in *Greenmantle*. He assumes the guise of a neutral South African pacifist in order to track and to destroy a diabolical German agent who heads a dangerous army of spies in *Mr. Standfast*. Knighted and living as a country gentleman at Fosse Manor with his wife, Mary (Lamington), and their son, he opposes the forces of destruction and irrationality exerted by the evil genius of the corrupt Dominick Medina in *The Three Hostages*. He narrates the introductory pages of *The Courts of the Morning*. He exerts a beneficent influence restoring order, sanity, and purpose to the island community in *The Island of Sheep*.

General Von Hanneken   The German officer whose forces occupy, pillage, and terrorize the villagers in Central Africa during World War I in C. S. Forester's *The African Queen*.

Mr. Hanover   Congregational minister at Rope Terrace when Sylvia Russell is a young, lonely mother; he reasons with people rather than preaches to them; though attracted to Sylvia, he is circumspect in friendship for her; his beautiful voice when preaching on Jacob persuades Sylvia to call her son Jacob rather than William after his father; years later at Sylvia's request he recommends Jacob for army commission; he encourages her to let Mary Hervey Russell enter university on fellowship at seventeen in Storm Jameson's *Farewell, Night; Welcome, Day.*

Hansel   Small boy who reports to his father that he overheard a conversation between Herr Koch and another shortly before Koch's murder in Graham Greene's *The Third Man and the Fallen Idol.*

Charlotte Garton Hansyke   Joint heir with her brother, Mark Garton, to the Garton shipbuilding business; she is the wife of Richard Hansyke and mother of Mary Garton Hansyke; selfish and irresponsible, unable to face financial reality, she depletes the Garton fortune and spoils the Hansyke family reputation with numbers of male admirers; she deserts her eight-year-old daughter and her husband in Storm Jameson's *The Lovely Ship.*

Mary Garton Hansyke   Daughter born in 1841 to Charlotte Garton Hansyke; after her mother's desertion, eight-year-old Mary becomes the ward of her uncle, Mark Henry Garton; despite her uncle's refusal to accept her business potential, she succeeds in building the Hansyke and Garton family shipbuilding operations into a modern steamship line; at age fifteen, angered at her uncle's refusal to make her a partner in the shipbuilding enterprise, she takes her father's advice and hopes to achieve freedom, money, and power by marrying the elderly Archibald Roxby; when he soon dies, she insists that their son, Richard Roxby, become the principal Roxby heir over the claims of the three surviving Roxby brothers; after deciding not to marry her coworker and lover, John Mempes, she marries Hugh Hervey; he leaves her soon after the birth of their daughters Clare and Sylvia, but she welcomes him back often during the remainder of his life in Storm Jameson's *The Lovely Ship.* The death of Mary Garton Hansyke Roxby Hervey is presented at the close of *A Richer Dust* and at the beginning of *Company Parade.*

Richard Hansyke   The husband of Charlotte Garton Hansyke, the father of Mary Garton Hansyke, and lord of Hansyke Manor; a careless spender, he resents his wife's relationships with other men and her failure to bear a son; he is deserted by his wife and later by his daughter in Storm Jameson's *The Lovely Ship.*

Nurse Hapgood   Care-giver to Eustace after his collapse following his paper-chase; she attempts to foster his sense of self-importance and tries to prevent him from worrying unduly in L. P. Hartley's *The Shrimp and the Anemone.*

Anna Haraldsen   Thirteen-year-old daughter of Valdemar Haraldsen; she shows her bravery and coolness when she rallies over a hundred islanders to join her father and his friends in achieving victory over their foes in John Buchan's *The Island of Sheep.*

Marius Haraldsen   Father of Valdemar; a twenty-year-old plot against him was foiled by Richard Hannay and Mr. Lombard; their pledge to aid his son, should vengeance be sought by the evildoers, is honored in John Buchan's *The Island of Sheep.*

Valdemar Haraldsen (alias James Smith)   Scholar and keen naturalist; threatened, pursued, and reduced to near physical and nervous collapse by Lancelot Troth and Jacques D'Ingraville, he is brought back to renewed health by the Richard Hannays and the Clanroydens; he determines to return home and face his enemies' attack and succeeds in killing D'Ingraville, the evil mastermind of the plot to destroy him, in John Buchan's *The Island of Sheep.*

Nancy, Lady Harben   Wife of Sir Thomas Harben; an elegant, wealthy elderly woman, she gives money to the right-wing publishers who dine with her, attend her parties, and head newspapers that advocate her husband's views in Storm Jameson's *Before the Crossing* and in *The Black Laurel.*

Sir Thomas Harben   Husband of Nancy Harben; he was born in 1864 and in 1920 holds nineteen doctorates, eight chairmanships or board memberships in companies which include the Midland Railway, English Stock Corporation, Lloyd's Bank, a petrol combine, a Canadian timber operation, and shipbuilding and engineering firms; he sees pacifism as a threat to his financial power and collaborates with William Gary in Storm Jameson's *Before the Crossing* and in *The Black Laurel.*

Harbin   Double agent who is the actual "accident" victim buried in Harry Lime's grave in Graham Greene's *The Third Man and the Fallen Idol.*

Claud Fresnay, Lord Harbinger   Wealthy nobleman of thirty-one years who courts Lady Barbara Carádoc in competition with Charles Courtier and marries her at the end in John Galsworthy's *The Patrician.*

Emily Harbour   Inelegant, grim-faced, loud-spoken Kentuckian; she informs Evelyn Orcham that, because of a Rajah's un-Christian harem next door, she and her husband, John L. Harbour, must immediately leave his hotel in Arnold Bennett's *Imperial Palace.*

John L. Harbour   Sixty-year-old American cigarette king; with his stout body, red face, mouth of gold-studded teeth, and firm handshake, he is, nevertheless, afraid of his wife in Arnold Bennett's *Imperial Palace.*

Captain Harcourt   Observant, honest, friendly captain, who chases the French Imperial Guard with Hornblower in C. S. Forester's *Hornblower in the West Indies.*

Mrs. Harcourt   A wealthy woman who takes an interest in Miriam Henderson in Dorothy Richardson's *Oberland.* Miriam reflects on their subsequent meeting in Switzerland, where Mrs. Harcourt offers to finance Miriam for six months of additional training in secretarial skills in *March Moonlight.*

Hardcastle   A regular-army recruit whose behavior after Percy Higgins's death prompts a fight with Mike Brady in David Lodge's *Ginger, You're Barmy.*

Fairy Hardcastle   Head of security at the N.I.C.E. (National Institute for Coordinated Experiments) who takes pleasure in tormenting her prisoners; she almost captured Jane Studdock before Jane found refuge at St. Anne's; she is killed in the destruction of the N.I.C.E. in C. S. Lewis's *That Hideous Strength.*

Sir Frederick Harden   Well-born father of Lucia and inheritor of the title, estate, and famous Harden library; he dissipates the family fortune, surreptitiously sells the library, and dies suddenly in France, leaving Lucia penniless in May Sinclair's *The Divine Fire.*

Lucia Harden   Beautiful, intelligent, and talented daughter of Sir Frederick Harden; she hires Keith Rickman to catalogue her father's library and sets in motion Rickman's moral and intellectual development; in spite of enormous obstacles, she finally marries Rickman in May Sinclair's *The Divine Fire.*

Mellicent (Milly) Hardisty   A plain-looking young woman, Sir Percy's older daughter; she writes better poetry than does Jermyn Haslam; she prefers spinsterhood to marriage to him in Ivy Compton-Burnett's *Men and Wives.*

Sir Percy Hardisty   A quiet man who usually does what his wife, Rachel, tells him to do; he supposedly still cherishes a special love for his first wife in Ivy Compton-Burnett's *Men and Wives.*

Polly Hardisty   Mellicent's younger sister, who attends Harriet Haslam's funeral; she accepts a proposal from Gregory Haslam in Ivy Compton-Burnett's *Men and Wives.*

Rachel, Lady Hardisty   The second wife of Sir Percy; a good friend of Harriet and Sir Godfrey Haslam, she is wise, clever, and kind in Ivy Compton-Burnett's *Men and Wives.*

Cyrus Bethman Hardman   Samuel Edward Ratchett's ineffectual American bodyguard; he was in love with the unfortunate daughter of Pierre Michel in Agatha Christie's *Murder on the Orient Express.*

Hardwick   Principal of the art school where Janos Lavin teaches; he disapproves of Lavin's teaching methods and drops some of his classes in John Berger's *A Painter of Our Time.*

Ben Hardy   A coach driver who ferries men between London and the Basic Training camp in David Lodge's *Ginger, You're Barmy.*

Salcome (Sally) Hardy   The newspaperman who alerts Lord Peter Wimsey to Harriet Vane's discovery of a corpse in Dorothy L. Sayers's *Have His Carcase.*

Captain Sir Thomas Hardy   Baronet and captain of the *Triumph* who is shocked at Hornblower's presence; his wealth and airs contrast with Hornblower's poverty in C. S. Forester's *Flying Colours.*

Charles Hare   A stiff over-prudent clergyman, who is not sympathetic to his parishioners at St. Athelstan's Anglican Church; he uses his daughter, Dorothy, as his assistant and housekeeper in George Orwell's *A Clergyman's Daughter.*

Dorothy Hare   A compulsively penitent, sexually frigid woman; she serves as her clergyman father's parish minister, assistant, and personal housekeeper; she loses her memory one night while making costumes for the church-school master, Victor Stone, and finds herself in London in pauper's rags; she is befriended by some street people and learns to pick hops; having regained her memory, she becomes a schoolteacher in a horrid private school and finally returns to her home to take over ministering to her father's parish and return to housekeeping in George Orwell's *A Clergyman's Daughter.*

Sir Thomas Hare   A "good hearted, chuckle-headed man" who is Dorothy's cousin and who finds her a position with the Ringwood House Academy for Girls in George Orwell's *A Clergyman's Daughter.*

Miss Hargreaves   A middle-aged typing instructor of RAC clerks at Catterick who despairs of Norman in David Lodge's *Ginger, You're Barmy.*

Alf Hargreaves   George's lazy, no-good brother, who helps him beat up his wife in Alan Sillitoe's *Her Victory.*

Bert Hargreaves   George's younger brother, who helps George beat up his wife in Alan Sillitoe's *Her Victory.*

Eric Hargreaves   Dentist whom Maureen Kirby regrets she cannot afford because of her declining economic condition following her boyfriend Len Wincobank's incarceration in Margaret Drabble's *The Ice Age.*

George Hargreaves   Factory owner whose wife leaves him for another life; he and his brothers beat her up to bring her home, but she is saved by her neighbor and lover, Thomas Phillips, in Alan Sillitoe's *Her Victory.*

Harry Hargreaves   George's lazy, no-good brother, who helps him beat up his wife in Alan Sillitoe's *Her Victory.*

Sir John Hargreaves (codename: "C")   Inept British aristocrat appointed intelligence-service director; he blindly agrees to Dr. Percival's accusations and murder of Arthur Davis in Graham Greene's *The Human Factor.*

Pam Hargreaves   Middle-class woman who begins to have a breakdown caused by boredom; she leaves her husband, George, to begin a new timid life; feeling that she has failed, she tries to kill herself by leaving on the gas; she is saved by Thomas Phillips, a roomer in the next flat; they become friends, fall in love, have a child, Rachael, and eventually live in Israel in Alan Sillitoe's *Her Victory.*

Mrs. Harker   Tom Harker's reputedly domineering mother in Isabel Colegate's *The Shooting Party.*

Tom Harker   Suspected poacher who is employed to flush game from the woods for the shooting party; substituting for Dan Glass, he is accidentally and fatally shot by Gilbert, Lord Hartlip in Isabel Colegate's *The Shooting Party.*

Chloe Harlech   Twice-married old acquaintance and potential lover of Ted Stennett; they meet on a flight from Bombay to London in Margaret Drabble's *The Middle Ground.*

Corporal Steve Harmon   Young midwestern army recruit who tells the narrator of Barney Barnes's death; he dies in a trap Dalby sets for the narrator in Len Deighton's *The Ipcress File.*

Edouard Harmost   Music teacher who is a friend and confidant of Gyp Winton Fiersen in John Galsworthy's *Beyond.*

Manou Harouni   Leslie Fowler's former lover in Isabel Colegate's *Statues in a Garden.*

Sir Maurice Harpenden   Father of Napier Harpenden; he was responsible for separating his son years before from the socially declassé Iris March (Storm); at his home Iris makes a last unsuccessful bid for freedom and happiness with Napier in Michael Arlen's *The Green Hat.*

Captain Napier (Naps) Harpenden   Young, shy, and handsome foreign service officer; three days before his marriage to his young lover, Venice Pollen, he involves himself in a brief yet ultimately devastating affair with his childhood sweetheart Iris Storm in Michael Arlen's *The Green Hat.*

Venice Pollen Harpenden   Newspaper heiress and loyal young wife of Napier Harpenden, the young aristocrat who betrays their conventional but childless union for the more passionate love of the doomed Iris Storm in Michael Arlen's *The Green Hat.*

Graham Harper   Furniture designer at Timberwork; he becomes Orlando King's good friend until Graham's political views supporting socialism cause problems; Graham volunteers to go to Spain and fight for his beliefs, and he is killed in battle in Isabel Colegate's *Orlando King.*

Peter Harranson   A fair-haired boy who was interested in Clara Maugham when they met in Paris during her secondary-school trip; she encounters him again when she goes to Paris with Gabriel Denham in Margaret Drabble's *Jerusalem the Golden.*

Harriet   Art teacher and fulfilling ex-lover of writer Giles Hermitage, who tortures himself with her memory when she abruptly leaves him after seven years in John Wain's *The Pardoner's Tale.*

Archduchess Harriet/ Archduke Harry of Roumania   A bestial woman who falls helplessly in love with the male Orlando, who escapes from her to Constantinople; transformed into a woman, Orlando returns, only to be pursued by Harriet, who has similarly undergone a sexual transformation into the obnoxious, even uglier Archduke Harry in Virginia Woolf's *Orlando: A Biography.*

Lieutenant Colonel Harriman (covername: Sergeant Murray)   Sharp-eyed investigator and espionage agent who assists the narrator and Colonel Ross in uncovering Dalby as a double agent, and who arrests Dalby in Len Deighton's *The Ipcress File.*

Frank Harrington   Head of Whitehall's Berlin Field Unit, who is Bernard Samson's surrogate father and Werner Volkmann's antagonist, having framed Werner in a past investigation; he is Zena Volkmann's lover and is suspected of divulging secrets in Len Deighton's *Berlin Game*. He assists Erich Stinnes's defection in *Mexico Set*. He turns field agent to assist Samson and Werner in *London Match*.

John Quincy Harrington Pompous, naïve, verbose, friendly, prejudiced American businessman in Russia; being an "expert" in all subjects, he infuriates and ingratiates Ashenden; a happily married family man, he is determined to do his business no matter what the cost in W. Somerset Maugham's *Ashenden: or The British Agent*.

Susan Harrington Kindly, solid, boring Englishwoman vacationing at the Santa Marina Hotel who cares for her invalid aunt, Mrs. Paley, and becomes engaged to Arthur Venning; the couple represents to Terence Hewet the kind of fossilized love in marriage he detests in Virginia Woolf's *The Voyage Out*.

Harris Lodging mate of Jerome who, with George, makes up the bachelor trio of young Londoners in Jerome K. Jerome's *Three Men in a Boat (To Say Nothing of the Dog)*.

Harris Cable censor and roommate of Wilson, who refuses to make friends with him in Graham Greene's *The Heart of the Matter*.

Harrison British government employee; a co-worker of Stella Rodney and her lover, Robert Kelway, he threatens to expose Kelway's treasonous activities if Stella refuses his sexual advances in Elizabeth Bowen's *The Heat of the Day*.

Harrison Aging boatswain who is showing the signs of his age, though they are ignored in C. S. Forester's *The Happy Return* and in *Ship of the Line*.

Joe Harrison A black American actor who works for Maurice Conchis and makes love to Lily DeSeitas while Nicholas Urfe is forced to watch in John Fowles's *The Magus*.

Mrs. Harrowdean Attention-demanding widowed mistress of Mr. Britling; she expresses hostility towards Edith Britling in H. G. Wells's *Mr. Britling Sees It Through*.

Harry Member of the smuggling gang who warns Francis Andrews not to return to Elizabeth's cottage, since the rest of the gang will be waiting for him in Graham Greene's *The Man Within*.

Harry Alcoholic and angry publisher of Janos Lavin's drawings; he hates the class system and Com-

munist Party edicts about art in John Berger's *A Painter of Our Time*.

Harry Wealthy, middle-aged, married Dublin man who tries to seduce Caithleen Brady; she despises him and rejects his advances in Edna O'Brien's *The Country Girls*.

Harry Man in Henneky's pub; he is a friend of Ida Arnold's in Graham Greene's *Brighton Rock*.

Harry A morose, secretive youth with sadistic fantasies; he plots to rape Bridget at knifepoint but fails and finds a gentler way to meet Jean at a rock-and-roll film at the Palladium in David Lodge's *The Picturegoers*.

Harry Anna Wulf's acquaintance who attempts to persuade her to change her novel, *Frontiers of War*, into a play dramatizing the superior white man trapped in the "mud" of Africa in Doris Lessing's *The Golden Notebook*.

Harry Three-year-old who is brought by his possibly abusive mother to the day-care center where Evelyn Morton Stennett volunteers some of her time in Margaret Drabble's *The Middle Ground*.

Mr. Harry The domineering headmaster of Brinsley Street School, where Ursula Brangwen teaches in D. H. Lawrence's *The Rainbow*.

Sir Harry Rich, elderly squire who seduces and impregnates the young Marion Yaverland, leaves his estate for about a year, and refuses to acknowledge paternity of Richard Yaverland upon his return; he can conceal Richard's paternity because his mother, Lady Teresa, and his business manager, Peacey, cruelly threaten and exert power over Marion in Rebecca West's *The Judge*.

Sir Harry Callow but decent young man running for Parliament who befriends Richard Hannay during his flight across Scotland in John Buchan's *The Thirty-Nine Steps*.

Hart Gangling, young, promising midshipman who has won the acknowledgement of his captain in C. S. Forester's *Ship of the Line*.

Hartbourne Bradley Pearson's former colleague at the tax-inspection office; he becomes Christian Evandale's third husband in Iris Murdoch's *The Black Prince*.

Tom Hartigan Young man who alerts the police to Alexander Bonaparte Cust in Agatha Christie's *The A.B.C. Murders*.

Leo Harting   Part-Jewish West-German (FRG) national patriotically serving the British as temporary Second Secretary in the Bonn Embassy; he disappears shortly after he verifies Klaus Karfeld's wartime atrocities and attempts to assassinate Karfeld to prevent his imposing neo-Nazi ideology on the FRG; sought by British investigator Alan Turner, he is intercepted and murdered by Ludwig Siebkron's police thugs in John le Carré's *A Small Town in Germany*.

Aline, Lady Hartlip   Wife of Gilbert, Lord Hartlip, who is aware of her affair with Charles Farquar in Isabel Colegate's *The Shooting Party*.

Gilbert, Lord Hartlip   Sportsman whose marriage to Aline was motivated by monetary gain; husband and wife are aware of each other's infidelities; he resents competition for his reputation as the finest shot in England in Isabel Colegate's *The Shooting Party*.

Ma Hartly   Mother of Isabel Winterbourne; an army wife, she bears many children all round the Empire in Richard Aldington's *Death of a Hero*.

Pa Hartly   Poor, retired Army man living with small means and supporting numerous children, including Isabel Winterbourne, in Richard Aldington's *Death of a Hero*.

Harvey   One of the captains who examine Hornblower for a lieutenant's commission in C. S. Forester's *Mr. Midshipman Hornblower*.

Admiral Harvey   Admiral who is to bring the *Atropos* news and information in C. S. Forester's *Hornblower and the Atropos*.

Cynthia Harwick   John's sister and a passionate devotee of his republican sympathies in the Irish situation in C. Day Lewis's *Child of Misfortune*.

John Harwick   Dorothea Green's second husband; a dogmatic, patronizing judge, he reinforces her reasoned approach to the external world; although a friend of his dead predecessor, he is impatient with the foibles of romancing that Arthur Green inherited from his father in C. Day Lewis's *Child of Misfortune*.

Diane Harwood   Victim of an attack by Molly Murray during a tantrum, as reported in a letter from Judy Channing to Molly's mother, Alison Murray, in Margaret Drabble's *The Ice Age*.

Hasele   Yuli's rescuer in the wilderness who arranges for him to go to Pannoval in Brian W. Aldiss's *Helliconia Spring*.

Sir Godfrey Haslam   A man with a nervous wife; he enjoys spending his wife's money on his children and his friends when she is hospitalized; he almost proposes to Camilla Bellamy after his wife, Harriet, dies in Ivy Compton-Burnett's *Men and Wives*.

Gregory Haslam   The younger son of Sir Godfrey and Harriet; of the children, he gets along best with his mother, but he also spends time with Agatha Calkin and his other "old ladies"; he finally is engaged to Polly Hardisty in Ivy Compton-Burnett's *Men and Wives*.

Griselda Haslam   The daughter of Sir Godfrey and Harriet; she becomes engaged to the rector Edward Bellamy and later to Dr. Anthony Dufferin in Ivy Compton-Burnett's *Men and Wives*.

Harriet, Lady Haslam   A high-minded woman who makes her family unhappy with her demands on them; she attempts suicide with a placebo and then has a nervous breakdown; she is given a fatal tablet by her son Matthew in Ivy Compton-Burnett's *Men and Wives*.

Jermyn Haslam   The second son of Sir Godfrey and Harriet; he wants to write poetry but has less talent than Mellicent Hardisty, the girl he unsuccessfully proposes to in Ivy Compton-Burnett's *Men and Wives*.

Matthew Haslam   The elder son of Sir Godfrey and Harriet; his mother disapproves of his aspirations both to do scientific research and to marry Camilla Bellamy; he gives his mother a fatal tablet in Ivy Compton-Burnett's *Men and Wives*.

Willie Haslip   Bart's friend who is interested in Ellie's sister Angie in Mary Lavin's *Mary O'Grady*.

Dr. Joseph Hasselbacher (codename: Captain Müller)   Aging informant and kindly German doctor living in Havana; he breaks his friend James Wormold's coding ruse and warns Wormold of an assassination plot but is murdered by unidentified enemy agents in Graham Greene's *Our Man in Havana*.

Pata Hassim   Nephew of one of the chiefs of Wajo; he saves Lingard's life and then is aided by Lingard in his unsuccessful attempt to claim the rule of Wajo, but he is destroyed with the explosion of the *Emma* in Joseph Conrad's *The Rescue: A Romance of the Shallows*.

Captain Arthur Hastings   A dim-witted, romantically susceptible army officer; during a period of convalescence in 1916, he encounters Hercule Poirot at Styles Court and narrates the investigation there in Agatha Christie's *The Mysterious Affair at Styles: A Detective Story*. He falls in love with and marries Dulcie Duveen in *The*

Murder on the Links. He returns often from his ranch in Argentina to assist Poirot and acts as his chronicler in five other novels before returning with him to Styles Court in *Curtain: Hercule Poirot's Last Case.*

Judith Hastings   Arthur Hastings's favorite daughter; she is Dr. John Franklin's research assistant and becomes his wife after he is widowed in Agatha Christie's *Curtain: Hercule Poirot's Last Case.*

Mrs. Hatch   One of Kate Brown's neighbors; upon Kate's returning to her neighborhood, Mrs. Hatch does not recognize her, thinking she is simply a strange woman walking the street in Doris Lessing's *The Summer Before the Dark.*

Mr. Hattersly   Colleague of Billy Fisher; he is expected to become the new Director of Information and Publicity for the Shepford District Council at the end of Keith Waterhouse's *Billy Liar on the Moon.*

Emma Hatton   The head nursemaid to the Sullivan children; she is beloved by Neville Sullivan and the other young children in Ivy Compton-Burnett's *Parents and Children.*

Hatty   Friend of Aunt Augusta Bertram from their younger days; formerly employed in a circus, Hatty reads tea leaves for a living and tells Henry Pulling what she sees in his future in Graham Greene's *Travels with My Aunt.*

George Haunslow   A sincere socialist in Mashopi treated with contempt by Willi Rodde because of his emotional and unstable nature as well as his inability to treat his black mistress and illegitimate child with detached coldness in Doris Lessing's *The Golden Notebook.*

Madame Hautchamp   Edouard's wife, who tells Marya Zelli that Stephan has been arrested in Jean Rhys's *Postures.*

Edouard Hautchamp   Owner of Hotel de l'Univers where Stephan and Marya Zelli reside until Stephan's arrest and subsequent jailing for theft in Jean Rhys's *Postures.*

Norah Hauxley   Intelligent, attractive reporter and widow; she attracts men but falls for Joe Lampton and tries to make him happy in John Braine's *Life at the Top.*

Brigadier Havelock   Inspector William Rigby's superior, who obstructs George Smiley's investigation into the murder of Stella Rode in John le Carré's *A Murder of Quality.*

Mr. Hawes   Embezzling curate at St. Mary Mead in Agatha Christie's *The Murder at the Vicarage.*

Nancy Hawkins   The narrator, who recalls her days as an overweight, capable young war widow making her way in a post-war publishing world populated by frauds like Hector Bartlett, who tries to destroy her because she terms him a "pisseur de copie"; as she gradually loses weight, she transforms herself from the motherly, advice-dispensing "Mrs. Hawkins" to the elegant and attractive "Nancy" in Muriel Spark's *A Far Cry from Kensington.*

Tom Hawkins   World War II casualty whose young widow narrates Muriel Spark's *A Far Cry from Kensington.*

Richard Hawk-Monitor   The tall, thoroughly normal young man whom Elfine Starkadder loves; he is interested only in such time-honored pursuits of an old established country family as riding to hounds in Stella Gibbons's *Cold Comfort Farm.*

Nicholas Hawkshaw   Uncle of Katrine Yester and wealthy Laird of Calidon, where Katrine and David Sempill meet in John Buchan's *Witch Wood.*

Haworth   Schoolboy at Seaforth House in Roy Fuller's *The Ruined Boys.*

Celia Hawthorne   Divorced mother of one; she is the lover of Paul Mason and is jealous of Susan Thirkill in C. P. Snow's *A Coat of Varnish.*

Henry Hawthorne (code identification: 59200)   Mysterious, bumbling Secret Service agent; he recruits the financially strapped, untested James Wormold in the men's washroom of Sloppy Joe's bar in Graham Greene's *Our Man in Havana.*

Emma Hay   Joyfully self-important playwright whose old acquaintance with the Provincial Lady is renewed at a writers' conference in Brussels in E. M. Delafield's *The Provincial Lady Goes Further.*

William (Bill Straw) Hay   Coalminer's son, ex-convict, and underworld character who introduces Michael Cullen to and partners him in smuggling in Alan Sillitoe's *A Start in Life.*

Mildred Haycock   The twice-widowed, well-to-do, handsome, fast, younger (by twenty years) sister of Bertha Conyers; she breaks her engagement to Kenneth Widmerpool because of his impotence in Anthony Powell's *At Lady Molly's.*

Dr. Haydock   Police surgeon at St. Mary Mead; he

appears in Agatha Christie's *Murder at the Vicarage,* in *Sleeping Murder,* and in two other novels.

Bill Haydon (codename "Tailor"; covername: Gerald) Elitist career British Intelligence officer, Commander of the London Station, and long-term Soviet double agent; he sacrifices his recruit and probable lover Jim Prideaux in Operation Testify to eliminate Control and sleeps with his cousin, Lady Ann Smiley, to discredit her husband, George, in John le Carré's *Tinker, Tailor, Soldier, Spy.*

Haydon-Smith Tory Cabinet Minister who accompanies Meinertzhagen to pressure Swaffield to withdraw support for Jenny Rastall's legal challenge in C. P. Snow's *In Their Wisdom.*

Emily Haye Stepmother of John Haye; her difficult relationship with her stepson undergoes a major change after his accidental blinding in Henry Green's *Blindness.*

John Haye Artistically inclined public-school student who is blinded by a freak accident while returning home on a train, has a short but important romantic friendship with Joan Entwhistle, and then moves with his stepmother Emily to London, where he first has a nervous collapse; he then recovers and hopes to become a writer in Henry Green's *Blindness.*

Ben Hayes A walk-on with his father Sam in Nick Ollanton's act; he keeps the magician's complicated gear in trim in J. B. Priestley's *Lost Empires.*

Sam Hayes Father of Ben; together they work as walk-ons and mechanics for Nick Ollanton's magic act in J. B. Priestley's *Lost Empires.*

Hayford Husband of Serena (Daintry) Gardner after she leaves Paul Gardner in Isabel Colegate's *Agatha.*

Susan Forsyte Haymon One of the four Forsyte sisters of Old Jolyon's generation; the stipulation in her will that her body be cremated causes family consternation when she dies in 1895 in John Galsworthy's *The Man of Property* and in *In Chancery.*

Sir Arthur Hayward Affectionate though undemonstrative father of Charles Hayward; he is an Assistant Commissioner of Scotland Yard in Agatha Christie's *Crooked House.*

Charles Hayward Sensible young man, formerly employed in the Diplomatic Service; he is in love with Sophia Leonides in Agatha Christie's *Crooked House.*

Podge Hayward Rude, impolite young man who annoys Olivia Curtis by telling her she is naïve and unsophisticated as he dances with her in Rosamond Lehmann's *Invitation to the Waltz.* When Rollo Spencer and Olivia are secretly spending a night in a hotel, Podge sees Rollo in the lobby in *The Weather in the Streets.*

Haywood The weak, pretentious young gentleman whose only merit is his genuine sensitivity to literature; he meets Philip Carey in Heidelberg, Paris, and London in W. Somerset Maugham's *Of Human Bondage.*

Hazel Rabbit pioneer and statesman; impelled by Fiver's visions, Hazel leads a group of buck rabbits from the doomed Sandleford warren and is gradually established as their Chief Rabbit; seeking doe rabbits at the police-state Warren of Efrafa, he becomes embroiled in war but prevails through skilled leadership, courage, and supernatural aid; at his death Hazel is taken into the Owsla (rabbit-warren militia) of the mythological Elahrairah in Richard Adams's *Watership Down.*

Lucy Hazell Beautiful, rich widow approaching middle age who practices prostitution for entertainment; she befriends Catherine Casement and James Churchill in Kingsley Amis's *The Anti-Death League.*

Dr. Headley A brawny, red-headed, sensually aggressive physician at the Islington Maternity Hospital, where Alvina Houghton studies to become a nurse in D. H. Lawrence's *The Lost Girl.*

Headmaster The wise old academician who recognizes that Sammy Mountjoy is intelligent and talented but also unscrupulous and selfish; he offers him the best advice he can in William Golding's *Free Fall.*

Bishop Thomas Heard Ecclesiastic who travels from Bampopo, Africa, to Nepenthe; he sometimes falters in discerning others' true natures and undergoes a change of character (which may be attributed to the island's siroccos) in which he comes to accept behavior he formerly would have condemned in Norman Douglas's *South Wind.*

Ronny Heaslop Mrs. Moore's conventional and arrogantly British son, who is city magistrate in Chandrapore, India; his engagement to Adela Quested brings her to India in E. M. Forster's *A Passage to India.*

Chief Inspector Heat Callous police official who enmeshes double-agent Adolf Verloc in a counter-espionage plot in Joseph Conrad's *The Secret Agent: A Simple Tale.*

George (Gordy) Heatherley   Guardian of Cicely and Mark Lennon; he consents to invite the Stormers to visit in John Galsworthy's *The Dark Flower*.

Mr. Heaton   The Cambridge-educated, shy, young Congregational clergyman who often visits Mrs. Morel for tea; he feels discomfited in the company of colliers such as Mr. Morel in D. H. Lawrence's *Sons and Lovers*.

Priscilla Heaven   Childhood friend of Harriet Frean; she marries Robert Lethbridge; her hysterical paralysis becomes the successful means of destroying the love her husband and Harriet Frean have for each other in May Sinclair's *Life and Death of Harriet Frean*.

Sir Ernest Heavyweather   Bullying, smug barrister employed in the defense of John Cavendish in Agatha Christie's *The Mysterious Affair of Styles: A Detective Story*.

Hebe   Lady Barbara Wellesey's Negro servant, who has a reputation for promiscuity in C. S. Forester's *The Happy Return*.

Hebridean cripple   Mute and limbless genius who loathes humanity and tries to destroy John Wainwright's mind by capturing it with his own in Olaf Stapledon's *Odd John: A Story Between Jest and Earnest*.

Mrs. Heccomb   Anna Quayne's former governess, the widowed stepmother of Daphne and Dickie Heccomb; Portia Quayne is sent to stay with her while Anna and Thomas Quayne holiday in Capri in Elizabeth Bowen's *The Death of the Heart*.

Daphne Heccomb   Loud, bad-mannered, flirtatious young woman; she is Mrs. Heccomb's stepdaughter and Portia Quayne's rival for Eddie's affections in Elizabeth Bowen's *The Death of the Heart*.

Dickie Heccomb   Uncouth, belligerent young man of twenty three; he is Mrs. Heccomb's stepson in Elizabeth Bowen's *The Death of the Heart*.

Charles Hecht   Easily goaded master teacher at Carne School; he falls prey to his wife Shane's and Terence Fielding's maliciously aimed jibes in John le Carré's *A Murder of Quality*.

Shane Hecht   Charles Hecht's spouse, who maliciously derides George Smiley for marrying above his station in John le Carré's *A Murder of Quality*.

Dr. Heddle   Country doctor; his chance meeting with Lord Raingo on a village walk draws him into attendance on Raingo through his decline and death from pneumonia in Arnold Bennett's *Lord Raingo*.

Simon Hegarty   Bailiff and rent collector for Jocelyn Chadwick and collector of his own annual fee from the farmers for protection in Liam O'Flaherty's *Famine*.

Miss Hei   Phuong's mercenary sister; she tries to broker Phuong and other women to the highest European male bidders in Graham Greene's *The Quiet American*.

Hugh Heidler   A tall, fair, fortyish Englishman, who is fresh and sturdy with an underlying sense of brutality; with his wife, Lois, he takes Marya Zelli into his home and seduces her, keeps her, and then abandons her in Jean Rhys's *Postures*.

Lois Heidler   Plump, dark woman who is younger than her husband, Hugh; she winces when he speaks to her and passively accepts his seduction of Marya Zelli in Jean Rhys's *Postures*.

Herr Heinrich   German tutor of the minor Britling sons; his sentimentality is expressed through his fondness for a squirrel, and his polite inquisitiveness first annoys and later impresses Mr. Britling; he asks Mr. Britling to send his violin to his parents before he is killed in the war in H. G. Wells's *Mr. Britling Sees It Through*.

Father Heironymous   Aged priest on Plakos; his people have left the church to follow pagan rituals that threaten Koré Arabin in John Buchan's *The Dancing Floor*.

Helen   Pete's attractive wife and Christopher Martin's mistress in William Golding's *Pincher Martin*.

Helen   A wealthy, bored woman with whom Colin Pasmore has an affair; her husband first tries to buy Colin off and then beats him up to get rid of him in David Storey's *Pasmore*.

Helen   Young, attractive, dutiful second wife of Dan Graveson's father; Dan responds to her with both indifference and resentment in Alan Burns's *Buster*.

Helen (alias Lady Helen de Waldebere)   Shamus's abused wife and Aldo Cassidy's ambivalent lover; she agrees to leave Shamus for Cassidy but, after a bizarre, sadistic confrontation with both men, disappears with Shamus, leaving Cassidy emotionally paralyzed in John le Carré's *The Naive and Sentimental Lover*.

Helena   A native English girl who marries the Roman career officer Constantius Chlorus and becomes the mother of the future Emperor Constantine; after her husband divorces her for a more politically advantageous marriage, she converts to Christianity and as the Empress Dowager seeks to find the cross on which

Christ was crucified, ultimately succeeding in her objective in Evelyn Waugh's *Helena*.

Helen Wills   Cat so named for its playful interest in a tennis ball; the difficulty of keeping its acquisition unknown to Robert is enhanced by its frequent production of kittens in E. M. Delafield's *The Diary of a Provincial Lady*.

Hemmings   Secretary for the New Collier Company who believes that Old Jolyon Forsyte, the Chairman of the Board, is getting too old in John Galsworthy's *The Man of Property*.

Gerald Hemmingway   Young actor who, posing as Stephens the window cleaner, gives testimony to entrap Dr. Roberts in Agatha Christie's *Cards on the Table*.

Henderson   London journalist who covers the Martian landing at Horsell Common; he dies when his parlaying deputation is slaughtered in H. G. Wells's *The War of the Worlds*.

General Henderson   The kindly, brave, and honest father of the Henderson family who nevertheless has the narrowness of his caste and calling in W. Somerset Maugham's *The Hour Before the Dawn*.

Mr. Henderson   Miriam's beloved Pater, with whose superior taste, cultural sophistication, and dislike of (if not contempt for) women she identifies in Dorothy Richardson's *Pointed Roofs*. His fortunes decline and his arrogance increases in *Backwater*. He is finally declared a bankrupt; Miriam's sympathies lie more and more with her mother in *Honeycomb*.

Mrs. Henderson   Miriam's mother, a shadowy figure alluded to affectionately but not visibly present in Dorothy Richardson's *Pointed Roofs*. She accompanies Miriam, who is clearly accustomed to lead her mother rather than be led by her, to north London for her job interview at the school; she falls ill and has surgery, from which she seems to recover in *Backwater*. She suffers from severe depression and is sent to the seaside with Miriam in the hope that she will rally there; convinced of her utter worthlessness, she kills herself during Miriam's brief absence one afternoon in *Honeycomb*.

Mrs. Henderson   The tall, handsome matriarch of the Henderson family whose dignity and breeding help her to bear the death of her sons in W. Somerset Maugham's *The Hour Before the Dawn*.

Barnabas Henderson   Blue-robed, long-ringletted, elaborately moustached disciple of Scorpio Murtlock, whose cult he partly supports; he eventually leaves Murtlock to operate a picture gallery, where the paintings of Bosworth Deacon are successfully exhibited in Anthony Powell's *Hearing Secret Harmonies*.

Dolly Henderson   Sue Brown's late mother, a much-adored music-hall singer in P. G. Wodehouse's *Fish Preferred* and in two other novels.

Ellie Henderson   Poor spinster cousin of Clarissa Dalloway; invited at the last minute to Clarissa's party this year, she is left alone among the guests and in life, yearning, observing, alienated, sad, in her cheap, pink flowers and shabby, old black dress in Virginia Woolf's *Mrs. Dalloway*.

Eve Henderson   Delicate, unadventurous older sister of Miriam in Dorothy Richardson's *Pointed Roofs* and in *Backwater*. She is Miriam's confidante and correspondent in *Honeycomb*. She works as governess for the wealthy Green family and shows signs of nervous tension and depression in *The Tunnel*. She moves to London to work as an assistant in a flower shop and take a course in floral decorations, but in the end returns to the Green family in *Interim*. She opens a specialty shop in the same seaside town where her youngest sister Harriett and her husband Gerald Ducayne are running a boarding house in *Deadlock*. She dies unexpectedly in *The Trap*.

Evelyn Henderson   One of the young socialites whose holiday is delayed by heavy fog in Henry Green's *Party Going*.

Harriett Henderson   Lively, irreverent younger sister and companion of Miriam Henderson in Dorothy Richardson's *Pointed Roofs* and in *Backwater*. She marries the wealthy Gerald Ducayne in *Honeycomb*. She and her husband are still affluent in *The Tunnel*. They suffer financial reverses and take to operating a boarding house in a seaside town; eventually they leave England in *Deadlock*.

Jamie Henderson   Imogene King's escort when she comes to Italy to visit her father, Orlando King, in Isabel Colegate's *Orlando at the Brazen Threshold*.

Jim Henderson   The tall, good-looking, idealistic twenty-one-year-old son of General Henderson; Jim's moral ideology causes him to become a conscientious objector when World War II breaks out but does not protect him from the machinations of Dora Friedberg, whom he marries and murders in W. Somerset Maugham's *The Hour Before the Dawn*.

John Henderson   One of the four Oxford chums; an evangelical parson's son, he has become a chemist and a puritanical socialist; he betrays his passion for the movement in order to maintain his job, which was obtained through the influence of his good friend's landed father, Sir Charles Neale; he marries Neale's daughter and becomes a typical family man while his spirit yearns to join the battle against the Spanish fascists in C. Day Lewis's *Starting Point.*

May Henderson   Honest, well-bred, and unhappily married wife of the enigmatic Roger; she falls deeply in love with Dick Murray but is forced to stay married because of the traumatic outbreak of World War II in W. Somerset Maugham's *The Hour Before the Dawn.*

Miriam Henderson   An inexperienced seventeen-year-old girl when, in the face of her father's financial difficulties, she decides she must earn her own living; without consulting anyone, she arranges to go to Hanover as a pupil-teacher in Dorothy Richardson's *Pointed Roofs.* Returned from Germany, virtually dismissed by Fraulein Pfaff, she takes a teaching position paying £20 a year at a private school for local girls in drab north London, where the pupils have distressingly limited futures, in *Backwater.* Finding the moral and physical strain too great, she leaves the school and takes a position as governess in the luxurious country home of the Corries, where she learns first-hand what upper-middle-class life is like in *Honeycomb.* The breakup of the Henderson family following her mother's suicide results in Miriam's move to London, where she works as a dental assistant and receptionist in the surgery on Wimpole Street and lives in an attic room on Tansley Street on the fringe of Bloomsbury in *The Tunnel.* Her personal relationships deepen and grow more complex in *Interim* and in *Deadlock.* Her political interests expand to include Socialism and anarchists in *Revolving Lights.* At twenty-eight she leaves the rooming house to share rooms with another woman in *The Trap.* She takes a much-needed holiday in the Burnese Alps in *Oberland.* Back in London and Tansley Street, she decides to give in to Hypo Wilson's pressures and accept him as a lover, but this relationship fails, too, in part because she has become emotionally involved with a young French girl named Amabel in *Dawn's Left Hand.* She feels herself too entangled in complex and emotionally draining relationships (with Wilson, Michael Shatov, and Amabel) and decides to cut loose, leave London, and attempt to write, as several people have been suggesting she do, in *Clear Horizon.* On the verge of a serious illness (physical and psychological), she has left the dental surgery and gone to live in Sussex among Quakers, whose beliefs and personalities strongly appeal to her; she hopes to write a new kind of prose fiction from the woman's point of view, but her first attempts do not satisfy her in *Dimple Hill.* She goes to Switzerland again, this time to Vaud, and here begins to write prose sketches for the *Friday Review;* she feels encour-

aged to try once more to find a way to express what to *her* was reality in *March Moonlight.*

Richard ("Dikko") Henderson   Hard-drinking friend and ally of James Bond; he gives Bond information about Japanese customs in Ian Fleming's *You Only Live Twice.*

Roger Henderson   The oldest son of General Henderson and the husband of May; he fails to inspirit his personality and his marriage with the warmth that he patriotically brings to his country in W. Somerset Maugham's *The Hour Before the Dawn.*

Roger Henderson   A wealthy Tory barrister from a good family; one of Rosamund Stacey's boyfriends, he has a crude, sometimes appealing charm in Margaret Drabble's *The Millstone.*

Sarah Henderson   Miriam Henderson's eldest sister, who plays a maternal role in Dorothy Richardson's *Pointed Roofs* and in *Backwater.* She marries Bennett Brodie in *Honeycomb.* She has a serious ailment requiring surgery, for which Miriam seeks help from her friend Dr. Densley in *Clear Horizon.* She looks after Miriam, who returns from Switzerland with the flu in *March Moonlight.*

Tommy Henderson   Innocent youngest son of General Henderson; his life is ended near the Hendersons' country home in an enemy attack on a hidden airfield made known to the Germans by Dora Friedberg in W. Somerset Maugham's *The Hour Before the Dawn.*

Henery   A handsome coast guard, with whom Evelyn Crane plays at Devonshire beach; she says that "his only subject of conversation is bait fish" in C. Day Lewis's *The Friendly Tree.*

Teddy Henfrey   Iping clock jobber who first voices suspicions about Griffin, believing him to be a fugitive from justice in H. G. Wells's *The Invisible Man: A Grotesque Romance.*

Mr. Heng   Asian importer, saboteur, and leader of the Vietnamese underground; he shows Thomas Fowler the moulds for plastic explosives Alden Pyle helped smuggle into Vietnam and, with Fowler's complicity, has Pyle murdered in Graham Greene's *The Quiet American.*

Henley   Homosexual fashion designer; he marries Suzette, who is many years his junior, in Colin MacInnes's *Absolute Beginners.*

Mrs. Henneker   Mother-in-law of Tom Wyndham;

she embarrasses Lewis Eliot with her requests for his help in publishing a biography of her husband in C. P. Snow's *Corridors of Power.*

Mrs. Henniker   Proprietress of "The Blue Danube," a bizarre brothel; she becomes the secretary of Iolanthe Samiou in Lawrence Durrell's *Tunc.*

Lisl (Tante Lisl) Henning   German matron whose hotel is Bernard Samson, Werner Volkmann, and Frank Harrington's hideout in Len Deighton's *Berlin Game,* in *Mexico Set,* and in *London Match.*

Henriques   Portuguese villain and murderer; he joins John Laputa in planning the uprising in order to steal the treasure of Prester John, shoots Laputa, and then is strangled by him in John Buchan's *Prester John.*

Henriques   Jewish solicitor who is introduced by Charles March to Lewis Eliot and in 1929 brings Eliot his first important law brief in C. P. Snow's *Time of Hope.*

Henry   The barber at Badmore who supplies condoms to Jonathan Browne during his last haircut before leaving the army in David Lodge's *Ginger, You're Barmy.*

King Henry (Tudor) VII   Monarch whose supporters rewrote history, attributing his crimes to his predecessor, King Richard III, according to Alan Grant's twentieth-century analysis in Josephine Tey's *The Daughter of Time.*

Henschell   A founder of Shangri-La; he was killed before Hugh "Glory" Conway arrived at Shangri-la in James Hilton's *Lost Horizon.*

Ellen Henshaw   Garrulous old woman who in her youth was a famous courtesan and later a proprietor of a chain of brothels; daughter of a poor musician, she is uneducated and given to frank and sometimes shocking but colorful reminiscences in Anthony Burgess's *The Pianoplayers.*

William (Billy) Henshaw   Father of Ellen; he is an unsuccessful piano player in pubs and movie houses; an affectionate but negligent father, he loves drink and women; he dies of heart failure in the fifteenth day of a piano-playing marathon in Anthony Burgess's *The Pianoplayers.*

Geraldine Hope Henson (Hennie)   Intelligent, thirty-three-year-old social scientist and criminologist; the second witness chosen by Frits Krom to substantiate the evidence against Paul Firman, she has been asked

by the CIA to record the interviews in Eric Ambler's *Send No More Roses.*

Captain Alexander Hepburn   A captain in the Scottish army, stationed in Germany; he loves the doll-maker Hannele zu Rassentlow but when she makes a too life-like doll of him, he comes to believe that he must have reverence and obedience from her in D. H. Lawrence's *The Captain's Doll.*

Evangeline Hepburn   Wife of Captain Hepburn; she travels to Germany to stop her husband from continuing in an affair with the doll-maker, Hannele zu Rassentlow, but she falls from her hotel room window to her death in D. H. Lawrence's *The Captain's Doll.*

Dr. Hepplewhite   Bulky referee of the duel between Hornblower and Simpson; though he is businesslike, he enjoys the activity in C. S. Forester's *Mr. Midshipman Hornblower.*

Cecil Hepworth   Real-estate developer whose friendship is cultivated by the ambitious mortgage manager of the Saddleford Building Society in Roy Fuller's *Image of a Society.*

Charles Herbert   Emotionally frustrated, physically and spiritually ailing father of Ianthe; Sibyl Jardine's first husband, he perversely keeps his daughter with him after Sibyl leaves him; he seeks consolation in religion in Rosamond Lehmann's *The Ballad and the Source.*

Ianthe Herbert   Morbid, self-absorbed daughter of Sibyl Anstey Herbert Jardine and her first husband, Charles Herbert; though Ianthe is intelligent and well educated, her abnormal childhood leads to insanity later in life in Rosamond Lehmann's *The Ballad and the Source.*

Sir Reuben Hergesheimer   A Jewish immigrant who is a businessman and a sportsman often invited to Sir Randolph Nettleby's estate to shoot in Isabel Colegate's *The Shooting Party.*

Angus Heriot   The witty and principled only son of Eliza and Sir Robert; he is heir to the family estate in Ivy Compton-Burnett's *The Last and the First.*

Eliza, Lady Heriot   The autocratic second wife of Sir Robert; she conceals Osbert Grimstone's proposal to Hermia, her stepdaughter, in Ivy Compton-Burnett's *The Last and the First.*

Hermia Heriot   The thirty-four-year-old eldest of Sir Robert's daughters; she requests money to buy a partnership in a school and inherits a fortune from Hamilton Grimstone, gives it to her family, and marries Osbert Grimstone in Ivy Compton-Burnett's *The Last and the First.*

Madeline Heriot   Sir Robert's second daughter, the younger stepdaughter of Eliza in Ivy Compton-Burnett's *The Last and the First.*

Sir Robert Heriot   An impressive old man, who loves his wife Eliza and her children but also his older daughters, despite Eliza's jealousy in Ivy Compton-Burnett's *The Last and the First.*

Roberta Heriot   The daughter and second child of Eliza and Sir Robert; she begins the pencil-and-paper games that lead to the discovery of Osbert Grimstone's proposal to her half sister Hermia in Ivy Compton-Burnett's *The Last and the First.*

Tony Heriot   A sophisticated young man from a neighboring family; polite and suave, he invites Kate Curtis to his family's hunt ball in Rosamond Lehmann's *Invitation to the Waltz.*

John Heritage   "Poet" in the Browning mode who meets Dickson McCunn at the Black Bull Inn; he risks his life to rescue Sakskia, loving but losing the beautiful Russian princess in John Buchan's *Huntingtower.*

Aunt Hermione   Dulcie Mainwaring's efficient, even bossy, churchgoing relation who keeps house for her brother, with the dubious assistance of Mrs. Sedge, in Barbara Pym's *No Fond Return of Love.*

Giles Hermitage   Successful but painfully lonely middle-aged novelist who constructs both happy and pathetic versions of a story about fictional counterpart Gus Howkins based on his own recent experiences with his lost lover Harriet, the dying Helen Chichester-Redfern, and his uncertain new relationship with Helen's daughter, Dinah, in John Wain's *The Pardoner's Tale.*

General Manuel Hernandez   Loyal, stubborn lieutenant general of El Supremo (Don Julian de Alvarada y Moctezuma) in C. S. Forester's *The Happy Return.*

Richard (Dick) Herncastle   Narrator, whose loss of innocence parallels a world's loss of innocence on the eve of World War I; as assistant on the variety stage to his magician uncle, Nick Ollanton, he learns to differentiate between illusion and reality both off stage and on; he leaves the music halls to join the army, becoming later a successful watercolorist in J. B. Priestley's *Lost Empires.*

Hernisarath   A friend of the Shokerandit family; he helps Luterin Shokerandit on his journey back to Karnahbar in Brian W. Aldiss's *Helliconia Winter.*

Kate Hernon   Old, wise woman of the valley who performs black magic and pagan rituals to protect the peasant farmers from evil in Liam O'Flaherty's *Famine.*

Kitty Hernon   Wife of Patch Hernon; evicted from her land, she sends several of her children to America to escape the impoverished conditions in Liam O'Flaherty's *Famine.*

Patch Hernon   Tenant farmer and neighbor of the Kilmartins; his crops are ruined by the blight and he eventually goes crazy in Liam O'Flaherty's *Famine.*

Herod Agrippa   Opportunistic, artful Jewish friend of Claudius; confirmed by Claudius as King of the Jews, he comes to believe himself the prophesied Messiah; he dies shortly before his plot to overthrow Roman rule is to be carried out in Robert Graves's *Claudius, the God and His Wife Messalina.*

Vincent Heron   Bird-faced rival at Belvedere School who mocks Stephen Dedalus's admiration for Lord Byron and his affections for Emma C. in James Joyce's *A Portrait of the Artist as a Young Man.*

Father Herrera   Young priest assigned to take over for Father Quixote during his vacation; Father Herrera has previously served as secretary to the local bishop in Graham Greene's *Monsignor Quixote.*

Emily Herrick   The twenty-years-younger half sister of Nicholas Herrick; she is an intelligent woman who pretends not to recognize her brother's deceit about the manuscript in Ivy Compton-Burnett's *Pastors and Masters.*

Nicholas Herrick   An impressive old man who is the owner of a school; he pretends to have written a manuscript he finds in old Crabbe's room in Ivy Compton-Burnett's *Pastors and Masters.*

Mrs. Herriton   Lilia Herriton's overbearing mother-in-law, who goes to great lengths to keep her daughter-in-law from embarrassing the family in E. M. Forster's *Where Angels Fear to Tread.*

Charles Herriton   Lilia Herriton's deceased husband in E. M. Forster's *Where Angels Fear to Tread.*

Harriet Herriton   Lilia Herriton's excitable, ill-judging sister-in-law; she kidnaps Lilia's baby from Gino Carella with immediately tragic consequences in E. M. Forster's *Where Angels Fear to Tread.*

Irma Herriton   The inquisitive daughter of Lilia and the late Charles Herriton in E. M. Forster's *Where Angels Fear to Tread.*

Lilia Herriton   Mrs. Herriton's flighty widowed daughter-in-law who travels to Italy, where she falls in love with and marries an unsuitable Italian, much to the dismay of her relations, and dies in childbirth in E. M. Forster's *Where Angels Fear to Tread.*

Philip Herriton   Romantic young lawyer who lets his sister and mother run his life; he goes to Italy to try to bring Lilia (Herriton) Carella's baby back to England in E. M. Forster's *Where Angels Fear to Tread.*

Julius P. Hersheimmer   Young American millionaire who seeks his cousin Jane Finn in Agatha Christie's *The Secret Adversary.*

Dr. Hervey   Physician who treats Sophia Willoughby's children; he writes to summon Frederick Willoughby home when his children are ill in Sylvia Townsend Warner's *Summer Will Show.*

Mrs. Hervey   Young doctor's wife who intercepts her husband's letter to Frederick Willoughby and delivers it to Sophia Willoughby in Sylvia Townsend Warner's *Summer Will Show.*

Hugh Hervey   Second husband of Mary Hansyke Roxby Hervey and father of Clara Hervey Roxby and Sylvia Hervey Russell; he deserts his family early in marriage, but frequently returns in Storm Jameson's *The Lovely Ship.* He avoids all strong emotion and refuses to look into the hearts of his children; at fifty-four he is astonished that, despite her alienation from her mother, Sylvia names her firstborn after her mother in *Farewell, Night; Welcome, Day.*

Richard Hervey   Son born in 1915 to Mary Hervey Russell during her marriage to Lieutenant Thomas Penn Vane; he is placed at age three in care of a woman in Yorkshire so his mother can work in London while his father is still in the air force after World War I in Storm Jameson's *Company Parade* and in *The Journal of Mary Hervey Russell.* Eight-year-old Richard and his mother, following the death of her grandmother, go to live with her lover/cousin, the younger Nicholas Roxby, in *Love in Winter.*

Harry Hesketh   Wealthy Devonshire husband of Five Towns girl Alicia Orgreave; in his enviably gracious home the visiting Hilda Lessways Clayhanger experiences the trauma consequent on her visit to Dartmoor prison, where her bigamous former husband is imprisoned in Arnold Bennett's *These Twain.*

Anton Hesse   A German Jewish refugee who is moody and disagreeable but nevertheless an effective communist leader in Zambesia; he marries Martha Quest in Doris Lessing's *A Ripple from the Storm.* She later divorces him in *Landlocked.*

Grete Hesse   Anton Hesse's deceased wife, about whom he constantly talks after marrying Martha Quest in Doris Lessing's *A Ripple from the Storm.*

Ulrica Hesse   One of the wealthiest German pupils in the Hanover school; she is regarded by Fraulein Pfaff and the other girls as specially privileged, in a class by herself, in Dorothy Richardson's *Pointed Roofs.*

Hethers   Simpson's second in his duel with Hornblower in C. S. Forester's *Mr. Midshipman Hornblower.*

Dr. Heve   A taciturn physician who attends Darius Clayhanger's final illness in Arnold Bennett's *Clayhanger.*

Mr. Heve   An unintellectual vicar; he is Dr. Heve's brother and a late admirer of Maggie Clayhanger; his death from influenza leaves Maggie a spinster in Arnold Bennett's *Clayhanger.*

Sir Hew   Red-faced, fussy old Major General who invites Hornblower to dinner in C. S. Forester's *Mr. Midshipman Hornblower.*

Terence Hewet   Rachel Vinrace's fiancé briefly before her death; an amiable, romantic would-be novelist, Terence brings Rachel's personal growth to fruition with the visionary power of love after a long, tentative, frustrating, subtle courtship that moves toward communication; their relationship provides a momentary union of fact and vision, a new order, and insight into the all-pervading pattern or meaning for which they seek; Rachel's death creates for Hewet that moment of perfect vision and unity for which both longed in Virginia Woolf's *The Voyage Out.*

Eric Hewson   Doctor at Toynton Grange, a private nursing home, married to Maggie Hewson in P. D. James's *The Black Tower.*

Maggie Hewson   Alcoholic, flirtatious, bored wife of Eric Hewson; she discovers that Wilfred Anstey's "miraculous" cure was only a misdiagnosis and is murdered in P. D. James's *The Black Tower.*

Axel Heyst   Reclusive Swede involved in Morrison's failed coal company; he retires to Samburan and befriends the traveling musician Lena, only to have her murdered by two gamblers, Jones and Ricardo, who have been led to believe, by the jealous hotel owner, Schomberg, that Heyst possesses a fortune; he dies by Lena's side in Joseph Conrad's *Victory: An Island Tale.*

T. S. Heywood   Bitter war veteran and scientist; he is the husband of Evelyn Lamb, but regrets the impulsive wartime marriage to a woman twelve years older than he and is bored by her newfound literary career and her entertaining of artistic devotees; in 1913 he shared a London flat with Hervey Russell and Philip Nicholson and, like Nicholson and David Renn, he has never recovered from unrequited love for Hervey in Storm Jameson's *Company Parade.* In 1939 T. S. avoids his wife, lives alone in a room next to his laboratory on the third floor of their home, and has loved and painfully lost the seductive and promiscuous Georgina Swan; he is seen variously as the only person brilliant enough to talk to Einstein, as a big, clumsy man with a peasant background, and as a "compassionate archangel living with the monster" he pretended to be in *Before the Crossing.*

Hrr-Anggl Hhrot   Hrr-Brahl Yprt's father in Brian W. Aldiss's *Helliconia Spring.*

Hibbert   Young, fresh-faced captain who attempts to drill Bush concerning Captain Sawyer's confinement during the court of inquiry; he is silenced in C. S. Forester's *Lieutenant Hornblower.*

Mr. Hibbert   Aging Baptist missionary to China who reared Drake and Nelson Ko and instilled in Drake the importance of family in John le Carré's *The Honourable Schoolboy.*

Doris Hibbert   Chinese-born, middle-aged spinster who cynically rejects the possibility of familial love as a motive for Drake Ko's actions in John le Carré's *The Honourable Schoolboy.*

Hickey   Unkempt farmhand who tends to the Brady farm; he is Caithleen Brady's childhood friend, but after the farm is mortgaged he starts life over as a watchman in England in Edna O'Brien's *The Country Girls.*

Hickson   Innkeeper and grocer whose store is rushed in H. G. Wells's *Mr. Britling Sees It Through.*

Mr. Hickson   Millionaire businessman and art collector who befriends Sara and Matt Monday and introduces them to Gulley Jimson; he later collects from Sara a number of Gulley's nudes, and upon his death they are given to the Nation in Joyce Cary's *Herself Surprised* and in *The Horse's Mouth.*

Doreen Higgins   A star-struck young usher at the Pal-

ladium; she has an affair with Maurice Berkley, her married employer, and becomes pregnant by him, leaving London to have her baby in the north in David Lodge's *The Picturegoers.*

Percy Higgins   A weak, devout National Service recruit befriended by Mike Brady; he is tormented by the recruits and Corporal Baker in Basic Training and dies trying to shoot off his trigger finger, leading to Mike Brady's attack on Baker in David Lodge's *Ginger, You're Barmy.*

Zoe Higgins   Prostitute who invites Leopold Bloom into the brothel in James Joyce's *Ulysses.*

Eric Higgs   Old boss of Humphrey Leigh in the security service; he helps Humphrey discover information about Tom Thirkill in C. P. Snow's *A Coat of Varnish.*

Charles Highway   An adolescent living with his sister and her husband and studying for the entrance exams to Oxford University; obsessed with himself as only an adolescent can be, he is also obsessed with sex and, in particular, with one girl, Rachel Noyes; Charles keeps indexed, cross-referenced, and highly self-conscious notes on everything, including his attempts to woo Rachel in Martin Amis's *The Rachel Papers.*

Gordon Highway   The rich, educated, and philandering father of Charles in Martin Amis's *The Rachel Papers.*

Claire Hignam   One of the wealthy socialites trapped in a fog-bound London railway station; she becomes annoyed by her ineffectual husband, Robert, in Henry Green's *Party Going.*

Robert Hignam   One of the wealthy socialites trapped in a fog-bound London railway station; his ineffectuality and frequent retreats to the bar annoy his wife, Claire, in Henry Green's *Party Going.*

Mr. Hilbery   Father of Katherine and husband of Maggie; he represents fact and lives by laws of mental accuracy in an abstract realm detached from the contradictions of the outside world; a scholar versed in the most minute details of the Romantic poets, he is editing a volume of Shelley "which scrupulously observed the poet's system of punctuation"; Mr. Hillbery is unable to become personally involved in any real-life situation in Virginia Woolf's *Night and Day.*

Cyril Hilbery   Katherine Hilbery's cousin who has had several children by a woman who is not his wife, much to Mrs. Milvain's dismay in Virginia Woolf's *Night and Day.*

Katherine Hilbery The young London heroine who has the potential for combining the ideologies of her visionary mother and fact-loving father and thus to integrate fact and vision; the daughter of a famous literary family, she pursues domestic interests which contrast sharply with her friend Mary Datchet, on whom she has a crush; initially engaged to William Rodney, she at last recognizes that she belongs with Ralph Denham after Mary's confession in Virginia Woolf's *Night and Day*.

Maggie Hilbery Visionary, profoundly influential mother of Katherine Hilbery; "beautifully adapted for life in another planet", she recognizes the false limitations of clocktime and is a seductive older woman married to her opposite in Virginia Woolf's *Night and Day*.

Hildegarde Former girlfriend of Ronald Bridges, whose independence is threatened by her mothering in Muriel Spark's *The Bachelors*.

Lady Abbess Hildegarde Abbess of Crewe whose death leads to the rivalry among nuns in Muriel Spark's *The Abbess of Crewe*.

Anna Hilfe Sister of Willi Hilfe, Austrian refugee, and agent of the spy ring "The Free Mothers"; she attempts to help Arthur Rowe covertly and visits him in the asylum, where he falls in love with her; after his escape, she helps him uncover the spy ring, eventually confessing her love for Rowe in Graham Greene's *The Ministry of Fear*.

Willi Hilfe Charismatic, ruthless Austrian refugee employed by the spy ring "The Free Mothers" and brother of Anna Hilfe; he gains the trust of Arthur Rowe, who thinks Hilfe is committed to helping him, and he commits suicide when his true mission and identity are discovered by Rowe in Graham Greene's *The Ministry of Fear*.

Mrs. Hill The science teacher at the secondary school Clara Maugham attends; though vague and a poor disciplinarian, she introduces Clara to the excitement of learning in Margaret Drabble's *Jerusalem the Golden*.

Sandra Hill One of Lynda Coldridge's good friends in Doris Lessing's *The Four-Gated City*.

Stephen Hilliard Eustace Cherrington's Oxford classmate who is preparing to become a solicitor; because of his common sense and realistic attitude he is viewed by Eustace as a potential suitor to his sister Hilda in L. P. Hartley's *The Sixth Heaven*. Stephen, now a solicitor, sends an angry, scornful letter to Eustace in Venice, accusing him of leaving Hilda without adequate male protection and suggesting that Lady Nelly Staveley may be implicated in Dick Staveley's seduction of Hilda in *Eustace and Hilda*.

Thomas Hilliard Superior officer of Revenue killed in the smuggling raid after Francis Andrews informs on the gang in Graham Greene's *The Man Within*.

Denis Hillier (alias Sebastian Jagger) English, middle-class Catholic who works for a nameless British intelligence service; he is given the job of bringing a British scientist back from defection in Russia; he is the stereotypical secret agent, urbane, dangerous, self-assured, but with an unusual vulnerability in Anthony Burgess's *Tremor of Intent*.

Eugene Dana Hilliot Nineteen-year-old son of a wealthy man; he signs aboard a ship to gain experience before going to Cambridge and has difficulty gaining the crew's acceptance but is eventually "promoted" from mess boy to fireman; he is the narrator of Malcolm Lowry's *Ultramarine*.

Sir Terence Hillman Distinguished barrister who gets D. released on bail in Graham Greene's *The Confidential Agent*.

Henry, Lord Hillmorton Earl who refuses to help his daughter, Elizabeth Fox-Milnes, with a gift of money before his death; he dies of cancer in C. P. Snow's *In Their Wisdom*.

Hilly Member of the auxiliary fire service; she has a very brief sexual affair with Richard Roe in Henry Green's *Caught*.

Miss Hillyard History Tutor at Shrewsbury College, Oxford: she has never liked Harriet Vane in Dorothy L. Sayers's *Gaudy Night*.

Gaija Hin The slave master who orders Myk to kill Datnil Skar in Brian W. Aldiss's *Helliconia Spring*.

Sappho Hinchcliffe An intelligent woman and part of an emotional romantic triangle with Stephen Halifax and John Connell during their Oxford days; she has since gone on to a successful career in acting in Margaret Drabble's *A Summer Bird-Cage*.

Thelma Hind Harry Sinton's former secretary, who now works directly for his brother; from her Harry learns the facts about the gun which was used to kill Max Callis in Roy Fuller's *Fantasy and Fugue*.

William Hingest Fellow in Physical Chemistry at Bracton College, University of Edgestow; an early recruit to the N.I.C.E. (National Institute for Coordinated Experiments), he decides to leave its employ; he is the first to hint to Mark Studdock that the N.I.C.E. have enormous power; he is murdered on the same night he leaves the N.I.C.E. in C. S. Lewis's *That Hideous Strength.*

Joe Hinkins   Rectory gardener and a Fenchurch St. Paul bellringer in Dorothy L. Sayers's *The Nine Tailors: Changes Rung on an Old Theme in Two Short Touches and Two Full Peals.*

Mr. Hinks   Fishbourne saddler given to gambling and to wearing checks and tight trousers who threatens Alfred Polly after learning that Polly badmouths him behind his back in H. G. Wells's *The History of Mr. Polly.*

Sir Francis Hinsley   A British gentleman who is employed in writing scripts and publicity for a major Hollywood studio; he befriends Dennis Barlow and later commits suicide when the studio unfeelingly fires him after more than twenty years' service in Evelyn Waugh's *The Loved One.*

Clarissa Hipper   Kind and generous older sister of Blanche Wilcher; she was to have married Loftus Wilcher until Blanche stole him away; she later befriends Sara Monday and encourages her to marry Tom Wilcher in Joyce Cary's *Herself Surprised* and in *To Be a Pilgrim.*

Countess Hippolyta   Society woman with an entourage of hangers on; she is enthralled by Felix Charlock's recording devices and introduces him to the Firm in Lawrence Durrell's *Tunc.*

Dr. Hippolyte   Haitian physician who assists Sigbjorn Wilderness after Sigbjorn cuts his wrists in Malcolm Lowry's *Dark as the Grave Wherein My Friend Is Laid.*

Hirsch   Hide merchant who accidentally stows away on the boat carrying the silver in Joseph Conrad's *Nostromo: A Tale of the Seaboard.*

St. John Hirst   Endearingly ugly vacationing "genius" (by his own description) and friend of Terence Hewet at the Santa Marina Hotel; the eldest son of a country parson, Hirst tries to decide between continuing at Cambridge and entering the law; with ludicrous crushes on Helen Ambrose and Rachel Vinrace, this obnoxious, unappealing young man serves as the sharp-cutting edge of intellectual fact against which Rachel Vinrace will measure herself in Virginia Woolf's *The Voyage Out.*

Norman Hislop   Nick Ollanton's assistant, whose place is taken, by mutual consent as Norman is unable to please his employer, by Dick Herncastle, Ollanton's nephew in J. B. Priestley's *Lost Empires.*

Adolf Hitler   The directionless, lazy, intellectual, penniless, and generally despised brother of Alois Hitler, whom he visits in Liverpool in 1912; he is a bigot who blames his problems and the problems of the world on racial deviance; sensitive and given to out-of-body experiences, Adolf is somewhat absurd and quite unremarkable in Beryl Bainbridge's *Young Adolf.* He is the "incredibly naïf yet . . . sometimes entrancing performing pet" of Putzi Hanfstaengl; a sexually repressed, fanatical visionary, he tries to claim authority by leading a march in Munich in 1923 and is imprisoned after its failure in Richard Hughes's *The Fox in the Attic.* He becomes focus and leader of burgeoning, euphoric Nazi Germany and establishes his authority in 1934 with a blood purge against his inconveniently powerful follower, Ernst Röhm, and others in *The Wooden Shepherdess.*

Alois Hitler   Egotistical, inconsiderate waiter and small-time salesman who calls himself a businessman; he feels frustrated that his brother, Adolf, is not like himself; Alois is friends with Meyer and Kephalus and ignores his wife, Bridget, in Beryl Bainbridge's *Young Adolf.*

Bridget Hitler   Alois's simple, clean, lonely wife, who knows Alois will leave her one day; her son, Pat, is everything to her, and she does not approve of her brother-in-law Adolf's being around her baby; nevertheless, she is helpful to Adolf, advising him to conceal a scar by combing his hair forward in Beryl Bainbridge's *Young Adolf.*

William Patrick Hitler   Son of Alois and Bridget; he is a good baby, well-behaved and generally beloved in Beryl Bainbridge's *Young Adolf.*

Hobbs   Paunchy acting gunner who acts as Captain Sawyer's snitch in C. S. Forester's *Lieutenant Hornblower.*

Sergeant Hobson   A soldier on Jonathan Browne's last guard duty in National Service in David Lodge's *Ginger, You're Barmy.*

Alan Hobson   An English artist; he is viewed by Frederick Tarr as a "crowd man" who vulgarizes the individual; he has his hat knocked off by Tarr in a symbolic display of his philosophy in Wyndham Lewis's *Tarr.*

Agatha Hoccleve   The archdeacon's wife, whose clothes and manner remind one and all that her father was a bishop in Barbara Pym's *Some Tame Gazelle.*

Archdeacon Henry Hoccleve Self-important, idle, intellectually pretentious vicar who accepts the devotion of both his wife and Belinda Bede as no more than his due in Barbara Pym's *Some Tame Gazelle*. He makes an appearance, much aged, in *Excellent Women*. His quotation-filled sermons are still recalled in *A Glass of Blessings*.

Henrietta Hodge Miss Pym's friend, headmistress of a girls' physical-education college; her favoritism motivates one student's murder of another in Josephine Tey's *Miss Pym Disposes*.

Mr. Hodges Grubby, foul-mouthed old man who desperately seeks any job he can get at Corker's employment agency; Corker despises him but nonetheless feels forced by Hodges to ponder his own ignorance and mortality in John Berger's *Corker's Freedom*.

Mrs. Hodges Lay midwife who realizes that Liza Kemp is having a miscarriage but idly gossips about funerals and insurance while Liza lies dying in W. Somerset Maugham's *Liza of Lambeth*.

Hodgkin British sales representative for a suit-cloth goods manufacturer; he helps Desmond Kenton evade the police and cross the Austrian frontier into Czechoslovakia in Eric Ambler's *Uncommon Danger*.

Bill Hodgkisson A friend of Walter Morel in D. H. Lawrence's *Sons and Lovers*.

Reinhold Hoffmann Rocket engineer with the US space program; he is in charge of building the space ship for the first US manned moon landing in Arthur C. Clarke's *Childhood's End*.

Sonia Hoffmann Woman engaged to the wrestler Schmule; she refuses to sign any marriage certificate without a dazzling diamond upon her finger in Wolf Mankowitz's *A Kid for Two Farthings*.

René Hoffmayer Loyal business manager of Honoré Burckheim's ironworks; he showers gifts upon Ernest Siguenau as if upon a beloved son; he is betrayed when Siguenau lies about him to Burckheim but is more puzzled than angry when he loses his job through this treachery in Storm Jameson's *Cousin Honoré*.

Mrs. Hogan Wife of Luke Hogan, with whom she hosts the party at which Philip Swallow first meets Desiree Zapp in David Lodge's *Changing Places: A Tale of Two Campuses*.

Josephine Hogan Rural cousin of the Hannafeys who is deeply in love with Frankie Hannafey in Sean O'Faolain's *Come Back to Erin*.

Luke Hogan Chair of the English Department at Euphoric State University; he and Mrs. Hogan host the party at which Philip Swallow first meets Desiree Zapp in David Lodge's *Changing Places: A Tale of Two Campuses*.

St. John Hogan-Hannafey Well-to-do owner of an American shoe company; plagued with guilt over his marriage outside the Roman Catholic church, he becomes a heavy drinker and lets his business decline; he sentimentally wishes to retire in Ireland and ultimately disappears overboard on a ship returning to the country of his birth in Sean O'Faolain's *Come Back to Erin*.

Andrew Hogarth Crippled son of Georgina Hogg and Melvyn Hogarth; he is a member of Louisa Jepp's band of smugglers in Muriel Spark's *The Comforters*.

Eleanor Hogarth Second, bigamous wife of Melvyn Hogarth, recently estranged mistress of Willi Stock, business partner of Ernest Manders, and friend of Caroline Rose in Muriel Spark's *The Comforters*.

Melvyn Hogarth Bigamist (husband of Georgina Hogg and Eleanor Hogarth) and member of Louisa Jepp's gang in Muriel Spark's *The Comforters*.

Tom Hogarth Bold, blond, challenging member of the War Cabinet; he is the most brilliant advocate in the House of Commons, successive leader of seven ministries including the Ministry of Munitions, and one of the finest polemical and descriptive writers in the country; he is, nevertheless, considered by Lord Raingo to have every gift except common sense in Arnold Bennett's *Lord Raingo*.

Georgina Hogg A professional housekeeper whose tyranny, greed, and enormous bosom are altogether repulsive; a "cradle Catholic", she wields her piety for extortion and blackmail; her death by drowning frees Caroline Rose to write her novel in Muriel Spark's *The Comforters*.

Charles Holland A son of Lord and Lady Slane; a retired general, he does not wish to have the responsibility of his widowed mother's living with him in Vita Sackville-West's *All Passion Spent*.

Charlotte (Carrie) Holland Eldest daughter of Lord and Lady Slane; she attempts to impose on her mother her ideas of the behavior befitting the aged widow of a prominent politician in Vita Sackville-West's *All Passion Spent*.

Deborah Holland Lady Slane's great-granddaughter; she reveals to Lady Slane her dream of becoming a musician; she refuses to marry and sacrifice herself to another's career in Vita Sackville-West's *All Passion Spent*.

Edith Holland The unmarried youngest daughter of Lord and Lady Slane; still living in her parents' house at Elm Court Place, she is freed by her father's death and her mother's retirement to Hampstead to live a life of her own in Vita Sackville-West's *All Passion Spent*.

Herbert Holland The eldest son of Lord and Lady Slane; he receives the family jewels after Lord Slane's death and Lady Slane's retirement to Hampstead in Vita Sackville-West's *All Passion Spent*.

Hubert Holland A tall, pale boy at Lucius Cassidy's school; he takes music lessons from Oliver Shelley in Ivy Compton-Burnett's *Two Worlds and Their Ways*.

Jack Holland Shopkeeper and spirits merchant who is in love with Mrs. Brady; after her death he turns his devotions, which are rejected, to her daughter, Caithleen Brady, in Edna O'Brien's *The Country Girls*.

Kay Holland A son of Lord and Lady Slane; a confirmed bachelor and an authority on globes, astrolabes, compasses, and such instruments, he does not want the responsibility of sharing his comfortable set of rooms with his widowed mother in Vita Sackville-West's *All Passion Spent*.

Lavinia Holland The avaricious wife of William Holland; the couple's occupation is to scrape and save and pare in Vita Sackville-West's *All Passion Spent*.

Mabel Holland Wife of Herbert Holland in Vita Sackville-West's *All Passion Spent*.

Selina Holland The woman of "high ends" and a vicarage upbringing with whom Miriam Henderson is sharing a flat in what she calls "a marriage of convenience" in Dorothy Richardson's *The Trap*.

William Holland The parsimonious son of Lord and Lady Slane; he and his wife will accept his widowed mother to live with them only if she is a paying guest in Vita Sackville-West's *All Passion Spent*.

Maud Hollebone A typical Englishwoman in the Swiss pension where Miriam Henderson is spending her recuperative holiday in Dorothy Richardson's *Oberland*.

Maggie Hollins Kitchen drudge of the Baines family; late in life she marries an Irish drunkard, has children, is widowed, and sinks forgotten into poverty in Arnold Bennett's *The Old Wives Tale*.

Geoffrey Hollis Pediatrician who is the first husband of Margaret; he joins Charles March in caring for Charles Eliot during his bout of meningitis in C. P. Snow's *Homecomings*.

Margaret Davidson Hollis Lewis Eliot's former lover, who turned from him to marry Geoffrey Hollis; she divorces Hollis after bearing a son, and then marries Lewis Eliot and bears another son in C. P. Snow's *Homecomings*. She dislikes the Howards but nevertheless supports their claim for justice in *The Affair*. She is a close friend of Caroline Quaife and sympathizes with her during Roger Quaife's affair and divorce in *Corridors of Power*. She helps her husband through the difficult period of his threatened blindness in *The Sleep of Reason*. She quarrels with Lewis about the offer of a post in government and informs him that their son will leave England to become a journalist in the Middle East in *Last Things*.

Maurice Hollis Child of Geoffrey and Margaret Hollis in C. P. Snow's *Homecomings*. A student at Cambridge, he is a concern to his mother, now Margaret Eliot, because he cannot pass his exams to study medicine in *The Sleep of Reason*. He fails medical-school exams a second time, begins doing charity work, and marries Diana Dobson in *Last Things*.

Captain Holly Captain of the Owsla (rabbit-warren militia) of the Sandleford Warren; he escapes to tell Bigwig of the warren's destruction in Richard Adams's *Watership Down*.

Dr. Holmes Blustering traditional medical doctor whose harsh therapy includes separating Septimus Smith from his wife and whose forced entry into Smith's room precipitates Smith's suicidal window leap in Virginia Woolf's *Mrs. Dalloway*.

Constance Holmes See Lily Montgomery DeSeitas.

Julie Holmes See Lily DeSeitas.

June Holmes See Rose DeSeitas.

William Holmes Acquaintance of Orlando King and Theodora Bates in Italy; he is known as Wicked Will in Isabel Colegate's *Orlando at the Brazen Threshold*.

Holroyd American financier who supports the foundation of the Occidental Republic in Joseph Conrad's *Nostromo: A Tale of the Seaboard*.

Mr. Holroyd Georgie Pillson's hairdresser, whose clandestine monthly professional visits to Georgie are so well observed and understood that they occasion no gossip at all in Riseholme in E. F. Benson's *"Queen Lucia"*.

Victor Holroyd   Bitter, malicious, wheelchair-bound patient at Toynton Grange; when he threatens to disclose that Wilfred Anstey's "miraculous" cure was simply a misdiagnosis, he is killed in P. D. James's *The Black Tower*.

Mr. Holt   Principal Bursley bookseller; his displays of Richard Larch's "eccentric" orders spread Richard's fame as a great reader in Arnold Bennett's *A Man From the North*.

Portman C. Holtman   A stranger whose undelivered letter, detailing an encounter with Eva Trout on an airplane, provides much of her personal history in Elizabeth Bowen's *Eva Trout, or Changing Scenes*.

Lady Homartyn   Hostess and mediator of political discussions in her home in H. G. Wells's *Mr. Britling Sees It Through*.

Mrs. Honeychurch   Freddy and Lucy Honeychurch's conventional mother, who is opposed to Lucy's marrying George Emerson in E. M. Forster's *A Room with a View*.

Freddy Honeychurch   Lucy Honeychurch's brother; his swimming invitation to George Emerson results in an encounter that, however ludicrous, assists Lucy's self-discovery in time to make the right marriage in E. M. Forster's *A Room with a View*.

Dr. Hazel Honeychurch   Sociology professor at Brockshire University who succeeds Cosmo Sultana and Owen Tuby as resident image maker in J. B. Priestley's *The Image Men*.

Lucy Honeychurch   Naïve middle-class heroine whose sensual awareness is awakened during a trip to Italy; her self-knowledge and independent spirit mature in time for her to break off her engagement with Cecil Vyse and to marry George Emerson in E. M. Forster's *A Room with a View*.

Hooker   Fourth lieutenant aboard the *Sutherland* in C. S. Forester's *Ship of the Line*.

Hooper   The banal and spiritually ignorant young platoon commander in Charles Ryder's unit in World War II; he is also casual and careless about military responsibilities in Evelyn Waugh's *Brideshead Revisited*.

Marcia Hooper   Mitchell Hooper's wife in John Fowles's *Daniel Martin*.

Mitchell Hooper   A young American computer expert living in Egypt; he is a fellow traveler with Daniel Martin and Jane Mallory on their Nile cruise in John Fowles's *Daniel Martin*.

Hopkins   Clyde Barstow's replacement as British Consul to Wallacia in Margaret Drabble's *The Ice Age*.

Hopkins   Manservant to the Nettleby family in Isabel Colegate's *The Shooting Party*.

Miss Hopkins   Avid young reader of sensational novels and a talkative patron of Mrs. Bedley's lending library in Ronald Firbank's *The Flower Beneath the Foot*.

Mr. Hopkins   Member of the Alpha and Omega Club who is of questionable character in Norman Douglas's *South Wind*.

Mr. Hopkins   Proprietor of a fish shop whose nearly nude posing for the painter Irene Coles causes consternation in Tilling in E. F. Benson's *Miss Mapp*.

The Fabulous Hoplite (Hop)   Handsome, witty homosexual friend of the narrator; he makes his living as a contact man for gossip columnists and poses for the narrator's photographs in Colin MacInnes's *Absolute Beginners*.

Hoppe   A technician from one of Sirius's colonized planets who is assigned by Ambien II to find out what is going on in the Canopian part of Rohanda (Shikasta); he travels northward on a journey lasting five years in Doris Lessing's *The Sirian Experiments*.

Frank Hopper   Family lawyer Julia Delmore calls to help negotiate with Jake Driver and Detective Ambrose what is to be done about the obnoxious Cliff Sanders after he is arrested for his brainless extortion scheme; he is a character in the novel Giles Hermitage writes in John Wain's *The Pardoner's Tale*.

James Horgan   Unsavory stockbroker with whom Philip Weston becomes involved as an apprentice; he loses a great deal of Edmund Weston's and Sir Aylmer Weston's money in Isabel Colegate's *Statues in a Garden*.

Horatio Hornblower   A lower-middle-class youth who finds his life at sea; at seventeen he begins a stint as a midshipman aboard the *Justinian* in C. S. Forester's *Mr. Midshipman Hornblower*. As a lieutenant aboard the *Indefatigable* he serves under an insane captain and experiences an emergency change in command in *Lieutenant Hornblower*. As Commander of the *Atropos* he suffers the tribulations of leadership in *Hornblower and the Atropos*. He is Commander of the

Hotspur and later promoted to Captain; well respected by his fellow seamen, he lives two lives, one at sea commanding his ship, and the other a more constricted life as breadwinner and husband of Mary Ellen (Mason) in *Hornblower and the Hotspur*. As a captain he constantly seeks seclusion, fearing to show weakness to his crew; he is a capable seaman with an ever-calculating mind; his wife dies in childbirth while he is at sea in *The Happy Return*, in *Ship of the Line*, and in *Flying Colours*. He has become Sir Horatio Hornblower; he is the reserved, compassionate, diplomatic commander of British naval forces in various oceans of the world; he loves his career but also loves his second wife, the former Lady Barbara Wellesley, and his son, Richard; he likes ceremonies, battles, and mysteries but hates music; he never forgets the people he is commanding in *Commodore Hornblower*, in *Lord Hornblower*, in *Hornblower in the West Indies*, and in *Hornblower And the Crisis: An Unfinished Novel.*

Little Horatio Hornblower   Infant son of Horatio; he celebrates the return of his part-time father; he is somewhat jealous of his newborn sister in C. S. Forester's *Hornblower and the Atropos*. Until his death by smallpox he is his father's strongest emotional bond to the land in *Hornblower and the Hotspur*.

Little Maria Hornblower   Newborn daughter of Horatio in C. S. Forester's *Hornblower and the Atropos*. She dies of smallpox in *Horatio and the Hotspur*.

Maria Ellen Mason Hornblower   A boarding-house operator's daughter in C. S. Forester's *Lieutenant Hornblower*. She becomes the strong, independent wife of Horatio Hornblower; she loyally endures poverty, suffering, and the deaths of her children in *Hornblower and the Atropos* and in *Hornblower and the Hotspur*. She is pregnant when Horatio sails as Captain in *The Happy Return*. She has died in the birth of their only surviving child, Richard, before he returns in *Flying Colours.*

Richard Arthur Horatio Hornblower   Hornblower's infant son, whose mother died when he was born; he is entrusted to the care of Lady Barbara (Wellesley) Leighton in C. S. Forester's *Flying Colours.*

Mrs. Horncle   Dictatorial and unsympathetic head nurse at the psychiatric hospital in Malcolm Lowry's *Lunar Caustic.*

Jason (Jay) Horner   Songwriter whose strange alliance with Edward, Lord Champneis points to both men as possible murder suspects in Josephine Tey's *A Shilling for Candles.*

Sol Horowitz ("Horror")   One of a pair of vicious thugs who intend to make Vivienne Michel a victim in

a scheme to burn down a remote, unprofitable motel for insurance money in Ian Fleming's *The Spy Who Loved Me.*

Horridge   Coroner who rules Rebecca de Winter committed suicide in Daphne Du Maurier's *Rebecca.*

Horrocks   Stupid midshipman aboard the *Atropos* in C. S. Forester's *Hornblower and the Atropos.*

Gladys Horrocks   Alfred Thipps's servant; she is also arrested on suspicion of murder in Dorothy L. Sayers's *Whose Body?.*

George Horsfield   A wasted but sensitive Englishman who travels about spending his legacy; he takes Julia Martin as a lover in Paris in Jean Rhys's *After Leaving Mr. Mackenzie.*

Miss Hortense   Aline, Lady Hartlip's lady's maid in Isabel Colegate's *The Shooting Party.*

Faltaus Hosnani   An anti-British Coptic Christian Egyptian and the elderly, dying husband of Leila and father of Nessim and Narouz; his encouragement of his wife's seduction of their young guest, David Mountolive, may be motivated by a far-sighted anticipation of Mountolive's increased authority in the British foreign service in Lawrence Durrell's *Mountolive.*

Justine Hosnani   Beautiful Jewish wife of the Coptic Christian Nessim Hosnani; she is an archetypal temptress, driven to promiscuity by a childhood rape until the death of her rapist liberates her to become a kibutzim in Palestine in Lawrence Durrell's *Justine.* Her affair with Pursewarden is explored in *Balthazar.* She is revealed to be her husband's confederate in providing guns to Palestinian Jews, her marriage and her sexual intrigues being politically motivated in *Mountolive.* Forcibly expatriated from Palestine, she remains under house arrest until released through her discovery of Memlik's appetite for acceptance into Alexandrian society in *Clea.*

Leila Hosnani   Mother of Nessim and Narouz Hosnani; she is mentioned in Lawrence Durrell's *Justine.* Her residence is described and her history expanded upon in *Balthazar.* She has an affair with young David Mountolive before her beauty is ravaged by smallpox in *Mountolive.*

Narouz Hosnani   Nessim's brother, violently passionate in nature but driven to almost monastic reclusiveness by his harelip; he manages and lives on the family estate; he is jealously and secretly in love with Clea Montis; when the homosexual Toto de Brunel makes advances to him at a masquerade, he kills Toto, whom he believes to be Nessim's wife, Justine, in Lawrence Durrell's *Balthazar*. Obsessed with messianism, he becomes a danger to his brother's political intrigues; he is murdered by their political opponents in *Mountolive*.

Nessim Hosnani A "spiritually impotent" Alexandrian banker, whose externally blissful marriage to Justine is marred by her compulsive infidelity in Lawrence Durrell's *Justine*. His tormenting jealousy is elaborated upon in *Balthazar*. His Coptic plot to support the Palestinian Jews is discovered by the British, but he survives by bribing the Egyptian minister Memlik in *Mountolive*. He has lost an eye, much money, and all his social and political power, but his fortunes are finally rising again in *Clea*.

Manna Host The attractively modern Swedish fiancée of Tom Sweetnan; she attends Hilda Lessways Clayhanger's party to view the house for rent in Arnold Bennett's *These Twain*.

Hotchkinson Solicitor who manages the case for the defence of George Passant, Jack Cotery, and Olive Calvert in C. P. Snow's *Strangers and Brothers*.

Hotchkinson Solicitor who represents Neil St. John; he advises Stephen Freer not to testify on behalf of Neil in C. P. Snow's *The Malcontents*.

Stéphanie Houdet Aunt of Marie Middleton; she is the live-in companion of Lilian Portway in Italy; she was in a Nazi concentration camp for two years and is abused by her beloved son, Yves; she is disappointed when she receives nothing from Lilian's will in Angus Wilson's *Anglo-Saxon Attitudes*.

Yves Houdet Handsome and vain son of Stéphanie; he is a reckless young man chasing women and fortunes; he beats his mother when he is drunk in Angus Wilson's *Anglo-Saxon Attitudes*.

Alvina Houghton The demure daughter of a neurotic invalid mother and an unsuccessful merchant; seemingly doomed to a repressed, isolated life in a dreary Midlands village, she achieves psychic rebirth through her union with the performer Ciccio and rebelliously travels with him to his mountain village in Italy in D. H. Lawrence's *The Lost Girl*.

Clariss Houghton The "petulant, heart-stricken" invalid mother who turns her daughter, Alvina, over to a governess's care in D. H. Lawrence's *The Lost Girl*.

James Houghton An entrepreneur who establishes Manchester House, a fashionable clothing emporium, in the middle of a dreary, unfashionable Midlands village; this "drapery dream" and all his other commer-

cial schemes fail; when he dies, he leaves only debts for his daughter, Alvina, to pay in D. H. Lawrence's *The Lost Girl*.

Sammikins, Lord Houghton Brother of Caroline Quaife; he votes against Roger Quaife in a crucial Parliamentary debate which leads to Quaife's resignation in C. P. Snow's *Corridors of Power*. He dies in 1966 after a long illness in *Last Things*.

Daniel House Poet, the "Tiresias-like" and virile persona of a collection of his erotically charged poems from the late twenties; though now in physical decline, he continues to show an ease in erotic experience which surprises his rather inhibited disciple and visitor, James Ross, in Roy Fuller's *The Carnal Island*.

Jack House Surgery patient in Clive Ward charged with killing a policeman; he stirs up protests among the other patients, who resent his being in the same ward with them in John Berger's *The Foot of Clive*.

Margaret House Unfashionable, illegitimate middle-aged daughter of the poet Daniel House in Roy Fuller's *The Carnal Island*.

Yvonne House Wife of Daniel; she is tolerant of her husband's unofficial family and his earlier amorous connections in Roy Fuller's *The Carnal Island*.

Housemartin Jay's burly, vicious espionage confidant, who snatches Raven from Lederers' coffeehouse but is killed by Dalby's agents in the Shoreditch Police Station after he is arrested for impersonating a Metropolitan Police chief inspector in Len Deighton's *The Ipcress File*.

Lord Hovenden Diffident aristocrat of egalitarian sympathies; becoming enamored of Irene Aldwinkle, he proposes to her during an outing to Rome in Aldous Huxley's *Those Barren Leaves*.

Howard Chief attendant to the sleeping Graham; Howard attempts to keep secret Graham's awakening and conceals his great status from Graham; he is ordered by the Council to poison Graham in H. G. Wells's *When the Sleeper Wakes: A Story of the Years to Come*.

Mr. Howard A candidate for the job that John Lewis wants; he is a young, intelligent, inexperienced Oxford graduate in Kingsley Amis's *That Uncertain Feeling*.

Donald Howard Physicist and Cambridge college fellow who is a Communist sympathizer; he is disliked even by his supporters; he has used false evidence in his published research; he appeals the loss of his fellowship to the Court of Seniors and resigns himself to their final decision in C. P. Snow's *The Affair*. He works as a member of Leonard Getliffe's faculty in *The Sleep of Reason*.

Evelyn (Evie) Howard   Emily Inglethorp's super-capable companion in Agatha Christie's *The Mysterious Affair at Styles: A Detective Story*.

Laura Howard   Donald's wife, who stridently urges her husband's cause to all listeners in C. P. Snow's *The Affair*.

Howells   The somewhat addled chair of the English department at Adam Appleby's college; he confuses Adam with Camel, saying he wants to offer Adam a job when he actually means Camel in David Lodge's *The British Museum Is Falling Down*.

Mary Howells   Friend of Arthur Piper and cook for Richard Roe's unit of the auxiliary fire service; she goes away without leave to care for her mentally disturbed daughter and to confront her worthless soldier son-in-law in Henry Green's *Caught*.

Reggie Howerton   Homosexual director of music who helps Piers Mosson with plans for production of the opera in Angus Wilson's *Setting the World on Fire*.

Beatrix Howick   Sixtyish widowed tutor in English literature at an Oxford women's college; she is mother of Emma, whose romantic life she hopes will be enlarged in Barbara Pym's *A Few Green Leaves*.

Emma Howick   Academic spinster in her thirties who comes to stay in her mother's cottage in a West Oxfordshire village to write up her anthropological field notes and characteristically to observe and study the villagers in Barbara Pym's *A Few Green Leaves*.

April Howkins   Unusually mature-acting adult daughter of the separated Gus and Daphne Howkins; she supports her father's future happiness with his new lover Julia Delmore; she is a character in one variant of the story novelist Giles Hermitage writes in John Wain's *The Pardoner's Tale*.

Augustus (Gus) Robert Howkins   Bored, middle-aged husband recently separated from his wife; he becomes infatuated with and pursues the mysterious, beautiful, and troubled Julia Delmore while on vacation in Wales from his small London article-clipping service; he is the central character of the story novelist Giles Hermitage writes in John Wain's *The Pardoner's Tale*.

Daphne Howkins   Estranged but still-dependent wife of the bored Gus Howkins, who seizes on her brief, meaningless affair as an opportunity to escape from their unsatisfying marriage and who later rejects her appeals to him for reconciliation; she is a character in the story novelist Giles Hermitage writes in John Wain's *The Pardoner's Tale*.

Mr. Hoylake   Personable, open boss to Joe Lampton; he tries to be friendly while maintaining his position in John Braine's *Room at the Top*.

Hrr-Tryhk Hrast   A phagor leader who is killed by the people of Oldorando; his death starts a war between the phagors and the humans in Brian W. Aldiss's *Helliconia Spring*.

Hsi Mei ("May")   Chinese girl subject to a violent struggle between two contending natures; she is one of the supernormals of John Wainwright's Pacific island colony in Olaf Stapledon's *Odd John: A Story Between Jest and Earnest*.

Caroline Martha Hubbard   Seemingly ridiculous American traveller; she is in fact the retired actress Linda Arden, grandmother of Daisy Armstrong in Agatha Christie's *Murder on the Orient Express*.

Hudig   Dutch merchant and father of Peter Willems's wife in Joseph Conrad's *An Outcast of the Islands*.

Bandsman Hudnutt   Naïve, dreamy musician, who uses his creative tendencies and has charges filed against him in C. S. Forester's *Hornblower in the West Indies*.

Hufsa   Mythological rabbit traitor sent to spy on Elahrairah by Prince Rainbow in Richard Adams's *Watership Down*.

Hugh   A Welsh actor and a friend of David Evans in Margaret Drabble's *The Garrick Year*.

Hughes   Wounded veteran of the Boer War who is infatuated with Ivy Barton; he is imprisoned for a month after stabbing his wife with a bayonet in John Galsworthy's *Fraternity*.

Mrs. Hughes   Seamstress employed by Cecilia Dallison; she is jealous of Ivy Barton and allows her baby to die of starvation in John Galsworthy's *Fraternity*.

Tubby Hughes   Pay Office clerk at Badmore in David Lodge's *Ginger, You're Barmy*.

Octavia, Duchess of Hull   A visitor at Chevron; a dowager with a sharp, witty tongue, she plays bridge admirably; no hostess dare omit her from a house party in Vita Sackville-West's *The Edwardians*.

The Widow Hullins   One of the last old women in Bursley who smoke a cutty; Denry Machin attempts to collect some of the rent owed by her and devises his scheme to lend rent payments with interest to those threatened with the bailiff in Arnold Bennett's *The Card: A Story of Adventure in the Five Towns*.

Hullo Central   Personal maid of Sylvia Tietjens, who has so named her because of the sound of her voice in Ford Madox Ford's *Some Do Not. . . .*

Hulme   Famous scientist who is Charles Sheriff's research professor; he offers kindly professional advice to Arthur Miles in C. P. Snow's *The Search*.

Human Echinoderms   An alien species whose minds are much like ours except that their methods of reproduction and social organization tend to repress individuality in favor of the "tribal mentality" in Olaf Stapledon's *Star Maker*.

Adrian Hume   The younger brother of Alice and Francis; he gives the tutor Mr. Pettigrew a hard time in Ivy Compton-Burnett's *Mother and Son*.

Alice Hume   Francis's thirteen-year-old sister, who says that she knew that Julius Hume had a special relationship to them in Ivy Compton-Burnett's *Mother and Son*.

Francis Hume   A fifteen-year-old whose support is begrudged by Miranda Hume; he is really the son and not the nephew of Julius Hume in Ivy Compton-Burnett's *Mother and Son*.

Harriet Hume   London concert pianist who is attracted to Arnold Condorex; she minimizes their differences — his lesser intellect, his failure to appreciate music and art, and his lack of interest in social change; her intuition is so keen that she seems to have extrasensory power and can identify his purposes and challenge his lies before they are spoken in Rebecca West's *Harriet Hume, A London Fantasy*.

Julius Hume   Miranda's husband; he is not Rosebery's father, but he is father — not uncle — to Francis, Alice, and Adrian; he proposes to Emma Greatheart and is accepted and then rejected in Ivy Compton-Burnett's *Mother and Son*.

Miranda Hume   The wife of Julius and mother of Rosebery; she dies when Julius tells her that Francis, Alice, and Adrian are his children by another woman in Ivy Compton-Burnett's *Mother and Son*.

Rosebery (Rosebud) Hume   Miranda's middle-aged son, whose feelings for womanhood are directed only toward his mother until her death in Ivy Compton-Burnett's *Mother and Son*.

Dr. Humphries   Old English teacher living in a northern Argentinian city; he plays chess with Dr. Eduardo Plarr and is unwilling to help him try to save Charley Fortnum in Graham Greene's *The Honorary Consul*.

Mr. Hunker   American movie producer and companion of Lord Barralonga; he tacitly supports Rupert Catskill's plan to overthrow Utopian rule in H. G. Wells's *Men Like Gods*.

Hunt   Manchester school teacher who studied economics at the University of London; he was a university friend of Arthur Miles and Charles Sheriff; he went into teaching because he did not excel in his university exams; he fails with women and with writing and continues to be a confidant to Miles in C. P. Snow's *The Search*.

Hunt   A man of indeterminate age and background whom Kate Fletcher Armstrong has found interesting for his rudeness and various circle of friends and acquaintances in Margaret Drabble's *The Middle Ground*.

Delia Hunt   Middle-aged housemate of Hervey Russell in London, 1918; she is haunted by having lived three years with a brutal husband almost thirty years earlier in Johannesburg; she wants Hervey to join her disreputable counseling-women-by-mail firm, in which she sells the names and addresses of the women to commercial advertisers in Storm Jameson's *Company Parade*. In 1939 she is referred to as Captain Tim Hunt's no-good former wife in Johannesburg in *Before the Crossing*.

Captain Tim Hunt   Delia Hunt's husband, whom she left years earlier in Johannesburg; he writes her in 1918 that he has changed and may move to London in Storm Jameson's *Company Parade*. At age sixty-eight he appears to be forty; he is praised for extreme courage in World War I; he is an obsessive hater of socialists; he pilots Julian Swan's airplane, and illegally ships munitions to Germany; he has taken poor and starving twenty-three-year-old Marie Duclos as his mistress, and he becomes David Renn's prime suspect in a murder case in *Before the Crossing*.

Hunter   Midshipman aboard the *Indefatigable*, the *La Reve*, and the *Marie Galante* in C. S. Forester's *Mr. Midshipman Hornblower*.

Captain Maximillan ("Max") Hunter   Heavy-drinking, pessimistic, thin, pale twenty-eight-year-old administrative officer for the top secret Operation Apollo mission; he is a bisexual with preference for homosexual relationships; he uses the alias Captain Vincent Lane in an unsuccessful plot to seduce Signalman Andy Pearse; he is the author of the Anti-Death League Manifesto in Kingsley Amis's *The Anti-Death League*.

Geoffrey Hunter-Payne   Alvina Smithers's distant relative who visits on vacation from the "Colonies"; Georgie Smithers's best hope for a husband, he is is seduced by Georgie's friend Margy Stuart in Richard Aldington's *The Colonel's Daughter*.

Huntley   Ballet master with the Isabel Cornwallis Ballet Company in Colin MacInnes's *City of Spades*.

Dr. Hurd   One of the Canadian doctors boarding with Mrs. Bailey while training in a London hostpiral in Dorothy Richardson's *Interim*.

Mr. Hurd   Dr. Hurd's father who comes with Mrs. Hurd to London to see their son; they stay in Mrs. Bailey's house and impress Miriam Henderson with their devotion in Dorothy Richardson's *Interim*.

Mrs. Hurd   Mr. Hurd's wife, who is similarly devoted to their son in Dorothy Richardson's *Interim*.

Mr. Hurlbird   Florence Dowell's uncle, a wealthy American entrepreneur, whose apparent life-long symptoms of a heart condition prove on his death at an advanced age to be a physical anomaly; he provides the pattern for his niece's feigned illness in Ford Madox Ford's *The Good Soldier: A Tale of Passion*.

Emily Hurlbird   An elderly maiden aunt of Florence Hurlbird Dowell in Ford Madox Ford's *The Good Soldier: A Tale of Passion*.

Florence Hurlbird   Florence Hurlbird (Dowell)'s elderly maiden aunt who, with her sister Emily, attempts to dissuade John Dowell from marrying her niece, though she refuses to tell him of the affair Florence had with a young American, Jimmy, in Ford Madox Ford's *The Good Soldier: A Tale of Passion*.

Joe Hurt   A writer and one of Rosamund Stacey's boyfriends; he has a rough magnetism and is erroneously suspected of being the father of Rosamund's baby in Margaret Drabble's *The Millstone*.

Denis Hussey   Young son of Johnny Hussey; he turns on his policeman father when he learns that Johnny has been an informer; Johnny then forces him to leave the family home in Sean O'Faolain's *A Nest of Simple Folk*.

Johnny Hussey   Nephew of Leo Foxe-Donnel and an opportunistic member of the Royal Irish Constabulary; he spies on Leo and informs the authorities of Leo's involvement in a gun-running rebel plot; as a result, Leo is once again arrested and imprisoned in Sean O'Faolain's *A Nest of Simple Folk*.

George Hutchins   Charles Lumley's college acquaintance, whom Charles remembers as an "unpleasantly dogged and humourless young man"; Charles later encounters him serving as the self-important president of a local literary society and as part-time tutor to wealthy Samuel Braceweight's son in John Wain's *Hurry On Down*.

Bertram Hutton   Dolores's brother, who secretly marries Elsa Blackwood; he refuses his uncle James's financial help to go to Oxford, accepts financial help from Dolores, and allows Perdita Kingsford to fall in love with him in Ivy Compton-Burnett's *Dolores*.

Cleveland Hutton   Dolores's father, the vicar of the parish; he marries three times and does not appreciate Dolores's devotion to him in Ivy Compton-Burnett's *Dolores*.

Cleveland Hutton (the younger)   Sophia's only son, who is educated and then adopted by his uncle James Hutton in Ivy Compton-Burnett's *Dolores*.

Dolores Hutton   The underappreciated victim of duty, who sacrifices her chances for happiness to what she sees as her responsibility to her father Cleveland, her brother Bertram, her friend Perdita Kingsford, and her stepsister Sophy in Ivy Compton-Burnett's *Dolores*.

Evelyn Hutton   Sophia's younger daughter, who grows up to marry Herbert Blackwood in Ivy Compton-Burnett's *Dolores*.

James Hutton   Cleveland's elder brother, who is made a Dean; he is willing to educate his nephew Bertram but instead pays to educate another nephew, the younger Cleveland, and adopts him in Ivy Compton-Burnett's *Dolores*.

Sophia Hutton   The second wife of Cleveland and the elder sister of Carrie Blackwood; she is an irritable, jealous, sensitive woman in Ivy Compton-Burnett's *Dolores*.

Sophy Hutton   Sophia's elder daughter, who marries

William Soulsby when Dolores, his first choice, steps aside out of pity in Ivy Compton-Burnett's *Dolores*.

Hwan Te (or Huan Te) Chinese boy with an extra thumb on each hand; he is one of the supernormals of John Wainwright's Pacific island colony in Olaf Stapledon's *Odd John: A Story Between Jest and Earnest*.

Père Hyacinthe Secular, Legitimist confessor of Great-aunt Léocadie in Sylvia Townsend Warner's *Summer Will Show*.

Jim Hylton Prisoner of war with Geoffrey Raingo; his escape and return to London make Adela Raingo believe her son has also escaped in Arnold Bennett's *Lord Raingo*.

Joe Hynes Newspaper reporter who owes Leopold Bloom three shillings in James Joyce's *Ulysses*.

Dr. Joe Hynes Son of Johnny Hynes; he vacillates between helping the poor and sickly and ignoring their pleas; he decides to leave the valley but is struck dead by the plague in Liam O'Flaherty's *Famine*.

Johnny Hynes Wealthy shopkeeper and son of an informer; he rises to wealth during the Repeal Movement and then uncharitably tries to increase his wealth during the blight in Liam O'Flaherty's *Famine*.

Thomsy Hynes Lazy drunkard who lives with the Kilmartins; he finally does good when he tries to help Mary Kilmartin find her fugitive husband, Martin; he later dies of the plague in Liam O'Flaherty's *Famine*.

Tony Hynes Son of Johnny Hynes; through an arranged marriage, he becomes a wealthy importer of Indian corn during the famine in Liam O'Flaherty's *Famine*.

Hyoi A hross, one of the native species of Malacandra (Mars), who is Ransom's first contact on Malacandra; he is killed by Weston and Devine in C. S. Lewis's *Out of the Silent Planet*.

Hyzenthlay ("shine-dew-fur") Visionary doe rabbit who conspires with Bigwig to lead other does out of Efrafa in Richard Adams's *Watership Down*.

I A voice that is relating "how it was I quote before Pim with Pim after Pim how it is three parts I say it as I hear it" in Samuel Beckett's *How It Is*.

Iain A man briefly involved with Kate Fletcher Armstrong in Margaret Drabble's *The Middle Ground*.

Ibrahim Indian servant to "Tusker" and Lucy Smalley; because he has visited his brother in England, he considers himself somewhat above the average servant; he is very concerned with proper "pukka" speech and behavior in Paul Scott's *Staying On*.

Ibum Sensitive young black servant whom Ahmadou Mouth overworks as she attempts to act the part of a Cunan society lady and who later serves the even more abusive Edna Mouth in Ronald Firbank's *Sorrow in Sunlight*.

Ichthyoids A highly developed species of intelligent marine life on another planet, more talented in theoretical than in practical matters, who eventually form a telepathic union with the Arachnoids to create a symbiotic species in Olaf Stapledon's *Star Maker*.

Mr. Ickeringway Fifty-year-old ex-naval man and chief hotel engineer; he presides proudly over the immense machinery which makes the hotel self-sufficient in water supply and electrical power in Arnold Bennett's *Imperial Palace*.

Ida Philip Weston's eventual wife, who soon divorces him in Isabel Colegate's *Statues in a Garden*.

Idwal A superior sheepdog created by Thomas Trelone and living on the Pughs' farm in Olaf Stapledon's *Sirius: A Fantasy of Love and Discord*.

Sir Edgar Iffley Senior historian among British medievalists and president of their professional association; he asks Gerald Middleton to become editor of their new journal and asks Gerald to replace him as president of the association after the Melpham fraud has been revealed in Angus Wilson's *Anglo-Saxon Attitudes*.

Beatrice Ifor A beautiful girl whose ruination Sammy Mountjoy helps bring about in William Golding's *Free Fall*.

Frank Illidge Weak-willed young socialist sympathizer who works as a laboratory assistant to Lord Edward Tantamount; an acquaintance of the cynical Maurice Spandrell, he becomes unwittingly an accomplice in Everard Webley's murder in Aldous Huxley's *Point Counter Point*.

Ilse Pessimistic Swedish prostitute; she provides sex for various members of the auxiliary fire service in Henry Green's *Caught*.

Immada Hassim's sister, who fights as bravely as a man for his rule of Wajo but is destroyed with the explosion of the *Emma* in Joseph Conrad's *The Rescue: A Romance of the Shallows*.

Frederick Gordon Immerson Quiet, restrained publicity manager on salary plus commission; he is the chief pet of Managing Director Evelyn Orcham for his shrewd promotion of the hotel and his capacity to discover the wily tactics of Sir Henry Savotte to buy the hotel in Arnold Bennett's *Imperial Palace*.

Albert Immonds Truckdriver who goes to Corker's employment agency looking for a job in London; awed and frightened by the city, he is anxious about the "transforming power of London" and what it may do to his wife in John Berger's *Corker's Freedom*.

Freddie Impiatt Hilary Burde's colleague and weekly drinks-and-dinner host; he and his wife, Laura, erroneously believe Hilary to be in love with her, and Freddie becomes convinced that they are lovers in Iris Murdoch's *A Word Child*.

Laura Impiatt Wife of Hilary Burde's higher-ranking colleague Freddie Impiatt; she carries on an unsuspected love affair with Christopher Cather in Iris Murdoch's *A Word Child*.

Lester Ince Cambridge college fellow who is one of the young reactionaries against Donald Howard in C. P. Snow's *The Affair*. He offers his country home to Lewis Eliot for convalescence after his cardiac arrest in *Last Things*.

Incent An agent who succumbs to a condition known as Undulant Rhetoric, thus falling victim to the wiles of the Shammat Empire; he does sometimes emerge from the disease, only to have severe relapses in Doris Lessing's *Documents Relating to the Sentimental Agents in the Volyen Empire*.

Individual One A claustrophobic who sees no difference between countries, continents and cities; she eventually loses her mind in Doris Lessing's *Re: Colonised Planet 5, Shikasta*.

Individual Two An eleven-year-old female gang leader, responsible for committing many crimes, not because of her own will, but because she has been the victim of indoctrination; she is killed eventually in a terrorist exploit in Doris Lessing's *Re: Colonised Planet 5, Shikasta*.

Individual Three   Innocent who cannot believe that humans could be so cruel as to have caused a holocaust in Doris Lessing's *Re: Colonised Planet 5, Shikasta*.

Individual Four   See the Brand.

Individual Five   Son of rich parents who knows no real family life, and who claims several citizenships before becoming a member in the International Police Force in Doris Lessing's *Re: Colonised Planet 5, Shikasta*.

Individual Six   Native of a concentration camp; he grew up never able to understand why people could blame atrocities on one country or why people could claim a nationality, because he sees all people and all countries contributing to crises and problems; he eventually commits suicide in Doris Lessing's *Re: Colonised Planet 5, Shikasta*.

Individual Seven   A neglected girl who finds elation in participating in riots; she treats herself with utter derision for being born into a wealthy family, attempting to gain acceptance by prostituting herself to other people's demands before she ends up committing suicide in Doris Lessing's *Re: Colonised Planet 5, Shikasta*.

Taynth Indredd   The prince of Pannoval and ambassador to Borlien; he pushes JandolAngand's divorce and planned marriage to Simdol Tal in Brian W. Aldiss's *Helliconia Summer*.

Madame Inez   Fortune teller who tells Pamela Pringle that she is a reincarnation of Helen of Troy in E. M. Delafield's *The Provincial Lady Goes Further*.

Miss Ingamells   Shop assistant at the Clayhanger printshop; she marries when past thirty and has three children in Arnold Bennett's *Clayhanger*.

Winifred Inger   The schoolteacher with whom Ursula Brangwen has a Lesbian affair; she marries Ursula's uncle Tom Brangwen in D. H. Lawrence's *The Rainbow*.

Inglebrecht   Revolutionary tract writer who enlists Sophia Willoughby to distribute leaflets, the *Communist Manifesto*, in Sylvia Townsend Warner's *Summer Will Show*.

Alfred Inglethorp   Evelyn Howard's supposed cousin; having quickly wooed and married her employer, Emily (Cavendish), he is disliked and resented

by the Cavendish family in Agatha Christie's *The Mysterious Affair at Styles: A Detective Story*.

Emily Cavendish Inglethorp   Imperious widowed septuagenarian stepmother of John and Lawrence Cavendish; she is poisoned after her marriage to Alfred Inglethorp in Agatha Christie's *The Mysterious Affair at Styles: A Detective Story*.

Arthur Inglewood   Amateur photographer and Innocent Smith's schoolmate, who assists in Smith's defense at his trial in G. K. Chesterton's *Manalive*.

Captain Jacques D'Ingraville (alias Pierre Blanc)   Famous french flying ace, superb pilot, and marksman in John Buchan's *Mr. Standfast*. He reappears as the most dangerous of Senor Castor's staff of Conquistadores in the Gran Seco in *The Courts of the Morning*. In his last appearance he is the evil intelligence behind Lancelot Troth's vendetta against Valdemar Haradsen in *The Island of Sheep*.

Tertius Inkpen   District Factory Inspector, amateur musician, and wise friend to Hilda and Edwin Clayhanger; he is injured in Albert Benbow's factory; he carries on a secret affair with a married woman in Arnold Bennett's *These Twain*.

Hesther Innes   An actress who tried to kill herself when she learned of her pregnancy, fearing it would ruin her career; rescued by her husband, she now brings the baby to rehearsals in Margaret Drabble's *A Summer Bird-Cage*.

Mary Innes   The top graduating senior of a physical-education college; after her successful rival for the top position is murdered, she refuses the post, realizing that she innocently motivated the murderer in Josephine Tey's *Miss Pym Disposes*.

Inspector   Fruit-drop-eating head of the Brighton Police Station; he is questioned by Ida Arnold about Hale's death and tracks Pinkie Brown down in Graham Greene's *Brighton Rock*.

Mr. Instone   Barrister for Clare Corven in the divorce proceedings brought by Sir Gerald Corven in John Galsworthy's *Over the River*.

Miss Insull   Respected spinster in John Baines's shop; having married ancient Mr. Critchlow after he bought the shop, she attempts to commit suicide as sales dwindle in Arnold Bennett's *The Old Wives Tale*.

The Interpreter   Stern enemy and interrogator of the Cartographer; he interprets for the Colonel in Nigel Dennis's *A House in Order*.

Ira   A sleazy, illiterate, thieving Yank, the object of the deluded Rita's infatuation; he does not talk to her but finds instant rapport with the younger of her aunts, Margo Bickerton, in Beryl Bainbridge's *The Dressmaker*.

Sister Irene of the Incarnation   Nun of the Flaming-Hood who accompanies Laura de Nazianzi from the Pisuergan palace to her new convent home and later indulges with other nuns in gossip about Prince Yousef's wedding ceremony in Ronald Firbank's *The Flower Beneath the Foot*.

Irina   Common-law wife of fellow Moscow Centre agent Boris; she is murdered by Karla's thugs for informing her Western lover, Ricki Tarr, of the presence of a Soviet double agent highly placed in British Intelligence in John Carré's *Tinker, Tailor, Soldier, Spy*.

Iris   An older woman who owns a café in London; she takes Martha Quest under her wing soon after she arrives in London in Doris Lessing's *The Four-Gated City*.

Grace Ironwood   Doctor and member of St. Anne's community; she confirms that Jane Studdock has the power of second sight in C. S. Lewis's *That Hideous Strength*.

Blackie Isaacs   Manager of the wrestler Schmule and father of Reen in Wolf Mankowitz's *A Kid for Two Farthings*.

Godfrey Isaacs   Client of James Horgan in Isabel Colegate's *Statues in a Garden*.

Reen Isaacs   Daughter of Blackie; she is Sonia Hoffmann's only competition for Schmule's affection in Wolf Mankowitz's *A Kid for Two Farthings*.

Princess Isabel   Great-niece of England's Queen Charlotte and friend of Olga Bracely; she snubs Lucia Lucas's repeated invitations in E. F. Benson's *Lucia in London*.

Isbister   American artist who makes Graham heir to his fortune, a legacy which Graham's estate executors parlay into enormous wealth and influence in H. G. Wells's *When the Sleeper Wakes: A Story of the Years to Come*.

Horace Isbister   Fashionable and eminent portrait painter and friend of St. John Clarke; his reputation is in decline at the time of his death in Anthony Powell's *The Acceptance World* but has risen in *Hearing Secret Harmonies*.

Iseult   Daughter figure in the archetypal family romance of James Joyce's *Finnegans Wake*.

Christopher (Herr Issyvoo, Christoph, Christophilis) Isherwood   Young English writer who narrates the story of his life and friends in pre-World War II Berlin; he slowly comes to understand the importance of the political changes taking place in Christopher Isherwood's *Goodbye to Berlin*. He later returns to expand on his German, as well as American, friends in *Down There on a Visit*.

Ishmael   Constance Maine and Charles Watkins's illegitimate son in Doris Lessing's *Briefing for a Descent into Hell*.

Isildur   King of Gondor who long ago defeated Sauron in battle and cut the One Ring from his finger in J. R. R. Tolkien's *The Fellowship of the Ring*.

Iskador   An archer who escapes from Pannoval with Yuli and becomes his wife in Brian W. Aldiss's *Helliconia Spring*.

Italian chum   The mistress of Wilfred Barclay; she ejects him from her villa because Barclay refuses to give credence to Padre Pio's stigmata in William Golding's *The Paper Men*.

Ernest Itterby   Prime Minister whose image is changed from that of dull politician to aggressive champion of the people to make his reelection more viable in J. B. Priestley's *The Image Men*.

Examining Magistrate Ivanov   Nicolas Rubashov's former college friend and battalion commander; he interrogates Rubashov, promising him imprisonment rather than death if Rubashov falsely confesses; he is executed by state officials for conducting the case negligently in Arthur Koestler's *Darkness at Noon*.

Boris Ivanovitch   Bolshevist whom Tuppence and Tommy Beresford encounter as Count Stepanov in Agatha Christie's *The Secret Adversary*. As Monsieur Krassine he is involved in a jewel theft investigated by Hercule Poirot in *The Mystery of the Blue Train*.

Peter Ivanovitch   Emigré Russian revolutionary in Joseph Conrad's *Under Western Eyes*.

Fanny Ivanovna   Nikolai Bursanov's mistress for many years; she is the motherly governess to his daughters, Sonia, Nina, and Vera Bursanov, and is a proud and devoted woman in William Gerhardie's *Futility: A Novel on Russian Themes*.

Moxon Ivery (Herr Graf von Schwabing) Head of the formidable German spy network in Great Britain and Europe; a fiendishly clever man of innumerable aliases and disguises, he is captured as the result of his passion for Mary Lamington; forced to witness firsthand the horrors of war, he is killed by German bullets in John Buchan's *Mr. Standfast.*

Ivor Anna Wulf's homosexual boarder who develops a friendship with Anna's daughter; his lover's coming to share his flat eventually causes Anna to ask them both to leave in Doris Lessing's *The Golden Notebook.*

Marcia Ivory Spinster clerk in her mid-sixties; she is insanely obsessive about certain domestic details but otherwise extremely negligent; she becomes infatuated with the National Health Surgeon who performed her mastectomy; she lives alone in her late parents' semi-detached house in Clapham, thinking about her dead cat Snowy and other disconnected topics in Barbara Pym's *Quartet in Autumn.*

Iyfilka Daughter of Si and Cretha, wife of Sar Gotth Den, and mother of Dresyl Den in Brian W. Aldiss's *Helliconia Spring.*

J

Jack A South African living in London with whom Martha Quest has a love affair; he later trains girls to work in his brothel in Doris Lessing's *The Four-Gated City*.

Jack Joyce's husband, who moves his family to the States, where he has been offered a faculty position in Doris Lessing's *The Diaries of Jane Somers*.

Jack Rita's father, a shy, socially insecure butcher; his affection for his daughter is remote in Beryl Bainbridge's *The Dressmaker*.

Jack Slow but steady factory worker and friend of Arthur Seaton, with whom his wife is having an affair in Alan Sillitoe's *Saturday Night and Sunday Morning*.

Jack Working-class man whose lodgings are upstairs from F. X. Enderby's; he believes mistakenly that Enderby is having an affair with his girlfriend; his peculiar conception of honor requires him to fight a reluctant and frightened Enderby in Anthony Burgess's *Inside Mr. Enderby*.

Dr. Harry Jackley Curator of the aquarium of the zoological garden who is off the premises during controversial times; he is chief candidate for directorship after the end of the Uni-European government in Angus Wilson's *The Old Men at the Zoo*.

Jackson Coxswain aboard the *Indefatigable*; he is second in command under Hornblower in the surprise attack by jolly boat of the *Papillin* in C. S. Forester's *Mr. Midshipman Hornblower*.

Jackson The Boothbys' African cook, who is befriended by Paul Blackenhurst in order to anger and frustrate Mrs. Boothby; he is eventually fired from his job in Doris Lessing's *The Golden Notebook*.

Mr. Jackson Widdrington's cousin, a scholarly schoolmaster at Sawston; he fights to keep the day-boys in his school in E. M. Forster's *The Longest Journey*.

Grant Jackson Tom Collander's close friend, who is serving five years for corruption at a different prison from that in which Tom is serving time in Margaret Drabble's *The Ice Age*.

Rathbone Jackson President of Ishmaelia who is briefly displaced when Dr. Benito and his Russian supporters stage an unsuccessful coup in Evelyn Waugh's *Scoop*.

Sally Jackson A woman who undergoes psychiatric treatment, after which Kate Fletcher Armstrong finds her a boring person in Margaret Drabble's *The Middle Ground*.

Molly Jacobs Anna Wulf's closest friend, a part-time actress and member of the British Communist Party; her life revolves around her attempting to liberate herself from traditional female roles as well as from her ex-husband and her son in Doris Lessing's *The Golden Notebook*.

Tommy Jacobs Molly Jacobs and Richard Portmain's emotionally troubled son, who rebels against his parents, attempts suicide, and is blinded in the process; he teams up with his father's wife to help the African revolutions for independence in Doris Lessing's *The Golden Notebook*.

Father Bernard Jacoby A God-hating, high-church Anglican priest, a convert of Jewish origin, who is Rozanov's philosophical disputant; after Rozanov's death he decamps to Greece, where he preaches anti-Christian doctrine in classical Greek to peasants who look after him, believing him mad in Iris Murdoch's *The Philosopher's Pupil*.

Jaffir The Malay chief Hassim's faithful messenger, who brings Hassim's ring to Lingard to initiate the bond between them and dies heroically bringing Lingard news of Jörgenson's end in Joseph Conrad's *The Rescue: A Romance of the Shallows*.

Jagger Tall, fat, red-haired, civilian-dressed late-arriving security officer who quickly resolves mysteries surrounding espionage threats against the security of top-secret Operation Apollo in Kingsley Amis's *The Anti-Death League*.

Alice Jago Wife of Paul; she is viewed as a liability to her husband in his candidacy for election to Master in C. P. Snow's *The Masters*.

Paul Jago Anglo-Irish fellow of the Cambridge college; as Senior Tutor he is the leading candidate for new Master, but he finally loses the election in a close vote in C. P. Snow's *The Masters*. He refuses to serve on the Court of Seniors hearing Donald Howard's case, and he makes a private appeal to Arthur Brown for justice in the case in *The Affair*.

Dr. Jagon Monarchist who after two years has exchanged his Royalist loyalties for allegiance to the new Juventus Party, which promises more democracy, in John Buchan's *The House of the Four Winds*.

Jahsper Miss Pankerton's tall, pale friend who

writes; Miss Pankerton declares that Bloomsbury can do nothing without him in E. M. Delafield's *The Diary of a Provincial Lady*.

Jakes   Former porter at Shrewsbury College, Oxford, who was dismissed for dishonesty; now a jobbing gardener, he supplements his income with minor blackmail; Harriet Vane, recognizing him at another Oxford college, foils and reports him in Dorothy L. Sayers's *Gaudy Night*.

Mrs. Jakes   Wife of the former Shrewsbury College porter; Annie Wilson's children board at her house in Dorothy L. Sayers's *Gaudy Night*.

Phil Jamaica   A fighter at Isaacs's gymnasium who teaches Joe a few self-defense steps in Wolf Mankowitz's *A Kid for Two Farthings*.

Dr. James   A physician at the Islington Maternity Hospital where Alvina Houghton studies to become a nurse; he tries futilely to woo her with sweets and flowers in D. H. Lawrence's *The Lost Girl*.

Miss James   The very thin, dark-haired matron at Lucius Cassidy's school; she accompanies Sefton Shelley's friends in their visit to his house in Ivy Compton-Burnett's *Two Worlds and Their Ways*.

Mrs. James   The proprietress of the Gainsborough Hotel in Mashopi, where Anna Wulf and her socialist friends are boarders; she is enamored of Willi Rodde, even though he patronizes her, in Doris Lessing's *The Golden Notebook*.

Joker James   Musician with Black Ice; Kate Fletcher Armstrong puts him on her list of possibly "marginal people" in Margaret Drabble's *The Middle Ground*.

Margaret James   Violet Weston-Moreton's best friend in Isabel Colegate's *Statues in a Garden*.

Marylin James   Ex-pupil of Romley Fourways', the school Kate Fletcher (Armstrong) attended; she is a plumber who is used in the television film Kate is making in Margaret Drabble's *The Middle Ground*.

Captain Ronny James   Officer from the Potential Officer wing at Catterick who is present at the interviews in which Jonathan Browne and Mike Brady announce that they don't wish to be officers in David Lodge's *Ginger, You're Barmy*.

Theo James   Elizabeth Gruffydd-Williams's friend who finds John Lewis trying to escape from Elizabeth's house after her husband comes home; Lewis pretends

to be a plumber in Kingsley Amis's *That Uncertain Feeling*.

W. Neil James   Julia Martin's former, early lover, to whom she turns for money; he is rich, kind, and cautious; he sends her the money in Jean Rhys's *After Leaving Mr. Mackenzie*.

Dr. Jameson   A kindly physician who attends Mrs. Morel before her death in D. H. Lawrence's *Sons and Lovers*.

Jamesu   Servant to Officer Rudbeck; he sees Johnson steal the key to the office safe but does not report the theft in Joyce Cary's *Mister Johnson*.

Jan   A bright and articulate London working girl; she and Mag live together in what they discover is a house of prostitution; they fascinate Miriam Henderson by their insouciance and unconventionality in Dorothy Richardson's *The Tunnel* and in *Interim*. Miriam comes to see her as Cynical Jan in *Dawn's Left Hand*.

Jan (Janet)   Fifteen-year-old granddaughter of Daniel House; despite a slight deformity of one leg, she has a nymph-like appearance to the visiting young poet James Ross in Roy Fuller's *The Carnal Island*.

JandolAngand   The king of Borlien; he divorces his wife in order to marry Simdol Tal, the princess of Oldorando, as part of his plan to rule Helliconia in Brian W. Aldiss's *Helliconia Summer*.

Jane   Imogene King's roommate in Isabel Colegate's *Agatha*.

Jane   Bensington's severe, overprotective cousin, whose constant disapproval keeps Bensington meek and reclusive in H. G. Wells's *The Food of the Gods, and How It Came to Earth*.

Old Jane   Portress at the gates of the convent of the Flaming-Hood who makes friendly conversation with the forlorn Laura de Nazianzi in Ronald Firbank's *The Flower Beneath the Foot*.

Bronson Jane   Impressive new type of American financier and sportsman; on behalf of powerful clients, he negotiates a sale of stocks with Arnold Tavanger, the majority stockholder, in John Buchan's *The Gap in the Curtain*. His description of the missing Francis Galliard sparks Sir Edward Leithen's imagination and a determination to find him in *Sick Heart River*.

Janet   Diva Plaistow's parlormaid in E. F. Benson's *Miss Mapp* and in *Mapp and Lucia*. She is Diva's assistant in a tea shop in *The Worshipful Lucia* and in *Trouble for Lucia*.

Janet   The resident housekeeper of the Tebricks at their Rylands home; Richard Tebrick dismisses her and instructs her to dismiss the servants in order to conceal his wife's transformation into a fox in David Garnett's *Lady Into Fox*.

Auntie Janey   Woman about whom the eleven-year-old Kate Fletcher (Armstrong) told some schoolmates an embarrassing story concerning her spaniel in Margaret Drabble's *The Middle Ground*.

Janis   One of a pack of young "summer people" in Connecticut; the young Englishman Augustine Penry-Herbert is shocked at her sexual overtures, and she is equally shocked at his expectation of consummation in Richard Hughes's *The Wooden Shepherdess*.

Janni   One-armed corporal devoted to Constantine Maris; he is the one other man who remains to aid Leithen in John Buchan's *The Dancing Floor*.

Mr. Janson   Conrad, Lord Field's butler at Wood Hill in Isabel Colegate's *Orlando King*.

Mrs. Janson   Mr. Janson's wife in Isabel Colegate's *Orlando King*.

Inspector James Japp   Police detective with whom Hercule Poirot maintains a cordial collaboration without respecting his abilities through six Agatha Christie novels, including *The Mysterious Affair at Styles: A Detective Story* and *The A.B.C. Murders*.

Peter Japp   Colonial-born old ruffian; an alcoholic storekeeper, he illegally sells liquor to the natives in John Buchan's *Prester John*.

John (Jacko) Jaques   An oily, malicious, happiness-hating abortionist with a classy clientele; the perfidious friend of Hugo Chesterton, he gives Hugo tips about his rich clients and gets vicarious thrills from the burglaries; jealous of Hugo, he covets Daisy Bland not from lust but for power; he manipulates her into giving evidence against her lover and then arranges Hugo's capture in Nicholas Blake's *A Tangled Web*.

Major Harry Jardine   Shy, gentlemanly second husband of Sibyl Anstey Herbert; kindly towards children, he is an alcoholic who accepts life matter-of-factly in Rosamond Lehmann's *The Ballad and the Source*.

Sibyl Anstey Herbert Jardine   Complex, individualistic mother of Ianthe Herbert; a believer in women's emancipation and, she is selfish and vicious even towards those she loves in expressing her independence and in violating conventions in Rosamond Lehmann's *The Ballad and the Source*. She is remembered by others on a Caribbean island where she spent the last years of her life, striking up intimate relationships before she died there in *A Sea-Grape Tree*.

Miss Jarman ("Jarvie")   One of three aging spinsters living at the May of Teck Club in Muriel Spark's *The Girls of Slender Means*.

Jarnti   Ben Ata's head commander of Zone Four's vast armies; he escorts Al-Ith to Zone Four; he is forced to confront his own savage ways when he comes face to face with her in Doris Lessing's *The Marriages Between Zones Three, Four, and Five*.

Catherine Jarrold   The spinster daughter of William Jarrold, Lord Orlestone; she is a practicing Christian full of virtuous complacency unrelieved by one ounce of true Christian charity; she is the recipient of her sister-in-law Hester Jarrold's confidences, especially about Evelyn Jarrold in Vita Sackville-West's *Family History*.

Dan Jarrold   Son of Thomas and Evelyn Jarrold; he inherits Orlestone estate at Newlands and the Jarrold coal fortune; educated at Eton and encouraged to think for himself by his tutor, Miles Vane-Merrick, he is influenced by Viola and Lionel Anquetil in Vita Sackville-West's *Family History*.

Evan Jarrold   Second and surviving son of William Jarrold, Lord Orlestone; he squires Evelyn Jarrold, his widowed sister-in-law, around London after Evelyn has broken off with Miles Vane-Merrick in Vita Sackville-West's *Family History*.

Evelyn Jarrold   Middle-class daughter of a county solicitor; the widow of Tommy Jarrold, she is the mother of Dan, heir to the Orlestone estate, title, and fortune; she is a woman of passionate feeling protected by her value for social conventions; she breaks off her affair with Dan's tutor, Miles Vane-Merrick, fearing the Jarrolds' disapproval in Vita Sackville-West's *Family History*.

Geoffrey Jarrold   A surviving son of William Jarrold; Hester's husband, he is Ruth's father in Vita Sackville-West's *Family History*.

Hester Jarrold   Wife of Geoffrey Jarrold, a surviving son of William Jarrold, Lord Orlestone; although critical of her attractive sister-in-law, Evelyn Jarrold, Hester comes to London to nurse Evelyn in her final illness in Vita Sackville-West's *Family History*.

Ruth Jarrold   Daughter of Geoffrey and Hester Jarrold and niece of Evelyn Jarrold, to whom she is devoted; she uses the family fortune to frequent a society not really her own; ambitious but harmless and silly, she loves Miles Vane-Merrick but loses him to Evelyn in Vita Sackville-West's *Family History*.

Tommy Jarrold   Elder son of William Jarrold, Lord Orlestone; he marries Evelyn and fathers a son, Dan, before he is killed in Flanders in 1916 in Vita Sackville-West's *Family History*.

William Jarrold   The Jarrold family patriarch; a self-made man who turned coal mines into a fortune, he bought into the landed gentry by acquiring Newlands, in Surrey; he is elevated to the peerage, becoming Lord Orlestone; his great sorrow is his rejection as a member of the Royal Yacht Squadron in Vita Sackville-West's *Family History*.

Mrs. Jarvis   Unpopular friend of Betty Flanders in Virginia Woolf's *Jacob's Room*.

Albert Jarvis   Lord Hartlip's gun loader, who is fiercely competitive with Percy Maidment in Isabel Colegate's *The Shooting Party*.

George Jarvis   Benditch man who travels on the train with D. in Graham Greene's *The Confidential Agent*.

Jasper   The object of Alice Mellings's devoted love; a homosexual, he puts up with her because he depends on her for basic necessities and comfort; he is badly injured when the bomb that he is transporting in a car goes off before he and his accomplices can find a place to park in Doris Lessing's *The Good Terrorist*.

Jay (covernames: Henry Carpenter, Christian Stakowski, Mr. Aristo; codename Box Four)   Bureaucratic villain who controls Dalby and is suspected of kidnapping Raven; however, he is rewarded with a civil-service position rather than punished when his Communist activities are unmasked in Len Deighton's *The Ipcress File*.

Robert Jeames (satirical portrait of Harold Monro)   Amiable and harmless editor who makes anthologies of all the worst authors and whom George Winterbourne encounters at a literary gathering in Richard Aldington's *Death of a Hero*.

Jean   A girl who dances with Harry at a rock-and-roll film and walks home with him in David Lodge's *The Picturegoers*.

Jean   The young woman at the pension in Vaud with whom Miriam Henderson becomes intensely and exclusively involved; she calls Miriam "Dick" and continues to occupy her mind in Dorothy Richardson's *March Moonlight*.

Father Jean   Tall, pale priest and former moral theologian in Graham Greene's *A Burnt-Out Case*.

Jean-Pierre   Elderly servant to Henry Breasley and husband of Mathilde in John Fowles's *The Ebony Tower*.

Lady Molly Jeavons   Daughter of an earl, sister-in-law of another, and widow of a marquess; now the childless wife of Ted Jeavons, she entertains a mixed social bag at her city house in Anthony Powell's *At Lady Molly's*. Charles Stringham's alcoholism cure under the supervision of Geraldine Weedon takes place in a flat in Lady Molly's house in *Casanova's Chinese Restaurant*. Lady Molly continues to distribute miscellaneous hospitality in *The Kindly Ones*. She dies in a bomb hit on her house in *The Soldier's Art*.

Ted Jeavons   Lady Molly's unemployable war-wounded second husband, who has to get away from his wife's parties from time to time; his brief affair with Mildred Haycock during the 1914 war has repercussions in Anthony Powell's *At Lady Molly's*. He is enlivened by World War II, serving as an air-raid warden in *The Kindly Ones*. He survives the bombing of his house in *The Soldier's Art*. His death is mentioned in *Hearing Secret Harmonies*.

Sergeant Jebb   Cambridge lecturer in history who at age fifty-two must decide whether to have a rare and previously unsuccessful surgical procedure or to face certain death without surgery; he seeks help from friends and relatives in making his decision, but their insensitive escapism and lack of concern for him convince him that neither his life nor his death matters to others or, consequently, to himself in Storm Jameson's *There Will Be a Short Interval*.

Simon Jebb   Sergeant Jebb's son, who was left at age three with Dame Rhetta Sergeant, his uncaring grandmother, while his father went to France to be with his dying Swiss wife; as an eighteen-year-old student, Simon is unmoved by the deaths of his mistress and his grandmother and by scandalous reports linking him to their deaths; he is unwilling to listen to his father's attempts to discuss his death-related dilemma; he is equally unwilling to acknowledge that he has any hopes or plans for his own living in Storm Jameson's *There Will Be a Short Interval*.

Jebedee   Oxford tutor and wartime recruiter for British Intelligence; with Adrian Fielding and Steed-Aspry he recruits George Smiley in John le Carré's *Call for the Dead*.

Charlie Jebson   Handsome, muscular young seller of the finest Scotch beef at the Smithfield Market; he drives a hard bargain for his meat with Jack Craddock, meat buyer for the hotel; he also owns and runs the "Shaftesbury" express lunch-and-supper counter which Evelyn Orcham and Gracie Savotte visit for a lark in Arnold Bennett's *Imperial Palace*.

Reginald Jeeves   Erudite, unflappable manservant of Bertie Wooster; his competence extends to the extrication of Bertie from romantic entanglements and a variety of other embarrassments in P. G. Wodehouse's *The Code of the Woosters* and in *Aunts Aren't Gentlemen*. He appears in eight other novels.

Constable Bobby Jeffers   Iping policeman whom Griffin nearly strangles when he tries to arrest him at the Coach and Horses in H. G. Wells's *The Invisible Man: A Grotesque Romance*.

Jeffrey   An American who left behind his job in advertising to come to Europe; though much younger than Kate Brown, he becomes romantically involved with her before becoming seriously ill on their trip to Spain in Doris Lessing's *The Summer Before the Dark*.

Vincent Jeffries   Walter's good-looking, blue-eyed, broad-shouldered, slim-hipped brother, who tries unsuccessfully to pick up Anna Morgan in Jean Rhys's *Voyage in the Dark*.

Walter Jeffries   Anna Morgan's comfortably well-off lover, nearly twenty years older than Anna; he backs out of his relationship with her by having his brother write to tell her in Jean Rhys's *Voyage in the Dark*.

Jehan   The chosen assistant of the master builder in William Golding's *The Spire*.

Cassandra (Cassie) Jekyll   Governess to Duncan Edgeworth's daughters; she marries him after his divorce from Alison and bears Duncan a son and heir, William, in Ivy Compton-Burnett's *A House and Its Head*.

Gretchen Jekyll   A good woman, Oscar's mother; she gets Emma Marshall to confess her murder of young Richard Edgeworth and to reveal Sibyl Edgeworth's bribes and threats in Ivy Compton-Burnett's *A House and Its Head*.

Oscar Jekyll   A clergyman with a slender income and a widowed mother to support; he proposes to Nance

Edgeworth when his mother dies in Ivy Compton-Burnett's *A House and Its Head*.

Jellamy   The butler of the Gavestons whom Blanche Gaveston does not want to witness the family's meals and private conversations in Ivy Compton-Burnett's *A Family and a Fortune*.

Jelli   Deformed but extremely sensitive Hungarian girl; she is one of the supernormals of John Wainwright's Pacific island colony in Olaf Stapledon's *Odd John: A Story Between Jest and Earnest*.

Jem   Humble member of the relief crew aboard the canal boat in C. S. Forester's *Hornblower and the Atropos*.

Jemmie   Anna Wulf's previous boarder from Ceylon, with whom she felt uncomfortable, much as she does with Ivor in Doris Lessing's *The Golden Notebook*.

Jen   Young girl who is hired to help Nanny care for the children in Isabel Colegate's *Orlando King*.

Peter Jenkin   Nervous, affected young man, a poet, who blinks and jerks; he does not dance but sulkily derides society as he converses with Olivia Curtis in Rosamond Lehmann's *Invitation to the Waltz*.

Jenkins   Servant in the Long Rooms who assists Hornblower in C. S. Forester's *Lieutenant Hornblower*.

Captain Jenkins   Nicholas's father, a regular soldier; his distaste for his brother Giles's affairs is mentioned in Anthony Powell's *A Question of Upbringing*. His familial background, army career, and character are analyzed in *The Kindly Ones* and in *Temporary Kings*.

Albert Jenkins   Dandified nineteen-year-old cockney with sallow skin, shallow chest, and small feet; he shares an office with Richard Larch and introduces him to good restaurants but disgusts Richard with his crudities in Arnold Bennett's *A Man From the North*.

Giles Jenkins   Uncle with whom Nicholas Jenkins dines from time to time; fey, egotistic, and contemptuous of all respectable behavior, he is so unreliable in his relations with women and in his financial dealings that he is always on the brink of disgrace in Anthony Powell's *A Question of Upbringing* and in *A Buyer's Market*. His relationship with Mrs. Erdleigh is introduced in *The Acceptance World*. He has become a keen supporter of Hitler; he dies leaving his money to Mrs. Erdleigh in *The Kindly Ones*.

Ieuan Jenkins   John Lewis's colleague at the library who, desperately needing the money because his wife is ill, applies for the job Lewis wants; he accuses Lewis of becoming friendly with Vernon Gruffydd-Williams to get the promotion; he gets the job in Kingsley Amis's *That Uncertain Feeling*.

Megan Jenkins   Chronically ill, paranoid wife of Ieuan Jenkins; she is Jean Lewis's friend but is disliked by John Lewis in Kingsley Amis's *That Uncertain Feeling*.

Nicholas (Nick) Jenkins   Narrator and protagonist; he is an army captain's son whose introduction to Society occurs at a weekend at Peter Templer's house, where he begins a long infatuation with Jean Templer in Anthony Powell's *A Question of Upbringing*. He works for a London publisher and attends debutante dances in *A Buyer's Market*. He becomes a published novelist; Jean (Templer) Duport becomes his lover in *The Acceptance World*. He meets his future wife, Lady Isobel Tolland, in *At Lady Molly's*. He mingles with artists and writers and aristocrats of British society as he seeks to establish himself as a writer in *Casanova's Chinese Restaurant*. He is married and unable to write as World War II approaches; he is trying to get a commission in *The Kindly Ones*. His Army career is for a while frustrated and made miserable by his condescending and detested superior, his old acquaintance Widmerpool, in *The Valley of Bones* and in *The Soldier's Art*. He moves up through Army ranks and is posted ultimately to General Staff Intelligence Corps, where he attains the rank of major; he meets Jean and does not recognize her in *The Military Philosophers*. He is demobilized and growing in literary reputation; he has a second son in *Books Do Furnish a Room*. He recognizes the advantages and disadvantages of increasing age in *Temporary Kings*. He is a distinguished writer in his sixties with far-flung, important connections throughout the literary and social world; changes he observes in his contemporaries increase his self examination in *Hearing Secret Harmonies*.

Sid Jenkins   Broad, shabby, easily genial former coal miner and street fighter; his colloquial oratory won him the leadership of the Labour Party and a place as Minister without Portfolio in the War Cabinet; he defends Lord Raingo in government skirmishes in Arnold Bennett's *Lord Raingo*.

Tom Jenkins   Steersman of the canal boat who is appreciative of Hornblower's assistance in C. S. Forester's *Hornblower and the Atropos*.

Ted Jenks   Artist-in-residence at Brockshire University in J. B. Priestley's *The Image Men*.

Miss Jennet   The maid for Sir Ransome Chace; she wants two thirds of a butler's salary for doing the job of a butler; she frequently exchanges gossip with the Lovats' servants in Ivy Compton-Burnett's *Darkness and Day*.

Mrs. Jennings   A friendly woman who adores babies; she watches Octavia Stacey twice a week while Rosamund Stacey goes to the library in Margaret Drabble's *The Millstone*.

Bill Jennings   A friendly American who, together with his brother-in-law, Hank Johnson, completes an incongruous team that is ahead of its time but manages to please an audience in J. B. Priestley's *Lost Empires*.

Liz Jennings   Twenty-nine-year-old single woman who hopes to marry John Pomfret; however, after he becomes re-involved with Jane Weatherby, she becomes involved with Jane's friend Richard Abbot in Henry Green's *Nothing*.

Maria (Jenny) Jennings   The housekeeper for the Donne family; spare and sturdy, with gentle eyes, she is especially kind to Reuben Donne in Ivy Compton-Burnett's *Elders and Betters*.

Jenny   Cousin of amnesiac soldier Chris Baldry, whom she has loved possessively since childhood; she envies his former lover, Margaret Allington, whom she describes as "a big trustworthy dog", and despises his wife, Kitty; she is the narrator of Rebecca West's *The Return of the Soldier*.

Enno Jensen   Sasha's husband, who leaves her temporarily, saying she doesn't know how to make love; he is incapable of earning a regular living by writing or doing public relations; he finally leaves her permanently in Jean Rhys's *Good Morning Midnight*.

Sasha (Sophia) Jensen   Woman in her forties on a downward slope; aided by a small inheritance, she tries to drink herself to death and fails; she becomes pregnant by Enno Jensen and aborts the child; she works part time as a saleswoman in a dress-house; she is a survivor who ultimately accepts her "little life" in Jean Rhys's *Good Morning Midnight*.

Jepp   Zoological laboratory assistant whose incorrect data lead Arthur Miles to a great mistake in his research in C. P. Snow's *The Search*.

Louisa Jepp   Part-Gypsy grandmother of Laurence Manders and leader of an unlikely but successful band of smugglers in Muriel Spark's *The Comforters*.

Jerry Jerningham   Leading juvenile who decides to settle for security and comfort instead of a life on the stage once the concert party disbands in J. B. Priestley's *The Good Companions*.

Jerome   One of three larky young city men on a fortnight's holiday on the Thames; the narrator of the boating adventures, he intersperses the humorous account with scraps of history and travel notes in Jerome K. Jerome's *Three Men in a Boat (To Say Nothing of the Dog)*.

Jerry   A "bohemian" who had lived in the room that Maureen rents to Kate Brown; he left to go live in Turkey in Doris Lessing's *The Summer Before the Dark*.

Sir Henry Jervoise   The dramatic and tricky Defense Counsel; he has a quizzical eye in Nicholas Blake's *A Tangled Web*.

Odi Jeseratabhar   The Priest-Militant Admiral of Sibornal; she plans to conquer Borlien; she becomes SatoriIrvrash's lover in Brian W. Aldiss's *Helliconia Summer*.

Miss Jessop   Mousey, subservient spinster, inexplicably tyrannized by the eccentric Mrs. Bone whom she frequently visits in Barbara Pym's *Excellent Women*. She appears briefly with her brother, a former Colonial administrator, in *Less Than Angels*.

Horace Jewdwine   Aristocratic cousin of Lucia Harden; he is an Oxford don who prostitutes himself intellectually to achieve popular success, evades his "understanding" to marry Lucia after the loss of her money, and betrays Keith Rickman both professionally and personally in May Sinclair's *The Divine Fire*.

Jewel   Eurasian girl in Patusan with whom Jim falls in love in Joseph Conrad's *Lord Jim*.

Arthur Jewell (Ortheris)   Orphaned private in Hugh Britling's regiment; his foul mouth and fighting are a curiosity to Hugh in H. G. Wells's *Mr. Britling Sees It Through*.

Jheserabhay   A painter of porcelain who worked for Eedap Mun Odin; he makes Odin want a simpler life in Brian W. Aldiss's *Helliconia Winter*.

Jill   Jane Somers's niece who comes to stay with Jane in London after finishing school; she takes a job with *Lilith*, becoming not only a success but one of Jane's closest friends in Doris Lessing's *The Diaries of Jane Somers*.

Big Jill   A pimp and a lesbian; she is the narrator's confidante on matters of the heart, especially concerning Suzette, in Colin MacInnes's *Absolute Beginners*.

Jim   A wholesome, well-reared clergyman's son, raised on adventure novels, who goes to sea to become a merchant-marine officer but is humiliated after he joins the group that quietly abandons the steamer *Patna* and eight hundred Muslim pilgrims in the mistaken belief that the ship is sinking; he wanders around the ports of the Far East until he becomes an agent for Stein in Patusan, where he is revered by the natives but again behaves immorally in a time of crisis; he accepts death in retribution for Gentleman Brown's murder of Dain Waris in Joseph Conrad's *Lord Jim*.

Jim   Friendly prison officer who trades stories with Len Wincobank on the best meal they had ever enjoyed; he also tells Wincobank the story of Alfred Collins in Margaret Drabble's *The Ice Age*.

Jim   A black youth who was living alone in the condemned house that Alice Mellings and her cronies move into and fix up in Doris Lessing's *The Good Terrorist*.

Jim   George's lover, whose death forces George to reevaluate his own life in Christopher Isherwood's *A Single Man*.

Little Jim   Black Jamaican child whom ten-year-old Emily Bas-Thornton has failed to teach to read in Richard Hughes's *A High Wind in Jamaica*.

Uncle Jim   Potwell Inn landlady's nephew; he is a reform-school lout who terrorizes his aunt and fights repeatedly with Alfred Polly; his decomposed body is misidentified as Polly's when he drowns while wearing Polly's clothes in H. G. Wells's *The History of Mr. Polly*.

Jimmy   An R.A.F. Communist Party member whose followers faction themselves off from Anton Hesse's Communist group in Doris Lessing's *A Ripple from the Storm*.

Jimmy   Morose, silent American boy, studying painting in Paris; he lives with John and Florence Dowell and continues an infidelity with Florence that began before the marriage; he is supplanted as Florence's lover by Edward Ashburnham in Ford Madox Ford's *The Good Soldier: A Tale of Passion*.

Jimmy   Iris's live-in lover, who manages the café where Martha Quest is renting a room in Doris Lessing's *The Four-Gated City*.

Jimmy   Anna Wulf's communist friend who organizes a teacher's delegation to the Soviet Union in Doris Lessing's *The Golden Notebook*.

Jimmy (Christina)   English girl and pupil in the Hanover school in Dorothy Richardson's *Pointed Roofs*.

Gulley Jimson   Aging, eccentric artist whose only salable paintings are nudes of Sara Monday; trying to repossess some from her, he causes her accidental death, suffers a stroke, and is taken away to jail, never completing his murals of the Fall and the Creation in Joyce Cary's *Herself Surprised*, in *To Be a Pilgrim*, and in *The Horse's Mouth*.

Nina Jimson   Gentle, sweet supposed wife of Gulley Jimson; she is abused by Gulley and dies young of the flu in Joyce Cary's *Herself Surprised*.

Jinny   Former lover and fiancée of Dougal Douglas; her developing a chronic illness drove him to abandon her in Muriel Spark's *The Ballad of Peckham Rye*.

Jinny   A sensual, sexual, music-loving girl, who represents the body in human motion; she bestows on Louis the kiss that condemns the children to leave Paradise and grow up in Virginia Woolf's *The Waves*.

Agatha Jixson   The head housekeeper's fluffy young secretary; she timidly serves first Mrs. O'Riordon, who leaves to marry, then Miss Maclaren, who must be hospitalized, and, finally, Violet Powler, who is the special protégé of Evelyn Orcham and recognizes Agatha's intelligence in Arnold Bennett's *Imperial Palace*.

Joan   Beautiful, passionate, intuitive woman; she loves George and wants a life with him and her father in Rex Warner's *The Wild Goose Chase: An Allegory*.

Joanna   One of Jack's many lovers, engaged to a wealthy second cousin whom she does not love, but who offers her security in Doris Lessing's *The Four-Gated City*.

Joanna   Foreign landlady who with her husband, Gustav, takes in Caithleen Brady and Bridget Brennan as tenants in Dublin; she later becomes Caithleen's confidante about sexual matters in Edna O'Brien's *The Country Girls*.

Jocelin   A methodical, unemotional, and extremely efficient terrorist member of Alice Mellings's group; she is an expert at building explosives in Doris Lessing's *The Good Terrorist*.

Dean Jocelin   An ecclesiastical chancellor who is obsessed with the desire to build an edifice for God and who is prepared to sacrifice almost anything, including himself, to accomplish his holy purpose in William Golding's *The Spire*.

Dr. Jochum   An emigré professor who loses his job at Hillesley College and moves to Benedict Arnold University in Malcolm Bradbury's *Stepping Westward*.

Cousin Jock   Clare Aubrey's cousin; he is a poet, flautist, and businessman but is unsuccessful and rude; he lives with his wife, Constance, and his daughter, Rosamund, in a poor section of London in Rebecca West's *The Fountain Overflows*.

Joe   The six-year-old boy who lives at 111 Fashion Street with his mother, his father being in Africa; reality and fantasy intermingle when he believes he has purchased a genuine unicorn that will grant him any wish once his horn develops in Wolf Mankowitz's *A Kid for Two Farthings*.

Joe   Black man in front of the Royal Oak doors (in London) in Graham Greene's *Brighton Rock*.

Joe   Intelligent, kind, friendly farmer; he rebels against the government, hoping for revenge and a better life in Rex Warner's *The Wild Goose Chase: An Allegory*.

Joe   Malarial, shell-shocked victim of the war; he is prone to periodic violence, but he is succored by the primitive love of the miser's servant Elsie Sprickett in Arnold Bennett's *Riceyman Steps*.

John   The Lovatts' garden boy, who becomes Ben Lovatt's greatest friend and influence until John leaves to join a job-training scheme in Manchester in Doris Lessing's *The Fifth Child*.

John   An admirer of Janos Lavin's work who unsuccessfully tries to get him an exhibition; John agrees with Lavin's political philosophies, and after Lavin's disappearance he publishes Lavin's journal and writes the commentary in it; he is narrator of John Berger's *A Painter of Our Time*.

John (Comrade John)   A member of the British Communist Party who helps Anna Wulf gain admission into the party's inner circle in Doris Lessing's *The Golden Notebook*.

Prince John   Young and handsome claimant to the throne of Evallonia; he is safely removed to London after leaving Dickson McCunn a gold ring as a memento of the adventure in John Buchan's *Castle Gay*. Kept safe by posing as Sir Archibald Roylance's manservant and later by traveling with the circus under Randall Glynde's protection, he wins the support of the Juventus party by saving the life of the Countess Araminta Troyos and killing the criminal Count Mastrovin in *The House of the Four Winds*.

Johnnie Nursery-group playmate of Laurie Gray, Jane and Malcolm Gray's son; Johnnie's mother, Denise, and Jane are unsuccessful in beginning a friendship in Margaret Drabble's *The Waterfall.*

Johnny Ted Brown and Stanley Lett's friend in Mashopi who is a jazz pianist, often furnishing the music for parties at the Mashopi Hotel in Doris Lessing's *The Golden Notebook.*

Johnny A young man partially paralyzed from war injuries; he has lived on a Caribbean island since he was taken there by the elderly Sibyl Jardine, who was emotionally involved with him before her death; an idyllic love affair with Rebecca Landon releases him from the tenacious hold of the dead Sibyl in Rosamond Lehmann's *A Sea-Grape Tree.*

Johns Assistant secretary and male nurse for Dr. Forester at the asylum; initially a great admirer of Forester, he befriends Arthur Rowe, becomes disillusioned in Forester and Poole when he observes their bizarre behavior, and kills them both in Graham Greene's *The Ministry of Fear.*

Johns A rooming-house resident with Jim Dixon, who is grudgingly impressed that Johns cuts his own hair; the Welches' friend, he is hostile towards Jim in Kingsley Amis's *Lucky Jim.*

Mrs. Johns A psychoanalyst who attempts to help Phoebe Coldridge with her two daughters; she believes Phoebe would be much happier if she would play traditional feminine roles in Doris Lessing's *The Four-Gated City.*

Stan Johns An egotistical man John Lewis meets at Elizabeth Gruffydd-Williams's beach party; he is proud of the speech he presented on the state of Welsh music and thinks his own Welsh music is the best in Kingsley Amis's *That Uncertain Feeling.*

Johnson Poet, dreamer, and government clerk who creates his own romantic destiny by any means: he steals, forges, and eventually commits a murder (for which he is later hanged) while trying to be a black man carrying the white man's burden in Joyce Cary's *Mister Johnson.*

Johnson Sly pirate who kidnaps Hornblower and Spendlove for a gubernatorial pardon in C. S. Forester's *Hornblower in the West Indies.*

Mr. (Dad) Johnson An old committee member of the local Rugby League who helps Arthur Machin get a position on the team in David Storey's *This Sporting Life.*

Johnson the Tapper Beggar for food in London restaurants in Colin MacInnes's *City of Spades.*

Carol Elvira (née Miller/Muller) Johnson Undercover Russian agent who is arrested by Frank Harrington's field unit and offers information on codenames of K.G.B. agents; she is later murdered in Len Deighton's *London Match.*

George Johnson Conrad, Lord Field's groom at Wood Hill in Isabel Colegate's *Orlando King.*

George Johnson (Huy Throvis-Mew) Blackmailing publisher and one of Jane Wright's part-time employers in 1945 in Muriel Spark's *The Girls of Slender Means.*

Hank Johnson An American who is billed with his brother-in-law, Bill Jennings, as a "Comedy Duo" in J. B. Priestley's *Lost Empires.*

Harold Johnson Alfred Polly's cousin who houses him and helps him considerably after Alfred's father dies; Harold believes Alfred was foolish to marry Miriam and to open a shop in Fishbourne in H. G. Wells's *The History of Mr. Polly.*

Jack Johnson World War II operative and amateur wireless enthusiast; he sells radios at Johnson's Fair Deal and ineptly trains Fred Leiser in Radio communications for his fatal incursion into East Germany in John le Carré's *The Looking-Glass War.*

Tiaré Johnson The cheerful Tahitian hotel proprietress who narrates events in Charles Strickland's life in Tahiti in W. Somerset Maugham's *The Moon and Sixpence.*

Johnston Felix Bacon's butler in Ivy Compton-Burnett's *More Women Than Men.*

Johor (George Sherban) The Canopus emissary who is sent to assist the people on Shikasta; he is undisputed leader during "The Trial" in Doris Lessing's *Re: Colonised Planet 5, Shikasta.* He is emissary to Planet 8 in *The Making of the Representative of Planet 8.* He is Agent Klorathy's adviser when Klorathy visits the Volyen empire in *Documents Relating to the Sentimental Agents in the Volyen Empire.*

Jojo A young Scottish girl Nicholas Urfe befriends but will not make love to after his return from Phraxos in John Fowles's *The Magus.*

Inigo Jolliphant   Former schoolteacher with a genuine talent for composing sprightly tunes; he is hopelessly in love with Susie Dean in J. B. Priestley's *The Good Companions.*

Mr. Jonas   A cruel schoolmaster ashamed of his Welsh ancestry who beats Huw Morgan for fighting and expells him from school when Huw attacks him for punishing a student for speaking Welsh in Richard Llewellyn's *How Green Was My Valley.*

Caleb Jonathan   Solicitor for the Crale family; he receives Hercule Poirot with expansive hospitality in Agatha Christie's *Five Little Pigs.*

Jones   Also known as A2, an assistant to Mr. Rennit; assigned to follow and protect Arthur Rowe, he is killed by the spy ring "The Free Mothers" in Graham Greene's *The Ministry of Fear.*

Major Jones   English con man who lives by his wits and is an accomplished liar; first arrested, then befriended by the Tontons Macoutes in Haiti, he tries to persuade Brown to come in on a mysterious deal, which turns sour; he finally joins the rebels and dies helping them to escape in Graham Greene's *The Comedians.*

Miss Jones   The tutor of Jane (Gray); she introduces Jane to her future husband, Malcolm Gray, at a party which follows a performance by Malcolm that causes Jane to fall in love with him in Margaret Drabble's *The Waterfall.*

Mr. Jones   Villainous, woman-hating gambler; tricked into thinking Axel Heyst is hiding a fortune and then enraged to discover his error, he kills Heyst's love, Lena, and his own partner, Martin Ricardo, in Joseph Conrad's *Victory: An Island Tale.*

Mr. Jones   A member of the Libraries Committee who interviews John Lewis and argues with Mr. Salter about the importance of drama in Kingsley Amis's *That Uncertain Feeling.*

Mr. Jones (satiric representation of the Czar)   The owner of Manor Farm; he is chased off his land by his animals when they decide to take over the management of the farm and turn it into a cooperative in George Orwell's *Animal Farm.*

Amelia Jones   Chester Nimmo's nurse who is thrown out of her job after she sees Chester sexually attacking Nina (Woodville) Latter; her story is heard by James Latter and confirms his suspicions about his wife in Joyce Cary's *Not Honour More.*

Arthur Jones   Welsh worker in the Dupret Foundry; his singing on the day after his son is born gladdens the hearts of his co-workers in Henry Green's *Living.*

Austin Jones   Able television interviewer assigned by Anthony Keating to interview Len Wincobank, successful property developer; he is present at the Mike Morgan comedy performance in Margaret Drabble's *The Ice Age.*

Bert Jones   Bench worker at the Dupret foundry; he falls in love with Lily Gates and plans to elope with her to Canada, but when he fails to find his parents in Liverpool he leaves Lily and is seen no more in Henry Green's *Living.*

Bessie Jones   Thirteen-year-old daughter of Bev Jones; she is physically and sexually precocious but mentally retarded; enticed by the promise of unlimited sweets and mindless television, she readily becomes the concubine of an Arab sheik in Anthony Burgess's *1985.*

Bev Jones   Well-educated schoolteacher who is intellectually opposed to the totalitarian socialist government of a future Great Britain; when his wife is killed in a hospital fire, he opts out of the system and reveals an unsuspected resourcefulness and capacity for violence and crime in Anthony Burgess's *1985.*

Carie Jones   A young secretary who joins the Communist Party, headed by Anton Hesse; she later drops out to get married in Doris Lessing's *A Ripple from the Storm.*

Dilys Jones   A young blonde woman who works with John Lewis; she is a junior assistant at the library in Kingsley Amis's *That Uncertain Feeling.*

Ernest Jones   British psychiatrist, a student of Dr. Sigmund Freud; he is responsible for Freud's escape from Vienna in Anthony Burgess's *The End of the World News.*

Gypsy Jones   Small, grubby, young pacifist whose attractiveness derives largely from her egotism; Widmerpool pays for her abortion but is sexually unrewarded; she sleeps with Nicholas Jenkins and others in Anthony Powell's *A Buyer's Market.* She is a ruthless leftist and Communist in *The Acceptance World* and in *The Kindly Ones.* She marries Craggs in *Books Do Furnish a Room* and is widowed in *Temporary Kings.* Her death is mentioned in *Hearing Secret Harmonies.*

James Jones   Brilliant lunatic who can express himself only through a music too subtle to be understood by normal human beings in Olaf Stapledon's *Odd John: A Story Between Jest and Earnest.*

John Jones Young and eager first lieutenant of the *Atropos* whom Hornblower trusts to lead the attack against the *Vengeance* and the *Amelia Jane*; eager to succeed, he stays aboard the *Atropos* as it is decommissioned and is promoted to captain in an ally's military in C. S. Forester's *Hornblower and the Atropos*.

R. (Dickie) Jones Enormously fat small-time bookmaker and money lender hired by Freddie Threepwood to retrieve love letters; he attempts to swindle his client in P. G. Wodehouse's *Something New*.

Shelley Jones The American gun-runner who enlists the help of Frank Dawley in Alan Sillitoe's *The Death of William Posters*. Dawley forces him into battle with the French in *A Tree on Fire*.

Jones-Wyatt Bands-and-Cabaret manager who arranged for the hotel the most innovative New Year's Eve entertainment to be found in London in Arnold Bennett's *Imperial Palace*.

Washingtonia Jong ("Washy") Chinese-American teen-age girl; she is one of the supernormals of John Wainwright's Pacific island colony in Olaf Stapledon's *Odd John: A Story Between Jest and Earnest*.

Jonothan Son of Daniel and Miriam; his grandmother, Kitty Friedman, feels he is being over-criticized by his father in Margaret Drabble's *The Ice Age*.

Captain Jonsen Pirate leader, who idealizes children; he tries to befriend the Bas-Thornton children, but he is confused and ultimately destroyed by the children's innocence in Richard Hughes's *A High Wind in Jamaica*.

Marmaduke ("Marmie") Jopley Scandal-monger, stockbroker, and adroit toady whose car and coat are appropriated as a disguise by Richard Hannay; he retaliates later by setting the London police on Hannay in John Buchan's *The Thirty-Nine Steps*.

Anne Jopling Gunnar's first wife, who died in an auto accident for which Hilary Burde, with whom she was having an affair, was responsible in Iris Murdoch's *A Word Child*.

Gunnar Jopling A top civil servant, formerly Hilary Burde's colleague at Oxford University, who unexpectedly becomes Hilary's department chief in Whitehall; he hates Hilary for the infidelity and death of his first wife, Anne, in Iris Murdoch's *A Word Child*.

Lady Kitty Jopling Gunnar Jopling's second wife, with whom Hilary Burde has an emotional entanglement that leads to her death in Iris Murdoch's *A Word Child*.

Tristram Jopling Son of Anne and Gunnar; four years old at the time of his mother's death, he kills himself at the age of sixteen in Iris Murdoch's *A Word Child*.

Jordan Coxswain appointed as officer of watch aboard the possibly plague-infested *Caroline* in C. S. Forester's *Mr. Midshipman Hornblower*.

Daphne Jordan Member of George Passant's group; his latest beloved, she remains with him throughout his trial in C. P. Snow's *Strangers and Brothers*.

Thomas Jordan Owner of the surgical appliances factory in Nottingham; he gives Paul Morel his first interview and his first job in D. H. Lawrence's *Sons and Lovers*.

Jörgenson A washed-up Dutch sea captain who lives with a native girl; he tries to dissuade Lingard from Hassim's cause but agrees to command the beached, heavily armed *Emma*, and dies when he explodes it in Joseph Conrad's *The Rescue: A Romance of the Shallows*.

José Monkeylike pirate, who plays with the children and is their favorite in Richard Hughes's *A High Wind in Jamaica*.

Jose Old blind man whose wife has died and who wants Leon Rivas, the ex-priest and guerrilla leader, to administer the last rites in Graham Greene's *The Honorary Consul*.

Father Jose Grandson of Senor Diego and formerly a priest of the local parish; Father Jose tells Father Quixote how the so-called Mexicans who have returned to Galicia have used their money to turn the eyes of the priests; he is visiting his grandfather, Senor Diego, when Father Quixote and Enrique Zancas stop to buy wine; after Father Jose reveals how the local priest has been seduced by money, Father Quixote confronts him in his full regalia as monsignor, interrupting the procession for the feast and overturning the statue of the Madonna in Graham Greene's *Monsignor Quixote*.

Padre Jose Obese priest who marries in order to escape a death sentence under anticlerical laws in Mexico; after forty years in the priesthood, he considers himself a buffoon when he marries and thinks he has "defiled God"; when he is asked by the police lieutenant to hear the whiskey priest's last confession, he refuses, afraid and cowardly in Graham Greene's *The Power and the Glory*.

Joseph   Orphaned Indian boy from Ranpur who becomes gardener for Lucy and "Tusker" Smalley; Frank Bhoolabhoy discovers him at St. John's Church where the young boy sometimes voluntarily tends the gravesites in Paul Scott's *Staying On*.

Joseph   Haitian servant and right hand of Brown at his hotel, the Trianon; crippled in an interrogation by the Tontons Macoutes, he is a central figure in a voodoo ceremony; he dies fighting with the rebels in Graham Greene's *The Comedians*.

Father Joseph   Early-middle-aged, level-headed carpenter/priest; he is responsible for the construction and repair of the buildings comprising the leproserie in Graham Greene's *A Burnt-Out Case*.

Josephine   A Paulist sister from Iowa who befriends Ruth (Sister Mary Joseph) after a peace demonstration in San Francisco in David Lodge's *How Far Can You Go?*.

King Jotifa   "Oriental" monarch of exotic Dateland who visits the kingdom of Pisuerga on a diplomatic mission in Ronald Firbank's *The Flower Beneath the Foot*.

Count Paul Jovian ("Ashie")   Former classmate of John Galt, "Jaikie", at St. Mark's College, Cambridge; he assumes his dead father's position of leadership in Juventus, a new political party in John Buchan's *The House of the Four Winds*.

Mr. Joyboy   The stuffy, pompous chief mortician at Hollywood's Whispering Glades cemetery; he awkwardly courts Aimée Thanatogenos and is stunned when she commits suicide in his embalming room; he pays Dennis Barlow to dispose of her body in the pet-cemetery crematorium in Evelyn Waugh's *The Loved One*.

Joyce   Jane Somers's closest friend during the period of her editorship and Jane's coeditorship of *Lilith*; she changes completely when she decides that she will save her marriage by giving up her career and moving with her husband to the States in order to become a faculty housewife for her husband in Doris Lessing's *The Diaries of Jane Somers*.

Joyce   A communist who ceased to be Anna Wulf's friend after she joined the Party, mainly because she has become a "comrade" rather than a sincere friend in Doris Lessing's *The Golden Notebook*.

Bob Joyce   The Father Confessor for the Imber Court

community; a cassocked Anglican priest, he has a bulging face and glittering eyes in Iris Murdoch's *The Bell*.

James Joyce   The writer, who is found alive and well in Skerries; he disclaims *Ulysses* as that "collection of smut" and expresses a desire to join the Jesuits in Flann O'Brien's *The Dalkey Archive*.

Robson Joyce   Commercial traveller for the publishers Tremlett & Grove's; he becomes engaged to Agatha Bright in Frank Swinnerton's *The Happy Family*.

Juan   A Spaniard with whom the Bolter returns to England at the outbreak of World War II; they settle with the gathered Radlett clan at Matthew Radlett's country house; a complete language barrier puts the family at a loss in dealing with Juan until it is discovered that he is an excellent professional cook in Nancy Mitford's *The Pursuit of Love*.

Lizzie Judd   Tom Judd's daughter who has become pregnant; her marriage to Ron Strutt, one of her lovers, is arranged by Henry Carrington, Reginald Purfleet, and others in Richard Aldington's *The Colonel's Daughter*.

Tom Judd   Chief foreman of a small factory; self-satisfied but judicious and prejudiced but honest, he represents the English upper working class in Richard Aldington's *The Colonel's Daughter*.

Judson   Freddie Threepwood's gossiping manservant; his discovery of a letter from R. Jones to Freddie helps Ashe Marson retrieve the missing scarab in P. G. Wodehouse's *Something New*.

Daniel Judson   One of Senor Castor's bodyguards who kidnaps Lady Roylance and who reports to General Lossberg the position of the enemy forces under Lord Clanroyden in John Buchan's *The Courts of the Morning*.

Judy   Scottish girl and pupil in the Hanover school in Dorothy Richardson's *Pointed Roofs*.

Judy   Wife to Billy, the boarding house owner where Pinkie Brown and crew live; she has casual sex with Dallow and serves as a contrast to the newly-married, naïve Rose Wilson in Graham Greene's *Brighton Rock*.

Judy   Young neighbor girl whom John Wainwright admires because she is so good at being herself in Olaf Stapledon's *Odd John: A Story Between Jest and Earnest*.

Horace Jules   Novelist and magazine editor; he is the figurehead Director of the N.I.C.E. (National Institute for Coordinated Experiments) in C. S. Lewis's *That Hideous Strength.*

Julia   An attractive woman who works in the Pornosec (pornography) division and devises ways to meet Winston Smith for sexual liaisons; she is captured with Smith by the Party in George Orwell's *Nineteen Eighty-Four.*

Julia   The long-time servant of Sigismund Claverhouse and his mother; Sigismund and William Soulsby gently tease her in Ivy Compton-Burnett's *Dolores.*

Julia   A character from Anna Wulf's manuscript, *The Shadow of the Third,* who in many ways reflects Molly Jacobs; the main protagonist, Ella, lives with Julia for a short while in Doris Lessing's *The Golden Notebook.*

Julian   A sensitive actor forever playing pageboys, princes, and younger brothers; he drowns himself to avoid making a decision between continuing his career or accepting Michael Fenwick's romantic overtures in Margaret Drabble's *The Garrick Year.*

Colonel Julyan   Kindly magistrate who finds distasteful the accusation of murder against Maxim de Winter in Daphne Du Maurier's *Rebecca.*

Carl Jung   Stiffly formal Swiss psychiatrist who attempts to persuade Dr. Sigmund Freud to change the Freudian conception of infantile sexuality in Anthony Burgess's *The End of the World News.*

Juno   A superior sheepdog created by Thomas Trelone and living on the Pughs' farm in Olaf Stapledon's *Sirius: A Fantasy of Love and Discord.*

Jupiter   Male ballet dancer with the Isabel Cornwallis Ballet Company in Colin MacInnes's *City of Spades.*

Sally Jupp   Opportunistic and ambitious maid who becomes engaged to Stephen Maxie despite her existing marriage and is murdered in P. D. James's *Cover Her Face.*

Edward (Ted) Justice   Romantic yet practical rookie plain-clothes policeman assigned to the conviction of pimps; he is in love but cannot marry his girlfriend because her father has a police record; he is suspended from the police force because he refuses to testify against Frankie Love in Colin MacInnes's *Mr. Love and Justice.*

Edward Justice's girlfriend   An ex-convict's daughter devoted to Edward; she wants to marry him; she has a miscarriage in Colin MacInnes's *Mr. Love and Justice.*

Edward Justice's girlfriend's father   An unnamed former convict who dislikes Edward Justice; the fact of his past crimes presents a roadblock to Edward's marriage to his daughter; he retires to Africa so that they may marry in Colin MacInnes's *Mr. Love and Justice.*

Justine   Infant daughter of Melissa Artemis by Justine Hosnani's husband, Nessim; Darley names her and takes her with him in his seclusion on a Greek island in Lawrence Durrell's *Justine* and in *Balthazar.* With perfect indifference he restores her to her father when he returns to Alexandria in *Clea.*

K

Mr. K. D.'s contact, an instructor of Entrenationo, who betrays his government and kills Else Crole; after D. shoots at him, he dies of a heart attack in Graham Greene's *The Confidential Agent.*

Prince K—— Father of the illegitimate Razumov, whom he betrays with the assassin Victor Haldin to the Russian Police in Joseph Conrad's *Under Western Eyes.*

Kaimakam Leader of the local Turkish militia and direct superior of the Mudir; he enters into the recovery area, catching the crew of the *Atropos* by surprise, in C. S. Forester's *Hornblower and the Atropos.*

Mr. Kalowsky An eighty-two-year-old Lithuanian Jew, committed to a psychiatric hospital by his brother as a threat to himself and others, who wants to be transferred to a sanatorium in Malcolm Lowry's *Lunar Caustic.*

Kalpurnia Beautiful dancer with whom the Count Ann-Jules of Pisuerga prefers to spend his time, rather than with his frustrated admirer Olga Blumenghast in Ronald Firbank's *The Flower Beneath the Foot.*

Monsieur Kamensky See Alexander Gregorievitch.

Mr. Kammell Anthony Keating's contact at Krusograd who receives and gives back some secret papers that Keating is to bring back to England in Margaret Drabble's *The Ice Age.*

Mr. Kandinsky A trousers-maker who fulfills several roles — father-figure, landlord, myth-maker — for the lonely and highly imaginative Joe in Wolf Mankowitz's *A Kid for Two Farthings.*

Betty Kane Charming, seemingly innocent and vulnerable adolescent who accuses Marion Sharpe and her mother of having kidnapped, imprisoned, and beaten her; she is proved to have lied in order to conceal a sexual escapade in Josephine Tey's *The Franchise Affair.*

Kangaroo See Benjamin Cooley.

Karden Former Nazi official; now a skilled, highly regarded East German attorney, he defends Hans-Dieter Mundt during his treason trial in John le Carré's *The Spy Who Came In from the Cold.*

Supervisor Karellen The leader of the Overlords; he makes the policies under which Earth is governed in Arthur C. Clarke's *Childhood's End.*

Dr. Klaus Karfeld Isolated, chauvinistic FRG Chancellor, former chemist, and Nazi war criminal now immune from prosecution; he publicly opposes Britain's entry into the Common Market while secretly plotting to ally West Germany with the Soviet bloc and arranging his accuser Leo Harting's murder in John le Carré's *A Small Town in Germany.*

Kargis A boy from the Caucasus; he is one of the supernormals of John Wainwright's Pacific island colony in Olaf Stapledon's *Odd John: A Story Between Jest and Earnest.*

Mr. Karkeck Legitimate but unimposing solicitor; for a short time he allows the imposing George Cannon to operate an illegal practice behind Karkeck's good name in Arnold Bennett's *Hilda Lessways.*

Karla (codename "The Sandman"; covername: Martin Brandt) Ruthless head of Moscow Centre's Thirteenth Directorate; he directs the previously recruited double agent to betray British and American secrets and to discredit Control and George Smiley in John le Carré's *Tinker, Tailor, Soldier, Spy.* He loses Chinese double agent Nelson Ko to Smiley's organization and to the American C.I.A. in *The Honourable Schoolboy.* He is forced to defect to the West when Smiley unearths Karla's misappropriations of Moscow Centre funds to protect his institutionalized daughter, Tatiana, in *Smiley's People.*

Ahmed Kasim Younger son of Mohammed Ali Kasim; he assists Dmitri Bronowsky, whose secret wish to unite Ahmed and the daughter of Sir Ahmed Bahadur, the Nawab of Mirat, ends with Ahmed's death at the hands of Hindus who attack the train on which he, Guy Perron, Sarah Layton, and other English travelers share a compartment in Paul Scott's *A Division of the Spoils.*

Mohammed Ali Kasim An outspoken member of the Congress Party; he is jailed for a time by the British in Paul Scott's *The Day of the Scorpion.* The father of Ahmed and Sayed Kasim, he also appears in *The Towers of Silence* and in *A Division of the Spoils.*

Sayed Kasim Eldest son of Mohammed Ali Kasim; he is one of several officers and men in the Indian Army who join the INA (the "Indian National Army"), a contingent who conspire with the Japanese in an attempt to free India from British rule in Paul Scott's *The Day of the Scorpion* and in *The Towers of Silence.*

Spike Kaspar Bill Haydon's protégé, known with

Nick de Silsky as "the Russians"; he carries messages for the British Intelligence Soviet networks in John le Carré's *Tinker, Tailor, Soldier, Spy* and in *The Honourable Schoolboy*.

Katchen A beautiful refugee in Ishmaelia with whom William Boot falls in love; she uses him as a money convenience until she can flee the country with her real lover in Evelyn Waugh's *Scoop*.

Kate Jane Somers's niece who wants to be a model; a very poor student, she comes to live with Jane but does nothing but sit on the couch or sleep until told to go live in Hannah Deloch's commune in Doris Lessing's *The Diaries of Jane Somers*.

Kate British Intelligence agent who confesses to her lover Jack Brotherhood that she protected her other lover Magnus Pym by removing incriminating evidence from his personnel files in John le Carré's *A Perfect Spy*.

Kate A Bournemouth barmaid, who enters into a loveless marriage with Herbert Gregory in Lawrence Durrell's *The Black Book*.

Kate The Trelones' trusted family servant in Olaf Stapledon's *Sirius: A Fantasy of Love and Discord*.

Kate The upper housemaid for the Clares; she has a trim figure and dark eyes and often agrees with Ainger, the butler, in Ivy Compton-Burnett's *The Present and the Past*.

Big Kate Large, noisy, honest woman; she shows "She" at age fifteen what to do with machines on her first day of work at the mill; after the women have crawled on their hands and knees on an ice-covered street before dawn to get to work, Kate kindly asks the foreman "How's your feet?"; an irrepressible woman, she prides herself on being able to pour a whole bottle of cold tea down her throat without swallowing once in Storm Jameson's *A Day Off*.

Katerina Co-proprietor of the Villa Sofia and of the half of Victor Pancev's body buried in her part of the garden in Muriel Spark's *Territorial Rights*.

Kati (Katinka) First wife of Janos Lavin; married to Lavin for two years while he is a student in Budapest, she ends up in an asylum in John Berger's *A Painter of Our Time*.

Emmanuel (Manny) Katz Poet and husband of Miriam Katz; his happy family life inspires the narrator to continue pursuing Suzette in Colin MacInnes's *Absolute Beginners*.

Miriam Katz Wife of Emmanuel Katz in Colin MacInnes's *Absolute Beginners*.

Saul Katz Young son of Emmanuel and Miriam Katz in Colin MacInnes's *Absolute Beginners*.

Alice Kauffman Desiree Zapp's feminist agent, who advises her during the kidnapping of Morris Zapp in David Lodge's *Small World*.

Betsy Kay Woman who took off her shirt during a violent summer rainstorm that occurred during a party at which Kate Fletcher Armstrong was present in Margaret Drabble's *The Middle Ground*.

Kayle Yuli's benefactor in Pannoval who finds him a place to live in Brian W. Aldiss's *Helliconia Spring*.

Alroy Kear Elegant, thrifty, organized, well-intentioned speaker and writer; being a master of social graces, Roy wrote his best novels as dramas of nobility and used his skills to raise his social status; critics and clubs love him for his good heart, although his unrealistic view of life is shown in his relationship with Edward Driffeld in W. Somerset Maugham's *Cakes and Ale: Or the Skeleton in the Cupboard*.

Mr. Keating Father of Anthony, Matthew, and Paul; he is a worldly churchmaster and schoolmaster; his death brings his estranged family together for an unsuccessful reunion in Margaret Drabble's *The Ice Age*.

Mrs. Keating Mother of Anthony Keating and two other sons; she is physically frail and is detached during the family reunion that occurs when her husband dies in Margaret Drabble's *The Ice Age*.

Anthony Keating Songwriter, television producer, property man, man of enforced leisure, and spy; following a mild heart attack at the age of thirty-eight, he unexpectedly experiences hope and joy while in prison in a foreign land; the father of four children, he is divorced from his wife, Babs, who has remarried; he is in love with Alison Murray in Margaret Drabble's *The Ice Age*.

Barbara (Babs) (Cockburn Keating) The thirty-eight-year-old, overweight ex-wife of Anthony Keating and mother of his four children; she is married to Stuart and has a child by him in Margaret Drabble's *The Ice Age*.

Mary Keating Eldest daughter of Anthony and Babs, who are divorced; she lives with her mother and her mother's husband, Stuart; she turns down a visit to her father's home because of its rural location in Margaret Drabble's *The Ice Age*.

Matthew Keating   Estranged barrister brother of Anthony Keating in Margaret Drabble's *The Ice Age*.

Paul Keating   Estranged barrister brother of Anthony Keating in Margaret Drabble's *The Ice Age*.

Peter Keating   Son of divorced parents Anthony Keating and Babs, who has remarried; he lives with his mother; he broke a leg at a school practice ski party in Margaret Drabble's *The Ice Age*.

Ruth Keating   One of two daughters of Anthony Keating and Babs, who has remarried; she lives with her mother; of the four children of Anthony and Babs, Ruth most resembles Anthony; she is fourteen and tall in Margaret Drabble's *The Ice Age*.

Stephen Keating   One of two sons of Anthony Keating and Babs, who are divorced; Stephen lives with his mother in Margaret Drabble's *The Ice Age*.

Helen Keats   The new young classics mistress with a degree from Oxford; she teaches in Josephine Napier's school and marries Felix Bacon in Ivy Compton-Burnett's *More Women Than Men*.

John Keats   Global Agency correspondent in Lawrence Durrell's *Justine*. He becomes increasingly involved with the Alexandrians and is reported killed in the desert "much later" in *Balthazar*. Pressured by Pursewarden's widow to expose her husband's incest in a biographical work in progress, he renounces the project in *Clea*.

Lydia Keats   Well-known astrologist who has foretold the death of Christine Clay in Josephine Tey's *A Shilling for Candles*.

Albert Keche   Middle-aged, tall, thin, stooped, secretive man; manager of the Reserve Hotel, he hides Emil Schimler from German agents and later assists Josef Vadassy's spy-hunting in Eric Ambler's *Epitaph for a Spy*.

Suzanne Keche   Shrewish, overbearing woman; she is the wife of Albert Keche and the owner of the Reserve Hotel in Eric Ambler's *Epitaph for a Spy*.

Sylvia Kedge   Crippled, bitter, but apparently devoted secretary to Maurice Seton in P. D. James's *Unnatural Causes*.

Lady Constance Keeble   Lord Emsworth's handsome, dictatorial widowed sister, who is determined to suppress her brother Galahad Threepwood's memoirs; she is opposed to the romantic attachments of her nephew Ronnie Fish and her niece Millicent

Threepwood in P. G. Wodehouse's *Fish Preferred*. She appears in seven other novels.

Mr. Keen   Douglas Knowell's boss in Doris Lessing's *A Proper Marriage*.

Keene   Crafty middle-aged captain of the *Justinian*; his fatherly treatment of Hornblower saves Hornblower from death in a duel of honor; he transfers Hornblower to the *Indefatigable* in C. S. Forester's *Mr. Midshipman Hornblower*.

Barbara Keene   Rich daughter of one of Henry Pulling's bank clients; she eventually moves to South Africa; she is a possible romantic interest of Pulling until he moves to Paraguay in Graham Greene's *Travels with My Aunt*.

Hunter Keepe   A journal editor and the ineffectual brother of Rosa Keepe in Iris Murdoch's *The Flight from the Enchanter*.

Rosa Keepe   A middle-class woman with a conscience who goes to work in a factory and falls under the baleful influence of the Lusiewicz brothers until she appeals to Mischa Fox for help in Iris Murdoch's *The Flight from the Enchanter*.

Kehaar   Injured black-headed gull rescued and restored to health by the rabbits; he helps Hazel locate rabbit does for his warren and fend off Efrafan attacks in Richard Adams's *Watership Down*.

Keightley   W.O.O.C.(P.) agent who discovers and gives the narrator a tape that helps him avoid Dalby's brainwashing attempt in Len Deighton's *The Ipcress File*.

Keith   Twenty-five-year-old lower-middle-class roommate and presumed lover of Piers Longridge in Barbara Pym's *A Glass of Blessings*. He makes a characteristic complaint about untidiness when he appears briefly in *No Fond Return of Love*.

Miss Keith   The middle-aged Scotswoman who is secretary to Princess Edna Novemali; she kindly allows Somerset Maugham to steal an invitation to the Princess's party to satisfy the dying wish of Elliott Templeton in W. Somerset Maugham's *The Razor's Edge*.

Mr. Keith   Radical older man who values an amoral lifestyle; he makes a career of bailing out prisoners, especially Amy Wilberforce; he occasionally bores his listeners in Norman Douglas's *South Wind*.

Cornelius (Corney) Kelleher   Undertaker at Paddy Dignam's funeral who comes across Leopold Bloom and Stephen Dedalus after their confrontation with the two English soldiers in James Joyce's *Ulysses*.

Dr. Kello   The local Medical Officer of Health; he convinces an army of reporters that Roylance will explain all in two days, thus giving "John Macnab" the time he needs to take his stag in John Buchan's *John Macnab*.

Alison Kelly   An Australian airline stewardess who falls in love with Nicholas Urfe; she spends several weeks with him in Athens and apparently commits suicide after he loses interest in her, but reappears after Nicholas returns to England in John Fowles's *The Magus*.

Celia Kelly   Good-natured prostitute in London who falls in love with, and is abandoned by, Murphy in Samuel Beckett's *Murphy*.

Bernard Kelshall   University student from a poor Jewish family who is brilliant in economics; he is identified as the spy in the Marxist group and kills himself under the influence of a drug planted in his drink by Mark Robinson in C. P. Snow's *The Malcontents*.

Robert Kelway   Stella Rodney's lover and government co-worker; at first he denies to Stella the truth of Harrison's accusations of treason; later, just before his probably intentional fall to his death, he admits their truth in Elizabeth Bowen's *The Heat of the Day*.

Kemi   A Finn, one of the supernormals of John Wainwright's Pacific island colony in Olaf Stapledon's *Odd John: A Story Between Jest and Earnest*.

Dr. Kemp   Port Burdock physician and former schoolmate of Griffin, whom, after sheltering, he attempts to turn in after discovering Griffin's murderous nature; Griffin hunts him in a climactic chase which ends in Griffin's death at the hands of a mob in H. G. Wells's *The Invisible Man: A Grotesque Romance*.

Mrs. Kemp   The gossipy, self-centered mother of Liza; she likes her beer and a drop of whiskey on the quiet and is mean both in purse and spirit, enjoying fussy self-important conversation with a neighbor about funeral arrangements while Liza dies in W. Somerset Maugham's *Liza of Lambeth*.

George Kemp   Exuberant, energetic, common merchant; his big ideas for the town went unsupported because of his lack of manners; "Lord George" loved Rose Driffield very much and finally left his wife for Rose in W. Somerset Maugham's *Cakes and Ale: Or the Skeleton in the Cupboard*.

Gordon Kemp   A London University graduate in English who is friends with Mike Brady and Jonathan Browne; he goes on for his commission in National Service and is shot in Cyprus in David Lodge's *Ginger, You're Barmy*.

Joan Kemp   A Charlotte Street bohemian, who is Nicholas Urfe's landlady after his return from Phraxos in John Fowles's *The Magus*.

Jonathan Kemp   The best student at Freddie Wentworth's actor-training academy, according to Freddie; he finally gets a part in a play and is rehearsing a fall at the end of Penelope Fitzgerald's *At Freddie's*.

Liza Kemp   The beautiful, vital young girl who refuses to marry Tom, instead alienating herself from her close-knit community by falling in love with a married man; the union results in her dying in great pain from a miscarriage in W. Somerset Maugham's *Liza of Lambeth*.

Ken   Widower of Norman's sister; he plans to marry his new girlfriend and set up a driving school and pities his brother-in-law's empty life in Barbara Pym's *Quartet in Autumn*.

Kendal   A sculpture teacher who uses electricity and light in his sculpture; he helps the principal clean out his water closet, which has been filled with stolen school property in David Storey's *A Temporary Life*.

Bill Kendrick   English airplane pilot who found the lost town of Shangri-La when he was blown off course during a flight between the gulf and the South Coast of Arabia; his body is discovered on a train bound for Scotland in Josephine Tey's *The Singing Sands*.

Kenilworth   An obese foreign-service professional; David Mountolive's less successful contemporary and disliked competitor, he gives unwelcome advice that Mountolive would be wiser to take in Lawrence Durrell's *Mountolive*. He is a consular official in Alexandria in *Clea*.

Kennedy   Midshipman aboard the *Indefatigable* who is sent on deck to summon Hornblower for dinner in the cabin in C. S. Forester's *Mr. Midshipman Hornblower*.

Dr. James Kennedy   Straight-laced half-brother of Helen Spenlove Kennedy Halliday in Agatha Christie's *Sleeping Murder*.

Mina Kennedy   Gold-haired, siren-like barmaid whom Leopold Bloom encounters at the Ormond Hotel in James Joyce's *Ulysses*.

Kenneth   Constantine Ormeau's friend who is head-master of The Castle, a short-lived school which Eva Trout attends and which Constantine persuades Willy Trout to support in Elizabeth Bowen's *Eva Trout, or Changing Scenes*.

Charles Kent   Drug addict and illegitimate son of Miss Russell, whom he visited at Fernly Park the night of Roger Ackroyd's death in Agatha Christie's *The Murder of Roger Ackroyd*.

Diane Kent   Woman with a black eye and stitches in her nose who brings her child to the day-care center where Evelyn Morton Stennett volunteers some of her time in Margaret Drabble's *The Middle Ground*.

Eduardo (Eddie) Kent   Proprietor of La Universal restaurant; he is a friend of Sigbjorn Wilderness and a good samaritan who is punished for coming to the aid of an accident victim in Malcolm Lowry's *Dark as the Grave Wherein My Friend Is Laid*.

Elaine Kent   Worker at Meadows, Meade & Grindley and friend of Dixie Morse in Muriel Spark's *The Ballad of Peckham Rye*.

Gloria Zsuzsu Kent   Executive Officer in Whitehall and Bernard Samson's lover and confidante in Len Deighton's *Mexico Set* and in *London Match*.

Desmond d'Esterre Kenton   Thin, intelligent, thirty-year-old English freelance journalist; he is in Nurenberg searching for an exclusive story; being broke, he reluctantly agrees to deliver Herman Sachs's "securities" (B2 documents) to the Hotel Josef and, through a convoluted series of events, is enlisted by the Zaleshoffs to recover the documents from Stefan Saridza in Eric Ambler's *Uncommon Danger*.

Dr. Kephalus   An intense coroner, who describes graphic accidents and deaths; he and Meyer are close friends, given to long discussions in Beryl Bainbridge's *Young Adolf*.

Darko Kerim   Gypsy-like, earring-wearing, romantic Secret Service agent in Istanbul; he assists James Bond before he is killed by KGB men in Ian Fleming's *From Russia, With Love*.

Mrs. Kerr   Attractive, experienced, and sophisticated upper-class English widow whose marked avoidance of the circle of other women her age and unsubtle preference for either solitude or the company of the younger Sydney Warren is a subject of gossip in Elizabeth Bowen's *The Hotel*.

Alison Kerr   One of a pair of sisters who teach sewing at the Marcia Blaine School in Muriel Spark's *The Prime of Miss Jean Brodie*.

Ellen Kerr   One of a pair of sisters who teach sewing at the Marcia Blaine School; they are incompetent both in teaching and in spying on Jean Brodie in Muriel Spark's *The Prime of Miss Jean Brodie*.

Mark Kerr ("Mark Riddell")   The Marquis of Montrose's trusted lieutenant, a "malignant", whom David Sempill, minister of Woodilee, shelters when Kerr is wounded and unable to escape with Montrose's defeated army; he departs from Scotland with Sempill in John Buchan's *Witch Wood*.

Ronald Kerr   Mrs. Kerr's twenty-year-old son in Elizabeth Bowen's *The Hotel*.

Henry Kerrison   Pathologist, widower, and father of two in P. D. James's *Death of an Expert Witness*.

Mrs. Kershaw   Ann Walton's landlady, who acts as a mother and a friend; William McClusky comes between them by seducing Mrs. Kershaw, but Mrs. Kershaw redeems her friendship with Ann in Beryl Bainbridge's *Sweet William*.

Derek Kershaw   Husband of Maureen; he is a friend of John Middleton and warns John away from Larrie Rourke in Angus Wilson's *Anglo-Saxon Attitudes*.

Frank Kershaw   Secretary at the Lancashire mill from which William Widgery vanished; he is run down by a truck in what is made to seem an accident in Roy Fuller's *The Second Curtain*.

Maureen Kershaw   Daughter of Harold Cressett; she hates her stepmother and advises John Middleton to abandon support for her father's cause in Angus Wilson's *Anglo-Saxon Attitudes*.

Reginald Kershaw   Son of a school friend of Charles Curtis; he is a guest at Curtis's home; entertaining and witty, he escorts Kate and Olivia Curtis to the Spencers' ball in Rosamond Lehmann's *Invitation to the Waltz*.

Adèle von Kessen   Wife of Walther and mother of Franz, Mitzi, and four younger children in Richard Hughes's *The Fox in the Attic*. After blind Mitzi's departure for a Carmelite convent, Adèle assuages her sorrow by creating a garden on the parapet below Mitzi's old room in *The Wooden Shepherdess*.

Franz von Kessen   Eldest of the children of Baron Walther von Kessen; without his family's awareness, he has for a long period kept hidden in the attics of the family castle the fanatical young Nazi fugitive Wolff Scheidemann; the dream of a reborn Germany he shares with his sister Mitzi influences his enthusiasm for Nazism in Richard Hughes's *The Fox in the Attic*. Married and a father, he continues to be a vocal supporter of Hitler in *The Wooden Shepherdess*.

Heinz von Kessen   One of Walther's youngest children; he and his twin, Rudi, are a pair of daredevil blond athletes in Richard Hughes's *The Fox in the Attic* and in *The Wooden Shepherdess*.

Irma von Kessen   Youngest daughter of Walther in Richard Hughes's *The Fox in the Attic* and in *The Wooden Shepherdess*.

Mitzi von Kessen   Beautiful German cousin of Augustine Penry-Herbert; preoccupied with her progressive blindness, she never suspects his romantic infatuation with her; she has a profound religious experience and enters a convent in Richard Hughes's *The Fox in the Attic*. Her religious nature expands in the isolation of the convent as her homeland changes during the 1930's in *The Wooden Shepherdess*.

Otto von Kessen   Younger brother of Walther; a retired German colonel, he lost a leg in World War I and now does government work in Richard Hughes's *The Fox in the Attic*. S.S. men beat him to death with his own artificial leg during the blood purge that consolidates Hitler's power in 1934 in *The Wooden Shepherdess*.

Rudi von Kessen   One of Walther's twin sons and youngest children in Richard Hughes's *The Fox in the Attic* and in *The Wooden Shepherdess*.

Trudl von Kessen   Ten-year-old daughter of Walther in Richard Hughes's *The Fox in the Attic*. She has a Hungarian fiancé in *The Wooden Shepherdess*.

Baron Walther von Kessen   Bavarian baron who acts as host to his young English cousin, Augustine Penry-Herbert, in Richard Hughes's *The Fox in the Attic*. He becomes a conventional though unenthusiastic supporter of Hitler in *The Wooden Shepherdess*.

Kevin   A man briefly involved with Kate Fletcher Armstrong in Margaret Drabble's *The Middle Ground*.

Nurse Kewley   Forty-five-year-old, tall, buxom, determined nurse; she seems to Lord Raingo to have the sense to respond to his moods and not worry him throughout his last illness in Arnold Bennett's *Lord Raingo*.

Muawiya Khaslat   Edgar Perry's outspoken student, who adores Perry but has been ordered by the Moslem Brotherhood to kill him because he is English; Khaslat's

half-hearted murder attempt during a picnic fails; to save face, Khaslat claims that Perry attempted suicide in P. H. Newby's *The Picnic at Sakkara*.

Elie Khoury   Deceased Lebanese husband of Ethel Khoury and former director of the Phoenician Shipping Line in Port Said; he smuggled arms to Cypriot rebels despite his wife's disapproval; Elie's death brings Jack Townrow back to Egypt in P. H. Newby's *Something to Answer For*.

Ethel Khoury   Practical and stubborn British wife of Elie Khoury; she believes Elie was murdered and asks Jack Townrow to investigate; she is most concerned about protecting Elie's wealth; she leaves Egypt for Britain with Elie's body in P. H. Newby's *Something to Answer For*.

Kidd   A homosexual henchman of Seraffimo Spang in Ian Fleming's *Diamonds Are Forever*.

Mrs. Kiddle   Joseph Kiddle's wife, who is driven insane by Ada's death in T. F. Powys's *Mr. Weston's Good Wine*.

Ada Kiddle   Joseph Kiddle's deceased oldest daughter, who drowned herself out of shame for her ruined maidenhood in T. F. Powys's *Mr. Weston's Good Wine*.

Ann Kiddle   Joseph Kiddle's ruined maiden daughter, who is tricked by Jane Vosper into sexual relations with John and Martin Mumby and accepts John Mumby's proposal of marriage in T. F. Powys's *Mr. Weston's Good Wine*.

Joseph Kiddle   Folly Down dealer in cattle who dreams of cheating Squire Mumby in T. F. Powys's *Mr. Weston's Good Wine*.

Phoebe Kiddle   Joseph Kiddle's ruined maiden daughter, who is tricked by Jane Vosper into sexual relations with John and Martin Mumby; she bears an illegitimate child and refuses Martin Mumby's marriage proposal in T. F. Powys's *Mr. Weston's Good Wine*.

Kid-from-Outer-Space   Schoolmate of the narrator; he works for the city of London and represents the Establishment in Colin MacInnes's *Absolute Beginners*.

(Prisoner No. 400; codename "Hare-Lip") Kieffer
Son of Nicholas Rubashov's friend, political associate, and professor of history; tortured by "steambath", he turns informer so that Gletkin can consolidate his case against Rubashov but is executed as a political liability in Arthur Koestler's *Darkness at Noon*.

Sam Kiever Alleged European journalist and Abteilung operative; he takes Alec Leamas from Bill Ashe to Amsterdam and delivers him to Peters in Leamas's supposed defection from Britain in John le Carré's *The Spy Who Came In from the Cold.*

C'Sarr Kilander IX The Father Supreme of the Church of Akhanaba and the final authority in religious matters in Borlien and Oldorando in Brian W. Aldiss's *Helliconia Summer.*

Jimmy Kilburn A recent millionaire for whom Owen Tuby and Cosmo Sultana form an image as a curmudgeonly altruist in J. B. Priestley's *The Image Men.*

Doris Kilman Special friend and teacher of Elizabeth Dalloway; a fanatic pacifist/activist, she is detested by Clarissa Dalloway for her hideous, smelly green macintosh and for her emotional kidnap of Elizabeth; petulant and sulky, Kilman loses Elizabeth in a department-store tea room to her own egotistic self-pity about her ugly body; she thinks "it is the flesh that she must control" in Virginia Woolf's *Mrs. Dalloway.*

Brian Kilmartin Tenant farmer who steadfastly clings to his land through tragedy, sickness, and famine in the valley; he always tries to do the right thing for his family in Liam O'Flaherty's *Famine.*

Maggie Kilmartin Wife of Brian Kilmartin; she dutifully stands by her husband, family, and farm until her death during the famine in Liam O'Flaherty's *Famine.*

Martin Kilmartin Son of Brian Kilmartin; accused of complicity in Jocelyn Chadwick's death, he flees the valley but is later reunited with his wife; they escape with their baby son to America in Liam O'Flaherty's *Famine.*

Mary Kilmartin Beautiful wife of Martin Kilmartin; she takes control of the Kilmartin farm during the famine; her strong will and determination to survive help her and her baby survive the plague; she is finally reunited with her husband, and they escape to America in Liam O'Flaherty's *Famine.*

Michael Kilmartin Youngest son of Brian Kilmartin; his prolonged consumptive illness, ending with his death, depletes the family wealth in Liam O'Flaherty's *Famine.*

Lily Kimble Former parlormaid; responding to Gwenda Reed's newspaper advertisement of inquiry about Helen Halliday, she is murdered in Agatha Christie's *Sleeping Murder.*

Ma Kin A simple, old-fashioned, forty-five-year-old Burmese native; she is U Po Kyin's wife; she reminds him over and over that he needs to build good deeds so that his reincarnation will be better than this life in George Orwell's *Burmese Days.*

Lord Kinarth Host of a party at which Anthony Keating was present; Tim tells an untrue story about Laura Blakely's behavior at the party; the false story leads Keating to believe Tim a liar in Margaret Drabble's *The Ice Age.*

Alice Kincaid One of the nurses treating Charles Watkins in Doris Lessing's *Briefing for a Descent into Hell.*

John Kincaid The "pricker", representative of the Kirk; he determined that Elspeth Todd is a witch, but, discredited by "Mark Riddell", he disappears from Woodilee village in John Buchan's *Witch Wood.*

Georgina ("Miss Georgie") Kinethmont Spinster aunt and acid-tongued traveling companion of Miss "Kirsty" Everdale; she warns Spencer Perceval, the Prime Minister, of the plot to assassinate him and thereby saves his life in John Buchan's *The Free Fishers.*

King of Bavaria Sally's admirer; he extends an invitation to her to visit him in Isabel Colegate's *Agatha.*

Professor King Respected scholar who persuades one of his students to allow him to adopt her illegitimate child (Orlando King) in seclusion; he abandons London in an attempt to escape society and make his own life; when Orlando becomes an adult, King sends him to London to seek his fortunes; King does not tell Orlando of his parentage before his unexpected heart attack in Isabel Colegate's *Orlando King.* Professor King is remembered by Orlando in *Orlando at the Brazen Threshold.* King is mentioned in *Agatha.*

Adolf (Dolly) King A musician at the sports club who had a brief affair with Martha Quest; he is quite scornful of her as well as of himself because, although Jewish, he is an anti-Semite in Doris Lessing's *Martha Quest.*

Agatha King Daughter of Orlando and Judith (Gardner) King; she is Orlando's favorite daughter in Isabel Colegate's *Orlando King.* She goes to Italy to visit Orlando and falls in love with her cousin Henry Field in *Orlando at the Brazen Threshold.* Having married Henry, she becomes the mother of two children; after Orlando's death she carries on the quest for understanding and knowledge that Professor King bequeathed Orlando in *Agatha.*

Imogene King Second daughter of Orlando King

and Judith (Gardner) King in Isabel Colegate's *Orlando King* and in *Agatha*.

Julius King An American biochemist; Tallis Browne's adversary, he is a mischief maker whose practical joke has the unintended effect of causing Rupert Foster's death; he nearly succeeds in destroying Axel Nilsson and Simon Foster's relationship in Iris Murdoch's *A Fairly Honourable Defeat*.

Orlando King Illegitimate child of Pauline and Leonard Gardner; he is raised by Professor King on a remote French island; Orlando is unaware that Leonard is his father when he applies for work with Timberwork furniture factory, which is managed by Leonard; Orlando becomes a keen businessman and surpasses Leonard's position; after Leonard's accidental death, Orlando unknowingly marries his own stepmother when he weds Leonard's widow, Judith; when the truth of Orlando's birth is disclosed by Sid, Judith is destroyed and is mentally incapacitated, and Orlando is devastated as well; Orlando, bereft of wife, volunteers in the war efforts as a rescue worker and is blinded and seriously injured in the line of duty in Isabel Colegate's *Orlando King*. Orlando moves to Italy and buys a villa where he entertains avidly and enjoys his daughters' visits; he dies suddenly of a heart attack in *Orlando at the Brazen Threshold*. Orlando's quest for knowledge and truth that was instilled in him by his adoptive father is continued by his daughter Agatha King in *Agatha*.

Mr. Kingcroft English farmer who loves Lilia Herriton in E. M. Forster's *Where Angels Fear to Tread*.

Arthur Kingfisher An aging, famous literary theorist and father of Angelica and Lily Pabst; he is cured of impotence when Persse McGarrigle asks his question at the Modern Language Association conference; he takes the UNESCO chair of literary criticism, and he becomes engaged to Song-Mi Lee in David Lodge's *Small World*.

Perdita Kingsford Dolores Hutton's friend at college who falls in love with Bertram Hutton but marries Sigismund Claverhouse because he loves her; she dies in childbirth nine months later in Ivy Compton-Burnett's *Dolores*.

Mrs. Kingsmead A woman at Global Foods whose praise of Kate Brown's ability to take care of all of the delegates' needs alerts Kate to the fact that she is treated by the delegates in the same way that her own family treats her in Doris Lessing's *The Summer Before the Dark*.

John ("Jock") Kinloch Popular and audacious un-

dergraduate student and an admirer of Anthony Lammas; he loves his childhood playmate Miss "Kirsty" Everdale and wins her admiration and love in John Buchan's *The Free Fishers*.

Millicent (Millie), Lady Kinnard An Irish patriot and widow who is loved by Christopher Bellman and Barnabus Drumm; she offers herself to her nephews Andrew Chase-White and Pat Dumay and declares that the latter is the only man she truly loves; she assists Pat's political cause by blackmailing Andrew with a threat to tell his mother that his dead father, her half brother, was her lover in Iris Murdoch's *The Red and the Green*.

Father Martin Kipling The aging, anxious parish priest of Our Lady of Perpetual Succour, Brickley; he starts a campaign against the cinema when he finds himself having lustful thoughts at a movie; he performs the marriage ceremony for Len and Bridget in David Lodge's *The Picturegoers*.

Mrs. Kipps Art Kipps's working-class aunt who raises him after his mother dies in H. G. Wells's *Kipps: The Story of a Simple Soul*.

Art Kipps Impressionable young draper who inherits a fortune and tries to become a gentleman, getting engaged at first to a manipulative upper-class girl, whose brother embezzles his money; instead Kipps marries his childhood sweetheart and invests in a play which later leaves him independently wealthy in H. G. Wells's *Kipps: The Story of a Simple Soul*.

James Kipps Art Kipps's shopkeeper uncle who raises him and apprentices him to the Folkestone Drapery Bazaar; he is forever finding junk for his nephew to "invest" in once he becomes wealthy in H. G. Wells's *Kipps: The Story of a Simple Soul*.

Kirby Security functionary who supplies Humphrey Leigh with information gathered on Tom Thirkill in C. P. Snow's *A Coat of Varnish*.

Mrs. Kirby Heavy-smoking, croaky-voiced mother of Maureen Kirby in Margaret Drabble's *The Ice Age*.

Marlene Kirby Sid's wife; her sister-in-law, Maureen Kirby, considers her a foul-tempered and abusive mother in Margaret Drabble's *The Ice Age*.

Maureen Kirby Attractive girlfriend-secretary to Len Wincobank; she leaves him for Derek Ashby during Wincobank's four-year imprisonment; she is a friend of Anthony Keating in Margaret Drabble's *The Ice Age*.

Sid Kirby Maureen Kirby's brother, who attends a

family get-together at their mother's on Christmas Eve in Margaret Drabble's *The Ice Age.*

Mrs. Kirk   The Morels' neighbor who tends the Morel children while Gertrude is in labor before Paul's birth in D. H. Lawrence's *Sons and Lovers.*

Barbara Kirk   Howard Kirk's wife and his partner in amoral hypocrisy; she attempts suicide at the end of Malcolm Bradbury's *The History Man.*

Howard Kirk   A teacher who is the embodiment of radical chic, an adept academic tactician, and a Marxist sociologist in Malcolm Bradbury's *The History Man.*

Otto Kirnberger   A German archaeologist and guide living in Egypt; he befriends Daniel Martin and Jane Mallory on their cruise up the Nile, helping them appreciate and understand what they are seeing in John Fowles's *Daniel Martin.*

Kite   Former leader of Pinkie Brown's mob; he is killed by Colleoni's mob in the waiting room at St. Pancras station in Graham Greene's *Brighton Rock.*

Big Klaus   One of the Hare Indians who accompanies Sir Edward Leithen in his search for the guide Lew Frizel and Francis Galliard; he tells Leithen that the death of the Hare tribe has been predicted in John Buchan's *Sick Heart River.*

Rosa Klebb   The ugly, sadistic head of Operations and Executions for the USSR espionage agency SMERSH; she fails to kill James Bond with poison-tipped knitting needles, but appears to have succeeded with a poison-tipped blade hidden in her shoe at the conclusion of Ian Fleming's *From Russia, With Love.*

Honor Klein   An anthropologist and Cambridge don, who is Georgie Hands's former tutor, Palmer Anderson's half sister and lover, and Martin Lynch-Gibbon's lover in Iris Murdoch's *A Severed Head.*

Suzanne Klein   Irving Macher's girlfriend who is persuaded by Macher to infuriate Roger Micheldene by enticing him and then stopping him short of having sex with her by biting him in Kingsley Amis's *One Fat Englishman.*

Kleister   Old business rival of Paul Firman and victim of Firman's shrewd "business" deals in Eric Ambler's *Send No More Roses.*

Klils   Laintal Ay's uncle, who rules Oldorando jointly with his brother, Nahkri, in Brian W. Aldiss's *Helliconia Spring.*

Klin   A top representative of Planet 8 who was a Fruit Maker before the Ice; he is chosen as part of a committee to make an information-gathering journey to the Cold Pole in Doris Lessing's *The Making of the Representative for Planet 8.*

Klorathy   A Canopian leader who spends his time journeying to other planets, attempting to help the governments and aid the citizens in becoming moral and wise individuals; he spends a great deal of his time on Shikasta, instructing Ambien II in Doris Lessing's *The Sirian Experiments.* On the colonies of Volyen he helps Incent and high officials in *Documents Relating to the Sentimental Agents in the Volyen Empire.*

Anton Kluber   The intellectual German commandant who befriends Maurice Conchis and later betrays him in Conchis's fictionalized account of the Nazi occupation of Phraxos in John Fowles's *The Magus.*

Kniaz   "Old Prince" who believes in his shares and offers support to Nikolai Bursanov for his gold mines in William Gerhardie's *Futility: A Novel on Russian Themes.*

Mrs. Knight   Sheila's wealthy mother, who is sensitive about her social status; she dotes on her husband and likes Lewis Eliot despite herself in C. P. Snow's *Time of Hope.* She devotes herself to caring for her ill husband and is inclined to blame Eliot for Sheila's suicide in *Homecomings.*

Henry Knight   Ethan Llewelyn's first client in a capital case; he is a maker of barrels for going over Niagara Falls; Ethan defends him successfully against charges of murdering a policeman; he reappears as Ethan's waiter in Malcolm Lowry's *October Ferry to Gabriola.*

Laurence Knight   Languid Anglican clergyman, insecure outside his home, who hopes to promote the welfare of his neurotic daughter, Sheila, by encouraging the help of the possessively devoted Lewis Eliot in C. P. Snow's *Time of Hope.* Very ill, he tries to relieve Eliot of guilt about the suicide of Sheila in *Homecomings.*

Sheila Knight   Neurotic, sexually frigid young woman, who attracts men and is the object of Lewis Eliot's obsessive love; she marries Eliot and becomes a social embarrassment to him; though the marriage is a torment to both, she holds to it as her last resort in C. P. Snow's *Time of Hope.* She makes an unwise investment in the publishing firm of R. S. Robinson, fights unsuccessfully against her mental depression, and commits suicide without leaving a note in *Homecomings.*

Mr. Knott   Owner of the house where Watt replaces Arsene as servant in Samuel Beckett's *Watt*.

Emma Knott   University student and daughter of a prosperous surgeon; a member of the Marxist group, she adores Neil St. John for his political idealism in C. P. Snow's *The Malcontents*.

Mrs. Knowell   Martha Quest's mother-in-law, who proves — instead of the intrusive pest Martha imagined — polite, kind, and noninterfering in Doris Lessing's *Martha Quest* and in *A Proper Marriage*.

Caroline Knowell   The daughter of Martha Quest's first marriage, to Douglas Knowell; her mother, not wanting Caroline to be subjected to the tortures that parents bring their children, abandons her when she leaves her husband in Doris Lessing's *A Proper Marriage*. She is raised by her father and his new wife, Elaine (Talbot), in *A Ripple from the Storm* and in *Landlocked*. She appears in *The Four-Gated City*.

Douglas Knowell   Martha Quest's first husband, a conventional man who assumes a job as a town civil servant; his careful adherence to the social rules of his class disturbs Martha in Doris Lessing's *Martha Quest* and in *A Proper Marriage*.

Knowles   Lame sailor on the *Narcissus* in Joseph Conrad's *The Nigger of the "Narcissus"*.

Drake Ko   Wealthy and respected Chinese smuggler whose attempts to save his only blood relative, his brother Nelson, exemplify honorable action and family love in John le Carré's *The Honourable Schoolboy*.

Nelson Ko (Sheng-hsiu; also Yao Kai-sheng)   Karla's Chinese mole, who attempts to defect from China and rejoin his brother, Drake, in Hong Kong but is captured by British Intelligence agents and the American C.I.A. in John le Carré's *The Honourable Schoolboy*.

John (nicknames: "Lange", "Lofty") Koby   Streetwise American ex-journalist turned CIA agent who divulges to Bernard Samson Bret Rensselaer's past and fingers him as a K.G.B. mole in Len Deighton's *London Match*.

Herr Koch   Head clerk at the mortuary whose throat is slit, probably by Harry Lime, after he has told Rollo Martins that he heard the sounds of the "accident" and then saw the actual participants, including a third man, in Graham Greene's *The Third Man and the Fallen Idol*.

Koepgen   A philosopher and poet; he thinks he can escape the clutches of the Firm, but ultimately he is bound by their contracts in Lawrence Durrell's *Tunc*.

KolobEktofer   Leader of JandolAngand's fifth army; he believes it is unwise to attack the Draits; he is killed in battle in Brian W. Aldiss's *Helliconia Summer*.

Kolynos   The Provincial Lady's family dog; it attached itself to Vicky on a picnic and was rescued by her pleas from threatened extermination in E. M. Delafield's *The Provincial Lady Goes Further*.

Captain Kondal   The first officer to the Gorshek General; although he is considered by the General to be the perfect officer, he is killed by the General after he has witnessed his superior disobey orders in Alan Sillitoe's *The General*.

Sabina Kordt (covernames: "Watchman One", Olga Kravitsky)   Axel's licentious Czechoslovakian double agent; while searching for Magnus Pym, Jack Brotherhood discovers that her work for British Intelligence explicitly connects Magnus to Axel in John le Carré's *A Perfect Spy*.

Michale Koresipoulis   Hypocritical, shallow, pompous ruler; he leads a state with no people in order to save himself in Rex Warner's *The Wild Goose Chase: An Allegory*.

George Kosinski   Bernard Samson's brother-in-law and Tessa Kosinski's husband; a car salesman, he is the contact between Harry Posh and Bernard in Len Deighton's *London Match*.

Tessa Kimber-Hutchinson Kosinski   Fiona Samson's sister, who sometimes takes care of the Samson children; she identifies Giles Trent as a K.G.B. agent in Len Deighton's *Berlin Game*. She is Bernard's and Fiona's go-between in *Mexico Set*. She causes Richard Cruyer's divorce in *London Match*.

Fraulein Kost   Prostitute and boarder at Fraulein Schroeder's in Christopher Isherwood's *Goodbye to Berlin*.

Willy Kost   A refugee scholar; he is loved by Mary Clothier; his guilt-induced impotence is cured by Jessica Byrd in Iris Murdoch's *The Nice and the Good*.

Kosti the Pole   Larry Darrell's hulking traveling companion in Germany; he will speak of philosophical reality and spiritual truth only when drunk, but he further ignites Larry's desire for knowledge in W. Somerset Maugham's *The Razor's Edge*.

Kostia   Revolutionary student who offers to help Razumov escape Russia in Joseph Conrad's *Under Western Eyes*.

Kramenin   A small, pale man who is the power behind the Russian Revolution in Agatha Christie's *The Secret Adversary.*

Kramer   Middle-aged businessman and co-conspirator with Paul Firman; blackmailed and swindled by Paul Firman and threatened with exposure for income-tax evasion, he suffers a fatal heart attack in Eric Ambler's *Send No More Roses.*

Frieda Kramer   Widow of M. Kramer; she exposes Firman as Oberholzer at her husband's funeral in Eric Ambler's *Send No More Roses.*

Peter Arsenievitch Krasnojabkin   Handsome young Russian whom Madame Steynlin befriends, much to the dismay of some of the islanders in Norman Douglas's *South Wind.*

Krassky   Soviet embassy courier who carries Karla's misappropriated funds and fatherly inquiries about Tatiana to Anton Grigoriev and takes George Smiley's blackmail ultimatum to Karla in John le Carré's *Smiley's People.*

Ernst Krebelmann   Thick-headed young son of Baron Walther von Kessen's man-of-business in Kammstadt; a Hitler youth, he is a patriotic, uncomprehending witness of several events in Richard Hughes's *The Wooden Shepherdess.*

Otto Kreisler   A self-obsessed and paranoid German painter; he is hounded by creditors, obsessed by Anastaysa Vasek, kills Louis Soltyk in a duel, and hangs himself in his cell in Wyndham Lewis's *Tarr.*

Claus Kretzschmar   West German nightclub owner and occasional espionage operative; he helps fellow agent Otto Leipzig blackmail Oleg Kursky for revenge and turns blackmail clues over to George Smiley so that Smiley will avenge his loyal friend's brutal death in John le Carré's *Smiley's People.*

Dr. C. V. Krishnan   President of the Eastern Division of the Freedom League; he believes the Overlords will not show themselves because their appearance would be totally alien and repulsive to humans in Arthur C. Clarke's *Childhood's End.*

Kristbjorg   Fisherman in British Columbia with whom Sigbjorn Wilderness regrets quarreling before his journey in Malcolm Lowry's *Dark as the Grave Wherein My Friend Is Laid.*

Kristin   A Stockholm barrister's daughter, who does domestic work at Mr. and Mrs. Bennett's home; she often weeps while doing her work in Margaret Drabble's *A Summer Bird-Cage.*

Sir Leicester Kroesig   The practical, wealthy banker father of Tony; he and Matthew Radlett hold each other in contempt; he believes that a wife should be a social and business asset to her husband, and he soon finds his daughter-in-law, Linda (Radlett), inadequate in Nancy Mitford's *The Pursuit of Love.*

Moira Kroesig   The child of Linda Radlett's marriage to Tony; Linda almost dies giving birth, and takes no interest in Moira before or after leaving Tony; Moira is reared by Tony's parents in Nancy Mitford's *The Pursuit of Love.*

Tony Kroesig   Linda Radlett's first husband, with whom she falls in love during her debutante season; a banker from a banking family, he is young, handsome, and rich; neglectful and selfish, he is disappointed in his marriage in Nancy Mitford's *The Pursuit of Love.*

Erik Krogh   Wealthy Swedish entrepreneur, factory-owner, household name in international business, and lover of Kate Farrant; he engages in unethical business ventures, including hostile takeovers, is obsessively private and secretive, and is responsible for the death of Anthony Farrant in Graham Greene's *England Made Me.*

Krolgul   A Shammat agent, expert at rhetorical trickery, who not only causes many near and ill-planned revolts against the Volyen Empire, but causes the Canopian agent, Incent, to side with him and his plans in Doris Lessing's *Documents Relating to the Sentimental Agents in the Volyen Empire.*

Frits Buhler Krom   Late-middle-aged criminologist and professor of Sociology and Social Administration; the leader of the team appointed to question Paul Firman, he discovers Firman's activities and blackmails him into disclosing the details of his criminal career in order to prove the existence of that criminal type in Eric Ambler's *Send No More Roses.*

Kronsteen   Strategist for the USSR espionage agency SMERSH; he plots to humiliate and destroy James Bond in Ian Fleming's *From Russia, With Love.*

Karl Kroop   Popular teacher of popular culture at Euphoric State University; he is initially denied tenure but then offered it in place of Howard Ringbaum; he organizes a faculty vigil during student unrest in David Lodge's *Changing Places: A Tale of Two Campuses.*

Betty Kruger   Boris Kruger's wife, also a member of Sympathizers of Russia, who resents people's constant fear of the "Left" in Doris Lessing's *A Proper Marriage* and in *A Ripple from the Storm*.

Boris Kruger   A Polish intellectual involved with socialism and organizer for a group called the Sympathizers of Russia in Doris Lessing's *A Proper Marriage* and in *A Ripple from the Storm*.

Kua-ko'   Runi's brother and chief hunter for the family; he tells Mr. Abel of Rima's death in W. H. Hudson's *Green Mansions*.

Hari Kumar   An Anglicized Indian who, returning to Mayapore upon completing his education, is shattered to find himself invisible to the English; Hari becomes extremely cautious of friendship and is slow to respond to Daphne Manners; their romance attracts police Superintendent Ronald Merrick's jealous hatred, and after they have become lovers, Hari is arrested for complicity in the gang attack on Daphne and himself in Paul Scott's *The Jewel in the Crown*. He breaks silence and exposes the injustice when the case is reopened; he is eventually released in *The Day of the Scorpion*.

Kunzor   The gene-father of one of Al-Ith's many children in Doris Lessing's *The Marriages between Zones Three, Four, and Five*.

Oleg Kursky ("the Ginger Pig"; covername: Kirov) Bullying, repulsive Moscow Centre agent; at Karla's secret order, he offers to reunite Maria Ostrakova with her illegitimate daughter but is following Karla's private orders to create a false history for Karla's daughter, Tatiana, using Ostrakova's daughter's identity; blackmailed by Otto Leipzig and General Vladimir into revealing Karla's secret, he is assassinated for his treachery in John le Carré's *Smiley's People*.

Kurtz   An international-relief-organization official who is actually working with Harry Lime in a penicillin-substitution racket; he is with Lime at the time of his supposed death in Graham Greene's *The Third Man and the Fallen Idol*.

Marty Kurtz (covernames: Gold, Raphael, Schulmann, Spielberg)   Nazi-concentration-camp survivor, Israel's super-patriotic spymaster, and Israeli Intelligence's maverick outsider; having wooed the physically and emotionally abused Charlie into his espionage "family" by promising her his fatherly love and the romantic love of Joseph (Gadi Becker), he uses her uncertainties in a complex anti-Palestinian operation that fails to resolve Middle East tensions but secures Salim's, Khalil's, Tayeh's, and Fatmeh's actual deaths and Charlie's and Gadi Becker's psychic deaths in John le Carré's *The Little Drummer Girl*.

U Po Kyin   A fat, power-hungry local magistrate; he is trying to gain the trust of and membership in the European Club; he deals in rumours and bribery to get them and defames Dr. Veraswami in George Orwell's *Burmese Days*.

L

L. The aristocratic agent who through bribery and a network of spies frustrates D.'s attempts to buy coal for his country in Graham Greene's *The Confidential Agent*.

Lady L. An arbiter of social practices for the aristocratic class of Edwardian society; she exercises the power to admit or exclude persons from intimate social gatherings on the basis of birth, dignity (virtue), and reserve in Vita Sackville-West's *The Edwardians*.

Hercule La Bataille Haitian drummer with the Isabel Cornwallis Ballet Company; he practices voodoo in Colin MacInnes's *City of Spades*.

Labib A Maronite Christian Lebanese taxi-driver with fierce capitalist views; he drives Jane Mallory and Daniel Martin from Beirut to Palmyra and back in John Fowles's *Daniel Martin*.

La Cecilia Italian in the German army and the inner circle of the Iron Hands, a group of violent German Nationalists who attempt to assassinate Chancellor Loeffler and Warren Creevey and are thwarted in both attempts by Adam Melfort in John Buchan's *A Prince of the Captivity*.

Emma Lacey Governess to the Calderone children; her private means give her some independence in Ivy Compton-Burnett's *Elders and Betters*.

Florence Lacey The young niece of Emma Lacey; she first accepts and then rejects Thomas Calderone's proposal and finally agrees to marry Desmond Donne in Ivy Compton-Burnett's *Elders and Betters*.

Norman Lacey Civil-service clerk who loves Vera Allen; he asks Lewis Eliot for testimony in the trial of his father in C. P. Snow's *Homecomings*.

Antony Lachish Cousin of the Staveleys who participates in the houseparty at Anchorstone Hall; upon seeing Dick Staveley naked, he says that there is something repellent in sheer masculinity in L. P. Hartley's *The Sixth Heaven*. He writes to Eustace Cherrington in Venice and gives him his first understanding that the romantic relationship Eustace envisioned between Dick and his sister Hilda may have turned out badly in *Eustace and Hilda*.

Elizabeth Lackersteen A young woman who longs for the life of the rich and travels to Burma to live with her aunt and uncle and ultimately find a husband; she courts and spurns John Flory and is the reason for his suicide in Goerge Orwell's *Burmese Days*.

Tom Lackersteen A forty-year-old timber manager; he drinks to excess and is a member of the European Club; he is Elizabeth's uncle and tries unsuccessfully to make love to her in George Orwell's *Burmese Days*.

Oliver Lacon Sometimes talkative, often intelligent senior Cabinet Office official, governmental adviser, and watchdog over intelligence affairs ("Whitehall's head prefect"); he unofficially recruits George Smiley to unearth the double agent in John le Carré's *Tinker, Tailor, Soldier, Spy*. He generously assists Smiley in reestablishing the London Station after Haydon's treachery ("the Fall") in *The Honourable Schoolboy*. He tries to limit Smiley's investigation of General Vladimir's murder in *Smiley's People*.

Beatrice Lacy Maxim de Winter's sister, known for her straightforward, direct manner; the second Mrs. de Winter is somewhat intimidated by her, but is gratified to learn that Beatrice was not a wholehearted admirer of Rebecca de Winter in Daphne Du Maurier's *Rebecca*.

Major Giles Lacy Beatrice's somewhat foolish husband in Daphne Du Maurier's *Rebecca*.

Laddy Boy Sailor and friend to Johnny Fortune; he helps Johnny get a job on a ship sailing to Nigeria in Colin MacInnes's *City of Spades*.

La Dolciquita Mistress of the Russian Grand Duke; she is a professional courtesan of whom Edward Ashburnham becomes enamored for a week at Monte Carlo; the affair costs Edward much of his fortune and puts him completely in the power of his wife, Leonora, in Ford Madox Ford's *The Good Soldier: A Tale of Passion*.

Ladyday Son of Lord Derrydown; Arnold Condorex calls him "the good, young Ladyday" and likens him and his father to sheep with long faces; targeting him for defeat, along with elder politicians, Condorex thinks him so vulnerable that "a touch of my ridicule will kill him" in Rebecca West's *Harriet Hume, A London Fantasy*.

Marianne Laffon French girl with extraordinary memory for French literature; she is one of the supernormals of John Wainwright's Pacific island colony in Olaf Stapledon's *Odd John: A Story Between Jest and Earnest*.

Lahitte A Frenchman proposing to lecture in English on Spanish literature; he asks Miriam Henderson to edit his lecture, which she regards as hopelessly beyond any such help in Dorothy Richardson's *Deadlock.*

Bandel Eith Lahl   A commander of the Boldoranian forces fighting with Pannoval against Sibornal; he is killed by Luterin Shokerandit in Brian W. Aldiss's *Helliconia Winter.*

Torress Lahl   The wife of Bandel Eith Lahl and a physician; she is taken captive by Luterin Shokerandit and tends him when he becomes ill; later she becomes his lover and has a son by him in Brian W. Aldiss's *Helliconia Winter.*

Pastor Lahmann   Swiss cleric and widower with four small boys; he teaches in the Hanover school and is jealously monitored by Fraulein Pfaff in Dorothy Richardson's *Pointed Roofs.*

Signe Laine   General Midwinter's sensual, marvellously beautiful yet murderous assistant; she lures Harvey Newbegin into the conspiracy and tries to lure the narrator away from his mission; Dawlish considers recruiting her in Len Deighton's *The Billion-Dollar Brain.*

Major Laird   Tall, red-faced, red-haired marine who is brimming with pride in C. S. Forester's *Ship of the Line.*

George Laird   A physician of Scottish descent who is married to Gratian Pierson; he becomes ill working at the battle fronts during World War I and returns to be nursed by his wife in John Galsworthy's *Saint's Progress.*

Gratian Pierson Laird   A nurse during World War I who provides a home for her sister Noel Pierson when Noel leaves London with her illegitimate baby in John Galsworthy's *Saint's Progress.*

Lakamba   Rajah of Sambir who sells gunpowder to Dain Maroola and helps Kaspar Almayer's daughter elope in Joseph Conrad's *Almayer's Folly: A Story of an Eastern River.* He thwarts Peter Willems and Almayer in *An Outcast of the Islands.*

Climbers Lake   Employee at the nursery run by David Parker and Gordon Paget; he feuds with Tim Rattray in Angus Wilson's *The Middle Age of Mrs. Eliot.*

Chandra Lal   Intelligent, evasive, honest, passionate Indian agitator and lawyer; responsible for bombings and riots, he escapes the British government until his love for Giulia Lazzari becomes his downfall in W. Somerset Maugham's *Ashenden: or The British Agent.*

Dr. Panna Lal   Dr. Aziz's unpleasant fellow assistant, who volunteers to testify against Aziz in E. M. Forster's *A Passage to India.*

Lalage   The daughter of Charles Smithson and Sarah Woodruff in John Fowles's *The French Lieutenant's Woman.*

Charles Merkland, Lord Lamancha   Scots Member of Parliament and Cabinet Minister; aware he has become bored and stale, he joins Sir Edward Leithen and John Palliser-Yeates to become the poacher "John Macnab" and succeeds in killing a stag on Haripol, the estate of Lord Claybody, before he is apprehended in John Buchan's *John Macnab.* He takes Sir Edward Leithen and Vernon Milburne cruising on his yacht to the Greek Isles in *The Dancing Floor.* He provides sanctuary on his estate for Hermann Loeffler, German Chancellor, in England to attend an important peace conference, in *A Prince of the Captivity.*

Dr. Lamb   Lynda Coldridge's psychoanalyst, whom Martha Quest also visits briefly in Doris Lessing's *The Four-Gated City.*

Dr. Lamb   The physician who treats Sophia Stace in her last illness in Ivy Compton-Burnett's *Brothers and Sisters.*

Avery Lamb   Horace and Charlotte's youngest child, who is afraid of his father; when he is caught taking comfits, he says that his brother Jasper takes things too, in Ivy Compton-Burnett's *Manservant and Maidservant.*

Charlotte Lamb   A woman who married Horace for love; she comes to value her children highest, even above Mortimer Lamb, whom she plans to run away with in Ivy Compton-Burnett's *Manservant and Maidservant.*

Emilia Lamb   The elderly aunt of Horace and Mortimer Lamb; she supervises the housekeeping and tries to moderate the excesses of the adult Lambs in Ivy Compton-Burnett's *Manservant and Maidservant.*

Evelyn Lamb   Essay writer, journalist, and editor of *London Review;* in 1918 she is a wealthy, haughty, insecure, and nerve-wracked woman, who in a fit of "war emotion" married the much younger soldier T. S. Heywood; he returns from war embittered and never able to love her; she funds right-wing publishers, writes an early positive essay on Hitler, cultivates a large following of literary "devotees", is frequently painted by young London artists, and has brief relationships with attractive but selfish and ambitious men, including William Ridley and Penn Vane, in Storm Jameson's

Company Parade. Evelyn Lamb in 1939 continues her fashionable entertaining of the London literati, but on the eve of war has a nervous crack-up after inviting a sexual encounter with brutal Captain Tim Hunt in *Before the Crossing.*

Horace Lamb   A penny-pinching and tyrannical father, who deposits his wife's money into his savings account and refuses to spend it on heat for the house or clothes for the children; he reforms when he learns that his wife, Charlotte, and her money plan to leave him in Ivy Compton-Burnett's *Manservant and Maidservant.*

Jasper Lamb   The twelve-year-old son of Horace and Charlotte; he has an almost pitiful look to him; he, along with Marcus, does not warn his father, Horace, about the unsafe bridge in Ivy Compton-Burnett's *Manservant and Maidservant.*

Lucius Lamb   An aging poet, who has become Gerda Marshalson's permanent houseguest and dependent in Iris Murdoch's *Henry and Cato.*

Marcus Lamb   Horace and Charlotte's eldest son, an eleven-year-old; he makes a wax image of his father to stick pins into; he hesitates and doesn't warn his father that the bridge is unsafe in Ivy Compton-Burnett's *Manservant and Maidservant.*

Mortimer Lamb   Cousin to Horace Lamb; he plans to set up housekeeping with Charlotte Lamb; he later agrees to marry Magdelen Doubleday until he discovers that she revealed his alliance with Charlotte to Horace Lamb in Ivy Compton-Burnett's *Manservant and Maidservant.*

Sarah Lamb   The oldest and best child of Horace and Charlotte; she tries to shield the younger children from hardships in Ivy Compton-Burnett's *Manservant and Maidservant.*

Tamasin Lamb   The ten-year-old daughter of Horace and Charlotte; she is the only child who has some affection for her father in Ivy Compton-Burnett's *Manservant and Maidservant.*

Terence Lambert   Twenty-seven-year-old interior decorator, who was once Bernard Sands's lover; he has an affair with Elizabeth Sands but drops her to live with Sherman Winter in Angus Wilson's *Hemlock and After.*

Wilfrid Lambert   Friend of Auberon Quin and James Barker; he becomes a commander in the West Kensington army and is killed in battle by Adam Wayne in G. K. Chesterton's *The Napoleon of Notting Hill.*

Frances Lamberton (satirical portrait of Brigit Patmore)   Married friend of Elizabeth Paston; George Winterbourne sees her at Shobbe's party in Richard Aldington's *Death of a Hero.*

Blanche de Lambese   Vain young lady of the court of Pisuerga and friend of Laura de Nazianzi in Ronald Firbank's *The Flower Beneath the Foot.*

Adam Lambsbreath   The dithering old manservant whose only interests in life are his little Elfine Starkadder and the dumb beasts in the cowshed in Stella Gibbons's *Cold Comfort Farm.*

Dido Lament   Owner and editor of a London tabloid; she hosts frequent parties for the local celebrities in Colin MacInnes's *Absolute Beginners.*

Mary Lamington   Adorable, golden-haired girl of nineteen, serving as a V.A.D. in the shell-shock hospital at Isham; she is Richard Hannay's contact in their intelligence assignment to uncover and destroy a diabolical network of enemy spies operated by a dangerous, elusive mastermind; her intelligence, courage, skill, and resourcefulness during the pursuit win the admiration and love of Hannay in John Buchan's *Mr. Standfast.* As Lady Hannay, charming young wife and mother of Peter John, she persuades Hannay to undertake the search for three young people kidnapped and being held as hostages in *The Three Hostages.* As the sympathetic and gracious hostess of Fosse Manor, she provides a refuge for guests Valdemar Haraldsen and his daughter, Anna, while Haraldsen is regaining his mental and physical health after being terrorized by villains determined to destroy him in *The Island of Sheep.*

Anthony ("Nanty") Lammas   A licensed minister of the kirk and a professor in the University of St. Andrews and former tutor to Harry, Lord Belses, eldest son of Lord Snowdoun, Minister of Scotland; he discovers the truth both of Squire Cranmer's evil conspiracy to attack England at home and abroad, using his wife as decoy, and of Gabriel Cranmer's courage and gallantry in John Buchan's *The Free Fishers.*

Antony Lamont   One of the three Dublin characters held in captivity by the fictional novelist Dermot Trellis; he is the brother of Sheila Lamont in Flann O'Brien's *At Swim-Two-Birds.*

Gerald (Jerry) Lamont   Chief suspect and roommate of Albert Sorrell; he is christened "The Levantine" by Detective-Inspector Alan Grant, who refuses to believe Lamont is guilty even though clues point unequivocally to him as the killer in Josephine Tey's *The Man in the Queue.*

Sheila Lamont   Antony Lamont's sister, who is raped by her creator, Dermot Trellis, and gives birth to Orlick Trellis in Flann O'Brien's *At Swim-Two-Birds*.

Madame Lamotte   Mother of Annette (Forsyte); she helps Soames Forsyte in his courtship in John Galsworthy's *In Chancery*.

Detective Lampeter   Melancholy American black man; he is in charge of the bomb-disposal unit that defuses the bomb sent to Robert Halliday by Karlis Zander in Eric Ambler's *The Care of Time*.

Joe Lampton   Amoral, manipulative, charming accountant; of working-class background, he gets what he wants by assimilating and socializing with the upper class; his love for Alice Aisgill is his last happiness in John Braine's *Room at the Top*. His marriage to Susan Brown provides a retreat to family responsibilities after affairs and anger in *Life at the Top*.

Alexander Lancaster   Businessman and cousin of Christopher Isherwood; he invites him to visit Germany, tries to warn him against human isolation, and later commits suicide in Christopher Isherwood's *Down There on a Visit*.

Damon Lancewood   Jake Richardson's friend and contemporary; in a conversation between them Jake realizes he has never liked women except as sex objects in Kingsley Amis's *Jake's Thing*.

Lieutenant-Colonel Algernon Lancing   Commanding Officer of Catterick; Jonathan Browne and Mike Brady inform him that they don't wish to be officers in David Lodge's *Ginger, You're Barmy*.

Nicholas P. (Niki) Landau   Polish-born, naïve British book salesman; he receives Yakov Savelyev's questionable manuscript from Katya Orlova at a Moscow bookfair and delivers it, after being turned away at British Intelligence offices, to a Foreign Office clerk rather than to Barley Blair in John le Carré's *The Russia House*.

Bernhard Landauer   Wealthy Jewish businessman who isolates himself in his villa and finally commits suicide in Christopher Isherwood's *Goodbye to Berlin*.

Natalia Landauer   Repressed daughter in a wealthy Jewish family; she is tutored by Christopher Isherwood; later she travels to Paris and finds love and happiness in Christopher Isherwood's *Goodbye to Berlin*.

Lander   Barrister who argues the case for Jenny Rastall's challenge to her father's will in C. P. Snow's *In Their Wisdom*.

Rebecca Landon   Naïve teen-aged neighbor of the Jardine family; as an adult in the 1940s she recalls her youthful memories before World War I of stories about Sibyl Jardine as told to her from several different viewpoints in Rosamond Lehmann's *The Ballad and the Source*. As a young woman, a visitor to a Caribbean island where she arrives alone when her lover does not appear on board ship, she has a passionate love affair with Johnny during her brief stay in *A Sea-Grape Tree*.

Stephen Lane   Clergyman obsessed with sexual evil in Agatha Christie's *Evil Under the Sun*.

Mrs. Lang   A Frenchwoman with an intellectual face; she is the mother of Christian Stace as well as of Gilbert and Caroline Lang in Ivy Compton-Burnett's *Brothers and Sisters*.

Caroline (Carrie) Lang   Gilbert's sister, who looks more English than he; she is proposed to by the younger Andrew Stace and then by Julian Wake in Ivy Compton-Burnett's *Brothers and Sisters*.

Gilbert Lang   A barrister who proposes to Dinah Stace before he discovers that his mother is also Christian Stace's mother; he proposes finally to Sarah Wake in Ivy Compton-Burnett's *Brothers and Sisters*.

Langatse   Blind Tibetan monk who, through telepathic contact, becomes the spiritual adviser to John Wainwright's colony of supernormals in Olaf Stapledon's *Odd John: A Story Between Jest and Earnest*.

Dr. Charles Langley-Beard   Veterinary surgeon at the zoological gardens who is nominal director after the resignation of Dr. Leacock; his interest in old records interrupts efficient administration in Angus Wilson's *The Old Men at the Zoo*.

Lankor   One of the supernormals of John Wainwright's Pacific island colony in Olaf Stapledon's *Odd John: A Story Between Jest and Earnest*.

Captain Lansen   Commercial pilot for Northern Air Services; his freelance reconnaissance flights from Düsseldorf to Finland endanger his innocent passengers in John le Carré's *The Looking-Glass War*.

Sperr Lansing   Vulgar comic host of a television talk show on which F. X. Enderby is interviewed about one of his poems that has been made into a movie in Anthony Burgess's *The Clockwork Testament: Or Enderby's End*.

Dr. Lanza   Italian professor and refugee who believes government and property are the source of all evil; his brilliant orations show Chester Nimmo the power of rhetoric in Joyce Cary's *Except the Lord.*

Isabel Lapford   Wife of the Vice-Chancellor of Brockshire University in J. B. Priestley's *The Image Men.*

Jayjay Lapford   Vice-Chancellor of Brockshire University; he is courted by Cosmo Sultana and Owen Tuby for university endorsement of their Institute of Social Imagistics in J. B. Priestley's *The Image Men.*

Madame La Pierre   Maria Ostrakova's greedy and inquisitive landlady who feeds Ostrakova after Moscow Centre's thugs brutalize her and lies to Karla's assassins to protect Ostrakova in John le Carré's *Smiley's People.*

John Laputa   Noble black leader, whose military skill, intellect, and spellbinding charisma as the reincarnation of "Prester John" enable him to lead his people into a mighty uprising against the whites; defeated, he plunges to his death into a chasm of underground waters, wearing Prester John's collar of rubies in John Buchan's *Prester John.*

Richard Larch   Young Northern man aspiring to be a London writer; he consistently ignores his real strengths and desires until his repeated failures to produce good writing and his failure to be sincere with the pretty heiress Adeline Aked cause him consciously to subside into bookkeeping and marriage to the working girl Laura Roberts in Arnold Bennett's *A Man From the North.*

Emilio Largo   Handsome, womanizing, ruthless owner of a yacht and member of a smuggling ring broken up by James Bond in Ian Fleming's *Thunderball.*

T. S. ("Timmy") Lariarty   Dapper Gran Seco magnate and old acquaintance of Lord Clanroyden; he warns Lord Clanroyden of the planned murders of the two women and of Castor by the Conquistadors, attacks Senor Cyril Romanes, and is killed in John Buchan's *The Courts of the Morning.*

Aunt Larkins   Alfred Polly's mother-in-law and mother of his cousins Annie, Minnie, and Miriam (Polly) in H. G. Wells's *The History of Mr. Polly.*

Annie Larkins   Alfred Polly's cheerful oldest cousin, who becomes Miriam Polly's business partner after Alfred Polly's supposed death in H. G. Wells's *The History of Mr. Polly.*

Minnie Larkins   Alfred Polly's youngest cousin, to

whom he hints misleadingly about marriage in H. G. Wells's *The History of Mr. Polly.*

Clifford Larr   Hilary Burde's senior colleague who alone of Burde's associates knows the story of Anne Jopling's death; a well-to-do upper-class homosexual, he prepares a weekly dinner for Hilary, for whom he yearns; his romantic idealization of Crystal Burde tempers his characteristic pessimism; eventually he makes good on his frequent promise of suicide in Iris Murdoch's *A Word Child.*

Larry   American G.I. from Ohio; he is a frequent customer of Dorothy Macpherson in Colin MacInnes's *City of Spades.*

Miss Larsen   Attractive, promiscuous Dutch mercenary; she successfully plants a bomb in the Israeli Labour Attaché's residence in Bad Godesberg that kills several innocent bystanders, including the Attaché's son Gabriel, and so initiates Marty Kurtz's operation to assassinate Khalil in John le Carré's *The Little Drummer Girl.*

Frederick Larson   An academic, knowledgeable about archeology, who suffers the same sorts of stammering problems that Dr. Charles Watkins suffered; he is also given sedatives in Doris Lessing's *Briefing for a Descent into Hell.*

Jacques Laruelle   French film-maker, boyhood friend of Geoffrey Firmin, and one-time lover of Yvonne Firmin; his recollection of the Consul (Geoffrey) on the Day of the Dead 1939 calls forth the recitation of the events that took place one year earlier in Malcolm Lowry's *Under the Volcano.*

Lord Lasswade   Husband of Kitty (Malone) Lasswade chosen for her by her mother, who decided her cousin Edward Pargiter "would not do"; his estate lies isolated and cold in the north; he becomes a governor-general and dies, widowing Kitty in Virginia Woolf's *The Years.*

Kitty Malone, Lady Lasswade   Daughter of an Oxford don and first cousin to Colonel Abel Pargiter's seven children; beloved by Edward Pargiter, she admires Jo Robson, who reminds her of a farmhand who once kissed her under a haywagon; at her mother's insistence, she marries Lord Lasswade and lives shiveringly in the north; she appears at the final Pargiter gathering in 1937 the widow of a governor-general in Virginia Woolf's *The Years.*

Brenda Last   Tony Last's aristocratic and beautiful wife, who engages in an adulterous love affair with John Beaver; after Beaver deserts her and Tony is declared legally dead, she marries Jock Grant-Menzies in Evelyn Waugh's *A Handful of Dust*.

John Andrew Last Brattish child of Tony and Brenda Last; hearing of his accidental death, Brenda weeps with relief that the deceased is not her lover, John Beaver, in Evelyn Waugh's *A Handful of Dust*.

Tony Last Young landowner whose wife, Brenda, carries on an adulterous affair and demands a divorce; he chivalrously assumes responsibility in the divorce proceedings, but when Brenda breaks their agreement with unreasonable financial demands he rebels and sets off on an expedition to South America; captured in the jungle by a deranged illiterate settler, he is forced to spend his days reading the novels of Charles Dickens aloud; in England he is declared dead in Evelyn Waugh's *A Handful of Dust*.

Doña Rita de Lastaola Basque peasant girl who is established in Paris society by the millionaire Henry Allègre, becomes committed to the Spanish royalist cause, chooses to marry the daring gunrunner Monsieur George over J. K. Blunt and José Ortega, nurses George after he is deceitfully wounded in a duel by Blunt, but then leaves George in Joseph Conrad's *The Arrow of Gold: A Story Between Two Notes*.

Laszlo "Activist scholar of Marxism" and a good friend of Janos Lavin, who was politically active with him in Hungary; Laszlo becomes an administrator in Eastern Europe and is executed for supposedly betraying the socialist cause; his death spurs Lavin to return to Eastern Europe and fight for the cause in John Berger's *A Painter of Our Time*.

Mildred Lathbury Unassuming thirty-year-old spinster; she is a keen observer of and commentator on the affairs of men and women in her limited circle of her London flat, her church, and her work for distressed gentlewomen in Barbara Pym's *Excellent Women*. Her subsequent life is discussed in *Jane and Prudence*.

Captain Bobby Latimer One of Senor Castor's guards; he helps "Sandy" (Lord Clanroyden) plan their military strategy in John Buchan's *The Courts of the Morning*.

Charles Latimer Mild-mannered, middle-aged former academic; a college professor turned mystery writer, he becomes fascinated with the apparently dead criminal Dimitrios Makropoulos and, while tracing his footsteps, becomes involved in a complicated, decadent criminal society in Eric Ambler's *The Mask of Dimitrios*.

Rose Latimer Secretary in the British Communist Party and one of the few persons whom Anna Wulf dislikes in Doris Lessing's *The Golden Notebook*.

Marquis de la Tour du Pin ("Turpin") Young French nobleman engaged to Adela Victor, one of the hostages; with Mary (Lamington) Hannay he goes in diguise to a suspicious dancing-club, where he, too, becomes a prisoner; he finds Adela, breaks the hypnotic power Dominick Medina has over her mind, and frees her by knocking out Odell, Medina's evil butler, in John Buchan's *The Three Hostages*.

Simone Latrelle (Solitaire) Haiti-raised expert in voodoo who is trusted by Mr. Big, though she is his prisoner; she becomes James Bond's lover and ally in Ian Fleming's *Live and Let Die*.

Miss La Trobe Complex, troubled, androgynous artist whose unified vision offers redemption from fragmented, alienated life; she writes and directs the village pageant produced at Pointz Hall one June morning in 1939; she drinks too much, tramps exuberantly alone over the downs, despises the intriguing members of the audience, and tries to give English history unity in her play, while twelve airplanes presaging World War II fly overhead in Virginia Woolf's *Between The Acts*.

Deveroux Latter Monocle-wearing playwright at Harriet Blair's parties; he enjoys cloak-and-dagger conversation in C. Day Lewis's *Starting Point*.

James Latter Retired captain who is Nina Woodville's first love and second husband; he searches for simple truths in the world and cannot accept the dishonesty in Chester Nimmo and his wife; as a result he tries to kill Chester and succeeds in killing his wife for honor in Joyce Cary's *Prisoner of Grace*, in *Except the Lord*, and in *Not Honour More* (told in James's voice).

May Latter Politically active and controlling woman who raises Nina Woodville and, after Nina is pregnant by James Latter, arranges her marriage to Chester Nimmo in Joyce Cary's *Prisoner of Grace*, in *Except the Lord*, and in *Not Honour More*.

Robert Latter Well-liked older brother of James Latter; he continually tries to find Jim a job and to keep him out of debt in Joyce Cary's *Prisoner of Grace*.

Robert Latter (the younger) Youngest child of Nina Woodville and James Latter; he is the only child recognized as Jim's, Tom and Sally having been reared as Chester Nimmo's in Joyce Cary's *Prisoner of Grace* and in *Not Honour More*.

Mrs. Lattimer Anna Wulf's friend, an attractive

woman, in Mashopi in Doris Lessing's *The Golden Notebook*.

Adrian Lauder   An English army chaplain who had been Edward Pierson's curate; he is embarrassed by Noel Pierson's unmarried pregnancy in John Galsworthy's *Saint's Progress*.

Henry Laugier   Buddha-shaped Directeur of the Hotel de la Concorde from Carcassonne in Arnold Bennett's *Imperial Palace*.

Laurel   Dulcie Mainwaring's niece who comes briefly to live at her aunt's suburban London house after leaving school; she complicates the romantic and social life in Barbara Pym's *No Fond Return of Love*.

Laurence   Disdainful Oxford student, nephew of Lady Naylor, in Elizabeth Bowen's *The Last September*.

Laurie   Purser's steward aboard the *Lydia* who is forced into the role of ship's surgeon; he is scared, but under pressure he comes through with the aid of Lady Barbara Wellesley and Captain Hornblower in C. S. Forester's *The Happy Return*.

Laurin   Trusted director of I.G.S., one of Erik Krogh's companies; Fred Hall is jealous of him in Graham Greene's *England Made Me*.

Mr. Lavater   Slim, pale, grey-haired man under Dominick Medina's evil control; until he became Medina's "disciple", he had been a friend of Lord Clanroyden in John Buchan's *The Three Hostages*.

Hezekiah Lavender   A gnarled old man and expert bell ringer who for sixty years has pulled the Tenor "Tailor Paul" in Dorothy L. Sayers's *The Nine Tailors: Changes Rung on an Old Theme in Two Short Touches and Two Full Peals*.

John Lavender   Fifty-eight-year-old English barrister; he has never practiced the law, but he is moved by newspapers to become a public man, and volunteers to speak to the nation on behalf of the war effort during World War I; he grows disillusioned, mounts a pile of books and journals to immolate himself for his patriotism, and falls into the arms of Isabel Scarlet where he believes he is in paradise in John Galsworthy's *The Burning Spear: Being the Experiences of Mr. John Lavender in Time of War*.

Henriette Lavendie   Wife of Pierre; she is ill from drug addiction in John Galsworthy's *Saint's Progress*.

Pierre Lavendie   Poor Belgian artist; he paints portraits of Edward Pierson and Noel Pierson in John Galsworthy's *Saint's Progress*.

Diana Lavin   Janos Lavin's attractive English wife, who marries Lavin because he is a refugee and because she believes she can "rescue" him by being his interpreter, guide, and financier; she grows bitter and disappointed as the years go by and Lavin's paintings are not recognized in John Berger's *A Painter of Our Time*.

Janos Lavin   Hungarian painter who flees Hungary, where he was active as a Marxist revolutionary, and moves to England; there he marries an Englishwoman who supports him while he paints; after painting for years without "success", he finally has a successful exhibition, only to disappear a week later, writing his friends back home that he has returned to Eastern Europe to resume his political activism in John Berger's *A Painter of Our Time*.

Fay Lavington   Socialite who, for a brief time, attracts Harry Sinton and to whom he turns for an alibi when he believes he has committed a murder in Roy Fuller's *Fantasy and Fugue*.

Eleanor Lavish   Gossipy writer of romance novels who reenacts Lucy Honeychurch's first romantic encounter with George Emerson in one of her novels in E. M. Forster's *A Room with a View*.

Dr. Lawrence   London medical man who acknowledges that one day his daughters, Ellen, Joan, and Veronica, must marry, but who makes clear his disapproval of the suitors they attract in Elizabeth Bowen's *The Hotel*.

Miss Lawrence   A partner in Lesbia Firebrace's school; she teaches the girls Latin and Greek in Ivy Compton-Burnett's *Two Worlds and Their Ways*.

Mr. Lawrence   Emma Evans's theologian father in Margaret Drabble's *The Garrick Year*.

Mrs. Lawrence   Mother of Emma Evans; she died of tuberculosis when Emma was a girl in Margaret Drabble's *The Garrick Year*.

Mrs. Lawrence   Mother of Ellen, Joan, and Veronica Lawrence; like her husband, Dr. Lawrence, she disapproves of the suitors her daughters attract in Elizabeth Bowen's *The Hotel*.

Ellen Lawrence   Attractive but shallow and flirtatious sister of Joan and Veronica Lawrence; the sisters' attitudes, aspirations, and behavior contrast sharply with those of Sydney Warren in Elizabeth Bowen's *The Hotel*.

George Lawrence   A cool, sarcastic Englishman, who is a member of His Majesty's Nigerian Civil Service; he is lovingly devoted to Lady Patricia Brandon as well as being the caretaker of John Geste and friend to Henri de Beaujolais in Percival Christopher Wren's *Beau Geste.*

Joan Lawrence   Sister of Ellen Lawrence, whom she resembles in being attractive, shallow, and flirtatious in Elizabeth Bowen's *The Hotel.*

Veronica Lawrence   Sister of Ellen Lawrence, whom she resembles in being attractive, shallow, and flirtatious in Elizabeth's Bowen's *The Hotel.*

Lawson   Student who studies at Amitrano's studio in Paris with Philip Carey; he is cheerful, agreeable, and mediocre, yet proves somewhat successful as an artist in W. Somerset Maugham's *Of Human Bondage.*

Raynil Laynan   Chief apprentice of the tanners and Datnil Skar's successor; he betrays Datnil to Aoz Roon in Brian W. Aldiss's *Helliconia Spring.*

Colonel John Layton   Husband of Mildred Layton and father of Sarah and Susan Layton; Commander of the Pankot Rifles, he is a prisoner of war in Germany throughout most of the war years in Paul Scott's *The Day of the Scorpion* and in *The Towers of Silence.* He returns to India and to his family in *A Division of the Spoils.*

Mabel Layton   The stepmother of Colonel John Layton and widow of the former District Commissioner of Pankot; she commands the respect, if not the admiration, of most of the upper-crust families in Pankot in Paul Scott's *The Day of the Scorpion.* Her daughter-in-law Mildred, coveting her residence Rose Cottage and angry that Mabel has allowed the retired missionary teacher Barbara Batchelor to live there with her as a companion, callously ejects Barbara almost without notice when Mabel dies in *The Towers of Silence.*

Mildred Layton   Daughter of a famous general and wife of Colonel John Layton, the Commanding Officer of the Pankot Rifles; she makes the most of her position as "senior" to nearly every other woman in Pankot; she is a tyrant to her daughters, Susan and Sarah Layton, in Paul Scott's *The Day of the Scorpion.* She is cruelly unfeeling toward Barbara Batchelor; in her husband's absence as prisoner of war, she drinks too much and has become Kevin Coley's lover in *The Towers of Silence.* Her power to make life miserable for those around her is diminished by the return of her husband in *A Division of the Spoils.*

Sarah Layton   The usually well-judging elder daughter of Colonel John Layton; her mother, Mildred, and her sister, Susan, look to her for support in Paul Scott's *The Day of the Scorpion.* A brief romance with Major Jimmy Clark, whom she meets while visiting her aunt and uncle in Calcutta, results in pregnancy and an abortion in *The Towers of Silence.* She and her new lover and future husband, Guy Perron, provide assistance to the wounded in the aftermath of a bloody massacre in the fighting that accompanies the partition of India in *A Division of the Spoils.*

Susan Layton   The unstable younger daughter of Colonel John Layton; Susan's engagement and marriage to Captain Edward (Teddie) Bingham are hurried by the war, and Teddie is killed before the birth of their son in Paul Scott's *The Day of the Scorpion.* She marries Ronald Merrick, who tried to save her husband's life and was himself badly wounded, in *The Towers of Silence.* Widowed again, she and her child are among the English aboard the ambushed train who witness the massacre of the Muslims in *A Division of the Spoils.*

Giulia Lazzari   Practical, jaded, immoral Spanish dancer; while traveling in Europe, she collects data for Chandra Lal, who is her lover and co-conspirator in W. Somerset Maugham's *Ashenden: or The British Agent.*

Dr. Edwin Leacock   Director of the zoological gardens in London who uses television to win support for an experimental animal reserve in Wales; he is tricked by Lord Godmanchester into transporting wild animals from London and resigns his position when the animals become a danger to citizens in Angus Wilson's *The Old Men at the Zoo.*

Harriet Leacock   Daughter of Edwin and Madge; a nymphomaniac, she is killed by her dog when she has sex with it in Angus Wilson's *The Old Men at the Zoo.*

Madge Leacock   Wife of Edwin; she goes to Wales with him and fails to ingratiate herself with Lady Godmanchester in Angus Wilson's *The Old Men at the Zoo.*

Mr. Leadbetter   Moviegoer too absorbed in the film to notice the murder of the man sitting in front of him in Agatha Christie's *The A.B.C. Murders.*

Leadbitter   The designated hangman of the *Atropos* in C. S. Forester's *Hornblower and the Atropos.*

Steven Leadbitter   Ex-sergeant major and disciplined, unemotional car-hire driver, who fabricates stories of his supposed married life to divert his grieving passenger, Lady Franklin, and to increase his income from her generosity; he falls in love with her only to be rebuffed, yet in his self-inflicted death he offers her a final message of love and restoration to health and sanity in L. P. Hartley's *The Hireling*.

Tom Leadbitter   Florence Marvell's Art Editor at Gimblett's; he brings Marvell and Trevor Hamburg together at a luncheon engagement in hopes that she will advise Trevor how to save his marriage in Frank Swinnerton's *Some Achieve Greatness*.

Nellie Leader   Cator's secretary at the Rasuka oil well; she is in love with Robert Winter in P. H. Newby's *A Journey to the Interior*.

Christopher Leaf   Former student of Albert Shore and father of Flip in Roy Fuller's *My Child, My Sister*.

Eve Leaf   Frances's stepmother; twenty years earlier, she had eloped from her husband, Albert Shore, with one of his students in Roy Fuller's *My Child, My Sister*.

Flip Leaf   Alienated, misunderstood, and finally deranged daughter of Eve and Christopher Leaf; a rebellious art student, she forms an alliance with Albert Shore in Roy Fuller's *My Child, My Sister*.

Frances Leaf   Fiancée and later wife of Fabian Shore and mother of Albert Shore's granddaughter in Roy Fuller's *My Child, My Sister*.

Mrs. Leak   Genial raconteur of the village of Great Mop; she takes Lolly Willowes to her first witches' sabbath in Sylvia Townsend Warner's *Lolly Willowes: or, the Loving Huntsman*.

Alec Leamas (covernames: Mr. Amies, Stephen Bennett, Robert Lang, Mr. Thomas, Alexander Thwaite)   Stubborn, wilful, brutally cynical long-term fieldman for British Intelligence; weary of the Cold War, he agrees to Control's scheme (Operation Rolling Stone) to eliminate Abteilung agent Hans-Dieter Mundt but finds himself and his lover Liz Gold caught in Control's double-doublecross that protects Mundt and condemns him, Liz, and loyal GDR intelligence officer Jens Fiedler in John le Carré's *The Spy Who Came In from the Cold*.

Elizabeth Leaming   Devoted, love-lorn assistant to Ronald Callendar in P. D. James's *An Unsuitable Job for a Woman*.

Anthea Leaver   Stay-at-home wife of Arnold Leaver; she prefers realistic fiction to realistic living in Muriel Spark's *Territorial Rights*.

Arnold Leaver   Headmaster of Ambrose College; his

attempt to holiday in Venice with his mistress is ruined by his son's blackmail in Muriel Spark's *Territorial Rights*.

Robert Leaver   Sometime art student and prostitute who finds his real creativity in blackmail and terrorism in Muriel Spark's *Territorial Rights*.

Lawrence Le Bas   Housemaster regarded as a lunatic to be humored or outwitted by Nicholas Jenkins and his friends at prep school in Anthony Powell's *A Question of Upbringing*. He collapses during a speech by Widmerpool at one of his annual Old Boys dinners in London in *The Acceptance World*. Jenkins last encounters him in the school library in *Books Do Furnish a Room*.

Jacques Lebon   Prizemaster of the privateer *Vengeance* and a pirate aboard the *Amelia Jane* in C. S. Forester's *Hornblower and the Atropos*.

Carlo Lech   Deceased Military Supply Officer and high-level white-collar con man; the operator who initiated Paul Firman into the world of high-level business espionage, he was Firman's boss until his death in Eric Ambler's *Send No More Roses*.

Le Chiffre   USSR agent, an undercover paymaster who is trying to win money by gambling to cover his embezzlements; a repulsive and perverted benzedrine-inhalant addict, he is defeated by James Bond at baccarat; his subsequent torture of Bond is interrupted by his assassination as a traitor in Ian Fleming's *Casino Royale*.

Leclerc   Director of the now-unimportant Department for unspecified military intelligence operations; his unrealistic desire to regain the Department's wartime glory prompts him to devise the disastrous Operation Mayfly in John le Carré's *The Looking-Glass War*.

Dr. Leddra   Baptist minister and friend of the Nimmos; he becomes one of the leaders in the miners' strike in Joyce Cary's *Except the Lord*.

Bee Lederer   Grant Lederer's ambitious and seductive wife in John le Carré's *A Perfect Spy*.

Grant Lederer III   Cynical, politically ambitious C.I.A. agent heading the Vienna Embassy's Legal Department; he suspects Magnus Pym's duplicity, tracks his movements over years, and presses Jack Brotherhood to expose and repudiate Magnus, but is reprimanded and demoted for his efforts in John le Carré's *A Perfect Spy*.

Hugh Lederer   Father of Isobel and sometime suitor

of the widowed Nancy Hawkins in Muriel Spark's *A Far Cry from Kensington.*

Isobel Lederer   Tenant in Milly Sanders's house who becomes pregnant and cannot be certain of her baby's paternity in Muriel Spark's *A Far Cry from Kensington.*

Alison Ledgard   A wealthy invalid looked after by her spinster daughter, Charlotte; she dies leaving everything to her granddaughter, Gracie Tisbourne, in Iris Murdoch's *An Accidental Man.*

Charlotte Ledgard   Clara Tisbourne's handsome, unmarried elder sister; her long-nursed love for Matthew Gibson Grey goes unrequited; her self-sacrificial care of her mother goes unrewarded; she recognizes that her liaison with Mitzi Ricardo is like an unhappy marriage and feels cheated of life in Iris Murdoch's *An Accidental Man.*

Helen Ledwidge   Spirited daughter of Mary Amberley; a series of disappointments with men, including her brief affair with Ekki Gesbrecht and her passionless marriage to Hugh Ledwidge, leads her through a period of spiritual growth and eventually to a reconciliation with her longtime lover, Anthony Beavis, in Aldous Huxley's *Eyeless in Gaza.*

Hugh Ledwidge   Insecure scholar whose casual affair with Helen Amberley (Ledwidge) leads to their eventual passionless marriage in Aldous Huxley's *Eyeless in Gaza.*

Mabel Lee   Efficient Asian secretary of the English Department at Euphoric State University in David Lodge's *Changing Places: A Tale of Two Campuses.*

Olive Lee   Elderly churchgoing spinster and volunteer local researcher, who shares her house with her poorer friend Miss Grundy and is always eager to savor memories of village life in the good old days in Barbara Pym's *A Few Green Leaves.*

Song-Mi Lee   Intelligent, beautiful Korean secretary and companion to Arthur Kingfisher; she meets Persse McGarrigle on the plane to Seoul and becomes engaged to Kingfisher in David Lodge's *Small World.*

Delphine Leeder   Dark, melancholic, voluptuous, twenty-nine-year-old mistress of Lord Raingo; she deeply loves him, but believing he should be free to marry a lady and believing she has indirectly caused a young soldier's death, she commits suicide, lessening Raingo's will to live as he battles pneumonia in Arnold Bennett's *Lord Raingo.*

Gwendolyn (Gwen) Leeder   Sister of Lord Raingo's mistress; she eventually becomes the fiancée of Raingo's son, Geoffrey, in Arnold Bennett's *Lord Raingo.*

Harry Leek   A curate and one of the twin sons of Henry Leek; they jointly accuse Priam Farll of bigamy in Arnold Bennett's *Buried Alive: A Tale of These Days.*

Henry Leek   Bold, dishonest, philandering valet of famous artist Priam Farll; his sudden death gives the shy Farll an opportunity to seize another identity with hilarious results in Arnold Bennett's *Buried Alive: A Tale of These Days.*

Mrs. Henry Leek   Battered, abandoned wife of Henry Leek; she is persuaded by her sons to accuse Priam Farll of bigamy in Arnold Bennett's *Buried Alive: A Tale of These Days.*

John Leek   Older, aggressive son of Henry Leek; he accompanies his twin brothers and mother to accuse Priam Farll of bigamy in Arnold Bennett's *Buried Alive: A Tale of These Days.*

Matthew Leek   A curate and the twin brother of Harry Leek in Arnold Bennett's *Buried Alive: A Tale of These Days.*

Guy Leet   Aged, acerbic critic and former lover of Charmian Piper in Muriel Spark's *Memento Mori.*

Ludwig Leferrier   An American student who becomes Gracie Tisbourne's fiancé; he renounces both her and an Oxford fellowship in order to return to the United States to face draft-evasion charges in Iris Murdoch's *An Accidental Man.*

Madame Lefranc   Monsieur Lefranc's plump, placid wife, who never takes sides in Jean Rhys's *Postures.*

Monsieur Lefranc   Owner of the restaurant frequented by Marya and the Heidlers; he distrusts Marya in Jean Rhys's *Postures.*

Kate Lefroy   Hospital administrator who has an unsatisfactory marriage with a feckless philosopher; she becomes Humphrey Leigh's lover in C. P. Snow's *A Coat of Varnish.*

Susan Leg   Pushy tourist who writes romances under the name of Rudolph da Vinci; Elizabeth Mapp's tenant and claimed property, she is deftly courted away by Lucia (Lucas) Pillson in E. F. Benson's *Trouble for Lucia.*

Charles Legge   Broadcaster and friend of Max Callis; he reveals to Harry Sinton details of Callis's past and most tellingly his earlier attempt at suicide, evidence which contributes to Harry's final recovery of a true understanding of his part in Callis's death in Roy Fuller's *Fantasy and Fugue.*

Raine Legge   Social butterfly and friend of Serena (Daintry, Gardner) Hayford in Isabel Colegate's *Agatha.*

Sir Thomas Legge   Assistant Commissioner of Scotland Yard; he and Inspector Maine understand the motives and accurately analyze the Indian Island murders but fail to identify the perpetrator in Agatha Christie's *And Then There Were None.*

Rory Leggett   Anthony Keating and Giles Peters's partner in a property development in Margaret Drabble's *The Ice Age.*

Legolas   Young elven prince who is a member of the fellowship who travel with Frodo Baggins to destroy the One Ring and its terrible power in J. R. R. Tolkien's *The Fellowship of the Ring,* in *The Two Towers,* and in *The Return of the King.*

Henri Legros   Mr. Mackenzie's solicitor, who sends weekly cheques to Julia Martin from Mr. Mackenzie in Jean Rhys's *After Leaving Mr. Mackenzie.*

Suzanne Legros   A Frenchwoman whose unclaimed letter further complicates the identification of a body found in the Fenchurch St. Paul churchyard in Dorothy L. Sayers's *The Nine Tailors: Changes Rung on an Old Theme in Two Short Touches and Two Full Peals.*

Sib Legru   See Dr. Z. Fonanta.

Miss Lehr   German-American who with her brother lives in Mexico; she and her brother clothe, feed, and shelter the whiskey priest for a time in Graham Greene's *The Power and the Glory.*

Mr. Lehr   Widowed German-American who lives with his sister in Mexico; defensive about his Lutheranism, he nonetheless takes in the whiskey priest and clothes, feeds, and shelters him in Graham Greene's *The Power and the Glory.*

Norman Leif   Norwegian galley boy aboard the *Oedipus Tyrannus* and friend of Dana Hilliot; his pet "mickey" (pigeon) falls into the harbor and cannot be saved in Malcolm Lowry's *Ultramarine.*

Humphrey Leigh   Widower in his sixties who is retired from national security service; he loves Kate Lefroy, helps Frank Briers in his investigation of the murder of his friend and kinswoman Lady Ashbrook,

and accepts a position to work for Briers in a special force of anti-terrorism in C. P. Snow's *A Coat of Varnish.*

Leighton   Emily Failing's friendly servant in E. M. Forster's *The Longest Journey.*

Admiral Sir Percy Gilbert Leighton   Forceful commander in C. S. Forester's *The Happy Return.* He weds Lady Barbara Wellesley before he is fatally wounded in *Ship of the Line.*

Ada Leintwardine   Editor of Sillery's memoirs who deserts him to join the publishing firm of Quiggin & Craggs; she marries Quiggin and becomes a successful novelist and the mother of twins in Anthony Powell's *Books Do Furnish a Room.* She tries to influence Glober to film a St. John Clarke novel in *Temporary Kings.* She brings off a TV documentary on Clarke in *Hearing Secret Harmonies.*

Otto Leipzig (codename "the magician")   Fiercely patriotic Estonian confidence man and occasional British Intelligence operative; he blackmails Oleg Kursky into revealing Karla's schizophrenic daughter, sends blackmail clues to General Vladimir, comforts Maria Ostrakova when Karla's agents beseige her, and refuses to reveal the blackmail information to Karla's agents who, through their brutal torture, murder him in John le Carré's *Smiley's People.*

Fred Leiser (covername: Fred Hartbeck)   Naïve World War II Polish spy for British Intelligence; his warm compassion promises a mature friendship for John Avery, but his fascination with British life and Leclerc's inept Department induces him to leave his King of Hearts garage and participate in an ill-conceived search for a non-existent GDR missile site in John le Carré's *The Looking-Glass War.*

Dr. Gustav Leist   Scholar of medical history and modern art; he draws crowds to his enraged speeches against the execration of art museums and stealing of paintings, particularly in Warsaw, in Storm Jameson's *The Black Laurel.*

Felix Leiter   A thirty-five-year-old, likeable, tough CIA agent from Texas in Ian Fleming's *Casino Royale.* He loses an arm and a leg in a shark attack and is let go by the CIA in *Live and Let Die.* He works for Pinkerton's Detective Agency in *Diamonds Are Forever.* He saves Bond's life in *Goldfinger.* He has been drafted back into the CIA in *Thunderball.*

Sir Edward Leithen   Brilliant London lawyer, Member of Parliament, and later Attorney-General and cabinet member; he is lured into exciting adventure in which he uncovers and thwarts a malevolent conspiracy to destroy civilization in John Buchan's *The Power-House*. Fatigued and bored with life, he leaves London for a vacation in Scotland, where he joins Mr. Palliser-Yeates and Lord Lamancha in a lighthearted scheme to rejuvenate themselves by poaching two stags and a salmon from three nearby estates as "John Macnab" in *John Macnab*. He becomes the confidant of two attractive young people, Vernon Milburne and Koré Arabin, and gains spiritual insight and faith in a benevolent, purposeful universe in *The Dancing Floor*. He attends a Whitsuntide houseparty at Flambard, a great house, and participates in a psychic experiment in the supernatural and acknowledges the danger of learning one's "Fate" without attaining the "power of Grace" in *The Gap in the Curtain*. His final journey, to find the missing Francis Galliard and to "make his soul", ends in triumphant success in *Sick Heart River*.

Mrs. Leivers   Miriam's intensely spiritual mother and a friend of Paul Morel's mother in D. H. Lawrence's *Sons and Lovers*.

Agatha Leivers   Miriam's older sister; she is a school teacher with an independent spirit in D. H. Lawrence's *Sons and Lovers*.

Edgar Leivers   The eldest son of the Leivers family at Willey Farm; he becomes Paul Morel's close friend in D. H. Lawrence's *Sons and Lovers*.

Hubert Leivers   The youngest child in the Leivers family whom Paul Morel often visits in D. H. Lawrence's *Sons and Lovers*.

Miriam Leivers   Paul Morel's shy, sensitive, mystical, puritanical, intensely romantic young lover; they share a life devoted to books and exploration of nature, but when Paul's sensual passion for her develops, Miriam fails to respond in kind; she is devastated when he leaves her at the end of D. H. Lawrence's *Sons and Lovers*.

Color Sergeant Lejaune   Cruel, unfeeling, well-versed Legionnaire; he is the "friend" of Francesco Boldini; he tries to control his violent temper while being a loyal soldier to the French flag; he enjoys punishing subordinates in Percival Christopher Wren's *Beau Geste*.

Alice Lejour   Philip Lejour's sister; she has long nursed an unrequited love for Effingham Cooper; her sudden appearance in her car on the narrow road foils Effingham Cooper and Marian Taylor's plan to rescue Hannah Crean-Smith from Gaze Castle in Iris Murdoch's *The Unicorn*.

Max Lejour   The owner of Riders, the only house in the neighborhood of Gaze Castle; he is a reclusive scholar and the father of Alice and Philip Lejour; Hannah Crean-Smith's will in his favor enrages Violet Ever-creech in Iris Murdoch's *The Unicorn*.

Philip (Pip) Lejour   Alice Lejour's brother, a journalist and poet; the suicide of his former lover Hannah Crean-Smith prompts his own in Iris Murdoch's *The Unicorn*.

Miss Lemaitre   The clever-faced, sad-eyed lecturer in French at the women's college that Dolores Hutton attends in Ivy Compton-Burnett's *Dolores*.

Carla (Crale) Lemarchant   Daughter of the murdered Amyas Crale and the convicted Caroline Crale; sixteen years after the trial she asks Hercule Poirot to investigate, hoping to clear her mother so that she may honorably marry her fiancé in Agatha Christie's *Five Little Pigs*.

Syd Lemon   Rick Pym's steadfast right-hand man who goes to prison for Rick and mourns at his funeral; he has tried to protect Magnus Pym from Rick and himself in John le Carré's *A Perfect Spy*.

Lemuel   Malone's fictional keeper in a mental institution; he has an alternately tender and cruel relationship with MacMann in Samuel Beckett's *Malone Dies*.

Minna Lemuel   Revolutionary "fairy-story-telling Jewess" and eastern-European refugee; she is Frederick Willougby's mistress but becomes Sophia Willoughby's lover after she and Sophia meet in Minna's Paris salon; she is bayoneted by Caspar in the Paris Uprising of 1848 in Sylvia Townsend Warner's *Summer Will Show*.

Len   Peter Granby's grandmother's lover in Alan Sillitoe's *Out of the Whirlpool*.

Len   The stocky, devoted fiancé of Bridget; he is depressed because the National Service and a domineering mother have prevented his marrying Bridget, but he finally does marry her in David Lodge's *The Picturegoers*.

Lena   Englishwoman who is rescued from a sleazy company of musicians by Axel Heyst in Sourabaya, resists rape by the gambler Martin Ricardo, and tries to save Heyst but is murdered by Ricardo's henchman, Jones, in Joseph Conrad's *Victory: An Island Tale*.

Georges Lengard   Companion of Captain Rupert Ling in London and Dieppe prior to Ling's abandonment of Sylvia Hervey Russell in Dieppe in order to enter investment partnership in Cape Town in Storm

Jameson's *The Voyage Home.* He is a passenger on the *North Star,* Captain William Russell's ship; he threatens to blackmail Sylvia eight years after her marriage by revealing her past to Captain Russell; he is a criminal whose arrival in New Orleans is awaited by police; he gains praise for heroism in a fever epidemic at Vera Cruz but is trampled to death by a cab horse just before a ceremony recognizing his heroism; a report of his death gladdens Sylvia Hervey Russell in *Farewell, Night; Welcome, Day.*

Jack Leningrad   Head of the gold-smuggling ring who employs Michael Cullen and William Hay in Alan Sillitoe's *A Start in Life.*

Cicely Lennon   Sister of Mark; her marriage causes Mark's return from vacation in the Alps in John Galsworthy's *The Dark Flower.*

Mark Lennon   Sculptor who at age nineteen is a student at Oxford in 1880; he is seduced by Anna Stormer and leaves Oxford to study art in Rome and Paris; having fallen in love with Olive Cramier, he nearly drowns with her while trying to flee her husband; he marries Sylvia Doone in 1891, falls in love with seventeen-year-old Nell Dromore, and flees to Rome with Sylvia in John Galsworthy's *The Dark Flower.*

Sylvia Doone Lennon   Childhood friend of Cicely and Mark Lennon; she marries Mark four years after his disastrous affair with Olive Cramier; she suffers greatly when she learns that Mark is infatuated with Nell Dromore in John Galsworthy's *The Dark Flower.*

Herr Lensch   German flying ace, rivaling Peter Pienaar in skill and heroism, until their final contest when Pienaar insures an Allied victory by crashing into Lensch's plane in John Buchan's *Mr. Standfast.*

Charles Lenton   Prime Minister who accepts Roger Quaife's resignation from his cabinet in C. P. Snow's *Corridors of Power.*

Great-aunt Léocadie   Elderly, selfish, conservative, independent French aunt of Sophia Willougby; she attempts to arrange a reconciliation between Sophia Willoughby and her husband Frederick in Sylvia Townsend Warner's *Summer Will Show.*

Leon   One of the gang hired to guard Sakskia, the Russia princess, in Huntingtower House; he by mistake tells Dickson McCunn the kidnappers will arrive by sea, and then is knocked out and kept prisoner by the Gorbals Die-Hards in John Buchan's *Huntingtower.*

Leonard   Annie Morel's suitor and husband in D. H. Lawrence's *Sons and Lovers.*

Captain P. B. ("Brian") Leonard   A military impostor working for British Intelligence as the security officer for top-secret Operation Apollo; aged forty, he is black-haired, sallow-complexioned, proud, meticulous, and self-centered; he begins an affair with the prostitute Lucy Hazell; he uses the aliases Mr. Lock and Padlock in Kingsley Amis's *The Anti-Death League.*

Aristide Leonides   Wealthy widowed businessman whose marriage to a young waitress shocks his children and grandchildren; she and the tutor are arrested for his murder in Agatha Christie's *Crooked House.*

Brenda Leonides   Poor and pregnant waitress rescued by marriage to Aristide Leonides; she is arrested after his death by poison in Agatha Christie's *Crooked House.*

Clemency Leonides   Austere daughter-in-law of Aristide Leonides; she is a scientist devoted to her research and to her husband, Roger, in Agatha Christie's *Crooked House.*

Eustace Leonides   Indolent, moody, and slightly lame sixteen-year-old grandson of Aristide Leonides in Agatha Christie's *Crooked House.*

Josephine Leonides   Ugly, precocious eleven-year-old granddaughter of Aristide Leonides, whom she resented because he prevented her studying ballet; her life is the ostensible object of three unsuccessful murder attempts in Agatha Christie's *Crooked House.*

Magda Leonides   Self-dramatizing actress and wife of Philip Leonides; she is the mother of Eustace, Josephine, and Sophia in Agatha Christie's *Crooked House.*

Philip Leonides   Son of Aristide, husband of Magda, and father of Eustace, Josephine, and Sophia; he is of reserved, self-doubting temperament in Agatha Christie's *Crooked House.*

Roger Leonides   The devoted elder son of Aristide and husband of Clemency; his repeated failures at business have disappointed but not soured him in Agatha Christie's *Crooked House.*

Sophia Leonides   Courageous, intelligent granddaughter of Aristide Leonides, whose secret will recognizes her superior qualities; she is engaged to Charles Hayward in Agatha Christie's *Crooked House.*

Anastasia Alexandrovna Leonidov   Emotional, sweet, warmhearted, adventurous woman; she is part of the "intelligentsia" through her husband, and she is close to John Harrington in W. Somerset Maugham's *Ashenden: or The British Agent.*

Luigi Leopardi   Maker of Italian B films and creator of Annabel Christopher as the "English Lady-Tiger" in Muriel Spark's *The Public Image*.

Leopold   Karen Michaelis's nine-year-old son by Max Ebhart; he has not seen his mother since he was an infant in Elizabeth Bowen's *The House in Paris*.

Leo Leopoldi   Youthful companion of Grace Gregory and companion of her adventures in Venice in Muriel Spark's *Territorial Rights*.

Father Leopoldo   Head of the Trappist Monastery at Osera; he assumes responsibility for Father Quixote and his friend Enrique Zancas (Sancho) when their automobile crashes just outside the monastery; he provides them sanctuary and prevents the Guardia (military police) from arresting and returning them to El Toboso in Graham Greene's *Monsignor Quixote*.

Anna le Page   Young, brown-haired, free-spirited feminist; sexually liberated and potentially bi-sexual, she tries unsuccessfully to seduce Jenny Bunn; she is British but effectively convinces everyone she is French in Kingsley Amis's *Take a Girl Like You*.

Dennis Lerner   Aide at Toynton Grange, a private nursing home, and friend and co-conspirator of Julius Court in P. D. James's *The Black Tower*.

Jean-Pierre le Rossignol   Attractive young Frenchman; an anthropology student at the Foresight Research Centre, he seems to regard all of English life as a subject for study in Barbara Pym's *Less Than Angels*.

Joseph Leroy   A black, six-foot Rastafarian who is injured along with Evelyn Morton Stennett during a domestic quarrel with "his woman" Irene Crowther in Margaret Drabble's *The Middle Ground*.

Dr. Lesage   Rachel Vinrace's physician during her fatal illness; he is unable to save her in Virginia Woolf's *The Voyage Out*.

Leslie   Husband of Dottie and lover of Fleur Talbot and Gray Mauser in Muriel Spark's *Loitering with Intent*.

General Davy Leslie   A commander of one of the troops of the Army of the Covenant allied against the Marquis of Montrose but a liberal, generous-hearted man in John Buchan's *Witch Wood*.

Kate Leslie   An Irish widow who becomes Malintzi (a green goddess) when Don Ramon Carrasco resurrects the old Aztec gods; she marries Don Cipriano Viedma, Ramon's general, in D. H. Lawrence's *The Plumed Serpent (Quetzalcoatl)*.

Simon Lessing   School-boy stepson of actress Clarissa Lisle in P. D. James's *The Skull Beneath the Skin*.

Carolyn Lessways   Emotional, widowed mother of Hilda Lessways; having accompanied her nervous, ailing friend Sarah Gailey to George Cannon's Brighton boarding house, she suddenly dies there, precipitating Hilda's entry into the boarding-house business, where she is drawn into a bigamous marriage with George Cannon in Arnold Bennett's *Hilda Lessways*.

Hilda Lessways   Dark, enigmatic, independent, surprising girl; her unusual behavior excites the love of Edwin Clayhanger in Arnold Bennett's *Clayhanger*. Desperately bored within her mother's placid Bursley domesticity, she first seeks excitement in newspaper employment; she is attracted both to Edwin Clayhanger, printer, and to George Cannon, prospective newspaper owner, but she allows herself to be bound to Cannon's Brighton boarding-house venture after her mother dies there; she drifts into a bigamous marriage with Cannon in *Hilda Lessways*. She is the passionate, impetuous wife of Edwin Clayhanger; her desire to be equal in all ways in her marriage constantly causes the tension-filled incidents which make the couple feel their life together is dangerously dramatic in *These Twain*.

Guy Lester   Tall, beautiful, willowy drunk; he calls Marya Zelli a hussy in Jean Rhys's *Postures*.

Mrs. Lestrange   Mysterious first wife of Colonel Lucius Protheroe; she is Lettice Protheroe's mother in Agatha Christie's *The Murder at the Vicarage*.

Gerald Lesworth   A young British army officer garrisoned in Ireland; he is killed in a skirmish shortly after Lady Naylor dismisses as totally unsuitable his proposed engagement to her husband's niece, Lois Farquar, in Elizabeth Bowen's *The Last September*.

Robert (Robin) Lethbridge   Rejected suitor of Harriet Frean and unwilling husband of Priscilla Heaven, to whose care he devotes his life; he becomes a selfish hypochondriac after her death and endangers the health of his second wife, Beatrice Walker, by his incessant demands in May Sinclair's *Life and Death of Harriet Frean*.

Stanley Lett   A friend of Ted Brown in Mashopi; he is presumably having an affair with Mrs. Lattimer in Doris Lessing's *The Golden Notebook*.

Letty (Mrs. Teddy)   Spite-filled wife of Mr. Britling's secretary and Cecily Corner's sister; she refuses to believe her husband has been killed, and she vows to kill those responsible for the war; she is soothed by Mr. Britling in H. G. Wells's *Mr. Britling Sees It Through*.

Leverett-Smith   Parliamentary Secretary who serves Roger Quaife and stands by him even when he disagrees on nuclear disarmament in C. P. Snow's *Corridors of Power*.

Lord Levering   Ninety-one-year-old Lancashire peer; he is married to his fourth young wife and has a ten-year-old daughter; he is a zealot for total abstinence and is the self-constituted leader of the opposition to the movement led by Evelyn Orcham for Licensing Reforms, but he chooses to stay in Orcham's hotel for the sittings of the Licensing Commission in Arnold Bennett's *Imperial Palace*.

John Leverrier   One of Nicholas Urfe's predecessors at the Lord Byron School and at Bourani; he lives at a monastery in Italy, where Urfe visits him to try to discover the truth about Maurice Conchis in John Fowles's *The Magus*.

Colonel Stanley Levin   An elegant, intelligent Jewish officer much preoccupied with his engagement to a well-connected Frenchwoman, Nanette de Bailly, in Ford Madox Ford's *No More Parades*.

Mr. Levinsohn   Jewish solicitor of the Imperial Palace Hotel Company; he cleverly maneuvers the shareholders to give a majority vote for a resolution limiting the highest individual voting power to ten no matter how many shares are owned in Arnold Bennett's *Imperial Palace*.

Julia Levison   Duchess Lucy's raucous-voiced and frizzy-blonde friend, who is an "arriviste" in society in Vita Sackville-West's *The Edwardians*. She attaches herself to Martha Denman for motives of self interest; she meets Evelyn Jarrold in the dress shop of Rivers and Roberts in *Family History*.

David Levkin   Otto Narraway's apprentice; Narraway's wife and daughter both become pregnant by him in Iris Murdoch's *The Italian Girl*.

Elsa Levkin   Otto Narraway's lover and David Levkin's sister; she dies accidentally in a house fire in Iris Murdoch's *The Italian Girl*.

Christine Ford, Lady Levy   Wife of the missing financier; her family wanted her to marry Julian Freke in Dorothy L. Sayers's *Whose Body?*.

Rachel Levy   Daughter of Christine and Sir Reuben Levy in Dorothy L. Sayers's *Whose Body?*. She becomes engaged to Freddy Arbuthnot in *Strong Poison*.

Sir Reuben Levy   A financier whose disappearance dramatically affects the value of certain stocks and coincides with the discovery of a body in Alfred Thipp's bathtub in Dorothy L. Sayers's *Whose Body?*.

Lewis   One of the crewmen aboard the *Indefatigable* involved in gambling on watch in C. S. Forester's *Mr. Midshipman Hornblower*.

Lord Lewis   An upright reptile of a man and a jealous god of the marketplace who decides as Chairman of the Board to suppress the product John Henderson has developed for the company in C. Day Lewis's *Starting Point*.

Miss Lewis   Operator of a small, hot, and drafty shop, where "She" clerks and stands so long behind a counter that her feet swell to double their normal size; Miss Lewis, though relatively indifferent to the needs of the women who work for her, finally gives "She" a sickly smile and offers to help her get home in Storm Jameson's *A Day Off*.

Boney Lewis   An aging actor who makes love to Hannah Graves in Penelope Fitzgerald's *At Freddie's*.

Cyfartha Lewis   A disreputable former prizefighter who is the constant companion of Dai Bando and becomes his eyes after Dai Bando loses his sight in Richard Llewellyn's *How Green Was My Valley*.

Jean Lewis   Wife of John Lewis and former schoolmate of Elizabeth Gruffydd-Williams; she lives in a sordid apartment with her two young children and husband and treats him coolly after suspecting that he is having an affair with Elizabeth in Kingsley Amis's *That Uncertain Feeling*.

John Lewis   A young, lower-middle-class Welsh assistant librarian who is restless and bored; he has an affair with Elizabeth Gruffydd-Williams so that she will influence her husband to promote him at work; feeling guilty and suffering from injured pride, he declines the rigged job offer, resolves to be hereafter faithful to his wife, and moves his family to his home town, where he takes a job in coal sales in Kingsley Amis's *That Uncertain Feeling*.

Meillyn Lewis   A young woman cruelly exposed as an adulteress by the deacons of the church in Richard Llewellyn's *How Green Was My Valley*.

Morgan Lewis   A Scottish stable groom who believes in a pantheistic world of "moon people"; he refuses Lou Witt's marriage proposal in D. H. Lawrence's *St. Mawr*.

Lex　A phagor who guards SatoriIrvrash; he arranges for Billy Xiao Pin to be kidnapped from prison in Borlien and taken to the phagor leader in Brian W. Aldiss's *Helliconia Summer*.

Johnny Leyland　A solicitor who fights with Colin Freestone and causes him to go to the hospital in David Storey's *A Temporary Life*.

Mr. Leyton　The youngest and most self-conscious and irascible of the dentists for whom Miriam Henderson works in Dorothy Richardson's *The Tunnel*.

Diana Leyton　Second cousin of Bryan Summerhay; she attracts him away from Gyp Winton Fiersen temporarily in John Galsworthy's *Beyond*.

Maxim Libnikov　The Russian friend of Julius Halliday in D. H. Lawrence's *Women in Love*.

Miss Lickerish　Elderly, outspoken, eccentric village spinster who keeps hedgehogs in her untidy cottage in Barbara Pym's *A Few Green Leaves*.

Major-General Liddament　Commander of Nicholas Jenkins's division during the war; an admirer of Trollope and a bit of an eccentric, he takes to Jenkins; he is furious at Widmerpool's intriguing in Anthony Powell's *The Soldier's Art*.

Frau Lieberman　German refugee who stays a while with Sukey Matthews and her family while waiting for her husband and second son to escape Nazi Germany; she angrily persuades Sukey to believe a war might break out in Angus Wilson's *No Laughing Matter*.

Renee Liepmann　Leader of the bourgeois bohemian set; she is one of many offended by Otto Kreisler's outrageous behavior in Wyndham Lewis's *Tarr*.

Bruno Liesecke　German who marries Frieda Mosebach, the Schlegels' cousin, in E. M. Forster's *Howards End*.

Lieutenant　Well-groomed, angry police officer who hunts the whiskey priest; embittered by his poverty-stricken upbringing and enraged by priests who took the poor's money with promises of glory in the afterlife, he is driven by his desire to rid his state in Mexico of all priests in Graham Greene's *The Power and the Glory*.

Ronson Lighter　Thief and Billy Whisper's right-hand man; he is jailed in Colin MacInnes's *City of Spades*.

Geoffrey Lightfoot　Owner of a chain of pet-food stores and a pet-food company who confronts Bill Fisher about Fisher's affair with his wife, Helen, in Keith Waterhouse's *Billy Liar on the Moon*.

Helen Lightfoot　The sexually voracious thirty-four-year-old wife of Geoffrey Lightfoot and lover of Billy Fisher; she is unfaithful to both in Keith Waterhouse's *Billy Liar on the Moon*.

Diane Lightowler　Art teacher at Petersons School who recognizes and promotes Bryan Morley's artistic gifts and introduces him to a very different, liberated way of life in David Storey's *A Prodigal Child*.

Liku　Lok's daughter; she is captured and eventually cannibalized by the opposing tribe of Homo sapiens in William Golding's *The Inheritors*.

Olivia, Lady Lilburn　Lord Lilburn's wife, who is in love with Lionel Stephens but remains faithful to her husband in Isabel Colegate's *The Shooting Party*.

Robert (Bob), Lord Lilburn　Mellow aristocrat invited to Sir Randolph Nettleby's shooting party; he is unaware that his wife's interest is held by Lionel Stephens in Isabel Colegate's *The Shooting Party*.

Rawdon Lilly　An intellectual writer who argues the virtues of leadership and power to Aaron Sisson; he wants Aaron to follow him in D. H. Lawrence's *Aaron's Rod*.

Tanny Lilly　Rawdon's headstrong wife in D. H. Lawrence's *Aaron's Rod*.

Lily　One of two girlfriends of Mark Armstrong in Margaret Drabble's *The Middle Ground*.

Lily　Young woman who has no illusions and "accepts human nature" as she invites the somewhat disreputable "She" to go to a bar with her and knows "She" needs other women to write fake testimonials to help her get household jobs; nevertheless, "She" finally hates Lily because of envy for a woman who gains independence while "She" continues to depend on men for new dresses and free beer in Storm Jameson's *A Day Off*.

Harry Lime　A charmer and leader of men, friend of Rollo Martins, and lover of Anna Schmidt; he betrays and uses them both; he is the head of a black-marketeering ring that substitutes fake drugs for penicillin, being thus responsible for the deaths of many children; supposedly dead, Lime is in fact the mysterious third man who resurfaces to, unwittingly, reveal the possibility of compassion and moral wisdom in a fragmented world as his once-naïve friend Rollo Martins fires the bullet that kills him in Graham Greene's *The Third Man and the Fallen Idol.*

Lionel Limpness Playful, campy school friend of Eddy Monteith serving as "honorable attache at the English Embassy" in Pisuerga in Ronald Firbank's *The Flower Beneath the Foot.*

Lord Tony Limpsfield London socialite in E. F. Benson's *Lucia in London.*

Amin Lin One of Shay Tal's followers; she goes into exile with her in Brian W. Aldiss's *Helliconia Spring.*

Lincoln Half brother to Ostrog and second in command in the revolutionary organization in H. G. Wells's *When the Sleeper Wakes: A Story of the Years to Come.*

John Lincoln Constance Ollerenshaw's long-dead lover, a well-intending, affectionate, vacillating seaman who did not keep his promise to leave his wife and who died three years after the death of his eighteen-month-old illegitimate child; his faithlessness contributed to Constance's lifelong reclusiveness in Margaret Drabble's *The Realms of Gold.*

Linda Repulsive, bloated mother of John Savage; she returns to futuristic London after years lost in the New Mexico wildernesss and is content to die in a drug-induced coma in Aldous Huxley's *Brave New World.*

Johnny Lindsay A militant socialist who more than any of the others has demolished the "Colour Bar" in his house and acts as a great leader for the Africans, in spite of his ever-increasing ill health and risk of arrest in Doris Lessing's *A Ripple from the Storm* and in *Landlocked.*

Rosa Lindsay Hereward Egerton's mistress both before he marries Ada Merton and after his illegitimate children are revealed; she refuses to marry Egerton in Ivy Compton-Burnett's *A God and His Gifts.*

Colin Lindsey One of Hari Kumar's closest friends at school in England; in India he passes Hari in the bazaar and appears not to recognize him in Paul Scott's *The Jewel in the Crown.*

Linford Young student from Shropshire who calls on Mr. Chips after other Brookfield boys tell him falsely that the retired master is looking for him; Mr. Chips, recognizing the old "leg-pull" on the boy, entertains him at tea; he says good-bye to Mr. Chips the night before Chips dies in James Hilton's *Good-bye, Mr. Chips.*

Jenny Ling Rich, immature, greedy, fun-loving, beautiful woman; she is the wartime lover and later wife of the younger Nicholas Roxby; she gets a divorce when he cannot endure the postwar social whirl she requires and when she cannot accept his resignation as manager of the shipping business and his intention to live only on the allowance received from the family estate in Storm Jameson's *A Richer Dust.*

Captain Rupert Ling Wealthy cousin and irresponsible lover of eighteen-year-old Sylvia Hervey Russell; he promises marriage but abandons her in Dieppe to pursue Cape Town gold-mining schemes with Georges Lengard in Storm Jameson's *The Voyage Home.* He dies two years after abandoning Sylvia, according to report in *Farewell, Night; Welcome, Day.*

Captain Tom (Tuan) Lingard Trader who rescues the future Mrs. Almayer from Sulu pirates in Joseph Conrad's *Almayer's Folly: A Story of an Eastern River.* He establishes Peter Willems in *An Outcast of the Islands.* He captains the brig *Lightning*, rescues the yacht *Hermit*, becomes stranded on the Shore of Refuge, and falls in love with a passenger, Edith Travers; he fails to support Hassim's coup; he concludes by sailing on the opposite bearing from the ship carrying Mrs. Travers in *The Rescue: A Romance of the Shallows.*

Viscount Lord Lingham Aged hero of agriculture and hunting fields; he moves the motion in the House of Lords which brings Lord Raingo under attack for his handling of propaganda and causes him to overtax his heart in Arnold Bennett's *Lord Raingo.*

Major Linklater Tall, thin retired army officer with a sense of humour; he flies to meet customers on liners at Southampton, Cherbourg, and Plymouth in Arnold Bennett's *Imperial Palace.*

Mark (Markie) Linkwater Manipulative, "brilliant", much-disliked London barrister with a vaguely reptilian appearance; he is drawn into a fateful affair with Emmeline Summers in Elizabeth Bowen's *To the North.*

Mr. Lintoff Russian revolutionary whom Miriam Henderson meets through Michael Shatov in Dorothy Richardson's *Revolving Lights.*

Mrs. Lintoff Mr. Lintoff's wife, also a Russian revolutionary in Dorothy Richardson's *Revolving Lights.*

Lion Utopian educational co-ordinator who explains the evolution of his society to the Earthlings, quoting the maxim "Our education is our government" in H. G. Wells's *Men Like Gods.*

Annie ("Lippsie") Lippschitz Rick Pym's Jewish mistress, who nurses Dorothy Pym and loves and rears young Magnus Pym; her death, Magnus claims, set his resolve to discredit Rick in John le Carré's *A Perfect Spy*.

Lise   Psychotic searcher who plans to control her own destiny by plotting her death at the hands of a sex criminal in Muriel Spark's *The Driver's Seat*.

Clarissa Lisle   Aging but still beautiful actress invited to make a comeback performance at Ambrose Gorringe's castle; she is killed in P. D. James's *The Skull Beneath the Skin*.

Wattie Lithgow   Middle-aged Border Scots who, using the name John Macnab, acts as strategist in the plot to poach two stags and a salmon in John Buchan's *John Macnab*.

Lizzy Little   Schoolmate to Kate Fletcher (Armstrong); she worked hard to become a hairdresser in Margaret Drabble's *The Middle Ground*.

Eddy Littlejohn   Friend of Adam Fenwick-Symes; he marries Nina Blount; much of his life has been spent in military service, and he is ultimately assigned to a desk position in the London war office in Evelyn Waugh's *Vile Bodies*.

Lucy Littlejohn   A nymphomaniac who has been to bed with Andy Adorno, Quentin Villiers, Giles Coldstream, and everyone those three can think of; she is one of the decadent weekend guests in Martin Amis's *Dead Babies*.

Shimon (covernames: Karman, Levene) Litvak   Emaciated Israeli operative and Marty Kurtz's loyal, pragmatic lieutenant; though suspicious of Charlie's instability, he assists Kurtz in her conversion and deployment as an Israeli operative in John le Carré's *The Little Drummer Girl*.

Edith Liversidge   Energetic, critical spinster who patronizes her poor relation Miss Aspinall while dictating to everyone else about housekeeping and sanitary arrangements for garden parties in Barbara Pym's *Some Tame Gazelle*.

Livia   Augustus's ambitious, scheming wife, who actually rules the Roman Empire and disposes of all who threaten her power in Robert Graves's *I, Claudius*.

Liz   The only person who understands and accepts Billy Fisher's need for imaginative escape; she becomes his third fiancée in Keith Waterhouse's *Billy Liar*.

Liz   Middle-aged divorcée who breeds Siamese cats;

she is a neighbor of Leonora Eyre in Barbara Pym's *The Sweet Dove Died*.

Lizzie   Wife of the prison officer Jim in Margaret Drabble's *The Ice Age*.

Llewellyn (Llew)   Crude, simple, and rather vicious identical twin brother of Miles Faber raised as a son by Aderyn the Bird Queen; after discovering each other by accident, Llew and Miles trade places for a time; Llew is killed by Miss Emmett for his attempted rape of Catherine Faber in Anthony Burgess's *MF*.

Alec Llewellyn   A shady character and friend of John Self, to whom he owes money; he eventually goes to jail in Martin Amis's *Money*.

David Llewellyn   University student who is one of the four defended by Lewis Eliot from threat of expulsion on account of sexual misconduct in C. P. Snow's *The Sleep of Reason*.

Mr. Llewelyn   Ethan Llewelyn's brutal and neglectful father, now dead, in Malcolm Lowry's *October Ferry to Gabriola*.

Ethan Llewelyn   Retired criminal lawyer, plagued by guilt and pursued by the element of fire, who with his wife Jacqueline takes a trip to Gabriola Island, British Columbia, in search of a new home in Malcolm Lowry's *October Ferry to Gabriola*.

Gywn Llewelyn   Ethan Llewelyn's younger brother who was lost at sea in Malcolm Lowry's *October Ferry to Gabriola*.

Jacqueline Llewelyn   Ethan Llewelyn's wife, who accompanies him to Gabriola Island, taking care of details while he drinks in a bar and ponders his fate in Malcolm Lowry's *October Ferry to Gabriola*.

Tommy Llewelyn   Son of Ethan and Jacqueline Llewelyn; he is now at boarding school in Vancouver in Malcolm Lowry's *October Ferry to Gabriola*.

Deidre Lloyd   Wife of Teddy Lloyd, the art master, and mother of numerous children in Muriel Spark's *The Prime of Miss Jean Brodie*.

Heron Lloyd   Noted explorer and authority on Arabia who is contacted by Bill Kendrick to participate in an expedition to Arabia to verify Kendrick's archeological find in Josephine Tey's *The Singing Sands*.

Teddy Lloyd   The one-armed, married art master at the Marcia Blaine School; his love for Jean Brodie is vicariously consummated with a member of "the Brodie set" but not exactly in accordance with Miss Brodie's years of preparation in Muriel Spark's *The Prime of Miss Jean Brodie*.

Owen Lloyd-Thomas Earnest but narrow-minded nonconformist minister who arouses public opinion against Sirius and Plaxy Trelone after they refuse to stop living together in Olaf Stapledon's *Sirius: A Fantasy of Love and Discord*.

Lo Supernormal girl whose experience with atrocities during the Russian Revolution and its aftermath leads her to appreciate the orderly domestic world of Jane Austen; among the members of John Wainwright's colony, she is the one emotionally closest to John in Olaf Stapledon's *Odd John: A Story Between Jest and Earnest*.

Lobo An aptly named Peruvian student and mapmaker who preys on women; he longs for his homeland in a self-pitying way in Lawrence Durrell's *The Black Book*.

Miss Lockhart Science teacher and Jean Brodie's rival for the admiration of her students and of Gordon Lowther in Muriel Spark's *The Prime of Miss Jean Brodie*.

Lockwood Bespectacled, self-consumed tutor at Charles Lumley's college whom Charles challenges while visiting his alma mater with Veronica Roderick in John Wain's *Hurry On Down*.

Alec Loding Professional actor of discreditable-roué parts; in boyhood an intimate neighbor of the Ashby family, he is struck by Brat Farrar's resemblance to Simon Ashby; he persuades Brat to present himself as Patrick Ashby and coaches him in the impersonation in Josephine Tey's *Brat Farrar*.

Hermann Loeffler German Chancellor who seeks peace in a world united by common values rather than nationalistic goals; he is saved from death many times by Adam Melfort in various disguises in John Buchan's *A Prince of the Captivity*.

Loerke The sinister, cynical artist who believes art is subservient to industry; his affair with Gudrun Brangwen helps bring about the final disaster in D. H. Lawrence's *Women in Love*.

Frances (Fanny) Logan Daughter of a runaway mother; she is brought up by her maternal aunt, Emily Warbeck; she spends her holidays with the family of another maternal aunt, Sadie Radlett; educated, a good listener, and a happy child, Fanny is Linda Radlett's closest friend and confidante; she marries Alfred Wincham; she is narrator of Nancy Mitford's *The Pursuit of Love*. She tells

the story of her contemporary and relation Polly Hampton in *Love in a Cold Climate*.

Sir Giles Logan Very successful businessman who champions Orlando King's continued success in Timberwork and various other business ventures in Isabel Colegate's *Orlando King*.

Louisa Loggerheads Proprietor of a pub, the Dragon; there Edwin Clayhanger executes the first important business deal given him by his father and first feels female attraction for the champion clogdancer Florence Simcox in Arnold Bennett's *Clayhanger*.

Loilanum Laintal Ay's mother, who tries to take control of the country when her father, Little Yuli, dies in Brian W. Aldiss's *Helliconia Spring*.

Queen Lois (Her Dreaminess) Self-centered and materialistic matron of Court life in Pisuerga who opposes her son Yousef's languid interest in young Laura de Nazianzi and encourages his marriage instead to the Princess Elsie of England in Ronald Firbank's *The Flower Beneath the Foot*.

Lok Good-natured and slow-witted leader of a tribe of small, red-haired hominids (supposedly Homo neanderthalensis) who are eventually eradicated by a Homo sapiens tribe in William Golding's *The Inheritors*.

Trevor Lomas Working-class lout and rival of Humphrey Place in Muriel Spark's *The Ballad of Peckham Rye*.

Lomax Purser aboard the *Renown* in C. S. Forester's *Lieutenant Hornblower*.

Mr. Lombard Friend of Richard Hannay from his mining years in Rhodesia; now a middle-aged suburbanite, he tells Hannay that Valdemar Haraldsen's son and his daughter, Anna, are being threatened, and with Hannay and "Sandy" Arbuthnot courageously defends them and their island; he determines to seek his own Island of Sheep and to "make his soul" in John Buchan's *The Island of Sheep*.

Ivor Lombard Attractive young dillettante who lives primarily by his poise and charm; after a brief visit at Henry Wimbush's Crome houseparty, he moves on to the next in a series of trivial entertainments at which he is in constant demand in Aldous Huxley's *Crome Yellow*.

Captain Philip Lombard Soldier accused of the deaths of twenty-one East Africans; he is shot with his own revolver in Agatha Christie's *And Then There Were None*.

Longley Gerard's nephew, a scared young boatswain's mate on his maiden voyage in the *Sutherland*; he shows signs of growth but is killed in the *Sutherland*'s final battle in C. S. Forester's *Ship of the Line*.

Piers Longridge Thirty-five-year-old brother of Wilmet and Rodney Forsyth's friend Rowena Talbot; he lives by scholarly odd jobs and features as a possible romantic object for Wilmet, though he seems to prefer his friend Keith, in Barbara Pym's *A Glass of Blessings*. His relationship to the Forsyths continues in *No Fond Return of Love*.

Elsie Longstaff Put-upon, old-time performer in J. B. Priestley's *The Good Companions*.

Curly Lonsdale Bookie, brother-in-law of January Marlowe, and sometime double for Tom Wells in Muriel Spark's *Robinson*.

Lopez (code identification: 59200/5/1) James Wormold's impatient Cuban assistant; he misunderstands his employer's instructions and is nearly killed when one of Wormold's fictions backfires in Graham Greene's *Our Man in Havana*.

Miss Lord Daily charwoman and commentator on the romantic and domestic affairs of Dulcie Mainwaring's household; she declares her disdain for women's education and "all this reading" in Barbara Pym's *No Fond Return of Love*.

Countess Loredan A member of the Venetian nobility who frequents the salon of Lady Nelly Staveley; she accepts Eustace Cherrington in his role as would-be writer in L. P. Hartley's *Eustace and Hilda*.

Jervis, Lord Lorimer Younger colleague and friend of Hillmorton and Ryle; he lives with and then marries Jenny Rastall in C. P. Snow's *In Their Wisdom*.

Rose Lorimer Medievalist historian who loses her sanity over the issue of the relationship of ancient Christianity and pre-Christian British religion; she is committed to an asylum when she becomes dangerous in Angus Wilson's *Anglo-Saxon Attitudes*.

Mrs. Lorrimer One of the murdered suspects of the death of Mr. Shaitana in Agatha Christie's *Cards on the Table*.

Edwin Lorrimer Arrogant, secretive pathologist at Hoggatt's Laboratory; he is murdered in P. D. James's *Death of an Expert Witness*.

Lancelot Loseby An Army captain who is the grandson of Lady Ashbrook; he is sexually licentious and is a suspect in the murder of his grandmother; he marries Susan Thirkill after his grandmother's death in C. P. Snow's *A Coat of Varnish*.

General Alexander Lossberg Lord Clanroyden's military antagonist in John Buchan's *The Courts of the Morning*.

Lo Tsen Manchu Princess who is close to a hundred years old but appears nineteen; she was an unwilling guest to Shangri-La some years before Hugh "Glory" Conway's party arrives in Tibet; Lo Tsen escapes Shangri-La with Captain Charles Mallison and dies shortly after she acquires her freedom; she is a talented musician in James Hilton's *Lost Horizon*.

James Loudon Hypocritical ringleader of the Bolshevick plot to keep Sakskia, the Russian princess, prisoner and to steal her jewels; he falls to his death battling Dickson McCunn and the Gorbals Die-Hards in John Buchan's *Huntingtower*.

Louis An outsider with an Australian accent whose father is a Brisbane banker; loving order, Louis is destined to draw the threads together, to create one permanent moment out of the present and historical many; his loving pursuit of the fearful Rhoda is unsuccessful in Virginia Woolf's *The Waves*.

Louis An elderly boatman dedicated to caring for Johnny in Rosamond Lehmann's *A Sea-Grape Tree*.

Louis A Swiss Frenchman in the Natcha-Kee-Tawara Troupe of travelling theatrical performers who work at Houghton's theater in D. H. Lawrence's *The Lost Girl*.

Sir Louis British ambassador to the Soviet Union and David Mountolive's superior and mentor during his posting there in Lawrence Durrell's *Mountolive*.

Louisa Old servant in George Cannon's boarding house; she is angered at the promiscuous behaviour of the young servant Florrie Bagster, and she makes known the bigamous nature of the marriage of Hilda Lessways and George Cannon in Arnold Bennett's *Hilda Lessways*.

Madame Louise Head saleswoman and one half of the formidable combination at the dress shop of Rivers and Roberts; a large woman tightly encased in black satin, she looks like an eighteenth-century gentleman with her gray hair cropped and brushed back in Vita Sackville-West's *Family History*.

Louisiana Young ballet dancer; she is the ingenue of

the Isabel Cornwallis Ballet Company in Colin MacInnes's *City of Spades*.

Mrs. Lousse (alias Sophie Loy)   Woman who accuses Molloy of running over and killing her dog; she takes Molloy home and keeps him drugged, clean, and shaven in a dark room in Samuel Beckett's *Molloy*.

Brigit Hallam Lovat   A woman with a secret sorrow; she believes that she is the daughter of her husband, Edmund Lovat; she is really the daughter of Sir Ransome Chace and Mrs. Spruce, the Lovats' cook, in Ivy Compton-Burnett's *Darkness and Day*.

Edmund Lovat   A short, broad man, the elder son of Selina, husband of Brigit, father of Rose and Viola (and secretly of Mildred Hallam); he believes he is the father of his wife, Brigit, in Ivy Compton-Burnett's *Darkness and Day*.

Gaunt Lovat   The younger, but still middle-aged, son of Selina Lovat; he stays with his mother and says he cannot afford to marry; he is a friend of Sir Ransome Chace in Ivy Compton-Burnett's *Darkness and Day*.

Rose Lovat   The elder daughter of Edmund and Brigit Lovat; she is the sister with the brains, who overhears her grandmother saying that Brigit is Edmund's daughter and their marriage incestuous in Ivy Compton-Burnett's *Darkness and Day*.

Selina Lovat   The tall, pale-faced mother of Edmund and Gaunt; her influence permeates the house in Ivy Compton-Burnett's *Darkness and Day*.

Viola Lovat   The younger daughter of Edmund and Brigit Lovat; she is the sister with the charm, according to Mildred Hallam, her governess and half sister, in Ivy Compton-Burnett's *Darkness and Day*.

Ben Lovatt   The "fifth child", who is a throwback to a more primitive age and is unable to adjust to his family; placed in an institution, he is rescued by his mother; he ultimately grows up to be a misfit in society but a success with friends who are much like him in Doris Lessing's *The Fifth Child*.

David Lovatt   An eccentric architect whose goal is to marry a "nice" woman and to settle down and have ten children; he becomes more and more estranged from his wife after the birth of their fifth child in Doris Lessing's *The Fifth Child*.

Deborah Lovatt   David Lovatt's sister, who has several problems with her love life and is rather cool and curious about her brother's family life in Doris Lessing's *The Fifth Child*.

Harriet Lovatt   David's wife, who wants nothing more than to have ten or more children; after the birth of her fifth child, Ben, she is seen by the family as a monster herself; she must learn to live with the problems that Ben causes in Doris Lessing's *The Fifth Child*.

Helen Lovatt   David and Harriet Lovatt's second child, who spends all her school holidays with her grandmother Molly Burke in order to stay away from her youngest brother, Ben, in Doris Lessing's *The Fifth Child*.

James Lovatt   David Lovatt's father, a wealthy boat builder ever generous in helping out his son's financially strapped family in Doris Lessing's *The Fifth Child*.

Jane Lovatt   Harriet and David Lovatt's third child, who is much like her grandmother; she eventually moves out of the house to live at a boarding school in order to avoid her youngest brother, Ben, in Doris Lessing's *The Fifth Child*.

Jessica Lovatt   David Lovatt's stepmother in Doris Lessing's *The Fifth Child*.

Luke Lovatt   David and Harriet Lovatt's first child, utterly scornful of his parents because they rescue his brother, Ben, from an institution; consequently he goes away to boarding school and spends all of his holidays with Grandfather James Lovatt in Doris Lessing's *The Fifth Child*.

Paul Lovatt   Harriet and David Lovatt's fourth child, who was completely neglected by his mother because she was busy dealing with his younger brother, Ben; his terrible behavior problems are due to his having to live with Ben in Doris Lessing's *The Fifth Child*.

Frankie Love   Shrewd merchant seaman; when he cannot find a job on land he agrees to be a pimp for his girlfriend, a prostitute; he is arrested by Edward Justice, but the two men become friends in Colin MacInnes's *Mr. Love and Justice*.

Frankie Love's girlfriend   An unnamed prostitute; she angers Frankie Love by aborting what could possibly be their child in Colin MacInnes's *Mr. Love and Justice*.

Frankie Love's girlfriend's mother   Unnamed gypsy faith healer; she practices her business from her daughter's apartment to divert attention from the prostitution going on inside in Colin MacInnes's *Mr. Love and Justice*.

Lovell   Francis's academic friend who takes Sarah

Bennett to the Tate in Margaret Drabble's *A Summer Bird-Cage.*

Chips Lovell   Pushy scriptwriter friend of Nicholas Jenkins and nephew by marriage of Lady Molly Jeavons in Anthony Powell's *At Lady Molly's.* He becomes a gossip columnist and is engaged to Priscilla Tolland in *Casanova's Chinese Restaurant.* His marriage to Priscilla is successful in *The Kindly Ones.* He joins the Marines in *The Valley of Bones.* He is distressed at Priscilla's infidelity with Odo Stevens but hopes to be reconciled with her when he is killed by a flying bomb at the Ardglass party at the end of the war in *The Soldier's Art.*

Mary Lovell   A young woman for whom Christopher Martin feels an obsessive lust; she marries Nathaniel Walterson in William Golding's *Pincher Martin.*

Lovesake   Sketch-writer for *The Daily Paper;* he was editor of a northern paper which Lord Raingo had bought and sold over his head, but he remains on friendly terms with Raingo and allows him his place in the Press Gallery when the Prime Minister is under attack in the House of Commons in Arnold Bennett's *Lord Raingo.*

Low   Surgeon aboard the *Indefatigable* in C. S. Forester's *Mr. Midshipman Hornblower.*

Sandy Lowe   World War II British staff sergeant, now a boxing instructor; he incompletely prepares Fred Leiser in hand-to-hand combat for Leclerc's abortive Operation Mayfly in John le Carré's *The Looking-Glass War.*

Mrs. Lowe-Island   One of the town matriarchs in Doris Lessing's *Martha Quest.*

Major-General George Arthur Frederick Lowerby (Smiler)   Man who married late and soon became a widower; he hesitates in 1945 to join William Gary in talks about peace; he chairs the Political Investigation Committee and the Berlin advance Control Commission for Allied Occupation; he has three sons at school and loves Humphrey Brent as he would a son in Storm Jameson's *The Black Laurel.*

Gordon Lowther   The bachelor singing master for the Marcia Blaine School; Jean Brodie enters into an affair with him in an unsuccessful attempt to suppress her passion for Teddy Lloyd in Muriel Spark's *The Prime of Miss Jean Brodie.*

Helen Lowther   A pretty, rich, young married American woman, friend of Mrs. de Bray Pape; she is adored by the boy Mark (Tommie, Michael) Tietjens in Ford Madox Ford's *The Last Post.*

P. Loxias   The pseudonymous editor of Bradley Pearson's *The Black Prince — A Celebration of Love* in Iris Murdoch's *The Black Prince.*

Emma Loy   Successful novelist who becomes intent on ruining Nancy Hawkins because she has called Loy's hanger-on, Hector Bartlett, a "pisseur de copie" in Muriel Spark's *A Far Cry from Kensington.*

Luard   Secondary-school science master who in 1914 raises Miles's interest in science through his explanations of modern chemistry in C. P. Snow's *The Search.*

Sir James Lubbock   Lord Peter Wimsey's friend, an expert chemical analyst, whom Lord Peter consults in Dorothy L. Sayers's *Unnatural Death* and in *The Unpleasantness at the Bellona Club.* His trial testimony is damaging to Harriet Vane in *Strong Poison.*

Amy Lucas   Philip Lucas's aunt, bedridden for seven years in a private lunatic asylum; her death at eighty-three is mourned with exemplary propriety by Philip and Lucia, especially as it results in doubling their income and providing them with a house in London in E. F. Benson's *Lucia in London.*

Emmeline (Lucia) Lucas   "Peppino" Lucas's wife, who makes liberal use of a few Italian phrases in her reign as queen and cultural leader of Riseholme society; she loses her preeminence upon the arrival of the acclaimed opera singer Olga Bracely, but Olga good-naturedly engineers Lucia's restoration in E. F. Benson's *"Queen Lucia".* Lucia amuses London's social leaders with the intrepidity and success of her social campaign, but she returns to reclaim Riseholme in *Lucia in London.* After being widowed she moves to Tilling, where she successfully challenges Elizabeth Mapp's social dominance in *Mapp and Lucia.* Large donations to civic organizations assist her Town Council membership and election to Mayor; she is Mrs. Georgie Pillson in *The Worshipful Lucia* and in *Trouble for Lucia.*

Philip (Peppino) Lucas   A wealthy retired barrister, solid and practical in business matters but the author of "prose poems" hand-printed by a press supported by himself; he is the indulgent, worshipful consort of Lucia Lucas in E. F. Benson's *"Queen Lucia".* He inherits a London house, from which Lucia launches a more ambitious social ascent, returning to Riseholme when he becomes ill in *Lucia in London.*

Wilfred Lucas-Dockery   A former college sociology professor who becomes a chief prison official and learns that his theories about penology and coddling the criminal do not work in Evelyn Waugh's *Decline and Fall.*

Professor Lucifer Inventor of a flying ship who debates the concept of good and evil with Father Michael and forces him out of the ship onto the dome of St. Paul's cathedral; he reappears as the Master, the superintendent of the insane asylum to which Turnbull and MacIan are sentenced in G. K. Chesterton's *The Ball and the Cross*.

Lawrence Lucifer Narrator whose memoirs comprise an examination of the sterile London society he designates "the English Death"; he retires to a Mediterranean island to ponder the significance of what he has learned in Lawrence Durrell's *The Black Book*.

Lucinda One of Wilfred Barclay's former mistresses — "a genius when it came to sex" — in William Golding's *The Paper Men*.

Lucy Irene Coles's six-foot-tall maid and artist's model in E. F. Benson's *Miss Mapp* and in *The Worshipful Lucia*.

Lucy A widowed duchess, who manages Chevron until her son, Sebastian, comes of age in Vita Sackville-West's *The Edwardians*.

Lucy Sir Henry Merriman's mistress; she offers herself to Francis Andrews in return for his testimony and succeeds in seducing him, despite his attempts to remain faithful to Elizabeth in Graham Greene's *The Man Within*.

Lucy One of two girlfriends of Mark Armstrong in Margaret Drabble's *The Middle Ground*.

Erich von Ludendorff German general who is arrested after leading Hitler's 1923 putsch in Munich in Richard Hughes's *The Fox in the Attic*.

Roy Ludlow Jonathan Browne's replacement as accounts-and-inventory clerk at Badmore in David Lodge's *Ginger, You're Barmy*.

Sister Ludmila A woman not in holy orders but called "sister" by courtesy who runs a clinic and shelter for the poor and homeless in Mayapore in Paul Scott's *The Jewel in the Crown*.

Paul Lufkin Industrialist who retains Lewis Eliot as his legal consultant; he unsuccessfully bids for a government contract in atomic-energy development and learns he will be given a peerage by Labor government in C. P. Snow's *Homecomings*. An ally of Roger Quaife, he goes after the blackmailer Hood and arranges for Quaife's economic needs after his resignation from government in *Corridors of Power*. He receives an honorary degree; he makes inquiries about Eliot's eye specialist in *The Sleep of Reason*.

Luke Emotionally scarred, alcoholic American journalist covering Southeast Asia; he discovers J. Frost's murder, assists Jerry Westerby's investigations, and is mistaken for Westerby and murdered by Drake Ko's bodyguard Tiu in John le Carré's *The Honourable Schoolboy*.

Nora Luke Mathematician and wife of Walter; she works with her husband in atomic-energy research in C. P. Snow's *The New Men*.

Theodora Luke A mistress in Josephine Napier's school who has a university degree; she is a special friend of Maria Rosetti in Ivy Compton-Burnett's *More Women Than Men*.

Walter Luke Physicist who is the youngest fellow in the Cambridge college and who makes a significant discovery in his work; he casts his vote for Paul Jago in the election of a new Master in C. P. Snow's *The Masters*. He leads British research in atomic energy; he is ill from exposure to atomic radiation, disapproves of use of the atomic bomb, recommends British development of the bomb for self-protection, and receives appointment as Chief Superintendent of atomic-energy research after Martin Eliot declines in *The New Men*. He negotiates with Cambridge officials for university research in atomic energy in *The Affair*. He is a member of Roger Quaife's advisory committee and is subjected to a security check in *Corridors of Power*. He accepts a ministerial post for the government after it was declined by Francis Getliffe and Lewis Eliot, and he speaks for the government on the issue of the security threat by Cambridge students in *Last Things*.

Andrew Lumley The mastermind behind the "Power-House"; he proves to Edward Leithen "how thin is the protection of civilisation," but his inhuman conspiracy is defeated by Leithen's visionary powers in John Buchan's *The Power-House*.

Charles Lumley Young college history graduate who attempts to escape his middle-class status and the expectations that accompany it through a disjointed series of unusual jobs and relationships in John Wain's *Hurry On Down*.

Janice Lumm Ex-pupil of Romley Fourways', the school Kate Fletcher (Armstrong) attended; she has cancer in Margaret Drabble's *The Middle Ground*.

Mamma Luna Aged mother of Bamboo, who supports her by his fishing; she later sends word of his death to the Mouth family in Ronald Firbank's *Sorrow in Sunlight*.

Bertha Lunken   Frederick Tarr's "official fiancé"; she is seduced and impregnated by Otto Kreisler and later marries and divorces Tarr in Wyndham Lewis's *Tarr*.

Alec Luria   American Jewish psychiatrist who is a friend of Humphrey Leigh in C. P. Snow's *A Coat of Varnish*.

Mr. Luscombe   The farmer father of Bill and Lewis; he directs the wheat mowing in the opening scene of John Fowles's *Daniel Martin*.

Bill Luscombe   Brother of Lewis Luscombe; he is the farmer helping with the mowing in the opening scene of John Fowles's *Daniel Martin*.

Lewis Luscombe   Brother of Bill Luscombe; he drives the reaper in the opening scene of John Fowles's *Daniel Martin*.

Janislav (Jan) Lusiewicz   The younger of two Polish brothers who bend Rosa Keepe to their will in Iris Murdoch's *The Flight from the Enchanter*.

Stefan Lusiewicz   The elder of two Polish brothers who bend Rosa Keepe to their will but are put to flight by Mischa Fox in Iris Murdoch's *The Flight from the Enchanter*.

Lusik   The mind-father of one of Al-Ith's children; the narrator, he chronicles Al-Ith's history in Doris Lessing's *The Marriages Between Zones Three, Four, and Five*.

Lüthy   Bavarian physicist who meets Arthur Miles at Cambridge and assists him in compiling data for research in crystallography; he confesses the problems of his love life to Miles in Munich in C. P. Snow's *The Search*.

Elizabeth Luton   Jane Weston's necessary maid; her engagement to Colonel Boucher's necessary manservant Atkinson results in the marriage of their employers in E. F. Benson's *"Queen Lucia"*.

Mr. Luttrell   Mrs. Cosway's neighbor and only friend; his property, Nelson's Rest, is left empty after he shoots his dog and swims out to sea to his death in Jean Rhys's *Wide Sargasso Sea*.

Daisy Luttrell   Sharp-tongued shrew whose disposition is improved by her husband's accidentally shooting her in Agatha Christie's *Curtain: Hercule Poirot's Last Case*.

Colonel George (Toby) Luttrell   Henpecked husband who, mistaking his wife for a rabbit, shoots her in Agatha Christie's *Curtain: Hercule Poirot's Last Case*.

Philip Luttrell   Reserved, careful rector and friend of Catherine Frobisher; he secretly loves Lise Grainger in his youth but in middle age falls in love with and marries Emily Crowne; after some months of unhappiness Philip and Emily are reconciled and happily conceive a child in Margaret Kennedy's *Red Sky at Morning*.

Mrs. Luxmore   Woman who embroiders a tale of murderous passion against Major John Despard in Agatha Christie's *Cards on the Table*.

Marina Luzzi   Wealthy Italian who is engaged to marry Hubert Mosson, quarrels with Hubert's mother, breaks her engagement because Hubert is a sexual pervert, helps Magda Sczekerny break from Primrose Lynmouth, and is invited to attend Piers Mosson's production of an opera which she had encouraged in Angus Wilson's *Setting the World on Fire*.

Miss Lyall   An elderly, rabbit-faced spinster; Lady Ambermere's companion, she exchanges slavish attention for her room and board in E. F. Benson's *"Queen Lucia"* and in *Lucia in London*.

Edward Lyall   Member of Parliament, local celebrity, and eligible bachelor heir to the major local estate whom Jane Cleveland imagines paired with Prudence Bates in Barbara Pym's *Jane and Prudence*.

Sir Oulstone Lyall   Historian who is an authority on Central Asia; he admires the work of Roy Calvert and is embarrassed by Calvert regarding Lyall's possible plagiarism in C. P. Snow's *The Light and the Dark*.

Lychnis   Maternal but intellectually inferior Utopian woman who nurses William Barnstaple back to health after the rebellion at Quarantine (Coronation) Crag in H. G. Wells's *Men Like Gods*.

David Lydell   Fortyish, hypochondriacal, and self-indulgent vicar, whose unexpected engagement to Letty Crowe's sixtyish friend Marjorie disrupts Letty's plan to share Marjorie's house upon her retirement in Barbara Pym's *Quartet in Autumn*.

Miss Lydgate   Harriet Vane's old English tutor at Shrewsbury College, Oxford; her scholarly integrity is equaled by her charitable goodwill; the manuscript of her years-in-progress scholarly work is disfigured and mutilated in Dorothy L. Sayers's *Gaudy Night*.

Alaric Lydgate   Middle-aged book reviewer and amateur anthropologist, invalided out of the Colonial Service, who returns from Africa with his trunks full of field notes to live near the Swans in a London suburb in Barbara Pym's *Less Than Angels.*

Gertrude Lydgate Sixtyish spinster, former missionary, and friend and roommate of Esther Clovis; she is expert in the African languages studied by Father Gemini in Barbara Pym's *Less Than Angels.*

Mad Jane (Janie) Lyn Retarded yet harmless woman who sees the murder of Stella Rode; her garbled report to Carne Police authorities makes her their chief suspect in John le Carré's *A Murder of Quality.*

Leila Lynch A nurse in a London hospital; she was once in love with her cousin Edward Pierson; married twice, she was divorced once and widowed in 1916; she becomes the lover of Jimmy Fort but leaves him so that he will be free to marry Noel Pierson in John Galsworthy's *Saint's Progress.*

Vincent Lynch Medical student who abandons Stephen Dedalus during the confrontation with the English soldiers in James Joyce's *Ulysses.*

Alexander Lynch-Gibbon Sculptor, brother of Martin Lynch-Gibbon, lover of Antonia Lynch-Gibbon, fiancé of Georgie Hands, and finally husband of Antonia in Iris Murdoch's *A Severed Head.*

Antonia Lynch-Gibbon Martin Lynch-Gibbon's wife, some five years older than he, and lover of both Alexander Lynch-Gibbon, whom she will eventually marry, and of Palmer Anderson in Iris Murdoch's *A Severed Head.*

Martin Lynch-Gibbon A wine merchant and a scholar *manqué* with a deep interest in military history; he is Antonia Lynch-Gibbon's husband and the lover first of Georgie Hands, then of Honor Klein; he is the narrator of Iris Murdoch's *A Severed Head.*

Vesper Lynd Russian secret agent; torn between her duty and her love for James Bond, she kills herself in Ian Fleming's *Casino Royale.*

Angela Lyne Basil Seal's wealthy mistress, who begins to drink heavily when Basil neglects her; after her husband is killed in World War II, she and Basil agree to marry in Evelyn Waugh's *Put Out More Flags.*

Cedric Lyne Gentle and chivalrous husband of Angela Lyne; he is killed in the British Norway campaign against the Germans in Evelyn Waugh's *Put Out More Flags.*

Primrose Lynmouth Librarian at Tothill House who is jealous of her Hungarian assistant, Magda Sczekerny, and quits her position during a quarrel provoked by Marina Luzzi in Angus Wilson's *Setting the World on Fire.*

Lynn Dennis's secretary at the electronics firm and a single mother; she writes him a love letter and helps to revive him after his daughter's death; she has an affair with him, but she ends up with Austin Brierly in David Lodge's *How Far Can You Go?.*

Lyons Property developer who fared worse than Anthony Keating's partnership during the 1970s property-market collapse in Margaret Drabble's *The Ice Age.*

Casimir Lypiatt Frustrated artist and admirer of Myra Viveash; following the failure of his art exhibition he argues with Mr. Mercaptan, who panned his work, and in the final scene he contemplates suicide in Aldous Huxley's *Antic Hay.*

Dr. Lyte Physician who treats and is blackmailed by Patrick Seton in Muriel Spark's *The Bachelors.*

M

M Head of the British Secret Service; he has a close but increasingly contentious relationship with his agent James Bond in Ian Fleming's *Casino Royale* and in succeeding novels, ending with *You Only Live Twice*.

Ma The broad-figured mother of Sammy Mountjoy; he always sees her in terms of the cloacal background of their slum life on Rotten Row in William Golding's *Free Fall*.

Henry Maartens Brilliant Nobel Prize-winning physicist and husband to Katy; egotistical and proud but emotionally immature, he demands the attention of all those closest to him, especially his wife; despite her death he goes on to remarry, and eventually to contribute to the development of the atom bomb in Aldous Huxley's *The Genius and the Goddess*.

Katy Maartens Henry's earthy, sensual wife, whose beauty, tact, and understanding complement his genius; she seduces her husband's young protégé John Rivers, bringing him into manhood, but is killed in an automobile accident, the result of an argument with her daughter, jealous for the young man's attentions in Aldous Huxley's *The Genius and the Goddess*.

Ruth Maartens Adolescent daughter of Henry and Katy Maartens; she develops a crush on family houseguest John Rivers, with whom her mother is having an affair; becoming aware of the relationship, she argues with her mother, causing an automobile accident in which both are killed in Aldous Huxley's *The Genius and the Goddess*.

Alcestic ("Allie") Mabbott Close friend to Brenda Richardson; she is seen as a bore by Jake Richardson; her husband, Geoffrey, leaves her for Brenda after they become close through a series of encounter-group workshops; she is sometimes referred to as "old Smudger" by Jake in Kingsley Amis's *Jake's Thing*.

Geoffrey Mabbott Affable, self-centered, eccentric dresser with a natural ability to get at cross purposes with others; he is husband to Brenda Richardson's close friend, Allie; he eventually leaves Allie for Brenda in Kingsley Amis's *Jake's Thing*.

Mabel Ferdinand Clegg's cousin, with whom he has been brought up in John Fowles's *The Collector*.

Mabel Distraught wife who accuses Nancy Hawkins of seducing her husband, Patrick, in Muriel Spark's *A Far Cry from Kensington*.

Macalister Philip Carey's acquaintance who enjoys expounding the philosophies of Kant in W. Somerset Maugham's *Of Human Bondage*.

Mrs. MacAnder Friend of Winifred Dartie; she tells the Forsyte aunts about seeing Irene Forsyte and Philip Bosinney in Richmond Park in John Galsworthy's *The Man of Property*.

Colonel MacAndrew Amy Strickland's military brother-in-law, who is both morally outraged and completely unable to comprehend the driving force behind Charles Strickland's desertion of his wife in W. Somerset Maugham's *The Moon and Sixpence*.

J. N. Macandrew (alias Meyer, Lassom) Member of British Intelligence who interviews and then trains Adam Melfort for service in Europe; he dies before a firing squad "with steady, smiling eyes" in John Buchan's *A Prince of the Captivity*.

Macarius Bishop of Aelia Capitolina (Jerusalem) who is of considerable assistance to Helena as she attempts to find the cross on which Christ was crucified in Evelyn Waugh's *Helena*.

General John Gordon MacArthur Commanding officer responsible for the apparently blundering but in fact deliberate sacrifice of a young officer; he is a murder victim in Agatha Christie's *And Then There Were None*.

Senhor MacBride-Pereira Self-satisfied, somewhat voyeuristic retired Brazilian diplomat who prides himself on his half-Scottish background and knowledge of British idiom; he rents a flat from Mrs. Beltane in suburban London from which he observes Dulcie Mainwaring and other neighbors in Barbara Pym's *No Fond Return of Love*. He makes an appearance in *The Sweet Dove Died*.

MacCann Political activist friend of Stephen Dedalus in James Joyce's *A Portrait of the Artist as a Young Man*.

Jeames MacConochie-Smith Conceited and unprincipled fellow who becomes a frequent visitor to the Verren household; he is acquainted with Bertram Verren because the latter has occasionally played accompaniment for him at local shows in Frank Swinnerton's *The Young Idea: A Comedy of Environment*.

Finn MacCool Hero of Old Ireland held in captivity by the fictional novelist Dermot Trellis; he tells the tale of Mad Sweeney and bores his listeners in Flann O'Brien's *At Swim-Two-Birds*.

Policeman MacCruiskeen Second policeman that

the narrator meets in hell; his series of Chinese boxes and other inventions fascinate the narrator in Flann O'Brien's *The Third Policeman*.

Kevin Macdermott   Barrister defending Marion Sharpe and her mother in Josephine Tey's *The Franchise Affair*. He is suspicious of the reappearance of Patrick Ashby in *Brat Farrar*.

Macdonald   Professor of Geology at Cambridge who is actually a physicist; he invites Arthur Miles to do research at Cambridge and promotes Miles for the directorship of the new National Institute in C. P. Snow's *The Search*.

Bob Macdonald   Sophie Macdonald's happily married husband; he is tragically killed in a freak car accident in W. Somerset Maugham's *The Razor's Edge*.

Ramsey MacDonald   Capable and experienced chief engineer of the hurricane-tossed *Archimedes*; relaxing alone on the poop deck as the crippled ship is towed to safety after the storm, he is overtaken by exhaustion and falls unnoticed into the ocean in Richard Hughes's *In Hazard*.

Sophie Macdonald   The dry-humored, shrewd young girl whose beloved husband Bob and their baby are tragically killed in a car crash, leaving her to anesthetize herself with alcohol until Larry Darrell begins to care for her in W. Somerset Maugham's *The Razor's Edge*.

Gerty MacDowell   Unmarried woman who sees her life through the lens of popular romances; she lifts her skirts while a dark stranger, Leopold Bloom, masturbates on the beach in James Joyce's *Ulysses*.

Mr. Macgillivray   Scotland Yard official who joins forces with Sir Walter Bullivant of the Foreign Office to enlist the undercover talents of Richard Hannay in John Buchan's *The Thirty-Nine Steps* and in *Mr. Standfast*. He works with Hannay to uncover the sinister villain and international combine believed to be responsible for the disappearance of the three young people in *The Three Hostages*. He gives Hannay valuable information about Mr. Lancelot Troth, a solicitor threatening Valdemar Haraldsen, son of the Haraldsen whom Hannay and other friends had vowed to help when endangered, in *The Island of Sheep*.

Sir Alexander MacGowan   Member of Parliament from Scotland who exchanges words and blows with Michael Mont; he is rejected by his fiancée Marjorie Ferrar after she loses the libel suit in John Galsworthy's *The Silver Spoon*.

Bill MacGrath   Homosexual clergyman who unsuccessfully tries to seduce Eric Craddock in London after the death of Bernard Sands in Angus Wilson's *Hemlock and After*.

Miss Macgregor ("Greggie")   One of three aging spinsters who live in the May of Teck Club; she functions as house historian and insists on the exsistence of a buried, unexploded German bomb in the garden in Muriel Spark's *The Girls of Slender Means*.

Mr. Macgregor   A large, heavy, tolerant Deputy Commissioner of Kyanktada District and the Secretary of the European Club; he tries to get the other members to admit a native into the membership as requested by his superiors in George Orwell's *Burmese Days*.

Mary Macgregor   The member of "the Brodie set" famous for her stupidity; she is used as a scapegoat by Jean Brodie and her girls in Muriel Spark's *The Prime of Miss Jean Brodie*.

Irving Macher   A young and brilliant but nasty American undergraduate novelist who is hated by Roger Micheldene; he advises Micheldene to be less rigid and more natural and impulsive, steals Micheldene's lecture notes and replaces them with a comic book, and has an affair with Micheldene's mistress, Helene Bang, in Kingsley Amis's *One Fat Englishman*.

Arthur Machin   A factory worker who becomes a professional football player; he lives with Mrs. Hammond until they argue and he is asked to leave; as a professional player he goes from ardent beginner to resigned old-timer in David Storey's *This Sporting Life*.

Edward Henry (Denry) Machin   Unconventional opportunist; his spontaneous response to every circumstance enables him from his youth to draw public attention which helps him rise from poverty-stricken clerk to wealthy businessman and Councillor of Bursley, always secretly amazed at his own exploits and exulting in his surprising successes in Arnold Bennett's *The Card: A Story of Adventure in the Five Towns*.

Eli Machin   Oldest employee at Henry Mynor's pottery; he recognizes the naïveté of Anna Tellwright's concern for workmen's safety in Arnold Bennett's *Anna of the Five Towns*.

Professor MacHugh   Narrator of Taylor's stirring speech in the newspaper office in James Joyce's *Ulysses*.

Evan MacIan   Roman Catholic Scottish Highlander who is extremely offended by James Turnbull's opinions of the Virgin Mary and challenges him to a duel which they attempt to fight many times, only to be constantly interrupted by the authorities; he and Turnbull are confined to an insane asylum and eventually escape by following Father Michael through the final conflagration in G. K. Chesterton's *The Ball and the Cross.*

Miss Mackay   Headmistress of the Marcia Blaine School; she is unsuccessful in forcing the retirement of the unorthodox Jean Brodie until Sandy Stranger gives her pursuit the necessary direction in Muriel Spark's *The Prime of Miss Jean Brodie.*

Steve Mackelvore   Long-term British Intelligence operative and often incompetent agent/controller; he is forced by Ricki Tarr to cable the message that exposes the double agent in John le Carré's *Tinker, Tailor, Soldier, Spy.* He recruits Lizzie Worthington in *The Honourable Schoolboy.* He receives Vladimir's request to identify the Soviet Commercial Secretary Kirov as Moscow Centre's agent Oleg Kursky in *Smiley's People.*

Mackenzie   Leader of a plot, by the Cartographer's compatriots, to escape from a nearby prison camp; he causes the Cartographer to fear for his life by involving him in the escape in Nigel Dennis's *A House in Order.*

General Mackenzie   A not-very-likable acquaintance of General Curzon, to whom he owes his job security; later he returns the favor by authorizing Curzon's unit to join the war campaign in France in C. S. Forester's *The General.*

Mr. Mackenzie   Shallow, financially comfortable, forty-eight-year-old most recent lover of Julia Martin; morally blind, selfish, and brutal, he is attracted reluctantly to the strange and bizarre for short periods in Jean Rhys's *After Leaving Mr. Mackenzie.*

Python Macklin   The "dreaded" nemesis whom Schmule must fight in order to win the £25 purse that will recall sunny weather to his relationship with Sonia in Wolf Mankowitz's *A Kid for Two Farthings.*

Maclean   Communist friend of Paul Gardner in Isabel Colegate's *Agatha.*

Maclintick   A music critic who greatly admires Hugh Moreland; when his wife, Audrey, leaves him, Maclintick commits suicide in Anthony Powell's *Casanova's Chinese Restaurant.*

Audrey Maclintick   The shrewish, discontented, angry wife of Maclintick; she leaves him and runs away with the violinist Carolo in Anthony Powell's *Casanova's Chinese Restaurant.* Abandoned by Carolo, she takes on Hugh Moreland, supervising, nursing,

and living with but never marrying him in *The Soldier's Art,* in *The Military Philosophers,* and in *Temporary Kings.*

MacMann   Malone's fictional character who lives in a madhouse and represents Malone's final anguish in Samuel Beckett's *Malone Dies.*

Vincent Macmaster   The ambitious, cautious son of a poor Scottish shipping clerk; his rise has been assisted by the intelligence, money, and social connections of his close friend Christopher Tietjens; he marries Edith Duchemin, holds evening parties for ambitious men of talent and influence, and is knighted for a brilliant financial evaluation that was the idea and work of Tietjens in Ford Madox Ford's *Some Do Not. . . .* He is McKechnie's uncle in *No More Parades* and in *A Man Could Stand Up —.*

"John Macnab"   See Sir Edward Leithen, John Palliser-Yeates, and Charles Merkland, Lord Lamancha.

Andrew MacPhee   Cynical member of St. Anne's community and long-time friend of Elwin Ransom in C. S. Lewis's *That Hideous Strength.*

The Pooka MacPhellimey   A devil with a civil tongue who helps devise tortures for the writer Dermot Trellis in Flann O'Brien's *At Swim-Two-Birds.*

Mr. Macpherson   Middle-aged and rheumatic Scots who organizes the defense to prevent "John Macnab" from killing a stag on Lord Claybody's property in John Buchan's *John Macnab.*

Mrs. Macpherson   Bitter mother of Muriel, Dorothy, and Arthur Macpherson, who is her son by David Macdonald Fortune; she has an intense dislike for blacks because David left her and never supported Arthur financially; she refuses to welcome Arthur home when he is released from prison in Colin MacInnes's *City of Spades.*

Arthur Macpherson   Lazy, gambling half brother to Johnny Fortune; he often asks Johnny and others for money and steals the money sent to his mother by David Fortune; he aids the police in Johnny's arrest on false pimping charges in Colin MacInnes's *City of Spades.*

Dorothy Macpherson   A prostitute and the daughter of Mrs. Macpherson; she lives with her pimp, Billy Whispers, until he is jailed; she moves in with Johnnny Fortune and her sister (Muriel Macpherson) and assumes their rent; she loves Johnny and wants him to be her pimp in Colin MacInnes's *City of Spades.*

Muriel Macpherson   Mrs. Macpherson's shy daughter, who falls in love with Johnny Fortune; she supports him on her wages as a tailor's assistant but leaves him when he has an affair with her sister, Dorothy Macpherson; she bears his child, William Macpherson Fortune; she refuses to stand in Johnny's defense in court and will not allow William to return to Africa with Johnny in Colin MacInnes's *City of Spades.*

Hector Willard MacQueen Samuel Edward Ratchett's private secretary; his father was the District Attorney for the Daisy Armstrong case in Agatha Christie's *Murder on the Orient Express.*

MacQuern A young Scot whose rivalry for the notice of Zuleika Dobson almost leads to a fight with the Duke of Dorset; he is one of the Oxford undergraduates to die for love in Max Beerbohm's *Zuleika Dobson; or An Oxford Love Story.*

Andrew George (Andy) Macready Dying jazz trumpeter and Barley Blair's father figure and guru on mortality; his love of individuals inspires Barley to betray all oppressing institutions in John le Carré's *The Russia House.*

Macrobes Spiritual beings with higher intelligence than man who are the evil force behind the N.I.C.E. (National Institute for Coordinated Experiments); they communicate with the inner circle of the N.I.C.E. by means of Alcasan's head in C. S. Lewis's *That Hideous Strength.*

Madam Owner of the brothel at which Frankie Love's girlfriend works; Madam dislikes Frankie and tries to get him arrested in Colin MacInnes's *Mr. Love and Justice.*

Madden Medical student who carouses with Stephen Dedalus in James Joyce's *Ulysses.*

Maddix Ascetic, short, middle-aged creator of unusual drinks in the hotel bar; he was persuaded by Evelyn Orcham to come to London after being for twenty years the best-known barman in New York in Arnold Bennett's *Imperial Palace.*

Harriet Maddock Mrs. John Baines's sister; she never reveals that her niece Sophia stole money to facilitate her elopement and she welcomes disillusioned Mrs. Baines to live with her in Arnold Bennett's *The Old Wives Tale.*

Dr. Maddox School physician; he is a bouncy little man exuding urbanity and antisepsis in Nicholas Blake's *A Question of Proof.*

Mr. Maddox Journalist and early friend of Keith

Rickman; he cares for him after Rickman nearly dies of starvation in May Sinclair's *The Divine Fire.*

Madeline A follower of the Christ-like figure who rises from the grave in D. H. Lawrence's *The Escaped Cock.*

Mademoiselle Vicky's governess and the Provincial Lady's general assistant; she is emotional but often shrewd, sensible, and outspoken, particularly where Vicky's education is considered; she resents losing control of Vicky when she is sent to boarding school in E. M. Delafield's *The Diary of a Provincial Lady* and in *The Provincial Lady Goes Further.*

Percival Wemys Madison The representative of the weak "little 'uns" who are abysmally lost in William Golding's *Lord of the Flies.*

Mad Worlds Alien races of a high order whose fixation on interstellar travel perverts their intelligence, causing them to engage in a destructive missionary enterprise in Olaf Stapledon's *Star Maker.*

Mag A bright and articulate London working girl; she and Jan live together in what they discover is a house of prostitution; they fascinate Miriam Henderson by their insouciance and unconventionality in Dorothy Richardson's *The Tunnel* and in *Interim.* Miriam comes to see her as Radical Mag in *Dawn's Left Hand.*

Magdalen (Madge) A typist and occasionally a photographer's model; she shares her apartment with her boyfriend Jake Donaghue and his hanger-on Peter O'Finney until she throws them out in order to be able to marry Sammy Starfield; she gives Sammy Jake's translation of a cinematic hot property in Iris Murdoch's *Under the Net.*

Maggie Giggly psychiatric nurse who prefers a ward of private cells in Malcolm Lowry's *Lunar Caustic.*

Dr. Magiot French-trained Haitian doctor, a Marxist, who treats Brown's mother and helps Brown deal with the death of Dr. Philipot; he sees Haiti's situation clearly and becomes a courier for the rebels; he is killed by the Tontons Macoutes in Graham Greene's *The Comedians.*

Maria Magistretti The last in the line of Italian girls employed in the Narraway household; Edmund Narraway falls in love with her in Iris Murdoch's *The Italian Girl.*

Mr. Magnate Stereotypical capitalist interviewed,

and later robbed, by John Wainwright in Olaf Stapledon's *Odd John: A Story Between Jest and Earnest*.

Mrs. Maguire Alice Maguire's domineering mother in Mary Lavin's *Mary O'Grady*.

Alice Maguire The girl next door, too shy to admit her love for Patrick O'Grady; she is left behind when he goes to America in Mary Lavin's *Mary O'Grady*.

Nelly Mahone Aged woman who preaches repentance outside pubs and who suspects the strange powers of Dougal Douglas in Muriel Spark's *The Ballad of Peckham Rye*.

Brendan Mahoney Mike Brady and Peter Nolan's fat Irish friend with whom Jonathan Browne has a brief drink in London in David Lodge's *Ginger, You're Barmy*.

Mahood See Basil.

Maisie Maidan A beautiful young married woman with a severe heart condition; she follows Edward Ashburnham from India to Bad Nauheim in Germany and dies of shock upon discovering that he does not love her in Ford Madox Ford's *The Good Soldier: A Tale of Passion*.

Sybil Maiden An elderly, dignified scholar from Girts College, Cambridge; she encounters Persse McGarrigle in Rummidge, in Hawaii, and in New York, and meets Philip Swallow and Joy Simpson in Delphi; she reveals that she is the mother of Angelica and Lily Pabst by Arthur Kingfisher in David Lodge's *Small World*.

Percy Maidment Lionel Stephens's gun loader, who is fiercely competitive with Albert Jarvis in Isabel Colegate's *The Shooting Party*.

Captain Mailler (Hollinder) Brutal, swarthy, ex-Black-and-Tan Scotsman wanted for murder; he is Robinson's (Stefan Saridza's) bully-boy and henchman; it is his roughing up of Desmond Kenton that persuades Kenton to join forces with the Zaleshoffs in Eric Ambler's *Uncommon Danger*.

Maillotte Christophine Dubois's best and only friend and Tia's mother in Jean Rhys's *Wide Sargasso Sea*.

Inspector Maine Scotland Yard investigator into the Indian Island murders in Agatha Christie's *And Then There Were None*.

Constance Maine Charles Watkins's ex-mistress, who writes letters to Charles's doctors at his mental ward, letting them know what she knew about the patient in Doris Lessing's *Briefing for a Descent into Hell*.

David Mainwaring One of two children of Judith (Street) and Hugo Mainwaring; he suffered permanent brain damage when the incorrect amount of anaesthetic was given him during an operation on lumps in his neck in Margaret Drabble's *The Middle Ground*.

Dulcie Mainwaring Pleasant spinster in her early thirties, a research assistant whose investigations extend voyeuristically into the lives of ordinary men and women — especially the Forbes family; she lets rooms in her suburban London house to Viola Dace and to her niece Laurel in Barbara Pym's *No Fond Return of Love*.

Felix Byron Mainwaring Handsome, smug, upper-class senior professor of anthropology, who flatters and persuades Mrs. Foresight into endowing some grants and purchasing a Georgian building in London, dubbed "Felix's Folly" by students, as the Foresight Research Centre; he then turns his charms toward an equally wealthy widow from the United States named Cornelia van Heep in Barbara Pym's *Less Than Angels*.

Hugo Mainwaring Estranged husband of Judith Street Mainwaring and father of their two children; he is a first cousin to Evelyn Morton Stennett and friend to Kate Fletcher Armstrong; he is a successful journalist/correspondent who suffered the loss of half an arm while a foreign correspondent in Margaret Drabble's *The Middle Ground*.

Judith Street Mainwaring Estranged wife of Hugo Mainwaring and mother of their two children; her life seems unalterably damaged because of her obsessive seeking of revenge against the hospital that is responsible for the brain damage to her son David; she is an art historian in Margaret Drabble's *The Middle Ground*.

Nancy ("Nan") Mainwaring Hugo Mainwaring's mother, whose relationship with her son is more that of stranger/lover than of mother/son in Margaret Drabble's *The Middle Ground*.

Mainwearing John Henderson's immediate boss; he is a disinterested scientist, patiently watching the world's movements in C. Day Lewis's *Starting Point*.

Alex Mair Brilliant scientist who runs a nuclear power station; he is about to take an important government post when former mistress Hilary Robarts complicates his life in P. D. James's *Devices and Desires*.

275

Alice Mair   Austere author of cookbooks and sister of Alex Mair in P. D. James's *Devices and Desires*.

Maisie   Innocent, young new waitress at Snow's restaurant; she is close in age to Rose Wilson in Graham Greene's *Brighton Rock*.

Lee Maitland   Woman whose 7:40 A.M. arrival from Virginia by train Geoffrey Firmin recalls awaiting in Malcolm Lowry's *Under the Volcano*.

Mary Makepeace   A young American pregnant by a priest; she meets Morris Zapp on a plane full of pregnant women bound for England to have abortions, but she decides to have the child; she meets Morris again in a Soho strip club, moves in with Hilary Swallow, and teaches her about the women's movement in David Lodge's *Changing Places: A Tale of Two Campuses*.

Clement Makin   An actress almost twenty years older than Charles Arrowby; their love affair was Charles's first in Iris Murdoch's *The Sea, the Sea*.

Dimitrios Makropoulos   Brutal, corrupt murderer and master criminal, ex-heroin addict, drug dealer, and white slaver; he is uncovered by Charles Latimer's innocent search for the history of the presumed-dead Dimitrios; now a respectable director of the Eurasian Credit Trust and threatened with exposure, he shoots Peters (Frederik Petersen) and is killed by him in Eric Ambler's *The Mask of Dimitrios*.

Mal   An aged patriarch who of all his Neanderthal folk has "the most pictures" in his head; he dies of natural causes, being drawn into the "womb of Oa" in William Golding's *The Inheritors*.

Lady Malden   Wife of Sir James; she tells Mrs. Pendyce about her husband George's accompanying Helen Bellew in John Galsworthy's *The Country House*.

Sir James Malden   A Justice of the Peace who holds reactionary views on the status of women in John Galsworthy's *The Country House*.

David Malevich   Daniel Martin's American film producer; he arranges for Dan's trip to Egypt in John Fowles's *Daniel Martin*.

Signor Malipizzo   Unjust magistrate who delights in jailing innocent citizens; he hates the Russians in Norman Douglas's *South Wind*.

Derek Mallaby   The unsatisfactory boyfriend to whom Vivienne Michel lost her virginity in Ian Fleming's *The Spy Who Loved Me*.

Sir Joshua Malleson   A dry, learned baronet, who is the guest of Hermione Roddice in D. H. Lawrence's *Women in Love*.

Mrs. Mallet   The only female member of the Identity Club; she pretends to be Captain Mallet's wife but is, in reality, Beaufort Mallet's lover in Nigel Dennis's *Cards of Identity*.

Captain Mallet   Pseudonymous member (and the eventual president) of the Identity Club; he is adept at transforming the identities of his subjects into identities of his own devising in Nigel Dennis's *Cards of Identity*.

Beaufort Mallet   Younger member of the Identity Club; he pretends to be the son of Captain and Mrs. Mallet but is actually Mrs. Mallet's lover in Nigel Dennis's *Cards of Identity*.

Captain Charles Mallinson   H.M. Vice-Consul who is very unhappy to be abducted on a highjacked plane and taken to the Tibetan monastery, Shangri-La, along with Hugh "Glory" Conway, Henry D. Barnard, and Miss Roberta Brinklow in James Hilton's *Lost Horizon*.

Mallory   Commander of the second gig in the *Indefatigable*'s surprise attack of the *Papillin* in C. S. Forester's *Mr. Midshipman Hornblower*.

Anne Mallory   Anthony and Jane Mallory's younger daughter in John Fowles's *Daniel Martin*.

Anthony Mallory   Daniel Martin's student-days friend, now an Oxford philosophy don; as he lies dying from cancer he insists on seeing Dan, with whom he has not spoken in many years; he asks Dan to befriend his wife, Jane, and immediately thereafter commits suicide in John Fowles's *Daniel Martin*.

Clare Mallory   An innocent and pious former novice, who has been forced to leave the convent because of an incident involving Hilda Syms; she succeeds in converting Mark Underwood, with whom she falls deeply in love, as she gradually loses her own interest in religion; when he leaves her, she finds a new mission in helping others in David Lodge's *The Picturegoers*.

Elizabeth (Bett) Mallory   The pious, Irish Catholic wife of Tom Mallory and mother of eight children, including Clare, Patrick, and Patricia Mallory; she creates a love-filled home that attracts Mark Underwood; she secretly nurses a fear that a lump in her breast may be cancerous in David Lodge's *The Picturegoers*.

Jane Mallory   Anthony Mallory's enigmatic, left-lean-ing wife and Nell Randall's sister; she had a brief Oxford romance with Daniel Martin before marrying Anthony; she cuts all ties with Dan after his divorce from Nell; travelling down the Nile with Dan after Anthony's death, she reluctantly renews their friendship and love in John Fowles's *Daniel Martin*.

Patricia Mallory   The somewhat alienated teenaged daughter of Tom and Elizabeth Mallory and sister of Clare Mallory; she wants to be a writer and develops an innocent crush on Mark Underwood, though she remains loyal to Clare in David Lodge's *The Picturegoers*.

Patrick Mallory   The young teenaged son of Tom and Elizabeth Mallory and younger brother of Patricia and Clare Mallory; he is just awakening to sexuality and is approached by a homosexual at the Palladium in David Lodge's *The Picturegoers*.

Paul Mallory   The glum, pedantic schoolboy son of Anthony and Jane Mallory in John Fowles's *Daniel Martin*.

Rosamund Mallory   Anthony and Jane Mallory's older daughter; she helps Daniel Martin persuade Jane to go to Egypt with him in John Fowles's *Daniel Martin*.

Tom Mallory   An easy-going car salesman, who is the Catholic-convert husband of Elizabeth Mallory and father of eight children, including Clare, Patrick, and Patricia Mallory; he is feeling some mid-life urges but still loves his family in David Lodge's *The Picturegoers*.

Captain Mallow   Efrafan rabbit killed by a fox that Bigwig decoyed away from Hazel's band in Richard Adams's *Watership Down*.

Miss Mallow   Typist who works with Gregory Vigil for the Society for the Regeneration of Women in John Galsworthy's *The Country House*.

Mr. Mallow   Constable and choir-member in Mary Webb's *The House in Dormer Forest*.

Giles Mallow   Tom's younger brother, who has remained at the impoverished Shropshire family estate and become engaged to Tom's old girlfriend's younger sister while Tom has gone off to Africa in Barbara Pym's *Less Than Angels*.

Naomi Mallow   Tom's eccentrically untidy widowed mother, an avid gardener, who lives on her run-down estate with her brother and younger son in Barbara Pym's *Less Than Angels*.

Tom Mallow   Twenty-nine-year-old, attractive, impoverished upper-class bachelor anthropologist who retains a tenderness for his tweedy childhood sweetheart, Elaine, although he is the somewhat careless live-in lover of Catherine Oliphant and the simultaneous beau of Dierdre Swan; he is finishing his doctoral thesis and engaged in field work in Africa in Barbara Pym's *Less Than Angels*.

Malone   The writer, who is telling stories to pass the time before he dies; his life will end when his story is finished — unless he runs out of paper or pencils — in Samuel Beckett's *Malone Dies*.

Julian Malory   Fortyish, ascetic, apparently celibate vicar of the high Anglican, Victorian-gothic St. Mary's, Mildred Lathbury's local church; he surprises the circle of "excellent" churchgoing women, including his sister and the heroine herself, by becoming engaged in Barbara Pym's *Excellent Women*. He appears as a guest preacher in *A Glass of Blessings*.

Winifred Malory   Older sister of the vicar; she is an eager, sentimental, selfless spinster devoted to good causes and "making a home" for her brother; she sometimes desperately depends upon her friendship with Mildred Lathbury in Barbara Pym's *Excellent Women*.

Mrs. Maltese   A friend who gives evidence against Fleur Forsyte Mont in the libel suit in John Galsworthy's *The Silver Spoon*.

Humphrey Maltravers   A government official who marries Margot Beste-Chetwynde for her money and social status; he helps get Paul Pennyfeather out of prison in Evelyn Waugh's *Decline and Fall*.

Lily, Lady Malvezin   Wife of a liberal peer; she gossips about Lady Barbara Carádoc's love affairs in John Galsworthy's *The Patrician*.

The Man   Helen's husband, who beats up Colin Pasmore to keep him away from his wife in David Storey's *Pasmore*.

Managa   Runi's sworn enemy; Mr. Abel joins his tribe after Rima's death in W. H. Hudson's *Green Mansions*.

Manager of the Banco Ejidal in Oaxaca   Official who tells Sigbjorn Wilderness that Juan Fernando Martinez, whom Sigbjorn has come to Mexico to see, died six years earlier in Malcolm Lowry's *Dark as the Grave Wherein My Friend Is Laid*.

Rosie Manasch   A lively Jewish heiress whose exoticism seems out of place at the debutante dances in

Anthony Powell's *A Buyer's Market*. Twice widowed, she resumes her maiden name and has become the anonymous backer of *Fission* and a society hostess for cultural events; she takes up Odo Stevens and withdraws her support of *Fission* in *Books Do Furnish a Room*. She marries Stevens in *Temporary Kings*.

Flora Manby   The frivolous and shallow girlfriend of Rico Carrington in D. H. Lawrence's *St. Mawr*.

Toni Mandel   Anton Hesse's possessive Austrian mistress in Doris Lessing's *A Ripple from the Storm*.

Mrs. Mander   A gossipy, sociable, party-giving, unwise woman; she worries openly about Rita while she gloats about her daughter Valerie's American fiancé in Beryl Bainbridge's *The Dressmaker*.

Valerie Mander   An outgoing, generous, somewhat spoiled girl with an American fiancé; she is patronizingly kind to Nellie and Rita in Beryl Bainbridge's *The Dressmaker*.

Miss Manders   The companion to Eliza Mowbray; she is a friend to Nigel, Rudolph, and Malcolm Mowbray in Ivy Compton-Burnett's *A Father and His Fate*

Sir Edwin Manders   Wealthy businessman and pious Catholic, whose serene life has become a series of religious retreats; he is father of Laurence Manders in Muriel Spark's *The Comforters*.

Ernest Manders   Sir Edwin Manders's homosexual brother; he and Eleanor Hogarth are partners in a floundering dance studio in Muriel Spark's *The Comforters*.

Helena, Lady Manders   Daughter of Louisa Jepp, wife of Sir Edwin Manders, and mother of Laurence Manders; she seeks to effect a reconciliation between her son and Caroline Rose in Muriel Spark's *The Comforters*.

Laurence Manders   Former lover of Caroline Rose; her conversion to his faith (Roman Catholicism) has ended their sexual relationship, although their affectionate reliance on each other persists in Muriel Spark's *The Comforters*.

Geoffrey Manifold   Young research assistant, colleague, and admirer of Prudence Bates in Barbara Pym's *Jane and Prudence*.

The Man in the Macintosh   Mysterious figure who appears in several episodes in James Joyce's *Ulysses*.

Merode Manley   Student at the state educational institute for women whose brief disappearance causes considerable consternation in Henry Green's *Concluding*.

Olive Mannering   Granddaughter of the poet Percy Mannering, indulgent friend of Eric Colston, and paid object of Godfrey Colston's ritualistic but unexacting sexual perversions; she unexpectedly elopes with the aged and deaf but well-to-do Ronald Sidebottome in Muriel Spark's *Memento Mori*.

Percy Mannering   Aged and out-of-fashion but still impassioned poet, who continues to be inspired by life in Muriel Spark's *Memento Mori*.

Daphne Manners   A sensitive, open-hearted young Indian-born Englishwoman, who returns to India from England after the death of her parents; she lives with Lady Chatterjee, an old friend of her one remaining relative, Lady Manners; her tender, gradual love affair with the England-educated Hari Kumar is happy until they are assaulted by several Indians, who knock Hari unconscious and rape Daphne; Hari is unjustly imprisoned for the rape, and Daphne dies giving birth to, she believes, Hari's daughter in Paul Scott's *The Jewel in the Crown*.

Ethel, Lady Manners   Widow of the ex-governor of the province and still an influential member of the British Raj; as Daphne Manners's aunt, she takes a personal interest in the charges against Hari Kumar, Daphne's lover and probable father of her child in Paul Scott's *The Jewel in the Crown*. Daphne having died in childbirth, Lady Manners raises the child; she is instrumental in getting Hari Kumar's case reviewed by Captain Nigel Rowan, ADC to the provincial governor, in *The Day of the Scorpion*. She appears in *The Towers of Silence* and in *A Division of the Spoils*.

Parvati Manners   The daughter of Daphne Manners and probably of Hari Kumar, Daphne's rape making the question possible; Daphne having died giving birth to the child, she is entrusted to the care of her great aunt Lady Manners in Paul Scott's *The Jewel in the Crown*. Her education and development are touched on in *The Day of the Scorpion*, in *The Towers of Silence*, and in *A Division of the Spoils*.

Ruth Manners   A young society girl whom Donovan Anderson dates after breaking up with Martha Quest in Doris Lessing's *Martha Quest* and in *A Proper Marriage*.

Mannie   The groom in the Mason household; he discovers the fire in Pierre Cosway's bedroom in Jean Rhys's *Wide Sargasso Sea*.

Miss Manning French teacher and inamorata of Mr. Carew at Sammy Mountjoy's school in William Golding's *Free Fall*.

Mr. Manning Handsome, talkative civil servant; he worships women as objects of beauty, not as people in H. G. Wells's *Ann Veronica: A Modern Love Story*.

Mr. Manning London journalist neighbor of Mr. Britling; he hides from Colonel Rendezvous's fitness hikes in H. G. Wells's *Mr. Britling Sees It Through*.

Lady Manningtree Short, good-humored, unpretentious woman who receives Lady Barbara Wellesley when the *Lydia* reaches home in C. S. Forester's *The Happy Return*.

Peter Kinloch, Lord Mannour Chief advisor to Lord Snowdoun (Minister of Scotland); he is the father of "Jock" Kinloch and sole trustee of Miss "Kirsty" Everdale's estate; he entrusts Anthony Lammas with the dangerous and delicate task of preserving Lord Belses from harm in John Buchan's *The Free Fishers*.

Man on Putney Hill (Artilleryman) Soldier who first meets the anonymous narrator after freakishly surviving the massacre at Horsell Common; he encounters him again in London, where the soldier outlines his pipedream of building an underground resistance movement to counter Martian rule in H. G. Wells's *The War of the Worlds*.

Mrs. Manresa Boisterous, jolly, crass woman of questionable background married to a wealthy Jew; she has a secret affair with Giles Oliver; she and her other "friend", William Dodge, arrive unannounced at Pointz hall on the day of the village pageant; she fancies herself Queen Elizabeth in the historical play in Virginia Woolf's *Between The Acts*.

Christopher Mansel Eye specialist who performs surgery for Lewis Eliot's detached retina in C. P. Snow's *The Sleep of Reason*. He saves Lewis Eliot's life when his heart stops during a second surgery on his eye in *Last Things*.

Ahmed Mansour Soldier and sergeant who accompanies Robert Winter into the desert; he is sympathetic to Winter's grief over Osman's death in P. H. Newby's *A Journey to the Interior*. He is a student of agriculture at Fouad University; he invited Edgar Perry to the ill-fated picnic in P. H. Newby's *The Picnic at Sakkara*.

Manus ("The Brother") Con man who invents, among other fantastic schemes and concoctions, the "gravid water" that causes Mr. Collopy's enormous weight gain in Flann O'Brien's *The Hard Life*.

The Man Who Died The Christ-like figure that rises from the grave, renounces abstract love and self-sacrifice, and travels to Egypt to have a sexual affair with the priestess of Isis, who takes him for the lost Osiris in D. H. Lawrence's *The Escaped Cock*.

Cissie Mapes Small-boned variety artist with little talent who manages to fit into a box that figures prominently in Nick Ollanton's illusionist act; she sleeps with her employer, who does not return her love; she seeks sympathy from an understanding Dick Herncastle in J. B. Priestley's *Lost Empires*.

Francis Maple Secretary of the Dolligner Society, a group of liberal Catholics whose meeting Adam Appleby attends in David Lodge's *The British Museum Is Falling Down*.

Elizabeth Mapp Malicious busybody despised and feared by her Tilling neighbors; her vigilant observations assist her matrimonial campaign upon Major Benjamin Flint in E. F. Benson's *Miss Mapp*. She is unseated after a long struggle with Lucia Lucas as Tilling's dominant social force but compensates by becoming engaged to Flint in *Mapp and Lucia*. As Mrs. Mapp-Flint she continues her combat with Lucia in *The Worshipful Lucia*. Mayor Lucia appoints her Mayoress to keep an eye on her, but Mrs. Mapp-Flint has occasional successes, handily defeating Georgie Pillson in a Town Council election; she triumphs in being recognizably portrayed in Irene Coles's prizewinning satiric painting in *Trouble for Lucia*.

Miss Marathon A partner in Lesbia Firebrace's school; she is a precise, kindly, critical teacher of mathematics in Ivy Compton-Burnett's *Two Worlds and Their Ways*.

Rae Marcable (Rosie Markham) Charismatic yet remote musical-comedy star; by rejecting her childhood sweetheart, Albert Sorrell, she sets the scene for his murder in Josephine Tey's *The Man in the Queue*.

Marcel Manager of the theatrical company and longtime friend and agent for the actress Rose Vibert Dillingham in David Garnett's *Aspects of Love*.

Marcel Haitian hotel manager for Brown's mother; he is also her lover and a one-third owner of the Trianon; he sells his share to Brown and hangs himself in Graham Greene's *The Comedians*.

Charles March Jewish barrister from a wealthy family; he befriends Lewis Eliot during their law examinations, introduces Eliot to influential people to advance Eliot's career, abandons the law to study medicine in 1930, and sends Eliot to a good physician to diagnose his strange illness in C. P. Snow's *Time of Hope.* He defies his father to give up the law and study for medicine, marries Ann Simon against his father's wishes, and completely alienates his father and loses his inheritance when he refuses to ask Ann to prevent the political ruin of Sir Philip March in *The Conscience of the Rich.* He examines Sheila (Knight) Eliot's body after her suicide and offers to sign a certificate that she died of natural causes; he attends the delivery of Charles Eliot's birth in *Homecomings.* He advises Lewis Eliot on the seriousness of Francis Getliffe's disease in *Last Things.*

David March   Barrister who defends Mrs. Underwood and Julian Underwood at the trial challenging the will of Mr. Massie in C. P. Snow's *In Their Wisdom.*

Gerald Haveleur March   Brooding, alcoholic "cavalier of low creatures" who reaches his nadir and finally commits suicide after a brief reunion with his twin sister, Iris Storm, whom he hates passionately for her role in the death of his pre-World War I idol, Boy Fenwick, in Michael Arlen's *The Green Hat.*

Katherine March   Daughter of Leonard; she defies her father to marry the gentile Francis Getliffe, wins back her father's affection, and joins her family in vowing to snub Charles March when he refuses to save Sir Philip March's political career in C. P. Snow's *The Conscience of the Rich.* She sends a telegram with news of her husband's death to Lewis Eliot in *Last Things.*

Leonard March   Retired Jewish banker, who is the wealthy father of Charles and Katherine; he overcomes his disapproval of Francis Getliffe as husband of Katherine; he is extremely disappointed when Charles gives up the law to become a doctor and is furiously unhappy when Charles marries Ann Simon; he disinherits Charles when Charles refuses to intervene with Ann to save Sir Philip March's political career in *The Conscience of the Rich.*

Nellie March   A "manly" woman who lives with her lover Jill Banford on a sterile chicken farm during World War I; she is mesmerized by an intruder, the soldier Henry Grenfel, whom she identifies with the fox that preys on the chickens; after Grenfel kills Banford, March marries him but remains troublingly unfulfilled by her erotic destiny in D. H. Lawrence's *The Fox.*

Sir Philip March   Parliamentary Secretary who is the elder brother of Leonard; he made money from privileged information in 1929 government defense con-

tracts; he asks help from Leonard to persuade Ann Simon to prevent further publication of embarrassing information, and loses his government position in C. P. Snow's *The Conscience of the Rich.*

Kenneth Marchal (Ken) Toomey   Self-educated, middle-class, British writer of novels and plays, who achieves fame and wealth for his work but not critical acclaim; persecuted and disdained for his notorious homosexuality and atheism, he remains an expatriate through most of his life, although more ascetic than libertine; his greatest fame comes from his family connection to Carlo Campanati in Anthony Burgess's *Earthly Powers.*

Marchant   Director of the Toybrook Industrial Complex, the institute where he and Felix Charlock labor to construct the android of Iolanthe Samiou in Lawrence Durrell's *Nunquam.*

Marchant   Christopher Tietjens's old nurse, who cares for Christopher's son, Tommie Tietjens, in Ford Madox Ford's *Some Do Not. . . .*

Lord Marchmain   Wealthy, aristocratic head of the Flyte family, who became a convert to Roman Catholicism upon his marriage; he leaves his wife and family after serving in World War I and moves to Italy, where he lives with a mistress; Lady Marchmain having died and politics on the Continent in turmoil, he returns to his English country house in failing health; on his deathbed he makes a sign of repentance in Evelyn Waugh's *Brideshead Revisited.*

Lady Marchmain   The deeply religious Roman Catholic mother of the Flyte family; the demands of her piety drive away her husband and two of her children, Julia and Sebastian Flyte, in Evelyn Waugh's *Brideshead Revisited.*

Marcias   Helena's tutor when she is a young princess in Britain; later he becomes a popular Gnostic philosopher on the Continent in Evelyn Waugh's *Helena.*

Alfred Marcon   The nephew of Charity and Stephen Marcon; he is hired as a tutor to the Ponsonby sons; later, having become a companion to Sabine Ponsonby, he believes that he will inherit her money in Ivy Compton-Burnett's *Daughters and Sons.*

Charity Marcon   The spinster twin of the physician Stephen Marcon; she does research at the British Museum and writes biographies in Ivy Compton-Burnett's *Daughters and Sons.*

Stephen Marcon   An obscure country doctor who wanted to be a medical researcher; he treats Sabine

Ponsonby at the end of her life in Ivy Compton-Burnett's *Daughters and Sons*.

Sir Marcus   Aged millionaire armaments-maker and owner of Midland Steele; he manufactures a war-scare by contriving the assassination of the Minister for War in Middle Europe but is murdered by his hired assassin James Raven in Graham Greene's *A Gun for Sale*.

Lewis Mardin   Courteous, persistent Jewish entrepreneur in Paris; he persuades Sophia Baines Scales to sell to him her much-prized boarding house when illness forces her to leave it in Arnold Bennett's *The Old Wives Tale*.

Margaret   Nicholas Urfe's downstairs neighbor in London; she introduces him to Alison Kelly in John Fowles's *The Magus*.

Margaret   One of Wilfred Barclay's former mistresses; she puts him to great trouble and expense to retrieve his sexually indiscreet letters in William Golding's *The Paper Men*.

Margaret   A sweet young girl who claims in her hallucinatory voice to be in love with Gilbert Pinfold in Evelyn Waugh's *The Ordeal of Gilbert Pinfold*.

Sister Margaret   Head of the convent where Caithleen Brady and Bridget Brennan attend school; her strict rules contribute to Caithleen and Bridget's decision to get themselves expelled in Edna O'Brien's *The Country Girls*.

Archie Margolin   A Jewish former salesman and Dan Boleyn's roommate; he kicks Dan out of their flat and replaces him as Zagreus's pupil in Wyndham Lewis's *The Apes of God*.

Margrit   Clever, ambitious, six-foot, blonde Austrian au pair girl who stayed with Anthony and Babs Keating for a time in Margaret Drabble's *The Ice Age*.

Maria   Mother of Brigitta from her single liaison with the whiskey priest in Graham Greene's *The Power and the Glory*.

Maria   Young prostitute at the Farolito with whom Geoffrey Firmin has sex in Malcolm Lowry's *Under the Volcano*.

Maria   Kate Brown's grandfather's housekeeper in Lourenco Marques in Doris Lessing's *The Summer Before the Dark*.

Maria   Maurice Conchis's Greek housekeeper at Bourani in John Fowles's *The Magus*.

Maria   Kate Leslie's servant in D. H. Lawrence's *The Plumed Serpent (Quetzalcoatl)*.

Marie   A Swiss Girl who fills in for Anya and Silvia while they are away from the hotel, thus taking over their roles of nurse to Kate Brown in Doris Lessing's *The Summer Before the Dark*.

Sister Marie Augustine   One of the nuns who genuinely care for Antoinette Cosway in the convent in Jean Rhys's *Wide Sargasso Sea*.

Marigold   Roger Saxe's mistress, a beautiful woman of thirty, in Iris Murdoch's *The Black Prince*.

Marina   Lecturer in Italian at Kent University; her friend Kate Fletcher Armstrong envies her for having a "proper job" in Margaret Drabble's *The Middle Ground*.

Mario   Neapolitan manservant to the sensual Eddy Monteith; he bathes his master and orders his dinner at the English Embassy in Pisuerga in Ronald Firbank's *The Flower Beneath the Foot*.

Helen Mariot   Wife of the British consul in Srem Panh; she helps to look after Meg Eliot when Bill Eliot is killed and does not get along well with Meg in Angus Wilson's *The Middle Age of Mrs. Eliot*.

Jimmie Mariot   British consul who looks after Meg Eliot when Bill Eliot is killed in Srem Panh in Angus Wilson's *The Middle Age of Mrs. Eliot*.

Constantine Maris   Greek agent in Athens who supplies Sir Edward Leithen with a boat, arms, and a crew in John Buchan's *The Dancing Floor*.

Marjorie   Widowed friend of Letty Crowe; her engagement to Father David Lydell upsets Letty's retirement plans in Barbara Pym's *Quartet in Autumn*.

Marjorie   Brenda Last's elder sister, who lives in London and acts as confidante and alibi for Brenda in her adultery in Evelyn Waugh's *A Handful of Dust*.

Dr. Marjorie   The narrator's sensible lover; she deserts him because he drives her away in Len Deighton's *Spy Story*.

Marjory   Miriam's sister, who joins her in her live-in affair with Daniel Martin in John Fowles's *Daniel Martin*.

Mark   A World War II veteran who is an Oxford friend of Andrew Randall in John Fowles's *Daniel Martin*.

Mark   A member of *Lilith*'s staff with whom Jane Somers's niece Jill moves in; Jane respects and admires Mark in Doris Lessing's *The Diaries of Jane Somers*.

Mark   Handsome, rude friend of Joe Lampton and close friend and family connection of Susan (Brown) Lampton in John Braine's *Life at the Top*.

Markey   Butler who works for Major Winton in John Galsworthy's *Beyond*.

Father Markey   Priest in charge of the Mission and the Concert; he dislikes Tarry Flynn and refuses to let him help with either event, keeping Tarry from being with his hoped-for girlfriend, Mary Reilly, in Patrick Kavanagh's *Tarry Flynn*.

Mrs. Markey   Wife of Markey; she cooks for Major Winton in John Galsworthy's *Beyond*.

Dorothy Markham   Debutante who lives at the May of Teck Club in 1945; she becomes a model-agency owner years later in Muriel Spark's *The Girls of Slender Means*.

Mrs. Marks (Mother Sugar)   Anna Wulf's psychoanalyst, to whom Anna unconsciously answers when attempting to justify or explain her feelings and actions; Mrs. Marks constantly attempts to help Anna see herself as an artist in Doris Lessing's *The Golden Notebook*.

Marl   A top representative for Planet 8 who helps invent an ice house; he acts as an inspiration for others, as well as a model of self-discipline in Doris Lessing's *The Making of the Representative for Planet 8*.

Marlan   The savagely cruel chief of the Homo sapiens tribe that triumphs over the Neanderthals in William Golding's *The Inheritors*.

Marleen   The maid/nanny of Rosamund Stacey and of Beatrice; she tells the girls about her romance with a park gardener and leaves the girls to play in the park while she visits with the gardener in Margaret Drabble's *The Millstone*.

Tom Marling   Judith (Gardner) King's ex-lover, with whom she renews her acquaintance in an effort to get even with her husband, Orlando King, after one of his numerous affairs in Isabel Colegate's *Orlando King*.

Francis Marloe   A self-styled psychoanalyst, struck off the medical registry for prescription-writing abuse; he is the homosexual brother of Christian Evandale in Iris Murdoch's *The Black Prince*.

Marlow   Garrulous narrator in Joseph Conrad's *Lord Jim* and in *Chance: A Tale in Two Parts*.

Brenda Marlow   A pretty young girl "aware of her own novelty" who applies for a job at Corker's employment agency and offends Corker with her impertinence and romantic notions regarding prospective employers in John Berger's *Corker's Freedom*.

Nicholas Marlow   Thirty-five-year-old, romantic, handsome production engineer and, as Sidney Arthur Ferning's replacement, the new manager of Spartacus's Milan office; a secret idealist, he reluctantly becomes involved in industrial-military espionage and then willingly becomes a double agent for the Zaleshoffs after being beaten by OVRA thugs in Eric Ambler's *Cause for Alarm*.

Dr. Marlowe   Family physician to the Gavestons in Ivy Compton-Burnett's *A Family and a Fortune*.

Brian Marlowe   Teenaged son of January Marlowe, temporarily orphaned by his mother's plane crash in Muriel Spark's *Robinson*.

January Marlowe   Catholic convert and journalist, stranded on the island of Robinson after a plan crash; she is the only woman in a group of three men and a boy in Muriel Spark's *Robinson*.

Lester Marlowe   Priscilla's brother, who has intellect, individuality, and eccentric charm; of his legitimate kindred, he is acquainted only with Daniel and Graham Sullivan in Ivy Compton-Burnett's *Parents and Children*.

Priscilla Marlowe   The eldest illegitimate daughter of Sir Jesse Sullivan; she lives in a cottage on the estate but is not received at the main house in Ivy Compton-Burnett's *Parents and Children*.

Susan Marlowe   The youngest Marlowe sibling; the Marlowe children are supposedly all orphans from South America whose late parents were Sir Jesse Sullivan's friends in Ivy Compton-Burnett's *Parents and Children*.

Dain Maroola   Malayan rajah, hunted by the Dutch for smuggling gunpowder, who promises to help Kaspar Almayer find his gold mine but elopes with Almayer's daughter, Nina, in Joseph Conrad's *Almayer's Folly: A Story of an Eastern River*.

Jane Marple   Intuitive, sharp-minded, and observant seventy-four-year-old spinster, who solves the murder of Colonel Lucius Protheroe in *The Murder at the Vicarage*. She applies her knowledge of village life in St.

Mary Mead to the solution of murder in ten other novels before, considerably aged, she employs her fondness for seemingly innocent gossip to solve an eighteen-year-old mystery in *Sleeping Murder.*

Captain James Marpole   Captain of the *Clorinda*; he seems an "ideal children's captain" but is actually a liar and a coward; he hides his cowardice with false accusations against the pirates in Richard Hughes's *A High Wind in Jamaica.*

Sylvia Marriott   A witness who testifies at Harriet Vane's trial for Philip Boyes's murder; she tells Lord Peter Wimsey that she thinks Norman Urquhart is the murderer in Dorothy L. Sayers's *Strong Poison.*

Mr. Marsden   Stoic ranking stategist to whom Hornblower reports with captured French papers; Marsden listens to Hornblower's plan to deceive French forces in C. S. Forester's *Hornblower And the Crisis: An Unfinished Novel.*

Marsh   One of the better gunners aboard the *Sutherland* in C. S. Forester's *Ship of the Line.*

Hilary Marsh   A spy friend of Margaret Patten; she works in the foreign office and is interested in finding out about Colin Coldridge's connections with the Soviet Union in Doris Lessing's *The Four-Gated City.*

Arlena Marshall   Glamorous, man-hungry woman; Hercule Poirot's perception of her as a type of victim is borne out by her murder in Agatha Christie's *Evil Under the Sun.*

Charlie Marshall   Cocaine-smoking Indocharter Aviation Company pilot and occasional C.I.A. operative; he helps Lizzie Worthington convince Drake Ko not to assassinate Tiny Ricardo, is blackmailed by Jerry Westerby, and agrees to pilot Sino-Soviet double agent Nelson Ko out of China in John le Carré's *The Honourable Schoolboy.*

Emma Marshall   Richard Edgeworth's first nurse, who reveals to the family that Grant Edgeworth is Richard's father; she kills Richard when she is bribed and threatened by Sibyl Edgeworth to do so in Ivy Compton-Burnett's *A House and Its Head.*

Captain Kenneth Marshall   Widower who married Arlena Marshall; generous pity was a component of his affection for both wives in Agatha Christie's *Evil Under the Sun.*

Linda Marshall   Kenneth Marshall's daughter; she is full of morbid hatred for her stepmother, Arlena, in Agatha Christie's *Evil Under the Sun.*

Alexander (Sandy) Marshalson   A fast-living young landowner whose death in a racing-car accident brings his younger brother and heir, Henry, home from America in Iris Murdoch's *Henry and Cato.*

Gerda Marshalson   Henry Marshalson's mother, whose preference for his elder brother shaped Henry's personality and career; Henry's quixotic — or retributive — plans threaten her comfort, but Henry at last makes the marital and property decisions of her wishes in Iris Murdoch's *Henry and Cato.*

Henry Marshalson   A second-rate British scholar who teaches in a small college in the United States; inheriting the family estate upon the accidental death of his elder brother, he plans to dispose of it and to live in relative poverty in the States with his brother's supposed mistress, Stephanie Whitehouse, as his wife; her jilting him changes his mind, and he decides instead to marry Colette Forbes and keep the property in Iris Murdoch's *Henry and Cato.*

Ashe Marson   A clergyman's athletic, energetic son, who has supported himself since University by writing detective stories under the pseudonym Felix Clovelly; he goes to Blandings Castle as the manservant of Mr. Peters, who has hired him to recover a valuable scarab in P. G. Wodehouse's *Something New.*

Mrs. Marston   Mother of Edward Marston and mother-in-law of Hazel Woodus; she condemns her son as a condoner of sin when he lives with and cares for Hazel after she is impregnated by Squire Reddin in Mary Webb's *Gone to Earth.*

Anthony Marston   Criminally irresponsible youth; he is an early murder victim in Agatha Christie's *And Then There Were None.*

Edward Marston   Hazel Woodus's husband, a preacher who believes her too childlike to consummate their marriage; he loses his religious faith when Hazel is somewhat willingly seduced by Squire Jack Reddin after Reddin's earlier attempted rape of her failed; Marston cares for Hazel during her pregnancy; he cannot find beauty — only satanic forces and danger — in nature in Mary Webb's *Gone to Earth.*

Tony Marston   An apprentice farmer in Africa appointed by Charlie Slatter to work on Richard Turner's farm; he finds Moses and Mary Turner together and ultimately discovers Mary's corpse in Doris Lessing's *The Grass Is Singing.*

Marta   Peasant wife of former priest Leon Rivas; she faithfully follows him during the kidnapping of the

Honorary Consul in Graham Greene's *The Honorary Consul.*

Marty Martello   American C.I.A. liaison to British Secret Service; he allegedly works with London Station agents to bring off Operation Dolphin but actually calls for Jerry Westerby's assassination and plots with fellow agents to replace George Smiley with Saul Enderby in John le Carré's *The Honourable Schoolboy.*

Edgar Marten   Young Jewish minerologist who competes with Denis Phipps for Angelina's affections in Norman Douglas's *South Wind.*

Great-Aunt Martha   Relative who took in Kate Fletcher (Armstrong) and Peter Fletcher when they fled London during the World War II bombings; Kate found her a frightful woman in Margaret Drabble's *The Middle Ground.*

Martians   Cloud-like beings from Mars who invade Earth and battle the Second Men in Olaf Stapledon's *Last and First Men: A Story of the Near and Far Future.*

Martin   Michael and Miriam's son, who is interested in astronomy in David Lodge's *How Far Can You Go?.*

Martin   Sarah Bennett's lover while she is in Paris after graduating from Oxford; he works in a bookstore and speaks perfect French in Margaret Drabble's *A Summer Bird-Cage.*

Martin   A quiet, prideless art dealer whose wife has left him and their infant son; he is in love with Clelia Denham and is a member by courtesy of the Denham household in Margaret Drabble's *Jerusalem the Golden.*

Mr. Martin   A country clergyman; he is the benign but distant father of Daniel Martin in John Fowles's *Daniel Martin.*

Sergeant Martin   Experienced and quick-witted assistant to Adam Dalgliesh in P. D. James's *Cover Her Face* and in *A Mind to Murder.*

Bertha Martin   One of a pair of English sisters and pupils in the Hanover school in Dorothy Richardson's *Pointed Roofs.*

Caroline Martin   Daughter of Nell Randall and Daniel Martin; she has been raised without much contact with Dan or interest in education; she becomes secretary and lover to Bernard Dillon; she finally achieves a good relationship with Dan in John Fowles's *Daniel Martin.*

Charles Martin   French mechanic who died on an

earlier Heron Lloyd expedition to Arabia in Josephine Tey's *The Singing Sands.*

Christopher Hadley ("Pincher") Martin   An officer in the British Royal Navy during World War II; he is the lonely protagonist who is seemingly shipwrecked on a tiny mid-Atlantic island when his ship is supposedly torpedoed in William Golding's *Pincher Martin.*

Daniel Martin   A country clergyman's son, now a middle-aged English playwright and screenwriter in retreat from his past; he has a love affair with actress Jenny McNeil in America; he returns to England for a deathbed visit with his estranged friend Anthony Mallory, who asks him to befriend his wife, Jane Mallory; Daniel takes Jane on a cruise down the Nile, during which they renew their old love for each other in John Fowles's *Daniel Martin.*

Julia Martin   Quiet, inoffensive, strained, anxious thirty-six-year-old former artist's model; divorced (or at least separated) from her husband, she lives on money given to her by various men and drinks to escape the harsh reality of her bedraggled existence in Jean Rhys's *After Leaving Mr. Mackenzie.*

Millie Martin   Daniel Martin's aunt, who raises Daniel in place of his dead mother in John Fowles's *Daniel Martin.*

Odette Martin   Painfully thin, blonde, passionate Frenchwoman and companion of Andre Roux (Verrue) in Eric Ambler's *Epitaph for a Spy.*

Solomon Martin   Sister and fellow pupil of Bertha in Dorothy Richardson's *Pointed Roofs.*

Roddy Martindale   Tedious, chatty homosexual; he serves as the Foreign Office representative to the Intelligence Steering Committee (the "Wise Men") in John le Carré's *Tinker, Tailor, Soldier, Spy* and in *The Honourable Schoolboy.*

Canon Martineau   Howard's brother, a churchman; he participates in the school-board meeting and worries that he will have to help support Howard after he gives away his law practice in C. P. Snow's *Strangers and Brothers.*

Howard Martineau   A solicitor who is partner with Harry Eden and is George Passant's employer but abandons his profession to become a religious tramp; he testifies at Passant's trial for fraud in C. P. Snow's *Time of Hope.* He gives his share of the partnership to Eden, sells the advertising firm to Passant and Cotery, gives them false circulation figures for the circular, and testifies during the trial that he had lied about the circulation figures in *Strangers and Brothers*.

Senor Martinez   The very religious proprietor of a small hotel in rural Spain who tolerates Jeffrey's and Kate Brown's affair only because of his affection for Kate and because of Jeffrey's illness in Doris Lessing's *The Summer Before the Dark*.

Senora Martinez   The wife of the proprietor of a small hotel in the rural part of Spain in Doris Lessing's *The Summer Before the Dark*.

Juan Fernando Martinez   Sigbjorn Wilderness's friend, a Zapotecan Indian in the employ of the Banco Ejidal and an advocate of la vida impersonal; Sigbjorn, having traveled to Mexico in order to meet him, discovers that he has been dead for six years in Malcolm Lowry's *Dark as the Grave Wherein My Friend Is Laid*. He is associated both with Dr. Arturo Vigil and with Juan Cerillo in *Under the Volcano*.

Mother Martinez de la Rosa   Aged abbess of the convent of the Flaming-Hood in Pisuerga who indulges with the other nuns in gossip about Prince Yousef's wedding ceremony in Ronald Firbank's *The Flower Beneath the Foot*.

Rollo Martins   Hack writer of westerns summoned to Vienna after World War II by Harry Lime, the friend he has hero-worshipped since their school days; informed by Colonel Calloway that Lime was a vicious black-marketeer responsible for many deaths, Martins attempts to prove his friend's innocence, only to discover that he too has been betrayed; his eventual shooting of Lime in the sewer underneath the city may be at once an act of mercy and an act of revenge — an act of criminal justice that releases a once-beloved friend from the evil that has infected his soul in Graham Greene's *The Third Man and the Fallen Idol*.

N. Marukakis   Dark, lean Greek newspaper correspondent; a political activist, he supplies Charles Latimer with information about Dimitrios Makropoulos's criminal and espionage activities in 1922–24 and introduces him to Irana Preveza in Eric Ambler's *The Mask of Dimitrios*.

Thomas Marvel   Top-hatted tramp (and later Port Stowe innkeeper) whose aid Griffin forcibly enlists and who later escapes with Griffin's money and the scientific notebooks containing his formula for invisibility in H. G. Wells's *The Invisible Man: A Grotesque Romance*.

Annabel Marvell   Unconventional younger sister of Florence Marvell; she makes a modest and uncertain

living as an actress in Frank Swinnerton's *Some Achieve Greatness*.

Florence Marvell   Fifty-one-year-old successful author and illustrator of children's books and magazine stories; her life has become a routine of drawing the delicate country scenes for her books, tending her cats, and visiting her neighbors; though she does not relish being drawn into the problems of the family members of her new neighbor Sir Roderick Patterson, a man she almost married thirty years ago, nearly everyone she touches is healed in some way; her nomination as one of the Women of the Year comes as no surprise in Frank Swinnerton's *Some Achieve Greatness*.

Marvellous Mister Mars   An Alsatian dog, star of the movies *Red Godfrey's Revenge* and *Five in a Flood*; Jake Donaghue steals him from Sammy Starfield with the intention of exchanging him for the return of a translated novel stolen from Jake but ends by buying Mars from Sammy in Iris Murdoch's *Under the Net*.

Bernard Marx   Highly intelligent human-genetic engineer who becomes enamored of his co-worker Lenina Crowne, taking her to the uncivilized New Mexico reservation where he discovers John Savage; returning to England, he exploits Savage for his advantage in Aldous Huxley's *Brave New World*.

Mary   Jen's sister in Isabel Colegate's *Orlando King*.

Mary   Student at the state educational institute for women whose never explained or resolved disappearance creates violent emotional undercurrents among the other characters in Henry Green's *Concluding*.

Mary   Girfriend of Mick Shaughnessy; her pregnancy is announced in the last line of Flann O'Brien's *The Dalkey Archive*.

Mary   Reggie's lover; she disapproves highly of the rest of the group's becoming involved with the making of bombs and gladly moves out of the house with Reggie in Doris Lessing's *The Good Terrorist*.

Mary-Ann   Hard-working, moral cook, whose friendship developed William Ashenden's propriety; she knew Rosie Driffeld when she was young in W. Somerset Maugham's *Cakes and Ale: Or the Skeleton in the Cupboard*.

Viola Masefield   A lecturer in the English department who has a brief affair with Professor Treece in Malcolm Bradbury's *Eating People Is Wrong*.

Oliver Maskelyne   A British intelligence officer and sworn enemy of the Hosnanis; his suspicion of their anti-British intrigues is at first disbelieved by David Mountolive, who transfers him to Palestine; there he discovers proof that the Hosnanis are supplying guns for the Jews in Lawrence Durrell's *Mountolive*. He dies in World War II in *Clea*.

Mason   Head gardener of Charleswood, the Westons' country estate, in Isabel Colegate's *Statues in a Garden*.

Corporal Mason   A sex-obsessed nineteen-year-old instructor of RAC clerks at Catterick in David Lodge's *Ginger, You're Barmy*.

Mr. Mason   Wealthy Briton who marries Antoinette's mother Mrs. Cosway; he repairs her estate, Coulibri, in Jean Rhys's *Wide Sargasso Sea*. See Jonas Mason in *Dictionary of British Literary Characters 18th- and 19th-Century Novels*.

Mrs. Mason   A hardworking, shrewd boarding-house keeper, whose daughter, Maria, marries Horatio Hornblower in C. S. Forester's *Lieutenant Hornblower*.

Paul Mason   Young banker who is Celia Hawthorne's love for a time; he is a friend of Humphrey Leigh and is involved with Tom Thirkill in international financial dealings in C. P. Snow's *A Coat of Varnish*.

Rachel Mason   The "dark-haired, dark-eyed and energetic" wife of the master builder, though more Mason's "sister than wife" in William Golding's *The Spire*.

Richard Mason   Son of Mr. Mason and stepbrother to Antoinette Cosway; he arranges the marriage between Antoinette and Mr. Rochester in Jean Rhys's *Wide Sargasso Sea*. See Richard Mason in *Dictionary of British Literary Characters 18th- and 19th-Century Novels*.

Roger Mason   The earthy master builder who helps in the pagan sacrifice of the much-abused cathedral servant, Pangall, after committing adultery with his wife, Goody Pangall, while pushing the spire to its limits for Dean Jocelin in William Golding's *The Spire*.

Caduta Massi   A middle-aged Italian actress worried about her cellulite thighs; she is recruited for John Self's movie in Martin Amis's *Money*.

Mr. Massie   Wealthy old man whose death and will are the occasions for legal disputes among his heirs in C. P. Snow's *In Their Wisdom*.

John Massingham   Detective-Inspector and Adam Dalgliesh's unadmiring assistant in P. D. James's *Death of an Expert Witness*. He has become Chief Inspector;

he and Dalgliesh develop mutual respect in *A Taste for Death*.

Masson   The chief Representative for Housing and Sheltering who is Marl's colleague and assists in experiments on how to live in ice houses in Doris Lessing's *The Making of the Representative for Planet 8*.

William Masson   A rich man who was a fellow at Nicholas Herrick's college; he is a man who does not much want to marry a woman, even Emily Herrick, in Ivy Compton-Burnett's *Pastors and Masters*.

Masterman   Sid Pornick's lodger, the tubercular socialist author who lectures Art Kipps on the uselessness of the wealthy classes; he is gratified by Kipps's elopement with working-class Anne Pornick in H. G. Wells's *Kipps: The Story of a Simple Soul*.

Edward Masterman   Samuel Edward Ratchett's valet, who shares Antonio Fascarelli's berth and provides his alibi; Masterman is proved a loyal connection of Daisy Armstrong's family in Agatha Christie's *Murder on the Orient Express*.

Fido Masterman   The muscle-bound physical training instructor at Wandicott House who participates in the kidnaping directed in part by his former army officer Gerry in William Golding's *Darkness Visible*.

Masters   Lieutenant aboard the *Justinian* who pleads with Hornblower not to duel in C. S. Forester's *Mr. Midshipman Hornblower*.

Major Masters   American C.I.A. military agent stationed in northeast Thailand; he neglects to file Jerry Westerby's timely report and ironically welcomes Westerby as a representative of moribund British influence into the club of second-class powers in John le Carré's *The Honourable Schoolboy*.

Conrad Masters   Discreet English surgeon, a "captain of men", who delivers Iris Storm's stillborn child in a dark Parisian prison hospital and cares for her through the resultant complications in Michael Arlen's *The Green Hat*.

Gordon Masters   The slightly crazed head of the English Department at the University of Rummidge; he goes berserk during student demonstrations and resigns, but later escapes from the psychiatric ward to hunt down Morris Zapp in David Lodge's *Changing Places: A Tale of Two Campuses*.

Sergeant Charles Masterson   Handsome, cold-hearted assistant to Adam Dalgliesh; he dislikes his boss and uses questionable methods to get information in P. D. James's *Shroud for a Nightingale*.

Jill Masterson   Auric Goldfinger's secretary; a good-time girl, she is killed when Goldfinger, having discovered her betrayal with James Bond, has her body completely painted with gold, leaving no unpainted skin to "breathe" in Ian Fleming's *Goldfinger*.

Tilly Masterson (alias Soames)   Jill Masterson's Lesbian sister; she tries to avenge Jill's murder but is herself killed by Oddjob in Ian Fleming's *Goldfinger*.

Maston   Minister's Advisor on Intelligence and head of the London espionage agency known as the Circus; of studied appearance, he is nicknamed "Marlene Dietrich"; his sycophantic hypocrisy threatens George Smiley's professional integrity in John le Carré's *Call for the Dead*.

Count Anton Mastrovin   One of the toughest Communists in Europe; a fanatic "maker of revolution", he is part of the present Republican administration of Evallonia in John Buchan's *Castle Gay*. He tries to bully John Galt, "Jaikie", and is killed by Prince John defending the life of the Countess Araminta Troyos in *The House of the Four Winds*.

Matchett   A capable and outspoken woman of unfailing good sense and sound perspective who is now the Quaynes' housekeeper but who previously managed Thomas Quayne's mother's household; she becomes by default both advocate for and adviser to the orphaned Portia Quayne in Elizabeth Bowen's *The Death of the Heart*.

Lillian Matfield   Head secretary in the Twigg and Dersingham firm who is attracted to James Golspie in J. B. Priestley's *Angel Pavement*.

Detective-Sergeant Mather   Officer who traces James Raven through stolen, counterfeit bank notes and, with Anne Crowder's information, kills him in Graham Greene's *A Gun for Sale*.

Reggie Mather   Banker who warns his friend Sir Aylmer Weston about James Horgan in Isabel Colegate's *Statues in a Garden*.

Phillip Mathers   Victim of murder for his money by the narrator and John Divney in Flann O'Brien's *The Third Policeman*.

Henry Matheson   A very conventional Tory relation of Mr. and Mrs. Maynard; he offers Martha Quest a job in his London law firm in Doris Lessing's *The Four-Gated City*.

Herbert Matheson   General manager of the Saddleford Building Society; he joined the company as an office boy and worked his way up to the top; his soon-to-be-vacated position is the cause of intense rivalry among the other executives of the company in Roy Fuller's *Image of a Society*.

Mathew   An old man who works for the Court; he is an informant for Mr. Maynard regarding white men in the Location in Doris Lessing's *A Ripple from the Storm*.

Andrew Mathews   Stella Mathews's Scottish husband, whose family had trouble adjusting to his having married a Jew; he is by nature quieter and more serious than his wife in Doris Lessing's *Martha Quest* and in *A Proper Marriage*.

Esther Mathews   Stella Mathews's infant in Doris Lessing's *A Proper Marriage*.

Harry Mathews   A dedicated teacher at a London school for poor, backward children; he participates in the teachers' delegation to the Soviet Union and returns disappointed in his lack of impact on communist politics in Doris Lessing's *The Golden Notebook*.

Murdoch Mathews   A communist R.A.F. man, who believes that the workers are not capable of education and thus causes Anton Hesse to believe that Murdoch is the victim of capitalist propaganda in Doris Lessing's *A Ripple from the Storm*.

Phil Mathews   A student at the art school where Colin Freestone teaches; he is the boyfriend of Rebecca Newman in David Storey's *A Temporary Life*.

Stella Mathews   A newly married Jewish woman, friendly with Martha Quest and Douglas Knowell in Doris Lessing's *Martha Quest*. She grows apart from them in *A Proper Marriage*.

Michael Mathewson   Insurance investigator whose enquiries concerning a lost ring upset the servants and lead to the climax of Henry Green's *Loving*.

Mr. Mathias   Personable young lawyer; he selects Emily Bas-Thornton to testify against the pirates and coaches her performance in Richard Hughes's *A High Wind in Jamaica*.

Mathilde   Elderly servant to Henry Breasley and wife of Jean-Pierre in John Fowles's *The Ebony Tower*.

René Mathis   James Bond's French counterpart and ally; sensible and humorous, he encourages the recovering Bond in Ian Fleming's *Casino Royale*. He apprehends Rosa Klebb after she has kicked Bond with a poison-tipped blade concealed in her shoe in *From Russia, With Love.*

Tom Mathlong   An imprisoned black leader whom Anna Wulf knew from Mashopi; the now idealistic Marion Portmain wants to help him in Doris Lessing's *The Golden Notebook.*

Matron   Nurse in charge of Clive Ward in John Berger's *The Foot of Clive.*

Matt   Dai Evans's boyhood friend who as a youth led a group of boys, including Dai, in killing a deer in John Berger's *The Foot of Clive.*

Matthew   Man briefly involved with Kate Fletcher Armstrong in Margaret Drabble's *The Middle Ground.*

Matthews   Eldest English seaman aboard the *Marie Galante*; he assumes the position of petty officer in C. S. Forester's *Mr. Midshipman Hornblower.*

Matthews   Servant at Wood Hill in Isabel Colegate's *Orlando King.*

Matthews   Gabriel Denham's homosexual boss, whose flattery and admiration of Gabriel are matter for Denham family mirth in Margaret Drabble's *Jerusalem the Golden.*

Clara (The Countess) Matthews   William's wife, who has sexual affairs with soldiers during World War I and hates her youngest child, Marcus; she dies with her husband in a country hotel during a bombing raid in World War II in Angus Wilson's *No Laughing Matter.*

David Matthews   Lawyer who is consulted about Paul Gardner's case in Isabel Colegate's *Agatha.*

Ethel Matthews   A fortyish, short, fat, deceptive woman; her success in manipulating Anna Morgan produces in Anna a continuing heavy burden of impotence; she sets up shop with Anna to entertain men in Jean Rhys's *Voyage in the Dark.*

George Matthews   A soft-spoken BBC announcer and a casual friend of Rosamund Stacey; he is not driven by intense ambition, nor committed to anything in particular; he is the father of Rosamund's baby in Margaret Drabble's *The Millstone.*

Gladys Matthews   William and Clara's eldest daughter, who tends to be fat; she is successful in business as the owner of an employment agency; she is the lover of London financial tycoon Alfred Pritchard; she loses money gambling, cheats an old German refugee cou-

ple out of money for a painting, and is sent to prison for four years in Angus Wilson's *No Laughing Matter.*

Granny Matthews   William's mother, who quarrels with her grandchildren over a litter of kittens and her dog; she leaves her small estate to Sukey Matthews instead of to her son in Angus Wilson's *No Laughing Matter.*

Marcus Matthews   Youngest child of William and Clara; he is disliked by his mother, who punishes him for bedwetting into his adolescence; a homosexual, he becomes a wealthy collector of art in Angus Wilson's *No Laughing Matter.*

Margaret Matthews   One of twin younger daughters of William and Clara; she becomes a very successful novelist, is remarried after a divorce, and joins brothers Quentin and Rupert on a platform to rally against fascists in Angus Wilson's *No Laughing Matter.*

Quentin Matthews   William and Clara's eldest son, who is wounded in World War I; he gives up tutoring at Oxford to become a London journalist, becomes a critic of communism and fascism, and goes down in an airplane crash en route to Singapore in 1967 in Angus Wilson's *No Laughing Matter.*

Rupert Matthews   Middle child of William and Clara; he becomes a successful stage actor, marries and has two children, joins his sister Margaret and brother Quentin on a stage to oppose fascism, and goes into movies after World War II in Angus Wilson's *No Laughing Matter.*

Sukey Matthews   One of twin younger daughters of William and Clara; she marries Hugh Pascoe and is bitter at God when her youngest and favorite son is killed during the founding of Israel after World War II in Angus Wilson's *No Laughing Matter.*

William (Billy Pop) Matthews   Unsuccessful writer and husband of Clara; he lives on a small annuity, drinks heavily, tolerates his wife's sexual infidelities with soldiers during World War I, fondles and borrows money from his daughter Gladys, and is killed with his wife in a country hotel during a bombing raid in World War II in Angus Wilson's *No Laughing Matter.*

Matumbi   Greedy, lazy, and abused lover of Sergeant Gollup; she extorts gifts from Ajali and Johnson by threatening to tell Gollup they are flirting with her in Joyce Cary's *Mister Johnson.*

Gray Maturin   The virile, simple, and pleasant young man from a good old brokerage family whom the pragmatic Isabel Bradley marries as a better prospect than

Larry Darrell in W. Somerset Maugham's *The Razor's Edge.*

Henry Maturin Gray Maturin's clever, competent, hard-nosed father, whose softer side shows in his love for his son; however, Henry cannot protect his son from the New York Stock Exchange disaster in 1929, which ruins the Maturin family in W. Somerset Maugham's *The Razor's Edge.*

Mr. Matushi An African member of the Social Democratic party who is involved with Martha Quest and other communists in trying to make life better for the Africans in Doris Lessing's *A Proper Marriage* and in *Landlocked.*

Uncle Matvey Katya Orlova's eccentric uncle in John Le Carré's *The Russia House.*

Maud A pupil at Lesbia Firebrace's school who is asked to look after Clemence Shelley; she takes first place in studies in Ivy Compton-Burnett's *Two Worlds and Their Ways.*

Nicola Maude Beautiful girlfriend of Rollo Spencer; she is shy, quiet, cool-acting, and unspoilt in Rosamond Lehmann's *Invitation to the Waltz.* Now the wife of Rollo, she is a frail, sickly woman in *The Weather in the Streets.*

Mr. Maudsley Correct and financially successful father of the Maudsley family in L. P. Hartley's *The Go-Between.*

Mrs. Maudsley Snobbish, interfering mother of the Maudsley family; she forces Leo Colston to disclose his role as go-between and, finally, in an outbuilding on the estate, to witness "two bodies moving like one" in L. P. Hartley's *The Go-Between.*

Denys Maudsley Oldest son of the Maudsley family; he demonstrates athletic prowess and contributes to leisure-class pursuits at Brandham Hall in L. P. Hartley's *The Go-Between.*

Marcus Maudsley Wealthy, early-adolescent classmate of Leo Colston from Southdown Hill School; he invites his less affluent friend to the family's summer estate in L. P. Hartley's *The Go-Between.*

Marian Maudsley A beautiful young woman, daughter of the Maudsleys, whose covert passion for Ted Burgess implicates Leo Colston and brings about the death of her lover and trauma for all at Brandham Hall; Leo sees her as the Virgin of the zodiac in L. P. Hartley's *The Go-Between.*

John Maufe Police officer who, having arrested the Communist Bill Pincomb, is framed by Chester Nimmo and is sent to prison for three years; his case conclusively shows James Latter that Chester Nimmo and his wife cannot be trusted in Joyce Cary's *Not Honour More.*

Alan Maugham Clara's brother who is a chemical-factory worker; though he lives in his native city he rarely sees his mother; Clara prefers him to their elder brother, Arthur, but their affection is limited to mutual good will in Margaret Drabble's *Jerusalem the Golden.*

Albert Maugham Clara's unsympathetic, respectable, hardworking father, moderately successful but obscurely embittered, who was killed on a pedestrian crossing when she was sixteen in Margaret Drabble's *Jerusalem the Golden.*

Arthur Maugham The elder of Clara's brothers; the Maugham family structure is so dilapidated that his emigration to Australia is inconsequential in Margaret Drabble's *Jerusalem the Golden.*

Clara Maugham Highly intelligent, emotionally venturesome young woman whose scholastic ability provides an escape from a restrictive, hateful home; her attraction to the lively, affectionate family of her friend Clelia Denham is a stimulus in her love affair with Gabriel Denham in Margaret Drabble's *Jerusalem the Golden.*

Kathie Maugham Alan's wife, a once-pretty girl admired by Clara Maugham; she has become heavy-hipped and untidy in Margaret Drabble's *Jerusalem the Golden.*

May Maugham Clara's joyless, censorious, undemonstrative widowed mother, whose undeveloped intellectual gifts have brought her no pleasure; her life and impending death are solitary in Margaret Drabble's *Jerusalem the Golden.*

W. Somerset Maugham The perceptive, shrewd narrator, who befriends Larry Darrell in W. Somerset Maugham's *The Razor's Edge.*

Virginia Maunciple Beautiful, childlike mistress of millionaire Jo Stoyte; exploited by him and seduced by Stoyte's physician Dr. Obispo, she remains innocently oblivious of her power over men in Aldous Huxley's *After Many a Summer.*

Maureen The young radical woman who is desperately afraid of growing up to become a replica of her mother — married, close-minded, and conventional;

she rents a room in her house to Kate Brown in Doris Lessing's *The Summer Before the Dark.*

Maureen   One of Gerald's many lovers of whom Emily Cartright is extremely jealous in Doris Lessing's *Memoirs of a Survivor.*

Maureen   Annie Reeves's new Home Help, who never does a proper job in caring for Annie; she steals money from Annie's pension in Doris Lessing's *The Diaries of Jane Somers.*

Maureen   A happy good-time girl whose affair with Bruno Greensleave ended when his wife discovered it in Iris Murdoch's *Bruno's Dream.*

Maurice   Quiet, polite young man in naval uniform; he intently accomplishes his duty of dancing and conversing with the girls in Rosamond Lehmann's *Invitation to the Waltz.*

Gray Mauser   Young poet and lover of Leslie in Muriel Spark's *Loitering with Intent.*

Mavis   Maureen Kirby's sister, whom Maureen views as "stuck with a lot of snotty kids" in Margaret Drabble's *The Ice Age.*

Mavis   The golden-hearted mother-figure for Joe; she provides the most sincere support for the boy's pet goat in Wolf Mankowitz's *A Kid for Two Farthings.*

Stella Mawson   Artist who knows too much about the murder of Edwin Lorrimer; she is murdered in P. D. James's *Death of an Expert Witness.*

Max   A German Swiss in the Natcha-Kee-Tawara Troupe of theatrical performers who work at Houghton's theater in D. H. Lawrence's *The Lost Girl.*

Max   Acquaintance of Penelope and Guy Waring; he is an international currency smuggler in Isabel Colegate's *Orlando at the Brazen Threshold.*

Max   "Incorrigible" friend of Janos Lavin from their Berlin days; he is loved but also detested by Lavin because he continues living in the "no-man's land" of the refugee, where he has "no sense of responsibility towards anything except his past" in John Berger's *A Painter of Our Time.*

Eleanor Maxie   Strong-willed, aristocratic mother of Stephen Maxie and Deborah Riscoe in P. D. James's *Cover Her Face.*

Stephen Maxie   Physician son of Eleanor Maxie and brother of Deborah Riscoe; his engagement to Sally Jupp precipitates her murder in P. D. James's *Cover Her Face.*

Father Maximilian   Jesuit confessor and ally of Sister Alexandra in Muriel Spark's *The Abbess of Crewe.*

Maxwell   Civilian officer in C. S. Forester's *Mr. Midshipman Hornblower.*

C. W. Maxwell   A fresh, blond youth who is acting Divisional Forest Officer and is killed in U Po Kyin's uprising in the jungle in George Orwell's *Burmese Days.*

Clarence Maxwell   Police superintendent who describes the case against Cora Ross and Kitty Pateman to Lewis Eliot in C. P. Snow's *The Sleep of Reason.*

Sidney Maxwell   An American tourist on Persse McGarrigle's tour to the Lake Isle of Innisfree; he confesses that he is the father of Bernadette McGarrigle's child and makes a good settlement for her and the child in David Lodge's *Small World.*

May   James Bond's motherly Scottish housekeeper in Ian Fleming's *From Russia, With Love.* She inveighs against health food in *Thunderball.*

Mr. May   A comic, effeminate, down-at-heel impresario, who becomes a business partner of theater-owner James Houghton in D. H. Lawrence's *The Lost Girl.*

Charles May   An Irishman who writes scientific articles about stars; he is one of Clifford Chatterley's circle of "mental-lifers" at Wragby Hall in D. H. Lawrence's *Lady Chatterley's Lover.*

Ma Hla May   A traditionally beautiful native Burmese girl; she is John Flory's mistress and is the reason for Elizabeth Lackersteen's rejection of Flory in George Orwell's *Burmese Days.*

Edgar Maybrick   Organist at St. John's Church in Pankot; on the night Mabel Layton dies, he accompanies Barbara Batchelor to the hospital morgue so that she can view Mabel one last time in Paul Scott's *The Towers of Silence.*

Diana Maybury   The wife of Maurice Allington's physician; she has an affair with Allington, helps him dig into Dr. Underhill's grave, and leaves Allington and her husband to go off with Allington's wife, Joyce, in Kingsley Amis's *The Green Man.*

Dr. Jack Maybury   Family physician and friend of Maurice Allington; he believes that Allington's visions of the supernatural are hallucinations caused by delirium tremens in Kingsley Amis's *The Green Man*.

Mayden   Lord Raingo's secretary-general; he was previously managing director of a hotel-owning company; he becomes Raingo's confidant in the ministry and later becomes Geoffrey Raingo's confidant when he searches for his father's lost love, Delphine Leeder, in Arnold Bennett's *Lord Raingo*.

Captain E. Maydew   Young Army officer who dances with Helen Bellew at a Pendyce dance in John Galsworthy's *The Country House*.

Mr. Maynard   The town magistrate; he dislikes his wife and is hypocritical as well as cruel in his actions, both private and public in Doris Lessing's *Martha Quest*. He tries to coerce his son Binkie into marrying in order to give his grandson a proper name in *A Proper Marriage* and in *A Ripple from the Storm*. He appears in *Landlocked* and in *The Four-Gated City*.

Binkie Maynard   A popular boy in the town; he treats the Africans with derision and shows an utter lack of responsibility and respect for people in Doris Lessing's *Martha Quest*. He is the father of Masie Gale's child, born while he is off fighting in World War II, in *A Proper Marriage*.

Myra Maynard   A conventional town matriarch, who hates the Africans and is overindulgent towards her spoiled son in Doris Lessing's *Martha Quest*. She constantly attempts to regain her grandchild from its mother, Masie Gale, in *A Proper Marriage* and in *The Four-Gated City*.

Luke Mayne   A Quaker intellectual, also in poor health, who has come to the Sussex farm; he develops an interest in Miriam Henderson in Dorothy Richardson's *Dimple Hill*.

David Mayot   A member of the Whitsuntide house party at Flambard who participates in Professor Moe's experiment to experience a moment of future time and learns the name of the new Prime Minister, Waldemar, a year in advance; during the year he allies himself with Waldemar's programs, but he is defeated when Waldemar changes his positions during the election in John Buchan's *The Gap in the Curtain*.

Fraulein Mayr   German light-opera singer and boarder at Fraulein Schroeder's in Christopher Isherwood's *Goodbye to Berlin*.

Alice McAdam   Scottish spinster and "veteran ballet mistress of the Opera-House" of Cuna-Cuna who over-

sees the erotic dances performed at Madame Ruiz's charity gala in Ronald Firbank's *Sorrow in Sunlight*.

Ravi McAndrews   The handler for monkeys doing simple chores on the *Endeavor*; he first realizes that a chemical plant on Rama is used to create life in Arthur C. Clarke's *Rendezvous with Rama*.

Hugh McBane   Cambridge scientist and younger colleague of Thomas Trelone in Olaf Stapledon's *Sirius: A Fantasy of Love and Discord*.

Mr. McBryde   District Superintendant of Police in Chandrapore, India; he has an affair with Nancy Derek in E. M. Forster's *A Passage to India*.

Maggie McBryde   Feisty, red-headed, middle-aged jobseeker, whom Mr. Corker considers as a possible housekeeper for himself in John Berger's *Corker's Freedom*.

Adam McCaffrey   The undersized eight-year-old son of Brian and Gabriel; he is almost as one with his similarly undersized dog in Iris Murdoch's *The Philosopher's Pupil*.

Alan McCaffrey   The now-deceased husband of Alexandra, whom he left for Fiona Gates; he never saw his youngest son, Tom, after Fiona's death, turning him over to Alexandra for upbring in Iris Murdoch's *The Philosopher's Pupil*.

Alexandra (Alex) McCaffrey   Mother of George and Brian; she retains from girlhood a dormant infatuation for the philosopher Rozanov in Iris Murdoch's *The Philosopher's Pupil*.

Brian McCaffrey   George's slightly younger brother, conventional and easy-going if only in comparison with George in Iris Murdoch's *The Philosopher's Pupil*.

Gabriel McCaffrey   Brian's sentimental, affectionate wife, who likes and assists her very different sister-in-law, Stella McCaffrey, in Iris Murdoch's *The Philosopher's Pupil*.

George McCaffrey   A local celebrity envied and lusted after because he represents liberation from morals; a museum curator who was fired for smashing a valuable glass collection in a fit of rage, he believes that he may have tried to kill his wife; rebuffed in his efforts to seek to reestablish himself with his revered old professor, the philosopher Rozanov, he drowns the suicidally drugged Rozanov and, unsuspected, achieves a degree of serenity in Iris Murdoch's *The Philosopher's Pupil*.

Rufus McCaffrey The long-dead child of George and Stella, who carries the guilt and blame for his accidental death in Iris Murdoch's *The Philosopher's Pupil*.

Stella McCaffrey George's clever and clear-sighted but entirely devoted wife; hospitalized after what may have been his attempt to kill her, she eventually returns home, George having become tractable after his unsuspected drowning of Professor Rozanov in Iris Murdoch's *The Philosopher's Pupil*.

Tom McCaffrey George's half brother, a London University student; the choice of him as a safe husband for Hattie Meynal motivates Rozanov's return to Ennistone; Tom is repudiated by Rozanov but does marry Hattie in Iris Murdoch's *The Philosopher's Pupil*.

Mrs. McCaird Alec Leamas's gossipy landlady, whose stories of Leamas's deterioration spread rapidly in John le Carré's *The Spy Who Came In from the Cold*.

Dr. McCall Cynical Scotchman and friend of Reginald Purfleet; the well-to-do of the district like him better than do the panel patients in Richard Aldington's *The Colonel's Daughter*.

Angus McCandless ("The McCandless") Jacqueline Llewelyn's biological and foster father, a cabbalist and white magician who adopted Jacqueline after her mother, Flora McClintock, committed suicide in Malcolm Lowry's *October Ferry to Gabriola*.

Graham McCintosh Single, physically unattractive, introspective college teacher who rooms with Patrick Standish; he tries unsuccessfully to seduce Jenny Bunn in Kingsley Amis's *Take a Girl Like You*.

Flora Jacqueline McClintock Jacqueline Llewelyn's mother, a Scottish student who had an affair with Angus McCandless while he was separated from his wife; without having told him of her pregnancy, she deposited the baby on his doorstep and committed suicide in Malcolm Lowry's *October Ferry to Gabriola*.

Edna McClusky William's wife and the mother of his children; she is his slave, helping him with his deceptions, letting him stay with her, and supporting his choices in Beryl Bainbridge's *Sweet William*.

William McClusky An exciting charmer, liar, and playwright; from the moment he meets Ann Walton, he is in control of their relationship; Ann finally doubts him, and William loses his power in Beryl Bainbridge's *Sweet William*.

Wally McConnachie Foreign officer and sometime lover of Fleur Talbot in Muriel Spark's *Loitering with Intent*.

Mr. McConnell Large and active editor of the *Hampshire Argus*, which publishes an insulting photograph of Elizabeth Mapp-Flint; Benjy Flint's reconsidered plan of punishment initiates the adventures of the tiger whip in E. F. Benson's *Trouble for Lucia*.

Millie McCraig Scottish widow and long-term British Intelligence operative; she entices Bill Haydon to the safehouse in John le Carré's *Tinker, Tailor, Soldier, Spy*. She eavesdrops for George Smiley during Operation Dolphin in *The Honourable Schoolboy*. She runs the Berne safehouse where Smiley interrogates and blackmails Anton Grigoriev in *Smiley's People*.

Liam McCreedy Persse McGarrigle's head of department at University College, Limerick, in David Lodge's *Small World*.

McCulloch Unassertive secret service technician; with Dennison he helps launch Leclerc's misguided operation in John le Carré's *The Looking-Glass War*.

William McCullum Wreck-master and salvage director of the Coromandel Coast in the East India Company; his expertise is required for the treasure-rescue mission; he is shot in a duel with the ship's surgeon, von Eisenbeiss, who then successfully treats him in C. S. Forester's *Hornblower and the Atropos*.

Mrs. McCunn Dickson McCunn's conventional wife; she is vacationing at a "hydropathic" while her husband pursues adventure in John Buchan's *Huntingtower* and in *The House of the Four Winds*.

Dickson McCunn Middle-aged, retired, adventuresome but sensible Glasgow grocer; with his allies, the high-spirited Gorbals Die-Hards, he defeats the evil Bolsheviks and saves an imprisoned Russian princess, Sakskia, and her jewels and "adopts" all six boys in John Buchan's *Huntingtower*. Aided by Dougal Crombie and John Galt, he prevents violence between two political factions in Evallonia in *Castle Gay*. He determines to help Prince John and guides the Royalist Party and Prince John to the throne, thus restoring the country's peace in *The House of the Four Winds*.

Hugh McFarlane Elizabeth Trant's suitor and later husband in J. B. Priestley's *The Good Companions*.

Mr. McFarline An elderly Scots miner who exploits his African workers and attempts to take sexual advantage of young Martha Quest in Doris Lessing's *Martha Quest*. He resents her and other communists for influencing the Social Democrats in *A Ripple from the Storm*.

Father McGahern Father Austin Brierly's parish priest, who is obsessed with fund-raising in David Lodge's *How Far Can You Go?*.

Bernadette McGarrigle Dr. Brendan O'Shea's Irish niece, who develops a crush on Morris Zapp in *Changing Places: A Tale of Two Campuses*. She has had a baby by Sidney Maxwell and works as a stripper; she meets her cousin, Persse McGarrigle, in the chapel at Heathrow Airport in *Small World*.

Persse McGarrigle The virginal, romantic Catholic lecturer at University College, Limerick; he attends a conference at Rummidge, where he meets Angelica Pabst, whom he then pursues all over the world, with the occasional help of Morris Zapp and Sybil Maiden; he asks the right question of panelists at a Modern Language Association convention in New York, thus restoring Arthur Kingfisher's potency in David Lodge's *Small World*.

Peter McGarrigle A brilliant young scholar engaged to Angelica Pabst; Persse McGarrigle was mistaken for him when he was invited to Limerick for his interview in David Lodge's *Small World*.

McGoff Crew member aboard the *Oediupus Tyrannus* who complains about the food in Malcolm Lowry's *Ultramarine*.

Jimmy McGrath A Scottish, middle-class bomber pilot stationed in Mashopi, who professes to be a communist; he has a homosexual relationship with Paul Blackenhurst in Doris Lessing's *The Golden Notebook*.

Judy McGrath Peter's opportunistic wife; she was involved with the late Joseph Radeechy, is Richard Biranne's lover, and attempts to seduce John Ducane; she elopes to Australia with "Ewan" (Gavin Fivey) in Iris Murdoch's *The Nice and the Good*.

Peter McGrath An office messenger whose self-interested schemes are frustrated; he replaces Gavin Fivey as John Ducane's manservant in Iris Murdoch's *The Nice and the Good*.

Miss McGregor A spinster and the domestic help of Louise and Stephen Halifax; her budgie dies, and she mourns it as if it were her child in Margaret Drabble's *A Summer Bird-Cage*.

Andrew McGrew An even-tempered facilitating corporal in the R.A.F., who balances Anton Hesse's bad temper during their communist meetings in Doris Lessing's *A Proper Marriage*. He marries Maisie Gale in order to give her child a father in *A Ripple from the Storm*. He appears in *Landlocked*.

Mr. McGuffog Sir Archibald Roylance's gamekeeper; he joins his master in the battle to save Sakskia, the Russian princess, in John Buchan's *Huntingtower*.

McGuire Middle-aged, dark, thickset, self-confident lawyer employed by the legal firm that represents Casa Editrice Pacioli, a subsidiary of Syncom-Sentinel; he persuades Robert Halliday to accept the proposed Pacioli-sponsored Luccio (Karlis Zander)-Halliday editorial collaboration on the Nechayev (Russian) memoir in Eric Ambler's *The Care of Time*.

Emily McHugh An underqualified teacher of French in a girls' school, who is partly supported by her lover, Blaise Gavender, by whom she has an eight-year-old son; her sexual power over Blaise makes it impossible for him to do more than pretend to renounce her; she becomes the second Mrs. Gavender after Harriet Gavender's death in Iris Murdoch's *The Sacred and Profane Love Machine*.

Luke (Luca) McHugh The eight-year-old retarded son of Emily McHugh and Blaise Gavender; emotionally repressed, he no longer speaks to his mother at all; he opens up immediately to Harriet Gavender and her dogs; Harriet takes him away with her, and he witnesses her death in the Hanover airport; he regresses altogether and is packed off to an institution by his parents after their marriage in Iris Murdoch's *The Sacred and Profane Love Machine*.

Nurse McInnes Rachel Vinrace's caretaker during her fatal fever in Virginia Woolf's *The Voyage Out*.

Captain James Grant McKechnie Vincent Macmaster's nephew, a dark, handsome, bemedaled officer and Latin Prize man; he suffers from shellshock and problems with his wife; his being put in the care of Christopher Tietjens on the Western Front creates problems for Tietjens in Ford Madox Ford's *No More Parades*. Constantly resentful of being Tietjens's second in command, he survives World War I but goes mad on Armistice Day in *A Man Could Stand Up —*.

Mr. McKecknie A rare-books-store and library owner; he is Gordon Comstock's employer until Comstock is arrested for being drunk and disorderly; McKecknie lets Comstock go but gives him the name of another bookseller who is looking for a clerk in George Orwell's *Keep the Aspidistra Flying*.

Babbie McKelvie Middle-aged housekeeper for Anthony Lammas in John Buchan's *The Free Fishers*.

Flora McLeod Henry Field's governess, who has an

affair with Orlando King in Isabel Colegate's *Orlando King*.

Mrs. McNab   The housekeeper and charwoman who restores the Ramsays' summer house in the Hebrides at the last possible moment before its irrevocable ruin in Virginia Woolf's *To the Lighthouse*.

Jenny McNeil   An intelligent young English actress becoming a film star who has an affair with Daniel Martin while in Hollywood; she embodies Dan's failure fully to engage in any relationship since his Oxford romance with Jane (Mallory); she writes three "contributions" to a novel he plans to write in John Fowles's *Daniel Martin*.

Mrs. McPhillip   Frankie McPhillip's gentle, sympathetic mother, who forgives Gypo Nolan's betrayal in Liam O'Flaherty's *The Informer*.

Frankie McPhillip   Rebel murderer who is killed by the police when his friend Gypo Nolan informs on him in Liam O'Flaherty's *The Informer*.

Mary McPhillip   Attractive, peace-loving office worker who falls in love with Dan Gallagher but is rejected by him in Liam O'Flaherty's *The Informer*.

Gwen, Lady McReith   A thin, overperfumed widow, who is Nicholas Jenkins's fellow houseguest at the Templers'; her dancing with the schoolboy Nicholas has an unsettling effect on him; during the visit she sleeps with Peter Templer in Anthony Powell's *A Question of Upbringing*. She is a Lesbian who runs a female operation that supplies drivers to Belgians or Poles in London during World War II in *The Kindly Ones* and in *The Military Philosophers*.

McWhist   Along with Norton, one of two mountain climbers who encounter John Wainwright in the mountains of Scotland in Olaf Stapledon's *Odd John: A Story Between Jest and Earnest*.

Corker Mead   Charley Summers's employer in Henry Green's *Back*.

Michael Meade   A failed schoolmaster and priest, now leader of the lay community at Imber Court; his homosexual involvement with Toby Gashe precipitates the crisis that results in the dissolution of the community in Iris Murdoch's *The Bell*.

Arthur Meadowes   Emotionally fragile Bonn Embassy Registrar who misguidedly views Leo Harting with love when Harting seduces his daughter, Myra Meadowes; he tries unsuccessfully to revenge himself on Alan Turner for past interrogations in John le Carré's *A Small Town in Germany*.

Felicity Meadowes   Daughter of Robin and Violet Meadowes in David Lodge's *How Far Can You Go?*.

Myra Meadowes   Sexually permissive daughter of Bonn Embassy Registrar Arthur Meadowes; though devastated by a mental breakdown she suffered from Alan Turner's earlier interrogations in Warsaw of her and her family, she is charmed by Leo Harting's gentleness in John le Carré's *A Small Town in Germany*.

Robin Meadowes   Violet Casey's tutor; he seduces and then marries Violet and becomes a classics professor at a northern university, where he has an affair with a student, Caroline, in David Lodge's *How Far Can You Go?*.

Mrs. Meadows   Seemingly upstanding cousin of Bishop Heard; she premeditates the murder of her legal husband, Mr. Muhlen, in Norman Douglas's *South Wind*.

Captain James Meadows   Desperate court-martialed captain; he dies in battle with a French brig in C. S. Forester's *Hornblower And the Crisis: An Unfinished Novel*.

Molly Meakin   Second-generation British Intelligence operative who beds Peter Guillam with surprising passion and assists George Smiley and the C.I.A. in identifying Tiny Ricardo in John le Carré's *The Honourable Schoolboy*.

Philip Meakin   Jonathan Browne's college acquaintance who has become a research assistant much sought after by female students and thus an object of jealousy to Jonathan in David Lodge's *Ginger, You're Barmy*.

Ursula Mecke   German dancer who is sent by Roy Calvert to meet Lewis Eliot when Eliot visits Berlin before the war in C. P. Snow's *The Light and the Dark*.

Dominick Medina   Gifted seductive villain, a poet with satanic pride who covets the subjugation of other men's souls; he masterminds a corrupt crime syndicate, kidnaps three young people of prestigious families, hypnotizes them, and holds them hostage; defeated by Richard and Mary (Lamington) Hannay and "Sandy" Arbuthnot, Medina stalks Richard Hannay at Machray, a deer-forest, determined to kill him, but himself dies on the mountain, again defeated by overweening pride, in John Buchan's *The Three Hostages*.

Felix Meecham   A British army officer, Mildred

Finch's younger half brother, who is in love with Ann Peronett; when it becomes clear that she will not divorce her errant husband, Randall Peronett, he leaves to take up a posting in India and perhaps to marry a French former girlfriend in Iris Murdoch's *An Unofficial Rose.*

Petey Meegan   Peasant-farmer and bachelor who tries to win the hand of Mary Flynn in Patrick Kavanagh's *Tarry Flynn.*

Mr. Meek   Small-shopkeeper who is the best listener in Folly Down in T. F. Powys's *Mr. Weston's Good Wine.*

Mrs. Meer   One of the poor whom Evelyn Morton Stennett tries to help; she is a widow with four grown children in Margaret Drabble's *The Middle Ground.*

Meg   Middle-aged spinster who devotes her social and emotional life to the thankless homosexual Colin and his series of lovers; she is a friend and former publishing colleague of Leonora Eyre in Barbara Pym's *The Sweet Dove Died.*

Considine Meggatt   Uncle of Rodney Meggatt; his once-scandalous affair with Lady Elfrida Tilney is still a subject of gossip in Meggatt-Tilney social circles and a cause of tension and disagreement between their families in Elizabeth Bowen's *Friends and Relations.*

Rodney Meggatt   Nephew of Considine Meggatt and husband of Janet Studdart, whose sister Laurel is married to Edward Tilney, in Elizabeth Bowen's *Friends and Relations.*

Mr. Mehta   An elderly Indian man living on the same floor of apartments as the narrator in Doris Lessing's *Memoirs of a Survivor.*

Mrs. Mehta   Mr. Mehta's wife, a neighbor of the narrator in Doris Lessing's *Memoirs of a Survivor.*

Meinertzhagen   Tory party spokesman who asks Reginald Swaffield to abandon support of Jenny Rastall's challenge to her father's will in C. P. Snow's *In Their Wisdom.*

Friedrech Meister   A German who supposedly disappeared near Tibet about the time that the German monk Meister appeared at Shangri-La; he is researched by Rutherford after Hugh "Glory" Conway's mysterious adventure in James Hilton's *Lost Horizon.*

Mel   An old stonecutter, typical of the common worker, in William Golding's *The Spire.*

Miss Meldrum   A too-friendly if not somewhat med-

dling fellow-guest in the Brighton house where Eve and Miriam Henderson and Harriett (Henderson) and Gerald Ducayne spend their holiday in Dorothy Richardson's *Backwater.*

Mr. Meldrum   Mr. Wetherby's successor as Head of Brookfield; he holds office for three decades, dying suddenly of pneumonia in James Hilton's *Good-bye, Mr. Chips.*

Mrs. Meldrum   F. X. Enderby's landlady; she is a local busybody and snoop, who turns Enderby out of his lodgings because of his slovenly living habits in Anthony Burgess's *Inside Mr. Enderby.*

Colonel Adam Melfort   Hero who has "made his soul" by a selfless act of generosity when he assumed the crime and punishment for his weak wife's forgery, and by unrelenting self-discipline; now embarked on a quest to find leaders of quality and of genius, he gambles his own life to effect in Warren Creevey the change that will redirect his powers toward universal good in John Buchan's *A Prince of the Captivity.*

Camilla Considine Melfort   Adam Melfort's pretty, weak wife, whose debts and expensive habits result in her act of forgery and in Adam's assuming the responsibility and punishment for her crime in John Buchan's *A Prince of the Captivity.*

Nigel Melfort   Adam Melfort's young son, who died of meningitis; his memory combined with the memory of the white sands and blue waters of the island Eilean Ban becomes Adam's only solace in John Buchan's *A Prince of the Captivity.*

Mélisande   Zuleika Dobson's attentive and loyal personal maid in Max Beerbohm's *Zuleika Dobson; or An Oxford Love Story.*

Rosa Mellendip   Astrologer friend of Lynda Coldridge; she also gives Martha Quest her predictions in Doris Lessing's *The Four-Gated City.*

Mr. Melling   An aged office clerk at the factory where Paul Morel works in D. H. Lawrence's *Sons and Lovers.*

Alice Mellings   A thirty-six-year-old "good" terrorist, who is a maternal figure for her group of comrades, constantly revolting against her mother's conventional ways while at the same time employing them; she unsuccessfully attempts to make her group of comrades into a family in Doris Lessing's *The Good Terrorist.*

Cedric Mellings   Alice Mellings's wealthy father, who is unsympathetic to her demands for money and understanding; he is ultimately responsible for kicking Alice and Jasper out of his ex-wife's house in Doris Lessing's *The Good Terrorist.*

Dorothy Mellings   Alice Mellings's middle-class, conventional mother, who is resentful of her daughter's using her university education to do only what Dorothy spent her life doing — cooking and nannying others — in Doris Lessing's *The Good Terrorist.*

Bertha Coutts Mellors   A common, sassy, working-class woman; she is the estranged wife of the gamekeeper, whom she has rendered psychically impotent with her sexual rapacity and willful ways in D. H. Lawrence's *Lady Chatterley's Lover.*

Oliver Mellors   A working-class gamekeeper who protects the remnants of Sherwood Forest on Sir Clifford Chatterley's estate; rendered psychologically impotent by his willful estranged wife, he is restored to phallic power through the ministrations of Lady Chatterley during their sexual unions in Wragby Wood, and in return he helps her achieve psychic rebirth in D. H. Lawrence's *Lady Chatterley's Lover.*

Mrs. Melville   Middle-aged, poor, worn-out mother of Ellen Melville; she prides herself on having pretty arms; she hates political conservatives and patriarchy; she had enjoyed pretending the infant Ellen was a boy as she sang her to sleep using "The Ride of the Valkyries" as a lullaby in Rebecca West's *The Judge.*

Ellen Melville   Typist and suffrage activist in Edinburgh; she is humorous, energetic, determined, and intense; deeply attached to her mother, she grieves after her death; Ellen gradually recognizes her fiancé Richard Yaverland's obsessive attachment to his mother, but both she and he fail to recognize the independence and strength of their mothers in Rebecca West's *The Judge.*

Mark Members   Successful poet, critic, and lecturer who has always succeeded in being slightly ahead of the latest fashion in writing and personal style; at University with Nicholas Jenkins, he is one of Sillery's young men in Anthony Powell's *A Question of Upbringing.* He becomes one of St. John Clarke's secretaries in *The Acceptance World.* He has organized a writers' conference in Venice in 1958 and is the fourth husband of an American journalist in *Temporary Kings.* He receives a prize for poetry in *Hearing Secret Harmonies.*

Hannah Membury   Harrison Membury's chatty wife, who succinctly characterizes Magnus Pym's betrayals for Jack Brotherhood in John le Carré's *A Perfect Spy.*

Harrison Membury   Retired librarian and former British Army Intelligence agent; he connects "Greensleeves" to Axel for Jack Brotherhood and explains why "Greensleeves" was a fraud in John le Carré's *A Perfect Spy.*

Memlik   Sexually perverse Egyptian Minister for Interior; his famous collection of Korans is a cover for his acceptance of bribes; as a sop to the British he arranges the assassination of Narouz Hasnani, who is useless to him, instead of the guilty — but bribe-yielding — Nessim Hosnani in Lawrence Durrell's *Mountolive.* He keeps Justine Hosnani under house arrest until she discovers he can also be bribed by inclusion in European-Alexandrian society in *Clea.*

John Mempes   Partner of Mark Henry Garton; he stays on in the Garton enterprise as an employee of Mary Garton Hansyke after Garton's death; he is elegant in manner and handsome but cynical; he loves Mary but refuses to take her administrative actions seriously because she is young and female; they clash because he wants to continue building clipper ships, while she favors converting the business to steam ships; he becomes her lover, but she suddenly decides to marry Hugh Hervey in Storm Jameson's *The Lovely Ship.*

First Men   Our present human species and its descendants, including two great future civilizations, the World State and the Patagonian culture, in Olaf Stapledon's *Last and First Men: A Story of the Near and Far Future.*

Second Men   A superior form of humanity that arises long after a nuclear disaster destroys the Patagonian civilization of the First Men, and that is itself virtually annihilated by a virus that it uses to repel Martian invaders in Olaf Stapledon's *Last and First Men: A Story of the Near and Far Future.*

Third Men   A diminutive and short-lived human species, especially adept at the biological sciences, that uses genetic engineering to produce the first artificial human beings, the Great Brains (Fourth Men), in Olaf Stapledon's *Last and First Men: A Story of the Near and Far Future.*

Great Brains (Fourth Men)   Highly intelligent but unemotional members of a futuristic human species, each consisting of brain matter that fills a concrete turret, with a pair of hands attached, created through genetic engineering by the Third Men in Olaf Stapledon's *Last and First Men: A Story of the Near and Far Future.*

Fifth Men   A massive and highly developed human species who create a utopian society on Earth but inadvertently cause the planet's destruction and have to migrate to Venus in Olaf Stapledon's *Last and First Men: A Story of the Near and Far Future*.

Sixth Men   A future human race living on Venus, evolved naturally from the Fifth Men; their fascination with flight leads them to create the Seventh (Flying) Men in Olaf Stapledon's *Last and First Men: A Story of the Near and Far Future*.

Seventh (Flying) Men   An avian species of human beings living on Venus who experience spiritual ecstasy while aloft but are unfitted for "pedestrian" life in Olaf Stapledon's *Last and First Men: A Story of the Near and Far Future*.

Eighth Men   A practical-minded form of humanity living on Venus nearly a billion years in the future in Olaf Stapledon's *Last and First Men: A Story of the Near and Far Future*.

Ninth Men   The first human species to live on Neptune in Olaf Stapledon's *Last and First Men: A Story of the Near and Far Future*.

Fourteenth Men   An advanced but imperfect human species living on Neptune in Olaf Stapledon's *Last and First Men: A Story of the Near and Far Future*.

Fifteenth Men   A highly evolved form of humanity living on Neptune in Olaf Stapledon's *Last and First Men: A Story of the Near and Far Future*.

Sixteenth Men   An artificially created human species living on Neptune; they attempt to resolve fundamental philosophical questions and create their own successors, who they hope will reach even higher levels of consciousness in Olaf Stapledon's *Last and First Men: A Story of the Near and Far Future*.

Seventeenth Men   An advanced but unstable Neptunian species of humanity in Olaf Stapledon's *Last and First Men: A Story of the Near and Far Future*.

Last (Eighteenth) Men   The most fully developed human species; its members include the narrator, who speaks to us from Neptune two billion years from now; both superior individuals and members of a group mind, the Last Men are doomed by a cosmic accident in Olaf Stapledon's *Last and First Men: A Story of the Near and Far Future*.

Inspector Mendel (covername: Arthur)   S p e c i a l Branch detective of vaguely Jewish heritage who, following his retirement, assists George Smiley in solving Samuel Fennan's murder by interrogating Adam Scarr and setting a trap for Dieter Frey in John le Carré's

Call for the Dead. He researches background on Thursgood Preparatory School's faculty in *A Murder of Quality*. He helps unearth British Intelligence's traitorous double agent in *Tinker, Tailor, Soldier, Spy*. He gathers information to blackmail Karla into defecting in *Smiley's People*.

Solly Mendelsohn   Gruff, good-hearted journalist and friend of Fleur Talbot in Muriel Spark's *Loitering with Intent*.

Bernard Mendizabal   A Spanish Jew with a disreputable air; Miriam Henderson is attracted to him because of his devil-may-care attitude and his spellbinding talk; she freely fraternizes with him in a way that raises eyebrows in Dorothy Richardson's *Interim*.

Marie Mendrill   Manager of D.'s hotel; an agent of L., she attempts to get D.'s papers from him and kills Else Crole in Graham Greene's *The Confidential Agent*.

Miss Menley   Neighbor of Sylvia Russell; she cares for and teaches Mary Hervey Russell when Sylvia goes on long sea voyages on her husband's ship in Storm Jameson's *Farewell, Night; Welcome, Day*.

Pastuer Mercaptan   Fatuous art critic whose sense of decorum is utterly removed from contemporary sensibilities in Aldous Huxley's *Antic Hay*.

Lieutenant Commander Karl Mercer   Authority on life support and second officer of the *Endeavor*; he first discovers that the atmosphere is breathable in Arthur C. Clarke's *Rendezvous with Rama*.

Lord Mercot   Heir to a dukedom; an Oxford undergraduate, he is kidnapped and held as one of the hostages in John Buchan's *The Three Hostages*.

Eden Mere   Wife of O. V. Mere, public-relations entrepreneur; she joins Owen Tuby and Cosmo Sultan in setting up their office as sellers of images in J. B. Priestley's *The Image Men*.

O. V. Mere   Public-relations man who helps establish Cosmo Sultana and Owen Tuby's credentials as image makers in J. B. Priestley's *The Image Men*.

Anne Meredith   A suspect of the murder of Mr. Shaitana; she is drowned in Agatha Christie's *Cards on the Table*.

Rose Meredith   Housekeeper for Harold and Fay Corrigan and substitute mother for Bryan Morley in David Storey's *A Prodigal Child*.

Otto Mergen   A sinister Czech; he is composer, pianist and manager for Lilly Farris, with whom he shares a taste for voyeurism in J. B. Priestley's *Lost Empires.*

Dr. Merivale   Mr. Chips's physician who reassures Chips that, despite his advanced age, he is fit and past the age when people get horrible diseases and so will die a natural death in James Hilton's *Good-bye, Mr. Chips.*

Merlin   Magician from King Arthur's time kept asleep under a spell; he is sought by the N.I.C.E. (National Institute for Coordinated Experiments) for the use of his magical powers; he allies himself with Elwin Ransom and the St. Anne's community and is empowered by the heavenly forces to defeat the evil N.I.C.E.; he is instrumental in the destruction of the N.I.C.E. in C. S. Lewis's *That Hideous Strength.*

Lord Merlin   The wealthy, eccentric, cultured neighbor whose property is contiguous to Alconleigh, the Radletts' estate; a great art collector with stylish friends, he is detested by Matthew Radlett; he becomes Linda Radlett's devoted friend, buying her a London house when she leaves her first husband; his attentive friendship lasts for years in Nancy Mitford's *The Pursuit of Love.*

Benedicta Merlin   An eerie mixture of evil and goodness; she seduces and marries Felix Charlock for the Firm's purposes in Lawrence Durrell's *Tunc.* She becomes his nurse and supporter in *Nunquam.*

Stephen Merriall   Social columnist for the *Evening Gazette* under the pseudonym Hermione; his and Lucia Lucas's charade of being lovers is the more useful socially because no one takes it seriously in E. F. Benson's *Lucia in London.*

Ronald Merrick   Superintendent of Police in Mayapore, whose courtship Daphne Manners rejects; he vengefully arrests and brutally questions Daphne's lover Hari Kumar in connection with Daphne's rape in Paul Scott's *The Jewel in the Crown.* Though Merrick later resigns from the police to accept a regular commission in the Army, the infamous case follows him wherever he goes; he is unexpectedly Teddie Bingham's best man when Teddie marries Susan Layton; he is badly burned and loses an arm in an unsuccessful attempt to save Bingham after a military ambush in *The Day of the Scorpion.* Though he is married to Susan, his sadistic impulses find release in his sexual exploitation of Indian boys; his savage murder at their hands may have an element of political as well as personal vengeance in *A Division of the Spoils.*

Jack Merridew   A natural hunter, warrior, and dem-

agogue who becomes Ralph's bloodthirsty antagonist in William Golding's *Lord of the Flies.*

Sir Henry Merriman   Barrister who leads the prosecution against the smugglers and loses the case despite the testimony of Francis Andrews in Graham Greene's *The Man Within.*

Mrs. Merry   Charles's mild-looking wife; she waters the marmalade and teaches scriptures at Mr. Herrick's school in Ivy Compton-Burnett's *Pastors and Masters.*

Charles Merry   A tall, thin schoolmaster at Mr. Herrick's school; he teaches the younger boys and does most of the work in Ivy Compton-Burnett's *Pastors and Masters.*

Egbert Merrymarsh   A deceased celebrated novelist, whose unfinished novel *Robert and Rachel* is in the possession of his mistress Amy Rottingdean in David Lodge's *The British Museum Is Falling Down.*

Ada Merton   A good-hearted, stable woman, who becomes Hereward Egerton's wife in Ivy Compton-Burnett's *A God and His Gifts.*

Alfred Merton   Ada's father, a scholar who is a friend of Sir Michael Egerton; he says that Hereward Egerton has not done his part as a husband in Ivy Compton-Burnett's *A God and His Gifts.*

Emmeline Merton   Ada's sister, who goes away when she becomes pregnant by Hereward Egerton; she returns years later with her daughter, Viola, in Ivy Compton-Burnett's *A God and His Gifts.*

Aunt Pauline Merton   Alfred Merton's sister; she is an unmarried woman who brings up Ada and Emmeline Merton when their mother dies in Ivy Compton-Burnett's *A God and His Gifts.*

Mrs. Merton-Vane   A comely, kindly, foolish widow, who marries the Reverend Cleveland Hutton after his wife Sophia dies in Ivy Compton-Burnett's *Dolores.*

Messalina   Claudius's young and beautiful but profligate wife, who dupes Claudius into allowing her to marry one of her lovers and pays for her incontinence and deceitfulness with her life in Robert Graves's *Claudius, the God and His Wife Messalina.*

Dr. Messinger   An explorer who hopes to find a lost city in the South American jungles; he persuades Tony Last to accompany him on the expedition; he is accidentally killed in a boating accident in a remote part of the jungle in Evelyn Waugh's *A Handful of Dust.*

MettyVasidol   A prostitute who saves JandolAngand's life after the battle of the Cosgatt; she is AbathVasidol's mother in Brian W. Aldiss's *Helliconia Summer*.

Mr. Meyer   A generous, know-it-all landlord; Alois Hitler's drinking buddy, he is kind to Adolf Hitler, lending him books and having long talks; Meyer teases Bridget Hitler and embarrasses her with questions while he cuddles her son, Pat, in Beryl Bainbridge's *Young Adolf*.

Harriet (Hattie) Meynell   Rozanov's granddaughter, an orphan brought up by, but not with, her grandfather, who has fallen obsessively in love with her; she marries Tom McCaffrey in Iris Murdoch's *The Philosopher's Pupil*.

Michael   Mr. Weston's thorough assistant, who proves himself to be Tamar Grobe's angel in T. F. Powys's *Mr. Weston's Good Wine*.

Michael   An Oxford friend of Sarah Bennett; he married Stephanie immediately after coming down from Oxford; he is committed to politics and seems to have a model marriage in Margaret Drabble's *A Summer Bird-Cage*.

Michael   A photographer at *Lilith* who has a brief romance with Jane Somers's coworker, Phyllis, in Doris Lessing's *The Diaries of Jane Somers*.

Michael   A sex-obsessed student who becomes an English scholar and teacher; he marries Miriam, does work on Graham Greene, becomes head of his English department, and joins the Catholics for an Open Church in David Lodge's *How Far Can You Go?*.

Michael   Anna Wulf's ex-lover; his leaving her throws Anna into a long depression that actually produces some of her best journal-writing, including her new manuscript, *The Shadow of the Third*, in Doris Lessing's *The Golden Notebook*.

Cousin Michael   Cousin of Sarah Bennett and Louise Bennett Halifax and the brother of Daphne; a close friend of Sarah, he often provided Sarah with a means of temporary independence from Louise while they were all growing up in Margaret Drabble's *A Summer Bird-Cage*.

Father Michael   Passenger in Professor Lucifer's flying ship; he and Lucifer debate the concept of good and evil; Lucifer forces him out of the ship, and he saves himself by clinging to the cross on top of St. Paul's cathedral; he later reappears as a prisoner in the deepest cell of the insane asylum to which

Turnbull and MacIan are sentenced and saves the inmates by leading them through the final conflagration in G. K. Chesterton's *The Ball and the Cross*.

Michaelis   Obese ex-convict anarchist acquaintance of Verloc in Joseph Conrad's *The Secret Agent: A Simple Tale*.

Michaelis (Mick)   A bounderish young Irish writer whose sexual affair with Lady Chatterley fails to provide the genuine connection with vital life that she needs in D. H. Lawrence's *Lady Chatterley's Lover*.

Mrs. Michaelis   Karen Michaelis's restrained but concerned mother in Elizabeth Bowen's *The House in Paris*.

Karen Michaelis   Upperclass English wife of Ray Forrestier; her past includes her earlier broken engagement to Ray, her subsequent affair with Max Ebhart, and her abandonment of Leopold, her son by Max, in Elizabeth Bowen's *The House in Paris*.

Dr. Roy Michaels   A geophysicist and the chief scientist of the Clavius Base; he briefs Dr. Floyd on the discovery of the Moon artifact, TMA-1, in Arthur C. Clarke's *2001: A Space Odyssey*.

Michel   Fisherman killed with Peyrol in Joseph Conrad's *The Rover*.

Michel   Exuberant and generous painter and friend of Janos Lavin from their Berlin days; despite Lavin's description of him as an "indifferent painter", he ends up in the "history-of-art books"; twenty years later, in London for an exhibition of his art, he visits Lavin and is instrumental in securing an exhibition for him in John Berger's *A Painter of Our Time*.

Pierre Michel   Conductor on the Orient Express; his daughter, a servant in Daisy Armstrong's family, died tragically in Agatha Christie's *Murder on the Orient Express*.

Vivienne Michel   A young woman wounded by her unsatisfactory, ego-bruising relationships with men; her temporary job of managing an isolated motel makes her the intended incidental victim of an arson scam; James Bond saves her life and restores her emotional health; she is the narrator of Ian Fleming's *The Spy Who Loved Me*.

Pamela Micheldene   Roger Micheldene's second wife, who left him; her writing him a letter asking him to get her brother's manuscript back from Strode Atkins leads Micheldene to find the Swinburne notebooks that Atkins stole in Kingsley Amis's *One Fat Englishman.*

Roger Micheldene   An overweight, snobbish, lustful, angry Englishman and publisher on a short visit to America; he has affairs with Helene Bang and Mollie Atkins, knows Irving Macher's novel is good but refuses to accept it because he dislikes Macher, and is prejudiced against Americans, Blacks, and Jews; on his journey home his unwelcome shipboard companion is the horrible Anglophile Strode Atkins in Kingsley Amis's *One Fat Englishman.*

Rosemary Michelis   Martin Lynch-Gibbon's sister, formerly married to a stockbroker; she assists others in their love affairs but is not sexually involved with anyone in Iris Murdoch's *A Severed Head.*

Michie   A former serviceman who commanded a tank troop at Anzio; he is a university student interested in taking a special subject from Jim Dixon, but Jim fears Michie's intelligence in Kingsley Amis's *Lucky Jim.*

Lord (Woof-dog) Middlesex   Londoner whose incriminating correspondence with Babs Shyton involves him in a divorce scandal in E. F. Benson's *Lucia in London.*

Agnes Middleton   The middle Middleton daughter, who tries to get approval from the adults by saying what they want to hear in Ivy Compton-Burnett's *The Mighty and Their Fall.*

Arthur Middleton   Middle-aged husband of Diana Middleton; he becomes infatuated with the much younger Annabel Paynton in Henry Green's *Doting.*

Diana Middleton   Wife of Arthur Middleton; she has a tepid affair with Arthur's oldest friend, Charles Addinsell, in response to her husband's equally tepid affair with Annabell Paynton in Henry Green's *Doting.*

Egbert Middleton   Lavinia's brother, who is studying at Oxford; he is witty, ironic, and supportive of his sister in Ivy Compton-Burnett's *The Mighty and Their Fall.*

Gerald Middleton   Aging, wealthy, retired professor of English medieval history who is alienated from his wife and children; he prefers collecting art to writing history and reluctantly accepts the editorship of a new journal; he reconstructs events of his past relationships with Gilbert Stokesay to discover a fraud on the historical community; he renews his friendship with Gilbert's widow, Dollie, once his lover, in Angus Wilson's *Anglo-Saxon Attitudes.*

Hengist Middleton   An ironic and rebellious boy, who punctures some of the adults' pretensions and hypocrisies in Ivy Compton-Burnett's *The Mighty and Their Fall.*

Hugo Middleton   The adopted son of Selina Middleton; he is attracted to Teresa Chilton but later proposes to Lavinia Middleton, his niece by courtesy, in Ivy Compton-Burnett's *The Mighty and Their Fall.*

Ingeborg (Thingy) Middleton   Danish-born wife of Gerald, from whom she lives estranged; she suffers from a guilty conscience for having caused her daughter to cripple her hand in a fire; she cares for her son John after his accident in Angus Wilson's *Anglo-Saxon Attitudes.*

John Middleton   Younger son of Gerald and Ingeborg; he gave up a seat in Parliament to become a journalist; he searches for citizens with causes of complaint against the government bureaucracy; he is the homosexual lover of Larrie Rourke and loses a leg in an automobile accident in Angus Wilson's *Anglo-Saxon Attitudes.*

Lavinia Middleton   Her father Ninian's companion; she jealously tries to prevent his marriage to Teresa Chilton and later accepts Hugo Middleton's proposal in order to become independent from her father in Ivy Compton-Burnett's *The Mighty and Their Fall.*

Leah Middleton   The youngest Middleton child, who is sometimes mischievous, unravelling the governess's skirt in Ivy Compton-Burnett's *The Mighty and Their Fall.*

Marie Hélène Middleton   Robin's wife, who won a law suit for property against her aunt; she refuses to divorce Robin because she is a Roman Catholic in Angus Wilson's *Anglo-Saxon Attitudes.*

Ninian Middleton   A pompous, autocratic, and egotistical father; he thinks that his marriage to Teresa Chilton, his power over everyone, and his control of everyone's money are for the best in Ivy Compton-Burnett's *The Mighty and Their Fall.*

Peter Middleton   Adolescent son of Diana and Arthur Middleton in Henry Green's *Doting.*

Ransome Middleton   Selina Middleton's son who comes home to die, leaving his fortune to his niece Lavinia Middleton after his brother, Ninian, fails a test of integrity in Ivy Compton-Burnett's *The Mighty and Their Fall.*

Robin Middleton   Older son of Gerald and Ingeborg; he administers the family business; the lover of Elvira Portway, he begins to give Roman Catholicism serious thought after his wife refuses him a divorce in Angus Wilson's *Anglo-Saxon Attitudes*.

Sarah Middleton   A friend of the Gavestons; she shelters Miss Griffin when Matilda Seaton turns her out in Ivy Compton-Burnett's *A Family and a Fortune*.

Selina Middleton   The widowed grandmother who leaves money to her adopted son Hugo so that he will not marry Lavinia Middleton in order to become independent in Ivy Compton-Burnett's *The Mighty and Their Fall*.

Thomas Middleton   Sarah's husband, a tactful and unobtrusive man, in Ivy Compton-Burnett's *A Family and a Fortune*.

Timothy Middleton   Intellectual son of Robin and Marie; he is discovering his first love in Angus Wilson's *Anglo-Saxon Attitudes*.

Arthur Middlewitch   Supercilious young man who, after losing an arm in World War II, returns to England where he gambles with other people's money; he acts as an intercessor among the confused romantics in Henry Green's *Back*.

General Midwinter   An American arch-right-wing reactionary who owns and controls his own spy network by means of a vast computer complex hidden in Texas; he plans to invade Latvia and weaken Communism by directing his tanks across the frozen sea in Len Deighton's *The Billion-Dollar Brain*.

Bob Midwinter   Proletarian author of a sociological study of Edgar Allan Poe; he is one of the people sought by Harry Sinton in his search for the facts of Max Callis's death in Roy Fuller's *Fantasy and Fugue*.

Mifanwy   Bitch who has a litter of puppies by Sirius in Olaf Stapledon's *Sirius: A Fantasy of Love and Discord*.

Miguel   Guarani Indian guerrilla who guards Charley Fortnum with a machine gun after his kidnapping in Graham Greene's *The Honorary Consul*.

Miguel   Ward of Robinson in Muriel Spark's *Robinson*.

Mike   A friend of Rosamund Stacey and Lydia Reynolds in Margaret Drabble's *The Millstone*.

Mike   Tall, blond Irishman introduced to Jane Gray by James Otford at a race track; Jane admires a tattoo

on the back of Mike's hand that reads "BOB" vertically and horizontally in Margaret Drabble's *The Waterfall*.

Mikhel   Former Estonian military officer, General Vladimir's adjunct, and proprietor of the Free Baltic Library; he receives and secrets Maria Ostrakova's first letter to General Vladimir and, jealous of his wife Elvira's love for the General, betrays Vladimir to Karla in John le Carré's *Smiley's People*.

Councilor Mikulin   Russian official who plans to use Razumov as a double agent in Joseph Conrad's *Under Western Eyes*.

Vernon Milburne   Hero of World War I with the rank of colonel; he confides to a sympathetic Sir Edward Leithen his haunting cycle of nightmares; later on the Greek island of Plakos he and Koré Arabin endure a test of faith, courage and love in John Buchan's *The Dancing Floor*.

Sister Mildred   Novice mistress and advisor/accomplice of Sister Alexandra in Muriel Spark's *The Abbess of Crewe*.

Miles   A former public-school boy and Catholic convert; he becomes a conservative Catholic academic at Cambridge and struggles with his homosexuality, but is helped by Bernard in David Lodge's *How Far Can You Go?*.

Mr. Miles   Secretary of a Trade Association who is the father of Arthur; he lifts his son's ambitions with speculations on the stars in C. P. Snow's *The Search*.

Arthur Miles   Physicist, born in 1899, who specializes in crystallography; he acquires professional fame, publishes an incorrect report, and loses directorship of the National Institute; he loves Audrey but does not marry her; he gives up science to write after he marries Ruth Elton, and he decides not to expose Charles Sheriff's professional duplicity in C. P. Snow's *The Search*.

Frank Miles   A mine worker and a friend of Arthur Machin; they play on the same football team in David Storey's *This Sporting Life*.

Henry Miles   Introverted, conscientious, gentle, unimaginative career civil servant, who loves his wife, Sarah Miles, but can't express it; he persuades Maurice Bendrix to engage the services of a private detective when he suspects Sarah of infidelity; after Sarah's death, he asks Bendrix to share his house in Graham Greene's *The End of the Affair*.

Sarah Miles   Beautiful, restless, kind, intelligent,

spiritually tormented wife of Henry Miles; deeply in love with Maurice Bendrix, she has an intense affair with him which she ends in obedience to her promise to God to do so, should Bendrix survive an air raid; she keeps a journal in which she reveals the ways and means of her affair and of her search for belief in God; she experiences a "dark night of the soul" when she realizes her belief; she dies of pneumonia; after her death, miracles are attributed to her which serve to point out the validity of her belief and the efficacy of her conversion in Graham Greene's *The End of the Affair*.

Miller   Business associate of James Horgan in Isabel Colegate's *Statues in a Garden*.

Brigadier-General Miller   An exemplary, loyal supporter of General Curzon in C. S. Forester's *The General*.

Dr. Miller   Pacifist physician and anthropologist who befriends Anthony Beavis in Mexico and becomes the chief instrument in his development toward non-violent action and basic human sympathy in Aldous Huxley's *Eyeless in Gaza*.

St. Quentin Miller   A family friend in whom Anna Quayne confides; he develops a kindly interest in Portia Quayne in Elizabeh Bowen's *The Death of the Heart*.

Millicent   The first mistress taken by Anton Hesse after he and his wife, Martha Quest, agree that their marriage is "in name only" in Doris Lessing's *Landlocked*.

Millie   English girl and pupil in the Hanover school who shares with Miriam Henderson a passionate fondness for Germany in Dorothy Richardson's *Pointed Roofs*.

John P. Milligan   A Yankee representative of a shipping and railroad company that stands to profit from Sir Reuben Levy's disappearance in Dorothy L. Sayers's *Whose Body?*.

Mr. Mills   Spanish royalist who introduces Doña Rita de Lastaola to Monsieur George in Joseph Conrad's *The Arrow of Gold: A Story Between Two Notes*.

Aubrey Mills   Stephen Dedalus's friend during his sojourn from school in James Joyce's *A Portrait of the Artist as a Young Man*.

Milly   The prostitute who accompanies Tony Last on a staged trip to the seashore so that their presence together can be taken as evidence of adultery, chivalrously protecting the reputation of Tony's adulterous wife in the divorce proceedings in Evelyn Waugh's *A Handful of Dust*.

Milly   May Quest's young South African friend whom she stays with in Cape Town before leaving to come to England to visit Martha Quest in Doris Lessing's *The Four-Gated City*.

Aunt Milly   Sister of Bertie Eliot; she urges Lewis Eliot to use his inheritance from Aunt Thirza to pay back his father's debts and lends Lewis money to subsidize his study of law in C. P. Snow's *Time of Hope*.

James Milton   Anglican clergyman whose easily aroused romantic inclinations lean at first toward the Lawrence sisters but settle on Sydney Warren, to whom he proposes in Elizabeth Bowen's *The Hotel*.

Eustace (Eusty) Carádoc, Lord Miltoun   Thirty-year-old eldest son of the Earl of Valleys; his political career is jeopardized by his infatuation with Audrey·Noel; he is saved from disaster when she leaves England in John Galsworthy's *The Patrician*.

Mrs. Milvain   Katherine Hilbery's aunt, whose single-sighted moralistic view makes a mountain of a molehill over Cassandra Otway and William Rodney as well as over Katherine's cousin Cyril's dilemma, causing Katherine to detest her in Virginia Woolf's *Night and Day*.

Mimi   Voluptuous Florentine prostitute, who is fondly recalled in the after-life musings of Eustace Barnack in Aldous Huxley's *Time Must Have a Stop*.

Mingo   Pierce Clothier's steadfast dog, whose presence assists in Pierce's rescue from drowning in Iris Murdoch's *The Nice and the Good*.

Miss Miniver   Liberated friend of Ann Veronica Stanley; she believes in women's rights in H. G. Wells's *Ann Veronica: A Modern Love Story*.

Mrs. Minkel   Professor Minkel's outspoken wife, whose moral condemnation of Israeli terrorism irks Marty Kurtz in John le Carré's *The Little Drummer Girl*.

Professor Minkel   Liberal Israeli intellectual who defends Palestinian rights and criticizes Israeli policy but becomes Khalil's target in his test of Charlie's commitment to terrorism in John le Carré's *The Little Drummer Girl*.

Minney   The old family nurse who cares for the Cherrington children at the family's modest seaside home in Anchorstone in L. P. Hartley's *The Shrimp and the Anemone*. She continues to serve them into adulthood in *The Sixth Heaven* and in *Eustace and Hilda*.

Minnie Layton household servant, who is ayah (nursemaid) to little Edward Bingham, son of Susan (Layton) and the late Teddie Bingham; when Susan, having suffered a nervous breakdown, pours a ring of petrol around the child and lights it, Minnie saves his life in Paul Scott's *The Day of the Scorpion*. An employee at the Bhoolabhoys' hotel, Minnie is a friend of Colonel "Tusker" and Lucy Smalley in *Staying On*.

Mino Rupert Birkin's cat in D. H. Lawrence's *Women in Love*.

Minton Sullen senior apprentice at the Folkestone Drapery Bazaar who warns Art Kipps how dismal their future in the drapery business will be; he quits to join a cavalry regiment, later to die in battle in the Terah Valley in H. G. Wells's *Kipps: The Story of a Simple Soul*.

Minty Introverted English newspaper reporter whose job is to obtain business and personal information about Erik Krogh; he constantly attempts to shadow Krogh and persuades Anthony Farrant to provide him with information for money in Graham Greene's *England Made Me*.

Mira Colonel Abel Pargiter's mistress, whose affections and ministrations are not enough to alleviate his cosmic angst in Virginia Woolf's *The Years*.

Miriam A young Cockney girl and aspiring actress with whom Daniel Martin has an affair; she is Marjory's sister in John Fowles's *Daniel Martin*.

Miriam Wife of Michael, who converts her to Catholicism; she becomes more and more devoted, through their marriage, to social and church causes, joining Adrian Walsh's Catholics for an Open Church in David Lodge's *How Far Can You Go?*.

Miriam Daniel's wife and Jonothan's mother; her mother, Kitty Friedman, is concerned about her because Miriam is losing weight and acting odd at the time of a Christmas Eve family get-together in Margaret Drabble's *The Ice Age*.

The Misery Kid Grubby bohemian jazz aficionado; a model for the narrator's photography, he and Dean Swift save the narrator from a beating in Colin MacInnes's *Absolute Beginners*.

Kate Miskin Police inspector who aids Adam Dalgliesh; her grandmother is killed in her presence in P. D. James's *A Taste for Death*.

Morton Mitcham Banjo player and imaginative raconteur; he is a member of the concert party in J. B. Priestley's *The Good Companions*.

Dr. Mitchell A wealthy Scottish physician to whom Alvina Houghton briefly becomes engaged — before she runs off with the passionate Italian, Ciccio — in D. H. Lawrence's *The Lost Girl*.

Joseph Mitchell Captain who champions the Costaguanan cause in Joseph Conrad's *Nostromo: A Tale of the Seaboard*.

Mrs. Mitchett Parishioner who brings her unmarried, pregnant daughter for advice from Edward Pierson in John Galsworthy's *Saint's Progress*.

Miss Mitford The governess for the older Sullivan children; she is a fairly satisfied and well-read person of intelligence in Ivy Compton-Burnett's *Parents and Children*.

Sandy Mitford One of Nicholas Urfe's predecessors at the Lord Byron School on Phraxos in John Fowles's *The Magus*.

Dr. Mitra Indian physician who takes care of "Tusker" Smalley; he is called in when "Tusker" has a fatal coronary in Paul Scott's *Staying On*.

Mitri Old Greek steward at the Arabin castle on Plakos who leads Vernon Milburne to the House in hopes the man can save his mistress, Koré Arabin, in John Buchan's *The Dancing Floor*.

Tabwinga (Sixpence) Mleli Mr. Maynard's African Court Messenger, hired by him to spy on white R.A.F. men's activities in the Location in Doris Lessing's *A Ripple from the Storm*.

M'ling Bear-dog-ox hybrid, who is the adoring servant of Montgomery and dies defending him from the other beast-men in H. G. Wells's *The Island of Doctor Moreau*.

Mnemjian Barbershop proprietor, triple-agent spy, and city "archivist", who knows the ancestry and income of everyone in Alexandria; a hunchbacked dwarf, he has acquired a fortune through his attractiveness to women in Lawrence Durrell's *Justine*. He is mentioned in *Balthazar*. He brings Darley up to date on Alexandrian gossip in *Clea*.

Ralph Moberly Mrs. Weston's personal chauffeur, who is in love with Ellen, the kitchenmaid, and is pursued relentlessly by Beatrice, the personal maid of Cynthia Weston, in Isabel Colegate's *Statues in a Garden*.

Professor August Moe Brilliant physicist and member of the Whitsuntide house party at Flambard; he appeals to Sir Edward Leithen to participate and to urge the participation of six other members of the party in an experiment to test a new theory of Time in which the trained participants experience a form of prevision, a glimpse for one instant of one section of a page of *The Times* of the next year; he dies at the climax of the experiment in John Buchan's *The Gap in the Curtain.*

Mr. Moffat A panama-hat wearer at Dunes Hotel who turns out to be a professor at Manchester University; because he is unperturbed by Mrs. Foljambres's display of hauteur, all the Greens are intrigued with this man who does not defer to accepted opinion in C. Day Lewis's *Child of Misfortune.*

Dr. H. E. Moffatt The National Health physican Rosamund Stacey first sees when she decides to keep her baby in Margaret Drabble's *The Millstone.*

Claud Moggerhanger Wealthy underworld kingpin who arranges Michael Cullen's ultimate downfall in Alan Sillitoe's *A Start in Life.*

Polly Moggerhanger Claud Moggerhanger's daughter; Michael Cullen's grand passion and lover, she betrays Michael to her father in Alan Sillitoe's *A Start in Life.*

Bert Moggerson Fiancé of Mabel Amerson; although he tries to break off his relationship with her, he is forced to accept his responsibility by Roger Dennett in Frank Swinnerton's *The Happy Family.*

Dr. Ernest Mohr An East German medical doctor and S.S. war criminal living in Spain; he sends untrustworthy information to the Bonn government and is finally exposed by Dawlish and the narrator in Len Deighton's *Funeral in Berlin.*

Dr. Dimitri Moisevitch An astronomer and member of the U.S.S.R. Academy of Science; he has heard rumors of a startling discovery on the Moon in Arthur C. Clarke's *2001: A Space Odyssey.*

Moishe Cap-maker and Kandinsky's friend with an irritatingly pretentious viewpoint on economics in Wolf Mankowitz's *A Kid for Two Farthings.*

Nathaniel Mold A deputy librarian and an eligible, if somewhat common, middle-aged bachelor who comes to visit the vicarage in Barbar Pym's *Some Tame Gazelle.*

Mole The good-natured, shy creature who ventures away from his natural underground home to a hole in the river bank with the Water Rat; he participates in rescuing Toad from the consequences of his numerous reckless adventures in Kenneth Grahame's *The Wind in the Willows.*

Moll Malone's fictional character who has an affair with MacMann in Samuel Beckett's *Malone Dies.*

Mollie (satiric representation of the upper classes) The "foolish, pretty white mare who drew Mr. Jones's trap"; she always wore ribbons in her mane; she ran away to the people in order to evade hard work with the animal cooperative in George Orwell's *Animal Farm.*

Molloy Lame, stone-sucking, and ill-smelling narrator, continually on the point of visiting his mother; he struggles to finish relating his story in the first section of Samuel Beckett's *Molloy.*

Dolly Molloy "Soapy" Molloy's young, beautiful wife and brainier confederate, who poses as his daughter for the purpose of attracting prospective pigeons in P. G. Wodehouse's *Money for Nothing.* She appears in four other novels.

Thos G. ("Soapy") Molloy A handsome, deceptive, middle-aged swindler, forced by circumstances to involve Alexander Twist in his scheme to doublecross Lester Carmody in P. G. Wodehouse's *Money for Nothing.* He appears in four other novels.

Molly A social worker assigned to assist Maudie Fowler whom Maudie dislikes because she senses the girl's disgust with herself and her poor living conditions in Doris Lessing's *The Diaries of Jane Somers.*

Sir James Molony Neurologist engaged by the British Secret Service; he rehabilitates James Bond after his near-death in Ian Fleming's *Dr. No.* He treats him for depression after Tracy di Vicenzo's murder in *On Her Majesty's Secret Service.* He has won a Nobel Prize in *You Only Live Twice.*

Moma Station headman who brings a suit against Johnson for holding back the station laborers' pay in Joyce Cary's *Mister Johnson.*

Mona Young woman who spends an evening with Charles Sheriff after a college dance; she is loved by Hunt, who fails to win her, and she marries another in C. P. Snow's *The Search.*

M. de Moncoutant, Lord of Muzillac Affluent officer under the Pouzauges who is picked up with marines for transport in C. S. Forester's *Mr. Midshipman Hornblower.*

Mustapha Mond   Banal "Resident Controller for Western Europe" who cynically allows Bernard Marx to bring the uncivilized John Savage to futuristic England in order to test the effect of his presence in Aldous Huxley's *Brave New World*.

Monday   Secretary of the General Council of the Anarchists of Europe and fourth member of the Council to reveal himself as a spy to Gabriel Syme; he joins the other Council members in the pursuit of Sunday in G. K. Chesterton's *The Man Who Was Thursday: A Nightmare*.

Matthew Monday   Sara's repressed husband; he is liberated by marriage until his jealousy of his wife and Gulley Jimson destroys his pride in Joyce Cary's *Herself Surprised*.

Sara Monday   Self-indulgent, good-hearted cook who marries the higher-class Matthew Monday; after his death she lives with Gulley Jimson and then with Tom Wilcher; she constantly gets herself into trouble and is accidently killed trying to stop Gulley from getting some of his old paintings in Joyce Cary's *Herself Surprised* (told in Sara's voice), in *To Be a Pilgrim*, and in *The Horse's Mouth*.

Miss Moneypenny   M's secretary and Loelia Ponsonby's good friend; she nurses a secret desire for James Bond in Ian Fleming's *Casino Royale* and in succeeding novels, ending with *You Only Live Twice*.

Count Andrea di Monfalcone   Handsome young Italian nobleman who visits Lady Nelly Staveley at her Venetian palazzo in L. P. Hartley's *Eustace and Hilda*.

Monique   A previous au pair for the Browns' children with whom Michael Brown became infatuated; she had had to have an abortion when she became pregnant by a Frenchman in Doris Lessing's *The Summer Before the Dark*.

Monkeys   Creatures with nearly human intelligence who become obsessed with the love of metal and who attack the Second Men in Olaf Stapledon's *Last and First Men: A Story of the Near and Far Future*.

Norman Monkley   A poor trailer-dweller and unpublished novelist; when his stepdaughter is killed by a car driven by Austin Gibson Grey, he seizes the occasion for blackmail; Austin's enraged attack on him leaves him permanently helpless and mindless from a head injury in Iris Murdoch's *An Accidental Man*.

Mr. Monsell   An American who stays briefly with Richard Lovat Somers in Cornwall during the war years in D. H. Lawrence's *Kangaroo*.

Catherine Mont   Baby daughter of Fleur and Michael in 1930 in John Galsworthy's *Flowering Wilderness*.

Christopher (Kit) Mont   Son of Fleur and Michael; he is a baby in 1924 in John Galsworthy's *The Silver Spoon*. He contracts measles in *Swan Song*. He tells his mother about Dinny Cherrell's encounter with Wilfred Desert in the park in *Flowering Wilderness*.

Emily, Lady Mont   Sister of General Conway Cherrell and Hilary Cherrell and wife of Sir Lawrence Mont; she is concerned more with her son Michael's appearance than with his politics in John Galsworthy's *The Silver Spoon*. She is fifty-nine when she entertains her niece Dinny Cherrell in *Maid In Waiting*. She counsels Dinny to make a modern arrangement with Wilfred Desert in *Flowering Wilderness*.

Fleur Forsyte Mont   Daughter of Soames and Annette Forsyte, born in 1901 at risk of her mother's life in John Galsworthy's *In Chancery*. She offers herself to Jon Forsyte in 1920 despite their parents' opposition; rejected by him, she marries Michael Mont in *To Let*. She flirts with Wilfred Desert but decides to be faithful to her husband, to whom she bears a son, Christopher, in 1923 in *The White Monkey*. She is insulted by Marjorie Ferrar in 1924, wins a libel suit brought by Soames, and loses public sympathy in *The Silver Spoon*. She organizes a railway canteen during the General Strike in 1926 and seduces Jon but loses him again to his wife; she is rescued by her father from a fire caused by her own cigarette in *Swan Song*. She drives Adrian and Hilary Cherrell into the country to search for Ronald Ferse in *Maid In Waiting*. She counsels Dinny Cherrell during her trials of love with Wilfred Desert in *Flowering Wilderness*. She pays the legal fees incurred by Tony Croom from Clare Corven's divorce in *Over the River*.

Sir Lawrence Mont   Ninth baronet, father of Michael; he is the author of a book about Gladstone and Disraeli in John Galsworthy's *The White Monkey*. He visits the Marquess of Shropshire in an effort to settle the libel suit in *The Silver Spoon*. He helps Michael organize the Slum Clearance Committee in *Swan Song*. He hosts the shooting party where Dinny Cherrell meets Edward Hallorsen and Lord Saxenden in *Maid In Waiting*. He urges Wilfred Desert to give up Dinny if Wilfred cannot resolve his quarrel with himself in *Flowering Wilderness*. He speaks to Gerald Corven on behalf of Clare Corven and suggests that Jack Muskham employ Tony Bicket in *Over the River*.

Michael Conway Mont   Twenty-four-year-old son of Sir Lawrence; he marries Fleur Forsyte in 1920 after she is rejected by Jon Forsyte in John Galsworthy's *To Let*. He is a junior partner in a London publishing firm; he rejoices at the birth of his son, Christopher, in *The White Monkey*. He quits the publishing firm, is a Tory Member of Parliament in 1924, and fights with Sir Alexander MacGowan in *The Silver Spoon*. As M.P., he turns his attention to a slum-clearance project in *Swan Song*. He arranges publication of Hubert Cherrell's diary in *Maid In Waiting*. He unsuccessfully opposes Wilfred Desert's plan to publish his confessional poem in *Flowering Wilderness*.

Montague   Level-headed and successful college friend of Dan Graveson; he stays in touch with Dan and helps him get a job when he is down on his luck in Alan Burns's *Buster*.

Harry Montague   Charles Smithson's solicitor and friend, who helps Charles find Sarah Woodruff in John Fowles's *The French Lieutenant's Woman*.

Lord Montdore   Popular and conscientious earl; though rich and powerful, he has relinquished domestic sway to his wife; a fair and honorable politician, he is dull and quiet at home in Nancy Mitford's *Love in a Cold Climate*.

Sonia, Lady Montdore   Lord Montdore's handsome, not high-born wife; a great planner, hostess, and thinker, she is also snobbish, self-centered, and greedy; the birth of her only child, Polly Hampton, occurs in the twentieth year of her marriage; her intolerance of weakness and her jealousy estrange her from Polly in Nancy Mitford's *Love in a Cold Climate*.

Laura Montefiore   Mother of Wyndham Farrar in Margaret Drabble's *The Garrick Year*.

Monteith   Security official who interrogates Lewis Eliot in C. P. Snow's *Corridors of Power*.

Eddy Monteith   Languid and affected Welsh aristocrat who rejects his capricious plans to enter the Jesuit monastery in favor of joining an archaeological expedition to Dateland, where he is eaten by a jackal while composing a sonnet in Ronald Firbank's *The Flower Beneath the Foot*.

Pedrito Montero   Secessionist rebel leader in Costaguana in Joseph Conrad's *Nostromo: A Tale of the Seaboard*.

Montgomery   Dissolute medical student who has fled London in disgrace to become Moreau's assistant; he revives Edward Prendick after having him rescued from his drifting lifeboat; Montgomery dies at the hands of the beast-men after getting drunk with them when Moreau is killed in H. G. Wells's *The Island of Doctor Moreau*.

Aggie Montgomery   Cheerful English governess of young Prince Olaf of Pisuerga; she enjoys novels and conducts with discretion an amorous involvement with court physician Dr. Cuncliffe Babcock in Ronald Firbank's *The Flower Beneath the Foot*.

Lily Montgomery   Maurice Conchis's invented boyhood love and fiancée in John Fowles's *The Magus*. See also Lily Montgomery DeSeitas.

Clea Montis   A beautiful, fair-haired Alexandrian painter, whose homosexual affair with Justine Hosnani is mentioned in Lawrence Durrell's *Justine*. She is the object of Narouz Hosnani's unwanted adoration in *Balthazar*. She appears in *Mountolive*. She becomes Darley's lover; she loses her right hand and nearly her life when impaled underwater by Balthazar's accidental firing of the late Narouz's harpoon in *Clea*.

Montmorency   The dog that reluctantly accompanies the vacationing trio on the river, chasing cats and generally being the perfect nuisance in Jerome K. Jerome's *Three Men in a Boat (To Say Nothing of the Dog)*.

Francie Montmorency   A semi-invalid and the pampered wife of Hugo Montmorency; she is the house guest of Sir Richard and Lady Naylor in Elizabeth Bowen's *The Last September*.

Hugo Montmorency   A family friend of Sir Richard and Lady Naylor; before each married another he was the lover of Sir Richard's late sister; now the oversolicitous husband of Francie, he is at the same time strongly attracted to younger women, especially Marda Norton, in Elizabeth Bowen's *The Last September*.

Mr. Montross   Wealthy Jewish neighbor of Wilfred Bentworth; he joins Michael Mont's slum-conversion committee in John Galsworthy's *Swan Song*.

Dr. Monygham   Friend of Charles Gould in Joseph Conrad's *Nostromo: A Tale of the Seaboard*.

Michael Moon   Intellectual journalist without ambition who organizes the Court of Beacon and leads the defense of Innocent Smith at his trial in G. K. Chesterton's *Manalive*.

Moon-Watcher   The leader of the man-ape tribe that first discovers the artifact on Earth; he becomes the first hunter, tool user, and murderer in Arthur C. Clarke's *2001: A Space Odyssey*.

Mrs. Moore   Wise old woman who chaperones her son Ronny Heaslop's fiancée, Adela Quested, to India; her experience of spiritual chaos in the Marabar Caves deprives Adela of necessary counsel; she regains her spirituality but dies on her journey home in E. M. Forster's *A Passage to India*.

Ralph Moore   Mrs. Moore's younger son in E. M. Forster's *A Passage to India*.

Stella Moore   Mrs. Moore's daughter, who marries Henry Fielding in E. M. Forster's *A Passage to India*.

Tanya Moore   Independent young governess to Mrs. Jardine's grandchildren; her artistic sensibility, her honesty, and her natural candour make her perfect with children in Rosamond Lehmann's *The Ballad and the Source*.

Mophtar   The leader of the FLN guerrillas in Algeria with whom Frank Dawley fights in Alan Sillitoe's *A Tree on Fire*.

Donald Mor   Son of William and Nan Mor; the strains in their marriage are reflected in his rebellious behavior in Iris Murdoch's *The Sandcastle*.

Felicity Mor   William Mor's teenaged daughter, home from boarding school; her emotional disturbance is manifested in practices of black magic; the resolution of her parents' crisis restores her balance, and she decides to continue her education in Iris Murdoch's *The Sandcastle*.

Nan Mor   The strong and intelligent wife of William Mor; she fights successfully to detach him from Rain Carter and to save her marriage in Iris Murdoch's *The Sandcastle*.

William Mor   Senior master at St. Bride's School; he falls in love with Rain Carter when she comes to paint Demoyte's portrait; he intends to leave his wife but is out-maneuvered and made to face up to his responsibilities in Iris Murdoch's *The Sandcastle*.

Jaques Moran   Molloy's antithesis, a secret agent, who nevertheless is a mirror image sharing the same physical defects as the other and who finally becomes another Molloy, or the only Molloy, writing the "report" that is really Molloy's story in the second section of Samuel Beckett's *Molloy*.

Maggie Moran   Attractive dancer who becomes Billy Henshaw's girlfriend; she introduces Ellen Henshaw to Lesbian sexuality when Ellen is a teenager in Anthony Burgess's *The Pianoplayers*.

Sluggsy Morant   The more durable of a pair of vicious thugs who torch an isolated, unprofitable motel for insurance money; he survives his presumed death

to be dispatched by James Bond a second time in Ian Fleming's *The Spy Who Loved Me*.

Arthur Morcom   Dentist who courts Olive Calvert; he is dropped by Olive for Jack Cotery; he privately warns Lewis Eliot about the questionable financial dealings of Passant and Cotery, and he offers money to help Cotery jump bond during the trial in C. P. Snow's *Strangers and Brothers*.

Dr. Moreau   Infamous island-dwelling scientist and surgeon who in an attempt to recreate human beings, uses vivisection on animals and schools them in morality and language; he rules them like a god and is ultimately killed by one of them, a resected cougar, in H. G. Wells's *The Island of Doctor Moreau*.

Lord Morecambe   Young member of the British aristocracy; about a year older than Eustace Cherrington, he visits Venice with his new wife and encourages Eustace's literary endeavors in L. P. Hartley's *Eustace and Hilda*.

Mrs. Morecambe   Alfred's wife and confidence-game partner; she gives Henry Weldon transportation the day of Paul Alexis Goldschmidt's murder in Dorothy L. Sayers's *Have His Carcase*.

Alfred Morecambe (aliases: William Bright, Simpson)   A confidence man who disguised himself as a tramp barber to acquire possession of the murder weapon in Dorothy L. Sayers's *Have His Carcase*.

Heloise, Lady Morecambe   The beautiful newly married American wife of Lord Morecambe; she visits Lady Nelly Staveley in Venice and takes kindly to Eustace Cherrington in L. P. Hartley's *Eustace and Hilda*.

Annie Morel   The second child of the Morels; she studies to be a teacher and later marries; she assists Paul in administering a fatal morphia overdose to their cancer-stricken mother in D. H. Lawrence's *Sons and Lovers*.

Arthur Morel   The fourth child born to the Morels; he differs from the other children because "he loved his father from the first"; Arthur is wild, restless, spontaneous, and very like his father, Walter, in D. H. Lawrence's *Sons and Lovers*.

Gertrude Morel   Paul's emotionally parasitic, puritanical mother; once overwhelmed by Walter Morel's "sensuous flame of life", she grows to detest his drunken, uneducated ways and their life in a shabby miners' village in the industrial Midlands; disillusioned, she tries to live through the lives of her sons and plays out a perverse Oedipal relationship, especially with Paul, the protagonist, in D. H. Lawrence's *Sons and Lovers*.

Paul Morel   The second son of the Morels; his relationship with his parents dramatizes the "Oedipal complex": Paul hates his alcoholic father and has a perversely sensual love for his parasitic mother; after a youth spent in a tense, unhappy home in a colliery village, he develops a relationship with a romantic, spiritually intense girl (Miriam Leivers), and later has a passionate union with an older woman (Clara Dawes), but neither meets his psychic needs; when his mother dies, he leaves to seek a new start in D. H. Lawrence's *Sons and Lovers*.

Walter Morel   A vital but illiterate and alcoholic coal miner, husband to Gertrude and father to four children; once handsome and life-loving, he has been wasted by a lifetime of working in the mines, and he feels unwelcome in his own household; he often shows tenderness and gentleness toward his children, but they favor their mother, and the household often erupts with violent domestic quarrels in D. H. Lawrence's *Sons and Lovers*.

William Morel   The oldest Morel child; he is the victim of his mother's smothering and perverse love before he goes off to work in a London shipping firm; not long after he gets to London, he becomes engaged to a frivolous woman, Lily Western; he develops pneumonia and dies, leaving his mother devastated in D. H. Lawrence's *Sons and Lovers*.

Hugh Moreland   Musician who becomes Nicholas Jenkins's closest friend; his involvement with Priscilla Tolland, his association with Maclintick, and his unconventional marriage to Matilda Wilson are recounted in Anthony Powell's *Casanova's Chinese Restaurant* and in *The Kindly Ones*. He is taken over by Audrey Maclintick in *The Valley of Bones*. He dies in *Temporary Kings*.

Don Giustino Morena   Parliamentary Representative of Nepenthe who appeals to his listeners' emotions and who defends criminals in Norman Douglas's *South Wind*.

Miss Moreton   Wilfred Moreton's rather plain sister in Isabel Colegate's *Statues in a Garden*.

Wilfred Moreton   Eldest son of a viscount; he marries Violet Weston and is killed in the war in 1915 in Isabel Colegate's *Statues in a Garden*.

Mrs. Morgan   Protective mother of Jimmy Morgan and the liberal publisher of *Forward*, a progressive weekly magazine; it is at her behest that Max Divver

travels as a correspondent to Poland in Nigel Dennis's *Boys and Girls Come Out to Play*.

Angharad Morgan   Gwilym Morgan's youngest daughter, who loves Mr. Gryffydd but makes an unhappy marriage with Yestin Evans in Richard Llewellyn's *How Green Was My Valley*.

Anna Morgan   Young chorus girl who drifts through and among small towns in England, haunted by warm and intense memories of the West Indies (her original home); she ends up in the throes of a botched abortion, hovering between life and death in Jean Rhys's *Voyage in the Dark*.

Beth Morgan   Gwilym Morgan's loyal wife and the devoted mother of eight children in Richard Llewellyn's *How Green Was My Valley*.

Bronwen Morgan   Ivor Morgan's wife and the lifelong love of Huw Morgan; she takes in Huw as a boarder after Ivor's death; she refuses Mathew Harries's marriage proposal when Huw reveals his love to her in Richard Llewellyn's *How Green Was My Valley*.

Ceridwen Morgan   Gwilym Morgan's oldest daughter, who marries Blethyn in a double ceremony with her brother Davey and has twins in Richard Llewellyn's *How Green Was My Valley*.

Dai Morgan   A soldier whose leave was denied by Christopher Tietjens on police advice to protect him from his wife's brutal lover; he takes a mortar hit and dies in Tietjens's arms in Ford Madox Ford's *No More Parades*.

Davey Morgan   Gwilym Morgan's third son, who becomes a leader of the socialist movement among the local miners and in London; after winning a law suit against the mine owner, he emigrates to New Zealand in Richard Llewellyn's *How Green Was My Valley*.

Gwilym Morgan   A hard-working coal miner whose conservative Christianity puts him at odds with the socialism and unionism of other miners and several of his sons in Richard Llewellyn's *How Green Was My Valley*.

Gwilym Morgan, the younger   Gwilym Morgan's headstrong fifth son, who marries Marged Evans after Owen Morgan breaks his engagement with her; he emigrates to America following Marged's suicide in Richard Llewellyn's *How Green Was My Valley*.

Hester Morgan   Anna's stepmother, who resents Anna and her father, Hester's husband; she dies with little or no money in Jean Rhys's *Voyage in the Dark*.

Huw (The Old Man) Morgan The sensitive, intelligent son and youngest brother in a family of coal miners divided over unionization; he refuses professional education to enter the colliery, but is fired after being arrested for assault; discontented with modern industrial life, he leaves the valley after his father's death in the mine in Richard Llewellyn's *How Green Was My Valley.*

Ianto Morgan Gwilym Morgan's second son, who marries and leaves the valley but returns after his wife's death to work in the colliery; fired from the mines for organizing unions, he becomes an ironworker and emigrates to Germany in Richard Llewellyn's *How Green Was My Valley.*

Ivor Morgan Gwilym Morgan's oldest son, who initially sides with his father and against his younger brothers on unionization but later becomes an active union organizer; he marries Bronwen, leads a choir in a command performance before Queen Victoria, and dies in a mine cave-in in Richard Llewellyn's *How Green Was My Valley.*

Jimmy Morgan Mrs. Morgan's sheltered, epileptic son; despite his mother's objections, he travels to Poland with Max Divver prior to the Nazi invasion; his experiences there transform him into a clear-eyed young man in Nigel Dennis's *Boys and Girls Come Out to Play.*

Mike Morgan Failed actor but brilliant comedian who has a sado-masochistic relationship with his audiences; he is a friend to Anthony Keating and Giles Peters in Margaret Drabble's *The Ice Age.*

Owen Morgan Gwilym Morgan's mechanically talented fourth son, who left the valley to work in the steel works after breaking his engagement to Marged Evans; he returns but emigrates to America after Marged's suicide in Richard Llewellyn's *How Green Was My Valley.*

Owen Morgan Professor of Forensic Science who assists Frank Briers in investigating the murder of Lady Ashbrook in C. P. Snow's *A Coat of Varnish.*

Uncle "Bo" Ramsay Morgan Ann Morgan's father's brother in the West Indies in Jean Rhys's *Voyage in the Dark.*

Ernesto Morgana A wealthy scholar and the husband of Fulvia Morgana in David Lodge's *Small World.*

Fulvia Morgana A rich, sexually adventurous Marxist Professor of Cultural Studies at the University of Padua; she and her husband, Ernesto Morgana, use

their connections with terrorists to get Morris Zapp released in David Lodge's *Small World.*

Miss Moriarty Schoolteacher who informs Caithleen Brady that she has received a scholarship to a convent in Edna O'Brien's *The Country Girls.*

Cyril Morland Young English soldier who is Noel Pierson's lover for a night; he dies in battle in 1916 in John Galsworthy's *Saint's Progress.*

Morley Schoolboy at Seaforth House in Roy Fuller's *The Ruined Boys.*

Alan Morley Eldest brother of Bryan and a novice prizefighter in David Storey's *A Prodigal Child.*

Arthur Morley Farm laborer, father of Alan and Bryan; a simple man, he believes in hard work and clean living in David Storey's *A Prodigal Child.*

Brian Morley A farm laborer's son with creative and intellectual gifts who attracts the sympathy and patronage of Fay Corrigan, the wealthy aunt of a friend; she and her husband pay his school tuition; his education and artistic training lead to a liberation that becomes dangerous in David Storey's *A Prodigal Child.*

Sarah Morley Arthur Morley's wife, who encourages her son Bryan to seek a better life when Fay Corrigan offers to help him go to a good, expensive school in David Storey's *A Prodigal Child.*

Crispin Mornu Sayren Stund's advisor, who prosecutes JandolAnganol for Simdol Tal's death in Brian W. Aldiss's *Helliconia Summer.*

Mrs. Morran ("Aunt Phemie") Elderly Scots woman who gives Dickson McCunn and John Heritage a room in her house in Dalquharter village; she bravely walks with Dougal Crombie out of the village so that he will be safe and shelters Sakskia and Cousin Eugenia after their escape form Huntingtower House in John Buchan's *Huntingtower.*

Jean Morrel George Greggson's wife, who is proved to have psychic powers; their children, Jeffrey and Jennifer Anne, begin a new human evolutionary stage in Arthur C. Clarke's *Childhood's End.*

Captain Morris Commander of the marines aboard the *Sutherland*; unlike Hornblower, he is one for details in appearance, not in substance in C. S. Forester's *Ship of the Line.*

Mr. Morris Old servant who, along with his wife, is

supplied by Sir Jesse Sullivan to the Marlowes in Ivy Compton-Burnett's *Parents and Children*.

Mrs. Morris Old servant who, along with her husband, is supplied by Sir Jesse Sullivan to the Marlowes in Ivy Compton-Burnett's *Parents and Children*.

Mrs. Morris Welsh charwoman who shares with her employers the occupation of scrutinizing the social and ecclesiastical lives of their neighbors in Barbara Pym's *Excellent Women*.

Arthur Morris Member of the Weatherby-Pomfret social set who slowly dies of a blood clot in Henry Green's *Nothing*.

Isaac Morris The arranger of the purchase and provisioning of Indian Island; a former drug dealer, he is the first murder victim in Agatha Christie's *And Then There Were None*.

Morrison English sea captain who dies after involvement in a failed coal venture with Axel Heyst in Joseph Conrad's *Victory: An Island Tale*.

Leslie Morrison Working-class lover of Elsie (Palmer) Williams; he impulsively kills Horace Williams, Elsie's husband, in a fight; he is executed with Elsie in E. M. Delafield's *Messalina of the Suburbs*.

Morrisse Friendly, dedicated interior decorator in partnership with Cornblow in Storm Jameson's *There Will Be a Short Interval*.

Jessie Morrow Satirical spinster who nonetheless cherishes romantic dreams; she is a poor relation and ladies' companion to the redoubtable Miss Doggett in Barbara Pym's *Jane and Prudence*.

Dixie Morse Affectionate but materialistic fiancée of Humphrey Place in Muriel Spark's *The Ballad of Peckham Rye*.

Mrs. Mortimer Inspector Mortimer's wife, greatly absorbed in the care of her young grandchildren; of the collection of aged Londoners, only she receives no warning telephone call from death in Muriel Spark's *Memento Mori*.

Henry Mortimer Agnostic, retired police inspector, whose sensitivity allows him to understand that death is in fact responsible for the outbreak of telephone calls warning a group of elderly Londoners that they must die in Muriel Spark's *Memento Mori*.

Mr. Mortlake Piano tuner and rival for power on the

Parochial Church Council in Barbara Pym's *Jane and Prudence*.

Mr. Morton Husband of Mrs. Morton and father of their two daughters, Evelyn Morton Stennett and Isobel (Morton); he is healthy and active in his retirement years in Margaret Drabble's *The Middle Ground*.

Mrs. Morton Wife of Mr. Morton and mother of their two daughters, Evelyn (Morton) Stennett and Isobel (Morton); she is active and healthy in her retirement years in Margaret Drabble's *The Middle Ground*.

Isobel (Morton) Wife of David and sister of Evelyn (Morton) Stennett; she is a lecturer in English Literature at Sussex in Margaret Drabble's *The Middle Ground*.

Frieda Mosebach The Schlegels' German cousin who marries Bruno Liesecke in E. M. Forster's *Howards End*.

Bill Moser Dean of Faculty at Euphoric State University; he arranges Morris Zapp's academic exchange with Philip Swallow in David Lodge's *Changing Places: A Tale of Two Campuses*.

Moses The Turners' native houseboy, who slowly gains control over Mary Turner and in the end kills her in Doris Lessing's *The Grass Is Singing*.

Moses (satiric representation of the Russian church) A raven at Manor Farm; he always talks of the wonders of Sugarcandy Mountain that wait for good animals who obey their masters in George Orwell's *Animal Farm*.

Pavel Moskvin K.G.B. Colonel who fails to exterminate Bernard Samson and halt Erich Stinnes's defection in Len Deighton's *Mexico Set*. He is Bernard and Fiona Samson's antagonist and is assassinated through Fiona's orders in *London Match*.

Sir Andrew Moss Judge presiding over the highly publicized Shyton vs. Shyton divorce case in E. F. Benson's *Lucia in London*.

Great Grandfather Mosson Ninety-year-old head of the family in Tothill House, London, who tells his great-grandsons the story of his visit to hell, and who instructs his grandson Hubert to reconcile with Piers and Tom Mosson in Angus Wilson's *Setting the World on Fire*.

(Sir) Hubert Mosson Wealthy baronet, the grandson of Great Grandfather Mosson; he breaks his engagement with Marina Luzzi, inherits Tothill House at his grandfather's death, approves production of the opera by Piers Mosson but prohibits it after learning of Rosemary Mosson's liaison with Jim Terrington, and dies from an accident incurred while enjoying his perverse sexual pleasures in Angus Wilson's *Setting the World on Fire*.

Jackie, Lady Mosson American-born daughter-in-law of Great Grandfather Mosson; her Puritanism had perverted her son Hubert's sexual habits; she drives away his fiancée, Marina Luzzi, and changes her values after the death of Hubert in Angus Wilson's *Setting the World on Fire*.

Piers (Van) Mosson Older son of Rosemary; he plans production of an opera in Vanbrugh hall of Tothill House when he is seventeen, inherits Tothill at the death of his Uncle Hubert, produces the opera with success at age twenty-eight, and discovers terrorists working under the cover of his production of a play by Ralph Tucker; his life is saved by his brother, Tom, in Angus Wilson's *Setting the World on Fire*.

Rosemary (Ma) Mosson War-widowed daughter-in-law of Lady Mosson; she is the mother of Piers and Tom; she fights her habits of gambling and drinking and alienates the Mosson family when she announces she will live unmarried with Jim Terrington in Angus Wilson's *Setting the World on Fire*.

Tom (Pratt) Mosson Younger brother of Piers; Rosemary's son, he chooses his mother over his grandmother and uncle Hubert, moves in to live with Piers after the death of Hubert, becomes a successful London barrister, and loses his life while saving Piers from the attack of Magda Sczekerny in Angus Wilson's *Setting the World on Fire*.

Nigel Mostyn Earnest, naïve British Intelligence operative and General Vladimir's inexperienced case officer, who fails to understand the import of Vladimir's call for Max (George Smiley) but, despite his superiors' warning to forget the call, gives Smiley the message that sets him on Karla's trail in John le Carré's *Smiley's People*.

Mother Superior The highborn, austere, and deeply respected nun who is in charge of the convent at Mei-tanfu; she perceives Kitty Fane's unhappiness and gently assists her on the road to self-knowledge in W. Somerset Maugham's *The Painted Veil*.

Rex Mottram A dashing, sexually compelling, morally inadequate financial speculator; the belated revelation that he is divorced prohibits the Catholic ceremony planned by Lady Marchmain, and Julia Flyte marries him

in a civil ceremony; he quickly proves to be an unfaithful husband; he becomes a cabinet minister during World War II in Evelyn Waugh's *Brideshead Revisited*.

Moub Uuundaamp's wife, whose rape by Harbin Fashnalgid is avenged by her husband in Brian W. Aldiss's *Helliconia Winter*.

Mould A somewhat simple groundskeeper in Nicholas Blake's *A Question of Proof*.

Captain Mound Polite, cool-headed, quick, reliable captain killed in battle; Hornblower is distressed at losing him in C. S. Forester's *Commodore Hornblower*.

Isobel Mound School headmistress; a college friend of Beatrix Howick, she visits the West Oxfordshire cottage where Emma Howick is staying in Barbara Pym's *A Few Green Leaves*.

Veronica Mount A cultivated widow of modest means who is an Openshaw family connection; of a generation older than Manfred North, she is emotionally bound to him and resorts to elaborate trickery for the purpose of keeping him single in Iris Murdoch's *Nuns and Soldiers*.

Mountain Impressive, rather exotic youth; an athlete and a dandy, he represents an ideal figure to Gerald Bracher at Seaforth School in Roy Fuller's *The Ruined Boys*.

Arthur Mounteney Nobel Prize-winning physicist who works on atomic-energy research with Walter Luke in C. P. Snow's *The New Men*. A member of Roger Quaife's advisory committee, he questions Michael Brodzinski's presence at their meetings after Brodzinski has raised questions of loyalty in *Corridors of Power*.

Henrietta Mountjoy Socially precocious eleven-year-old girl who spends the day in the Fishers' house in Paris on her way to visit her grandmother; there she meets and talks frankly with Leopold in ways that reveal the strength and resilience of both children in Elizabeth Bowen's *The House in Paris*.

Sammy Mountjoy The artist-protagonist whose mental quest is to discover the specific time in his life when he fell from God's grace in William Golding's *Free Fall*.

Taffy Mountjoy Sammy Mountjoy's attractive but neglected wife in William Golding's *Free Fall*.

Mountolive (the elder) David's father, formerly a judge in the foreign service in India; on his retirement, he has remained there in scholarly pursuits instead of joining his wife in England; his son was eleven when he last saw him in Lawrence Durrell's *Mountolive*.

Mrs. Mountolive   David's mother; she maintains a comfortable home in England for a husband who she knows will never see it in Lawrence Durrell's *Mountolive*.

David Mountolive   An able and intelligent innocent among political and sexual intriguers; his youthful love affair with Leila Hosnani dangerously blinds him to the anti-British intrigues of her family in Lawrence Durrell's *Mountolive*. He marries Pursewarden's sister, Liza, in *Clea*.

Beatrice Mourre   Mother of Simone Mourre, who is the fiancée of Mujid; she is half French, half Lebanese; she met Kate Fletcher Armstrong while both women were in hospital giving birth to sons in Margaret Drabble's *The Middle Ground*.

Simone Mourre   Daughter to Beatrice Mourre; she is the fiancée of Mujid in Margaret Drabble's *The Middle Ground*.

Mr. Mouth   Evasive, worried, pious father of Miami, Edna, and Charlie Mouth; he is opposed to their move to the vice-filled city of Cuna-Cuna but reluctantly gives in to his wife's ambitious plans in Ronald Firbank's *Sorrow in Sunlight*.

Ahmadou Mouth   Persistent, ambitious matron who convinces her husband and family to move from her native village of Mediaville to Cuna-Cuna, the capital city of their island nation, for the improved social opportunities she feels her daughters will have there in Ronald Firbank's *Sorrow in Sunlight*.

Charlie Mouth   Charming, distracted, independent young son of Ahmadou and Mr. Mouth; he immerses himself in sensual pleasures when he moves to Cuna-Cuna with his family in Ronald Firbank's *Sorrow in Sunlight*.

Edna Mouth   Vain, precocious younger daughter of Ahmadou and Mr. Mouth; she is seduced in Cuna-Cuna by the aristocratic Vitti Ruiz and becomes hardened against her previous life and family in Ronald Firbank's *Sorrow in Sunlight*.

Miami Mouth   Sensual older daughter of Ahmadou and Mr. Mouth; she reluctantly leaves her home and her lover Bamboo for the social opportunities her mother anticipates in the city of Cuna-Cuna and later enters a charismatic convent when Bamboo is killed

and her siblings corrupted in Ronald Firbank's *Sorrow in Sunlight*.

Audrey Mowbray   The youngest daughter of Miles and Ellen; she is bewildered by the loss of her mother and by her father's plan to marry Verena Gray in Ivy Compton-Burnett's *A Father and His Fate*.

Constance Mowbray   The second daughter of Miles and Ellen; she often takes her father's part in family discussion in Ivy Compton-Burnett's *A Father and His Fate*.

Eliza Mowbray   The widow of Miles Mowbray's brother and the mother of Malcolm, Rudolph, and Nigel; she dramatizes herself and tries to order her nieces around when Ellen and Miles Mowbray are absent in Ivy Compton-Burnett's *A Father and His Fate*.

Ellen Mowbray   Wife of Miles; she is the emotional and moral center of the family in Ivy Compton-Burnett's *A Father and His Fate*.

Malcolm Mowbray   Miles Mobray's nephew who will inherit Miles's entailed estate; he quarrels with his mother, Eliza, becomes engaged to Verena Gray, and finally is to marry his cousin Ursula Mowbray in Ivy Compton-Burnett's *A Father and His Fate*.

Miles Mowbray   The egotistical father who tests his daughters; he becomes engaged to young Verena Gray when his wife, Ellen, is missing in a shipwreck and does not want to give her up when his wife returns in Ivy Compton-Burnett's *A Father and His Fate*.

Nigel Mowbray   Malcolm's youngest brother; he confides everything to Miss Manders, his mother's companion, in Ivy Compton-Burnett's *A Father and His Fate*.

Rudolf Mowbray   His mother Eliza's favorite son; he is a young man who annoys his uncle Miles Mowbray with low-voiced, ironic comments in Ivy Compton-Burnett's *A Father and His Fate*.

Ursula Mowbray   The eldest daughter of Miles and Ellen; she is often in sympathy with her mother and her cousin Malcolm in Ivy Compton-Burnett's *A Father and His Fate*.

Mowlem   Day head-porter of the hotel who presided with grandeur at the revolving doors of the great hall; he is understood to be writing, with expert assistance, a book of reminiscences of his post in Arnold Bennett's *Imperial Palace*.

Charles Moyne   Old down-and-out man who is dispossessed by the firm of Carter & Galloway; Ida Arnold gives him money in Graham Greene's *Brighton Rock*.

Mr. Muckerji Indian who lives in D.'s London hotel; his quiet investigations are both hindrance and help to D. in Graham Greene's *The Confidential Agent*.

Mudir Harbor master of the harbor near the crash sight of the *Speedwell*, whose treasure was to be recovered; he cunningly deceives the *Atropos* into believing that there were no armies in the area in C. S. Forester's *Hornblower and the Atropos*.

Muggridge Drunkard surgeon's mate aboard the *Indefatigable* involved in gambling on watch in C. S. Forester's *Mr. Midshipman Hornblower*.

Muhlen Contemptible blackmailer whose real name is Mr. Retlow and whose legal wife is Mrs. Meadows in Norman Douglas's *South Wind*.

Major Muir Cockney officer in charge of the educational unit of the British Army in Gibraltar and, therefore, Sgt. Richard Ennis's commander; Muir's incompetence and self-importance make him the butt of Ennis's literate insults and lofty contempt in Anthony Burgess's *A Vision of Battlements*.

Mungo Muirhead Fanatic minister of Kirk Aller, a neighboring town to Woodilee village; he chastises David Sempill for sheltering Mark Kerr, one of Montrose's lieutenants, in John Buchan's *Witch Wood*.

Mujid Iraqui refugee from Bagdad, where he had been teaching and pursuing a doctorate at the university until he appeared at a demonstration in favor of Kurdish independence; he is the fiancé of Simone Mourre; he comes to London seeking the aid of Kate Fletcher Armstrong in Margaret Drabble's *The Middle Ground*.

Boy Mulcaster A boorish aristocrat, who is an acquaintance of Charles Ryder and Sebastian Flyte at Oxford and the brother of Charles's future wife; he is arrested with Charles and Sebastian for drunkenness in Evelyn Waugh's *Brideshead Revisited*.

Bartly Mulholland Sly, cruel right-hand man to Dan Gallagher in the Irish revolutionary organization in Liam O'Flaherty's *The Informer*.

Cornelius Muller Bigoted South African security head who blackmailed Maurice Castle in Pretoria, may have killed Communist agent Carson, and suspects Castle as a double agent in Graham Greene's *The Human Factor*.

Bertha Mullet The red-haired nursemaid of the Sullivan family; she tells the children stories of her family's fall from prosperity in Ivy Compton-Burnett's *Parents and Children*.

Malachi (Buck) Mulligan Satiric, conformist medical student who shares the tower with Stephen Dedalus and takes his keys in James Joyce's *Ulysses*.

Rat Mulligan Timid tailor who is falsely accused of informing the police of the whereabouts of Frankie McPhillip in Liam O'Flaherty's *The Informer*.

Jenny Mullion Deaf but perceptive guest at the Crome estate; she parodies other guests in her closely guarded journal in Aldous Huxley's *Crome Yellow*.

Mr. Mulvatey Popular journalist who becomes acquainted with Bertram Verren and is invited to read some of Gladys Verren's work; he tries to convince her to satisfy the public taste to win acceptance for her writing in Frank Swinnerton's *The Young Idea: A Comedy of Environment*.

Lieutenant Mulvey Molly Bloom's first lover from the time she was a girl in Gibraltar in James Joyce's *Ulysses*.

Mum The narrator's mother; the flirtatious owner of a boarding house, she gives attention to her male boarders but does not show love to her son or her husband in Colin MacInnes's *Absolute Beginners*.

Squire Mumby Hard-bargaining farmer who considers himself socially superior to his Folly Down neighbors in T. F. Powys's *Mr. Weston's Good Wine*.

John Mumby Squire Mumby's sexually insatiable, miserly son, who is frightened by Mr. Weston's lion and proposes to Ann Kiddle in T. F. Powys's *Mr. Weston's Good Wine*.

Martin Mumby John's equally caddish brother, who is frightened by Mr. Weston's lion and proposes to Phoebe Kiddle in T. F. Powys's *Mr. Weston's Good Wine*.

Munday The butler at Miles Vane-Merrick's castle in Kent; a grizzled old man, he has been with Miles a long time in Vita Sackville-West's *Family History*.

Mrs. Munday Housekeeper-cook at Miles Vane-Merrick's castle in Kent; she first appears to Evelyn Jarrold, arriving for a visit, as the incarnation of Ceres, prepared to take all family and visitors into her welcoming embrace in Vita Sackville-West's *Family History*.

Emmeline Munday The senior mistress at Josephine

Napier's school; she is a short, ponderous woman with drab hair and vague eyes in Ivy Compton-Burnett's *More Women Than Men*.

Hans-Dieter Mundt (covername: Mundt Freitag) Hitler Youth member and later counter-subversion agent for the GDR Intelligence Service, Abteilung; with Dieter Frey, he persuades Elsa Fennan to betray her husband and her adopted country in John le Carré's *Call for the Dead*. He is captured by Peter Guillam, betrays Abteilung to become a British double agent, and effects Alec Leamas's and Liz Gold's deaths in *The Spy Who Came In from the Cold*.

James Munster Solicitor and long-time friend of Sir Roderick Patterson; he extricates Saul Patterson, Sir Roderick's son, from an embarrassing criminal case involving a thief and confidence man intent on getting even with Sir Roderick for sending him to prison in Frank Swinnerton's *Some Achieve Greatness*.

Juley Munt The Schlegels' aunt, who tries to help her nieces in E. M. Forster's *Howards End*.

Dr. Walter (codename "Brahms Four") von Munte High-level East German officer at the Deutsche Emissions und Girobank and Silas Gaunt's and Bret Rensselaer's longtime inside source; he defects with Bernard Samson's help in Len Deighton's *Berlin Game*. He is Bernard Samson's information source in *London Match*.

Div Muntras Krillio Muntras's son, who steals Billy Xiao Pin's watch and tries to kill RobaydayAnganol in Brian W. Aldiss's *Helliconia Summer*.

Immyat Muntras Krillio Muntras's daughter and chief medical practitioner in Lordryardry; she tends Billy Xiao Pin when he is sick in Brian W. Aldiss's *Helliconia Summer*.

Captain Krillio Muntras An ice trader who helps MettyVasidol save JandolAnganol in Brian W. Aldiss's *Helliconia Summer*.

Mr. Murbles Solicitor for the Duke of Denver and Lord Peter Wimsey in Dorothy L. Sayers's *Clouds of Witness,* in *Unnatural Death,* and in *The Unpleasantness at the Bellona Club*.

Joan Murchison A secretary who infiltrates Norman Urquhart's office to get information for Lord Peter Wimsey in Dorothy L. Sayers's *Strong Poison*.

Miss Murdoch The partner in the school with Hermia Heriot; she is a spare, elderly woman, who does not want

any changes and who uses Hermia's money to pay her own debts in Ivy Compton-Burnett's *The Last and the First*.

Cynthia Murdoch Styles Court resident; a Red Cross Hospital worker, she mixes Emily Inglethorp's sleeping powders in Agatha Christie's *The Mysterious Affair at Styles: A Detective Story*.

Count Casimir Muresco Competent and vital representative of the Nationalist or Monarchist Party of Evallonia; he seeks Thomas Carlyle Craw's influence to insure the neutrality of Britain in John Buchan's *Castle Gay*. He is devoted to restoring the rightful monarch, Prince John, to the throne in *The House of the Four Winds*.

E. Jimpson Murgatroyd A "gloomy old buster" but a capable physician, who prescribes country relaxation for Bertie Wooster in P. G. Wodehouse's *Aunts Aren't Gentlemen*. He appears in *Full Moon*.

Evelyn Murgatroyd A flamboyant, melodramatic vacationer who fancies herself a *femme fatale* as she searches desperately for attention, intimacy, and social activity at the Santa Marina hotel in Virginia Woolf's *The Voyage Out*.

Senor Murillo Wealthy businessman father of Conception Gomez; he hires Sgt. Richard Ennis to teach guitar to Conception, thus creating the opportunity for their attachment in Anthony Burgess's *A Vision of Battlements*.

Charles Murley A womanizing government official, who warns Bernard Sands he needs help running Vardon Hall; after Sands's death, Murley agrees to take his place on the committee and begins a program of economizing in Angus Wilson's *Hemlock and After*.

Murphy Self-loving Irish egoist and "seedy solipsist" in search of annihilation who instead finds accidental death by immolation; his ashes are strewn on the barroom floor; he is the central figure in Samuel Beckett's *Murphy*.

Serjeant Murphy Serjeant-at-law who officiates at the meeting between Charles Smithson and Ernest Freeman following the jilting of Ernestina Freeman in John Fowles's *The French Lieutenant's Woman*.

D. B. Murphy Sailor who tells tall tales during the dissipated narrative in the cabman's shelter in James Joyce's *Ulysses*.

Alison Murray A beautiful, unhappy former actress of promise who fails in her close relationships with others; she is the ex-wife of Donnell Murray; she is alienated from her elder daughter, Jane; her younger daughter, Molly, has cerebral palsy; Alison is having a difficult time in her relationship with Anthony Keating in Margaret Drabble's *The Ice Age*.

Dick Murray   The loving, decent man who has all the qualities of warmth that Roger Henderson lacks and is unable to prevent himself from falling in love with May Henderson, who loves him deeply in return in W. Somerset Maugham's *The Hour Before the Dawn*.

Donnell Murray   A successful actor, who is Alison Murray's ex-husband and father of Molly and Jane Murray; he is liked by Anthony Keating in Margaret Drabble's *The Ice Age*.

Felicia Murray   A new student at the women's college who becomes Dolores Hutton's friend; she is a daughter of a parson with eleven children in Ivy Compton-Burnett's *Dolores*.

Jane Murray   The alienated eighteen-year-old daughter of Alison and Donnell Murray; she is sentenced to prison for two years after a fatal traffic accident in Wallacia, a Balkan country, in Margaret Drabble's *The Ice Age*.

Molly Murray   Ten-year-old daughter of Alison and Donnell Murray; she suffers from cerebral palsy and is given to violent behavior in Margaret Drabble's *The Ice Age*.

Murti   Al-Ith's sister and confidante in Doris Lessing's *The Marriages Between Zones Three, Four, and Five*.

Leslie (Scorpio) Murtlock   The leader of a cult devoted to Harmony with high overtones of black magic and ritual sex; he eventually gets Widmerpool in his power in Anthony Powell's *Hearing Secret Harmonies*.

Bob Muschat   Important member of the Free Fishers who has been sent by the British Government to Yonderdale and to the area near Hungrygrain to watch and to report on any secret service activity with France in John Buchan's *The Free Fishers*.

Freddie Mush   Pretentious, monacle-wearing secretary to Rupert Catskill; he opposes the Utopians because their eugenic and environmental policies contradict his naturalist ideals in H. G. Wells's *Men Like Gods*.

Coral Musker   Emotional, penniless virgin traveling to a dancing job in Constantinople; she is befriended by Carleton Myatt and, out of gratitude, becomes his mistress; she is falsely arrested as Richard Czinner's

accomplice and betrayed when Joseph Günlich lies to Myatt in Graham Greene's *Stamboul Train*.

Jack Muskham   First cousin of Sir Lawrence Mont; he brawls with Wilfred Desert after trying to horsewhip him in John Galsworthy's *Flowering Wilderness*.

My mother   Unloving woman whom Molloy is on his way to visit by bicycle when he is arrested for loitering, and in whose room he lives after her death in Samuel Beckett's *Molloy*.

Carleton Myatt   Shrewd but emotionally sensitive young Jewish merchant; he charms and seduces Coral Musker and tries briefly to rescue her but abandons her to pursue Janet Pardoe in Graham Greene's *Stamboul Train*.

Mr. Mybug   A chubby intellectual bent on proving that Branwell Brontë rather than Emily Brontë really wrote *Wuthering Heights* in Stella Gibbons's *Cold Comfort Farm*.

Myk   A phagor slave belonging to Aoz Roon; he is forced to execute Datnil Skar; he is a member of the other intelligent race on Helliconia in Brian W. Aldiss's *Helliconia Spring*.

Henry Mynors   Most eligible bachelor; he is a successful businessman and an active churchman, is kind toward children, is boldly able to cope with the miser Ephraim Tellwright's crotchets, and genuinely loves Anna Tellwright, but he is limited in general human compassion; Anna realizes she can never love him as she does Willie Price, although she will be all he wants in a wife in Arnold Bennett's *Anna of the Five Towns*.

Myra   Nursemaid who looks after Pierre Cosway and then deserts him during the blacks' riot and the ensuing fire in Jean Rhys's *Wide Sargasso Sea*.

ConegUndunory MyrdemInggala   Queen of Borlien; although greatly loved by the people, she is divorced by her husband for political reasons in Brian W. Aldiss's *Helliconia Summer*.

Willard Myron   Technical sergeant on the *Endeavor* and a mechanical genius; he develops a way to transport materials in Rama in Arthur C. Clarke's *Rendezvous with Rama*.

Mr. Myson   Founder, proprietor and editor of the *Five Towns Weekly*; he battles with the established *Staffordshire Signal*, loses, and is bought out; thus Denry Machin is taught to avoid any financial risks with newspapers in Arnold Bennett's *The Card: A Story of Adventure in the Five Towns*.

N

"N" The mysteriously omniscient narrator, who identifies himself as a secret presence and a student of human nature in Iris Murdoch's *The Philosopher's Pupil.*

Naab A rebel leader who is sacrificed in Brian W. Aldiss's *Helliconia Spring.*

Mother Felicity Nadezhda Russian Catholic nun who controls Karla's schizophrenic daughter Tatiana at the private clinic she heads near Berne in John le Carré's *Smiley's People.*

Peter Nagle Opportunistic painter who works at the Steen Clinic in P. D. James's *A Mind to Murder.*

Nahkri Laintal Ay's uncle, who rules Oldorando jointly with his brother, Klils, in Brian W. Aldiss's *Helliconia Spring.*

Captain Moti Naidu Indian whose duty is "to provide certain ancillary information" for top-secret Operation Apollo; he is very considerate and respectful of others but philosophically impotent in Kingsley Amis's *The Anti-Death League.*

Chief Inspector Nailsworth The huge, good-humored friend of the murdered Inspector Stone; clumsy and direct, he is called "Elephant" because he never forgets in Nicholas Blake's *A Tangled Web.*

Naipundeg A captain in the Sibornalese army who is killed in a duel with Harbin Fashnalgid in Brian W. Aldiss's *Helliconia Winter.*

Prek Namh Minister for Education who is the Badai government official Bill Eliot dies to save in Srem Panh in Angus Wilson's *The Middle Age of Mrs. Eliot.*

Nancy Charles Watkins's wife (in his alternate reality) and a resident of the West Indies; she is perhaps a hallucinatory version of Nancy Thorpe in Doris Lessing's *Briefing for a Descent into Hell.*

Councillor Joseph Patrick Nannetti Newspaper manager who employs Leopold Bloom in James Joyce's *Ulysses.*

Nanny The child Bernard's nursemaid whose sponge showered drops upon him while bathing, awakening the eloquent child to sensation, a luminous epiphany of an experience recalled by the adult Bernard in Virginia Woolf's *The Waves.*

Nanny The Gardners' nursemaid, who cares for the children of Orlando and Judith (Gardner) King as well as for Stephen and Paul Gardner in Isabel Colegate's *Orlando King.*

Nanny The Nettleby family nursemaid who is in charge of Violet and Osbert Nettleby in Isabel Colegate's *The Shooting Party.*

Lady Nantley Pamela Brune's mother; she and Lord Nantley confide in Sir Edward Leithen, Pamela's godfather, their hope that Pamela and Charles Ottery will marry in John Buchan's *The Gap in the Curtain.*

Lord Nantley Father of Pamela Brune; he is a member of the Whitsuntide house party at Flambard and friend of Sir Edward Leithen in John Buchan's *The Gap in the Curtain.*

Mollie Nantley Old friend who warns Sir Edward Leithen that he is not being fair to Koré Arabin by paying her so much attention and that he is too old to marry her in John Buchan's *The Dancing Floor.*

Helena Napier Pretty, fashionable, disorganized anthropologist who, with her husband, lets the flat beneath Mildred Lathbury's and helps to widen her circle, partly by carrying on a flirtation with her colleague Everard Bone in Barbara Pym's *Excellent Women.* She is mentioned in *Less Than Angels.*

Josephine Napier The head of a girls' school, jealous of her adopted son Gabriel Swift's wife, Ruth (Giffard); she lets her stand in a draft when Ruth is delirious, hastening Ruth's death in Ivy Compton-Burnett's *More Women Than Men.*

Rockingham Napier Handsome, sociable aesthete and ex-Flag Lieutenant in the Navy, who makes friends and flirts mildly with Mildred Lathbury; the two of them take up a hobby of "observing the anthropologists" after his wife takes a Pimlico flat near Mildred Lathbury's in Barbara Pym's *Excellent Women.* He is rapturously discussed in *A Glass of Blessings*

Simon Napier The husband of Josephine and the former beloved of Elizabeth Giffard; he dies from a fall when Elizabeth lets go of the ladder he is standing on in Ivy Compton-Burnett's *More Women Than Men.*

Napoleon Member of the Gorbals Die-Hards; he assists Dickson McCunn in freeing Sakskia, the Russian princess, in John Buchan's *Huntingtower.*

Napoleon (satiric representation of Joseph Stalin) A pig on Mr. Jones's farm; he takes over leadership of the animals after the hero, Snowball, has been ousted and the leader, Major, has died in George Orwell's *Animal Farm*.

B. Napur   Indian solicitor and barrister in an African colony; he is a friend of Giles Colmore, whom he attempts, without success, to represent at Giles's trial in Roy Fuller's *The Father's Comedy*.

Narcissus   Greek freedman and loyal servant to Claudius; he is slain at Agrippinilla's orders following Claudius's death in Robert Graves's *Claudius, the God and His Wife Messalina*.

Narrator (covernames: Edmond Dorf, Liam Dempsey, Patrick Armstrong)   A tough-minded, wisecracking, morally decent, working-class espionage agent; he unmasks Dalby, his supervisor, as a double agent; he is the anonymous narrator of Len Deighton's *The Ipcress File*. Using the covername Edmond Dorf, he is assigned to smuggle a Russian defector out of Berlin in *Funeral in Berlin*. He thwarts General Midwinter's reactionary plots in *The Billion-Dollar Brain*. He is used as a decoy and *agent provocateur* by his agency so it can attempt to salvage Nazi-counterfeited currency from a sunken German submarine in *Horse Under Water*. As Patrick Armstrong he rejoins his agency as a computer whiz working for an Anglo-American naval warfare committee intent on securing a Russian defector and his nuclear submarine in *Spy Story*.

Narrator   Unnamed Englishman who goes on a mental voyage through the cosmos as a "disembodied, wandering viewpoint", combining with alien minds to form the Cosmic Spirit in search of the Star Maker in Olaf Stapledon's *Star Maker*.

Narrator   An unnamed man who, fascinated with the scientific theories of the mad De Selby, departs this life to narrate his experiences in a mechanized hell where De Selby's skewed theories are in force in Flann O'Brien's *The Third Policeman*.

Narrator   Open-minded, intelligent teenager living and working in London in the 1950's as a free-lance photographer; he is at odds with the Establishment and a defender of the independence and lifestyles of teenagers and of his friends, who include prostitutes, hustlers, and homosexuals; disgusted by racism in the city, he aids endangered blacks during racial riots; he is in love with Suzette and devoted to his father in Colin MacInnes's *Absolute Beginners*.

Narrator   Unnamed college student with literary pretensions who creates the novelist Dermot Trellis and numerous other characters who get out of control in Flann O'Brien's *At Swim-Two-Birds*.

Narrator   An anonymous journalist and amateur philosopher who experiences first-hand the Martian landing and conquest, being humbled by the omnipotent aliens and undergoing many adventures while fleeing from them in H. G. Wells's *The War of the Worlds*.

Narrator's Brother   The anonymous journalist's unnamed brother, who rescues the Elphinstones from bandits and, while fleeing with them to France, witnesses the mass exodus from London and the suicidal attack on the Martians by the ramship *Thunder Child* in H. G. Wells's *The War of the Worlds*.

Edmund Narraway   A wood-engraver; Otto Narraway's ascetic brother, he is the narrator of Iris Murdoch's *The Italian Girl*.

Flora Narraway   The only child of Otto and Isabel Narraway and the lover of David Levkin, by whom she becomes pregnant; she has an abortion in Iris Murdoch's *The Italian Girl*.

Isabel Narraway   Wife of Otto and lover of David Levkin, whose child she conceives and intends to keep in Iris Murdoch's *The Italian Girl*.

Lydia Narraway   The violent mother whose destructive love alternated between her sons, Otto and Edmund, in their youth; her death brings Edmund back to the family home in Iris Murdoch's *The Italian Girl*.

Otto Narraway   A stonemason; he is Isabel's husband, Flora's father, Edmund's brother, and Elsa Levkin's lover in Iris Murdoch's *The Italian Girl*.

Nasar   A Canopian who Ambien II believes is a misfit, and whom she meets while visiting the Shikastan city of Koshi, where Nasar has been stationed as an official for twenty-five years in Doris Lessing's *The Sirian Experiments*.

Nash   Chief gunner and friend of Captain Bennett on the search for Nazi gold; he is killed by Bennett when the gold is loaded onto the flying boat in Alan Sillitoe's *The Lost Flying Boat*.

Nash   Bully from the Belvedere School who interrogates Stephen Dedalus in James Joyce's *A Portrait of the Artist as a Young Man*.

Nash   Master's mate aboard the *Atropos* in C. S. Forester's *Hornblower and the Atropos*.

Nash   A psychiatrist for the Firm; he treats Benedicta Merlin for her psychoses and attends Felix Charlock through his illness and surgery in Lawrence Durrell's *Nunquam*.

Pamela (Beau) Nash   A handsome, wealthy girl used to having her own way; she is Mary Innes's devoted friend in Josephine Tey's *Miss Pym Disposes*.

Abe Nathan   Mildred's husband, a retired American scriptwriter; he is a close friend and mentor of Daniel Martin, who lives in a cabin behind Nathan's Hollywood home in John Fowles's *Daniel Martin*.

Bethesda Nathan   Young woman whom Philip Weatherby begins to see after he ends his engagement to Mary Pomfret in Henry Green's *Nothing*.

Mildred Nathan   Abe Nathan's wife; she is a friend of Daniel Martin and Jenny McNeil in John Fowles's *Daniel Martin*.

Nathaniel   A bishop's son and a friend of Charles Smithson; he accompanies him on a night of debauchery in John Fowles's *The French Lieutenant's Woman*.

Nautiloids   A mollusk-like alien species whose history illustrates the importance of nurture rather than nature in Olaf Stapledon's *Star Maker*.

Navah   A technician from one of Sirius's colonized planets who is assigned by Ambien II to find out what is happening in the Canopian part of Rohanda (Shikasta) and ends up settling down in the southern part of an isolated northern continent in Doris Lessing's *The Sirian Experiments*.

Myra, Lady Naylor   Wife of Sir Richard Naylor; she is Laurence's aunt and aunt by marriage of Lois Farquar, the orphaned daughter of Sir Richard's sister; like her husband she seems determined to ignore the Anglo-Irish War (1919–21) and to deny its significance to Ireland's Ascendancy class in Elizabeth Bowen's *The Last September*.

Sir Richard Naylor   Husband of Lady Naylor and uncle and guardian of Lois Farquar, his late sister's daughter; he insists to anyone who will listen that the quarrel between the native Irish and the English that disturbs the peace outside the walls of his estate is of no concern to Irish Big House society; his myopia extends also to the romantic behavior of his friend Hugo Montmorency in Elizabeth Bowen's *The Last September*.

Laura Lita Carmen Etoile (Rara) de Nazianzi   Maid and companion to Queen Lois of Pisuerga and niece of the Duchess of Cavaljos; the ardent lover of Prince Yousef, Laura is stricken with grief and joins a convent, where she is eventually sainted, when Yousef marries Princess Elsie of England in Ronald Firbank's *The Flower Beneath the Foot*.

Anthony Neale   Leader of the four Oxford chums; unable to leap the gap between thought and action, he wonders what he seeks in life; he sympathizes with the socialists but accepts his position as heir to landed property as a way of being closer to the people; when the land is lost, he becomes a schoolmaster until Mrs. Appleton's complaint leads to his resignation and self-recognition and he joins the battle against the Spanish fascists in C. Day Lewis's *Starting Point*.

Bill Neale   Janos Lavin's friend who sees art in general as frivolous because to him "the Party is a kind of work of art in itself" in John Berger's *A Painter of Our Time*.

Brenda Neale   Anthony's lively, flippant younger sister; she becomes the wife of John Henderson, who is surprised that an expensive education did not spoil her; she supports his sinking spirits after he confesses that he crawled to keep his job in C. Day Lewis's *Starting Point*.

Sir Charles Neale   A landed aristocrat and Member of Parliament; he is incisive in speech and movement; he arranges a job for John Henderson; having lost his property in the depression, he is left prostrate, an old man whose ideal civilization has passed, a ghost in his own house in C. Day Lewis's *Starting Point*.

Neary   Murphy's philosophic mentor, in love with Miss Counihan in Samuel Beckett's *Murphy*.

Nebulae   The earliest forms of intelligence and spirit in the universe in Olaf Stapledon's *Star Maker*.

Ned   Small, neat, rather spiteful twenty-nine-year-old homosexual assistant professor from the United States who takes up with James Boyce, deliberately in competition with Leonora Eyre and to a lesser extent Phoebe Sharpe in Barbara Pym's *The Sweet Dove Died*.

Ned   Decent and questioning British Intelligence spymaster; he directs the Russia House operations, coaches Barley Blair in patriotism and honor, and alone understands Barley's motives for betrayal in John le Carré's *The Russia House*. He narrates highlights of his fading espionage career in *The Secret Pilgrim*.

Mr. Neiman   Mrs. Neiman's spouse, regarded by Ethan Llewelyn as a model of husbandly solicitude in Malcolm Lowry's *October Ferry to Gabriola*.

Mrs. Neiman   Elderly woman on the ferry to Gabriola Island whose mouth bleeds badly after she has all her teeth extracted in Malcolm Lowry's *October Ferry to Gabriola*.

Nella Italian peasant, a servant of Orlando King in Isabel Colegate's *Orlando at the Brazen Threshold*.

Nellie Maggie Winter's younger sister; she is overmastered by grief following the death of her child, Rachel; the birth of her son brings no consolation in Richard Hughes's *The Fox in the Attic*. Widowed, she can barely keep herself and her son alive by giving lessons, being aided by neighbors almost as poor as she in *The Wooden Shepherdess*.

Nellie Rita's proper, possessive, dominant elder aunt; a talented dressmaker and a good housekeeper, she exhibits odd behavior and occasional bursts of rage; she perceives Ira as a threat in Beryl Bainbridge's *The Dressmaker*.

Nelson An American communist who has a brief affair with Anna Wulf; he has a split personality — demonic and rational — and is obsessed with talking about his wife, who supposedly "castrates" him, in Doris Lessing's *The Golden Notebook*.

Horatio, Lord Nelson Admiral who receives the forged papers from Captain Vincent in Joseph Conrad's *The Rover*. Horatio Hornblower assists in coordinating his funeral procession in C. S. Forester's *Hornblower and the Atropos*.

Nero Son of Agrippinilla; he is adopted by Claudius in Robert Graves's *Claudius, the God and His Wife Messalina*.

Norah Nesbitt A cheerful woman; separated from her husband, she supports herself and her child by writing cheap novelettes; she is the first woman genuinely to love the adult Philip Carey, but perversely he rejects her love for the cheap and shallow Mildred Rogers in W. Somerset Maugham's *Of Human Bondage*.

Nethilta Young, rash Efrafan doe rabbit whose jibe at an officer attracts the Council's suspicion and complicates Bigwig's escape attempt in Richard Adams's *Watership Down*.

Cicely Nettleby Nineteen-year-old granddaughter of Sir Randolph Nettleby; her mother, Ida Nettleby, finds her flirtatious behavior unsuitable to her station; Cicely takes a liking to Tibor Rakassyi until he shows his utter disdain for the lower classes in Isabel Colegate's *The Shooting Party*.

Ida Nettleby Sir Randolph Nettleby's daughter-in-law, whose husband is reported to be out on business; Ida is a nonchalant mother except for her concern over the manners of her daughter Cicely in Isabel Colegate's *The Shooting Party*.

Marcus Nettleby Fifteen-year-old grandson of Sir Randolph Nettleby and brother of Cicely; he is included in Sir Randolph's shooting parties in Isabel Colegate's *The Shooting Party*.

Minnie, Lady Nettleby Sir Randolph Nettleby's wife, who is concerned mostly with entertaining and appearances; unlike Sir Randolph, she prefers London to the country; she is a doting grandmother and a considerate hostess in Isabel Colegate's *The Shooting Party*.

Osbert Nettleby Youngest grandson of Sir Randolph Nettleby; his mother, Ida, leaves him in the care of his schoolmaster in Isabel Colegate's *The Shooting Party*.

Sir Randolph Nettleby Baronet and country gentleman; his great fear is the dissolution of the social-class system in England; though he treats his servants and tenants with consideration and does not resent the lower classes, he does not want his way of life to disintegrate with the onslaught of industrialism in Isabel Colegate's *The Shooting Party*.

Violet Nettleby Youngest daughter of Ida Nettleby and granddaughter of Sir Randolph Nettleby in Isabel Colegate's *The Shooting Party*.

Neuville Captain of the *Pique*; he is a hospitable French privateer who picks up the crew of the sunk *Marie Galante* in C. S. Forester's *Mr. Midshipman Hornblower*.

Neville A bookish, interior-dwelling, poetic boy, passionately in love with Percival; after Percival's death, Neville is always on the lookout for a new beloved; he is indifferent to nature except as a vehicle for what he seeks; as Neville grows older, he celebrates the moment, the life that love and poetry give him in Virginia Woolf's *The Waves*.

Hank Newbegin Harvey Newbegin's boisterous young son in Len Deighton's *The Billion-Dollar Brain*.

Harvey Newbegin A former U.S. State Department official, General Midwinter's buffoonish agent, and the narrator's old friend; he violates Midwinter's order to assassinate the narrator, defects to Russia, and is eventually murdered outside a Russian train in Len Deighton's *The Billion-Dollar Brain*.

Mercy Newbegin Harvey Newbegin's muddle-headed spouse in Len Deighton's *The Billion-Dollar Brain*.

Lieutenant-General Patrick Newell Greying, healthy British NATO Strike Force South official; he negotiates the details of the Abra Bay project with The Ruler, using Robert Halliday and Dieter Schelm as intermediaries in Eric Ambler's *The Care of Time.*

Dr. M. Newhover Corrupt medical doctor in wicked association with Dominick Medina; he prescribes a treatment for Richard Hannay which will make him more susceptible to Medina's hypnotic suggestions in John Buchan's *The Three Hostages.*

Miss Newland A vulnerable, unhappy student at Shrewsbury College, Oxford; she is driven to attempt suicide by malicious anonymous letters in Dorothy L. Sayers's *Gaudy Night.*

Elizabeth Newman Rebecca's mother and Colin Freestone's lover; the wife of a wealthy industrialist, she has a perverse relationship with her husband that includes infidelity, beating, and forgiveness in David Storey's *A Temporary Life.*

Hal Newman Young man who gently pursues Agatha King while she is in Italy in Isabel Colegate's *Orlando at the Brazen Threshold.*

Rebecca Newman A student at the art school where Colin Freestone teaches; she befriends him and then catches him in bed with her mother; she gets a boyfriend at the school and remains friends with Colin in David Storey's *A Temporary Life.*

The New One Nil's otherwise undesignated infant-child who, together with Liku, is kidnapped by the Homo sapiens in William Golding's *The Inheritors.*

Mrs. Newsome Former house mistress at Molly Murray's school; she was dismissed for her insincere affection in Margaret Drabble's *The Ice Age.*

Bill Newsome Artist and friend of Kay and Colin Pasmore; he and his wife introduce Kay to Norman Fowler in David Storey's *Pasmore.*

Marjorie Newsome Friend of Kay and Colin Pasmore; she and her artist husband introduce Kay to Norman Fowler in David Storey's *Pasmore.*

Ng-Gunko Twelve-year-old East African boy; he is one of the supernormals of John Wainwright's Pacific island colony in Olaf Stapledon's *Odd John: A Story Between Jest and Earnest.*

Earl of Ngumo Head of an important and militarily strong Azanian tribe; together with General Connolly he plays a significant role in the successful revolt against Emperor Seth in Evelyn Waugh's *Black Mischief.*

Nicholas Lover of Lucy Goldsmith (later Lucy Otford); he unhappily discovers her half undressed with another man when he visits her Cambridge dorm rooms with her cousin Jane Gray in Margaret Drabble's *The Waterfall.*

Nicholas The oldest son of Beatrice and Hallam and the nephew of Rosamund Stacey; his constant playing with war toys annoys his pacifist mother in Margaret Drabble's *The Millstone.*

Captain Nichols The roguish, shifty sea-captain whose narration of events that occur in Charles Strickland's life includes his painful death in Tahiti in W. Somerset Maugham's *The Moon and Sixpence.*

Mrs. Nichols A servant in the home of Yestin Evans; she spreads gossip about the Evanses' marital problems in Richard Llewellyn's *How Green Was My Valley.*

Alexander Nicholson ("Alexis Nicolaevitch") Russian aristocrat and Sakskia's fiancé; mistakenly attacked by Dickson McCunn, he subsequently joins McCunn in freeing Sakskia, whose love he wins in John Buchan's *Huntingtower.*

Anna Nicholson A landscape painter; Lois Heidler's friend and confidante, she acts as messenger to Marya Zelli from the Heidlers in Jean Rhys's *Postures.*

Philip Nicholson Young man with a shock of thick blond hair, clear blue eyes, and a ridiculous wild laugh, who attracts devoted friends; he and David Renn are the only survivors from a battalion of five; they were critically wounded on consecutive days in 1917; Philip plans to establish a pacifist newspaper with the aid of T. S. Heywood, Hervey Russell, and Renn, but he dies soon after discharge from the army in Storm Jameson's *Company Parade.* In 1938 David Renn and T. S. Heywood still grieve for him in *Before the Crossing.*

Richard Nicholson Nephew of Mr. Sutcliffe; a scholar and writer who hires Mary Olivier to be his secretary, he falls in love with her and after a brief affair accepts Mary's refusal of marriage because of her obligation to her senile mother; he marries another woman just ten days before Mrs. Olivier dies in May Sinclair's *Mary Olivier: A Life.*

Nick Simon Camish's long-time friend, who like Simon has forged a career through intellect and industry; he is host of the party at which Simon meets Rose Vassiliou in Margaret Drabble's *The Needle's Eye.*

Tam Nickson Old friend of the society of the Free Fishers whose home in Yonderdale near Hungrygrain is the military headquarters of Jock Kinloch, Bob Muschat, Eben Garnock, and "Nanty" Lammas in John Buchan's *The Free Fishers.*

Nicole   Daughter of Angela and Dennis; she has Down's Syndrome in David Lodge's *How Far Can You Go?.*

Nigel   Jack Brotherhood's right-hand man; he handles the details of the intelligence service's investigation into Magnus Pym's betrayal in John le Carré's *A Perfect Spy.*

Nigel   Would-be helpful neighbor of Marcia Ivory; he wonders at her odd behavior in Barbara Pym's *Quartet in Autumn.*

Ronald Nightingale   Chemist and fellow of the Cambridge college who is bitter over his failure to be elected to the Royal Society; he supports Redvers Crawford for election as new college Master and is responsible for a circular which insults Alice Jago in C. P. Snow's *The Masters.* Bursar of the college, he is suspected of removing crucial photographic evidence in the affair of Donald Howard's fraudulent research; he casts the lone dissenting vote in the final decision on Howard's fellowship in *The Affair.*

Nikita   Murderous Russian revolutionary who cripples Razumov for betraying Victor Haldin in Joseph Conrad's *Under Western Eyes.*

Nil   Neanderthal mother of Liku and of an infant male called "the new one"; she is killed by the Homo sapiens enemy in William Golding's *The Inheritors.*

Nildro-hain ("song of blackbird")   Doe rabbit whose death impels her mate, Strawberry, to leave the Warren of the Snares and join Hazel's pioneers in Richard Adams's *Watership Down.*

Nils   Assistant to the newspaper reporter Minty in Graham Greene's *England Made Me.*

Axel Nilsson   A civil servant who is Rupert Foster's colleague and Simon Foster's lover in Iris Murdoch's *A Fairly Honourable Defeat.*

Mrs. Nimmo   Beautiful, unselfish, loving mother of Chester Nimmo; she tragically dies soon after the family is forced to leave their farm in Joyce Cary's *Except the Lord.*

Chester Nimmo   Son of a rigidly moral stableman and

preacher; aided by his marriage to the gentry-class Nina Woodville, he rises to political greatness; throughout his political and personal life he finds it difficult to balance the morally right and the politically necessary in Joyce Cary's *Prisoner of Grace,* in *Except the Lord* and in *Not Honour More.*

Dorothy Nimmo   Infant youngest sister of Chester Nimmo; her death occurrs five months after her mother's in Joyce Cary's *Except the Lord.*

Georgina Nimmo   Beautiful, stubborn, pragmatic older sister of Chester Nimmo; she sacrifices her dreams of marriage and happiness to help keep the Nimmo family together in Joyce Cary's *Except the Lord.*

Richard Nimmo   Scholarly older brother of Chester Nimmo; he graduates from Oxford but disappointingly returns to the family home in Joyce Cary's *Except the Lord.*

Ruth Nimmo   Younger sister of Chester Nimmo; forced by family poverty into servitude at the Slapton House, she falls in love and elopes with a rake of a gentleman, Geoffrey Simnel, in Joyce Cary's *Except the Lord.*

Sally Nimmo   Second child of Nina Woodville and James Latter; raised to believe she is the daughter of Chester Nimmo, she adores Chester and aids him throughout his political and private life in Joyce Cary's *Prisoner of Grace* and in *Not Honour More.*

Tom Nimmo   Generous, self-educated farmer and evangelical preacher who raised his children under a rigid moral code; when he mistakenly calculates the wrong day of the Second Coming, his influence on his son Chester fades, but it is later restored in Joyce Cary's *Except the Lord.*

Tom Nimmo (the younger)   Oldest son of Nina Woodville and James Latter but brought up to believe his father is Chester Nimmo; an aspiring actor, he continually gets into trouble with women and the law and eventually is forced to flee the country to Germany, where he commits suicide in Joyce Cary's *Prisoner of Grace.*

Nina   A foreign dressmaker working in Britain illegally; when she is threatened with exposure as an unintended effect of Mischa Fox's device for routing the Lusiewicz brothers, she commits suicide in Iris Murdoch's *The Flight from the Enchanter.*

Ninette   Robert de Quincey's partner at the Garden Gallery; she turns down Janos Lavin's paintings as a "bit unimaginative" in John Berger's *A Painter of Our Time.*

Gilbert Niven ("Daft Gibbie")   Deformed village

idiot of Woodilee; he warns David Sempill against entering the Wood in John Buchan's *Witch Wood*.

Eleanor Nixey (Lady Harndean) Wife of Malcolm Nixey in J. B. Priestley's *Bright Day*.

Malcolm Nixey (Lord Harndean) Unscrupulous business entrepreneur who brings financial ruin to the Alingtons in J. B. Priestley's *Bright Day*.

Mrs. Nixon Old housekeeper for Darius Clayhanger; her young niece stirs Darius's libido, an embarrassing symptom of his decline from "softening of the brain," in Arnold Bennett's *Clayhanger*.

Dr. Julius No Very tall, bald, skull-faced, chinless half-Chinese, half-German villain; he plans to use a new radio beam to deflect the course of American test missiles; he has an exotically fortified and armed private island in Ian Fleming's *Dr. No*.

Beatrice Noakes Plump, middle-aged, garrulous chambermaid who loves to gossip; with her ingenuous helpfulness, she reassures Violet Powler on her first day as housekeeper at the hotel in Arnold Bennett's *Imperial Palace*.

Noaks A squat, bespectacled youth; he is the last of the Oxford undergraduates to kill himself for Zuleika Dobson; ashamed of having been afraid of the water, he defenestrates from Mrs. Batch's boarding house in Max Beerbohm's *Zuleika Dobson; or An Oxford Love Story*.

Nobby A carefree thief and street fellow who befriends Dorothy when she finds herself in London, having lost her memory; he takes her to pick hops and protects her for a while in George Orwell's *A Clergyman's Daughter*.

Mr. Noble A gentleman lodger in the house in St. John's Wood, London, where Miriam Henderson goes to live after a brief stay in the residence run by the Young Woman's Bible Association in Dorothy Richardson's *March Moonlight*.

Audrey (Anonyma) Lees Noel Estranged wife of a vicar; separated from him, she falls in love with Lord Miltoun and gives him up after an appeal by Lady Casterley in John Galsworthy's *The Patrician*.

Denis Nolan A resourceful, expert, independent Gaze Castle workman with unexpected attractiveness for women; he is briefly intimate with Marian Taylor; he rescues Effingham Cooper from the bog and becomes the executioner of Hannah Crean-Smith's husband in Iris Murdoch's *The Unicorn*.

Gypo Nolan Powerfully built but mentally deficient ex-policeman who informs on his friend Frankie McPhillip in order to obtain money for food and lodging in Liam O'Flaherty's *The Informer*.

John Wyse Nolan One of the patriotic drinkers in Barney Kiernan's Pub in James Joyce's *Ulysses*.

Peter Nolan An Irish friend of Mike Brady involved in a politically motivated art theft, as well as in Mike's joining the Irish Republican Army in David Lodge's *Ginger, You're Barmy*.

Nonni An eleven-year-old boy who goes with a small committee on an early journey to the Cold Pole, but later dies after severely injuring his arm in Doris Lessing's *The Making of the Representative for Planet 8*.

Norah Red-haired, spirited, resourceful ten-year-old member of a large family; she often performs necessary services for her neighbor, Rachel, and looks after Sylvanus in Richard Hughes's *The Wooden Shepherdess*.

Noreen Rose Vassiliou's severe, unbending nanny, who taught Rose to take Biblical injunctions against wealth literally in Margaret Drabble's *The Needle's Eye*.

Mr. Norfolk A master of the lowest form at Seaforth House; he is nicknamed "the Jacket" in Roy Fuller's *The Ruined Boys*.

Norman The Caliban-like regular-army recruit who does his basic training with Jonathan Browne, joins Mike Brady and Jonathan at the Clerk's Course, and ends up in charge of pigs at Badmore in David Lodge's *Ginger, You're Barmy*.

Norman Sixtyish bachelor clerk who resides alone in a bed-sitting room near Kilburn Park thinking occasionally about his coworkers, especially Marcia Ivory, in Barbara Pym's *Quartet in Autumn*.

Beatrice Normandy A distant cousin of Lady Drew; she plays with George Ponderevo at Bladesover when they are children and becomes his lover later; she rejects George's marriage proposal because she is Carnaby's mistress in H. G. Wells's *Tono-Bungay*.

Mrs. Norris The hostess of the party in which Kate Leslie first talks with Don Ramon Carrasco and Don Cipriano Viedma in D. H. Lawrence's *The Plumed Serpent (Quetzalcoatl)*.

Arthur Norris Neurotic and devious entrepreneur, masochist, crook, and spy, who educates William Bradshaw about the underside of life in Berlin's demimonde; he reflects the amorality of the Weimar Republic in Christopher Isherwood's *Mr. Norris Changes Trains.*

Manfred North   Guy Openshaw's second cousin, who works in the family bank; he is expected to court Guy's widow, Gertrude, but his undisclosed passion is for Anne Cavidge in Iris Murdoch's *Nuns and Soldiers.*

Norton   Along with McWhist, one of two mountain climbers who encounter John Wainwright in the mountains of Scotland in Olaf Stapledon's *Odd John: A Story Between Jest and Earnest.*

Marda Norton   Accident-prone, affianced, and unaccompanied house guest of Sir Richard and Lady Naylor; she is several years older than the admiring Lois Farquar, Livvy Thompson, and Laurence but considerably younger than Hugo Montmorency; all compete for her attention in Elizabeth Bowen's *The Last September.*

Stephen Norton   Amateur naturalist whose shooting death is called a suicide in Agatha Christie's *Curtain: Hercule Poirot's Last Case.*

Commander William Norton   Captain of the space ship *Endeavor,* leader of the Rama expedition, and the first to enter Rama in Arthur C. Clarke's *Rendezvous with Rama.*

Father Nostradamus   Confessor to the Countess Yvorra; he accompanies her to the royal court's summer retreat, indulges her religious affectations, and assists her in grooming Laura de Nazianzi for religious life in Ronald Firbank's *The Flower Beneath the Foot.*

(Nostromo) Gian' Battista   Dark captain of the dock workers who rescues and hides a cache of silver ingots during the revolution in Costaguana and then keeps it as his own; he proposes to Linda Viola but realizes he loves her sister, Giselle; he dies after being mistaken by Giorgio Viola for Ramirez, taking his secret to the grave in Joseph Conrad's *Nostromo: A Tale of the Seaboard.*

Princess Edna Novemali   An upper-class woman of exemplary pretension in W. Somerset Maugham's *The Razor's Edge.*

Frau Nowak   Tubercular mother of Otto Nowak; oblivious to changes occurring around her, she gives Christopher Isherwood a place to stay in Christopher Isherwood's *Goodbye to Berlin.*

Otto Nowak   Young, German working-class hustler and friend of Christopher Isherwood in Christopher Isherwood's *Goodbye to Berlin.*

Rachel Noyes   The twenty-year-old "older woman" who becomes the object of Charles Highway's desire; in his eyes she is perfect, but even he begins to see that she is shallow, pretentious, and sexually unremarkable in Martin Amis's *The Rachel Papers.*

Nuflo   Rima's grandfather in W. H. Hudson's *Green Mansions.*

Jimmy Nunn   Comedian and old-time performer in J. B. Priestley's *The Good Companions.*

Nurse   Slender, twenty-three-year-old with dark, twinkling eyes; she impresses Richard Larch with her cheerful competence, but he finds her self-reliance chafing and her publication of poetry intimidating in Arnold Bennett's *A Man From the North.*

Nurse   A spare and upright woman, whom the Lamb children trust and respect in Ivy Compton-Burnett's *Manservant and Maidservant.*

Nursemaid   A young, pretty servant in the household of an important county family; she screams when Edward Ashburnham, perceiving her to be unhappy, kisses her in a train; the family takes him to court and attempts to harm him politically in Ford Madox Ford's *The Good Soldier: A Tale of Passion.*

O

Lady O.   A rigidly territorial aristocrat; she plans that her daughter Alice make a good match by marrying Sebastian, master of Chevron, in Vita Sackville-West's *The Edwardians*.

Oa   The earth-mother goddess perceived as both womb and tomb by the Neanderthal tribe in William Golding's *The Inheritors*.

Mrs. Oakley   One of the "old guard" at the day-care center where Evelyn Morton Stennett volunteers some of her time; she is rigid and controlling with children in Margaret Drabble's *The Middle Ground*.

Mrs. Oakroyd   Jess Oakroyd's shrewish wife in J. B. Priestley's *The Good Companions*.

Jess Oakroyd   Kindly Yorkshireman who joins Miss Trant in the management of the concert party which she names The Good Companions in J. B. Priestley's *The Good Companions*.

Lily Oakroyd   Jess Oakroyd's daughter, whom he joins in Canada once the concert party has disbanded in J. B. Priestley's *The Good Companions*.

Constable Eustace Oates   Police officer whose helmet is stolen by "Stinker" Pinker at the instigation of "Stiffy" Byng in P. G. Wodehouse's *The Code of the Woosters*. He appears in *Stiff Upper Lip, Jeeves*.

Major O'Bally   Talkative shareholder who attends the General Meeting of the New Collier Company in John Galsworthy's *The Man of Property*.

Dr. Sigmund Obispo   Cynical and exploitative physician to Jo Stoyte; his chief duties involve his research into methods to prevent aging; he demonstrates his contempt for Stoyte by his quack treatments and his seduction of his employer's mistress in Aldous Huxley's *After Many a Summer*.

Mr. Obo-King   Owner of the Blake Street gambling house in Colin MacInnes's *City of Spades*.

Pat O'Brian   American soldier, the member of the International Patrol that arrests Anna Schmidt, for whom he feels sympathy in Graham Greene's *The Third Man and the Fallen Idol*.

O'Brien   An upper Party member with an urbane manner; he befriends Winston Smith and convinces him to join the Brotherhood against the Party, in reality so that he can "retrain" him in the Ministry of Love by torturing him and manipulating his mind through Smith's terror of rats until he betrays Julia in George Orwell's *Nineteen Eighty-Four*.

Billy O'Brien   Friend and hanger-on of the Christophers; his attempt to blackmail Annabel Christopher after her husband's suicide fails in Muriel Spark's *The Public Image*.

Damien O'Brien   The prudish, humorless, deeply repressed, ugly, and excessively devout Irish Catholic second cousin to Clare Mallory; he has left the seminary and wants to marry Clare, who is repelled by him, and he is fiercely jealous of Mark Underwood in David Lodge's *The Picturegoers*.

Edward O'Brien   A Catholic medical student with a rubbery face who marries Tessa; he becomes a successful general practitioner; he tells Dennis that Dennis's daughter has Down's Syndrome in David Lodge's *How Far Can You Go?*.

Marylin O'Brien   Ex-pupil of Romley Fourways', the school Kate Fletcher (Armstrong) attended; she has six children in Margaret Drabble's *The Middle Ground*.

Matt O'Brien   Aged inmate of an insane asylum and Lisa Brooke's long-forgotten surviving husband in Muriel Spark's *Memento Mori*.

Tessa O'Brien   A nurse who converts to Catholicism and marries Edward O'Brien; she attends a summer course where she receives sexual advances from several men and where she discovers that Robin Meadowes is having an affair in David Lodge's *How Far Can You Go?*.

'Obson   One of three English road laborers mistaken by John Lavender for German prisoners of war in John Galsworthy's *The Burning Spear: Being the Experiences of Mr. John Lavender in Time of War*.

Mrs. Ockham   Sentimental, middle-aged widow and heiress to Eustace Barnack's estate; her gushing attentions to Sebastian Barnack, whom she emotionally identifies with her own dead son, greatly complicate his rightful interest in a small legacy from his uncle in Aldous Huxley's *Time Must Have a Stop*.

Earl of Ockleford   Magnificent Lord President of the Council; his advice was not solicited by the Prime Minister when he chose Sam Raingo as new Minister of Records; consequently, he takes sides against Raingo in the House of Lords attack in Arnold Bennett's *Lord Raingo*.

John O'Connell   Cemetery caretaker who jokes during Paddy Dignam's funeral in James Joyce's *Ulysses*.

Mr. O'Connor   Private detective of the Imperial Palace Hotel; he discovers the criminal background of a guest who had made a scene over collecting furs from the cloakroom in Arnold Bennett's *Imperial Palace*.

Paddy O'Conor   Uncouth, semi-literate lampman at the Tennant estate who loves the housemaid Kate Armstrong in Henry Green's *Loving*.

Bonaparte O'Coonassa   Irish-speaking narrator, who is bemused by outsiders' interest in the peasants of the Gaeltacht; he finds a treasure that leads to his arrest and imprisonment in Flann O'Brien's *The Poor Mouth*.

Prince Odalchini   A fanatical Monarchist who comes to England to seek the support of newspaper magnate Thomas Carlyle Craw in restoring the hereditary monarchy of Evallonia in John Buchan's *Castle Gay*.

Oddjob   Auric Goldfinger's paid assassin; a Korean karate expert, he uses a steel-rimmed bowler hat to dispatch Goldfinger's enemies; he is himself killed by James Bond in Ian Fleming's *Goldfinger*.

Mr. Odell   An evil colleague in the crime syndicate ruled by Dominick Medina, whom he serves as butler in John Buchan's *The Three Hostages*.

Danby Odell   Bruno Greensleave's widower son-in-law and manager of Bruno's printing works; he is attractive to women and liked by men; he becomes Lisa Watkins's lover at the end of Iris Murdoch's *Bruno's Dream*.

Gwen Odell   Bruno Greensleave's daughter and Danby Odell's wife; she died years ago attempting to rescue from drowning a child who could swim in Iris Murdoch's *Bruno's Dream*.

Eedap Mun Odin   A wealthy merchant in Koriantura who hides the deserters Harbin Fashnalgid and Luterin Shokerandit and kills Major Gardeterark; he arranges escape to Shivenink for his family, Harbin, Luterin, and Torress Lahl in Brian W. Aldiss's *Helliconia Winter*.

Odirin Nan Odin   Eedap Mun Odin's brother, who provides safe haven for the refugees in Brian W. Aldiss's *Helliconia Winter*.

Sir Charles Odmore   An old friend of George and Clara Tisbourne; he has a country house in Iris Murdoch's *An Accidental Man*.

Hester, Lady Odmore   Wife of Sir Charles and mother of Sebastian and Ralph; she is a country-house hostess in Iris Murdoch's *An Accidental Man*.

Ralph Odmore   Sebastian's younger brother; he is at school with Patrick Tisbourne, who is in love with him in Iris Murdoch's *An Accidental Man*.

Sebastian Odmore   Gracie Tisbourne's former suitor; after she is jilted by Ludwig Leferrier, her parents are disappointed to learn of the announcement of Sebastian's engagement to Karen Arbuthnot in Iris Murdoch's *An Accidental Man*.

Frankie O'Donnell   Leo Foxe-Donnel's uncle, who runs a tavern in Limerick where rebel discussions are a frequent topic; there Leo first becomes interested in the rebel cause in Sean O'Faolain's *A Nest of Simple Folk*.

John (Johno) O'Donnell   Leo Foxe-Donnel's wild, illegitimate son, who participates in Irish rebel activity in Sean O'Faolain's *A Nest of Simple Folk*.

Judith Foxe O'Donnell   Leo Foxe-Donnel's mother, who encourages her son's upringing as a gentleman and dotes on him until he becomes involved in Irish rebel activities in Sean O'Faolain's *A Nest of Simple Folk*.

Julie Keene O'Donnell   Leo Foxe-Donnel's wife, who does all she can to help her husband, even though she is severely disillusioned when she learns of his secretive rebel actions in Sean O'Faolain's *A Nest of Simple Folk*.

Long John O'Donnell   Judith Foxe O'Donnell's hard-working and cantankerous farmer husband, who makes life unduly harsh for his wife and children in Sean O'Faolain's *A Nest of Simple Folk*.

Nicholas O'Donnell   Leo Foxe-Donnel's erudite and sympathetic uncle, who is very much involved in rebel actions in Sean O'Faolain's *A Nest of Simple Folk*.

Pattie O'Driscoll   Half-Jamaican, half-Irish housekeeper and mistress of Carel Fisher; she is liberated from her thralldom by learning that Elizabeth Fisher is also his lover in Iris Murdoch's *The Time of the Angels*.

Emily Offenbach   Rose Vassiliou's well-educated, highly intelligent friend from girlhood; she remains Rose's loyal but ineffectual friend in Margaret Drabble's *The Needle's Eye*.

Officer in White Uniform   The unnamed Royal Navy officer who rescues the boys from their island and who, completely misunderstanding what has occurred there, cheerily congratulates the boys by saying "Jolly good show" at the conclusion of William Golding's *Lord of the Flies*.

Peter (Finn) O'Finney   Irish friend, distant cousin, self-designated factotum, and fellow conspirator of Jake Donaghue in Iris Murdoch's *Under the Net*.

Ogden   Gardener to the Nettleby family; he dislikes any challenge to his authority in Isabel Colegate's *The Shooting Party*.

Ogilvy   Astronomer who first investigates the landing sight on Horsell Common and who dies when his parlaying deputation is slaughtered in H. G. Wells's *The War of the Worlds*.

Angie O'Grady   Third child and second daughter of Mary and Tom O'Grady; she is a shy, quiet girl wooed by Willy Haslip; she and Willie both die with Ellie O'Grady and Bart in the crash of an airplane that has been offering afternoon rides to the curious in Phoenix Park in Mary Lavin's *Mary O'Grady*.

Ellie O'Grady   Second child and eldest daughter of Mary and Tom O'Grady; she is an outgoing, assertive girl engaged to Bart; both die with Angie O'Grady and Willie Haslip in the crash of an airplane that has been offering afternoon rides to the curious in Phoenix Park in Mary Lavin's *Mary O'Grady*.

Larry O'Grady   Fourth child and second son of Mary and Tom O'Grady; dismissed from the seminary, he becomes a missionary in Mary Lavin's *Mary O'Grady*.

Mary O'Grady   Country-bred wife of Tom and mother of Patrick, Ellie, Angie, Larry, and Rosie; she loves her family so passionately that their life in the Dublin of the 1920s and 1930s is fraught with imagined dangers, but her real problems are those she cannot foresee in Mary Lavin's *Mary O'Grady*.

Patrick O'Grady   Eldest son of Mary and Tom O'Grady; he goes to America shortly after the death of his father and there succeeds in business only to lose everything in the Wall Street crash of 1929; he returns to Ireland so clinically depressed as to require institutionalization in Mary Lavin's *Mary O'Grady*.

Rosie O'Grady   Youngest child and third daughter of Tom and Mary O'Grady; to Mary's dismay, she refuses a university education so that she may be free to marry Frank Esmay; the marriage is not happy, but at last it provides Rosie with the experience that Mary regards, despite everything, as one of the true joys of life — motherhood — in Mary Lavin's *Mary O'Grady*.

Tom O'Grady   Mary O'Grady's sensitive, kind, and industrious husband; a conductor on the tramline, he dies suddenly just as their eldest child, Patrick, is about to go to America in Mary Lavin's *Mary O'Grady*.

Patsy O'Hanlon   Squatter and husband of Sally O'Hanlon; he becomes the first victim of the plague in the valley in Liam O'Flaherty's *Famine*.

Sally O'Hanlon   Wife of Patsy O'Hanlon; after her husband's death, she kills her own starving children in Liam O'Flaherty's *Famine*.

General O'Hara   A drunken, foolish officer whose blustering interference resulting from his misunderstanding of an incident in Sylvia Tietjens's hotel room ultimately improves General Campion's respect for Christopher Tietjens in Ford Madox Ford's *No More Parades*.

Greta Ohlsson   Swedish missionary-school matron, who shares sleeping accomodations with Mary Debanham; she was once Daisy Armstrong's nurse in Agatha Christie's *Murder on the Orient Express*.

Sheriff Hank O'Keene   Miranda County officer who becomes the archenemy of the People's Garden group in David Lodge's *Changing Places: A Tale of Two Campuses*.

Prince Olaf (His Lankiness)   Boy prince of Pisuerga and younger brother of Prince Yousef; he enjoys slumming and eavesdropping among the crowds of common people with his governess Mrs. Montgomery in Ronald Firbank's *The Flower Beneath the Foot*.

Gil Olafson   An inspired, intelligent sculptor; hired by Mrs. Jardine, he eventually marries Tanya Moore to the consternation of Mrs. Jardine, who felt an attachment to him in her last attempt at renewing her youth in Rosamond Lehmann's *The Ballad and the Source*.

Jacob Olatunde   Nigerian evangelical minister who comes to live and conduct noisy services beneath Letty Crowe's bed-sitting room in London in Barbara Pym's *Quartet in Autumn*.

An Old Blind Woman   Matriarchal visionary figure who "sat in a camp-stool . . . clasping a brown mongrel tight in her arms and singing . . . from the depths of her gay, wild heart" in Virginia Woolf's *Jacob's Room*.

The Old Grey Fellow   Bonaparte O'Coonassa's grandfather, who capitalizes on the city folks' fascination with peasant life and language in Flann O'Brien's *The Poor Mouth*.

Oldham   Evelyn Orcham's valet; he disappoints Orcham by requesting to leave his service upon winning a little money, but he quickly begs to be reinstated in Arnold Bennett's *Imperial Palace*.

Old Major (satiric representation of Karl Marx or Vladimir Ilich Lenin)   The oldest pig on Mr. Jones's farm; he organizes the farm animals to rid themselves of the farmer and run the farm as a collective and after his success is the leader of the farm cooperative in George Orwell's *Animal Farm*.

Oldroyd   A crewman caught gambling while on watch in C. S. Forester's *Mr. Midshipman Hornblower*.

The Old Woman   Mal's mate, the oldest of the Neanderthal females and keeper of the sacred fire; she is killed along with Nil by the Homo sapiens enemy in William Golding's *The Inheritors*.

Old Woman with Chicken   Unnamed domino player in a bar in Malcolm Lowry's *Under the Volcano*.

Gordon O'Leary   A man posing as an American; he attempts to scare Alice Mellings into storing IRA gun parts in her house in Doris Lessing's *The Good Terrorist*.

Mary O'Leary   A poor woman who lives in the basement, helps Meyer with small jobs, and babysits for Bridget; she wasted her youth waiting for her runaway husband in Beryl Bainbridge's *Young Adolf*.

Olga   Sexually sadistic friend of Arthur Norris in Christopher Isherwood's *Mr. Norris Changes Trains*.

Olga   Official Soviet interpreter for the British Teacher's Delegation in Moscow who is infinitely patient and polite — especially to Harry Mathews — in Doris Lessing's *The Golden Notebook*.

Olga   American socialist who befriends Leon Trotsky (Lev Davidovich Bronstein) during his stay in New York in Anthony Burgess's *The End of the World News*.

Mr. Oliphant   Dignified, unflappable butler of Strathlarrig House, where a dead salmon is delivered with the compliments of "John Macnab" in John Buchan's *John Macnab*.

Catherine Oliphant   Small, vulnerable-looking though emotionally strong, thirty-one-year-old writer for women's magazines; she shares her flat with the ungrateful Tom Mallow and entertains his fellow anthropologists Mark Penfold and Digby Fox, even befriending her apparent rival Dierdre Swan, before becoming interested in the lonely Alaric Lydgate in

Barbara Pym's *Less Than Angels*. One of her stories is being read in a hairdresser's in *A Glass of Blessings*.

Peter ("Jumbo") Oliphant   Newly knighted chairman of Lupus Books; he takes Barley Blair to Peredelkino writers' village where Blair first meets "Goethe" (Yakov Savelyev) in John le Carré's *The Russia House*.

General Olivarez   Commander of one of the Gran Seco forces; he surrenders to Lord Clanroyden and testifies to the defeat of his and General Lossberg's forces to the President and Cabinet of Olifa in John Buchan's *The Courts of the Morning*.

Oliver   Land agent for Robin Hill, the site chosen by Soames Forsyte for his country house in John Galsworthy's *The Man of Property*.

Oliver   Devoted suitor whose marriage proposals Mrs. Harrowdean threatens to accept in H. G. Wells's *Mr. Britling Sees It Through*.

Oliver   Protagonist who learns his lessons in life from various mentors — including Miss Dawlish, Evie Babbacombe, Henry Williams, and Evelyn de Tracey — and succeeds eventually in becoming a fine scientist in William Golding's *The Pyramid*.

Oliver's Father   Parent who uses binoculars to watch his son make love to Evie Babbacome on an open escarpment within full view of the town in William Golding's *The Pyramid*.

Ariadne Oliver   Outspoken feminist author of forty-six successful, much-translated detective novels; she becomes associated with Hercule Poirot in Agatha Christie's *Cards on the Table*. She appears in six other novels, ending with *Elephants Can Remember*.

Bartholomew Oliver   Cantankerous, self-absorbed patriarch retired from the Indian Civil Service; he owns Pointz Hall, the English estate on which the village pageant is performed one June morning in 1939 in Virginia Woolf's *Between The Acts*.

Caro Oliver   Baby daughter of Giles and Isa Oliver; she spends most of her time in her perambulator in Virginia Woolf's *Between The Acts*.

Lady Edwina Oliver   Perceptive aged mother of Sir Quentin Oliver and free spirit who blossoms when Fleur Talbot treats her like a person in Muriel Spark's *Loitering with Intent*.

Francis Oliver   Bank clerk who reads the Lessons and partakes in disputes of the Parochial Church

Council at the Clevelands' church in Barbara Pym's *Jane and Prudence.*

George Oliver   Young son of Giles and Isa Oliver; he gives hints of what the future may bring when in his small green net he catches white cabbage butterflies in Virginia Woolf's *Between The Acts.*

Giles Oliver   Son of Bartholomew; he is a would-be farmer and London stockbroker who lives and quarrels with his wife, Isa, at Pointz Hall; while the planes presaging World War II fly overhead, Giles returns from London and is less than pleased to find his secret lover, Mrs. Manresa, and her friend William Dodge at Pointz Hall to attend the play in Virginia Woolf's *Between The Acts.*

Isa Oliver   Wife of Giles Oliver; quarreling incessantly with her husband, Isa writes poetry, suspects Giles of infidelity, and fancies herself in love with Rupert Haines in Virginia Woolf's *Between The Acts.*

Sir Quentin Oliver   Snob and egomaniacal center of the Autobiographical Association; he preys on the weaknesses of his followers in Muriel Spark's *Loitering with Intent.*

Caroline Olivier   Mother of Mary Olivier; she dominates the family through her religious purity, using it to punish and control her husband and her children, especially Mary, who spends her life unsuccessfully trying to win her mother's love and approval in May Sinclair's *Mary Olivier: A Life.*

Charlotte Olivier   Sister of Emilius, Victor, and Lavinia Olivier; her insanity, exacerbated by her forced isolation, creates in Victor and Lavinia an obsessive fear of the disease in May Sinclair's *Mary Olivier: A Life.*

Dan (Dank) Olivier   Second of the sons of Emilius and Caroline Olivier; he defeats both alcohol and his parents' wishes by escaping on a cattle ship to Canada to become a farmer in May Sinclair's *Mary Olivier: A Life.*

Emilius Olivier   Father of Mary Olivier; his jealousy of his wife Caroline's love for her sons and his failure in business reduce him to a dejected, drunken, ineffectual old man in May Sinclair's *Mary Olivier: A Life.*

Lavinia (Lavvy) Olivier   Sister of Emilius, Victor, and Charlotte; she gives up her life to care for Charlotte and Victor and is tormented by Emilius for her Unitarian beliefs in May Sinclair's *Mary Olivier: A Life.*

Mark Olivier   Eldest child of Emilius and Caroline Olivier; he is the mother's favorite but escapes her domination and control by enlisting in The Royal Field Artillery and serving in India, where he dies of a heart attack in May Sinclair's *Mary Olivier: A Life.*

Mary (Minx, Minky) Olivier   Only daughter of Emilius and Caroline Olivier; she must struggle with both her family and organized religion; she develops her own mystic philosophy which gives her the strength to endure sacrifices and the solitary life in May Sinclair's *Mary Olivier: A Life.*

Rodney (Roddy) Olivier   Youngest of the sons of Emilus and Caroline Olivier; although he has heart disease, he is sent to farm in Canada, where his health is ruined, and he ultimately dies in May Sinclair's *Mary Olivier: A Life.*

Victor Olivier   Brother of Emilius, Charlotte, and Lavinia, who becomes his nurse in May Sinclair's *Mary Olivier: A Life.*

Albert Edward (Nick) Ollanton   A superb showman; a magician whose stage name is Ganga Dun, he considers himself an honest illusionist whose act offers an audience a temporary respite from the horrors of a world at the brink of war, a world in which public figures and politicians are illusionists of a more sinister sort, in J. B. Priestley's *Lost Empires.*

Alice Ollerenshaw   Sister of Hugh and of Frances (Wingate); the subject of her suicide several years earlier is suppressed at family gatherings in Margaret Drabble's *The Realms of Gold.*

Beata Ollerenshaw   Stephen's young, waiflike wife; an anorexia-nervosa victim, she accepts his spoonfeeding throughout her pregnancy but lapses thereafter into a state requiring permanent hospitalization; she is indifferent even to the murder/suicide of her baby and husband in Margaret Drabble's *The Realms of Gold.*

Constance Ollerenshaw   Sir Frank's aunt, whose reclusive, embittered, eccentric behavior leads to the neglect that contributes to her death by starvation and that causes a short-lived public scandal in Margaret Drabble's *The Realms of Gold.*

David Ollerenshaw   A self-sufficient geologist, whose work takes him to parts of the world visited by Frances Wingate; their friendship is cemented by the discovery that they are second cousins in Margaret Drabble's *The Realms of Gold.*

Sir Frank Ollerenshaw   Frances Wingate's intellectual, capable father, who has risen in academia from unpropitious origins; his domestic stance is benign but aloof in Margaret Drabble's *The Realms of Gold.*

Hugh Ollerenshaw Frances Wingate's functioning-alcoholic brother, a financier; he cannot combat the emotional problems that claim his sensitive son Stephen in Margaret Drabble's *The Realms of Gold.*

Natasha Ollerenshaw Hugh's handsome, capable wife; Frances Wingate envies her flair for domestic creativity, but Natasha is devastated by the tragedy that overtakes her family in Margaret Drabble's *The Realms of Gold.*

Stella, Lady Ollerenshaw Frances Wingate's mother, a birth-control-crusading gynecologist perpetually embarrassed by the fecundity of her descendants in Margaret Drabble's *The Realms of Gold.*

Stephen Ollerenshaw A serious university student given to pessimistic philosophical musing; Hugh's son, he confides much in his aunt, Frances Wingate; he is an obsessively devoted father, even in the deliberate act of making his infant daughter a fellow victim of his suicide plan in Margaret Drabble's *The Realms of Gold.*

Ern Ollershaw Tough but secretive older laborer, who approaches Charles Lumley about sharing their window-cleaning business; the arrangement is profitable until Ern is arrested for drug-running in John Wain's *Hurry On Down.*

Herr Ollinger Magnus Pym's Berne, Switzerland, landlord at whose boarding house Magnus meets, befriends, and first betrays Axel in John le Carré's *A Perfect Spy.*

Osborne O'Loonassa Schoolmaster who christens all the Gaelic-speaking children Jams O'Donnell in Flann O'Brien's *The Poor Mouth.*

Anthony (Olly) Olorenshaw Cambridge student who is the leader of the group which breaks into an office for documents dealing with biological warfare in C. P. Snow's *Last Things.*

Father Finbar O'Malley A priest who repatriates young Irish people from Rummidge in David Lodge's *Small World.*

Omar A silent boatman who takes Daniel Martin and Jane Mallory to Kitchener's Island in John Fowles's *Daniel Martin.*

Sally O'Mears Cactus-award winner who is featured in the television film Kate Fletcher Armstrong is making in Margaret Drabble's *The Middle Ground.*

J. J. (Jack) O'Molloy Unsuccessful barrister who encounters Leopold Bloom in Barney Kiernan's Pub in James Joyce's *Ulysses.*

Countess Olympia d'Omptyda Shy, nervous lady of court noted for her "excellent principles and birth" who presents the queen with the archaeologists' report from Dateland in Ronald Firbank's *The Flower Beneath the Foot.*

No. 1 Head of Nicolas Rubashov's political party who creates an illogical, nearly religious mystique rather than a solid power base by having his followers imprisoned, tortured, and liquidated in Arthur Koestler's *Darkness at Noon.*

One on his back in the dark One referred to as "he", desirous of company in his loneliness, who hears a voice which is not companionable but which relates past events in Samuel Beckett's *Company.*

Oolava Runi's sister; she is promised as a bride to Mr. Abel in W. H. Hudson's *Green Mansions.*

Oover An American Rhodes Scholar; in emulation of the Duke of Dorset he fulfills his pledge to commit suicide, but he "respect(s) Rhodes' intentions" by attending lectures while life lasts in Max Beerbohm's *Zuleika Dobson; or An Oxford Love Story.*

Gertrude McCluskie Openshaw Guy's wife, a teacher who after her husband's death falls in love with the younger and somewhat directionless Tim Reede and eventually marries him in Iris Murdoch's *Nuns and Soldiers.*

Guy Openshaw Gertrude's well-to-do husband and "Count" Szczepanski's mentor and friend, an affectionate, philosophical, inquisitive member of a close-knit Christianized-Jewish extended family; his protracted death from cancer occurs at the beginning of Iris Murdoch's *Nuns and Soldiers.*

Janet Openshaw Stanley's Anglican wife; her expectation of her children's inheriting Guy Openshaw's money is understood to affect her resentment of Gertrude Openshaw's marriage to Tim Reede in Iris Murdoch's *Nuns and Soldiers.*

Stanley Openshaw Guy Openshaw's first cousin, a "right-wing Labour" Member of Parliament in Iris Murdoch's *Nuns and Soldiers.*

Gilbert Opian A homosexual actor whose living arrangement with Lizzie Scherer is disturbed by her renewed yearning for Charles Arrowby in Iris Murdoch's *The Sea, the Sea.*

Maeldoon O'Poenassa Legendary character whose hidden treasure is found by Bonaparte O'Coonassa in Flann O'Brien's *The Poor Mouth*.

Tom Orbell Historian and Cambridge college fellow who is volatile in his anti-establishment opinions; he joins the group pressing for a reconsideration of Donald Howard's fellowship in C. P. Snow's *The Affair*.

Evelyn Orcham Boyish, restrained, middle-aged, brilliant Managing Director of the Imperial Palace Hotel; he is fascinated with organization and genuinely interested in people; his talents for attending to detail and to personalities make his hotel thrive; he is drawn into a brief disturbing affair with Gracie Savotte, fails her test for a relationship, and finds his suitable mate in his hotel protégé Violet Powler in Arnold Bennett's *Imperial Palace*.

Lord Oresby President, twice, of the zoological society after the death of Lord Godmanchester; he supports Simon Carter against Jackley for the directorship after the downfall of the Uni-European government in Angus Wilson's *The Old Men at the Zoo*.

Orfik The father of Little Yuli in Brian W. Aldiss's *Helliconia Spring*.

Alicia Orgreave Tennis-playing, coltish youngest child of Osmond Orgreave in Arnold Bennett's *Clayhanger*. She is Harry Hasketh's wife and a relaxed young mother; her comfortable, gracious way of living in Devonshire makes Hilda Lessways Clayhanger discontented with her lot in the Five Towns in *These Twain*.

Charlie Orgreave Best school friend of Edwin Clayhanger and later a struggling doctor; his early representation of Edwin's distinction interests the Orgreave family to encourage the shy young man in Arnold Bennett's *Clayhanger*. Having attended Miss Sarah Gailey's dancing school with Hilda Lessways, he encourages his family to invite her to their home, where she meets Edwin in *Hilda Lessways*.

Janet Orgreave Beautiful second daughter of Osmond Orgreave, architect of the Clayhangers' new home; Bursley people assume she will marry Edwin Clayhanger, and she waits patiently for him to propose to her in Arnold Bennett's *Clayhanger*. The sedate, accomplished sister of Charlie Orgreave, she still hopes Edwin Clayhanger will marry her although she recognizes the mutual attraction of Edwin and Hilda Lessways in *Hilda Lessways*. A fortyish, attractive spinster, she loses her niche when her parents die; she moves to her younger sister's Hesketh estate before she finds her place in London with her bachelor brother, Charlie, in *These Twain*.

Osmond Orgreave A liberal-spending, assiduous architect and the indulgent father of seven; his influence first broadens his neighbor Edwin Clayhanger's views in Arnold Bennett's *Clayhanger*. His home is a cultural magnet for Hilda Lessways and Edwin Clayhanger in *Hilda Lessways*. His indigent death leaves his beloved daughter Janet in difficulties in *These Twain*.

Mrs. O'Riordon ("mother") A widowed Yorkshire gentlewoman and Head Housekeeper of the hotel; her accomplished, flirtatious ways attract Managing Director Evelyn Orcham's indulgence during a difficulty with one of her housekeepers; she announces her imminent marriage in Arnold Bennett's *Imperial Palace*.

Orlando Androgynous hero/heroine whose life spans three centuries; a man in 1588, Orlando favors writing poetry and swooning over the strenuous activities of his aristocratic ancestors; sent as ambassador to Constantinople, Orlando sleeps for seven days and wakes up as a woman, who then travels with the Gypsies to get her bearings and notices the differences in attitude on the ship as she returns to England; there she is hounded once again by the now-male Archduke Harry; during the Victorian era, she marries Marmaduke Bonthrop Shelmerdine, Esquire, and ruminates over her long life, celebrating the androgynous, unified vision she has experienced through living in both male and female bodies in one lifetime in Virginia Woolf's *Orlando: A Biography*.

Sergey Orlov Katya Orlova's son in John le Carré's *The Russia House*.

Anna Orlova Katya Orlova's daughter in John le Carré's *The Russia House*.

Yekaterina Borisova Orlova (Katya; codenames: Alina, Mariya) Yakov ("Goethe") Savelyev's former mistress and Barley Blair's incredibly beautiful lover; despite her fears for her family's well-being, she smuggles "Goethe's" manuscript ("a gift of trust") to Niki Landau and tries to protect Barley from Soviet and British intelligence in John le Carré's *The Russia House*.

Mr. Orly The mild-mannered senior dentist in the Wimpole Street surgery, where he and his wife live on the upper floor and provide both lunch and tea to Mr. Hancock, Mr. Leyton, and Miriam Henderson in Dorothy Richardson's *The Tunnel*.

Mrs. Orly The garrulous, good-hearted wife of the senior dentist in Dorothy Richardson's *The Tunnel*.

Ormarin Resident of the colony of Volyendesta where his rebellious party has built a hospital for Rhetorical Diseases; he has prepared his colony for the invasion from the Planet Maken in Doris Lessing's *Documents Relating to the Sentimental Agents in the Volyen Empire.*

Constantine Ormeau Willy Trout's influential companion, especially after the death of Cissy Trout; although Eva Trout dislikes, distrusts, and resents him and knows him to be manipulative, upon Willy's death he becomes Eva's guardian, for Willy's shrewdness in business did not extend to a clear assessment of Constantine in Elizabeth Bowen's *Eva Trout, or Changing Scenes.*

Julian Ormerod Wealthy, charming, sophisticated playboy, who befriends Patrick Standish; he claims to have many wives throughout the world and tries unsuccessfully to seduce Jenny Bunn in Kingsley Amis's *Take a Girl Like You.*

Philip Ormston Gentleman neighbor of the Nettlebys in Isabel Colegate's *The Shooting Party.*

The Orphan Jerry Westerby's young Tuscany mistress, who deeply loves Westerby but who loses him to the intrigue espionage promises in John le Carré's *The Honourable Schoolboy.*

Mrs. Orr A quiet, helpful woman at Sawston who refuses to marry Herbert Pembroke; she provides lodging for A. C. Varden in E. M. Forster's *The Longest Journey.*

Colonel Ortega A youthful, slender Spanish officer and an honorable soldier; he leads the fort prior to its siege in C. S. Forester's *Lieutenant Hornblower.*

José Ortega Spaniard who insists, unsuccessfully, on marrying Doña Rita de Lastaola because of a childhood pledge in Joseph Conrad's *The Arrow of Gold: A Story Between Two Notes.*

Ramon Ortega A Spanish hired assassin and courier; sent to steal the photographs from Herman Sachs (Boranovsky), he stabs him and through Andreas Zaleshoff's manipulations is later arrested in Eric Ambler's *Uncommon Danger.*

Orual Eldest daughter of Trom, King of Glome, sister of Redival, and half sister of Psyche; she is educated in Greek philosophy by the Fox, but never totally rejects her native paganism; she protests the sacrifice of Psyche and meets with Psyche after she is given to the God of the Grey Mountain; she convinces Psyche to shine a light on the god when he comes to her at night, which results in Psyche's wandering of the earth; Orual spends much of the rest of her life haunted by the memory of Psyche and trying to find out what happened to her, along with her quest for the true Ungit in C. S. Lewis's *Till We Have Faces.*

Sitric O'Sanassa Poverty-stricken peasant who goes to live with the seals in Flann O'Brien's *The Poor Mouth.*

Douglas Osbaldiston Government civil-service official who serves on the committee that refuses a permanent appointment to George Passant in C. P. Snow's *Homecomings.* He serves Roger Quaife, disagrees with Quaife's nuclear policy, and quarrels with Lewis Eliot over Quaife's policy; his wife is dying in *Corridors of Power.*

Captain Osborn Tall and bony captain of the *Lord Mornington* in C. S. Forester's *Ship of the Line.*

Dr. Brendan (or Milo) O'Shea A prudish general practitioner who is landlord of Morris Zapp in Rummidge and who enjoys Morris's TV and car; he is the uncle of Bernadette McGarrigle, whom he punishes for watching pops programs and reading *Playboy* in Morris's room in David Lodge's *Changing Places: A Tale of Two Campuses.* He is called Dr. Milo O'Shea in *Small World.*

Osman Young, likeable soldier who accompanies Robert Winter on his journey into the desert; his murder jolts Winter into accepting the death of his wife in P. H. Newby's *A Journey to the Interior.*

Neville Osmand French and Latin teacher at the school Hilary Burde attended; he was responsible for Hilary's intellectual awakening; Hilary remembers him with gratitude and affection but ultimately, though unintentionally, fails him in Iris Murdoch's *A Word Child.*

Lady Osprey Beatrice Normandy's stepmother; she is a shallow and silly representative of Victorian pretension in H. G. Wells's *Tono-Bungay.*

Alexander (Tom) Ossipon Womanizing ex-medical student and self-styled anarchist, who plans to elope with Winnie Verloc but robs and abandons her when he learns she has murdered her husband in Joseph Conrad's *The Secret Agent: A Simple Tale.*

Igor Ostrakov Former Soviet military officer turned Baltic resister and close friend of General Vladimir; he urges his wife, Maria, to defect and to contact Vladimir for assistance but dies shortly after joining Maria in Paris in John le Carré's *Smiley's People.*

Alexandra Ostrakova The probably deceased

illegitimate daughter of Maria Ostrakova and Jewish dissident Joseph Glikman; Karla has used her name to build a false history for his daughter, Tatiana, in John le Carré's *Smiley's People*.

Maria Andreyevna Rogova Ostrakova Guilt-ridden, middle-aged Russian defector, who is unwittingly responsible for Karla's defection when she writes to General Vladimir for help in ascertaining the sincerity of a Soviet KGB offer to reunite her with her illegitimate daughter, Alexandra, in John le Carré's *Smiley's People*.

Ostrog Chief Wind-Vane attendant and revolutionary leader; he is an immensely powerful man who uses Graham's cult of personality to overthrow the Council and to establish himself as shadow ruler with Graham as his puppet, but he becomes his enemy when Graham asserts his authority and democratic ideals in H. G. Wells's *When the Sleeper Wakes: A Story of the Years to Come*.

Charlotte Otford Daughter to Lucy and James Otford; when Jane Gray thinks back to the times she took notice of James, she recalls a Christmas dinner at which she observed James's great care in feeding and tending to Charlotte's needs in Margaret Drabble's *The Waterfall*.

James Otford The husband of Lucy and the father of their three children; his love affair with Jane Gray transforms her life; he is a silent partner in an automobile garage and a sports-car enthusiast; his near death in a freak auto accident causes his affair with Jane to be discovered by Lucy in Margaret Drabble's *The Waterfall*.

Lucy Goldsmith Otford Cousin to Jane Gray, who thinks of Lucy as a sister; Lucy is the wife of James Otford and mother of their three children; although Jane and James have an intense affair, Lucy's marriage endures in Margaret Drabble's *The Waterfall*.

Simon Otford Son of Lucy and James Otford in Margaret Drabble's *The Waterfall*.

Other Men Inhabitants of the Other Earth, a humanoid species with highly developed senses of smell and taste, used to satirize various social and political problems in Olaf Stapledon's *Star Maker*.

James O'Toole Anxious American CIA agent and father of Lucinda (Tooley); he meets Henry Pulling on a boat to Asuncion; O'Toole cuts a deal with Mr. Visconti in which he lets Mr. Visconti go free in exchange for a valuable piece of art in Graham Greene's *Travels with My Aunt*.

Lucinda (Tooley) O'Toole Teenaged girl on the Orient Express traveling to Istanbul to meet her boyfriend; she meets Henry Pulling on the train and confides in him regarding her distress over a possible pregnancy, and she introduces him to the pleasures of marijuana in Graham Greene's *Travels with My Aunt*.

Otter The generous, sometimes elusive creature who lives on the river bank and is a good friend of Water Rat, Mole, and Badger in Kenneth Grahame's *The Wind in the Willows*.

Mrs. Otter The provincial yet kindly Englishwoman who introduces Philip Carey to Amitrano's studio in Paris in W. Somerset Maugham's *Of Human Bondage*.

Captain Charles Ottery Member of the Whitsuntide house party at Flambard where Ottery participates in Professor Moe's psychic experiment in prevision and learns that in one year he will be dead; faced with Pamela Brune's sudden critical illness, he forgets his own torment in concern and love for her and wins peace and serenity in John Buchan's *The Gap in the Curtain*.

Otto First mate of the pirate ship in Richard Hughes's *A High Wind in Jamaica*.

Otto A German dentist who is married to an English woman; he is ostracized by the English public during the Great War, and he elicits the pity of John Lavender in John Galsworthy's *The Burning Spear: Being the Experiences of Mr. John Lavender in Time of War*.

Cassandra Otway Young woman whose companionship with Katherine Hilbery's fiancé William Rodney scandalizes Katherine's aunt, Mrs. Milvain, in Virginia Woolf's *Night and Day*.

Mrs. Oulsnam Plump, laughing, self-confident housekeeper; she is transferred from the Majestic Hotel to replace Miss Venables, who thought she should have been considered for Head Housekeeper of the Imperial Palace when Violet Powler gained the position in Arnold Bennett's *Imperial Palace*.

Our Vicar Village clergyman, whose wife urges him to intervene in Mrs. Blenkinsop's attempt to cancel her daughter's wedding; he only intones with dignity that a mother's love is sacred, that self-sacrifice is beautiful, and that the love of a good man should not be relinquished in E. M. Delafield's *The Diary of a Provincial Lady*.

Our Vicar's Wife A village gossip who is always busy with projects that are full of impracticable ideas; she feels faint if she senses the presence of a cat in the room; though childless, she gives much advice on child-rearing; she has status in the village because she lives with a "holy man" in E. M. Delafield's *The Diary of a Provincial Lady*. She reappears in *The Provincial Lady Goes Further*.

Owen   Officer aboard the *Atropos* in C. S. Forester's *Hornblower and the Atropos*.

Owen   Welshman who is punished for spitting on deck despite Hornblower's disdain for violence in C. S. Forester's *The Happy Return*.

Mr. Oxford   Suave, manipulating Jewish art dealer; he recognizes that Priam Farll is not dead and speculates a fortune by selling Farll's recent paintings to an American collector in Arnold Bennett's *Buried Alive: A Tale of These Days*.

Oyarsa of Malacandra   Spiritual ruler of Malacandra (Mars), known as Oyarsa only on his own planet, known as Malacandra on other planets; Oyarsa explains the spiritual nature of the universe to Elwin Ransom in C. S. Lewis's *Out of the Silent Planet*. Oyarsa transports Ransom from Thulcandra (Earth) to Perelandra (Venus) to fight the evil that is assaulting the newly created world in *Perelandra*.

Oyarsa of Perelandra   Spiritual ruler of Perelandra (Venus); he meets with Elwin Ransom after Ransom's defeat of Edward Weston and explains the spiritual nature of the universe in C. S. Lewis's *Perelandra*.

Oyre   Aoz Roon's daughter, who is in love with Laintal Ay; she finds a telescope, with which Vry Tal studies the stars in Brian W. Aldiss's *Helliconia Spring*.

Ozzie   Interior decorator and Orlando King's house guest in Isabel Colegate's *Orlando at the Brazen Threshold*.

P

Mr. de P— A fanatical and hated government official whose assassination is investigated in Joseph Conrad's *Under Western Eyes.*

Marquis of P. Landowner who is persuaded by Paul Trent to lease Glastonbury land to the Communists; he is father to the illegitimate Will Zoyland in John Cowper Powys's *A Glastonbury Romance.*

Hans P A critic who knows James Schafter; he comes to London to meet him and later writes a review of James's work (the part from Anna Wulf's journal) in Doris Lessing's *The Golden Notebook.*

Pablo Owner of the hut in which the guerrilla band holds Charley Fortnum after his kidnapping in Graham Greene's *The Honorary Consul.*

Angelica Pabst Brilliant, beautiful scholar of romance and twin sister of Lily Pabst; she is pursued all over the world by Persse McGarrigle, whom she meets at a conference in Rummidge, but she is engaged to marry Peter McGarrigle; she discovers that she is the daughter of Sybil Maiden and Arthur Kingfisher in David Lodge's *Small World.*

Lily Pabst Twin sister of Angelica Pabst and daughter of Sybil Maiden and Arthur Kingfisher; she is a strip-tease dancer and sex-club performer whom Persse McGarrigle mistakes for Angelica; she makes love to Persse at the Modern Language Association convention in David Lodge's *Small World.*

James Tayper Pace A straightforward and honest member of the lay community at Imber Court who confronts Michael Meade with Toby Gashe's confession of their affair in Iris Murdoch's *The Bell.*

Theodora Pace Reporter for the BBC and a good friend to Montgomery Pew; she falls in love with Johnny Fortune and becomes pregnant by him but has a miscarriage and a nervous breakdown; she speaks in Johnny's defense in court in Colin MacInnes's *City of Spades.*

Renaldo Pacioli Early-middle-aged, tall, thin, blond, ethical Italian; the son of the founder of Casa Pacioli and a member of the board of directors, he (under orders from Syncom) serves as Pacioli's representative to Robert Halliday in Eric Ambler's *The Care of Time.*

Miss Packer Stylish, thirty-six-year-old, efficient personal secretary to the Prime Minister; she accompanies him everywhere, and her demeanor indicates the latest status of government members circulating around the Prime Minister in Arnold Bennett's *Lord Raingo.*

Geoffrey Paddington Boy Dougdale's consultant for his research on the peerage; because of Geoffrey's dislike of Lady Montdore, he is not introduced to Polly Hampton until after Polly's marriage to Boy; he has become Polly's lover at the end of Nancy Mitford's *Love in a Cold Climate.*

Paddock Richard Hannay's efficient and devoted manservant in John Buchan's *The Thirty-Nine Steps* and in *The Three Hostages.*

Paddy Huge tanner in Clive Ward for surgery for a rupture; he is fearful about the surgery and is reassured by the other patients in John Berger's *The Foot of Clive.*

Padgett Conscientious Shrewsbury College porter in Dorothy L. Sayers's *Gaudy Night.*

Mr. Paganotti Vittorio's uncle, who is owner of the bottle factory; his manners are detached and businesslike in Beryl Bainbridge's *The Bottle Factory Outing.*

Mrs. Page John Page's wife and Flo's mother in Isabel Colegate's *The Shooting Party.*

Ellen Page Maid to the Nettleby family, companion to Cicely Nettleby, and sweetheart of John Siddons in Isabel Colegate's *The Shooting Party.*

Flo Page John Page's daughter, who is employed by the Nettlebys as a maid; she is liked by Dan Glass in Isabel Colegate's *The Shooting Party.*

John Page Game-beater for Sir Randolph Nettleby and father of Flo Page in Isabel Colegate's *The Shooting Party.*

Mary Page Ellen Page's younger sister, also employed by the Nettleby family as a maid; she takes a particular liking to Master Osbert Nettleby in Isabel Colegate's *The Shooting Party.*

Melodie Page Young British Intelligence operative who is allegedly trying to buy armaments and who dies after sending vital coded information to Charlie in Len Deighton's *Yesterday's Spy.*

Paget Rich pupil in Herbert Getliffe's chambers, who is training in law to become manager of his family's estates in C. P. Snow's *Time of Hope.*

Mrs. Paget Mother of Gordon; she suffers strokes which cripple her and goes to live with David Parker after Gordon's death and Meg Eliot's departure in Angus Wilson's *The Middle Age of Mrs. Eliot.*

Gordon Paget Partner with David Parker in running a nursery; he is David's lover, writes books on gardening with David, loves music, and dies of cancer in Angus Wilson's *The Middle Age of Mrs. Eliot.*

Paine A British soldier; Colonel Calloway's driver, he protects his superior officer from a drunken Rollo Martins by knocking out the writer in Graham Greene's *The Third Man and the Fallen Idol.*

Lieutenant James Pak Man who flies by glider to the southern hemisphere of Rama and first discovers life on Rama in Arthur C. Clarke's *Rendezvous with Rama.*

Emma Paley Invalid, deaf, cantankerous aunt of Susan Harrington; she pays for their vacation at the Santa Marina Hotel in Virginia Woolf's *The Voyage Out.*

Henry Pallender Affluent military-ceremony expert who coordinates the funeral procession for Vice Admiral Lord Viscount Nelson with Hornblower in C. S. Forester's *Hornblower and the Atropos.*

Contessa Pallestra An Italian countess who is the guest of Hermione Roddice in D. H. Lawrence's *Women in Love.*

John Palliser-Yeates Great banker and financier; he is a member of the Thursday Club at which Richard Hannay dines with Dominick Medina, evil genius, in John Buchan's *The Three Hostages.* Tired and depressed, he joins Sir Edward Leithen and Lord Lamancha in using the name "John Macnab" to issue the challenge of poaching two stags and a salmon from three Scots estates in John Buchan's *John Macnab.*

Grengo Pallos A friend of Krillo Muntras; he takes in Billy Xiao Pin when he is sick in Brian W. Aldiss's *Helliconia Summer.*

Mrs. Palmer Mother of Elsie and Geraldine; she runs a boarding house; she worries about Elsie's childlike playing with neighborhood boys; she is triumphant when Elsie marries her "so generous" employer in E. M. Delafield's *Messalina of the Suburbs.*

David Palmer Maurice Allington's young trainee assistant; he takes charge of the Green Man inn when Allington is out having adventures with women and ghosts in Kingsley Amis's *The Green Man.*

Elsie Palmer Seventeen-year-old, naïve London typist who has no sense of cause and effect and lacks intelligence, imagination, sympathy, and passion; to her, war means only inconvenience in shopping; she is foolishly surprised that her husband, Horace Williams, and her lover, Leslie Morrison, become antagonists; she is executed with the latter for killing the former in E. M. Delafield's *Messalina of the Suburbs.*

Geraldine Palmer Elsie's hypochondriac, jealous, self-pitying, and overbearing sister from whom Elsie escapes by early marriage in E. M. Delafield's *Messalina of the Suburbs.*

Pamela Giles Peters's companion on a visit to Anthony Keating's residence; Keating notes particularly unattractive qualities in her in Margaret Drabble's *The Ice Age.*

Pamela Ann Walton's selfish, jealous, shallow cousin, whom Ann dislikes but to whom she is always cordial; Pamela has an affair with William McClusky and treats Ann as a pawn for her schemes in Beryl Bainbridge's *Sweet William.*

Panagiotis Handsome young Greek actor with whom Balthazar falls self-destructively in love in Lawrence Durrell's *Clea.*

Panayotis Former monk and schoolteacher whose tongue was cut out; he is watchman and gardener of Justine Hosnani's "oasis" in Lawrence Durrell's *Justine.*

Lina Pancev Bulgarian defector whose involvement in the lives of American and British tourists in Venice leads her to return to a more ordered life behind the Iron Curtain in Muriel Spark's *Territorial Rights.*

Serge Pancev Cousin and fiancé of Lina Pancev; he brings her back to Bulgaria in Muriel Spark's *Territorial Rights.*

Victor Pancev A missing Bulgarian; his daughter, Lina Pancev, has come to Venice to search for his grave in Muriel Spark's *Territorial Rights.*

Pancrazio An inhabitant of the primitive Abruzzi Mountains in Italy; he offers his house to Alvina Houghton and his nephew Ciccio in D. H. Lawrence's *The Lost Girl.*

Pangall The crippled church caretaker who is the butt of all the builders' jokes and is eventually cuckholded by his wife, Goody, in William Golding's *The Spire.*

Goody Pangall The temptress wife of the cathedral

servant Pangall; she miscarries Roger Mason's child and dies miserably in William Golding's *The Spire*.

Miss Pankerton   A new neighbor; of martial appearance and self-proclaimed unconventionality, she is received with persistent dread by the Provincial Lady in *The Diary of a Provincial Lady*. The Provincial Lady has become enured to her in *The Provincial Lady Goes Further*.

Sylvia Pankhurst   Suffragette to whom Kitty Weston writes for a position in the movement in Isabel Colegate's *Statues in a Garden*.

Pantaleon (Panta)   Venezuelan trader who arranges Mr. Abel's visit to the Maquiritari Indian village to recuperate from an illness in W. H. Hudson's *Green Mansions*.

Molly Panton   Young farm-girl who has a child by Robert Brown; she eventually joins Robert and his wife, Molly, in one household in Joyce Cary's *To Be a Pilgrim*.

Millicent de Bray Pape   An American eccentric whose husband is immensely wealthy; she rents Groby House from Sylvia Tietjens and has the Groby great tree cut down in Ford Madox Ford's *The Last Post*.

Mike Papini   An American novelist and journalist and an old friend of Emma Evans; he journeys to Hereford from London to see the opening performances at the Garrick Theatre and asks Emma to run away with him in Margaret Drabble's *The Garrick Year*.

Mr. Pappleworth   A supervisor at the surgical appliances factory; he tries to intimidate Paul Morel when the youngster puts in his first day of work as a clerk in D. H. Lawrence's *Sons and Lovers*.

Father Paradis   Member of the Quebec clergy who speaks the French of France though he is Canadian; he nurses Sir Edward Leithen on his arrival in Canada in John Buchan's *Sick Heart River*.

Miss Paradise   Spinster sister of Henry Paradise; she is convinced by "Captain Mallet" that she is the widowed Mrs. Florence Paradise, his longtime family housekeeper, in Nigel Dennis's *Cards of Identity*.

Henry Paradise   A parasite who attempts to find favor with the "Mallets"; he is transformed by "Captain Mallet" into Jellico, their butler with a profligate past, in Nigel Dennis's *Cards of Identity*.

Edmund Paramor   London solicitor who represents Helen Bellew and George Pendyce in the divorce suit in John Galsworthy's *The Country House*.

Janet Pardoe   Mabel Warren's vapid, calculating "companion"; she leaves Warren and attempts to seduce Carleton Myatt in Graham Greene's *Stamboul Train*.

Johnny Pardoe   Eligible, propertied, hearty ensign, popular at the debutante dances; he becomes engaged to Barbara Goring in Anthony Powell's *A Buyer's Market*. He is a melancholy, difficult husband in *At Lady Molly's*.

Nigel Pargeter   An Englishman who has been in America for two weeks and is working on his Ph.D.; he dislikes the class distinctions and materialism in England but admits that America is not perfect either in Kingsley Amis's *One Fat Englishman*.

Richard Pargeter   A very rich bachelor with a yacht; he has been pursued by husband-hunting girls long enough to have no trouble brushing off Karen Arbuthnot, but he succumbs to Ann Colindale in Iris Murdoch's *An Accidental Man*.

Colonel Abel Pargiter   The patriarch of the upper-middle-class English family whose cycle, 1880–1937, is described; his wife dies of cancer; neither his mistress, Mira, nor his daughter Eleanor, who cares for him after his stroke, suffices to dissipate his cosmic angst in Virginia Woolf's *The Years*.

Celia Pargiter   Wife of Morris Pargiter; she is mother of Peggy and North Pargiter in Virginia Woolf's *The Years*.

Delia Pargiter   Colonel Abel Pargiter's fourth child; resentful of her dying mother, Delia leaves home for independence until she marries Patrick, an Irishman; in 1937 she is hostess of a final party; there the Pargiter clan gather meaningfully and Eleanor Pargiter experiences epiphany in Virginia Woolf's *The Years*.

Sir Digby Pargiter   Brother of Colonel Abel Pargiter; "in politics", Sir Digby marries pretty, frivolous Eugenie, fathers Maggie and Sara, and dies in early middle age in Virginia Woolf's *The Years*.

Edward Pargiter   Second child of the Pargiter clan; a bachelor don and poet at Oxford, Edward loved unrequitedly his cousin Kitty Malone (Lasswade) and translated the *Antigone* in Virginia Woolf's *The Years*.

Eleanor Pargiter   Oldest daughter of Colonel Abel Pargiter and "angel of the house" in Abercorn Terrace, London; Eleanor sacrifices her life to her family, caring for her mortally ill mother, her stroke-afflicted father, and her soldier-brother Martin's laundry; finally at fifty-five she meets again the man she thinks she might have married, the homosexual Nicholas Pomjalovsky; her suffering is at last alleviated by the experience of a luminous epiphany in Virginia Woolf's *The Years.*

Eugenie Pargiter   Pretty, frivolous wife of Sir Digby Pargiter; she is the mother of Maggie and Sara Pargiter in Virginia Woolf's *The Years.*

Maggie Pargiter   Daughter of Sir Digby; she lives in a shabby house in Hyams Place with her sister, Sara, after their parents' death; she marries a Frenchman; she hosts a dinner in 1917 at which her cousin Eleanor Pargiter meets Nicholas Pomjalovsky in Virginia Woolf's *The Years.*

Martin Pargiter   Colonel Abel Pargiter's sixth child; a soldier in India, he returns as Captain Pargiter but is no longer active; his sister Eleanor takes care of his socks and laundry when all her other charges have left or died; dreading cancer, he employs his niece Peggy as physician in Virginia Woolf's *The Years.*

Milly Pargiter   Colonel Abel Pargiter's fifth child; she marries Hugh Gibbs, her brother Edward's Oxford friend interested in horses and women; she grows fat and reminds her nephew North Pargiter of an animal munching in its stall at her sister Delia's 1937 Pargiter reunion party in Virginia Woolf's *The Years.*

Morris Pargiter   Third child of the upper-middle-class English family; a lawyer, Morris married Celia and has two children, Peggy and North, in Virginia Woolf's *The Years.*

North Pargiter   Son of Morris Pargiter; having sold his farm in Africa to return to London, in 1937 he accompanies his cousin Sara to his aunt Delia's reunion party, at which he muses philosophically on the old looking at the young, who return their gaze in Virginia Woolf's *The Years.*

Peggy Pargiter   Daughter of Morris Pargiter; she becomes a doctor in a London hospital, cares for her uncle Martin and his fear of cancer, and accompanies her aunt Eleanor to her aunt Delia's reunion gathering of the family in 1937 in Virginia Woolf's *The Years.*

Sara Pargiter   Daughter of Sir Digby; having been dropped as a child, Sara has a crooked back and cannot dance; she ends up alone in a shabby flat in London in Virginia Woolf's *The Years.*

Violet Pargiter   Wife of Colonel Abel Pargiter and

mother of the original seven Pargiter children; she dies of cancer, leaving her eldest daughter, Eleanor, to run the dysfunctional household in Virginia Woolf's *The Years.*

Parker   Shifty-eyed butler at Fernly Park; he is supposed to have blackmailed his former employer; he and Dr. James Sheppard together discover Roger Ackroyd's body in Agatha Christie's *The Murder of Roger Ackroyd.*

Mrs. Parker   Old neighbor at Mount Sorrel in Isabel Colegate's *Agatha.*

Charles Parker   A Scotland Yard officer who freely consults and collaborates with Lord Peter Wimsey in Dorothy L. Sayers's *Whose Body?,* in *Clouds of Witness,* in *Unnatural Death,* and in *The Unpleasantness at the Bellona Club.* He is Chief Detective-Inspector Parker; he becomes engaged to Lady Mary Wimsey in *Strong Poison.*

David Parker   Younger brother of Meg Eliot; He is homosexual, loves Gordon Paget, runs a nursery, and cannot persuade Meg to live with him after her convalescence in Angus Wilson's *The Middle Age of Mrs. Eliot.*

Freddy Parker   Unlucky, unscrupulous, and unpaid Financial Commissioner for South-Eastern Europe; he concocts the dreadful alcoholic "Parker's poison" and hates the Russians in Norman Douglas's *South Wind.*

Jessie Parker   A woman featured in the television film Kate Fletcher Armstrong is making; she speaks of her son who joined the British Army and died at eighteen years of age in Ireland in Margaret Drabble's *The Middle Ground.*

Kate Parker   Practical district nurse and tenant in Milly Sanders's house in Muriel Spark's *A Far Cry from Kensington.*

Lola Parker   Scandalmongering invalid stepsister/"lady" of Mr. Freddy Parker; she proves herself to be an adept liar in Norman Douglas's *South Wind.*

Sir Peter Parker   Admiral of the Fleet; he is Chief Mourner in the Nelson funeral procession in C. S. Forester's *Hornblower and the Atropos.*

Gordon Parkinson   Bryan Morley's friend at Petersons School who teaches Bryan about another type of life in the city; at the Phoenix Theatre Bryan meets actors and plays hookey from school in David Storey's *A Prodigal Child.*

Montagu Parkinson   Fat, unethical, middle-aged,

self-serving, corrupt journalist; another burnt-out case, he prints a highly fictionalized series of stories about Querry; after seeing Marie Rycker's combs in Querry's hotel room, he tells Maurice Rycker and is therefore indirectly responsible for Querry's murder in Graham Greene's *A Burnt-Out Case.*

Rudyard Parkinson   Famous and crotchety Regius Professor of Belles-Lettres at All Saints' College, Oxford; he reviews Morris Zapp's book unfavorably but lavishly praises Philip Swallow's book on Hazlitt, thus giving Philip's career a boost in David Lodge's *Small World.*

Mr. Parkis   Methodical, conscientious, widowed, scrupulous private detective; hired to shadow Sarah Miles, he becomes almost an intimate of Maurice Bendrix and is ultimately convinced of Sarah's goodness in Graham Green's *The End of the Affair.*

Lance Parkis   Twelve-year-old son of Mr. Parkis; he assists his father in shadowing Sarah Miles; he almost dies of acute appendicitis but is saved, he believes, by the miraculous intervention of the dead Sarah in Graham Greene's *The End of the Affair.*

Vincent C. Parkman (code indentification: 59200/5/4)   See James Wormold.

Sidney Parks   Cyril's friend who wins the carrots-and-beets category ten times straight in the vegetable show they both enter yearly in John Berger's *The Foot of Clive.*

Parlingeltig   Priest-Chaplain of the Church of the Formidable Peace; he advocates overthrowing the Oligarchy that governs Sibornal and is executed by the Supreme Oligarch in Brian W. Aldiss's *Helliconia Winter.*

Nicholas Parnell   A friend of Belinda Bede and Archdeacon Hoccleve from their undergraduate years; now Librarian at their old university, he comes to visit their village in Barbara Pym's *Some Tame Gazelle.*

Augustus Parr   Christopher Isherwood's spiritual guru, who tries to help him save Paul from fatal despair in Christopher Isherwood's *Down There on a Visit.*

Bob Parrinder   A boarder in Paul's house in the country who often sees psychiatrists; he works on and off in the film industry; he offers Martha Quest a good deal of advice about her inner life in Doris Lessing's *The Four-Gated City.*

Professor Maynard Parrish   The author of a book on Melville published by Roger Micheldene; he asks

Micheldene to present a lecture on the book trade in Britain and America, and Micheldene accepts because this gives him an excuse to be near Helene Bang by spending the weekend in her house in Kingsley Amis's *One Fat Englishman.*

Mr. Parrow   A young white-collar workingman on holiday in Brighton; he pairs off with Miriam Henderson and introduces her to the social and economic limitations, not to mention the prejudices, of a lower-middle-class male in Dorothy Richardson's *Backwater.*

Admiral Lord Parry   Powerful upper-class military man who plays whist with Hornblower shortly before the return to action in C. S. Forester's *Lieutenant Hornblower.*

Diane Parry   One of the weekend guests of Celia and Quentin Villiers; she is the girlfriend of Andy Adorno and a victim of one of his bizarre pranks in Martin Amis's *Dead Babies.*

Helena Parry   Clarissa Dalloway's ancient cousin from summers at Bourton who shows up faithfully at Clarissa's party; she recognizes Peter Walsh, is amazed at Elizabeth Dalloway's beauty, and is intrigued by the recurring melodrama in Virginia Woolf's *Mrs. Dalloway.*

Owen Parry   Man who shoots at Sirius and then claims that Sirius attacked him without provocation in Olaf Stapledon's *Sirius: A Fantasy of Love and Discord.*

Sir Gregory Parsloe-Parsloe   Neighbor and unscrupulous pig-raising competitor of Lord Emsworth; his hiring away Lord Emsworth's pigman George Cyril Wellbeloved is unforgiven in P. G. Wodehouse's *Fish Preferred.* He appears in four other novels.

Parsons   Tubby, boisterous, good-humored lover of literature; he, Platt, and Alfred Polly are the fraternal Three P's at the Port Burdock Drapery Bazaar; Parsons's dismissal for a foolish window-decorating project makes Alfred feel genuine loss in H. G. Wells's *The History of Mr. Polly.*

Tom Parsons   A mild-mannered, happy man, who lives next door to Winston Smith and is turned in to the Thought Police by his daughter, one of the Party's Junior Spies, for saying "Down with Big Brother" in his sleep; he shares a cell in the Ministry of Love with Smith for a short while in George Orwell's *Nineteen Eighty-Four.*

Jenny Partiger   Chancery staff secretary qua Information Officer; acting from naïve love and emotional starvation, she gives Leo Harting keys to the Bonn

Embassy's restricted desks and files in John le Carré's *A Small Town in Germany*.

Vendice Partners   Cold, sarcastic advertising executive who agrees to sponsor an exhibition of the narrator's photographs in Colin MacInnes's *Absolute Beginners*.

Partridge   Bosun's mate of the *Indefatigable* involved in gambling on watch in C. S. Forester's *Mr. Midshipman Hornblower*.

Pascal   The French housekeeper/nanny of the Evans family in Margaret Drabble's *The Garrick Year*.

Hugh Pascoe   Latin teacher who marries Sukey Matthews; he becomes part owner of a public school; he persuades Sukey to allow a German refugee to stay with their family just before World War II in Angus Wilson's *No Laughing Matter*.

Dienu Pasharatid   Io Pasharatid's wife, who defends him against charges of selling arms to Borlien enemies and later conspires with Odi Jeseratabhar and SatoriIrvrash to invade Borlien; she dies at the battle of Keevasian Sandbar in Brian W. Aldiss's *Helliconia Summer*.

Io Pasharatid   Ambassador to Borlien from Sibornal; he flees home when he is suspected of plotting to overthrow JandolAngand and later leads forces against Borlien in Brian W. Aldiss's *Helliconia Summer*.

Colin Pasmore   Middle-class college teacher who is going through a breakdown; he finds himself bored, then disgusted, with his wife and family, hates his research, and almost by accident takes a flat so that he can have an affair with a bored, wealthy woman; finally, after having been beaten by the woman's husband, he goes home to his wife in David Storey's *Pasmore*.

Dad Pasmore   Colin Pasmore's coal-miner father, who becomes very angry and repudiates Colin when Colin tells him that his marriage is over; he follows Colin home to his rented flat to see the woman with whom Colin is having an affair; he dies of cancer in David Storey's *Pasmore*.

Kay Pasmore   Very conventional, stable wife of Colin Pasmore; at first depressed, she brightens up and takes a lover when her husband leaves her for another woman; she eventually welcomes him back in David Storey's *Pasmore*.

Mom Pasmore   Colin's mother, a hardworking, lower-class woman; Colin visits her to tell about his separation from his wife, Kay, in David Storey's *Pasmore*.

Charlie Pass   Sir Randolph Nettleby's gun loader in Isabel Colegate's *The Shooting Party*.

George Passant   Solicitor who teaches law courses in night school, encourages Lewis Eliot to study law, and tutors him for exams; he leads group discussions about social idealism with youths at a farm retreat; he is acquitted of charges of fraud in C. P. Snow's *Time of Hope*. He speaks to the school board in defense of Jack Cotery, lends money to start Jack in business, enters into questionable financial arrangements with Jack and Olive Calvert, and lives a life of sexual freedom with members of his group; he is fired from his position at the school during his trial and is distressed when Herbert Getliffe wins his acquittal at the expense of his self-respect in *Strangers and Brothers*. He works for Lewis Eliot in government civil service for three years and is angry and disappointed when he is refused a permanent appointment; he returns to his home town to practice law in *Homecomings*. Cora Ross's uncle, he asks Lewis Eliot to inquire about the legal defense for her; he announces his intention to leave his home town after the trial is over in *The Sleep of Reason*.

Peter Passer   Former chorister and petty thief at the Church of the Blue Jesus in Pisuerga who accompanies his master Count Cabinet into exile on St. Helena island, where he serves as his valet and errand-boy in Ronald Firbank's *The Flower Beneath the Foot*.

Elizabeth Paston (satirical portrait of Hilda Doolittle)   Attractive, intellectual, modern woman who becomes George Winterbourne's wife when she abandons her ideas of free love on thinking she is pregnant; she approves of married couples having lovers until George takes up with Fanny Welford in Richard Aldington's *Death of a Hero*.

George Paston   A middle-aged artist who has fallen in love with and become a teacher to Miranda Grey; his guidance in matters of art and life form the basis of her growth in John Fowles's *The Collector*.

Pat   A twenty-six-year-old woman who is Bert's lover; Alice Mellings feels a great liking for her before Pat leaves the house in Doris Lessing's *The Good Terrorist*.

Patagonians   A species of short-lived human beings whose culture flourishes for about 15,000 years and then is demolished through a nuclear accident in Olaf Stapledon's *Last and First Men: A Story of the Near and Far Future*.

Dr. Patarescu   Semiretired Rumanian medical man

on Phraxos; he treats Nicholas Urfe's venereal disease in John Fowles's *The Magus.*

Patchway   A dirty-looking local farm laborer who does gardening for the Imber Court community in Iris Murdoch's *The Bell.*

Mrs. Pateman   Mother of Dick and Kitty; she protects her husband's sensitive ego and tells Lewis Eliot that she is grateful for his kindness in C. P. Snow's *The Sleep of Reason.*

Dick Pateman   University student who is one of four students defended by Lewis Eliot against threat of dismissal for sexual misconduct; he is the brother of Kitty in C. P. Snow's *The Sleep of Reason.*

Kitty Pateman   Young woman who is convicted with Cora Ross of torturing and murdering an eight-year-old boy in C. P. Snow's *The Sleep of Reason.*

Percy Pateman   Father of Dick and Kitty; he is rude and ungrateful to Lewis Eliot, demands that Eliot help him find work, and runs up telephone bills with reverse charges to the Eliots after the trial in C. P. Snow's *The Sleep of Reason.*

Paterson   Jarrold family butler; he prefers Mrs. Tommy (Evelyn Jarrold) and Mr. Dan (her son) to the rest of the Jarrold clan and judges these two the type of aristocrat he has been trained to serve in Vita Sackville-West's *Family History.*

Dorothy Paterson   Timid, devoted lover of Richard Pulling; the relationship was not consummated because Pulling died unexpectedly in France; she visits his grave constantly and is seen there by Henry Pulling and Aunt Augusta Bertram in Graham Greene's *Travels with My Aunt.*

Peter Paterson ("Peer Pairson")   Burly young member of the Gorbals Die-Hards; he assists Dickson McCunn in freeing Sakskia, the Russian princess, in John Buchan's *Huntingtower.*

Patmore   Scotland Yard detective who discusses a murder case with Conder in Graham Greene's *It's a Battlefield.*

Miss (Patty) Patmore   Andrew Stace's nurse, who promises to stay on with his daughter Sophia and becomes the beloved nurse of Sophia's children; she is a woman of kindness, faithfulness, and curiosity in Ivy Compton-Burnett's *Brothers and Sisters.*

Captain Ralph Paton   Handsome estranged stepson of Roger Ackroyd; he is engaged to Flora Ackroyd and

clandestinely married to the parlormaid Ursala Bourne in Agatha Christie's *The Murder of Roger Ackroyd.*

Patrick   An outsider at the factory who is liked by Brenda; an Irishman with a temper, he undergoes behavior shifts as situations change in Beryl Bainbridge's *The Bottle Factory Outing.*

Patrick   Delia Pargiter's Irish husband, who grows hard of hearing in Virginia Woolf's *The Years.*

Patrick   A man briefly involved with Kate Fletcher Armstrong in Margaret Drabble's *The Middle Ground.*

Patrick   Nancy Hawkins's co-worker at the Ullswater press whose wife constantly suspects him of infidelity in Muriel Spark's *A Far Cry from Kensington.*

Graham Patten   John Patten's son by a former marriage; he goes through several jobs as a jazz musician, a screenplay writer, and ultimately a government official; he is killed in the Catastrophe in Doris Lessing's *The Four-Gated City.*

John Patten   Margaret Patten's husband, who is a member of the Labour Party; he is later arrested because of his supposed homosexuality in Doris Lessing's *The Four-Gated City.*

Margaret Patten   Mark Coldridge's mother, who loves more than anything else to be a hostess; she dislikes her son because he refuses to defend her husband against charges of homosexuality and because he does defend his brother Colin's actions in Doris Lessing's *The Four-Gated City.*

Evelyn, Lady Patterson   Eldest daughter of a wealthy family who, by her own private admission, married her husband because she saw in him the vehicle for her own rather high ambitions; even as he is recovering from a stroke, she is still calculating his chances for high office in Frank Swinnerton's *Some Achieve Greatness.*

Sir Roderick Patterson   Prominent sixty-one-year-old barrister and Member of Parliament; though he appears to be a confident and uncompromising character, he has secret doubts as to his own worth; driven to succeed, first by his mother and later by his wife, Sir Roderick has devoted his life to his work; beset by the troubles of his children, realizing that he has little future in the current government or a subsequent one, and even worried that he may lose his seat in the House of Commons, he suffers a stroke in Frank Swinerton's *Some Achieve Greatness.*

Saul Patterson   Son of Sir Roderick Patterson; he becomes involved with a confidence man bent on embarassing his father; at his wits' end, Saul reveals his troubles to Florence Marvell, then a complete stranger, on the train ride back to Slocumbe; her advice leads to his improved relationship with his father and to his undying admiration for Florence in Frank Swinnerton's *Some Achieve Greatness*.

Syd Patterson   A self-proclaimed artist and the trouble-prone younger brother of Sir Roderick; bitter about his brother's success as compared to his own meager life, and galled by a publisher's rejection of his autobiographical novel, he attacks and unintentionally kills a stranger who has praised Sir Roderick in Frank Swinnerton's *Some Achieve Greatness*.

Paul   Magnetic male prostitute who seeks spiritual guidance from Augustus Parr and encourages Christopher Isherwood to pursue spiritual discipline; he dies from drug addiction in Christopher Isherwood's *Down There on a Visit*.

Fat Paul   John Self's *real* father in Martin Amis's *Money*.

Father Paul   Priest in charge of the dynamo in Graham Greene's *A Burnt-Out Case*.

Papy Paul   Elderly neighbor of the Mouth family in Mediaville who helps Mr. and Mrs. Mouth celebrate their Pearl Anniversary just before they move to Cuna-Cuna in Ronald Firbank's *Sorrow in Sunlight*.

Peter Pay Paul   Phony drug dealer who sells an asthma cure as if it were marijuana in Colin MacInnes's *City of Spades*.

Pauline   Student seeking to abort the illegitimate child (Orlando King) she conceived with Leonard Gardner; she is persuaded to let Professor King adopt the child instead; she never tells Leonard of the child, but she leaves a large sum of money in Orlando's name and disappears in Isabel Colegate's *Orlando King*.

Pauline   Julian Tower's niece and ward who is "controlled by a committee of relatives" in Elizabeth Bowen's *To the North*.

Sergeant Pavel   Fat, womanizing Czech Army Intelligence operative who, by Axel and Magnus Pym's devices, becomes the traitor "Greensleeves" to boost Pym's standing with his service and loyalty to Axel in John le Carré's *A Perfect Spy*.

Angela Payne   News reporter who has an affair with

Orlando King in Isabel Colegate's *Orlando King*. She is remembered in *Orlando at the Brazen Threshold*.

Annabell Paynton   Young woman who first has a brief romantic friendship with Arthur Middleton, then with his oldest friend, Charles Addinsell, in Henry Green's *Doting*.

Paula Paynton   Mother of Annabel Paynton in Henry Green's *Doting*.

Pryor Paynton   Father of Annabel Paynton in Henry Green's *Doting*.

Peacey   Artful business manager of Sir Harry; having rescued Marion Yaverland from a mob stoning her because she is pregnant and unmarried, he arranges a secret but legal marriage ceremony, claiming it will protect her and her unborn child from further violence in the squire's absence; he thus earns Sir Harry and Lady Teresa's gratitude, and his threats to demand custody of the child, Richard Yaverland, give him lasting power over Marion; he later brutally rapes and impregnates her and becomes the custodian and abuser of her second son, Roger Yaverland, in childhood and adolescence in Rebecca West's *The Judge*.

Peacock   Neighbor who is humbled when the Squire helps put out a barn fire on his farm in John Galsworthy's *The Country House*.

Enoch Peake   Chairman of the Bursley Mutual Burial Club and owner of Cochnage Gardens, a sporting resort; he is the new husband of pub-owner Louisa Loggerheads in Arnold Bennett's *Clayhanger*.

Potty Peake   A harmless village imbecile who hangs around the Fenchurch St. Paul churchyard in Dorothy L. Sayers's *The Nine Tailors: Changes Rung on an Old Theme in Two Short Touches and Two Full Peals*.

Pearce   Friend of Art Kipps from the Folkestone Drapery Bazaar; he is snubbed by Kipps's snobbish mentor, Chester Coote, at a concert in H. G. Wells's *Kipps: The Story of a Simple Soul*.

Heather Pearce   Homely, power-hungry nursing student who enjoys blackmail; she is murdered in P. D. James's *Shroud for a Nightingale*.

Pearl   Fleshy, gaudy, drunken, deceased wife of the guilt-ridden Cyril, who time after time rescued her from her drunken stupors in John Berger's *The Foot of Clive*.

Signalman Andy Pearse   Young soldier who, perhaps because he is depressed over the death of a fellow soldier who dies in a freak automobile accident, resists the seduction attempt of Max Hunter, who is using the alias Captain Vincent Lane at the time, in Kingsley Amis's *The Anti-Death League*.

Bradley Pearson   A fifty-eight-year-old retired tax inspector and writer of modest success; his ex-wife Christian Evandale, her brother Francis Marloe, and Arnold and Rachel Baffin are variously and unsatisfactorily attracted to him; his love affair with the young woman Julian Baffin is brief, joyous, and doomed; wrongly convicted of Arnold Baffin's murder, he is sent to prison, where he writes *The Black Prince — A Celebration of Love*, which forms the bulk of Iris Murdoch's *The Black Prince*.

Eric Pearson   Electrical engineer who works with Walter Luke in atomic-energy research and displays little concern over American use of atomic bombs in C. P. Snow's *The New Men*.

George Pearson   Newspaper reporter who unwittingly breaks the news of his son's arrest and pending trial to the boy's father, Harold Colmore, in Roy Fuller's *The Father's Comedy*.

Sergeant George Pearson   Superintendent Armstrong's assistant; an innocent, blue-eyed officer, he is a favorite of middle-aged ladies in Nicholas Blake's *A Question of Proof*.

Jack Pearson   Stout, bearded literary editor of the *New Watchman*, a left-wing Fleet Street paper where Alan Percival works after the war in Roy Fuller's *The Perfect Fool*.

Mary Pearson   Wife of Eric; she is angry with her husband because he is not outraged by American use of atomic bombs in C. P. Snow's *The New Men*.

Abel Peartree   Worldly preacher; though he was despised by the young Edwin Clayhanger for zealously instituting a Saturday afternoon Bible Class for schoolboys, he is wryly respected for his casual, business-like behaviour when he appears at the mature Edwin's "At Home" in Arnold Bennett's *These Twain*.

Clara Pease-Henneky   Suffragette and political activist in Isabel Colegate's *Statues in a Garden*.

Mr. Peck   Schoolteacher who embarrasses Lewis Eliot over the war-effort contribution in C. P. Snow's *Time of Hope*.

George Peck   Country rector who realizes that Brat Farrar is not Patrick Ashby; Brat consults him about Simon Ashby in Josephine Tey's *Brat Farrar*.

Nancy Ledingham Peck   Neighbor of the Ashby family; once a top debutante, she stunned society by becoming the wife of a country clergyman in Josephine Tey's *Brat Farrar*.

Sebastian Pedigree   A former teacher of Matty Septimus at the Greenfield foundling school and an inveterate pederast; he provides commentary on the events in William Golding's *Darkness Visible*.

Pedro   Brutish servant of the rapacious gamblers who murder Lena in Joseph Conrad's *Victory: An Island Tale*.

Pedug   The Planet 8 representative in charge of the Education of the Young before the Ice struck in Doris Lessing's *The Making of the Representative for Planet 8*.

Margaret Peel   A university lecturer and a stultifying manipulator who fakes a suicide attempt to elicit Jim Dixon's sympathy; she is a hypocrite who plays the role of the tortured woman in her love affairs, and Jim rejects her in Kingsley Amis's *Lucky Jim*.

Matthew Peel-Swynnerton   Cyril Povey's friend; to reduce expenses in Paris, he stays at Pension Frensham, recognizes its proprietor as Cyril's long lost Aunt Sophia Baines, and informs the Baines family in Arnold Bennett's *The Old Wives Tale*.

Inspector Peerson   Finnish Police Inspector; he investigates Wilf Taylor's death and easily discredits John Avery's lame cover as Taylor's brother in John le Carré's *The Looking-Glass War*.

Mr. Peeve   Gloomy chief editor of the *Liberal*, a socialist newspaper; he allows his sub-editor Mr. Barnstaple to take the fateful holiday which leads him into the perfect world of Utopia in H. G. Wells's *Men Like Gods*.

Jocas Pehlevi   Mild-mannered brother of Julian Pehlevi and Benedicta Merlin; he oversees the Eastern branch of the Firm in Lawrence Durrell's *Tunc*. He dies of cancer in *Nunquam*.

Julian Pehlevi   Director of the Merlin Firm; he deflowers his sister Benedicta Merlin in Lawrence Durrell's *Tunc*. Shattered by the death of Iolanthe Samiou, he becomes obsessed with the creation of her android; he is finally murdered by his own creation in *Nunquam*.

pelado   Unnamed thief with "conquistador's hands" who steals the dying Indian's money in Malcolm Lowry's *Under the Volcano*.

Alfred Pelcher Managing Director of the Spartacus Machine Tool Company; he unknowingly convinces Nicholas Marlow to spy for Andreas Zaleshoff and to pretend to work solely for General Vagas when Pelcher instructs Marlow to make new business contacts in Eric Ambler's *Cause for Alarm*.

Pellew Captain on the *Indefatigable* and a whist player, with a reputation for success in both roles in C. S. Forester's *Mr. Midshipman Hornblower*. He is promoted to Rear Admiral; Hornblower accepts his criticism and orders but is somewhat jealous of his advancement in *Hornblower and the Hotspur*.

Mr. Pemberton Headmaster of Seaforth House; he is a cleric given to sermonizing about morality and school honor, yet he trades upon his pupils' feelings of inadequacy and guilt and is ultimately shown to have been involved in a dubious financial relationship with a local merchant in Roy Fuller's *The Ruined Boys*.

Dicky Pemberton Assistant District Commissioner whose suicide Henry Scobie investigates and reflects upon repeatedly in Graham Greene's *The Heart of the Matter*.

Thomas Pemberton Physician who is a distant relative of Lord Hillmorton; he inherits the title when Hillmorton dies in C. P. Snow's *In Their Wisdom*.

Herbert Pembroke Rickie Elliott's ambitious brother-in-law; the headmaster of Dunwood House at Sawston, he forces Rickie to help him try to remove the day-boys from the school in E. M. Forster's *The Longest Journey*.

Ralph Pembroke An angry, violent, self-pitying black man and Kenneth Toomey's larcenous secretary-lover for many years in Anthony Burgess's *Earthly Powers*.

Dr. Walter Penberthy Physician who signs General Fentiman's death certificate; a pioneer of the glandular theory of crime, he needs money for a clinic; Ann Dorland is his devoted friend in Dorothy L. Sayers's *The Unpleasantness at the Bellona Club*.

Bill Pendlebury Ella Sands's brother, who is writing a book on Cecil Rhodes and is constantly in debt; he helps Ella prosecute the case against Vera Curry in Angus Wilson's *Hemlock and After*.

Shanks Pendleton One of Judith (Gardner) King's friends in Isabel Colegate's *Orlando King*.

Bee Pendyce Eldest daughter of Horace; she is attracted to young Cecil Tharp in John Galsworthy's *The Country House*.

General Charles Pendyce Younger brother of Squire Horace; he is retired from the army; he enquires about Margery Pendyce when she leaves her husband in John Galsworthy's *The Country House*.

George Pendyce Eldest son of Horace; he loses money gambling on horses and is humiliated when Helen Bellew ceases caring for him in John Galsworthy's *The Country House*.

Gerald Pendyce Younger son of Horace; he is a captain in the army in John Galsworthy's *The Country House*.

Horace Pendyce Squire of Worsted Skeynes, an English country estate, who threatens to disinherit his son George for gambling and refusing to surrender Helen Bellew in John Galsworthy's *The Country House*.

Margery Pendyce Wife of Horace, aged fifty-two in 1891, who leaves her husband when he threatens to disinherit their son George; she discovers that Helen Bellew has ceased to care for George, and she persuades Jaspar Bellew to drop his divorce suit in John Galsworthy's *The Country House*.

Norah Pendyce Younger daughter of Horace in John Galsworthy's *The Country House*.

Mark Penfold Third-year anthropology student who shares a flat with Digby Fox and competes for a Foresight Fellowship; he is not above the allure of courting a Belgravia debutante in Barbara Pym's *Less Than Angels*.

Penk Mr. Burleigh's thuggish chauffeur, who is beaten up by the Utopian woman whom he molests; he rebuffs William Barnstaple for opposing Rupert Catskill's plan to overthrow Utopian rule in H. G. Wells's *Men Like Gods*.

Nancy Penkethman Beautiful society gossip columnist; she is an accomplished companion to the wealthy and usually accompanies Lord Watlington in Arnold Bennett's *Imperial Palace*.

Peter Pennecuik One of the ruling elders and session-clerk of the Kirk in Woodilee; he is a sanctimonious egoist who opposes David Sempill and who is among the first to die of the plague in John Buchan's *Witch Wood*.

David Pennistone Tall, thin, hook-nosed intellectual whose interest in Descartes and Gassendi creates an intellectual bond with Nick Jenkins during their military service in Anthony Powell's *The Valley of Bones* and in *The Soldier's Art*. He joins Finn's firm after the war and marries a French girl in *The Military Philosophers* and in *Books Do Furnish a Room*.

Penny Pert, protective, orange-haired personal secretary to actor Jake Driver; Gus Howkins must negotiate with her in his attempts to obtain more information about Julia Delmore; she is a character in the story novelist Giles Hermitage writes in John Wain's *The Pardoner's Tale*.

Mrs. Penny A selfish, seventy-year-old woman living in Jane Somers's apartment hours; she wants Jane to befriend her in Doris Lessing's *The Diaries of Jane Somers*.

Paul Pennyfeather A timid Oxford student unfairly expelled; he becomes a schoolmaster, gets engaged to a wealthy socialite, and is unjustly arrested as the head of the white-slavery ring actually controlled by his fiancée, Margot Best-Chetwynde; after being spirited out of prison through financial and political influence, he returns to Oxford to continue his studies in Evelyn Waugh's *Decline and Fall*.

Dr. Penrose Major Kelvin Halliday's psychiatrist, who gives Halliday's diary to Gwenda Reed in Agatha Christie's *Sleeping Murder*.

Mr. Penrose Tutor to Aubrey Gaveston; he is a little man with spectacles in Ivy Compton-Burnett's *A Family and a Fortune*.

Augustine Penry-Herbert A young Englishman who finds a drowned child on his estate in Wales; to avoid village suspicion he travels to cousins in Germany, where his visit coincides with the collapse of the Deutschmark; he is there when Hitler leads his 1923 Munich putsch; he falls in love with his beautiful cousin Mitzi von Kessen in Richard Hughes's *The Fox in the Attic*. Shanghaied aboard a rum-running ship, he is stranded without identification in Connecticut, where he falls in with a crowd of hard-drinking teenaged "summer people"; he eventually escapes to Canada and home; he falls tepidly in love with Joan Dibden, and postpones committing himself by accompanying Ludovic Corcos to Morocco; he and Ludo eventually join Joan and her new husband, Anthony Fairfax, in Germany in *The Wooden Shepherdess*.

Uncle Pentstemon Acerbic old man who disrupts both his great-nephew Alfred Polly's wedding and the funeral of Alfred's father with his bad-tempered outbursts in H. G. Wells's *The History of Mr. Polly*.

Arthur Peplow Minister of St. John's Church who attends to the religious needs of most of the military and civilian families in Pankot; he conducts the memorial service for Teddie Bingham in Paul Scott's *The Day of the Scorpion*. He counsels the Laytons after the death of Mabel Layton in *The Towers of Silence*.

Clarissa Peplow Arthur's wife, who allows Barbara Batchelor to take a room in her home after Barbara is ejected from Rose Cottage following the death of Mabel Layton in Paul Scott's *The Towers of Silence*.

Mr. Pepper Tedious scholarly friend of Ridley Ambrose; he voyages across the Atlantic with Rachel Vinrace to South America and portends the final tragedy by moving from the Ambroses' villa to the hotel while yammering about typhoid in Virginia Woolf's *The Voyage Out*.

Spencer Perceval Prime Minister of England, cousin and guardian of Gabriel Perceval Cranmer, and the principal target of Squire Cranmer's mad plot in John Buchan's *The Free Fishers*.

Percival The unifying mythic and human mock-epic hero whose accidental death in India variously affects his six childhood friends; Percival was Neville's beloved although Percival loved Susan, who secretly loved Bernard in Virginia Woolf's *The Waves*.

Percival The boy servant of the Middletons; he refuses to be called James for the convenience of Selina Middleton but later becoems servile in the hope of rising to the rank of butler in Ivy Compton-Burnett's *The Mighty and Their Fall*.

Dr. Percival Coldly insensitive, unprincipled physician, attached to British Intelligence community; he wrongly suspects and murders Arthur Davis in Graham Greene's *The Human Factor*.

Uncle Percival Senior partner to the solicitor chosen to defend Hugo Chesterton; more daring and imaginative than his "stick in the mud" partner, Bruce Rogers, he pressures Bruce to fight rather than to go through the motions of a trial in Nicholas Blake's *A Tangled Web*.

Alan Percival Handsome youth who grows to maturity between 1912 and 1947; he is a journalist who wants to be a cartoonist; serving in the war as a radar technician, he meets and marries an attractive and ambitious woman, who finally leaves him for a more successful and ambitious man in Roy Fuller's *The Perfect Fool*.

Carl Percival Alan Percival's father; he is a mill

owner forced into early retirement by ill health in Roy Fuller's *The Perfect Fool.*

Enid Percival   Alan Percival's mother in Roy Fuller's *The Perfect Fool.*

Percy   Georgie's brother who is the town surveyor in E. F. Benson's *The Worshipful Lucia.*

Mr. Percy   A sensitive teacher at Seaforth House who, like some of the boys, is painfully conscious of being trapped in a mediocre world; as a teacher he exerts an influence on Gerald Bracher, arousing Bracher's interest in music and literature; he is involved in a rather tentative romantic affair with Mr. Pemberton's niece in Roy Fuller's *The Ruined Boys.*

Dr. Carlisle Perera   An ex-biologist and member of the Rama committee; he first identifies Rama as a space ark, first realizes the potential effect of warming on Rama, and discovers a way to save Lieutenant Pak in Arthur C. Clarke's *Rendezvous with Rama.*

Colonel Perez   Chief of police in a small northern Argentianian city and friend of Dr. Eduardo Plarr; he tracks down the kidnappers of Charley Fortnum, the Honorary Consul, and falsifies his report of the death of Dr. Plarr in Graham Greene's *The Honorary Consul.*

Perfetta   Gino Carella's slatternly Italian servant in E. M. Forster's *Where Angels Fear to Tread.*

Marcelle Periscope   Film star and coveted party guest in E. F. Benson's *Lucia in London.*

Perkins   A timid hiker whom Harriet Vane encounters after her discovery of Paul Alexis Goldschmidt's body in Dorothy L. Sayers's *Have His Carcase.*

Jerry Perkins   Teen-aged admirer of twenty-three-year-old Elsie Sprickett; he runs important errands for her and is rewarded with an unreserved kiss in Arnold Bennett's *Riceyman Steps.*

Tim Perkins   Cynical, academically slow student at Carne School who is murdered in John le Carré's *A Murder of Quality.*

Tom Perkins   The talented, charismatic headmaster at Philip Carey's school who recognizes his talents but does not quite manage to persuade him to go up to Oxford in W. Somerset Maugham's *Of Human Bondage.*

William Esse Perkins   A wealthy American philanthropist who wants to finance Mark Coldridge's rescue colonies in North Africa in Doris Lessing's *The Four-Gated City.*

Deborah Perne   The eldest of the three spinster sisters who run Wordsworth House, the north London school where Miriam Henderson teaches in Dorothy Richardson's *Backwater.*

Haddie Perne   The youngest and — to Miriam Henderson — most appealing of the Perne sisters; she comes to represent a genuine threat to Miriam's emotional independence in Dorothy Richardson's *Backwater.*

Jenny Perne   The least adept of the Perne sisters at handling adolescent girls, who are prone to tease and make fun of her; she encourages Miriam Henderson to read newspaper "leaders" on education in *Backwater.*

Ann Peronett   The conventional, loyal wife of Randall Peronett; she is disgracefully treated by him but refuses other men's offers in the hope that Randall will return to her; she discovers after she has rejected Felix Meecham that her daughter's hostility to him was a mask for jealous love in Iris Murdoch's *An Unofficial Rose.*

Fanny Peronett   The wife of Hugh Peronett; a wealthy art dealer's daughter, she inherited the magnificent Tintoretto nude; her funeral occurs at the beginning of Iris Murdoch's *An Unofficial Rose.*

Hugh Peronett   A retired civil servant passed over "by the terror and the glory of life"; determined that his son, Randall Peronett, will not suffer the same fate for lack of funds, he sells his Tintoretto to enable Randall to elope with his lover Lindsay Rimmer in Iris Murdoch's *An Unofficial Rose.*

Miranda Peronett   The teenaged daughter of Randall and Ann Peronett; she sees to it that Felix Meecham, with whom she is in love herself, will not marry her mother after her father's desertion in Iris Murdoch's *An Unofficial Rose.*

Randall Peronett   A famous rosegrower married to Ann Peronett; his elopement with his lover Lindsay Rimmer is financed by his father's sale of a Tintoretto nude in Iris Murdoch's *An Unofficial Rose.*

Steve Peronett   Randall and Ann's charming, beloved son, who died at fourteen of polio; since his death there has been no happiness in his parents' marriage in Iris Murdoch's *An Unofficial Rose.*

Mr. Perosi   Jealous head of about thirty waiters; this Frechman born in Milan is flattered by Violet Powler's demeanour as a new housekeeper and her request to be taught to speak French in Arnold Bennett's *Imperial Palace.*

Major Wilfrid (Potty) Perowne The lover with whom Sylvia Tietjens decamped for an adulterous affair before returning to her husband in *Some Do Not. . . .* He is used by Sylvia in a scheme to humiliate and discredit her husband before his superior officers in *No More Parades.* He is killed in the trenches in *A Man Could Stand Up —.*

Mr. Perr A statistician who is a leader in the various socialist activities going on in Zambesia in Doris Lessing's *Martha Quest*, in *A Proper Marriage*, and in *A Ripple from the Storm.*

Mrs. Perr A faintly malicious woman, who like her husband is involved in socialist or leftist politics in Doris Lessing's *Martha Quest* and in *A Proper Marriage.*

Perrance A repairer of Greek statues with a "studio" in Flaxman's Court and an elaborate manner, full of rhetorical flourishes, as well as a hot temper usually directed at his young woman-companion in Dorothy Richardson's *The Trap.*

Perrault A founder of Shangri-La; he is 200 years old when he greets Hugh "Glory" Conway as his replacement in 1933; Perrault treasures the paradise of Shangri-La and devised the method of highjacking a plane to bring new people to his community in order to avoid the extinction of the monastery in James Hilton's *Lost Horizon.*

Miss Perrin Secretary for Michael Mont; she translates his letters for him in John Galsworthy's *The White Monkey.*

Guy Perron Cambridge-educated sergeant assigned to British Field Security; he becomes Sarah Layton's lover and future husband; through Sarah he meets Dmitri Bronowsky, becoming Bronowsky's confidant and privy to the details of Ronald Merrick's history and many other events; Perron is with Sarah and several other members of an English party on a train that is ambushed in a Hindu attack on Muslims in Paul Scott's *A Division of the Spoils.*

Perrot Boastful but nonconfrontational District Commissioner of police and Henry Scobie's immediate superior; he claims that Scobie is the only subordinate he can trust in Graham Greene's *The Heart of the Matter.*

Alfred Perrott One of Evelyn Murgatroyd's English suitors vacationing at the Santa Marina Hotel in Virginia Woolf's *The Voyage Out.*

George Perrott Wealthy man posing as an industrialist and art patron but actually the head of a mysteri-ous and powerful criminal association responsible for two murders in Roy Fuller's *The Second Curtain.*

Perry One of the "boys" with whom Martha Quest has a brief, meaningless fling in Doris Lessing's *Martha Quest.*

Edgar Perry Innocent, idealistic English professor at Fouad University in Cairo who is briefly imprisoned for his crusade to improve student housing; he is an English tutor to Tureiya Pasha; Edgar does not reveal Muawiya Khaslat's attempt to murder him but presents it as a suicide attempt; he and his wife return to England in P. H. Newby's *The Picnic at Sakkara.*

Mary Perry Wife to Edgar Perry; she is disenchanted with her marriage and travels to Cairo to tell Edgar the falsehood that she is leaving him for another man; in the end she becomes pregnant and falls in love with her husband again in P. H. Newby's *The Picnic at Sakkara.*

Ralph Perryman Physician who attended Lady Ashbrook; he served as her financial messenger and is believed to be her murderer in C. P. Snow's *A Coat of Varnish.*

The Personage Private secretary of the private secretary of IT, whom John Lavender takes to be the Unseen Power in John Galsworthy's *The Burning Spear: Being the Experiences of Mr. John Lavender in Time of War.*

Eugene Peshkov A Russian émigré, porter at the rectory; he is loved by Muriel Fisher, whom he dislikes, and by Pattie O'Driscoll, whom he is no longer keen to marry after Muriel reveals Pattie's affair with Carel Fisher in Iris Murdoch's *The Time of the Angels.*

Leo Peshkov Eugene's handsome son, a "troublemaker of genius"; he cons money from both Marcus Fisher and Anthea Barlow and steals and pawns his father's icon in Iris Murdoch's *The Time of the Angels.*

Pete The director of the troupe of players that Pincher Martin belongs to in civilian life; Martin almost openly cuckholds him in William Golding's *Pincher Martin.*

Peter One of Jen's brothers in Isabel Colegate's *Orlando King.*

Peters Ideologically committed Abteilung agent who begins Alec Leamas's debriefing and delivers Leamas to the East German border and Abteilung officials in John le Carré's *The Spy Who Came In from the Cold.*

Sergeant Peters   A man appointed by the camp commander to attend all the "Red" meetings, which many R.A.F. pilots attend, in order to identify the pilots for transfer in Doris Lessing's *A Ripple from the Storm.*

Aline Peters   An American millionaire's daughter who, having become engaged to Freddie Threepwood, for a while resists the importunities of her more personable, energetic suitor, George Emerson, in P. G. Wodehouse's *Something New.*

Giles Peters   Wealthy, longtime friend of Anthony Keating; they become partners in the property-development business with Rory Leggett; Giles is a womanizer in Margaret Drabble's *The Ice Age.*

Harriet Peters   The leading actress slated to appear in Wyndham Farrar's next film and reported by Wyndham to look a little like Emma Evans in Margaret Drabble's *The Garrick Year.*

J. Preston Peters   A dyspeptic American millionaire who has become a collector of precious Egyptian scarabs, one of which is absentmindedly abstracted by Lord Emsworth; Peters's daughter's engagement to a son of Lord Emsworth complicates the recovery in P. G. Wodehouse's *Something New.*

Frederik Petersen (Mr. Peters)   Fat, fiftyish, corrupt, middle-aged drug smuggler and white slaver; one of Dimitrios Makropoulos's Council of Seven drug lords in 1931, he was betrayed by him and follows Charles Latimer in an attempt to find Dimitrios in Eric Ambler's *The Mask of Dimitrios.*

Peterson   An Etonian who obtains his commission as an army officer in David Lodge's *Ginger, You're Barmy.*

Petey   Broke traveler and uncle to Tarry Flynn; he persuades Tarry to leave the farm and seek a new life on his own in Patrick Kavanagh's *Tarry Flynn.*

Father Petrus   Parish priest whose understanding of Nazi aims and strategies is better than the von Kessens' but who is too sensible to argue; he discovers Otto von Kessen's body in Richard Hughes's *The Wooden Shepherdess.*

Mrs. Pettican   Philip Boyes's cook, who prepared his last meal and shared much of it in Dorothy L. Sayers's *Strong Poison.*

Miss Petticott   The governess of Clemence and Sefton Shelley; she likes the visiting school matrons but not the schoolmistress Miss Chancellor in Ivy Compton-Burnett's *Two Worlds and Their Ways.*

Claudia Pettifer   Oxford graduate in her mid-thirties who busily renovates an Islington house; she is temporarily abandoned by her husband, Graham, while he is working on his book and flirting with Emma Howick in Barbara Pym's *A Few Green Leaves.*

Graham Pettifer   Fortyish married anthropologist; the former lover of Emma Howick, he comes to stay near and impose on Emma in West Oxfordshire while finishing his book in Barbara Pym's *A Few Green Leaves.*

Mr. Pettigrew   Intelligent, upper-middle-class director of a criminal rehabilitation center where Bev Jones is sent after his conviction for petty theft; a committed socialist, Pettigrew attempts relentlessly to persuade or force Jones into conforming in Anthony Burgess's *1985.*

Mr. Pettigrew   The tutor of Adrian, Alice, and Francis Hume; he is a small, neat man, who eavesdrops on the children to hear the Hume family secrets in Ivy Compton-Burnett's *Mother and Son.*

Mabel Pettigrew   Caretaker of Charmian Piper, blackmailer of Godfrey Colston, and eventual inheritor of Lisa Brooke's fortune in Muriel Spark's *Memento Mori.*

Eddie Pettrie   A factory owner and friend of the Newmans; he helps Colin Freestone get to the hospital and tries to explain the strange lifestyle of the Newmans to Colin in David Storey's *A Temporary Life.*

Joe Petty   Chauffeur for John Lavender; his cynicism drives Lavender to search for the Unseen Power in John Galsworthy's *The Burning Spear: Being the Experiences of Mr. John Lavender in Time of War.*

John Petty   Jimmy Morgan's tutor, who is sleeping with Mrs. Morgan's secretary; he leaves to join a group which studies "problems people read about in newspapers" in Nigel Dennis's *Boys and Girls Come Out to Play.*

Marian Petty   Housekeeper for John Lavender; she nurses him back to health after his great fall in John Galsworthy's *The Burning Spear: Being the Experiences of Mr. John Lavender in Time of War.*

Michel Pevsner   A Polish professor living on the Sterns' farm; he has a close relationship with Thomas Stern's wife and child in Doris Lessing's *Landlocked.*

Montgomery Pew   Amiable, impressionable assistant welfare officer with the Colonial Department in London until he is fired for fraternizing with the black immigrants; a good friend to Johnny Fortune, he gives him money and lodging and aids in his acquittal in Colin MacInnes's *City of Spades*.

Peyrol   Old swashbuckling master gunner who returns from the Indian Seas with gold to retire on Scevola Bron's farm, becomes a lookout for Lieutenant Réal, and is killed by Captain Vincent, carrying papers meant to deceive the British concerning Napoleon's Egyptian invasion in Joseph Conrad's *The Rover*.

Lily Pfaff   North German who runs her Hanover "finishing" school with fanatical strictness and a watchful eye for signs of erotic behavior, forbidding any physical contact between girls; she resents the slightest attention paid by Pastor Lahmann to any of the girls and is critical of naïve Miriam Henderson for her lack of social awareness and her earnest manner in Dorothy Richardson's *Pointed Roofs*.

Professor Pforzheim   German medievalist historian esteemed by his English colleagues; he gives a lecture to their association and is studying a tomb in Europe with similarities to those of Melpham in Angus Wilson's *Anglo-Saxon Attitudes*.

Mrs. Phancy   A gray, mistrustful woman who, with her husband, is in charge of an unprofitable, isolated motel; they hire Vivienne Michel to replace them as end-of-season manager in Ian Fleming's *The Spy Who Loved Me*.

Ted Phancy   Mrs. Phancy's crude, falsely genial husband in Ian Fleming's *The Spy Who Loved Me*.

Cheme Phar   A woman who strives to enter the makers corps which is open only to men; she is a follower of Shay Tal in Brian W. Aldiss's *Helliconia Spring*.

Felicity Phee   A student lover of Howard Kirk and the Kirks' lodger in Malcolm Bradbury's *The History Man*.

Marjorie Phelps   A maker of pottery figurines; she is Lord Peter Wimsey's Bohemian contact in Dorothy L. Sayers's *The Unpleasantness at the Bellona Club* and in *Strong Poison*.

Phil   An artist's model whom Sebastian meets at Viola's in London; the fourth of Sebastian's "experiments" in love, she breaks down his conventions, loosens his rigidity, and introduces him to disorder and truancy in Vita Sackville-West's *The Edwardians*.

Albert Philby   Ex-convict and odd-job man at Toynton Grange, a private nursing home; he is killed in P. D. James's *The Black Tower*.

Philip   A very politically active young man who has asked Maureen to marry him in Doris Lessing's *The Summer Before the Dark*.

Philip   A small, weak-looking man who fixes the toilets and the electricity in the condemned house that Alice Mellings takes over; he moves into the house but later dies in Doris Lessing's *The Good Terrorist*.

Dr. Philipot   Haitian Secretary for Social Welfare who has fallen from favor and kills himself at the Trianon, Brown's hotel, in Graham Greene's *The Comedians*.

Madame Philipot   Brave wife of the Haitian Secretary for Social Welfare, who has committed suicide; she stands up to the Tontons Macoutes when they take her husband's body in Graham Greene's *The Comedians*.

Henri Philipot   Haitian poet and nephew of Dr. Philipot, the Secretary for Social Welfare who kills himself; he forms a rebel group and is joined by Major Jones; he saves Jones and Brown by killing Captain Concasseur, but is forced to leave Haiti for the Dominican Republic in Graham Greene's *The Comedians*.

Brother Phillipe   Practical religious brother; he works as a carpenter and is in charge of the dynamo which provides electricity for the leproserie in Graham Greene's *A Burnt-Out Case*.

Phillips   Maintopman on the *Pluto* who after capture tells the prisoners of the major battle that the English mounted to free them in C. S. Forester's *Flying Colours*.

Phillips   Ship's boy who believes himself indifferent to death because he is disappointed in love in Richard Hughes's *In Hazard*.

Mr. Phillips   Julie Camish's prosperous businessman father, who was willing to give his daughter anything except an education; he was pleased at her marriage to Simon Camish in Margaret Drabble's *The Needle's Eye*.

Ceinwen Phillips   Huw Morgan's first and only lover; she disappears without telling Huw she is pregnant in Richard Llewellyn's *How Green Was My Valley*.

James Phillips   Husband of Charley Summers's lost love, Rose, in Henry Green's *Back*.

Mervyn Phillips   Brother of Ceinwen Phillips; a bully, he harasses Huw Morgan until Huw learns to box in Richard Llewellyn's *How Green Was My Valley*.

Ridley Phillips   Young son of James and Rose Phillips in Henry Green's *Back*.

Rose Grant Phillips   Dead lover of Charley Summers; her memory haunts and obsesses the disoriented returning soldier in Henry Green's *Back*.

Thomas Phillips   Newly retired sailor who saves the life of Pam Hargreaves when she tries to kill herself; he hires her to help him go through his Aunt Clara's estate, falls in love with her, saves her from her husband and his brothers, and fathers her child; learning that he is Jewish when he goes through the estate, he leaves for Israel in Alan Sillitoe's *Her Victory*.

Nurse Philliter   An attractive, competent young woman who is hired to share Agatha Dawson's care with Mary Whittaker but is dismissed before Agatha's death; she has become engaged to Dr. Carr in Dorothy L. Sayers's *Unnatural Death*.

Aunt Lucy Philps   The widowed, stolidly conventional guardian of the Broom sisters in Dorothy Richardson's *Backwater* and in *Interim*.

Philstrom   Newspaper reporter who joins forces with Professor Hammerstein in his pursuit of information about Erik Krogh in Graham Greene's *England Made Me*.

Phi-oo   Selenite administrator who serves as Cavor's principal monitor and guide, as well as his liason with the Grand Lunar, and who enlightens him about Selenite culture in H. G. Wells's *The First Men in the Moon*.

Denis Phipps   Nineteen-year-old poet who, in spite of agonizing over the vast amount of knowledge he has yet to learn, comes to have a better understanding of himself in Norman Douglas's *South Wind*.

Raymond Phipps   Art historian invited to Italy by Orlando King in Isabel Colegate's *Orlando at the Brazen Threshold*.

Madame Phiri   A French woman who is part of the Global Foods delegation meeting in Istanbul in Doris Lessing's *The Summer Before the Dark*.

Elias Phiri   An African member of the Communist Party who stands as a symbol of the rest of the group's high-minded goals of racial equality; he is being paid by Mr. Maynard to spy on the group and report specific information to him in Doris Lessing's *A Ripple from the Storm*.

Phoebe   Housekeeper for Daniel Martin's country house, Thorncombe; she is Ben's wife in John Fowles's *Daniel Martin*.

Phoenix   A Native American stable groom; his boss, Rachel Witt, resists the primitive attraction of his sexual overtures in D. H. Lawrence's *St. Mawr*.

Phuong ("Phoenix")   Thomas Fowler's exploited Annamite mistress; she leaves Fowler for Alden Pyle but returns to him and his falsely promised economic security when Pyle is murdered in Graham Greene's *The Quiet American*.

Phyllis   A young, ambitious worker for *Lilith* who is promoted to assistant editor but suddenly leaves the profession to marry the editor of the magazine and have children in Doris Lessing's *The Diaries of Jane Somers*.

Phyllis   Girlfriend, later fiancée, of Malcolm Swan in Barbara Pym's *Less Than Angels*.

Commander Picton   British Intelligence official and counterterrorist whose presence reminds Marty Kurtz of the amiable British officers who brutalized him and murdered fellow Jews after World War II but whose shrewdness penetrates Kurtz's assumed charm to expose the Israeli's dedication to violence in John le Carré's *The Little Drummer Girl*.

Peter Pienaar   Independent South African scout, big-game hunter, and prospector; he and Richard Hannay journey as two South African neutrals across enemy territory to decipher a mysterious code and prevent the German conspiracy from succeeding in John Buchan's *Greenmantle*. Despite his age, he makes a great success as a fighter pilot and rival to Lensch, the great German flying ace; wounded and taken prisoner, he endures heroically; his last act, after downing five enemy planes, is to crash into the sixth, Lensch's craft, in heroic self-sacrifice in *Mr. Standfast*.

Pierce   Surgeon's mate aboard the *Renown* in C. S. Forester's *Lieutenant Hornblower*.

Carroll Pierce   A boring and shy poor teacher at Freddie Wentworth's school who makes love to Hannah Graves one time and tries to make her fall in love with him forever in Penelope Fitzgerald's *At Freddie's*.

Pierino   Theodora Bates's acquaintance, who appears with Mimi Piero in Isabel Colegate's *Orlando at the Brazen Threshold*.

Mimi Piero   An American heiress and an acquaintance of Theodora Bates in Isabel Colegate's *Orlando at the Brazen Threshold*.

Pierpoint Omniscient off-screen philosopher whose encyclical on "apery" warns of the stifling and "societification" of art by large numbers of people with money but no talent, the so-called "Apes of God", in Wyndham Lewis's *The Apes of God*.

Petit Pierre Haitian journalist who seems always in high good humor and who always knows the latest news; he warns Brown at critical moments in Graham Greene's *The Comedians*.

Piers A fellow art student and boyfriend of Miranda Grey in John Fowles's *The Collector*.

Edward Pierson Anglican vicar of a London parish who has been a widower for fifteen years in 1916; he resigns his parish rather than repudiate his unmarried daughter, Noel, when she has a baby; he accepts an assignment as a chaplain in Egypt in John Galsworthy's *Saint's Progress*.

Noel (Nolly) Pierson Eighteen-year-old daughter of Edward in 1916; she has a love affair with the young soldier Cyril Morland, has his baby after he is killed in battle, moves to the country to work on a farm, and marries Jimmy Fort in John Galsworthy's *Saint's Progress*.

Robert (Bob) Pierson Brother of Edward; he goes to London to be with Edward during Noel's confinement in Wales in John Galsworthy's *Saint's Progress*.

Thirza Pierson Wife of Robert; she gives motherly advice to Noel Pierson and provides her a place where she can have her baby in Wales, away from London, in John Galsworthy's *Saint's Progress*.

Piggy A fat boy who is at once intellectual and ineffectual; he serves as the thoughtful guide of the leader Ralph in William Golding's *Lord of the Flies*.

Dr. Felix Pike An American agent working for a secret organization, Facts for Freedom, who steals medical secrets from his government and is unearthed by the narrator in Len Deighton's *The Billion-Dollar Brain*.

Piker Pinkie Brown's old schoolmate, now a waiter at a Peacehaven hotel; his and Pinkie's account of their school acquaintance provides additional background to Pinkie's life in Graham Greene's *Brighton Rock*.

Miss Pilbeam The new governess for the younger Sullivan children; she is slower at mathematics and Latin than her pupils in Ivy Compton-Burnett's *Parents and Children*.

Professor Pilbeam Professor of Hispanic studies and an authority on Cervantes's *Don Quixote* from the University of Notre Dame; Pilbeam happens to be visiting Osera, the Trappist Monastery near Orense where Enrique Zancas and Father Quixote go for refuge in Graham Greene's *Monsignor Quixote*.

P. Frobisher (Percy) Pilbeam Sue Brown's sleazy, unencouraged admirer; as manager of a private-inquiry agency he is hired by Sir Gregory Parsloe-Parsloe to steal and destroy Galahad Threepwood's memoirs in P. G. Wodehouse's *Fish Preferred*. He appears in five other novels.

Eustace Pilbrow Fellow of the Cambridge college who originally supports Paul Jago for election as new Master but changes his vote to Redvers Crawford because of Jago's conservative politics in C. P. Snow's *The Masters*.

Max Pilgrim Professional pianist and singer of suggestive songs in Anthony Powell's *A Buyer's Market*, in *At Lady Molly's*, and in *Casanova's Chinese Restaurant*. He is living with Hugo Tolland in *The Kindly Ones*. His popularity gets a revival during wartime in *The Soldier's Art*.

Mr. Pilkington (satiric representation of the British government) The farmer of Foxwood farm; instead of helping the people try to restore Manor Farm to Mr. Jones, he went into trade agreements with the pigs who had control of Manor Farm in George Orwell's *Animal Farm*.

Richard (Dicky) Pilkington "Financial Agent of Shaftesbury Avenue" who profits from the financial ruin of both Sir Frederick Harden and Isaac Rickman and nearly kills Keith Rickman by viewing his effort to redeem the Harden library for Lucia Harden as a game of "pluck" in May Sinclair's *The Divine Fire*.

Georgie Pillson Personally vain bachelor whose favorite hobby is needlework; he serves as Lucia Lucas's devoted squire but is subverted by his unexpected infatuation for Olga Bracely in E. F. Benson's *"Queen Lucia"*. Bored by the inept leadership of Daisy Quantock, he welcomes Lucia's return from London in *Lucia in London*. When Lucia moves to Tilling, after her husband's death, he takes a house there rather than separate from his housemaid Foljambe, who is engaged to Lucia's chauffeur in *Mapp and Lucia*. His marriage to Lucia constitutes a vow of celibacy in *The Worshipful Lucia*. He loyally assists and encourages her social intrigues, but he becomes tired of her mayoral posturing in *Trouble for Lucia*.

Hermione (Hermy) Pillson One of Georgie Pillson's

two hearty, strapping sisters and occasional visitors; their recognition of Daisy Quantock's yoga-expert Guru as a curry cook from an Indian restaurant prompts his sudden departure in E. F. Benson's *"Queen Lucia"*.

Ursula (Ursy) Pillson　Hearty, athletic sister of Hermione and Georgie Pillson in E. F. Benson's *"Queen Lucia"*.

Pim　Tormented character created by the "I" in Samuel Beckett's *How It Is*.

Mrs. Pimlott　Housekeeper who cleans writer Giles Hermitage's apartment once a week but whom Giles avoids because of her incessant chatter in John Wain's *The Pardoner's Tale*.

Pimp　Unnamed sinister man whom Geoffrey Firmin meets in the toilet after his encounter with the prostitute Maria in Malcolm Lowry's *Under the Volcano*.

Pimpernel　Rabbit refugee from Sandleford Warren killed by Cowslip and his followers at the Warren of the Snares in Richard Adams's *Watership Down*.

Billy Xiao Pin　A member of the crew of the Earth spaceship *Avernus* that studies Helliconia; he falls in love with MyrdemInggala and lands on Helliconia to attempt to meet her; it is his watch which becomes the talisman of evil for JandolAngand in Brian W. Aldiss's *Helliconia Summer*.

Rose Yi Pin　Billy Xiao Pin's girlfriend, who pleads with him not to go to Helliconia in Brian W. Aldiss's *Helliconia Summer*.

Bill Pincomb　Communist leader during the General Strike who strikes a bargain with Chester Nimmo; he is arrested, but the arresting police officer is set up and sent to prison in Joyce Cary's *Not Honour More*.

Angel Pineda　Young son of Martha and Luis, an ambassador to Haiti; he is much hated by Brown for occupying his mother's time and devotion in Graham Greene's *The Comedians*.

Luis Pineda　South American ambassador to Haiti and husband of Martha Pineda, Brown's mistress; Brown never knows whether he is aware of the affair; he provides a safe haven for Major Jones in Graham Greene's *The Comedians*.

Martha Pineda　German wife of a Latin American ambassador to Haiti; she has a long-running affair with Brown, is devoted to her son Angel, and finally befriends Major Jones; she is unjustly mistrusted by the jealous Brown and leaves Haiti estranged from him in Graham Greene's *The Comedians*.

Pine-tree　Homo sapiens tribe member who is so designated according to a botanical resemblance by Lok and Fa in William Golding's *The Inheritors*.

Gilbert Pinfold　A famous middle-aged novelist who suffers a frightening series of hallucinations while traveling on a ship in the Mediterranean in Evelyn Waugh's *The Ordeal of Gilbert Pinfold*.

Mrs. Gilbert Pinfold　The kindly wife of the famous novelist; her chief interest is farming on their large country estate in Evelyn Waugh's *The Ordeal of Gilbert Pinfold*.

Molly Pink　Young, self-important, fat secretary for Carter & Galloway, she is picked up by Charles Hale and used by him for protection against the Mob in Graham Greene's *Brighton Rock*.

Harold P. ("Stinker") Pinker　Bertie Wooster's Oxford friend, a lumbering, intrepid curate engaged to "Stiffy" Byng in P. G. Wodehouse's *The Code of the Woosters*. His continued Rugby prowess and his marriage to Stiffy are reported in *Aunts Aren't Gentlemen*. He appears in *Stiff Upper Lip, Jeeves*.

Constance Pinn　Emily McHugh's former charwoman and current lodger, who works as a secretary at the school from which Emily was fired; she forms an intimacy with Kiki St. Loy and provides David Gavender with his sexual initiation in Iris Murdoch's *The Sacred and Profane Love Machine*.

Miss Pinnegar　A commonplace woman who serves as a surrogate wife to James Houghton; she barely keeps Manchester House and his other commercial schemes afloat in D. H. Lawrence's *The Lost Girl*.

Pino　Commander of the French forces along the coast attacked on shore by the crew of the *Sutherland* joined by Spanish land forces in C. S. Forester's *Ship of the Line*

Padre Pio　A holy man who is supposed to have what Wilfred Barclay himself claims to have — four of Christ's five stigmata — in William Golding's *The Paper Men*.

Arthur Piper　Elderly member of the auxiliary fire service; he spends most of his time indulging in malicious gossip and currying favor with his superiors until he is killed during the first London air raid in Henry Green's *Caught*.

Charmian Piper Roman Catholic convert and aged novelist, whose wisdom alows her to respond without fear to death's telephone call, and whose renewed fame through the revival of her books arouses the antagonism of her husband, Godfrey Colston, and the jealousy of her son, Eric, in Muriel Spark's *Memento Mori.*

Pipkin (Hlaoroo) Small, weak rabbit in Hazel's band from the doomed Sandleford Warren; his handicaps give Hazel's band early practice in solving problems they will need to solve later on a larger scale; his small size also has uses in Richard Adams's *Watership Down.*

Brandon Pirbright Young anthropologist from the United States who studies at the new Research Centre in Barbara Pym's *Less Than Angels.*

James Pirbright George Cyril Wellbeloved's successor as Lord Emsworth's pigman in P. G. Wodehouse's *Fish Preferred.*

Melanie Pirbright Young wife of Brandon Pirbright; she is an anthropologist from the United States who studies at the new Research Centre in Barbara Pym's *Less Than Angels.*

Captain Pirie Jonathan Browne's kind-hearted, vague commanding officer at Badmore, who attempts to help him leave on time for his vacation with Pauline Vickers in David Lodge's *Ginger, You're Barmy.*

Tom Pirie Twenty-two-year-old son of Lady Viola; he tries to rape Meg Eliot in Angus Wilson's *The Middle Age of Mrs. Eliot.*

Lady Viola Pirie Friend of Meg Eliot; she serves with her on the Committee for Aid to the Elderly; she invites Meg to live with her after Bill Eliot's death and urges Meg to leave after Tom Pirie's attempt to rape her in Angus Wilson's *The Middle Age of Mrs. Eliot.*

Mr. Pitt Labour Exchange official and possible former operative for British Intelligence; he gets Alec Leamas a job at the Bayswater Library for Psychic Research in John le Carré's *The Spy Who Came In from the Cold.*

Ebenezer Pittendreich ("Pitten") Butler of Miss "Kirsty" Everdale and a passenger in the wrecked mail coach in John Buchan's *The Free Fishers.*

Pitter Dickensian clerk, the humble assistant to Bosenby, Nick Ollanton's agent in J. B. Priestley's *Lost Empires.*

Dot Pitter Charley Summers's secretary; Charley takes her for a weekend in the country, where she ends up sleeping with James Phillips in Henry Green's *Back.*

Charles Pitt-Heron Young married man whose sudden flight from London prompts his wife, Ethel, to seek Edward Leithen's counsel, precipitating Leithen's uncovering of the evil conspiracy and the rescue of Pitt-Heron in John Buchan's *The Power-House.*

Ethel Pitt-Heron Distraught young wife of the missing Charles Pitt-Heron; she appeals for aid to Edward Leithen in John Buchan's *The Power-House.*

Humphrey Place Factory worker whose association with Dougal Douglas almost frees him from marriage with the materialistic Dixie Morse in Muriel Spark's *The Ballad of Peckham Rye.*

Godiva (Diva) Plaistow Rotund and energetic Tilling widow; she is Elizabeth Mapp's social rival who triumphs in sartorial one-upmanship in E. F. Benson's *Miss Mapp.* She alternates in allegiance to Elizabeth Mapp and to Lucia Lucas in *Mapp and Lucia* and in *The Worshipful Lucia.* She opens a tea shop in *Trouble for Lucia.*

Major ("Barmy") Plank Former African explorer whose confusion is attributable to malaria; Mr. Cook's friend and houseguest, he threatens and maligns Bertie Wooster in P. G. Wodehouse's *Aunts Aren't Gentlemen.* He appears in *Stiff Upper Lip, Jeeves.*

Maitre Planquet Chief Chef of the Imperial Palace restaurant kitchen; he believes he has reached his zenith in the hotel and proudly demonstrates both the modernity of cooking and the preservation of ancient ways for special dishes to Evelyn Orcham's guests in Arnold Bennett's *Imperial Palace.*

Bill Plantagenet Alcoholic sailor and failed musician; he is committed to City Hospital in New York suffering from delirium tremens but is eventually discharged because he is an Englishman; he is last seen curled in a foetal position in a bar in Malcolm Lowry's *Lunar Caustic.*

Plant Men Alien beings with a dual nature — an active "animal" side that is dominant at night and a spiritual "plant" side that emerges in daylight — who are eventually doomed by an imbalance between their two natures in Olaf Stapledon's *Star Maker.*

Senora Plarr Dr. Eduardo Plarr's Paraguayan mother, who lives in Buenos Aires, getting fat on sweets and forgetting Plarr's father in Graham Greene's *The Honorary Consul.*

Dr. Eduardo Plarr   Physician son of an English political-activist father and Paraguayan mother; he is torn between rational skepticism and the urge to love; he has an affair with Clara Fortnum and assists the guerrillas — including childhood friend Leon Rivas — who have kidnapped Charley Fortnum, the Honorary Consul, finally dying in the attempt in Graham Greene's *The Honorary Consul*.

Platt   Transparent follower of fashion and romance; he, Parsons, and Alfred Polly are the fraternal Three P's at the Port Burdock Drapery Bazaar in H. G. Wells's *The History of Mr. Polly*.

Plautus   The cat belonging to Hester Wolsey and Emma Greatheart; it is made much of by Hester in Ivy Compton-Burnett's *Mother and Son*.

Mr. Player   One of the wealthiest men — considered "a legend" — in Martha Quest's town; he shocks his entire community by his beliefs that the Africans should be treated like human beings lest they revolt in Doris Lesing's *Martha Quest* and in *A Proper Marriage*.

Bertha Pledge   Neighbor of Florence Marvell; although a bit of a gossip, she is a sensitive friend to Florence in Frank Swinnerton's *Some Achieve Greatness*.

Ralph Pledge   Invalid neighbor of Florence Marvell; he and his wife, Bertha, are great admirers of Florence in Frank Swinnerton's *Some Achieve Greatness*.

Arthur Plimpton   Wealthy young American who is rigidly conservative in his political views; he courts Penelope Getliffe but marries someone else in C. P. Snow's *Corridors of Power*.

Mr. Plimsing   Efficient hotel detective, formerly of Scotland Yard; he flourishes his watch and other jewelry with royal insignia as reminders of his former speciality in the protective surveillance of distinguished visitors and his accompaniment of British princes abroad; he discreetly solves the mystery of Ceria's disappearance in Arnold Bennett's *Imperial Palace*.

Sergeant Pluck   First policeman that the narrator meets in hell; his Atomic Theory of the transference of atoms from bicycles to humans is propounded in Flann O'Brien's *The Third Policeman*.

Colonel Plum   Assistant Deputy Director of Internal Security at the English Ministry of Information; he wishes to retain Susie as his mistress, but Basil Seal outwits him and puts Plum's war security measures into doubt in Evelyn Waugh's *Put Out More Flags*.

Dr. Plunkett   Blunt, gin-drinking medical doctor for the employees of the Rasuka oil well in P. H. Newby's *A Journey to the Interior*.

Anna Livia (ALP) Plurabelle   Archetypal fecund alluvial mother figure, author of the "mamafesto," which is James Joyce's *Finnegans Wake*.

Uncle Podger   One of the type who can fix anything if everyone attends him; he disastrously hangs a picture on the living-room wall; Harris is accused of resembling him in Jerome K. Jerome's *Three Men in a Boat (To Say Nothing of the Dog)*.

Wanda Podolak   Polish refugee, seamstress, and tenant in Milly Sanders's house; her suicide is brought on by blackmail and by her terrified belief in radionics in Muriel Spark's *A Far Cry from Kensington*.

Jack Pohlen   Rich German Jew who is the life-long lover of Marcus Matthews and trains Marcus in art collection in Angus Wilson's *No Laughing Matter*.

Hercule Poirot   Eccentric, fastidious Belgian detective, who uses his "little gray cells" to solve the murder of a despotic dispenser of charity in Agatha Christie's *The Mysterious Affair at Styles: A Detective Story*. He makes use of a physician, Dr. James Sheppard, to play the role of "Dr. Watson", but he is alert to evidence of Dr. Sheppard's dual role in *The Murder of Roger Ackroyd*. Contradictory testimony leads him to the unpublicized solution of the justifiable assassination of a kidnap-murderer in *Murder on the Orient Express*. He recognizes that all but one of a series of apparently lunatic murders are red herrings to divert inquiry from that one in *The A.B.C. Murders*. His association with Ariadne Oliver begins in *Cards on the Table*. He is on an island holiday when he is required to solve the murder of a vacationing actress in *Evil Under the Sun*. He investigates a sixteen-year-old murder in *Five Little Pigs*. He acts as detective in twenty-seven other novels before returning to Styles Court to track down a multiple murderer; there he supplies the solution to the mystery of his own death as well in *Curtain: Hercule Poirot's Last Case*.

Millicent Pole   A working girl who is acquitted in a trial for sexual solicitation in John Galsworthy's *Maid In Waiting*.

Pollack   Gordon-Nasmyth's cousin who accompanies George Ponderevo on the disastrous "quap" expedition to Africa in H. G. Wells's *Tono-Bungay*.

Esdras Pollock   A rural boatman hostile to the police; he grudgingly testifies that he witnessed from his boat Harriet Vane's discovery of Paul Alexis

Goldschmidt's body in Dorothy L. Sayers's *Have His Carcase*.

Polly   One of Maudie Fowler's sisters; their childhood relationship was very close; her later strong dislike of Maudie was caused mainly by Maudie's good relationship with children in Doris Lessing's *The Diaries of Jane Somers*.

Polly   A feisty but kind woman; she is in charge of the machinists at Jordan's factory where Paul Morel works in D. H. Lawrence's *Sons and Lovers*.

Alfred Polly   Working-class Englishman with mixed ideals, mangled syntax, and a habit of labeling people with bizarre epithets, who leads a disappointing life as a draper, an unsuccessful shopkeeper, and an unsatisfied husband; however, he finally learns that he can remake his world and abandons his home and wife to become a handyman at the Potwell Inn, where he discovers peace of mind at last in H. G. Wells's *The History of Mr. Polly*.

Miriam Larkins Polly   Alfred Polly's cousin and morose wife of fifteen years; she uses her widow's insurance to open a tea shop after her husband's supposed drowning, though she never believes him dead in H. G. Wells's *The History of Mr. Polly*.

Sharon Polsen   Ex-pupil at Romely Fourways', the school Kate Fletcher (Armstrong) attended; she is married to a bookie in Margaret Drabble's *The Middle Ground*.

Claude Polteed   Head of a London detective agency who is hired by Soames Forsyte to watch his wife, Irene, for a lover in John Galsworthy's *In Chancery*.

Polwheal   Hornblower's quiet and respectful servant in C. S. Forester's *The Happy Return* and in *Ship of the Line*.

Georges Gaston Pombal   A consular official who is actually a spy for the French; he shares an apartment with Darley in Lawrence Durrell's *Justine*. He appears in *Balthazar*. He is Pursewarden's friend and apartment sharer in *Mountolive*. He accidentally causes the death of his lover Fosca in *Clea*.

John Pomfret   Well-to-do, middle-aged widower in postwar London; he is the father of Mary Pomfret and former lover of Jane Weatherby, whom he finally agrees to marry in Henry Green's *Nothing*.

Mary Pomfret   Daughter of John Pomfret; she becomes engaged to Philip Weatherby until their parents

subtly cause the engagement to end in Henry Green's *Nothing*.

Reggie Pomfret   A second-year student at Jesus College, Oxford; rescued by Harriet Vane from Jakes's extortion attempt, he develops a crush on her and tries to fight Lord Peter Wimsey in Dorothy L. Sayers's *Gaudy Night*.

Nicholas Pomjalovsky   Eleanor Pargiter's Polish friend, whom she meets at her cousin Maggie Pargiter's dinner party in 1917; he attempts to explain his hopes for the new world and to make a speech at Delia Pargiter's reunion dinner in 1937; Eleanor might have married him, she thinks, but Nicholas loves men in Virginia Woolf's *The Years*.

Sir Mucho Pomposo   Rear Admiral of the Red, a military man with little grasp of the arts of seamanship in C. S. Forester's *Ship of the Line*.

Lilah Pomprey   Popular London hostess who seeks to undermine Adam Melfort's influence on Frank Alban and to dominate the saintly young minister in John Buchan's *A Prince of the Captivity*.

George Pond   An English-teacher friend of Adam Appleby; he lives comfortably with his wife Sally and lies to Adam and Camel about his sex life in David Lodge's *The British Museum Is Falling Down*.

Mrs. Ponderevo   George's mother; she is Lady Drew's housekeeper at Bladesover when George is growing up in H. G. Wells's *Tono-Bungay*.

Edward (Teddy) Ponderevo   Susan's husband and George's uncle; first a chemist at Wimblehurst, he invents "tono-bungay", a phony health-giving elixir, that along with other scams and a genius for advertising makes him wealthy; in the end he dies in France after escaping bankruptcy court in George's airship in H. G. Wells's *Tono-Bungay*.

George Ponderevo   Teddy's nephew, who loves Beatrice Normandy both as a child and as an adult; he marries and divorces Marion Ramboat; he rises in financial status by assisting his uncle in tono-bungay and other such projects; he has an aptitude for science and engineering and builds an airship which he uses to help his uncle escape the country; he is the narrator of H. G. Wells's *Tono-Bungay*.

Susan Ponderevo   Teddy's good-humored and charming wife; she and her nephew George are very fond of each other; she is always somewhat skeptical of her husband's various moneymaking scams in H. G. Wells's *Tono-Bungay*.

Mickey Pondoroso   United Nations diplomat visiting England to conduct a study of British society; he is photographed by the narrator in Colin MacInnes's *Absolute Beginners*.

Ponsonby   The cheery, chubby lieutenant of Stephens, the "Dictator" of the boys' secret society, The Black Spot, in Nicholas Blake's *A Question of Proof.*

Chilton Ponsonby   The eldest son of John Ponsonby; he makes ironic comments to his sister Clare, teases his brother Victor, and mimics his grandmother's gait in Ivy Compton-Burnett's *Daughters and Sons.*

Clare Ponsonby   The eldest of John Ponsonby's daughters; courageous and outspoken, she accepts proposals from Alfred Marcon under some duress and later from Sir Rowland Seymour in Ivy Compton-Burnett's *Daughters and Sons.*

Frances Ponsonby   John Ponsonby's daughter, the pseudonymous author of a novel that he disparages but that wins a literary prize in Ivy Compton-Burnett's *Daughters and Sons.*

Henrietta (Hetty) Ponsonby   The sister of John; she runs his household and thinks she is indispensable; she pretends suicide, insults John's wife, Edith (Hallam), and spitefully tells family secrets at a dinner party in Ivy Compton-Burnett's *Daughters and Sons.*

John Ponsonby   A novelist with the popular touch who nevertheless has money problems; he marries the governess Edith Hallam, thinking that she has sent him money as a tribute to his literary gifts in Ivy Compton-Burnett's *Daughters and Sons.*

Loelia Ponsonby   The Double-0 Section secretary, who worries whenever James Bond and the two other 00 agents are in danger in Ian Fleming's *Moonraker* and in subsequent novels. She has married and is replaced by Mary Goodnight in *On Her Majesty's Secret Service.*

Muriel Ponsonby   Daughter of John Ponsonby; an easy-tempered child, she has three successive governesses and has to start at the beginning in her education with each change in Ivy Compton-Burnett's *Daughter and Sons.*

Sabine Ponsonby   An autocratic grandmother who surreptitiously reads the letters that the family governesses send and receive; she instructs her son John to marry Edith Hallam, the present governess, in Ivy Compton-Burnett's *Daughters and Sons.*

Victor Ponsonby   John Ponsonby's seventeen-year-old son, who has a close bond with his brother Chilton and his three sisters but feels despair at living with his autocratic grandmother, Sabine, in Ivy Compton-Burnett's *Daughters and Sons.*

Poole   An apparently physically deformed agent of the spy ring "The Free Mothers"; he attempts to get film hidden in a prize cake from Arthur Rowe and appears later as a sick-bay attendant in the asylum, where he is killed by Johns in Graham Greens's *The Ministry of Fear.*

Frank Poole   Astronaut and crew member of the space ship *Discovery*; he goes outside the space ship to make repairs and is murdered by HAL in Arthur C. Clarke's *2001: A Space Odyssey.*

Grace Poole   The woman Rochester hires to care for his wife, Bertha (Antoinette Cosway), in the attic of his English house; she becomes drunk, allowing Antoinette the opportunity to set fire to the house in Jean Rhys's *Wide Sargasso Sea.* See Grace Poole in *Dictionary of British Literary Characters 18th- and 19th-Century Novels.*

Stanley Poole   Office boy at Twigg and Dersingham who plays detective in J. B. Priestley's *Angel Pavement.*

Charles Poore   Cab driver who is an eyewitness to the shooting of Inspector Stone outside of Princess Popescu's residence on Queen's Parade in Nicholas Blake's *A Tangled Web.*

Mrs. Pope   Elderly but formidable parish acquaintance of Edwin Braithwaite, who persuades her to let a spare room in her West Hampstead house to Letty Crowe in Barbara Pym's *Quartet in Autumn.*

Princess Popescu   A flamboyant celebrity of Southbourne, related to the former royal family of Romania; Hugo Chesterton is attempting to steal her jewels when he is interrupted and shoots the inspector in Nicholas Blake's *A Tangled Web.*

Princess Popoffski   Daisy Quantock's second important acquisition, a spiritualist whom Daisy successfully keeps from Lucia Lucas's takeover attempts; after Popoffski's departure Daisy discovers and burns "apparition" props, and Robert Quantock buys up and burns newspapers exposing Popoffski as the con woman Marie Lowenstein in E. F. Benson's *"Queen Lucia".*

Isabel Poppitt   Young woman who lives with her wealthy widowed mother and is a relative newcomer to Tilling bridge-playing society in E. F. Benson's *Miss Mapp.* Her enthusiasm for living in a primitive beach cottage permits Georgie Pillson's extended occupancy of her house in *Mapp and Lucia*.

Susan Poppitt   Wealthy widow whose "Royce" motorcar and sables are held in resentful contempt by Elizabeth Mapp, as is her receiving the Order of the British Empire from his Majesty; a two-years newcomer in Tilling, she still conciliates the dominant Miss Mapp; she becomes engaged to Algernon Wyse in E. F. Benson's *Miss Mapp*. She is Mrs. Wyse in *Mapp and Lucia* and in *The Worshipful Lucia*. Algernon and Lucia (Lucas) Pillson conspire to dispose of the stuffed corpse of her budgerigar when she becomes unhinged with spiritualist communion in *Trouble for Lucia*.

Mr. Poppleham   Urbane Member of Parliament and principal secretary to the Prime Minister, Andrew Clyth, in Arnold Bennett's *Lord Raingo*.

Hans Popplereuter   German sailor from another ship who meets Dana Hilliot in port and goes on a drunken spree with him in Malcolm Lowry's *Ultramarine*.

Jeremy Pordage   Passive British scholar who is hired by millionaire Jo Stoyte to catalogue his rare book collection; in the course of his work he stumbles across an obscure manuscript that promises to offer his employer the secret of eternal youth in Aldous Huxley's *After Many a Summer*.

Anne Pornick   Art Kipps's childhood sweetheart and future wife, who elopes with him after he discovers her working as a maid at Mrs. Bindon Botting's house, but who finds it harder than he does to adapt to upperclass society in H. G. Wells's *Kipps: The Story of a Simple Soul*.

Sid Pornick   Art Kipps's childhood friend and future brother-in-law, a bicycle maker and socialist who frowns on Kipps's inherited wealth but welcomes him into his family in H. G. Wells's *Kipps: The Story of a Simple Soul*.

Ronald Porson   Barrister who is the leader for the prosecution in the trial of George Passant, Jack Cotery, and Olive Calvert in C. P. Snow's *Strangers and Brothers*. He loves Ann Simon and envies Herbert Getliffe's professional successes; he raises questions about Getliffe's involvement in financial scandals of government contracts and drunkenly confides his disappointments to Lewis Eliot in *The Conscience of the Rich*. He asks for Eliot's help and needs Eliot's financial assistance when he is arrested for immoral behavior in *Corridors of Power*. He shows up to gloat over the mortality of Eliot after Eliot's cardiac arrest in *Last Things*.

Mr. Porteous   Faithful friend to the elder Theodore Gumbril and an expert in Latin poetry; his son runs up ruinous gambling debts in Aldous Huxley's *Antic Hay*.

Orlo J. Porter   An irritable police-scuffling demonstrator whose devotion to communist principles diminishes as he contemplates the reality of his inherited wealth; his engagement to Vanessa Cook is marred by his jealousy of Bertie Wooster in P. G. Wodehouse's *Aunts Aren't Gentlemen*.

Marion Portmain   Richard Portmain's unhappily married, alcoholic wife and mother of his three children; she gains courage to leave Richard and become a companion of Tommy Jacobs in Doris Lessing's *The Golden Notebook*.

Richard Portmain   Molly Jacobs's ex-husband, a successful businessman, who, unlike Molly, is very conservative in his politics and traditional in what he believes to be the role of women in Doris Lessing's *The Golden Notebook*.

Lord Port Scatho   Benevolent bankowner who learns that his bank has been the instrument of a scheme by his nephew, Mr. Brownlie, to discredit Christopher Tietjens; he endeavors to correct the injustice in Ford Madox Ford's *Some Do Not. . . .*

Canon Portway   Dead antiquarian who was owner of the property on which the Melpham discoveries were made; he was blackmailed by Barker and Barker's daughter when they threatened to reveal Gilbert Stokesay's secret in Angus Wilson's *Anglo-Saxon Attitudes*.

Elvira Portway   Granddaughter of Lilian Portway; she resigns as secretary to John Middleton and is the lover of Robin Middleton; she tells Gerald Middleton about John's homosexuality; her inheriting the estate of her grandmother makes her feel guilty in Angus Wilson's *Anglo-Saxon Attitudes*.

Lilian Portway   Aging ex-actress who is the grandmother of Elvira; she is visited by Gerald Middleton in Italy to enquire what she may know about the Melpham artifacts, and she dies leaving her estate to Elvira in Angus Wilson's *Anglo-Saxon Attitudes*.

Harry Posh   American C.I.A. media source who suspects Bret Rensselaer as a K.G.B. mole; he is Bernard Samson's liaison with the K.G.B. in prisoner exchange in Len Deighton's *London Match*.

Alan Post   A friend of Michael Brown; his asking Kate Brown to fill in as a Portuguese translator at the

Global Food conference inadvertently sets Mary Finchley off on her quest for personal identity in Doris Lessing's *The Summer Before the Dark.*

Flora Poste   The decisive young woman with plenty of sound common sense who descends upon her eccentric rural relatives and decides to bring order out of chaos in Stella Gibbons's *Cold Comfort Farm.*

Miss Postman   The overprotective, possessive companion of Charlotte Volley and the dedicatee of her most admired book in E. M. Delafield's *The Provincial Lady Goes Further.*

Potato Chip   A racehorse owned by Mr. Cook that is the only serious competition for Colonel Briscoe's; its neurotic affection for a black-and-white cat complicates its training in P. G. Wodehouse's *Aunts Aren't Gentlemen.*

Potini   The Italian Ambassador to the court of Edward VII; while a guest at Chevron he chides Sebastian, just returned from Oxford, for the English lack of interest in "Woman" in Vita Sackville-West's *The Edwardians.*

Kenneth (Kenny) Potter   George's student who, through questioning him about his experiences of life, allows George to emerge from his grief in Christopher Isherwood's *A Single Man.*

Thomas Potter   Businessman and friend of James Latter; his business is singled out for destruction during the General Strike in Joyce Cary's *Not Honour More.*

Ianthe Potts   School friend of Emma Howick; she is a disappointed spinster who comes to visit the village for a weekend in Barbara Pym's *A Few Green Leaves.*

Alice Poulshot   Mother of Susan and sister of Eustace Barnack and of John Barnack, whose frequent travelling has resulted in her responsibility for the upbringing of his son, Sebastian, in Aldous Huxley's *Time Must Have a Stop.*

Susan Poulshot   Kindly cousin of Sebastian Barnack, with whom she was in love as an adolescent; in later life she attempts to console him after his many years of bitter experience in Aldous Huxley's *Time Must Have a Stop.*

Poulson   Property developer who fared worse than Anthony Keating's partnership during the 1970s property-market collapse in Margaret Drabble's *The Ice Age.*

Mrs. Poulteney   A rich, domineering, Puritanical widow; she hires Sarah Woodruff as a supposed good deed, and then fires her when she is seen walking once too often on the Undercliff in John Fowles's *The French Lieutenant's Woman.*

Marquis of Pouzauges   Affluent, gaudily attired aristocrat picked up with marines for transport in C. S. Forester's *Mr. Midshipman Hornblower.*

Cyril Povey   Clever, dilettante artist and negligent son of Constance Baines Povey; he inherits all the wealth created with such suffering by his Aunt Sophia Baines and the money so frugally saved by his mother in Arnold Bennett's *The Old Wives Tale.*

Daniel Povey   Samuel Povey's cousin; his sexual knowledge helps Samuel and his wife Constance to conceive their son Cyril; his sentence of death for the murder of his wife causes Samuel to die in exhaustion from trying to prevent the execution in Arnold Bennett's *The Old Wives Tale.*

Dick Povey   Daniel Povey's son; his exploits on his "bone-shaker" down St. Luke's Square bring his father together with Samuel Povey in a relationship that costs Samuel his life in Arnold Bennett's *The Old Wives Tale.*

Samuel Povey   Unimposing, honest clerk in John Baines's store; he wins Baines's eldest daughter, Constance, and achieves dignity in business, marriage, and parenthood; he rises to heroism in the cause of his cousin Daniel Povey's trial for murder in Arnold Bennett's *The Old Wives Tale.*

Powell   Second mate of the *Ferndale* who discovers de Barral's attempt to poison Captain Anthony in Joseph Conrad's *Chance: A Tale in Two Parts.*

Milly Powell   Laura Roberts's matronly married sister; Richard Larch first sees her on a bus, judges her to be slipping quickly into a dull unlovely domesticity, and fears Laura will soon be like that in Arnold Bennett's *A Man From the North.*

Violet Powler   Dark-haired, dark-eyed, sedate, competent young laundry worker; she is removed from a conflict with her boss, Cyril Purkin, to the position of housekeeper at the Imperial Palace Hotel, where her discreet authority wins her the approval of most of the employees she must work with and wins her the love of the Managing Director, Evelyn Orcham, in Arnold Bennett's *Imperial Palace.*

Colonel Powys   The Irish-Catholic father of Leonora Ashburnham; he causes the first rift between Leonora and her husband, Edward Ashburnham, by suggesting that Edward is too generous to his tenants in Ford Madox Ford's *The Good Soldier: A Tale of Passion.*

Mrs. Powys An impoverished Irish-Catholic gentlewoman who, together with Mrs. Ashburnham, arranges the marriage of her daughter Leonora to Edward Ashburnham in Ford Madox Ford's *The Good Soldier: A Tale of Passion.*

Monsieur Pozzi Thirty-one-year-old, slim, sinuous, elegant Parisian, assistant manager of the hotel, and new protégé of the manager Mr. Cousin; he impresses Managing Director Evelyn Orcham with his naturalness and vivacity so that Orcham realizes by contrast how much he lives in a world of constraint in Arnold Bennett's *Imperial Palace.*

Mrs. Ppynrryn Friend who gives evidence against Fleur Forsyte Mont in the libel suit in John Galsworthy's *The Silver Spoon.*

Harry Praschko Leo Harting's fellow war refugee turned politically pragmatic member of the FRG's Bundestag; he betrays Harting to Ludwig Siebkron in John le Carré's *A Small Town in Germany.*

Marjorie Pratt A school teacher who very much admires Martha Quest for her belonging to unpopular movements; like Martha, she quickly becomes a part of socialist and communist activities in Zambesia in Doris Lessing's *A Ripple from the Storm.*

Walter Pratt Bachelor art critic in Muriel Spark's *The Bachelors.*

Walter Pratt The youngest of the Fenchurch St. Paul bellringers in Dorothy L. Sayers's *The Nine Tailors: Changes Rung on an Old Theme in Two Short Touches and Two Full Peals.*

Prause Navigator who conducts the ship from port to port under the direction of the Captain; he is always competing for Hornblower's attention in C. S. Forester's *Hornblower and the Hotspur.*

Baron (Kuno) von Pregnitz Wealthy, homosexual government official who commits suicide after being blackmailed by Schmidt in Christopher Isherwood's *Mr. Norris Changes Trains.*

Prendergast A teaching colleague of Paul Pennyfeather at Llanabba School; he becomes a prison chaplain and meets a horrible death at the hands of a crazed maniac in Evelyn Waugh's *Decline and Fall.*

Edward Prendick Young naturalist who is marooned on a tropical island populated by surgically altered animals who believe themselves human; he tries to live among them but ultimately flees back to sea as they revert to their bestial states; the experiences make him forever doubtful of humanity's civilized nature in H. G. Wells's *The Island of Doctor Moreau.*

Mr. Prentice Scotland Yard policeman who helps Arthur Rowe in his initial attempts to uncover the spy ring "The Free Mothers" in Graham Greene's *The Ministry of Fear.*

Mrs. Prentice A fortuneteller who tells young Adolf Hitler that he holds the globe in his fingers in Beryl Bainbridge's *Young Adolf.*

Robert Prentice Innocent member of Woodilee village who confirms David Sempill's account of the Satanic rites in the Wood in John Buchan's *Witch Wood.*

Miss Prentiss Tall, gaunt, aridly sweet, accomplished mistress of dark hints; she feels overworked and jealous of Miss Maclaren's gaining the position of Head Housekeeper, angrily argues with Violet Powler when she later becomes Head Housekeeper, then furiously resigns in Arnold Bennett's *Imperial Palace.*

The President Identity Club president; he falls into disfavor with and is eventually fallen upon and dispatched by the members of the club in Nigel Dennis's *Cards of Identity.*

President of the World State An American member of the Financial Directorate that controls the world government; he out-maneuvers his Chinese counterpart for political power and, inadvertently, for the affections of the Daughter of Man in Olaf Stapledon's *Last and First Men: A Story of the Near and Far Future.*

Preston Master's mate aboard the *Justinian* who acts as Hornblower's second at his duel with Simpson in C. S. Forester's *Lieutenant Hornblower.*

Judith Preston Young dentist's receptionist and girlfriend of Giles Colmore; she becomes involved with Giles's father in a complex relationship which offers him an "unforeseen extension of his youth" in Roy Fuller's *The Father's Comedy.*

Irana Preveza Greek-born, blowzy, full-figured, middle-aged woman; now the proprietess of "La Vierge St. Marie", a bawdy-house, she once served as a letter-drop for Dimitrios Makropoulos in Eric Ambler's *The Mask of Dimitrios.*

Price Master-at-arms aboard the *Sutherland*; his rigid disciplinarianism contrasts with Hornblower's style of leadership in *Ship of the Line.*

Eiluned Price A witness who testifies at Harriet Vane's trial for Philip Boyes's murder; she tells Lord

Peter Wimsey that she thinks Boyes killed himself in Dorothy L. Sayers's *Strong Poison*.

Fanny Price   The unwashed, unpopular, and untalented starving girl who studies art with Philip Carey, falls in love with him, and hangs herself in despair in W. Somerset Maugham's *Of Human Bondage*.

Matthew Price   Curator of birds at the zoological garden who is killed by a hungry mob trying to take birds to eat after the war in Angus Wilson's *The Old Men at the Zoo*.

Dr. Thelma Price   Archaeologist and member of the Rama committee in Arthur C. Clarke's *Rendezvous with Rama*.

Titus Price   Wesleyan Sunday School Superintendent in Bursley; his façade of piety and prosperity crumbles when, after condemning a child for the theft of a Bible, he embezzles School funds, approves his son's forgery, and hangs himself at his work, knowing the facts will be revealed in Arnold Bennett's *Anna of the Five Towns*.

Willie Price   Faithful, loving, ingenuous son of Titus; his daily humble sincerity and dignity in crisis win Anna Tellwright's unspoken love and generous aid toward a life in Australia; her act overwhelms him with a sense of all his losses, so that he commits an undiscovered suicide in a mine pit in Arnold Bennett's *Anna of the Five Towns*.

Martha Price Ridley   Trouble-making gossip at St. Mary Mead in Agatha Christie's *The Murder at the Vicarage*. She appears in *The Body in the Library*.

Augusta Prideaux   Elderly spinster gentlewoman in reduced circumstances who regales her acquaintances, including Wilmet Forsyth and her mother-in-law Sybil, with her exploits as a governess in Europe in Barbara Pym's *A Glass of Blessings*.

Jim Prideaux ("Rhino"; covernames: Vladimir Hajeck, Jim Ellis)   Linguist employed as a French instructor at Thursgood's Preparatory School; formerly a British Intelligence fieldman, he was recruited by Bill Haydon; he was betrayed in Control's Czechoslovakian Operation Testify in John le Carré's *Tinker, Tailor, Soldier, Spy*.

Mitchka, Baroness Annamaria von Prielau-Carolath   The friend of Hannele zu Rassentlow, the doll-maker, in D. H. Lawrence's *The Captain's Doll*.

The Priestess of Isis   Cult practitioner who believes that the "Man Who Died" is the lost Osiris; she sexually and spiritually heals the Christ-like title character of D. H. Lawrence's *The Escaped Cock*.

Adam Prince   Epicene, middle-aged food critic; he is a former Church-of-England priest who has "gone over" to Roman Catholicism; he is a neighbor to the heroine Emma Howick in the village in Barbara Pym's *A Few Green Leaves*.

Princess   Vivacious and quick-witted Egyptian princess who is fond of Edgar and Mary Perry and involves herself in their lives in P. H. Newby's *The Picnic at Sakkara*.

Pring   Marxist unionist who calls for the Lilmouth Strike; he is initially admired by the young Chester Nimmo but later despised because he advocates violence in Joyce Cary's *Except the Lord*.

Mr. Pring   Stone cracker who recognizes Mr. Weston as the Devil or God in T. F. Powys's *Mr. Weston's Good Wine*.

Pamela Pringle   Scandalously promiscuous and self-justifying old schoolfriend of the Provincial Lady; she and her third husband, Waddell Pringle, entertain the Provincial Lady; she makes repeated appearances attended by different men in E. M. Delafield's *The Provincial Lady Goes Further*.

Rowena Pringle   A "sanctimonious Christian bitch" who competes with Nick Shales in the education of Sammy Mountjoy in William Golding's *Free Fall*.

Waddell Pringle   Third and present husband of Pamela; she requires the Provincial Lady's assistance in his deception in E. M. Delafield's *The Provincial Lady Goes Further*.

Priscilla   Would-be-helpful neighbor of Marcia Ivory; she wonders about Marcia's odd behavior in Barbara Pym's *Quartet in Autumn*.

Priscilla   The "band and line" saucer painter; her work represents a stupendous monotony in Henry Mynors's pottery in Arnold Bennett's *Anna of the Five Towns*.

Prison Chaplain   Chaplain from Jim Drover's prison who comes to tell the Assistant Commissioner that he will resign because of what he considers the inhumane reprieve of Drover in Graham Greene's *It's a Battlefield*.

Prisoner No. 402   Unnamed man imprisoned in the cell adjoining Nicolas Rubashov's; tapping out the "quadratic alphabet" on the prison walls, he communicates information along the line of cells to Rubashov in Arthur Koestler's *Darkness at Noon*.

Canon Pritchard   Previous incumbent of Nicholas Cleveland's current parish; he comes to visit the vicarage unannounced to notice and comment on his successor's management (or mismanagement) of parish affairs in Barbara Pym's *Jane and Prudence*.

Mrs. Pritchard   Canon Pritchard's socially prominent wife, who makes an unannounced visit with her husband to notice and comment on her successor's management (or mismanagement) of domestic affairs in Barbara Pym's *Jane and Prudence*.

Alfred Pritchard   London business tycoon who is Gladys Matthews's life-long lover and conspires with her to raise money on a painting belonging to a German refugee couple in Angus Wilson's *No Laughing Matter*.

Conwy Pritchard   Postmaster's son whose youthful affair with Plaxy Trelone arouses Sirius's jealousy in Olaf Stapledon's *Sirius: A Fantasy of Love and Discord*.

Pritt   Scientist from Cambridge University who announces the errors of Arthur Miles's latest research to prevent Miles's appointment as Director of the new National Institute in C. P. Snow's *The Search*.

Privett   Dedicated and trustworthy personal maid of Evelyn Jarrold in Vita Sackville-West's *Family History*.

Mrs. Privett   The kind, good-natured proprietress of a seaside hotel; she hires young Maudie Fowler for a summer to work as a maid in Doris Lessing's *The Diaries of Jane Somers*.

Gareth Probert   An office worker who writes poetry and the verse play *The Martyr* for amateur theater; pretentious and rude, he represents cultural affectation to John Lewis in Kingsley Amis's *That Uncertain Feeling*.

Stan Proctor   Pork butcher and childhood friend of Fay Corrigan; she sleeps with him because of a threat of blackmail in David Storey's *A Prodigal Child*.

The "Professor"   Supplier of explosives; he boasts that he does not fear arrest because of the explosives and detonator he is known to carry on his person in Joseph Conrad's *The Secret Agent: A Simple Tale*.

Mr. Professor   Young Norwegian geometry teacher in Norman Douglas's *South Wind*.

Prosper Profond   A wealthy Belgian, who is familiar with Annette Forsyte; he tells Fleur Forsyte (Mont) the truth about Soames and Irene Forsyte in John Galsworthy's *To Let*.

William Propter   Philosophical retired professor whose boyhood loyalty to the millionaire Jo Stoyte renders permissible his frequent sarcasm; he becomes an especial confidant to Pete Boone, whose fatal action is largely a result of their conversations in Aldous Huxley's *After Many a Summer*.

Dr. Protheroe   The specialist who sees the critically ill Octavia Stacey; an old friend of Rosamund Stacey's father, he informs Rosamund's parents that Rosamund has had a baby in Margaret Drabble's *The Millstone*.

Anne Protheroe   Young second wife of Colonel Lucius Protheroe; she admits that she and Lawrence Redding are lovers in Agatha Christie's *The Murder at the Vicarage*.

Edith Rhys Protheroe   One of the premier hostesses in John Lewis's home town and the owner of a butcher shop; she invites Lewis and his wife to her cocktail party in Kingsley Amis's *That Uncertain Feeling*.

J. R. Prothero   Sleek, clever, polished Member of Parliament who turns a deliberately deaf ear to Bev Jones in Anthony Burgess's *1985*.

Lettice Protheroe   Daughter of Colonel Lucius Protheroe by his first wife; she hates her stepmother, Anne Protheroe, in Agatha Christie's *The Murder at the Vicarage*.

Colonel Lucius Protheroe   Village magistrate and property owner; he is found murdered in Agatha Christie's *The Murder at the Vicarage*.

Percy Protheroe   A butcher and former War Reserve constable who is married to Edith Protheroe in Kingsley Amis's *That Uncertain Feeling*.

Ebenezer Proudfoot   Uncharitable minister of the moorland village of Bold, where he leads a fiery revival; he chastises David Sempill in John Buchan's *Witch Wood*.

Edna Prout   A woman writer Miriam Henderson meets at the Wilson home who shocks her by revealing that she puts "real" people into her books in Dorothy Richardson's *Revolving Lights*.

The Provincial Lady   Nameless self-deprecating narrator; she lives on a country estate, from which she observes the behavior of villagers, family members, and tyrannical servants in E. M. Delafield's *The Diary* *of a Provincial Lady.* Having become a popular novelist, she is more independent and assertive; she manages her own flat and finances in London but retains her concern for her husband, Robert, and her children, Vicky and Robin, who have been sent to boarding schools in *The Provincial Lady Goes Further.* She is exuberantly observant of celebrities she meets after she is a popular author in America as well as in England during her lecture tour in *The Provincial Lady in America.* She turns her critical eye on Russia in the mid-1930s in *Straw Without Bricks: I Visit Soviet Russia.* She is concerned with home-front volunteer efforts and the needs of refugees in World War II; her comic sensibility is tempered with appropriate outrage in *The Provincial Lady in Wartime.*

Prudence Prostitute attracted to men in uniform; she has a brief fling with Albert Pye but soon becomes bored and dumps him in Henry Green's *Caught.*

Bernie Pryde Ex-C.I.D. detective who worked for Adam Dalgliesh and commits suicide, leaving his young partner Cordelia Gray to run his new detective agency in P. D. James's *An Unsuitable Job for a Woman.*

Psyche (Istra) Daughter of Trom, King of Glome, and half sister of Orual and Redival; she is the youngest and most beautiful daughter of the king; when the land is under famine, lots are cast for a sacrifice and the lot falls to Psyche; she is taken to the Grey Mountain and left for the Shadowbrute; when Orual comes to bury Psyche's bones, Orual finds Psyche alive; Orual convinces Psyche to shine a light on the god when he comes to her at night, resulting in a curse on Psyche to wander the earth in C. S. Lewis's *Till We Have Faces.*

Hanna Puchwein Wife of Kurt; she divorces her husband and is under some suspicion as a security leak because of her Communist sympathies in C. P. Snow's *The New Men.* She is G. S. Clark's wife and disapproves of his political hostility to Donald Howard in *The Affair.*

Kurt Puchwein German-Jewish chemist who was smuggled out of Berlin in 1938 by Roy Calvert; he goes to America to work in atomic research in C. P. Snow's *The New Men.*

Captain Puffin Golf and drinking partner of Benjamin Flint; after an argument and a rashly agreed-upon duel, their amity is restored when they encounter each other escaping by the same early-morning train; Puffin has a stroke and drowns in a bowl of oxtail soup in E. F. Benson's *Miss Mapp.*

Mrs. Pugh Wife of Llewelyn Pugh in Olaf Stapledon's *Sirius: A Fantasy of Love and Discord.*

Jane Pugh Daughter of Llewelyn and Mrs. Pugh in Olaf Stapledon's *Sirius: A Fantasy of Love and Discord.*

Llewelyn Pugh Welsh sheep farmer, a sympathetic man for whom Sirius works in Olaf Stapledon's *Sirius: A Fantasy of Love and Discord.*

Mrs. Pullbody Woman sent by Isabel Scarlet to John Lavender; she wishes her sister's husband's sister's husband to be interned as a threat because he is German in John Galsworthy's *The Burning Spear: Being the Experiences of Mr. John Lavender in Time of War.*

Angelica Pulling Henry Pulling's stepmother; distressed by the numerous affairs of her husband, Richard Pulling, she often searched for him while he was "napping"; at her funeral Henry establishes contact with Aunt Augusta Bertram in Graham Greene's *Travels with My Aunt.*

Henry Pulling Cautious, middle-aged bank manager who upon retirement spends his time growing dahlias, writing his friend Miss Keene in Australia, and chatting with his neighbor Major Charge; his life changes abruptly when his Aunt Augusta Bertram comes into it, and as he leaves to travel with her he realizes just how boring his whole life has been and what a pleasure it is to travel with his aunt and listen to her stories; he finally joins her in Paraguay, where he discovers that she is actually his mother, and he remains there, where he helps Mr. Visconti in his smuggling operation and plans to marry the daughter of the Chief of Customs in Graham Greene's *Travels with My Aunt.*

Jo Pulling Henry Pulling's uncle who, afraid of dying early, wants to travel to "slow life up"; he has a stroke and is unable to travel the usual way, so with Aunt Augusta Bertram's help he moves into a huge mansion in Italy with 52 rooms and travels from room to room, thereby slowing life up to his satisfaction; he dies shortly before reaching the last room in Graham Greene's *Travels with My Aunt.*

Richard Pulling Henry Pulling's lazy, handsome, deceased father; a building contractor, Richard had numerous affairs, was fond of napping in odd places, loved to read Sir Walter Scott, and considered that "nothing was really worth a fight"; Henry thinks of him often and wonders about his father's relationship with his stepmother in Graham Greene's *Travels with My Aunt.*

Puppeteer Performer of a Punch-and-Judy show at

the psychiatric hospital in Malcolm Lowry's *Lunar Caustic*.

Mr. Purcey Wealthy businessman who spends his time riding his new automobile around London in John Galsworthy's *Fraternity*.

James Purchase Billy Fisher's colleague who shaves his nose; he vies for a promotion Billy wants in Keith Waterhouse's *Billy Liar on the Moon*.

Jerry Purdy A collier who neglects his consumptive wife and children; he is a drinking buddy of Walter Morel in D. H. Lawrence's *Sons and Lovers*.

Mina Purefoy Woman who gives birth at the Holles Street hospital in James Joyce's *Ulysses*.

Reginald Purfleet The local pedant, dilettante, and busybody; masked as an idealist, he is realistic where his own good is concerned and escapes Georgie Smithers by running away in Richard Aldington's *The Colonel's Daughter*.

Detective-Inspector Purity Crooked policeman who frames Johnny Fortune for living off the earnings of Dorothy Macpherson, a prostitute; he frames Johnny on hemp charges and also arrests Billy Whispers and Ronson Lighter; he unsuccessfully tries to convince Montgomery Pew to be an informant in Colin MacInnes's *City of Spades*.

Cyril Purkin Thirty-eight-year-old Midlander who is Managing Director of the laundry; short, with suspicious eyes and prominent nose, he was formerly a chemical engineer, who, having gained his position by writing to Evelyn Orcham, modernizes the laundry, organizes social benefits for employees, and adds a research department, but he fails to impose himself upon Violet Powler, who is then transferred to hotel housekeeping and wins Orcham's love in Arnold Bennett's *Imperial Palace*.

Mrs. Purrett Secretary of the zoological gardens who threatens to quit during the harassing administration of Langley-Beard in Angus Wilson's *The Old Men at the Zoo*.

Liza Pursewarden The blind sister and incestuous lover of the poet-novelist in Lawrence Durrell's *Mountolive*. After his death she burns his magnificent letters to protect his reputation; she marries David Mountolive in *Clea*.

Percy (penname: Ludwig) Pursewarden A celebrat-

ed poet-novelist and British-embassy "contract officer"; his suicide is mentioned in Lawrence Durrell's *Justine*. He is revealed to have been Justine Hosnani's preferred lover and to have had an affair with his own sister, Liza, in *Balthazar*. His suicide is proved to have been motivated by his discovery of the political treachery of Nessim Hosnani, whom he trusted, in *Mountolive*. His writings and his literary and personal reputations receive attention in *Clea*.

Captain Purvis An officer in charge of Guy Perron's security assignments; Perron foils his suicide attempt in Paul Scott's *A Division of the Spoils*.

Mr. Purvis Master's mate aboard the *Renown* in C. S. Forester's *Lieutenant Hornblower*.

Mrs. Purvis Arthur Row's overweight landlady and his only companion in Graham Greene's *The Ministry of Fear*.

Pushkov A thinking, talented speaker; a leader of the revolt and a good friend to Joe and George, he tries to talk the people into action in Rex Warner's *The Wild Goose Chase: An Allegory*.

Albert Pye Sub Chief of Richard Roe's auxiliary fire service unit; disturbed by his sudden elevation to authority and tormented by the possibility that he might have mistakenly had sex with his sister Amy when they were children, he kills himself by putting his head in a gas oven in Henry Green's *Caught*.

Amy Pye Mentally disturbed sister of Albert Pye; after briefly abducting Richard Roe's son Christopher, she is sent to a mental asylum in Henry Green's *Caught*.

Mr. Pyecroft A schoolmaster actively involved in the leftist political activities in Zambesia in Doris Lessing's *Martha Quest*, in *A Proper Marriage*, and in *A Ripple from the Storm*.

Mrs. Pyecroft A woman interested in leftist politics but torn between the matronly and feminine roles which she must play and the need to appear an educated and informed woman in Doris Lessing's *Martha Quest*.

Alden Pyle Idealistic, quiet American attached to the Economic Aid Mission in Saigon; he naïvely supplies Asiatic terrorists with plastic (diolacton) explosives and saves Thomas Fowler from Vietminh guerrillas, but is betrayed by a cynical Fowler for allowing innocent bystanders to be murdered and for falling in love with Fowler's mistress Phuong in Graham Greene's *The Quiet American.*

Belinda Pym   Magnus Pym's first wife, who loves Magnus but blames Jack Brotherhood and the secret service for encouraging Magnus's need to betray in John le Carré's *A Perfect Spy.*

Dr. Cyrus Pym   American criminologist and friend of Dr. Herbert Warner; he documents the past criminal history of Innocent Smith and is the chief prosecutor at his trial in G. K. Chesterton's *Manalive.*

Dorothy Godchild (Dot) Watermaster Pym   Sir Makepeace Watermaster's fragile sister, Rick Pym's much-abused wife, and Magnus Pym's loving mother; she surrenders her place in her son's heart to her husband's many lovers in John le Carré's *A Perfect Spy.*

Laetitia (Lucy) Pym   Spinster whose sleuthing results in the shocking identification of the murderer of a physical-education college student in Josephine Tey's *Miss Pym Disposes.*

Magnus Richard Pym ("Titch", "Sir Magnus"; cov- ernames: **Pym Canterbury, Pembroke, Mr. Sanderstead)**   Charming, amoral senior British/Czechoslovakian double agent; he exonerates his professional and personal betrayals in a lengthy suicide letter to his son that fixes his motivations on his father's duplicitous heritage in John le Carré's *A Perfect Spy.*

Mary (Mabs) Pym   Ambitious, aristocratic former British agent; Jack Brotherhood's former mistress, she is now Magnus Pym's second wife; she finds Axel in her desperate search for Magnus, but eventually leads Jack Brotherhood to Pym in John le Carré's *A Perfect Spy.*

Richard Thomas (Rick) Pym   Magnus Pym's charismatic, Micawber-like father; he cheats everyone he meets, launches impossible business scams, hides his secrets from his friends and family, but loves his son above all in John le Carré's *A Perfect Spy.*

Thomas (Tom) Pym   Magnus and Mary Pym's handsome son, who has already begun to follow his father's duplicitous life when Magnus commits suicide in John le Carré's *A Perfect Spy.*

Miss Pyme   Secretary to Leonard Gardner in London in Isabel Colegate's *Orlando King.*

Q

Quaggan Friend in British Columbia who will take care of the Wildernesses' cat while they are on vacation in Malcolm Lowry's *Dark as the Grave Wherein My Friend Is Laid*.

Lady Caroline (Caro) Quaife First wife of Roger Quaife; she stands by her husband even after she learns of his affair with Ellen Smith in C. P. Snow's *Corridors of Power*.

Roger Quaife Parliamentary Secretary who pursues a policy of nuclear disarmament; he resigns after a narrow Parliamentary vote on his policy; he marries Ellen Smith after he divorces Lady Caroline in C. P. Snow's *Corridors of Power*.

Daisy Quantock A plump, dumpy Riseholme matron who lives in "ecstatic pursuit of some idea which those who do not share it call a fad"; vegetable diets and Christian Science are succeeded by yoga, seances, and lozenges to increase height; she is Lucia Lucas's resentful social rival in E. F. Benson's *"Queen Lucia"*. Her temporary ascendancy does not survive Lucia's return to Riseholme in *Lucia in London*. She vacillates in her rebellion against Lucia in *Mapp and Lucia*. She appears in *Trouble for Lucia*.

Robert Quantock Comfort-loving husband of Daisy Quantock; he is a wealthy speculator in Rumanian oil; he proposes hiring his wife's yoga Guru as a cook in E. F. Benson's *"Queen Lucia"*. He appears in *Lucia in London* and in *Mapp and Lucia*.

Elinor Quarles Temperamental daughter of John Bidlake, and wife of Philip Quarles; guilt-ridden in her emotional ambivalence toward her husband and son, she briefly contemplates an affair with Everard Webley and is devastated by the death of her child in Aldous Huxley's *Point Counter Point*.

Philip Quarles Circumspect novelist and husband of Elinor; returning with his wife from abroad, he heartlessly plots a new novel based on the unhappiness and foibles of his close acquaintances in Aldous Huxley's *Point Counter Point*.

Philip (Little Philip) Quarles Precocious son of Philip and Elinor; he abruptly dies after seeming to recover from a bout of meningitis in Aldous Huxley's *Point Counter Point*.

Rachel Quarles Long-suffering wife of Sidney Quarles, whose many indiscretions and failures she accepts with patient resignation in Aldous Huxley's *Point Counter Point*.

Sidney Quarles Self-important but non-productive aging historian; a failure at politics and business, he is successful only in seducing his social inferiors, one of whom causes trouble when she becomes pregnant in Aldous Huxley's *Point Counter Point*.

Quarrel Cayman Islander who becomes James Bond's ally in Ian Fleming's *Live and Let Die*. He goes with Bond to Crab Key, where he is killed by a flame-thrower in *Dr. No*.

Lord Quarryman Landowner whose estate neighbors Worsted Skeynes; he is smugly satisfied with his life in John Galsworthy's *The Country House*.

Quartermaster Unnamed ship's officer aboard the *Oedipus Tyrannus* who has one green eye and one brown eye; he is a homosexual who makes a pass at Dana Hilliot in Malcolm Lowry's *Ultramarine*.

Gridley Quayle Periodical-detective-story hero whose adventures enthrall Freddie Threepwood; he is the creation of Ashe Marson in P. G. Wodehouse's *Something New*.

Anna Quayne Beautiful, selfish, self-centered wife of Thomas; she encourages the attentions of Eddie and of St. Quentin Miller, and she resents the intrusion of sixteen-year-old Portia Quayne to her elegant, childless London home in Elizabeth Bowen's *The Death of the Heart*.

Portia Quayne Penniless sixteen-year-old half sister of Thomas Quayne; her father's affair with her mother precipitated the divorce of Thomas's parents; now orphaned after a life spent abroad in off-season resorts and modest hotels, she has been sent to live with Thomas and Anna in accordance with the elder Quayne's last wishes in Elizabeth Bowen's *The Death of the Heart*.

Thomas Quayne Upper-class, exceedingly correct, and pompously reserved husband of Anna and half brother of Portia Quayne; his intention is always to do "the right thing", but he is often in a quandary as to exactly what, in relation to Portia, the right thing actually is in Elizabeth Bowen's *The Death of the Heart*.

Anna Quentin A nightclub folksong singer and

mime actress loved unrequitedly by Jake Donaghue and unrequitedly in love herself with Hugo Belfounder in Iris Murdoch's *Under the Net.*

Dorothy Quentin   Lynda Coldridge's friend from the mental hospital who moves into Lynda's apartment to take care of her but really needs Lynda's care; she eventually commits suicide in Doris Lessing's *The Four-Gated City.*

Sadie Quentin   Anna Quentin's sister, a "glossy and dazzling" movie star loved unrequitedly by Hugo Belfounder and unrequitedly in love herself with Jake Donaghue in Iris Murdoch's *Under the Net.*

Querry   Spiritually and morally bankrupt but brutally honest middle-aged man; a famous church architect, he becomes disillusioned with his career and his life, flees civilization, and comes to live at the mission; he befriends Dr. Colin, designs a new hospital, and slowly begins to be cured of his spiritual aridity; ironically, just as the cure has taken effect, he is falsely accused of fathering Marie Rycker's child and is killed by an irrational Maurice Rycker in Graham Greene's *A Burnt-Out Case.*

Alfred Quest   Martha Quest's poverty-stricken farmer father, who cuts himself off from his wife and children; he cannot forget his time fighting in World War I in Doris Lessing's *Martha Quest,* in *A Proper Marriage,* in *A Ripple from the Storm,* and in *Landlocked.*

Bessie Quest   Jonathan Quest's young wife, who Jonathan's mother believes shuns her help with their dairy farm in Doris Lessing's *The Four-Gated City.*

Jonathan Quest   Martha Quest's conventional younger brother, who is educated at an expensive private school in Doris Lessing's *Martha Quest.* He leaves it to fight in World War II; returning to Africa, he marries and starts a dairy farm in *Landlocked* and in *The Four-Gated City.*

Martha Quest   A woman who grows up in a closed-minded Central African community and struggles for self-realization through two marriages, a membership in the Communist Party, and a persistently unconventional outlook on life in Doris Lessing's *Martha Quest,* in *A Proper Marriage,* in *A Ripple from the Storm,* and in *Landlocked.* She is able to leave behind Africa for England and ultimately to come to terms with herself and her past in *The Four-Gated City.*

May Quest   Martha Quest's overbearing mother,

who is disappointed with the development of both of her children; she perpetually attempts to mold her daughter into a conventional, well-behaved woman in Doris Lessing's *Martha Quest,* in *A Proper Marriage,* in *A Ripple from the Storm,* in *Landlocked,* and in *The Four-Gated City.*

Adela Quested   Ronny Heaslop's well-intentioned naïve fiancée, whose distaste for the arrogant behavior of the British officials in India contributes to her decision not to marry him; overwhelmed, disoriented, and sexually stimulated by the sudden terror she experiences in the Marabar Caves, she accuses Dr. Aziz of attempted rape; the British community rallies around her, but ostracizes her after she withdraws her testimony at his trial; she returns to England in E. M. Forster's *A Passage to India.*

Amanda Quiggin   One of the unattractive identical twin daughters of Ada (Leintwardine) and J. C. Quiggin in Anthony Powell's *Temporary Kings.* As radical university undergraduates they are notorious for assaulting Widmerpool on public occasions with red paint and a stink bomb in *Hearing Secret Harmonies.*

Belinda Quiggin   Amanda's identical twin and fellow trouble maker in Anthony Powell's *Temporary Kings* and in *Hearing Secret Harmonies.*

J. G. Quiggin   One of Sillery's leftist young men at University in Anthony Powell's *A Question of Upbringing.* He converts both St. John Clarke and Lord Erridge to Marxism; he lives with Mona Templer and prepares to start a magazine with Lord Erridge in *The Acceptance World.* Mona leaves him for Erridge in *At Lady Molly's.* He founds a publishing company and marries Ada Leintwardine in *Books Do Furnish a Room.* His publishing company has failed, and his anarchic university-age twin daughters are a constant anxiety to him in *Hearing Secret Harmonies.*

Nurse Quigley   Nurse who quiets the medical students at the maternity hospital in James Joyce's *Ulysses.*

Ned Quilley   Charlie's sometimes drunken theatrical agent, who provides Marty Kurtz and Shimon Litvak valuable information about Charlie's past and capricious allegiances that strengthens the Israelis' manipulation in John le Carré's *The Little Drummer Girl.*

Auberon Quin   Government official who becomes King of England and establishes the "Charter of the Cities" as a joke, but is taken seriously by Adam Wayne in G. K. Chesterton's *The Napoleon of Notting Hill.*

Mr. Quincey   Retired walnut grower from the U.S. who cultivates his garden and disapproves of Geoffrey Firmin's drinking in Malcolm Lowry's *Under the Volcano*.

Monsignor Quixote   Parish priest of El Toboso; he is reputed to be a descendant of the great Don Quixote; when he meets the Bishop of Motopo, the Bishop is so impressed with Father Quixote's talent and intelligence that he recommends him for promotion to monsignor; granted permission for a brief holiday, Father Quixote travels across Spain with Enrique Zancas, whom he calls Sancho, having many adventures which parallel those of Cervantes's Don Quixote; kidnapped by his own Bishop and returned to El Toboso under guard, Father Quixote escapes with the help of Zancas and eventually travels to a Trappist Monastery at Osera in northwestern Spain, where he dies while performing a symbolic mass in Graham Greene's *Monsignor Quixote*.

R

R. Playful, sarcastic, pessimistic, prodding supervisor to Ashenden; he likes to make aspects of espionage as basic but fascinating as possible, and R. banters with Ashenden to test his mettle in W. Somerset Maugham's *Ashenden: or The British Agent.*

Lady R One of the physically affectionate adults who curl young Joe's nerves in Wolf Mankowitz's *A Kid for Two Farthings.*

Mr. Rabb A pious Christian and a likable, courteous officer who commands instant respect in spite of his badly bitten fingernails; he becomes paralyzed by fear during the hurricane in Richard Hughes's *In Hazard.*

James Rabbit Shopkeeper who makes an agreement with Johnny Hynes to buy Indian corn and sell it at a high price to the poor farmers during the blight in Liam O'Flaherty's *Famine.*

Rabscuttle Mythological rabbit, captain of El-ahrairah's Owsla (rabbit-warren militia), in Richard Adams's *Watership Down.*

Colonel Johnny Race One of the four sleuths invited to Mr. Shaitana's fatal bridge party, where he meets Hercule Poirot in Agatha Christie's *Cards on the Table.* He appears in three other novels.

Rachel Doted-on daughter of Nellie and Gwilym; out shooting in the marsh at his estate in Wales, Augustine Penry-Herbert finds and carries home her body; though her death is natural and his action necessary, he becomes the focus of unpleasant speculation that motivates his leaving to visit cousins in Germany in Richard Hughes's *The Fox in the Attic.*

Rachid Robert Winter's obsequious servant in P. H. Newby's *A Journey to the Interior.*

Peter Rackman (alias: Philip Rogers) A temporary mill worker with literary tastes who is implicated in the disappearance and later murder of William Widgery in Roy Fuller's *The Second Curtain.*

Claudia Radeechy The late wife of the suicide Joseph Radeechy; her fatal fall from a window was wrongly ruled accidental in Iris Murdoch's *The Nice and the Good.*

Joseph Radeechy One of Octavian Gray's subordi-

nates; his suicide is investigated in Iris Murdoch's *The Nice and the Good.*

Agatha Raden Elder daughter of Colonel Alastair Raden of Glenraden; she becomes engaged to Junius Bandicott in John Buchan's *John Macnab.*

Colonel Alastair Raden Highlander, the last male of an ancient family line, who is challenged when "John Macnab" proposes to kill a stag and remove it from his estate; he behaves with admirable sportsmanship in John Buchan's *John Macnab.*

Janet Raden (Lady Roylance) Resourceful younger daughter of Colonel Alastair Raden of Glenraden; she anticipates "John Macnab's" strategy to kill a stag on their estate, catches John Palliser-Yeates, and hires Fish Benjie Bogle to deliver the stag to her home, defeating "John Macnab"; she becomes engaged to and marries Sir Archibald Roylance in John Buchan's *John Macnab.* Honeymooning with Roylance in Olifa City, South America, she takes part in Lord Clanroyden's plot to restore freedom in the republic in *The Courts of the Morning.* She joins Archie in yet another adventure in Evallonia in *The House of the Four Winds.*

Mrs. Radford Clara Dawes's mother; after leaving her husband, Baxter, Clara comes to live at Mrs. Radford's house in D. H. Lawrence's *Sons and Lovers.*

Jassy Radlett One of the eight children of Matthew and Sadie Radlett; at the age of seven she begins to save her money so that she can run away from home; at the start of her debutante season she does run away to Hollywood, having fallen in love with a movie actor in Nancy Mitford's *The Pursuit of Love.* She and her sister Victoria are gossiping girls in *Love in a Cold Climate.*

Linda Radlett Second daughter of Matthew and Sadie and Fanny Logan's closest confidante; intense and distracted, Linda is an extremist about anything she believes in, be it animals, society, Communism, or love; beautiful and impulsively romantic, she makes bad marriages to Tony Kroesig and Christian Talbot before she falls in love with Fabrice de Sauveterre; she dies giving birth to his child in Nancy Mitford's *The Pursuit of Love.* She appears in *Love in a Cold Climate.*

Louisa Radlett The conventional eldest of Matthew and Sadie's eight children; during her debutante season she makes a successful marriage to the thirty-nine-year-old Lord Fort William in Nancy Mitford's *The Pursuit of Love.*

Matt Radlett A son of Matthew and Sadie Radlett; he runs away from Eton to participate in the Spanish Civil War in Nancy Mitford's *The Pursuit of Love*.

Matthew Radlett Uncle by marriage of Fanny Logan, whom he openly dislikes; the terrifying and stubborn father of eight, he is an impulsive, devoted, and self-righteous country gentleman in Nancy Mitford's *The Pursuit of Love*. He has become Lord Alconleigh in *Love in a Cold Climate*.

Sadie Radlett Matthew's wife and the loving, somewhat distracted mother of eight, including Louisa, Linda, Jassy, and Matt; she is an affectionate aunt and hostess to Fanny Logan in Nancy Mitford's *The Pursuit of Love* and in *Love in a Cold Climate*.

Victoria Radlett A younger daughter of Sadie and Matthew Radlett; she appears in Nancy Mitford's *The Pursuit of Love* and in *Love in a Cold Climate*.

Mr. Raeburn Dower House frequentor and political discussionist who always loses his trousers playing hockey in H. G. Wells's *Mr. Britling Sees It Through*.

Rafael Memlik's barber, procurer, and co-conspirator in Lawrence Durrell's *Mountolive*.

Mrs. Raikes A farmer's pretty young wife; her association with Alfred Inglethorp arouses suspicion in Agatha Christie's *The Mysterious Affair at Styles: A Detective Story*.

Reggie Rainbell (Pisspot) The alcoholic department head at Shepford District Council who takes an early retirement in Keith Waterhouse's *Billy Liar on the Moon*.

John Rainborough A public servant, the departmental chief in the organization regulating immigrant labor permits in Iris Murdoch's *The Flight from the Enchanter*.

Prince Rainbow Mythological being, regent for Lord Frith the sun god, in Richard Adams's *Watership Down*.

Kurt Rainer Vivienne Michel's former employer and lover, who treated her badly in Ian Fleming's *The Spy Who Loved Me*.

Adela, Lady Raingo Independent, undomesticated, impulsive, loving mother, misunderstood wife, and dignified aristocrat; she pursues a lonely course to her accidental death in a car accident in Arnold Bennett's *Lord Raingo*.

Geoffrey Raingo Traumatized escaped prisoner of war; he returns to his father's mansion where he regains his health while restoring the mansion; he falls in love with the sister of his father's mistress and wins his father's trust and admiration as his heir in Arnold Bennett's *Lord Raingo*.

Samuel, Lord Raingo of Eccles Intelligent, sensitive, benevolent, middle-aged millionaire; he is confident in commercial enterprise and shrewd in politics, but he suffers from class inferiority and sexual insecurity; he accepts the powerful government post of Minister of Records, which brings about a series of public and private crises, overtaxing his damaged heart, increasing his serious depression, and causing his death in Arnold Bennett's *Lord Raingo*.

Tibor, Count Rakassyi Member of the Hungarian royalty; he has caught Cicely Nettleby's favor while attending one of Sir Randolph Nettleby's shooting parties; he has little regard for "peasants" and scoffs at the attention given to the wounded Tom Harker; his lack of concern for humanity averts Cicely's attentions in Isabel Colegate's *The Shooting Party*.

Ralph Handsome and capable twelve-year-old public-school boy; he has the role of leader thrust upon him from the moment he uses a conch shell to sound the first assembly of the castaway boys in William Golding's *Lord of the Flies*.

Ralph The son of a merchant; he woos and wins Mandy, the daughter of Albert Handley, by stealing one of Albert's paintings in *A Tree on Fire*.

Mr. Ralston Pontifical Head of Brookfield who is appointed after Meldrum; he raises the status of Brookfield but is not very likable and earns the wrath of the Governors, alumni, and students when he demands that Mr. Chips retire at age sixty in James Hilton's *Good-bye, Mr. Chips*.

Mr. Ramage Conversational, obsessive, manipulative married man; he loves Ann Veronica Stanley in H. G. Wells's *Ann Veronica: A Modern Love Story*.

Evelyn Ramage Old girlfriend of Charles Murley; she gives parties that Terence Lambert attends to meet important people in Angus Wilson's *Hemlock and After*.

Miss Ramboat Marion's shy maiden aunt, who does

not approve of George Ponderevo in H. G. Wells's *Tono-Bungay*.

Mr. Ramboat   Marion's father; he is a clerk in the Walham Green Gas Works and has an avocation as a gardener in H. G. Wells's *Tono-Bungay*.

Mrs. Ramboat   Mr. Ramboat's wife and Marion's mother; George Ponderevo sees that Marion will become much like her conventional mother in H. G. Wells's *Tono-Bungay*.

Marion Ramboat   An attractive but shallow young woman who copies designs; George Ponderevo falls in love with her and marries her, but she is ultimately too conventional and unintelligent for George, and they are divorced in H. G. Wells's *Tono-Bungay*.

Abdul Ramdez   Cosmopolitan blue-eyed Palestinian Arab living between Arab and Israeli worlds; with his sister, Suzi Ramdez, he assists Barbara Vaughan and Freddy Hamilton in Muriel Spark's *The Mandlebaum Gate*.

Joe Ramdez   A lordly, unscrupulous Jordanian businessman; he is father of Abdul and Suzi by one of his wives and seducer and eventual husband of Miss Rickward in Muriel Spark's *The Mandlebaum Gate*.

Suzi Ramdez   Cosmopolitan, clever, blue-eyed Arab women living in Jordan; she works for her father's tourist business but thwarts his schemes by assisting in conspiring with Barbara Vaughan and Freddy Hamilton in Muriel Spark's *The Mandlebaum Gate*.

Ramdson   Anthony Neale's headmaster, who gets to the heart of the matter and sympathetically leads Anthony to choose resignation in C. Day Lewis's *Starting Point*.

Ramirez   Vagabond rival of Nostromo (Gian' Battista) for the hand of Linda Viola in Joseph Conrad's *Nostromo: A Tale of the Seaboard*.

Frank Rammage   Fat and aging London landlord who rents rooms to castaways, opposes Larrie Rourke's departure to live with John Middleton's mother, and is suspected of blackmail to become the beneficiary of the estate of Canon Portway, his patron, in Angus Wilson's *Anglo-Saxon Attitudes*.

Mark Rampion   Painter and critic of modern culture; having risen from a modest background, he has developed a philosophy of life that skillfully balances

his art, marriage, and personal relationships in Aldous Huxley's *Point Counter Point*.

Mary Rampion   Contented wife of Mark and loving mother of two children; she blithely rejects her upper-class upbringing for the fulfilling rewards of her marriage in Aldous Huxley's *Point Counter Point*.

Rampole   Grouchy co-owner of a publishing firm; he is, through Basil Seal's machinations, arrested for publishing an alleged fascist magazine in Evelyn Waugh's *Put Out More Flags*.

Rampound   Politician and target of Arnold Condorex's conspiracy to topple his "elders"; he provides Condorex's easy excuse for all misdeeds: when found out, Condorex repeats the refrain "Rampound has done far worse than this" in Rebecca West's *Harriet Hume, A London Fantasy*.

Mr. Ramsay   Neurotic, egotistical, eccentric philosopher and writer; Mrs. Ramsay nurtures him into believing in the intellectual prowess he doubts and coddles him into denying his lack of ultimate professional success; surrounded by his eight children and admiring students, he paces and pontificates and worries about never getting past "R" in the alphabet in spite of his absolute belief in the empiric-theoretical view; his wife's death destroys him emotionally and generates his obsessive need to be mothered by every woman with whom he comes in contact; his free-floating hostility surfaces frequently; finally he takes his son James and daughter Cam to the lighthouse twenty years too late in Virginia Woolf's *To the Lighthouse*.

Mrs. Ramsay   An excessive maternalist and hostess, who holds court, offering friends, guests, and family "communion" without religion in the form of *boeuf au daube*, nurturance, and conditional love in return for adoration and obedience; her death leaves the remaining characters devastated, confused, and ultimately stronger as they search for identity and relationship without her; she promises James, the youngest of her eight children, an expedition "to the lighthouse" tomorrow, at their vacation home in the Isle of Sky, Hebrides; the boat sails twenty years later, after her death in Virginia Woolf's *To the Lighthouse*.

Andrew Ramsay   Oldest son and second child of the Ramsays; he enlists in the army and is killed in France by an exploding shell in Virginia Woolf's *To the Lighthouse*.

Camilla (Cam) Ramsay   Second-youngest child of Mr. and Mrs. Ramsay; denied by her mother in favor of her brother James, Cam fears the stuffed boar on the wall which Mrs. Ramsay covers with a green shawl; she experiences James's acceptance of his father on the fateful boat trip to the lighthouse postponed twenty years in Virginia Woolf's *To the Lighthouse*.

James Ramsay   Youngest child and favorite son of Mrs. Ramsay; James must enact his mother's promise that they go "to the lighthouse tomorrow" twenty years later with his father and sister Cam; after World War I as well as three crucial deaths in his family, James pilots that small boat to find his own identity, liberate himself from his mother, and recognize, forgive, and accept his father, whom he has despised and feared since childhood in Virginia Woolf's *To the Lighthouse*.

Prue Ramsay   Beautiful oldest daughter of Mr. and Mrs. Ramsay; she is most influenced by her mother's expectations that she marry and relinquish "the manliness in her girlish heart"; her death in childbirth is mentioned in Virginia Woolf's *To the Lighthouse*.

Charles Ramsbottom   Eccentric, charming millionaire; he is a rebel in C. S. Forester's *Hornblower in the West Indies*.

Mr. Randall   Farmer, gratified that Oliver Green, who lives with him, is "one of us" in C. Day Lewis's *Child of Misfortune*.

Andrew Randall   A wealthy, aristocratic Oxford friend of Daniel Martin; he marries Dan's former wife, Nell, the sister of Jane Mallory; Dan visits him at his country estate following Anthony Mallory's death in John Fowles's *Daniel Martin*.

Eve Randall   The flirtatious sixteen-year-old daughter with whose family Oliver Green resides; she has a charming restlessness that attracts him in C. Day Lewis's *Child of Misfortune*.

Louie Randall   Young woman friend of Isobel Sands; she is an active worker for the Communist Party and wants Isobel to keep her professorship in Angus Wilson's *Hemlock and After*.

Nell Randall   Daniel Martin's former wife, sister of Jane Mallory, and mother of Daniel's daughter, Caroline; somewhat superficial, she finds her perfect niche as Lady Randall, wife of Andrew Randall and hostess at Compton, his country estate, in John Fowles's *Daniel Martin*.

Penelope Randall   Andrew and Nell Randall's daughter in John Fowles's *Daniel Martin*.

Father Rank   Unhappy, intelligent Catholic priest in an African port; he confides in Henry Scobie, who later confesses his love affair with Helen Rolt to him; he cannot absolve him, but after Scobie's suicide he is angry with Louise Scobie for assuming that God will not forgive Scobie in Graham Greene's *The Heart of the Matter*.

Elwin Ransom   Philologist and Cambridge don who is kidnapped and taken to Malacandra (Mars) by Edward Weston and Dick Devine; while there he learns of the spiritual relationship between Malacandra and Thulcandra (Earth); he returns to Earth and is commanded by Oyarsa of Malacandra to observe the activities of Weston and Devine in C. S. Lewis's *Out of the Silent Planet*. Transported to Perelandra (Venus) to thwart the appearance of evil on the new-formed world by shielding the Green Lady, Perelandra's first woman, from the evil temptations of Weston, he engages Weston in a prolonged struggle in which Weston, as the embodiment of evil, dies and then returns to Earth in *Perelandra*. As head of the community at St. Anne's Manor he is also known as Mr. Fisher-King and the Pendragon of Logres; after he communicates with the spiritual beings whom he has met during his journeys to Mars and Venus and acts as their agent on Earth, monitoring the evil activities of the N.I.C.E. (National Institute for Coordinated Experiments) and successfully directing its destruction, he returns to Perelandra where he will live forever in C. S. Lewis's *That Hideous Strength*.

Rear Admiral Henry Ransome   Stern, sensible, jealous, independent commander-in-chief in C. S. Forester's *Hornblower in the West Indies*.

Father Marius Ransome   Handsome new assistant priest at St. Luke's with rumored "leanings" toward Roman Catholicism, who comes to stay with Mary Beamish and her invalid mother in Barbara Pym's *A Glass of Blessings*.

RantanOboral   The last warlord of Borlien to defy JandolAngand; he is the father of YeferOboral and MyrdemInggala in Brian W. Aldiss's *Helliconia Summer*.

Ranulf   A "small, and dry and wrinkled" mason who is one of those who defect, stealing away from Salisbury cathedral in William Golding's *The Spire*.

Mr. Raper   Friend of Tom Judd and bookkeeper at

the small factory where both work in Richard Aldington's *The Colonel's Daughter*.

Countess Medusa Rappa Gossipy and "easily disturbable" lady of the court of Pisuerga and friend of Countess Violet of Tolga in Ronald Firbank's *The Flower Beneath the Foot*.

Rashaverak One of the Overlords; he reads all of Rupert Boyce's books on the occult in Arthur C. Clarke's *Childhood's End*.

Rashenko Ill, tall, thin, white-haired Soviet agent; tortured and rendered mute by Stefan Saridza's agents, he assists the Zaleshoffs and Desmond Kenton in Eric Ambler's *Uncommon Danger*.

Lieutenant Rashid Jovial police officer whom Edgar Perry meets at a dinner party given by Ronald Colt; he is pursuing Muawiya Khaslat in P. H. Newby's *The Picnic at Sakkara*.

Hannele, Countess Johanna Zu Rassentlow A talented doll-maker who makes a too realistic doll of her lover, Captain Hepburn, over which they separate before reuniting at the end of D. H. Lawrence's *The Captain's Doll*.

Jenny Rastall Widowed daughter of Massie; she is disinherited by his will; she works for Reginald Swaffield; she disputes the will and loses, and marries Lorimer after living with him in C. P. Snow's *In Their Wisdom*.

Dr. Raste Overworked, seemingly unsympathetic young doctor; he attempts to save the starving Earlforward couple in spite of themselves and gives employment to the displaced young servant Elsie Sprickett and her shell-shocked love, Joe, in Arnold Bennett's *Riceyman Steps*.

Miss Raste Dr. Raste's young daughter, who carries a message to the Earlforward home; her instant love for the mothering Elsie Sprickett persuades her father to employ Elsie and her fiancé, Joe, after the Earlforward couple's death in Arnold Bennett's *Riceyman Steps*.

Samuel Edward Ratchett Rich American murdered on the Calais Coach; Hercule Poirot discovers that he was the kidnap-murderer Cassetti, arrested for the murder of Daisy Armstrong but acquitted on a technicality in Agatha Christie's *Murder on the Orient Express*.

Simon Rathbone An Oxford friend of Sarah Bennett; he joins Ildiko Bates and David Vesey in throwing a party, at which Sarah meets Jackie Almond in Margaret Drabble's *A Summer Bird-Cage*.

Julius (the Split-Man) Ratner A second-rate Jewish writer and Zagreus's associate; he is Pierpoint's illustration of an Ape of God in Wyndham Lewis's *The Apes of God*.

Mrs. Rattery A wealthy, restless American divorcée, who is the mistress of Jock Grant-Menzies; she is helpful and considerate at the time of Tony Last's son's death; she rejects John Beaver's attempts to become her lover in Evelyn Waugh's *A Handful of Dust*.

John Rattery Carla Lemarchant's fiancé; she fears that she should not marry unless she can clear her late mother of the stain of murder in Agatha Christie's *Five Little Pigs*.

Eileen Rattray Wife of Tim; a former nurse, she disappoints David Parker when he asks her to help him watch after Meg Eliot when Meg has her nervous breakdown in Angus Wilson's *The Middle Age of Mrs. Eliot*.

Tim Rattray Horticulturalist who works for David Parker and Gordon Paget; he tries to help Meg Eliot adjust to life after her nervous breakdown in Angus Wilson's *The Middle Age of Mrs. Eliot*.

Charley Raunce Butler at an Anglo-Irish estate who is disturbed by the changes brought about by World War II; he elopes to England with the housemaid Edith, with whom he lives "happily ever after" in Henry Green's *Loving*.

Ravelston A wealthy editor of the leftist publication *Antichrist*; he publishes Gordon Comstock's poetry and takes care of him after he gets arrested and fired in George Orwell's *Keep the Aspidistra Flying*.

Dr. Eric Ravelston Young American specialist who confirms Sir Edward Leithen's terminal illness and reveals he has been troubled by Francis Galliard's neurological well-being in John Buchan's *Sick Heart River*.

Raven Mysteriously missing chemical-warfare biochemist and supposed British defector who is the key to Jay's scheme to discredit the narrator; he is rescued by the narrator and de-programmed by W.O.O.C.(P.) psychiatrists in Len Deighton's *The Ipcress File*.

James Raven Emotionally tormented, harelipped assassin; betrayed by Davis and others, he escapes the police and sets off to take revenge on Davis and Sir Marcus but is betrayed by Anne Crowder, the women whose life he saves, and killed in Graham Greene's *A Gun for Sale.*

Magdalen Raven Widowed mother of Avice Shrubsole; she comes to live with and be rather exploited by her daughter's family and to be fitted into the village society in Barbara Pym's *A Few Green Leaves.*

Dame Patricia Raven The long-time friend of John Forbes's late wife; her affair with Forbes has been motivated by compassion for his grief, and she ends it to make way for the woman with whom she intends to share her life in Iris Murdoch's *Henry and Cato.*

Rawcliffe British popular poet and wastrel on the downslope of his career; attaching himself to F. X. Enderby in Rome, he steals Enderby's long poem and turns it into a film script in Anthony Burgess's *Inside Mr. Enderby.*

Ray A younger man who makes a pass at Tessa O'Brien during her summer course in David Lodge's *How Far Can You Go?.*

Geoffrey Raymond Secretary of Roger Ackroyd, whose will leaves him £500 in Agatha Christie's *The Murder of Roger Ackroyd.*

Rayner Third lieutenant aboard the *Sutherland* in C. S. Forester's *Ship of the Line.*

Kirylo Sidorovitch Razumov Conformist student at St. Petersburg University who betrays Victor Haldin, is interrogated by the Russian police, and goes abroad to become a double agent, but reveals himself to the revolutionary underground, is crippled, and ends his life in a cottage in the south of Russia in Joseph Conrad's *Under Western Eyes.*

Michael Reagan Lifelong friend of Colin Saville; he gets an education and manages to escape the almost inevitable poverty of a coalmine family in David Storey's *Saville.*

Eugene Réal Lieutenant whose parents are executed in the Terror; he arranges for Peyrol to deliver false papers to the English and marries the orphan Arlette in Joseph Conrad's *The Rover.*

Francis Rebbing A little, vivacious man; in earlier

years he had made electioneering speeches for Sam Raingo and, upon a chance encounter with Raingo near the House of Lords, he reassures the nervous Raingo by affirming the powerful impression Raingo had made upon him in Arnold Bennett's *Lord Raingo.*

Rebecca Artificial-flower maker and hat trimmer; she is Joe's mother in Wolf Mankowitz's *A Kid for Two Farthings.*

Rector Clergyman whose interest in gemology results in the naming of Jasper, Ruby, and Amber Darke; Solomon Darke rebels at calling his second son Garnet and names him Peter in Mary Webb's *The House in Dormer Forest.*

Rector Good, sensitive, religious man and father; his secrets burden his attempts at goodness in Rex Warner's *The Aerodrome: A Love Story.*

Rector's wife Strong, affectionate, thoughtful mother; she hides her resentment of her husband in Rex Warner's *The Aerodrome: A Love Story.*

Redacteur Newspaper editor and boss of the reporter Minty; he pressures Minty to obtain personal and business information on Erik Krogh in Graham Greene's *England Made Me.*

Hattie Redburn Good-hearted woman who helps Richard Lovat Somers and his wife Harriet when they are being persecuted as spies in Cornwall during the war years in D. H. Lawrence's *Kangaroo.*

Jack Reddin Squire whose attempt to rape Hazel Woodus fails but who later seduces her in Mary Webb's *Gone to Earth.*

Lawrence Redding Young artist whose apparent courtship of Lettice Protheroe masks his involvement with Anne Protheroe in Agatha Christie's *The Murder at the Vicarage.*

Mrs. Redfern A well-known campaigner for the cause of women in Dorothy Richardson's *Dawn's Left Hand.*

Christine Redfern Seemingly frail and bookish wife of Patrick; she avoids the sun and behaves with open jealousy of Arlena Marshall in Agatha Christie's *Evil Under the Sun.*

Patrick Redfern A handsome adventurer apparently

infatuated with Arlena Marshall in Agatha Christie's *Evil Under the Sun.*

Keith Redington   Thirty-year-old widowed captain of a small yacht who has been on his own since the age of fifteen; like Jenny Blanchard he is a free spirit, unshackled by the conventions that rule most people in Frank Swinnerton's *Nocturne.*

Redival   Daughter of Trom, King of Glome, sister to Orual, and half sister to Psyche; immature and vain, she is neglected by Orual after the birth of Psyche; Orual eventually learns that her neglect contributed to Redival's unhappiness in C. S. Lewis's *Till We Have Faces.*

Carol Redman   An American acquaintance of Laurie Gaynor; she becomes Anna Morgan's lover in Jean Rhys's *Voyage in the Dark.*

Mrs. Redwood   Dandy Redwood's overwrought wife, who grows to love and mother their Boomfood son, Edward, even though she plays the martyr while doing it in H. G. Wells's *The Food of the Gods, and How It Came to Earth.*

Professor Dandy Redwood   Bensington's unsung partner who sees belatedly both herakleophorbia's dangers and Winkles's selfish motives; Redwood helps the Boomfood babies, including his son, adapt to civilization, and endures house arrest during the Giant rebellion to become negotiator for them with Caterham's government in H. G. Wells's *The Food of the Gods, and How It Came to Earth.*

Edward Ronson (Pantagruel) Redwood   The Redwoods' Boomfood son, who grows up to become a leader in the Giant rebellion and the lover of the lone Giant woman, the Princess of Weser Dreiburg, in H. G. Wells's *The Food of the Gods, and How It Came to Earth.*

Selina Redwood   The acknowledged beauty among the May of Teck Club residents; she juggles selfish affairs with both Colonel Felix Dobell and Nicholas Farringdon, who loves her; her action of reentering the burning building — passing the girls still trapped by their larger sizes — in order to rescue and appropriate a Schiaparelli evening dress contributes to the religious conversion of Nicholas Farringdon in Muriel Spark's *The Girls of Slender Means.*

Mr. Reed   Father of Nancy Reed and son of Old Mr. Reed, tenant of Thorncombe in John Fowles's *Daniel Martin.*

Mrs. Reed   Mother of Nancy Reed; she puts a stop to Nancy's friendship with Daniel Martin in John Fowles's *Daniel Martin.*

Old Mr. Reed   An elderly farmer; he is Nancy Reed's grandfather in John Fowles's *Daniel Martin.*

Giles Reed   Gwenda's lately married husband; he supports his wife's investigation of an old mystery, but his job often keeps him away from home in Agatha Christie's *Sleeping Murder.*

Gwenda Reed   Newly married woman who, having grown up in New Zealand following a family tragedy, returns to live in the house of her early childhood; haunted by a tragedy in the past, she investigates the mystery in Agatha Christie's *Sleeping Murder.*

Nancy Reed   A young country girl, Daniel Martin's first love, who lives at Thorncombe; she returns with her husband years later when Dan is staying at Thorncombe in John Fowles's *Daniel Martin.*

Tim Reede   A thirtyish painter of limited talent and industry but ardent and innocent in his approach to life and art; he falls in love with Gertrude Openshaw and eventually marries her in Iris Murdoch's *Nuns and Soldiers.*

Reeves   Colonel Lucius Protheroe's quarrelsome butler in Agatha Christie's *The Murder at the Vicarage.*

Annie Reeves   An elderly woman in Maudie Fowler's neighborhood whom Jane Somers also befriends because Annie is completely abandoned, having no family or other friend, in Doris Lessing's *The Diaries of Jane Somers.*

Harry Reeves   Middle-aged, well-to-do farmer who becomes enamoured of Bess Wrigley and runs away with her in Richard Aldington's *The Colonel's Daughter.*

Reggie   Mary's lover, whose departure with Mary from Alice Mellings's house is hastened by their discovery of an instruction manual for building bombs in Doris Lessing's *The Good Terrorist.*

Herr Regierungsrat   An artistocratic German who after World War I briefly becomes engaged to Hannele von Rassentlow in D. H. Lawrence's *The Captain's Doll.*

Reginald   Middle-aged Dublin bachelor who becomes the boyfriend of the much younger Bridget Brennan in Edna O'Brien's *The Country Girls.*

Hilda Reid Connie Chatterley's sister; she marries a rich, older Cambridge government official who writes essays; a headstrong "amazon" who has dismissed "that sex business" forever, Hilda is unwilling to accept the abandonment of self that would provide her psychic rebirth in D. H. Lawrence's *Lady Chatterley's Lover*.

Sir Malcolm Reid A once well-known painter in the Royal Academy; he seems "Scotch and lewd" when he meets the lover, Mellors, of his daughter Connie Chatterley in D. H. Lawrence's *Lady Chatterley's Lover*.

Reilly Groom of Jocelyn Chadwick; he tells the police, after Chadwick's death, of his master's plot to ruin the Kilmartin family in Liam O'Flaherty's *Famine*.

Mary Reilly A semi-gentleman farmer's beautiful daughter whose alleged sexual attack prompts the Church to hold a Mission in town; she is the true love of Tarry Flynn, but their relationship never materializes in Patrick Kavanagh's *Tarry Flynn*.

Rear-Admiral Vanya Mikhail Remoziva Russian antisubmarine warfare commander who is to be secretly transferred from the Arctic to a remote Scottish island to further a British Intelligence operation in Len Deighton's *Spy Story*.

Renata Pregnant wife of Pepino (Giuseppe Baldino); she is living in Italy and ready to give birth while her husband, a patient in Clive Ward, worries about her and hopes that she will bear him a son in John Berger's *The Foot of Clive*.

Colonel Rendezvous Fitness-crazed neighbor of Mr. Britling; he is used to commanding men in H. G. Wells's *Mr. Britling Sees It Through*.

René A gigolo of about thirty who takes money from Sasha Jensen; he calls himself a "mauvais garçon" in Jean Rhys's *Good Morning Midnight*.

Renee Johor's friend who has helped save refugees from the whirlpools and with whom Johor travels in Doris Lessing's *Re: Colonised Planet 5, Shikasta*.

David Renn Former soldier, editor, and novelist; he supervises Mary Hervey Russell in a London publishing house in 1918 and appears cold, stoical, hot-tempered, and sarcastic; though left in pain and badly crippled from his nearly fatal war injury, he refuses to return to the village of Hitchins to be cared for by his mother, Kathy Renn, in Storm Jameson's *Company Parade*. He becomes a member of the London secret police to hunt down the killer of his old friend, Henry Smith, in 1938 and 1939 in *Before the Crossing*. In 1945 Renn opposes William Gary in intelligence operations when both deal with international political betrayals and murders connected with the planned governance of the British Zone in newly occupied East Germany; sparing no effort, Renn goes about Europe persistently trying to locate and help Marie Duclos; he adopts her young son to take him to safety in England and to provide warmth and love for him in *The Black Laurel*.

Kathy Renn Mother of David Renn; she wishes he would give up his independence and his work because of his war-related physical disabilities and pain but acknowledges that he knows best about his decisions in Storm Jameson's *Company Parade*. David, having returned home briefly in 1939, may be talking only to his mother's ghost and to the chair that still holds her impression in the old village house that is for sale in *Before the Crossing*.

Mr. Rennit Private detective for the Orthotex Agency; he is employed by Arthur Rowe to find out about the mysterious prize cake in Graham Greene's *The Ministry of Fear*.

Tom Renshaw A worthy young farmer whose suit eventually rewards the gentle patience of Emily Saxton in D. H. Lawrence's *The White Peacock*.

Bret Rensselaer An American whose empire is the British Economics Intelligence Committee; he is "Brahms Four's" later contact and Dicky Cruyer's boss in Len Deighton's *Berlin Game*. He loses his empire and is framed as a K.G.B. mole; he asks Bernard Samson's assistance and is shot in the chase of Pavel Moskvin in *London Match*.

Jules Reuss Manager of Burckheim ironworks; he conspires with Siguenau and distant German cousins to replace French workers with Germans in Burckheim's factory; he lies to Honoré Burckheim about René Hoffmayer and Edward Berthelin to destroy his trust in them; he believes that France cannot survive in economic or military strength without collaboration with Germany in Storm Jameson's *Cousin Honoré*.

Sidney Revel Pudgy, dumpy romance novelist who elopes with Helen Walshingham after Art Kipps breaks off his engagement with her in H. G. Wells's *Kipps: The Story of a Simple Soul*.

Rex Editor of a British leftist newspaper and a friend of Anna Wulf; he also acts as a literary critic for the

Communist Party in Doris Lessing's *The Golden Notebook*.

Reyer Fair, pale, bored young night-manager; his quickness in offering his coat to Evelyn Orcham for an impromptu night walk impresses the Managing Director, who intends to oversee the young man's progress in Arnold Bennett's *Imperial Palace*.

Professor Reynolds Ragged, fifty-nine-year-old professor of literature, now a voluntary outcast and an articulate opponent of the state; he lives by shoplifting, a skill he attempts to teach Bev Jones in Anthony Burgess's *1985*.

Barbara Reynolds Efficient, intelligent American professional woman; she is Robert Halliday's literary agent in Eric Ambler's *The Care of Time*.

Lydia Reynolds A novelist and Rosamund Stacey's roommate; her latest novel is a semi-biographical account of Rosamund's pregnancy in Margaret Drabble's *The Millstone*.

Rhoda A shy, dreamy, poetic girl who represents the unconscious and unbalanced creativity; she swims in the mystic, wild, ungrounded imagination and carries a brown bowl of petals, a flotilla which she drowns as she throws herself into the ocean; in contrast to Bernard, Rhoda cannot write and has trouble staying in the body and relating to other people's physicality in Virginia Woolf's *The Waves*.

Rhoda Small-headed, tall, birdlike parlormaid at the Marshalson estate; only Gerda Marshalson can understand her speech; Colette Forbes tells Henry Marshalson that she once years ago happened upon a sexual encounter between Rhoda and Sandy Marshalson in Iris Murdoch's *Henry and Cato*.

Rhodia A female, originally from Lelanos, who is Ambien II's helpful jailor when she is taken prisoner by the leaders of Grakconkranpatl; Rhodia eventually leads Ambien II to Lelanos in Doris Lessing's *The Sirian Experiments*.

Owen Rhys An American who, along with Bud Villiers and Kate Leslie, is disgusted by the bullfight which they attend together; Kate leaves, but Rhys and Villiers stay on for the "experience" in D. H. Lawrence's *The Plumed Serpent (Quetzalcoatl)*.

Konstantina Riber A woman with whom Charles Watkins professes to have fallen in love while he was stationed in Yugoslavia; she is later killed in Doris Lessing's *Briefing for a Descent into Hell*.

Don Vincente Ribiera Costaguanan dictator in Joseph Conrad's *Nostromo: A Tale of the Seaboard*.

Margaret (Mitzi) Ricardo A middle-aged woman of lower-class Jewish origin; her remarkable career as an athlete was ended by injury, but she is a cheerful, affectionate, helpful friend; Ludwig Leferrier's landlady, she is disliked by Gracie Tisbourne; she loves Charlotte Ledgard, with whom she shares a cottage and a dog at the end of Iris Murdoch's *An Accidental Man*.

Martin Ricardo Depraved gambler who, misled into thinking Axel Heyst has a fortune, nearly rapes Lena; he is shot by his jealous partner, Jones, in Joseph Conrad's *Victory: An Island Tale*.

Tiny (Ric) Ricardo Occasional C.I.A. pilot and Lizzie Worthington's abusive lover; he runs drugs for Drake Ko, interferes with Nelson Ko's escape from China, trades Lizzie to Drake Ko for his life, and attempts to murder Jerry Westerby in John le Carré's *The Honourable Schoolboy*.

Ricarlo An Italian juggler on the variety circuit; he is a pleasant, quiet chap whose one weakness is women in J. B. Priestley's *Lost Empires*.

Mr. Ricci A founding member of the new political party, Juventus, with Count Jovian in John Buchan's *The House of the Four Winds*.

Ricciardo Pale, young, Italian manservant to General and Mrs. Vagas in Eric Ambler's *Cause for Alarm*.

J. J. Riceyman Henry Earlforward's fat old uncle; he one evening dramatically tells his newly discovered nephew of the disasters of building the underground railway in Clerkenwell, suffers a stroke from the telling, and dies before morning; Henry finds himself proprietor of the bookstore in Arnold Bennett's *Riceyman Steps*.

Richard Reformed sex criminal whom Lise pursues, having selected him as her murderer in Muriel Spark's *The Driver's Seat*.

King Richard III The last Plantagenet monarch, maligned by historians currying favor with his usurper, King Henry VII, in Josephine Tey's *The Daughter of*

Time. See Richard of Gloucester in *Dictionary of British Literary Characters 18th- and 19th-Century Novels.*

Mr. Richards Despicable Vice President of the Alpha and Omega Club who burglarizes the Duchess of San Martino; he hates the Russians in Norman Douglas's *South Wind.*

Miss Richards The nurse on duty when Rosamund Stacey attempts to visit her hospitalized daughter; she must tell Rosamund that her daughter cannot have visitors in Margaret Drabble's *The Millstone.*

Brenda Richardson Forty-seven-year-old overweight third wife of Jake Richardson; she leaves Jake after sex therapy is unsuccessful in reviving his interest in her; she finds happiness with her best friend's husband, Geoffrey Mabbott, in Kingsley Amis's *Jake's Thing.*

Jaques Cecil ("Jake") Richardson Cynical fifty-nine-year-old history professor at Oxford University whose declining sex drive leads to psychological therapy which leads him to the realization that he has never appreciated women except as sex objects; he decides to give up any and all interest in women at the conclusion of Kingsley Amis's *Jake's Thing.*

Miss (Mouse) Rickard Unmarried sister of Clara Matthews; she quarrels with her nieces and nephews over a litter of kittens and her parrot and leaves her estate to her niece Margaret Matthews in Angus Wilson's *No Laughing Matter.*

Terry Rickards Former Scotland Yard detective now a provincial chief inspector with a pregnant wife; he heads the investigation of serial killings and the murder of Hilary Robarts in P. D. James's *Devices and Desires.*

Kitty Ricketts Prostitute in the brothel where Leopold Bloom and Stephen Dedalus meet in James Joyce's *Ulysses.*

Isaac Rickman Keith Rickman's father, who is a second-hand book dealer; he purchases the Harden library at far less than its true value through collusion with Richard Pilkington, thus precipitating Keith Rickman's departure from the business in May Sinclair's *The Divine Fire.*

Savage Keith (Razors, Rickets, Ricky-Ticky) Rickman Cockney poet and genius who struggles with his poetry and his own moral code and with his estrangements from his father, from Horace Jewdwine, from friends, and from financial supporters; he grows as a man and a poet in May Sinclair's *The Divine Fire.*

Miss Rickward ("Ricky") Middle-aged spinster, headmistress, and domineering friend of Barbara Vaughan in Muriel Spark's *The Mandlebaum Gate.*

Nancy Riddle A clergyman's daughter and a resident of the May of Teck Club in Muriel Spark's *The Girls of Slender Means.*

Rider Former employee of the Rasuka oil well who disappeared into the desert and is assumed to be dead; a character of mythic proportions, he is remembered with reverence by the natives and with outrage by the Europeans; accounts of his behavior and exploits greatly influence Robert Winter in P. H. Newby's *A Journey to the Interior.*

Honeychile Rider Naïve, pure-hearted, self-educated girl; her knowledge of nature enables her to save herself and James Bond in Ian Fleming's *Dr. No.*

Gregory Riding An impossibly beautiful young man of wealth and breeding; he has an easy job at an art gallery, all the women and men and money that he wants, and time to enjoy it all; Gregory has an adopted brother, Terry Service, whom he despises, and a sister, Ursula Riding, whom he adores; Gregory has it made, but finds his fortune and self-confidence declining when Ursula commits suicide and Terry begins to rise in the world in Martin Amis's *Success.*

Henry Riding A dotty aristocrat, Gregory and Ursula Riding's father; he adopts Terry Service in Martin Amis's *Success.*

Ursula Riding Gregory's sister; she is a pampered and wealthy young lady who, after having sex with her adopted brother, Terry Service, commits suicide in Martin Amis's *Success.*

Ridley Lord Barralonga's jockey-like chauffeur, who wounds the Utopian scientist Cedar after trying to kidnap him, and who loudly rebuffs William Barnstaple for opposing Rupert Catskill's plan to overthrow Utopian rule in H. G. Wells's *Men Like Gods.*

Miss Ridley The governess to the Clare children; she has a degree and wants to learn all she can in Ivy Compton-Burnett's *The Present and the Past.*

William Ridley Conceited, patronizing new writer about to be discharged from the military in 1918; although he has not read it, he cruelly disparages Hervey Russell's first novel when he is introduced to her at Evelyn Lamb's home the day after the book's publication; he boasts that his forefathers were peasants without recognizing the irony of his elitism; he uses Evelyn Lamb as someone who can help him meet influential rich people, but she is attracted by his air of toughness and superiority in Storm Jameson's *Company Parade*.

Karl (codename "Mayfair") Riemeck Interior Ministry official, secretary to the SED Praesidium, head of the Coordinating Committee for the Protection of the People, and secret informant for British Intelligence; he is murdered while defecting to West Berlin because his concern for his mistress allowed Hans-Dieter Mundt time to find him in John le Carré's *The Spy Who Came In from the Cold*.

Inspector William (Bill) Rigby Detective in Carne Police Service who directs the investigation into Stella Rode's murder and ensures, despite his superior Brigadier Havelock's petulant interference, that the murderer is brought to justice by aiding George Smiley in John le Carré's *A Murder of Quality*.

Riggs Chauffeur to Soames Forsyte; he drives Soames to visit the site of his family's origins in John Galsworthy's *Swan Song*.

Ted Riley British field officer who assists Bernard Samson in uncovering Erich Stinnes as a K.G.B. plant and is killed when stealing files to prove it in Len Deighton's *London Match*.

Rilla A refugee saved from the whirlpool by Jahor; she is unable to emerge from her shocked state in Doris Lessing's *Re: Colonised Planet 5, Shikasta*.

Rima Young girl who is believed by the Maquiritari Indians to be an evil spirit called a daughter of the Didi; Mr. Abel falls in love with her, and she is killed by the tribe in W. H. Hudson's *Green Mansions*.

William Rimall Proprietor of a bookshop near St. Paul's who sells More's *Utopia* to Lord Miltoun in John Galsworthy's *The Patrician*.

Clarence Rimmer Hearty bon vivant and a novelist and critic; he believes in Harry Sinton's innocence and offers him pieces of information about the late Max Callis in Roy Fuller's *Fantasy and Fugue*.

Kay Rimmer Milly Drover's sister; she goes to the

Communist Party meeting, has a brief affair with Philip Surrogate, and spends the night with Jules Briton, who intends to ask her to marry him in Graham Greene's *It's a Battlefield*.

Lindsay Rimmer Emma Sands's beautiful secretary-companion; motivated by greed, she is Emma's conspirator in a scheme of revenge against Hugh Peronett; her elopement with Randall Peronett is conditional on his acquisition of capital in Iris Murdoch's *An Unofficial Rose*.

Howard Ringbaum Augustan specialist at Euphoric State University who is denied tenure because he has not read Hamlet; he sends an anonymous letter exposing Philip Swallow's affair with Melanie Byrd to Morris Zapp and to Hilary Swallow in David Lodge's *Changing Places: A Tale of Two Campuses*. Now at Southern Illinois University, he travels to England with his wife, trying to make love to her in odd places in order to join a men's club in *Small World*.

Thelma Ringbaum Frustrated wife of Howard Ringbaum; she leaves Howard and has an affair with Morris Zapp in David Lodge's *Small World*.

Ringwraith A dreaded chief whom Merry Brandybuck kills in battle in J. R. R. Tolkien's *The Two Towers*.

Effie Rink George Ponderevo's happy, sensual mistress during the time he is unhappily married to Marion; she is a typist for his uncle Teddy Ponderevo in H. G. Wells's *Tono-Bungay*.

Dante Riordan Stephen Dedalus's aunt who renounces the nationalist politician Charles Stuart Parnell because of his infidelity in James Joyce's *Ulysses*.

Marie Léonie (Charlotte) Riotor A blonde, tall, talkative Frenchwoman; she is a former ballet dancer who becomes the mistress of the younger Mark Tietjens for over twenty years until he marries her shortly before his death; she is referred to in Ford Madox Ford's *Some Do Not. . . .* Her history is detailed in *The Last Post*.

Deborah Riscoe Intelligent and independent daughter of Eleanor Maxie, sister of Stephen Maxie, and love interest of Adam Dalgliesh in P. D. James's *Cover Her Face*, in *A Mind to Murder*, and in *Unnatural Causes*.

Ed Ristow Senior agent for Drug Enforcement Administration in Southeast Asia; he is forced to resign when he fails to accept Tiny Ricardo's deal for Sino-

Soviet agent Nelson Ko in John le Carré's *The Honourable Schoolboy*.

Rita   A bookish, sheltered, sad, lifeless girl until she falls in love with the American Ira, whom she completely misunderstands, imagining him to be romantic and exotic in Beryl Bainbridge's *The Dressmaker*.

Rita   A waitress at the Kit-Cat café who constantly thinks and speaks in clichés; she becomes one of Billy Fisher's three fiancées in Keith Waterhouse's *Billy Liar*.

Madame Rita   Owner of the hat shop where Joe's mother works in Wolf Mankowitz's *A Kid for Two Farthings*.

Amos Ritchie   Blacksmith of Woodilee village; he warns David Sempill to ignore the Satanic rites he has witnessed but, after his wife dies of the plague, helps Sempill nurse the other villagers in John Buchan's *Witch Wood*.

Leon Rivas   Paraguayan former priest and boyhood friend of Eduardo Plarr and leader of a leftist band that kidnaps Charley Fortnum, the Honorary Consul, mistaking him for the American Ambassador; he dies trying to save Dr. Plarr in Graham Greene's *The Honorary Consul*.

Mr. Rivers   Owner of the fashionable London dress shop of Rivers and Roberts; small of stature and finicky, with long expressive hands and tiny feet in patent leather shoes, he complements Madame Louise, the head saleswoman, in Vita Sackville-West's *Family History*.

Isobel Rivers   Patricia, Lady Brandon's niece and the childhood companion of the Geste brothers; she becomes the sweet, quiet, faithful love of John Geste in Percival Christopher Wren's *Beau Geste*.

John Rivers   Retired physicist who recalls for a colleague the story of his acquaintance with Henry Maartens, his Nobel Prize-winning mentor: as a young man he spent a summer with Maartens and his family, a witness to the dynamic relationship of the scientist with his wife, to whom the young man lost his virginity in Aldous Huxley's *The Genius and the Goddess*.

Sir John Rivers   Chairman of the Governors who assures Mr. Chips that he has a place at Brookfield until he is a hundred years old in James Hilton's *Good-bye, Mr. Chips*.

Bill ("Jumbo") Roach   Pudgy, unsociable, mostly ignored student at Thursgood Preparatory School; his friendship and admiration are restorative to Jim Prideaux in John le Carré's *Tinker, Tailor, Soldier, Spy*.

Hilary Robarts   Abrasive, passionate administrative assistant to Alex Mair; she tries to marry him but is murdered in P. D. James's *Devices and Desires*.

RobaydayAnganol   JandolAngand's son, who lives with the Madis, a nomadic people, and murders Simdol Tal in order to hurt his father in Brian W. Aldiss's *Helliconia Summer*.

Nehemiah Robb   Church bellman, gravedigger, and beadle in John Buchan's *Witch Wood*.

Joan Robbins   The resentful next-door neighbor of the abandoned house that Alice Mellings and her comrades take over; Alice makes her overtures of friendship in Doris Lessing's *The Good Terrorist*.

Robert   Thirty-year-old alcoholic boss of Kate Fletcher Armstrong before she left him and rose to a better position in Margaret Drabble's *The Middle Ground*.

Robert   A footman at Manderly in Daphne Du Maurier's *Rebecca*.

Robert   Novelist, civil servant, one-time lover (as well as future husband) of Plaxy Trelone, and narrator of Olaf Stapledon's *Sirius: A Fantasy of Love and Discord*.

Robert   Phlegmatic, detached, and gratifyingly reliable husband of the Provincial Lady; he is an expert of the silent complaint: about servants, cold toast, running out of hot water, and adapting to changes in household routine in E. M. Delafield's *The Diary of a Provincial Lady*. He adjusts with patience to his wife's new independence, although when she talks of her book, he changes the subject to household finances or the difficulty of getting satisfactory raspberries; his eventual admission that her book is funny is characteristically dry in *The Provincial Lady Goes Further*.

Roberta   Faye's masculine, parent-like lover who watches out for Fay, comforts her, and becomes crazy with sorrow when Fay is killed in Doris Lessing's *The Good Terrorist*.

Roberto   Italian servant in the Sanger household who is devoted to the Sangers and does all the work in the house; when Albert Sanger dies, Roberto accompanies the Sanger children to England, where he continues to keep house for them in Margaret Kennedy's *The Constant Nymph.*

Roberts Kind and easy-going second lieutenant who is implicated as a conspirator in C. S. Forester's *Lieutenant Hornblower.*

Chief Petty Officer Roberts A rum-guzzling and hypocritical non-commissioned officer who serves at sea under Pincher Martin and who resents Nathaniel Walterson in William Golding's *Pincher Martin.*

Dr. Roberts Prosperous, agreeable physician; the number of his patients to die is less "reasonable" than he proclaims in Agatha Christie's *Cards on the Table.*

Mr. Roberts The colliery manager in John Lewis's home town who is Lewis's father's friend; he goes to Mrs. Protheroe's party in Kingsley Amis's *That Uncertain Feeling.*

Dai Roberts Elusive rural shooting companion of Augustine Penry-Herbert; his avoidance of the inquest into their accidental discovery of Rachel's body makes possible the suspicion that drives Augustine away from home in Richard Hughes's *The Fox in the Attic.*

Laura Roberts Friendly young restaurant cashier with warm eyes and glowing red hair; she is chosen by Richard Larch to be his wife after he recognizes the falsity of his relationship to Adeline Aked and accepts his attraction to Laura in Arnold Bennett's *A Man From the North.*

Norman Roberts Traveling salesman who is baffled when young Elsie Palmer whispers in the dark that she loves him because she can think of nothing to say about the movie that they are watching and that she does not understand in E. M. Delafield's *Messalina of the Suburbs.*

Sir John Robertson A specialist and dealer in old furniture whose offer to take Christopher Tietjens into partnership is rejected in Ford Madox Ford's *Some Do Not. . . .* He refuses to help Christopher after the war because of the false rumors of the latter's infidelities in *A Man Could Stand Up* — and in *The Last Post.*

Robin Son of the Provincial Lady, who usually refers to him as "the boy" because she does not want him to discover how attached to him she really is; she worries about his colds and about the cost of his boarding school in E. M. Delafield's *The Diary of a Provincial Lady.* The Provincial Lady finds his schoolfriends indistinguishable one from another in *The Provincial Lady Goes Further.*

Fred Robins Sara Monday's lover, a worker at the railroad; he is the man Sara chooses to stay with when Tom Wilcher asks her to marry him in Joyce Cary's *To Be a Pilgrim* and in *The Horses Mouth.*

Robinson Oliver Green's colleague; he has a cocky, confiding manner and a genius for using people in C. Day Lewis's *Child of Misfortune.*

Robinson Lapsed Catholic on whose solitary island (also named Robinson) January Marlowe is stranded after a plane crash in Muriel Spark's *Robinson.*

Robinson Terminally ill bank manager who refuses to lend Henry Scobie the money to send his wife, Louise Scobie, to South Africa in Graham Greene's *The Heart of the Matter.*

Mr. Robinson The youngest, most important partner in the legal firm where Martha Quest gains a job as a secretary until she quits the firm to marry in Doris Lessing's *Martha Quest* and in *A Proper Marriage.* Having rehired her, he continues to be her employer in *A Ripple from the Storm* and in *Landlocked.*

Arthur Robinson A scholar, now dead, who committed library theft to conceal a crucial error of fact in his brilliant book; the fraud was recognized and exposed by Miss de Vine in Dorothy L. Sayers's *Gaudy Night.*

Mark Robinson Cambridge University student who confesses to Stephen Freer that he is the source of the drug that may have caused Bernard Kelshall to jump to his death; he declares he will abandon his studies and go into exile in India in C. P. Snow's *The Malcontents.*

Phyllis Robinson An eighteen-year-old whose variety turn is a frank imitation of Lily Farris's more successful act; she is rescued by Dick Herncastle from a sordid intrigue involving Lily and Otto Mergen in J. B. Priestley's *Lost Empires.*

Red Robinson A Cockney who is one of the "Commune conspirators"; he possesses a monomaniacal " 'atred" for Philip Crow; he proposes Johnny Geard for mayor of Glastonbuy and becomes a foreman in the "Municipal", the communist factory in John Cowper Powys's *A Glastonbury Romance.*

R. S. Robinson Small-time publisher who persuades Sheila (Knight) Eliot to make an investment in his firm and who spreads malicious gossip about her shortly before her suicide in C. P. Snow's *Homecomings.*

Jo Robson Oxford chum of Edward Pargiter and Hugh Gibbs; he is admired by Kitty Lasswade because of his resemblance to a farmhand who once kissed her under a rick in Virginia Woolf's *The Years*.

Poll Robson Dumpy, middle-aged friend of Meg Eliot; she sponges on her acquaintances and suddenly comes into money in Angus Wilson's *The Middle Age of Mrs. Eliot*.

Commendatori Rocco A big man with a deep voice, always in gleaming white professional dress; he is chief of the grill kitchens of the hotel and invents six new hors d'oeuvre each day in Arnold Bennett's *Imperial Palace*.

Madame Rochard The mother-figure of the Natcha-Kee-Tawara Troupe, the five absurdly histrionic, second-rate *artistes* who perform at Houghton's theater in D. H. Lawrence's *The Lost Girl*.

Father John Roche Charitable parish priest who gives everything he has to help the poor and hungry in Liam O'Flaherty's *Famine*.

Nasty Roche Snobbish student at the Clongowes Woods School who questions Stephen about his father's profession in James Joyce's *A Portrait of the Artist as a Young Man*.

Mr. Rochester Tall, handsome, rich Englishman; England is real to him and Jamaica a dream; selfish and unyielding in temperament, he is initially infatuated with the beautiful Antoinette Cosway but becomes ultimately cold and distrusting of the blacks and of Antoinette, accelerating her descent into madness; he renames her Bertha and imprisons her in the attic of his English house in Jean Rhys's *Wide Sargasso Sea*. See Edward Fairfax Rochester in *Dictionary of British Literary Characters 18th- and 19th-Century Novels*.

Bertha Rochester See Antoinette Cosway.

Mr. Rock Famous scientist who in his youth developed an important theory but in old age fights to protect his cottage, his mentally disturbed granddaughter, and his dignity from the malevolence of the two directors of a state educational institution for women in Henry Green's *Concluding*.

Elizabeth Rock Mentally disturbed granddaughter of Mr. Rock and lover of Sebastian Birt in Henry Green's *Concluding*.

Wilhelm (Willi) Rodde A German expatriate, very intellectual and emotionally detached, who becomes Anna Wulf's lover in Mashopi, Africa, and triggers her interest in communism in Doris Lessing's *The Golden Notebook*.

Hermione Roddice An overintellectual aristocrat who is Rupert Birkin's lover until he leaves her for the more substantial Ursula Brangwen in D. H. Lawrence's *Women in Love*.

Stanley Rode Junior science teacher at Carne School whose working-class background and manners make him an obvious dupe for his spouse's hypocritical nature and a ready suspect in her murder in John le Carré's *A Murder of Quality*.

Stella Glaston Rode Samuel Glaston's daughter and Stanley Rode's spouse; she shrewishly blackmails various Carne School faculty members and is murdered at North Fields, her house, in John le Carré's *A Murder of Quality*.

Bernard Roderick Plump, wealthy factory manager and businessman who, for the sake of discretion, presents himself as the uncle of his traveling companion and lover Veronica (Roderick); he later pays Charles Lumley's hospital bills as a final gesture before ending Charles's relationship with the girl in John Wain's *Hurry On Down*.

Veronica Roderick Attractive young companion of wealthy Bernard Roderick; she poses as his niece to hide the fact they are lovers; ignorant of this liaison, Charles Lumley falls in love with her and enters Teddy Bunder's drug-running operation against his better judgment in order to indulge Veronica's expensive tastes in John Wain's *Hurry On Down*.

Jan Rodericks Rupert Boyce's brother-in-law and a doctoral candidate in engineering physics and astronomy; he is the only human to go to the Overlords' home planet; he is the last man in Arthur C. Clarke's *Childhood's End*.

Boris Roderigo The communications officer of the *Endeavor* and member of the Fifth Church of Christ Cosmonaut; he believes Rama is an ark sent to save the faithful from the Judgement and disarms the missile sent by the Mercury government to destroy Rama in Arthur C. Clarke's *Rendezvous with Rama*.

Mr. Rodkin A former lodger at Mrs. Bailey's whose return from travels round the world happens to coincide with Eleanor Dear's brief stay in the Tansley Street house in Dorothy Richardson's *Interim*. He marries her in *Revolving Lights*.

Roderick Rodney Stella Rodney's college-age son in Elizabeth Bowen's *The Heat of the Day*.

Stella Rodney Fortyish English divorcée, a government employee engaged in secret work during World

War II; after Robert Kelway's death she retrospectively surveys the events of her own life, the climate of wartime London, and the ways in which these connect with what she has been able to learn about Kelway's life and family in Elizabeth Bowen's *The Heat of the Day*.

William Rodney   Katherine Hilbery's first fiancé, a mentally alert, physically twisted inhabitant of the scholarly realm; William is perfectly suited to Katherine's mathematical mind; with him she could have achieved practical compromise but not a spiritual union in Virginia Woolf's *Night and Day*.

Dr. Rodriguez   Rachel Vinrace's first, incompetent physician during her fatal visionary fever in Virginia Woolf's *The Voyage Out*.

Christopher Roe   Five-year-old son of Richard Roe; after being briefly abducted by the mentally disturbed Amy Pye, he is sent to the country to avoid the blitz in Henry Green's *Caught*.

Richard Roe   Widowed father of Christopher Roe and member of the Auxiliary Fire Service at the beginning of World War II; his experience with the other members of the fire service transform him from a self-pitying businessman into a competent though still disturbed fireman in Henry Green's *Caught*.

George, Earl of Roehampton   A landowner more comfortable at his Norfolk estate or at the Newmarket races than in London society; discovering his wife Sylvia's affair with Sebastian, he exiles her to the country estate to avoid scandal in Vita Sackville-West's *The Edwardians*. He appears in *Family History*.

Lady Margaret Roehampton   Unattractive daughter of Lord and Lady Roehampton; she is enamored briefly of a young painter, but her parents arrange her engagement to the socially acceptable Tony Wexford in Vita Sackville-West's *The Edwardians*.

Sylvia, Lady Roehampton   A professional beauty who initiates an affair with Sebastian, his first "experiment" in love and her last challenge to the encroaching years in Vita Sackville-West's *The Edwardians*. She and Lord Roehampton participate in the London Season in *Family History*.

Roger   The dictatorial Jack Merridew's henchman, who possesses all the sadistic attributes of the hangman underling in William Golding's *Lord of the Flies*.

Rogers   Servant to the Nettleby family in Isabel Colegate's *The Shooting Party*.

Miss Rogers   Employee of the Committee for Aid to the Elderly who is corrected by Meg Eliot for refusing to allow the elderly to enjoy alcoholic beverages in Angus Wilson's *The Middle Age of Mrs. Eliot*.

Mrs. Rogers   A social worker who is more of a nuisance than a help to Maudie Fowler in Doris Lessing's *The Diaries of Jane Somers*.

Bruce Rogers   A conventional-minded solicitor whose business is "conveyancing, testaments, briefs"; he is disappointed in the legal system; he is retained by Hugo Chesterton in Nicholas Blake's *A Tangled Web*.

Ethel Rogers   Cook at Indian Island; culpable with her husband, Thomas, in the death of a former employer, she is an early victim of murder in Agatha Christie's *And Then There Were None*.

Mildred Rogers   The deceitful, commonplace, and essentially stupid woman who exerts a powerful hold over Philip Carey despite her torment of his generous spirit in W. Somerset Maugham's *Of Human Bondage*.

Thomas Rogers   Butler at Indian Island; he and his wife, Ethel, jointly caused the death of an old woman whose trusted servants they were; he is murdered while chopping firewood in Agatha Christie's *And Then There Were None*.

Vera Rogers   A welfare officer whom Maudie Fowler detests but who is dutiful and hardworking in Doris Lessing's *The Diaries of Jane Somers*.

Ernst Röhm   Head of the increasingly out-of-control S.A.; accused of disloyalty, he dies in a blood purge engineered by Hitler to consolidate power in Richard Hughes's *The Wooden Shepherdess*.

Jimmy Roland   Tim Reede's old friend; his telling Ed Roper of Tim and Daisy Barrett's "plot" to have Tim marry for money is taken seriously in Iris Murdoch's *Nuns and Soldiers*.

Marcus Rolf   Young unpublished American writer, wandering through Europe; he transcribes the recollective narrative of Ellen Henshaw in Anthony Burgess's *The Pianoplayers*.

Mr. Rolovsky   A man in the millinery business for whom Maudie Fowler used to work in Doris Lessing's *The Diaries of Jane Somers*.

Helen Rolt   Strong, self-assured, newly married and widowed survivor of a shipwreck and a forty-day ordeal in an open boat; she settles in the African port where Henry Scobie is Assistant Police Commissioner and has an affair with him, vacillating between contempt and loving concern for him until his death in Graham Greene's *The Heart of the Matter.*

Cyril Romanes Noted figure in the hunting-field and a polo-player of international fame; in command of the camp where Lady Roylance (Janet Raden) is held hostage, he plots to get revenge by murdering the two women and Castor, but kills Castor and then is killed himself in John Buchan's *The Courts of the Morning.*

Tatiana (Tania) Romanova Patriotic Russian agent; she is enlisted to betray James Bond but instead falls in love with him in Ian Fleming's *From Russia, With Love.*

Willy Romantowski Young German who is used by Nazis to try to lure Roy Calvert to Germany after the War begins in C. P. Snow's *The Light and the Dark.*

Sir Ronald Poet and diplomat, minister at the British legation in Stockholm; he occasionally hosts Erik Krogh in Graham Greene's *England Made Me.*

Ronnie Ivor's homosexual lover, an out-of-work actor, who covertly challenges Anna Wulf's temper and her own fears of homophobia in Doris Lessing's *The Golden Notebook.*

Ronny Christopher Isherwood's friend who introduces him to Paul in Christopher Isherwood's *Down There on a Visit.*

Bruno Rontini Philosophical Florentine art dealer and devoted friend and distant relation of Eustace Barnack; an unselfish friend to all, he helps save Sebastian Barnack from a great social embarrassment by recovering a disputed valuable drawing, but — incurring the anger of a competing dealer — he is betrayed to the fascist authorities, who imprison him; released after many years, he is nursed in his final days by a repentant Sebastian in Aldous Huxley's *Time Must Have a Stop.*

Aoz Roon A hunter who becomes ruler of Oldorando by murdering Nahkri and Klils, Laintal Ay's uncles, in Brian W. Aldiss's *Helliconia Spring.*

Professor Arnold Root Elderly archaeologist friend of Sybil Forsyth in Barbara Pym's *A Glass of Blessings.*

Brigitte Weidegrunde Roper Handsome, blowsily sexy German-born wife of Edmund Roper; she leaves

him voluntarily to become a prostitute in Anthony Burgess's *Tremor of Intent.*

Ed Roper An art dealer who is Guy Openshaw's "honorary cousin"; Tim Reede's old friend and occasional benefactor, he is a connection for Tim with the Openshaw circle after Guy's death; he spreads a story which is for a time damaging to Tim's marriage to Gertrude Openshaw in Iris Murdoch's *Nuns and Soldiers.*

Edmund Roper Schoolboy friend of Denis Hillier; he is placidly mediocre except for extraordinary ability in theoretical science; a defector to Russia, he is the object of Hillier's mission in Anthony Burgess's *Tremor of Intent.*

Rosa A woman of the South American Macushi tribe who is the spokesperson for her people as they lead Tony Last and Dr. Messinger deep into the jungle; she and her tribe desert the pair, thus leading to the tragic fate of the two explorers in Evelyn Waugh's *A Handful of Dust.*

Rosa A chambermaid suspected of collaboration in murder; a "hot piece of goods," she is involved with schoolmaster Cyril Wrench in Nicholas Blake's *A Question of Proof.*

Rosa Shy hospital worker with whom Charles Lumley begins a highly traditional but refreshingly simple and honest relationship he later recognizes as a period of emotional healing in John Wain's *Hurry On Down.*

Rosalie A previous au pair for the Browns' children; she was addicted to drugs in Doris Lessing's *The Summer Before the Dark.*

Cousin Rosamund (Rose) Little daughter of Constance and Jock and cousin of the Aubrey children, who enjoy playing with her; she has curly clean blonde hair, and her dreamy behavior and speech impediment set her apart from other children, except for little Richard Quin Aubrey, with whom she feels secure; although most people dismiss her as retarded, her comments are startling but thoughtful in Rebecca West's *The Fountain Overflows.*

Mrs. Roscorla The old mother who rules the family behind the scenes and disapproves of Miriam Henderson in Dorothy Richardson's *Dimple Hill.*

Alfred Roscorla The younger brother in the family

of Quakers who run the Sussex fruit-farm where Miriam Henderson has arranged to stay in Dorothy Richardson's *Dimple Hill.*

Rachel Mary Roscorla   The sister, housekeeper, and confidante of her brothers; she hopes to acquire Miriam Henderson as a sister-in-law in Dorothy Richardson's *Dimple Hill.* With this aim in mind, after her mother's death she invites Miriam back to the Sussex farm in *March Moonlight.*

Richard Roscorla   The elder brother and major male figure in the hosuehold; he has a history of unsatisfactory relations with women in Dorothy Richardson's *Dimple Hill.* His feelings for Miriam Henderson being still unclear, she comes to realize that "apart from his surroundings", he is, for her, "almost nothing" in *March Moonlight.*

Rose   Navigator of the flying boat who kills himself with Sparks Adcock's revolver to avoid Captain Bennett's anger on the day the boat is scheduled to return with the gold in Alan Sillitoe's *The Lost Flying Boat.*

Dear Rose   Vicky's godmother, who has just returned from America praising central heating, telephone service, and the drinking of cold water at breakfast; she helps in the search for a school for Vicky in E. M. Delafield's *The Diary of a Provincial Lady.* She assists the Provincial Lady in acquiring a London apartment for her literary life in *The Provincial Lady Goes Further.*

Archibald Rose   Barrister who is the nephew of Hector Rose; he is junior to Bosanquet in the prosecution of Cora Ross and Kitty Pateman in C. P. Snow's *The Sleep of Reason.*

Caroline Rose   Roman Catholic convert and author of a critical work in progress; her conversion and her interrupted love affair with Laurence Manders are elements in her emotional breakdown; fearing madness, she discovers herself to be a character in a novel in progress; she achieves her cure by investigating its plot and becoming its author in Muriel Spark's *The Comforters.*

George Arthur Rose (Hadrian VII)   Misanthropic English Pope whose earlier (unjust) expulsion from two seminaries and subsequent indigence scandalize his papacy; refusing to succumb to blackmail or to abdicate, he is assassinated by Jerry Sant on the first anniversary of his papacy in Frederick William Rolfe's *Hadrian the Seventh.*

Hector Rose   Permanent secretary in Civil Service who works for Thomas Bevill and with Lewis Eliot and joins with Bevill after the war to offer appointment of Martin Eliot as head of atomic-energy research in C. P. Snow's *The New Men.* He employs George Passant at Eliot's insistence but successfully opposes a permanent appointment for Passant in *Homecomings.* He dissuades Eliot from immediate resignation when Roger Quaife leaves government in *Corridors of Power.* He advises Eliot not to accept the offer of a ministerial post in government in *Last Things.*

Hubert Rose   Wealthy old friend of Bernard Sands; forced by Bernard to abandon his plans to seduce a child, he hangs himself when exposed in Angus Wilson's *Hemlock and After.*

Count Rosek   A music-loving Pole who lives in London; though he is a friend of Gustav Fiersen, he tries to seduce Gyp Winton Fiersen; unsuccessful, he sends Daphne Wing (Daisy Wagge) to tempt Fiersen; he helps Fiersen kidnap the baby in John Galsworthy's *Beyond.*

Rosemary   An art drafter in the New Albion advertising firm where Gordon Comstock worked a short time; she remains his girlfriend and finally becomes pregnant and marries Comstock in George Orwell's *Keep the Aspidistra Flying.*

Rosemary   Alison Murray's older sister, who has cancer of the breast; Alison believes Rosemary hates and resents her in Margaret Drabble's *The Ice Age.*

Mr. Rosenbaum   Sallow, squat member of the Republican Party and Government in Evallonia in league with Count Mastrovin in John Buchan's *The House of the Four Winds.*

Proinsias ("Frank") Rosenberg   Young-looking, short Irish psychiatrist who treats Jake Richardson; after several frustrating months of treatment, Jake leaves him in Kingsley Amis's *Jake's Thing.*

Maria Rosetti   The clever and cynical birth mother of Gabriel Swift; she is a teacher who becomes Josephine Napier's partner only after she has seen Josephine hasten Ruth (Giffard) Swift's death and has been revealed as Gabriel's mother in Ivy Compton-Burnett's *More Women Than Men.*

Colonel Ross   Head of military intelligence at the War Office; he suspects that Dalby is a double agent and masterminds the plot to uncover him, but his obsession with his country residence and cultivation of roses threatens to impede the narrator's work uncovering Dalby in Len Deighton's *The Ipcress File.*

Albert Ross   Captain of infantry whom Ellen Henshaw marries at the beginning of World War II; a smug, priggish man, he divorces Ellen when he learns that she has been a prostitute in Anthony Burgess's *The Pianoplayers.*

Cora Ross   Young woman who is the niece of George Passant; she is convicted with Kitty Pateman of torturing and murdering an eight-year-old boy in C. P. Snow's *The Sleep of Reason.*

James Ross   A young poet and an admirer of the aging literary giant Daniel House; he visits House on a remote island where a series of experiences, including House's death in a boating accident, link Ross to the elder poet's island and its influence in Roy Fuller's *The Carnal Island.*

Captain Alistair Ross-Donaldson   Amiable adjutant for top-secret Operation Apollo who introduces new members of the unit to prostitute Lucy Hazell in Kingsley Amis's *The Anti-Death League.*

Lady Rosseter   See Sally Seton.

Mr. Rossi   The bottle-factory manager who, though a family man, persistently intimidates Brenda with sexual advances in Beryl Bainbridge's *The Bottle Factory Outing.*

Signor Rossi   Italian acquaintance of Orlando King and Theodora Bates in Isabel Colegate's *Orlando at the Brazen Threshold.*

Albert (covernames: Luigi, Mario) Rossino   Italian national and a Palestinian mercenary; he controls Charlie in Italy and, with his lover Astrid Berger, destroys a bourgeois house in Verona as an act of supposed liberation in John le Carré's *The Little Drummer Girl.*

Adrian Rossiter   Effeminate draft dodger who, while on the run from the authorities for evading his National Service, stays in Laurence Sinton's house in Roy Fuller's *Fantasy and Fugue.*

Rotherham   Lieutenant aboard the flagship in C. S. Forester's *Hornblower and the Atropos.*

Amy Rottingdean   The dotty, old-fashioned former

mistress of the long-deceased author Egbert Merrymarsh; she keeps her daughter, Virginia Rottingdean, under strict control, invites Adam to inspect Merrymarsh's papers, and demands an exorbitant price for them in David Lodge's *The British Museum Is Falling Down.*

Virginia Rottingdean   The sexually curious but inexperienced young daughter of Amy Rottingdean, who keeps her strictly supervised; she attempts to seduce Adam Appleby, reveals that her mother was the mistress of the long-deceased author Egbert Merrymarsh, and shows Adam the manuscript of *Robert and Rachel,* an unpublished novel by Merrymarch, in David Lodge's *The British Museum Is Falling Down.*

Father Roughton   Thin, dark-featured clergyman who conducts the burial service for Helen Chichester-Redfern at the request of her daughter, Dinah, in John Wain's *The Pardoner's Tale.*

Mr. Round   Editor of the *Courier* who wrote a damaging article about Chester Nimmo concerning the Brome incident; he is subsequently dismissed in Joyce Cary's *Prisoner of Grace.*

Larrie Rourke   Young Irish homosexual who is the lover of John Middleton; he steals jewelry from John's mother and is killed in an automobile accident while in Europe to escape criminal prosecution in Angus Wilson's *Anglo-Saxon Attitudes.*

Barbara Rouse   A physical-education-college graduating senior; the headmistress's favorite, she is resented and disliked by the other students even before she is given the top appointment that motivates her murder in Josephine Tey's *Miss Pym Disposes.*

Sergeant Pieter Rousseau   The space-reconnaissance instrumentation expert who keeps track of the members of the expedition in Arthur C. Clarke's *Rendezvous with Rama.*

Josiah Routh (also "Mr. Tuke")   Embezzler who as Tuke, the ruthless but bland butler employed in evil conspiracies by Mr. Julius Pavia/Andrew Lumley, comes to Edward Leithen's notice in a hit-and-run accident; he is in murderous pursuit of Charles Pitt-Heron in Bokhara, but is killed after his attempt to murder Pitt-Heron in John Buchan's *The Power-House.*

Suzanne Rouvier   The practical, good-natured artist's model turned artist in W. Somerset Maugham's *The Razor's Edge.*

Andre Roux (Arsene Marie Verrue) Dark, bad-tempered, strong, dangerous thirty-five-year-old French-born superspy for hire; posing as a vacationer accompanied by a lady-friend, he photographs the top-secret French military installations using a Zeiss Contax camera identical to Josef Vadassy's and attempts to retrieve the photographs from Vadassy in Eric Ambler's *Epitaph for a Spy*.

General Rovira Commander of the Spanish land forces that join with the *Sutherland*'s crew to take the Rosas Bay in C. S. Forester's *Ship of the Line*.

Edward Rowan Member of Parliament; the father of Laura and of two older sons, he is estranged from his wife, Tania; his mistress is Sue Staunton, his wife's best friend, in Rebecca West's *The Birds Fall Down*.

Laura Eduarevna Rowan Eighteen-year-old who comes from London with mother, Tania Rowan, for a fortnight's visit in France with her grandparents, Nikolai and Sofia Diakanov; she grows in independence but also in cynical and destructive pragmatism as the marriage of her parents fails and her grandfather dies betrayed; she is introduced to the intricacies of espionage, and she survives the intrigue designed to victimize her as she joins the conspirators in murder and, instead of soaring, falls down in Rebecca West's *The Birds Fall Down*.

Captain Nigel Rowan An aide to the Provincial Governor after service in Burma; as aide he reviews several legal cases involving Indians accused of political crimes, one being the accusation of rape against Hari Kumar; Rowan recommends that Kumar be released in Paul Scott's *The Day of the Scorpion*.

Tania Rowan Mother of Laura and wife of Edward Rowan; she is the daughter of Nikolai and Sofia Diakanov in Rebecca West's *The Birds Fall Down*.

Mrs. Rowbotham Thin, anxious Forewoman of the Upholstery; she unconsciously loves difficulties in Arnold Bennett's *Imperial Palace*.

Mrs. Rowbottham Diminutive old landlady with a crinkled face and warm smile; she disarmingly blushes as she welcomes the young country hopeful Richard Larch to her London rooming house in Arnold Bennett's *A Man From the North*.

Lily Rowbottham Young, beautiful daughter of Richard Larch's London landlady; her engagement and obvious happiness accentuate Richard's loneliness in Arnold Bennett's *A Man From the North*.

Steven Rowcliffe Physician who loves Gwendolen Cartaret; he is tricked into marriage by Mary Cartaret; he allows Mary to make him comfortable and complacent, denying both his ideals of socially responsible medicine and Gwendolen's love in May Sinclair's *The Three Sisters*.

Alice Rowe Arthur Rowe's deceased wife; he is haunted by his having committed euthanasia on her in Graham Greene's *The Ministry of Fear*.

Arthur Rowe Introverted, alienated former journalist who euthanized his wife; injured by a bomb set by a spy ring during World War II, he suffers amnesia, escapes from a suspicious asylum where he is known as "Digby", and with the help of Anna Hilfe, whom he loves, aids police in uncovering the spy ring, meanwhile recovering his memory in Graham Greene's *The Ministry of Fear*.

Janet Rowe The Leonides family nanny, who supposes that Aristide Leonides was murdered by Communists; she dies of poison apparently intended for Josephine Leonides in Agatha Christie's *Crooked House*.

Mr. Rowlands Librarian at Aberdarcy Public Library who is not well liked by the members of the Libraries Committee; Vernon Gruffydd-Williams tries to hire John Lewis to be Rowlands's second in command to spite Rowlands in Kingsley Amis's *That Uncertain Feeling*.

Rowsby Woof A dog, victim of one of El-ahrairah's tricks; his story, told at a critical moment, suggests an important stratagem to Hazel in Richard Adams's *Watership Down*.

Roxanne Six-foot redhead with remarkable breasts; Roxanne is a member of the social and sexual trio of Americans who visit Celia and Quentin Villiers for a weekend of decadence in Martin Amis's *Dead Babies*.

Archibald (Archie) Roxby First husband of Mary Garton Hansyke, who marries him at age fifteen when he is ill and in his sixties; he is a clumsy lover and later an apologetic and humble man; the couple live in a wing of the Roxby mansion owned by the four Roxby brothers; Archie soon dies and his inheritance goes to their infant son, Richard Roxby; the marriage gives Mary Garton Hansyke her chance to enter the shipbuilding business in Storm Jameson's *The Lovely Ship*.

Clara Hervey Roxby Gentle, intuitive, shy older daughter of Mary Garton Hansyke Roxby Hervey and Hugh Hervey; she marries rich Nicholas Roxby after her sister, Sylvia, rejects him; widowed early, she is the mother of the younger Nicholas Roxby and Georgina Roxby in Storm Jameson's *The Voyage Home*. She recognizes Sylvia's envy of her wealth and unbroken connection with their mother and sees that Sylvia has become like their domineering, unhappy mother in *Farewell, Night; Welcome, Day*.

Nicholas Roxby A shipbuilding-family member born in 1868; his marriage to his wealthy cousin Clare Hervey reunites two powerful shipbuilding families in the late nineteenth century; upon his death at the age of thirty-four, his ten-year-old son, also named Nicholas, succeeds to Mary Hansyke Roxby Hervey's estate and the management of the Roxby shipping enterprise in Storm Jameson's *The Voyage Home*.

Nicholas Roxby (the younger) Son of Clare Hervey Roxby and Nicholas Roxby; fatherless at age ten, he is the principal heir of his grandmother Mary Hansyke Roxby Hervey; he marries Jenny Ling; he serves in the army in World War I; he meets his cousin Mary Hervey Russell at the death of their grandmother in Storm Jameson's *A Richer Dust*. He resents his grandmother's penurious monthly allowance, disappoints her with plans to enter the army at the urging of a friend, and arouses her determination to exclude his current wife from inheriting any of her estate in *The Voyage Home*. Following his divorce and release from the army, he decides to give up management of the shipping business; he lives with Hervey Russell and her eight-year-old son, Richard, for a winter of coldness, fear, and bitterness in an affair reflecting the disillusionment of the postwar generation about war and about failed marriages in *Love in Winter*.

Richard Roxby Son of Archibald Roxby and Mary Hansyke; when Richard's elderly father dies soon after marriage to fifteen-year-old Mary, she insists that their infant son become the chief heir of the Roxby shipyard fortune, taking precedence over the three surviving Roxby brothers in Storm Jameson's *The Lovely Ship*.

Roy Maturing, good-hearted, proud, searching young man, who thinks about important things in life in Rex Warner's *The Aerodrome: A Love Story*.

Joan Royce Daughter of the Master and Lady Muriel; she loves Roy Calvert, is crushed when he refuses to marry her, and continues to love him after his marriage to Rosalind Wykes in C. P. Snow's *The Light and the Dark*.

Lady Muriel Royce Wife of the Master; she is Roy Calvert's intimate friend but does not realize that her daughter is in love with Calvert in C. P. Snow's *The Light and the Dark*.

Vernon Royce Master of a Cambridge college; he supports the election of Roy Calvert to a fellowship in C. P. Snow's *The Light and the Dark*. His death in 1937 forces the election of a new college Master in *The Masters*.

General Royer French general who urges Richard Hannay to attempt to stop the three enemy conspirators from sailing from England with their stolen intelligence plans in John Buchan's *The Thirty-Nine Steps*.

Sir Archibald ("Archie") Roylance Well-bred, ebullient young Scots laird; he enlists in the Lennox Highlanders under Richard Hannay in World War I, then transfers to the Flying Corps, where he meets and admires Peter Pienaar in John Buchan's *Mr. Standfast*. Lame from a flying accident in the War, he joins Dickson McCunn and the Gorbals Die-Hards in defeating Sakskia's persecutors in *Huntingtower*. In London he meets Hannay and becomes an ally in discovering the whereabouts of the hostages and in warning Hannay about Dominick Medina's arrival for hunting in *The Three Hostages*. He meets and falls in love with Janet Raden, who inspires him to achieve the first success in his fledgling political career in *John Macnab*. Honeymooning with Janet in Olifa, South America, he joins in liberating the country from the corrupt dictatorship of Mr. Castor in *The Courts of the Morning*. After two years as a member of the House of Commons and parliamentary private secretary to the Under-Secretary for Foreign Affairs, he is obliged to go to a conference in Geneva, where he aids the Evallonian Royalists by providing a hiding place as his new manservant, "McTavish", for their leader, Prince John, in *The House of the Four Winds*.

John Robert Rozanov A celebrated philosopher who returns to Ennistone, where he fell in love with his long-dead wife, to settle his granddaughter, for whom he lusts, safely in marriage; unconscious from a suicidal overdose of sleeping pills, he is drowned by George McCaffrey, an old disciple whose friendship he has scorned in Iris Murdoch's *The Philosopher's Pupil*.

Nicolas Salmanovitch (Prisoner No. 404) Rubashov Ex-Commissar of the People now a state prisoner; accused of political divergencies, he is arrested and executed even though he is a good and faithful servant of the Party and its leader No. 1 [One] in Arthur Koestler's *Darkness at Noon*.

Linda Rubenstein   British-born wife of American Tom Rubenstein, who is a friend to Paul Armstrong in Margaret Drabble's *The Middle Ground*.

Tom Rubenstein   Husband of Linda Rubenstein; a friend of Paul Armstrong, he is a historian in Margaret Drabble's *The Middle Ground*.

David Rubin   American scientist who advises Roger Quaife on nuclear-weapons policy; he suggests to Quaife that he should abandon his attempts to shape a policy of disarmament in C. P. Snow's *Corridors of Power*.

Ruby   A three-year-old West Indian child who is forced to finish her lunch by rigid Mrs. Oakley at the day-care center where Evelyn Morton Stennett donates some of her time in Margaret Drabble's *The Middle Ground*.

Celia Rudbeck   Initially kind and considerate wife of Officer Rudbeck; she comes to Africa hoping to be enchanted by its wildness but becomes bored and hopes for a change in Joyce Cary's *Mister Johnson*.

Harry Rudbeck   Assistant District Officer in Fada whose only real desire is to build a road; he later questions the value of the road as well as of his part in signing the execution order of his friend Johnson in Joyce Cary's *Mister Johnson*.

Rudd   Physicist who leads a team of researchers competing with Walter Luke in atomic-energy research in C. P. Snow's *The New Men*.

Rudolph   An adventurous, slow-thinking, good man; he cares for people but does not think about what he should do; he simply acts on impulse in Rex Warner's *The Wild Goose Chase: An Allegory*.

Rudy   Fumbling M.I. 6 radio operator and photographer sent as James Wormold's assistant; he muddles various radio transmissions, compromising Wormold, Beatrice Severn, and himself in Graham Greene's *Our Man in Havana*.

Dr. Rüedi   Swiss psychiatrist who incompletely explains to George Smiley the tortured double nature of his patient Tatiana in John le Carré's *Smiley's People*.

Nancy Rufford   Leonora Ashburnham's ward, with whom Edward Ashburnham falls in love; although she is an innocent child, she is in league with Leonora to torture Edward; after Edward's suicide, she goes mad with guilt and grief and becomes the charge of John Dowell in Ford Madox Ford's *The Good Soldier: A Tale of Passion*.

Ruggles   The younger Mark Tietjens's closest friend; his scandalous, false reports of Christopher Tietjens's relationships with women estrange the two brothers and contribute to their father's death in Ford Madox Ford's *Some Do Not. . . .* and in *No More Parades*.

Contessa Ruhl   A Russian frequenter of the best hotels in the best seasons; she invites Denry Machin and his bride to tea; then Denry disguises himself to resemble her to humiliate Captain Deverax in Arnold Bennet's *The Card: A Story of Adventure in the Five Towns*.

Gunter Ruhling   A German who listens to Corker's speech in the park and is invited by Corker to tea; Corker deserts him and leaves him to pay the bill in John Berger's *Corker's Freedom*.

Camilla Ruiz   Wealthy, vain, cosmopolitan widow and center of aristocratic society in Cuna-Cuna who rents an apartment to the Mouth family; at her charity gala Edna Mouth is seduced by her lustful son Vittorio in Ronald Firbank's *Sorrow in Sunlight*.

Vittorio (Vitti) Ruiz   Passionate, impetuous son of the aristocratic Madame Ruiz; he seduces young Edna Mouth, indulges her developing taste for luxury and her increasing callousness toward others, and humors her security in their relationship, which he does not take seriously, in Ronald Firbank's *Sorrow in Sunlight*.

The Ruler   Eccentric, possibly schizophrenic Persian Gulf potentate; he wishes to engineer a defense pact with either America or her Allies in which his port, Abra Bay, would serve as a secret Allied base designed to offset Soviet buildup in the Middle East; Robert Halliday "interviews" him in Eric Ambler's *The Care of Time*.

Mr. Rumbold   Fishbourne china dealer whose aunt Alfred Polly rescues from "the great Fishbourne fire" in H. G. Wells's *The History of Mr. Polly*.

Bill Rumm   A former thief and safecracker; his reformation to locksmith was assisted by Lord Peter Wimsey, who consults him as to break-ins and locks in Dorothy L. Sayers's *Strong Poison*.

Agatha Runcible   An irresponsible society girl who is much involved in wild parties and eccentric behavior; she is eventually killed while driving in an automobile race in Evelyn Waugh's *Vile Bodies*.

Runi   Maquiritari Indian who accepts Mr. Abel into

his family to recuperate from illness in W. H. Hudson's *Green Mansions*.

Canon Rushbourne   College friend of Edward Pierson; he advises Edward to choose between his London parish and his daughter Noel in John Galsworthy's *Saint's Progress*.

Naomi Rushworth   An aggressive woman who becomes engaged to Dr. Penberthy in Dorothy L. Sayers's *The Unpleasantness at the Bellona Club*.

Mr. Rusper   Glottal, oval-headed Fishbourne ironmonger who gets into a street brawl with Alfred Polly; he loses his whole stock of hoses in "the great Fishbourne fire" in H. G. Wells's *The History of Mr. Polly*.

Miss Russell   Housekeeper at Fernly Park; Roger Ackroyd's will leaves her £1000; Charles Kent is her illegitimate son in Agatha Christie's *The Murder of Roger Ackroyd*.

Carlin Russell   Daughter of Captain William Russell and Sylvia Hervey Russell; she is sister of Mary Hervey Russell and Jacob Russell; born seventeen years after Jacob, she has little connection to the grown siblings; her mother finds her relationship with Carlin more comfortable than her relationship with her older daughter in Storm Jameson's *Farewell, Night; Welcome, Day*.

Mrs. Edward Russell   Captain William Russell's beloved stepmother; she sent him to serve his apprenticeship aboard a vessel in the North Sea when only thirteen; a neighbor of lonely young Sylvia Russell at Rope Terrace, she criticizes Sylvia for attending Congregational church; she is poor but gives away her money and silverware; rumored to be alcoholic, she fails to wash her hands, leans too close to babies, forces cake into the mouth of a new baby, and consequently is banished from her grandchildren by Sylvia Russell in Storm Jameson's *Farewell, Night; Welcome, Day*.

George Russell ("A. E.")   Theosophic Irish poet who criticizes Stephen Dedalus's interpretation of Shakespeare in the Irish National Library in James Joyce's *Ulysses*.

Jacob Russell   Only son of Sylvia Hervey Russell and Captain William Russell; he is brother of Mary Hervey Russell and Carlin Russell; he is bullied by his cruel father when apprenticed on his ship; he writes a long series of letters to his mother while serving in the air force in World War I; he wins medals for bravery and dies heroically in Storm Jameson's *Farewell, Night; Wel-*

come, Day. His heroism is further detailed in *A Richer Dust* and in *Love in Winter*. His memory is honored at a postwar ceremony in *Company Parade*.

Mary Hervey Russell (Hervey Russell)   Eldest child of Sylvia Hervey Russell and Captain William Russell and granddaughter of Mary Garton Hansyke; like her mother, Hervey hates domesticity; following the armistice, she works in a London editorial and advertising office and is forced to leave her three-year-old son, Richard, in the care of a woman in Yorkshire as her marriage with Thomas Penn Vane disintegrates and her husband remains in the military for several months in Storm Jameson's *Company Parade*. She fails in an attempt to mend the long alienation between her mother and her grandmother by arriving at her grandmother's deathbed just after she has slipped into a coma in *A Richer Dust*. Following her divorce from Penn Vane, Hervey takes her cousin, the younger Nicholas Roxby, as lover and lives with him and her eight-year-old son, Richard, in *Love in Winter*. From 1937 to 1943 she records her wartime travels and contacts with political and literary colleagues in France, Germany, Czechoslovakia, and the Netherlands and also looks back intermittently to her youth in Yorkshire and the disintegration of her marriage in London in *The Journal of Mary Hervey Russell*.

Sylvia Hervey Russell   Daughter born in 1868 to Mary Garton Hansyke Roxby Hervey and Hugh Hervey in Storm Jameson's *The Lovely Ship*. She is favored by her mother over her older sister, Clara, until disowned at eighteen because she rejects marriage to Nicholas Roxby; she elopes to London with Captain Rupert Ling, is deserted by him, lives impoverished and disgraced on the streets of Dieppe, and impetuously marries Captain William Russell without love; she demands that her mother give Captain Russell a job in *The Voyage Home*. Sylvia becomes the stern and possessive mother of Mary Hervey Russell, Jacob Russell, and Carlin Russell; she is the recipient of a long series of letters from her air-force son, Jacob, during World War I in *Farewell, Night; Welcome, Day*. Sylvia appears briefly as the grieving mother of her son at a military service and is a steadying support for her daughter Hervey, whose marriage has failed, in *Company Parade*.

Captain William Russell   Garrulous husband of Sylvia Hervey Russell and father of Mary Hervey, Jacob, and Carlin Russell; he sees his children so seldom that he can remember the name of only the eldest and calls all three by the same name; he is on sea voyages about nine months of each year; he wants his unappreciative wife to accompany him on voyages; sent to sea at age thirteen, he works over fifty-seven years and then is denied his full pension by the shipping company; he seeks to harden his son by bullying and by refusing praise, even when Jacob wins medals for bravery in war; he begins a happier life after the death of Sylvia, although he misses her familiar scoldings; his oldest daughter tears up the folios he kept during the years at sea in her bitterness for his failure to share himself with his family in Storm Jameson's *The Voyage Home*, in *Farewell, Night; Welcome, Day*, and in *The Journal of Mary Hervey Russell*.

The Russian   One of a series of lovers Sasha Jensen takes in Paris; he is gentle, resigned, and melancholy in Jean Rhys's *Good Morning Midnight*.

Ruth   Former lover of Sigbjørn Wilderness; she left him at the Hotel Cornada in Mexico City because he would not stop drinking in Malcolm Lowry's *Dark as the Grave Wherein My Friend Is Laid*.

Ruth   Bill Plantagenet's lost wife or lover in Malcolm Lowry's *Lunar Caustic*.

Ruth (or Edith)   Molloy's "true love" (who paid him); she died taking a bath in Samuel Beckett's *Molloy*.

Ruth (Sister Mary Joseph)   A plain, devout Catholic who becomes a nun; she teaches biology in a girls' grammar school and helps reform her order; she travels through the United States, attending peace rallies, and becomes a charismatic Catholic in David Lodge's *How Far Can You Go?*.

Rutherford   Friend who supplies Woodford Green with an account of Hugh Conway's story; his research lends circumstantial support to the existence of an inaccessible and previously unknown Tibetan paradise in James Hilton's *Lost Horizon*.

June Ryan   Emily Cartright's eleven-year-old friend, who is also her rival for Gerald's attention; June is one of an alcoholic couple's eleven self-relying children; she joins a pack of women traveling away from the city and leaves Emily without saying good-bye in Doris Lessing's *Memoirs of a Survivor*.

Marie Rycker   Pretty, young, naïve subjugated wife of Maurice Rycker; confined in a loveless marriage, she fantasizes an affair with Querry after he tells her his life story; after she discovers she is pregnant, she wrongly names Querry as the father, thereby causing

her husband to shoot Querry and kill him in Graham Greene's *A Burnt-Out Case*.

Maurice Rycker   Cold, tall, self-important, class-conscious, social-climbing French colonial; an ex-seminarian and a scrupulous man, he is also a religious hypocrite who confines God's love to Church law, prescribed ritual, and philosophy, thereby classifying love as form rather than substance; desperate to befriend Querry because he regards him as important, he later shoots him because he believes that Querry impregnated his wife in Graham Greene's *A Burnt-Out Case*.

Celia Ryder   Charles Ryder's shallow, unfaithful wife, whose social contacts and artificial enthusiasm have helped in promoting her husband's career as a painter; after Charles's involvement with Julia Flyte, she divorces him and quickly remarries in Evelyn Waugh's *Brideshead Revisited*.

Charles Ryder   A middle-class Oxford student who is socially elevated by his close friendship with Sebastian Flyte; he has had a successful career as a painter by the time he falls in love with Sebastian's sister Julia and divorces his wife; although deeply hurt by Julia's renouncing their love in order to return to the Catholic church, he himself becomes a Catholic; he serves as a captain in the British army in World War II in Evelyn Waugh's *Brideshead Revisited*.

Edward Ryder   Charles Ryder's wealthy and eccentric father, who spends his time collecting antiquities; he is remote and ironic in his relationship with his son in Evelyn Waugh's *Brideshead Revisited*.

Francis Ryle   Son of Lord Ryle; he is a principal at the Treasury and warns his father away from womanizing in C. P. Snow's *In Their Wisdom*.

James, Lord Ryle   Historian and member of the House of Lords; he is a friend of Hillmorton in C. P. Snow's *In Their Wisdom*.

Alf Rylett   Sensitive if somewhat awkward young man who tries to court Jenny Blanchard; after taking her sister, Emmy, to the theater, he finds Emmy a less exciting but more appropriate object of his affections in Frank Swinnerton's *Nocturne*.

S

Madame de S—— Emigrée Russian revolutionary in Joseph Conrad's *Under Western Eyes.*

Jorge Julio Saavedra Argentine novelist who writes novels of "machismo" and does research at the brothel with Dr. Eduardo Plarr; he offers himself as a hostage for Charley Fortnum after Dr. Plarr asks his help in Graham Greene's *The Honorary Consul.*

Ahmed Sabry An Egyptian satirical playwright and performer who entertains at a party in Cairo attended by Daniel Martin and Jane Mallory in John Fowles's *Daniel Martin.*

Connie Sachs (covername: Constance Salinger) Arthritic, overweight former Oxford don employed as Soviet expert for British Intelligence; her expertise has earned her the nickname "mother Russia"; after she has been dismissed for her knowledge of Moscow Centre, she reveals to George Smiley suppressed information that contributes to the exposure of the double agent in John le Carré's *Tinker, Tailor, Soldier, Spy.* After Smiley reinstates her, she profiles Sino-Soviet double agent Nelson Ko in *The Honourable Schoolboy.* She provides Smiley with the information on Oleg Kursky and Tatiana that sets up Karla's defection in *Smiley's People.*

Herman Sachs (Borovansky) Small, dark, brown-eyed, middle-aged Russian agent-turncoat; posing as a German Jew, he persuades Desmond Kenton to smuggle securities (Russian B2 mobilization instructions) and deliver them to him at the Hotel Josef, where he is killed by Ramon Ortega in Eric Ambler's *Uncommon Danger.*

Elias Sacrapant An agent of the Firm; he helps to ensnare Felix Charlock in Lawrence Durrell's *Tunc.* He later commits suicide by leaping from a building in *Nunquam.*

Saddler One of the landing party at Scotchman's Bay who acts as a scout; he is a petty officer who is in charge of heating the shot as the landing party open fire on escaping ships in C. S. Forester's *Lieutenant Hornblower.*

Sadie The unlovely eldest of a pack of rum-running American young people in Connecticut during Prohibition; the mistress and "kinda the niece" of a blacksmith, she shares with Augustine Penry-Herbert a hair-raising escape from pursuing police and rewards him with his sexual initiation in Richard Hughes's *The Wooden Shepherdess.*

Nikolai Sadoff (covername Erich Stinnes) K.G.B. major and Fiona Samson's chief assistant in Len Deighton's *Berlin Game.* He defects to England in *Mexico Set.* He identifies Bret Rensselaer as a mole in *London Match.*

Lady St. Cloud Brenda Last's mother; she sends sympathetic regrets that she cannot attend her grandson's funeral; she advises Brenda in her divorce proceedings in Evelyn Waugh's *A Handful of Dust.*

Reggie St. Cloud Brenda Last's pompous brother, who insists that his sister receive an unreasonable amount of alimony from Tony; his handling of this situation is a factor in Tony's rejection of his wife's demands and his subsequent trip to South America in Evelyn Waugh's *A Handful of Dust.*

Marquis de Sainte-Croix Affluent, generous benefactor of Hornblower; he is a short, plump, ageless man, who provides Hornblower with a means for survival during the tough times ashore with no naval pay in C. S. Forester's *Lieutenant Hornblower.*

Marquis de St. Eustache Wednesday of the General Council of the Anarchists of Europe; in dueling with Gabriel Syme, he reveals himself as Inspector Ratcliffe, a Scotland Yard detective, and joins the other Council members in the pursuit of Sunday in G. K. Chesterton's *The Man Who Was Thursday: A Nightmare.*

Gerald Wimsey, Lord Saint-George Lord Peter Wimsey's handsome, extravagant nephew, an Oxford undergraduate; he has glimpsed and, it is hoped, can identify the Shrewsbury College mischief maker in Dorothy L. Sayers's *Gaudy Night.*

Neil St. John Twenty-year-old university student of sociology from a working-class background who is a member of the Marxist group; he is tried for possession of drugs after the death of Bernard Kelshall and will be dismissed from the university in C. P. Snow's *The Malcontents.*

Johnny St. John John A homosexual wit and writer who is something of a friend of Wilfred Barclay, to whom he relates that he is being eaten alive by the worms of conscience in William Golding's *The Paper Men.*

Kiki St. Loy An oversexed, beautiful, popular, intelligent seventeen-year-old French girl, whose appearance in Emily McHugh's French class exposed Emily's incompetence; Constance Pinn takes her up in the hope that she can be manipulated into an affair with Blaise and/or David Gavender; instead she provides therapeutic sex for Monty Small in Iris Murdoch's *The Sacred and Profane Love Machine*.

St. Mawr A horse possessing almost supernatural power and virtue that attracts Rachel Witt in D. H. Lawrence's *St. Mawr*.

Mistress Saintserf ("Aunt Grizel") Katrine Yester's aunt and companion at Calidon; she is sympathetic to the love between Katrine and David Sempill and grieves for Katrine's death in John Buchan's *Witch Wood*.

Akira Sakazaki Japanese translator of the novels of Ronald Frobisher; he meets Persse McGarrigle in a bar in Tokyo in David Lodge's *Small World*.

Dol Sakil Rol Sakil's daughter, who becomes Aoz Roon's wife in Brian W. Aldiss's *Helliconia Spring*.

Rol Sakil A midwife and storyteller who relates the history of the generations from Si to Little Yuli in Brian W. Aldiss's *Helliconia Spring*.

Sakskia Beautiful young Russian princess of great family who is persecuted and imprisoned with her cousin Eugenia at Huntingtower House on the Scottish coast; her courage and gallantry, with the help of Dickson McCunn and Gorbals Die-Hards, save her jewels, overcome her enemies, and unite her with her lover, Alexis Nicolaevitch (Alexander Nicholson), in John Buchan's *Huntingtower*.

Mrs. Salad Old, working-class former servant of Gerald Middleton when he was the lover of Dollie Stokesay; she is fined for theft with a warning of imprisonment in Angus Wilson's *Anglo-Saxon Attitudes*.

Vin Salad Grandson of Mrs. Salad; he is a waiter who moves in the London circle of homosexuals and warns Gerald Middleton about the bad influence Larrie Rourke has on John Middleton in Angus Wilson's *Anglo-Saxon Attitudes*.

Dr. David Salaman Jewish physician and friend of Sergeant Jebb; when the two men in 1945 found themselves walking on dead bodies at an abandoned Nazi labor camp, Salaman's face reflected pity, anger, and curiosity; Jebb perceptively recognizes the same expression on the doctor's face when Salaman tells him of the choice he must make in a "short interval" in Storm Jameson's *There Will Be a Short Interval*.

Saleh The Waziri's boy who initially has the Waziri's blessings; he is later beaten and thrown in prison when his usefulness ends in Joyce Cary's *Mister Johnson*.

Salim (covernames: Yanuka, Michel) Khalil's treacherous younger brother and a Palestinian terrorist qua exchange student in Munich; he becomes Charlie's phantom lover and another brutally murdered victim in Marty Kurtz's operation to assassinate Palestinian bomb makers in John le Carré's *The Little Drummer Girl*.

Salisbury Barrister who is beginning his practice out of Herbert Getliffe's chambers when Lewis Eliot becomes a pupil there in C. P. Snow's *Time of Hope*.

Marc Sallafranque Wealthy French auto manufacturer, compulsive gambler, and second husband of Isabelle Terry; short, fat, candid, and humble, Marc is reunited with her after she rethinks her decision to divorce in Rebecca West's *The Thinking Reed*.

Sally Henry Field's mistress in Isabel Colegate's *Agatha*.

Sally A doctor who is envied by her friend Kate Fletcher Armstrong because she has a "proper job" in Margaret Drabble's *The Middle Ground*.

Norbert Salt Highly nervous American ballet dancer with the Isabel Cornwallis Ballet Company; he temporarily lives with Montgomery Pew in Colin MacInnes's *City of Spades*.

Mr. Salter A lecturer on constitutional history at the local university who interviews John Lewis for the sub-librarian job and argues with Mr. Jones about the importance of drama in Kingsley Amis's *That Uncertain Feeling*.

Saltoun Colleague who Arnold Condorex thinks despises him because of his less advantaged background and whom he in turn despises for coming from a privileged class in Rebecca West's *Harriet Hume, A London Fantasy*.

Mr. Salvatini The boss at the dress-house who fires Sasha Jensen in Jean Rhys's *Good Morning Midnight*.

Sam Half of "Sam 'n Eric", a pair of twins always mentioned in tandem; they typify people of good will who behave as decently as possible but eventually capitulate to evil in William Golding's *Lord of the Flies*.

Sam Watt's fellow insane-asylum inmate, to whom Watt tells his adventures in Samuel Beckett's *Watt*.

Lame-Foot Sam Elderly Jamaican who entertains the Bas-Thornton children with stories; he is killed by lightning during the hurricane as they watch in Richard Hughes's *A High Wind in Jamaica*.

Sambo African baby and one of the supernormals of John Wainwright's Pacific island colony in Olaf Stapledon's *Odd John: A Story Between Jest and Earnest.*

Iolanthe Samiou A young prostitute who has an affair with Felix Charlock; she becomes a film star before dying of cancer resulting from paraffin injections in her breasts in Lawrence Durrell's *Tunc.*

Iolanthe Samiou (2) An android created in the image of Iolanthe Samiou; she becomes a seducer and murderess before leaping to her death with Julian Pehlevi from the top of St. Paul's Cathedral in *Nunquam.*

Samson Richard Turner's elderly native house servant, who resigns shortly after Turner's marriage because of Mary Turner's terrible temper and rudeness in Doris Lessing's *The Grass Is Singing.*

Bernard (Bernie) Samson A second-generation British espionage officer who exposes his wife, Fiona, as a K.G.B. colonel and assists Dr. Munte's defection in Len Deighton's *Berlin Game.* He persuades K.G.B. major Erich Stinnes to defect in *Mexico Set.* He discovers a mole in the London Office and exonerates Bret Rensselaer and liberates Werner Volkmann in *London Match.*

Fiona Kimber-Hutchinson Samson (codenames: "Gusseisen", "Pig Iron", "Ironfoot") A K.G.B. colonel who is exposed by her husband and fellow British espionage agent Bernard Samson while working in Whitehall Intelligence Department as a mole in Len Deighton's *Berlin Game.* She is Bernard's opponent in Major Stinnes's defection in *Mexico Set.* She orders Pavel Moskvin's death and plans Stinnes's return in *London Match.*

Patty Samuals A politically involved woman who became a communist when she was twenty but later abandoned that cause; she has an intimate relationship with Mark Coldridge and ultimately has a nervous breakdown in Doris Lessing's *The Four-Gated City.*

Samuel Young racetrack employee who pays Spicer his winnings just before Pinkie Brown kills Spicer in Graham Greene's *Brighton Rock.*

Captain Samuels Psychiatrist who treats Susan (Layton) Bingham when she has a nervous breakdown after the death of her husband, Edward, in Paul Scott's *The Day of the Scorpion.*

Fructuoso Sanabria ("Chief of Gardens") Along with the Chief of Rostrums and the Chief of the Municipality (Zuzugoitea), one of the three militiamen who persecute Geoffrey Firmin at the Farolito in Malcolm Lowry's *Under the Volcano.*

Senora Sanchez The madam of a brothel in a small northern Argentianian city; Clara Fortnum, wife of the Honorary Consul, worked for her in Graham Greene's *The Honorary Consul.*

Professor Luis Sanchez (code identification: 59200/5/3) See James Wormold.

Mr. Sandal Ashby family solicitor; he is the first to be taken in by Brat Farrar's impersonation of Patrick Ashby in Josephine Tey's *Brat Farrar.*

Lady Claudine Sandbach Sister of Edward, Lord Campion and wife of Paul Sandbach in Ford Madox Ford's *Some Do Not. . . .*

Paul Sandbach Dark, bull-dog-faced, violent-mannered, lame husband of Lady Claudine; flagrantly unfaithful to his wife, he spreads rumors about Christopher Tietjens's supposed infidelities in Ford Madox Ford's *Some Do Not. . . .*

Agnes (Aggie) Sandeman Cousin of Lucia Lucas and of Adele, Lady Brixton; she introduces Lucia to London society in E. F. Benson's *Lucia in London.*

Sanders Young pilot who tells Rutherford and Woodford Green about a highjacked plane that was never recovered in James Hilton's *Lost Horizon.*

Clifford Sanders Small, nervous, petty-criminal brother of Julia Delmore; he lives on Jake Driver's income and tries to extort money from both Jake and Gus Howkins by claiming Julia is kidnapped; he is a character in the story Giles Hermitage writes in John Wain's *The Pardoner's Tale.*

Milly Sanders Kindly Irish landlady to Nancy Hawkins and other tenants in Muriel Spark's *A Far Cry from Kensington.*

Sanderson Curator of the insect house at the zoological gardens who is arrested and jailed during the government of the Uni-Europeans after the war in Angus Wilson's *The Old Men at the Zoo.*

Trixie Sanderson One of the adolescent girls in the north London school in Dorothy Richardson's *Backwater.*

Colonel Sandmeyer Member of the US Technical Intelligence who reveals to Reinhold Hoffmann that Konrad Schneider is still alive in Arthur C. Clarke's *Childhood's End.*

Sandra   A little girl living in the Midlands, whom Beatrice forbids her children to play with because she uses vulgar words, plays in the outside lavatory, and speaks in an incomprehensible accent; Rosamund Stacey briefly considers naming her daughter after her in Margaret Drabble's *The Millstone.*

Bernard Sands   A famous English novelist; he is a fifty-seven-year-old ex-schoolteacher who has begun to practice homosexuality with young men; he celebrates his success in securing a government endowment for Vardon Hall, a writers' commune, before he dies of heart failure in Angus Wilson's *Hemlock and After.*

Elizabeth Sands   Daughter of Bernard and Ella; she works for a women's fashion magazine, falls in love with Terence Lambert, her father's ex-lover, and wishes to marry him in Angus Wilson's *Hemlock and After.*

Emma Sands   A famous detective-story writer, who is the much-regretted former lover of Hugh Peronett; she takes revenge for Hugh's cowardice in not having left his wife by engineering his son Randall's helpless passion for Lindsay Rimmer, and makes her triumph clear to Hugh after he has sold his beloved Tintoretto nude to finance Randall's elopement in Iris Murdoch's *An Unofficial Rose.*

Evelyn (Ella) Sands   Wife of Bernard; she suffers from a mental breakdown, suspects her husband has begun to practice homosexuality, and after his death acts to carry out his wishes in Angus Wilson's *Hemlock and After.*

Isobel Sands   Bernard's sister, who is a professor of English literature; she sits on a Communist political committee and announces her intention to resign her professorship in Angus Wilson's *Hemlock and After.*

James Sands   Son of Bernard and Ella; he is a lawyer who disapproves of his father's life and opinions and abets his wife in raising their children contrary to his parents' wishes in Angus Wilson's *Hemlock and After.*

Sir Lewis Sands   A historian and member of the Rama committee; he advocates calm in studying Rama in Arthur C. Clarke's *Rendezvous with Rama.*

Nicholas Sands   Young son of James and Sonia; he enjoys disobeying his parents in Angus Wilson's *Hemlock and After.*

Rachel Sands   Member of George Passant's group; she is fired from her job because of her association with Passant and because of the group's life-style in C. P. Snow's *Strangers and Brothers.*

Sonia Sands   Wife of James; she dislikes her mother-in-law, Ella, and punishes Ella with public announcement of Bernard's homosexuality in Angus Wilson's *Hemlock and After.*

Sanford   Director of administration for Leclerc's nostalgic but absurd Department; he assumes control of Registry while Adrian Haldane works on Operation Mayfly in John le Carré's *The Looking-Glass War.*

Albert Sanger   Brilliant composer of grandiose operas who leaves his native England and roves the world acquiring three wives, various lovers, and seven (known) children before dying in the Karindehutte, a chalet in the Austrian Tyrol; jealous, vulgar, and possessing a "naphtha-flare genius", he dies and leaves the world his musical works, his talented children, and a devoted and gifted disciple, Lewis Dodd, in Margaret Kennedy's *The Constant Nymph.*

Antonia (Tony) Sanger   Beautiful, proud, reckless, and generous daughter of Albert Sanger and his second wife; wildly independent and intelligent, she captures the heart of Jacob Birnbaum and marries him, later bearing his child in Margaret Kennedy's *The Constant Nymph.*

Caryl Sanger   Handsome, even-tempered son of Albert Sanger and his first wife; Caryl writes music, handles his father's business affairs, and together with his sister Kate manages the household in Margaret Kennedy's *The Constant Nymph.*

Kate Sanger   Daughter of Albert Sanger and his first wife; Kate runs the Sanger household and is honest, hard-working, and liked by all; she has a promising voice in Margaret Kennedy's *The Constant Nymph.*

Paulina (Lina) Sanger   Wild, gay, brilliant daughter of Albert Sanger and his second wife in Margaret Kennedy's *The Constant Nymph.*

Sebastian Sanger   Small, fair, polite, ten-year-old son of Albert Sanger and his second wife; of Sanger's wild children, he has managed to retain some manners and gentlemanly ways in Margaret Kennedy's *The Constant Nymph.*

Teresa (Tessa) Sanger   Quick-witted, thin, pale daughter of Albert Sanger and his second wife; Teresa loves Lewis Dodd devotedly and is heartbroken when he marries another, but she later runs away with him, only to die shortly after from a heart condition in Margaret Kennedy's *The Constant Nymph.*

Maung (Ko S'la) San Hla   A lazy and dirty native

manservant who is devoted to John Flory in George Orwell's *Burmese Days.*

Sankey Gossip-mongering, white-haired, skinny surgeon who takes Bush to hospital in C. S. Forester's *Lieutenant Hornblower.*

Sankey Old Jolyon Forsyte's servant who presents an unconventional appearance in John Galsworthy's *The Man of Property.*

Duchess of San Martino A permanent resident of Nepenthe; she is an indiscriminate American who depends on Don Francesco's "guidance" and makes plans to join the Catholic church in Norman Douglas's *South Wind.*

Jerry Sant Fatuous socialist and past object of George Arthur Rose's public derision who, failing in his attempt to blackmail Hadrian, assassinates him in Frederick William Rolfe's *Hadrian the Seventh.*

Sarah A London prostitute who reminds Charles Smithson of Sarah Woodruff in John Fowles's *The French Lieutenant's Woman.*

Sarah A Cambridge friend of Rosamund Stacey; she is now a wife and mother in Margaret Drabble's *The Millstone.*

Sarah Maid for the Darke family; always sulky, she becomes hostile in the presence of Rachel Darke in Mary Webb's *The House in Dormer Forest.*

Sarah Harriet Lovatt's sister, suffering from marital problems, whose fourth child, Amy, is born with Down's syndrome in Doris Lessing's *The Fifth Child.*

Dr. Sargent Regular attendee at Corker's slide shows and lectures who loves them because they are full of facts in John Berger's *Corker's Freedom.*

Stefan Saridza (Colonel Robinson) Stiff-elbowed, balding, moustached, cruel Bulgarian man; a longtime powerful political saboteur, he is employed by Pan-Eurasian Petroleum to steal the B2 mobilization plans for the company and is thwarted by Desmond Kenton and the Zaleshoffs in Eric Ambler's *Uncommon Danger.*

Mrs. Sarn Widowed mother of Prue and Gideon, who poisons her with foxglove as an economy measure in Mary Webb's *Precious Bane.*

Gideon Sarn Greedy, cruel Shropshire farmer; although he is sole heir of the farm after his father's death, he poisons his mother to save the cost of her food and care; he causes the suicide of Jancis Beguildy,

who drowns with their baby, and he makes a slave of his sister, Prudence Sarn, by promising he will eventually help her get surgery for her harelip; his precious bane is the love of riches which finally destroys everyone close to him, and he dies a suicide in Mary Webb's *Precious Bane.*

Prudence (Prue) Sarn Gideon Sarn's sister, who serves as his slave for years in hope that he will pay for surgical repair of her harelip; the deformity makes her an outcast but also gives her sensitivity and inner strength; superstitious villagers view the harelip as punishment for satanic elements in her or her mother; she loves Kester Woodseaves from the moment she sees him; she is narrator of Mary Webb's *Precious Bane.*

Saruman the White Powerful head of the wizards' council; he is consumed by the desire to possess the power of the One Ring and leads evil men and dwarves in an attack on those who keep the ring in J. R. R. Tolkien's *The Fellowship of the Ring.* He is deposed from power by Gandalf and sent from the Shire by Frodo Baggins in *The Two Towers.* He is killed by his own evil servant in *The Return of the King.*

Sasha The Russian princess with whom the male Orlando falls in love during the Great Frost on the Thames, 1604; when the thaw melts the Thames, Sasha breaks Orlando's heart, betraying him by sailing back to Russia in Virginia Woolf's *Orlando: A Biography.*

Sass (Disastrous) Black servant boy who leaves the Cosway family in Jean Rhys's *Wide Sargasso Sea.*

Sataal A priest who teaches Yuli the ways of civilization in Brian W. Aldiss's *Helliconia Spring.*

SatoriIrvrash Ex-chancellor of Borlien; he believes old documents are more credible than church doctrine and reveals the truth about religious belief and human history on Helliconia in Brian W. Aldiss's *Helliconia Summer.*

SatoriIrvrash (the younger) An Earth philosopher named for the Borlienese Chancellor on Helliconia; he determines the true nature of mankind in Brian W. Aldiss's *Helliconia Winter.*

Mrs. Satterthwaite The wealthy widowed mother of Sylvia Tietjens, about whom she has no illusions in Ford Madox Ford's *Some Do Not. . . .*

Mr. Saunter Reclusive World War I veteran who raises poultry in the village of Great Mop and serves as an example to Lolly Willowes of a self-sufficient man in Sylvia Townsend Warner's *Lolly Willowes: or, the Loving Huntsman.*

Sauron Most powerful force of evil who searches for and leads men to war in an attempt to gain the One Ring which would bring him ultimate, all-encompassing power in J. R. R. Tolkien's *The Fellowship of the Ring,* in *The Two Towers,* and in *The Return of the King.*

Fabrice de Sauveterre A wealthy French duke who aids Linda Radlett when she is stranded in Paris after leaving her second husband; Linda becomes his contented mistress in Paris until he sends her to England at the outbreak of World War II; he is straightforward, passionate, and the love of Linda's life; he is shot by Nazis at about the time of Linda's death in childbirth in Nancy Mitford's *The Pursuit of Love.* He is a Montdore houseguest in *Love in a Cold Climate.*

Savage Midshipman aboard the *Sutherland* in C. S. Forester's *Ship of the Line.*

Mr. Savage Self-assured professional man; he is head of the detective agency from which Maurice Bendrix employs a detective to follow Sarah Miles in Graham Greene's *The End of the Affair.*

John (the Savage) Savage Biological son of Linda and Thomas; his ignorant awe of civilization compels him to visit the "brave new world"; taken to England by Bernard Marx, he quickly becomes disenchanted, eventually seeking isolation; after murdering Lenina Crowne he kills himself in a moment of self-loathing in Aldous Huxley's *Brave New World.*

Yakov Yefremovich Savelyev ("Goethe"; codenames: Pyotr, Daniil, Bluebird) Distinguished dissident Russian physicist; he is inspired to humanitarian treason by Barley Blair's drunken statements at a writer's *dacha* in Peredelkino; his rambling manuscript, sent to Blair but intercepted by British Intelligence bureaucrats, claims that the East-West balance of terror is a bluff because Soviet telemetry and missiles are defective and Soviet officials have lied to their political superiors to protect their status and privileges in John le Carré's *The Russia House.*

Colin Saville A coal miner's son who is sent to college and becomes a teacher; he neither enjoys his education nor likes his work, but he feels responsible for his brothers and their success; his attempt to become a poet also gives him no satisfaction in David Storey's *Saville.*

Ellen Saville Mother of Colin Saville and wife of Harry, a poor coal miner, in David Storey's *Saville.*

Harry Saville Poor, working-class coal miner who is determined that Colin, the eldest of his three living sons, will have a college education in David Storey's *Saville.*

Quin Savory Self-congratulatory author of *The Great Gay Round* who is interviewed by Mabel Warren and thus provides her cover as she stalks Richard Czinner in Graham Greene's *Stamboul Train.*

Gracie Savotte Beautiful, vivacious, intelligent young daughter of the millionaire Sir Henry Savotte; determined not to be a frivolous socialite, she attracts Evelyn Orcham into a brief affair because she thinks his instincts in all things match hers; she abandons him because he fails her test of his priorities, publishes an impressive book of her thoughts, and marries an aristocrat who is devoted to her in Arnold Bennett's *Imperial Palace.*

Sir Henry Savotte Small, spry, decisive baronet and millionaire; he accepts his beloved daughter Gracie's independent, unorthodox ways; he accepts only total success in his business ventures and wins in bringing about the merger of the Imperial Palace with a group of other luxury hotels under his control in Arnold Bennett's *Imperial Palace.*

Eric Sawbridge Young physicist from the same town as Martin and Lewis Eliot; he works with Martin and Walter Luke on atomic energy research and confesses to spying for Communists in C. P. Snow's *The New Men.*

Captain Sawyer Shaggy, long-haired, paranoid, insane Captain of the *Renown*; mysteriously injured in a fall through the hatchway attempting to catch "mutineers", he becomes a terror-ridden invalid; he dies at the hands of a Spanish prisoner during the prison break aboard the *Renown* in C. S. Forester's *Lieutenant Hornblower.*

Priscilla Saxe Bradley Pearson's younger sister; unskilled and spoiled, she left school early, becoming a second-rate society tart; she marries the father of her aborted child and leaves him after a childless marriage of many years; she kills herself with sleeping pills in Iris Murdoch's *The Black Prince.*

Roger Saxe The unaffectionate, mindlessly selfish husband of Priscilla; after her suicide he marries his pregnant mistress Marigold in Iris Murdoch's *The Black Prince.*

Lord Saxenden (Snubby Bantham) Public-school chum of Hilary Cherrell; he fails to be effective in helping Hubert Cherrell in John Galsworthy's *Maid In Waiting.*

Mr. Saxton Farmer who in desperation begins to shoot at the armies of wild rabbits that are his landlord's livelihood and that are devouring his crops; losing his lease, he emigrates with his wife to Canada, leaving his grown-up children, George and Emily, in England in D. H. Lawrence's *The White Peacock.*

Emily Saxton George's independent, gentle, beautiful sister, a schoolteacher sensitive to life's tragedies; after years as the object of Cyril Beardsall's tepid admiration she makes a happy marriage with Tom Renshaw in D. H. Lawrence's *The White Peacock.*

George Saxton Handsome, muscular, sensitive son of a farmer; he can never bring forth the assertiveness which would win his beloved Lettie Beardsall from her richer suitor; his initially successful marriage to his cousin sours, and his revived unsatisfied passion for Lettie drives him to drink in D. H. Lawrence's *The White Peacock.*

Gertie Saxton George Saxton's only daughter, whom he greatly prefers to his sons; her infancy is the happiest period of his married life; her later alliance with her mother in contempt of him contributes to his decline in D. H. Lawrence's *The White Peacock.*

Meg Saxton George Saxton's handsome, gregarious, prosperous cousin, who operates and later inherits a pub; he marries her soon after the marriage of Lettie Beardsall, and they are at first happy; her children and business eventually occupy her affections in D. H. Lawrence's *The White Peacock.*

Henrietta Sayce The ten-year-old daughter of Penny Sayce; she gassed a neighbor's cat "in the interest of science", is reported to be a user of LSD, and is blackmailing her brother; she is asked to be one of Gracie Tisbourne's bridesmaids; she dies in an auto accident in Iris Murdoch's *An Accidental Man.*

Oliver Sayce Henrietta's older brother and blackmail victim; he is a homosexual antiques dealer in Iris Murdoch's *An Accidental Man.*

Penny Sayce A generally unlucky recent widow and country neighbor of Sir Charles Odmore in Iris Murdoch's *An Accidental Man.*

Rose Sayer The spinster sister and assistant of a missionary in Central Africa at the outbreak of World War I; after his death, motivated by patriotic fervor for England, she and the initially reluctant Charlie Allnutt travel down the Ulanga River by boat on a mission to bombard a German vessel with a hand-made torpedo in C. S. Forester's *The African Queen.*

Samuel Sayer The staunchly religious missionary brother of Rose, who has been his assistant for ten years until his death in war-ravaged Central Africa in C. S. Forester's *The African Queen.*

Miss Sayers An American agent who wants to handle Mark Coldridge's new novels, as long as he does not write anything offensive about politics or social issues in Doris Lessing's *The Four-Gated City.*

Arthur Saywell The cold, bookish, mother-dominated Rector of Papplewick whose wife, Cynthia, the mother of Yvette and Lucille, ran off with a passionate younger man in D. H. Lawrence's *The Virgin and the Gipsy.*

Cissie Saywell A pale, pious, vitriolic woman of suppressed emotions; although over forty, she dedicates her life fully to her mother and consequently makes life miserable for her nieces, Yvette and Lucille Saywell, in D. H. Lawrence's *The Virgin and the Gipsy.*

Cynthia Saywell The scandalously unrestrained and beautiful wife of Arthur, the Rector of Papplewick; she abandoned her daughters Yvette and Lucille and her husband to run off with a poor but passionate younger man; her presence is deeply felt in the Saywell housewell throughout D. H. Lawrence's *The Virgin and the Gipsy.*

Fred Saywell A selfish, life-denying, unvital old bachelor, who is Arthur's brother and Yvette's uncle; he lives unhappily with his family at the Papplewick rectory in D. H. Lawrence's *The Virgin and the Gipsy.*

Granny Saywell A repressive matriarch in her seventies; crippled and failing in health, she dominates the lives of her three adult children and her granddaughters, Yvette and Lucille; she is washed away in a flood at the close of D. H. Lawrence's *The Virgin and the Gipsy.*

Lucille Saywell The more practical, more repressed, and more morally conventional of the two daughters of clergyman Arthur Saywell in D. H. Lawrence's *The Virgin and the Gipsy.*

Yvette Saywell A rebel against life at the repressive, unvital Papplewick rectory; she slips off to befriend an older couple who live together out of wedlock and visits a caravan of Gypsies; a handsome, insouciant Gypsy, Joe Boswell, stirs Yvette's passions, and after he rescues her from a flood, she spends the night with him; she learns his name only after he has fled in D. H. Lawrence's *The Virgin and the Gipsy.*

Nini Scagg Old acquaintance who moved from the

village of Mediaville to the city of Cuna-Cuna long before the Mouths; Ahmadou Mouth's hopes that she will be of assistance socially are dashed by the discovery that she has become an exotic dancer in a brothel in Ronald Firbank's *Sorrow in Sunlight*.

Mr. Scaife Scotland Yard agent and former Navy man sent by his chief, Mr. Macgillivray, to assist Richard Hannay in his search for the location of the crucial thirty-nine steps in John Buchan's *The Thirty-Nine Steps*.

Gerald Scales Profligate, insensitive salesman; he seduces Sophia Baines into an elopement, speedily wastes his inheritance, abandons her in Paris, wanders to South America, and returns to die a pauper at his cousin's door in Arnold Bennett's *The Old Wives Tale*.

Ma Scantion Midwife and first female member of the apothecary corps; she tends the first victims of bone fever in Oldorando in Brian W. Aldiss's *Helliconia Spring*.

Major Scarlet Father of Isabel; he is a militarist whose patriotic enthusiasm causes Lavender to hallucinate that he is in the presence of a Prussian in John Galsworthy's *The Burning Spear: Being the Experiences of Mr. John Lavender in Time of War*.

Isabel (Aurora) Scarlet Nurse who is a neighbor of John Lavender; she is interrogated by Aunt Rose about Lavender's sanity; she calls Lavender "Don Pickwixote", and catches him in her arms when he attempts self-immolation in John Galsworthy's *The Burning Spear: Being the Experiences of Mr. John Lavender in Time of War*.

Emmanuel (Emma) Scarlett-Taylor A university student who is Tom McCaffrey's friend; a gifted countertenor, he has decided against a career as a professional singer and is trying to stop singing; sexually ambivalent, he is attracted to the thin, boyish Pearl Scotney in Iris Murdoch's *The Philosopher's Pupil*.

Adam Scarr Used-car dealer who secretes Hans-Dieter Mundt's car in Battersea, London; he is drowned by Mundt to draw George Smiley off Mundt's trail in John le Carré's *Call for the Dead*.

Reinhold Schäder Nazi official who likes Roy Calvert; he sends Romantowski to Switzerland to try to lure Calvert to Germany after the war begins in C. P. Snow's *The Light and the Dark*.

Wilbur Schäfer Brash, robust, informal American ambassador; he has no sensitivity for intrigue even though his wartime affair with a Swedish countess

might be an information leak in W. Somerset Maugham's *Ashenden: or The British Agent*.

James Schafter An American writer who gets a section of Anna Wulf's journal published in a small American magazine in Doris Lessing's *The Golden Notebook*.

Mr. Schatzweiler An American Jewish businessman who goes into the old-furniture business with Christopher Tietjens after World War I and embezzles most of the profits in Ford Madox Ford's *The Last Post*.

Ed Schaumwein The stereotypical, vulgar American film producer; he hires Ronald Beard to write a film script in Los Angeles in Anthony Burgess's *Beard's Roman Women*.

Lothar Scheidemann Younger brother of Wolff; an ardent, idealistic young Nazi, he takes part in the Munich putsch in Richard Hughes's *The Fox in the Attic*. He is astonished in the moments before his execution by firing squad during the blood bath of "reprisals" against Ernst Röhm in *The Wooden Shepherdess*.

Wolff Scheidemann Young Nazi and political assassin who hides out in the von Kessins' attics, where he plans the murders of everyone who offends him — especially Augustine Penry-Herbert and Mitzi von Kessen — but finally hangs himself in Richard Hughes's *The Fox in the Attic*.

Dieter Schelm Intelligent senior official of West German Intelligence on loan to NATO's Combined Intelligence Service Bureau; he recruits Robert Halliday as a liaison between Karlis Zander and his people and NATO Intelligence in order to facilitate the Abra Bay port negotiations in Eric Ambler's *The Care of Time*.

Eleazer Schenk Self-complacent leader of the California "Big Oak Band"; he plays upon a green and yellow grand piano in the main restaurant of the hotel in Arnold Bennett's *Imperial Palace*.

Lizzie Scherer An appealing, inept actress who became a successful performer under Charles Arrowby's direction; her passionate devotion to Charles has long outlasted their affair, though she has become the companionate housemate of the homosexual Gilbert Opian in Iris Murdoch's *The Sea, the Sea*.

Azik Schiff Wealthy Jewish businessman who is married to Rosalind (Wykes) Calvert; he invites Lewis and Margaret (Hollis) Eliot to a theater party in C. P. Snow's *The Sleep of Reason*. He dotes on his son David in *Last Things*. He is a guest at the wedding of Jenny Rastall and Lord Lorimer in *In Their Wisdom*.

David Schiff   Son of Azik and Rosalind (Wykes) Schiff; he is in day school; he is reported in the obituary as dying in 1967 from an accident in C. P. Snow's *Last Things.*

Emil Schimler (alias Paul Heinberger)   Middle-aged, hollow-cheeked German; a former newspaper editor and concentration-camp survivor hiding from the Gestapo because of his free-press newspaper-smuggling activities and befriended by Albert Keche, he is discovered and taken back to Germany in Eric Ambler's *Epitaph for a Spy.*

Colonel Charles Schlegel III   A retired U.S. Marine Corps Air Wing colonel and the narrator's new American superior; he suspects Steve Champion in Len Deighton's *Yesterday's Spy.* He takes over the War Games center and directs the submarine commander to risk his vessel and its classified machinery in a mission under the Arctic ice in *Spy Story.*

Helen Schlegel   Margaret Schlegel's clever but quixotic sister; her earlier engagement to Paul Wilcox lasted one night; moral outrage leads to the expression of pity that is her sexual relationship with Leonard Bast; she bears his child in E. M. Forster's *Howards End.*

Margaret (Meg) Schlegel   The more sensible of a pair of sisters whose unconventional bent for culture is attributable to their half-German ancestry; she becomes Ruth Wilcox's sympathetic friend and marries the widowed Henry Wilcox in E. M. Forster's *Howards End.*

Theobald (Tibby) Schlegel   Helen and Margaret Schlegel's aloof and unsympathetic brother in E. M. Forster's *Howards End.*

Schmidt   Arthur Norris's blackmailing secretary in Christopher Isherwood's *Mr. Norris Changes Trains.*

Anna Schmidt   Uninspired member of the acting company at the Josefstadt Theatre; a Hungarian whose father was a Nazi, she has falsified papers supplied by her lover Harry Lime; at first rejecting Rollo Martins's advances, she goes off with him after the second funeral — the actual one — for Lime at the end of Graham Greene's *The Third Man and the Fallen Idol.*

Hans Schmidt   Waldemar's friend who invites him and Christopher Isherwood to visit at Ambrose's in Christopher Isherwood's *Down There on a Visit.*

Joy Schmidt   Karel's miserable, sometimes violently destructive wife; her leaving her family for a Lesbian commune facilitates the permanent union of Karel and Frances Wingate in Margaret Drabble's *The Realms of Gold.*

Karel Schmidt   Frances Wingate's former lover, a patient and self-sacrificing history professor constitutionally unable to resist his students' importunities; his marriage is violently unhappy; he cannot understand Frances's suspension of a loving relationship that gave happiness to both in Margaret Drabble's *The Realms of Gold.*

Schmule   Wrestler also known as the "Hammer" and "Maccabeus" among his athletically enthusiastic friends; he prides himself on physical development and blames his obscurity upon his betrothed lover, Sonia, in Wolf Mankowitz's *A Kid for Two Farthings.*

Knorad Schneider   Brilliant rocket engineer in charge of creating the space ship for the first Russian manned moon landing in Arthur C. Clarke's *Childhood's End.*

Eva Schnerb   Gossip columnist who describes in the popular gazettes the activities and raiment of the court society of Pisuerga at their many parties and events and who thereby indulges the fantasy of common reader Madame Wetme in Ronald Firbank's *The Flower Beneath the Foot.*

Bernie Schnitz   A fat American with a cigar whom Adam Appleby encounters at the British Museum; he is buying a library for his college in Colorado and offers Appleby a part-time job as an assistant in David Lodge's *The British Museum Is Falling Down.*

Anthony Schofield   The young gardener who represents to Ursula Brangwen an old, traditional, and stifling way of life; Ursula rejects his marriage proposal in D. H. Lawrence's *The Rainbow.*

Maggie Schofield   Anthony's sister, who is Ursula Brangwen's girlhood friend in D. H. Lawrence's *The Rainbow.*

Mr. Schomberg   Corrupt hotel owner in Sourabaya who, jealous over Lena's affection for Axel Heyst, misinforms a pair of rapacious gamblers that Heyst has a fortune, resulting in the gamblers' murder of Lena in Joseph Conrad's *Victory: An Island Tale.*

Myra Schoonmaker   American heiress whom Lady Constance Keeble has not met but imagines to be suitable matrimonial material for Ronnie Fish; Sue Brown takes Myra's identity in visiting Blandings Castle in P. G. Wodehouse's *Fish Preferred.*

Herr Schraub   Teacher of history to the pupils in the Hanover school in Dorothy Richardson's *Pointed Roofs.*

Fraulein Schroeder   Adaptable, formerly well-off landlady of the boarding house where William Bradshaw lives in Christopher Isherwood's *Mr. Norris Changes Trains.* Christopher Isherwood lives in her boardinghouse in *Goodbye to Berlin.*

Max Schurer   Foreign chef who wants to leave England; he warns that a war is coming in J. B. Priestley's *Lost Empires.*

Schwartz   A small-minded, unforgiving German Legionnaire; he leads the plot to kill Color Sergeant Lejaune in Percival Christopher Wren's *Beau Geste.*

Hezekiah Schwarz   Secretary and accomplice of the bogus spiritualist "Princess Popoffski" in E. F. Benson's *"Queen Lucia".*

Henry Scobie   Conscientious, troubled Catholic Assistant Police Commissioner in an African port; he is married to Louise Scobie, whose ill health he blames on himself; he has an affair with Helen Rolt, becomes entangled with Yusef, a merchant involved in illicit trade, and suffers from an increasing sense of guilt; he cannot accept his long-sought promotion because of his angina and he commits suicide in Graham Greene's *The Heart of the Matter.*

Lieutenant-Commander Josh Scobie   An Alexandrian policeman who is also a transvestite; he is beaten to death by sailors in Lawrence Durrell's *Balthazar.* As "El Scob" he has become a bizarre local saint in *Clea.*

Louise Scobie   Disappointed, staunchly Catholic wife of Henry Scobie; she suffers social humiliation from Henry's lack of advancement, goes to South Africa, hears rumors of his affair with Helen Rolt, and returns more content and relaxed until Henry's death in Graham Greene's *The Heart of the Matter.*

Mr. Scogan   Cynical friend and former schoolmate of Henry Wimbush; his thoughts about the ideals of a rational human society are undercut by his cunning exploitation of others in Aldous Huxley's *Crome Yellow.*

Tom Rodney Sonnenschein   A trendy rector who does not believe in immortality of the soul; he performs an exorcism service at Maurice Allington's request to destroy the evil spirits of Dr. Underhill and the green man in Kingsley Amis's *The Green Man.*

Scoraw   A rebel who escapes from Pannoval with Yuli, Iskador, and Usilk in Brian W. Aldiss's *Helliconia Spring.*

Scorchington   One of many targets of Arnold Condorex's conspiracy to overthrow all elder politicians for his own advantage in Rebecca West's *Harriet Hume, A London Fantasy.*

Pearl Scotney   The young part-Gypsy cousin of both Ruby Doyle and Diane Sedleigh; she is hired by Rozanov to be maid and companion for his granddaughter, Hattie Meynell, in Iris Murdoch's *The Philosopher's Pupil.*

Mr. Scott   Father of Mary Scott Summers; he attends the opening-night performance at the Garrick Theatre with his wife, encounters Emma Evans, and tells his daughter of Emma's whereabouts in Margaret Drabble's *The Garrick Year.*

Mrs. Scott   Mother of Mary Scott Summers; she attends the opening night performance at the Garrick Theatre with her husband, encounters Emma Evans, and tells her daughter of Emma's whereabouts in Margaret Drabble's *The Garrick Year.*

Pauline Scott   Ex-pupil at Romley Fourways', the school Kate Fletcher (Armstrong) attended; she fell in love with an abusive man who escaped from prison and fled with Pauline to Canada in Margaret Drabble's *The Middle Ground.*

Shirley ("Marylou") Scott   Ex-pupil at Romley Fourways', the school Kate Fletcher (Armstrong) attended, and sister of Pauline Scott; she was a popular actress during the 1960s in Margaret Drabble's *The Middle Ground.*

Gerald Scottow   Peter Crean-Smith's employee and long-time lover; he serves as Hannah Crean-Smith's jailer and is shot dead by her in Iris Murdoch's *The Unicorn.*

Screwtape   Senior Devil who instructs his nephew Wormwood, a junior devil, in the art of tempting human beings in C. S. Lewis's *The Screwtape Letters.*

Scrodd   Stern old college headmaster who reacts angrily when alumnus Charles Lumley returns to offer the college his window-washing services in John Wain's *Hurry On Down.*

Elton Scrope   The brother of Catherine Scrope Clare; he is clever, aloof, and eccentric in Ivy Compton-Burnett's *The Present and the Past.*

Theophilus Scrope   Psychologist and philosopher who interviews Adam Melfort for the intelligence service and becomes both counselor and friend in John Buchan's *A Prince of the Captivity.*

Ursula Scrope The clever sister of Catherine Scrope Clare; she does not want to marry and would like the restoration of her usual life with Elton and without Catherine in Ivy Compton-Burnett's *The Present and the Past.*

Scrubsdale Old shareholder who attends the General Meeting of The New Collier Company in John Galsworthy's *The Man of Property.*

Helen Scrymgeour Edward Ponderevo's mistress during the peak of his success in H. G. Wells's *Tono-Bungay.*

Alec Scudder Clive Durham's uncivilized gamekeeper, who becomes involved in a homosexual relationship with Maurice Hall in E. M. Forster's *Maurice.*

Franklin P. Scudder American journalist; he appeals to Richard Hannay for refuge, confides a villainous plot by German agents to destroy the power of British coastal defenses, and is murdered in Hannay's apartment in John Buchan's *The Thirty-Nine Steps.*

Joyce Scully Headmistress at Romley Fourways' whom Kate Armstrong interviews for the television film she is making in Margaret Drabble's *The Middle Ground.*

ScufBar MyrdemInggala's major domo; he smuggles a letter from the queen to the religious leader but betrays her by giving it to Alam Esomber in Brian W. Aldiss's *Helliconia Summer.*

Magda Sczekerny Librarian at Tothill House who is a Hungarian refugee; she does the research for Piers Mosson's production of the opera, marries Ralph Tucker, is a terrorist, and causes the death of Tom Mosson when she attacks Piers in Angus Wilson's *Setting the World on Fire.*

Basil Seal A well-born but crude and unprincipled British aristocrat who takes an important post in Emperor Seth's government in Azania; his foolish new rules and insensitive activities help the rebels to form and group against Seth, and when Seth is overthrown and murdered Basil returns to England in Evelyn Waugh's *Black Mischief.* Basil stays at his sister Barbara Sothill's country home while seeking a military position in World War II; he works at military headquarters in London and finally volunteers for a commando unit in *Put Out More Flags.*

Cynthia, Lady Seal Basil's much-tried mother in Evelyn Waugh's *Put Out More Flags.*

Sea-Rat Adventurer The sea-faring rat who meets Water Rat and Mole and tells them of his wonderful adventures travelling the world; his fascinating stories tempt the Water Rat to leave his comfortable home until the sensible Mole dissuades him in Kenneth Grahame's *The Wind in the Willows.*

Captain Searle Harbor master at Kerrith, near Maxim de Winter's estate, Manderly; he informs Mrs. de Winter that Rebecca de Winter's body has been found in a boat with holes in the bottom in Daphne Du Maurier's *Rebecca.*

Leslie Searle American photographer who disappears after a spat with his host and co-author, Walter Whitmore; Searle turns out to be a woman who assumed a disguise to murder Whitmore in revenge for a friend's suicide but changed her mind in Josephine Tey's *To Love and Be Wise.*

Eric Sears Paula Biranne's lover, whose possible return she awaits with misgiving; he left her after he lost a foot, crushed by a billiard table in a jealous attack by her unfaithful then-husband, Richard, in Iris Murdoch's *The Nice and the Good.*

Arthur Seaton Young factory worker who wants to live fully, has many encounters with women — especially the married sisters Brenda and Winnie — fights at any chance, and drinks too much; he finally decides to marry Doreen Greatton, a young woman with little life experience, in Alan Sillitoe's *Saturday Night and Sunday Morning.*

Matilda (Aunt Matty) Seaton Daughter of Oliver; lame from a fall from a horse, she is a woman who is manipulative and malicious to the Gavestons and cruel to her companion, Miss Griffin, in Ivy Compton-Burnett's *A Family and a Fortune.*

Oliver Seaton Blanche Gaveston's impoverished father, who comes with his daughter Matty to live in the Gavestons' lodge in Ivy Compton-Burnett's *A Family and a Fortune.*

Sebastian Heir to the vast ducal estate of Chevron; he loves the tradition represented by Chevron and hates the heartless society of Edwardian London; he plans to travel with Leonard Anquetil to "contact life" and be a better master to Chevron in Vita Sackville-West's *The Edwardians.* Established as master at Chevron, he is described by Miles Vane-Merrick as the model landlord in *Family History.*

Sebastian The perhaps permanently LSD-incapacitated once-witty friend to whom Stephen Ollerenshaw pays duty visits that contribute to Stephen's dangerous depression in Margaret Drabble's *The Realms of Gold.*

Father Sebastian The slated replacement for the Reverend Stephen Ambedkar at St. John's Church in Pankot; some members of the congregation find Sebastian a bit too Roman in demeanor and in the conduct of his services in Paul Scott's *Staying On.*

Secretary of State Haitian government official bribed by Brown to allow William Smith to see Major Jones in prison in Graham Greene's *The Comedians.*

Secretary for Social Welfare The successor to Dr. Philipot in the Haitian government; he takes William Smith and Brown on a disillusioning tour of Duvalierville in Graham Greene's *The Comedians.*

Mrs. Sedge Incompetent, although Viennese, cook for Dulcie Mainwaring's Aunt Hermione and Uncle Bertram in Barbara Pym's *No Fond Return of Love.*

Bill Sedge Immigrant bachelor knitwear buyer who sucessfully combines an easiness with English ways with residual Continental gallantry in his acquaintance with Dulcie Mainwaring and especially Viola Dace, despite his being brother to a household servant in Barbara Pym's *No Fond Return of Love.*

Adam Sedgwick Scientist and member of the House of Lords who suffers from Parkinson's disease; he undergoes successful surgery and becomes a friend of Thomas Pemberton in C. P. Snow's *In Their Wisdom.*

Diamond (Diane) Sedleigh A prostitute; love has made her the reserved property of George McCaffrey; she accompanies Father Jacoby when he departs suddenly, but she goes only to Paris; there she is set up as a mistress by a rich philanthropist who saves prostitutes and occasionally saves one for himself in Iris Murdoch's *The Philosopher's Pupil.*

Captain Segura (nickname: Red Vulture) Middle-aged, lecherous officer in the Cuban security police; he unsuccessfully woos Milly Wormold and investigates her father's supposed intelligence agents in Graham Greene's *Our Man in Havana.*

Prince of Seitz-Bunau (Mr. Prince, Prince) German prince who joins the *Atropos* crew as a midshipman and accepts his role as subordinate to Hornblower in C. S. Forester's *Hornblower and the Atropos.*

Sejanus Tiberius's ruthless henchman, who coldly carries out executions while seeking to establish himself as ruler of Rome before being executed himself in Robert Graves's *I, Claudius.*

Mrs. Selden The cook for the Lambs; she sings Chapel hymns and frowns on Miriam Biggs and George in Ivy Compton-Burnett's *Manservant and Maidservant.*

Barry Self John's ostensible father, who puts out a contract for John to be hurt, but not killed; the man he hires is John's real father, Fat Paul; Barry marries Vera, a "mature" centerfold model, in Martin Amis's *Money.*

John Self Whiz-kid producer of TV ads; he is addicted to alcohol, pornography, and masturbation; he is given a lot of money to make a movie which for mysterious reasons his chief backer sabotages; John is obsessed with Selina Street because she likes his money and eventually begins an emotional relationship with Martina Twain; John is narrator in Martin Amis's *Money.*

Selim Nessim Hosnani's servant, who informs Nessim about the infidelities of Justine Hosnani in Lawrence Durrell's *Justine* and in *Balthazar.* He is revealed to be spying for the Egyptian officials upon the Hosnanis' political intrigues in *Mountolive.*

Poppy Sellers Typist at Twigg and Dersingham who is attracted to the firm's junior clerk, Howard Turgis, in J. B. Priestley's *Angel Pavement.*

Viscount Sellings A former guinea-pig director of one of Lord Raingo's early enterprises; Sellings is despised by Raingo but accepted as a dinner companion at the Savoy when Raingo, devastated by jealousy, seeks his absent mistress, Delphine Leeder, at the great hotel in Arnold Bennett's *Lord Raingo.*

Selwyn A director in the Hereford company; he gives little advice or direction to the actors in Margaret Drabble's *The Garrick Year.*

David Sempill Young Scots minister; a Platonist and humanist, he is aware that many of his parishioners are practicing pagan rites in the Wood and is unable to convince them of their sin; he is shunned by the villagers and censured and excommunicated by the Presbytery for sheltering Mark Kerr and for denouncing the villagers for their blasphemy; he meets and loves Katrine Yester and with her nurses the villagers during the plague; when Katrine dies, he leaves Woodilee with Mark Kerr to sail to Europe in John Buchan's *Witch Wood.*

Mr. Semple Prudent staff-manager of the hotel; he does not support Mrs. O'Riordon's request for consideration of provocation for one of her housekeepers in a contretemps with a guest in Arnold Bennett's *Imperial Palace.*

Mrs. Semprill　A bitter gossip who tells the newspaper that Dorothy Hare and Mr. Warburton had been having an affair and have run off to Paris to elope or maybe just live in sin when Dorothy disappears and Mr. Warburton goes to Europe for six months; her gossip causes Dorothy to be afraid to return home in George Orwell's *A Clergyman's Daughter.*

Shalini Gupta Sen　Hari Kumar's widowed aunt; Hari lives with her for a time when he returns to India in Paul Scott's *The Jewel in the Crown.*

Howard Send　American expatriate editor of *The Highgate Review* and employer of Nancy Hawkins in Muriel Spark's *A Far Cry from Kensington.*

Matthew (Matty) Septimus (Windy, Wandgrave, Windrap, Wildwort, Windwort, Wildwave, Windgrove, Windrove)　A kind of idiot savant or prophet whose seemingly mad ramblings, full of apocalyptical force, contain much truth about modern society in William Golding's *Darkness Visible.*

Serafina　Luscious, dark-eyed, young, and incompetent typist in the Spartacus Milan office; she in reality works for Arturo Bellinetti in Eric Ambler's *Cause for Alarm.*

Serapamoun　An Egyptian "Cotton king"; a Coptic Christian, he is Nessim Hosnani's co-conspirator against the British; he warns Nessim of danger from the unpredictable Narouz Hosnani in Lawrence Durrell's *Mountolive.*

Miles Sercombe　Lady Ann Smiley's cousin, a slow-witted, pretentious Cabinet official who signs off on Oliver Lacon's and George Smiley's plans in John le Carré's *Tinker, Tailor, Soldier, Spy.*

Serge　A friend of the Russian in Jean Rhys's *Good Morning Midnight.*

Dame Rhetta Sergeant　Mother of Sergeant Jebb; she is a caricatured, evil figure, bald beneath a red wig; she selfishly rejected her husband and eight-year-old son, took her maiden name, and became a noted writer of popular romances; she dies of a heart attack while raging at her grandson, Simon Jebb, when he attempts to regain love letters written to him by his dead mistress — letters his grandmother callously planned to use in her novels in Storm Jameson's *There Will Be a Short Interval.*

Serpentine　Utopian scientist who befriends the Earthlings but whom they murder in their failed attempt to take him hostage at Quarantine (Coronation) Crag in H. G. Wells's *Men Like Gods.*

Terry Service　An orphan whose father killed his mother and sister; Terry is adopted by the aristocratic Ridings, but is never fully accepted, especially by the children, Gregory and Ursula; as a young man, he is a repulsive mass of neuroses, but when he begins work as a union organizer in his office, he gains both wealth and self confidence, becoming somewhat vicious, in Martin Amis's *Success.*

Emperor Seth　The young Oxford-educated Emperor of Azania; his attempts to make alleged progressive reforms in the country cause much hostility and initiate a rebellion in which Seth is ultimately murdered in Evelyn Waugh's *Black Mischief.*

Digby Seton　Spendthrift, dissipated brother of Maurice Seton in P. D. James's *Unnatural Causes.*

Maurice Seton　Rich, successful mystery writer; he is murdered in P. D. James's *Unnatural Causes.*

Patrick Seton　Confidence man and ex-convict who exploits a genuine gift as a spiritualist; though altogether without conscience, he is diminished as a threat to others by his conviction for fraud in Muriel Spark's *The Bachelors.*

Sally Seton　Clarissa Dalloway's childhood friend with whom Clarissa had been in love one summer at the family's house at Bourton; Sally resurfaces unexpectedly at Clarissa's party as the discontented Lady Rosseter; she married a titled *nouveau riche* miner's son, with whom she lives opulently with her five sons in a Manchester suburb in Virginia Woolf's *Mrs. Dalloway.*

Mr. Settlewhite　Solicitor who represents Marjorie Ferrar in her libel suit against Fleur Mont in John Galsworthy's *The Silver Spoon.*

Beatrice Severn　Loving, open-hearted Secret Service operative; she poses as James Wormold's secretary, presses him to follow Intelligence procedures, falls in love with him, and, despite his daughter's resistance, returns with him to England in Graham Greene's *Our Man in Havana.*

Seward of Denethor II　Leader of the Gondors, who are at war with the forces of the evil Sauron in J. R. R. Tolkien's *The Two Towers.*

Tivvyriah Sexton　Foolish, unlovely hired girl in love with the handsome Gideon Sarn; she has evidence of his poisoning his mother and hopes to blackmail him into marrying her in Mary Webb's *Precious Bane.*

Prince Seyid　Emperor Seth's father, who leads an

unsuccessful revolt against Seth's Azanian rule; General Connolly leads Seth's army effectively in this first revolt in Evelyn Waugh's *Black Mischief.*

Evelyn Seymour   Thirty-four-year-old son of Sir Rowland; he mischievously tells Alfred Marcon that he will inherit Sabine Ponsonby's money in Ivy Compton-Burnett's *Daughters and Sons.*

Humphrey Seymour   Communist editor of the *Note,* a news sheet that publishes the reports that lead to the political embarrassment of Sir Philip March in C. P. Snow's *The Conscience of the Rich.*

Jane Seymour   The sister of Sir Rowland; she is Hetty Ponsonby's friend and the opinionated maiden aunt of Evelyn Seymour in Ivy Compton-Burnett's *Daughters and Sons.*

Sir Rowland Seymour   The father of Evelyn Seymour; he proposes to Clare Ponsonby and is accepted by her in Ivy Compton-Burnett's *Daughters and Sons.*

Shadowbrute   Son of Ungit and god of the Grey Mountain, also known as the Brute, to whom the Great Offerings are made; Psyche is brought to him as an offering; when Psyche shines a light on him to discover who he is, she is condemned to wander the earth in C. S. Lewis's *Till We Have Faces.*

Norah Shadox-Brown   A sturdy, middle-aged retired headmistress, who "regards all subtleties as falsehoods"; she is Marcus Fisher's intrusive, ineffectual friend in Iris Murdoch's *The Time of the Angels.*

Shadrack   The younger partner in the undertaking firm of Shadrack and Duxbury; he discovers Billy's careless disregard of business matters in Keith Waterhouse's *Billy Liar.*

Shahin   A Turkish boy and one of the supernormals of John Wainwright's Pacific island colony; he kills Hsi Mei out of mercy and later kills himself to prevent the dissolution of the colony in Olaf Stapledon's *Odd John: A Story Between Jest and Earnest.*

Mr. Shaitana   Bridge-party host whose collection of guests includes four sleuths and, after his murder, four suspects in Agatha Christie's *Cards on the Table.*

Nick Shales   The atheistic science teacher whose humane decency influences Sammy Mountjoy's life in William Golding's *Free Fall.*

Mr. Shalford   Art Kipps's employer at the Folkestone Drapery Bazaar, a bald, energetic man with a peculiarly condensed style of English who advocates his vague "System" as a means of business efficiency in H. G. Wells's *Kipps: The Story of a Simple Soul.*

Shamus (alias Lord de Waldebere)   Dogmatically eccentric brute, failed novelist, womanizer, and professed sentimental lover; he drowns his limited talent in liquor and selfishness, abuses his wife, Helen, lusts after Sandra Cassidy, and lives off Aldo Cassidy's largesse until crushing Cassidy emotionally by his and Helen's sudden disappearances in John le Carré's *The Naive and Sentimental Lover.*

Paul Shanahan   One of the Dublin characters held in captivity by the fictional novelist Dermot Trellis; he also appeared in the novels of the fictional William Tracy, and he recites "A Pint of Plain is Your Only Man" in Flann O'Brien's *At Swim-Two-Birds.*

Shannana   MyrdemInggala's mother, whose spirit advises MyrdemInggala in Brian W. Aldiss's *Helliconia Summer.*

Mrs. Sharkey   Rose Vassiliou's poor and desperate but hardworking neighbor and friend; she has successfully reared several children and finds herself saddled with much of the care of an illegitimate grandchild in Margaret Drabble's *The Needle's Eye.*

Eileen Sharkey   Mrs. Sharkey's unlucky, uneducated, misfit daughter; her adolescent dreams of a life of glamour are extinguished by unwed motherhood in Margaret Drabble's *The Needle's Eye.*

Mrs. Sharpe   Marion's mother, also falsely accused of kidnapping in Josephine Tey's *The Franchise Affair.*

James Sharpe   A young Scot who visits the Somerses while they live in Cornwall and are persecuted by local authorities during World War I in D. H. Lawrence's *Kangaroo.*

Marion Sharpe   Intelligent young woman who with her mother is falsely accused of kidnapping and imprisoning Betty Kane in Josephine Tey's *The Franchise Affair.*

Phoebe Sharpe   Recent university graduate who is editing literary remains in a country cottage and becomes briefly the girlfriend of James Boyce until Leonora Eyre discovers the fact in Barbara Pym's *The Sweet Dove Died.*

Michael Shatov   A new young boarder in Mrs. Bailey's house; a highly educated Russian Jew to whom Miriam Henderson gives English lessons, he becomes her importunate suitor as well as a major figure in her life in Dorothy Richardson's *Deadlock,* in *The Trap,* and in *Clear Horizon*. It is he who suggests that she stay with his Quaker friends in Sussex in *Dimple Hill*. He marries Amabel, and they have a child in *March Moonlight*.

Mick Shaughnessy Civil servant who deals with the mad scientist De Selby and the repentant author James Joyce in Flann O'Brien's *The Dalkey Archive*.

Shaun the Postman (Kevin) Extroverted, worldly son figure, rival of Shem; he appears under many names in the archetypal family romance of James Joyce's *Finnegans Wake*.

Shaw Grumpy mate of Lingard's brig the *Lightning* in Joseph Conrad's *The Rescue: A Romance of the Shallows*.

Mr. Shaw Instructing attorney in the defense of Giles Colmore in Roy Fuller's *The Father's Comedy*.

Mr. Shaw Reclusive and rather mysterious Chinese who provides the capital and becomes a silent partner in Ellen Henshaw's chain of brothels in Anthony Burgess's *The Pianoplayers*.

Arnold Shaw University Vice-Chancellor in Lewis Eliot's home town; he is forced to resign under pressure of rebellious faculty in C. P. Snow's *The Sleep of Reason*.

Lord Osmund Willoughby Finnian Shaw Host of a chaotic lenten dinner and costume party, at which his bohemian guests are robbed of their possessions in Wyndham Lewis's *The Apes of God*.

Vicky Shaw Arnold's daughter, a physician; she is in love with Pat Eliot and is angry with Lewis Eliot for telling her that Pat no longer cares for her in C. P. Snow's *The Sleep of Reason*. After Pat's divorce from Muriel Calvert he and Vicky marry in *Last Things*.

Dr. Philip Shawcross The medical officer in Kuala Kangsar, a British settlement in Malaya; friendly and generous, he allows Kenneth Toomey to live in his house while the latter writes a book; he and Toomey become close but remain platonic friends in Anthony Burgess's *Earthly Powers*.

Queen Shazvin A brave and prosperous woman who commands a small mountain kingdom on the verge of being pillaged; in spite of the brief period of aid given by Ambien II in directing her decisions, she is later killed by the horsemen in Doris Lessing's *The Sirian Experiments*.

She A forty-six-year-old poor woman who has repeatedly loved and depended on men but considers herself respectable because she has only one client at a time and maintains long relationships; her day's wandering through London manifests her keen observation of people and situations, insightful recall of memories, and possible ability finally to stop romanticizing untrustworthy men and to depend on her wits and audacity, her hard work, and a few disreputable women like herself in order to survive the bleak future in Storm Jameson's *A Day Off*.

James Shearwater Distracted physiologist whose energies go into his esoteric experiments; feeling a sense of loss, he develops an interest in Myra Viveash, ignoring his wife, Rose, and failing to see her indiscretions in Aldous Huxley's *Antic Hay*.

Rosie Shearwater Promiscuous young wife of James; unsatisfied with her husband, she has an affair with the younger Theodore Gumbril and is then herself seduced by Coleman in Aldous Huxley's *Antic Hay*.

Sheffield Miriam Henderson's landlord in Flaxman's Court, from whom the genteel Miss Holland shrinks in Dorothy Richardson's *The Trap*.

Poppy, Duchess of Sheffield Eccentric cousin of Dorothea Cortese; her infatuation with the bearded Georgie Pillson is a dangerous social advantage to Lucia (Lucas) Pillson and highly alarming to him in E. F. Benson's *Trouble for Lucia*.

Sheila Charles Lumley's college girlfriend, whose stuffy, critical relatives he finds unbearable in John Wain's *Hurry On Down*.

Sheldon Personal maid of Sylvia, Lady Roehampton in Vita Sackville-West's *The Edwardians*.

Monica Sheldon Homespun "bachelor-girl" and sports enthusiast who is invited to the houseparty at Achorstone Hall to be a companion for Dick Staveley in L. P. Hartley's *The Sixth Heaven*. She is the fiancée of Dick Staveley, whose engagement is announced in *Eustace and Hilda*.

Clemence Shelley The daughter of Sir Roderick and his second wife, Maria; she cheats at Lesbia Firebrace's school to take second place in her studies in Ivy Compton-Burnett's *Two Worlds and Their Ways*.

Maria, Lady Shelley Sir Roderick's second wife; she takes and sells Oliver Firebrace's earring to give the money to Sir Roderick to buy back the farm in Ivy Compton-Burnett's *Two Worlds and Their Ways*.

Mary, Lady Shelley The deceased first wife of Sir

Roderick and the mother of Oliver in Ivy Compton-Burnett's *Two Worlds and Their Ways.*

Oliver Shelley   The son of Sir Roderick and his deceased first wife, Mary; he becomes the music master at Lucius Cassidy's school and forms a conspicuous friendship with Oliver Spode in Ivy Compton-Burnett's *Two Worlds and Their Ways.*

Sir Roderick Shelley   The blue-eyed father of his first wife Mary's son, Oliver, of his second wife Marie's daughter, Clemence, and son, Sefton, and of Mrs. Aldom's son, the family butler, in Ivy Compton-Burnett's *Two Worlds and Their Ways.*

Sefton Shelley   The son of Sir Roderick and his second wife, Maria; he cheats at Lucius Cassidy's school to satisfy his mother's ambition for his success in Ivy Compton-Burnett's *Two Worlds and Their Ways.*

Marmaduke Bonthrop Shelmerdine   Husband of the female Orlando; Orlando marries Marmaduke under the pressues of the Victorian age and much against her better judgment in Virginia Woolf's *Orlando: A Biography.*

Shelob   A hideous giant spider to whom Gollum betrays Frodo Baggins and Sam Gamgee; Shelob's bite paralyzes Frodo in J. R. R. Tolkien's *The Two Towers.*

Shem the Penman (Jerry)   Introverted, artistic son figure, rival of Shaun; he appears under many names in the archetypal family romance of James Joyce's *Finnegans Wake.*

Shen Kuo   Chinese boy and one of the supernormals of John Wainwright's Pacific island colony in Olaf Stapledon's *Odd John: A Story Between Jest and Earnest.*

Caroline Sheppard   Sharp-witted, insightful, gossipy spinster sister of Dr. James Sheppard in Agatha Christie's *The Murder of Roger Ackroyd.*

Dr. James Sheppard   Physician, neighbor, and co-discoverer of the late Roger Ackroyd; pressed into service as chronicler by Hercule Poirot in the absence of Captain Hastings, he is scrupulously though incompletely truthful in Agatha Christie's *The Murder of Roger Ackroyd.*

George Sherban   See Johor.

Rachel Sherban   George Sherban's young sister, whose journal documents some events in Doris Lessing's *Re: Colonised Planet 5, Shikasta.*

Charles Sheriff   Chemist who trains with Arthur

Miles at King's College, University of London; he excels in his exams, pursues women, declines into professional mediocrity, and marries Audrey; he knowingly publishes a paper with false data to secure his fame in C. P. Snow's *The Search.*

Russell Sheriton   Former Cold War brawler now head of the C.I.A.'s Soviet operations; his acknowledged flair for surviving political power plays fails when he disregards Ned's warnings and misreads Barley Blair's humanism in John le Carré's *The Russia House.*

Mrs. Sherman   The mother of Colin Freestone's mentally ill wife; the doctor seems to blame her for Mrs. Freestone's problems in David Storey's *A Temporary Life.*

Shiek   Calm old Arab of sanctified demeanor who is a known brothel-keeper of child prostitutes, one probably having been Justine Hosnani's lost child, in Lawrence Durrell's *Balthazar.* He leads the inebriated but innocently unsuspecting David Mountolive into the decaying brothel, where Mountolive is assaulted and robbed by the children in *Mountolive.*

Miss Shillingford   The woman who pays a visit to the Roscorla farm when Miriam Henderson is present and who angers her by insisting that, although she wants women to have the vote, she herself is not prepared to "scream for it" in Dorothy Richardson's *Dimple Hill.*

Andrew Shillinglaw ("Reiverslaw")   Morose man of mystery; he is a farmer at Reiverslaw who accompanies David Sempill, the minister of Woodilee, to the Black Wood on Lammas Eve to witness the Satanic revels in John Buchan's *Witch Wood.*

Shillitoe   Young tailor of Bursley; Denry Machin makes a deal to provide him with a ticket for the Countess of Chell's ball in exchange for a tuxedo for himself; at the ball he dares Denry to dance with the Countess of Chell in Arnold Bennett's *The Card: A Story of Adventure in the Five Towns.*

Shingler   Young Detective Inspector who works under Frank Briers in investigating the murder of Lady Ashbrook in C. P. Snow's *A Coat of Varnish.*

Keith Shipley   A successful advertising executive who is Pat Shipley's husband in Alan Sillitoe's *The Death of William Posters.*

Pat Shipley   A country nurse with whom Frank Dawley stays and falls in love after leaving his wife and children in Alan Sillitoe's *The Death of William Posters.*

Mrs. Shobbe   Shobbe's wife, who married to escape the tyranny of a Victorian home and family; she becomes her husband's means to escape working for a living in Richard Aldington's *Death of a Hero.*

Herr Shobbe (satirical portrait of Ford Madox Ford)   Periodical editor at whose studio George Winterbourne meets Elizabeth Paston in Richard Aldington's *Death of a Hero.*

Colin Shoe   Editor in charge of Names at Mackintosh & Tooley in Muriel Spark's *A Far Cry from Kensington.*

Lobanster Shokerandit   Luterin's father and Keeper of the Wheel; he is revealed as the Supreme Oligarch in Brian W. Aldiss's *Helliconia Winter.*

Luterin Shokerandit   The younger son of the Keeper of the Wheel in Sibornal; he becomes an army officer and kills Bandal Eith Lahl in battle and takes his wife captive; after becoming a deserter, he kills his father and is imprisoned for ten years; his trust and innocence are what the people of Helliconia must have in order to survive in Brian W. Aldiss's *Helliconia Winter.*

Albert Shore   Sixty-year-old novelist living in North Oxford who must confront people from his past as a result of his son's intended marriage to the daughter of his former wife in Roy Fuller's *My Child, My Sister.*

Fabian Shore   Son of Albert; he becomes unexpectedly engaged to marry Frances Leaf in Roy Fuller's *My Child, My Sister.*

Mrs. Shortman   Typist who works with Gregory Vigil; she edited objectionable material from the publications of the Society for the Regeneration of Women in John Galsworthy's *The Country House.*

The Marquess of Shropshire   Old friend of Sir Lawrence Mont's father; he advises his granddaughter Marjorie Ferrar to abandon her libel suit and pays her debts for her when she loses it in John Galsworthy's *The Silver Spoon.* He eagerly joins Michael Mont's slum-conversion committee to advance ideas of electrification in *Swan Song.* He speaks to his nephew Bobbie Ferrar on behalf of Hubert Cherrell in *Maid In Waiting.*

Lady Agatha Carádoc Shropton   Eldest daughter of the Earl of Valleys; she is appalled by the amorous affairs of her brother, Lord Miltoun, and her sister, Lady Barbara Carádoc, in John Galsworthy's *The Patrician.*

Ann Shropton   Six-year-old daughter of Lady Agatha; she plays with her pets in the home of her grandparents, Lord and Lady Valleys, in John Galsworthy's *The Patrician.*

Avice Shrubsole   Energetic, social-climbing former social worker; a doctor's wife and mother of three, she tries to dominate village social life and longs to purchase a grander house in Barbara Pym's *A Few Green Leaves.*

Martin Shrubsole   Young, materialistic junior village physician combining general practice with geriatrics; he is nonetheless unnerved by the undamped passions of the aged and frustrated by the presence of his mother-in-law in his cramped house in Barbara Pym's *A Few Green Leaves.*

Dr. Shubunkin   Sex-obsessed psychiatrist and member of the Identity Club; he presents a case history to the club illustrating the importance of sex in determining identity in Nigel Dennis's *Cards of Identity.*

Mr. Shushions   Oldest Sunday School teacher in the Five Towns; he taught many of the townsmen to read and write; he saved young Darius Clayhanger and his family from the workhouse and started Darius on his successful career as a printer, but his own death in the workhouse so shocks Darius that it speeds his decline in Arnold Bennett's *Clayhanger.*

George Shuttleworth   Husband of Olga Bracely in E. F. Benson's *"Queen Lucia"* and in *Lucia in London.*

Colonel (Stinkpot) Shyton   Irate husband who sues his wife, Babs, for divorce in E. F. Benson's *Lucia in London.*

Babs Shyton   Wife of Colonel Shyton; her indiscreet letters lead her husband to sue her for divorce in E. F. Benson's *Lucia in London.*

Si   Yuli's and Iskador's son in Brian W. Aldiss's *Helliconia Spring.*

Siantos   White-haired Greek government official; a friend of Charles Latimer, he provides Latimer with a letter of introduction to N. Marukakis and with some additional information about Dimitrios Makropoulos's whereabouts in 1922 in Eric Ambler's *The Mask of Dimitrios.*

Sid   Old friend of Professor King and Orlando King; through him the truth of Orlando's parentage is revealed in Isabel Colegate's *Orlando King.* He sends brief messages to Orlando in Italy in *Orlando at the Brazen Threshold.*

John Siddons Footman to the Nettleby family and sweetheart of Ellen Page in Isabel Colegate's *The Shooting Party.*

Janet Sidebottome Sister of Lisa Brooke in Muriel Spark's *Memento Mori.*

Ronald Sidebottome Old, deaf brother of Lisa Brooke and husband of Tempest Sidebottome, after whose death he elopes with his contemporary's granddaughter, Olive Mannering, in Muriel Spark's *Memento Mori.*

Tempest Sidebottome Social reformer, hospital committee-woman of imperious temper, and wife of Ronald Sidebottome; her death dissipates the family's enthusiasm for continuing a suit over Lisa Brooke's estate in Muriel Spark's *Memento Mori.*

Sidi "Olive-skinned Armenian youth" and friend of Bachir; he reads a newspaper account of Princess Elsie's arrival in Kairoulla to Bachir and his friends as they fill orders in the Countess of Varna's flower shop in Ronald Firbank's *The Flower Beneath the Foot.*

Ludwig Siebkron Bonn's Chief of Police and senior Interior Ministry official; he aids Klaus Karfeld by secretly initiating a police manhunt and murdering Leo Harting in John le Carré's *A Small Town in Germany.*

Father Sifans The priest who trains Yuli in the priesthood in Brian W. Aldiss's *Helliconia Spring.*

Zesty-Boy Sift Singer and writer of songs about London teenagers in Colin MacInnes's *Absolute Beginners.*

Sigrid Swedish girl who cures herself of consumption; she is one of the supernormals of John Wainwright's Pacific island colony; she sacrifices herself to prevent the dissolution of the colony in Olaf Stapledon's *Odd John: A Story Between Jest and Earnest.*

Blanche Siguenau British wife of Ernest; she lives zestfully, rides horseback, dries herbs for teas, and loves to garden; she sympathizes with René Hoffmayer when her ambitious husband betrays him; she is murdered by Henry Eschelmer as she tries to save her husband in Storm Jameson's *Cousin Honoré.*

Ernest Siguenau Distant cousin of Honoré Burckheim; he is assigned by Jules Reuss to manage the behavior of Burckheim and to report to Reuss on the activities of René Hoffmayer as Reuss and Siguenau become conspirators in favor of merging interests of the Burckheim ironworks with those of German industrialists in Storm Jameson's *Cousin Honoré.*

Fanny Siguenau Daughter of Ernest and Blanche Siguenau; her fiancé, Robert Berthelin, has just left the village to fight Germans when her parents are murdered; she leaves for Bordeaux to assist refugees in Storm Jameson's *Cousin Honoré.*

Silas Martha Quest's African garden boy in Doris Lessing's *A Proper Marriage.*

Silk Powerful bosun's mate who commands a section of seamen in Bush's division; his strength brings down the door to the fort in C. S. Forester's *Lieutenant Hornblower.*

Ambrose Silk Homosexual aesthete and writer who works for the British Ministry of Information in World War II; falsely accused of being a fascist, he flees to Ireland while Basil Seal takes over his apartment and possessions in Evelyn Waugh's *Put Out More Flags.*

Sillery (Sillers) University don whose thirst for power and intrigue, rather than his homosexual leanings, motivate his cultivation of a leftist student coterie in Anthony Powell's *A Question of Upbringing.* Intrigue is Sillery's forte as he maneuvers among his acquaintances at his Sunday teas; he leads a march in Hyde Park in *The Acceptance World.* Retired, he still lives in his University rooms; he has been made a peer by the Labour Government in *Books Do Furnish a Room.* His ninetieth birthday is celebrated in *Temporary Kings.* He has died in *Hearing Secret Harmonies.*

The Silts Rickie Elliott's poor relations in E. M. Forster's *The Longest Journey.*

Silver Member of the Sandleford Owsla (rabbit-warren militia) who joins Hazel's pioneers in Richard Adams's *Watership Down.*

Silverweed Morbid rabbit poet whose performance helps alert Fiver to the deeply hidden evil in the Warren of the Snares in Richard Adams's *Watership Down.*

Silvia An Italian woman working in the expensive London hotel where Kate Brown stays; she ministers to all of the hotel's guests, having like Kate been trained to be nanny and nurturer in Doris Lessing's *The Summer Before the Dark.*

Florence Simcox (Mrs. Offlow) Champion clog-dancer; her surprise appearance at the Dragon pub startles young Edwin Clayhanger's dormant sexuality in Arnold Bennett's *Clayhanger.*

Mr. Sime One-armed butler of Sir Archibald Roylance; he joins his master in the battle to rescue

Sakskia, the Russian princess, in John Buchan's *Huntingtower*.

Simmonds Lady Nelly Staveley's English maid who serves her in Venice; she is "like the negation of personality, her presence was so self-effacing" in L. P. Hartley's *Eustace and Hilda*.

Miss Simmons Teacher at Romley Fourways' school when Kate Fletcher (Armstrong) was a student there in Margaret Drabble's *The Middle Ground*.

Tommy Simmons Littlestone boy who unintentionally launches the Cavorite vessel back into space, ending both his life and Bedford's chances of returning to the moon in H. G. Wells's *The First Men in the Moon*.

Geoffrey Simnel Rake who elopes with Ruth Nimmo in Joyce Cary's *Except the Lord*.

Simon The page boy for the Clares; he left school, believing that money is power and wanting to become a butler in Ivy Compton-Burnett's *The Present and the Past*.

Simon A frail, prescient boy, who undergoes a mystical illumination when he perceives — just before his sacrificial death — that a pig's head on a stick is an emblem of Beelzebub in William Golding's *Lord of the Flies*.

Mr. Simon A sarcastic young African who sees the humor and worthlessness of those whites, like Martha Quest, working to liberate the Africans in Doris Lessing's *Landlocked*.

Ann Simon Jewish daughter of a doctor; a member of the Communist Party, she is invited by Katherine March to meet Lewis Eliot, but she falls in love instead with Charles March and marries Charles over the outraged opposition of Charles's father; she could have prevented publication of reports that ruin the career of Sir Philip March in C. P. Snow's *The Conscience of the Rich*.

Simone An eclectic Oxford friend of Sarah Bennett; the daughter of a French opera singer and an Italian general, she wanders the world wearing old clothes she has gathered from various parts of Europe; she has no talent for daily realities such as cooking, utility bills, and the weather; through her Sarah Bennett sees the past in Margaret Drabble's *A Summer Bird-Cage*.

Jack Simons Honest, serious, middle-aged automobile-export delivery driver who tries to warn Charles Lumley against getting mixed up in Teddy Bunder's drug-smuggling racket in John Wain's *Hurry On Down*.

Simpson Brawny, good-looking, middle-aged midshipman, who returns to the *Justinian* bitter after losing his commission as lieutenant; a stubborn, jealous tyrant, he insults Hornblower, accusing him of cheating, and brings about a duel to the death in C. S. Forester's *Mr. Midshipman Hornblower*.

Mrs. Simpson Secretary for Mayor Lucia (Lucas) Pillson in E. F. Benson's *Trouble for Lucia*.

Amy Simpson Aging, angry, and nagging but solicitous housekeeper of the Assistant Commissioner in Graham Greene's *It's a Battlefield*.

Joy Simpson Widow of a British diplomat and mother of two; she has an extended affair with Philip Swallow in Turkey, Greece, and Israel, but is disillusioned when Philip goes back to his wife in David Lodge's *Small World*.

Miranda Simpson Daughter of Joy Simpson and Philip Swallow in David Lodge's *Small World*.

Sims Builder-decorator hired by Gwenda Reed to renovate her house in Agatha Christie's *Sleeping Murder*.

Sims A colorless, rejected schoolmaster; the puritanical offspring of intolerant missionaries, he gravitated to education; mentally enslaved by the headmaster's contemptuous treatment, he righteously plots revenge in Nicholas Blake's *A Question of Proof*.

Sinclair A member of the spy ring "The Free Mothers", with the cover of a clergyman; he first encounters Arthur Rowe at a fete where Rowe wins a cake containing film; he becomes known to Rowe as "the vicar" at the asylum in Graham Greene's *The Ministry of Fear*.

Sinclair One of Evelyn Murgatroyd's English suitors vacationing at the Santa Marina Hotel in Virginia Woolf's *The Voyage Out*.

Old Singleton Weather-beaten sailor on the *Narcissus* in Joseph Conrad's *The Nigger of the "Narcissus"*.

Aunt Rosie Sinkin Old lady who, hearing one of John Lavender's speeches, thinks he may be insane; she notifies her nephew, Wilfred Sinkin, to investigate in John Galsworthy's *The Burning Spear: Being the Experiences of Mr. John Lavender in Time of War*.

Wilfred Sinkin Rosie Sinkin's forty-five-year-old nephew, who serves on the Board of Guardians; he makes enquiries after the sanity of John Lavender in John Galsworthy's *The Burning Spear: Being the Experiences of Mr. John Lavender in Time of War*.

Harry Sinton Director of his brother's publishing firm; during a period of mental breakdown he becomes convinced that he has killed an acquaintance and possibly also his father and seeks to establish the facts through his own investigations in Roy Fuller's *Fantasy and Fugue.*

Laurence Sinton Publishing-house director who, after poisoning his father, tries to persuade his brother, Harry, to take an overdose of sleeping pills and attempts to implicate him in the death of Max Callis in Roy Fuller's *Fantasy and Fugue.*

Sipple A drunken, homosexual professional clown; he is mistakenly accused of murdering Iolanthe Samiou's brother before escaping to Turkey in Lawrence Durrell's *Tunc.*

Sirius An extraordinarily intelligent dog, called Bran while he is working on Mr. Pugh's farm, who examines human nature and culture from an alien perspective; his frustration over the split in his psyche between his "wolf-nature" and his "human" side, and over his lack of hands, leads to a deepening alienation from humanity that ends only with his death in Olaf Stapledon's *Sirius: A Fantasy of Love and Discord.*

Aaron Sisson Inarticulate working-class man who leaves his wife and children in England and travels through Europe in search of a meaning to life; he plays the flute (his "rod") and resists all of the theories of those he encounters with the possible exception of Rawdon Lilly's in D. H. Lawrence's *Aaron's Rod.*

Sister The nurse in charge of the ward where Rosamund Stacey's daughter is hospitalized; she wages a losing battle against Rosamund's determined efforts to see her daughter in Margaret Drabble's *The Millstone.*

Datnil Skar A master tanner who shows Shay Tal the secret history book of Oldorando in Brian W. Aldiss's *Helliconia Spring.*

Inspector Skarrett Policeman investigating Paul Gardner in Isabel Colegate's *Agatha.*

Terry Skate Young, trendy, devout Anglo-Catholic florist who loses his faith while attending to the de Tankerville mausoleum in Barbara Pym's *A Few Green Leaves.*

Julian Skeffington Scientist and Cambridge college fellow who forces reopening of the case for Donald Howard's fellowship; he first voices suspicion of Ronald Nightingale in C. P. Snow's *The Affair.*

Eric Skelding Solicitor who prepared and reads the will of Mr. Massie to Katherine Underwood and Julian Underwood in C. P. Snow's *In Their Wisdom.*

Mr. Skellorn Rent collector whose probity drives his married daughter to take time to deliver promptly the collected rents to Carolyn Lessways, even though he has been stricken with paralysis in Arnold Bennett's *Hilda Lessways.*

Mary Skelton Young, attractive American woman; she poses as the sister of her actual cousin, Warren Skelton, to whom she is secretly engaged; they assist Josef Vadassy in his spying in Eric Ambler's *Epitaph for a Spy.*

Warren Skelton Ebullient, young, handsome American man; he is engaged to his cousin, Mary Skelton, but poses as her brother; he assists Josef Vadassy in Eric Ambler's *Epitaph for a Spy.*

Diana Skidmore Recent widow of a wealthy American; she provides social occasions for political discussions in C. P. Snow's *Corridors of Power.*

Skinner Aged, untidy butler of Moze Hall, Lord Raingo's estate; under Miss Thorping, he has to preside at the table in spite of his appearance in Arnold Bennett's *Lord Raingo.*

Mr. Skinner Shiftless, lazy, lisping manager of Bensington's and Redwood's Experimental Farm; he is presumed eaten by the giant rats that result from his sloppy handling of the Boomfood in H. G. Wells's *The Food of the Gods, and How It Came to Earth.*

Mrs. Skinner Skinner's dirty, large-nosed wife, an equally irresponsible manager of the Experimental Farm; she spreads the Bigness and makes her grandson, Albert Edward Caddles, Big by stealing and opening two cans of Boomfood when she abandons the Farm in H. G. Wells's *The Food of the Gods, and How It Came to Earth.*

Felix Skinner The middle-aged publisher of Philip Swallow's book on Hazlitt; while making love to his secretary he discovers that review copies were never sent in David Lodge's *Small World.*

Skip One of the trio of Americans who visit Celia and Quentin Villiers for a decadent weekend; Skip is a drug-eating sex object for Roxanne and Marvell Buzhardt, who rescued him from an abusive childhood and retained him as a primarily sexual companion in Martin Amis's *Dead Babies.*

Skitosherill Captain of the guard in New Ashkitosh;

he helps Laintal Ay and Aoz Roon escape from there in Brian W. Aldiss's *Helliconia Spring.*

Anton Skrebensky   Ursula Brangwen's maternal cousin and lover, a young soldier defined by his "conservative materialism"; his and Ursula's intense love affair ultimately fails, and he goes abroad to be a colonial administrator in D. H. Lawrence's *The Rainbow.*

Skrumppabowr   The brutal leader of the Kace with whom JandolAngand signs a peace treaty in Brian W. Aldiss's *Helliconia Summer.*

Inspector Slack   Overbearing police detective in charge of the investigation into Lucius Protheroe's death in Agatha Christie's *The Murder at the Vicarage.* He continues at odds with Jane Marple in *The Body in the Library.*

Slade   A weedy young student at Seaforth House; he is at first mildly persecuted by Gerald Bracher for his lack of athletic prowess and then adopted by him as a friend in a relationship which is misunderstood by the school's principal in Roy Fuller's *The Ruined Boys.*

Alice Slade   Secretary of the English Department at the University of Rummidge; she is unhelpful when Morris Zapp first arrives at Rummidge in David Lodge's *Changing Places: A Tale of Two Campuses.*

Deborah, Lady Slane   Wife of Henry, Lord Slane; she forsakes her dream of an artistic career to devote herself to her diplomat husband; widowed many years later, she declines to be any longer an appendage and moves to a small house in Hampstead to live her own life in Vita Sackville-West's *All Passion Spent.*

Henry Lyuleph Holland, first Earl of Slane   A distinguished politician whose dominant personality forces everyone into his shadow in Vita Sackville-West's *All Passion Spent.*

SlanjivalIptrekira   JandolAngand's royal armorer; he attempts to make matchlock guns similar to those used by the Sibornalese army in Brian W. Aldiss's *Helliconia Summer.*

Antony Slater   An orphan and an artist who is married to Gill Slater; he devotes himself to paints and canvas but never bothers with providing food, shelter, and warmth to his wife; he is doing well and dating happily after his marital separation in Margaret Drabble's *A Summer Bird-Cage.*

Gill Slater   Oxford friend and London roommate of Sarah Bennett; she has recently left her artist husband, Antony Slater; often depressed, she realizes her par-

ents were right when they warned her against Antony, who began to treat her as his personal maid, failing to realize she too had a need for accomplishment in Margaret Drabble's *A Summer Bird-Cage.*

Mrs. Slatter   Charlie Slatter's wife; she makes several attempts to befriend Mary Turner but is constantly rebuffed because of Mary's pride and scorn of her; in the end she ceases to defend the Turners against the community's spiteful gossip in Doris Lessing's *The Grass Is Singing.*

Charlie Slatter   A very rich farmer and neighbor of the Turners; he wants their land for cattle grazing and in the end persuades Richard Turner to sell his land to him in Doris Lessing's *The Grass Is Singing.*

Miss Slaughter   Strong-willed elderly woman who, wanting a lasting memorial, commissions Gulley Jimson to paint a wall in a new town hall in Joyce Cary's *Herself Surprised.*

General Slessing   A Colonial officer, over sixty and high up in the "Cables" department; Lord Raingo wishes to chastise him for trying to interfere in the compositions of the nightly world-message in Arnold Bennett's *Lord Raingo.*

Slingsby   Blandings Castle chauffeur whose social status among the servants is permanently elevated by his having witnessed the elopement of Aline Peters and George Emerson in P. G. Wodehouse's *Something New.*

Mr. Sloan   One of Squire Cranmer's henchmen in John Buchan's *The Free Fishers.*

Maria Sloane   A guest of Matty Seaton; her simplicity and humor make first Dudley Gaveston and then Edgar Gaveston fall in love with her; she becomes the second Mrs. Edgar Gaveston in Ivy Compton-Burnett's *A Family and a Fortune.*

Slomer   Very wealthy, deformed, crippled patron and committee member on the local Rugby League who hires Arthur Machin in David Storey's *This Sporting Life.*

Slubgob   Principal of the Tempters' Training College in C. S. Lewis's *The Screwtape Letters.*

Mr. Slump   A cynical alcoholic journalist who is one of the writers of an advice-to-the-lovelorn newspaper column; his advice ultimately leads to Aimée Thanatogenos's suicide in Evelyn Waugh's *The Loved One.*

Slumtrimpet   Tempter assigned to the fiancée of

Wormwood's subject in C. S. Lewis's *The Screwtape Letters*.

Robert ("Coz") Smale   Elderly relative of Alvina Smithers living with the Smitherses; he teases Georgie Smithers endlessly and is disgraced when he makes sexual advances to Lizzie Judd in Richard Aldington's *The Colonel's Daughter*.

Julia (Juley) Forsyte Small   Seventy-two-year-old widow, who lives with her sisters Ann and Hester Forsyte and her brother, Timothy; her gossip causes the jealous Soames Forsyte to rape his wife in John Galsworthy's *The Man of Property*.

Léonie Small   Monty's mother, who insisted that he address her by her first name after the death of Monty's father; she writes Monty love letters in which her regret for Sophie Small's death is clearly artificial in Iris Murdoch's *The Sacred and Profane Love Machine*.

Montague (Monty) Small   A successful detective-story writer, who, though he likes his neighbor Harriet Gavender, aids the long-enduring infidelity of her husband, Blaise, with an invented patient as alibi; he is mourning the recent death of his wife in Iris Murdoch's *The Sacred and Profane Love Machine*.

Sophie Small   A Swiss ex-actress whose recent death is mourned by her husband, Monty Small; he is still tormented by jealousy and uncertainty as to her love affairs in Iris Murdoch's *The Sacred and Profane Love Machine*.

Lucy Smalley   The perennial "secretary" to the senior military wives in Paul Scott's *The Day of the Scorpion*, in *The Towers of Silence*, and in *A Division of the Spoils*. Thirty years later she and Colonel Smalley, now retired, live quietly in Pankot, having stayed on in India after 1947, when independence was granted to India and Pakistan; Lucy, nearly seventy, daydreams about moments of imagined glory; after the death of her husband, her last connection to England and to her former life in India, Lucy feels desolate and abandoned in *Staying On*.

"Tusker" Smalley   A major who fleetingly appears in Paul Scott's *The Day of the Scorpion*, in *The Towers of Silence*, and in *A Division of the Spoils*. Thirty years later he is a retired colonel; he and his wife, Lucy, represent the last vestiges of the old Raj in India; having stayed on instead of returning to England, he spends his days savoring a few gins, upbraiding his one servant, Ibrahim, and complaining about the sad state of world

and local affairs; he dies at seventy-one of a coronary in *Staying On*.

Mrs. Tallents Smallpeace   Secretary of the League for Educating Orphans; she offers to help find assistance for Ivy Barton in John Galsworthy's *Fraternity*.

Captain Buffy Smallpiece   Conventional, unthinking, upper-class youth who is almost Philip Weston's only friend in his regiment in Isabel Colegate's *Statues in a Garden*.

Smaug   Merciless, cruel dragon who kills all of the inhabitants near the Misty Mountains, including the family of Thorin Oakenshield; he stole the treasures of the Oakenshield family and began living in their castle; he is driven from the castle by Thorin and his companions and is killed by Bard of Lake-town Esgaroth in J. R. R. Tolkien's *The Hobbit; or There and Back Again*.

Olga Smedoff   Aged, overweight, clever female Soviet agent and woman of the world; the owner of a safe house in Prague where Andreas Zaleshoff and Desmond Kenton take refuge, she shares information vital to the B2 documents' recovery in Eric Ambler's *Uncommon Danger*. She is identified as French born in *Epitaph for a Spy*.

Wilfred Smee   One of Stephen Halifax's oldest friends; he follows Sarah Bennett after a party to warn her that Stephen Halifax is on the verge of a nervous breakdown in Margaret Drabble's *A Summer Bird-Cage*.

Herbert Smeeth   Head bookkeeper at Twigg and Dersingham; he is overjoyed at being given a raise by James Golspie, and later bewildered when the firm goes bankrupt after Golspie's departure in J. B. Priestley's *Angel Pavement*.

Smiley   Ambitious midshipman aboard the *Atropos* whose fighting skills are tested in the boarding of the *Castilla* in C. S. Forester's *Hornblower and the Atropos*.

Lady Ann (Sercomb[e]) Smiley   George Smiley's aristocratic wife and Bill Haydon's cousin and lover; she takes lovers to show her independence and to console herself for her dissatisfaction in her marriage in John le Carré's *Call for the Dead*. Her faithlessness affords Shane Hecht endless derision in *A Murder of Quality* and allows Soviet spymaster Karla to discredit Smiley professionally in *Tinker, Tailor, Soldier, Spy*. Her presence haunts Smiley constantly in *The Honourable Schoolboy*. Her repeated attempts to reconcile with him finally end in rejection in *Smiley's People*.

George Smiley (codename "Beggerman"; covernames: **Alan Angel, Barraclough, Carmichael, Adrian Hebden, Herr Lachman, Leber, Lorimer, Max, Oates, Sampson, Savage, Mr. Standfast**) German-literature scholar, espionage recruiter, and reluctant spymaster who solves Samuel Arthur Fennan's murder in John le Carré's *Call for the Dead.* He solves Stella Rode's murder in *A Murder of Quality.* He launches with British Intelligence head Control a complex double-doublecross to protect Hans-Dieter Mundt that ends in Alec Leamas's and Liz Gold's deaths in *The Spy Who Came In from the Cold.* He warns John Avery against Leclerc's fantasy to revitalize the nearly defunct wartime military operations department that ends in Avery's spiritual death and Fred Leiser's assassination in *The Looking-Glass War.* He uncovers British Intelligence's traitorous double agent in *Tinker, Tailor, Soldier, Spy.* He traces this long-term double agent back to his Soviet controller Karla and resurrects the espionage agency through Operation Dolphin in *The Honourable Schoolboy.* Forcibly retired, he is later recalled to active service by Labour Government Cabinet Minister Oliver Lacon to solve the murder of his former Estonian recruit, General Vladimir, and to force Karla's defection, his culminating but morally questionable personal triumph, in *Smiley's People.*

Mary Smiling Flora Poste's London friend whose two interests in life are the imposing of reason and moderation upon her admirers and the collection of brassières in Stella Gibbons's *Cold Comfort Farm.*

Sebastian Smiss Bachelor co-director with Reggie Dacker of the Imperial Palace Hotel; he is winner of the secret competition between them for a place on the newly formed Board of the Orcham Merger of eight luxury hotels; his success is due to his tireless application and attention to detail in Arnold Bennett's *Imperial Palace.*

Smith James Horgan's senior clerk, who feels threatened by Philip Weston's position as an apprentice in Isabel Colegate's *Statues in a Garden.*

Captain Smith Officer in British internal security who investigates intelligence leaks in atomic-energy research; he works with Martin Eliot to secure a confession from Eric Sawbridge in C. P. Snow's *The New Men.*

Mrs. Smith William Smith's wife; forceful and somewhat more realistic, she stands up to the Tontons Macoutes; she finally leaves Haiti with her husband for Santo Domingo in Graham Greene's *The Comedians.*

Ellen Smith Wife of a mentally ill government official; she has a secret love affair with Roger Quaife and marries him after his resignation from government in C. P. Snow's *Corridors of Power.*

Gabrielle Smith London University Professor of Literature and mistress of Simon Jebb; at age thirty-five she kills herself and leaves a note for Simon which police investigate, as they shortly afterwards investigate the relationship between the theft of her love letters and the death of Dame Rhetta Sergeant in Storm Jameson's *There Will Be a Short Interval.*

Gerald Smith A Marxist historian whose wife's psychiatric hospitalization is due to her inability to stand being ostracized from the community because of her husband's political affiliations in Doris Lessing's *The Four-Gated City.*

Henry Smith Socialist Member of Parliament; he is the victim of murder in 1938 because he knows of espionage involving the sale of arms to Germany on the eve of World War II; his World War I friend David Renn investigates the murder; suspects include Stephen Coster, Julian Swan, Louis Earlham, Captain Tim Hunt, and Captain Will Ford in Storm Jameson's *Before the Crossing.*

Hugh Smith Weak youth who, being the only man ever loved by Sheila Knight, is her only hope for happiness; he decides not to marry her after his possessive rival Lewis Eliot warns him about her emotional instability in C. P. Snow's *Time of Hope.*

Innocent Smith An old schoolmate of Arthur Inglewood; he mysteriously appears at Beacon House and influences the boarders with his behavior; some think him eccentric, others crazy; he is acquitted of all the charges of burglary, desertion, bigamy, and attempted murder in G. K. Chesterton's *Manalive.*

Katherine Smith A "goodthinkful" person (someone who is incapable of bad thoughts, naturally orthodox, and sexually frigid); she married Winston Smith to produce children; childless, she lives apart from him in George Orwell's *Nineteen Eighty-Four.*

Rezia Smith Italian wife of the suicidal Septimus Smith; she is a seamstress and the creator of beautiful hats; she can cope with her English war-veteran husband's hallucinations and states of mind only with deep, blind love and patience in Virginia Woolf's *Mrs. Dalloway.*

Septimus Warren Smith World War I veteran and victim of "delayed stress syndrome"; Septimus is the Dostoevskian double and shadow twin of Clarissa Dalloway; able neither to live in the moment, nor to accept change and flux, nor to cope with his failure —

society provides him no place nor value — Septimus communes with his dead friend Evan and the singing swallows and writes exquisite, poetic "orts and frags" on the meaning of life; afflicted with the "terrible beauty" of madness, he is a victim of insensitive medical doctors; Dr. Holmes's violent intrusion nudges Septimus's suicidal leap from the window and impalement on railings below in Virginia Woolf's *Mrs. Dalloway*.

William Abel Smith   American vegetarian and former presidential candidate from Wisconsin who tries to establish a vegetarian center in Haiti but leaves, disillusioned, for Santo Domingo; he is a kind, dignified idealist finally much admired by Brown in Graham Greene's *The Comedians*.

Wily Smith   A black Euphoric State University student; he takes Philip Swallow's novel-writing class, writes a glowing report of him in the Course Bulletin, is arrested for spray-painting slogans, and is the cause for Philip's arrest for brick-stealing in David Lodge's *Changing Places: A Tale of Two Campuses*.

Winston Smith   A smallish Party worker; he begins to feel a need to join the Brotherhood against Big Brother and the Party; he falls in love and has a sexual liason with another member of the Party and is finally tortured and beaten into proclaiming his love for Big Brother in George Orwell's *Nineteen Eighty-Four*.

Smither   Housekeeper for Timothy Forsyte in John Galsworthy's *To Let*. She joins the household staff of Winifred Dartie in *Swan Song*.

Smither   Aunt Ann Forsyte's maid who prepares her hair each morning in John Galsworthy's *The Man of Property*.

Smithers   A fat boy sent up to Sudeley Hall by parents looking for social elevation; he is taunted, bullied, and tormented by the others in Nicholas Blake's *A Question of Proof*.

Alvina Smithers   An Amazon who terrified quiet men; she married Fred Smithers because he was a sportsman and soldier; discontented and narrow-minded, she only adds to the miseries of her daughter, Georgie, in Richard Aldington's *The Colonel's Daughter*.

Lieutenant Colonel Frederic Smithers   Retired career army man with small means; his vices include an occasional London tart and losing racehorse bets; living in the past, he fails to provide a future for his daughter, Georgie, in Richard Aldington's *The Colonel's Daughter*.

Georgina Smithers   Naïve, homely, earnest young woman who is left in post-World War I England with little prospect of marriage; she strives to deal with her plight and with her pukka army mother and father in Richard Aldington's *The Colonel's Daughter*.

Smithson   Secondary-school headmaster who awards Arthur Miles a university scholarship in C. P. Snow's *The Search*.

Constable Smithson   Policeman and friend of John Wainwright; he is murdered by John after catching John robbing Mr. Magnate's house in Olaf Stapledon's *Odd John: A Story Between Jest and Earnest*.

Charles Smithson   A young gentleman and amateur zoologist who falls in love with the mysterious Sarah Woodruff while visiting his fiancée, Ernestina Freeman, in Lyme Regis; after making love to Sarah, he breaks his engagement; then unable to find Sarah, he travels until she is found living with the Rossetti group; they do and do not marry in the alternative endings of John Fowles's *The French Lieutenant's Woman*.

Sir Robert Smithson   Charles Smithson's uncle, who frustrates Charles's hopes of inheriting his estate by marrying Bella Tompkins in John Fowles's *The French Lieutenant's Woman*.

Dr. Fabian Smollett   A clever man, whose skill as a physician Duncan Edgeworth does not completely trust; he attends Ellen Edgeworth in her last illness in Ivy Compton-Burnett's *A House and Its Head*.

Florence Smollett   Cousin and wife of Fabian, and friend of the Edgeworths in Ivy Compton-Burnett's *A House and Its Head*.

Mrs. Smythe   Nosy landlady who pesters the newly graduated Charles Lumley with questions about his nonexistent "job" while he decides what he wants to do next in John Wain's *Hurry On Down*.

Mrs. Smythe   Unobtrusive, silent woman and sister to Richard Smythe in Graham Greene's *The End of the Affair*.

Albert Smythe   Abrupt, fidgety second partner in Curpet's law firm; he approves Richard Larch's promotion to bookkeeper for the firm in Arnold Bennett's *A Man From the North*.

Richard Smythe   Driven, birthmark-disfigured, truth-seeking rationalist; a professed atheist who tries to find a faith in his unbelief, he sees Sarah Miles weekly for counseling sessions, in which he tries to convince her that God doesn't exist, until he declares his love for her; he attributes the sudden disappearance of his birthmark to the dead Sarah's ministrations in Graham Greene's *The End of the Affair.*

Snape minor   Schoolboy at Seaforth House in Roy Fuller's *The Ruined Boys.*

Snedding   Dense and disregarded pupil in Herbert Getliffe's chambers in C. P. Snow's *Time of Hope.*

Snowball (satiric representation of Leon Trotsky) Pig organizer on Mr. Jones's farm; he is a hero in the uprising against people when the animals take over Manor Farm; he is run off by Major when Major wants to change the rules to benifit pigs over other farm animals in George Orwell's *Animal Farm.*

Lord Snowdoun   His Majesty's Secretary of State and Minister of Scotland; he seeks Anthony Lammas's aid in persuading his son, Harry Lord Belses, to renounce his friendship for the notorious Mrs. Cranmer and to assume his familial responsibilities in John Buchan's *The Free Fishers.*

Julie Snowflake   An American student with whom James Walker has a love affair and goes on a trip west in Malcolm Bradbury's *Stepping Westward.*

Soames   Ship's master and lieutenant aboard the *Indefatigable* who assists Hornblower in preparing to board the *Marie Galante*; his death in battle precedes Hornblower's promotion to Acting Lieutenant in C. S. Forester's *Mr. Midshipman Hornblower.*

Father Socket   Confidence man cum medium who competes with Patrick Seton in Muriel Spark's *The Bachelors.*

Socrates the Greek (Sock)   A man in the village neighboring the Quests' farm who owns a shoddy store and hotel; he treats people according to their social status in Doris Lessing's *Martha Quest.*

Olga Sologub   Russian emigrée prostitute last seen dancing with Andy Bredahl, Dana Hilliot's enemy, after Dana abandons her in Malcolm Lowry's *Ultramarine.*

Abe Solomon   One of the circle of Hunt's friends whom Kate Fletcher (Armstrong) found interesting when she was aged sixteen; he was one of the few people who could put Hunt in his place in Margaret Drabble's *The Middle Ground.*

Louis Soltyk   A Pole who is seen by Otto Kreisler as a "tool of fate" always coming between him and his desires;

he is unintentionally killed by Kreisler in a duel in Wyndham Lewis's *Tarr.*

Etty Somers   Flighty, independent cousin of Olivia and Kate Curtis in Rosamond Lehmann's *Invitation to the Waltz.* She has never married and allows Olivia to live with her in *The Weather in the Streets.*

Harriet Somers   Richard Lovat Somers's spunky wife, who boils when he shows interest in "revolutions or governments or whatnot" rather than attending to their marriage; she more than holds her own against his foolish notion that he is her "lord and master" in D. H. Lawrence's *Kangaroo.*

Jane Somers   A middle-aged editor of a fashion magazine; caring for an elderly friend and for her sister's teen-age daughters and embarking on a new romance, she comes to terms with her fears of loneliness and the isolation that old age brings with it in Doris Lessing's *The Diaries of Jane Somers.*

Richard Lovat Somers   A small, bearded man who writes poems and essays; he travels with his wife, Harriet, from England to Australia following World War I; desiring action in the "world of men", he is attracted to the Diggers, a revolutionary Australian group, but ultimately he avoids commitments to political and social groups and to any individuals other than his wife; he journeys toward New Zealand at the close of D. H. Lawrence's *Kangaroo.*

Ivy Something   Shy daughter of Sir Somebody and Lady Something; she is rumored by gossip columnist Eva Schnerb to be engaged to a member of the archaeological expedition to Dateland in Ronald Firbank's *The Flower Beneath the Foot.*

Rosa Bark, Lady Something   Vacuous, chatty wife of the British Ambassador; she is teased irreverently by King William of Pisuerga; she attracts the assertively expressed sexual interest of Queen Thleeanouhee of Dateland in Ronald Firbank's *The Flower Beneath the Foot.*

Sir Somebody Something   Somewhat rugged but sensitive English Ambassador to Pisuerga, who patiently tolerates his wife's often-confused ramblings and behavior in Ronald Firbank's *The Flower Beneath the Foot.*

Jan ("The Swede") Sondersheim   Swedish birth-control expert in Margaret Drabble's *The Middle Ground.*

Susan Sondersheim   Jan Sondersheim's wife, who appears to suffer a breakdown at a dinner party at Evelyn (Morton) and Ted Stennett's; she is later reported to have been a victim of a hostage/police shoot-out affair in Geneva in Margaret Drabble's *The Middle Ground*.

Max Sonnenheim The visiting friend of Ted Burton; he monopolizes Miriam Henderson at the Hendersons' summer party, alienates Ted, and dies abroad in Dorothy Richardson's *Backwater*.

Sonny Sontage A forger who outfits the narrator as "Liam Dempsey" for his first mission in Finland in Len Deighton's *The Billion-Dollar Brain*.

Onny Soraghan Servant girl in the Coniffe home who shares with Gabriel Galloway an infatuation that leads to their running off to Dublin together; there, caught up in the Bohemian world of Sylvester and Telman Young, she takes lovers, becomes pregnant, rejects Gabriel's marriage proposals, and seeks a back-alley abortion that costs her her life in Mary Lavin's *The House in Clewe Street*.

Albert (Bert) Sorrell Bookmaker and childhood lover of actress Rae Marcable; he is stabbed as he waits in line to buy theater tickets in Josephine Tey's *The Man in the Queue*.

Barbara Sothill Basil Seal's sister and for a time the billeting officer for war-evacuee children in her rural district; she is overfond of her brother in Evelyn Waugh's *Put Out More Flags*.

General Sotillo Cruel Monterist general in Joseph Conrad's *Nostromo: A Tale of the Seaboard*.

William Soulsby Sigismund Claverhouse's friend, who is also an old school friend of Cleveland Hutton; he wants to marry Dolores Hutton but marries Sophy Hutton when Dolores refuses him in Ivy Compton-Burnett's *Dolores*.

Mr. Soutar Engineer aboard the *Archimedes*; understanding no Chinese, he becomes mistakenly convinced that the Chinese firemen are plotting rebellion during the hurricane in Richard Hughes's *In Hazard*.

Stephen Southernwood Shepherd and former preacher, who has rejected intellectually his Christian faith but suffers great emotional emptiness; he abandons his pregnant wife, Deborah Arden, and later their newborn child but grows enough spiritually to pity the imperfections of one other human being and to love Deborah's spirit and body; he experiences no religious renewal or sexual ecstasy in their reunion, though he finally accepts the inseparable nature of joy and pain in the human condition and recognizes the value of pity in Mary Webb's *The Golden Arrow*.

Sozy Homeless, elderly woman who becomes a loyal servant to Johnson in Joyce Cary's *Mister Johnson*.

Maurice Spandrell Cynical social parasite whose bitterness toward life eventually leads him to murder Everard Webley and to arrange his own death in Aldous Huxley's *Point Counter Point*.

Jack Spang (alias Rufus B. Saye) European head of "The Spangled Mob" of diamond smugglers; he is Seraffimo Spang's twin brother in Ian Fleming's *Diamonds Are Forever*.

Seraffimo Spang Jack Spang's twin brother, who runs the Las Vegas end of the diamond-smuggling enterprise in Ian Fleming's *Diamonds Are Forever*.

Spargus One of Cavor's laborers who let the laboratory furnaces die, thereby accidentally producing Cavorite amidst a devastating wind-storm in H. G. Wells's *The First Men in the Moon*.

Ben Sparrow Decent, hard-working Special Branch Police official who knows George Smiley from their wartime intelligence days; he assigns Inspector Mendel to the Samuel Fennan murder case in John le Carré's *Call for the Dead*. He provides Smiley an introduction to Carne Police Inspector Rigby in *A Murder of Quality*.

Spascock The Volyen Defender of the Public who defends the government against Lord Grice's indictment of it in Doris Lessing's *Documents Relating to the Sentimental Agents in the Volyen Empire*.

Dave Spear An idealistic communist, who is organizer of the Glastonbury "Commune" and leader of strikes against the capitalist Philip Crow; the employees of the communistic factory turn against him despite his fervent claim to be "the voice of the Future" in John Cowper Powys's *A Glastonbury Romance*.

Persephone (Percy) Spear The boyish-looking wife of the communist Dave Spear; despite her revulsion for sexual contact with males, she is the lover both of Philip Crow and of Will Zoyland; herself a communist, she leaves Glastonbury for Russia in John Cowper Powys's *A Glastonbury Romance*.

Dr. John Spedding Physician with a practice in South Kensington who takes his wife, Teresa, to Covent Garden opera; he treats Sebastian for a sprained ankle and is later invited to Chevron, Sebastian's country estate, in Vita Sackville-West's *The Edwardians*.

Teresa Spedding Dr. John Spedding's wife, who is dazzled by the glittering society and Christmas celebration at Chevron; she refuses to betray her husband and flees from Sebastian's attempted seduction in Vita Sackville-West's *The Edwardians*.

Dr. Speedwell The kindly, overworked small-town physician who attends to the medical needs of the denizens of Anchorstone in L. P. Hartley's *The Shrimp and the Anemone*.

Elsa Speier One of the German pupils in the Hanover school in Dorothy Richardson's *Pointed Roofs*.

Freddie Spencer Owner of the farm on which Arthur Morley works and through whom Bryan Morley meets Fay Corrigan in David Storey's *A Prodigal Child*.

Sir John Spencer Father of Marigold and Rollo; he spends the party secluded in the library, where Olivia Curtis has a friendly conversation with him in Rosamond Lehmann's *Invitation to the Waltz*. He seems bewildered and senile in *The Weather in the Streets*.

Margaret Spencer Friend and companion of Bryan Morley; she keeps up her friendship throughout their growing up in David Storey's *A Prodigal Child*.

Marigold Spencer Vivacious, happy daughter of Sir John and Lady Spencer; she is a friend of Olivia Curtis, whom she rescues from an unpleasant dance partner in Rosamond Lehmann's *Invitation to the Waltz*. Married with two children, she is rather flighty and unsettled in *The Weather in the Streets*.

Mary Spencer Wife of Freddie Spencer and mother of Margaret Spencer, Bryan Morley's friend, in David Storey's *A Prodigal Child*.

Rollo Spencer Handsome son of Sir John and Lady Spencer; he politely dances with various girls, is amused at Olivia Curtis's naïveté, and moodily talks to Olivia at the dance about his girl Nicola Maude in Rosamond Lehmann's *Invitation to the Waltz*. The husband of Nicola, he enters into a back-street sexual affair with Olivia who, after eight months, breaks off the affair at the insistence of Lady Spencer in *The Weather in the Streets*.

Sibyl, Lady Spencer Mother of Marigold and Rollo; she gives a ball in her home and graciously mixes with her guests but forgets decorum briefly when she does a fast reel in Rosamond Lehmann's *Invitation to the Waltz*. She tactfully tells Olivia Curtis that her affair with Rollo must end, as she will tolerate no scandal, in *The Weather in the Streets*.

Miss Spencer-Haigh A British Council employee who finds Nicholas Urfe a teaching job on Phraxos in John Fowles's *The Magus*.

Erasmus Spendlove Precise, well-informed secretary and companion to Hornblower; Spendlove is kidnapped with Hornblower by pirates in C. S. Forester's *Hornblower in the West Indies*.

Noel Spens Dora Greenfield's London lover, a journalist who brings adverse publicity to Imber Court by his reporting of the bell incident in Iris Murdoch's *The Bell*.

Spicer Ageing, fearful, nervous, marginally thoughtful man; a member of Pinkie Brown's mob, he witnessed Pinkie's killing of Charles Hale; he posed as Hale in Snow's Restaurant; deluded into thinking that Pinkie is looking out for him, he plans a hideaway trip to become part owner of the Blue Anchor pub in Nottingham; after he is beaten by Colleoni's mob, Pinkie pushes him down the stairs at Billy's in Graham Greene's *Brighton Rock*.

Spidel Member of the evil gang hired to guard Sakskia, the Russian princess, until her captor arrives to claim her in John Buchan's *Huntingtower*.

Mrs. Sammy Spillikins Supervisor at the women's lodging where the nurses live in Margaret Drabble's *The Millstone*.

Sidney Spinks Resident of Keith Rickman's boarding house; he relieves Rickman of the obligation to marry Flossie Walker by marrying her himself in May Sinclair's *The Divine Fire*.

Spiro A young Greek student trying to get into Oxford or Cambridge; he is tutored by Rosamund Stacey in Margaret Drabble's *The Millstone*.

Spittle Lame caretaker hired to guard Sakskia, the Russian princess imprisoned in Huntingtower House; he is captured by the Gorbals Die-Hards and made prisoner in the wine cellar in John Buchan's *Huntingtower*.

Oliver Spode The master of mathematics at Lucius Cassidy's school; he and Oliver Shelley are reproved for their conspicuous friendship; Oliver Spode is unaware that he is the natural son of Oliver Firebrace, Oliver Shelley's maternal grandfather, in Ivy Compton-Burnett's *Two Worlds and Their Ways*.

Roderick Spode Would-be dictator who heads the Black Shorts, a fascist mob; he aspires to the hand of Madeline Bassett; his enmity for Bertie Wooster is neutralized by Jeeves's discovery that he secretly designs ladies' undergarments in P. G. Wodehouse's *The Code of the Woosters*. His having become the Earl of Sidcup is mentioned in *Aunts Aren't Gentlemen*. He appears in three other novels.

Dominic Spong   A sententious, wealthy lawyer, whose wife dies; a frequent visitor at Sir Godfrey Haslam's house, he becomes engaged to Camilla Bellamy in Ivy Compton-Burnett's *Men and Wives*.

Elsie Sprickett   Twenty-three-year-old, strongly built, blue-eyed, black-haired, widowed servant of the miser Henry Earlforward; she has the primitive power and dignity of an ancient votaress in spite of her poverty; her unselfconscious, warm responses have a healing power for her beloved shell-shocked Joe and a soothing power for others in Arnold Bennett's *Riceyman Steps*.

Mrs. Spruce   The Lovats' cook, beloved by young Rose and Viola Lovat; she is secretly the mother of Brigit Lovat; she sends an anonymous letter to Brigit's father, Sir Ransome Chace, when it is rumored that Brigit is Edmund Lovat's daughter in Ivy Compton-Burnett's *Darkness and Day*.

Mr. Spurr   Editor of the *Zambesia News*; he offers Martha Quest a job writing for the woman's page, which she indignantly turns down in Doris Lessing's *Martha Quest*.

Squealer (satiric representation of a propagandist)   A pig; he talks all the animals back to work, explains changes, and mollifies the animals whenever trouble seems near in George Orwell's *Animal Farm*.

Squire   Conscience-driven estate owner and the rector's friend; he can be cruel to his sister Florence in Rex Warner's *The Aerodrome: A Love Story*.

Andrew Stace   The squire of Moreton Edge, who is the unacknowledged natural father of his adopted son, Christian; Andrew does not want Christian to marry his daughter Sophia in Ivy Compton-Burnett's *Brothers and Sisters*.

Andrew Stace (the younger)   Dinah's tall young brother; he expects to inherit Moreton Edge but leaves the land to live in London after his parents' incest is discovered in Ivy Compton-Burnett's *Brothers and Sisters*.

Christian Stace   Andrew's unacknowledged illegitimate son, a physician; he falls in love with Andrew's daughter, Sophia Stace, marries her, and has three children in Ivy Compton-Burnett's *Brothers and Sisters*.

Christiana (Dinah) Stace   Christian and Sophia's daughter; three young men propose to her, but she expects to live celibately with her brother in Ivy Compton-Burnett's *Brothers and Sister*.

Robin Stace   The younger brother of the younger Andrew and Dinah; educated at Oxford and employed in a government office, he is sardonic about his mother's domination of the family in Ivy Compton-Burnett's *Brothers and Sisters*.

Sophia Stace   Andrew's beautiful daughter, who always gets her way; she unknowingly marries her half brother; she tyrannizes over their three children in Ivy Compton-Burnett's *Brothers and Sisters*.

Mrs. Stacey   Rosamund Stacey's mother; she worked at a probation center when Rosamund was growing up in Margaret Drabble's *The Millstone*.

Andrew Stacey   Rosamund Stacey's brother; not as bright as his two sisters, he leads a conventional life full of bridge and dinner parties in Margaret Drabble's *The Millstone*.

Clare Stacey   Andrew Stacey's wife; she is a dim, conventional woman interested in dinner parties, trips to the beauty parlor, and cleanliness in Margaret Drabble's *The Millstone*.

Herbert Stacey   Rosamund Stacey's father; he and his wife are fairly wealthy yet vote Labour and try to instill Labour values in their children; they conveniently extend their trip abroad when they learn of Rosamund's pregnancy in Margaret Drabble's *The Millstone*.

Octavia Stacey   Rosamund Stacey's baby; she becomes very ill and almost dies in Margaret Drabble's *The Millstone*.

Rosamund Stacey   A Cambridge student who has neglected sexual experience while working to complete her thesis; she gets experience, becomes pregnant, and decides to keep the child, finish her thesis, and become a scholar in Margaret Drabble's *The Millstone*. Her "neighbourly gin and tonic" with Ted Stennett is interrupted by a frantic Irene Crowther in *The Middle Ground*.

Henry Stack   Wilfred Desert's batman during World War I; he serves as butler in Wilfred's London rooms in John Galsworthy's *Flowering Wilderness*. He notifies Dinny Cherrell that Wilfred has drowned in Siam in *Over the River*.

Herr Staefel   Master of German descent who, while

visiting his family, is caught in Germany at the outbreak of the War and is subsequently killed on the Western Front; Mr. Chips's eulogizing of him along with the British boys from Brookfield causes a small stir among the students in James Hilton's *Good-bye, Mr. Chips.*

Neville Stafford   Upper-middle-class student at Colin Saville's school whose family owns a mill; he seems to be Colin's friend until he steals Colin's only love in David Storey's *Saville.*

Stagruk   A delegate from Planet 2 who persists in seeing Canopus as an enemy and believes that the Sirians should pull out of Shikasta (Rohanda) in Doris Lessing's *The Sirian Experiments.*

Abigail de Mordell Staines-Knight   Secretary to Ian Tooley, keeper of the box, and friend of Nancy Hawkins in Muriel Spark's *A Far Cry from Kensington.*

Aubrey Stainford   Impoverished public-school acquaintance of Val Dartie; he steals a valuable snuffbox from Winifred Dartie and forges a check in Val's name in John Galsworthy's *Swan Song.*

Mr. Stairforth   Enthusiastic, loquacious manager of the Stocks Department; he is father of seventeen children in Arnold Bennett's *Imperial Palace.*

Stamp   Billy Fisher's obnoxious office mate in the undertaking firm in Keith Waterhouse's *Billy Liar.*

Harry Stamp   Gentleman neighbor of Sir Randolph Nettleby in Isabel Colegate's *The Shooting Party.*

Mildred Stamp   Harry Stamp's vulgar wife and a barely tolerated neighbor of Minnie, Lady Nettleby in Isabel Colegate's *The Shooting Party.*

Stan   Unpleasant, "Americanized" younger brother of Charles Lumley's girlfriend Rosa; his job as a hairdresser makes him the center of family discussion because of the gossip he brings home in John Wain's *Hurry On Down.*

Stan (Stanislaus)   Open-hearted bartender at the Prague Restaurant Sport; he instructs his nephew to tip Jerry Westerby off to Jim Prideaux's betrayal in Operation Testify in John le Carré's *Tinker, Tailor, Soldier, Spy.*

Patrick Standish   Handsome thirty-year-old unscrupulous playboy and college teacher; he relentlessly and at last successfully pursues Jenny Bunn in Kingsley Amis's *Take a Girl Like You.*

John Stanford   Sinister figure out of Sigbjorn Wilderness's past; Sigbjorn encounters him in Oaxaca despite his attempt to avoid being recognized in Malcolm Lowry's *Dark as the Grave Wherein My Friend Is Laid.*

Sophy Stanhope   A brilliant, beautiful young woman who is evil incarnate; she is devoted to "weirdness" and the need to control others by force of will in William Golding's *Darkness Visible.*

Toni Stanhope   The twin sister of Sophy; she is a professional terrorist trained by Arabs; she assists in a kidnaping and fire-bombing in William Golding's *Darkness Visible.*

Ivan Stanitski   Nikolai Bursanov's book-keeper who falsified reports and ledgers yet seems remorseful and is allowed to stay on as a dependent in William Gerhardie's *Futility: A Novel on Russian Themes.*

Stanley   Adjutant under Lord Edrington's command who is thrown from his horse in C. S. Forester's *Mr. Midshipman Hornblower.*

Stanley   A calm, plodding farmer; although slow to move, he is an activist and a devoted friend to the farmers in Rex Warner's *The Wild Goose Chase: An Allegory.*

Stanley   A young liberal man who has dated Maureen in Doris Lessing's *The Summer Before the Dark.*

Stanley   Iris's lorry-driving cousin whom Iris would like Martha Quest to marry in Doris Lessing's *The Four-Gated City.*

Ann Veronica Stanley   Independent, scientific, social woman; she is searching for freedom, happiness, and her place in the world; her study of comparative anatomy mirrors her use of certain social rules and disregard of others in H. G. Wells's *Ann Veronica: A Modern Love Story.*

Mollie Stanley   Aristocratic, disciplined, considerate aunt; she tells Ann Veronica Stanley what she should be thinking, but does not consult Ann in H. G. Wells's *Ann Veronica: A Modern Love Story.*

Peter Stanley   Salesman, chauvinist, hobbyist, and Ann's father; he thinks of Ann as property more than as a thinking person in H. G. Wells's *Ann Veronica: A Modern Love Story.*

Rose Stanley   The member of "the Brodie set" who becomes "famous for sex"; her "instinct" inspires Jean

Brodie to cast her in the role of Teddy Lloyd's lover in Muriel Spark's *The Prime of Miss Jean Brodie.*

Christopher Stannix Adam Melfort's best friend, who, upon hearing Adam pronounced guilty of forgery, dismisses it as a lie to save his weak wife, Camilla, in John Buchan's *A Prince of the Captivity.*

Dr. William Stanton The astronomer who first identifies Rama as an artifact in Arthur C. Clarke's *Rendezvous with Rama.*

Stanton-Browne Giggling young woman who is introduced by Charles Sheriff to Arthur Miles and Audrey as his latest conquest in C. P. Snow's *The Search.*

Mélie Staple-Craven Julia Corrie's friend, who entertains her with spiritualist games in Dorothy Richardson's *Honeycomb.*

Percy Staple-Craven The doting husband of Mélie in Dorothy Richardson's *Honeycomb.*

Batista Staretti Brother of Maria Clandon-Hartley; he swindles Herbert Clandon-Hartly out of four thousand pounds and persuades his father to disinherit Maria if she marries Clandon-Hartley; he is responsible for the couple's wanderings and financial embarrassment in Eric Ambler's *Epitaph for a Spy.*

Sammy Starfield A bookmaker whom Madge plans to marry; he gives Jake Donaghue good advice that allows Jake to place lucrative bets on horses; he appropriates a translation by Jake of a French novel that is a likely movie prospect in Iris Murdoch's *Under the Net.*

Amos Starkadder Husband of Judith and father of Elfine, Reuben, and Seth; he has been chained to Cold Comfort Farm by years of toil and grime, but his real passion lies in lay preaching, an ambition quickly utilized by Flora Poste in Stella Gibbons's *Cold Comfort Farm.*

Elfine Starkadder The startled-bird daughter of Amos and Judith; her natural beauty and charms are fostered by Flora Poste, who undertakes to mastermind the marriage of a more civilized Elfine to Dick Hawk-Monitor in Stella Gibbons's *Cold Comfort Farm.*

Ezra Starkadder A horsey cousin of the Starkadders in Stella Gibbons's *Cold Comfort Farm.*

Judith Starkadder The strong-boned wife of Amos and mother of Elfine, Reuben, and Seth; she spends her time contemplating a nebulous grief; she invites Flora Poste to Cold Comfort Farm to atone for the

mysterious wrong her husband did to Flora's father in Stella Gibbons's *Cold Comfort Farm.*

Micah Starkadder A half cousin of the Starkadders; he is one of the many relatives who are bound to Cold Comfort Farm by a mysterious curse in Stella Gibbons's *Cold Comfort Farm.*

Rennet Starkadder A Starkadder relative thought of by the rest as a bit "daft"; she resembles a baby bird but captures the heart of Mr. Mybug in Stella Gibbons's *Cold Comfort Farm.*

Reuben Starkadder Son who truly loves the land and is eager to comply with Flora Poste's idea of encouraging his father, Amos, to go about the country preaching, thus leaving the management of Cold Comfort Farm to his own capable hands in Stella Gibbons's *Cold Comfort Farm.*

Seth Starkadder The village Romeo who, though he throbs with animal sexuality, is really interested in the movies, a fascination which is quickly fostered by his perceptive cousin Flora Poste in Stella Gibbons's *Cold Comfort Farm.*

Urk Starkadder Elfine Starkadder's cousin who is determined to marry her; he is obsessed with watervoles in Stella Gibbons's *Cold Comfort Farm.*

Miss Starkie The Middletons' governess, who disapproves of Lavinia Middleton's plan to marry Hugo, her supposed uncle, in Ivy Compton-Burnett's *The Mighty and Their Fall.*

Corporal Starling British member of the International Patrol arresting Anna Schmidt; he notifies Colonel Calloway that she is being taken away by the Russians in Graham Greene's *The Third Man and the Fallen Idol.*

Star Maker The Prime Mover of a succession of universes (including our own), whose creations are motivated by a desire for aesthetic fulfillment rather than by love or justice; the Star Maker is the object of the search by the narrator and the other components of the Cosmic Spirit in Olaf Stapledon's *Star Maker.*

Starnberg Second conductor in Evart's orchestra; he is Evart's confidential friend in Alan Sillitoe's *The General.*

Star Ponce Former seaman who teaches Frankie Love how to be a pimp but in the end stabs Frankie in the groin in Colin MacInnes's *Mr. Love and Justice.*

Bertram (Blackshirt) Starr-Smith Pierpoint's business manager and a British fascist who attacks Julius Ratner while attending Lord Osmund Shaw's costume party in Wyndham Lewis's *The Apes of God*.

Stars   Intelligent cosmic masses who find it difficult to imagine that intelligent life can exist on planets in Olaf Stapledon's *Star Maker*.

Star Sleuth   Mistrustful plain-clothes policeman and supposed mentor to Edward Justice; he dislikes Justice and bashes him on the head with a truncheon in Colin MacInnes's *Mr. Love and Justice*.

Susie Staunton   Edward Rowan's mistress and Tania Rowan's closest friend in Rebecca West's *The Birds Fall Down*.

Anne Staveley   Eighteen-year-old sister of Richard, who chides her for not having encouraged him to speak to Miss Fothergill as Eustace Cherrington did at his sister Hilda's urgings in L. P. Hartley's *The Shrimp and the Anemone*. She appears as colorless as her brother Dick is flamboyant at the Anchorstone Hall houseparty in *The Sixth Heaven*.

Edie, Lady Staveley   Wife of Sir John, hostess of Anchorstone Hall, and mother of Richard and Anne; she plies Eustace Cherrington with brandy following her son's rescue of him in L. P. Hartley's *The Shrimp and the Anemone*. She and her husband host the eventful houseparty in *The Sixth Heaven*. She writes a long letter to Lady Nelly Staveley describing the class differences between her son and Hilda Cherrington, whom she describes as "a handicap on any occasion that didn't involve life or death" in *Eustace and Hilda*.

Sir John Staveley   Aristocratic owner of Anchorstone Hall and father of Richard and Anne in L. P. Hartley's *The Shrimp and the Anemone*. He and Lady Staveley host the eventful houseparty in *The Sixth Heaven*.

Lady Nelly Staveley   The worldly and attractive fifty-ish relative by marriage of the Staveley family in L. P. Hartley's *The Sixth Heaven*. She befriends Eustace Cherrington and hosts him for a summer in her rented Venetian residence; she tells him that women often "like men to be rather helpless . . . even a little ridiculous and pathetic", and she advises him to keep some necessary distance between himself and his sister Hilda in *Eustace and Hilda*.

Richard (Dick) Staveley   Aristocratic scion of Anchorstone Hall who rescues Eustace Cherrington following the latter's overexertion in his paper-chase with Nancy Steptoe in L. P. Hartley's *The Shrimp and the Anemone*. He is known for his heroic exploits as a pilot in the Great War; while Eustace sees him as the ideal romantic escort for his sister Hilda, he seduces her in *The Sixth Heaven*. He is transformed from romantic hero to destroyer as Eustace begins to understand the darker reality Richard represents in *Eustace and Hilda*.

Clementina Stay   Manageress of a Caribbean tourist island; she believes she is psychic and can restore Johnny in Rosamond Lehmann's *A Sea-Grape Tree*.

Stebbings   Grey-haired and bearded impressed hand from the East India convoy in C. S. Forester's *Ship of the Line*.

Steed-Aspry   Oxford don and wartime recruiter for British Intelligence; with Jebedee and Adrian Fielding he recruits George Smiley; he suggests that Smiley marry Lady Ann and later gives him a porcelain figurine as a wedding present in John le Carré's *Call for the Dead*. He founds a men's club in Manchester Square which will cease when its original forty members die in *Tinker, Tailor, Soldier, Spy*.

Captain Steerforth   The efficient and dignified captain of the cruise ship Gilbert Pinfold sails on in Evelyn Waugh's *The Ordeal of Gilbert Pinfold*.

"Mama" Stefano   Greedy, conniving Tuscany postal employee and gossip; she sizes up Jerry Westerby's character accurately and, without intentional flattery, gives the agent the ironic sobriquet "the honourable schoolboy" in John le Carré's *The Honourable Schoolboy*.

Stein   Benevolent English trader who befriends Jim and helps him start his life over again in Patusan in Joseph Conrad's *Lord Jim*.

Stella   A Gypsy-like woman whom Martha Quest meets shortly after arriving in London; she lets her a room in her house in Doris Lessing's *The Four-Gated City*.

Stella   Evelyn Morton Stennett's friend; she is a part-time physiotherapist who lives in the country in Margaret Drabble's *The Middle Ground*.

Lady Stella   Genteel and compassionate aristocrat who finds the Utopians' immodesty shocking but who at first sides with Mr. Barnstaple in opposing Rupert Catskill's plan to overthrow Utopian rule in H. G. Wells's *Men Like Gods*.

Evelyn Morton Stennett   Ted Stennett's wife, who tolerates his many infidelities, including a long affair with her good friend Kate Fletcher Armstrong; she donates a great deal of her time to working with the less fortunate in Margaret Drabble's *The Middle Ground*.

James Stennett Brother of Ted Stennett, who claims that James is the "most boring man in Britain"; he lives with his parents in Margaret Drabble's *The Middle Ground*.

Sebastian Stennett Eldest of the three children of Evelyn (Morton) and Ted Stennett; he is a troubled, rebellious child in Margaret Drabble's *The Middle Ground*.

Ted Stennett Husband of Evelyn Morton Stennett; he is a very successful zoologist turned international advisor on epidemics; he is a womanizer who has had a long affair with Kate Fletcher Armstrong in Margaret Drabble's *The Middle Ground*.

Vicky Stennett Second of the three children of Evelyn (Morton) and Ted Stennett in Margaret Drabble's *The Middle Ground*.

Stent Astronomer Royal who supervises the final investigation of the Horsell Common landing site and who dies when his parlaying deputation is slaughtered in H. G. Wells's *The War of the Worlds*.

Stephanie The child of a family of politicians; Sarah Bennett's Oxford friend, she married Michael immediately after coming down from Oxford; she is committed to politics and seems to have a model marriage in Margaret Drabble's *A Summer Bird-Cage*.

Stephanie Jeffrey's old girlfriend, with whom he had lived for a summer in Spain after finishing college in Doris Lessing's *The Summer Before the Dark*.

Stephen Schoolyard bully who beats John Wainwright and then is beaten by him; Stephen later becomes John's friend in Olaf Stapledon's *Odd John: A Story Between Jest and Earnest*.

Stephens The "Dictator" of the Black Spot, a boys' secret society bent on discrimination and personal insult, especially against Smithers; he inadvertently helps Nigel Strangeways in solving the murders in Nicholas Blake's *A Question of Proof*.

James Stephens Fiery Irish rebel leader who is instrumental in finally persuading Leo Foxe-Donnel to join the rebel cause in Sean O'Faolain's *A Nest of Simple Folk*.

Lionel Stephens Gentleman who falls in love with Olivia, Lady Lilburn; being an excellent sportsman, he is resented and despised by Lord Hartlip in Isabel Colegate's *The Shooting Party*.

Lady Anne Stepney Pretty, contentious, untidy debutante in Anthony Powell's *A Buyer's Market*. She becomes Dicky Umfraville's fourth wife in *The Acceptance World*. As Sir Magnus Donners's mistress, she plays hostess at a party during which the players depict the seven deadly sins; she has affairs with Peter Templer and J. C. Quiggin in *The Kindly Ones*.

Lady Peggy Stepney Elder sister of Lady Anne Stepney; Charles Stringham thinks of marrying her in Anthony Powell's *A Question of Upbringing* and does so in *A Buyer's Market*. They are divorced in *The Acceptance World*. She has married again in *The Military Philosophers*.

Major Steptoe Nancy's father; the Steptoes are the Cherringtons' somewhat competitive neighbors in Anchorstone in L. P. Hartley's *The Shrimp and the Anemone*.

Mrs. Steptoe Nancy and Gerald Steptoe's mother in L. P. Hartley's *The Shrimp and the Anemone*.

Gerald Steptoe Son of Major and Mrs. Steptoe; a year older than Eustace Cherrington and physically robust, he serves as a contrast to Eustace, although his sister, Nancy, admits he is hopeless and reports she has given up on him, unlike Hilda with Eustace, in L. P. Hartley's *The Shrimp and the Anemone*.

Nancy Steptoe Daughter of Major and Mrs. Steptoe; she offers Eustace Cherrington the chance for a healthy physical experience and a non-subservient relationship with her in L. P. Hartley's *The Shrimp and the Anemone*. After being married to Captain Alberic, she divorces him and meets Eustace again during his Venetian sojourn; she offers him a chance for a love affair, which he declines, offering her money instead in *Eustace and Hilda*.

Stern Property developer who fared worse than Anthony Keating and his partnership during the 1970s property-market collapse in Margaret Drabble's *The Ice Age*.

Dr. Stern Martha Quest's impersonal and apathetic doctor, who does little to aid her in preventing pregnancy in her marriage to Douglas Knowell in Doris Lessing's *A Proper Marriage*.

Esther Stern Thomas Stern's three-year-old daughter; she does not seem to know or like her father in Doris Lessing's *Landlocked*.

Rachel Stern Thomas Stern's wealthy Polish wife, who has nothing in common with her husband in Doris Lessing's *Landlocked*.

Sarah Stern   Thomas Stern's brother's wife; she highly disapproves of the love affair between Thomas and Martha Quest in Doris Lessing's *Landlocked*.

Thomas Stern   Probably the only man with whom Martha Quest experiences true love; he is a Polish refugee, married to a woman of higher social class; he leaves to go to Israel, returns, and ultimately dies of Blackwater in the Zambesi in Doris Lessing's *Landlocked*.

Dr. Reinhold Steuckel   Munich jurist with whom Augustine Penry-Herbert becomes friendly; he explains the political situation to Augustine in Richard Hughes's *The Fox in the Attic*. He continues to supply intelligent analysis of Adolf Hitler's political success in *The Wooden Shepherdess*.

General Stevcek   Czechoslovakian military intelligence officer whose knowledge of and position in the Praesidium deceives Control and lures Jim Prideaux to his betrayal in John le Carré's *Tinker, Tailor, Soldier, Spy*.

Steven   A twelve-year-old African servant on Jonathan and Bessie Quest's farm; he is the first black African that May Quest ever sees as an actual human being in Doris Lessing's *The Four-Gated City*.

Herbert (Odo) Stevens   Costume jeweler who trains with Jenkins during the war; he is cheerful, intelligent, and narcissitic in Anthony Powell's *The Valley of Bones*. He has an affair with Priscilla Tolland in *The Soldier's Art* and with Pamela Flitton in *The Military Philosophers*. His book, *Sad Majors,* is published, thanks to Rosie Manasch's backing, in *Books Do Furnish a Room*. He is married to Rosie in *Temporary Kings*.

Stevie   Mentally childlike brother of Winnie Verloc, whose love for him rules her life; employed in an espionage plot by Adolf Verloc without malice but with reckless contempt, Stevie is killed by a terrorist bomb he is delivering in Joseph Conrad's *The Secret Agent: A Simple Tale*.

Matthew (Mattie) Stewart   The very mischievous and successful child actor in Freddie Wentworth's training school who befriends Jonathan Kemp in Penelope Fitzgerald's *At Freddie's*.

Madame Steynlin   Musically inclined, childless Dutchwoman who enjoys mothering others and who takes a special interest in the Russians, particularly Peter Krasnojabkin, on Nepenthe in Norman Douglas's *South Wind*.

Stifford (Stiff)   Young paper boy; he grows to manage the Clayhanger printshop under Edwin Clayhanger in Arnold Bennett's *Clayhanger*.

Stil   A completely self-sufficient and self-disciplined Motzen who is amazed by Lord Grice's mannerisms and weaknesses in Doris Lessing's *Documents Relating to the Sentimental Agents in the Volyen Empire*.

Still   Second lieutenant aboard the *Atropos* in C. S. Forester's *Hornblower and the Atropos*.

Sir Horace Stimms   War profiteer whose titles, wealth, and land have been gained at England's expense in Richard Aldington's *The Colonel's Daughter*.

Erich Stinnes   See Nikolai Sadoff.

Julia Stitch   A wealthy socialite who uses her influence with Lord Copper to have author John Courteney Boot sent as a war correspondent to Ishmaelia, not imagining that the wrong Boot will be assigned to the story in Evelyn Waugh's *Scoop*.

Willi Stock (The Baron)   Bookseller, man about town, and dabbler in the occult; he proves to be the London contact for Louisa Jepp's gang of smugglers in Muriel Spark's *The Comforters*.

Colonel Alexeyevitch (covernames: Captain Maylev, Professor Eberhard Lebowitz) Stok   A Red Army operative, Dawlish's K.G.B. counterpart, who is a spokesperson for humane concerns; as "Johnnie Vulkan's" (Paul Louis Broum's) official but extracurricular contact he changes from avuncular figure to mechanical K.G.B. thug in Len Deighton's *Funeral in Berlin*. He uses a corpse disguised in Admiral Vanya Remoziva's uniform in a conspiracy to thwart German reunification in *Spy Story*.

Henrietta (Regan) Stoker   Cockney cook in the Matthewses' London house who is constantly drunk and is hit by a car and paralyzed when drunk in Angus Wilson's *No Laughing Matter*.

Stokes   Surly servant in the Corrie household in Dorothy Richardson's *Honeycomb*.

Jill Stokes   Oldest friend of Meg Eliot; she is disliked by Bill Eliot and turns furiously against Meg after learning Meg tried to mediate between her and her son-in-law in Angus Wilson's *The Middle Age of Mrs. Eliot*.

Jim Stokes   Lord Lamancha's former orderly and troop sergeant in the war; one of the unemployed men hired by Charles Johnson Claybody to apprehend "John Macnab", he spots Lamancha, fights with him, and suffers a broken leg in John Buchan's *John Macnab*.

Leonard Stokes   Arrogant British canal pilot who turns in his resignation when the Suez Canal is nationalized; he is romantically interested in Leah Strauss in P. H. Newby's *Something to Answer For*.

Professor Stokesay   Long-dead expert in Anglo-Saxon history whose reputation is undone by Gerald Middleton's discovery that the Melpham affair was a fraud in Angus Wilson's *Anglo-Saxon Attitudes*.

Dollie Stokesay   Aging widow of Gilbert Stokesay; she was once Gerald Middleton's lover; she has overcome a life-long drinking affliction; she directs Gerald to the documents which conclude his investigation into the Melpham fraud in Angus Wilson's *Anglo-Saxon Attitudes*.

Gilbert Stokesay   Dead son of Professor Stokesay and husband of Dollie; his writings as essayist and poet have become popular; he disclosed once to Gerald Middleton the secret of his practical joke in the Melpham affair in Angus Wilson's *Anglo-Saxon Attitudes*.

Major Stone   A disoriented but non-violent mental patient at the asylum kept with severe cases after observing Poole and Dr. Forester burying the remains of Jones; he provides clues to Arthur Rowe as Rowe attempts to discover the true nature of the asylum in Graham Greene's *The Ministry of Fear*.

Denis Stone   Sensitive, young, ineffectual poet and guest at Crome estate; unhappy in his literary achievements, he is also frustrated in his devotion to Anne Wimbush, whose attentions to the painter R. Gombauld cause him to depart abruptly his host's houseparty in a moment of bitter indecisiveness in Aldous Huxley's *Crome Yellow*.

Martin Stone   Young physician, nephew of Cecilia Dallison and Bianca Dallison; he spends much energy in sanitation and child-rescue causes in London tenements in John Galsworthy's *Fraternity*.

Sylvanus Stone   Eighty-year-old father of Bianca Dallison and Cecilia Dallison; he lives with Bianca and Hilary Dallison; he is writing an endless book on universal brotherhood in John Galsworthy's *Fraternity*.

Victor Stone   A cheery schoolmaster who he tries to convince Dorothy Hare to talk her Rector father into allowing pageants and musical celebration in church; he would like to court Dorothy but has been refused in George Orwell's *A Clergyman's Daughter*.

Police Captain Stoner   Fatherly officer who, investigating the motel arson and the deaths of the two arsonists, advises Vivienne Michel to dissociate herself from the James Bonds as well as from criminals in Ian Fleming's *The Spy Who Loved Me*.

Iris March Fenwick Storm   Self-destructive, aristocratic young widow; she is a self-styled "shameless, shameful lady of the green hat" whose sophistication and independence combined with vulnerability attract the romantic attention of several men from her aristocratic circle in Michael Arlen's *The Green Hat*.

Anna Stormer   Thirty-six-year-old Austrian wife of Harold; she is attracted to the young student Mark Lennon and seduces him while vacationing in the Alps in John Galsworthy's *The Dark Flower*.

Harold Stormer   Forty-eight-year-old Oxford tutor who invites his student Mark Lennon to vacation in the Alps, where his wife, Anna, seduces Mark in John Galsworthy's *The Dark Flower*.

Rikki Stormgren   The Secretary General of the United Nations; he is for many years the only human to have contact with the Overlords; he attempts to discover their nature in Arthur C. Clarke's *Childhood's End*.

Jo Stoyte   Boorish multi-millionaire California oil tycoon; his fear of death causes him to support outlandish schemes to restore and prolong youth in Aldous Huxley's *After Many a Summer*.

Margaret Strafford   Imber Court community member who welcomes Dora Greenfield and officiously reminds her of the community's rules in Iris Murdoch's *The Bell*.

Mark Strafford   Margaret's bearded, sarcastic, indolent husband in Iris Murdoch's *The Bell*.

Mark Straithes   Wealthy schoolmate of Anthony Beavis; his love of adventure and violence leads him into the service of revolutionary causes; he loses a leg in Mexico in Aldous Huxley's *Eyeless in Gaza*.

Sandy Stranger   The member of the Brodie set "notorious for her small, almost non-existent, eyes"; cast by Jean Brodie as witness to the vicarious consummation of her love for Teddy Lloyd, Sandy becomes both lover and witness; eventually she betrays Jean Brodie and converts to Catholicism, becoming a nun and a celebrated moral psychologist in Muriel Spark's *The Prime of Miss Jean Brodie*.

Jack Strangeways   One of the Wragby Hall "mental-lifers" who argue the supremacy of the mind over the body in D. H. Lawrence's *Lady Chatterley's Lover*.

Commander John Strangeways   Agent whose disappearance on Crab Key initiates James Bond's investigation in Ian Fleming's *Dr. No*.

Nigel Strangeways   A quick-witted private agent who calls himself an "amateur"; an Oxford friend of Michael Evans, he was sent down for answering exams with limericks; his uncanny knack for "fitting in" and his genuine interest in people conceal his scientific curiosity; Michael calls him to help solve the campus murder in Nicholas Blake's *A Question of Proof*. He appears in fifteen subsequent novels.

Olive Strangeways   Advanced thinker at Wragby Hall who speaks about a book she has read concerning the possibility that babies could be bred in bottles; she champions a future time when "a woman needn't be dragged down by her *functions*" in D. H. Lawrence's *Lady Chatterley's Lover*.

Leah Strauss   Loyal daughter of Abravanel and wife to Robert Strauss; she thinks she is to blame for the mental condition of her husband, whom she left behind in the United States; she becomes romantically involved with Jack Townrow in P. H. Newby's *Something to Answer For*.

Robert Strauss   Husband to Leah Strauss; he is living in the United States and undergoing drug therapy for his depression in P. H. Newby's *Something to Answer For*.

Strawberry   Rabbit originally from the Warren of the Snares who joins Hazel's pioneers after his mate is killed in Richard Adams's *Watership Down*.

Strawson   Head keeper of the zoological gardens who is held responsible by Old Filson for the death of his son in Angus Wilson's *The Old Men at the Zoo*.

Sir Herbert Street   Art adviser to Mr. van Koppen in Norman Douglas's *South Wind*.

Selina Street   A gorgeous, thirtyish blonde sexual mercenary; she is John Self's unfaithful whore — until she finds someone more useful — in Martin Amis's *Money*.

Harriet Streeter   Larry Streeter's maltreated wife, who sleeps with Jimmy Morgan to get revenge on her husband; she later borrows money from Jimmy to return to America in Nigel Dennis's *Boys and Girls Come Out to Play*.

Larry Streeter   Tyrannical expatriate American and

director of Poland's gold mines, who refuses to flee the oncoming Nazis; he murders Max Divver when he returns to Mell in search of him in Nigel Dennis's *Boys and Girls Come Out to Play*.

Heinz Strehler   Half-Jewish Viennese son of a famous novelist; he lives briefly with Kenneth Toomey and proves to be a remarkably greedy, corrupt, and shifty petty criminal in Anthony Burgess's *Earthly Powers*.

Jakob Strehler   Austrian-Jewish, Nobel Prize-winning novelist much admired by Kenneth Toomey, who devises a doomed attempt to secure Strehler's escape from the Nazis in Anthony Burgess's *Earthly Powers*.

Amy Strickland   Charles Strickland's pragmatic wife, who is completely shocked when he suddenly disappears and cannot believe he has left for an ideal rather than for a woman in W. Somerset Maugham's *The Moon and Sixpence*.

Ata Strickland   The young native Tahitian girl who falls deeply in love with Charles Strickland, bears his son, and nurses him until he dies mutilated and blind from leprosy in W. Somerset Maugham's *The Moon and Sixpence*.

Charles Strickland (modified portrait of Paul Gauguin)   A single-minded stockbroker who suddenly abandons family and career to become a painter in Paris, leaving eventually for Tahiti where he dies a lingering death from leprosy in W. Somerset Maugham's *The Moon and Sixpence*.

Stringer   Colin Saville's childhood friend, who does not escape the poverty of the coalmine family in David Storey's *Saville*.

Charles Stringham   Good-natured but weak youth, Nicholas Jenkins's schoolfellow, whose early alcoholism interrupts his University career; he is sent by his hated stepfather, Buster Foxe, to his father's farm in Kenya; his changed personality and increasing drinking on his return are bewildering to friends in Anthony Powell's *A Question of Upbringing*. He marries his former fiancée, Lady Peggy Stepney, in *A Buyer's Market* and is divorced in *The Acceptance World*. He becomes the virtual prisoner of his sister's former governess, Geraldine Weedon, in *Casanova's Chinese Restaurant*. His habitual ridicule of Widmerpool works to his disadvantage when, as an army private, he is transferred by Major Widmerpool to a Mobile Laundry Unit in the far East in *The Soldier's Art*. He dies in a Japanese POW camp in *The Military Philosophers*.

Flavia Stringham   Melancholic elder sister of Charles

Stringham; Pamela Flitton, the daughter of her marriage to Cosmo Flitton, is probably Cosmo's, although rumored to be Dicky Umfraville's, in Anthony Powell's *A Buyer's Market*. Divorced also from her second husband, the American businessman and alcoholic Harrison Wisebite, Flavia is the mistress of the much younger Robert Tolland until he is killed in action in *The Valley of Bones*. She detests her son-in-law Kenneth Widmerpool in *Hearing Secret Harmonies*.

Jasper Stringwell-Anderson   Young historian of medieval Britain who expresses no surprise about the Melpham fraud; he supports the position that Gerald Middleton should continue as editor of the new journal in Angus Wilson's *Anglo-Saxon Attitudes*.

Babs Stripling   Peter Templer's elder sister, who left her first husband for Jimmy Stripling in Anthony Powell's *A Question of Upbringing*. She marries again after her divorce in *The Acceptance World*.

Jimmy Stripling   Husband of Peter Templer's elder sister, Babs; prevented by physical problems from service in World War I, he resents all those who did serve in Anthony Powell's *Question of Upbringing*. Divorced from Babs, he is obsessed with the occult and dominated by Mrs. Erdleigh; Jean Templer tells Nicholas Jenkins that she had an affair with Stripling in *The Acceptance World*. Stripling is still under Mrs. Erdleigh's control, but the object of his obsession has shifted to old cars in *Temporary Kings*.

Blanche Stroeve   Dirk Stroeve's reserved but deeply passionate wife, who falls in love with Charles Strickland, leaves her husband, and chooses a painful death by poison when Strickland leaves her in W. Somerset Maugham's *The Moon and Sixpence*.

Dirk Stroeve   A sweet-natured buffoon with no artistic talent but with the perception to see the genius of Charles Strickland; his support endures despite Strickland's callous seduction of his wife, Blanche, in W. Somerset Maugham's *The Moon and Sixpence*.

Mr. Strong   Harley Street surgeon with a grand house in Dulwich who has operated on Marcia Ivory and become the focus of her wandering imagination in Barbara Pym's *Quartet in Autumn*.

Steward Stroud   Vice-Chancellor of the University of Rummidge; he asks Morris Zapp to decide whether Philip Swallow or Robin Dempsey should get the senior lectureship, and he offers Morris the chairmanship of the department in David Lodge's *Changing Places: A Tale of Two Campuses*.

Willie Struthers   A passionate Communist who leads the Australian Socialist Party; he tries unsuccessfully to get the writer Richard Lovat Somers to lend his voice to the Party's cause in D. H. Lawrence's *Kangaroo*.

Tom Strutt   One of Lizzie Judd's lovers; he marries her when she becomes pregnant in Richard Aldington's *The Colonel's Daughter*.

Stuart   Civil servant who is husband to Babs, Anthony Keating's ex-wife; he and Babs have one child together in Margaret Drabble's *The Ice Age*.

Margery Stuart   Attractive flapper, the antithesis of Georgie Smithers, with plenty of money and her own car; she entertains frequently at her wealthy parents' home in Richard Aldington's *The Colonel's Daughter*.

Charlotte Stubbs   One of the typical teen-aged girls in the north London school in Dorothy Richardson's *Backwater*.

Janet Studdart   Young woman secretly in love with Edward Tilney, who marries her sister, Laurel; Janet's passion for her brother-in-law does not wane even after ten years of marriage to Rodney Meggatt in Elizabeth Bowen's *Friends and Relations*.

Laurel Studdart   Janet Studdart's sister, who marries Edward Tilney; through ten years of marriage she remains unaware of the depth of Janet's passion for Edward in Elizabeth Bowen's *Friends and Relations*.

Jane Tudor Studdock   Wife of Mark Studdock and graduate student in English Literature; she has the gift of second sight and is able to discern the plots of the N.I.C.E. (National Institute for Coordinated Experiments); she is sought by the N.I.C.E. for her powers in the hope that she may guide them to the sleeping Merlin; after much soul searching she allies herself with the St. Anne's community and participates in the overthrow of the N.I.C.E. and is reunited with her husband in C. S. Lewis's *That Hideous Strength*.

Mark Studdock   Fellow in Sociology at Bracton College, University of Edgestow; ambitious to become part of the inner circle at Bracton, he is recruited by the leaders of the N.I.C.E. (National Institute for Coordinated Experiments) because of his wife's powers of second sight; when Augustus Frost attempts to initiate Mark to the inner circle of the N.I.C.E., he rejects the control of the Macrobes; he escapes the final destruction of N.I.C.E. headquarters and is reunited with his wife in C. S. Lewis's *That Hideous Strength*.

Colonel von Stumm   Arrogant German villain of enormous size and strength; Richard Hannay's antagonist, he is killed by the victorious Cossacks in John Buchan's *Greenmantle.*

Sayren Stund   King of Oldorando and Simdol Tal's father; he plots the downfall of JandolAngand in Brian W. Aldiss's *Helliconia Summer.*

Colin Sturgeon   A short, rosy boy at Lucius Cassidy's school; he cannot stomach the fat on the potted meat in Ivy Compton-Burnett's *Two Worlds and Their Ways.*

Sturgis   Helpful Rudge Hall butler of stupendously boring conversation from whom words "flutter . . . like bats out of a barn" in P. G. Wodehouse's *Money for Nothing.*

Styles   Seaman aboard the *Indefatigable* who is disfigured by facial boils, the result of rat gambling aboard ship in C. S. Forester's *Mr. Midshipman Hornblower.*

Rubia Subhan   Child mature beyond her eight years; she comes to Evelyn Morton Stennett's aid when Evelyn is injured during a domestic quarrel between Irene Crowther and Joseph Leroy in Margaret Drabble's *The Middle Ground.*

Inspector Sugg   A rude, stupid Scotland Yard officer who arrests Alfred Thipps and Gladys Horrocks; he mistrusts and resents Lord Peter Wimsey in Dorothy L. Sayers's *Whose Body?.*

Sukie   Sixteen-year-old Norfolk, Virginia, girl with whom Dick Watchett, on shore leave, falls in love when she passes out drunk at a party; after the hurricane he imagines her admiration of his heroism but recognizes that he no longer cares in Richard Hughes's *In Hazard.*

Sullivan   Red-haired Irishman whose fiddling comforts the crew of the *Lydia* in C. S. Forester's *The Happy Return.*

Professor Sullivan   Jan Rodericks's helper in stowing away in one of the Overlords' starships in Arthur C. Clarke's *Childhood's End.*

Mrs. Sullivan   A woman seated next to Rosamund Stacey in the maternity waiting room at St. Andrews; she has a shabby-looking two-year-old boy, a tired infant, and a new baby on the way; she has an exhausted, glazed expression and is a living model of endurance in Margaret Drabble's *The Millstone.*

Lucia Sullivan   The eldest daughter of Fulbert and Eleanor; she is honest and kind and sympathetic to the younger children in Ivy Compton-Burnett's *Parents and Children.*

Daniel Sullivan   The eldest son of Fulbert and Eleanor; his grandfather begrudges the cost of his education even though he earns a first at Cambridge in Ivy Compton-Burnett's *Parents and Children.*

Eleanor Sullivan   The wife of Fulbert and the mother of nine children; she becomes engaged to Ridley Cranmer when Fulbert is reported to have died in Ivy Compton-Burnett's *Parents and Children.*

Fulbert Sullivan   The father of nine children; he is reported dead in South America but returns just in time to prevent Eleanor's marriage to Ridley Cranmer in Ivy Compton-Burnett's *Parents and Children.*

Gavin Sullivan   The favorite child of his mother, Eleanor; he is a nine-year-old who recognizes his father in town and insists that he be sought in Ivy Compton-Burnett's *Parents and Children.*

Graham Sullivan   The second son of Fulbert and Eleanor; his grandfather threatens to apprentice him to a bootmaker in Ivy Compton-Burnett's *Parents and Children.*

Honor Sullivan   Ten-year-old daughter of Fulbert and Eleanor; she is closest to her brother Gavin and her nursemaid, Emma Hatton, but misses her father when he is in South America in Ivy Compton-Burnett's *Parents and Children.*

Isabel Sullivan   Fifteen-year-old daughter who challenges her mother, Eleanor, when she opens Isabel's letter from her father without asking permission in Ivy Compton-Burnett's *Parents and Children.*

James Sullivan   Nurse Emma Hatton's favorite pupil; he is thought to have no aptitude for books, but he secretly writes poetry in Ivy Compton-Burnett's *Parents and Children.*

Sir Jesse Sullivan   The penny-pinching grandfather who houses the Marlowes, his illegitimate children, in a cottage on the estate in Ivy Compton-Burnett's *Parents and Children.*

Neville Sullivan   The youngest child of Fulbert and Eleanor; he loves his nursemaid, Emma Hatton, best and entertains everyone with his winsome behavior in Ivy Compton-Burnett's *Parents and Children.*

Regan, Lady Sullivan   Sir Jesse's wife, a grandmother who loves only her blood relatives in Ivy Compton-Burnett's *Parents and Children.*

Venetia (Venice) Sullivan   The confidante of her sister Isabel in Ivy Compton-Burnett's *Parents and Children*.

Sultan   Self-complacent ruler of Rasuka; he respectfully tolerates the European presence in his region but fears its growth; he orders that Hebechi Effendi be executed in P. H. Newby's *A Journey to the Interior*.

Professor Cosmo Sultana   Somewhat sinister philosophy teacher who with Owen Tuby begins the Institute for Social Imagistics in J. B. Priestley's *The Image Men*.

Cheryl Summerbee   A bright, romantic British Airways clerk; she falls for Persse McGarrigle, learns about his romances from Angelica Pabst, is fired from her job, and becomes the object of Persse's new quest at the end of David Lodge's *Small World*.

Lady Summerhay   Country neighbor of Major Winton; she is unable to dissuade her son from living with Gyp Winton Fiersen in John Galsworthy's *Beyond*.

Bryan Summerhay   Junior barrister who falls in love with Gyp Winton Fiersen; he lives unmarried with her and her baby, raises Gyp's jealousy when he is attracted to Diana Leyton, and dies from an injury while riding a horse in John Galsworthy's *Beyond*.

Cecelia Summers   Aimless, restless, twenty-nine-year-old widow, who shares a house with her younger sister-in-law, Emmeline Summers, while she moves slowly and uncertainly toward a decision to marry Julian Tower; it is she who introduces Mark Linkwater, whom she has met on a train, to Emmeline in Elizabeth Bowen's *To the North*.

Charley Summers   Soldier who, after losing a leg and spending much of World War II in a prison camp, returns to England to find "everything the same . . . and at the same time different"; in his shell-shocked state he first confuses Nancy Whitmore with her half sister and his dead lover, Rose Phillips, but partially recovers from his nervous condition and ultimately marries Nancy in Henry Green's *Back*.

Emmeline (Angel) Summers   Slim, blonde, ethereal, and unmarried sister-in-law of Cecelia Summers; an unconventional but successful travel agent, she unwisely allows herself to be drawn ever deeper into a fateful affair with Mark Linkwater in Elizabeth Bowen's *To the North*.

Henry Summers   Husband of Mary Scott Summers in Margaret Drabble's *The Garrick Year*.

Mary Scott Summers   The proper and conventional childhood friend of Emma Evans; she visits Emma in

Hereford and later encounters Emma and Wyndham Farrar having dinner in a restaurant in Margaret Drabble's *The Garrick Year*.

Sunday   Mysterious figure who is the President of the General Council of the anarchists of Europe and also the invisible Chief of the special Scotland Yard detective force to combat anarchism; he reveals himself as "the Sabbath, . . . the peace of God", at the end of the Council members' pursuit of him in G. K. Chesterton's *The Man Who Was Thursday: A Nightmare*.

Sungold   Aging Utopian who arranges for the isolated William Barnstaple to return to Earth to plant the seeds of Utopia there in H. G. Wells's *Men Like Gods*.

The Superior   Cheroot-smoking, unworldly, wise priest; the head of the mission post, he respects Dr. Colin and Querry and understands his congregation; he helps rather than condemns; his summons to the Order's main house paves the way for Father Thomas's unintentional destruction of Querry in Graham Greene's *A Burnt-Out Case*.

Philip Surrogate   Egotistical political writer and influential Communist; he speaks at the party meeting about Jim Drover, has a brief affair with Kay Rimmer, and asks Caroline Bury to help Drover in Graham Greene's *It's a Battlefield*.

The Survivor   See "Emily".

Susan   The domestic and pragmatic girl who wants to hold on with her two red, rough hands; she makes and molds and possesses what she sees; she loves and hates ferociously; associated with water, she adores fresh fields and season; she marries, raises a family, stays home, and seethes; she is jealous when Jinny kisses Louis in Virginia Woolf's *The Waves*.

Susan (Susie)   Janos Lavin's ex-student who occasionally poses for him in John Berger's *A Painter of Our Time*.

Susie   A beautiful woman's-army-corps member who is Colonel Plum's mistress; Basil Seal eventually wins her for his paramour in Evelyn Waugh's *Put Out More Flags*.

Susie   Fourteen-year-old servant at the boarding house where Horatio Hornblower resides ashore; he gives her half a crown in return for her promise to get something to eat; she, like Maria Mason (Hornblower), adores him in C. S. Forester's *Lieutenant Hornblower*.

Mr. Sutcliffe   Wealthy landowner who falls secretly in love with the youthful Mary Olivier, teaches her to play tennis and to dance, and provides her with books from the London library in May Sinclair's *Mary Olivier: A Life.*

Rupert Sutcliffe   Acting head of the Englsih Department at the University of Rummidge after the resignation of Gordon Masters; he fearfully asks Morris Zapp about Hilary Swallow's application as a postgraduate student in David Lodge's *Changing Places: A Tale of Two Campuses.* An aging member of the English Department, he bemoans the changing times in *Small World.*

Mr. Sutherland   British Consul in Finland; he becomes rightly irritated by John Avery's ineptly designed cover as Wilf Taylor's brother in John le Carré's *The Looking-Glass War.*

Alderman Sutton   Successful businessman, lobbyist abreast of advances in geology, generous husband, and indulgent father; he respects Anna Tellwright's strength in Arnold Bennett's *Anna of the Five Towns.*

Mrs. Sutton   A benevolent, active churchwoman; she is a member of the second family of Bursley society; an old "flame" of Ephraim Tellwright, she promotes the match between the Tellwrights' daughter Anna and Henry Mynors by persuading the miser to let Anna join her family's annual excursion to the Isle of Man, where Henry proposes in Arnold Bennett's *Anna of the Five Towns.*

Beatrice Sutton   Artistic, stylish, spoiled daughter of Alderman Sutton; she hoped to marry Henry Mynors, but she befriends Anna Tellwright, who does marry him in Arnold Bennett's *Anna of the Five Towns.*

Suzette (Suze, Crepe Suzette)   Seventeen-year-old secretary to Henley, whom she marries for money and status despite her love for the narrator in Colin MacInnes's *Absolute Beginnners.*

Kissy Suzuki   James Bond's beautiful Japanese lover and ally; she attempts to keep him with her after he loses his memory, not revealing what she knows of his past; she is pregnant with his child when he finally leaves in Ian Fleming's *You Only Live Twice.*

Tilly Svoboda   Outspoken, observant cockney, formerly maid to the Landon family; she relates tales about Sibyl Jardine to the Landon children in Rosamond Lehmann's *The Ballad and the Source.*

Reginald Swaffield   Wealthy property developer who employs Jenny Rastall in his charitable organization

and finances her legal suit to challenge her father's will in C. P. Snow's *In Their Wisdom.*

Swain   Unemployed hair-dresser who accepts Michael Mont's offer to work on an experimental poultry farm in John Galsworthy's *The Silver Spoon.*

Hilary Swallow   The intelligent, conservative, shy wife of Philip Swallow; she begins to learn about the women's movement from Mary Makepeace and has a brief affair with Morris Zapp, Philip's counterpart in an academic exhange; she decides to apply as a postgraduate student to the English Department in David Lodge's *Changing Places: A Tale of Two Campuses.* She becomes a successful marriage counsellor and wins back her husband from Joy Simpson in *Small World.*

Matthew Swallow   Son of Hilary and Philip Swallow; he encounters Philip and Joy Simpson in Israel, precipitating Philip's return to Hilary in David Lodge's *Small World.*

Philip Swallow   A diffident English lecturer, married to Hilary Swallow; he participates in an exchange between his University of Rummidge and Euphoric State University in the United States, and has two affairs: one with Desiree Zapp, the wife of his counterpart, Morris Zapp, and one with student Melanie Byrd, who is Morris's daughter; his health improves, and the new experiences of student unrest and sexual freedom give him a new outlook on life in David Lodge's *Changing Places: A Tale of Two Campuses.* He becomes head of the English Department at the University of Rummidge; he has an extended affair with Joy Simpson, has his book on Hazlitt favorably reviewed, becomes a candidate for a UNESCO chair of literary criticism, and goes back abashedly to Hilary in *Small World.*

Dierdre Swan   Tall, thin, attractive, nineteen-year-old first-year anthropology student who lives in a London suburb with her mother and aunt in Barbara Pym's *Less Than Angels.* She is mentioned in *No Fond Return of Love.*

Georgina Swan   Unhappy middle-aged and seductive woman who is the wife of Julian Swan; she is emotionally abused by her husband and has several affairs; she dies of shock, rejection, and depression after Julian announces his intention to divorce her and after she tries to prevent his arrest for involvement in espionage in Storm Jameson's *Before the Crossing.*

Julian Swan   Cruel husband of promiscuous Georgina Swan and an enemy of David Renn and Henry Smith; Swan is publisher of *Order,* a right-wing weekly designed to attack socialism and pacifism and to further the power of big business; he dines with and flatters Evelyn Lamb and Nancy, Lady Harben to gain abundant funding for his publication in Storm Jameson's *Before the Crossing*.

Mabel Swan The widowed mother of Dierdre and Malcolm; she shares her suburban house with her sister Rhoda Wellcome and takes a benevolent, anxious interest in the affairs of young people, including Catherine Oliphant, in Barbara Pym's *Less Than Angels*.

Malcolm Swan Conventional twenty-five-year-old businessman who lives at home with his mother, aunt, and sister and becomes engaged to his girlfriend Phyllis in Barbara Pym's *Less Than Angels*.

Claire Swann Wife of Douglas; she is Ann Peronett's attentive, hostile neighbor in Iris Murdoch's *An Unofficial Rose*.

Douglas Swann Anglican priest and counsellor of patient fidelity to Ann Peronett; he is thought to be somewhat enamored of her in Iris Murdoch's *An Unofficial Rose*.

Barbara Swayne Beautiful, somewhat vacuous, and unfaithful wife of Paul Berowne and sister of Dominic Swayne in P. D. James's *A Taste for Death*.

Dominic Swayne Debonair and psychotic brother of Barbara Swayne in P. D. James's *A Taste for Death*.

Sweeney The factotum, a querulous and disappointed man, in Nicholas Blake's *A Question of Proof*.

Mad King Sweeney Legendary Irish figure whose tale of exile is told by Finn MacCool; he becomes one of the judges of the fictional novelist Dermot Trellis in Flann O'Brien's *At Swim-Two-Birds*.

Swells Jockey who is dismissed when he wins too convincingly on George Pendyce's horse in John Galsworthy's *The Country House*.

Sweny Druggist who sells Leopold Bloom a bar of lemon soap on credit in James Joyce's *Ulysses*.

Thomas (Tom) Swetnam Short, stocky cockney; he has been inherited as senior employee by Lord Raingo from his father; Swetnam's loyalty to Raingo and long service permit him to express his realist's views and modify Raingo's enthusiasms in Arnold Bennett's *Lord Raingo*.

Miss Swift Aging, increasingly senile nanny to Violet Tennant's children in Henry Green's *Loving*.

Dean Swift Drug addict and jazz aficionado who is often in jail for robbing chemists' shops; he models for the narrator's camera; he and the Misery Kid save the narrator from a beating during the racial riots in Colin MacInnes's *Absolute Beginners*.

Gabriel Swift A handsome young man who marries Ruth Giffard; he leaves the house of his adopted mother, Josephine Napier, to live with his father, Jonathan Swift, and mother-in-law, Elizabeth Giffard, in Ivy Compton-Burnett's *More Women Than Men*.

Jonathan Swift Josephine Napier's brother and Gabriel Swift's father; he is a man whose writing could not be published in Ivy Compton-Burnett's *More Women Than Men*.

Mr. Swindon Dairyman who becomes the Provost of West Kensington in G. K. Chesterton's *The Napoleon of Notting Hill*.

Lucy Swithin Widowed sister of Bartholomew Oliver; she also lives at Pointz Hall; interrupted perpetually in reading her favorite book, *Outline of History*, she encourages and assists the production of the village pageant on the lawn to raise money for church electric lights; bullied and belittled by her brother, she is a mild-mannered link among the fragmented relationships in Virginia Woolf's *Between The Acts*.

Ernest Swyndle Fat, arrogant, and foolish preacher, who marries Ruby Darke in Mary Webb's *The House in Dormer Forest*.

Sybil Mark's quiet, plain, domestic wife; she is Susan (Brown) Lampton's cousin in John Braine's *Life at the Top*.

Sylvanus (Syl) Infant son of Nellie and Gwilym; his mother blames him for the death, before he is born, of Rachel and, before he is weaned, of Gwilym in Richard Hughes's *The Fox in the Attic*. His presence makes real employment an impossibility for Nellie in *The Wooden Shepherdess*.

Sylvester Boyhood friend of Gabriel Galloway; he goes to Dublin to study art, becomes a member of a colony of young Bohemians, urges Gabriel to join him, and provides living space for both Gabriel and Onny Soraghan when they run away from Castlerampart; after Onny's death he confesses his sexual involvement with her to Gabriel and implicates Telman Young as well in Mary Lavin's *The House in Clewe Street.*

Sylvester   Young, capable flag lieutenant on the *Sutherland* in C. S. Forester's *Ship of the Line.*

Sylvie   Fair, young, promiscuous, shallow girl; the late Spicer's girlfriend, she goes with Pinkie Brown to make love in a Lancia motorcar the day after Spicer's death in Graham Greene's *Brighton Rock.*

Syme   A tiny, unorthodox member of the Party; he works in the research Department writing the eleventh edition of the Newspeak Dictionary and disappears (Winston Smith thinks) because of his high intelligence in George Orwell's *Nineteen Eighty-Four.*

Gabriel Syme   Poet and spy attached to the Scotland Yard Special Force Detective investigating anarchist activities; he infiltrates the General Council of the Anarchists of Europe by getting elected to the post of Thursday; he investigates the Council and determines that all the other members of the Council, except Sunday, are also Scotland Yard Detectives; he eventually discovers that Sunday was responsible for appointing all the Council members as detectives in G. K. Chesterton's *The Man Who Was Thursday: A Nightmare.*

Alison Symington   Wife of Leslie; she decides she wants a third child in her middle age in C. P. Snow's *In Their Wisdom.*

Leslie Symington   Solicitor who carries Jenny Rastall's challenge of her father's will into court in C. P. Snow's *In Their Wisdom.*

Symons   British sailor captured by Peyrol in Joseph Conrad's *The Rover.*

Hilda Syms   An obsessive young girl in constant mourning for James Dreme, a dead teen movie-idol; her school-girl crush on Clare Mallory was the cause of Clare's dismissal from the convent; Clare visits but cannot help her in David Lodge's *The Picturegoers.*

Margaret Syms   Mother of the troubled Hilda Syms; she calls Clare Mallory to ask her for help in David Lodge's *The Picturegoers.*

Wojciech ("the Count", "Peter") Szczepanski   A tall, thin, pale, abstracted-looking Polish emigré, who falls in love with Gertrude Openshaw but is loved by Anne Cavidge in Iris Murdoch's *Nuns and Soldiers.*

Teresa Szigmondy   Friend of Mr. Hancock and niece of a Hungarian poet; she takes a fancy to Miriam Henderson and provides her with new aesthetic experiences in Dorothy Richardson's *The Tunnel.*

T

General T—— Russian official who interrogates Razumov in Joseph Conrad's *Under Western Eyes*.

Sir Connell T Famous doctor and friend of Chester Nimmo; sent by Chester to examine Nina (Woodville), he subtly forces her to return home in Joyce Cary's *Prisoner of Grace*.

Mr. Tabb Boatmaker who constructed the boat Rebecca de Winter sailed in the day of her death; he contends that the holes in the bottom were intentionally made in Daphne Du Maurier's *Rebecca*.

Tabby The cat whose violent death during the hurricane disturbs Emily Bas-Thornton far more than the death of Lame-Foot Sam in Richard Hughes's *A High Wind in Jamaica*.

Tabitha (Tabby) The Lovats' underhousemaid, who is cheerful and willing to be directed; she is liked very much by Rose and Viola Lovat in Ivy Compton-Burnett's *Darkness and Day*.

Tafta The head Grakconkranpatl priest who desires to sacrifice Ambien II, although she escapes; he is not only a leading enemy of Canopus, but the head of a School of Rhetoric in Shikasta in Doris Lessing's *The Sirian Experiments* and in *Documents Relating to the Sentimental Agents in the Volyen Empire*.

Asurr Tal Little Yuli's guide to the lands north of Oldorando; he tries to teach Yuli to speak with the dead in Brian W. Aldiss's *Helliconia Spring*.

Milna Tal Simdol Tal's younger sister, who secretly marries JandolAngand in Brian W. Aldiss's *Helliconia Summer*.

Shay Tal Loilanum's friend who is in love with Aoz Roon; she inspires the people of Oldorando to learn and question in order to improve their lives in Brian W. Aldiss's *Helliconia Spring*.

Simdol Tal The daughter of Sayren Stund; she is murdered before her marriage to JandolAngand in Brian W. Aldiss's *Helliconia Summer*.

Vry Tal A woman whom Shay Tal teaches; she wants to learn the movements of the stars; she creates a calendar and a star map in Brian W. Aldiss's *Helliconia Spring*.

Dr. Francis Talacryn (Bishop of Caerleon) Young prelate who serves as assistant to and is appointed to the cardinalate by Hadrian VII in Frederick William Rolfe's *Hadrian the Seventh*.

Mrs. Talbot A town matriarch who takes a strong liking to Martha Quest; she later comes to applaud the fact that Martha leaves Douglas Knowell, because she wants her daughter for him in Doris Lessing's *Martha Quest* and in *A Proper Marriage*.

Mrs. Talbot Sarah Woodruff's first employer in John Fowles's *The French Lieutenant's Woman*.

Christian Talbot The handsome upperclass Communist for whom Linda Radlett runs away from Tony Kroesig; after their marriage Linda and Christian go to help the Spanish in the Perpignan refugee camps, where Linda leaves him in Nancy Mitford's *The Pursuit of Love*.

Elaine Talbot Mrs. Talbot's pretty, dutiful daughter, who, after her young husband is killed in the war, marries Douglas Knowell and becomes stepmother to Martha Quest's daughter in Doris Lessing's *A Proper Marriage*.

Fleur Talbot Successful novelist who retells her experiences writing her first work, *Warrender Chase*, while she worked as a ghost writer for the members of the Autobiographical Association and their manipulative leader, Sir Quentin Oliver, in Muriel Spark's *Loitering with Intent*.

Florry Talbot Prostitute in the brothel where Leopold Bloom and Stephen Dedalus meet in James Joyce's *Ulysses*.

Harry Talbot Middle-aged commuting businessman and father of three; he flirts with his and his wife's old friend Wilmet Forsyth in Barbara Pym's *A Glass of Blessings*.

Rowena Talbot Friend of the heroine Wilmet Forsyth; she is a country-dwelling mother of three, happily married to the vaguely errant Harry in Barbara Pym's *A Glass of Blessings*.

Mr. Tallis Middle-aged antiquary and globe-trotter who is "Reggie" Daker's means of escape from a loveless, suffocating marriage in John Buchan's *The Gap in the Curtain*.

Tallit Syrian businessman and competitor of Yusef; he is more highly regarded by the police than Yusef, who provides Henry Scobie with information about his illegal activities; he is interrogated by Scobie and complains to his superiors in Graham Greene's *The Heart of the Matter.*

Talu   Tibetan pilot who highjacks the plane and abducts Hugh "Glory" Conway, Captain Charles Mallinson, Roberta Brinklow, and Henry D. Barnard, taking them to Shangri-La in Tibet; Talu dies in the plane's crash landing in James Hilton's *Lost Horizon.*

Mr. Tamberlaine   A part-time pimp and construction worker from the West Indies; he is Johnny Fortune's gambling partner; he invites Johnny to a voodoo party in Colin MacInnes's *City of Spades.*

Lord Tamworth   Husband of Enid and close friend of the Westons in Isabel Colegate's *Statues in a Garden.*

Enid, Lady Tamworth   Close friend of the Westons in Isabel Colegate's *Statues in a Garden.*

Luigi Tan   Shady Hong Kong merchant who arranges for a boat for Jerry Westerby and Lizzie Worthington to rendezvous with Nelson Ko and Drake Ko in John le Carré's *The Honourable Schoolboy.*

Tiger Tanaka   Head of the Japanese Secret Service; he enlists James Bond's help in destroying a "garden of death" created by Ernst Blofeld in Ian Fleming's *You Only Live Twice.*

Tanakil   A Homo sapiens girl who is driven mad by the knowledge that her people have cannibalized Liku, her little female friend from the Neanderthal tribe, in William Golding's *The Inheritors.*

Miles Tangin   A pesky journalist who attempts to harass Mark Coldridge and his family about the details of Colin Coldridge's fleeing to the Soviet Union and Sally Coldridge's suicide in Doris Lessing's *The Four-Gated City.*

Bill Tanner   M's Chief of Staff and James Bond's "best friend in the Service"; his surname is revealed in Ian Fleming's *You Only Live Twice.*

Paul Tanner   A character from Anna Wulf's manuscript, *The Shadow of the Third;* a married psychiatrist and Ella's lover, he mirrors Anna's own ex-lover Michael in Doris Lessing's *The Golden Notebook.*

Charles Tansley   Tedious young scholar/student in awe of Mr. Ramsay and in love with Mrs. Ramsay; a guest at the Ramsays' summer home in the Hebrides Islands, Charles pontificates at dinner that "women can't paint; women can't write" because he wants it to be true, much to the annoyance of Lily Briscoe in Virginia Woolf's *To the Lighthouse.*

Lord Edward Tantamount   Distracted aristocrat who has devoted his life to biology and consciously avoids relationships except in the most clinical manner in Aldous Huxley's *Point Counter Point.*

Hilda, Lady Edward Tantamount   Socially conscious wife of Lord Edward and one-time lover of the painter John Bidlake; she provides lavish entertainment in her fashionable London house in Aldous Huxley's *Point Counter Point.*

Lucy Tantamount   Promiscuous daughter of Lord and Lady Edward Tantamount; a frank sensualist, she takes and then abandons lovers, including Walter Bidlake, purely as a matter of whim in Aldous Huxley's *Point Counter Point.*

Countess Kattie Soderini Taosay   Mercenary Cunan society lady who effectively works the crowd collecting donations during Madame Ruiz's charity gala and who operates a booth selling rosaries during a religious street festival in Ronald Firbank's *Sorrow in Sunlight.*

Tapling   Unsympathetic, jaded, mistrustful member of the diplomatic service; he serves as a cook's mate aboard the *Caroline* under protest in C. S. Forester's *Mr. Midshipman Hornblower.*

Sir Arthur Tappitt   Tall Canadian physician to the Royal Family; he presides over Lord Raingo's last illness in Arnold Bennett's *Lord Raingo.*

Reginald Tarburcke   A television agent who tries to persuade Anna Wulf to have her novel *Frontiers of War* made into a watered-down television film in Doris Lessing's *The Golden Notebook.*

Michel Tardieu   A homosexual Professor of Narratology at the Sorbonne; he tries to help Persse McGarrigle track down Angelica Pabst at an Eliot Conference in Lausanne in David Lodge's *Small World.*

Major General Tarporley   Head of Military Intelligence; he is the newest star of the War Office Secret Service; Lord Raingo suspects he gave an order forbidding his people to enter Raingo's ministry in Arnold Bennett's *Lord Raingo.*

Tarquin   A dandified homosexual who bemoans his unrequited love for Clare; he is an acquaintance of Herbert Gregory in Lawrence Durrell's *The Black Book.*

Frederick Tarr   An English philosopher-critic with negative views on love and humor; he honorably marries Bertha Lunken, his "official fiancée", after she becomes pregnant by Otto Kreisler in Wyndham Lewis's *Tarr.*

Ricki Tarr (covernames: Tony Thomas, Trench, Poole)   Malayan-born gunrunner and assassin for British Intelligence; he informs George Smiley that his lover, a Soviet agent he knows as Irina, confirmed the presence of a double agent in the London Station in John le Carré's *Tinker, Tailor, Soldier, Spy.*

John Tarver   Chief designer at the Dupret foundry; his youth and progressive ideas annoy the older workers but impress Richard Dupret in Henry Green's *Living.*

Alan Tasburgh   Naval Captain who at twenty-eight loves Dinny Cherrell and plans to help Hubert Cherrell escape extradition in John Galsworthy's *Maid In Waiting.*

Abraham Taskerson   English poet who had been foster father to Geoffrey Firmin in Malcolm Lowry's *Under the Volcano.*

Tasuki   Chief bridgeman who aids Officer Rudbeck in completing the Fada road in Joyce Cary's *Mister Johnson.*

Mr. Tate   Belvedere teacher who objects to what he sees as heresy in Stephen Dedalus's essay in James Joyce's *A Portrait of the Artist as a Young Man.*

Jim Tate   Large, hoarse-voiced man and Ida Arnold's bookie in Kemp Town, Brighton; he is behind in payments to Pinkie Brown's mob; his conversation with Colleoni is overheard by Ida Arnold, thereby giving her access to more information in her quest to find out what happened to Charles Hale in Graham Greene's *Brighton Rock.*

Tatiana (Sasha; covername: Alexandra Ostrakova) Karla's rebellious, mentally ill daughter confined without Moscow Centre's knowledge in a private sanitarium in Berne; she confirms for George Smiley through her twisted, polarized psyche that she is Karla's daughter and Smiley's vehicle for the defeat of Karla in John le Carré's *Smiley's People.*

TatromanAdala   The daughter of Queen Myrdem-Inggala and King JandolAngand in Brian W. Aldiss's *Helliconia Summer.*

Taufiq   One of the few people on Shikasta who attempt to better the billions of oppressed people through speeches, exchanges of information, and good intention; he is later captured and unable to stem corruption in Doris Lessing's *Re: Colonised Planet 5, Shikasta.*

Mr. Taunton   An innocent, unsuspecting young cu-

rate, who is nearly trapped into marriage by Eleanor Dear in Dorothy Richardson's *The Tunnel.*

Arnold Tavanger   Member of the Whitsuntide house party at Flambard who succeeds during Professor Moe's experiment in gaining a preview of future time; he learns one fact about a worldwide merger, and, acting on it, loses the opportunity to make thousands of pounds of profit but learns how wisely ordained is man's ignorance of the future in John Buchan's *The Gap in the Curtain.*

Chief Inspector Tavener   Scotland Yard man who heads the investigation into Aristide Leonides's murder in Agatha Christie's *Crooked House.*

Captain Tayeh   Palestinian terrorist and Khalil's pragmatic lieutenant; he instructs Charlie in the Palestinian guerilla camp and receives her report on another terrorist's counterrevolutionary attitudes in John le Carré's *The Little Drummer Girl.*

Mrs. Taylor   Wilf Taylor's widow; when contacted by Leclerc and John Avery, she accurately discredits Leclerc's self-deceptive justification for her husband's death in John le Carré's *The Looking-Glass War.*

Dora Taylor   Miriam Henderson's new friend, a vegetarian and a simple-lifer in Dorothy Richardson's *The Trap.*

George Taylor   Dora Taylor's husband, also a vegetarian and a simple-lifer in Dorothy Richardson's *The Trap.*

Jean Taylor   Former companion-maid to Charmian Piper, former lover of Alec Warner, resident patient of the old women's hospital ward, and Roman Catholic convert, whose meditations on the last things free her from the terror of death in Muriel Spark's *Memento Mori.*

Marian Taylor   Hannah Crean-Smith's companion and French tutor at Gaze Castle; she fails in an attempt to rescue Hannah by force in Iris Murdoch's *The Unicorn.*

Mary Taylor   Matron of a teaching hospital, formerly German nurse Irmgard Grobel in P. D. James's *Shroud for a Nightingale.*

Wilf Taylor (covername: Malherbe)   Fantasy-driven, overanxious courier for British Intelligence; his accidental death in Finland sparks Leclerc's misguided Operation Mayfly in John le Carré's *The Looking-Glass War.*

Richard Tebrick   Faithful husband of Silvia; he hides

her transformation into a fox from the world and cares for her as if she were still herself by administering her daily toilet, dressing her in her favorite dressing-jackets, serving her tea, and taking exercise with her in the garden, but he is unable to hold her to the vows she took as a woman and releases her through the garden door after her repeated attempts to escape the garden by tunneling under the wall in David Garnett's *Lady Into Fox*.

Silvia Fox Tebrick   Richard Tebrick's well-bred young wife who is suddenly transformed into a small, bright red fox during an afternoon outing; her husband unsuccessfully attempts to arrest her evolution into a wild vixen, and she is mauled to death by hunting dogs while seeking refuge in the arms of her still-devoted husband in David Garnett's *Lady Into Fox*.

Teddy   Mr. Britling's secretary and Letty's husband; he is reported missing in the war in H. G. Wells's *Mr. Britling Sees It Through*.

Teddy   Mrs. Lousse's dog, run over and killed by Molloy on his way to visit his mother in Samuel Beckett's *Molloy*.

Teddywegs   Affectionate lap-dog sent from Princess Elsie of England to the royal family of Pisuerga as an early step toward her arranged marriage to Prince Yousef in Ronald Firbank's *The Flower Beneath the Foot*.

Tekla   Revolutionary Russian emigrée who nurses Razumov after his exposure and crippling in Joseph Conrad's *Under Western Eyes*.

Mavis Telford   Tommy Telford's wife, who lives for her annual invitation to an Embassy party in Lawrence Durrell's *Clea*.

Tommy Telford   Darley's censorship-department office colleague, a source of information about Pursewarden, Mountolive, and others in Lawrence Durrell's *Clea*.

Agnes Tellwright   Candid, biddable child; she adores her more independent half sister, Anna, but she docilely accepts her own helplessness under her father's regime in Arnold Bennett's *Anna of the Five Towns*.

Anna (Sis) Tellwright   Intelligent, sensitive, quietly rebellious young heiress; she is forced to live penuriously, but she dares to defy her tyrannous father by destroying evidence which would imprison Willie Price for forgery; she recognizes in the act her love for Willie, but she stoically accepts her commitment to Henry Mynors when her father abandons her in Arnold Bennett's *Anna of the Five Towns*.

Ephraim Tellwright   Shrewd, wealthy miser; he is former treasurer of the Hanley Methodist circuit and a twice-married domestic tyrant with a wry sense of humor; his harsh business practices are respected, although his demands for rent help precipitate the Prices' crisis; he believes his rule at home natural and just, although his daughters feel oppressed; Anna's need to help Willie Price by deceiving her father provokes his implacable animosity toward her in Arnold Bennett's *Anna of the Five Towns*.

Percy Temperton   Partner at Barclay and Bowley, the firm where Hilda Verren works; although he tries to use his position to pressure Hilda to become engaged to him, she rejects him; he is finally put in his place by Eric Galbraith, Hilda's fiancé, in Frank Swinnerton's *The Young Idea: A Comedy of Environment*.

Leslie Tempest   Insecure, rich, possessive, uncharismatic young industrialist, who wins Lettie Beardsall from George Saxton; he becomes successful as businessman, politician, and husband, but his wife's heart is never entirely his in D. H. Lawrence's *The White Peacock*.

Temple   Anti-clerical university companion of Stephen Dedalus in James Joyce's *Ulysses*.

Eadred Templecombe   A husband who threatens to divorce his wife when he finds Harry Tremaine in her bedroom; Lady L. and the Duchess of D. intervene to remind him that "people of their class" do not divorce in Vita Sackville-West's *The Edwardians*.

Betty (Taylor or Porter) Templer   Second wife of Peter Templer, who cannot remember her surname when he begins to take her to nightclubs after Mona leaves him in Anthony Powell's *At Lady Molly's*. His unkindness as a husband and his affair with Lady Anne Stepney cause Betty's emotional breakdown and institutionalization in *The Kindly Ones*. Her recovery after Peter's death and her subsequent happy marriage to a Foreign Office diplomat are reported in *Hearing Secret Harmonies*.

Jean Templer   Sister of Peter and an early love of Nicholas Jenkins in Anthony Powell's *A Question of Upbringing*. She marries Robert Duport in *A Buyer's Market*. She has a daughter, Polly; her marriage is in trouble, and she begins her affair with Jenkins in *The Acceptance World*. She has broken with Jenkins and begins an affair with Widmerpool in *At Lady Molly's*. She is divorced; her old affair with Jimmy Brent is analyzed in *The Kindly Ones* and in *The Valley of Bones*. Jenkins meets her without emotion in *Books Do Furnish a Room*. She is the widow of an assassinated Latin American dictator when she meets Jenkins in *Temporary Kings*.

Mona Templer Peter Templer's tall, beautiful wife, who leaves him to run off with Quiggin in Anthony Powell's *The Acceptance World.* Introduced earlier as an artist's model in *A Buyer's Market,* she is divorced from Templer and leaves Quiggin for Lord Erridge, with whom she sails to China in *At Lady Molly's.* She has left Erridge in *Casanova's Chinese Restaurant,* but she appears at his funeral in *Books Do Furnish a Room.*

Peter Templer Unintellectual, worldly, melancholic preparatory-school friend who enlarges Nick Jenkins's social world in Anthony Powell's *A Question of Upbringing.* He goes into "the City" instead of to University; his dissipations progress in *A Buyer's Market.* His marriage to Mona ends in her leaving him in *The Acceptance World.* He is divorced and involved with Betty in *At Lady Molly's.* His marriage to Betty collapses and he becomes grim and dejected in *The Kindly Ones* and in *The Valley of Bones.* He is infatuated with Pamela Flitton; his death on a secret-service mission is blamed on Widmerpool in *The Military Philosophers.*

Donald Templeton Friend of Bill Eliot; a barrister, he handles Meg's legal affairs after Bill's death and is disliked by Meg in Angus Wilson's *The Middle Age of Mrs. Eliot.*

Elliott Templeton Elegant, sophisticated, and terribly snobbish but nonetheless kind uncle of Isabel Bradley; he lives in Paris and gives his niece and her husband, Gray Maturin, a home when they are financially ruined in the stock-market crash in W. Somerset Maugham's *The Razor's Edge.*

Robert Templeton The detective invented by mystery-writer Harriet Vane in Dorothy L. Sayers's *Have His Carcase.*

Mr. Tench Weak-minded dentist who leaves his wife and child in England to practice dentistry in Mexico; at one point he meets and drinks with the whiskey priest; later he sees the priest being executed and feels overwhelmingly lonely in Graham Greene's *The Power and the Glory.*

Tengga A native on the Shore of Refuge who in his effort to gain power challenges Belarab's authority in Joseph Conrad's *The Rescue: A Romance of the Shallows.*

Mrs. Tennant Upper-class Anglo-Irishwoman who is confused by changing times and confounded by the wayward and amorous antics of her servants in Henry Green's *Loving.*

Violet Tennant Wife of Jack Tennant; while her husband is at war she has an affair with Dermot Davenport in Henry Green's *Loving.*

Teresa A Mexican peasant who marries Don Ramon Carrasco and follows him reverently in his efforts to resurrect the old Aztec gods in D. H. Lawrence's *The Plumed Serpent (Quetzalcoatl).*

Teresa Housekeeper for Father Quixote; because she is antagonistic toward the Bishop of El Toboso, she helps Father Quixote escape for his second trip to the mountains of northwestern Spain and the culmination of his journey in Graham Greene's *Monsignor Quixote.*

Teresa See James Wormold.

Lady Teresa Mother of Sir Harry; she dresses in layers of black cloth to identify herself as a widow and as an enthusiastic follower of Queen Victoria; she puts her big face threateningly close to Marion Yaverland as she speaks to her, thus magnifying her beak nose, baggy chin, and loud "strangulated contralto" as she warns her against revealing Richard Yaverland's paternity; she collaborates with cruel Peacey in Rebecca West's *The Judge.*

Teria Friend of Ruth Armstrong in Margaret Drabble's *The Middle Ground.*

Jim Terrington Army colonel; the best friend of Rosemary Mosson's late husband, he has been Rosemary's lover since before her widowhood; he helps Piers Mosson plan his production of the opera; his living with Rosemary is the cause of a rift in the Mosson family in Angus Wilson's *Setting the World on Fire.*

Isabelle Terry Rich, beautiful twenty-six-year-old American woman in high society in Cannes and Paris, 1928; at first naïve, romantic, and self-centered, she grows to a degree in her struggle to become notably rational; she considers marriage to Andre de Verviers, Lawrence Vernon, Alan Fielding, and Marc Sallafranque; she finally sees that all men are, in part, woman's enemy and that perfect reconciliation is beyond rational resolution; she remains a weak reed, but now a *thinking* reed, as she returns to Marc, whom she loves, in Rebecca West's *The Thinking Reed.*

Dr. Lois Terry Mournful teacher at Brockshire University attracted to Owen Tuby in J. B. Priestley's *The Image Men.*

Roy Terry Isabelle Terry's first husband, a famous daredevil pilot, whose death initiates her maturation in Rebecca West's *The Thinking Reed.*

Philip Tewby A dwarf whom Nick Ollanton uses in a ruse to enable Barney, another dwarf, to escape from the police after the murder of Nonie Colmar in J. B. Priestley's *Lost Empires*.

Jacques Textel   A famous anthropologist and Assistant Director General of UNESCO who is sought after by competitors for the UNESCO chair of literary criticism in David Lodge's *Small World*.

Father Oswald Thames   Upper-class, seventyish, somewhat smug celibate vicar of the Anglo-Catholic St. Luke's in Barbara Pym's *A Glass of Blessings*. The grand days of that parish under Father Thames are recalled in *Quartet in Autumn*.

Aimée Thanatogenos   A naïve cosmetician at Hollywood's Whispering Glades cemetery; courted by both Dennis Barlow and Mr. Joyboy, she finds it difficult to choose one over the other; her confusion ultimately leads to her decision to commit suicide in Evelyn Waugh's *The Loved One*.

Edith Tharkles   Loud and critical older sister of Charles Lumley's college girlfriend Sheila; Edith's verbal attacks on Charles's lack of direction, along with those of her husband, Robert, represent for Charles the unbearably banal and stifling essence of middle-class life in John Wain's *Hurry On Down*.

Robert Tharkles   Stereotypically prim and narrow middle-class brother-in-law of Charles Lumley's college girlfriend Sheila; Robert's blunt criticism of Charles finally provokes the young man to insult him openly and to set out on a survey of working-class society in John Wain's *Hurry On Down*.

Cecil Tharp   Son of a neighbor; he courts Bee Pendyce in John Galsworthy's *The Country House*.

General Thé   Dissident Vietnamese Chief of Staff turned terrorist leader of a shadowy outlaw army; he kills fifty innocent Saigonese women and children with the plastic explosives Alden Pyle provides in Graham Greene's *The Quiet American*.

Mrs. Theobald   Lilia Herriton's weak, elderly mother in E. M. Forster's *Where Angels Fear to Tread*.

Theoden   King of the Mark; he fights against the forces of Sauron in the War of the Ring in J. R. R. Tolkien's *The Two Towers*.

R. Theodorescu   Immensely fat, mysterious, urbane pederast and *soi disant* "information broker"; he is loyal to no one and nothing; he drugs Denis Hillier to obtain information from him for sale to the highest bidder in Anthony Burgess's *Tremor of Intent*.

Theresa   Alice Mellings's well-off aunt, who helps Alice financially; Alice somewhat dislikes her because of her love of sexual pleasure in Doris Lessing's *The Good Terrorist*.

Major Tufty Thesinger   Former major in Her Majesty's Rifles and now a British Intelligence operative in Hong Kong and head of Inter Services Liaison Staff; his incompetence and stupidity threaten to thwart George Smiley and Operation Dolphin in John le Carré's *The Honourable Schoolboy*.

Thethuthinang ("movement of leaves")   Doe rabbit, friend of Hyzenthlay, with whom she petitions the Efrafan Council for permission to emigrate in Richard Adams's *Watership Down*.

Mr. Thicknesse   Family lawyer whom Jane Weatherby is almost afraid to visit in Henry Green's *Nothing*.

Guy Thin   Pale, bespectacled, and articulate young friend of the flower-shop manager Bachir; he has newly arrived from England in hope of establishing a grocery business; he has "private designs" on the reluctant Harry Cummings in Ronald Firbank's *The Flower Beneath the Foot*.

Mrs. Thipps   Alfred's mildly querulous, deaf old mother; she thinks problems involving the bathroom demand the attention of the landlord, not the police in Dorothy L. Sayers's *Whose Body?*.

Alfred Thipps   An inoffensive church architect who is arrested on suspicion of murder after a dead body is discovered in his bathtub in Dorothy L. Sayers's *Whose Body?*.

Theodora Thirdman   A precocious and difficult adolescent who becomes an assertive and socially awkward young adult; she delights in manipulating confidences and meddling in the personal lives of others in Elizabeth Bowen's *Friends and Relations*.

Susan Thirkill   Daughter of Tom; she is Loseby's lover and provides him with an alibi during the investigation of his grandmother's murder; she is herself a suspect; she marries Loseby in C. P. Snow's *A Coat of Varnish*.

Tom Thirkill   Member of Parliament and entrepreneur; he is the father of Susan; he wishes for her marriage with Loseby; he is investigated as a possible suspect in the murder of Lady Ashbrook; he accepts a post in government in C. P. Snow's *A Coat of Varnish*.

Aunt (Za) Thirza　Aunt of Lena Eliot; she leaves £300 to Lewis Eliot in C. P. Snow's *Time of Hope.*

Queen Thleeanouhee　Sensual, androgynous queen of Dateland who makes a diplomatic visit to Pisuerga with her husband and takes a sexual interest in Lady Somebody, wife of the British Ambassador, in Ronald Firbank's *The Flower Beneath the Foot.*

James Thoday　Co-conspirator with William Thoday in disposing of a body in Dorothy L. Sayers's *The Nine Tailors: Changes Rung on an Old Theme in Two Short Touches and Two Full Peals.*

Mary Russell Deacon Thoday　William Thoday's wife, who was Jeff Deacon's wife and a housemaid in the Thorpe residence at the time of the theft of a necklace from a houseguest in Dorothy L. Sayers's *The Nine Tailors: Changes Rung on an Old Theme in Two Short Touches and Two Full Peals.*

William Thoday　Mary Russell Deacon's second husband; ringer of the number two bell "Sabaoth", he falls ill with influenza and is replaced for the nine-hour New Year's ringing-in by the accidental visitor Lord Peter Wimsey in Dorothy L. Sayers's *The Nine Tailors: Changes Rung on an Old Theme in Two Short Touches and Two Full Peals.*

Thomas　Officious "Director of Hatcheries" in the futuristic factory producing genetically engineered humans; he is driven from his position in humiliation when his subordinate Bernard Marx reveals him to be the biological father of John Savage in Aldous Huxley's *Brave New World.*

Father Thomas　Anxiety-ridden, overscrupulous, tunnel-visioned, youngish priest, supervisor of the mission school; uncertain of his vocation, he pesters Querry, seeing him as a saint despite Querry's brutal honesty as to his lack of belief and his shortcomings; temporarily in charge of the mission, Father Thomas is the first to believe that Querry had an affair with Marie Rycker and thus shares in the responsibility for Querry's death in Graham Greene's *A Burnt-Out Case.*

Father Thomas　Jesuit priest and lover of Sister Felicity in Muriel Spark's *The Abbess of Crewe.*

Mr. Thomas　Eurasian manager of the New Electric Cinema in Pankot; like Frank Bhoolabhoy, Thomas is a lay-preacher and assistant warden at St. John's Church, Pankot, in Paul Scott's *Staying On.*

Thompson　Somewhat violent officer of the *Sutherland* in C. S. Forester's *Ship of the Line.*

Thompson　Stereotypical Englishman whom Townrow meets in the yacht club in P. H. Newby's *Something to Answer For.*

Dr. Thompson　Psychiatric consultant who suggests an "alphabetical complex" motivating the killer in Agatha Christie's *The A.B.C. Murders.*

Ada Thompson　Suffragette and political activist in Isabel Colegate's *Statues in a Garden.*

Fleance Thompson　A shepherd in Wiltshire in E. M. Forster's *The Longest Journey.*

Livvy Thompson　Gushing young woman eager to fall in love who, being the Naylors' nearest Ascendancy-class neighbor of Lois Farquar's age, is a frequent visitor at Danielstown; her father's handling of her engagement to David Armstrong contrasts with Lady Naylor's handling of the proposed engagement between Lois and Gerald Lesworth in Elizabeth Bowen's *The Last September.*

Richard ("Dick") Haines Thompson　Middle-aged manager of the boarding house where Jenny Bunn stays; he claims to be an auctioneer and has an ambiguous connection with Julain Ormerod; he tries unsuccessfully to seduce Jenny Bunn in Kingsley Amis's *Take a Girl Like You.*

Maisie Thomson　Independent daughter of Ianthe (Herbert) and Robert Thomson; she has a violent sense of ownership and is jealous of her friends; she is passionate and disillusioned as she tells Rebecca Landon of her hatred for her grandmother Sibyl Jardine in Rosamond Lehmann's *The Ballad and the Source.* As a middle-aged doctor she goes to a Caribbean island where she is called to care for the elderly Sibyl Jardine at the end of Sibyl's life in *A Sea-Grape Tree.*

Robert Thomson　Ailing, destitute schoolteacher and husband of Ianthe Herbert; he appeals to his mother-in-law, Sibyl Jardine, to care for his children after his death in Rosamond Lehmann's *The Ballad and the Source.*

Kzahhn Ghht-Yronz Thorl　The leader of the phagors in hiding in Brian W. Aldiss's *Helliconia Summer.*

Thorne　Detective inspector from Scotland Yard; colorless but brainy, he has a "long questing nose" in Nicholas Blake's *A Tangled Web.*

Jeremy Thorne　Head of the classics department at Cambridge who helped Charles Watkins gain a job in the same department; he admits that he does not like Charles in Doris Lessing's *Briefing for a Descent into Hell.*

Ewart Thornton　Schoolteacher and séance participant whose "mounds of homework" keep him from human demands in Muriel Spark's *The Bachelors.*

Joseph Thornton　Author of a book on superstitions, ghosts, and magicians of which part of one chapter is devoted to Dr. Thomas Underhill; Maurice Allington learns from this book that some of Underhill's papers were buried with him and that Underhill's journal is in a Cambridge library in Kingsley Amis's *The Green Man.*

Sir Charles Thorpe　Landowner who died some fifteen years earlier following the theft of jewels from a houseguest in Dorothy L. Sayer's *The Nine Tailors: Changes Rung on an Old Theme in Two Short Touches and Two Full Peals.*

Sir Henry Thorpe　Sir Charles's son and Hilary's father; he impoverished himself by compensating Mrs. Wilbraham for the loss of her necklace; his burial preparations result in the unearthing of an unidentified body in the Fenchurch St. Paul churchyard in Dorothy L. Sayers's *The Nine Tailors: Changes Rung on an Old Theme in Two Short Touches and Two Full Peals.*

Hilary Thorpe　Sir Henry's intelligent teenaged daughter; she becomes Lord Peter Wimsey's helpful friend in Dorothy L. Sayers's *The Nine Tailors: Changes Rung on an Old Theme in Two Short Touches and Two Full Peals.*

Nancy Thorpe　A woman who believes that Charles Watkins deliberately attempts to make her feel worthless and make her marital problems seem insignificant in Doris Lessing's *Briefing for a Descent into Hell.*

Miss Thorping　Experienced housekeeper; she is hired by Lord Raingo's son, Geoffrey, to take charge of Moze Hall, which she efficiently orders in a way never achieved by Lord Raingo's late wife, Adela, in Arnold Bennett's *Lord Raingo.*

Threarah ("Lord Rowan Tree")　Chief rabbit, revered for the leadership that enabled the Sandleford Warren to survive an epidemic of disease; he cannot be persuaded of the danger foretold in Fiver's vision; he perishes with his subjects when the warren is gassed by men in preparation for real-estate development in Richard Adams's *Watership Down.*

Freddie Threepwood　A goggle-eyed, slack-jawed, spendthrift younger son of Lord Emsworth; his engagement to Aline Peters has restored him to his father's good will; his only passion is for detective stories featuring Gridley Quayle in P. G. Wodehouse's *Something New.* He appears in eight other novels.

Galahad Threepwood　Monocle-wearing, dapper younger brother of Lord Emsworth; the prospective publication of his scandalous memoirs is matter for widespread anxiety; he was in his youth prevented from marrying Dolly Henderson in P. G. Wodehouse's *Fish Preferred.* He appears in seven other novels.

Millicent Threepwood　Lord Emsworth's tall, blue-eyed, good-humored niece; she and Hugo Carmody combat Threepwood-family opposition to their romance in P. G. Wodehouse's *Fish Preferred.*

Dr. Thring　A callous man who is Maudie Fowler's physician; he tries to convince her that the best place for her to live is in a rest home in Doris Lessing's *The Diaries of Jane Somers.*

Mary Thriplow　Intelligent novelist who adopts a demure pose in order to seduce Mr. Calamy, with whom she has a passionate affair in Aldous Huxley's *Those Barren Leaves.*

Huy Throvis-Mew　See George Johnson.

Tilly Throvis-Mew　Wife of Jane Wright's employer; her visit to the May of Teck Club leads to her being stuck in an upstairs window just before an unrecovered German bomb explodes in Muriel Spark's *The Girls of Slender Means.*

Thursday　See Gabriel Syme.

J. Temple Thurston　Playwright, author of a dramatic adaptation of *The Wandering Jew,* whose death by fire Ethan Llewelyn finds significant and threatening in Malcolm Lowry's *October Ferry to Gabriola.*

Thwaites　Cumberland shepherd who treats Sirius so brutally that Sirius kills him in self-defense in Olaf Stapledon's *Sirius: A Fantasy of Love and Discord.*

Veronica Thwale　Seductive and predatory companion of the elderly Mrs. Gamble; setting her ambitions on the wealthy Paul de Vries, she nonetheless seduces young Sebastian Barnack, with whom she later continues the affair after her marriage in Aldous Huxley's *Time Must Have a Stop.*

Tia　Antoinette Cosway's best girlhood friend and Maillotte's daughter; she has small, deeply set black eyes in Jean Rhys's *Wide Sargasso Sea.*

Albert Tibbets　Journalist of the opposition press; he

investigates Thomas Carlyle Craw's "mysterious disappearance" and is granted an interview with Dickson McCunn impersonating Craw; the published story enrages Craw in John Buchan's *Castle Gay*.

Tibby   Dickson McCunn's aged maid, who cares for the house and keeps McCunn's absence a secret in John Buchan's *Huntingtower*.

Tiberius   Stepson of Augustus; he grows increasingly lascivious and tyrannical following his accession to emperor in Robert Graves's *I, Claudius*.

Irene Tidmarsh   Young, worldly friend who informs the surprised Elsie Palmer of a possible connection between sex and pregnancy; she advises that marriage is safer than weekends in the country with her employer in E. M. Delafield's *Messalina of the Suburbs*.

Mrs. Tietjens   The saintly, Anglican second wife of Mark Tietjens and mother of Christopher; she dies of a broken heart when Christopher takes back his estranged and cruel wife, Sylvia, in Ford Madox Ford's *Some Do Not. . . .* She is reverently remembered by General Campion in *No More Parades*.

Christopher Tietjens   Fourth son of a propertied Yorkshireman; he lives by the antiquated code of a Tory gentleman; despite his deep love for Valentine Wannop, he refuses to divorce or to malign his vindictive and unfaithful wife, Sylvia Tietjens, since it would bring her dishonor, and he endures slander with stoicism in Ford Madox Ford's *Some Do Not. . . .* His rectitude and his wife's malice get him into further difficulty in *No More Parades*. He is in charge of a battalion and proves himself under fire, but his wife's mischief injures him professionally; after the war and serious injury, he decides to live with Valentine in *A Man Could Stand Up —*. He refuses the Groby inheritance and becomes an antique-furniture dealer in *The Last Post*.

Lydia Tietjens   Female student of F. X. Enderby; she interviews him for a magazine and attempts to seduce him apparently out of malice rather than concupiscence in Anthony Burgess's *The Clockwork Testament; Or Enderby's End*.

Mark Tietjens (the elder)   A propertied Yorkshireman and father of several children, including the younger Mark and Christopher; after the death of his other two sons and a daughter in war, he kills himself when he is told plausible but false rumors about Christopher's immoral relationships with women in Ford Madox Ford's *Some Do Not. . . .* Christopher reveals to General Campion upon interrogation that his repudiation of his inheritance is motivated by shame

that his father would be so base as to commit suicide in *No More Parades*.

Mark Tietjens (the younger)   The reticent, stubborn, propertied, childless elder brother of Christopher; he becomes heir to the estate when his other brothers are killed in Ford Madox Ford's *Some Do Not. . . .* Mark is Transport Minister during the war in *No More Parades*. After hearing the terms on Armistice Day, he refuses to speak or move until he is dying in *The Last Post*.

Sylvia Tietjens   Christopher Tietjens's beautiful, hateful wife, who married him thinking she was pregnant with another man's child; she is bound to him in a destructive love-hate relationship in Ford Madox Ford's *Some Do Not. . . .* She torments and frustrates him professionally with slander and deceit in *No More Parades*. To further wound him she engineers the cutting down of the Groby great tree on the family property but realizes that her power and malice are exhausted in *The Last Post*.

Tommie (Mark, Michael) Tietjens   Son of Sylvia Tietjens and probably Christopher as well, though the circumstances of their marriage make both parents uncertain in Ford Madox Ford's *Some Do Not. . . .* Christopher's love for him in absentia is his strongest emotion in *No More Parades*. Tommie's resemblance to Christopher removes suspicion about his paternity in *The Last Post*.

Mr. Tiffield   Smart, bargaining, gluttonous businessman, who likes Joe Lampton and offers him a job in John Braine's *Life at the Top*.

Grigory Nasayan Tigranovich   Overbearing, newly appointed non-fiction editor at Katya Orlova's small publishing house, October; he is a possible K.G.B. agent in John le Carré's *The Russia House*.

Mary Tiller   Former cook at Ambrose College whose tryst in Venice with Arnold Leaver, headmaster of Ambrose, is disrupted by his son's blackmail in Muriel Spark's *Territorial Rights*.

Mr. Tilliard   One of Rickie Elliott's Cambridge friends in E. M. Forster's *The Longest Journey*.

Edward Tilney   Very proper, highly placed civil servant, husband of Laurel (Studdart) and son of Lady Elfrida Tilney; his anger with Considine Meggatt, his mother's lover, has never cooled, yet he is himself nearly drawn into an affair with his sister-in-law, Janet (Studdart) Meggatt, in Elizabeth Bowen's *Friends and Relations*.

Lady Elfrida Tilney   Sophisticated and still beautiful mother of Edward Tilney; her affair with Considine Meggatt caused the breakup of her marriage when Edward was a child; it now strains relations with her daughter-in-law, Laurel (Studdart), but not with Laurel's sister, Janet Studdart, in Elizabeth Bowen's *Friends and Relations*.

Marion Tilton   Sympathetic, competent, stylish secretary to Hotel Manager Emile Cousin; she befriends Violet Powler and proves to be the best dancer of the four women included in the banquet held by the officials involved in the Orcham Merger of luxury hotels in Arnold Bennett's *Imperial Palace*.

Tim   A mostly out-of-work actor who comes to Anthony Keating's residence to help care for Molly Murray; he is a good cook and a boring conversationalist who makes up lies in Margaret Drabble's *The Ice Age*.

Sir Horace Timberlake   Wealthy industrialist who makes a large endowment to the Cambridge college out of gratitude for the success of its tutors in the education of his nephew in C. P. Snow's *The Masters*.

Time Traveller   Compassionate, earnest scientist who travels into Earth's distant future and is grieved to discover that the human race has split into two breeds, the childish, surface-dwelling Eloi and the cannibalistic, subterranean Morlocks; he resumes time-travelling after returning home to recount his adventures in H. G. Wells's *The Time Machine: An Invention*.

Sir Ernest Timmerman   Self-important second in command to Lord Raingo in the Ministry of Records; he would like to command but is intimidated and placatory in Arnold Bennett's *Lord Raingo*.

Tims   Slow-witted former servant to Francis Andrews's father and friend to Andrews; he is caught and tried with the smugglers, but so badly treated by them that he nearly goes without representation in Graham Greene's *The Man Within*.

Beryl Tims   Housekeeper for Sir Quentin Oliver; Fleur Talbot calls her "the English Rose type" in Muriel Spark's *Loitering with Intent*.

Timzra   Loud, vulgar young singer introduced by the diplomats of Dateland during their visit to the Court of Pisuerga, where she becomes known as "Tropical Molly" in Ronald Firbank's *The Flower Beneath the Foot*.

Mrs. Tinckham   A cat-loving newsvendor and the discreet depositary of everything from manuscripts to personal confidences in Iris Murdoch's *Under the Net*.

Archie Tingley   Doris Tingley's ne'er-do-well husband, who cannot hold down a job yet becomes a millionaire when he gets into the distribution end of the moving-picture business that he realizes is the wave of the future in J. B. Priestley's *Lost Empires*.

Doris Tingley   A permanently angry woman who is nonetheless quick and conscientious as the replacement for Cissie Mapes in Nick Ollanton's act in J. B. Priestley's *Lost Empires*.

Tin Tin   A prostitute at Mère Catherine's brothel in Port-au-Prince; Brown's favorite girl at the brothel, she entertains Major Jones in Graham Greene's *The Comedians*.

Tipping   Jockey who rides George Pendyce's horse in the losing race in John Galsworthy's *The Country House*.

Angela Tirrit   Wealthy mistress of Edward Wilcher; after her husband dies she marries Edward in a plan to settle his debts in Joyce Cary's *To Be a Pilgrim*.

Clara Tisbourne   Gracie's mother, an attractive matron; she accepts Gracie's engagement to Ludwig Leferrier but would prefer that she marry Sebastian Odmore in Iris Murdoch's *An Accidental Man*.

George (Pinkie) Tisbourne   Gracie's father, a well-off family man in Iris Murdoch's *An Accidental Man*.

Gracie Tisbourne   A young heiress punished for her selfishness by Ludwig Leferrier's breaking of their engagement; she is rewarded with a happy marriage to Garth Gibson Grey for bravely enduring her misery in Iris Murdoch's *An Accidental Man*.

Patrick Tisbourne   Younger brother of Gracie, in whom he freely confides his passion for Ralph Odmore in Iris Murdoch's *An Accidental Man*.

Robert (Robin) Tisdall (Stannaway)   Likeable young man who has dissipated a large fortune; Christine Clay's alteration to her will, leaving him a sizeable inheritance, makes him the chief suspect in her murder in Josephine Tey's *A Shilling for Candles*.

Tiu   Drake Ko's bodyguard and business associate; he murders J. Frost and Luke and is beaten severely by Jerry Westerby when Drake and Nelson Ko reunite in John le Carré's *The Honourable Schoolboy*.

Tiverton   The spinsterish assistant headmaster and a born cricket player; an enthusiast who turned Commonroom cynic, he loves his comforts in Nicholas Blake's *A Question of Proof*.

Toad Generous, foolhardy creature whose wealth allows him to indulge his taste for novelty; his adventures with motor cars land him in a great deal of trouble; rescued by Badger, Water Rat, and Mole, he finally promises to mend his ways in Kenneth Grahame's *The Wind in the Willows*.

Tobias Martha Quest's elderly African cook; she respects Martha but very much dislikes her mother in Doris Lessing's *A Proper Marriage*.

Stephen Todberry Friend of Bertram Verren; he becomes infatuated with Gladys, Bertram's younger sister, but is rejected by her in Frank Swinnerton's *The Young Idea: A Comedy of Environment*.

Mr. Todd The eccentric and deranged leader of a group of South American natives; he speaks English but cannnot read the language; when Tony Last wanders into his territory, he keeps Tony a prisoner, forcing him to read Charles Dickens's novels incessantly in Evelyn Waugh's *A Handful of Dust*.

Elspeth Todd ("Bessie") Feeble-minded gray-haired villager of Woodilee; a member of the Satanic coven, she is tortured by John Kincaid, the "pricker", into an admission of her guilt; despite the ministrations of David Sempill, the minister, she dies in John Buchan's *Witch Wood*.

Lefty Todd The eccentric leader of the New Independent Socialists and a friend of Jake Donaghue and Hugo Belfounder; he makes a speech on a movie set that ends with a police raid and the destruction of a plastic Rome in Iris Murdoch's *Under the Net*.

Ron Todd Marxist and folk musician who promotes folk music as an art of protest in Colin MacInnes's *Absolute Beginners*.

William Todd Medical student, tenant in Milly Sanders's house, and lover (later husband) of Nancy Hawkins in Muriel Spark's *A Far Cry from Kensington*.

Daniel Tokenhouse Contemporary and friend of Captain Jenkins; he abandoned an army career to become a publisher of art books; an anti-religious puritan, he became an expatriate painter; his conversion to communism and subsequent nervous collapse are remembered by Nicholas Jenkins in Anthony Powell's *Temporary Kings*.

Countess Violet Tolga Trusted, soon-to-retire "Woman of the Bedchamber" for Queen Lois of Pisuerga; her sensuality and exasperation with her boorish husband the Count lead her to initiate an affair at the Summer-Palace with the attractively androgynous Ma-

demoiselle Olga Blumenghast in Ronald Firbank's *The Flower Beneath the Foot*.

Ben Toliver Businessman, bon vivant, Member of Parliament, and breakaway politician with ambiguous political motives; his interference threatens Colonel Schlegel's mission in Len Deighton's *Spy Story*.

Alfred Tolland Lord Warminster's younger brother and uncle of Lord Erridge and his nine Tolland siblings; Alfred is a family-history expert; he is much the oldest at Le Bas's Old Boy reunions in Anthony Powell's *The Acceptance World*. He appears in *At Lady Molly's*, in *Casanova's Chinese Restaurant*, and in *The Kindly Ones*. He rises from his sickbed to attend Lord Erridge's funeral in *Books Do Furnish a Room*.

Hugo Tolland The youngest, most amusing, and most gossiped about of Lord Warminster's sons in Anthony Powell's *At Lady Molly's* and in *Casanova's Chinese Restaurant*. He lives with Max Pilgrim in *The Kindly Ones*. After the war he operates an antiques shop in *Books Do Furnish a Room*.

Lady Isobel Tolland The highbrow eighth of Lord Warminster's ten children; Nicholas Jenkins, meeting her, knows immediately that he will marry her in Anthony Powell's *At Lady Molly's*. She recovers from a miscarriage in *Casanova's Chinese Restaurant*. Pregnant, she stays with her sister Lady Frederica Budd in *The Kindly Ones*. She and Jenkins have a son in *The Valley of Bones*. She attends her eldest brother's funeral and has a second son in *Books Do Furnish a Room*. She appears in *Temporary Kings* and in *Hearing Secret Harmonies*.

Lady Priscilla Tolland The musical youngest of Lord Warminster's ten children; she is pursued by Chips Lovell in Anthony Powell's *At Lady Molly's*. When her unconsummated affair with Hugh Moreland is ended, she becomes engaged to Lovell in *Casanova's Chinese Restaurant*. They marry in *The Kindly Ones*. She becomes interested in Odo Stevens in *The Valley of Bones*. Her affair with Stevens distresses Lovell; she is killed at a party when a flying bomb lands on the Jeavonses' house in *The Soldier's Art*.

Robert Tolland The seventh of Lord Warminster's ten children and the brother-in-law preferred by Nicholas Jenkins in Anthony Powell's *Casanova's Chinese Restaurant* and in *The Kindly Ones*. His affair with the somewhat older Flavia (Stringham) Wisebite is cut short by his death in France in World War II in *The Valley of Bones*.

Lady Susan Tolland The fifth of Lord Warminster's ten children; she is engaged to Roddy Cutts in Anthony Powell's *At Lady Molly's*. Her impeccable behavior over her husband's wartime infidelity in *The Military Philosophers* enables her to dominate over him; she has a daughter, her youngest child, Fiona, in *Books Do Furnish a Room*. She appears in *Hearing Secret Harmonies*.

Finn Toller   An imbecilic rogue induced by Mad Bet Chinnock to murder her beloved John Crow; he accidentally murders Tom Barter instead and, fleeing the scene, is in turn killed by Mad Bet in John Cowper Powys's *A Glastonbury Romance*.

George Tolley   Driver who wrecks The Fly-by-Night, a royal mail coach; his humiliation is compounded when Sir Turnour Wyse drives up to rescue Miss "Kirsty" Everdale and "Miss Georgie" Kinethmont in John Buchan's *The Free Fishers*.

Mrs. Tolputt   Sister-in-law of Teresa Spedding; she comes up from Dorking on the day Sebastian drops by the Speddings' for tea in Vita Sackville-West's *The Edwardians*.

General Hanra TolramKetinet   JandolAngand's general leading forces against the western countries; he is the brother of Mai TolramKetinet and becomes MyrdemInggala's lover in Brian W. Aldiss's *Helliconia Summer*.

Mai TolramKetinet   Hamra TolramKetinet's sister, who is MyrdemInggala's lady-in-waiting and best friend in Brian W. Aldiss's *Helliconia Summer*.

Tom   Angela's brother, a priest who is leaving the priesthood to marry in David Lodge's *How Far Can You Go?*.

Tom   Boyish, pleasant, shy young man in love with Liza Kemp; despite knowing of Liza's affair with Jim Blakeston and of her pregnancy, he still wants to marry her in W. Somerset Maugham's *Liza of Lambeth*.

Tom   Ida Arnold's estranged husband frequently referred to by Ida in Graham Greene's *Brighton Rock*.

Tom   Worker at Timberwork who quarrels with another worker, Geoffrey; Orlando King is able to help the two workers reach a compromise in Isabel Colegate's *Orlando King*.

Charles Tombs   Cambridge "professor", member of a group in Glasgow protesting the War as part of the social injustices suffered by the lower classes; he is suspected by Richard Hannay of being a pawn in the deadly German spy ring operating in Great Britain and Europe in John Buchan's *Mr. Standfast*. He reappears

in Birkpool pursuing a political career in *A Prince of the Captivity*.

Tompkin   Young surgeon who successfully operates on Adam Sedgwick for Parkinson's disease in C. P. Snow's *In Their Wisdom*.

Tompkins   One of three English road laborers mistaken by John Lavender for German prisoners of war in John Galsworthy's *The Burning Spear: Being the Experiences of Mr. John Lavender in Time of War*.

Bella Tompkins   A middle-class widow whose marriage to Sir Robert Smithson frustrates Charles Smithson's hopes of inheriting his uncle's estate in John Fowles's *The French Lieutenant's Woman*.

Ibrahim Tondapo   Simple-minded Nigerian acquaintance of Johnny Fortune; Ibrahim is beaten by Johnny for insulting him in Colin MacInnes's *City of Spades*.

Tonio   Barman who serves Eustace Cherrington and Nancy Steptoe Alberic during their reunion in Venice in L. P. Hartley's *Eustace and Hilda*.

Jean Tonnesen   Beautiful, multilingual espionage agent and the narrator's casual love interest; she is transferred to W.O.O.C.(P.) to aid him in uncovering the division's double agent in Len Deighton's *The Ipcress File*. She sets up the narrator's cover as Edmond Dorf in *Funeral in Berlin* and continues to work with him in *The Billion-Dollar Brain*.

Peregrin (Pippin) Took   Young, irrepressible hobbit who is a member of the fellowship who travel with Frodo Baggins to destroy the One Ring in J. R. R. Tolkien's *The Fellowship of the Ring*. Separated from the others, he joins forces with Seward of Denethor II; he fights a battle and saves Beregond, his human friend, in *The Two Towers*. Having rejoined the other fellowship members after the destruction of the ring, he assists in the rebellion against the invading men in *The Return of the King*.

Sir Alec Tooley   Father of Ian Tooley and director of Mackintosh & Tooley in Muriel Spark's *A Far Cry from Kensington*.

Ian Tooley   Director of Mackintoch & Tooley whose interest in radionics (the Box) and astrology fascinates his employee Nancy Hawkins in Muriel Spark's *A Far Cry from Kensington*.

Nappa Toomey   Daughter of Brian Kilmartin; she and her husband are among the first to leave the valley and sail to America to escape the poverty in Liam O'Flaherty's *Famine*.

Peter Topglass   A tall, balding naturalist, Michael Meade's old college friend, who is a member of the lay community at Imber Court in Iris Murdoch's *The Bell*.

Canon Topling   Friend of Mrs. Bellair and agent of the spy ring "The Free Mothers" in Graham Greene's *The Ministry of Fear*.

Tor-Oyarsa-Perelendri   First man of Perelandra; he becomes King of Perelandra after Elwin Ransom defeats Edward Weston, the embodiment of evil, in C. S. Lewis's *Perelandra*.

Torquemada   Catholic priest and enemy of Signor Malipizzo; his foolish cousin is unfairly questioned about Mr. Muhlen's murder in Norman Douglas's *South Wind*.

Torten   Old business rival of Paul Firman and victim of Firman's shrewd "business" deals in Eric Ambler's *Send No More Roses*.

Julian Tower   Thirty-nine-year old bachelor businessman, set in his ways but attracted to Cecelia Summers; they eventually conclude that they should marry in Elizabeth Bowen's *To the North*.

James (Jack) Farrer Townrow   Cynical opportunist who plans to rob Mrs. Khoury of her inheritance from her husband; having experienced a beating and suffering short-term amnesia, having become romantically involved with Leah Strauss, and having been accused of murder and espionage, he abandons his intention of robbing Mrs. Khoury and seeks an honorable life in P. H. Newby's *Something to Answer For*.

Charlie Townsend   The charming, vain, and self-centered Government official who is happy to conduct a clandestine affair with Kitty Fane; however, when the relationship begins to threaten his own marital harmony and status quo, he is covertly relieved to find that Kitty's husband is forcing her to accompany him on a dangerous mission to a cholera-infested area of China in W. Somerset Maugham's *The Painted Veil*.

Dorothy Townsend   Well-bred, courteous, and able wife of Charlie Townsend; she tolerates her husband's weaknesses and considers his conquests slightly common in W. Somerset Maugham's *The Painted Veil*.

Pixie Townsend   Tony Kroesig's second wife; she accompanies Moira Kroesig to America during World War II to escape the bombing and is therefore held more deeply in contempt by Moira's mother, Linda (Radlett), in Nancy Mitford's *The Pursuit of Love*.

Hilary Townshend   Gloomy aristocratic bachelor and Liberal politician who, as a "warrior of conduct", often frowns on the younger members of his class for their instabilities in Michael Arlen's *The Green Hat*.

Dr. Towzer   Medical man whom "Captain Mallet" transforms into Herbert Towzer, gardener and lover of roses, in Nigel Dennis's *Cards of Identity*.

Professor Edward Tracy   "Treacherous friend" of Sergeant Jebb; he refuses to use his power to get Jebb the academic chair he expected and undercuts Jebb's self-esteem by calling his scholarly writing arrogant, frivolous, old-fashioned, and useless in Storm Jameson's *There Will Be a Short Interval*.

William Tracy   Writer of westerns and one of the cast of characters held captive in the Red Swan Hotel by the fictional novelist Dermot Trellis in Flann O'Brien's *At Swim-Two-Birds*.

Poppy Traherne   "A lady in innumerable petticoats" who can "whirl herself into anything you like" (from a lily to a rainbow); she signs on as a performer for Houghton's theater in D. H. Lawrence's *The Lost Girl*.

Charlie Trainor   Unscrupulous calf-dealer who fulfils his sexual appetite with many women; he is constantly antagonizing Tarry Flynn in Patrick Kavanagh's *Tarry Flynn*.

Giulietta, Marchesa Trampani   Italian widow who first becomes a close friend and admirer of Sir George Dillingham; after his death she is attracted to Alexis Golightly and encourages him to return to Italy with her in David Garnett's *Aspects of Love*.

Elizabeth Trant   Provincial domestic drudge who is released by her father's death and a small inheritance to discover romance and adventure; she befriends a group of down-and-out actors who call themselves the Dinky Doos, renaming the group the Good Companions and managing their booking and, to some extent, their lives in J. B. Priestley's *The Good Companions*.

Ann Tranter   Sister of Ernest Freeman and aunt of Ernestina Freeman, who stays at her house in Lyme Regis in John Fowles's *The French Lieutenant's Woman*.

Francis X. Trapnel   Talkative novelist, whose magnum opus is destroyed by Pamela Flitton, his latest mistress, in Anthony Powell's *Books Do Furnish a Room*. He declines thereafter and dies after a drunken night in a saloon in *Temporary Kings*. He is the subject of a prizewinning biography by Russell Gwinnett in *Hearing Secret Harmonies.*

Mr. Travers Owner of the schooner *Hermit;* a proper gentleman, he remains remarkably uninvolved in his wife and Lingard's affair in Joseph Conrad's *The Rescue: A Romance of the Shallows.*

Dahlia Travers Bertie Wooster's aunt, publisher of the unprofitable weekly paper *Milady's Boudoir*; she manipulates Bertie's compliance in reckless and illegal schemes through the necessity of retaining her French cook, Anatole, in P. G. Wodehouse's *The Code of the Woosters* and in *Aunts Aren't Gentlemen.* She appears in five other novels.

Edith Travers The wife of the owner of the stranded *Hermit,* immediately drawn to the intensity and straightforward, heroic grandeur of Lingard; she comes close to abandoning her proper husband for Lingard but in the end leaves Lingard in Joseph Conrad's *The Rescue: A Romance of the Shallows.*

Louie Travers One of the working girls at the factory where Paul Morel works; she briefly becomes Baxter Dawes's mistress in D. H. Lawrence's *Sons and Lovers.*

Tom Travers Dahlia's husband, whose obsessive collecting of rare silver imperils Bertie Wooster in P. G. Wodehouse's *The Code of the Woosters.* His letter to Bertie in New York reveals the denouement in *Aunts Aren't Gentlemen.* He appears in five other novels.

Janet Traversa (variously, Rohtraut) Cheshire girl, fiancée of Dana Hilliot; Dana believes he is unworthy of her in Malcolm Lowry's *Ultramarine.*

Dr. Travis Physician who diagnoses Henry Scobie's angina and advises him to retire in Graham Greene's *The Heart of the Matter.*

Blanche Tray Erstwhile nurse of Dr. Towzer; she is transformed by "Captain Mallet" into the Mallets' gardener's assistant in Nigel Dennis's *Cards of Identity.*

"Shady" Tree A hunchback employed by "The Spangled Mob" in New York in Ian Fleming's *Diamonds Are Forever.*

Professor Stuart Treece The "good and liberal" head of the English Department who has affairs with a colleague, Viola Masefield, and with one of his students, Emma Fielding, in Malcolm Bradbury's *Eating People Is Wrong.*

Rowena Trefusis Thirty-six-year-old attractive sex researcher who leads Jake Richardson through a series of sex-response tests in a theater with eight observers in Kingsley Amis's *Jake's Thing.*

Dr. Trelawney A long-haired, white-robed, egotistical crackpot who leads a cult of disciples in pursuit of Oneness at an institute near the Jenkins home in 1914; meeting him again in 1939, Nick Jenkins continues to feel menaced by the latent sinister evil in Trelawney in Anthony Powell's *The Kindly Ones.* His death occurs in *The Military Philosophers.* His creed is revived in *Hearing Secret Harmonies.*

Dermot Trellis Bedridden novelist, created by the unnamed narrator; he severely restricts the freedom of his fictional characters until they turn on him and punish him in Flann O'Brien's *At Swim-Two-Birds.*

Orlick Trellis Offspring of the fictional novelist Dermot Trellis and one of his female characters; Orlick writes a novel within the novel within the novel in which he plots the punishment of his father in Flann O'Brien's *At Swim-Two-Birds.*

Elizabeth Trelone Wife of Thomas Trelone in Olaf Stapledon's *Sirius: A Fantasy of Love and Discord.*

Giles Trelone One of Plaxy Trelone's older brothers; his reporting of what Sirius has said to him is Mr. Pugh's first clue to Sirius's level of intelligence in Olaf Stapledon's *Sirius: A Fantasy of Love and Discord.*

Maurice Trelone One of Plaxy Trelone's older brothers; the sinking of his ship during World War II causes the death of his mother, Elizabeth, before it is discovered that he has survived in Olaf Stapledon's *Sirius: A Fantasy of Love and Discord.*

Plaxy Trelone Daughter of Elizabeth and Thomas Trelone; she is raised with Sirius and becomes his soul mate in Olaf Stapledon's *Sirius: A Fantasy of Love and Discord.*

Thomas Trelone Cambridge scientist whose physiological experiments are responsible for Sirius's great intelligence; Sirius regards him as a father figure in Olaf Stapledon's *Sirius: A Fantasy of Love and Discord.*

Thomasina ("Tamsy") Trelone Plaxy Trelone's older sister in Olaf Stapledon's *Sirius: A Fantasy of Love and Discord.*

Harry Tremaine The perfect courtier; he serves briefly as Sylvia, Lady Roehampton's lover in Vita Sackville-West's *The Edwardians.*

Mr. Tremayne An ultra-conventional friend of Gerald Ducayne; Miriam Henderson believes him to be scandalized by her passionate playing of Beethoven on the piano in Dorothy Richardson's *The Tunnel.*

Tremlin   Lecturer at King's College, University of London, who is a biochemist with interest in crystallography; he supervises Arthur Miles's research at King's In C. P. Snow's *The Search.*

Trent   District officer in charge of Richard Roe's auxiliary fire service unit; he becomes disgusted with Albert Pye's running of the unit and plans to fire him in Henry Green's *Caught.*

George Trent   Working-class painter known as one of the New Young Realists who admires Janos Lavin's work and learns from him; at an exhibit of his work he dedicates one of his paintings to Lavin in John Berger's *A Painter of Our Time.*

Giles Trent   British Secret Intelligence officer who is discovered as a mole to K.G.B. agent Chlestakon by Bernard Samson; he turns double agent to capture the agent in Len Deighton's *Berlin Game.*

June Trent   The supportive wife of artist George Trent in John Berger's *A Painter of Our Time.*

Paul Trent   A philosophical anarchist and lawyer come to Glastonbury to aid in the establishment of the "Commune"; he succeeds in securing from Lord P. the lease for the bulk of Glastonbury's land for the Communists in John Cowper Powys's *A Glastonbury Romance.*

Sergeant Tressell   Thomas Stern's sergeant while in the army; Thomas was in charge of carrying out this man's careless and indifferent demands, and develops an insatiable hatred of him in Doris Lessing's *Landlocked.*

Bobbie Trevor   Brother of Catherine Frobisher; he raises pigs but has no business sense and so lives in debt in the family home; he lives with a married woman, Lise Grainger, who later becomes his wife in Margaret Kennedy's *Red Sky at Morning.*

William James (Jaz) Trewhella   A young Cornishman who is a coal and wood merchant; he supports "Kangaroo" (Benjamin Cooley) and the Diggers and wants them to join forces with the "Reds" to bring about a violent revolution in Australia in D. H. Lawrence's *Kangaroo.*

Mrs. Tribe   "Bohemian" mother of Julie Tribe and neighbor to the Nimmos; she attempts to blackmail Nina (Woodville) Nimmo after her daughter and the

younger Tom Nimmo have an affair in Joyce Cary's *Prisoner of Grace.*

Julie Tribe   Daughter of the "Bohemian" Mrs. Tribe; she becomes engaged to the younger Tom Nimmo, but their relationship falls through in Joyce Cary's *Prisoner of Grace.*

J. F. Trigg   A solicitor whom Mary Whittaker consulted to inquire about the effects of inheritance-law changes; he tells Inspector Parker of being drugged by a mysterious woman in Dorothy L. Sayers's *Unnatural Death.*

Senora Trigo   Sigbjorn and Primrose Wilderness's landlady in Cuernavaca in Malcolm Lowry's *Dark as the Grave Wherein My Friend Is Laid.*

Kiril Trigorin   Fat, wealthy, and urbane but modest Russian ballet arranger who wanted to be a composer but had no talent for it; Trigorin is a great fan of Albert Sanger and visits him in Austria, where he eventually takes up with Sanger's mistress, Linda Cowlard, in Margaret Kennedy's *The Constant Nymph.*

Edward Winlove, Eleventh Viscount Trimingham
Grandson of Marian Maudsley and descendant of Ted Burgess; following the devastation of his family and others as a result of World War II, he feels he is living under a curse which the aged Leo Colston hopes to dispel, acting once more at the behest of Marian, by assuring the young man "there is no spell or curse except an unloving heart" in L. P. Hartley's *The Go-Between.*

Hugh Francis Winlove, Ninth Viscount Trimingham
Aristocratic veteran of the Boer War and ancestral owner of Brandham Hall who marries the pregnant Marian Maudsley after the death of her lover, Ted Burgess; he always insists that "nothing is ever a lady's fault" in L. P. Hartley's *The Go-Between.*

Robin Trimmle   Expert driver of the Rover Mail, which Sir Turnour Wyse appropriates for the wild drive to the Merry Mouth Inn in a desperate effort to defeat Squire Cranmer's plot to assassinate the Prime Minister in John Buchan's *The Free Fishers.*

J. S. Tring   Young, initially popular Resident Officer in Fada who realizes Rudbeck has been misusing funds for his road; he fires Johnson for complicity in the forgeries in Joyce Cary's *Mister Johnson.*

Trivett   Elderly family retainer; though a dangerous and incompetent driver, he is established as chauffeur to remove him from responsibility for the precious horses in Richard Hughes's *The Fox in the Attic.*

Trom   King of Glome and father of Orual, Redival, and Psyche; he is a ruthless, barbaric king; when the lot falls to Psyche to be sacrificed to save the kingdom, he is more than willing to let her be killed in C. S. Lewis's *Till We Have Faces*.

Alymer Troth   London solicitor who was involved twenty years earlier in a financial swindle culminating either in suicide or murder, but who was not himself convicted; one of the men intent on robbing Marius Haraldsen in Rhodesia, he was killed in John Buchan's *The Island of Sheep*.

Lancelot Troth   Son of Alymer Troth; determined to avenge his father's death, he writes to Valdemar Haraldsen submitting a claim against his inheritance and terrorizing him by threatening vengeance in John Buchan's *The Island of Sheep*.

Leon Trotsky   See Lev Davidovich Bronstein.

Sir Trotter-Stormer   Permanent resident of the upscale Ritz hotel in Pisuerga whose innocent note to Lady Something reinforces her confused and litigious belief that the establishment is infested with fleas in Ronald Firbank's *The Flower Beneath the Foot*.

Cissy Trout   Eva's mother, who died in a plane crash when Eva was an infant in Elizabeth Bowen's *Eva Trout, or Changing Scenes*.

Eva Trout   An unusually tall and large-boned girl, whose unconventional childhood was spent traveling the world with her wealthy father and his companion, Constantine Ormeau, after the early death of her mother; upon coming of age Eva inherits a fortune which she determines to use by giving herself, in order, a home of her own, a child, and a husband in Elizabeth Bowen's *Eva Trout, or Changing Scenes*.

Jeremy Trout   Eva's precocious but deaf-mute son, adopted as an infant from questionable sources in the midwestern United States in Elizabeth Bowen's *Eva Trout, or Changing Scenes*.

Willy Trout   Eva's wealthy widower father, shrewd in business but overtrusting of his companion, Constantine Ormeau; after his wife's early death he travels with Constantine and Eva; his suicide puts Eva in Constantine's guardianship in Elizabeth Bowen's *Eva Trout, or Changing Scenes*.

Jim Troyes   A middle-aged trade-unionist from Bradford who is engaged to Phoebe Coldridge until Jill and Gwen, Phoebe's daughters, help to break their engagement in Doris Lessing's *The Four-Gated City*.

Countess Arminta Troyos   Beautiful young Evallonian noblewoman; the dynamic soul of the Juventus Party in Evallonia, she is determined to put the next ruler on the throne in John Buchan's *The House of the Four Winds*.

Miss Truebody   Terence R. Fielding's housekeeper; her call to Stella Rode permits the murderer to hide evidence incriminating him in Rode's murder in John le Carré's *A Murder of Quality*.

Truelove   One of the most famous and successful prize agents in England; he is in business with Wilson in C. S. Forester's *Lieutenant Hornblower*.

Eric Trumbull   Tall, thin, forty-five-year-old American aesthete; he becomes a British citizen in charge of French propaganda and plans to inform the French intelligentsia about English gardens, much to the amazement and disgust of Lord Raingo, new Minister of Records, who nevertheless uneasily wonders if Trumbull's subtleties will work in Arnold Bennett's *Lord Raingo*.

Victor Trumpington   Guest from the Foreign Office at the Anchorstone Hall houseparty who plays tennis with Eustace Cherrington and suggests that mysticism can be grown out of; he also represents a commitment to reality which eludes Eustace in L. P. Hartley's *The Sixth Heaven*.

Truscott   Signal midshipman of the *Renown* in C. S. Forester's *Lieutenant Hornblower*.

Tsi-puff   Erudite Selenite who memorizes all aspects of Earthly culture which Cavor imparts in H. G. Wells's *The First Men in the Moon*.

Tsomotre   An apparently neckless Tibetan boy; he is one of the supernormals of John Wainwright's Pacific island colony in Olaf Stapledon's *Odd John: A Story Between Jest and Earnest*.

Mathew Williamson Tuakana   Unscrupulous Eurasian accountant and white-collar criminal, who becomes Chief Minister of Placid Island; in order to avoid exposure as Paul Firman's employer and co-criminal, he attempts the murder of Paul, his associates, and the three criminologists by beseiging the Villa Lipp in Eric Ambler's *Send No More Roses*.

Tuami   An artist and seer of the Homo sapiens tribe who opposes the cruel chief, Marlan, vies with him for the favors of the lusty Vivani, and seeks some point of light with which to combat the darkness of ignorance and superstition in William Golding's *The Inheritors*.

Waldo Tubbe (satirical portrait of T. S. Eliot)   A guest at Shobbe's "Sunday evening", where George Winterbourne meets London's artistic elite and their hangers-on in Richard Aldington's *Death of a Hero*.

Owen Tuby   English teacher who with Cosmo Sultana founds the Institute of Social Imagistics in J. B. Priestley's *The Image Men*.

Fred Tucher   American expatriate editor of *The Highgate Review* who employs Nancy Hawkins in Muriel Spark's *A Far Cry from Kensington*.

Edie Tucker   Woman interviewed in the television film Kate Fletcher Armstrong is making; she is a "registered childminder" in Margaret Drabble's *The Middle Ground*.

Mary Lou Tucker   The beautiful wife of Richard Lindbergh Tucker; he uses her as sexual bait first with Wilfred Barclay and then with the mysterious, omnipresent Mr. Halliday in William Golding's *The Paper Men*.

Ralph Tucker   Gardener and steward at Tothill House who writes plays of violence, marries Magda Sczekerny, and provides the lighting effects for Piers Mosson's production of the opera; his play based on the history of the Mossons and produced by Piers is a cover for his terrorist activities in Angus Wilson's *Setting the World on Fire*.

Professor Richard Lindbergh Tucker   A six-foot-three, two-hundred-and-twenty-five-pound sycophant; he hounds Wilfred Barclay in order to become the biographer of someone who belongs, as he believes, to the "Pageant of English Literature" in William Golding's *The Paper Men*.

Mr. Tuckles   An elderly and defenseless man who lives on the grounds of the Villiers estate; he and his wife are tormented by Andy Adorno and Quentin Villiers for amusement in Martin Amis's *Dead Babies*.

Mrs. Tuckles   An elderly and defenseless woman who lives on the grounds of the Villiers estate; she and her husband are tormented by Andy Adorno and Quentin Villiers for amusement in Martin Amis's *Dead Babies*.

Miss Tuke   The matron at Lesbia Firebrace's school; she is a pale, preoccupied woman with spontaneous affection for the girls in Ivy Compton-Burnett's *Two Worlds and Their Ways*.

Effie Tuke   Flesh-loathing, highly intellectual woman whom Alvina Houghton serves as maternity nurse in D. H. Lawrence's *The Lost Girl*.

Father Laurence Tulliver   Vicar of the Swans' suburban church who enlists Rhoda Wellcome to wash his vestments while his wife is ill in Barbara Pym's *Less Than Angels*.

Henry Tung   Boastful, garrulous Christian Chinese fireman aboard the *Archimedes*; understanding nothing of his language, Mr. Soutar believes him to be fomenting mutiny in Richard Hughes's *In Hazard*.

Tureiya Pasha   Good-natured Egyptian prince married to the Princess, who is twenty-five years his senior; he receives English lessons from Edgar Perry, whom the Pasha sees as a menace when he attempts to improve student housing; he is intrigued by Perry's apparent suicide attempt in P. H. Newby's *The Picnic at Sakkara*.

Howard Turgis   Junior clerk at Twigg and Dersingham made obsessively jealous by Lena Golspie's rejection in J. B. Priestley's *Angel Pavement*.

Mr. Turnbull   Toy-shop keeper who becomes the commander-in-chief of the Notting Hill army and dies in the last battle in G. K. Chesterton's *The Napoleon of Notting Hill*.

Alexander Turnbull   Drunken roadman in Scotland whose job and clothing Richard Hannay assumes to elude his pursuers; he then nurses Hannay during a bout of malaria in John Buchan's *The Thirty-Nine Steps*.

James Turnbull   Editor of *The Atheist* newspaper who seriously offends Evan MacIan by blaspheming the Virgin Mary; Turnbull and MacIan vow to duel each other for their beliefs; their attempted duel is constantly interrupted by the authorities; Turnbull and MacIan are captured and committed to an insane asylum where they encounter everyone who took their differences seriously; he and MacIan escape by following Father Michael through the final conflagration in G. K. Chesterton's *The Ball and the Cross*.

Regimental Sgt. Major Turner   Large, handsome, and very fit senior noncommissioned officer with the British Army in Gibraltar; he is the successful rival of Sgt. Richard Ennis for the love and sexual favors of Lavinia Grantham in Anthony Burgess's *A Vision of Battlements*.

Alan Turner   Abrasive, working-class counterintelligence officer for the Security Department; despite the Embassy's hypocritical rituals, he searches for the alleged traitor Harting and uncovers Karfeld's political betrayals, Ludwig Siebkron's murderous plots, and Leo Harting's unwarranted loyalty in John le Carré's *A Small Town in Germany*.

George Turner Sailing master whose familiarity with Turkish waters and experience with the fleet in Marmorice lands him aboard the Atropos in C. S. Forester's *Hornblower and the Atropos*.

Mary Turner A city girl who works as a secretary and leads an active life until her friends begin to question her failure to marry; she feels constrained to marry a farmer; out of boredom and loneliness, she turns to the companionship of her black servant, who in the end murders her in Doris Lessing's *The Grass Is Singing*.

Richard (Dick) Turner A poor farmer in Southern Rhodesia (Ngesi) who marries out of loneliness; he does not have the resources or the mentality to support his young, city-bred wife, and his farm eventually fails in Doris Lessing's *The Grass Is Singing*.

Seigfried von Turpitz A German literary theorist competing for the UNESCO chair of literary criticism; he wears one black glove over a perfectly normal hand and plagiarizes Persse McGarrigle's idea about the influence of T. S. Eliot on Shakespeare in David Lodge's *Small World*.

Mr. Turton English Collector in Chandrapore, India; he hosts an unsuccessful "bridge party" for the English and the Indians; his attitude to the Indians is typically and arrogantly English in E. M. Forster's *A Passage to India*.

Tusca Kyale's wife, who takes care of Yuli in Brian W. Aldiss's *Helliconia Spring*.

Tuss The street-smart black leader of a violent gang of teenage toughs; he befriends Bev Jones because the latter, knowing Greek and Latin, is admired as a link to the past in Anthony Burgess's *1985*.

Jayne Tuthill Ex-pupil of Romley Fourways', the school Kate Fletcher (Armstrong) attended; she is a worker at the hospital where Kate was born in Margaret Drabble's *The Middle Ground*.

Martina Twain An American friend of John Self; her

husband is having an affair with John's girlfriend; she tries to help John with his various problems and ends by falling in love with him in Martin Amis's *Money*.

Twal The Homo sapiens mother of Tanakil in William Golding's *The Inheritors*.

Mrs. Tweetyman Married daughter of Nicholas Soames; she and Euphemia Forsyte see June Forsyte and Philip Bosinney alone at the theatre in John Galsworthy's *The Man of Property*.

Mrs. Twemlow The apoplectic-looking housekeeper of Blandings Castle; her appearance complements that of the butler Beach as "one of a pair of vases . . . goes with its fellow" in P. G. Wodehouse's *Something New*.

Mr. Twinny After-hours workman at Milly Sanders's house in Muriel Spark's *A Far Cry from Kensington*.

"Dr." Alexander ("Chimp") Twist An American con man whose success as the proprietor of the diet-and-fitness establishment "Healthward Ho" is jeopardized by his renewed involvement with his old confederate "Soapy" Molloy in P. G. Wodehouse's *Money for Nothing*. He appears in four other novels.

Mr. Twistevant Tilling greengrocer and slumlord who serves on the Town Council in E. F. Benson's *The Worshipful Lucia*. He appears in *Miss Mapp*, in *Mapp and Lucia*, and in *Trouble for Lucia*.

Young Twistevant The Tilling greengrocer's son, whose horse-race-gambling losses inspire Mayor Lucia (Lucas) Pillson's utterly unsuccessful attempts to reform Tilling society's custom of playing bridge for threepence a hundred in E. F. Benson's *Trouble for Lucia*.

Tessa Tye Pretty, ineffectual, pregnant maid of Gracie Savotte, whose resourceful responses to Tessa's condition and attempted suicide in the hotel impress the Managing Director Evelyn Orcham in Arnold Bennett's *Imperial Palace*.

Tom Tyler Young man who is loved by Hannah Glossop; he finds her stupid and uninteresting in Henry Green's *Living*.

U

Ralph Udal Anglican churchman who asks Roy Calvert to help secure a living for him from his Cambridge college; he receives a living from Lord Bocastle but is humiliated when Rosalind Wykes breaks her engagement with him to marry Calvert in C. P. Snow's *The Light and the Dark*.

Thomasina (Tommy) Uhlmeister A drama teacher who has been Hilary Burde's lover and is constantly begging him to marry her; her anonymous letter to Gunnar Jopling warning him of Hilary's involvement with Kitty Jopling precipitates the catastrophe in Iris Murdoch's *A Word Child*.

Guaddl Ulbobeg Taynth Indredd's advisor and a friend of JandolAngand in Brian W. Aldiss's *Helliconia Summer*.

Umberto Young, intelligent, efficient typist and assistant to Nicholas Marlow in the Spartacus Milan branch office; he refuses to cooperate with OVRA (Italian secret police) and consequently saves Marlow's life in Eric Ambler's *Cause for Alarm*.

Dicky Umfraville Gentleman rider whose basic melancholy and dissatisfaction with life balance his frivolity; elegant, friendly, and witty, he is a veteran of the first World War and of many romantic entanglements; the fourth of his five marriages is to Lady Anne Stepney in Anthony Powell's *The Acceptance World*. He marries Lady Frederica Budd; his and Buster Foxe's mutual detestation is elaborated upon in *The Valley of Bones*. He claims to be Pamela Flitton's father in *The Military Philosophers*. He encounters Pamela's mother, Flavia (Stringham) Wisebite, in *Hearing Secret Harmonies*.

Inspector Umpelty The police officer in charge of investigating Paul Alexis Goldschmidt's murder in Dorothy L. Sayers's *Have His Carcase*.

Unchpin Stableman at Edwin Clayhanger's printshop; he misses his Christmas dinner because Edwin's wife, Hilda Lessways, makes the old man wait for their return from a visit, thereby creating another in the multitude of incidents angering Edwin about his wife's wilfulness in Arnold Bennett's *These Twain*.

The Uncle The narrator's uncle, who nags him about his studies and his laziness but who is reconciled with him at the end of Flann O'Brien's *At Swim-Two-Birds*.

Dr. Thomas Underhill A seventeenth-century resident of the house that became the Green Man inn; he performed supernatural feats, seduced adolescent girls, and allegedly murdered his wife; his spirit communicates with Maurice Allington, who is interested in Underhill's evidence that there is life after death in Kingsley Amis's *The Green Man*.

Julian Underwood Middle-aged son of Mrs. Underwood; he is anxious to inherit the estate of Mr. Massie and refuses to settle the dispute over the will out of court; he puts off marriage with Elizabeth Fox-Milnes in C. P. Snow's *In Their Wisdom*.

Katherine Underwood Woman in her mid-sixties who cared for the dying Mr. Massie; she persuaded him to leave his estate to her son, Julian, and dislikes Elizabeth Fox-Milnes in C. P. Snow's *In Their Wisdom*.

Mark Underwood An initially cynical student, would-be writer, and lapsed Catholic; he grows increasingly fond of the Mallory family, with whom he boards; he attempts to seduce Clare Mallory, who in turn tries to bring him back to the church; he converts, becomes more devout than she is, and decides to join the Dominican order, leaving Clare heartbroken in David Lodge's *The Picturegoers*.

Ungit Deity worshipped in Glome; according to the Fox, she is the local manifestation of the Greek goddess Aphrodite; Orual spends most of her life seeking the true Ungit in C. S. Lewis's *Till We Have Faces*.

The Unnamable Dislocated and unnamed writer whose raison d'etre is consideration of the impossibility of fiction in Samuel Beckett's *The Unnamable*.

Unndreid the Hammer Driat leader who attacks Borlien in Brian W. Aldiss's *Helliconia Summer*.

Frank Upjohn (satirical portrait of Ezra Pound) George Winterbourne's friend and sponsor; he introduces a new school of painting every season in Richard Aldington's *Death of a Hero*.

Nicholas Urfe An Oxford graduate who gets a job teaching English on the Greek island of Phraxos; he becomes the focus of an elaborate "god-game" orchestrated by Maurice Conchis; he learns through his mysterious and often frightening experiences and his hopeless love for one of the players, Lily DeSeitas; he finally returns to Alison Kelly; he is narrator of John Fowles's *The Magus*.

James Urkuhart A solicitor and the fraudulent co-trustee for Wemyss's estate, which he had been embezzling; he is killed as a result of a car accident during a chase in Nicholas Blake's *A Question of Proof.*

Norman Urquhart   A solicitor who is Rosanna Wrayburn's nephew, heir, and man of business; he was the late Phillip Boyes's cousin, roommate, and last-meal sharer in Dorothy L. Sayers's *Strong Poison.*

Sister Ursula   Anglican nun, who is extern sister for the invisible nuns of the Benedictine convent in Iris Murdoch's *The Bell.*

Sister Ursula   Masochistic, marriage-denouncing nun of the Flaming-Hood who begins to capture the affections and loyalty of Laura de Nazianzi in Ronald Firbank's *The Flower Beneath the Foot.*

Urthred   Utopian historian who explains his race's eugenic and environmental policies to the stranded Earthlings in H. G. Wells's *Men Like Gods.*

Mark Ury   One of the delegates to the conference of the planets who are to decide on the fate of Earth; he is preparing for another descent to Earth, along with other members of the delegation, in Doris Lessing's *Briefing for a Descent into Hell.*

Usilk   A prisoner in Pannoval whom Yuli befriends because of his parents, Kyale and Tusca; Usilk and Yuli escape from Pannoval together in Brian W. Aldiss's *Helliconia Spring.*

Joe Utlaw   Charismatic union organizer and Labour leader in Birkpool; his loss in the election underlines his moral failure even as a lucrative job with Warren Creevey assures his financial success in John Buchan's *A Prince of the Captivity.*

Uuundaamp   A sledge-dog driver who takes Luterin Shokerandit, Torress Lahl, and Harbin Fashnalgid north to Karnahbar; he abandons Harbin in a winter storm because Harbin raped his wife in Brian W. Aldiss's *Helliconia Winter.*

V

Josef Vadassy Thirty-two-year-old, polite Hungarian language teacher and amateur photographer; the unknowing recipient of photographs of top-secret artillery because of an inadvertent camera switch, he is forced by the French Government to identify the person to whom the photographs belong and to spy for them in Eric Ambler's *Epitaph for a Spy*.

Elsa Vagas Tall, imposing, unhappy, tense wife of General Vagas; coerced by OVRA into spying on her husband (whom she hates), she slips a note to Nicholas Marlow about Sidney Arthur Ferning's killing, tells Vagas that she has told OVRA that he is a German agent (thereby blowing Marlow's cover), and is later killed or commits suicide in Eric Ambler's *Cause for Alarm*.

General Johann Luitpold Vagas German military intelligence agent posing as a supporter of the Yugoslav government; he blackmails Nicholas Marlow into taking Sidney Arthur Ferning's place as a paid supplier of information about Spartacus's shell-production machinery in Eric Ambler's *Cause for Alarm*.

Hero Vale Wife of the headmaster and lover of Michael Evans; having married in fit of absent-mindedness, she is reckless in assignations, arranging to make love in a open hayfield where a boy is murdered later that same day in Nicholas Blake's *A Question of Proof*.

Percival ("Pedantic Percy") Vale A clergyman and pompous headmaster, who is husband of Hero; he is a stickler for the manifestation of discipline and contemptuous of failure; a co-trustee of his murdered nephew's estate, he is also murdered in Nicholas Blake's *A Question of Proof*.

Joan Valentine Intrepid, resourceful young woman who since her father's death has supported herself; she goes to Blandings Castle pseudonymously as the servant of Aline Peters, who has hired her to recover a scarab belonging to Aline's father; Joan, who once received unwanted love letters from Freddie Threepwood, is Ashe Marson's romantic interest in P. G. Wodehouse's *Something New*.

Geoffrey Carádoc, Earl of Valleys Nobleman who discourages his son, Lord Miltoun, and daughter, Lady Barbara Carádoc, from ruining their prospects by marrying beneath their social station in John Galsworthy's *The Patrician*.

Gertrude, Lady Valleys Wife of the Earl of Valleys; she rescues her son, Lord Miltoun, from the nursing of Audrey Noel, and she discourages her daughter, Lady Barbara Carádoc, from her attraction to Charles Courtier in John Galsworthy's *The Patrician*.

Doreen ("Granny") Valvona Astrology-reading resident patient of the old women's hospital ward in Muriel Spark's *Memento Mori*.

Rosina Vamburgh Peregrine Arbelow's first wife, a famous and temperamental actress, who left him for Charles Arrowby; she visits Charles in his retirement to threaten violent retaliation if he breaks his promise to her never to settle down permanently with another woman in Iris Murdoch's *The Sea, the Sea*.

Vande Brother of Ali and house steward of Helen Rolt; he is paid by Wilson to get information from Ali about Henry Scobie in Graham Greene's *The Heart of the Matter*.

Marguerite (Rita) Vandemeyer Bolshevist agent and Sir James Peel Edgerton's former lover; she is poisoned in Agatha Christie's *The Secret Adversary*.

Mrs. Van der Bylt A major figure in the Labour Party, who becomes a motherly figure for Martha Quest in Doris Lessing's *A Ripple from the Storm*, in *Landlocked*, and in *The Four-Gated City*.

Van der Pant Belgian refugee boarder at Dower House; he searches England for his family and wears Herr Heinrich's slippers in H. G. Wells's *Mr. Britling Sees It Through*.

Captain Vandervoor A Dutch captain captured by the pirates and killed in fear and misunderstanding by Emily Bas-Thornton; Jonsen is blamed and hanged for his murder in Richard Hughes's *A High Wind in Jamaica*.

Captain Van Donck Bigoted South African security official minimally censured by Cornelius Muller for brutalizing Sarah Castle in Pretoria in Graham Greene's *The Human Factor*.

Betty Vane Long-time friend of Lewis Eliot; she secretly marries Gilbert Cooke in C. P. Snow's *Homecomings*.

Harriet Vane A writer of detective novels whose first trial for the murder of Philip Boyes ends with a hung jury; Lord Peter Wimsey falls in love with her and discovers the identity of the real murderer in Dorothy L. Sayers's *Strong Poison*. Taking a solitary sea-side hike, Harriet finds the body of a murdered man in *Have His Carcase*. Returning to Shrewsbury College, Oxford, she becomes one of many targets of vengeance in *Gaudy Night*.

Lieutenant Thomas Penn Vane   Ground officer in the air force after the close of World War I; he assumes that his estranged wife, Mary Hervey Russell, considers him a failure because he is not a pilot; he has a mistress at the air base while poor and lonely Hervey waits for his postponed discharge; he divorces Hervey eighteen months after she moves to London to support herself and their child, and he begins reviewing books as friend and employee of Evelyn Lamb in *Company Parade* and in *The Journal of Mary Hervey Russell*.

Miles Vane-Merrick   The influential tutor of Dan Jarrold at Eton; he owns a castle in Kent and plans a political career; his affair with Evelyn Jarrold, fifteen years his senior, is broken off because of anxiety that the Jarrolds will find out; Miles becomes engaged to Lesley Anquetil but is with Evelyn at the end of her fatal illness in Vita Sackville-West's *Family History*.

Cornelia van Heep   Wealthy American widow courted for professional purposes by Felix Byron Mainwaring in Barbara Pym's *Less Than Angels*.

Mrs. Van Hopper   Overbearing, vulgar woman from whose employment Maxim de Winter rescues his second wife in Daphne Du Maurier's *Rebecca*.

Cornelius Van Humperdinck   A rich American for whom Simone Vonderaa leaves Denis Cathcart in Dorothy L. Sayers's *Clouds of Witness*.

Cornelius van Koppen   American millionaire who knowingly purchases the art fraud, *Locri Faun*, from his friend Count Caloveglia and keeps this knowledge a secret, even from the Count himself in Norman Douglas's *South Wind*.

Mrs. Van Rensberg   The Quests' Dutch neighbor, who is not as concerned about social games and etiquette as Mrs. Quest is; the Quests discontinue their friendship with her because of conflicting Dutch/British interests in Doris Lessing's *Martha Quest*.

Billy Van Rensberg   Marnie Van Rensberg's brother; he is Martha Quest's first true date in Doris Lessing's *Martha Quest*.

Marnie Van Rensberg   Martha Quest's friend whose chief interest is in finding an attractive husband in Doris Lessing's *Martha Quest*.

Pieter Van Ryberg   The assistant Secretary General of the United Nations; he speculates about the Overlords' purpose in Arthur C. Clarke's *Childhood's End*.

Tilli Van Tuyl   Half French, half Polish divorcée with an "exotic ugliness" who lives frugally as an actress in London; in love with Trevor Frobisher, she meets William Crowne, arranges to act a part in his play, and later marries him for his wealth and a country home; regretting her marriage to William, she dallies with Trevor in Margaret Kennedy's *Red Sky at Morning*.

A. C. Varden   A much-bullied day-boy at Sawston who becomes ill and is sent home in E. M. Forster's *The Longest Journey*.

Varguennes   The French lieutenant who, according to Sarah Woodruff's first account, seduced and abandoned her in John Fowles's *The French Lieutenant's Woman*.

Mr. Varity   Elderly, lonely gentleman who dances with the young girls; he is distasteful to Olivia Curtis and difficult to bear in Rosamond Lehmann's *Invitation to the Waltz*.

Duchess of Varna   Popular, attractive, but financially unstable lady of the court of Pisuerga who is forced to support herself by profits from her secretly owned flower shop and by peddling social introductions to middle-class Madame Wetme before she finally flees the country to escape her creditors in Ronald Firbank's *The Flower Beneath the Foot*.

Fred Varney   Honorable sergeant who is a friend of James Latter; he sets the moral example that Jim finds missing in his wife, Nina (Woodville), and Chester Nimmo in Joyce Cary's *Not Honour More*.

VarpolAnganol   JandolAngand's father, who is imprisoned after being deposed by his son; he advises JandolAngand to frame MyrdemInggala for treason as an excuse to divorce her in Brian W. Aldiss's *Helliconia Summer*.

Garibaldi Vasallo   A shifty speculator who is forced to sell half of a bombed-out London house to Jack, who has refurbished it, in Doris Lessing's *The Four-Gated City*.

Anastasya Vasek   A classically beautiful Russian; she "was bespangled and accoutred like a princess in the household of Peter the Great"; she becomes Frederick Tarr's lover in Wyndham Lewis's *Tarr*.

Vashi   The Warrior Queen of Zone Five who is told by the Providers that she must marry Benata, King of

Zone Four, in Doris Lessing's *The Marriages Between Zones Three, Four, and Five.*

Barba Vassili Gatekeeper of the Lord Byron School on Phraxos in John Fowles's *The Magus.*

Christopher Vassiliou Rose's violent, passionate ex-husband; of working-class Greek origin, he married Rose for her wealth but could not prevent her from giving away whatever sums came into her power of disposal; his vengeful legal proceedings to gain custody of their children are unsuccessful, but Rose's exaggerated sense of justice allows him to return to them and her in Margaret Drabble's *The Needle's Eye.*

Konstantin Vassiliou Rose's eldest child; a mature, refined, intelligent, conscientious student, he is Rose's special ally in Margaret Drabble's *The Needle's Eye.*

Marcus Vassiliou The easygoing middle child of Rose Vassiliou in Margaret Drabble's *The Needle's Eye.*

Maria Vassiliou The five-year-old youngest of Rose Vassiliou's three children in Margaret Drabble's *The Needle's Eye.*

Rose Bryanston Vassiliou A divorced mother of three who seeks Simon Camish's advice in preventing her ex-husband from taking her children; a guilt-ridden and independent yet helpless heiress, she is regarded with suspicion because her vows of poverty have resulted in her renunciation of her inheritance; she eventually compromises, retaining some wealth and allowing her husband to return in Margaret Drabble's *The Needle's Eye.*

Barbara Vaughan Half-Jewish, half-Protestant, Roman Catholic convert and spinster school teacher whose desire to see the Holy Places and to be near her archaeologist lover brings her to Israel and Jordan during the Eichmann trial in Muriel Spark's *The Mandlebaum Gate.*

Miles Vaughan Barbara Vaughan's Protestant cousin in Muriel Spark's *The Mandlebaum Gate.*

Ryland Vaughan The late Philip Boyes's sycophantic friend and heir to his copyrights in Dorothy L. Sayers's *Strong Poison.*

June Veeber Plump, spiteful, and flirtatious lover of the self-important George Hutchins, whom she accompanies on his literary-society business, arousing the contempt of Edwin Froulish's lover Betty in John Wain's *Hurry On Down.*

Isobel Veitch Kind, motherly widow who keeps house for David Sempill in John Buchan's *Witch Wood.*

Mrs. Velindre Rachel Darke's petulant, irritable, thin-voiced mother in Mary Webb's *The House in Dormer Forest.*

Catharine Velindre Distant relative of the Darke family; she is a "paying guest" but calls Solomon and Rachel Darke uncle and aunt; Jasper's beloved, she appears demure, but her restless eyes and sneaky look suggest her behavior as a troublemaker, a torturer, and almost a murderer in Mary Webb's *The House in Dormer Forest.*

Velma Princess Popescu's Italian maid, suspected of collaborating with Hugo Chesterton in Nicholas Blake's *A Tangled Web.*

Miss Venables Thirtyish, dark, plump housekeeper with a carefully cultivated voice; she is insubordinate to the new Head Housekeeper, Violet Power, but she later apologizes and is placed in another hotel in Arnold Bennett's *Imperial Palace.*

Agnes Venables Practical, sensible wife of the Rector of Fenchurch St. Paul in Dorothy L. Sayers's *The Nine Tailors: Changes Rung on an Old Theme in Two Short Touches and Two Full Peals.*

Theodore Venables Rector of Fenchurch St. Paul; he persuades Lord Peter Wimsey, his accidental New Year's guest, to substitute for a sick bell ringer; later he requests Lord Peter's assistance in solving the mystery of an unidentified body unearthed in the churchyard in Dorothy L. Sayers's *The Nine Tailors: Changes Rung on an Old Theme in Two Short Touches and Two Full Peals.*

Venerians An intelligent race of beings living in the oceans of Venus who are destroyed during the Fifth Men's attempts to make Venus inhabitable for human life in Olaf Stapledon's *Last and First Men: A Story of the Near and Far Future.*

Arthur Venning Likable if dull Englishman vacationing at the Santa Marina Hotel who becomes engaged to Susan Harrington and tries to avoid her following him around with a sweater after divulging that his brother died of pneumonia in Virginia Woolf's *The Voyage Out.*

Vera One of the primeval women inhabiting the forest where Charles Watkins finds himself after his shipwreck in Doris Lessing's *Briefing for a Descent into Hell.*

Vera A "mature" centerfold model who marries Barry Self in Martin Amis's *Money*.

Dr. Veraswami A kind-hearted medical man in the Burmese town of Kyauktada; he tries to help the native population in spite of their poverty; he is defamed and ruined by U Po Kyin because of his friendship with John Flory in George Orwell's *Burmese Days*.

Dr. William Vere Anthropology professor in Barbara Pym's *Less Than Angels*.

Miss Vereker Elderly former governess; she comes unannounced from retirement in West Kensington to visit her friends at the West Oxfordshire village in Barbara Pym's *A Few Green Leaves*.

Harry Vereker The Cambridge-educated organizer of sports at the Swiss pension; he impresses Miriam Henderson with his playing of a Chopin ballade in Dorothy Richardson's *Oberland*.

Verity A tall, pale pupil at Lesbia Firebrace's school; she comes with the group to visit Clemence Shelley at home in Ivy Compton-Burnett's *Two Worlds and their Ways*.

Adolf Verloc Seedy, bungling foreign agent whose cover is a novelties shop in London; his implementation of the staging of a phony terrorist bombing of the Greenwich observatory backfires when the bomb destroys his retarded brother-in-law; in vengeance, Verloc is murdered by his wife, Winnie, in Joseph Conrad's *The Secret Agent: A Simple Tale*.

Winnie Verloc Wife of the self-important, harried foreign agent Adolf Verloc, whom she married in order to provide a home for her brother, Stevie; she murders her husband after he accidentally causes Stevie's death in a bombing incident; cheated of her savings by the anarchist Ossipon, she kills herself in Joseph Conrad's *The Secret Agent: A Simple Tale*.

Vernon (Vern, Jules) Lonely, lazy, elder half brother to the narrator; he lives in his mother's boarding house and appears during the Napoli racial riots to tell the narrator that his father is on his deathbed; he is entrusted by his stepfather to give the unnamed narrator his savings and uncompleted manuscript in Colin MacInnes's *Absolute Beginners*.

Mrs. Clayton Vernon Stately, wealthy, middle-aged cousin-in-law of Richard Larch; she welcomes Richard to her home after the death of his sister Mary Larch Vernon and impresses her great expectations upon him in Arnold Bennett's *A Man From the North*. She presides over Bursley society in *Anna of the Five Towns*.

Lawrence Vernon Quiet, unaggressive lover of Isabelle Terry and owner of a Virginia plantation; he goes to France to win her from Andre de Verviers; she longs for the avenue of cypresses near his quiet home and assumes him to be like herself; he aims to develop the South economically without introducing the "conscienceless" industrialism of the Yankee North; she finally recognizes violence in his passive coldness in Rebecca West's *The Thinking Reed*.

Mary Larch Vernon Mild, serious older sister of Richard Larch, whom she brought up; in mid-life she marries William Vernon and within a year dies in childbirth in Arnold Bennett's *A Man From the North*.

William Vernon Sedate, middle-aged science master at the Wedgewood Institute and new husband of Richard Larch's sister Mary; his tender manifestations of affection for his wife are touching to Richard, who formulates a plan to go to London in order not to be an intruder in Arnold Bennett's *A Man From the North*.

Lieutenant Verrall A young, cocky gentleman Military Police Officer; he courts Elizabeth Lackersteen and then jilts her in George Orwell's *Burmese Days*.

Bertram Verren Twenty-four-year-old somewhat conceited, struggling, and frustrated artist saddled with his sisters and prevented from pursuing his genius as a pianist; his break comes when he is invited to tour with Charlie Barrett, but he becomes embroiled in an affair with his employer's wife in Frank Swinnerton's *The Young Idea: A Comedy of Environment*.

Gladys Verren Bertram's youngest sister, only eighteen as the novel opens; she keeps house for the family and tries, with little success, to write short stories for publication in Frank Swinnerton's *The Young Idea: A Comedy of Environment*.

Hilda Verren Twenty-two-year-old who plays the part of elder sister almost to a fault as she mothers both her older brother, Bertram, and younger sister, Gladys; working as a clerk at Barclay and Bowley, Hilda is relentlessly pursued by Percy Temperton, who has a share of the business; she is saved from Temperton by Eric Galbraith, a young man who has moved in next door and with whom she falls in love in Frank Swinnerton's *The Young Idea: A Comedy of Environment*.

Vervain Cruel and hated head of Efrafan Council Police; he deserts and disappears during Campion's retreat back to Efrafa in Richard Adams's *Watership Down*.

Andre de Verviers French aristocrat; in spite of his

romantic and sexual appeal, Isabelle Terry eventually recognizes his unacceptable violence, impulsiveness, unreason, and hysteria and rejects him in Rebecca West's *The Thinking Reed*.

Mr. Vesey   Senior clerk in the town-hall education office who is envious of Lewis Eliot in C. P. Snow's *Time of Hope*.

David Vesey   An Oxford friend of Sarah Bennett; he joins Ildiko Bates and Simon Rathbone in throwing a party, at which Sarah Bennett meets Jackie Almond in Margaret Drabble's *A Summer Bird-Cage*.

Dr. Veslovski   A Polish chess-player with whom Michael Shatov plays — often through the night — in Dorothy Richardson's *Deadlock*.

Wesley Vial   A homosexual barrister; he has total contempt for weakness and fair play; he hosts a voodoo party in Colin MacInnes's *City of Spades*.

Vibart   A publisher; he sells out his principles to the Firm in return for success, but he never achieves happiness in Lawrence Durrell's *Tunc* and in *Nunquam*.

Vic   Old business rival of Paul Firman and victim of Firman's shrewd "business" deals; he conspires with Mathew Williamson Tuakana in an attempt to liquidate Firman in Eric Ambler's *Send No More Roses*.

Vic   Vicky Stennett's boyfriend, who works as a guard on the Underground; Vicky says he is a "hopeless case" in Margaret Drabble's *The Middle Ground*.

Vic   One of the circle of Hunt's people whom Kate Fletcher (Armstrong) found interesting when she was aged sixteen in Margaret Drabble's *The Middle Ground*.

Vicar   Cheasing Eyebright's ponderous, opinionated clergyman, who shares Albert Edward Caddles's education with Lady Wondershot in H. G. Wells's *The Food of the Gods, and How It Came to Earth*.

Vicar   Conservative and ineffectual vicar of St. Thomas; he disapproves of Corker's remarks at a slide show but lets Corker continue his talk in John Berger's *Corker's Freedom*.

Teresa (Tracy) di Vicenzo   The beautiful half-English, half-Corsican ex-wife of a count; she is the attractively neurotic and reckless daughter of Marc-Ange Draco; James Bond's initial romance with her is prolonged as a form of therapy, at her father's behest, but — having escaped together from Ernst Stavro Blofeld — they fall in love and marry; Tracy is killed by Blofeld as the honeymoon begins in Ian Fleming's *On Her Majesty's Secret Service*.

Vice-President of the World State   The Chinese rival of the President of the World State in Olaf Stapledon's *Last and First Men: A Story of the Near and Far Future*.

Chloe Vickers   One of the most pursued women at Oxford; she became involved with Giles Peters; years later, she appears at the comedy performance of Mike Morgan, at which Anthony Keating is present in Margaret Drabble's *The Ice Age*.

Pauline Vickers   The librarian girlfriend first of Mike Brady, then of Jonathan Browne; she is the focal point of Jonathan's leaves from National Service and finally marries him in David Lodge's *Ginger, You're Barmy*.

Vicky   The Provincial Lady's attractively bright and independent though gratifyingly unextraordinary daughter, for whom a boarding school is sought in E. M. Delafield's *The Diary of a Provincial Lady*. She is periodically home or travelling with her family during school holidays in *The Provincial Lady Goes Further*.

Adele Victor   Julius's daughter, who is engaged to the Marquis de la Tour de Pin; she is kidnapped and held hostage until the Marquis rescues her in John Buchan's *The Three Hostages*.

Julius Victor   American banker, one of the richest, most powerful men in the world, whose only daughter, Adela, has been kidnapped and held as one of the hostages in John Buchan's *The Three Hostages*.

Victor Emanuel III   King of Italy who indignantly refuses to attend Hadrian VII's first anniversary celebration; he is appeased when Hadrian condescends to walk to the palace to visit him in Frederick William Rolfe's *Hadrian the Seventh*.

Victor Hugo   A Siamese cat belonging to Amy Allington; it becomes instinctively fearful whenever an apparition is nearby; it is killed by the green man, who is chasing Amy, in Kingsley Amis's *The Green Man*.

General Vidal   Proud yet understanding governor of the fortress where Hornblower is held prisoner in C. S. Forester's *Flying Colours*.

Don Cipriano Viedma   Don Ramon Carrasco's general; he marries the Irish woman Kate Leslie, and when Ramon resurrects the old Aztec gods, Cipriano assumes the persona of Huitzilopochtli, a death dealing god, in D. H. Lawrence's *The Plumed Serpent (Quetzalcoatl)*.

Jean-Pierre Vielle Imposing, stern, fiftyish Frenchman; the European Director of the Pax Foundation and the trusted employee of Karlis Zander for twenty years, he supervises all Zander's European operations and is a key factor in the success of the Abra Bay port negotiations in Eric Ambler's *The Care of Time*.

Vigeon Butler at Chevron in Vita Sackville-West's *The Edwardians*.

Dr. Arturo Diaz Vigil Advocate of la vida impersonal; the friend and physician of the Consul (Geoffrey Firmin), Vigil goes out drinking with him the night before the Consul's death in Malcolm Lowry's *Under the Volcano*. He is associated with Juan Fernando Martinez in *Dark as the Grave Wherein My Friend Is Laid*.

Gregory (Grig) Vigil Cousin of Margery Pendyce and Helen Bellew; he works in London for the Society for the Regeneration of Women and wishes Helen to divorce her husband in John Galsworthy's *The Country House*.

Gino Vignoli One of London's theater-going elite; he attends the Mike Morgan performance at which Anthony Keating is present in Margaret Drabble's *The Ice Age*.

Monsieur Vigot World-weary head of the French Sûreté in Saigon; he rightly suspects Thomas Fowler's complicity in Alden Pyle's death but refuses to act on his suspicions in Graham Greene's *The Quiet American*.

Colonel Gregor Viktorov (covernames: Aleksey Aleksandrovich Polyakov, Mr. Jefferson) Soviet Cultural Attaché and Moscow Centre agent exposed by Brod to Irina as Karla's agent to debrief the double agent Gerald; he is unmasked in George Smiley's investigation in John le Carré's *Tinker, Tailor, Soldier, Spy*.

Villanueva Spanish officer who is in command of entire armies in Scotchman's Bay in C. S. Forester's *Lieutenant Hornblower*.

Colonel Jose Gonzalez de Villena y Danvila Young leader of a scattered Spanish light-cavalry unit; very talkative, he bothers Hornblower to the extent that Hornblower leaves him on the Admiral's ship in C. S. Forester's *Ship of the Line*.

M. de Villers Dinner-party participant in Muzillac after the mass execution in C. S. Forester's *Mr. Midshipman Hornblower*.

Bud Villiers An American who, along with Owen Rhys and Kate Leslie, is disgusted by the bullfight that they attend together; Kate leaves, but Villiers and Rhys stay on for the "experience" in D. H. Lawrence's *The Plumed Serpent (Quetzalcoatl)*.

Celia Villiers Wife of Quentin; she is the hostess of a weekend of decadence and is one of the victims of the perverse pranks that occur in Martin Amis's *Dead Babies*.

Quentin Villiers The tall, blond, urbane, despicable, unscrupulous editor of a London University Literary Journal; he hosts a weekend of decadence at his country house which ends in murder in Martin Amis's *Dead Babies*.

Vilthuril Efrafan doe rabbit who becomes the mate of Fiver in Richard Adams's *Watership Down*.

Vincent Twenty-year-old lover of Rose Vibert Dillingham; initially he lives with her at her studio in Paris, but eventually — as her husband, Sir George Dillingham, does not object — he begins to spend more time at the vineyard near Chinon where Rose and Sir George live with their daughter, Jenny; Vincent is present the night Sir George has a fatal coronary in David Garnett's *Aspects of Love*.

Vincent Quiet young signaller of the *Sutherland* in C. S. Forester's *Ship of the Line*.

Captain Vincent Captain of the English sloop *Amelia* blockading Toulon during the French Revolution; he kills Peyrol and delivers his false papers to Admiral Nelson in Joseph Conrad's *The Rover*.

Rachel Vinrace Willoughby Vinrace's impressionable twenty-four-year-old musical daughter, who journeys on her father's ship to South America with her aunt and uncle, Helen and Ridley Ambrose; Rachel travels from the sheltered life of Victorian society into her own inner artistic world as well as into Life with all inherent terrors and pleasure; she dies of typhoid fever after a short engagement to Terence Hewet in Virginia Woolf's *The Voyage Out*.

Willoughby Vinrace Rachel Vinrace's brusque, hearty, probably incestuous father; he is the captain and owner of the *Euphrosyne*, the ship which carries Rachel to South America in Virginia Woolf's *The Voyage Out*.

Viola One of the actresses performing in Hereford in Margaret Drabble's *The Garrick Year*.

Viola The natural daughter of Emmeline Merton and Hereward Egerton; supposedly adopted by Emmeline and her unnamed deceased husband, she is in love with Salomon Egerton, her half brother, in Ivy Compton-Burnett's *A God and His Gifts*.

Viola   Younger sister of Sebastian, master of Chevron; she dislikes her aristocratic inheritance and leaves Chevron for an independent life in London; she becomes engaged to Leonard Anquetil in Vita Sackville-West's *The Edwardians*. She and her husband, Leonard, visit Miles Vane-Merrick in Kent, where they meet Evelyn Jarrold and her son, Dan; Viola takes charge of Evelyn in her last illness in *Family History*.

Giorgio Viola   Old Italian-revolutionary hotel keeper who befriends Nostromo, the lover of his daughter Giselle but fiancé of his daughter Linda; after becoming a lighthouse keeper, he shoots Nostromo mistaking him for Ramirez, Linda's spurned lover, in Joseph Conrad's *Nostromo: A Tale of the Seaboard*.

Giselle Viola   Giorgio Viola's daughter, who loves Nostromo although he is betrothed to her sister, Linda, in Joseph Cornad's *Nostromo: A Tale of the Seaboard*.

Linda Viola   Daughter of Giorgio Viola and fiancée of Nostromo; she discovers that Nostromo loves her sister Giselle in Joseph Conrad's *Nostromo: A Tale of the Seaboard*.

Teresa Viola   Wife of Giorgio in Joseph Conrad's *Nostromo: A Tale of the Seaboard*.

Violet   Young girl who marries Peter Granby and cares for him when he is blind in Alan Sillitoe's *Out of the Whirlpool*.

Mr. Visconti   Short, fat, bald lover of Aunt Augusta Bertram; always trying to establish a fortune, he swindled many people and used much of Augusta's money, but his dealings with cardinals and sheiks kept her entertained, and she genuinely loves him; he winds up in Paraguay involved in smuggling, and Augusta and Henry Pulling join him there in Graham Greene's *Travels with My Aunt*.

Visitor from Rome   A papal emissary sent to investigate the state of the construction project and the state of Dean Jocelin's soul in William Golding's *The Spire*.

Manus Visser   Dutch drug trafficker employed by Dimitrios Makropoulos and arrested in 1931 after Dimitrios betrayed him; it is his body, not Dimitrios's, that Charles Latimer sees in the Istanbul morgue in Eric Ambler's *The Mask of Dimitrios*.

Domino Vitali   Emilio Largo's mistress, a beautiful,

dark girl with a limp; she is persuaded to help James Bond and becomes a brave and resourceful ally, saving Bond's life in Ian Fleming's *Thunderball*.

Vittorio   The nephew of the bottle-factory owner; educated and polite, he is angling for marriage to Mr. Rossi's niece; he is an object of elaborate pursuit by Freda, who imagines him to be romantic and sexy in Beryl Bainbridge's *The Bottle Factory Outing*.

Vivani   A buxom early-day sexpot, a kind of Astarte figure, who tantalizes and seduces the Homo sapiens men in William Golding's *The Inheritors*.

Myra Viveash   Seductive socialite whose frenetic sensuality only masks her sense of loss and despair; Myra and the younger Theodore Gumbril wander aimlessly through a nightmare vision of Central London at the end of Aldous Huxley's *Antic Hay*.

Vladimir   Openly contemptuous embassy official employing Verloc in Joseph Conrad's *The Secret Agent: A Simple Tale*.

General Vladimir (covernames: Gregory, Vladimir Miller, Voldemar)   Ideologically committed Estonian exile, former British Intelligence operative, and freedom fighter with the Baltic Independence Movement and Riga Group; he reaches into the past to blackmail, with Otto Leipzig and Claus Kretzschmar's help, Oleg Kursky into revealing Karla's darkest secret but is betrayed by fellow Estonian Mikhel and murdered by Karla's thugs before he can pass the information through the bureaucracy to his trusted former contact Max (George Smiley) in John le Carré's *Smiley's People*.

Sarah Vodrey   The Prices' aged, loyal housekeeper; she likes to pray out loud in church, but she dies in loneliness and poverty almost as the removers come to claim the few remnants in the bankrupt Price home in Arnold Bennett's *Anna of the Five Towns*.

Hulde Vogel   Very fat, middle-aged, untidy Swiss woman; the wife of Walter Vogel and a former German singer, she is an undercover German agent in Eric Ambler's *Epitaph for a Spy*.

Walter Vogel   Short, very fat, middle-aged Swiss; he is the husband of Hulde Vogel; he is an undercover German agent who searches for and finds Emil Schimler and takes him back to Germany in Eric Ambler's *Epitaph for a Spy*.

A voice   One who talks to the "he" on his back in the dark (addressing him as "you"), relating a series of past events from the other's life, and finally commenting on the other's solitude in Samuel Beckett's *Company*.

Volivia Exotic dancer employed for the New Year fete at the hotel; her performance appears exciting and shameless to many but stirs Gracie Savott's candor about acceptance of the flesh in Arnold Bennett's *Imperial Palace*.

Werner Volkmann Former British Intelligence agent turned unauthorized field man for Bernard Samson; he arranges "Brahms Four's" escape in Len Deighton's *Berlin Game*. He is Erich Stinnes's Western contact and keeper in *Mexico Set*. He is the K.G.B.'s captured bargaining chip in *London Match*.

Zena Volkmann Werner Volkmann's wife and assistant, who gathers information from her lover Frank Harrington in Len Deighton's *Berlin Game*. She assists Erich Stinnes's enrollment in *Mexico Set*. She provides information about Whitehall's mole in *London Match*.

Charlotte (Carina) Volley A successful writer whose elegant country house is the setting for a luncheon attended by Dear Rose and the Provincial Lady; the only man of whom there is any trace about the property is the gardener in E. M. Delafield's *The Provincial Lady Goes Further*.

Mrs. Von Blerke American financial backer of the Garrick Theatre; she drowns in an airplane accident en route to the opening-night performance at the theater in Margaret Drabble's *The Garrick Year*.

Simone Vonderaa Denis Cathcart's expensive French mistress in Dorothy L. Sayers's *Clouds of Witness*.

Dr. Von Heber The most attractive and conventional of the Canadian doctors living at Mrs. Bailey's; he finds Miriam Henderson's behavior with Bernard Mendizabal totally unacceptable in Dorothy Richardson's *Interim*.

Mr. Vosper Jane Vosper's husband, who is banished to the kitchen while his wife entertains in the parlor in T. F. Powys's *Mr. Weston's Good Wine*.

Jane Vosper Mr. Vosper's wife, who, shamed on her wedding night, entertains herself by inciting and viewing the ruin of Folly Down maidens in her parlour in T. F. Powys's *Mr. Weston's Good Wine*.

Mr. Voules Friend of Aunt Larkins; he presides over the wedding of Alfred Polly and Miriam Larkins (Polly), apparently to prevent the uncertain bridegroom from changing his mind at the altar in H. G. Wells's *The History of Mr. Polly*.

Henry Voyce The fourth Oxford chum, insecure and bullied by the others, whose friendships mean everything to him; an apparent homosexual, he directs the Boys Club; to him, as to Harriet Blair, who perversely takes him as her lover, the economic slump is an overworked subject; his love imparts a sense of manhood, and he assumes guilt for the tragedy of Harriet and Theo Follett in C. Day Lewis's *Starting Point*.

John August Vulkan A German concentration-camp guard who died during World War II in Len Deighton's *Funeral in Berlin*. See also Paul Louis Broum.

Dean Vyner The hypocritical clergyman who, along with his wife, tries to see to it that the great stallion St. Mawr is gelded in D. H. Lawrence's *St. Mawr*.

Mrs. Vyner A clergyman's prudish wife; the Vyners try to assure that the great stallion St. Mawr is gelded in D. H. Lawrence's *St. Mawr*.

Mrs. Vyse Cecil's mother, a cultured Londoner who wants to mold Lucy Honeychurch to fit into her own society in E. M. Forster's *A Room with a View*.

Cecil Vyse Bright but pompous young Londoner who is pleased with his engagement to the ornamental and charming Lucy Honeychurch, perceiving her impulsiveness as needing only the check of his propriety in E. M. Forster's *A Room with a View*.

W

Miss Wace (Wacey) Personal secretary to Duchess Lucy at Chevron in Vita Sackville-West's *The Edwardians*.

Gilbert Wadamy Husband of Augustine Penry-Herbert's sister, Mary; an ambitious young Liberal Member of Parliament, he runs his life and marriage according to party principles in Richard Hughes's *The Fox in the Attic*. His party out of power, he spends his time after Mary's accident nursing her and lusting after Joan Dibden in *The Wooden Shepherdess*.

Mary Wadamy Wife of Gilbert, sister of Augustine Penry-Herbert, and mother of Polly in Richard Hughes's *The Fox in the Attic*. After the birth of her second daughter she is permanently paralyzed in a fall from a horse; attentively nursed by her husband, she is astonished to find that she has been impregnated; she gives birth to a son and heir in *The Wooden Shepherdess*.

Polly Wadamy Somewhat lonely only child of Mary and Gilbert Wadamy; she dotes on her uncle, Augustine Penry-Herbert, in Richard Hughes's *The Fox in the Attic*. She becomes the eldest of three children; travelling in Germany in 1934, she develops a crush on Adolf Hitler in *The Wooden Shepherdess*.

Waddington The boyish, charmingly ugly Deputy Commissioner for Mei-tan-fu who becomes a friend to Kitty Fane and helps her recognize her own strengths and weaknesses in W. Somerset Maugham's *The Painted Veil*.

Bill Wade Cabaret star whose career was launched by a musical written by Anthony Keating and backed by Giles Peters in Margaret Drabble's *The Ice Age*.

George Wade The Rugby League chairman who hires and supervises the local team for which Arthur Machin plays in David Storey's *This Sporting Life*.

Daisy (Daphne Wing) Wagge Young dancer, who has an affair with Gustav Fiersen, bears a dead child, and is befriended by his wife, Gyp Winton Fiersen; she begins to see Fiersen again after Gyp leaves him, and she persuades Fiersen to return the baby to Gyp in John Galsworthy's *Beyond*.

Maria Wagge Mother of Daphne Wing; she watches over Daphne during her pregnancy and near death in delivering a dead baby in John Galsworthy's *Beyond*.

Robert Wagge Undertaker who is the father of Daphne Wing; he threatens legal action against Gustav Fiersen for his daughter's pregnancy and relents when Gyp Winton Fiersen pays costs in John Galsworthy's *Beyond*.

Alexander Wainwright The leader of the Freedom League, an organization of humans opposed to the world federation demanded by the Overlords in Arthur C. Clarke's *Childhood's End*.

Anne Wainwright John Wainwright's sister; she is a normal human being in Olaf Stapledon's *Odd John: A Story Between Jest and Earnest*.

John ("Odd John") Wainwright Supernormal boy, first thought to be retarded but then recognized as far above genius level, who rebels against conventional wisdom and morality, discovers other supernormals, and founds a Pacific island colony of supernormals who eventually commit suicide rather than break up the colony in Olaf Stapledon's *Odd John: A Story Between Jest and Earnest*.

"Pax" Wainwright Understanding mother (and, briefly, lover) of John Wainwright in Olaf Stapledon's *Odd John: A Story Between Jest and Earnest*.

Rodney Wainwright Lecturer at the University of North Queensland; he interviews Ronald Frobisher on the radio, is seduced and blackmailed by Sandra Dix, and is saved from delivering his nonexistent paper for Morris Zapp's conference by a rumor about Legionnaire's Disease in David Lodge's *Small World*.

Thomas Wainwright ("Doc") Suburban physician, father of John Wainwright in Olaf Stapledon's *Odd John: A Story Between Jest and Earnest*.

Tom Wainwright John Wainwright's brother, a normal human being, in Olaf Stapledon's *Odd John: A Story Between Jest and Earnest*.

James Wait Black sailor who develops a mysterious illness on the voyage of the British freighter *Narcissus* and provokes both pity and suspicion in the crew; he survives the near sinking of the ship at the Cape of Good Hope but dies in sight of the Flores islands in Joseph Conrad's *The Nigger of the "Narcissus"*.

Waites Fearless impressed sailor aboard the *Sutherland* who develops into a worthy seaman in C. S. Forester's *Ship of the Line*.

Julian Wake A clever, witty, and very well-off man; he proposes to Dinah Stace so that she won't feel ostracized but then proposes to and is accepted by Caroline Lang in Ivy Compton-Burnett's *Brothers and Sisters*.

Launcelot Wake Mountain-climbing conscientious objector whom Richard Hannay meets at Fosse Manor; an unsuccessful rival for Mary Lamington's affection, he serves on the battlefront as a non-combatant carrying vital messages to and from Corps Headquarters, is mortally wounded, and dies affirming an even deeper commitment to peace in John Buchan's *Mr. Standfast*.

Sarah Wake Julian's sister, who is closest to him but agrees to marry Gilbert Lang in Ivy Compton-Burnett's *Brothers and Sisters*.

Wal Member of the regular fire brigade; he is assigned to Richard Roe's auxiliary-fire-service unit in Henry Green's *Caught*.

Sister Walburga Prioress of Crewe and advisor/accomplice of Sister Alexandra in Muriel Spark's *The Abbess of Crewe*.

Waldemar German youth who introduces Christopher Isherwood to the sexual freedoms of Germany and travels with him to Ambrose's island; he later enters England as the boyfriend of Dorothy and finally returns to Germany and marries in Christopher Isherwood's *Down There on a Visit*.

Waldron Officer of the watch at which rat gambling takes place aboard the *Indefatigable* in C. S. Forester's *Mr. Midshipman Hornblower*.

Wales Seaman with vast weapons knowledge aboard the *Indefatigable* in C. S. Forester's *Mr. Midshipman Hornblower*.

Jack Wales Polite, muscular, rich gentleman who loves Susan Brown and does not like Joe Lampton's advances in John Braine's *Room at the Top*.

Beatrice Walker Priscilla (Heaven) Lethbridge's nurse, who marries Robin Lethbridge after Priscilla's death in May Sinclair's *Life and Death of Harriet Frean*.

Flossie Walker Keith Rickman's fiancée, who briefly liberates Rickman, although their planned domestic life threatens to stifle his poetic genius in May Sinclair's *The Divine Fire*.

James Walker A British novelist invited to spend a year as creative-writing fellow at Benedict Arnold University; he returns home to his wife and daughter in Nottingham after only six months in Malcolm Bradbury's *Stepping Westward*.

Varvara Wall A Russian woman who, together with her English husband, runs "digs", lodgings for theatrical types; she wants Dick Herncastle to know that his relationship with Julie Blane is, for him, a mistake in J. B. Priestley's *Lost Empires*.

Nikolai Wallae Ship's fireman aboard the *Oedipus Tyrannus* who demonstrates his acceptance of Dana Hilliot by allowing him to become a fireman in Malcolm Lowry's *Ultramarine*.

Mrs. Wallis Real mother of actress Rae Marcable in Josephine Tey's *The Man in the Queue*.

Eleanor Walpole-Wilson The large, awkward only child of Sir Gavin, who is somewhat embarrassed at her unsuitability as a debutante; she breeds dogs and behaves in London as she does in the country in Anthony Powell's *A Buyer's Market*. She enrolls as a driver in World War II; Nicholas Jenkins finds her in charge after the bomb on the Jeavonses' house in *The Kindly Ones*.

Sir Gavin Walpole-Wilson Retired member of the diplomatic corps who is touchy regarding his inglorious career; he is the affectionate, vexed father of Eleanor; he enjoys the captive audience of young men supplied by the debutante dinner parties given for Eleanor in Anthony Powell's *A Buyer's Market*. He appears in *The Acceptance World*, in *At Lady Molly's*, and in *The Kindly Ones*. His death is mentioned in *The Military Philosophers*.

Walsh Pessimistic and therefore counter-productive surgeon aboard the *Sutherland* in C. S. Forester's *Ship of the Line*.

Adrian Walsh A bespectacled, repressed, authoritarian Catholic; he marries Dorothy Walsh and tries to help Father Austin Brierly by organizing Catholics for an Open Church in David Lodge's *How Far Can You Go?*.

Dorothy Walsh A provincial Catholic who marries Adrian Walsh and becomes more and more independent in David Lodge's *How Far Can You Go?*.

Peter Walsh Clarissa Dalloway's old childhood love during summers at Bourton; Clarissa rejected him angrily for Richard Dalloway; traumatized, Peter fled to India; never having married or written, he now returns ostensibly to report his sordid relationship with Daisy, a young married mother of two; he shares failure with the suicidal Septimus Smith, whose progress intersects his in London; Walsh reluctantly attends Clarissa's party in Virginia Woolf's *Mrs. Dalloway*.

Mrs. Walshingham Art Kipps's would-be mother-in-law, who dotes on her children and expects Kipps to finance them in their endeavors in H. G. Wells's *Kipps: The Story of a Simple Soul.*

Young Walshingham Brother of Art Kipps's fiancée, Helen; he is a budding solicitor, who fancies himself the embodiment of Nietzsche's Non-Moral Overman, and who embezzles and squanders Kipps's fortune once it has been entrusted to his care in H. G. Wells's *Kipps: The Story of a Simple Soul.*

Helen Walshingham Class-conscious young woodworking teacher who becomes engaged to her student Art Kipps and attempts to remold him into her ideal husband by erasing his lower-class background; however, she elopes with writer Sidney Revel after Kipps breaks off their engagement in H. G. Wells's *Kipps: The Story of a Simple Soul.*

Walter Eccentric, Falstaffian British Intelligence bureaucrat; he debriefs Niki Landau, starts Barley Blair's training, and is dismissed from Operation Bluebird so he won't embarrass Clive before the crass but wealthy American agents in John le Carré's *The Russia House.*

Walter British Home Secretary of State who intervenes to prevent Hubert Cherrell's extradition in John Galsworthy's *Maid In Waiting.*

Nathaniel Walterson A truly religious man and Pincher Martin's one real friend; Martin nevertheless tries to kill him at sea because Nathaniel marries Mary Lovell in William Golding's *Pincher Martin.*

Mrs. Walton Ann's hard, respectable, disapproving mother; she belittles Ann by blaming herself for her failure in child-rearing in Beryl Bainbridge's *Sweet William.*

Ann Walton Trusting, affectionate woman who works at the BBC; her dream of finding true love with someone who needs her turns into a nightmare when she falls under William McClusky's spell; she misunderstands him for a long time in Beryl Bainbridge's *Sweet William.*

Wang Axel Heyst's Chinese servant, who flees during Martin Ricardo's assault on his master in Joseph Conrad's *Victory: An Island Tale.*

Mrs. Wannop The middle-aged widowed mother of Valentine Wannop; a free-lance writer whose one novel is "the only good novel published since the eighteenth century", she is admired and given financial support by the elder Mark Tietjens until his death; the younger Mark resumes the financial assistance in Ford Madox Ford's *Some Do Not. . . .* She argues against but refuses to forbid the illegal union of Valentine and Christopher Tietjens in *A Man Could Stand Up —.*

Professor Wannop An admired classicist scholar and a close friend of the elder Mark Tietjens; his death leaves his wife and children penniless in Ford Madox Ford's *Some Do Not. . . .* That the actual writing of his work was done by his wife, whom his adoring women students resented, is revealed in *A Man Could Stand Up —.*

Edward Wannop Valentine's brother, a brilliant, radical youth; a conscientious objector, he works aboard a mine sweeper in the war in Ford Madox Ford's *Some Do Not. . . .*

Valentine Wannop Suffragette, pacifist, and well-educated daughter of Professor Wannop; her family's impoverishment has forced her to work as a housemaid; she falls selflessly in love with Christopher Tietjens in Ford Madox Ford's *Some Do Not. . . .* At the end of the war she decides to live with him in *A Man Could Stand Up —.* She is pregnant with his child and still being hounded by Sylvia Tietjens in *The Last Post.*

Miss Wanostrocht One of a group of former students collectively in love with the late Professor Wannop; she is headmistress of the school where Valentine Wannop teaches physical education during World War I in Ford Madox Ford's *A Man Could Stand Up —.*

Wantage Conservative butler to the Wadamy family who is disturbed by the rapidly changing times and standards in Richard Hughes's *The Fox in the Attic* and in *The Wooden Shepherdess.*

Dr. Wapenshaw Arrogant, solipsistic psychiatrist who treats F. X. Enderby after the breakup of his marriage to Vesta Bainbridge; he persuades Enderby that giving up writing poetry would be therapeutic in Anthony Burgess's *Inside Mr. Enderby.*

Peter Wappit Former member of the Scots Fusiliers, now game-keeper, body-servant, and companion to Dickson McCunn in John Buchan's *The House of the Four Winds.*

Captain Davey Warbeck The husband of Fanny Logan's Aunt Emily; capable, amusing, talkative, worldly, a great gossip, and a profound hypochondriac, Davey mediates between the loving, volatile Radlett family and the outside world in Nancy Mitford's *The Pursuit of Love.* He is an expert on human behavior in *Love in a Cold Climate.*

Emily Warbeck   Fanny Logan's aunt, who becomes her adoptive mother; organized and logical, Emily insists Fanny be educated, unlike her cousins the Radlett children; Emily provides a stable, loving environment in Nancy Mitford's *The Pursuit of Love* and in *Love in a Cold Climate*.

Mr. Warburton   A humorous and scandalous older gentleman, who wants to marry Dorothy Hare and is seen kissing her by Mrs. Semprill the evening before Dorothy disappears in George Orwell's *A Clergyman's Daughter*.

Sir Arthur Warcliff   Widower whose only child, ten-year-old David, has been kidnapped and held as one of the hostages in John Buchan's *The Three Hostages*.

David ("Davie") Warcliffe   Ten-year-old only child and heir of Sir Arthur Warcliffe; kidnapped and disguised as the little servant girl "Gerda" in Madame Bredda's household, he is held as one of the hostages; his soul is saved from the hypnotic power of the evil Dominick Medina by the courage and ingenuity of Mary (Lamington) Hannay in John Buchan's *The Three Hostages*.

Iris Ward   Onetime member of George Passant's group; she invested in Passant's farm scheme and testifies for the prosecution in Passant's trial in C. P. Snow's *Strangers and Brothers*.

Milton J. Ward   American soldier in England during World War I who is the latest lover of Clara Matthews in Angus Wilson's *No Laughing Matter*.

The Warden   Zuleika Dobson's grandfather, Warden for thirty years of Judas College, Oxford, whose dismay on learning from Zuleika that all the young men of Judas College have died for her changes to pride when he understands that the undergraduates of all the other Oxford colleges have perished too in Max Beerbohm's *Zuleika Dobson; or An Oxford Love Story*.

Mr. Wardlaw   Schoolmaster whom David Crawfurd meets journeying to Africa; he aids Crawfurd in suppressing John Laputa's uprising and heads the native college that Crawfurd establishes in John Buchan's *Prester John*.

Ware   The librarian in charge of manuscript collections at Cambridge; he is reluctant to allow Maurice Allington access to Dr. Thomas Underhill's journal in Kingsley Amis's *The Green Man*.

Lawrence Wargrave (alias: Ulick Norman Owen)   A reputed "hanging judge"; using the Owen alias, he purchases Indian Island through Isaac Morris; he is one of the ten mysteriously dead in Agatha Christie's *And Then There Were None*.

Guy Waring   Penelope Waring's well-connected husband, who takes Orlando King under his protection when Orlando first arrives in London as a young man with no connections or experience in Isabel Colegate's *Orlando King*.

Penelope Waring   Guy Waring's wife, who takes Orlando as her lover while he is living with her and her husband in Isabel Colegate's *Orlando King*.

Dain Waris   Son of the Malay chief Doramin; he befriends Jim but is killed by the rapacious pirate Gentleman Brown in Joseph Conrad's *Lord Jim*.

Jacqueline ("Jackie") Armine, Lady Warmestre   Hostess, wife, and mother who selfishly guards her safe and privileged existence and that of her son by fighting the influence Adam Melfort exerts over her husband; she finds her deepest joy in making restitution, in joining with Adam in his last, greatest enterprise in John Buchan's *A Prince of the Captivity*.

Kenneth Armine, Lord Warmestre   Nobleman with the makings of an apostle and the capacity for selfless leadership Adam Melfort is seeking; he is turned from a role as crusader through the influence of his charming wife, Jacqueline, in John Buchan's *A Prince of the Captivity*.

Warming   Graham's cousin, the lawyer and developer of Eadhamite; he wills his fortune to the comatose man's estate, which he also organizes into the trust that later becomes the world-ruling Council in H. G. Wells's *When the Sleeper Wakes: A Story of the Years to Come*.

Hugo, Lord Warminster   Father by his first wife of the ten Tolland children, including Nicholas Jenkins's wife, Lady Isobel; he spends much of his life big-game hunting in remote parts of the world in Anthony Powell's *At Lady Molly's*. His death of blood poisoning in Kashmir is reported in *Casanova's Chinese Restaurant*.

Katherine, Lady Warminster   Lady Molly Jeavons's sister, who is Lord Warminster's second wife and stepmother of his ten children; she writes enthusiastic, unimportant historical biography while mothering "with witch-like detachment" the Tolland children in Anthony Powell's *At Lady Molly's* and in *Casanova's Chinese Restaurant*. She has died in *The Kindly Ones*.

Warmson   Butler of James and Emily Forsyte; he reveals to Soames Forsyte that he has a son in the army in John Galsworthy's *In Chancery*.

Alec Warner   Friend and former lover of Jean Taylor, whose low social status kept him from marrying her; he is a rational sociologist whose pursuit of facts blinds him to supra-natural truths; a fire ends his monumental investigation of aging in Muriel Spark's *Memento Mori*.

Dr. Herbert Warner   Physician and alleged victim of attempted murder by Innocent Smith in G. K. Chesterton's *Manalive*.

Angela Warren   Caroline Crale's half-sister; her practical joke sixteen years earlier proves significant in the solution of the mystery in Agatha Christie's *Five Little Pigs*.

Mabel Warren   Aggressive Lesbian journalist; she impulsively boards her lover Janet Pardoe's train when she recognizes Richard Czinner and, by stalking him, betrays him to Subotican authorities in Graham Greene's *Stamboul Train*.

Sydney Warren   Serious and naïve yet idealistic and intellectual young woman, who interrupts her studies to winter with Tessa Bellamy, an ailing cousin, at a resort in northern Italy and there tries to sort out, under the gaze of her fellow guests, her conflicting ideas about how her life should be lived in Elizabeth Bowen's *The Hotel*.

Haji Wasub   The elderly leader of the native crew of the *Lightning* in Joseph Conrad's *The Rescue: A Romance of the Shallows*.

Dick Watchett   Junior officer of the *Archimedes* who finds life at sea a purifying experience and comes of age by meeting his terrifying responsibilities during the hurricane in Richard Hughes's *In Hazard*.

Waterbuck, Q.C.   Barrister who provides a legal opinion for the case brought by Soames Forsyte against Philip Bosinney in John Galsworthy's *The Man of Property*.

Peter Waterbury   Self-important, patronizing writer commissioned to write an article on Maurice Bendrix's work in Graham Greene's *The End of the Affair*.

Jimmie Waterford   Robinson's kinsman, who is stranded on his island after a plane crash, and who acts as January Marlowe's knight-errant in Muriel Spark's *Robinson*.

Stephen Fenwick Waterhouse   Chairman of the Funded Debt Commission in Ford Madox Ford's *Some Do Not. . . .* That he has forced Christopher Tietjens's

office to falsify the statistics in a politically sensitive governmental matter is revealed in *No More Parades*.

"Little Nell", Lady Watermaster   Sir Makepeace Watermaster's shrivelled, witch-like wife; her stupidity and prejudices help Rick Pym betray her husband and bed her sister-in-law Dorothy in John le Carré's *A Perfect Spy*.

Sir Makepeace Watermaster   Narrow-minded parsimonious minister, Liberal Member of Parliament, and Rick Pym's unwilling brother-in-law; he falls for Rick's scams and gives Rick church funds to marry his sister Dorothy in John le Carré's *A Perfect Spy*.

Water Rat   Good-natured common-sensical creature who hospitably shares his river-bank home with the Mole, is a good friend of the Badger, and participates in rescuing Toad from the consequences of his numerous reckless adventures in Kenneth Grahame's *The Wind in the Willows*.

Georgina, Lady Waters   Gossipy, well-meaning meddler who constantly involves herself in the lives of others, especially her family connections Cecilia Summers and Emmeline Summers in Elizabeth Bowen's *To the North*.

Sir Robert Waters   Kindly second husband of Georgina; he dutifully tries to entertain the oddly assorted guests whom his wife introduces to Farradays, their country cottage, in Elizabeth Bowen's *To the North*.

Mr. Watkin   Defense attorney for the pirates; his persistent questioning of Emily Bas-Thornton elicits the hysterical testimony that condemns his clients to death in Richard Hughes's *A High Wind in Jamaica*.

Lisa Watkin   A married woman who tries to seduce John Lewis at a party; by rejecting her, he shows that he has reformed in Kingsley Amis's *That Uncertain Feeling*.

Miss Watkins   Governess to Viola; she still resides at Chevron in Vita Sackville-West's *The Edwardians*.

Mr. Watkins   Paul Gardner's headmaster at Eton; he often calls upon Orlando King to discipline Paul in Isabel Colegate's *Orlando King*.

Charles Watkins   A man taken to a London mental ward after he is found wandering the streets hallucinating and living in an alternate reality where he believes himself to have been on a sea voyage and to have lived in the ruins of a deserted city; after shock therapy he finally sees himself once again as Professor Charles

Watkins in Doris Lessing's *Briefing for a Descent into Hell.*

Deirdre Watkins Attractive Welsh girl with whom Dan Graveson begins a short and immediately intimate relationship while on his army leave, during which he receives word of his brother's premature death in Alan Burns's *Buster.*

Felicity Watkins Charles Watkins's wife, who knows very little about her husband because of her fear of interfering with his personal life; she has a difficult time seeing her husband as a victim of amnesia in Doris Lessing's *Briefing for a Descent into Hell.* See Felicity.

Lisa Watkins Diana Greensleave's sister, a former nun, with whom both Miles Greensleave and Danby Odell fall in love; she confesses her love for Miles but rejects his advances and at last is happily united with Danby in Iris Murdoch's *Bruno's Dream.*

Harry Matcham, Lord Watlington Forty-eight-year-old peer whose "public services" had earned him his peerage; from pride and on principle, he never makes reservations anywhere; he arrives with his group to attend the New Year fete at the Imperial Palace and is forced to accept the favor of dining at Evelyn Orcham's table in Arnold Bennett's *Imperial Palace.*

Alf Watson Famous pugilist/flautist in E. F. Benson's *Lucia in London.*

Helmholtz Watson Insincere writer of propaganda and pornographic scenarios and confidant to genetic engineer Bernard Marx in Aldous Huxley's *Brave New World.*

Watt Enigmatic protagonist, formerly a servant in Mr. Knott's house, who questions meaning without finding answers; he ends in poverty and isolation, relating his adventures in an insane asylum in Samuel Beckett's *Watt.*

Father Watts-Watt A kindly cleric who provides the youthful and orphaned Sammy Mountjoy with a home in William Golding's *Free Fall.*

Lieutenant-General Sir Charles Wayland-Leigh ("the Buffalo") British commander during World War I; he is venerated by General Curzon in C. S. Forester's *The General.*

Adam Wayne Provost of Notting Hill; he first met President Quin as a child; as an adult he embraces the principles of Quin's "Charter of the Cities" and organizes the Empire of Notting Hill; he leads Notting Hill into battle against the other boroughs and establishes an independent dominion which lasts for twenty years in G. K. Chesterton's *The Napoleon of Notting Hill.*

The Waziri Tribal minister who serves the Emir; he befriends and then bribes Johnson to gain important information but later turns on Johnson when he is no longer useful in Joyce Cary's *Mister Johnson.*

Leo Weatherall A conventional young man who, during a car trip to Bonsall Head, tries futilely to woo Yvette Saywell, who considers him a mere "house-dog" in D. H. Lawrence's *The Virgin and the Gipsy.*

Jane Weatherby Middle-aged widow and mother of Philip; she eventually entices John Pomfret, with whom she had an affair years earlier, to marry her in Henry Green's *Nothing.*

Penelope Weatherby Nervous and sensitive seven-year-old daughter of Jane Weatherby in Henry Green's *Nothing.*

Philip Weatherby Snobbish, overserious son of Jane Weatherby; he becomes engaged to Mary Pomfret until their parents subtly break off the match in Henry Green's *Nothing.*

Weaver The wealthy industrialist who puts up money and is on the committee of the local Rugby League team; he hires Arthur Machin in David Storey's *This Sporting Life.*

Brigadier-General Webb An insubordinate loudmouth dismissed from his duty by General Curzon right in the heat of military action in C. S. Forester's *The General.*

Weber A semi-fascist American who seems inadvertently to shadow Geoffrey Firmin in Malcolm Lowry's *Under the Volcano.*

Elena Weber Rick Pym's aristocratic friend and Magnus Pym's first lover; her name becomes Magnus and Axel's coded signal in John le Carré's *A Perfect Spy.*

Everard Webley Fascist political leader who is in love with Elinor Quarles; he is murdered by Maurice Spandrell in Elinor's home in Aldous Huxley's *Point Counter Point.*

Mr. Webster Benign, elderly baker and member of Louisa Jepp's gang of smugglers in Muriel Spark's *The Comforters.*

Margaret (Meg) Wedderburn A young suburban girl in Dorothy Richardson's *Backwater.*

Mr. Weedin   Personnel manager at Meadows, Meade and Grindley in Muriel Spark's *The Ballad of Peckham Rye.*

Connie Weedin   Typist daughter of the personnel manager at Meadows, Meade & Grindley in Muriel Spark's *The Ballad of Peckham Rye.*

Geraldine (Tuffy) Weedon   Tall, dark, unattractive secretary and confidante of Amy Stringham Foxe; she is unrequitedly in love with Charles Stringham in Anthony Powell's *A Question of Upbringing.* She takes care of Charles during his alcoholic period in *At Lady Molly's* and has custodial care of him in *Casanova's Chinese Restaurant.* His escape from her is recounted in *The Soldier's Art.* She marries General Conyers in *The Kindly Ones* and Sunny Farebrother in *The Military Philosophers.* Her death is mentioned in *Hearing Secret Harmonies.*

Mr. Weekley   Real-estate manager who serves as a role model for Michael Cullen but fires him for engineering a shady house sale in Alan Sillitoe's *A Start in Life.*

Weena   Young Eloi woman who becomes devoted to the Time Traveller after he saves her from drowning; she dies in a forest fire while fleeing with him from the cannibalistic Morlocks in H. G. Wells's *The Time Machine: An Invention.*

Walter Weir   Drunken game beater in Isabel Colegate's *The Shooting Party.*

Lady Pandora Weir-Scott   Barley Blair's wealthy but distracted aunt, who misdirects Ned's search for Barley in John le Carré's *The Russia House.*

Inspector Welch   Official who participates in the investigation of Rebecca de Winter's death in Daphne Du Maurier's *Rebecca.*

Mrs. Welch   Cook at the Tennant estate whose visiting nephew causes much consternation among both servants and masters in Henry Green's *Loving.*

Bertrand Welch   A pretentious pacifist painter and the son of Professor Welch; he is a self-absorbed snob who has an affair with a married woman while simultaneously dating Christine Callaghan; he uses Christine to get closer to her uncle, Julius Gore-Urquhart, for whom he would like to work in Kingsley Amis's *Lucky Jim.*

Michel Welch   An effeminate writer and the son of Professor Welch; he represents cultural affectation to Jim Dixon in Kingsley Amis's *Lucky Jim.*

Professor "Neddy" Welch   The eccentric head of the Department of History at a provincial university; he is forgetful, evasive, stifling, and pompous in Kingsley Amis's *Lucky Jim.*

Flora Weldon   A haggard, overpainted fiftyish widow whose marriage plans are destroyed by the death of Paul Alexis Goldschmidt in Dorothy L. Sayers's *Have His Carcase.*

Henry Weldon (alias Haviland Martin)   Flora Weldon's apparently stupid son; he was disguised as the camper Haviland Martin at the time of Paul Alexis Goldschmidt's murder in Dorothy L. Sayers's *Have His Carcase.*

Fanny Welford   Charming young woman whose beautiful eyes cause men to fall hopelessly in love; she is first Reggie Burnside's friend, but she becomes George Winterbourne's lover in Richard Aldington's *Death of a Hero.*

Wellard   Young volunteer "conspirer"; having no friends or family, he falls victim to the captain's abuse aboard the *Renown*; he becomes the aspiring understudy of Horatio Hornblower; after promotion he perishes in the line of duty aboard the *Rapid* in C. S. Forester's *Lieutenant Hornblower.*

George Cyril Wellbeloved   Pugilistic, broken-nosed, frequently inebriated pigman whose professional services are the object of competition between Lord Emsworth and Sir Gregory Parsloe-Parsloe in P. G. Wodehouse's *Fish Preferred* and in three other novels.

Rhoda Wellcome   Spinster in her mid-fifties who shares her sister Mabel Swan's house, mildly tyrannizing her about domestic affairs in Barbara Pym's *Less Than Angels.* She makes an appearance in *No Fond Return of Love.*

Lady Barbara Wellesley   Stubborn aristocrat who forces passage on Captain Horatio Hornblower's ship *Lydia*; she gallantly nurses the battle-wounded sailors and arouses Hornblower's desire in C. S. Forester's *The Happy Return.* Her good nature and attractiveness, combined with ambition, lead to her marriage to Admiral Leighton in *Ship of the Line.* She is generously kind to Hornblower's child after the death of his mother in *Flying Colours.* Widowed, she has become Lady Barbara Hornblower and is a regal, fashionable, pleasant wife and an affectionate stepmother in *Commodore Hornblower,* in *Lord Hornblower,* and in *Hornblower in the West Indies.*

Wells   Clongowes Woods School bully who shoulders

Stephen Dedalus into a ditch in James Joyce's *A Portrait of the Artist as a Young Man.*

Mr. Wells   Small-job printer in Muriel Spark's *A Far Cry from Kensington.*

Tom Wells   Purveyor of lucky charms and a blackmailer; he is stranded with others after a plane crash physically threatens and psychologically challenges the faith of January Marlowe in Muriel Spark's *Robinson.*

Lord Welterfield   Stuffy, blustery Englishman; he is the member of the Pan-Eurasian Petroleum Board of Directors responsible for hiring strikebreakers in Eric Ambler's *Uncommon Danger.*

Algernon Wyvern Wemyss   A rich, upperclass schoolboy and the nephew of headmaster Percival Vale; a tormenter of the weaker and less affluent, he is called "a worm, a human wart, a squit"; he is murdered in Nicholas Blake's *A Question of Proof.*

Fritz Wendel   Wealthy German-American playboy who worries about being mistaken for a Jew in Christopher Isherwood's *Mr. Norris Changes Trains.* He introduces Christopher Isherwood to Sally Bowles in *Goodbye to Berlin.*

Julius Wendigee   Marconi-esque Dutch scientist, who receives Cavor's lunar radio transmissions that Bedford includes in his final account of his adventures in H. G. Wells's *The First Men in the Moon.*

Lord Wensleydale   Sylvia Roehampton's dance partner at the first court ball of the season; he unwittingly helps Sylvia avoid Sebastian in Vita Sackville-West's *The Edwardians.*

Miss Wentworth   Schoolmistress who once employed Maria Hornblower but dismissed her for giving free lessons to students in C. S. Forester's *Ship of the Line.*

Baby Wentworth   A dark, sly divorcée who preserves a social style popular in the 1920s; credited with the breaking up of several marriages, she has become the companion and presumed mistress of Sir Magnus Donners in Anthony Powell's *A Buyer's Market.* She has parted from Sir Magnus and is blissfully happy with an Italian husband in *The Acceptance World.* Again free and engaged in sexual intrigue, she ages and hardens until her death in *Hearing Secret Harmonies.*

Frieda (Freddie) Wentworth   The eccentric owner and manager of a children's resident actor-training academy specializing in Shakespeare who had worked

with the greats at the Old Vic in Penelope Fitzgerald's *At Freddie's.*

John Reginald Wentworth   Margaret Wentworth's husband, who is beguiled and fleeced by Rick Pym, but who dies believing Rick is a saviour in John le Carré's *A Perfect Spy.*

Margaret (Peggy) Wentworth   Rick Pym's fiery Irish nemesis; at Magnus Pym's contrivance, she prevents Rick's election to Parliament by publicly denouncing him for stealing her family's farm and causing her husband's death in John le Carré's *A Perfect Spy.*

Father Wentzal   The Oblate who spends the summer with the Hare Indians and who succors the terminally ill Sir Edward Leithen in John Buchan's *Sick Heart River.*

Princess of Weser Dreiburg   Boomfood baby who becomes the first Giant woman and Edward Redwood's lover; their outlawed relationship provides the spark for the Giant rebellion in H. G. Wells's *The Food of the Gods, and How It Came to Earth*

Dr. West   Physician called when Tom Harker is accidentally shot in the face in Isabel Colegate's *The Shooting Party.*

Lieutenant Edward West   Professional soldier who is made assistant to General Lowerby after a relatively minor injury disables him from other service; he is a pleasure-loving companion of Arnold Coster after the war and is the lover of Mary Brett for four years, until he infuriates Arnold Coster and Mary Brett by trying to seduce her daughter, Lise; he then quickly marries into a wealthy aristocratic British family in Storm Jameson's *The Black Laurel.*

Gertrude West   A relative of Mr. Bowley, managing partner of Barclay and Bowley; the unhappy and pessimistic Gertrude works with Hilda Verren as a clerk in the firm in Frank Swinnerton's *The Young Idea: A Comedy of Environment.*

Raymond West   Celebrated modernist poet and novelist; his knowledge of the world outside St. Mary Mead assists his aunt, Jane Marple, in Agatha Christie's *The Murder at the Vicarage.* He appears in *Sleeping Murder.*

Catherine (Cat) Westerby   Jerry Westerby's beloved teenage daughter, whose only contacts with her father beyond child-support are occasional rambling phone calls from him in John le Carré's *The Honourable Schoolboy.*

Clive Gerald (Jerry) Westerby Journalist and occasional operative for British Intelligence; his information confirms the betrayal of Operation Testify in John le Carré's *Tinker, Tailor, Soldier, Spy*. He searches out Karla's Chinese double agent Nelson Ko and, following his misguided conception of romanticism, is murdered by Fawn while attempting to rescue his unworthy love, Lizzie Worthington, in *The Honourable Schoolboy*.

"Pet", Lady Westerby Sir Samuel Westerby's alcoholic third wife and Jerry's stepmother; she loves Jerry but emotionally abuses him in John le Carré's *The Honourable Schoolboy*.

Sir Samuel (Sambo) Westerby Jerry Westerby's father; addicted to race horses, he ran his family's estate into bankruptcy before his death; his life is Jerry's worst model for love and family in John le Carré's *The Honourable Schoolboy*.

R. Westerfield A District Superintendent of Police; he is soldierly and has a melancholy sense of humour and is a member of the European Club in George Orwell's *Burmese Days*.

Louisa Lily Denys ("Gipsy") Western William Morel's London girlfriend; realizing that Gipsy is not the intellectual or spiritual match of his mother, he derides her for understanding "nothing but love-making and chatter" in D. H. Lawrence's *Sons and Lovers*.

Hannah Westlock Philip Boyes's maid, who served at his fatal dinner in Dorothy L. Sayers's *Strong Poison*.

Corporal Weston The obscene, conscienceless driver of the commanding officer of Catterick in David Lodge's *Ginger, You're Barmy*.

Mr. Weston Divine wine merchant and author who brings wine, marriage, and faith to the residents of Folly Down in T. F. Powys's *Mr. Weston's Good Wine*.

Mrs. Weston Sir Aylmer Weston's mother, who lives with his family; she is a radical intellectual; Aylmer's death kills her in 1914 after she informs her grandson, Edmund Weston, of his mother's illicit affair with his adopted brother and cousin, Philip Weston, in Isabel Colegate's *Statues in a Garden*.

Sir Aylmer Weston Respected politician and husband of Cynthia; he is unable to cope with the affair his wife has with his adopted son and nephew, Philip Weston, and kills himself in 1914 in Isabel Colegate's *Statues in a Garden*.

Cynthia, Lady Weston Sir Aylmer Weston's devoted, supportive wife, who is seen as a model of decorum in London in 1914; she has a sudden, intense affair with her adopted son, her husband's nephew, Philip; she finds herself in love with Philip and beseeches Aylmer to help her cope with the ordeal; in the years following Aylmer's suicide and Philip's abandonment of her, her behavior becomes increasingly notorious in Isabel Colegate's *Statues in a Garden*.

Edmund Weston Son of Cynthia and Sir Aylmer Weston; he is in love with Alice Benedict and despises his cousin and adopted brother, Philip Weston; he volunteers in the Army and is killed in the war in 1917 in Isabel Colegate's *Statues in a Garden*.

Edward Rolles Weston Physicist and professor who is the embodiment of evil; he designs a spaceship and travels to Malacandra (Mars) and back with Dick Devine; he and Devine return to Malacandra after kidnapping Elwin Ransom; Ransom escapes from Weston and Devine, and in their search for Ransom, they are captured by inhabitants of Malacandra and delivered to Oyarsa of Malacandra; he and Devine are expelled from Malacandra and return to Earth with Ransom in C. S. Lewis's *Out of the Silent Planet*. He travels to Perelandra (Venus) to seduce the Green Lady, the first woman in the new-created world; after a prolonged struggle, he is killed by Ransom in *Perelandra*.

Jane Weston A lame widow requiring, but not greatly restricted by, a Bath chair; the engagement of her maid to Colonel Boucher's manservant results in the engagement of their employers in E. F. Benson's *"Queen Lucia"*. As Mrs. Boucher she is a shrewd observer of Riseholme life in *Lucia in London*. She appears in *Mapp and Lucia* and in *Trouble for Lucia*.

Kitty Weston Younger daughter of Cynthia and Sir Aylmer Weston; she aspires to become an independent woman by pursuing politics and supporting women's suffrage against her father's advice in Isabel Colegate's *Statues in a Garden*.

Philip Weston Cynthia and Sir Aylmer Weston's adopted son and Sir Aylmer's nephew; he has an illicit affair with Cynthia that results in Sir Aylmer's suicide; a successful stockbroker, he marries Ida after the scandal; he dies an early death in 1938 in Isabel Colegate's *Statues in a Garden*.

Violet Weston Elder daughter of Cynthia and Sir Aylmer Weston; her engagement and wedding to Wilfred Moreton parallel Cynthia's affair with Philip Weston in Isabel Colegate's *Statues in a Garden*.

Nancy Westringham The editor of *Lilith* during wartime; she is much like Jane Somers's sister, Georgiana —

competent, dutiful, and superficially agreeable — in Doris Lessing's *The Diaries of Jane Somers*.

Alison Westwater   Charming young lady whose family property includes Castle Gay; spending the summer with her aunt, Harriet Brisbane-Brown, she meets and joins Dougal Crombie and John Galt, "Jaikie", in rescuing Thomas Carlyle Craw and in protecting Prince John from attack by his political enemies in John Buchan's *Castle Gay*. She joins the Archibald Roylances, Dougal, Jaikie, and Dickson McCunn in restoring Prince John to the throne of Evallonia in *The House of the Four Winds*.

Mr. Wetherby   Headmaster at Brookfield who hires the young Mr. Chips as a master at the school and counsels him to take a firm attitude toward discipline in James Hilton's *Good-bye, Mr. Chips*.

Wetheridge   An everlastingly grumbling Bellona Club member; he complains about the out-of-order notice on the library phone in Dorothy L. Sayers's *The Unpleasantness at the Bellona Club*.

Madame Wetme   Ambitious cafe owner who takes advantage of the Duchess of Varna's known financial trouble to bargain for an introduction into the Court circles of Pisuerga in Ronald Firbank's *The Flower Beneath the Foot*.

Harry E. Wexler   Politically ambitious buffoon who, as second in command at the C.I.A., pulls every string possible to censure the British publicly for Magnus Pym's intelligence betrayals in John le Carré's *A Perfect Spy*.

Barbara Wheatley   Desmond Wheatley's wife; she disapproves of Corker's slide show and lecture in John Berger's *Corker's Freedom*.

Desmond Wheatley   Efficient arranger of activities at St. Thomas's Social Club; after finding one particularly offensive, he decides that Corker will never give another slide show and lecture at the club in John Berger's *Corker's Freedom*.

Paul Whetstone   Elizabeth Gruffydd-Williams's party-going friend, who dislikes John Lewis in Kingsley Amis's *That Uncertain Feeling*.

Whiskey Priest   Small, giggling priest, self-described as "cowardly" and "useless to anyone"; he hides in various places in southern Mexico so as not to be imprisoned and killed because of anticlerical laws; he passes through a time of despair, fathers a bastard daughter, and neglects aspects of his Catholicism, but rather than fleeing from the purge he stays in his state,

dodging the police, administering the sacraments and helping people along the way until he is finally caught and executed in Graham Greene's *The Power and the Glory*.

Billy Whispers   Violent thief and drug dealer, who is Johnny Fortune's enemy and Dorothy Macpherson's pimp; he is eventually jailed in Colin MacInnes's *City of Spades*.

Hugh Whitbread   Obsequious bureaucrat who "polishes the King's boots" and assists the Court and Prime Minister in Virginia Woolf's *Mrs. Dalloway*.

Marcia, Duchess of Whitby   Friend of Olga Bracely; initially resistant, she sucumbs to Lucia Lucas's intrepid attempts at intimacy in E. F. Benson's *Lucia in London*.

Captain White   Officer in charge of the initial military inquiry into Giles Colmore's assault on an officer in Roy Fuller's *The Father's Comedy*.

Mr. White   Member of the Alpha and Omega Club in Norman Douglas's *South Wind*.

Professor White   The narrator's neighbor whose family represents the higher, much more privileged administrative circles in the country; he finally leaves with his family for Scotland in Doris Lessing's *Memoirs of a Survivor*.

Sister White   The middle-aged head of the hospital ward where Maudie Fowler spends her last days; she treats patients with respect and dignity in Doris Lessing's *The Diaries of Jane Somers*.

Chalky White   A friendly private in charge of Q.M. stores at Badmore; he rides back to camp from London with Jonathan Browne in David Lodge's *Ginger, You're Barmy*.

Connie White   The wife of the Deputy Commissioner of Mayapore; she tries vainly to elicit from Daphne Manners the details of her assault in the Bibighar Gardens in Paul Scott's *The Jewel in the Crown*.

Felicity White   One of the actresses performing in Hereford in Margaret Drabble's *The Garrick Year*.

Janet White   Professor White's daughter, who goes to one of the few schools for privileged children of administrators and therefore can not easily become friends with Emily Cartright, a child of a different social order, in Doris Lessing's *Memoirs of a Survivor*.

Robin White   Deputy Commissioner of Mayapore,

who conducts the initial investigation into the assault on Daphne Manners in Paul Scott's *The Jewel in the Crown*.

Mr. Whitehead Judith (Gardner) King's psychologist's assistant in Isabel Colegate's *Orlando King*.

Kevin Whitehead A child-abuse victim; physically repulsive with a personality to match, he is the butt of cruel and even dangerous jokes for the amusement of his "friends" in Martin Amis's *Dead Babies*.

Stephanie Whitehouse A forty-year-old woman who pretends to be younger; Henry Marshalson finds her in residence at the London flat of his late brother, whose mistress she claims to have been; she becomes Henry's lover and fiancée, but jilts him when she cannot persuade him to keep the family property; she confesses that she was his brother's charwoman, not his mistress in Iris Murdoch's *Henry and Cato*.

Dr. Whitelaw Local physician who attends Ralph Pledge and who is called in when Sir Roderick Patterson has a stroke in Frank Swinnerton's *Some Achieve Greatness*.

Hermione Whitfield A woman working in Geriatrics who is much like Jane Somers in clothing and personality; she dislikes Jane's interference with Maudie Fowler, Annie Reeves, and other elderly women in Doris Lessing's *The Diaries of Jane Somers*.

Whiting Captain of marines killed during a Spanish prison break in C. S. Forester's *Lieutenant Hornblower*.

Nancy Whitmore Natural daughter of Gerald Grant and half sister of Rose Phillips; she is first confused and angered by Charley Summers's confusing her with Rose but eventually takes Rose's place in Charley's affections and marries him in Henry Green's *Back*.

Walter Whitmore Journalist and radio broadcaster; after a tiff with Leslie Searle in a local pub he is suspected of pushing Searle into the river in Josephine Tey's *To Love and Be Wise*.

George Whitney A pennypinching, childless Irish landholder, a great joker, and a heavy drinker; he is kidnapped and executed by the I.R.A. for having divulged secrets in C. Day Lewis's *Child of Misfortune*.

Joyce Whitney Confidante of her sister, Dorothea Green, and her nephew Arthur Green; enthusiastically content, she does not anticipate any future kingdom in which men would be cured of their arrogance; after her husband George's execution she keeps house for Arthur in C. Day Lewis's *Child of Misfortune*.

Clara Whittaker Deceased spinster great aunt of Mary Whittaker; she made money and left it to her friend and companion, Agatha Dawson, in Dorothy L. Sayers's *Unnatural Death*.

Mary Whittaker The pleasant, self-possessed niece and heir of the wealthy Agatha Dawson; she gives up her job as a nurse to care for her terminally ill great aunt, whose death occurs earlier than expected in Dorothy L. Sayers's *Unnatural Death*.

Dick Whittingdon Nephew and heir to the Follett fortune; he is a wealthy playboy and an artistic failure, who is usurped of the inheritance by his cousin Horace Zagreus in Wyndham Lewis's *The Apes of God*.

Wickenden Head carpenter at Chevron; he reports to Sebastian that his son, Frank, wants to go into the motor trade in London, thus threatening to break the tradition of Wickenden family service to Chevron in Vita Sackville-West's *The Edwardians*.

Frank Wickenden A youth whose preference for the motor trade in London threatens the family tradition of service at Chevron in Vita Sackville-West's *The Edwardians*.

Jane Wickenden Housekeeper at the country estate of Chevron; she made her way up by promotion from maid in Vita Sackville-West's *The Edwardians*.

Martha Wickenden Wife of the head carpenter at the country estate of Chevron; she is the confidante of Chevron's housekeeper, Jane Wickenden, in Vita Sackville-West's *The Edwardians*.

Mrs. Wicket Formerly custodian of the linen room at Brookfield School; she lets a room to the retired Mr. Chips and tends to his meals and arranges the details for his teas with the new boys and new masters in James Hilton's *Good-bye, Mr. Chips*.

Felicity Wickham Bookstore proprietor and employer of Agatha (King) Field; she is a political activist who drags Henry Field to a political demonstration that nearly lands both in jail in Isabel Colegate's *Agatha*.

Leonard Carl (Len) Wicklow British Intelligence agent posing on Ned's orders as Abercrombie & Blair Publishing House's Russian-speaking editor; he guides Barley Blair through most of his rendezvous with Russian contacts in John le Carré's *The Russia House*.

Sylvia Oppenheim Wicks An Openshaw relation who, having already been swindled by her absconding husband, was swindled of her subsequent savings by a woman friend; Anne Cavidge helps her through a family crisis in Iris Murdoch's *Nuns and Soldiers*.

Mr. Wickstead   Lord Burdock's steward whom Griffin beats to death after Wickstead unwittingly corners him at a gravel quarry in H. G. Wells's *The Invisible Man: A Grotesque Romance*.

Melanie Wicky-Frey   Attractive, middle-aged secretary, associate, brilliant analyst, and lover of Paul Firman; she is the voice of reason and is instrumental in saving Firman from exposure in Eric Ambler's *Send No More Roses*.

Mr. Widdrington   One of Rickie Elliott's Cambridge friends; he is Mr. Jackson's cousin in E. M. Forster's *The Longest Journey*.

Father Luke Widgery   Social-climbing Roman Catholic convert from the Church of England; his fashionable sermons pack the pews, and his socialite mentor wishes him to help promote the burial of Priam Farll in Westminster Abbey in Arnold Bennett's *Buried Alive: A Tale of These Days*.

Viola Widgery   Sister of William Widgery; she initiates the investigation into her brother's sudden and mysterious disappearance in Roy Fuller's *The Second Curtain*.

William Widgery   George Garner's former school friend; the discoverer of an indestructible filament that he refuses to offer to a powerful company, he disappears and is later found floating in the Thames in Roy Fuller's *The Second Curtain*.

Mrs. Widmerpool   Kenneth Widmerpool's well-preserved, determined widowed mother, who is altogether devoted to him and to his career in Anthony Powell's *A Question of Upbringing*, in *A Buyer's Market*, in *At Lady Molly's*, and in *The Kindly Ones*. His marriage, which she opposes, results in her exile to Scotland in *The Military Philosophers*. Her death is unmourned by her son in *Temporary Kings*.

Kenneth Widmerpool   Ugly, boorish, irritatingly assiduous schoolmate of Nicholas Jenkins in Anthony Powell's *A Question of Upbringing*. He goes to work for Donners-Brebner and pursues and swears off women in *A Buyer's Market*. He becomes a bill broker and has acquired authority in *The Acceptance World*. He is briefly engaged to Mildred Haycock in *At Lady Molly's*. His political views are significant in *Casanova's Chinese Restaurant* and in *The Kindly Ones*. He achieves power in his military career and contracts a disastrous marriage to Pamela Flitton in *The Military Philosophers*. He becomes a Labour Member of Parliament in *Books Do*

Furnish a Room. A Cabinet Minister, he becomes a life peer; his leftist leanings are subject to an investigation in the House; he becomes a widower in *Temporary Kings*. He becomes Chancellor of a new university but finally drops out of society to become a pitiful member of Murtlock's cult in *Hearing Secret Harmonies*.

Wiggerson   Friendly, warm-hearted servant in the Corrie household who tries to help Miriam Henderson adjust to her role as governess in Dorothy Richardson's *Honeycomb*.

Amy Wilberforce   Wealthy, outspoken dipsomaniac, who comes to be pitied for her alcoholic bouts and periodic imprisonments in Norman Douglas's *South Wind*.

Mr. Wilbraham   Stern overseer of Cadover farms in E. M. Forster's *The Longest Journey*.

Mrs. Wilbraham   A family relation and houseguest on the occasion of (Sir) Henry Thorpe's marriage some fifteen years earlier; her valuable necklace was stolen and never recovered in Dorothy L. Sayers's *The Nine Tailors: Changes Rung on an Old Theme in Two Short Touches and Two Full Peals*.

Amy Sprott Wilcher   Devoted and loving wife of Bill Wilcher; she refuses to accept family charities after Bill's death and decides to go forth on her own in Joyce Cary's *To Be a Pilgrim*.

Ann Wilcher   Tom Wilcher's niece, an emancipated, modern young doctor; she treats Tom during his illness and marries Robert Brown in Joyce Cary's *To Be a Pilgrim*.

Bill Wilcher   Tom and Edward Wilcher's brother; he is a military man who settles down with his wife, Amy, supports Edward's lavish spending until it drives him broke, and later dies of cancer in Joyce Cary's *To Be a Pilgrim*.

Blanche Wilcher   Tom Wilcher's niece who aids in stopping him from marrying Sara Monday by having Sara arrested for stealing in Joyce Cary's *Herself Surprised* and in *To Be a Pilgrim*.

Edward Wilcher   Tom Wilcher's brother, a wild-spending politician whose affairs and debts continually drain the family's money in Joyce Cary's *To Be a Pilgrim*.

Gladys Wilcher   Wife of Jon Wilcher; an emancipated, modern woman, she enjoys money and continually has affairs in Joyce Cary's *To be a Pilgrim*.

Jon Wilcher   Son of Bill and Amy; as a soldier he becomes disillusioned by the Great War; he marries an adulterous woman and is tragically killed by an automobile in Joyce Cary's *To Be a Pilgrim.*

Lucy Wilcher   Tom Wilcher's sister and Robert Brown's mother; a charming, strong-willed woman, she marries the adulterous Puggy Brown and joins his Benjamite congregation in Joyce Cary's *To Be a Pilgrim.*

Tom Wilcher   Aristocratic bachelor and owner of Tolbrook Manor; most of his life is spent handling family affairs; he decides to marry Sara Monday in hopes of living a settled life, but Sara is imprisoned for stealing; after her later rejection of him he returns home to die in Joyce Cary's *Herself Surprised,* in *To Be a Pilgrim* (told in Tom's voice) and in *The Horse's Mouth.*

Wilcox   Flight engineer on the search for Nazi gold who is drowned when the gold is being loaded onto the flying boat in Alan Sillitoe's *The Lost Flying Boat.*

Charles Wilcox   Henry and Ruth's elder son, who despises the Schlegels; his punishment of Helen Schlegel's "seducer" ends with Leonard Bast's death, and Charles is sent to prison in E. M. Forster's *Howards End.*

Dolly Wilcox   Charles Wilcox's foolish, selfish, pretty wife in E. M. Forster's *Howards End.*

Evie Wilcox   Henry Wilcox's doting daughter in E. M. Forster's *Howards End.*

Henry Wilcox   A former school friend of Arthur Rowe; he is the only friend Rowe can recall when he is trying to hide from the police after the seance; Rowe encounters him again after the asylum escape, but he cannot remember him in Graham Greene's *The Ministry of Fear.*

Henry Wilcox   Ruth's prosperous, acquisitive, self-assured husband, who is pleasant but unfaithful; he marries Margaret Schlegel after the death of his first wife and unintentionally contributes to Leonard Bast's failure; the events surrounding the death of Leonard Bast destroy his self-confidence and improve his values in E. M. Forster's *Howards End.*

Paul Wilcox   Henry and Ruth's younger son; he almost immediately rescinds his impulsive — and accepted — proposal to Helen Schlegel in E. M. Forster's *Howards End.*

Robert Norman (Skipper) Wilcox   The art-school principal, who is a kleptomaniac, and who collects his own bodily fluids; generally crazy, he considers himself the personification of the college in David Storey's *A Temporary Life.*

Ruth Wilcox   Wise, spiritually integrated owner of Howards End and wife of Henry Wilcox; her family destroy her handwritten dying request that the property go to her friend Margaret Schlegel in E. M. Forster's *Howards End.*

Primrose Wilderness   Long-suffering wife of Sigbjorn Wilderness; she accompanies him to Mexico in Malcolm Lowry's *Dark as the Grave Wherein My Friend Is Laid.*

Sigbjorn Wilderness   Alcoholic writer who travels to Mexico, scene of his rejected novel *The Valley of the Shadow of Death,* in search of his friend Juan Fernando Martinez, only to find that Juan is dead in Malcolm Lowry's *Dark as the Grave Wherein My Friend Is Laid.*

Ezra Wilderspin   The blacksmith and biggest man among the Fenchurch St. Paul bell ringers; he pulls the smallest bell in Dorothy L. Sayers's *The Nine Tailors: Changes Rung on an Old Theme in Two Short Touches and Two Full Peals.*

Father Bill Wildfire   A priest who is informal advisor to the Dollinger Society, a group of liberal Catholics whose meeting Adam Appleby attends in David Lodge's *The British Museum Is Falling Down.*

Wilf   Mr. Cool's white half brother; he is not allowed to join Flikker's gang because Cool is black; he saves Cool from a beating by rioters in Colin MacInnes's *Absolute Beginners.*

Nancie Wilkie   One of the adolescent girls in the north London school in Dorothy Richardson's *Backwater.*

Frank Wilkins   Neighbor and friend of Diana Delacroix; he shares her fantasies and participates in her rituals of unearthing and burying items in a nearby cave in Elizabeth Bowen's *The Little Girls.*

Corporal Wilkinson   An instructor of RAC clerks at Catterick in David Lodge's *Ginger, You're Barmy.*

Peter Wilkinson   Neurotic, intellectual English homosexual who takes up with Otto Nowak in Christoper Isherwood's *Goodbye to Berlin.*

Mrs. Wilks   Member of the Autobiographical Association in Muriel Spark's *Loitering with Intent.*

Joanna Willems   Hudig's half-caste daughter, whom

Peter Willems marries, despises, and abandons for Aïssa in Joseph Conrad's *An Outcast of the Islands*.

Louis Willems   Son of Joanna and Peter Willems in Joseph Conrad's *An Outcast of the Islands*.

Peter Willems   Scheming Dutch trader who marries Hudig's half-caste daughter, Joanna, despises her, fails as a partner of Kaspar Almayer, takes a mistress, Aïssa, and is murdered by her in a jealous rage in Joseph Conrad's *An Outcast of the Islands*.

Robert Courtland Willett   Valentine Brodie's friend, a huge man, fond of drinking, partying, and fighting; in disaster, he reveals a considerable resourcefulness and capacity for action in Anthony Burgess's *The End of the World News*.

William   Sarah's husband; although physically disabled himself, he is appalled by his youngest child's retardation in Doris Lessing's *The Fifth Child*.

William   A younger son from an aristocratic British family who asks Maureen to marry him in Doris Lessing's *The Summer Before the Dark*.

William   The gardener for the Clare family; he is kind especially to Toby Clare in Ivy Compton-Burnett's *The Present and the Past*.

King William (Willie)   Languid, ambivalent, often witty monarch of Pisuerga who toys with Lady Something's sycophantic manner in Ronald Firbank's *The Flower Beneath the Foot*.

Weedy William   Graham Harper's associate who helps convince him to go to Spain in Isabel Colegate's *Orlando King*.

Williams   Chauffeur employed by Alan Percival's parents to drive him to school in Roy Fuller's *The Perfect Fool*.

Williams   Worker in Bill Pincomb's office who overhears an agreement between Chester Nimmo and his boss; he is accused of lying about the agreement by James Latter, but he later proves he was telling the truth, causing Jim to doubt his wife even more in Joyce Cary's *Not Honour More*.

Sergeant Williams   Large, slow-moving, tenacious assistant to Detective-Inspector Alan Grant in Josephine Tey's *The Man in the Queue*, in *A Shilling for Candles*, in *To Love and Be Wise*, in *The Daughter of Time*, and in *The Singing Sands*.

Beth Williams   Wife and former student of the painter David Williams in John Fowles's *The Ebony Tower*.

Cecilia Williams   Angela Warren's governess at the time of the murder of Amyas Crale; when Poirot interviews her sixteen years later, her belief in Caroline Crale's guilt is unshaken in Agatha Christie's *Five Little Pigs*.

Cliff Williams   Motorcyclist who dies possibly because of Ken Adamson's involvement in the accident that puts Ken in the hospital in John Berger's *The Foot of Clive*.

David Williams   A successful young abstract painter and art historian who visits Henry Breasley at his home in France in order to write a book about him; David nearly has an affair with Breasley's companion, Diana, but backs away, seeing his failure as indicative of his safe, pallid life and work in John Fowles's *The Ebony Tower*.

Evan Williams   Sandra's ambitious, sluggish husband, who has "the political history of England at his fingertips" in Virginia Woolf's *Jacob's Room*.

Henry Williams   An itinerant Welsh mechanic who succeeds in raising himself socially and financially by using the love of a lonely spinster, Miss Dawlish, to his advantage in William Golding's *The Pyramid*.

Horace Williams   Middle-aged lawyer; he is a widower who is self-conscious about balding; he is the employer and later the husband of Elsie Palmer; after ten years of marriage, he is murdered by Elsie's lover in E. M. Delafield's *Messalina of the Suburbs*.

Mary Williams   Wife of Henry Williams; she mysteriously appears in Stilbourne one day with their child in William Golding's *The Pyramid*.

Pandora Williams   Young woman who becomes engaged to Titus Willowes and will one day become the new mistress of Lady Place in Sylvia Townsend Warner's *Lolly Willowes: or, the Loving Huntsman*.

Sandra Wentworth Williams   Wife of Evan; she travels briefly with Jacob Flanders in Greece; they climb the Acropolis together and experience not only epiphany but a brief dalliance, Jacob's last before his death in Virginia Woolf's *Jacob's Room*.

Susy Williams   Daughter of a Eurasian hairdresser and a Welsh sergeant and herself a hairdresser in Pankot; like most Anglo-Indians, who belong neither to English nor Indian society, she exists on the fringe;

she plays the piano at St. John's in Paul Scott's *Staying On*.

Willingford   Manager of the Duncannon, a hotel drawn into the Orcham merger of luxury hotels; he commits suicide because of difficulties with his interfering wife over the merger in Arnold Bennett's *Imperial Palace*.

Mr. Willis   Managing director of Drover Willis, competitor of Meadows, Meade & Grindley; he hires Douglas Dougal (Dougal Douglas) to do research into the morals of his factory workers in Muriel Spark's *The Ballad of Peckham Rye*.

Grace Willison   Middle-aged, wheelchair-bound woman devoted to Toynton Grange and murdered in P. D. James's *The Black Tower*.

Grace Williton   Prim, conventional, suburban mother-in-law to Aylwin Forbes; she is rather outclassed by him as well as distressed by the marital trouble between him and her daughter, Marjorie, in Pym's *No Fond Return of Love*.

Augusta Willoughby   Haughty, prissy daughter of Sophia Willoughby; she dies of smallpox in Sylvia Townsend Warner's *Summer Will Show*.

Carey Willoughby   A coarse, dishonest novelist, who takes advantage of Professor Treece's kindliness during a "Poetry Weekend" in Malcolm Bradbury's *Eating People Is Wrong*.

Damian Willoughby   Effeminate, charming, affectionate son of Sophia Willoughby; he dies of smallpox in Sylvia Townsend Warner's *Summer Will Show*.

Frederick Willoughby   Sophia Willoughby's pleasure-loving, errant, aristocratic husband; he attempts to force Sophia to resume her position as his wife by cutting off her money from her father's estate in Sylvia Townsend Warner's *Summer Will Show*.

Sophia Willoughby   Sensible, strong-willed heiress of the Aspen family estate, Blandamer House, married to Frederick Willoughby; she travels to Paris in 1848 to have children by her husband after the death of their son and daughter from smallpox but falls in love with Minna Lemuel, his mistress, and becomes a courier for communists in Sylvia Townsend Warner's *Summer Will Show*.

Caroline Willowes   Religious, methodical, sensible, dutiful wife of Henry Willowes in Sylvia Townsend Warner's *Lolly Willowes: or, the Loving Huntsman*.

Everard Willowes   Indulgent father of Lolly Willowes in Sylvia Townsend Warner's *Lolly Willowes: or, the Loving Huntsman*.

Frances D'Urfey Willowes   Sickly Victorian mother of Lolly Willowes in Sylvia Townsend Warner's *Lolly Willowes: or, the Loving Huntsman*.

Henry Willowes   Eldest patriarchal brother of Lolly Willowes and a successful London barrister in Sylvia Townsend Warner's *Lolly Willowes: or, the Loving Huntsman*.

James Willowes   Lolly's brother and double; he studies chemistry but becomes head of the family brewery, inheriting the Willowes family home in Sylvia Townsend Warner's *Lolly Willowes: or, the Loving Huntsman*.

Laura (Lolly) Willowes   The once-independent mistress of Lady Place and its environs who has become the spinster Aunt Lolly, a resident of her brother Henry Willowes's house in London; she rebels at forty, moving to the secluded Chiltern village Great Mop and becoming a witch to maintain her independence in Sylvia Townsend Warner's *Lolly Willowes: or, the Loving Huntsman*.

Sibyl Willowes   Fashionable wife of James Willowes and mother of Titus in Sylvia Townsend Warner's *Lolly Willowes: or, the Loving Huntsman*.

Titus Willowes   Beloved nephew of Lolly Willowes and son of James and Sibyl; he threatens Lolly's independence when he comes to stay in Great Mop in Sylvia Townsend Warner's *Lolly Willowes: or, the Loving Huntsman*.

Captain Wilmot   An officer and a gentleman wounded in World War I; he undergoes an inversion of social status, being a mere clerk upon his return to civilian life in William Golding's *The Pyramid*.

Francis Wilmot   A young American from South Carolina whose sister is married to Jon Foysyte; he visits England in September 1924 and returns to America after being rejected by Marjorie Ferrar in John Galsworthy's *The Silver Spoon*.

Aunt Jane Wilshire   Elderly distant cousin of Mr. Britling; she is fatally injured in a German air raid in H. G. Wells's *Mr. Britling Sees It Through*.

Wilson   One of the most famous prize agents in England; he and his partner Truelove are employed by one fourth of the navy fleet in C. S. Forester's *Lieutenant Hornblower*.

Wilson   Undercover agent investigating police activities in an African port; he falls in love with Louise Scobie, spies on Henry Scobie's private and business affairs, is a secret reader and writer of poetry, and declares his love to Louise after Henry's death in Graham Greene's *The Heart of the Matter.*

Mr. Wilson   Sweet-stuff-shop owner who becomes the Provost of Bayswater and is killed by Adam Wayne in the last battle in G. K. Chesterton's *The Napoleon of Notting Hill.*

Mr. Wilson   Evelyn Jarrold's father, a retired solicitor living on an adequate income on two acres of ground in Vita Sackville-West's *Family History.*

Mr. Wilson   Mean-spirited, greedy, lower-class old man; father to Rose Wilson, he gives his permission for Pinkie Brown to marry Rose in return for money in Graham Greene's *Brighton Rock.*

Mrs. Wilson   Wife to Mr. Wilson and mother of Rose Wilson, Pinkie Brown's girlfriend, in Graham Greene's *Brighton Rock.*

Alma (Susan) Wilson   School friend who writes to Miriam Henderson when Miriam moves to London after her mother's suicide in Dorothy Richardson's *The Tunnel.* She welcomes Miriam's visits on weekends and holidays in *Revolving Lights.*

Annie (Robinson) Wilson   A widow with two young children who works as a maid at Shrewsbury College, Oxford; her surname was changed after her husband admitted academic fraud and theft and lost his university position in Dorothy L. Sayers's *Gaudy Night.*

Hypo Wilson (a version of H. G. Wells)   Alma's husband, a rising critic and writer who opens up a fascinating world of new ideas to Miriam Henderson in Dorothy Richardson's *The Tunnel.* Miriam finds herself immensely attracted to the man and yet in disagreement with his scientific approach to everything, including sex, in *Revolving Lights.* After several years of parrying and two unsuccessful attempts at love-making in London, he and Miriam finally consummate their strange affair at the Wilson home in *Dawn's Left Hand.* Delighted to learn that Miriam may be pregnant, he plans a "green solitude" for her, where she can gestate in comfort and where he can easily visit her, all of which makes Miriam feel enormous relief when she learns she is *not* expecting a child in *Clear Horizon.*

Jamie Wilson   Barrister who defends Kitty Pateman in her trial for murder in C. P. Snow's *The Sleep of Reason.*

Matilda Wilson   Tall, handsome, forceful actress, born Betty Updike, who becomes the mistress of Sir Magnus Donners in Anthony Powell's *The Acceptance World.* She and Hugh Moreland have an unconventional marriage in *Casanova's Chinese Restaurant.* They divorce in order for her to marry Sir Magnus in *The Kindly Ones.* She is an energetic hostess who enjoys power in *The Soldier's Art,* in *The Military Philosophers,* and in *Temporary Kings.* After Donners's death she organizes a grand literary prize in his honor in *Hearing Secret Harmonies.*

Rose Wilson   Sixteen-year-old, sentimental, loyal, essentially good, naïve cockney waitress at Snow's Restaurant; because she knows that Spicer posed as Charles Hale, she is seduced by and married to Pinkie Brown; she comes from the same neighborhood (Nelson Place), background, and religious faith (Roman Catholicism) as Pinkie and is the only one who appears to elicit human feelings from him; by failing to commit suicide at Pinkie's instigation, she demonstrates her love for him and the remnants of her religious faith in Graham Greene's *Brighton Rock.*

Schuler Wilson   American director of a mining company in the Dominican Republic who interviews Brown for a job as his catering manager but turns him down in Graham Greene's *The Comedians.*

Willy Wilson   Determined and strongwilled friend of the Nimmos; his hoped-for marriage to Georgina Nimmo is tragically prevented by her death in Joyce Cary's *Except the Lord.*

Anne Wimbush   Flirtatous young niece of Henry Wimbush; she seems resigned to life's disappointments; leading on R. Gombauld and Denis Stone, she ultimately rebuffs them both in Aldous Huxley's *Crome Yellow.*

Henry Wimbush   Aristocratic owner of the Crome estate and a seemingly convivial host; in a moment of honest reflection he reveals to Denis Stone his preference for bloodless scholarship and his distaste of personal human relationships in Aldous Huxley's *Crome Yellow.*

Priscilla Wimbush   Eccentric wife of Henry Wimbush; she is more interested in her astrological observations than in her guests in Aldous Huxley's *Crome Yellow.*

Colonel Dietrich Wimmel   An SS officer in Maurice Conchis's invented story who commits atrocities during the war against the people of Phraxos in John Fowles's *The Magus.*

Lady Mary Wimsey Foolish but spirited sister of Lord Peter and of the Duke of Denver; her family having broken up her romance with George Goyles, she becomes engaged to Denis Cathcart as a matter of convenience in Dorothy L. Sayers's *Clouds of Witness*. She becomes engaged to Chief Detective-Inspector Parker in *Strong Poison*.

Lord Peter Wimsey The elegant, wealthy, humorous, disarmingly sympathetic younger brother of the Duke of Denver; he is intelligent and highly if somewhat eccentrically educated; he solves the disappearance of a financier and identifies a body in a bathtub in Dorothy L. Sayers's *Whose Body?*. He saves his brother from a murder conviction in *Clouds of Witness*. He tracks down a multiple murderer as a result of an intriguing story anonymously told him in a restaurant in *Unnatural Death*. He is present when the death of General Fentiman is discovered in *The Unpleasantness at the Bellona Club*. He investigates and clears Harriet Vane of murder charges and falls in love with her in *Strong Poison*. He solves the mystery of a corpse discovered by Harriet on a rock by the sea in *Have His Carcase*. He identifies a superfluous body in a recent grave and locates a necklace stolen fifteen years earlier in *The Nine Tailors: Changes Rung on an Old Theme in Two Short Touches and Two Full Peals*. He exposes the vengeful perpetrator of a series of malicious anonymous assaults and averts a murder at an Oxford woman's college, and he successfully proposes to Harriet in *Gaudy Night*.

Alfred Wincham Fanny Logan's husband, an intellectual Oxford don in Nancy Mitford's *The Pursuit of Love* and in *Love in a Cold Climate*.

Len Wincobank Anthony Keating's inspirational friend; he is a property developer who is in prison for fraud; he is a man of genius and vision, but he is also ruthless and lacking in human warmth in Margaret Drabble's *The Ice Age*.

Maud Winderly Member of the Weatherby-Pomfret social set whose gossip causes great inconvenience to the other characters in Henry Green's *Nothing*.

Gibbie Winfortune Malevolent follower of Squire Cranmer and attacker of "Nanty" Lammas at the Merry Mouth Inn in John Buchan's *The Free Fishers*.

Anthony Wingate Frances's unregretted ex-husband, the father of her four children, in Margaret Drabble's *The Realms of Gold*.

Frances Ollerenshaw Wingate An ambitious archaeologist, renowned for her discovery of a lost Phoenician city; she is an energetic, sexually avid divorced mother of four; she worries about family members whose depressive bouts are more serious than her own; she regrets having broken off with her devoted — but married — lover, Karel Schmidt, in Margaret Drabble's *The Realms of Gold*.

Sister Winifrede Bumbling assistant of Sister Alexandra in Muriel Spark's *The Abbess of Crewe*.

Dr. Winkler Harry Lime's friend and medical adviser who arrives at the scene of the accident shortly after Lime is supposedly run over by a car in Graham Greene's *The Third Man and the Fallen Idol*.

Dr. Winkles Greedy, manipulative medical practitioner who learns of herakleophorbia while caring for the infant Edward Redwood; he perceives its economic and political possibilities, manipulates the media and the government until he is considered the authority on Boomfood, and reignites the public's fear of it when he unwittingly spills it into the pond behind his summer cottage on Keston Common while secretly attempting to analyze it in H. G. Wells's *The Food of the Gods, and How It Came to Earth*.

Geoffrey Winlow A member of the Pendyce shooting party who gossips to Hussell Barter about George Pendyce's selling his horse in John Galsworthy's *The Country House*.

Winnie Bill's wife and Brenda's sister; she is having an affair with Arthur Seaton in Alan Sillitoe's *Saturday Night and Sunday Morning*.

Winnie Milly's eight-year-old daughter, who accompanies her mother and Tony Last on their staged divorce-evidence intimacy; her presence gives Tony evidence to rescind the divorce proceedings when his wife, Brenda, becomes greedy in Evelyn Waugh's *A Handful of Dust*.

Godfrey Winslow Cambridge fellow and college bursar who opposes the election of Roy Calvert; he eventually becomes friendly to Calvert in C. P. Snow's *The Light and the Dark*. He resigns his office as bursar when he is excluded from negotiations with Sir Horace Timberlake for a college endowment; he actively supports the candidacy of Crawford for election as Master in *The Masters*. He is pleased to vote for reinstatement of Donald Howard's fellowship in opposition to Ronald Nightingale in *The Affair*.

Wint A homosexual henchman of Seraffimo Spang in Ian Fleming's *Diamonds Are Forever*.

Herr Winter Teacher of botany and geography in

the Hanover school in Dorothy Richardson's *Pointed Roofs*.

Joyce Winter   Robert Winter's wife, who died in the delivery of a stillborn baby in P. H. Newby's *A Journey to the Interior*.

Squire Leslie Winter   A benevolent mine owner who is the wealthy godfather of Sir Clifford Chatterley in D. H. Lawrence's *Lady Chatterley's Lover*.

Maggie Winter   Housekeeper at the Wadamy country house and aunt of Rachel in Richard Hughes's *The Fox in the Attic*. Her desire to help her sister, Nellie, is frustrated by the existence of baby Sylvanus and by Nellie's pride in *The Wooden Shepherdess*.

Natalie Winter   A genuine actress of ordinary appearance and shy personality; she is the star of the company gathered at Hereford in Margaret Drabble's *The Garrick Year*.

Robert Winter   Employee of an oil company who is sent to work in Rasuka while recovering from typhoid; he is anguished by the death of his wife, Joyce, but refuses to come to terms with his grief until he takes a trip into the desert where he confronts death and is finally able to love Nellie Leader in P. H. Newby's *A Journey to the Interior*.

Sherman Winter   Old acquaintance of Bernard Sands; a homosexual who looks much younger than his age, he takes Terence Lambert in to live with him in Angus Wilson's *Hemlock and After*.

Mr. Winterbourne   Broad churchman and classical scholar who inspires Oliver Green to enter the ministry in C. Day Lewis's *Child of Misfortune*.

Dear Manna Winterbourne   Dominating grandmother of George Winterbourne; she is responsible for wrecking her son's life in Richard Aldington's *Death of a Hero*.

Dear Pappa Winterbourne   The middle-class grandfather of George Winterbourne; he never did much with his life in Richard Aldington's *Death of a Hero*.

George Winterbourne   An artist and rebel against the Victorian cant and hypocrisy that force his generation into the blood-letting of World War I; something of an innocent, he marries Elizabeth Paston when she thinks herself pregnant, and he believes that her ideas of free love permit his affair with Fanny Welford; he dies in battle willfully to escape a world he cannot accept in Richard Aldington's *Death of a Hero*.

George Augustus Winterbourne   The protagonist's father, an inadequate sentimentalist with a genius for messing up other people's lives; he takes refuge in religion in Richard Aldington's *Death of a Hero*.

Isabel Hartly Winterbourne   George Augustus's domineering and unfaithful wife and the protagonist's despised and pitied mother in Richard Aldington's *Death of a Hero*.

Mrs. Winterby   An organizing woman of the "new society", considered a cultured lady by Edward Charteris in C. Day Lewis's *The Friendly Tree*.

Tom Winters   Anna Wulf's acquaintance, a member of the Communist Party, in Doris Lessing's *The Golden Notebook*.

Harry Winterslow   A Wragby "mental-lifer" who argues that "nothing but the spirit in us is worth having"; he hopes that civilization will evolve so that men can "get rid of our bodies altogether" in D. H. Lawrence's *Lady Chatterley's Lover*.

Lady Emily Winter-Willoughby   The daughter of the Duke and Duchess of Bude and wife to General Curzon; she tolerates the harangues of her mother, endures an often coldly formal marriage, and survives a still-born child with great strength and patience in C. S. Forester's *The General*.

Lord George Winter-Willoughby   Lady Emily's uncle; he is responsible for the dinner party at which his niece and General Curzon first meet in C. S. Forester's *The General*.

Lieutenant Horatio Winter-Willoughby   Lady Emily's cousin whose dismissal from his staff position by General Curzon is the source of the Duchess of Bude's acrimony regarding her son-in-law's callousness in C. S. Forester's *The General*.

Neil Wintney   Artist who paints a portrait of Dinny Cherrell in John Galsworthy's *Maid In Waiting*.

Charles Clare Winton   Retired army major, who fell in love with a married woman, had a natural child, Gyp (Fiersen), by her, raised Gyp openly as his own, and provides her safe haven during her trials of love in John Galsworthy's *Beyond*.

Rosamund Winton   Sister of Major Winton; she befriends her niece, Gyp (Fiersen), and helps to look after her in John Galsworthy's *Beyond*.

Winyatt   Master's mate aboard *Le Reve*; he is

Hornblower's independent command in C. S. Forester's *Mr. Midshipman Hornblower*.

Hunter Wisbech   A British archaeologist whom Frances Wingate encounters on her lecture tour; his casual mention of Karel Schmidt leads to a revelation that impels Frances to contact Karel in Margaret Drabble's *The Realms of Gold*.

Harrison Wisebite   Alcoholic American second husband of Flavia (Stringham) in Anthony Powell's *The Valley of Bones* and in *The Military Philosophers*.

Albert Witham   A tall, thin, chilly-mannered Oxford student, who tries unsuccessfully to woo Alvina Houghton in D. H. Lawrence's *The Lost Girl*.

Arthur Witham   An uneducated but relatively well-to-do married plumber, for whom Alvina Houghton feels a brief sensual attraction in D. H. Lawrence's *The Lost Girl*.

John Wither   Deputy Director of the N.I.C.E. (National Institute for Coordinated Experiments); he directs the operations of the N.I.C.E. in consultation with the Macrobes; his major goals are to capture Jane Studdock and Merlin so that the Macrobes can use Jane's and Merlin's special powers; he is killed by Elwin Ransom's pet bear just before N.I.C.E. headquarters is destroyed in C. S. Lewis's *That Hideous Strength*.

Withers   Elizabeth Mapp's parlormaid in E. F. Benson's *Miss Mapp*, in *Mapp and Lucia*, in *The Worshipful Lucia*, and in *Trouble for Lucia*.

Sir Herbert Witherspoon   Proper, cold, capable British ambassador; he appears inhuman in his perfect-fitting clothes and impeccable manners, although his stories reveal otherwise in W. Somerset Maugham's *Ashenden: or The British Agent*.

Archie Witt   Philip's stolid father, the proprietor of an ironmonger's shop in Saddleford, who takes his only recreation in playing cards with his family and in hiding behind the newspaper in Roy Fuller's *Image of a Society*.

Emily Witt   Philip's well-meaning but clinging mother, who contrives by various forms of emotional pressure to keep her middle-aged son living at home in Roy Fuller's *Image of a Society*.

Lou Witt   Rachel Witt's willful mother; she helps her daughter take the horse St. Mawr to New Mexico in D. H. Lawrence's *St. Mawr*.

Philip Witt   Solicitor with the Saddleford Building Society; he is also a frustrated writer who lives a stupifyingly dull home life with his tedious parents and has a brief affair with Rosie Blackledge in Roy Fuller's *Image of a Society*.

Rachel Witt   A young American woman who, at the height of her disillusionment with life, discovers a great stallion, St. Mawr, takes him to New Mexico, and then removes herself to a remote ranch high in the mountains in D. H. Lawrence's *St. Mawr*.

Whitney Witt   Aged American art collector, particularly of Priam Farll's work; he believes he has been swindled with imitations and launches the lawsuit that proves Farll to be alive in Arnold Bennett's *Buried Alive: A Tale of These Days*.

Wizard (Wiz)   Selfish, argumentative teenage hustler and pimp with a dislike for adults; his white-supremacist attitude horrifies the narrator in Colin MacInnes's *Absolute Beginners*.

Wolf   Yvonne Browning's boyfriend, a professional burglar of businesses and residence; he successfully robs Corker's employment agency, and after Yvonne goes to jail, he takes up with another woman in John Berger's *Corker's Freedom*.

Hester Wolsey   A woman hired as a companion by Miranda Hume; she tells Julius Hume's and Rosebery Hume's romantic secrets when Julius fails to propose to her in Ivy Compton-Burnett's *Mother and Son*.

Lady Wondershot   Cheasing Eyebright aristocrat and Albert Edward Caddles's grudging benefactor, an insufferable snob who regards working-class people as ungrateful serfs; she eventually dies an impoverished gambler in Monaco in H. G. Wells's *The Food of the Gods, and How It Came to Earth*.

Stephen (Podge) Wonham   Rickie Elliott's illegitimate half brother, a cheerful drunkard, who is reared by his aunt Emily Failing in E. M. Forster's *The Longest Journey*.

Wood   Violent-tempered purser of the *Sutherland* in C. S. Forester's *Ship of the Line*.

Mrs. Wood   Timberwork secretary who is first in hire to Leonard Gardner, then becomes Orlando King's secretary in Isabel Colegate's *Orlando King*.

Jimmy Wood   Mark Coldridge's partner in an electronics factory; he writes space-fiction novels and invents instruments designed to kill off part of the human brain; he is unable to see the moral and ethical dilemmas that his inventions raise in Doris Lessing's *The Four-Gated City*.

Ann-Marie ("Ree") Woodcock   Young American girl who develops a deep but sexually confused friendship with Augustine Penry-Herbert in Richard Hughes's *The Wooden Shepherdess*.

Bramber Woodcock   Devoted father who commutes from New York City to weekend with his family, summering in Connecticut; his affection for his youngest daughter, "Ree", is not entirely innocent; he is wiped out financially in the stock-market crash in Richard Hughes's *The Wooden Shepherdess*.

George Woodrow   Quack headmaster of Cavendish Academy, the third-rate school where Art Kipps receives his childhood miseducation in H. G. Wells's *Kipps: The Story of a Simple Soul*.

Sarah Woodruff   A melancholy young governess apparently seduced and deserted by a French lieutenant; she is known as the French lieutenant's whore in Lyme Regis, where she works as a companion to Mrs. Poulteney; she seeks the assistance of Charles Smithson and makes love to him; she disappears, and is finally found at the Rossetti home; she does and does not marry Charles in the alternative endings of John Fowles's *The French Lieutenant's Woman*.

Kester Woodseaves   Weaver and prize wrestler; new in the village, he lives independently; he weaves the wedding dress for Jancis Beguildy which instead becomes her shroud; he faces an angry mob that has tied Prudence Sarn's legs and plans to drown her as a witch; he wrestles the leader, grasps her in his arms as he calls her "Prue Woodseaves", and sweeps her up into the saddle of his horse; they gallop away to happiness in Mary Webb's *Precious Bane*.

Bumper Woodsman   Former boxer who now works as a bouncer at the Moonbeam nightclub in Colin MacInnes's *City of Spades*.

Abel Woodus   Superstitious father of Hazel Woodus; widower, bee-keeper, coffin maker, and harpist, he is a silent man who shares his grief for the death of his wife only with his bees; he tells the bees about each order for new coffins but believes household worries should be told to bees only if the events involve death in Mary Webb's *Gone to Earth*.

Hazel Woodus   Naïve wife of Edward Marston; she talks and sings hypnotically to animals and plants; she loves and nurses hurt wild creatures; she is despised by Edward's mother first as an evil influence and because she has no religion and later because she has

become pregnant through adultery or seduction; she dies trying to save her pet fox from the Squire's death-pack of hounds in Mary Webb's *Gone to Earth*.

Nina Woodville   Loyal wife of, first, Chester Nimmo and then of James Latter; she tries to balance her relationships with both men by being a mediator and comforter; she spiritually loves James but cannot escape her imprisonment by Chester and as a result is compromised by both men and eventually killed by James for her lack of honor in Joyce Cary's *Prisoner of Grace* (told in Nina's voice), in *Except the Lord*, and in *Not Honour More*.

Mr. Wooles   Senior member of a property-development company who tries to influence a Government minister to cooperate in a lucrative hotel deal in Roy Fuller's *The Perfect Fool*.

Dr. Herbert Wooley   Bumbling physician who fails to recognize the extent of Elsie Palmer's naïveté, passivity, and boredom as he initiates a half-comic, highly unromantic sexual encounter with this new household employee in E. M. Delafield's *Messalina of the Suburbs*.

Babs Woolford   Bruce Woolford's sexually promiscuous wife; her lovers include Jimmy Gorton in John le Carré's *The Looking-Glass War*.

Bruce Woolford   Back-biting Department operative; seeking his share of the agency's lost glory, he locates wireless expert Jack Johnson, the hapless agent Fred Leiser, and boxing instructor Sandy Lowe for Operation Mayfly in John le Carré's *The Looking-Glass War*.

Mr. Woolgar   Tilling real-estate agent in E. F. Benson's *Mapp and Lucia* and in *The Worshipful Lucia*.

Woolton   Rear guard of the attack party in the second attack on Scotchman's Bay in C. S. Forester's *Lieutenant Hornblower*.

Agatha Wooster   Bertie Wooster's aunt whose ferocity is reflected upon as a contrast to the jollier lawlessness of her sister, Dahlia Travers, in P. G. Wodehouse's *The Code of the Woosters* and in *Aunts Aren't Gentlemen*. She appears in two other novels.

Bertram Wilberforce (Bertie) Wooster   Oxford-educated gentleman of leisure who frequently borrows apt phrases from the major poets in the belief that he is quoting his manservant, Jeeves; his romantic chivalry and his susceptibility to the threat of culinary deprivation involve him in entanglements from which he is rescued by Jeeves's ingenuity in P. G. Wodehouse's *The Code of the Woosters* and in *Aunts Aren't Gentlemen*. He is narrator of eight other novels.

Zachary Wordsworth Aunt Augusta Bertram's simple, kind, black lover and companion, who loves her and lives with her until she leaves him for Mr. Visconti; heartbroken, Wordsworth searches for Augusta but is killed after trying to visit her once more in Graham Greene's *Travels with My Aunt*.

Worm A fictional larval entity created by the Unnamable when he reaches impasse in telling Mahood's story in Samuel Beckett's *The Unnamable*.

James Wormold (codenames: Luke Penny, Henry Leadbetter; code identification: 59200/5) Weak, fairly honorable, unheroic vacuum-cleaner salesman in Havana; he becomes an agent for British Intelligence (M.I.6), and, having invented the agents Engineer Cifuentes, Raul Dominguez, Vincent Parkman, Professor Luis Sanchez, and nude dancer Teresa, he fabricates reports of their activities to pay for his daughter Milly's expensive tastes in Graham Greene's *Our Man in Havana*.

Milly Wormold James Wormold's lovely but selfish teenage daughter; unable to differentiate parental indulgence and the power of prayer, she spends her father into near bankruptcy, thus causing him to accept British Intelligence's lucrative but misguided offer in Graham Greene's *Our Man in Havana*.

Professor de Worms Friday of the General Council of the Anarchists of Europe who tails Gabriel Syme after a Council meeting and is the first Council member to reveal himself to Syme as a Scotland Yard Detective; he travels to France with Gabriel Syme and Dr. Bull to prevent the assassination of the Czar and the King of France and joins the other Council members in the pursuit of Sunday in G. K. Chesterton's *The Man Who Was Thursday: A Nightmare*.

Wormwood Junior devil who is under the tutelage of his uncle Screwtape, a senior devil, and is attempting to lead his subject on the road to Hell in C. S. Lewis's *The Screwtape Letters*.

Elizabeth (Lizzie) Pelling Worthington Peter Worthington's wife and Tiny Ricardo's lover; she runs drugs with Ricardo, works unofficially for agent Sam Collins, willingly becomes Drake Ko's lover to save Ricardo, and tries to help her rejected suitor Jerry Westerby save Sino-Soviet agent Nelson Ko, but is caught and jailed for narcotics trafficking in John le Carré's *The Honourable Schoolboy*.

Peter Worthington Weak-willed, mission-driven schoolteacher, who marries Lizzie Worthington but is left by her to raise their son in John le Carré's *The Honourable Schoolboy*.

Helen Wotton Ostrog's beautiful niece, who shares an unconsummated attraction with Graham; Helen encourages Graham to use his position to bring about the promised Utopia in H. G. Wells's *When the Sleeper Wakes: A Story of the Years to Come*.

General Woundwort Rabbit dictator who founded the overcrowded totalitarian warren at Efrafa; he makes war upon Hazel's youthful colony; after his presumed death he becomes a terror-tale antagonist for young rabbits, likened to the Black Rabbit of Inlé in Richard Adams's *Watership Down*.

Julia Wray One of the wealthy socialites trapped in a fog-bound London railway station; she loves and hopes to marry Max Adey in Henry Green's *Party Going*.

Rosanna Wrayburn (Cremorna Garden) An age-incapacitated invalid who was a successful music-hall star; her nephews and heirs are Norman Urquhart and the late Philip Boyes in Dorothy L. Sayers's *Strong Poison*.

Cyril Wrench A schoolmaster from Oxford; an aesthete by choice, he is incurably petty-bourgeois; he carries on an affair with Rosa and is suspected of the murders in Nicholas Blake's *A Question of Proof*.

Wrenkin Forty-seven-year-old, grumbling factotum of the estate of Lord Raingo; he is proud of his employer's achievements and, desperately wanting to do something as his master lies dying, activates the electric power for Moze Hall, raising the fading lights to brilliance at the moment of Raingo's death in Arnold Bennett's *Lord Raingo*.

Colonel Wright M.I.5 official who interrogates Henry Scobie about his relationship with Yusef as a result of Tallit's complaint about Scobie in Graham Greene's *The Heart of the Matter*.

Cliff Wright First husband of Yvonne Firmin and father of Geoffrey Wright in Malcolm Lowry's *Under the Volcano*.

Edwina Wright An agent from Blue Bird Television Plays; seeking "clean" books to turn into family movies, he pesters Anna Wulf to sell her novel, *Frontiers of War*, in Doris Lessing's *The Golden Notebook*.

Geoffrey Wright Son of Yvonne Constable Wright (Firmin) and Cliff Wright; he died at the age of six months in Malcolm Lowry's *Under the Volcano*.

Jane Wright Aspiring writer and an overweight, unattractive resident of the May of Teck Club in the period just after Germany's surrender in 1945; she introduces Nicholas Farringdon to the women's residence and witnesses his infatuation with Selina Redwood; she is among the girls whose larger dimensions delay their escape from the fire that destroys the building; years later, now a successful gossip columnist, she reports Farringdon's martyrdom to the middle-aged women who had known him at the club in Muriel Spark's *The Girls of Slender Means.*

Shiner Wright   One of the few experienced firemen in Richard Roe's unit of the auxiliary fire service; he is killed during the first attack on London in Henry Green's *Caught.*

Mrs. Wrigley   Ron Wrigley's mother, who gets drunk at the opening celebration of Vardon Hall, likes Gilbert and Sullivan, and advises Celia Craddock not to have more children in Angus Wilson's *Hemlock and After.*

Bert Wrigley   Dishonest, shifty little man who fathers numerous children; he overlooks his Gypsy wife's "mercenary siren trade" in Richard Aldington's *The Colonel's Daughter.*

Bess Wrigley   Gypsy wife of Bert Wrigley; she trades her physical charms for various favors; her principal victim is Farmer Reeves in Richard Aldington's *The Colonel's Daughter.*

Ron Wrigley   A young homosexual prostitute who works for Vera Curry, supplies Bernard Sands with information about the plan to help Hubert Rose seduce a girl, and finds sexual happiness in prison after his conviction of crimes with Mrs. Curry in Angus Wilson's *Hemlock and After.*

Valentine (Val) Wrigley   Minor British poet in residence at an American college, and later archbishop of a cult religion in California; in his teens he was the lover of Kenneth Toomey in Anthony Burgess's *Earthly Powers.*

Sir Wigmore Wrinching   Prosecutor in the Duke of Denver's murder trial in Dorothy L. Sayers's *Clouds of Witness.*

Wriste   Undercover spy working as a steward on the cruise ship taking Denis Hillier to a Russian destination; in port he reveals himself as another secret agent with an upper-class accent whose mission is to kill Hillier and Edmund Roper in Anthony Burgess's *Tremor of Intent.*

Anna (Freeman) Wulf   A novelist attempting to overcome a writer's block while at the same time keeping a series of notebooks that record her experiences as a woman, an artist, a member of the British Communist Party, and an objective participant in the world around her in Doris Lessing's *The Golden Notebook.*

Janet Wulf   Anna Wulf's daughter, a conventional but intelligent child, who desires to escape her mother's ideas and life style by going to boarding school in Doris Lessing's *The Golden Notebook.*

Steven Wulf   Anna Wulf's ex-husband; she travelled with him to the African colony Mashopi to live as a tobacco farmer's wife but divorced him after the birth of their daughter, Janet, in Doris Lessing's *The Golden Notebook.*

Baron Wunderhausen   Very cunning and adaptable and multilingual man; he is involved with the Ministry of Foreign Affairs and married to Sonia Bursanov in William Gerhardie's *Futility: A Novel on Russian Themes.*

Miss Wyatt   Middle-aged, small, determined, competent nurse to Julia Martin's and Nora Griffiths's mother in Jean Rhys's *After Leaving Mr. Mackenzie.*

Lord Wychwood   Swedish strategic official with whom Hornblower sails to Russia in C. S. Forester's *Commodore Hornblower.*

Rosalind Wykes   Successful businesswoman who pursues Roy Calvert; she becomes engaged to Ralph Udal when Calvert declines to marry her but drops Udal and marries Calvert when he changes his mind; she bears a daughter, Muriel, to Calvert before he dies in World War II in C. P. Snow's *The Light and the Dark.* Having become the wife of Azik Schiff, she scrutinizes the clothing of Jenny Rastall at a party given by Swaffield in *In Their Wisdom.*

Tertius Wyland   Diplomat and politician; he is a friend of Rutherford, Woodford Green, and Sanders in James Hilton's *Lost Horizon.*

Beatrice Wyld   A spunky, flirtatious young woman; she is Paul Morel's friend and marries his brother Arthur, by whom she is pregnant in D. H. Lawrence's *Sons and Lovers.*

Wylie   A former fellow pupil of Murphy, also in love with Miss Counihan in Samuel Beckett's *Murphy.*

Tom Wyndham   Parliamentary Private Secretary who serves Roger Quaife and proves to be a very able ally to Quaife during his political battle to shape a new policy on nuclear weapons in C. P. Snow's *Corridors of Power.*

Sir Tremlett Wynes   Surgeon; he is called by Royal Family physician Sir Arthur Tappitt to insert drainage tubes into Lord Raingo's chest in the last attempts to save his life in Arnold Bennett's *Lord Raingo.*

Algernon Wyse   Wealthy and overcourteous gentleman whose returns home from the Continent agitate Tilling; he becomes engaged to Susan Poppitt in E. F. Benson's *Miss Mapp.* He is one of Lucia Lucas's social conquests in *Mapp and Lucia,* in *The Worshipful Lucia,* and in *Trouble for Lucia.*

Sir Turnour Wyse   Baronet of Wood Rising Hall; he becomes involved in the Free Fishers' successful efforts to thwart the depraved conspiracy of Squire Cranmer and bring to justice his gang; in saving the life of Prime Minister Spencer Perceval, he earns the gratitude of both Perceval and his Majesty's Government in John Buchan's *The Free Fishers.*

Colonel Meredith Wyvern   Neighbor and long-time friend of the parsimonious Lester Carmody, whom he is suing in retaliation for an act of cowardice that endangered his life; the quarrel is ended through the ingenuity and generous intercession of John Carroll, who loves Wyvern's daughter, in P. G. Wodehouse's *Money for Nothing.*

Patricia Wyvern   Daughter of Colonel Wyvern; she has long loved John Carroll but doubts his romantic commitment in P. G. Wodehouse's *Money for Nothing.*

X

Dr. X The psychiatrist whom Charles Watkins insists he cannot see; he believes drugs and shock therapy to be the only means of curing the patient in Doris Lessing's *Briefing for a Descent into Hell.*

Y

Dr. Y The psychiatrist to whom Charles Watkins seems to respond much better than to Dr. X; he is humane in his therapy and is opposed to giving the patient large amounts of drugs in Doris Lessing's *Briefing for a Descent into Hell.*

Frank Yamatoku Intelligent Japanese accountant and businessman; Mathew Williamson Tuakana's right-hand man, he works with Williamson to entrap Paul Firman in Eric Ambler's *Send No More Roses.*

Yang Chung Chinese boy killed by a shark; he is one of the supernormals of John Wainwright's Pacific island colony in Olaf Stapledon's *Odd John: A Story Between Jest and Earnest.*

Big James Yarlett Huge, dignified, benign compositor, who has been at the Clayhanger printshop for twenty years; he vows never again to raise his magnificent voice in song when Darius Clayhanger dies in Arnold Bennett's *Clayhanger.* He becomes General Manager of Edwin Clayhanger's Printshop; his negligent treatment by Hilda Lessways Clayhanger forms for Edwin another of his many grievances against his wife in *These Twain.*

Peter Yates One of the actors performing in Hereford in Margaret Drabble's *The Garrick Year.*

Marion Yaverland Middle-aged country woman; in her youth she gave birth in quick succession to Richard Yaverland, in consequence of a brief affair with the rich and powerful squire Sir Harry, and to Roger Yaverland, in consequence of her rape by Peacey, business manager for the squire; in her last years, she regrets that her preference for Richard and her fear of his being claimed as a son by Peacey persuaded her to give custody of Roger to the abusive Peacey; she drowns herself in order to free Richard of his obsessive, protective love for her in Rebecca West's *The Judge.*

Richard Yaverland Older son of Marion Yaverland; he is a successful businessman recently returned to Edinburgh from Rio de Janeiro; engaged to Ellen Melville, he is sexually and emotionally inhibited by his excessive concern for his mother, his hatred for the people who mistreated her from her youth, and his resentment of his half brother, Roger, with whom he has had to share his mother; he finally becomes his brother's murderer in an irrational attempt to avenge Marion's rape by killing the product of the rape in Rebecca West's *The Judge.*

Roger Yaverland Marion Yaverland's younger son, conceived as the result of rape; he suffers in infancy from his brother Richard's resentment and from his mother's struggle to love him; in childhood and adolescence he suffers abuse in the custody of the rapist, Peacey, to whom Marion has reluctantly transferred him because of her fear of losing her older son; his pitifully limited human potential is committed to Richard, who ironically becomes his murderer in Rebecca West's *The Judge.*

YeferalOboral MyrdemInggala's brother, who is killed by Io Pasharatid; after his death he is accused of treason to bolster the charges against MyrdemInggala in Brian W. Aldiss's *Helliconia Summer.*

Katrine Yester Beautiful young girl who loves and is loved by David Sempill; an ethereal, romantic presence, she loves the Wood and transforms it by day into "Paradise"; she sacrifices her life during the plague by helping Sempill nurse the villagers in John Buchan's *Witch Wood.*

Yhamm-Whrrmar A phagor who wounds Aoz Roon and later saves him in Brian W. Aldiss's *Helliconia Spring.*

Yori A man living near the frontier of Zones Three and Four who confirms for Al-Ith that there have been drastic declines in the birth rates of the animals and people of Zone Three in Doris Lessing's *The Marriages Between Zones Three, Four, and Five.*

Martin York Co-owner of a failing publishing company and an employer of Nancy Hawkins in Muriel Spark's *A Far Cry from Kensington.*

Youdi The voice of authority who has, perhaps, insisted that Moran write his "report" in Samuel Beckett's *Molloy.*

Krikor Youkoumian A shifty Azanian businessman who becomes part of the Emperor Seth's new government; he makes frequent use of his office in shady commercial ventures; he survives the various Azanian political changes and continues to prosper as a café owner in Evelyn Waugh's *Black Mischief.*

Dr. Young   An Islington hospital physician who flirts casually with Alvina Houghton while she studies there to become a nurse in D. H. Lawrence's *The Lost Girl.*

Bob Young   Son of Dora and Stanley Young; he is working at a garage, training to become a mechanic, in Margaret Drabble's *The Middle Ground.*

Dora Young   Wife of Stanley Young and mother of Bob and Patsy Young; she is interviewed in the television film Kate Fletcher Armstrong is making; she went to work full time after her children grew older in Margaret Drabble's *The Middle Ground.*

Maisie Young   Pretentiously intellectual member of the Autobiographical Association in Muriel Spark's *Loitering with Intent.*

Patsy Young   Daughter of Dora and Stanley Young; she works in a mental hospital in Margaret Drabble's *The Middle Ground.*

Stanley Young   Husband of Dora Young and father of their children, Patsy and Bob Young; he moves from job to job in Margaret Drabble's *The Middle Ground.*

Telman Young   Sylvester's friend, a Dublin artist, who pays Onny Soraghan to pose for him and becomes sexually involved with her in Mary Lavin's *The House in Clewe Street.*

Prince Yousef (His Weariness)   Young, handsome, and bored heir to the throne of Pisuerga whose marriage to Princess Elsie of England and forsaking of Laura de Nazianzi casts Laura into a profound grief in Ronald Firbank's *The Flower Beneath the Foot.*

Thomas Yownie   The Chief of Staff of the Gorbals Die-Hards; his boast, "Ye'll no' fickle Thomas Yownie", is proved when he throws the bomb that saves Sakskia, the Russian princess, in John Buchan's *Huntingtower.*

Hrr-Brahl Yprt   The leader of the phagor forces which march on Oldorando; he is also Hrr-Tryhk Hrast's grandson in Brian W. Aldiss's *Helliconia Spring.*

Telfourd Yule   Acquaintance of Jack Muskham; he warns Sir Lawrence Mont and Dinny Cherrell of Muskham's anger after Wilfred Desert's insult in John Galsworthy's *Flowering Wilderness.*

Yuli   A barbarian youth from the north of Helliconia; he becomes a priest of Akha and founder of Oldorando in Brian W. Aldiss's *Helliconia Spring.*

Yuli [the runt]   A phagor who is JandolAngand's personal servant in Brian W. Aldiss's *Helliconia Summer.*

Little Yuli   Laintal Ay's grandather and Yuli's great-grandson; he is king of Oldorando in Brian W. Aldiss's *Helliconia Spring.*

Karl Yundt   Toothless old terrorist with whom Adolf Verloc conspires in Joseph Conrad's *The Secret Agent: A Simple Tale.*

Yusef   Syrian merchant engaged in legitimate and illegal trade in West Africa; he ensnares Henry Scobie by lending him money to send Louise Scobie to South Africa, treats Scobie with suffocating friendliness, and is the cause of considerable suspicion cast on Scobie as well as, probably, the murder of Scobie's servant Ali in Graham Greene's *The Heart of the Matter.*

Yvonne   Janos Lavin's girlfriend when he lived in Eastern Europe; she believed Lavin impossible to love because he was "a political machine" in John Berger's *A Painter of Our Time.*

Countess Yvorra   Affected lady aristocrat with a "masculine form" and "would-be indulgent face" who heads a religious social clique of "some six, or so, ex-Circes" at the Court of Pisuerga, keeps a "menagerie" of various pets in her bedroom, and sympathizes with Laura de Nazianzi during her "difficult time of spiritual distress" in Ronald Firbank's *The Flower Beneath the Foot.*

Z

Dr. Z A therapist who knew Charles Watkins during his stammering crisis and who gives the patient's history to Dr. Y in Doris Lessing's *Briefing for a Descent into Hell.*

Horace Zagreus A disciple of Pierpoint, mentor of Dan Boleyn, and inheritor of the Follett fortune; he calls himself "Pierpoint's Plato" and conducts Dan on a tour of the London art world in Wyndham Lewis's *The Apes of God.*

Andreas Prokovitch Zaleshoff Broad-shouldered, early-middle-aged, and emotional but likeable American-born Russian spy; he rescues Desmond Kenton from Stefan Saridza's men and enlists his aid in recovering the stolen B2 plans in Eric Ambler's *Uncommon Danger.* Posing as an American businessman of Soviet parentage, he appeals to Nick Marlow's sense of right and wrong and persuades him to spy for him and his sister, thereby thwarting the evil General Vagas's plans for German war supremacy in *Cause for Alarm.*

Tamara Prokovna Zaleshoff Beautiful, sprightly, intelligent young woman; the sister of Andreas Zaleshoff, she and her brother work in tandem as idealistic Soviet agents; she rescues Desmond Kenton and her brother from an oil storage drum in Eric Ambler's *Uncommon Danger.* She appears in *Cause for Alarm.*

Enrique Zancas Former mayor of El Toboso and friend of Father Quixote; he travels with Father Quixote, ostensibly to Madrid to purchase purple socks on the occasion of the father's elevation to monsignor; though Zancas is a Communist, he had formerly been a student of religion at Salamanca; during their travels, he finds that he and the father have much in common in Graham Greene's *Monsignor Quixote.*

Karlis Zander (Dr. Luccio) Clever Northern European physican and an intelligent, well-preserved, middle-aged man; a powerful behind-the-scenes international contract-management consultant, he uses Robert Halliday as a front for the Abra Bay port negotiations in return for guaranteed anonymity and American citizenship in Eric Ambler's *The Care of Time.*

Darcy Zapp Nine-year-old son of Desiree and Morris Zapp and twin brother of Elizabeth Zapp in David Lodge's *Changing Places: A Tale of Two Campuses.*

Desiree Zapp The forceful, independent, estranged wife of Morris Zapp; she has an affair with his British exchange-scholar counterpart, Philip Swallow, in David Lodge's *Changing Places: A Tale of Two Campuses.* Divorced from Morris, she is a best-selling feminist author; she has an affair with novelist Ronald Frobisher and dickers with the terrorists who hold Morris for ransom in *Small World.*

Elizabeth Zapp Nine-year-old daughter of Desiree and Morris Zapp and twin sister of Darcy Zapp in David Lodge's *Changing Places: A Tale of Two Campuses.*

Morris Zapp The egotistical, brash Jewish American scholar of Jane Austen from Euphoric State University; he participates in an exchange with the University of Rummidge in England, has an affair with Hilary Swallow, the wife of counterpart Philip Swallow, helps to deal with student unrest at Rummidge, and undergoes a little softening through helping Hilary and Mary Makepeace; he wants to get his wife, Desiree, back in David Lodge's *Changing Places: A Tale of Two Campuses.* Newly incarnated as a deconstructionist, he befriends Persse McGarrigle, quests after the UNESCO chair of literary criticism, and is kidnapped by terrorists in Zurich; he loses some of his ambition after the experience and is philosophical over his failure to get the chair in *Small World.*

Zelda The sister of Miriam's husband, Daniel, in Margaret Drabble's *The Ice Age.*

Marya (Mado) Zelli A solitary, dispossessed, demeaned, reckless, lazy, twenty-eight-year-old ex-chorus girl from London who is married to Stephan Zelli; she lives in Montmartre in straitened circumstances with the Heidlers in a ménage à trois and is abused and ultimately deserted by Stephan in Jean Rhys's *Postures.*

Stephan Zelli Thin and secretive liar and thief in his late thirties; married to Marya, he abuses her and deserts her; he is a weak, aimless man in Jean Rhys's *Postures.*

Zena A runaway from Birmingham who marries Paul Coldridge; she dies because she has remained in a contaminated area after the Catastrophe in Doris Lessing's *The Four-Gated City.*

Zerbuchen A champion skier whose performance in the Sports Fest strikes Miriam Henderson as ravishingly beautiful in Dorothy Richardson's *Oberland.*

"Commercial Boris" Zimin (covernames: Kursky, Smirnov) Moscow Centre agent who sets up "gold seam" for double agent Nelson Ko in John le Carré's *The Honourable Schoolboy.*

Zina Pretty peasant girl of Sonia Bursanov's age; she is Nikolai Bursanov's mistress in William Gerhardie's *Futility: A Novel on Russian Themes*.

Mr. Zlentli A major African leader who refuses any help from white sympathizers in Doris Lessing's *Landlocked*.

Nell Zoyland The lover of Sam Dekker and the mother of his child, though she is maried to Will Zoyland; Sam's renunciation of her sends her reluctantly back to Will in John Cowper Powys's *A Glastonbury Romance*.

Will Zoyland Illegitimate son of the Marquis of P.; he is husband of Nell Zoyland and assistant to Philip Crow at Wookey Hole cave; his roguish conduct at his wife's child's christening drives her back to Sam Dekker in John Cowper Powys's *A Glastonbury Romance*.

Mr. Zuss-Amour Intelligent but crooked lawyer who prepares Johnny Fortune's court case; he doesn't believe Johnny will win and offers to bribe the policeman involved in Colin MacInnes's *City of Spades*.

Zuzugoitea (Chief of the Municipality) Along with the Chief of the Gardens (Fructuoso Sanabria) and the Chief of Rostrums, one of the three militiamen who persecute Geoffrey Firmin at the Farolito in Malcolm Lowry's *Under the Volcano*.

Cumulative Index of Novels

A Roman numeral I at the end of an entry indicates that the novel is included in *Dictionary of British Literary Characters 18th- and 19th-Century Novels*. Entries without the numeral indicate that the novel is included in this volume.

1985 (Anthony Burgess)

2001: A Space Odyssey (Arthur C. Clark)

Aaron's Rod (D. H. Lawrence)

The Abbess of Crewe (Muriel Spark)

The Abbot (Sir Walter Scott) I

The A.B.C. Murders: A New Poirot Mystery (Agatha Christie)

The Absentee (Maria Edgeworth) I

Absolute Beginners (Colin MacInnes)

The Acceptance World (Anthony Powell)

An Accidental Man (Iris Murdoch)

Adam Bede (George Eliot) I

The Adventures of David Simple in Search of a Faithful Friend (Sarah Fielding) I

Adventures of Eovaai, Princess of Ijaveo (Eliza Haywood) I

The Adventures of Ferdinand Count Fathom (Tobias Smollett) I

The Adventures of Harry Richmond (George Meredith) I

The Adventures of Hugh Trevor (Thomas Holcroft) I

The Adventures of Mr. George Edwards, a Creole (John Hill) I

The Adventures of Peregrine Pickle (Tobias Smollett) I

The Adventures of Philip on His Way through the World (William Makepeace Thackeray) I

The Adventures of Roderick Random (Tobias Smollett) I

The Adventures of Sir Launcelot Greaves (Tobias Smollett) I

The Aerodrome: A Love Story (Rex Warner)

The Affair (C. P. Snow)

The African Queen (C. S. Forester)

After Leaving Mr. Mackenzie (Jean Rhys)

After Many a Summer (Aldous Huxley)

After Many a Summer Dies the Swan See *After Many a Summer.*

Agatha (Isabel Colegate)

Agnes Grey (Anne Brontë) I

The Alexandria Quartet See *Justine, Balthazar, Mountolive,* and *Clea.*

Alice (Edward Bulwer-Lytton) I

Alice's Adventures in Wonderland (Lewis Carroll) I

All Passion Spent (Vita Sackville-West)

Allan Quatermain (H. Rider Haggard) I

Almayer's Folly: A Story of an Eastern River (Joseph Conrad)

Alton Locke (Charles Kingsley) I

The Amazing Marriage (George Meredith) I

Amelia (Henry Fielding) I

The American Senator (Anthony Trollope) I

And Then There Were None (Agatha Christie)

Angel Pavement (J. B. Priestly)

Anglo-Saxon Attitudes (Angus Wilson)

Animal Farm (George Orwell)

Annals of the Parish (John Galt) I

Anna of the Five Towns (Arnold Bennett)

Anna St. Ives (Thomas Holcroft) I

Anne of Geierstein (Sir Walter Scott) I

Ann Veronica: A Modern Love Story (H. G. Wells)

Antic Hay (Aldous Huxley)

The Anti-Death League (Kingsley Amis)

Anti-Pamela: or, Feign'd Innocence Detected (Eliza Haywood) I

The Antiquary (Sir Walter Scott) I

The Apes of God (Wyndham Lewis)

An Apology for the Life of Mrs. Shamela Andrews (Henry Fielding) I

Armadale (Wilkie Collins) I

The Arrow of Gold: A Story between two Notes (Joseph Conrad)

Ashenden: or The British Agent (W. Somerset Maugham)

Aspects of Love (David Garnett)

At Freddie's (Penelope Fitzgerald)

At Lady Molly's (Anthony Powell)

At Swim-Two-Birds (Flann O'Brien)

At the Back of the North Wind (George MacDonald) I

Aunts Aren't Gentlemen (P. G. Wodehouse)

The Autobiography of Christopher Kirkland (Mrs. Lynn Linton) I

The Autobiography of Mark Rutherford (Mark Rutherford) I

Ayala's Angel (Anthony Trollope) I

Azemia (William Beckford) I

The Bachelors (Muriel Spark)

Back (Henry Green)

Background to Danger See *Uncommon Danger.*

Backwater (Dorothy Richardson)

The Ballad and the Source (Rosamond Lehmann)

The Ballad of Peckham Rye (Muriel Spark)

The History of Ophelia (Sarah Fielding) I

The History of Pendennis (William Makepeace Thackeray) I

The History of Pompey the Little (Francis Coventry) I

The History of Rasselas, Prince of Abissinia (Samuel Johnson) I

The History of Samuel Titmarsh and the Great Hoggarty Diamond (William Makepeace Thackeray) I

The History of the Adventures of Mr. Joseph Andrews and of his Friend Mr. Abraham Adams (Henry Fielding) I

The History of the Countess of Dellwyn (Sarah Fielding) I

The History of the Nun (Aphra Behn) I

The History of Tom Jones (Henry Fielding) I

The Hobbit; or There and Back Again (J. R. R. Tolkien)

The Hole in the Wall (Arthur Morrison) I

Homecoming
    See *Homecomings.*

Homecomings (C. P. Snow)

Honeycomb (Dorothy Richardson)

The Honorary Consul (Graham Greene)

The Honourable Schoolboy (John le Carré)

Hopes and Fears (Charlotte Yonge) I

Hornblower and the Atropos (C. S. Forester)

Hornblower And the Crisis: An Unfinished Novel (C. S. Forester)

Hornblower and the Hotspur (C. S. Forester)

Hornblower in the West Indies (C. S. Forester)

The Horse's Mouth (Joyce Cary)

The Hotel (Elizabeth Bowen)

The Hound of the Baskervilles (Arthur Conan Doyle) I

The Hour Before the Dawn: A Novel (W. Somerset Maugham)

A House and Its Head (Ivy Compton-Burnett)

The House by the Churchyard (J. Sheridan Le Fanu) I

The House in Clewe Street (Mary Lavin)

The House in Dormer Forest (Mary Webb)

A House in Order (Nigel Dennis)

The House in Paris (Elizabeth Bowen)

The House of the Four Winds (John Buchan)

The House on the Beach (George Meredith) I

Howards End (E. M. Forster)

How Far Can You Go? (David Lodge)

How Green Was My Valley (Wyndham Lewis)

How It Is (Samuel Beckett)

The Human Factor (Graham Greene)

The Human Predicament
    See *The Fox in the Attic* and *The Wooden Shepherdess.*

Huntingtower (John Buchan)

Hurry on Down (John Wain)

Hypatia (Charles Kingsley) I

The Ice Age (Margaret Drabble)

I, Claudius (Robert Graves)

The Image Men (J. B. Priestly)

Image of a Society (Roy Fuller)

Imperial Palace (Arnold Bennett)

In Chancery (John Galsworthy)

Incognita (William Congreve) I

The Informer (Liam O'Flaherty)

In Hazard (Richard Hughes)

The Inheritors (William Golding)

The Injur'd Husband; or, the Mistaken Resentment (Eliza Haywood) I

The Innocent Voyage
    See *A High Wind in Jamaica.*

Inside Mr. Enderby (Anthony Burgess)

Interim (Dorothy Richardson)

In Their Wisdom (C. P. Snow)

In the Year of Jubilee (George Gissing) I

The Invisible Man: A Grotesque Romance (H. G. Wells)

Invitation to the Waltz (Rosamond Lehmann)

The Ipcress File (Len Deighton)

Isabel Clarendon (George Gissing) I

Is He Popenjoy? (Anthony Trollope) I

The Island of Dr. Moreau (H. G. Wells)

The Island of Sheep (John Buchan)

The Italian (Ann Radcliffe) I

The Italian Girl (Iris Murdoch)

It is Never Too Late to Mend (Charles Reade) I

It's a Battlefield (Graham Greene)

Ivanhoe (Sir Walter Scott) I

Jack Sheppard (William Harrison Ainsworth) I

Jacob's Room (Virginia Woolf)

Jake's Thing (Kingsley Amis)

Jane and Prudence (Barbara Pym)

Jane Eyre (Charlotte Brontë) I

Jerusalem the Golden (Margaret Drabble)

The Jewel in the Crown (Paul Scott)

John Caldigate (Anthony Trollope) I

John Inglesant, A Romance (J. Henry Shorthouse) I

John Macnab (John Buchan)

Jonathan Wild
    See *The Life of Mr. Jonathan Wild the Great.*

Jorrock's Jaunts and Jollities (Robert Surtees) I

Joseph Andrews
    See *The History and Adventures*

The Tragic Comedians (George Meredith) I

The Trap (Dorothy Richardson)

Travels for the Heart (S. J. Pratt) I

Travels into Several Remote Nations of the World. In Four Parts. By Lemuel Gulliver (Jonathan Swift) I

Travels With My Aunt: A Novel (Graham Greene)

Treasure Island (Robert Louis Stevenson) I

A Tree on Fire (Alan Sillitoe)

Tremor of Intent (Anthony Burgess)

The Trial (Charlotte Yonge) I

Trilby (George Du Maurier) I

Tristram Shandy
    See *The Life and Opinions of Tristram Shandy, Gentleman.*

The Triumph of Time
    See *The Lovely Ship, The Voyage Home,* and *A Richer Dust.*

Trouble for Lucia (E. F. Benson)

The Trumpet-Major (Thomas Hardy) I

Tunc (Lawrence Durrell)

The Tunnel (Dorothy Richardson)

Tutor of Truth (S. J. Pratt) I

The Two Deaths of Christopher Martin
    See *Pincher Martin.*

Two on a Tower (Thomas Hardy) I

The Two Sides of the Shield (Charlotte Yonge) I

The Two Towers (J. R. R. Tolkien)

Two Worlds and Their Ways (Ivy Compton-Burnett)

Ultramarine (Malcolm Lowry)

Ulysses (James Joyce)

The Unclassed (George Gissing) I

Uncle Silas (J. Sheridan Le Fanu) I

Uncommon Danger (Eric Ambler)

Under the Greenwood Tree (Thomas Hardy) I

Under the Net (Iris Murdoch)

Under the Volcano (Malcolm Lowry)

Under Two Flags (Ouida) I

Under Western Eyes (Joseph Conrad)

The Unicorn (Iris Murdoch)

Unknown to History (Charlotte Yonge) I

The Unnamable (Samuel Beckett)

Unnatural Causes (P. D. James)

Unnatural Death (Dorothy Sayers)

An Unofficial Rose (Iris Murdoch)

The Unpleasantness at the Bellona Club (Dorothy Sayers)

An Unsuitable Job for a Woman (P. D. James)

Vain Fortune (George Moore) I

The Valley of Bones (Anthony Powell)

The Valley of Fear (Arthur Conan Doyle) I

Valperga (Mary Shelley) I

Vanity Fair (William Makepeace Thackeray) I

Vathek (William Beckford) I

Venetia (Benjamin Disraeli) I

Veranilda (George Gissing) I

The Vicar of Bullhampton (Anthony Trollpe) I

The Vicar of Wakefield (Oliver Goldsmith) I

Victory: An Island Tale (Joseph Conrad)

Vile Bodies (Evelyn Waugh)

The Village on the Cliff (Anne Thackeray Ritchie) I

Villette (Charlotte Brontë) I

The Virgin and the Gipsy (D. H. Lawrence)

The Virginians (William Makepeace Thackeray) I

A Vision of Battlements (Anthony Burgess)

Vittoria (George Meredith) I

Vivian Grey (Benjamin Disraeli) I

The Voyage Home (Storm Jameson)

Voyage in the Dark (Jean Rhys)

The Voyage Out (Virginia Woolf)

The Wanderer (Frances Burney) I

The Warden (Anthony Trollope) I

The War of the Worlds (H. G. Wells)

The Water-Babies (Charles Kingsley) I

The Waterfall (Margaret Drabble)

The Water of the Wondrous Isles (William Morris) I

Watership Down (Richard Adams)

Watt (Samuel Beckett)

The Waves (Virginia Woolf)

The Way of All Flesh (Samuel Butler) I

The Way We Live Now (Anthony Trollope) I

The Weather in the Streets (Rosamond Lehmann)

Weir of Hermiston: An Unfinished Romance (Robert Louis Stevenson) I

The Well at the World's End (William Morris) I

The Well-Beloved (Thomas Hardy) I

Westward Ho! (Charles Kingsley) I

The West Window
    See *The Shrimp and the Anemone.*

What Will He Do With It? by Pisistratus Caxton (Edward Bulwer-Lytton) I

When the Sleeper Wakes: A Story of the Years to Come (H. G. Wells)

Where Angels Fear to Tread (E. M. Forster)

The Whirlpool (George Gissing) I

The White Monkey (John Galsworthy)

The White Peacock (D. H. Lawrence)

Whose Body? (Dorothy Sayers)

Wide Sargasso Sea (Jean Rhys)

The Wife and Woman's Reward (Caroline Norton) I

Index to 20th-Century Novelists, Novels, and Characters

The initials following each title identify the contributor who provided the character entries.

Richard Adams (1920–)

Watership Down (1972) — GH
Dr. Adams
Bigwig (Thlayli)
Blackavar
Blackberry
Black Rabbit of Inlé
Bluebell
Campion
Lucy Cane
Clover
Cowslip
Dandelion
El-ahrairah (Prince with a
    Thousand Enemies)
Fiver (Hrairoo)
Frith
Groundsel
Hazel
Captain Holly
Hufsa
Hyzenthlay ("shine-dew-fur")
Kehaar
Captain Mallow
Nethilta
Nildro-hain ("song of black-
    bird")
Pimpernel
Pipkin (Hlaoroo)
Rabscuttle
Prince Rainbow
Rowsby Woof
Silver
Silverweed
Strawberry
Thethuthinang ("movement
    of leaves")
Threarah ("Lord Rowan
    Tree")
Vervain
Vilthuril
General Woundwort

Richard Aldington (1892–1962)

The Colonel's Daughter, A Novel
    (1931) — NC
Bim
Bom
Mr. Brock
Henry Carrington, M.A.
Dolly Casement
Constant Craige

Mrs. Eastcourt
Martin Eastcourt
Mr. Empson-Courtney
Mrs. Empson-Courtney
Jeremiah Gould
Geoffrey Hunter-Payne
Lizzie Judd
Tom Judd
Dr. McCall
Reginald Purfleet
Mr. Raper
Harry Reeves
Robert ("Coz") Smale
Alvina Smithers
Lieutenant Colonel Frederic
    Smithers
Georgina Smithers
Sir Horace Stimms
Tom Strutt
Margery Stuart
Bert Wrigley
Bess Wrigley

Death of a Hero, A Novel (1929)
    — NG
Comrade-Editor Bobbe
Sam Browne
Reggie Burnside
Lieutenant Evans
Ma Hartly
Pa Hartly
Robert Jeames
Frances Lamberton
Elizabeth Paston
Mrs. Shobbe
Herr Shobbe
Waldo Tubbe
Frank Upjohn
Fanny Welford
Dear Manna Winterbourne
Dear Pappa Winterbourne
George Winterbourne
George Augustus Winter-
    bourne
Isabel Hartly Winterbourne

Brian W. Aldiss (1925–)

Helliconia Spring (1982) — KD
Alehaw
Laintal Ay
Father Bondorlonganon
Loil Bry
Calary

Cretha
Dathka
Dresyl Den
Sar Gotth Den
Dravog
Captain Ebron
Faralin Ferd
Festibariyatid
Hasele
Hrr-Anggl Hhrot
Gaija Hin
Hrr-Tryhk Hrast
Iskador
Iyfilka
Kayle
Klils
Raynil Laynan
Amin Lin
Loilanum
Myk
Naab
Nahkri
Orfik
Oyre
Cheme Phar
Aoz Roon
Dol Sakil
Rol Sakil
Sataal
Ma Scantion
Scoraw
Si
Father Sifans
Datnil Skar
Skitosherill
Asurr Tal
Shay Tal
Vry Tal
Tusca
Usilk
Yhamm-Whrrmar
Hrr-Brahl Yprt
Yuli
Little Yuli

Helliconia Summer (1983) — KD
AbathVasidol
AbstrogAthenat
Bathkaarnet-she
Archpriest BranzaBaginut
Bull
Bardol CaraBansity
Ghht-Mlark Chzarn

Lord Welterfield
Andreas Prokovitch Zaleshoff
Tamara Prokovna Zaleshoff

Kingsley Amis (1922–)

The Anti-Death League (1966)
— JM'n
Major William ("Willie")
Ayscue
Dr. Best
Catherine Casement
Captain James Churchill
Private Deering
Lucy Hazell
Captain Maximillan ("Max")
Hunter
Jagger
Captain P. B. ("Brian") Leon-
ard
Captain Moti Naidu
Signalman Andy Pearse
Captain Alistair Ross-Donald-
son

The Green Man (1969) — PM
Mr. Allington
Amy Allington
Joyce Allington
Lucy Allington
Margaret Allington
Maurice Allington
Nick Allington
John Duerinckx-Williams
God
The Green Man
Diana Maybury
Dr. Jack Maybury
David Palmer
Tom Rodney Sonnenschein
Joseph Thornton
Dr. Thomas Underhill
Victor Hugo
Ware

Jake's Thing (1978) — JM'n
Miss Calvert
Dr. Curnow
Ed
Janet ("Kelly") Gambeson
Evelyn ("Eve") Greenstreet
Damon Lancewood
Alcestic ("Allie") Mabbott
Geoffrey Mabbott
Brenda Richardson
Jaques Cecil ("Jake") Richard-
son
Proinsias ("Frank") Rosenberg

Rowena Trefusis

Lucky Jim (1954) — PM
Bill Atkinson
Alfred Beesley
Christine Callaghan
Catchpole
Dr. L. S. Caton
Jim Dixon
Carol Goldsmith
Cecil Goldsmith
Julius Gore-Urquhart
Johns
Michie
Margaret Peel
Bertrand Welch
Michel Welch
Professor "Neddy" Welch

One Fat Englishman (1963) — PM
Mollie Atkins
Strode Atkins
Arthur Bang
Dr. Ernst Bang
Helene Bang
Mr. Castlemaine
Father Colgate
Grace Derlanger
Joe Derlanger
Sue Greene
Suzanne Klein
Irving Macher
Pamela Micheldene
Roger Micheldene
Nigel Pargeter
Professor Maynard Parrish

Take a Girl Like You (1960)
— JM'n
Jenny Bunn
Anna le Page
Graham McCintosh
Julian Ormerod
Patrick Standish
Richard ("Dick") Haines
Thompson

That Uncertain Feeling (1955)
— PM
O. Killa Beynon
Mr. Davies
Edna Davies
Ken Davies
Bill Evans
Elizabeth Gruffydd-Williams
Vernon Gruffydd-Williams
Mr. Howard
Theo James
Ieuan Jenkins

Megan Jenkins
Stan Johns
Mr. Jones
Dilys Jones
Jean Lewis
John Lewis
Gareth Probert
Edith Rhys Protheroe
Percy Protheroe
Mr. Roberts
Mr. Rowlands
Mr. Salter
Lisa Watkin
Paul Whetstone

Martin Amis (1949–)

Dead Babies (1975) — DK
(U.S.A. title: *Dark Secrets*)
Andy Adorno
Marvell Buzhardt
Giles Coldstream
Lucy Littlejohn
Diane Parry
Roxanne
Skip
Mr. Tuckles
Mrs. Tuckles
Celia Villiers
Quentin Villiers
Kevin Whitehead

Money (1984) — DK
Martin Amis
Spunk Davis
Fielding Goodney
Lorne Guyland
Alec Llewellyn
Caduta Massi
Fat Paul
Barry Self
John Self
Selina Street
Martina Twain
Vera

The Rachel Papers (1973)
— DK
Norman Entwhistle
Charles Highway
Gordon Highway
Rachel Noyes

Success (1978) — DK
Gregory Riding
Henry Riding
Ursula Riding
Terry Service

Michael Arlen (1895–1956)

The Green Hat (1924) — J J
Mr. Cherry-Marvel
Hugo Cypress
Shirley Cypress
Guy de Travest
Colonel Victor Duck
Boy Fenwick
Sir Maurice Harpenden
Captain Napier (Naps)
   Harpenden
Venice Pollen Harpenden
Gerald Haveleur March
Conrad Masters
Iris March Fenwick Storm
Hilary Townshend

Beryl Bainbridge (1933–   )

The Bottle Factory Outing (1974)
— MK
Brenda
Freda
Mr. Paganotti
Patrick
Mr. Rossi
Vittorio

The Dressmaker (1973) — MK
(U.S.A. title: *The Secret Glass*)
Margo Bickerton
Ira
Jack
Mrs. Mander
Valerie Mander
Nellie
Rita

Sweet William (1976) — MK
Gerald
Mrs. Kershaw
Edna McClusky
William McClusky
Pamela
Mrs. Walton
Ann Walton

Young Adolf (1978) — MK
Mr. Dupont
Adolf Hitler
Alois Hitler
Bridget Hitler
William Patrick Hitler
Dr. Kephalus
Mr. Meyer
Mary O'Leary
Mrs. Prentice

Samuel Beckett (1906–1989)

Company (1980) — ST
(French title, 1979: *Companie*)
Bom
One on his back in the dark
A voice

How It Is (1964) — ST
(French title, 1961: *Comment c'est*)
I
Pim

Malone Dies (1955) — ST
(French title, 1951: *Malone meurt*)
Lemuel
MacMann
Malone
Moll

Molloy (1955; France: 1951) — ST
Gaber
Mrs. Lousse (alias Sophie Loy)
Molloy
Jaques Moran
My mother
Ruth (or Edith)
Teddy
Youdi

Murphy (1938) — ST
Miss Counihan
Mr. Endon
Celia Kelly
Murphy
Neary
Wylie

The Unnamable (1958) — ST
(French title, 1953:
L'Innommable)
Basil [Mahood]
The Unnamable
Worm

Watt (1953) — ST
Arsene
Mr. Knott
Sam
Watt

Max Beerbohm (1872–1956)

*Zuleika Dobson; or An Oxford Love
   Story* (1911) — AFB
Mrs. Batch
Clarence Batch
Katie Batch
Max Beerbohm
Edward Joseph Craddock
Zuleika Dobson
John Tanville-Tankerton,
   Duke of Dorset
MacQuern
Mélisande
Noaks
Oover
The Warden

Arnold Bennett (1867–1931)

Anna of the Five Towns (1902)
— OB
Miss Dickinson
Eli Machin
Henry Mynors
Titus Price
Willie Price
Priscilla
Alderman Sutton
Mrs. Sutton
Beatrice Sutton
Agnes Tellwright
Anna (Sis) Tellwright
Ephraim Tellwright
Sarah Vodrey

Buried Alive: A Tale of These Days
   (1908) — OB
Dr. Cashmore
Alice Challice
Miss Cohenson
Charlie Docksey
Lady Sophia Entwistle
Duncan Farll
Priam Farll
Harry Leek
Henry Leek
Mrs. Henry Leek
John Leek
Matthew Leek
Mr. Oxford
Father Luke Widgery
Whitney Witt

*The Card: A Story of Adventure in
   the Five Towns* (1911) — OB
(U.S.A. title: *Denry the Auda-
cious*)
Herbert Calvert
Countess of Chell (Interfering
   Iris)
Major Clutterbuck
Mrs. Codlyne
Councillor Cotterill
Nellie Cotterill
Sir Jehoshophat Dain

Kenneth (Padre) Bartlett
Olga Bracely
Irene Coles
Signor Cortese
Dorothea Cortese
Major Benjamin Flint
Foljambe
Grovesnor
Janet
Susan Leg
Emmeline (Lucia) Lucas
Mr. McConnell
Elizabeth Mapp
Georgie Pillson
Godiva (Diva) Plaistow
Susan Poppitt
Daisy Quantock
Poppy, Duchess of Sheffield
Mrs. Simpson
Mr. Twistevant
Young Twistevent
Jane Weston
Withers
Algernon Wyse

The Worshipful Lucia (1935) — CJ
Evie Bartlett
Kenneth (Padre) Bartlett
Cadman
Irene Coles
Amelia, Contessa di Faraglione
Major Benjamin Flint
Foljambe
Georgie
Grovesnor
Janet
Emmeline (Lucia) Lucas
Lucy
Elizabeth Mapp
Percy
Georgie Pillson
Godiva (Diva) Plaistow
Susan Poppitt
Withers
Algernon Wyse

John Berger (1926–   )

Corker's Freedom (1964) — RS
Jackie Armstrong
Bertha Brand
Yvonne (Velvet) Browning
Irene Corker
William Tracey Corker
Alec Gooch
Mr. Hodges
Albert Immonds
Brenda Marlow

Maggie McBryde
Gunter Ruhling
Dr. Sargent
The Vicar
Barbara Wheatley
Desmond Wheatley
Wolf

The Foot of Clive (1962) — RS
Ken Adamson
Maevis (Maeve) Adamson
Guiseppe (Pepino) Baldino
Harry Cole
Peter Cole
Phyl Cole
Cyril
Dorothy
Eileen
Eleanor
David (Dai) Evans
Robin Garton
Jack House
Matron
Matt
Paddy
Sidney Parks
Pearl
Renata
Cliff Williams

A Painter of Our Time (1958) — RS
Marcus Aurelius
Sir Gerald Banks
Berkeley-Tyne
Robert de Quincey
Erno
Leonard Gough
Henry H—
Len Hancock
Vee Hancock
Hardwick
Harry
John
Kati (Katinka)
Laszlo
Diana Lavin
Janos Lavin
Max
Michel
Bill Neale
Ninette
Susan (Susie)
George Trent
June Trent
Yvonne

Nicholas Blake See C. Day Lewis.

Elizabeth Bowen (1899–1973)

The Death of the Heart (1938) — JD
Eric E. J. Brutt
Eddie
Mrs. Heccomb
Daphne Heccomb
Dickie Heccomb
Matchett
St. Quentin Miller
Anna Quayne
Portia Quayne
Thomas Quayne

Eva Trout, or Changing Scenes
(1968) — JD
Bettie Mae Anapoupolis
Applethwaite
Eric Arble
Iseult (Smith) Arble
Dr. Gerard Bonnard
Mrs. Gerard Bonnard
Tony Clevering-Haight
Mrs. Dancey
Alaric Dancey
Andrew Dancey
Catrina Dancey
Henry Dancey
Louise Dancey
Mr. Denge
Elsinore
Portman C. Holtman
Kenneth
Constantine Ormeau
Cissy Trout
Eva Trout
Jeremy Trout
Willy Trout

Friends and Relations (1931) — JD
Considine Meggatt
Rodney Meggatt
Janet Studdart
Laurel Studdart
Theodora Thirdman
Edward Tilney
Lady Elfrida Tilney

The Heat of the Day (1949) — JD
Harrison
Robert Kelway
Roderick Rodney
Stella Rodney

The Hotel (1927) — JD
Tessa Bellamy
Colonel Duperrier
Mrs. Duperrier
Mrs. Kerr

Valentine (Val) Wrigley

Enderby Outside (1968) — FG
Miss Boland
Vesta Bainbridge
Yod Crewsy
F. X. Enderby
Easy Walker

The End of the World News (1983)
— FG
Paul A. Bartlett
Valentine Brodie
Vanessa Frame Brodie
Lev Davidovich Bronstein
[Leon Trotsky]
Hubert Frame
Sigmund Freud
Nat Goya
Calvin Gropius
Ernest Jones
Carl Jung
Olga
Robert Courtland Willett

Inside Mr. Enderby (1963) — FG
'Arry
Vesta Bainbridge
Yod Crewsy
F. X. Enderby
Jack
Mrs. Meldrum
Rawcliffe
Dr. Wapenshaw

MF (1971) — FG
Aderyn the Bird Queen
Dunkel
Miss Emmett
Catherine (Kitty) Faber
Miles Faber
Dr. Z. Fonanta [Sib Legru]
Dr. Gonzi
Llewellyn (Llew)

The Pianoplayers (1986) — FG
Frederick (Fred) Gosport
Ellen Henshaw
William (Billy) Henshaw
Maggie Moran
Marcus Rolf
Albert Ross
Mr. Shaw

Tremor of Intent (1966) — FG
Miss Devi
Denis Hillier (alias Sebastian
Jagger)
Brigitte Weidegrunde Roper
Edmund Roper

R. Theodorescu
Wriste

A Vision of Battlements (1965) — FG
Sgt. Julian Agate
Senor Barasi
Laurel Ennis
Sgt. Richard Ennis
Conception Gomez
Lavinia Grantham
Major Muir
Senor Murillo
Regimental Sgt. Major Turner

Alan Burns (1929–)

Buster (1961) — JJ
Bert
Lieutenant Crabbe
Lieutenant Gerson
Bryan Graveson
Daniel Graveson
Helen
Montague
Deirdre Watkins

Joyce Cary (1888–1957)

Except the Lord (1953) — RL
Brodribb
Mrs. Coyte
Fred Coyte
Dr. Dolling
Ted Goold
Dr. Lanza
James Latter
May Latter
Dr. Leddra
Mrs. Nimmo
Chester Nimmo
Dorothy Nimmo
Georgina Nimmo
Richard Nimmo
Ruth Nimmo
Tom Nimmo
Pring
Geoffrey Simnel
Willy Wilson
Nina Woodville

Herself Surprised (1941) — RL
Rozina (Rozzie) Balmforth
Robert Brown
Julie Eeles
Mr. Hickson
Clarissa Hipper
Gulley Jimson
Nina Jimson

Matthew Monday
Sara Monday
Miss Slaughter
Blanche Wilcher
Tom Wilcher

The Horse's Mouth (1944) — RL
Professor Alabaster
Rosina (Rozzie) Balmforth
Nosy Barbon
Lady Beeder
Sir William Beeder
Coker
Julie Eeles
Mr. Hickson
Gulley Jimson
Sara Monday
Fred Robins
Tom Wilcher

Mister Johnson (1939) — RL
Ajali
Aliu
Mallam Audu
Bamu
Benjamin
Blore
Brimah
Bulteel
Emir
Gollup
Jamesu
Johnson
Matumbi
Moma
Celia Rudbeck
Harry Rudbeck
Saleh
Sozy
Tasuki
J. S. Tring
The Waziri

Not Honour More (1955) — RL
A. M. Brightman
Brome
Clint
Drew
Bootham Goold
Amelia Jones
James Latter
May Latter
Robert Latter (the younger)
John Maufe
Chester Nimmo
Sally Nimmo
Bill Pincomb
Thomas Potter

Ransome Middleton
Selina Middleton
Percival
Miss Starkie

More Women Than Men (1933)
— KBe
Adela
Felix Bacon
Sir Robert Bacon
Mrs. Chattaway
William Fane
Mrs. Faulkner
Elizabeth Giffard
Ruth Giffard
Johnston
Helen Keats
Theodora Luke
Emmeline Munday
Josephine Napier
Simon Napier
Maria Rosetti
Gabriel Swift
Jonathan Swift

Mother and Son (1955) — KBe
Adela
Bates
Miss Burke
Emma Greatheart
Adrian Hume
Alice Hume
Francis Hume
Julius Hume
Miranda Hume
Rosebery (Rosebud) Hume
Mr. Pettigrew
Plautus
Hester Wolsey

Parents and Children (1941)
— KBe
Faith Cranmer
Hope Cranmer
Paul Cranmer
Ridley Cranmer
Emma Hatton
Lester Marlowe
Priscilla Marlowe
Susan Marlowe
Miss Mitford
Mr. Morris
Mrs. Morris
Bertha Mullet
Miss Pilbeam
Daniel Sullivan
Eleanor Sullivan
Fulbert Sullivan

Gavin Sullivan
Graham Sullivan
Honor Sullivan
Isabel Sullivan
James Sullivan
Sir Jesse Sullivan
Lucia Sullivan
Neville Sullivan
Regan, Lady Sullivan
Venetia (Venice) Sullivan

Pastors and Masters (1925) — KBe
Miss Badsen
Delia Bentley
Henry Bentley
Richard (Dickie) Bumpus
Mr. Burgess
Crabbe
Francis Fletcher
Lydia (Aunt Lyddie) Fletcher
Peter Fletcher
Theresa Fletcher
Emily Herrick
Nicholas Herrick
William Masson
Mrs. Merry
Charles Merry

The Present and the Past (1953)
— KBe
Alfred Ainger
Miss Bennet
Mr. Clare
Cassius Clare
Catherine Clare
Fabian Clare
Flavia Clare
Guy Clare
Henry Clare
Megan Clare
Tobias (Toby) Clare
Mrs. Frost
Thomas Halliday
Kate
Miss Ridley
Elton Scrope
Ursula Scrope
Simon
William

Two Worlds and Their Ways (1949)
— KBe
Adela
Aldom
Mrs. Aldom
Francis Bacon
Mr. Bigwell
Juliet Cassidy

Lucius Cassidy
Miss Chancellor
Mr. Dalziel
Esther
Lesbia Firebrace
Oliver Firebrace
Gwendolen
Hubert Holland
Miss James
Miss Lawrence
Miss Marathon
Maud
Miss Petticott
Clemence Shelley
Maria, Lady Shelley
Mary, Lady Shelley
Oliver Shelley
Sir Roderick Shelley
Sefton Shelley
Oliver Spode
Colin Sturgeon
Miss Tuke
Verity

Joseph Conrad (Józef Teodor Konrad Korzeniowski, 1857–1924)

Almayer's Folly: A Story of an Eastern River (1895) — CF
Mrs. Almayer
Kaspar Almayer
Nina Almayer
Babalatchi
Lakamba
Captain Tom (Tuan) Lingard
Dain Maroola

The Arrow of Gold: A Story Between Two Notes (1919) — CF
Henry Allègre
Captain J. K. Blunt
Dominic
Monsieur George
Doña Rita de Lastaola
Mr. Mills
José Ortega

Chance: A Tale in Two Parts (1913)
— CF
Flora de Barral Anthony
Roderick Anthony
de Barral
Mrs. de Barral
Mr. Fyne
Mrs. Fyne
Marlow
Powell

E. M. Delafield (Edmée Elizabeth Monica de la Pasture Dashwood, 1890–1943)

The Diary of a Provincial Lady (1930) — MM
Barbara Blenkinsop
Mrs. Blenkinsop
Lady Boxe
Crosbie Carruthers
Cook
Cissie Crabbe
Felicity Fairmead
Lady Frobisher
Helen Wills
Jahsper
Mademoiselle
Our Vicar
Our Vicar's Wife
Miss Pankerton
The Provincial Lady
Robert
Robin
Dear Rose
Vicky

Messalina of the Suburbs (1924) — MM
Leslie Morrison
Mrs. Palmer
Elsie Palmer
Geraldine Palmer
Norman Roberts
Irene Tidmarsh
Horace Williams
Dr. Herbert Wooley

The Provincial Lady Goes Further (1932) — MM
(U.S.A. title: *The Provincial Lady in London*)
Mr. Blamington
Mrs. Blamington
Mrs. Blenkinsop
Cousin Maud Blenkinsop
Casabianca
Cissie Crabbe
Distinguished Professor
Felicity Fairmead
Lady Frobisher
Young Frobisher
Emma Hay
Madame Inez
Kolynos
Mademoiselle
Our Vicar's Wife
Miss Pankerton
Miss Postman

Pamela Pringle
Waddell Pringle
The Provincial Lady
Robert
Robin
Dear Rose
Vicky
Charlotte (Carina) Volley

Nigel Dennis (1912–1989)

Boys and Girls Come Out to Play (1949) — JO
Lily Divver
Max Divver
Mrs. Morgan
Jimmy Morgan
John Petty
Harriet Streeter
Larry Streeter

Cards of Identity (1955) — JO
Mrs. Chirk
Captain Mallet
Mrs. Mallet
Beaufort Mallet
Miss Paradise
Henry Paradise
The President
Dr. Shubunkin
Dr. Towzer
Blanche Tray

A House in Order (1966) — JO
The Agronomist
The Cartographer
The Colonel
The Interpreter
Mackenzie

Norman Douglas (1868–1952)

South Wind (1917) — KBa
Andrea
Angelina
Bazhakuloff (Messiah)
Count Caloveglia
Charlie
Ernest Eames
Don Francesco
Bishop Thomas Heard
Mr. Hopkins
Mr. Keith
Peter Arsenievitch Krasnojab-kin
Signor Malipizzo
Edgar Marten
Mrs. Meadows
Don Giustino Morena

Muhlen
Freddy Parker
Lola Parker
Denis Phipps
Mr. Professor
Mr. Richards
Duchess of San Martino
Madame Steynlin
Sir Herbert Street
Torquemada
Cornelius van Koppen
Mr. White
Amy Wilberforce

Margaret Drabble (1939–   )

The Garrick Year (1964) — TD
Bob
Sophy Brent
Edmund Carpenter
David Evans
Emma Lawrence Evans
Flora Evans
Joseph Evans
Marjorie Farrar
Percy Edward Farrar
Wyndham Farrar
Michael Fenwick
Don Franklin
Rockie Goldenberg
Neville Grierson
Hugh
Julian
Mr. Lawrence
Mrs. Lawrence
Laura Montefiore
Mike Papini
Pascal
Harriet Peters
Mr. Scott
Mrs. Scott
Selwyn
Henry Summers
Mary Scott Summers
Viola
Mrs. Von Blerke
Felicity White
Natalie Winter
Peter Yates

The Ice Age (1977) — JM'n
Derek Ashby
Evelyn Ashby
Hattie Baines
Clyde Barstow
Bill
Laura Blakely
Mr. Boot

Mrs. Boxer
Ned Buckton
Sally Buckton
Mrs. Bunney
Mrs. Chalfont
Judy Channing
Humphrey Clegg
Sylvia Clegg
Tom Collander
Alfred Collins
Daniel
Jim Eaves
Eloise
Enid
Evie
Auntie Evie
Michael Eyam
Stanley Flood
Kitty Friedman
Max Friedman
Bert Gifford
Dr. Gobian
Auntie Grace
Harriet Hancox
Linton Hancox
Eric Hargreaves
Diane Harwood
Hopkins
Grant Jackson
Jim
Austin Jones
Jonothan
Mr. Kammell
Mr. Keating
Mrs. Keating
Anthony Keating
Barbara (Babs) (Cockburn Keating)
Mary Keating
Matthew Keating
Paul Keating
Peter Keating
Ruth Keating
Stephen Keating
Lord Kinarth
Mrs. Kirby
Marlene Kirby
Maureen Kirby
Sid Kirby
Rory Leggett
Lizzie
Lyons
Margrit
Mavis
Miriam
Mike Morgan
Alison Murray

Donnell Murray
Jane Murray
Molly Murray
Mrs. Newsome
Pamela
Giles Peters
Poulson
Rosemary
Stern
Stuart
Tim
Chloe Vickers
Gino Vignoli
Bill Wade
Len Wincobank
Zelda

Jerusalem the Golden (1967) — AFB
Walter Ash
Margarita Cassell
Peter de Salis
Amelia Denham
Annunciata (Nancy) Denham
Candida Gray Denham
Clelia Denham
Gabriel Denham
Magnus Denham
Phillippa Denham
Sebastian Denham
Miss Haines
Peter Harranson
Mrs. Hill
Martin
Matthews
Alan Maugham
Albert Maugham
Arthur Maugham
Clara Maugham
Kathie Maugham
May Maugham

The Middle Ground (1980) — JM'n
Adrian
Albert
Amarylis
Alex Armstrong
Kate Fletcher Armstrong
Luisa Armstrong
Mark Armstrong
Michael Armstrong
Paul Armstrong
Reuben Armstrong
Ruth Armstrong
Stuart Armstrong
Janice Ash
Ayesha
Tracy Baker
Denise (Scooter) Ball

Terry Ball
June Barnes
Miss Bates
Danny Blick
Mr. Bly
Mr. Carey
Fiona Macfarlane Carey
Clifford
Conroy
Irene Crowther
David
Clelia Denham
Danny Denham
Gabriel Denham
Jessica Denham
Marcus Denham
Phillippa Denham
Mabel Eddison
Emilio
Bob (Uncle Bob) Fletcher
Florrie Fletcher
June Fletcher
Peter Fletcher
Walter Fletcher
Julie Girtin
Mrs. Goldman
Sam Goldman
Chloe Harlech
Harry
Hunt
Iain
Sally Jackson
Joker James
Marylin James
Auntie Janey
Betsy Kay
Diane Kent
Kevin
Joseph Leroy
Lily
Lizzy Little
Lucy
Janice Lumm
David Mainwaring
Hugo Mainwaring
Judith Street Mainwaring
Nancy ("Nan") Mainwaring
Marina
Great-Aunt Martha
Matthew
Mrs. Meer
Mr. Morton
Mrs. Morton
Isobel (Morton)
Beatrice Mourre
Simone Mourre
Mujid

Mrs. Oakley
Marylin O'Brien
Sally O'Mears
Jessie Parker
Patrick
Sharon Polsen
Robert
Linda Rubenstein
Tom Rubenstein
Ruby
Sally
Pauline Scott
Shirley ("Marylou") Scott
Joyce Scully
Miss Simmons
Abe Solomon
Jan Sondersheim
Susan Sondersheim
Rosamund Stacey
Stella
Evelyn Morton Stennett
James Stennett
Sebastian Stennett
Ted Stennett
Vicky Stennett
Rubia Subhan
Teria
Edie Tucker
Jayne Tuthill
Vic
Vic
Bob Young
Dora Young
Patsy Young
Stanley Young

The Millstone (1965) — TD
Alex
Alexandra
Hamish Andrews
Beatrice
Bessie
Dr. Cohen
Dick
Elaine
Miss Ellis
Dr. Esmond
Frank
Hallam
Sister Hammond
Roger Henderson
Joe Hurt
Mrs. Jennings
Marleen
George Matthews
Mike
Dr. H. E. Moffatt

Nicholas
Dr. Protheroe
Lydia Reynolds
Miss Richards
Sandra
Sarah
Sister
Mrs. Sammy Spillikins
Spiro
Mrs. Stacey
Andrew Stacey
Clare Stacey
Herbert Stacey
Octavia Stacey
Rosamund Stacey
Mrs. Sullivan

The Needle's Eye (1972) — MK
Jeremy Alford
Mr. Bryanston
Mrs. Camish
Julie Camish
Simon Camish
Diana
Nick
Noreen
Emily Offenbach
Mr. Phillips
Mrs. Sharkey
Eileen Sharkey
Christopher Vassiliou
Konstantin Vassiliou
Marcus Vassiliou
Maria Vassiliou
Rose Bryanston Vassiliou

The Realms of Gold (1975) — AFB
Joe Ayida
Harold Barnard
Janet Ollerenshaw Bird
Mark Bird
Mr. Fox
John Lincoln
Alice Ollerenshaw
Beata Ollerenshaw
Constance Ollerenshaw
David Ollerenshaw
Sir Frank Ollerenshaw
Hugh Ollerenshaw
Natasha Ollerenshaw
Stella, Lady Ollerenshaw
Stephen Ollerenshaw
Joy Schmidt
Karel Schmidt
Sebastian
Anthony Wingate
Frances Ollerenshaw Wingate
Hunter Wisbech

A Summer Bird-Cage (1963) — TD
Jackie Almond
Ildiko Bates
Mr. Bennett
Mrs. Bennett
Sarah (Sal) Bennett
Aunt Betty
John Connell
Bill Conroy
Stella Conroy
Cousin Daphne
Francis
Louise (Lulu) Bennett Halifax
Stephen Halifax
Sappho Hinchcliffe
Hesther Innes
Kristin
Lovell
Martin
Miss McGregor
Michael
Cousin Michael
Simon Rathbone
Simone
Antony Slater
Gill Slater
Wilfred Smee
Stephanie
David Vesey

The Waterfall (1969) — JM'n
Brenda
Catherine
Denise
Bridget Goldsmith
Bianca Gray
Jane Gray
Laurie Gray
Malcolm Gray
Johnnie
Miss Jones
Mike
Nicholas
Charlotte Otford
James Otford
Lucy Goldsmith Otford
Simon Otford

Daphne Du Maurier (1907–1989)

Rebecca (1938) — SPh
Alice
Baker
Ben
Clarice
Frank Crawley
Lady Crowan
Mrs. Danvers

Mrs. de Winter
Maxim de Winter
Rebecca de Winter
Jack Favell
Frith
Grandmother
Horridge
Colonel Julyan
Beatrice Lacy
Major Giles Lacy
Robert
Captain Searle
Mr. Tabb
Mrs. Van Hopper
Inspector Welch

Lawrence Durrell (1912–1990)

Balthazar (1958) — MB
(The second novel of *The Alexandria Quartet*)
[Child] Arnauti
Jacob Arnauti
Melissa Artemis
S. Balthazar
Toto de Brunel
Paul Capodistria
L. G. Darley
Hamid
Justine Hosnani
Leila Hosnani
Narouz Hosnani
Nessim Hosnani
Justine
John Keats
Mnemjian
Clea Montis
Georges Gaston Pombal
Percy (penname: Ludwig)
   Pursewarden
Josh Scobie
Selim
Shiek

The Black Book (1938) — MB
Clare
Gracie
Herbert ("Death") Gregory
Kate
Lobo
Lawrence Lucifer
Tarquin

Clea (1960) — MB
(The fourth novel of *The Alexandria Quartet*)
Claude Amaril
Semira Amaril

[Child] Arnauti
Jacob Arnauti
Melissa Artemis
S. Balthazar
Paul Capodistria
L. G. Darley
Fosca
Griskin
Hamid
Justine Hosnani
Nessim Hosnani
Justine
Kenilworth
John Keats
Oliver Maskelyne
Memlik
Mnemjian
Clea Montis
David Mountolive
Panagiotis
Georges Gaston Pombal
Liza Pursewarden
Percy (penname: Ludwig)
   Pursewarden
Josh Scobie
Mavis Telford
Tommy Telford

Justine (1957) — MB
(The first novel of *The Alexandria Quartet*)
[Child] Arnauti
Jacob Arnauti
Melissa Artemis
S. Balthazar
Paul Capodistria
Cohen
L. G. Darley
Hamid
Justine Hosnani
Leila Hosnani
Nessim Hosnani
Justine
John Keats
Mnemjian
Clea Montis
Panayotis
Georges Gaston Pombal
Percy (penname: Ludwig)
   Pursewarden
Selim

Mountolive (1958) — MB
(The third novel of *The Alexandria Quartet*)
Claude Amaril
Semira Amaril
Jacob Arnauti

Melissa Artemis
S. Balthazar
Paul Capodistria
Cohen
L. G. Darley
Errol
Angela Errol
Griskin
Faltaus Hosnani
Justine Hosnani
Leila Hosnani
Narouz Hosnani
Nessim Hosnani
Kenilworth
Sir Louis
Oliver Maskelyne
Memlik
Clea Montis
Mountolive (the elder)
Mrs. Mountolive
David Mountolive
Georges Gaston Pombal
Liza Pursewarden
Percy (penname: Ludwig)
   Pursewarden
Rafael
Selim
Serapamoun
Shiek

Nunquam (1970) — MB
(The second novel of *The Revolt of Aphrodite*)
Felix Charlock
Cyrus P. Goytz
Marchant
Benedicta Merlin
Nash
Jocas Pehlevi
Julian Pehlevi
Elias Sacrapant
Iolanthe Samiou (2)
Vibart

Tunc (1968) — MB
(The first novel of *The Revolt of Aphrodite*)
Count Banubula
Caradoc
Felix Charlock
Mark Charlock
Graphos
Mrs. Henniker
Countess Hippolyta
Koepgen
Benedicta Merlin
Jocas Pehlevi
Julian Pehlevi

Elias Sacrapant
Iolanthe Samiou
Sipple
Vibart

Ronald Firbank (1886–1926)

The Flower Beneath the Foot (1923)
—J J
Abou
Count Ann-Jules
Dr. Arthur Amos Cuncliffe Babcock
Bachir
Bessie Barleymoon
Mrs. Bedley
Olga Blumenghast
Count Cabinet
Duchess Cavalojos (Her Gaudiness)
Harold Chilleywater
Victoria Gellybone Frinton Chilleywater
Harry Cummings
Lazari Demitraki
Effendi
Archduchess Elizabeth
Princess Elsie
Queen Glory
Miss Hopkins
Sister Irene of the Incarnation
Old Jane
King Jotifa
Kalpurnia
Blanche de Lambese
Lionel Limpness
Queen Lois (Her Dreaminess)
Mario
Mother Martinez de la Rosa
Eddy Monteith
Aggie Montgomery
Laura Lita Carmen Etoile (Rara) de Nazianzi
Father Nostradamus
Prince Olaf (His Lankiness)
Countess Olympia d'Omptyda
Peter Passer
Countess Medusa Rappa
Eva Schnerb
Sidi
Ivy Something
Rosa Bark, Lady Something
Sir Somebody Something
Teddywegs
Guy Thin
Queen Thleeanouhee
Timzra

Countess Violet Tolga
Sir Trotter-Stormer
Sister Ursula
Duchess of Varna
Madame Wetme
King William (Willie)
Prince Yousef (His Weariness)
Countess Yvorra

Sorrow in Sunlight (1924) — J J
(U.S.A. title: *Prancing Nigger*)
Bamboo
Eurydice Edwards
Ibum
Mamma Luna
Alice McAdam
Mr. Mouth
Ahmadou Mouth
Charlie Mouth
Edna Mouth
Miami Mouth
Papy Paul
Camilla Ruiz
Vittorio (Vitti) Ruiz
Nini Scagg
Countess Kattie Soderini
Taosay

Penelope Fitzgerald (1916–)

At Freddie's (1982) — SAP
Hannah Graves
Jonathan Kemp
Boney Lewis
Carroll Pierce
Matthew (Mattie) Stewart
Frieda (Freddie) Wentworth

Ian Fleming (1908–1964)

Casino Royale (1953) — JR
James Bond
Le Chiffre
Felix Leiter
Vesper Lynd
M
René Mathis
Miss Moneypenny

Diamonds Are Forever (1956) — JR
James Bond
Tiffany Case
Ernest Curco
Kidd
Felix Leiter
M
Miss Moneypenny
Loelia Ponsonby
Jack Spang

Seraffimo Spang
"Shady" Tree
Wint

Dr. No (1958) — JR
(U.S.A. title: *Doctor No*)
James Bond
Major Boothroyd
M
Sir James Molony
Miss Moneypenny
Dr. Julius No
Loelia Ponsonby
Honeychile Rider
Commander John Strangeways

From Russia, With Love (1957)
—JR
James Bond
Tiffany Case
Red Grant
Darko Kerim
Rosa Klebb
Kronsteen
M
René Mathis
May
Sir James Molony
Miss Moneypenny
Loelia Ponsonby
Tatiana (Tania) Romanova

Goldfinger (1959) — JR
James Bond
Pussy Galore
Auric Goldfinger
Felix Leiter
M
Jill Masterson
Tilly Masterson
Miss Moneypenny
Oddjob
Quarrel

Live and Let Die (1954) — JR
Mr. Big
James Bond
Simone Latrelle (Solitaire)
Felix Leiter
M
Miss Moneypenny
Quarrel

Moonraker (1955) — JR
(U.S.A. title: *Too Hot to Handle*)
James Bond
Gala Brand
Sir Hugo Drax
M

Buckland
William Bush
Carberry
Chapman
Clive
Cogshill
Coleman
Cope
Cray
Duff
Dutton
Greenwood
Hart
Hibbert
Hobbs
Horatio Hornblower
Mary Ellen Mason Hornblower
Jenkins
Lomax
Mrs. Mason
Colonel Ortega
Admiral Lord Parry
Pierce
Preston
Purvis
Roberts
Saddler
Marquis de Sainte-Croix
Sankey
Captain Sawyer
Silk
Susie
Truelove
Truscott
Villanueva
Wellard
Whiting
Wilson
Woolton

Lord Hornblower (1946) — MK
Brown
William Bush
Captain Freeman
Lucien Antoine de Ladon,
　Count de Gracay
Marie, Vicomtesse de Gracay
Horatio Hornblower
Lady Barbara Wellesley

Mr. Midshipman Hornblower (1950)
　— MW
Bolton
Bowles
Bromley
Caldwell
Carson
Chadd

Chalk
M. de Charette
Clay
Cleveland
Clough
Clynes
Kitty Cobham
George Crome
Cutler
Lady Dalrymple
Danvers
Duras (His Britannic Majesty
　Consul)
Eccles
Earl of Edrington
Finch
Foster
Franklin
Carlos Leonardo Luis Manuel
　de Godoy y Boegas
Griffin
Hales
Black Charlie Hammond
Harvey
Dr. Hepplewhite
Hethers
Sir Hew
Horatio Hornblower
Hunter
Jackson
Jordan
Keene
Kennedy
Lewis
Low
Mallory
Masters
Matthews
Maxwell
M. de Moncoutant, Lord of
　Muzillac
Muggridge
Neuville
Oldroyd
Partridge
Pellew
Marquis of Pouzauges
Simpson
Soames
Stanley
Styles
Tapling
M. de Villers
Waldron
Wales
Winyatt

Ship of the Line (1938) — MW
Bolton
Mrs. Bolton
Brown
William Bush
Cavendish
Colonel Juan Claros
Lord Cochrane
Duddingstone
Lord Eastlake
Captain Elliot
Gerard
Harrison
Hart
Hooker
Horatio Hornblower
Major Laird
Admiral Sir Percy Gilbert
　Leighton
Longley
Marsh
Captain Morris
Captain Osborn
Pino
Polwheal
Sir Mucho Pomposo
Price
Rayner
General Rovira
Savage
Stebbings
Sylvester
Thompson
Colonel Jose Gonzalez de
　Villena y Danvila
Vincent
Waites
Walsh
Lady Barbara Wellesley
Miss Wentworth
Wood

E. M. Forster (1879–1970)

Howards End (1910) — CH
Miss Avery
Jacky Bast
Leonard Bast
Percy Cahill
Crane
Bruno Liesecke
Frieda Mosebach
Juley Munt
Helen Schlegel
Margaret (Meg) Schlegel
Theobald (Tibby) Schlegel
Charles Wilcox

Jack Cardigan
Holly Forsyte Dartie
Montague (Monty) Moses
    Dartie
Publius Valerius (Val) Dartie
Winifred (Freddie) Dartie
Annette Lamotte Forsyte
George Forsyte
Irene Heron Forsyte
Jolyon (Young Jolyon, Jo)
    Forsyte
Jolyon (Jon) Forsyte
June Forsyte
Soames Forsyte
Timothy Forsyte
Gradman
Fleur Forsyte Mont
Michael Conway Mont
Prosper Profond
Smither

The White Monkey (1924) — RMc
    (The first novel of *A Modern
    Comedy*)
Anthony (Tony) Bicket
Victorine (Vic) Collins Bicket
Butterfield
Lady Alison (Charwell)
    Cherrell
Lionel (Charwell) Cherrell
Philip Norman Danby
Holly Forsyte Dartie
Publius Valerius (Val) Dartie
Winifred (Freddie) Dartie
Wilfred Desert
Dumetrius
Robert Elderson
Annette Lamotte Forsyte
George Forsyte
June Forsyte
Very Young Nicholas Forsyte
Very Young Roger Forsyte
Soames Forsyte
Gradman
Aubrey Greene
Fleur Forsyte Mont
Sir Lawrence Mont
Michael Conway Mont
Miss Perrin

David Garnett (1892–1981)

Aspects of Love (1955) — DC
Sir George Dillingham
Jeanne (Jenny) Dillingham
Rose Vibert Dillingham
Alexander (Alexis) Golightly
Marcel

Giulietta, Marchesa Trampani
Vincent

Lady Into Fox (1922) — BM-A
Mrs. Cork (Nanny)
Polly Cork
Simon Cork
Canon Fox
Janet
Richard Tebrick
Silvia Fox Tebrick

William Gerhardie (1895–1977)

Futility: A Novel on Russian Themes
    (1922) — SPr
Andrei Andreiech
Magda Nikolaevna Bursanov
Nikolai Vasilievich Bursanov
Nina Bursanov
Sonia Bursanov
Vera Bursanov
Admiral Butt
Cecedek
Eisenstein
Uncle Frostia
Fanny Ivanovna
Kniaz
Ivan Stanitski
Baron Wunderhausen
Zina

Stella Gibbons (1902–1989)

Cold Comfort Farm (1932) — AC
Mrs. Beetle
Agony Beetle
Meriam Beetle
Luke Dolour
Mark Dolour
Aunt Ada Doom
Charles Fairford
Richard Hawk-Monitor
Adam Lambsbreath
Mr. Mybug
Flora Poste
Mary Smiling
Amos Starkadder
Elfine Starkadder
Ezra Starkadder
Judith Starkadder
Micah Starkadder
Rennet Starkadder
Reuben Starkadder
Seth Starkadder
Urk Starkadder

William Golding (1911–   )

Darkness Visible (1979) — BO
Edwin Bell
Bill
Arthur Frankly
Gerry
Sim Goodchild
Fido Masterman
Sebastian Pedigree
Matthew (Matty) Septimus
Sophy Stanhope
Toni Stanhope

Free Fall (1959) — BO
Philip Arnold
Benjie
Mr. Carew
Commandant of German Pris-
    oner-of-war Camp
Dr. Kenneth Enticott
Evie
Dr. Halde
Headmaster
Beatrice Ifor
Ma
Miss Manning
Sammy Mountjoy
Taffy Mountjoy
Rowena Pringle
Nick Shales
Father Watts-Watt

The Inheritors (1955) — BO
Bush
Chestnut-head
Fa
Liku
Lok
Mal
Marlan
The New One
Nil
Oa
The Old Woman
Pine-tree
Tanakil
Tuami
Twal
Vivani

Lord of the Flies (1954) — BO
Eric
Percival Wemys Madison
Jack Merridew
Officer in White Uniform
Piggy
Ralph
Roger
Sam

Tom Tyler

Loving (1945) — JR
Kate Armstrong
Agatha Burch
Captain Dermot Davenport
Edith
Eldon
Michael Mathewson
Paddy O'Conor
Charley Raunce
Miss Swift
Mrs. Tennant
Violet Tennant
Mrs. Welch

Nothing (1950) — JR
Richard Abbot
Liz Jennings
Arthur Morris
Bethesda Nathan
John Pomfret
Mary Pomfret
Mr. Thicknesse
Jane Weatherby
Penelope Weatherby
Philip Weatherby
Maud Winderly

Party Going (1939) — JR
Robin Adams
Max Adey
Alex Alexander
Amabel
Angela Crevy
Richard Cumberland
May Fellowes
Evelyn Henderson
Claire Hignam
Robert Hignam
Julia Wray

Graham Greene (1904–1991)

Brighton Rock (1938) — JC
Ida Arnold
Barman
Bill
Bill
Billy
Brewer
Pinkie Brown (The Boy)
Clarence (the ghost)
Mr. Colleoni
Phil Corkery
Crab
Old Crowe
Cubitt
Dallow

Delia
Doris
Mr. Drewitt
Charles Hale
Harry
Inspector
Joe
Judy
Kite
Maisie
Charles Moyne
Piker
Molly Pink
Samuel
Spicer
Sylvie
Jim Tate
Tom
Mr. Wilson
Mrs. Wilson
Rose Wilson

A Burnt-Out Case (1961) — JC
Bishop
Captain/Priest
Dr. Colin
Deo Gratias
Father Jean
Father Joseph
Montagu Parkinson
Father Paul
Brother Phillipe
Querry
Marie Rycker
Maurice Rycker
The Superior
Father Thomas

The Comedians (1966) — V V
Mr. Baxter
Brown
Yvette Brown (the Comtesse
    de Lascot-Villiers)
Mère Catherine
Captain Concasseur
Clement Dupont
Hercule Dupont
Mr. Fernandez
Hamit
Major Jones
Joseph
Dr. Magiot
Marcel
Dr. Philipot
Madame Philipot
Henri Philipot
Petit Pierre
Angel Pineda

Luis Pineda
Martha Pineda
Secretary for Social Welfare
Secretary of State
Mrs. Smith
William Abel Smith
Tin Tin
Schuler Wilson

The Confidential Agent (1939) — V V
Joe Bates
Dr. Bellows
Lord Benditch
Mrs. Bennett
Brigstock
Mrs. Carpenter
Chauffeur
Clara
Crikey
Else Crole
Rose Cullen
Captain Currie
D.
Lord Fetting
First Secretary
Forbes
Fortescue
Sir Terence Hillman
George Jarvis
Mr. K.
L.
Marie Mendrill
Mr. Muckerji

The End of the Affair (1951) — JC
Alfred
Maurice Bendrix
Mrs. Bertram
Sylvia Black
Father Compton
Dunstan
Henry Miles
Sarah Miles
Mr. Parkis
Lance Parkis
Mr. Savage
Mrs. Smythe
Richard Smythe
Peter Waterbury

England Made Me (1935) — V V
Calloway
Lucia ("Loo") Davidge
Anthony Farrant
Kate Farrant
Gullie
Fred Hall
Professor Hammersten

Jo Stoyte

Antic Hay (1923) — PC
Mr. Bojanus
Mr. Boldero
Coleman
Emily
Theodore Gumbril (the elder)
Theodore Gumbril (the younger)
Casimir Lypiatt
Pastuer Mercaptan
Mr. Porteous
James Shearwater
Rosie Shearwater
Myra Viveash

Brave New World (1932) — PC
Lenina Crowne
Linda
Bernard Marx
Mustapha Mond
John (the Savage) Savage
Thomas
Helmholtz Watson

Crome Yellow (1921) — PC
Mr. Barbecue-Smith
Mary Bracegirdle
R. Gombauld
Ivor Lombard
Jenny Mullion
Mr. Scogan
Denis Stone
Anne Wimbush
Henry Wimbush
Priscilla Wimbush

Eyeless in Gaza (1936) — PC
Mary Amberley
Anthony Beavis
Brian Foxe
Ekki Giesbrecht
Helen Ledwidge
Hugh Ledwidge
Dr. Miller
Mark Straithes

The Genius and the Goddess (1955) — PC
Henry Maartens
Katy Maartens
Ruth Maartens
John Rivers

Point Counter Point (1928) — PC
Mrs. Bidlake
John Bidlake
Walter Bidlake
Denis Burlap

Marjorie Carling
Beatrice Gilray
Frank Illidge
Elinor Quarles
Philip Quarles
Philip (Little Philip) Quarles
Rachel Quarles
Sidney Quarles
Mark Rampion
Mary Rampion
Maurice Spandrell
Lord Edward Tantamount
Hilda, Lady Tantamount
Lucy Tantamount
Everard Webley

Those Barren Leaves (1925) — PC
Irene Aldwinkle
Lillian Aldwinkle
Mr. Calamy
Mr. Cardan
Francis Chelifer
Grace Elver
Mr. Falx
Lord Hovenden
Mary Thriplow

Time Must Have a Stop (1944) — PC
Eustace Barnack
John Barnack
Sebastian Barnack
Paul de Vries
Mrs. Gamble
Mimi
Mrs. Ockham
Alice Poulshot
Susan Poulshot
Bruno Rontini
Veronica Thwale

Christopher Isherwood (1904–1986)

Down There on a Visit (1962) — RL
Ambrose
Maria Constantinescu
Dorothy
Geoffrey
Christopher Isherwood
Alexander Lancaster
Augustus Parr
Paul
Ronny
Hans Schmidt
Waldemar

Goodbye to Berlin (1939) — RL
Bobby
Sally Bowles

Clive
Christopher Isherwood
Fraulein Kost
Bernhard Landauer
Natalia Landauer
Fraulein Mayr
Frau Nowak
Otto Nowak
Fraulein Schroeder
Fritz Wendel
Peter Wilkinson

Mr. Norris Changes Trains (1935) — RL
(U.S.A. title: *The Last of Mr. Norris*)
Ludwig Bayer
William Bradshaw
Arthur Norris
Olga
Schmidt
Fraulein Schroeder
Baron (Kuno) von Pregnitz
Fritz Wendel

A Single Man (1964) — RL
Charlotte (Charley)
Doris
George
Jim
Kenneth (Kenny) Potter

P. D. James (1920–)

The Black Tower (1975) — DGB
Wilfred Anstey
Father Michael Baddeley
Julius Court
Adam Dalgliesh
Inspector Daniel
Eric Hewson
Maggie Hewson
Victor Holroyd
Dennis Lerner
Albert Philby
Grace Willison

Cover Her Face (1962) — DGB
Adam Dalgliesh
Sally Jupp
Sergeant Martin
Eleanor Maxie
Stephen Maxie
Deborah Riscoe

Death of an Expert Witness (1977) — DGB
Adam Dalgliesh
Inspector Doyle

Jemmy Carlin
Tom Carlin
Eusebius Cassidy
Father Daly
Joe Finnegan
Larry Finnegan
Mrs. Flynn
Aggie Flynn
Bridie Flynn
Mary Flynn
Tarry Flynn
Father Markey
Petey Meegan
Petey
Mary Reilly
Charlie Trainor

Margaret Kennedy (1896–1967)

The Constant Nymph (1924) — RS
Jacob (Ikey Mo) Birnbaum
Charles Churchill
Evelyn Churchill
Florence Churchill
Robert Churchill
Linda Cowlard
Lewis Dodd
Millicent Dodd
Roberto
Albert Sanger
Antonia (Tony) Sanger
Caryl Sanger
Kate Sanger
Paulina (Lina) Sanger
Sebastian Sanger
Teresa (Tessa) Sanger
Kiril Trigorin

Red Sky at Morning (1927) — RS
Emily Crowne
Norman Crowne
William Crowne
Nigel Cuff
Catherine Frobisher
Charles Frobisher
Charlotte Frobisher
Trevor Frobisher
Lise Grainger
Sally Green
Bertha Hackbutt
Mandy Hackbutt
Philip Luttrell
Bobbie Trevor
Tilli Van Tuyl

Arthur Koestler (1905–1983)

Darkness at Noon (1940) — LB

Arlova
Michael (Prisoner No. 38)
  Bogrov
Comrade Gletkin
Examining Magistrate Ivanov
  (Prisoner No. 400; codename
  "Hare-Lip") Kieffer
No. 1
Prisoner No. 402
Nicolas Salmanovitch (Pris-
  oner No. 404) Rubashov

Mary Lavin (1912–)

The House in Clewe Street (1945)
  — ML
Theodore Coniffe
Katherine Coniffe
Lily Coniffe
Sara Coniffe
Theresa Coniffe
Cornelius Galloway
Gabriel Galloway
Onny Soraghan
Sylvester
Telman Young

Mary O'Grady (1950) — ML
Bart
Frank Esmay
Willie Haslip
Mrs. Maguire
Alice Maguire
Angie O'Grady
Ellie O'Grady
Larry O'Grady
Mary O'Grady
Patrick O'Grady
Rosie O'Grady
Tom O'Grady

D. H. Lawrence (1885–1930)

Aaron's Rod (1922) — KH
James Argyle
Francis Dekker
Marchesa Del Torre
Marchese Del Torre
Josephine Ford
Sir William Franks
Angus Guest
Rawdon Lilly
Tanny Lilly
Aaron Sisson

The Captain's Doll (1923) — KH
Captain Alexander Hepburn
Evangeline Hepburn

Mitchka, Baroness Annamaria
  von Prielau-Carolath
Hannele, Countess Johanna
  Zu Rassentlow
Herr Regierungsrat

The Escaped Cock (1929) — KH
  (U.S.A. title: *The Man Who
  Died*)
Madeline
The Man Who Died
The Priestess of Isis

The Fox (1923) — DJ
Jill Banford
Henry Grenfel
Nellie March

Kangaroo (1923) — DJ
John Thomas Buryan
Jack Callcott
Victoria Callcott
Benjamin ("Kangaroo")
  Cooley
Dug
Mr. Monsell
Hattie Redburn
James Sharpe
Harriet Somers
Richard Lovat Somers
Willie Struthers
William James (Jaz) Trewhella

Lady Chatterley's Lover (1928)
  — DJ
Lady Eva Bennerley
Berry
Ivy Bolton
Sir Clifford Chatterley
Constance (Connie), Lady
  Chatterley
Sir Geoffrey Chatterley
Daniele
Tommy Dukes
Duncan Forbes
Giovanni
Arnold B. Hammond
Charles May
Bertha Coutts Mellors
Oliver Mellors
Michaelis (Mick)
Hilda Reid
Sir Malcolm Reid
Jack Strangeways
Olive Strangeways
Squire Leslie Winter
Harry Winterslow

The Lost Girl (1920) — DJ

Sir John Spencer
Marigold Spencer
Rollo Spencer
Sibyl, Lady Spencer

Doris Lessing (1919–   )

Briefing for a Descent into Hell
(1971) — AB
Rosemary Bains
Miles Bovey
Charlie
Constance
Minna Erve
Felicity
George
Ishmael
Alice Kincaid
Frederick Larson
Constance Maine
Nancy
Konstantina Riber
Jeremy Thorne
Nancy Thorpe
Mark Ury
Vera
Charles Watkins
Felicity Watkins
Dr. X
Dr. Y
Dr. Z

The Diaries of Jane Somers (1984)
— AB
Eliza Bates
Boris
Brian
Bridgett
Charlie
John Curtis
Kathleen Curtis
Mathew Curtis
Richard Curtis
Sylvia Curtis
Hannah DeLoch
Felicity
Johnnie Fowler
Laurie Fowler
Maudie Fowler
Freddie
Georgiana (Georgie)
Jack
Jill
Joyce
Kate
Mark
Maureen
Michael

Molly
Mrs. Penny
Phyllis
Polly
Mrs. Privett
Annie Reeves
Mrs. Rogers
Vera Rogers
Mr. Rolovsky
Jane Somers
Dr. Thring
Nancy Westringham
Sister White
Hermione Whitfield

*Documents Relating to the Sentimen-
tal Agents in the Volyen Empire*
(1983) — AB
(The fifth novel of *Canopus in
Argos: Archives*)
Calder
Lord Grice
Incent
Johor (George Sherban)
Klorathy
Krolgul
Ormarin
Spascock
Stil
Tafta

The Fifth Child (1988) — AB
Alice
Amy
Angela
Dr. Brett
Bridgett
Frederick Burke
Molly Burke
Derik
Dorothy
Dr. Gilly
John
Ben Lovatt
David Lovatt
Deborah Lovatt
Harriet Lovatt
Helen Lovatt
James Lovatt
Jane Lovatt
Jessica Lovatt
Luke Lovatt
Paul Lovatt
Sarah
William

The Four-Gated City (1969) — AB

(The fifth novel of *Children of
Violence*)
Nick (Nicky) Anderson
Bob
Terence Boles
Harold Butts
Mary Butts
Jasmine Cohen
Joss Cohen
Amanda Coldridge
Arthur Coldridge
Colin Coldridge
Elizabeth Coldridge
Francis Coldridge
Galina Coldridge
Gwen Coldridge
Jill Coldridge
Lynda Coldridge
Mark Coldridge
Paul Coldridge
Phoebe Coldridge
Sally (Sarah Koenig) Coldridge
Rita Gale
Molly Grinham
Sandra Hill
Iris
Jack
Jimmy
Joanna
Mrs. Johns
Caroline Knowell
Dr. Lamb
Hilary Marsh
Henry Matheson
Mr. Maynard
Myra Maynard
Rosa Mellendip
Milly
Bob Parrinder
Graham Patten
John Patten
Margaret Patten
William Esse Perkins
Dorothy Quentin
Bessie Quest
Jonathan Quest
Martha Quest
May Quest
Patty Samuals
Miss Sayers
Gerald Smith
Stanley
Stella
Steven
Miles Tangin
Jim Troyes
Mrs. Van der Bylt

Akira Sakazaki
Joy Simpson
Miranda Simpson
Felix Skinner
Cheryl Summerbee
Rupert Sutcliffe
Hilary Swallow
Matthew Swallow
Philip Swallow
Michel Tardieu
Jacques Textel
Seigfried von Turpitz
Rodney Wainwright
Desiree Zapp
Morris Zapp

Malcolm Lowry (1909–1957)

Dark as the Grave Wherein My Friend Is Laid (1968) — PAM
borracho ("drunkard")
Juan Cerillo
Daniel
Erikson
Miss Gleason
Dr. Hippolyte
Eduardo (Eddie) Kent
Kristbjorg
Manager of the Banco Ejidal in Oaxaca
Juan Fernando Martinez
Quaggan
Ruth
John Stanford
Senora Trigo
Dr. Arturo Diaz Vigil
Primrose Wilderness
Sigbjorn Wilderness

Lunar Caustic (1968) — PAM
Battle
Dr. Claggart
Garry
Mrs. Horncle
Mr. Kalowsky
Maggie
Bill Plantagenet
Puppeteer
Ruth

October Ferry to Gabriola (1970) — PAM
Angela d'Arivée
boy
Richard Chapman
Peter Cordwainer
Captain Duquesne
Monsieur Grigorovitch

Madame Grigorovitch
Henry Knight
Mr. Llewelyn
Ethan Llewelyn
Gywn Llewelyn
Jacqueline Llewelyn
Tommy Llewelyn
Angus McCandless ("The McCandless")
Flora Jacqueline McClintock
Mr. Neiman
Mrs. Neiman
J. Temple Thurston

Ultramarine (1933) — PAM
Andersen ("Andy") Marathon Bredahl
Eugene Dana Hilliot
Norman Leif
McGoff
Hans Popplereuter
Quartermaster
Olga Sologub
Janet Traversa (variously, Rohtraut)
Nikolai Wallae

Under the Volcano (1947) — PAM
A Few Fleas
Lazarus Bolowski
Senor Bustamente
cartero
Juan Cerillo
Cervantes
Chief of Rostrums
Concepta
Captain Constable
Ramon Diosdado (the Elephant)
Dying Indian
Englishman
Geoffrey Firmin (the Consul)
Hugh Firmin
Yvonne Constable Firmin
Senora Gregorio
Dr. Guzman
Jacques Laruelle
Lee Maitland
Maria
Juan Fernando Martinez
Old woman with chicken
pelado
Pimp
Mr. Quincey
Fructuoso Sanabria ("Chief of Gardens")
Abraham Taskerson
Dr. Arturo Diaz Vigil

Weber
Cliff Wright
Geoffrey Wright
Zuzugoitea (Chief of the Municipality)

Colin MacInnes (1914–1976)

Absolute Beginners (1959) — SE
Call-me-Cobber
Mr. Cool
Dad
Amberly Drove
Edward the Ted (Ed)
Ex-Deb-of-Last-Year
Flikker
Henley
The Fabulous Hoplite (Hop)
Big Jill
Emmanuel (Manny) Katz
Miriam Katz
Saul Katz
Kid-from-Outer-Space
Dido Lament
The Misery Kid
Mum
Narrator
Vendice Partners
Mickey Pondoroso
Zesty-Boy Sift
Suzette (Suze, Crepe Suzette)
Dean Swift
Ron Todd
Vernon (Vern, Jules)
Wilf
Wizard (Wiz)

City of Spades (1957) — SE
Mr. Lord Alexander
Hamilton Ashinow
Karl Marx Bo
Alfy Bongo
Bushman
Jimmy Cannibal
Nat King Cole
Isabel Cornwallis
Hippolyte Dieudonne
Mrs. Fortune
Christmas Fortune
David MacDonald Fortune
John (Johnny) MacDonald Fortune
Peach Fortune
William Macpherson Fortune
Moscow Gentry
Huntley
Johnson the Tapper
Jupiter

Norma Cozens
Harvey (Boy) Dougdale
Lady Patricia Dougdale
Joyce Fleetwood
Cedric Hampton
Leopoldina (Polly) Hampton
Frances (Fanny) Logan
Lord Montdore
Sonia, Lady Montdore
Geoffrey Paddington
Jassy Radlett
Linda Radlett
Matthew Radlett
Sadie Radlett
Victoria Radlett
Fabrice de Sauveterre
Captain Davey Warbeck
Emily Warbeck
Alfred Wincham

The Pursuit of Love (1945) — MK
The Bolter
Lavender Davis
John, Lord Fort William
Juan
Sir Leicester Kroesig
Moira Kroesig
Tony Kroesig
Frances (Fanny) Logan
Lord Merlin
Jassy Radlett
Linda Radlett
Louisa Radlett
Matt Radlett
Matthew Radlett
Sadie Radlett
Victoria Radlett
Fabrice de Sauveterre
Christian Talbot
Pixie Townsend
Davey Warbeck
Emily Warbeck
Alfred Wincham

Iris Murdoch (1919–)

An Accidental Man (1971) — JF
Karen Arbuthnot
Mavis Argyll
Ann Colindale
Austin Gibson Grey
Betty Gibson Grey
Dorina Gibson Grey
Garth Gibson Grey
Matthew Gibson Grey
Alison Ledgard
Charlotte Ledgard
Ludwig Leferrier

Norman Monkley
Sir Charles Odmore
Hester, Lady Odmore
Ralph Odmore
Sebastian Odmore
Richard Pargeter
Margaret (Mitzi) Ricardo
Henrietta Sayce
Oliver Sayce
Penny Sayce
Clara Tisbourne
George (Pinkie) Tisbourne
Gracie Tisbourne
Patrick Tisbourne

The Bell (1958) — JF
The Abbess
Mother Clare
Catherine Fawley
Nick Fawley
Toby Gashe
Dora Greenfield
Paul Greenfield
Bob Joyce
Michael Meade
James Tayper Pace
Patchway
Noel Spens
Margaret Strafford
Mark Strafford
Peter Topglass
Sister Ursula

The Black Prince (1973) — JF
Arnold Baffin
Julian Baffin
Rachel Baffin
Oscar Belling
Christian Evandale
Hartbourne
P. Loxias
Marigold
Francis Marloe
Bradley Pearson
Priscilla Saxe
Roger Saxe

Bruno's Dream (1969) — JF
Auntie
Nigel Boase
Wilfred (Will) Boase
Adelaide de Crecy
Bruno Greensleave
Diana Greensleave
Janie Greensleave
Miles Greensleave
Parvati Greensleave
Maureen

Danby Odell
Gwen Odell
Lisa Watkins

A Fairly Honourable Defeat (1970)
—JF
Leonard Browne
Morgan Browne
Tallis Browne
Hilda Foster
Peter Foster
Rupert Foster
Simon Foster
Julius King
Axel Nilsson

The Flight from the Enchanter
(1956) — JF
Calvin Blick
Annette Cockeyne
Mischa Fox
Hunter Keepe
Rosa Keepe
Janislav (Jan) Lusiewicz
Stefan Lusiewicz
Nina
John Rainborough

Henry and Cato (1976) — JF
Beautiful Joe Beckett
Father Brendan Craddock
Bella Fischer
Russell Fischer
Cato Forbes
Colette Forbes
John Forbes
Giles Gosling
Lucius Lamb
Alexander (Sandy) Marshalson
Gerda Marshalson
Henry Marshalson
Dame Patricia Raven
Rhoda
Stephanie Whitehouse

The Italian Girl (1963) — JF
David Levkin
Elsa Levkin
Maria Magistretti
Edmund Narraway
Flora Narraway
Isabel Narraway
Lydia Narraway
Otto Narraway

The Nice and the Good (1968) — JF
Edward Binanne
Henrietta Biranne
Paula Biranne

James Stephens

Liam O'Flaherty (1896–1984)

Famine (1937) — RL
Jocelyn Chadwick
Mr. Coburn
Jack Crompton
Chief Constable Edwards
Father Thomas Geelan
Barney Gleeson
Ellen Gleeson
Ellie Gleeson
Patrick Gleeson
Simon Hegarty
Kate Hernon
Kitty Hernon
Patch Hernon
Dr. Joe Hynes
Johnny Hynes
Thomsy Hynes
Tony Hynes
Brian Kilmartin
Maggie Kilmartin
Martin Kilmartin
Mary Kilmartin
Michael Kilmartin
Patsy O'Hanlon
Sally O'Hanlon
James Rabbit
Reilly
Father John Roche
Nappa Toomey

The Informer (1925) — PD
Maggie Connemara
Katie Fox
Dan Gallagher
Mrs. McPhillip
Frankie McPhillip
Mary McPhillip
Bartly Mulholland
Rat Mulligan
Gypo Nolan

George Orwell (Eric Arthur Blair, 1903–1950)

Animal Farm (1945) — SAP
Boxer
Mr. Fredrick
Mr. Jones
Old Major
Mollie
Moses
Napoleon
Mr. Pilkington
Snowball
Squealer

Burmese Days (1934) — SAP
P. W. Ellis
John Flory
Ma Kin
U Po Kyin
Elizabeth Lackersteen
Tom Lackersteen
Mr. Macgregor
C. W. Maxwell
Ma Hla May
Maung (Ko S'la) San Hla
Dr. Veraswami
Lieutenant Verrall
R. Westerfield

A Clergyman's Daughter (1935) — SAP
Mrs. Creevy
Charles Hare
Dorothy Hare
Sir Thomas Hare
Nobby
Mrs. Semprill
Victor Stone
Mr. Warburton

Coming Up for Air (1939) — SAP
George Bowling
Hilda Bowling
Elsie Cookson

Keep the Aspidistra Flying (1936) — SAP
Mr. Cheeseman
Gordon Comstock
Julia Comstock
Mr. McKecknie
Ravelston
Rosemary

Nineteen Eighty-Four (1949) — SAP
Charrington
Julia
O'Brien
Tom Parsons
Katherine Smith
Winston Smith
Syme

Anthony Powell (1905–   )

The Acceptance World (1955) — DT
(The third novel of *A Dance to the Music of Time*)
Milly Andriadis
Bijou, Countess of Ardglass
Ralph Barnby

Lady Frederica Budd
St. John Clarke
Edgar Bosworth Deacon
Sir Magnus Donners
Robert (Bob) Duport
Myra Erdleigh
Alfred, Lord Erridge
Amy Foxe
Werner Guggenbühl
Horace Isbister
Giles Jenkins
Nicholas Jenkins
Gypsy Jones
Lawrence Le Bas
Mark Members
J. C. Quiggin
Sillery (Sillers)
Lady Anne Stepney
Lady Peggy Stepney
Charles Stringham
Babs Stripling
Jimmy Stripling
Jean Templer
Mona Templer
Peter Templer
Alfred Tolland
Dicky Umfraville
Baby Wentworth
Sir Gavin Walpole-Wilson
Kenneth Widmerpool
Matilda Wilson

At Lady Molly's (1957) — DT
(The fourth novel of *A Dance to the Music of Time*)
St. John Clarke
General Aylmer Conyers
Bertha Conyers
Roddy Cutts
Robert (Bob) Duport
Alfred, Lord Erridge
Amy Foxe
Buster Foxe
Mildred Haycock
Lady Molly Jeavons
Ted Jeavons
Nicholas (Nick) Jenkins
Chips Lovell
Johnny Pardoe
Max Pilgrim
J. C. Quiggin
Betty (Taylor or Porter) Templer
Jean Templer
Mona Templer
Peter Templer
Alfred Tolland

Heather Blenkinsop
Esther Clovis
Daphne Dagnall
Tom Dagnall
Fabian Driver
Mrs. Dyer
Digby Fox
Christabel Gellibrand
Dr. Luke Gellibrand
Flavia Grundy
Beatrix Howick
Emma Howick
Olive Lee
Miss Lickerish
Isobel Mound
Claudia Pettifer
Graham Pettifer
Ianthe Potts
Adam Prince
Magdalen Raven
Avice Shrubsole
Martin Shrubsole
Terry Skate
Miss Vereker

A Glass of Blessings (1959) — DJK
Wilfred Bason
Prudence Bates
Mary Beamish
Sister Blatt
Father Bode
Walter ("Bill") Coleman
Rodney Forsyth
Sybil Forsyth
Wilmet Forsyth
Sir Denbigh Grote
Archdeacon Henry Hoccleve
Keith
Piers Longridge
Julian Malory
Rockingham Napier
Catherine Oliphant
Augusta Prideaux
Father Marius Ransome
Professor Arnold Root
Harry Talbot
Rowena Talbot
Father Oswald Thames

Jane and Prudence (1953) — DJK
Prudence Bates
William Caldicote
Flora Cleveland
Jane Cleveland
Nicholas Cleveland
Miss Doggett
Fabian Driver
Mrs. Glaze

Arthur Grampian
Mildred Lathbury
Edward Lyall
Geoffrey Manifold
Jessie Morrow
Mr. Mortlake
Francis Oliver
Canon Pritchard
Mrs. Pritchard

Less Than Angels (1955) — DJK
Mrs. Beddoes
Mrs. Bone
Everard Bone
Esther Clovis
Primrose Cutbush
Vanessa Eaves
Elaine
Professor Gervase Fairfax
Minnie Foresight
Digby Fox
Father Egidio Gemini
Miss Jessop
Jean-Pierre le Rossignol
Alaric Lydgate
Gertrude Lydgate
Felix Byron Mainwaring
Giles Mallow
Naomi Mallow
Tom Mallow
Helena Napier
Catherine Oliphant
Mark Penfold
Phyllis
Brandon Pirbright
Melanie Pirbright
Dierdre Swan
Mabel Swan
Malcolm Swan
Father Laurence Tulliver
Cornelia van Heep
Dr. William Vere
Rhoda Wellcome

No Fond Return of Love (1961) — DJK
Mrs. Beltane
Paul Beltane
Uncle Bertram
Maurice Clive
Viola Dace
Aylwin Forbes
Horatia Forbes
Marjorie Forbes
Neville Forbes
Wilmet Forsyth
Digby Fox
Aunt Hermione

Keith
Laurel
Piers Longridge
Miss Lord
Senhor MacBride-Pereìra
Dulcie Mainwaring
Mrs. Sedge
Bill Sedge
Dierdre Swan
Rhoda Wellcome
Grace Williton

Quartet in Autumn (1977) — DJK
Father Bode
Janice Brabner
Edwin Braithwaite
Letty Crowe
Beth Doughty
Father Gellibrand
Luke Gellibrand
Marcia Ivory
Ken
David Lydell
Marjorie
Nigel
Norman
Jacob Olatunde
Mrs. Pope
Priscilla
Mr. Strong
Father Oswald Thames

Some Tame Gazelle (1950) — DJK
Connie Aspinall
Belinda Bede
Harriet Bede
Count Ricardo Bianco
Edgar Donne
Theodore Grote, Bishop of
    Mbawawa
Agatha Hoccleve
Archdeacon Henry Hoccleve
Edith Liversidge
Nathaniel Mold
Nicholas Parnell

The Sweet Dove Died (1978) — DJK
Humphrey Boyce
James Boyce
Mrs. Caton
Colin
Leonora Eyre
Miss Foxe
Liz
Senhor Macbride-Pereìra
Meg
Ned
Phoebe Sharpe

Herbert Getliffe
Marion Gladwell
Percy Hall
Henriques
Margaret Davidson Hollis
Mrs. Knight
Laurence Knight
Sheila Knight
Howard Martineau
Milly
Paget
George Passant
Mr. Peck
Salisbury
Hugh Smith
Snedding
(Za) Thirza
Mr. Vesey

Muriel Spark (1918–   )

The Abbess of Crewe (1974) — MR
Sister Alexandra
Father Baudouin
Sister Felicity
Sister Gertrude
Lady Abbess Hildegarde
Father Maximilian
Sister Mildred
Father Thomas
Sister Walburga
Sister Winifrede

The Bachelors (1960) — MR
Isobel Billows
Martin Bowles
Ronald Bridges
Chloe
Marlene Cooper
Alice Dawes
Francis Eccles
Detective Inspector Fergusson
Matthew Finch
Dr. Fleischer
Freda Flower
Elsie Forrest
Dr. Mike Garland
Hildegarde
Dr. Lyte
Walter Pratt
Patrick Seton
Father Socket
Ewart Thornton

The Ballad of Peckham Rye (1960)
— MR
Beauty
Maria Cheeseman

Merle Coverdale
Arthur Crewe
Leslie Crewe
Mavis Crewe
Dougal Douglas (Douglas Dougal)
Vincent Druce
Miss Frierne
Collie Gould
Jinny
Elaine Kent
Trevor Lomas
Nelly Mahone
Dixie Morse
Humphrey Place
Mr. Weedin
Connie Weedin
Mr. Willis

The Comforters (1957) — MR
Andrew Hogarth
Eleanor Hogarth
Melvyn Hogarth
Georgina Hogg
Louisa Jepp
Sir Edwin Manders
Ernest Manders
Helena, Lady Manders
Laurence Manders
Caroline Rose
Willi Stock (The Baron)
Mr. Webster

The Driver's Seat (1970) — MR
Bill
Carlo
Mrs. Fiedke
Lise
Richard

A Far Cry from Kensington (1988)
— MR
Hector Bartlett
Basil Carlin
Eva Carlin
Cathy
Connie
Gretta
Nancy Hawkins
Tom Hawkins
Hugh Lederer
Isobel Lederer
Emma Loy
Mabel
Kate Parker
Patrick
Wanda Podolak
Milly Sanders

Howard Send
Colin Shoe
Abigail de Mordell Staines-Knight
William Todd
Sir Alec Tooley
Ian Tooley
Fred Tucher
Mr. Twinny
Mr. Wells
Martin York

The Girls of Slender Means (1963)
— MR
Anne Baberton
Rudi Bittesch
Joanna Childe
Miss Coleman ("Collie")
Colonel G. Felix Dobell
Gareth Dobell
Nicholas Farringdon
Pauline Fox
Miss Jarman ("Jarvie")
George Johnson (Huy Throvis-Mew)
Miss Macgregor ("Greggie")
Dorothy Markham
Selina Redwood
Nancy Riddle
Tilly Throvis-Mew
Jane Wright

Loitering with Intent (1981) — MR
Warrender Chase
Father Egbart Delaney
Revission Doe
Dottie
Baronne Clotilde du Loiret
Sir Eric Findlay
Lady Bernice Gilbert ("Bucks")
Leslie
Gray Mauser
Wally McConnachie
Solly Mendelsohn
Lady Edwina Oliver
Sir Quentin Oliver
Fleur Talbot
Beryl Tims
Mrs. Wilks
Maisie Young

The Mandlebaum Gate (1965)
— MR
Michael Aaronson
"Benny" Bennett
Joanna Cartwright
Matt Cartwright
Harry Clegg

Eustace Gordon
Reggie Howerton
Marina Luzzi
Primrose Lynmouth
Great Grandfather Mosson
Sir Hubert Mosson
Jackie, Lady Mosson
Piers (Van) Mosson
Rosemary (Ma) Mosson
Tom (Pratt) Mosson
Magda Sczekerny
Jim Terrington
Ralph Tucker

P. G. Wodehouse (1881–1975)

Aunts Aren't Gentlemen (1974)
— AFB
(U.S.A. title: *The Cat-Nappers*)
Anatole
Colonel Jimmy Briscoe
Stephanie Byng
Mr. Cook
Vanessa Cook
Herbert Graham
Reginald Jeeves
E. Jimpson Murgatroyd
Harold P. Pinker
Major Plank
Orlo J. Porter
Potato Chip
Roderick Spode
Dahlia Travers
Tom Travers
Agatha Wooster
Bertram Wilberforce Wooster

Fish Preferred (1929) — AFB
(U.S.A. title: *Summer Lightning*)
Rupert Baxter
Sebastian Beach
Sue Brown
Empress of Blandings
Hugo Carmody
Clarence Threepwood, Lord
   Emsworth
Julia Fish
Ronald Overbury Fish
Dolly Henderson
Constance Keeble
Gregory Parsloe-Parsloe
P. Frobisher Pilbeam
James Pirbright
Myra Schoonmaker
Galahad Threepwood
Millicent Threepwood
George Cyril Wellbeloved

Money for Nothing (1928) — AFB
Bolt
Hugh Carmody
Lester Carmody
John Carroll
Ronald Overbury Fish
Egbert Flannery
Dolly Molloy
Thos G. Molloy
Sturgis
"Dr." Alexander Twist
Meredith Wyvern
Patricia Wyvern

Something New (1915) — AFB
(U.S.A. title: *Something Fresh*)
Rupert Baxter
Sebastian Beach
Clarence Threepwood, Lord
   Emsworth
George Emerson
R. (Dickie) Jones
Judson
Ashe Marson
Aline Peters
J. Preston Peters
Gridley Quayle
Slingsby
Freddie Threepwood
Twemlow
Joan Valentine

The Code of the Woosters (1938)
— AFB
Anatole
Madeline Bassett
Sir Watkyn Bassett
Stephanie Byng
Augustus Fink-Nottle
Reginald Jeeves
Constable Eustace Oates
Harold P. Pinker
Roderick Spode
Dahlia Travers
Tom Travers
Agatha Wooster
Bertram Wilberforce Wooster

Virginia Woolf (1882–1941)

Between The Acts (1941) — AH
William Dodge
Rupert Haines
Miss La Trobe
Mrs. Manresa
Bartholomew Oliver
Caro Oliver
George Oliver

Giles Oliver
Isa Oliver
Lucy Swithin

Jacob's Room (1922) — AH
Richard (Nick) Bonamy
Clara Durrant
Timothy Durrant
Julia Eliot
Fanny Elmer
Betty Flanders
Jacob Flanders
Florinda
Andrew Floyd
Mrs. Jarvis
An Old Blind Woman
Evan Williams
Sandra Wentworth Williams

Mrs. Dalloway (1925) — AH
Sir William Bradshaw
Millicent, Lady Bruton
Daisy
Clarissa Dalloway
Elizabeth Dalloway
Richard Dalloway
Evan
Ellie Henderson
Dr. Holmes
Doris Kilman
Helena Parry
Sally Seton [Lady Rosseter]
Rezia Smith
Septimus Warren Smith
Peter Walsh
Hugh Whitbread

Night and Day (1919) — AH
Mary Datchet
Ralph Denham
Mr. Fortescue
Mr. Hilbery
Cyril Hilbery
Katherine Hilbery
Maggie Hilbery
Mrs. Milvain
Cassandra Otway
William Rodney

Orlando: A Biography (1928) — AH
Nicholas Greene
Archduchess Harriet/ Arch-
   duke Harry of Roumania
Orlando
Sasha
Marmaduke Bonthrop
   Shelmerdine

To the Lighthouse (1927) — AH

William Bankes
Lily Briscoe
Augustus Carmichael
Mrs. McNab
Mr. Ramsay
Mrs. Ramsay
Andrew Ramsay
Camilla (cam) Ramsay
James Ramsay
Prue Ramsay
Charles Tansley

The Voyage Out (1915) — AH
Miss Allan
Helen Ambrose
Ridley Ambrose
Clarissa Dalloway
Richard Dalloway
Hughling Elliot
Mrs. Hughling Elliot
Mr. Flushing
Alice Flushing
Susan Harrington
Terence Hewet
St. John Hirst
Dr. Lesage
Nurse McInnes
Evelyn Murgatroyd
Emma Paley
Mr. Pepper
Alfred Perrott

Dr. Rodriguez
Sinclair
Arthur Venning
Rachel Vinrace
Willoughby Vinrace

The Waves (1931) — AH
Bernard
Jinny
Louis
Nanny
Neville
Percival
Rhoda
Susan

The Years (1937) — AH
Crosby
Hugh Gibbs
Lasswade
Kitty Malone, Lady Lasswade
Mira
Colonel Abel Pargiter
Celia Pargiter
Delia Pargiter
Sir Digby Pargiter
Edward Pargiter
Eleanor Pargiter
Eugenie Pargiter
Maggie Pargiter
Martin Pargiter
Milly Pargiter

Morris Pargiter
North Pargiter
Peggy Pargiter
Sara Pargiter
Violet Pargiter
Patrick
Nicholas Pomjalovsky
Jo Robson

Percival Christopher Wren (1885–1941)

Beau Geste (1924) — MK
Henri de Beaujolais
Francesco Boldini
Augustus (Gussie) Brandon
Sir Hector Brandon
Patricia, Lady Brandon
Buddy
Maurice Ffolliot
Digby Geste
John Geste
Michael (Beau) Geste
Hank
George Lawrence
Color Sergeant Lejaune
Isobel Rivers
Schwartz

Contributors

AB Andrea Broomfield
AFB Arlyn Bruccoli
DB Dawn Black
DGB David G. Brailow
LB Lynne Beene
MB Michael Begnal
OB Olga R. R. Broomfield
KBa Karen Ball
KBe Kate Begnal
BB't Barbara Brothers
BB'w Barbara Brown
AC Alison Martin Cunnar
DC Douglas Catron
JC Juliette Cunico
MC Martin Cavanaugh
PC Paul Carlton
AD A. A. Devitas
DD David Durr
JD Janet Egleson Dunleavy
KD Krystan Douglas
PD Paul A. Doyle
TD Tammilyn Duncan
GD-M Gareth Davies-Morris
SE Sharon Elliott
DE-M Dawn Elmore-McCrary
CF Charles Ford

GF Gloria Fromm
JF J. Fletcher
MF Mary Lou Fisk
RF Ruth Faurot
FG Frederic Gale
JG John R. Greenfield
MG Michael Goldberg
NG Norman Gates
RG Rene Greenlee
AH Abigail Helmstreet
CH Carolyn Hughes
GH Gwenyth Hood
KH Karl Henzy
CJ Catherine Jurca
DJ Dennis Jackson
EJ Edward T. Jones
JJ John Jones
AK Albert Kalson
DK Dennis Kearney
DJK Deborah J. Knuth
EK Ellen King
MK Melissa Kaegel
ML Michele Marsee Loeblich
RL Rich Lloyd
DM Daniel Marder
MM Margaret McDowell

PM Patricia Mandia
PAM Patrick A. McCarthy
BM-A Barbara Millard-Anderson
RMa Rebecca Mayer
RMc Richard McGhee
JM'n Jim Mang
JM'r Joan Markey
BO Bernard Oldsey
CO Christopher Orlet
JO John Orlet
MO Mary O'Toole
SAP Susan Anthony Proctor
SPh Susan Philp
SPr Sheryl Prange
JR John H. Rogers
MR Margaret Rowe
LS Lisa Schwerdt
RS Rene Sykes
MS-D Michelle Stacey-Doyle
DT Dorothea Thompson
MT Maureen Thum
ST Sheila Tombe
VV Vita Viviano
DW Danyelle Warden
MW Michele Whiting
TW Todd White